Less managing. More teaching. Greater learning.

INSTRUCTORS...

Would you like your **students** to show up for class more **prepared**? *(Let's face it, class is much more fun if everyone is engaged and prepared...)*

Want ready-made application-level **interactive assignments,** student progress reporting, and auto-assignment grading? *(Less time grading means more time teaching...)*

Want an **instant view of student or class performance** relative to learning objectives? *(No more wondering if students understand...)*

Need to **collect data and generate reports** required for administration or accreditation? *(Say goodbye to manually tracking student learning outcomes...)*

Want to **record and post your lectures** for students to view online?

With McGraw-Hill's *Connect™ Management,*

INSTRUCTORS GET:

- Interactive Applications – **book-specific interactive assignments** that require students to APPLY what they've learned.
- Simple **assignment management,** allowing you to spend more time teaching.
- **Auto-graded** assignments, quizzes, and tests.
- **Detailed Visual Reporting** where student and section results can be viewed and analyzed.
- Sophisticated **online testing** capability.
- A **filtering and reporting** function that allows you to easily assign and report on materials that are correlated to accreditation standards, learning outcomes, and Bloom's taxonomy.
- An easy-to-use **lecture capture** tool.

Click a subcategory to view **section** details

expand all | collapse all — export to excel

AACSB	# questions	# times submitted	# students submitted	category score
▼ **AACSB: Analytic**	15	2727	25/25	46.11%
Cumulative Quiz-Chapters 1,2,3 (Graded)	6	450	25/25	14.27%
Homework-Chapter 3 Part 2 (Graded)	6	1512	25/25	63.17%
Homework-Chapter 3 Part 1 (Graded)	3	765	25/25	59.2%
▶ AACSB: Reflective Thinking	26	4995	25/25	39.65%

Bloom's	# questions	# times submitted	# students submitted	category score
▼ **Bloom's: Analysis**	21	4074	25/25	28.42%
Cumulative Quiz-Chapters 1,2,3 (Graded)	7	525	25/25	13.96%
Homework-Chapter 3 Part 2 (Graded)	7	1764	25/25	41.74%
Homework-Chapter 3 Part 1 (Graded)	7	1785	25/25	24.99%
▶ Bloom's: Application	1	255	25/25	58.43%
▶ Bloom's: Comprehension	7	1239	25/25	58.0%
▶ Bloom's: Knowledge	12	2154	25/25	43.39%

STUDENTS...

Want an online, **searchable version** of your textbook?

Wish your textbook could be **available online** while you're doing your assignments?

Connect™ Plus Management eBook

If you choose to use *Connect™ Plus Management*, you have an affordable and searchable online version of your book integrated with your other online tools.

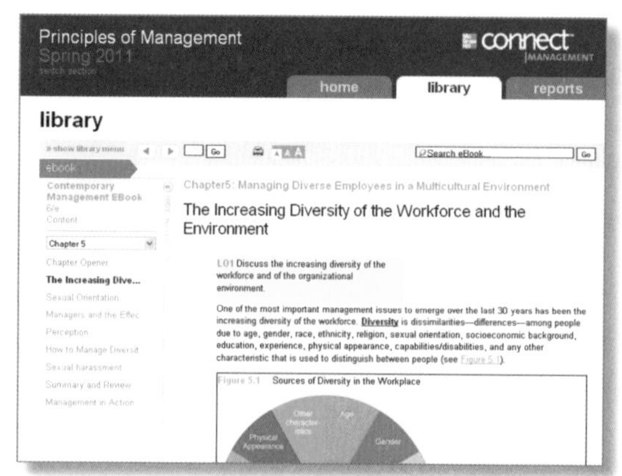

Connect™ Plus Management eBook offers features like:

- Topic search
- Direct links from assignments
- Adjustable text size
- Jump to page number
- Print by section

STUDENTS...

Want to get more **value** from your textbook purchase?

Think learning management should be a bit more **interesting**?

Check out the STUDENT RESOURCES section under the *Connect™* Library tab.

Here you'll find a wealth of resources designed to help you achieve your goals in the course. You'll find things like **quizzes, PowerPoints, and Internet activities** to help you study. Every student has different needs, so explore the STUDENT RESOURCES to find the materials best suited to you.

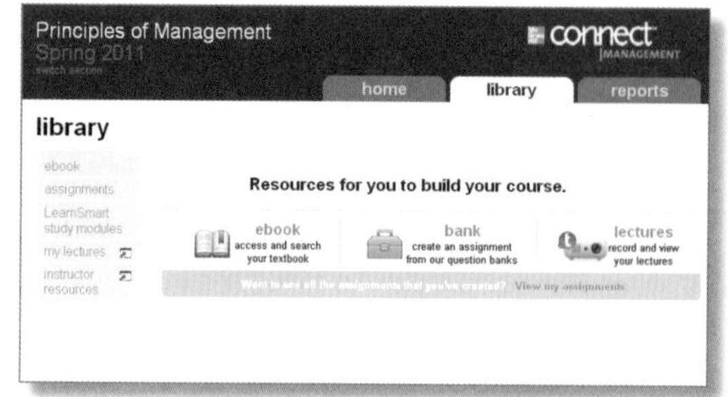

Contemporary Management

Seventh Edition

Gareth R. Jones
Mays Business School
Texas A&M University

Jennifer M. George
Jesse H. Jones Graduate School of Business
Rice University

CONTEMPORARY MANAGEMENT

Published by McGraw-Hill/Irwin, a business unit of The McGraw-Hill Companies, Inc., 1221 Avenue of the Americas, New York, NY, 10020.

Some ancillaries, including electronic and print components, may not be available to customers outside the United States.

This book is printed on acid-free paper.

1 2 3 4 5 6 7 8 9 0 DOW/DOW 1 0 9 8 7 6 5 4 3 2 1 0

ISBN 978-0-07-811269-0
MHID 0-07-811269-9

Vice president and editor-in-chief: *Brent Gordon*
Editorial director: *Paul Ducham*
Executive editor: *Michael Ablassmeir*
Director of development: *Ann Torbert*
Senior development editor: *Trina Hauger*
Editorial assistant: *Andrea Heirendt*
Vice president and director of marketing: *Robin J. Zwettler*
Marketing director: *Amee Mosley*
Executive marketing manager: *Anke Braun Weekes*
Vice president of editing, design, and production: *Sesha Bolisetty*
Senior project manager: *Bruce Gin*
Senior buyer: *Michael R. McCormick*
Interior designer: *Cara Hawthorne, cara david DESIGN*
Senior photo research coordinator: *Jeremy Cheshareck*
Photo researcher: *Allison Grimes*
Media project manager: *Jennifer Lohn*
Cover design: *Cara Hawthorne, cara david DESIGN*
Interior design: *Cara Hawthorne, cara david DESIGN*
Typeface: *10.25/12 Baskerville*
Compositor: *Laserwords Private Limited*
Printer: *R. R. Donnelley*

Library of Congress Cataloging-in-Publication Data

Jones, Gareth R.
Contemporary management / Gareth R. Jones, Jennifer M. George.
p. cm.
Includes index.
ISBN-13: 978-0-07-811269-0 (alk. paper)
ISBN-10: 0-07-811269-9 (alk. paper)
1. Management. I. George, Jennifer M. II. Title.
HD31.J597 2011
658–dc22

2010020430

www.mhhe.com

BRIEF CONTENTS

CONTENTS

Part One | Management

Chapter 1 Managers and Managing 2

A MANAGER'S CHALLENGE

What Is High-Performance Management? 3

Topics

Chapter 2 The Evolution of Management Thought 38

A MANAGER'S CHALLENGE

Finding Better Ways to Make Cars 39

Topics

Examples

Management in Action

Examples

Management in Action

Chapter 3 Values, Attitudes, Emotions, and Culture: The Manager as a Person 72

A MANAGER'S CHALLENGE

Values of a Founder Live On at PAETEC 73

Topics

Chapter 4 Ethics and Social Responsibility 104

A MANAGER'S CHALLENGE

Unethical Managers and the Perils of Peanut Butter 105

Topics

Examples

Management in Action

Examples

Management in Action

Chapter 5 Managing Diverse Employees in a Multicultural Environment 142

A MANAGER'S CHALLENGE

Topics

Chapter 6 Managing in the Global Environment 176

A MANAGER'S CHALLENGE

Topics

Examples

Management in Action

Examples

Management in Action

Chapter 7 Decision Making, Learning, Creativity, and Entrepreneurship 210

Chapter 8 The Manager as a Planner and Strategist 244

Part Three | Decision Making, Planning, and Strategy

Chapter 9

Value Chain Management: Functional Strategies for Competitive Advantage 280

A MANAGER'S CHALLENGE

Dell Is Battling with HP and Apple to Create Value for Customers 281

Topics

Part Four | Organizing and Controlling

Chapter 10

Managing Organizational Structure and Culture 312

A MANAGER'S CHALLENGE

Andrea Jung Reorganizes Avon's Global Structure 313

Topics

Chapter 11 Organizational Control and Change 352

A MANAGER'S CHALLENGE

Toyota Needs a Major Fix to Its Quality Control System 353

Topics

Chapter 12 Human Resource Management 388

A MANAGER'S CHALLENGE

Happy Employees Provide Exceptional Service at Zappos 389

Topics

Examples

Management in Action

Examples

Management in Action

Chapter 13 Motivation and Performance

426

A MANAGER'S CHALLENGE

Keeping Employees Highly Motivated at SAS 427

Topics

Chapter 14 Leadership

460

A MANAGER'S CHALLENGE

Judy McGrath Leads MTV Networks 461

Topics

Examples

Management in Action

Examples

Management in Action

Part Five | Leading Individuals and Groups

Chapter 15 Effective Groups and Teams 492

A MANAGER'S CHALLENGE
Teams Innovate at Cisco 493

Topics

Part Six | Managing Critical Organizational Processes

Chapter 16 Promoting Effective Communication 526

A MANAGER'S CHALLENGE
Managers in Diverse Industries Need Feedback from Employees 527

Topics

Examples

Management in Action

Examples

Management in Action

Part Six | Managing Critical Organizational Processes

Chapter 17 Managing Conflict, Politics, and Negotiation 562

Chapter 18 Using Advanced Information Technology to Increase Performance 590

PREFACE

In the seventh new edition of our book, *Contemporary Management*, we continue with our mission to provide students the most current and up-to-date account of the changes taking place in the world of business management. The fast-changing domestic and global environment continues to pressure organizations and their managers to find new and improved ways to respond in order to maintain and increase their performance. In particular, the recent global recession and financial meltdown have profoundly affected the management of both large and small companies as their managers have sought ways to increase their efficiency and effectiveness to survive in an increasingly competitive global environment.

In revising our book, we also continue our focus on making our text relevant and interesting to students–something that we know from instructor and student feedback engages them and encourages them to make the effort necessary to assimilate the text material. We continue to mirror the changes taking place in management practices by incorporating recent developments in management theory and research into our text and by providing vivid, current examples of how managers of companies large and small have responded to the changes taking place. Indeed, we have made the way managers and organizations have responded to recent economic events a focus of the new edition, and following the last edition many more examples of the opportunities and challenges facing founders, managers, and employees in small businesses are integrated into the text.

The number and complexity of the strategic, organizational, and human resource challenges facing managers and all employees has continued to increase throughout the 2000s. In most companies, managers at all levels are playing catch-up as they work toward meeting these challenges by implementing new and improved management techniques and practices. Today relatively small differences in performance between companies, such as in the speed at which they can bring new products or services to market or in how they motivate their employees to find ways to reduce costs or improve performance, can combine to give one company a significant competitive advantage over another. Managers and companies that use proven management techniques and practices in their decision making and actions increase their effectiveness over time. Companies and managers that are slower to implement new management techniques and practices find themselves at a growing competitive disadvantage that makes it even more difficult to catch up. Thus many industries have widening gaps between weaker competitors and the most successful companies, whose performance reaches new heights because their managers have made better decisions about how to use a company's resources in the most efficient and effective ways.

The challenges facing managers continue to mount as changes in the global environment, such as increasing global outsourcing and rising commodity prices, impact organizations large and small. For example, we extend our treatment of global outsourcing and examine the many managerial issues that must be addressed when millions of functional jobs in information technology, customer service, and manufacturing are sent to countries overseas. Similarly, increasing globalization means managers must respond to major differences in the legal rules and regulations and ethical values and norms that prevail in countries around the globe. Many companies and their managers, for example, have been accused of ignoring "sweatshop" working conditions under which the products they sell are manufactured abroad.

Moreover, the revolution in information technology (IT) has transformed how managers make decisions across all levels of a company's hierarchy and across all its functions and global divisions. This edition of our book continues to address these ongoing challenges as IT continues to evolve rapidly, especially in the area of mobile digital devices such as smartphones and tablet computers that can access ever more sophisticated software applications that increase their functionality. Other major challenges we continue to expand on in the new edition include the impact of the steadily increasing diversity of the workforce on companies, and how this increasing diversity makes it imperative for managers to understand how and why people differ so they can effectively manage and reap the performance benefits of diversity. Similarly, across all functions and levels, managers and employees must continuously search out ways to "work smarter" and increase performance. Using new IT to improve all aspects of an organization's operations to boost efficiency and customer responsiveness is a vital part of this process. So too is the continuing need to innovate and improve the quality of goods and services, and the ways they are produced, to allow an organization to compete effectively. We have significantly revised the seventh edition of *Contemporary Management* to address these challenges to managers and their organizations.

Major Content Changes

Once again, encouraged by the increasing number of instructors and students who are using our book with each new edition, and based on the reactions and suggestions of both users and reviewers, we have revised and updated our book in the following ways. First, just as we have included pertinent new research concepts in each chapter, so too have we been careful to eliminate outdated or marginal management concepts. As usual, our goal has been to streamline our presentation and keep the focus on the changes that have been taking place that have the most impact on managers and organizations. Our goal is to avoid presenting students with excessive content in too many and too long chapters just for the sake of including outmoded management theory. In today's world of video downloads, sound bites, text messaging, and twitters, providing the best content is much more important than providing excessive content–especially when some of our students are burdened by time pressures stemming from the need to work long hours at paying jobs and personal commitments and obligations.

Second, we have added significant new management content, and have reinforced its importance by using many new relevant small and large company examples that are described in new chapter opening cases titled "A Manager's Challenge"; in the many boxed examples featuring managers and employees in companies both large and small in each chapter; and in the new (from 2009 and 2010) "Case in the News" closing cases.

Chapter 1, for example, contains additional material on planning, with particular reference to how changing IT is affecting competition among companies; the chapter includes a new opening case about Steve Jobs and Apple, which is compared to Dell to highlight the four functions of management. It also contains an expanded discussion of outsourcing and its advantages and disadvantages and coverage of ethics and social responsibility using examples from the not-for-profit sphere. There is also new material about global crisis management, including a new box discussing how BP handled a major explosion at an oil refinery in Texas–something particularly relevant given the explosion of its drilling rig and the resulting huge oil spill in the Gulf of Mexico in 2010. Chapter 2 has updated coverage of changing manufacturing practices in the carmaking industry and of the way traditional management theories, such as Theory X and Theory Y, are being modified to suit changing conditions today.

Chapter 3 has additional material about the manager as a person and how personal characteristics of managers (and all members of an organization) influence organizational culture and effectiveness. New and updated material about, for example, changing work attitudes and job satisfaction, the importance of handling layoffs in a compassionate manner, and recent research on moods and emotions and their implications highlights the contemporary landscape of management.

Public concern over the ethical behavior of managers has continued to increase as a result of the major problems caused by the mortgage crisis that started in 2007 and the resulting financial crisis of 2008–2009. Chapter 4 contains updated material about the ethical issues that produced these crises and how regulators are trying to find new ways to manage and reduce the likelihood of such unethical behavior in the future. We have expanded our coverage of the many issues involved in acting and managing ethically throughout the book and especially in Chapter 4, which focuses on "Ethics and Social Responsibility." For example, we discuss new issues in ethics and ethical dilemmas, and provide more conceptual tools to help students understand better how to make ethical decisions. We have expanded coverage of issues relating to the high pay of CEOs, increased coverage of issues concerning regulations to protect consumer safety, and of problems caused by bribery and corruption in companies at home and overseas. Finally, we have expanded coverage of the ethics of nonprofits and their managers. Additionally, the ethical exercise at the end of every chapter continues to be a popular feature of our book.

Chapter 5, "Managing Diverse Employees in a Multicultural Environment," focuses on the effective management of the many faces of diversity in organizations for the good of all stakeholders. We have updated the text material and examples for such issues as gender and the implications of disabilities, sexual orientation, and religion in the workplace; the way the recession has affected poverty and unemployment; and how managers can take advantage of the increasing diversity of the population and workforce to reap the performance benefits that stem from diversity while ensuring that all employees are treated fairly and are not discriminated against. To address current issues in an era when many companies face discrimination lawsuits involving hundreds of millions of dollars, we discuss ways to effectively manage diversity.

Chapter 6 contains an integrated account of forces in both the domestic and global environments. It has also been revised and updated to reflect the way increasing global competition and free trade have changed the global value creation process; the chapter uses competition in the global electronics industry to illustrate these issues. The chapter also has expanded discussion of issues related to global outsourcing and of the movement to insource production back to the United States. Finally, it has new treatment of the dynamics of global competition–particularly in relation to how companies have updated their strategies to customize products to the tastes of customers in countries abroad.

Chapter 7, "Decision Making, Learning, Creativity, and Entrepreneurship," discusses new developments in these important issues. For example, we have expanded our discussion of social entrepreneurs who seek creative ways to address social problems to improve well-being by, for example, reducing poverty, increasing literacy, and protecting the natural environment. More generally, we discuss how managers in organizations large and small can improve decision making, learning, and creativity in their organizations. For example, we discuss using contests and rewards to encourage creativity and examples of current companies that use them.

As in the last edition, Chapter 8 focuses on corporate-, global-, and business-level strategies, and Chapter 9 discusses functional strategies for managing value chain activities. These two chapters make clear the links between the different levels of strategy while maintaining a strong focus on managing operations and processes. Chapter 8 contains an updated discussion of planning and levels of strategy and a revised treatment of business-level strategy that focuses on the importance of low-cost strategies in a recession. It also contains more information about vertical integration and how companies can use forward vertical integration to raise long-term profitability. In Chapter 9 we continue to explore how companies can develop new functional-level strategies to improve efficiency, quality, innovation, and responsiveness to customers. For example, beyond increased coverage of TQM, including the Six Sigma approach, we include an expanded discussion of the importance of customer relationship management and the need to retain customers during hard economic times.

In Chapters 10 and 11 we offer new coverage of organizational structure and control and discuss how companies are confronting the need to reorganize their hierarchies and ways of doing business as the environment changes and competition increases. In Chapter 10, for example, we discuss how companies such as Avon and Pier 1 have reorganized to improve their domestic performance–just as Nokia has reorganized its global operating structure to increase its global sales. There is increased emphasis on designing global organizational structure and the management issues surrounding it–including more coverage of organizational culture. In Chapter 11 we continue this theme by looking at how companies are changing their control systems to increase efficiency and quality, for example. The new opening case highlights Toyota's recent problems and why it lost control over its global quality standards; how to use control systems to increase quality is used as a theme throughout the chapter.

We have updated and expanded our treatment of the many ways in which managers can effectively manage and lead employees in their companies. For example, Chapter 12 includes a discussion of how treating employees well can lead to exceptional customer service, such as at Zappos, profiled in the opening case. The chapter also discusses best practices to recruit and attract outstanding employees, the importance of training and development, pay differentials, and family-friendly benefit programs. As another example, in light of the recent recession, Chapter 13 contains new coverage of how tough economic times can propel people to learn new skills and behaviors but also can lead to cuts in benefits and pay and thus limit managers' ability to provide merit pay and other performance inducements. This chapter also discusses prosocially motivated behavior and examples of people who are prosocially motivated to benefit others by a variety of factors, and more generally, discusses the many steps managers and organizations can take to create a highly motivated workforce.

Chapter 14 highlights the critical importance of effective leadership in organizations and factors that contribute to managers being effective leaders, including an updated discussion of servant leadership using the example of Zingerman's. The chapter also discusses how emotional intelligence may help leaders respond appropriately when they realize they have made a mistake, and has updated examples of how they can use reward and expert power to increase motivation and performance. Expanded and updated coverage of the effective management of teams, including virtual teams, is provided in Chapter 15. The chapter also has new coverage of the problems that arise because of a lack of leadership in teams, especially ethical issues. Chapter 16 includes updated coverage of effective communication and how, given the multitude of advances in IT, it is important to create opportunities for face-to-face communication. There is also a new discussion of social networking sites and why some managers attempt to limit employees' access to them while at work.

Chapter 17 includes an updated discussion of the vital task of effectively managing conflict and politics in organizations and how to negotiate effectively on a global level. There are many new examples of how managers can create a collaborative work context and avoid competition between individuals and groups, such as by building alliances as Indra Nooyi does at PepsiCo.

Finally, Chapter 18 has been substantially revised and updated to discuss the changing nature of companywide total computing solutions–including a new opening case that discusses the growing importance of cloud computing and the use of mobile storage server containers to create companywide remote data centers. There is also an expanded discussion of the nature of server computers and how they can be used to connect to mobile digital devices such as tablet computers and smartphones to enhance competitive advantage. The chapter also contains increased coverage of the ethical issues involved in the decision to outsource computer component and assembly operations to companies in China that do not follow the guidelines established by companies such as Apple.

We feel confident that the major changes we have made to the seventh edition of *Contemporary Management* reflect the changes that are occurring in management and the workplace; we also believe they offer an account of management that will stimulate and challenge students to think about their future as they look for opportunities in the world of organizations.

Unique Emphasis on Contemporary, Applied Management

In revising our book, we have kept at the forefront the fact that our users and reviewers are supportive of our attempts to integrate contemporary management theories and issues into the analysis of management and organizations. As in previous editions, our goal has been to distill new and classic theorizing and research into a contemporary framework that is compatible with the traditional focus on management as planning, leading, organizing, and controlling but that transcends this traditional approach.

Users and reviewers report that students appreciate and enjoy our presentation of management–a presentation that makes its relevance obvious even to those who lack exposure to a real-life management context. Students like the book's content and the way we relate management theory to real-life examples to drive home the message that management matters both because it determines how well organizations perform and because managers and organizations affect the lives of people inside and outside the organization, such as employees, customers, and shareholders.

Our contemporary approach has led us to discuss many concepts and issues that are not addressed in other management textbooks and is also illustrated by the way we organize and discuss these management issues. We have gone to great lengths to bring the manager back into the subject matter of management. That is, we have written our chapters from the perspective of current or future managers to illustrate, in a hands-on way, the problems and opportunities they face and how they can effectively meet them. For example, in Chapter 3 we provide an integrated treatment of personality, attitudes, emotions, and culture; in Chapter 4, a focus on ethics from a student's and a manager's perspective; and in Chapter 5, an in-depth treatment of effectively managing diversity and eradicating sexual harassment. In Chapters 8 and 9, our integrated treatment of strategy highlights the multitude of decisions managers must make as they perform their most important role–increasing organizational efficiency, effectiveness, and performance.

Our applied approach can also be clearly seen in the last three chapters of the book, which cover the topics of promoting effective communication; managing organizational conflict, politics, and negotiation; and using information technology in ways that increase organizational performance. These chapters provide a student-friendly, behavioral approach to understanding the management issues entailed in persuasive communication, negotiation, and implementation of advanced information systems to build competitive advantage.

Flexible Organization

Another factor of interest to instructors is how we have designed the grouping of chapters to allow instructors to teach the chapter material in the order that best suits their needs. For example, the more micro-oriented instructor can follow Chapters 1 through 5 with Chapters 12 through 16 and then use the more macro chapters. The more macro-oriented professor can follow Chapters 1 and 2 with Chapters 6 through 11, jump to 16 through 18, and then use the micro chapters, 3 through 5 and 12 through 15. Our sequencing of parts and chapters gives instructors considerable freedom to design the course that best suits their needs. Instructors are not tied to the planning, organizing, leading, and controlling framework, even though our presentation remains consistent with this approach.

ACKNOWLEDGMENTS

Finding a way to integrate and present the rapidly growing literature about contemporary management and make it interesting and meaningful for students is not an easy task. In writing and revising the various drafts of *Contemporary Management*, we have been fortunate to have the assistance of several people who have contributed greatly to the book's final form. First, we are grateful to Michael Ablassmeir, our senior sponsoring editor, for his ongoing support and commitment to our project and for always finding ways to provide the resources that we needed to continually improve and refine our book. Second, we are grateful to Trina Hauger, our developmental editor, for so ably coordinating the book's progress; and to her and Anke Braun Weekes, our senior marketing manager, for giving us concise and timely feedback and information from professors and reviewers that have allowed us to shape the book to the needs of its intended market. We also thank Cara Hawthorne for executing an awe-inspiring design; Bruce Gin for coordinating the production process; Margaret Richardson de Sosa (Rice University) and Patsy Hartmangruber (Texas A&M University) for providing excellent word-processing and graphic support; and Iliya Atanasov (Rice University) for his assistance with research. We are also grateful to the many colleagues and reviewers who gave us useful and detailed feedback and perceptive comments and valuable suggestions for improving the manuscript.

Producing any competitive work is a challenge. Producing a truly market-driven textbook requires tremendous effort beyond simply obtaining reviews of a draft manuscript. Our goal was simple with the development of *Contemporary Management*: to be the most customer-driven principles of management text and supplement package ever published! With the goal of exceeding the expectations of both faculty and students, we executed one of the most aggressive product development plans ever undertaken in textbook publishing. Hundreds of faculty have taken part in developmental activities ranging from regional focus groups to manuscript and supplement reviews and surveys. Consequently, we're confident in assuring you and your students, our customers, that every aspect of our text and support package reflects your advice and needs. As you review it, we're confident that your reaction will be, "They listened!"

We extend our special thanks to the faculty who gave us detailed chapter-by-chapter feedback during the development of the seventh edition:

Jerry Alley, Aspen University

Charles W. Beem, Bucks County Community College

Jennifer P. Bott, Ball State University

Professor Murray Brunton, Central Ohio Technical College

Judith G. Bulin, PhD, Monroe Community College, Rochester, New York

Cheryl Cunningham, Embry-Riddle Aeronautical University–Daytona Beach

Tom Deckelman, Owens Community College

Max E. Douglas, Indiana State University

Richard Estrella, California Polytechnic University

Valerie Evans, Kansas State University

Andrea Foster, John Tyler Community College

Travis Lee Hayes, Chattanooga State Technical Community College

Samuel Hazen, Tarleton State University

Irene Joanette-Gallio, Western Nevada College

Dr. Carol Larson Jones, Professor, Cal Poly Pomona, California

Coy A. Jones, The University of Memphis

Dr. Jordan J. Kaplan, Long Island University School of Business

Renee N. King, MBA, Eastern Illinois University

Mike Knudstrup, Florida Southern College

Jim Long, Southwestern Oklahoma State University

Margaret Lucero, Texas A&M–Corpus Christi

Christy McLendon Corey, University of New Orleans

Chrisann Merriman, University of Mary Hardin–Baylor

Sandra Jeanquart Miles, DBA, SPHR, Professor, Murray State University

Carol T. Miller, Community College of Denver

Bahaudin G. Mujtaba, Nova Southeastern University

Catherine Nowicki, International Business College

John Overby, The University of Tennessee at Martin

Professor KE Overton, Houston Community College, Houston, Texas

Fernando A. Pargas, James Madison University

Marc Pendel, SPHR, Instructor, Miller College of Business, Ball State University

Susan A. Peterson, Professor of Business, Scottsdale Community College

Gregory J. Schultz, Carroll University

Marc Siegall, California State University–Chico

Randi L. Sims, Professor, Nova Southeastern University

Professor Gerald Smith, University of Northern Iowa

Marjorie Smith, Mountain State University

Dr. Susan D. Steiner, The University of Tampa

Cynthia L. Sutton, Metropolitan State College of Denver

And our thanks also go to the faculty who contributed greatly to the fourth, fifth, and sixth editions of *Contemporary Management*:

M. Ruhul Amin, Bloomsburg University of Pennsylvania

Gerald Baumgardner, Pennsylvania College of Technology

James D. Bell, Texas State University

Danielle R. Blesi, Hudson Valley Community College

Charley Braun, Marshall University

Barry Bunn, Valencia Community College

Gerald Calvasina, Southern Utah University

Bruce H. Charnov, Hofstra University

Jay Christensen-Szalanski, University of Iowa

Brad Cox, Midlands Technical College

Marian Cox Crawford, University of Arkansas–Little Rock

Teresa A. Daniel, Marshall University

Thomas W. Deckelman, Owens Community College

Richard S. DeFrank, University of Houston

Fred J. Dorn, University of Mississippi

D. Harold Doty, University of Southern Mississippi

Sandra Edwards, Northeastern State University

Scott Elston, Iowa State University

Kim Hester, Arkansas State University

Anne Kelly Hoel, University of Wisconsin–Stout

Robert C. Hoell, Georgia Southern University

Carol Larson Jones, Cal Poly Pomona, California

Gwendolyn Jones, University of Akron

Kathleen Jones, University of North Dakota

Joanne E. Kapp, Siena College

Nicholas Mathys, DePaul University

Daniel W. McAllister, University of Nevada–Las Vegas

Douglas L. Micklich, Illinois State University

Don C. Mosley Jr., University of South Alabama

Clive Muir, Stetson University

Karen Overton, Houston Community College

Gary Renz, Webster University

L. Jeff Seaton, University of Tennessee–Martin

Fred Slack, Indiana University of Pennsylvania

M. James Smas, Kent State University

Sabine Turnley, Kansas State University

Isaiah O. Ugboro, North Carolina A&T State University

Please note that these lists do not include the more than 160 faculty members who reviewed or contributed to earlier editions of the text.

Finally, we are grateful to two incredibly wonderful children, Nicholas and Julia, for being all that they are and for the joy they bring to all who know them.

Gareth R. Jones
Mays Business School
Texas A&M University

Jennifer M. George
Jesse H. Jones Graduate School of Business
Rice University

Rich and Relevant Examples An important feature of our book is the way we use real-world examples and stories about managers and companies to drive home the applied lessons to students. Our reviewers praised the sheer range and depth of the rich, interesting examples we use to illustrate the chapter material and make it come alive. Moreover, unlike boxed material in other books, our boxes are seamlessly integrated into the text; they are an integral part of the learning experience and are not tacked on or isolated from the text itself. This is central to our pedagogical approach.

A Manager's Challenge opens each chapter, posing a chapter-related challenge and then discussing how managers in one or more organizations responded to that challenge. These vignettes help demonstrate the uncertainty and excitement surrounding the management process.

Our box features are not traditional boxes; that is, they are not disembodied from the chapter narrative. These thematic applications are fully integrated into the reading. Students will no longer be forced to decide whether or not to read boxed material. These features are interesting and engaging for students while bringing the chapter contents to life.

A MANAGER'S CHALLENGE

Values of a Founder Live On at PAETEC

How can managers create and sustain a caring culture while ensuring their organization's growth and effectiveness? PAETEC Communications is a broadband telecommunications company that provides local and long distance voice, data, and broadband Internet services to businesses in 84 markets across the United States.[1] When PAETEC was founded in 1998, it had fewer than 20 employees and revenues of only $150,000; today it has over 3,600 employees and over $1 billion in revenues.[2] Moreover, this phenomenal rate of growth occurred while the telecommunications industry lost hundreds of thousands of jobs.[3] PAETEC's amazing growth trajectory has not gone without notice; the company recently was included on Deloitte's 2009 Fast 500™ Ranking, which ranks the technology industry's top 500 fastest-growing companies in North America.[4]

PAETEC's growth and ongoing success are a tribute to the values of its five founders and the culture they created.[5] In particular, Arunas Chesonis, one of the founders and its current chairman and CEO, ensures that PAETEC's values are upheld by using them to guide the way he manages every day. The four core values of PAETEC are "a caring culture, open communication, unmatched service, and personalized solutions."[6] The ways in which these values are enacted daily result in a satisfied, motivated, and loyal workforce whose members have developed a unique and distinct approach to the way they perform their jobs.[7]

An overarching principle at PAETEC is that people—employees and customers—come first.[8] Chesonis believes that when a company takes good care of its employees, they

PAETEC founder and current CEO Arunas Chesonis believes that when a company takes good care of its employees, they will take good care of their customers.

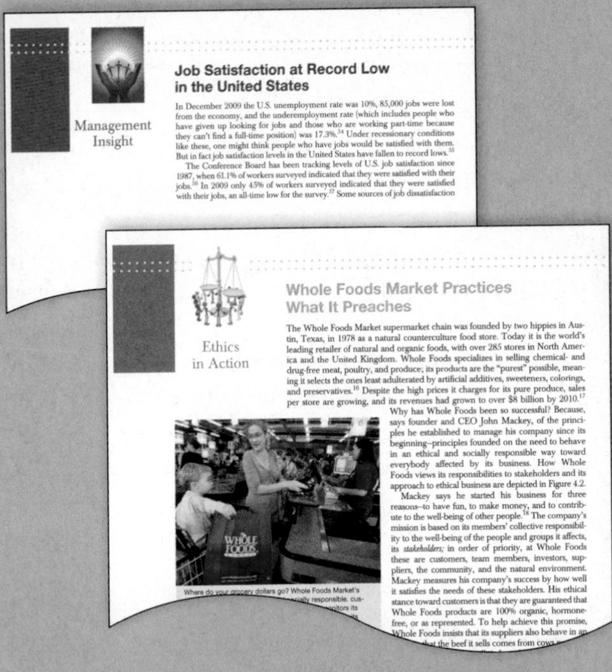

Management Insight

Job Satisfaction at Record Low in the United States

In December 2009 the U.S. unemployment rate was 10%, 85,000 jobs were lost from the economy, and the underemployment rate (which includes people who have given up looking for jobs and those who are working part-time because they can't find a full-time position) was 17.3%.[54] Under recessionary conditions like these, one might think people who have jobs would be satisfied with them. But in fact job satisfaction levels in the United States have fallen to record lows.[55]

The Conference Board has been tracking levels of U.S. job satisfaction since 1987, when 61.1% of workers surveyed indicated that they were satisfied with their jobs.[56] In 2009 only 45% of workers surveyed indicated that they were satisfied with their jobs, an all-time low for the survey.[57] Some sources of job dissatisfaction

Ethics in Action

Whole Foods Market Practices What It Preaches

The Whole Foods Market supermarket chain was founded by two hippies in Austin, Texas, in 1978 as a natural counterculture food store. Today it is the world's leading retailer of natural and organic foods, with over 285 stores in North America and the United Kingdom. Whole Foods specializes in selling chemical- and drug-free meat, poultry, and produce; its products are the "purest" possible, meaning it selects the ones least adulterated by artificial additives, sweeteners, colorings, and preservatives.[16] Despite the high prices it charges for its pure produce, sales per store are growing, and its revenues had grown to over $8 billion by 2010.[17]

Why has Whole Foods been so successful? Because, says founder and CEO John Mackey, of the principles he established to manage his company since its beginning–principles founded on the need to behave in an ethical and socially responsible way toward everybody affected by its business. How Whole Foods views its responsibilities to stakeholders and its approach to ethical business are depicted in Figure 4.2.

Mackey says he started his business for three reasons–to have fun, to make money, and to contribute to the well-being of other people.[18] The company's mission is based on its members' collective responsibility to the well-being of the people and groups it affects, its *stakeholders;* in order of priority, at Whole Foods these are customers, team members, investors, suppliers, the community, and the natural environment. Mackey measures his company's success by how well it satisfies the needs of these stakeholders. His ethical stance toward customers is that they are guaranteed that Whole Foods products are 100% organic, hormone-free, or as represented. To help achieve this promise, Whole Foods insists that its suppliers also behave in an ... the beef it sells comes from cows ...

Where do your grocery dollars go? Whole Foods Market's ... responsible. cus- ... itors its

Additional in-depth examples appear in boxes throughout each chapter. **Management Insight** boxes illustrate the topics of the chapter, while the **Ethics in Action, Managing Globally, Focus on Diversity, and Information Technology Byte** boxes examine the chapter topics from each of these perspectives.

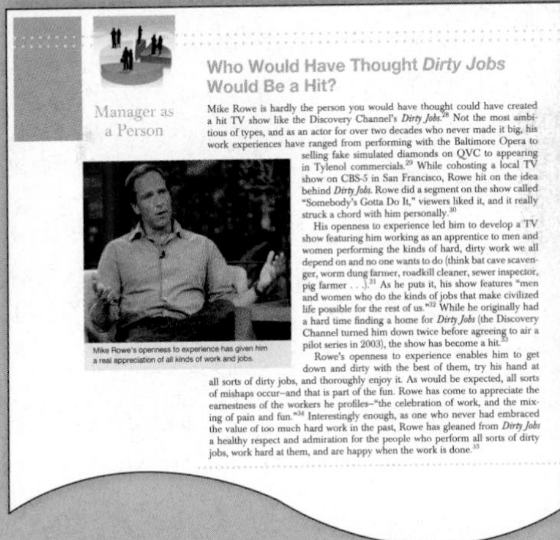

Manager as a Person

Who Would Have Thought *Dirty Jobs* Would Be a Hit?

Mike Rowe is hardly the person you would have thought could have created a hit TV show like the Discovery Channel's *Dirty Jobs.*[28] Not the most ambitious of types, and as an actor for over two decades who never made it big, his work experiences have ranged from performing with the Baltimore Opera to selling fake simulated diamonds on QVC to appearing in Tylenol commercials.[29] While cohosting a local TV show on CBS-5 in San Francisco, Rowe hit on the idea behind *Dirty Jobs.* Rowe did a segment on the show called "Somebody's Gotta Do It," viewers liked it, and it really struck a chord with him personally.[30]

His openness to experience led him to develop a TV show featuring him working as an apprentice to men and women performing the kinds of hard, dirty work we all depend on and no one wants to do (think bat cave scavenger, worm dung farmer, roadkill cleaner, sewer inspector, pig farmer . . .).[31] As he puts it, his show features "men and women who do the kinds of jobs that make civilized life possible for the rest of us."[32] While he originally had a hard time finding a home for *Dirty Jobs* (the Discovery Channel turned him down twice before agreeing to air a pilot series in 2003), the show has become a hit.[33]

Rowe's openness to experience enables him to get down and dirty with the best of them, try his hand at all sorts of dirty jobs, and thoroughly enjoy it. As would be expected, all sorts of mishaps occur–and that is part of the fun. Rowe has come to appreciate the earnestness of the workers he profiles–"the celebration of work, and the mixing of pain and fun."[34] Interestingly enough, as one who never had embraced the value of too much hard work in the past, Rowe has gleaned from *Dirty Jobs* a healthy respect and admiration for the people who perform all sorts of dirty jobs, work hard at them, and are happy when the work is done.[35]

Mike Rowe's openness to experience has given him a real appreciation of all kinds of work and jobs.

Further emphasizing the unique content covered in Chapter 3, Values, Attitudes, Emotions, and Culture: The Manager as a Person, the **Manager as a Person** boxes focus on how real managers brought about change within their organizations. These examples allow us to reflect on how individual managers dealt with real-life, on-the-job challenges related to various chapter concepts.

Small Business Examples To ensure that students see the clear connections between the concepts taught in their Principles of Management course and the application in their future jobs in a medium or small business, Jones and George have expanded the number of examples of the opportunities and challenges facing founders, managers, and employees in small businesses.

Experiential Learning Features

We have given considerable time and effort to developing state-of-the-art experiential end-of-chapter learning exercises that drive home the meaning of management to students. These exercises are grouped together at the end of each chapter in a section called "Management in Action." The following activities are included at the end of every chapter:

- **Topics for Discussion and Action** are a set of chapter-related questions and points for reflection. Some ask students to research actual management issues and learn firsthand from practicing managers.
- **Building Management Skills** is a self-developed exercise that asks students to apply what they have learned from their own experience in organizations and from managers or from the experiences of others.
- **Managing Ethically** is an exercise that presents students with an ethical scenario or dilemma and asks them to think about the issue from an ethical perspective to better understand the issues facing practicing managers.
- **Small Group Breakout Exercise** is designed to allow instructors in large classes to use interactive experiential exercises.
- **Exploring the World Wide Web** requires students to actively search the Web to find the answers to a problem.
- **Be the Manager** presents a realistic scenario where a manager or organization faces some kind of challenge, problem, or opportunity. These exercises provide students with a hands-on way of solving "real" problems by applying what they've just learned in the chapter.

Each chapter ends with a

- **Case in the News** that is an actual or shortened version of a *BusinessWeek* or *Wall Street Journal* article. The concluding questions encourage students to think about how real managers deal with problems in the business world.

Assurance of Learning Ready

Many educational institutions today are focused on the notion of assurance of learning, an important element of some accreditation standards. *Contemporary Management, Seventh Edition,* is designed specifically to support your assurance of learning initiatives with a simple yet powerful solution.

Each test bank question for *Contemporary Management* maps to a specific chapter learning outcome/objective listed in the text. You can use our test bank software, EZ Test and EZ Test Online, or *Connect Management* to easily query for learning outcomes/objectives that directly relate to the learning objectives for your course. You can then use the reporting features of EZ Test to aggregate student results in similar fashion, making the collection and presentation of assurance of learning data simple and easy.

AACSB Statement

The McGraw-Hill Companies are a proud corporate member of AACSB International. To support the importance and value of AACSB accreditation, *Contemporary Management, Seventh Edition,* recognizes the curricula guidelines detailed in the AACSB standards for business accreditation by connecting selected questions in the text and/or the test bank to the six general knowledge and skill guidelines in the AACSB standards.

The statements contained in *Contemporary Management, Seventh Edition,* are provided only as a guide for the users of this textbook. The AACSB leaves content coverage and assessment within the purview of individual schools, the mission of the school, and the faculty. While *Contemporary Management* and the teaching package make no claim of any specific AACSB qualification or evaluation, we have within *Contemporary Management* labeled selected questions according to the six general knowledge and skill areas.

Integrated Learning System

Great care was used in the creation of the supplementary material to accompany *Contemporary Management.* Whether you are a seasoned faculty member or a newly minted instructor, you'll find our support materials to be the most thorough and thoughtful ever created:

- **Instructor's Resource CD-ROM** The IRCD allows instructors to easily create their own custom presentations using the following resources: Instructor's Manual, Test Bank, EZ Test, and PowerPoint® presentations.
- **Instructor's Manual (IM)** The IM supporting this text has been completely updated to save instructors' time and support them in delivering the most effective course to their students. For each chapter, this manual provides a chapter overview and lecture outline with integrated PowerPoint® slides, lecture enhancers, notes for end-of-chapter materials, video cases and teaching notes, and more.
- **PowerPoint® Presentation** 40 slides per chapter feature reproductions of key tables and figures from the text as well as original content. Lecture-enhancing additions such as quick polling questions and company or video examples from outside the text can be used to generate discussion and illustrate management concepts.
- **Test Bank and EZ Test** The test bank has been thoroughly reviewed, revised, and improved. There are approximately 100 questions per chapter, including true/false, multiple-choice, and essay. Each question is tagged with learning objective, level of difficulty (corresponding to Bloom's taxonomy of educational objectives), AACSB standards, the correct answer, and page references. The new AACSB tags allow instructors to sort questions by the various standards and create reports to help give assurance that they are including recommended learning experiences in their curricula.

McGraw-Hill's flexible and easy-to-use electronic testing program **EZ Test** (found on the IRCD) allows instructors to create tests from book-specific items. It accommodates a wide range of question types, and instructors may add their own questions. Multiple versions of the test can be created, and any test can be exported for use with course management systems such as WebCT or BlackBoard. And now **EZ Test Online** (**www.eztestonline.com**) allows you to access the test bank virtually anywhere at any time, without installation, and it's even easier to use. Additionally, it allows you to administer EZ Test–created exams and quizzes online, providing instant feedback for students.

McGraw-Hill *Connect Management*

Less Managing. More Teaching. Greater Learning.

McGraw-Hill *Connect Management* is an online assignment and assessment solution that connects students with the tools and resources they'll need to achieve success.

McGraw-Hill *Connect Management* helps prepare students for their future by enabling faster learning, more efficient studying, and higher retention of knowledge.

McGraw-Hill *Connect Management* Features

Connect Management offers a number of powerful tools and features to make managing assignments easier, so faculty can spend more time teaching. With *Connect Management,* students can engage with their coursework anytime and anywhere, making the learning process more accessible and efficient. *Connect Management* offers you the features described below.

Diagnostic and Adaptive Learning of Concepts: LearnSmart

Students want to make the best use of their study time. The LearnSmart adaptive self-study technology within *Connect Management* provides students with a seamless combination of practice, assessment, and remediation for every concept in the textbook. LearnSmart's intelligent software adapts to every student response and automatically delivers concepts that advance the student's understanding while reducing time devoted to the concepts already mastered. The result for every student is the fastest path to mastery of the chapter concepts. LearnSmart

- Applies an intelligent concept engine to identify the relationships between concepts and to serve new concepts to each student only when he or she is ready.
- Adapts automatically to each student, so students spend less time on the topics they understand and practice more those they have yet to master.
- Provides continual reinforcement and remediation, but gives only as much guidance as students need.
- Integrates diagnostics as part of the learning experience.
- Enables you to assess which concepts students have efficiently learned on their own, thus freeing class time for more applications and discussion.

Online Interactive Applications

Online Interactive Applications are engaging tools that teach students to apply key concepts in practice. These Interactive Applications provide them with immersive, experiential learning opportunities. Students will engage in a variety of interactive scenarios to deepen critical knowledge of key course topics. They receive immediate feedback at intermediate steps throughout each exercise, as well as comprehensive feedback at the end of the assignment. All Interactive Applications are automatically scored and entered into the instructor gradebook.

Student Progress Tracking

Connect Management keeps instructors informed about how each student, section, and class is performing, allowing for more productive use of lecture and office hours. The progress-tracking function enables you to

- View scored work immediately and track individual or group performance with assignment and grade reports.
- Access an instant view of student or class performance relative to learning objectives.
- Collect data and generate reports required by many accreditation organizations, such as AACSB.

Smart Grading

When it comes to studying, time is precious. *Connect Management* helps students learn more efficiently by providing feedback and practice material when they need it, where they need it. When it comes to teaching, your time also is precious. The grading function enables you to

- Have assignments scored automatically, giving students immediate feedback on their work and side-by-side comparisons with correct answers.
- Access and review each response; manually change grades or leave comments for students to review.
- Reinforce classroom concepts with practice tests and instant quizzes.

Simple Assignment Management

With *Connect Management,* creating assignments is easier than ever, so you can spend more time teaching and less time managing. The assignment management function enables you to

- Create and deliver assignments easily with selectable end-of-chapter questions and test bank items.
- Streamline lesson planning, student progress reporting, and assignment grading to make classroom management more efficient than ever.
- Go paperless with the eBook and online submission and grading of student assignments.

Instructor Library

The *Connect Management* Instructor Library is your repository for additional resources to improve student engagement in and out of class. You can select and use any asset that enhances your lecture. The *Connect Management* Instructor Library includes

- Instructor Manual.
- PowerPoint® files.
- TestBank.
- Management Asset Gallery.
- eBook.

Student Study Center

The *Connect Management* Student Study Center is the place for students to access additional resources. The Student Study Center

- Offers students quick access to lectures, practice materials, eBooks, and more.
- Provides instant practice material and study questions, easily accessible on the go.
- Give students access to self-assessments, video materials, Manager's Hot Seat, and more.

Lecture Capture via Tegrity Campus

Increase the attention paid to lecture discussion by decreasing the attention paid to note taking. For an additional charge, Lecture Capture offers new ways for students to focus on the in-class discussion, knowing they can revisit important topics later.

McGraw-Hill *Connect Plus Management*

McGraw-Hill reinvents the textbook learning experience for the modern student with *Connect Plus Management.* A seamless integration of an eBook and *Management, Connect Plus Management* provides all of the *Connect Management* features plus the following:

- An integrated eBook, allowing for anytime, anywhere access to the textbook.
- Dynamic links between the problems or questions you assign to your students and the location in the eBook where that problem or question is covered.
- A powerful search function to pinpoint and connect key concepts in a snap.

In short, *Connect Management* offers you and your students powerful tools and features that optimize your time and energies, enabling you to focus on course content, teaching, and student learning. *Connect Management* also offers a wealth of content resources for both instructors and students. This state-of-the-art, thoroughly tested system supports you in preparing students for the world that awaits.

For more information about *Connect,* go to **www.mcgrawhillconnect.com**, or contact your local McGraw-Hill sales representative.

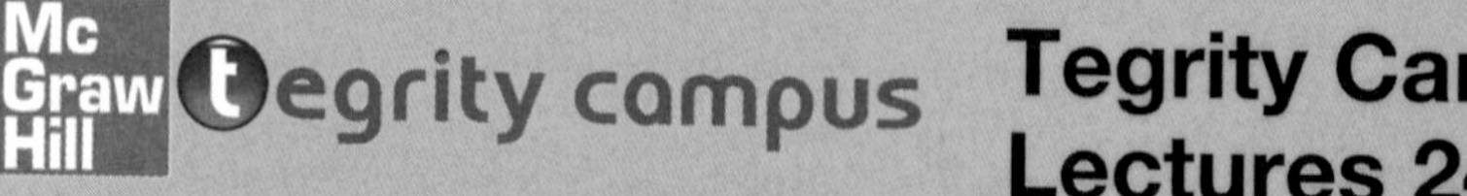

Tegrity Campus: Lectures 24/7

Tegrity Campus is a service that makes class time available 24/7 by automatically capturing every lecture in a searchable format for students to review when they study and complete assignments. With a simple one-click start-and-stop process, you capture all computer screens and corresponding audio. Students can replay any part of any class with easy-to-use browser-based viewing on a PC or Mac.

Educators know that the more students can see, hear, and experience class resources, the better they learn. In fact, studies prove it. With Tegrity Campus, students quickly recall key moments by using Tegrity Campus's unique search feature. This search helps students efficiently find what they need, when they need it, across an entire semester of class recordings. Help turn all your students' study time into learning moments immediately supported by your lecture.

Lecture Capture enables you to

- Record and distribute your lecture with a click of button.
- Record and index PowerPoint® presentations and anything shown on your computer so it is easily searchable, frame by frame.
- Offer access to lectures anytime and anywhere by computer, iPod, or mobile device.
- Increase intent listening and class participation by easing students' concerns about note taking. Lecture Capture will make it more likely you will see students' faces, not the tops of their heads.

To learn more about Tegrity, watch a two-minute Flash demo at **http://tegritycampus.mhhe.com.**

McGraw-Hill Customer Care Contact Information

At McGraw-Hill, we understand that getting the most from new technology can be challenging. That's why our services don't stop after you purchase our products. You can e-mail our product specialists 24 hours a day to get product training online. Or you can search our knowledge bank of Frequently Asked Questions on our support Web site. For customer support, call **800-331-5094,** e-mail **hmsupport@mcgraw-hill.com**, or visit **www.mhhe.com**/support. One of our technical support analysts will be able to assist you in a timely fashion.

SUPPORT MATERIALS

McGraw-Hill's Expanded Management Asset Gallery!

McGraw-Hill/Irwin Management is excited to now provide a one-stop shop for our wealth of assets, making it quick and easy for instructors to locate specific materials to enhance their courses.

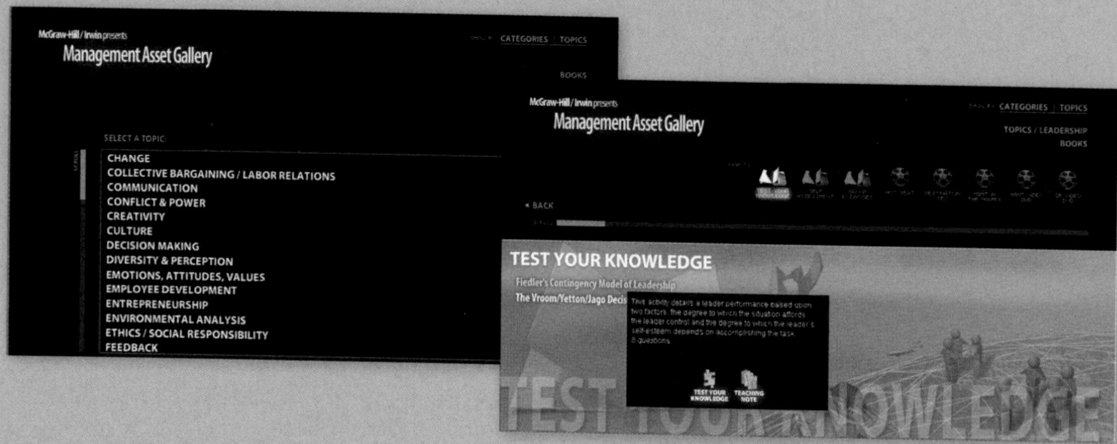

All of the following can be accessed within the Management Asset Gallery:

Manager's Hot Seat

This interactive, video-based application puts students in the manager's hot seat, builds critical thinking and decision-making skills, and allows students to apply concepts to real managerial challenges. Students watch as 15 real managers apply their years of experience when confronting unscripted issues such as bullying in the workplace, cyber loafing, globalization, intergenerational work conflicts, workplace violence, and leadership versus management.

Self-Assessment Gallery Unique among publisher-provided self-assessments, our 23 self-assessments give students background information to ensure that they understand the purpose of the assessment. Students test their values, beliefs, skills, and interests in a wide variety of areas, allowing them to personally apply chapter content to their own lives and careers.

Every self-assessment is supported with PowerPoints® and an instructor manual in the Management Asset Gallery, making it easy for the instructor to create an engaging classroom discussion surrounding the assessments.

Test Your Knowledge To help reinforce students' understanding of key management concepts, Test Your Knowledge activities give students a review of the conceptual materials followed by application-based questions to work through. Students can choose practice mode, which gives them detailed feedback after each question, or test mode, which provides feedback after the entire test has been completed. Every Test Your Knowledge activity is supported by instructor notes in the Management Asset Gallery to make it easy for the instructor to create engaging classroom discussions surrounding that materials that students have completed.

Management History Timeline This Web application allows instructors to present and students to learn the history of management in an engaging and interactive way. Management history is presented along an intuitive timeline that can be traveled through sequentially or by selected decade. With the click of a mouse, students learn the important dates, see the people who influenced the field, and understand the general management theories that have molded and shaped management as we know it today.

Video Library DVDs McGraw-Hill/Irwin offers the most comprehensive video support for the Principles of Management classroom through course library video DVDs. This discipline has library volume DVDs tailored to integrate and visually reinforce chapter concepts. The library volume DVDs contain more than 70 clips! The rich video material, organized by topic, comes from sources such as *BusinessWeek* TV, PBS, NBC, BBC, SHRM, and McGraw-Hill. Video cases and video guides are provided for some clips.

Destination CEO Videos

BusinessWeek produced video clips featuring CEOs on a variety of topics. Accompanying each clip are multiple-choice questions and discussion questions to use in the classroom or assign as a quiz.

Online Learning Center (OLC)

www.mhhe.com/jonesgeorge7e

Find a variety of online teaching and learning tools that are designed to reinforce and build on the text content. Students will have direct access to the learning tools while instructor materials are password protected.

eBook Options

eBooks are an innovative way for students to save money and to "go green." McGraw-Hill's eBooks are typically 40% off the bookstore price. Students have the choice between an online and a downloadable CourseSmart eBook.

Through CourseSmart, students have the flexibility to access an exact replica of their textbook from any computer that has Internet service without plug-ins or special software via the online version, or to create a library of books on their hard drive via the downloadable version. Access to the CourseSmart eBooks lasts for one year.

Features CourseSmart eBooks allow students to highlight, take notes, organize notes, and share the notes with other CourseSmart users. Students can also search for terms across all eBooks in their purchased CourseSmart library. CourseSmart eBooks can be printed (five pages at a time).

More info and purchase Please visit **www.coursesmart.com** for more information and to purchase access to our eBooks. CourseSmart allows students to try one chapter of the eBook, free of charge, before purchase.

Mc Graw Hill create

Create Craft your teaching resources to match the way you teach! With McGraw-Hill Create, **www.mcgrawhillcreate.com**, you can easily rearrange chapters, combine material from other content sources, and quickly upload content you have written, like your course syllabus or teaching notes. Find the content you need in Create by searching through thousands of leading McGraw-Hill textbooks. Arrange your book to fit your teaching style. Create even allows you to personalize your book's appearance by selecting the cover and adding your name, school, and course information. Order a Create book and you'll receive a complimentary print review copy in three to five business days or a complimentary electronic review copy (eComp) via e-mail in about one hour. Go to **www.mcgrawhillcreate.com** today and register. Experience how McGraw-Hill Create empowers you to teach *your* students *your* way.

AUTHORS

Gareth Jones is a Professor of Management in the Lowry Mays College and Graduate School of Business at Texas A&M University. He received his BA in Economics/Psychology and his PhD in Management from the University of Lancaster, U.K. He previously held teaching and research appointments at the University of Warwick, Michigan State University, and the University of Illinois at Urbana–Champaign. He is a frequent visitor and speaker at universities in both the United Kingdom and the United States.

He specializes in strategic management and organizational theory and is well known for his research that applies transaction cost analysis to explain many forms of strategic and organizational behavior. He is currently interested in strategy process, competitive advantage, and information technology issues. He is also investigating the relationships between ethics, trust, and organizational culture and studying the role of affect in the strategic decision-making process.

He has published many articles in leading journals of the field, and his recent work has appeared in the *Academy of Management Review,* the *Journal of International Business Studies,* and *Human Relations.* An article about the role of information technology in many aspects of organizational functioning was published in the *Journal of Management.* One of his articles won the *Academy of Management Journal's* Best Paper Award, and he is one of the most prolific authors in the *Academy of Management Review.* He is, or has served, on the editorial boards of the *Academy of Management Review,* the *Journal of Management,* and *Management Inquiry.*

Gareth Jones has used his academic knowledge to craft leading textbooks in management and three other major areas in the management discipline: organizational behavior, organizational theory, and strategic management. His books are widely recognized for their innovative, contemporary content and for the clarity with which they communicate complex, real-world issues to students.

Jennifer George is the Mary Gibbs Jones Professor of Management and Professor of Psychology in the Jesse H. Jones Graduate School of Business at Rice University. She received her BA in Psychology/Sociology from Wesleyan University, her MBA in Finance from New York University, and her PhD in Management and Organizational Behavior from New York University. Prior to joining the faculty at Rice University, she was a professor in the Department of Management at Texas A&M University.

Professor George specializes in organizational behavior and is well known for her research on mood and emotion in the workplace, their determinants, and their effects on various individual and group-level work outcomes. She is the author of many articles in leading peer-reviewed journals such as the *Academy of Management Journal,* the *Academy of Management Review,* the *Journal of Applied Psychology, Organizational Behavior and Human Decision Processes, Journal of Personality and Social Psychology,* and *Psychological Bulletin.* One of her papers won the Academy of Management's Organizational Behavior Division Outstanding Competitive Paper Award, and another paper won the Human Relations Best Paper Award. She is, or has been, on the editorial review boards of the *Journal of Applied Psychology, Academy of Management Journal, Academy of Management Review, Administrative Science Quarterly, Journal of Management, Organizational Behavior and Human Decision Processes, Organization Science, International Journal of Selection and Assessment,* and *Journal of Managerial Issues;* was a consulting editor for the *Journal of Organizational Behavior;* and was a member of the SIOP *Organizational Frontiers Series* editorial board. She is a fellow in the American Psychological Association, the American Psychological Society, and the Society for Industrial and Organizational Psychology and a member of the Society for Organizational Behavior. Professor George recently completed a six-year term as an associate editor for the *Journal of Applied Psychology.* She also has coauthored a widely used textbook titled *Understanding and Managing Organizational Behavior.*

Contemporary Management

CHAPTER 1

Managers and Managing

Learning Objectives

After studying this chapter, you should be able to:

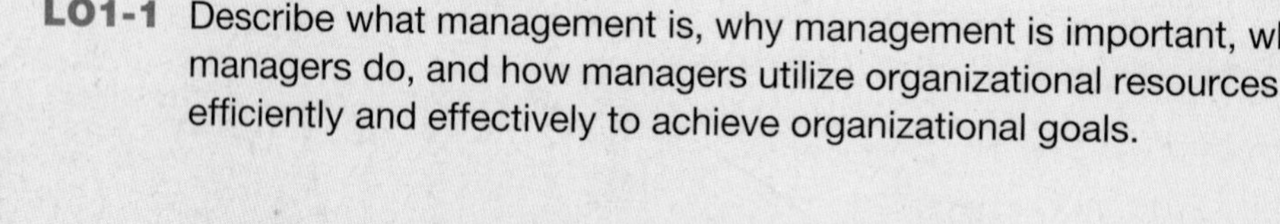

LO1-1 Describe what management is, why management is important, what managers do, and how managers utilize organizational resources efficiently and effectively to achieve organizational goals.

LO1-2 Distinguish among planning, organizing, leading, and controlling (the four principal managerial tasks), and explain how managers' ability to handle each one affects organizational performance.

LO1-3 Differentiate among three levels of management, and understand the tasks and responsibilities of managers at different levels in the organizational hierarchy.

LO1-4 Distinguish between three kinds of managerial skill, and explain why managers are divided into different departments to perform their tasks more efficiently and effectively.

LO1-5 Discuss some major changes in management practices today that have occurred as a result of globalization and the use of advanced information technology (IT).

LO1-6 Discuss the principal challenges managers face in today's increasingly competitive global environment.

A MANAGER'S CHALLENGE

Steve Jobs has Changed His Approach to Management

What is high-performance management? In 1976 Steven P. Jobs sold his Volkswagen van, and his partner Steven Wozniak sold his two programmable calculators, and they used the proceeds of $1,350 to build a circuit board in Jobs's garage. So popular was the circuit board, which developed into the Apple II personal computer (PC), that in 1977 Jobs and Wozniak founded Apple Computer to make and sell it. By 1985 Apple's sales had exploded to almost $2 billion, but in the same year Jobs was forced out of the company he founded. Jobs's approach to management was a big part of the reason he lost control of Apple.

Jobs saw his main task as leading the planning process to develop new and improved PCs. Although this was a good strategy, his management style was often arbitrary and overbearing. For example, Jobs often played favorites among the many project teams he created. His approach caused many conflicts and led to fierce competition, many misunderstandings, and growing distrust among members of the different teams.

Jobs's abrasive management style also brought him into conflict with John Sculley, Apple's CEO. Employees became unsure whether Jobs (the chairman) or Sculley was leading the company. Both managers were

Apple's CEO Steve Jobs proudly shows off his company's new iPad tablet computer in March 2010. More than 1 million iPads were sold within a month.

so busy competing for control of Apple that the task of ensuring its resources were being used efficiently was neglected. Apple's costs soared, and its performance and profits fell.

Apple's directors became convinced Jobs's management style was the heart of the problem and asked him to resign. After he left Apple, Jobs started new ventures. First he founded PC maker NEXT to develop a powerful new PC that would outperform Apple's PCs. Then he founded Pixar, a computer animation company, which become a huge success after it made blockbuster movies such as *Toy Story* and *Finding Nemo,* both distributed by Walt Disney.

In both these companies Jobs developed a clear vision for managers to follow, and he built strong management teams to lead the project teams developing the new PCs and movies. Jobs saw his main task as planning the companies' future product development strategies. However, he left the actual tasks of leading and organizing to managers below him. He gave them the autonomy to put his vision into practice. In both companies he encouraged a culture of collaboration and innovation to champion creative thinking.

Meanwhile Apple was struggling to compete against Michael Dell's new, low-cost PCs loaded with Microsoft's Windows software. Its performance was plummeting, and to help his old company survive, in 1996 Jobs convinced Apple to buy NEXT for $400 million and use its powerful operating system in new Apple PCs. Jobs began working inside Apple to lead its turnaround and was so successful that in 1997 he was asked to become its CEO. Jobs agreed and continued to put the new management skills he had developed over time to good use.

The first thing he did was create a clear vision and goals to energize and motivate Apple employees. Jobs decided that to survive, Apple had to introduce state-of-the-art, stylish PCs and related digital equipment. He instituted an across-the-board planning process and created a team structure that allowed programmers and engineers to pool their skills to develop new PCs. He delegated considerable authority to the teams, but he also established strict timetables and challenging "stretch" goals, such as bringing new products to market as quickly as possible, for these groups. One result of these efforts was Apple's sleek new line of iMac PCs, which were quickly followed by a wide range of futuristic PC-related products.[1]

In 2003 Jobs announced that Apple was starting a new service called iTunes, an online music store from which people could download songs for 99 cents. At the same time Apple introduced its iPod music player, which can store thousands of downloaded songs, and it quickly became a runaway success. Apple continually introduced new generations of the iPod, each more compact, powerful, and versatile than previous models. By 2006 Apple had gained control of 70% of the digital music player market and 80% of the online music download business, and its stock price soared to a new record level.

The next milestone in Jobs's managerial history came in 2007 when he announced that Apple would introduce the iPhone to compete directly with the popular BlackBerry. Once again he assembled a team of engineers not only to develop the new phone but to create an online iPhone applications platform where users would be able to download iPhone applications to make their phones more useful—able to surf the Web and interact with their friends. By 2010 over 2 million iPhone applications had been developed, over 2 billion applications had been downloaded by iPhone users, and Apple was the leader in the smartphone market.

In 2010 Jobs announced that Apple planned to introduce its new iPad tablet computer, which he claimed would be the best way to experience the Web, e-mail, and photos and would also have a wireless reading function to compete directly against Amazon.com's successful Kindle wireless reader.[2] Jobs organized a new engineering unit to pioneer the development of applications for its new iPad, and in spring 2010 analysts and customers were eagerly awaiting its innovative new digital tablet that could potentially revolutionize yet another industry and make Apple the most profitable company in global computers and electronics. When Apple announced on March 5 that the iPad would be released for sale on April 13, 2010, its stock rose to a record high of $219, and analysts claimed the company's stock might become worth more than Walmart's!

Overview

The history of Steve Jobs's ups and downs as founder and manager of Apple and his other companies illustrates many challenges facing people who become managers: Managing a company is a complex activity, and effective managers must possess many kinds of skills, knowledge, and abilities. Management is an unpredictable process. Making the right decision is difficult; even effective managers often make mistakes, but the most effective managers, like Jobs, learn from their mistakes and continually strive to find ways to increase their companies' performance.

In this chapter we look at what managers do and what skills and abilities they must develop to manage their organizations successfully. We also identify the different kinds of managers that organizations need and the skills and abilities they must develop to succeed. Finally, we identify some challenges managers must address if their organizations are to grow and prosper.

What Is Management?

When you think of a manager, what kind of person comes to mind? Do you see someone who, like Steve Jobs, can determine the future prosperity of a large for-profit company? Or do you see the administrator of a not-for-profit organization, such as a community college, library, or charity, or the person in charge of your local Walmart store or McDonald's restaurant, or the person you answer to if you have a part-time job? What do all these people have in common? First, they all work in organizations. **Organizations** are collections of people who work together and coordinate their actions to achieve a wide variety of goals, or desired future outcomes.[3] Second, as managers, they are the people responsible for supervising and making the most of an organization's human and other resources to achieve its goals.

organizations Collections of people who work together and coordinate their actions to achieve a wide variety of goals or desired future outcomes.

management The planning, organizing, leading, and controlling of human and other resources to achieve organizational goals efficiently and effectively.

Management, then, is the planning, organizing, leading, and controlling of human and other resources to achieve organizational goals efficiently and effectively. An organization's *resources* include assets such as people and their skills, know-how, and experience; machinery; raw materials; computers and information technology; and patents, financial capital, and loyal customers and employees.

LO1-1 Describe what management is, why management is important, what managers do, and how managers utilize organizational resources efficiently and effectively to achieve organizational goals.

Achieving High Performance: A Manager's Goal

One of the most important goals that organizations and their members try to achieve is to provide some kind of good or service that customers value or desire. The principal goal of CEO Steve Jobs is to manage Apple so it creates a continuous stream of new and improved goods and services–such as more powerful PCs, more versatile iPods and iPhones, and the ability to easily download diverse kinds of digital content from the Internet–that customers are willing to buy. In 2010 Apple led the field in many of these areas; its managers are currently working to make its new iPad the industry leader. Similarly, the principal goal of doctors, nurses, and hospital administrators is to increase their hospital's ability to make sick people well–and to do so cost-effectively. Likewise, the principal goal of each McDonald's restaurant manager is to produce burgers, salads, fries, and shakes that people want to pay for and eat so they become loyal return customers.

organizational performance A measure of how efficiently and effectively a manager uses resources to satisfy customers and achieve organizational goals.

efficiency A measure of how well or how productively resources are used to achieve a goal.

Organizational performance is a measure of how efficiently and effectively managers use available resources to satisfy customers and achieve organizational goals. Organizational performance increases in direct proportion to increases in efficiency and effectiveness (see Figure 1.1). What are efficiency and effectiveness?

Efficiency is a measure of how productively resources are used to achieve a goal.[4] Organizations are efficient when managers minimize the amount of input resources (such as labor, raw materials, and component parts) or the amount of time needed to produce a given output of goods or services. For example, McDonald's develops ever more efficient fat fryers that not only reduce the amount of oil used in cooking, but also speed up the cooking of french fries. UPS develops new work routines to reduce delivery time, such as instructing drivers to leave their truck doors open when going short distances. Steve Jobs instructed Apple's engineers not only to develop

Figure 1.1
Efficiency, Effectiveness, and Performance in an Organization

	EFFICIENCY: LOW	EFFICIENCY: HIGH
EFFECTIVENESS: HIGH	**Low efficiency/ high effectiveness** Manager chooses the right goals to pursue, but does a poor job of using resources to achieve these goals. Result: A product that customers want, but that is too expensive for them to buy.	**High efficiency/ high effectiveness** Manager chooses the right goals to pursue and makes good use of resources to achieve these goals. Result: A product that customers want at a quality and price they can afford.
EFFECTIVENESS: LOW	**Low efficiency/ low effectiveness** Manager chooses wrong goals to pursue and makes poor use of resources. Result: A low-quality product that customers do not want.	**High efficiency/ low effectiveness** Manager chooses inappropriate goals, but makes good use of resources to pursue these goals. Result: A high-quality product that customers do not want.

High-performing organizations are efficient *and* effective.

ever more compact, powerful, and multipurpose models of its iPod and iPhone but also to find cost-effective ways to do so, such as by outsourcing manufacturing to China. A manager's responsibility is to ensure that an organization and its members perform as efficiently as possible all the activities needed to provide goods and services to customers.

effectiveness A measure of the appropriateness of the goals an organization is pursuing and the degree to which the organization achieves those goals.

Effectiveness is a measure of the *appropriateness* of the goals that managers have selected for the organization to pursue and the degree to which the organization achieves those goals. Organizations are effective when managers choose appropriate goals and then achieve them. Some years ago, for example, managers at McDonald's decided on the goal of providing breakfast service to attract more customers. The choice of this goal has proved smart: Sales of breakfast food now account for more than 30% of McDonald's revenues and are still increasing. Jobs's goal is to create a continuous flow of innovative PC and digital entertainment products. High-performing organizations, such as Apple, McDonald's, Walmart, Intel, Home Depot, Accenture, and Habitat for Humanity are simultaneously efficient and effective. Effective managers are those who choose the right organizational goals to pursue and have the skills to utilize resources efficiently.

Why Study Management?

Today more students are competing for places in business courses than ever before; the number of people wishing to pursue Master of Business Administration (MBA) degrees–today's passport to an advanced management position–either on campus or from online universities and colleges is at an all-time high. Why is the study of management currently so popular?[5]

First, in any society or culture resources are valuable and scarce; so the more efficient and effective use that organizations can make of those resources, the greater the relative well-being and prosperity of people in that society. Because managers decide how to use many of a society's most valuable resources–its skilled employees, raw materials like oil and land, computers and information systems, and financial assets–they directly impact the well-being of a society and the people in it. Understanding what managers do and how they do it is of central importance to understanding how a society creates wealth and affluence for its citizens.

Second, although most people are not managers, and many may never intend to become managers, almost all of us encounter managers because most people have jobs and bosses. Moreover, many people today work in groups and teams and have to deal with coworkers. Studying management helps people deal with their bosses and their coworkers. It reveals how to understand other people at work and make decisions and take actions that win the attention and support of the boss and coworkers. Management teaches people not yet in positions of authority how to lead coworkers, solve conflicts between them, achieve team goals, and thus increase performance.

Third, in any society, people are in competition for a very important resource–a job that pays well and provides an interesting and satisfying career; and understanding management is one important path toward obtaining this objective. In general, jobs become more interesting the more complex or responsible they are. Any person who desires a motivating job that changes over time might therefore do well to develop management skills and become promotable. A person who has been working for several years and then returns to school for an MBA can usually, after earning the degree, find a more interesting, satisfying job that pays significantly more than the previous job. Moreover, salaries increase rapidly as people move up the organizational hierarchy, whether it is a school system, a large for-profit business organization, or a not-for-profit charitable or medical institution.

Indeed, the salaries paid to top managers are enormous. For example, the CEOs and other top executives or managers of companies such as Apple, Walt Disney, GE, and McDonald's receive millions in actual salary each year. However, even more staggering is the fact that many top executives also receive bonuses in the form of valuable stock or shares in the company they manage, as well as stock options that give them the right to sell these shares at a certain time in the future.[6] If the value of the stock goes up, the managers keep the difference between the price at which they obtained the stock option (say, $10) and what it is worth later (say, $33). When Steve Jobs became CEO of Apple again in 1997 he accepted a salary of only $1 a year. However, he was also awarded stock options that, with the fast rise in Apple's stock price throughout the 2000s, are worth billions of dollars today (he was also given the free use of a $90 million jet).[7] In 2010 Goldman Sachs paid its top managers stock bonuses worth $16.2 billion, and its CEO Lloyd Blankfein received Goldman Sachs stock worth over $8 billion–but this was only half the value of the stock that JPMorgan Chase CEO Jamie Dimon received from his company![8] These incredible amounts of money provide some indication of both the responsibilities and the rewards that accompany the achievement of high management positions in major companies–and go to anybody who successfully creates and manages a small business. What is it that managers actually do to receive such rewards?[9]

Essential Managerial Tasks

The job of management is to help an organization make the best use of its resources to achieve its goals. How do managers accomplish this objective? They do so by performing four essential managerial tasks: *planning, organizing, leading,* and *controlling.* The arrows linking these tasks in Figure 1.2 suggest the sequence in which managers typically perform them. French manager Henri Fayol first outlined the nature of these managerial activities around the turn of the 20th century in *General and Industrial Management,* a book that remains the classic statement of what managers must do to create a high-performing organization.[10]

Managers at all levels and in all departments–whether in small or large companies, for-profit or not-for-profit organizations, or organizations that operate in one country or throughout the world–are responsible for performing these four tasks, which we look at next. How well managers perform these tasks determines how efficient and effective their organizations are.

Figure 1.2
Four Tasks of Management

Planning
Choose appropriate organizational goals and courses of action to best achieve those goals.
Organizing
Establish task and authority relationships that allow people to work together to achieve organization goals.
Leading
Motivate, coordinate, and energize individuals and groups to work together to achieve organizational goals.
Controlling
Establish accurate measuring and monitoring systems to evaluate how well the organization has achieved its goals.

LO1-2 Distinguish among planning, organizing, leading, and controlling (the four principal managerial tasks), and explain how managers' ability to handle each one affects organizational performance.

Planning

To perform the **planning** task, managers identify and select appropriate organizational goals and courses of action; they develop *strategies* for how to achieve high performance. The three steps involved in planning are (1) deciding which goals the organization will pursue, (2) deciding what strategies to adopt to attain those goals, and (3) deciding how to allocate organizational resources to pursue the strategies that attain those goals. How well managers plan and develop strategies determines how effective and efficient the organization is–its performance level.[11]

planning Identifying and selecting appropriate goals; one of the four principal tasks of management.

As an example of planning in action, consider the situation confronting Michael Dell, founder and CEO of Dell Computer, who by 2010 was in a major contest with Steve Jobs to retain leadership in the PC and digital device market. In 1984 the 19-year-old Dell saw an opportunity to enter the PC market by assembling PCs and selling them directly to customers. Dell began to plan how to put his idea into practice. First, he decided that his goal was to sell an inexpensive PC, to undercut the prices charged by companies like Apple, Compaq, and HP. Second, he had to choose a course of action to achieve this goal. He decided to sell PCs directly to customers by telephone and so bypass expensive computer stores that sold Compaq and Apple PCs. He also had to decide how to obtain low-cost components and how to tell potential customers about his products. Third, he had to decide how to allocate his limited funds (he had only $5,000) to buy labor and other resources. He hired three people and worked with them around a table to assemble his PCs.

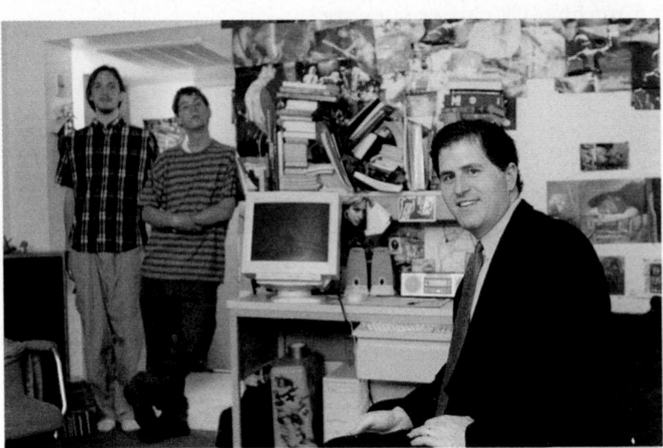

Michael Dell sits in the dorm room at the University of Texas–Austin, where he launched his personal computer company as a college freshman. When he visited, the room was occupied by freshmen Russell Smith (left) and Jacob Frith, both from Plano, Texas.

Thus to achieve his goal of making and selling low-price PCs, Dell had to plan, and as his organization grew, his plans changed and became progressively more complex. After setbacks during the 2000s that saw HP, Apple, and a new Taiwanese company, Acer, achieve competitive advantage over Dell in performance, styling, or pricing, Dell and his managers actively searched for new strategies to better compete against agile rivals and help the company regain its position as the highest-performing PC maker. In 2010 Dell was still locked in a major battle with its competitors, and its performance had not recovered despite attempts to introduce innovative new models of laptops and digital devices such as its own music player (which flopped). Dell needed a new approach to planning to compete more effectively; and new strategies Dell announced in 2010 included more powerful, customized lines of new laptops, and a plan to introduce its own smartphone and tablet computer.

As the battle between Dell, HP, Acer, and Apple suggests, the outcome of planning is a **strategy,** a cluster of decisions concerning what organizational goals to pursue, what actions to take, and how to use resources to achieve these goals. The decisions that were the outcome of Michael Dell's original planning formed a *low-cost strategy*. A low-cost strategy is a way of obtaining customers by making decisions that allow an organization to produce goods or services more cheaply than its competitors so it can charge lower prices than they do. Throughout its history, Dell has continuously refined this strategy and explored new ways to reduce costs; Dell became the most profitable PC maker as a result of its low-cost strategy, but when HP and Acer also lowered their costs it lost its competitive advantage and its profits fell. By contrast, since its founding Apple's strategy has been to deliver to customers new, exciting, and unique computer and digital products, such as its iPods, iPhones, and its new iPads–a strategy known as *differentiation.*[12] Although this strategy almost ruined Apple in the 1990s when customers bought inexpensive Dell PCs rather its premium-priced PCs, today Apple's sales have boomed as customers turn to its unique PCs

strategy A cluster of decisions about what goals to pursue, what actions to take, and how to use resources to achieve goals.

and digital products. To fight back, Dell has been forced to offer more exciting, stylish products–hence its decision to introduce a new smartphone to compete with the iPhone.

Planning strategy is complex and difficult, especially because planning is done under uncertainty when the result is unknown so that success or failure are both possible outcomes of the planning process. Managers take major risks when they commit organizational resources to pursue a particular strategy. Dell enjoyed great success in the past with its low-cost strategy; but presently Apple is performing spectacularly with its differentiation strategy, and HP has enjoyed a major turnaround because by lowering its costs it now can offer customers attractive, stylish PCs at prices similar to Dell's. In Chapter 8 we focus on the planning process and on the strategies organizations can select to respond to opportunities or threats in an industry. The story of Anne Mulcahy's rise to the top at Xerox and her decision to give control of the company to its new CEO, Ursula Burns, illustrates how important the abilities to plan and create the right strategies are to a manager's career success.

Manager as a Person

Ursula Burns "Copies" Anne Mulcahy as CEO of Xerox

By the early 2000s Xerox, the well-known copier company, was near bankruptcy. The combination of aggressive Japanese competitors, which were selling low-priced copiers, and a shift toward digital copying, which made Xerox's pioneering light-lens copying process obsolete, was resulting in plummeting sales. Losing billions of dollars, Xerox's board searched for a new CEO who could revitalize the company's product line. The person they chose to plan the company's transformation was Anne Mulcahy, a 26-year Xerox veteran. Mulcahy began her career as a Xerox copier salesperson, transferred into human resource management, and then used her considerable leadership skills to work her way up the company's hierarchy to become its president.

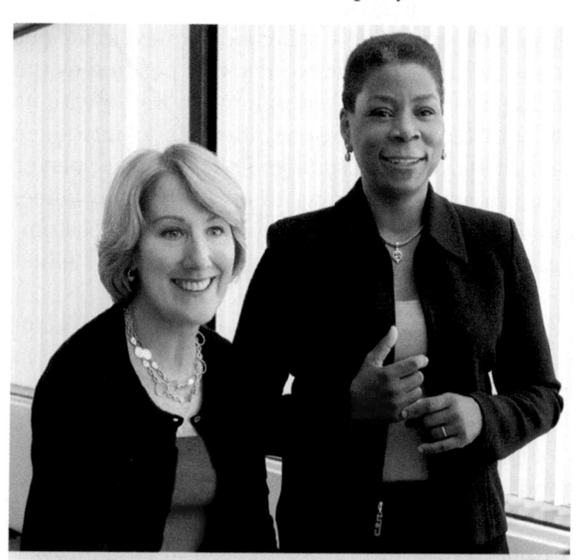

Former Xerox CEO Anne Mulcahy with her handpicked successor, Ursula Burns, who became the first female African-American manager to take charge of a major U.S. corporation.

As the new CEO, the biggest management challenge Mulcahy faced was deciding how to reduce Xerox's high operating costs. At the same time, however, she had to plan the best strategies for Xerox. Specifically, she had to decide how to best invest the company's remaining research dollars to innovate desperately needed new kinds of digital copiers that would attract customers back to the company and generate new revenues and profits. Simultaneously achieving both these objectives is one of the biggest challenges a manager can face, and how well she performed these tasks would determine Xerox's fate–indeed its survival.

To find a solution to this problem, Mulcahy, known as an unassuming CEO who prefers to stay in the background, focused her efforts on involving and listening to Xerox's managers, employees, and customers. Mulcahy began a series of "town hall" meetings with Xerox employees, asked them for all kinds of creative input and their best efforts, but told them that tough times were ahead and that layoffs would be necessary. At the same time she emphasized that only their hard work to find ways to reduce costs could save the company. To help discover how the company should best invest its R&D budget, Mulcahy made reaching out to customers her other main priority. She insisted that managers and engineers at all levels should visit, meet, and talk to customers to uncover what they most wanted from new digital copiers–and from Xerox. During one of her initiatives, called "Focus 500," which required Xerox's top 200 managers to visit its top 500 customers, she came to increasingly appreciate the skills of Ursula Burns, who had joined Xerox four years after her and was quickly establishing her own reputation as a manager. Burns, who had started her career as a mechanical engineer, was then the manager in charge of its manufacturing and supply chain activities.

By listening closely to both employees and customers, Mulcahy and Xerox's managers and engineers gained insights that led to the development of new strategies that transformed the company's product line. Mulcahy's strategy was to spend most of the R&D budget on developing two new kinds of digital copiers: a line of digital color copying machines for use by medium-sized and large businesses and a line of low-end copiers offering print quality, speed, and prices that even Japanese competitors could not match. To shrink costs Mulcahy also reduced the number of levels in Xerox's management hierarchy, cutting 26% from corporate overhead, and streamlined its operating units, reducing the number of employees from 95,000 to 55,000. By 2007 it was clear that Mulcahy and her managers–in particular Ursula Burns, who was now Mulcahy's second in command–had devised a successful turnaround plan to save Xerox.

Continuing to work closely with customers, Mulcahy and Burns developed new strategies for Xerox based on improved products and services. In talking to Xerox customers, for example, it became clear they wanted a combination of copying software and hardware that would allow them to create highly customized documents for their own customers. Banks, retail stores, and small businesses needed personalized software to create individual client statements, for example. Mulcahy decided to grow the customized services side of Xerox's business to meet these specialized needs. She also decided to replicate Xerox's sales and customer service operations around the globe and customize them to the needs of customers in each country. The result was soaring profits.

In 2009 Mulcahy decided she would leave the position of CEO to become Xerox's chairperson, and her hand-picked successor Ursula Burns would become its next CEO. The move to transfer power from one woman CEO to another at the same company is exceptional, and Burns is also the first African-American woman to head a public company as large as Xerox. Ursula Burns became Xerox's CEO in July 2009, and within six months she announced a new major planning initiative. Xerox would acquire Affiliated Computer Services for $6.4 billion so Xerox could increase its push to provide highly customized customer service. Burns said the acquisition would be a major game changer because it would triple Xerox's service revenue to over $10 billion and increase total company revenues to $22 billion. Also, $400 million in cost savings were expected. Xerox's shares have climbed 40% since Burns took over as CEO, and she is busily looking for further strategies to increase Xerox's growth. Indeed, Mulcahy decided that with Burns at the helm, Xerox's future looks bright, and she decided to retire in May 2010, at which time Burns will also become its chairman.

Organizing

organizing Structuring working relationships in a way that allows organizational members to work together to achieve organizational goals; one of the four principal tasks of management.

Organizing is structuring working relationships so organizational members interact and cooperate to achieve organizational goals. Organizing people into departments according to the kinds of job-specific tasks they perform lays out the lines of authority and responsibility between different individuals and groups. Managers must decide how best to organize resources, particularly human resources.

organizational structure A formal system of task and reporting relationships that coordinates and motivates organizational members so they work together to achieve organizational goals.

The outcome of organizing is the creation of an **organizational structure,** a formal system of task and reporting relationships that coordinates and motivates members so they work together to achieve organizational goals. Organizational structure determines how an organization's resources can be best used to create goods and services. As his company grew, for example, Michael Dell faced the issue of how to structure his organization. Early on he was hiring 100 new employees a week and deciding how to design his managerial hierarchy to best motivate and coordinate managers' activities. As his organization grew to become one of the largest global PC makers, he and his managers created progressively more complex forms of organizational structure to help it achieve its goals. We examine the organizing process in detail in Chapters 10 through 12.

Leading

leading Articulating a clear vision and energizing and enabling organizational members so they understand the part they play in achieving organizational goals; one of the four principal tasks of management.

An organization's *vision* is a short, succinct, and inspiring statement of what the organization intends to become and the goals it is seeking to achieve–its desired future state. In **leading,** managers articulate a clear organizational vision for the organization's members to accomplish, and they energize and enable employees so everyone understands the part he or she plays in achieving organizational goals. Leadership involves managers using their power, personality, influence, persuasion, and communication skills to coordinate people and groups so their activities and efforts are in harmony. Leadership revolves around encouraging all employees to perform at a high level to help the organization achieve its vision and goals. Another outcome of leadership is a highly motivated and committed workforce. Employees responded well to Michael Dell's hands-on leadership style, which has resulted in a hardworking, committed workforce. Managers at Apple now appreciate Steve Jobs's new leadership style, which is based on his willingness to delegate authority to project teams and his ability to help managers resolve differences that could easily lead to bitter disputes and power struggles. We discuss the issues involved in managing and leading individuals and groups in Chapters 13 through 16.

Ken Chenault, pictured here, is the president and CEO of American Express Company. Promoted in 1997, he climbed the ranks from its Travel Related Services Company thanks to his even temper and unrelenting drive. Respected by colleagues for his personality, most will say they can't remember him losing his temper or raising his voice. His open-door policy for subordinates allows him to mentor AmEx managers and encourages all to enter and speak their minds.

Controlling

controlling Evaluating how well an organization is achieving its goals and taking action to maintain or improve performance; one of the four principal tasks of management.

In **controlling,** the task of managers is to evaluate how well an organization has achieved its goals and to take any corrective actions needed to maintain or improve performance. For example, managers monitor the performance of individuals, departments, and the organization as a whole to see whether they are meeting desired performance standards. Michael Dell learned early in his career how important this is; it took Steve Jobs longer. If standards are not being met, managers seek ways to improve performance.

The outcome of the control process is the ability to measure performance accurately and regulate organizational efficiency and effectiveness. To exercise control, managers must decide which goals to measure–perhaps goals pertaining to productivity, quality, or responsiveness to customers–and then they must design control systems that will provide the information necessary to assess performance–that is, determine to what degree the goals have been met. The controlling task also helps managers evaluate how well they themselves are performing the other three tasks of management–planning, organizing, and leading–and take corrective action.

Michael Dell had difficulty establishing effective control systems because his company was growing so rapidly and he lacked experienced managers. In the 1990s Dell's costs suddenly soared because no systems were in place to control inventory, and in 1994 poor quality control resulted in a defective line of new laptop computers–some of which caught fire. To solve these and other control problems, Dell hired hundreds of experienced managers from other companies to put the right control systems in place. As a result, by 2000 Dell was able to make computers for over 10% less than its competitors, which created a major source of competitive advantage. At its peak, Dell drove competitors out of the market because it had achieved a 20% cost advantage over them.[13] However, we noted earlier that through the 2000s rivals such as HP and Acer also learned how to reduce their operating costs, and this shattered Dell's competitive advantage. Controlling, like the other managerial tasks, is an ongoing, dynamic, always-changing process that demands constant attention and action. We cover the most important aspects of the control task in Chapters 10, 11, 17, and 18.

The four managerial tasks–planning, organizing, leading, and controlling–are essential parts of a manager's job. At all levels in the managerial hierarchy, and across all jobs and departments in an organization, effective management means performing these four activities successfully–in ways that increase efficiency and effectiveness.

Performing Managerial Tasks: Mintzberg's Typology

Our discussion of managerial tasks may seem to suggest that a manager's job is highly orchestrated and that management is an orderly process in which managers rationally calculate the best way to use resources to achieve organizational goals. In reality, being a manager often involves acting emotionally and relying on gut feelings. Quick, immediate reactions to situations, rather than deliberate thought and reflection, are an important aspect of managerial action.[14] Often managers are overloaded with responsibilities and do not have time to analyze every nuance of a situation; they therefore make decisions in uncertain conditions not knowing which outcomes will be best.[15] Moreover, top managers face constantly changing situations, and a decision that seems right today may prove to be wrong tomorrow. The range of problems that managers face is enormous; managers usually must handle many problems simultaneously; and they often must make snap decisions using the intuition and experience gained through their careers to perform their jobs to the best of their abilities.[16] Henry Mintzberg, by following managers and observing what they actually *do*–hour by hour and day by day–identified 10 kinds of specific roles, or sets of job responsibilities, that capture the dynamic nature of managerial work.[17] He grouped these roles according to whether the responsibility was primarily decisional, interpersonal, or informational; they are described in Table 1.1.

Given the many complex, difficult job responsibilities managers have, it is no small wonder that many claim they are performing their jobs well if they are right just half of the time.[18] And it is understandable that many experienced managers accept failure by their subordinates as a normal part of the learning experience and a rite of passage to becoming an effective manager. Managers and their subordinates learn from both their successes and their failures.

Table 1.1
Managerial Roles Identified by Mintzberg

Type of Role	Specific Role	Examples of Role Activities
Decisional	Entrepreneur	Commit organizational resources to develop innovative goods and services; decide to expand internationally to obtain new customers for the organization's products.
	Disturbance handler	Move quickly to take corrective action to deal with unexpected problems facing the organization from the external environment, such as a crisis like an oil spill, or from the internal environment, such as producing faulty goods or services.
	Resource allocator	Allocate organizational resources among different tasks and departments of the organization; set budgets and salaries of middle and first-level managers.
	Negotiator	Work with suppliers, distributors, and labor unions to reach agreements about the quality and price of input, technical, and human resources; work with other organizations to establish agreements to pool resources to work on joint projects.
Interpersonal	Figurehead	Outline future organizational goals to employees at company meetings; open a new corporate headquarters building; state the organization's ethical guidelines and the principles of behavior employees are to follow in their dealings with customers and suppliers.
	Leader	Provide an example for employees to follow; give direct commands and orders to subordinates; make decisions concerning the use of human and technical resources; mobilize employee support for specific organizational goals.
	Liaison	Coordinate the work of managers in different departments; establish alliances between different organizations to share resources to produce new goods and services.
Informational	Monitor	Evaluate the performance of managers in different tasks and take corrective action to improve their performance; watch for changes occurring in the external and internal environments that may affect the organization in the future.
	Disseminator	Inform employees about changes taking place in the external and internal environments that will affect them and the organization; communicate to employees the organization's vision and purpose.
	Spokesperson	Launch a national advertising campaign to promote new goods and services; give a speech to inform the local community about the organization's future intentions.

Levels and Skills of Managers

To perform the four managerial tasks efficiently and effectively, organizations group or differentiate their managers in two main ways–by level in hierarchy and by type of skill. First, they differentiate managers according to their level or rank in the organization's hierarchy of authority. The three levels of managers are first-line managers, middle managers, and top managers–arranged in a hierarchy. Typically first-line managers report to middle managers, and middle managers report to top managers.

Second, organizations group managers into different departments (or functions) according to their specific job-related skills, expertise, and experiences, such as a manager's engineering skills, marketing expertise, or sales experience. A **department,** such as the manufacturing, accounting, engineering, or sales department, is a group of managers and employees who work together because they possess similar skills and experience or use the same kind of knowledge, tools, or techniques to perform their jobs. Within each department are all three levels of management. Next we examine why organizations use a hierarchy of managers and group them, by the jobs they perform, into departments.

department A group of people who work together and possess similar skills or use the same knowledge, tools, or techniques to perform their jobs.

LO1-3 Differentiate among three levels of management, and understand the tasks and responsibilities of managers at different levels in the organizational hierarchy.

Levels of Management

Organizations normally have three levels of management: first-line managers, middle managers, and top managers (see Figure 1.3). Managers at each level have different but related responsibilities for using organizational resources to increase efficiency and effectiveness.

At the base of the managerial hierarchy are **first-line managers,** often called *supervisors*. They are responsible for daily supervision of the nonmanagerial employees who perform the specific activities necessary to produce goods and services. First-line managers work in all departments or functions of an organization.

first-line manager A manager who is responsible for the daily supervision of nonmanagerial employees.

Examples of first-line managers include the supervisor of a work team in the manufacturing department of a car plant, the head nurse in the obstetrics department of a hospital, and the chief mechanic overseeing a crew of mechanics in the service

Figure 1.3
Levels of Managers

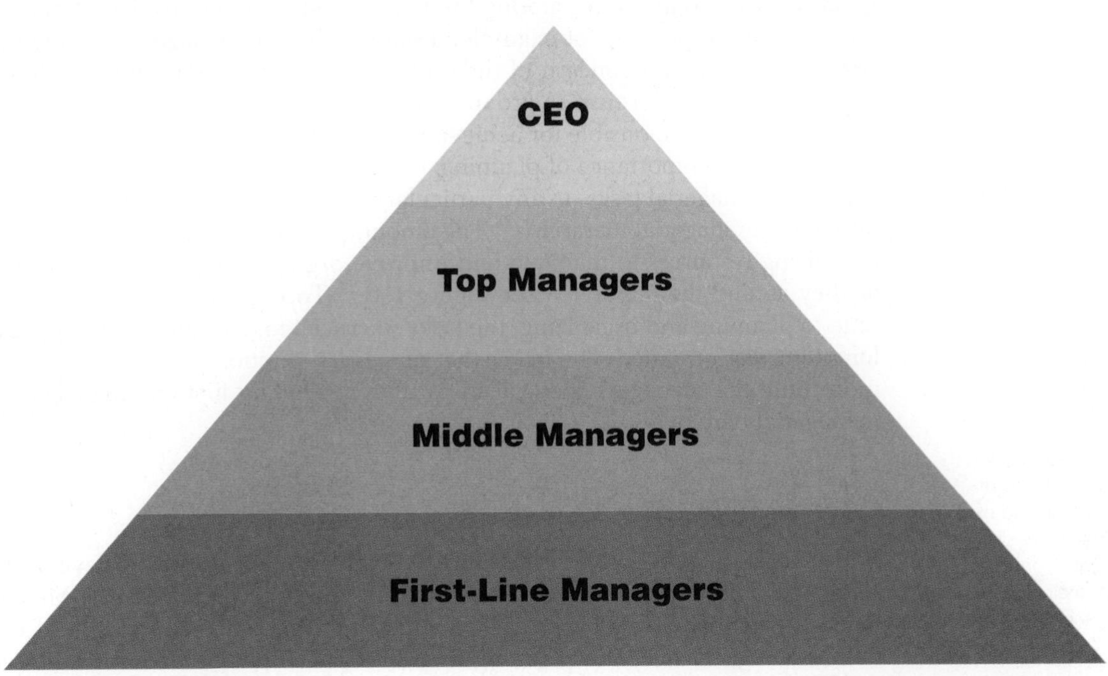

function of a new car dealership. At Dell, first-line managers include the supervisors responsible for controlling the quality of its computers or the level of customer service provided by telephone salespeople. When Michael Dell started his company, he personally controlled the computer assembly process and thus acted as a first-line manager or supervisor.

middle manager A manager who supervises first-line managers and is responsible for finding the best way to use resources to achieve organizational goals.

Supervising the first-line managers are **middle managers,** responsible for finding the best way to organize human and other resources to achieve organizational goals. To increase efficiency, middle managers find ways to help first-line managers and nonmanagerial employees better use resources to reduce manufacturing costs or improve customer service. To increase effectiveness, middle managers evaluate whether the organization's goals are appropriate and suggest to top managers how goals should be changed. Often the suggestions that middle managers make to top managers can dramatically increase organizational performance. A major part of the middle manager's job is developing and fine-tuning skills and know-how, such as manufacturing or marketing expertise, that allow the organization to be efficient and effective. Middle managers make thousands of specific decisions about the production of goods and services: Which first-line supervisors should be chosen for this particular project? Where can we find the highest-quality resources? How should employees be organized to allow them to make the best use of resources?

Behind a first-class sales force, look for the middle managers responsible for training, motivating, and rewarding the salespeople. Behind a committed staff of high school teachers, look for the principal who energizes them to find ways to obtain the resources they need to do outstanding and innovative jobs in the classroom.

top manager A manager who establishes organizational goals, decides how departments should interact, and monitors the performance of middle managers.

In contrast to middle managers, **top managers** are responsible for the performance of *all* departments.[19] They have *cross-departmental responsibility.* Top managers establish organizational goals, such as which goods and services the company should produce; they decide how the different departments should interact; and they monitor how well middle managers in each department use resources to achieve goals.[20] Top managers are ultimately responsible for the success or failure of an organization, and their performance (like that of Michael Dell or Ursula Burns) is continually scrutinized by people inside and outside the organization, such as other employees and investors.[21]

The *chief executive officer (CEO)* is a company's most senior and important manager, the one all other top managers report to. Today the term *chief operating officer (COO)* often refers to the top manager who is being groomed to take over as CEO when the current CEO, such as Anne Mulcahy, becomes the chair of the board, retires, or leaves the company. Together the CEO and COO are responsible for developing good working relationships among the top managers of various departments (manufacturing and marketing, for example); usually these top managers have the title "vice president." A central concern of the CEO is the creation of a smoothly functioning **top management team,** a group composed of the CEO, the COO, and the vice presidents most responsible for achieving organizational goals.[22]

top management team A group composed of the CEO, the COO, the president, and the heads of the most important departments.

The relative importance of planning, organizing, leading, and controlling–the four principal managerial tasks–to any particular manager depends on the manager's position in the managerial hierarchy.[23] The amount of time managers spend planning and organizing resources to maintain and improve organizational performance increases as they ascend the hierarchy (see Figure 1.4).[24] Top managers devote most of their time to planning and organizing, the tasks so crucial to determining an organization's long-term performance. The lower that managers' positions are in the hierarchy, the more time the managers spend leading and controlling first-line managers or nonmanagerial employees.

LO1-4 Distinguish between three kinds of managerial skill, and explain why managers are divided into different departments to perform their tasks more efficiently and effectively.

Managerial Skills

Both education and experience enable managers to recognize and develop the personal skills they need to put organizational resources to their best use. Michael Dell realized from the start that he lacked sufficient experience and technical expertise in marketing, finance, and planning to guide his company alone. Thus he recruited

Figure 1.4
Relative Amount of Time That Managers Spend on the Four Managerial Tasks

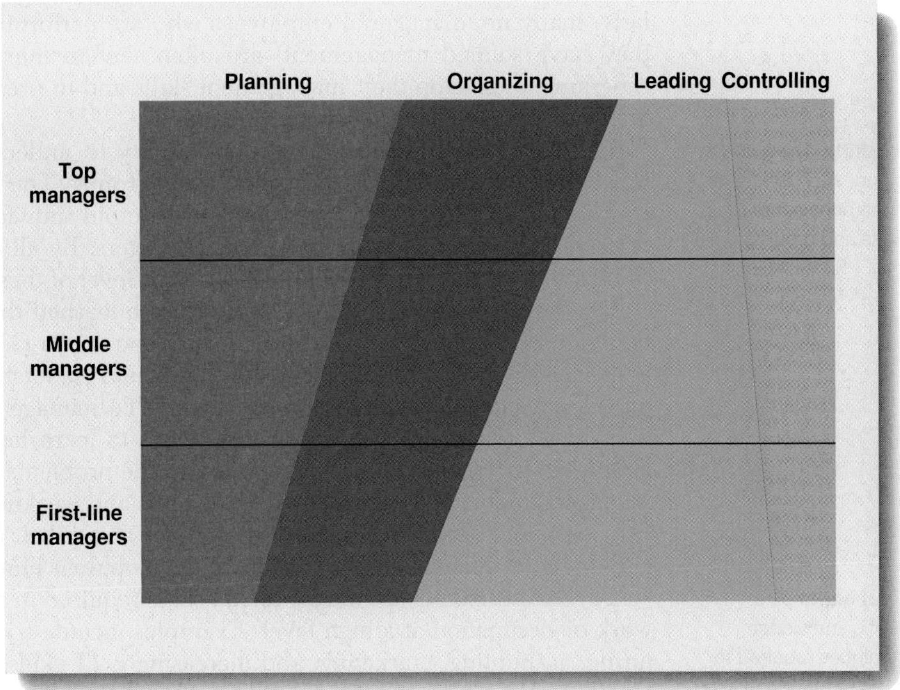

experienced managers from other IT companies, such as IBM and HP, to help build his company. Research has shown that education and experience help managers acquire and develop three types of skills: *conceptual, human,* and *technical.*[25]

conceptual skills The ability to analyze and diagnose a situation and to distinguish between cause and effect.

Conceptual skills are demonstrated in the general ability to analyze and diagnose a situation and to distinguish between cause and effect. Top managers require the best conceptual skills because their primary responsibilities are planning and organizing.[26] By all accounts, Steve Jobs was chosen as CEO to transform Apple, and Anne Mulcahy was chosen to revive Xerox, because of their ability to identify new opportunities and mobilize managers and other resources to take advantage of those opportunities.

Formal education and training are important in helping managers develop conceptual skills. Business training at the undergraduate and graduate (MBA) levels provides many of the conceptual tools (theories and techniques in marketing, finance, and other areas) that managers need to perform their roles effectively. The study of management helps develop the skills that allow managers to understand the big picture confronting an organization. The ability to focus on the big picture lets managers see beyond the situation immediately at hand and consider choices while keeping in mind the organization's long-term goals.

Today continuing management education and training, including training in advanced IT, are an integral step in building managerial skills because new theories and techniques are constantly being developed to improve organizational effectiveness, such as total quality management, benchmarking, and Web-based organization and business-to-business (B2B) networks. A quick scan through a magazine such as *BusinessWeek* or *Fortune* reveals a host of seminars on topics such as advanced marketing, finance, leadership, and human resources management that are offered to managers at many levels in the organization, from the most senior corporate executives to middle managers. Microsoft, IBM, Oracle, and many other organizations designate a portion of each manager's personal budget to be used at the manager's discretion to attend management development programs.

In addition, organizations may wish to develop a particular manager's abilities in a specific skill area–perhaps to learn an advanced component of departmental skills, such as international bond trading, or to learn the skills necessary to implement total quality management. The organization thus pays for managers to attend specialized programs to develop these skills. Indeed, one signal that a manager is performing well is an organization's willingness to invest in that manager's skill development. Similarly, many nonmanagerial employees who are performing at a high level (because they have studied management) are often sent to intensive management training programs to develop their management skills and to prepare them for promotion to first-level management positions.

human skills The ability to understand, alter, lead, and control the behavior of other individuals and groups.

Human skills include the general ability to understand, alter, lead, and control the behavior of other individuals and groups. The ability to communicate, to coordinate, and to motivate people, and to mold individuals into a cohesive team, distinguishes effective from ineffective managers. By all accounts, Steve Jobs, Anne Mulcahy, and Michael Dell all possess a high level of these human skills.

Like conceptual skills, human skills can be learned through education and training, as well as be developed through experience.[27] Organizations increasingly utilize advanced programs in leadership skills and team leadership as they seek to capitalize on the advantages of self-managed teams.[28] To manage personal interactions effectively, each person in an organization needs to learn how to empathize with other people–to understand their viewpoints and the problems they face. One way to help managers understand their personal strengths and weaknesses is to have their superiors, peers, and subordinates provide feedback about their job performance. Thorough and direct feedback allows managers to develop their human skills.

technical skills The job-specific knowledge and techniques required to perform an organizational role.

Technical skills are the *job-specific* skills required to perform a particular type of work or occupation at a high level. Examples include a manager's specific manufacturing, accounting, marketing, and increasingly, IT skills. Managers need a range of technical skills to be effective. The array of technical skills managers need depends on their position in their organizations. The manager of a restaurant, for example, may need cooking skills to fill in for an absent cook, accounting and bookkeeping skills to keep track of receipts and costs and to administer the payroll, and aesthetic skills to keep the restaurant looking attractive for customers.

As noted earlier, managers and employees who possess the same kinds of technical skills typically become members of a specific department and are known as, for example, marketing managers or manufacturing managers.[29] Managers are grouped into different departments because a major part of a manager's responsibility is to monitor, train, and supervise employees so their job-specific skills and expertise increase. Obviously this is easier to do when employees with similar skills are grouped into the same department because they can learn from one another and become more skilled and productive at their particular jobs.

Figure 1.5 shows how an organization groups managers into departments on the basis of their job-specific skills. It also shows that inside each department, a managerial hierarchy of first-line, middle, and top managers emerges. At Dell, for example, Michael Dell hired experienced top managers to take charge of the marketing, sales, and manufacturing departments and to develop work procedures to help middle and first-line managers control the company's explosive sales growth. When the head of manufacturing found he had no time to supervise computer assembly, he recruited experienced manufacturing middle managers from other companies to assume this responsibility. At Xerox, Anne Mulcahy nurtured many of her managers to develop the required functional skills, such as Ursula Burns, who used her engineering expertise to rise to become CEO.

core competency The specific set of departmental skills, knowledge, and experience that allows one organization to outperform another.

Today the term **core competency** is often used to refer to the specific set of departmental skills, knowledge, and experience that allows one organization to outperform its competitors. In other words, departmental skills that create a core competency give an organization a *competitive advantage.* Dell, for example, was the first PC maker to develop a core competency in materials management that allowed it to produce PCs at a much lower cost than its competitors–a major source of competitive advantage. Similarly, 3M is well known for its core competency in research and development (R&D) that allows it to innovate new products at a faster rate than its competitors, and Xerox has been working to develop a competency to provide a full-range service that is customized to the needs of each of the companies it serves.

Figure 1.5
Types and Levels of Managers

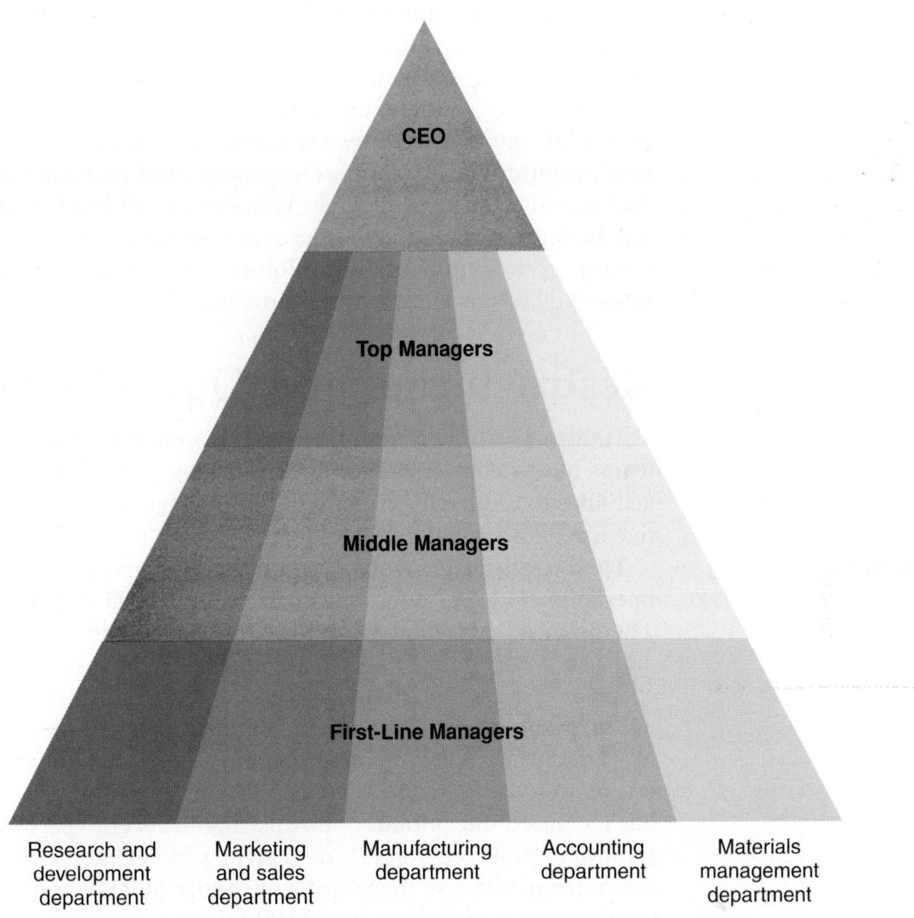

Effective managers need all three kinds of skills–conceptual, human, and technical–to help their organizations perform more efficiently and effectively. The absence of even one type of managerial skill can lead to failure. One of the biggest problems that people who start small businesses confront, for example, is their lack of appropriate conceptual and human skills. Someone who has the technical skills to start a new business does not necessarily know how to manage the venture successfully. Similarly, one of the biggest problems that scientists or engineers who switch careers from research to management confront is their lack of effective human skills. Ambitious managers or prospective managers are constantly in search of the latest educational contributions to help them develop the conceptual, human, and technical skills they need to perform at a high level in today's changing and increasingly competitive global environment.

Developing new and improved skills through education and training has become a priority for both aspiring managers and the organizations they work for. As we discussed earlier, many people are enrolling in advanced management courses; but many companies, such as Microsoft, GE, and IBM, have established their own colleges to train and develop their employees and managers at all levels. Every year these companies put thousands of their employees through management programs designed to identify the employees who the company believes have the competencies that can be developed to become its future top managers. Most organizations closely link promotion to a manager's ability to acquire the competencies that a particular company believes are important.[30] At Apple and 3M, for example, the ability to successfully lead a new product development team is viewed as a vital requirement for promotion; at Accenture and IBM, the ability to attract and retain clients is viewed as a skill its consultants must possess. We discuss the various kinds of skills managers need to develop in most of the chapters of this book.

Recent Changes in Management Practices

The tasks and responsibilities of managers have been changing dramatically in recent years. Two major factors that have led to these changes are global competition and advances in information technology (IT). Stiff competition for resources from organizations both at home and abroad has put increased pressure on all managers to improve efficiency and effectiveness. Increasingly, top managers are encouraging lower-level managers to look beyond the goals of their own departments and take a cross-departmental view to find new opportunities to improve organizational performance, as Steve Jobs and Anne Mulcahy did. Modern IT gives managers at all levels and in all areas access to more and better information and improves their ability to plan, organize, lead, and control. IT also gives employees more job-related information and allows them to become more skilled, specialized, and productive.[31]

Restructuring and Outsourcing

To utilize IT to increase efficiency and effectiveness, CEOs and top management teams have been restructuring organizations and outsourcing specific organizational activities to reduce the number of employees on the payroll and make more productive use of the remaining workforce.

restructuring Downsizing an organization by eliminating the jobs of large numbers of top, middle, and first-line managers and nonmanagerial employees.

Restructuring involves simplifying, shrinking, or downsizing an organization's operations to lower operating costs, as both Dell and Xerox have been forced to do. The financial crisis that started in 2009 has forced most companies–large and small, and profit and nonprofit–to find ways to reduce costs because their customers are spending less money, so their revenues decrease. Restructuring can be done by eliminating product teams, shrinking departments, and reducing levels in the hierarchy, all of which result in the loss of large numbers of jobs of top, middle, or first-line managers, as well as nonmanagerial employees. Modern IT's ability to improve efficiency has increased the amount of downsizing in recent years because IT makes it possible for fewer employees to perform a given task. IT increases each person's ability to process information and make decisions more quickly and accurately, for example. U.S. companies are spending over $100 billion a year to purchase advanced IT that can improve efficiency and effectiveness. We discuss the many dramatic effects of IT on management in Chapter 18 and throughout this book.

Restructuring, however, can produce some powerful negative outcomes. It can reduce the morale of remaining employees, who worry about their own job security–something Anne Mulcahy had to deal with at Xerox. And top managers of many downsized organizations realize that they downsized too far when their employees complain they are overworked and when increasing numbers of customers complain about poor service.[32] Dell faced this charge in the 2000s as it continued to reduce the number of its customer service representatives and outsource their jobs to India to lower costs.

outsourcing Contracting with another company, usually abroad, to have it perform an activity the organization previously performed itself.

Outsourcing involves contracting with another company, usually in a low-cost country abroad, to have it perform a work activity the organization previously performed itself, such as manufacturing, marketing, or customer service. Outsourcing increases efficiency because it lowers operating costs, freeing up money and resources that can be used in more effective ways–for example, to develop new products.

The need to respond to low-cost global competition has speeded outsourcing dramatically in the 2000s. Over 3 million U.S. jobs in the manufacturing sector have been lost since 2000 as companies have moved their operations to countries such as China, Taiwan, and Malaysia. Tens of thousands of high-paying IT jobs have also moved abroad, to countries like India and Russia, where programmers work for one-third the salary of those in the United States. Dell employs over 12,000 customer service reps in India, for example.[33]

Large for-profit organizations today typically employ 10% to 20% fewer people than they did 10 years ago because of restructuring and outsourcing. Ford, IBM, AT&T, HP, Dell, and DuPont are among the thousands of organizations that have

LO1-5 Discuss some major changes in management practices today that have occurred as a result of globalization and the use of advanced information technology (IT).

streamlined their operations to increase efficiency and effectiveness. The argument is that the managers and employees who have lost their jobs will find employment in new and growing U.S. companies where their skills and experience will be better utilized. For example, the millions of manufacturing jobs that have been lost overseas will be replaced by higher-paying U.S. jobs in the service sector that are made possible because of the growth in global trade.

LO1-6 Discuss the principal challenges managers face in today's increasingly competitive global environment.

Empowerment and Self-Managed Teams

empowerment The expansion of employees' knowledge, tasks, and decision-making responsibilities.

self-managed team A group of employees who assume responsibility for organizing, controlling, and supervising their own activities and monitoring the quality of the goods and services they provide.

The second principal way managers have sought to increase efficiency and effectiveness is by empowering lower-level employees and moving to self-managed teams. **Empowerment** is a management technique that involves giving employees more authority and responsibility over how they perform their work activities. The way in which John Deere, the well-known tractor manufacturer, empowered its employees illustrates how this technique can help raise performance. The employees who assemble Deere's vehicles possess detailed knowledge about how Deere products work. Deere's managers realized these employees could become persuasive salespeople if they were given training. So groups of these employees were given intensive sales training and sent to visit Deere's customers and explain to them how to operate and service the company's new products. While speaking with customers, these newly empowered "salespeople" also collect information that helps Deere develop new products that better meet customers' needs. The new sales jobs are temporary; employees go on assignment but then return to the production line, where they use their new knowledge to find ways to improve efficiency and quality.

Often companies find that empowering employees can lead to so many kinds of performance gains that they use their reward systems to promote empowerment. For example, Deere's moves to empower employees were so successful that the company negotiated a new labor agreement with its employees to promote empowerment. The agreement specifies that pay increases will be based on employees' learning new skills and completing college courses in areas such as computer programming that will help the company increase efficiency and quality. Deere has continued to make greater use of teams throughout the 2000s, and its profits have soared because its competitors cannot match its user-friendly machines that are the result of its drive to respond to its customers' needs.

Lonnie Love, an Illinois farmer, checks out the custom wiring job on his John Deere tractor. Technicians, such as the one working on Love's tractor, add irreplaceable know-how to help John Deere's sales force.

IT is being increasingly used to empower employees because it expands employees' job knowledge and increases the scope of their job responsibilities. Frequently IT allows one employee to perform a task that was previously performed by many employees. As a result, the employee has more autonomy and responsibility. IT also facilitates the use of a **self-managed team,** a group of employees who assume collective responsibility for organizing, controlling, and supervising their own work activities.[34] Using IT designed to give team members real-time information about each member's performance, a self-managed team can often find ways to accomplish a task more quickly and efficiently. Moreover, self-managed teams assume many tasks and responsibilities previously performed by first-line managers, so a company can better utilize its workforce.[35] First-line managers act as coaches or mentors whose job is not to tell employees what to do but to provide advice and guidance and help teams find new ways to perform their tasks more efficiently.[36] Using the same IT, middle managers can easily monitor what is happening in these teams and make better resource allocation decisions as a result. We discuss self-managed teams in more detail in Chapters 2, 10, and 15.

Challenges for Management in a Global Environment

Because the world has been changing more rapidly than ever before, managers and other employees throughout an organization must perform at higher and higher levels.[37] In the last 20 years, rivalry between organizations competing domestically (in the same country) and globally (in countries abroad) has increased dramatically. The rise of **global organizations,** organizations that operate and compete in more than one country, has pressured many organizations to identify better ways to use their resources and improve their performance. The successes of the German chemical companies Schering and Hoechst, Italian furniture manufacturer Natuzzi, Korean electronics companies Samsung and LG, Brazilian plane maker Embraer, and Europe's Airbus Industries are putting pressure on companies in other countries to raise their level of performance to compete successfully against these global organizations.

global organizations Organizations that operate and compete in more than one country.

Even in the not-for-profit sector, global competition is spurring change. Schools, universities, police forces, and government agencies are reexamining their operations because looking at how activities are performed in other countries often reveals better ways to do them. For example, many curriculum and teaching changes in the United States have resulted from the study of methods that Japanese and European school systems use. Similarly, European and Asian hospital systems have learned much from the U.S. system–which may be the most effective, though not the most efficient, in the world.

Today managers who make no attempt to learn from and adapt to changes in the global environment find themselves reacting rather than innovating, and their organizations often become uncompetitive and fail.[38] Five major challenges stand out for managers in today's world: building a competitive advantage, maintaining ethical standards, managing a diverse workforce, utilizing new information systems and technologies, and practicing global crisis management.

Building Competitive Advantage

What are the most important lessons for managers and organizations to learn if they are to reach and remain at the top of the competitive environment of business? The answer relates to the use of organizational resources to build a competitive advantage. **Competitive advantage** is the ability of one organization to outperform other organizations because it produces desired goods or services more efficiently and effectively than its competitors. The four building blocks of competitive advantage are superior *efficiency; quality; speed, flexibility,* and *innovation;* and *responsiveness to customers* (see Figure 1.6).

competitive advantage The ability of one organization to outperform other organizations because it produces desired goods or services more efficiently and effectively than they do.

Organizations increase their efficiency when they reduce the quantity of resources (such as people and raw materials) they use to produce goods or services. In today's competitive environment, organizations continually search for new ways to use their resources to improve efficiency. Many organizations are training their workforces in the new skills and techniques needed to operate heavily computerized assembly plants. Similarly, cross-training gives employees the range of skills they need to perform many different tasks; and organizing employees in new ways, such as in self-managed teams, lets them make good use of their skills. These are important steps in the effort to improve productivity. Japanese and German companies invest far more in training employees than do American or Italian companies.

Managers must improve efficiency if their organizations are to compete successfully with companies operating in Mexico, China, Malaysia, and other countries where employees are paid comparatively low wages. New methods must be devised either to increase efficiency or to gain some other competitive advantage–higher-quality goods, for example–if outsourcing and the loss of jobs to low-cost countries are to be prevented.

The challenge from global organizations such as Korean electronics manufacturers, Mexican agricultural producers, and European design and financial companies also

Figure 1.6
Building Blocks of Competitive Advantage

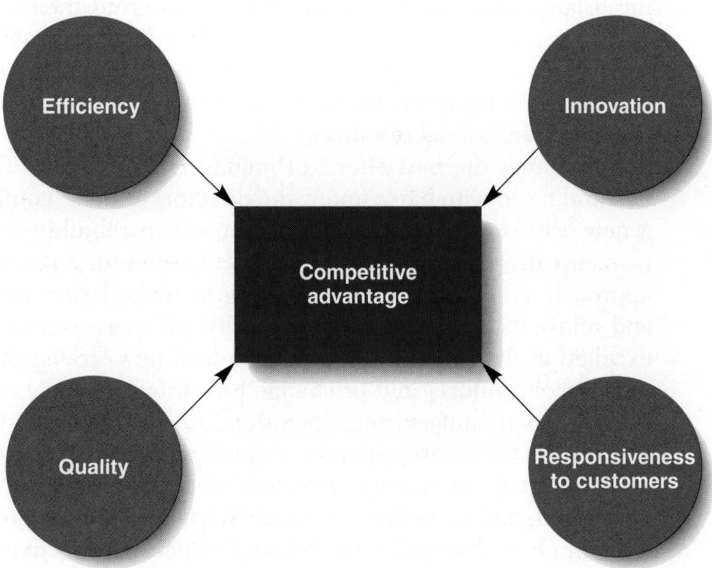

has increased pressure on companies to develop the skills and abilities of their workforces in order to improve the quality of their goods and services. One major thrust to improving quality has been to introduce the quality-enhancing techniques known as *total quality management (TQM)*. Employees involved in TQM are often organized into quality control teams and are responsible for finding new and better ways to perform their jobs; they also must monitor and evaluate the quality of the goods they produce. We discuss ways of managing TQM successfully in Chapter 9.

Today companies can win or lose the competitive race depending on their *speed*–how fast they can bring new products to market–or their *flexibility*–how easily they can change or alter the way they perform their activities to respond to actions of their competitors. Companies that have speed and flexibility are agile competitors: Their managers have superior planning and organizing abilities; they can think ahead, decide what to do, and then speedily mobilize their resources to respond to a changing environment. We examine how managers can build speed and flexibility in their organizations in later chapters. Michael Dell and Ursula Burns are working hard to make Dell and Xerox agile companies that can react to the technological changes taking place in a digital world–their problem is how to maintain their competitive advantage against HP, Apple, Kodak, and Canon.

innovation The process of creating new or improved goods and services or developing better ways to produce or provide them.

Innovation, the process of creating new or improved goods and services that customers want or developing better ways to produce or provide goods and services, poses a special challenge. Managers must create an organizational setting in which people are encouraged to be innovative. Typically innovation takes place in small groups or teams; management decentralizes control of work activities to team members and creates an organizational culture that rewards risk taking. For example, a team composed of Apple and Nike employees came up with the idea for a new model of iPod that would be able to record and measure the distance its owner had run, among other things, and the companies formed an alliance to make it.[39] Managing innovation and creating a work setting that encourages risk taking are among the most difficult managerial tasks. Innovation is discussed in depth in Chapter 9.

Organizations compete for customers with their products and services, so training employees to be responsive to customers' needs is vital for all organizations, but particularly for service organizations. Retail stores, banks, and hospitals, for example, depend entirely on their employees to perform behaviors that result in high-quality service at a reasonable cost.[40] As many countries (the United States, Canada, and

Switzerland are just a few) move toward a more service-based economy (in part because of the loss of manufacturing jobs to China, Malaysia, and other countries with low labor costs), managing behavior in service organizations is becoming increasingly important. Many organizations are empowering their customer service employees and giving them the authority to take the lead in providing high-quality customer service. As noted previously, empowering nonmanagerial employees and creating self-managed teams change the role of first-line managers and lead to more efficient use of organizational resources.

Sometimes the best efforts of managers to revitalize their organization's fortunes fail; and faced with bankruptcy, the directors of these companies are forced to appoint a new CEO who has a history of success in rebuilding a company. **Turnaround management** is the creation of a new vision for a struggling company using a new approach to planning and organizing to make better use of a company's resources and allow it to survive and eventually prosper–something Apple's Steve Jobs has excelled at. It involves developing radical new strategies such as how to reduce the number of products sold or change how they are made and distributed, or close corporate and manufacturing operations to reduce costs. Organizations that appoint turnaround CEOs are generally experiencing a crisis because they have become inefficient or ineffective; sometimes this is because of poor management over a continuing period, and sometimes it occurs because a competitor introduces a new product or technology that makes their own products unattractive to customers. For example, when Apple introduced the iPhone in 2007, sales of the former best-selling Motorola Razr cell phone plummeted because customers demand state-of-the-art products. Motorola has not recovered because it has no smartphone to compete with Apple, although it introduced new phones using Google's Android platform in 2009. BlackBerry seems to be holding its own and Nokia is fighting back, but Palm was suffering in 2010 when Dell and Microsoft announced plans to introduce their own new smartphones. What strategies will be required to make a new smartphone that can compete with the iPhone or BlackBerry?

turnaround management The creation of a new vision for a struggling company based on a new approach to planning and organizing to make better use of a company's resources and allow it to survive and prosper.

Achieving a competitive advantage requires that managers use all their skills and expertise, as well as their companies' other resources, to find new and improved ways to improve efficiency, quality, innovation, and responsiveness to customers. We revisit this theme often as we examine the ways managers plan strategies, organize resources and activities, and lead and control people and groups to increase efficiency and effectiveness.

Maintaining Ethical and Socially Responsible Standards

Managers at all levels, especially after the recent economic crisis, are under considerable pressure to make the best use of resources to increase the level at which their organizations perform.[41] For example, top managers feel pressure from shareholders to increase the performance of the entire organization to boost its stock price, improve profits, or raise dividends. In turn, top managers may pressure middle managers to find new ways to use organizational resources to increase efficiency or quality and thus attract new customers and earn more revenues–and then middle managers hit on their department's supervisors.

Pressure to increase performance can be healthy for an organization because it leads managers to question how the organization is working, and it encourages them to find new and better ways to plan, organize, lead, and control. However, too much pressure to perform can be harmful.[42] It may induce managers to behave unethically, and even illegally, when dealing with people and groups inside and outside the organization.[43]

A purchasing manager for a nationwide retail chain, for example, might buy inferior clothing as a cost-cutting measure or ignore the working conditions under which products are made to obtain low-priced products. These issues faced the managers of companies that make footwear and clothing in the 1990s, when customers learned about the sweatshop conditions in which garment and shoe workers around the world labored. Today companies such as Nike, Walmart, and Apple are trying to stop sweatshop practices and prevent managers abroad from adopting work practices that harm their workers. They now employ hundreds of inspectors who police the factories overseas that make the products they sell and who can terminate contracts with suppliers when they behave in an unethical or illegal way. Nevertheless, in a 2010 report Apple revealed that its investigations showed that sweatshop conditions still existed in some of the factories it used abroad. Apple said that at least 55 of the 102 factories were ignoring Apple's rule that staff cannot work more than 60 hours a week, for example. Apple is continuing its efforts to reduce these abuses.[44]

Similarly, to secure a large foreign contract, a sales manager in a large company, such as in the defense or electronics industry, might offer bribes to foreign officials to obtain lucrative contracts–even though this is against the law. In 2010, for example, German electronic equipment maker Siemens agreed to pay $1.4 billion in fines to settle claims that it paid bribes and kickbacks to organizations around the world between 2001 and 2007. Securities and Exchange Commission (SEC) Chairman Christopher Cox alleged, "Siemens paid staggering amounts of money to circumvent the rules and gain business. Now, they will pay for it with the largest settlement in the history of the Foreign Corrupt Practices Act since it became law in 1977."[45]

The issue of social responsibility, discussed in Chapter 4, centers on deciding what obligations a company has toward the people and groups affected by its activities–such as employees, customers, or the cities in which it operates. Some companies have strong views about social responsibility; their managers believe they should protect the interests of others. But some managers may decide to act in an unethical way and put their own interests first, hurting others in the process. A recent example showing why managers must always keep the need to act in an ethical and socially responsible way at the forefront of their decision making is profiled in the following "Ethics in Action" box.

Ethics in Action

"What Goes Around Comes Around": How Dishonest Top Managers Can Corrupt Any Organization—Even a Court

Court judges at the federal, state, or county level are expected to possess the highest ethical standards and abide by the rule of law; they are the top managers who organize and control the legal system and the courts. Why should ordinary citizens believe they are protected by the legal system and their individual rights will be upheld fairly and objectively if they cannot trust their judges? Then imagine the shock citizens of Luzerne County in the heart of Pennsylvania's struggling coal country experienced in 2009 when an FBI investigation revealed that two respected county judges, Mark Ciavarella and Michael Conahan, had conspired to use the managerial power of their office to profit financially by sending thousands of teenagers to jail.

How these managers controlled the county's judicial organization for this unethical and illegal purpose was revealed when investigators found that the number of youths entering detention in Luzerne County was two to three times higher than in similar counties–and these teens were being jailed for trivial violations. A boy who shoplifted a $4 bottle of nutmeg was jailed, for example, and so was the boy with him, who was charged with conspiracy to shoplift because

Pictured are disgraced former judges Mark Ciavarella and Michael Conahan as they leave the courtroom building during their trial, which accused them of giving thousands of teenagers illegal jail terms in order to benefit financially.

he was physically present. A girl who created a MySpace page that taunted her school administrator was also incarcerated.

Judges Ciavarella and Conahan's plan to subvert the court's organization and control system worked as follows. At that time Conahan controlled the county court and its budget, and Ciavarella controlled sentencing in the juvenile court. As the top managers of the court system, they were largely unsupervised. Over time they worked together to shut down the old county-run juvenile detention center by refusing to send teens there and cutting off its funding. Meanwhile they created their own organization, a privately owned detention center built by the judges' corrupt associates, to replace the facility. Then the judges contracted with the county to pay $58 million to use their detention center for 10 years. The judges admitted they took "at least" $2.6 million in payoffs from their private youth detention center and tried to hide this dishonest income by creating false income tax records.

Most of the teens sentenced were on trial for minor first offenses, and their time in court to defend themselves often lasted for only minutes. Most were unrepresented because their parents were told it was "unnecessary to have a lawyer"; as a consequence one boy remained locked up for over two years. The Pennsylvania Supreme Court has expunged the records of over 2,000 youths who were sent into detention by Ciavarella because of his unethical behavior. "They sold their oath of offices to the highest bidders and engaged in ongoing schemes to defraud the public of honest services that were expected from them," said Deron Roberts, chief of the FBI's Scranton office.[46]

In 2009 these corrupt ex-justices agreed to a plea bargain stating that they would spend seven years in jail and pay back millions of dollars. This plea bargain collapsed in October 2009 when the presiding judge decided it was too lenient, and in spring 2010 they faced 64 charges that could lead them to spend decades in jail.[47] Unethical managers eventually face the consequences of their unsavory actions.

Managing a Diverse Workforce

A major challenge for managers everywhere is to recognize the ethical need and legal requirement to treat human resources fairly and equitably. Today the age, gender, race, ethnicity, religion, sexual preference, and socioeconomic composition of the workforce presents new challenges for managers. To create a highly trained and motivated workforce, as well as to avoid lawsuits, managers must establish human resource management (HRM) procedures and practices that are legal, are fair, and do not discriminate against any organizational members.[48] Today most organizations understand that to motivate effectively and take advantage of the talents of a diverse workforce, they must make promotion opportunities available to each and every employee.[49] Managers must recognize the performance-enhancing possibilities of a diverse workforce, such as the ability to take advantage of the skills and experiences of different kinds of people.[50] Accenture provides a good example of a company that has utilized the potential of its diverse employees, as discussed in the following "Focus on Diversity" box.

Managers who value their diverse employees not only invest in developing these employees' skills and capabilities but also succeed best in promoting performance

Focus on Diversity

Accenture's Global Diversity Initiatives

Accenture is a global management consulting company that serves the IT needs of thousands of client companies located in over 120 countries around the world. A major driving force behind Accenture's core organizational vision is to manage and promote diversity in order to improve employee performance and client satisfaction. At Accenture, managers at all levels realize consultants bring distinct experiences, talents, and values to their work, and a major management initiative is to take advantage of that diversity to encourage collaboration between consultants to improve the service Accenture provides to each of its clients. Because Accenture's clients are also diverse by country, religion, ethnicity, and so forth, it tries to match its teams of consultants to the attributes of its diverse clients.

Global consulting company Accenture is a first-mover in taking advantage of the diverse skills and knowledge of its consultants to create teams that can provide the customized solutions needed to best satisfy clients such as large overseas companies.

Accenture provides hundreds of diversity management training programs to its consultants each year using its 13 teams of global human capital and diversity experts, who collaborate to create its programs. Accenture also encourages each of its consultants to pursue opportunities to "work across different geographies, workforces, and generations to create agile global leaders."[51] In 2010 one-third of its global workforce was composed of women, who also hold 16% of its management positions at all levels. Accenture chooses to buy from suppliers who can also demonstrate their commitment to diversity, and in 2010 nearly $300 million or 15% of Accenture's purchasing came from small minority- or women-owned suppliers. The firm also provides diversity training programs to its suppliers and prospective suppliers around the world to show them how diversity can increase their efficiency and effectiveness. In all these ways, Accenture uses its expertise in managing diversity to promote individual and organizational performance–one reason it has become the most successful and fast-growing consultancy company in the world.

over the long run. Today more organizations are realizing that people are their most important resource and that developing and protecting human resources is the most important challenge for managers in a competitive global environment. Kevin Rollins, a former CEO of Dell, commented, "I've seen firsthand the power of a diverse workforce. Leveraging the similarities and differences of all team members enables Dell to develop the best products, provide a superior customer experience, and contribute in meaningful ways to the communities where we do business."[52] And as Takahiro Moriguchi of Union Bank of California said when accepting a national diversity award for his company when he was its CEO, "By searching for talent from among the disabled, both genders, veterans, gay, all ethnic groups and all nationalities, we gain access to a pool of ideas, energy, and creativity as wide and varied as the human race itself."[53] We discuss the many issues surrounding the management of a diverse workforce in Chapter 5.

Utilizing IT and E-Commerce

As we have discussed, another important challenge for managers is to continually utilize efficient and effective new IT that can link and enable managers and employees to better perform their jobs–whatever their level in the organization. One example

UPS Dispatch Coordinator Jim McCauley shows driver Muamer Pleh how many stops he will be making in his next delivery run—all made possible by the company's new software that allows each driver to plan the most efficient delivery route each day, which saves the company time and money.

of how IT has changed the jobs of people at all organizational levels comes from UPS, where, until 2006, its drivers relied on maps, note cards, and their own experience to plan the fastest way to deliver hundreds of parcels each day. This changed after UPS invested over $600 million to develop a computerized route optimization system that each evening plans each of its 56,000 drivers' routes for the next day in the most efficient way by, for example, minimizing the number of left turns that waste both time and gas. The program has been incredibly successful and has been continuously updated so that by 2010 UPS drivers covered tens of million fewer miles each month while they delivered ever-increasing numbers of packages faster.

Increasingly, new kinds of IT enable not just individual employees but also self-managed teams by giving them important information and allowing virtual interactions around the globe using the Internet. Increased global coordination helps improve quality and increase the pace of innovation. Microsoft, Hitachi, IBM, and most companies now search for new IT that can help them build a competitive advantage. The importance of IT is discussed in detail in Chapters 16 and 18, and throughout the text you will find icons that alert you to examples of how IT is changing the way companies operate.

Practicing Global Crisis Management

Today another challenge facing managers and organizations is global crisis management. The causes of global crises or disasters fall into two main categories: natural causes and human causes. Crises that arise because of natural causes include the hurricanes, tsunamis, earthquakes, famines, and diseases that have devastated so many countries in the 2000s; hardly any country has been untouched by their effects. In 2010 both Haiti and Chile experienced severe earthquakes that killed thousands of people and left tens of thousands more homeless. Despite the extensive foreign aid they have received, both these countries will probably need years to recover from these crises and rebuild their economies and infrastructure.

Human-created crises result from factors such as industrial pollution, poor attention to worker and workplace safety, global warming and the destruction of the natural habitat or environment, and geopolitical tensions and terrorism. Human-created crises, such as global warming due to emissions of carbon dioxide and other gases, may intensify the effects of natural disasters. For example, increasing global temperatures and acid rain may have increased the intensity of hurricanes, led to unusually strong rains, and contributed to lengthy droughts. Scientists believe that global warming is responsible for the rapid destruction of coral reefs, forests, animal species, and the natural habitat in many parts of the world. The shrinking polar ice caps are expected to raise the sea level by a few critical inches.

Increasing geopolitical tensions, which are partly the result of the speed of the globalization process itself, have upset the balance of world power as different countries and geographic regions attempt to protect their own economic and political interests. Rising oil prices, for example, have strengthened the bargaining power of oil-supplying countries. This has led the United States to adopt global political strategies, including its war on terrorism, to secure the supply of oil vital to protecting its national interest. In a similar way, countries in Europe have been forming contracts and allying with Russia to obtain its supply of natural gas, and Japan and China have been negotiating with Iran and Saudi Arabia. The rise of global terrorism and terrorist groups is to a large degree the result of changing political, social, and economic conditions that have made it easier for extremists to influence whole countries and cultures.

Finally, industrial pollution and limited concern for the health and safety of workers have become increasingly significant problems for companies and countries. Companies in heavy industries such as coal and steel have polluted millions of acres of land around major cities in eastern Europe and Asia; billion-dollar cleanups are necessary. The 1986 Chernobyl nuclear power plant meltdown released over 1,540 times as much radiation into the air as occurred at Hiroshima; over 50,000 people died as a result, while hundreds of thousands more have been affected. In the area of worker health and safety, one example of a company whose managers paid too little attention to preventing crises is oil refiner British Petroleum, which is discussed in the following "Managing Globally" box.

Managing Globally

A Concern for Safety Explodes at BP

In 2009 a U.S. judge finally approved British Petroleum's (BP) plea agreement to pay $50 million–the largest U.S. criminal environmental fine ever–after pleading guilty to charges stemming from a 2005 explosion that killed 15 workers and injured 180 workers at BP's Texas City oil refinery, the third largest in the United States, situated 40 miles from Houston. The explosion was the third largest ever in the United States and the fifth largest globally. "We deeply regret the harm that was caused by this terrible tragedy. We take very seriously the commitments we've made as part of the plea agreement," said BP spokesman Daren Beaudo.

The remains of BP's Texas City oil refinery after the huge explosion that killed 15 workers, and injured hundreds more. BP faces billions in penalties, fines, and punitive damages from this debacle, and its woes continue on in the wake of the April 2010 Gulf of Mexico oil spill.

An investigation revealed that the 2005 explosion occurred because BP had relaxed safety procedures at its Texas City refinery to reduce operating costs. The U.S. Occupational Health and Safety Association (OSHA) decided the 2005 explosion was caused by defective pressure relief systems and by poor safety management programs. Consequently, in 1997 OSHA issued its largest fine up to that date, $21 million, against BP for the lapses that led to the refinery explosion because BP sacrificed safety at the refinery to cut costs. The judgment also required the U.S. unit of London-based BP to serve three years on probation while the company tried to solve more than 500 serious safety violations that had been discovered during the investigation.

Beyond the formal fines, however, BP faced hundreds of lawsuits stemming from the explosion from workers and their families and the people and organizations that had been affected by the blast, which was felt miles from the refinery. It is estimated that BP spent over *$2 billion* to settle these claims, most of which were settled privately outside the courts. After paying so much in legal costs and fines, and given the bad publicity it experienced globally, you might think a company like BP would immediately move to improve its safety procedures. However, while it paid these costs, it also earned $21 billion in profit during the same year; so how did its top management respond?

Not in a highly responsive way. In 2009 OSHA issued a new record $87 million fine against the oil giant for failing to correct the safety violations identified after the 2005 explosion. The 2007 agreement between BP and OSHA included a detailed list of ways in which BP should improve safety procedures at the plant–something its managers vowed to do. But a six-month inspection revealed hundreds of violations of the 2007 agreement to repair hazards at the refinery, and OSHA decided BP had failed to live up to the terms of its commitment to protect employees and that another catastrophe was possible because BP had a major safety problem in the "culture" of this refinery.

BP responded strongly to these accusations, arguing that it had spent hundreds of millions of dollars to correct the safety problems. BP also said that after it reviewed safety procedures at its four U.S. refineries and found that its Cherry Point refinery had the best process safety culture, the head of that refinery had been promoted to oversee better implementation of process safety across BP's U.S. operations. In 2007, however, another serious incident occurred when 10 workers claimed they were injured when a toxic substance was released at the Texas City plant, which BP denied. (A jury subsequently decided in favor of these workers, who were awarded over $200 million in punitive damages in 2009.)

In any event, in 2007 BP's board of directors decided to move quickly. They fired its CEO and many other top managers and appointed a new CEO, Anthony Hayward, who was instructed to make global refinery safety a key organizational priority. The board also decided to make a substantial portion of the future stock bonuses for the CEO and other top managers dependent on BP's future safety record, and the board committed over $5 billion to improving safety across the company's global operations.

Hayward's efforts seemed to be working, but in April 2010 the Deepwater Horizon oil-drilling platform that BP had leased from its U.S.-based owner Transocean exploded, killing 11 employees and the fractured oil pipe began to release millions of barrels of oil into the Gulf of Mexico. Despite all of BP's attempts to use its expertise to stop the oil gushing from the pipe, a mile below the sea, oil continued to flow into the gulf. In June 2010, the only hope to stop the flow of oil seemed to be from two relief wells that BP was drilling that would be completed by August 2010.

Management has an important role to play in helping people, organizations, and countries respond to global crises; such crises provide lessons in how to plan, organize, lead, and control the resources needed to both forestall and respond effectively to a crisis. Crisis management involves making important choices about how to (1) create teams to facilitate rapid decision making and communication, (2) establish the organizational chain of command and reporting relationships necessary to mobilize a fast response, (3) recruit and select the right people to lead and work in such teams, and (4) develop bargaining and negotiating strategies to manage the conflicts that arise whenever people and groups have different interests and objectives. How well managers make such decisions determines how quickly an effective response to a crisis can be implemented, and it sometimes can prevent or reduce the severity of the crisis itself.

Summary and Review

WHAT IS MANAGEMENT? A manager is a person responsible for supervising the use of an organization's resources to meet its goals. An organization is a collection of people who work together and coordinate their actions to achieve a wide variety of goals. Management is the process of using organizational resources to achieve organizational goals effectively and efficiently through planning, organizing, leading, and controlling. An efficient organization makes the most productive use of its resources. An effective organization pursues appropriate goals and achieves these goals by using its resources to create goods or services that customers want.

LO1-1

LO1-2 **MANAGERIAL TASKS** The four principal managerial tasks are planning, organizing, leading, and controlling. Managers at all levels of the organization and in all departments perform these tasks. Effective management means managing these activities successfully.

LO1-3, 1-4 **LEVELS AND SKILLS OF MANAGERS** Organizations typically have three levels of management. First-line managers are responsible for the day-to-day supervision of nonmanagerial employees. Middle managers are responsible for developing and utilizing organizational resources efficiently and effectively. Top managers have cross-departmental responsibility. Three main kinds of managerial skills are conceptual, human, and technical. The need to develop and build technical skills leads organizations to divide managers into departments according to their job-specific responsibilities. Top managers must establish appropriate goals for the entire organization and verify that department managers are using resources to achieve those goals.

LO1-5 **RECENT CHANGES IN MANAGEMENT PRACTICES** To increase efficiency and effectiveness, many organizations have altered how they operate. Managers have restructured and downsized operations and outsourced activities to reduce costs. Companies are also empowering their workforces and using self-managed teams to increase efficiency and effectiveness. Managers are increasingly using IT to achieve these objectives.

LO1-6 **CHALLENGES FOR MANAGEMENT IN A GLOBAL ENVIRONMENT** Today's competitive global environment presents many interesting challenges to managers. One of the main challenges is building a competitive advantage by increasing efficiency; quality; speed, flexibility, and innovation; and customer responsiveness. Other challenges are behaving in an ethical and socially responsible way toward people inside and outside the organization; managing a diverse workforce; utilizing new IT; and practicing global crisis management.

Management in Action

Topics for Discussion and Action

Discussion

1. Describe the difference between efficiency and effectiveness, and identify real organizations that you think are, or are not, efficient and effective. [LO1-1]
2. In what ways can managers at each of the three levels of management contribute to organizational efficiency and effectiveness? [LO1-3]
3. Identify an organization that you believe is high-performing and one that you believe is low-performing. Give five reasons why you think the performance levels of the two organizations differ so much. [LO1-2, 1-4]
4. What are the building blocks of competitive advantage? Why is obtaining a competitive advantage important to managers? [LO1-5]
5. In what ways do you think managers' jobs have changed the most over the last 10 years? Why have these changes occurred? [LO1-6]

Action

6. Choose an organization such as a school or a bank; visit it; then list the different organizational resources it uses. How do managers use these resources to maintain and improve its performance? [LO1-2, 1-4]
7. Visit an organization, and talk to first-line, middle, and top managers about their respective management roles in the organization and what they do to help the organization be efficient and effective. [LO1-3, 1-4]
8. Ask a middle or top manager, perhaps someone you already know, to give examples of how he or she performs the managerial tasks of planning, organizing, leading, and controlling. How much time does he or she spend in performing each task? [LO1-3]
9. Like Mintzberg, try to find a cooperative manager who will allow you to follow him or her around for a day. List the roles the manager plays, and indicate how much time he or she spends performing them. [LO1-3, 1-4]

Building Management Skills

Thinking about Managers and Management [LO1-2, 1-3, 1-4]

Think of an organization that has provided you with work experience and the manager to whom you reported (or talk to someone who has had extensive work experience); then answer these questions:

1. Think about your direct supervisor. Of what department is he or she a member, and at what level of management is this person?
2. How do you characterize your supervisor's approach to management? For example, which particular management tasks and roles does this person perform most often? What kinds of management skills does this manager have?
3. Do you think the tasks, roles, and skills of your supervisor are appropriate for the particular job he or she performs? How could this manager improve his or her task performance? How can IT affect this?
4. How did your supervisor's approach to management affect your attitudes and behavior? For example, how well did you perform as a subordinate, and how motivated were you?
5. Think about the organization and its resources. Do its managers use organizational resources effectively? Which resources contribute most to the organization's performance?
6. Describe how the organization treats its human resources. How does this treatment affect the attitudes and behaviors of the workforce?
7. If you could give your manager one piece of advice or change one management practice in the organization, what would it be?
8. How attuned are the managers in the organization to the need to increase efficiency, quality, innovation, or responsiveness to customers? How well do you think the organization performs its prime goals of providing the goods or services that customers want or need the most?

Managing Ethically [LO1-1, 1-3]

Think about an example of unethical behavior that you observed in the past. The incident could be something you experienced as an employee or a customer or something you observed informally.

Questions

1. Either by yourself or in a group, give three reasons why you think the behavior was unethical. For example, what rules or norms were broken? Who benefited or was harmed by what took place? What was the outcome for the people involved?
2. What steps might you take to prevent such unethical behavior and encourage people to behave in an ethical way?

Small Group Breakout Exercise [LO1-2, 1-3, 1-4]

Opening a New Restaurant

Form groups of three or four people, and appoint one group member as the spokesperson who will communicate your findings to the entire class when called on by the instructor. Then discuss the following scenario:

You and your partners have decided to open a large, full-service restaurant in your local community; it will be open from 7 a.m. to 10 p.m. to serve breakfast, lunch, and dinner. Each of you is investing $50,000 in the venture, and together you have secured a bank loan for $300,000 to begin operations. You and your partners have little experience in managing a restaurant beyond serving meals or eating in restaurants, and you now face the task of deciding how you will manage the restaurant and what your respective roles will be.

1. Decide what each partner's managerial role in the restaurant will be. For example, who will be responsible for the necessary departments and specific activities? Describe your managerial hierarchy.
2. Which building blocks of competitive advantage do you need to establish to help your restaurant succeed? What criteria will you use to evaluate how successfully you are managing the restaurant?
3. Discuss the most important decisions that must be made about (a) planning, (b) organizing, (c) leading, and (d) controlling to allow you and your partners to use organizational resources effectively and build a competitive advantage.
4. For each managerial task, list the issues to solve, and decide which roles will contribute the most to your restaurant's success.

Exploring the World Wide Web [LO1-2]

Go to the General Electric (GE) Web site at www.ge.com, click on "our company," then "company information," and then "Jeffrey Immelt," GE's CEO. You will see a list of articles that discuss his management style; click on articles such as "GE: Why The Company Still Has Spark, 2010" in *The Guardian* and "How to Build Great Leaders" in *Fortune*.

Search these articles or others for information that describes Immelt's approach to planning, organizing, leading, and controlling GE. What is his approach to managing? What effects has this approach had on GE's performance?

Be the Manager [LO1-2, 1-5]

Problems at Achieva

You have just been called in to help managers at Achieva, a fast-growing Internet software company that specializes in business-to-business (B2B) network software. Your job is to help Achieva solve some management problems that have arisen because of its rapid growth.

Customer demand to license Achieva's software has boomed so much in just two years that more than 50 new software programmers have been added to help develop a new range of software products. Achieva's growth has been so swift that the company still operates informally, its organizational structure is loose and flexible, and programmers are encouraged to find solutions to problems as they go along. Although this structure worked well in the past, you have been told that problems are arising.

There have been increasing complaints from employees that good performance is not being recognized in the organization and that they do not feel equitably treated. Moreover, there have been complaints about getting managers to listen to their new ideas and to act on them. A bad atmosphere is developing in the company, and recently several talented employees left. Your job is to help Achieva's managers solve these problems quickly and keep the company on the fast track.

Questions

1. What kinds of organizing and controlling problems is Achieva suffering from?
2. What kinds of management changes need to be made to solve them?

Case in the News

How Four Rookie CEOs Handled the Great Recession

Timing, as comics say, is everything. So what do you do when it's your first time on stage, and you're getting killed up there, with the audience booing and heckling and calling for the hook? Ask John Donahoe, who became the CEO of eBay in March 2008. Not only did Donahoe take the reins of the online retailer from one of the star CEOs of the dot-com era—the current California gubernatorial hopeful Meg Whitman—he did so at a time when the U.S. economy was imploding and eBay's business model was under assault. Suddenly the new guy was getting pounded from all sides. One employee wrote an online post arguing that "Donahoe has made eBay a miserable debacle and it's getting worse every day." The owner of a company that sells on the auction site called his strategy a "concentrated effort to destroy the eBay marketplace." Jim Cramer weighed in on his *Mad Money* television show with this vote of confidence: "EBay has lost touch with reality . . . the company is hapless," he said in September 2008. "They ought to sell themselves to someone." You might call it CEO hell, but Donahoe didn't kid himself. "It's going to get worse before it gets better," he kept saying.

While the Great Recession was tough on just about everyone, rookie CEOs were faced with what will likely be the biggest crisis of their careers. Employees, investors, and board members looked to them for guidance, but their task was complicated by swooning stock prices and, often, mass layoffs. "It's easy to look like a great leader when everything is going well," says executive coach Marshall Goldsmith. "The real great leader shows up in hard times."

Not all the newly minted chief executives made it through the flames. Frederick A. "Fritz" Henderson stepped down in December after eight months in the top job at General Motors as the automaker continued to struggle. Owen Van Natta lost his CEO spot at the social networking site MySpace on February 10, after nine months. A record high 1,482 chief executives resigned, retired, or stepped down from public and private U.S. companies in 2008, according to Challenger, Gray & Christmas, which helps laid-off executives find work. An additional 1,227 left their jobs in 2009.

The latest recession was particularly treacherous because it was so broad, hitting Wall Street, Detroit, the housing industry, and other pillars of the economy. Yet the challenges in particular sectors may have been more severe in the past—say, in the tech industry after the dot-com bust or in manufacturing during the oil crisis of the 1970s. Robert Crandall got his first chief executive job at American Airlines in time for the tumult of airline deregulation and oil price swings in the 1980s. "Desperation is the mother of invention," says Crandall, who is now retired. To compete with new low-cost rivals, he came up with the first national frequent-flier program and a two-tiered labor system. "Sure, it seemed challenging," he says. "But on the other hand, [becoming CEO] was the thing that I had been trying to achieve for many years."

Rookie chiefs from downturns past say starting the job in crisis forever affects how you lead. Ron Sargent was named to the top job at office supplies retailer Staples weeks before the September 11 attacks and in the midst of recession. "The thing that changed in me was the willingness to make tough decisions quickly," he says. After the terrorist attacks, Sargent had to choose between cutting payroll or trimming product lines to save money. He speedily worked out a back-to-basics strategy that eliminated consumer-oriented products like Britney Spears backpacks. It hurt margins in the short term, but it saved jobs and helped keep customer service strong.

First-timers from this recession such as Donahoe and T. Rowe Price's James A.C. Kennedy agreed to talk about how they managed through the downturn and about what they learned. Among the lessons seared into their hides was this one: Resist the inclination to hunker down and wait out the troubles. Remaining proactive and decisive improved their competitive positions as the economy began to recover. John Thompson, vice chairman of the headhunting firm Heidrick & Struggles, says it's particularly important in a downturn for CEOs "to bring an extraordinary sense of urgency."

Many of the new CEOs solicited counsel from veteran leaders; Donahoe consulted with Cisco Systems' John T. Chambers. Yet leaders know they bear sole responsibility for the decisions they make. "At the end of the day the CEO has to pick a path and take it," says Jeffrey A. Stoops, chief executive of the wireless phone tower company SBA Communications.

Servant Leadership

Donahoe's early months as eBay CEO incited such widespread vitriol in large part because he picked a path that was far different from that of Whitman. Coming into the job after three years at the San Jose company, he carried out the first round of layoffs ever at eBay. He reorganized the company's Web site in a way that gave less visibility to some small sellers, long eBay's bread and butter. And he cut a deal to acquire a consumer credit business called Bill Me Later for $945 million in the middle of the credit crunch, sending eBay's stock downward.

Although Donahoe had led the privately held Bain & Co. consulting firm before moving to eBay, he says running his first public company, with so many constituencies, required a different approach. It's not a popularity contest: You do what you think is right for the company and resist the attacks from those who prefer the status quo. "When I became CEO, there was an opportunity to take the next step," says Donahoe, 49. "And the next step was making changes that we knew were going to be unpopular in the short term." Donahoe, in fact, found that many employees and investors were more open to dramatic change than they might have been otherwise. "In a crisis, people were scared enough and uncertain enough that I could take action," he says. Donahoe is winning over at least some of his critics now. After falling below 12 at the end of 2008, eBay's stock has risen to 23. The company is earning steady profits again, and analysts say eBay is better positioned to compete with fast-growing rivals such as Craigslist and Amazon.com.

Donahoe's strategy is born of an approach he calls "servant leadership." He thinks of eBay's customers first, specifically the companies and entrepreneurs who sell goods on the site. Then he visualizes a chain of command through which the CEO can deliver what customers need. On trips around the world he takes along a Flip Video camera and films interviews with eBay sellers to share their opinions with his staff. He has even tied managers' compensation to customer loyalty, measured through regular surveys. Far from resenting the tough circumstances of his first job atop a large public company, Donahoe calls the experience a gift. "I will be such a better leader having gone through that, versus having had a lot of early success."

Swimming to Confidence

T. Rowe Price's Kennedy prides himself on balancing the demands of office and home. But over the second weekend of September 2008, as Lehman Brothers was crumbling to dust, he worked the phones from his Baltimore headquarters, trying to ease investor concerns about his own firm. Promoted to the top post at T. Rowe Price in January 2007, Kennedy had a seat precariously close to the biggest financial meltdown since the Great Depression. His firm is the sixth largest mutual fund manager in the United States, with more than $350 billion in assets under management. "The world seemed to be collapsing around us," he says of his first two years. All the while he was trying to learn to cope with the demands of a challenging new role in an organization where he had worked for more than three decades.

That meant learning new areas of the business. When Kennedy was named CEO, he left the equities department he had been running to set up shop on the fixed-income floor. His timing was fortunate: Fixed-income analysts were just starting to spot the dangers of mortgage-backed securities in mid-2007. Alarmed by the "ugly" possibilities, the new CEO ratcheted back on growth and trimmed expenses, such as hiring, advertising, and IT. When Lehman Brothers filed for bankruptcy on a Monday morning in September 2008, Kennedy's strategy looked prescient. T. Rowe Price had steered clear of many of the complex financial instruments that blew up in the aftermath. Profits dipped to a 12-year low that December, but the firm bounced back faster than almost all of its peers, in part because of Kennedy's preemptive cost cutting. In 2009 T. Rowe Price's assets under management increased 41%, to $391.3 billion, compared with a 16% rise for U.S. mutual funds overall, according to research firm Strategic Insights.

Kennedy made time for his personal life throughout the challenging months. He got married last year, for the second time, and kept up regular golf games with his new wife, Maureen. He also swam laps three times a week. Periodic checkups with his executive coach, Marty Seldman, helped Kennedy keep perspective on his life and career. "If leaders look like they are unraveling, it can create a vicious cycle of more fear and more stress in the company," says Seldman. "Jim stayed calm and confident."

Diamonds Are Forever

Diane M. Irvine had no time to celebrate getting the chief executive job at online jewelry retailer Blue Nile. Hours after her appointment in February 2008 she had to tell investors that sales from the previous holiday season had been worse than expected—and the credit crunch would probably mean a dreadful next year. The company's shares sank 20% the next day. "It was very daunting," she says. Irvine had to come up with a plan, and fast. She surprised many by using the recession as an excuse to go on the offensive. "We can gain market share," she told investors during a March 2008 presentation. She argued that Blue Nile had an edge on brick-and-mortar jewelry brands like Tiffany's and Zales in a downturn because it required little overhead and virtually no inventory. Competitors would struggle and close stores; Blue Nile would invest and expand.

The strategy had its doubters. "We were selling luxury goods in what was probably the worst economy in 75 years, so I think there was tremendous skepticism about how the company would weather the storm," says Mark Vadon, who founded Blue Nile in 1999 and led the company until Irvine took over. Adding to the challenge of waning consumer demand were diamond prices, which remained at boom-year levels. Irvine doubled down on technology that would help bring in new customers. Blue Nile's site underwent a year-long revamp, adding new tools to help buyers search for diamonds by budget, shape, and quality. The new CEO also pushed into overseas markets, tweaking the Web site to accept 23 different forms of currency. Credit was a barrier to many potential sales. So the Seattle company joined up with Bill Me Later (the company eBay would later acquire) to offer customers no-interest financing for six months on large purchases.

Although Irvine, now 51, worked as chief financial officer at the company almost since its founding, her buttoned-down demeanor as CEO has been a turnaround from the blue-jeans vibe of founder Vadon, 11 years her junior. "She added discipline to that company from the day she walked through the door," says Scott Devitt, analyst at Morgan Stanley. It's a work ethic Irvine says she developed in her youth, growing up on a farm and working summer jobs in the cornfields of Illinois. Irvine's offensive is beginning to pay off. In October Blue Nile posted its first year-over-year growth in revenues since mid-2008. "She's done a great job of stabilizing the business," says Deutsche Bank analyst Herman Leung. Meanwhile three of the top traditional jewelry retailers have filed for bankruptcy, and competitor Zale appears poised for a major restructuring.

Yammering Is Good

Molson Dry. Coors Light. Miller Genuine Draft. Carling. Just reading all the beer brands sold by Molson Coors could make you tipsy. The company, jointly headquartered in Denver and Montreal, has grown into one of the world's largest brewers through a series of 10 acquisitions and joint ventures over the past decade. Yet all the deal activity left a mishmash of workforces when Peter Swinburn became head of the company in June 2008. So even as sales began to slide going into the downturn, he decided his priority would be forging a cohesive corporate culture. "If you spend five years developing a brand, why shouldn't you spend five years developing a culture?" asks Swinburn, 57.

The challenge was getting a staff of 15,000 workers on three continents to think as one. There were different languages and work practices. The U.S. and British operations even disagreed over the proper size for a beer barrel. (It was 117 liters in the United States and 163 in the United Kingdom.) "You had people who were focused on their individual businesses and their own regions," says Rob Borland, a top marketing executive. Swinburn spent his first six months as CEO sketching out a framework for the new approach. In conversations with senior executives and in town hall meetings with employees, he came up with an unofficial motto—"Challenge the expected"—that he hoped would entice employees at all levels to think outside their roles. Swinburn also made sure employees had better tools to interact with one another. On the suggestion of one worker, he signed the company up for Yammer, a site for short messages similar to Twitter that would be visible only to colleagues. Some 2,000 employees now utilize the site to provide updates and collaborate on projects. Employees are also getting together in person more frequently. Benoit Maillette, the brewery manager in Toronto, says he meets with counterparts from around the world once or twice a year to socialize and share business ideas. One January gathering was in the company suite at a Montreal Canadiens hockey game, with a lot of time "around the bar," says Maillette. Swinburn's efforts appear to be having an impact.

Swinburn, who started working at Bass Brewers in his 20s, takes the beer business personally. "When Peter goes to the grocery store with his wife, he typically wanders off after just a few minutes," says Leo Kiely, who heads a joint venture Molson Coors has with SABMiller. "He's gone off to the beer aisle, and he's over there rearranging the shelves, making sure his beer is displayed properly and there are no torn packages." The brewer is eyeing more deals in the fast-consolidating beer market. Last May it bought Cobra Beer, a British brand popular in curry restaurants. Swinburn intends to keep expanding through acquisitions. "Our balance sheet is strong, so if the right opportunities come around, we can move," the CEO says.

For these new chief executives, survival was the first test. Still, their trials are far from over. As the economy recovers, they have to shift out of crisis mode and focus on long-term strategy and investments. If you come of age in a firestorm, your job has to change when the flames die out.

Questions for Discussion

1. Use the chapter material to decide what different kinds of management challenges these four CEOs faced as they took control of managing their different companies.
2. In what kinds of ways did these managers respond to these challenges—for example, in their approaches to planning, leading, organizing and controlling?
3. Search the Web. How are these managers and their companies currently performing?

Source: D. MacMillan, "How Four Rookie CEOs Handled the Great Recession," *BusinessWeek*, February 18, 2010. Reprinted from February 18, 2010 issue of *Bloomberg Businessweek* by special permission, copyright © 2010 by Bloomberg L.P.

CHAPTER 2

The Evolution of Management Thought

Learning Objectives

After studying this chapter, you should be able to:

LO2-1 Describe how the need to increase organizational efficiency and effectiveness has guided the evolution of management theory.

LO2-2 Explain the principle of job specialization and division of labor, and tell why the study of person–task relationships is central to the pursuit of increased efficiency.

LO2-3 Identify the principles of administration and organization that underlie effective organizations.

LO2-4 Trace the changes in theories about how managers should behave to motivate and control employees.

LO2-5 Explain the contributions of management science to the efficient use of organizational resources.

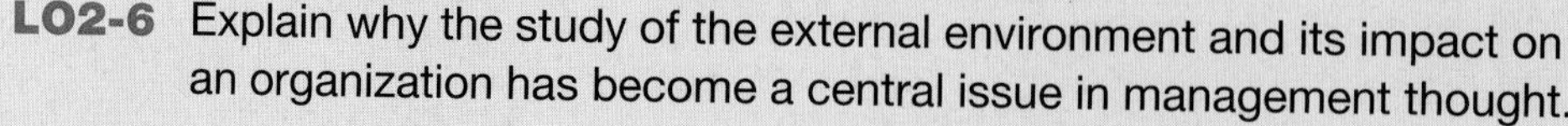

LO2-6 Explain why the study of the external environment and its impact on an organization has become a central issue in management thought.

A MANAGER'S CHALLENGE

Finding Better Ways to Make Cars

What is the best way to manage the work process? Car production has changed dramatically over the years as managers have applied different management principles to organize and control work activities. Prior to 1900, small groups of skilled workers cooperated to hand-build cars with parts that often had to be altered and modified to fit together. This system, a type of *small-batch production,* was expensive; assembling just one car took considerable time and effort, and skilled workers could produce only a few cars per day. Although these cars were of high quality, they were too expensive for most customers. Managers needed better methods to increase efficiency, reduce costs, and sell more cars.

Henry Ford revolutionized the car industry. In 1913 Ford opened the Highland Park car plant in Detroit to produce the Model T Ford, and his team of manufacturing managers pioneered the development of *mass-production manufacturing,* which made small-batch car production inefficient. In mass production, moving conveyor belts bring the cars to the workers, and each worker performs a single assigned task along the production line. Ford experimented to discover the most efficient way for each worker to perform an assigned task; and this was that each worker

(a) The photo on top, taken in 1904 inside a Daimler Motor Company factory, is an example of the use of small-batch production, a production system in which small groups of people work together and perform all the tasks needed to assemble a product. (b) In 1913 Henry Ford revolutionized car production by pioneering mass-production manufacturing, in which a conveyor belt brings each car to the workers, and each individual worker performs a single task along the production line. Cars are still built using this system, as shown in the photo of workers along a modern computerized automobile assembly line.

should perform one narrow, specialized task, such as bolting on the door or attaching the door handle. As a result, jobs in the Ford car plant became repetitive because they required little use of a worker's skills.[1] Ford's management approach increased efficiency and reduced costs so much that by 1920 he was able to reduce the price of a car by two-thirds and sold more than 2 million cars a year.[2] Ford became the leading car company in the world, and competitors rushed to adopt its new mass-production techniques.

The next major change in management thinking about car assembly occurred in Japan when Ohno Taiichi, a Toyota production engineer, pioneered the development of *lean manufacturing* in the 1960s after touring the U.S. factories of GM, Ford, and Chrysler. The management philosophy behind lean manufacturing is to continuously find methods to improve the efficiency of the production process to reduce costs, increase quality, and reduce car assembly time. Lean production is based on the idea that if workers have input and can participate in the decision-making process, their knowledge can be used to increase efficiency.

In lean manufacturing, workers work on a moving production line, but they are organized into small teams, each of which is responsible for a particular phase of car assembly, such as installing the car's transmission or electrical wiring system. Each team member is expected to learn the tasks of all members of that team, and each work group is responsible not only for assembling cars but also for finding ways to increase quality and reduce costs. By 1970 Japanese managers had applied the new lean production system so efficiently that they were producing higher-quality cars at lower prices than U.S. carmakers. By 1980 Japanese carmakers dominated the global market.

To compete, managers of U.S. carmakers visited Japan to learn the new manufacturing principles of lean production. All the Big Three U.S. carmakers spent billions of dollars implementing lean manufacturing; GM established its Saturn car division as a way to experiment with this new way of involving workers. In the 1990s U.S. carmakers also increased the number of robots they used on the assembly line and their use of IT to build and track the quality of cars being produced. Indeed, for a time it seemed that robots rather than employees would be building cars in the future. However, Toyota discovered something interesting at its first fully roboticized car plant. When only robots build cars, efficiency does not continually increase because, unlike people, robots cannot provide input to improve the work process. The optimum manufacturing methods must continuously work to find the right balance between using people, machinery, computers, and IT.

In the 2000s global car companies continued to compete fiercely to improve and perfect ways to make cars. Toyota remained the leader in pioneering new ways to manage its assembly lines to increase quality and efficiency; but other carmakers such as Honda, Nissan, and Hyundai, as well as Ford and GM, also made major strides to close the quality gap with Japanese carmakers. Nevertheless, U.S. carmakers steadily lost ground to their Japanese and European competitors because they could not make cars with the styling, quality, and price their customers demanded. It seemed that the future of all the Big Three U.S. carmakers was in doubt as they lost billions of dollars throughout the 1990s, and it seemed they might go out of business.

Everything changed in the carmaking business in 2009 after the economic and financial crisis led car sales to plummet, and every carmaker, including Toyota, lost billions of dollars. To stay afloat, most global carmakers had to rely on billions of dollars in assistance from their governments to stay in business because they could not pay their employees or finance their customers. At the same time the crisis showed that U.S. carmakers were essentially bankrupt because outdated contracts with their car dealers, unions, and workers had raised their overhead costs so high they could not compete globally. After borrowing billions from the U.S. government, GM was forced into bankruptcy to reduce its costs; Ford and Chrysler were able to form new contracts to reduce their costs; by spring 2010 it seemed that that all three would survive after Ford and GM reported profits.

To achieve this all U.S. carmakers had been forced to shut down hundreds of inefficient factories, lay off hundreds of thousands of car workers, and reduce the range of vehicles they produced. To survive, they focused their resources on the vehicles that managers believed would have the greatest appeal to customers in the future. Their managers raced to develop the cars customers wanted to buy today and to make them reliably and cost-effectively—which was especially important when Toyota overtook GM to become the largest global carmaker in 2008.

However, another milestone in carmaking history came in the spring of 2010 when Toyota—known as the quality leader—came under intense scrutiny because of claims that some of its cars suffered from uncontrolled acceleration due to brake defects and that it had been late in responding to owner complaints despite many accidents. Other carmakers also admitted defects, and the issue of how to better measure quality and safety to improve performance was a leading concern of carmakers in 2010. All carmakers were trying to find better ways to use the hundreds of computer sensors inside each vehicle to understand how to make a car more efficiently and effectively.

Overview

As this sketch of the evolution of management thinking in global car manufacturing suggests, changes in management practices occur as managers, theorists, researchers, and customers look for ways to increase how efficiently and effectively cars are made. The driving force behind the evolution of management theory is the search for better ways to use organizational resources to make goods and services. Advances in management thought typically occur as managers and researchers find better ways to perform the principal management tasks: planning, organizing, leading, and controlling human and other organizational resources.

In this chapter we examine how management thought has evolved in modern times and the central concerns that have guided ongoing advances in management theory. First we examine the so-called classical management theories that emerged around the turn of the 20th century. These include scientific management, which focuses on matching people and tasks to maximize efficiency, and administrative management, which focuses on identifying the principles that will lead to the creation of the most efficient system of organization and management. Next we consider behavioral management theories developed both before and after World War II; these focus on how managers should lead and control their workforces to increase performance. Then we discuss management science theory, which developed during World War II and has become increasingly important as researchers have developed rigorous analytical and quantitative techniques to help managers measure and control organizational performance. Finally we discuss changes in management practices from the middle to the late 1900s and focus on the theories developed to help explain how the external environment affects the way organizations and managers operate.

By the end of this chapter you will understand how management thought and theory have evolved over time. You will also understand how economic, political, and cultural forces have affected the development of these theories and how managers and their organizations have changed their behavior as a result. In Figure 2.1 we summarize the chronology of the management theories discussed in this chapter.

Scientific Management Theory

LO2-1 Describe how the need to increase organizational efficiency and effectiveness has guided the evolution of management theory.

The evolution of modern management began in the closing decades of the 19th century, after the industrial revolution had swept through Europe and America. In the new economic climate, managers of all types of organizations–political, educational, and economic–were trying to find better ways to satisfy customers' needs. Many major economic, technical, and cultural changes were taking place at this time. The introduction of steam power and the development of sophisticated machinery and equipment changed how goods were produced, particularly in the weaving and clothing industries. Small workshops run by skilled workers who produced hand-manufactured products (a system called *crafts production*) were being replaced by large factories in which sophisticated machines controlled by hundreds or even thousands of unskilled or semiskilled workers made products. For example, raw cotton and wool, which in the past had been spun into yarn by families or whole villages working together, were now shipped to factories where workers operated machines that spun and wove large quantities of yarn into cloth.

Owners and managers of the new factories found themselves unprepared for the challenges accompanying the change from small-scale crafts production to large-scale mechanized manufacturing. Moreover, many managers and supervisors in these workshops and factories were engineers who had only a technical orientation. They were unprepared for the social problems that occur when people work together in

Figure 2.1
The Evolution of Management Theory

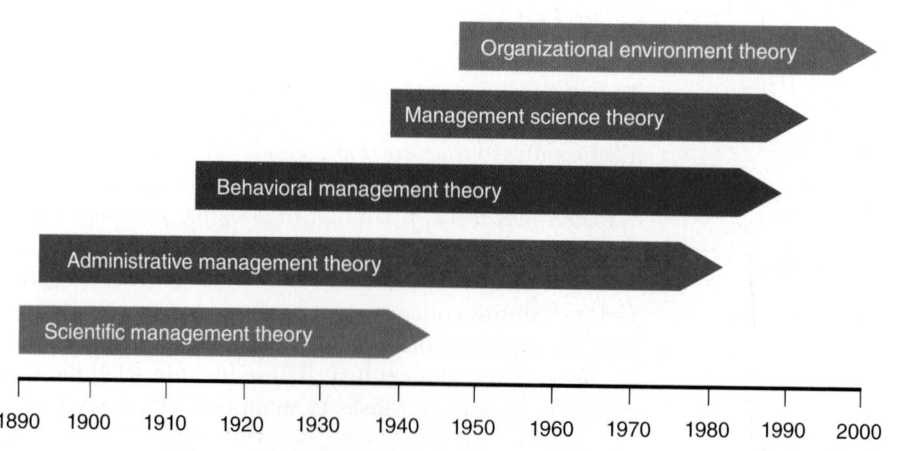

large groups in a factory or shop system. Managers began to search for new techniques to manage their organizations' resources, and soon they began to focus on ways to increase the efficiency of the worker–task mix.

Job Specialization and the Division of Labor

LO2-2 Explain the principle of job specialization and division of labor, and tell why the study of person–task relationships is central to the pursuit of increased efficiency.

Initially management theorists were interested in why the new machine shops and factory system were more efficient and produced greater quantities of goods and services than older, crafts-style production operations. Nearly 200 years before, Adam Smith had been one of the first writers to investigate the advantages associated with producing goods and services in factories. A famous economist, Smith journeyed around England in the 1700s studying the effects of the industrial revolution.[3] In a study of factories that produced various pins or nails, Smith identified two different manufacturing methods. The first was similar to crafts-style production, in which each worker was responsible for all the 18 tasks involved in producing a pin. The other had each worker performing only one or a few of these 18 tasks.

Smith found that the performance of the factories in which workers specialized in only one or a few tasks was much greater than the performance of the factory in which each worker performed all 18 pin-making tasks. In fact, Smith found that 10 workers specializing in a particular task could make 48,000 pins a day, whereas those workers who performed all the tasks could make only a few thousand.[4] Smith reasoned that this performance difference occurred because the workers who specialized became much more skilled at their specific tasks and as a group were thus able to produce a product faster than the group of workers who each performed many tasks. Smith concluded that increasing the level of **job specialization**—the process by which a division of labor occurs as different workers specialize in tasks—improves efficiency and leads to higher organizational performance.[5]

job specialization The process by which a division of labor occurs as different workers specialize in different tasks over time.

scientific management The systematic study of relationships between people and tasks for the purpose of redesigning the work process to increase efficiency.

Armed with the insights gained from Adam Smith's observations, other managers and researchers began to investigate how to improve job specialization to increase performance. Management practitioners and theorists focused on how managers should organize and control the work process to maximize the advantages of job specialization and the division of labor.

Frederick W. Taylor, founder of scientific management, and one of the first people to study the behavior and performance of people at work.

F. W. Taylor and Scientific Management

Frederick W. Taylor (1856–1915) is best known for defining the techniques of **scientific management,** the systematic study of relationships between people and tasks for the purpose of redesigning the work process to increase efficiency. Taylor was a manufacturing manager who eventually became a consultant and taught other managers how to apply his scientific management techniques. Taylor believed that if the amount of time and effort that each worker expends to produce a unit of output (a finished good or service) can be reduced by increasing specialization and the division of labor, the production process will become more efficient. According to Taylor, the way to create the most efficient division of labor could best be determined by scientific management techniques rather than by intuitive or informal rule-of-thumb knowledge. Based on his experiments and observations as a manufacturing manager in a variety of settings, he developed four principles to increase efficiency in the workplace:

- Principle 1: *Study the way workers perform their tasks, gather all the informal job knowledge that workers possess, and experiment with ways of improving how tasks are performed.*

To discover the most efficient method of performing specific tasks, Taylor studied in great detail and measured the ways different workers went about performing their tasks. One of the main tools he used was a time-and-motion study, which involves the careful timing and recording of the actions taken to perform a particular task. Once Taylor understood the existing method of performing a task, he then experimented to increase specialization. He tried different methods of dividing and coordinating the various tasks necessary to produce a finished product. Usually this meant simplifying jobs and having each worker perform fewer, more routine tasks, as at the pin factory or on Ford's car assembly line. Taylor also sought to find ways to improve each worker's ability to perform a particular task–for example, by reducing the number of motions workers made to complete the task, by changing the layout of the work area or the type of tools workers used, or by experimenting with tools of different sizes.

- Principle 2: *Codify the new methods of performing tasks into written rules and standard operating procedures.*

Once the best method of performing a particular task was determined, Taylor specified that it should be recorded so this procedure could be taught to all workers performing the same task. These new methods further standardized and simplified jobs–essentially making jobs even more routine. In this way efficiency could be increased throughout an organization.

- Principle 3: *Carefully select workers who possess skills and abilities that match the needs of the task, and train them to perform the task according to the established rules and procedures.*

To increase specialization, Taylor believed workers had to understand the tasks that were required and be thoroughly trained to perform the tasks at the required level. Workers who could not be trained to this level were to be transferred to a job where they were able to reach the minimum required level of proficiency.[6]

- Principle 4: *Establish a fair or acceptable level of performance for a task, and then develop a pay system that rewards performance above the acceptable level.*

To encourage workers to perform at a high level of efficiency, and to give them an incentive to reveal the most efficient techniques for performing a task, Taylor advocated that workers benefit from any gains in performance. They should be paid a bonus and receive some percentage of the performance gains achieved through the more efficient work process.[7]

By 1910 Taylor's system of scientific management had become nationally known and in many instances was faithfully and fully practiced.[8] However, managers in many organizations chose to implement the new principles of scientific management selectively. This decision ultimately resulted in problems. For example, some managers using scientific management obtained increases in performance, but rather than sharing performance gains with workers through bonuses as Taylor had advocated, they simply increased the amount of work that each worker was expected to do. Many workers experiencing the reorganized work system found that as their performance increased, managers required that they do more work for the same pay. Workers also learned that performance increases often meant fewer jobs and a greater threat of layoffs because fewer workers were needed. In addition, the specialized, simplified jobs were often monotonous and repetitive, and many workers became dissatisfied with their jobs.

Scientific management brought many workers more hardship than gain and a distrust of managers who did not seem to care about workers' well-being.[9] These dissatisfied workers resisted attempts to use the new scientific management techniques and at times even withheld their job knowledge from managers to protect their jobs and pay. It is not difficult for workers to conceal the true potential efficiency of a work system to protect their interests. Experienced machine operators, for example, can slow their machines in undetectable ways by adjusting the tension in the belts or by misaligning the gears. Workers sometimes even develop informal work rules that discourage high

Charlie Chaplin tries to extricate a fellow employee from the machinery of mass production in this scene from *Modern Times.* The complex machinery is meant to represent the power that machinery has over the worker in the new work system.

performance and encourage shirking as work groups attempt to identify an acceptable or fair performance level (a tactic discussed in the next section).

Unable to inspire workers to accept the new scientific management techniques for performing tasks, some organizations increased the mechanization of the work process. For example, one reason why Henry Ford introduced moving conveyor belts in his factory was the realization that when a conveyor belt controls the pace of work (instead of workers setting their own pace), workers can be pushed to perform at higher levels–levels that they may have thought were beyond their reach. Charlie Chaplin captured this aspect of mass production in one of the opening scenes of his famous movie *Modern Times* (1936). In the film Chaplin caricatured a new factory employee fighting to work at the machine-imposed pace but losing the battle to the machine. Henry Ford also used the principles of scientific management to identify the tasks that each worker should perform on the production line and thus to determine the most effective division of labor to suit the needs of a mechanized production system.

From a performance perspective, the combination of the two management practices–(1) achieving the right worker–task specialization and (2) linking people and tasks by the speed of the production line–makes sense. It produces the huge cost savings and dramatic output increases that occur in large, organized work settings. For example, in 1908 managers at the Franklin Motor Company using scientific management principles redesigned the work process, and the output of cars increased from 100 cars a *month* to 45 cars a *day;* workers' wages, however, increased by only 90%.[10] From other perspectives, however, scientific management practices raise many concerns. The definition of workers' rights not by the workers themselves but by the owners or managers raised an ethical issue, which we examine in the following "Ethics in Action" box.

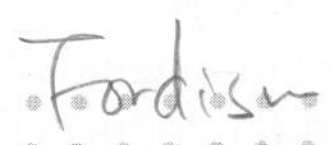

Ethics in Action

Fordism in Practice

From 1908 to 1914, through trial and error, Henry Ford's talented team of production managers pioneered the development of the moving conveyor belt and thus changed manufacturing practices forever. Although the technical aspects of the move to mass production were a dramatic financial success for Ford and for the millions of Americans who could now afford cars, for the workers who actually produced the cars many human and social problems resulted.

With simplification of the work process, workers grew to hate the monotony of the moving conveyor belt. By 1914 Ford's car plants were experiencing huge employee turnover–often reaching levels as high as 300% or 400% per year as workers left because they could not handle the work-induced stress.[11] Henry Ford recognized these problems and made an announcement: From that point on, to motivate his workforce, he would reduce the length of the workday from nine hours to eight hours, and the company would *double* the basic wage from $2.50 to $5.00 per day. This was a dramatic increase, similar to an announcement today of an overnight doubling of the minimum wage. Ford became an internationally famous figure, and the word *Fordism* was coined for his new approach.[12]

Ford's apparent generosity, however, was matched by an intense effort to control the resources–both human and material–with which his empire was built.

Henry Ford sits in an early model Ford outside a showroom in Detroit, Michigan, shortly after the corporation was formed in 1903. By 1914 Ford's car plants were experiencing huge employee turnover as workers left because they could not handle the work-induced stress.

He employed hundreds of inspectors to check up on employees, both inside and outside his factories. In the factory, supervision was close and confining. Employees were not allowed to leave their places at the production line, and they were not permitted to talk to one another. Their job was to concentrate fully on the task at hand. Few employees could adapt to this system, and they developed ways of talking out of the sides of their mouths, like ventriloquists, and invented a form of speech that became known as the "Ford Lisp."[13] Ford's obsession with control brought him into greater and greater conflict with managers, who often were fired when they disagreed with him. As a result, many talented people left Ford to join a growing number of rival car companies.

Outside the workplace, Ford went so far as to establish what he called the "Sociological Department" to check up on how his employees lived and spent their time. Inspectors from this department visited the homes of employees and investigated their habits and problems. Employees who exhibited behaviors contrary to Ford's standards (for instance, if they drank too much or were always in debt) were likely to be fired. Clearly Ford's efforts to control his employees led him and his managers to behave in ways that today would be considered unacceptable and unethical and in the long run would impair an organization's ability to prosper.

Despite the problems of worker turnover, absenteeism, and discontent at Ford Motor Company, managers of the other car companies watched Ford reap huge gains in efficiency from the application of the new management principles. They believed their companies would have to imitate Ford if they were to survive. They followed Taylor and used many of his followers as consultants to teach them how to adopt the techniques of scientific management. In addition, Taylor elaborated his principles in several books, including *Shop Management* (1903) and *The Principles of Scientific Management* (1911), which explain in detail how to apply the principles of scientific management to reorganize the work system.[14]

Taylor's work has had an enduring effect on the management of production systems. Managers in every organization, whether it produces goods or services, now carefully analyze the basic tasks that must be performed and try to devise work systems that allow their organizations to operate most efficiently.

The Gilbreths

Two prominent followers of Taylor were Frank Gilbreth (1868–1924) and Lillian Gilbreth (1878–1972), who refined Taylor's analysis of work movements and made many contributions to time-and-motion study.[15] Their aims were to (1) analyze every individual action necessary to perform a particular task and break it into each of its component actions, (2) find better ways to perform each component action, and (3) reorganize each of the component actions so that the action as a whole could be performed more efficiently–at less cost in time and effort.

The Gilbreths often filmed a worker performing a particular task and then separated the task actions, frame by frame, into their component movements. Their goal was to maximize the efficiency with which each individual task was performed so that gains across tasks would add up to enormous savings of time and effort. Their attempts to develop improved management principles were captured–at times quite humorously–in the movie *Cheaper by the Dozen,* a new version of which appeared

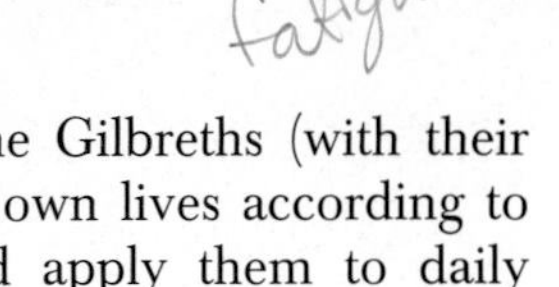

This scene from *Cheaper by the Dozen* illustrates how "efficient families," such as the Gilbreths, use formal family courts to solve problems of assigning chores to different family members and to solve disputes when they arise.

in 2004, which depicts how the Gilbreths (with their 12 children) tried to live their own lives according to these efficiency principles and apply them to daily actions such as shaving, cooking, and even raising a family.[16]

Eventually the Gilbreths became increasingly interested in the study of fatigue. They studied how physical characteristics of the workplace contribute to job stress that often leads to fatigue and thus poor performance. They isolated factors that result in worker fatigue, such as lighting, heating, the color of walls, and the design of tools and machines. Their pioneering studies paved the way for new advances in management theory.

In workshops and factories, the work of the Gilbreths, Taylor, and many others had a major effect on the practice of management. In comparison with the old crafts system, jobs in the new system were more repetitive, boring, and monotonous as a result of the application of scientific management principles, and workers became increasingly dissatisfied. Frequently the management of work settings became a game between workers and managers: Managers tried to initiate work practices to increase performance, and workers tried to hide the true potential efficiency of the work setting to protect their own well-being.[17] The story of how Andrew Carnegie created the most successful industrial company of his day, Carnegie Steel, illustrates the kind of management thinking that was sweeping through the United States at that time, the looming battles between management and workers, and the growing number of trade unions that were springing up to represent workers' interests (see the accompanying "Manager as a Person" box).

Manager as a Person

Andrew Carnegie Creates the New Industrial Company

Andrew Carnegie, born in Scotland in 1835, was the son of a master handloom weaver who, at that time, employed four apprentices to weave fine linen tablecloths. His family was well-to-do, yet 10 years later they were living in poverty. Why? Advances in weaving technology had led to the invention of steam-powered weaving looms that could produce large quantities of cotton cloth at a much lower price than was possible through handloom weaving. Handloom weavers could not compete at such low prices, and Carnegie's father was put out of business.

In 1848 Carnegie's family, like hundreds of thousands of other families in Europe at the time, emigrated to the United States to find work and survive. They settled near Pittsburgh, where they had relatives, and Carnegie's father continued to weave tablecloths and sell them door-to-door for around $6 a week. Carnegie found a job as a "bobbin boy," replacing spools of thread on power looms in a textile factory. He took home $1.20 for working a 60-hour week.

After his employer found out he could read and write, a rare skill at that time, Carnegie became a bookkeeper for the factory. In his spare time he became a telegraph messenger and learned telegraphy. He began to deliver telegrams to Tom Scott, a top manager at the Pennsylvania Railroad, who came to appreciate Carnegie's drive and talents. Scott made him his personal telegrapher for an astonishing sum of $35 a week. Carnegie was now 17; only seven years later,

Andrew Carnegie, depicted here in later life. His legacy is a complicated one of hard work as an immigrant, a rise to power and wealth through hardnosed management, accusations of monopolistic business practices, and a dedication to philanthropy that caused him to avow that "no one should die rich."

when he was 24, he was promoted to Scott's job, superintendent of the railroad's western division. At 30 he was offered the top job of superintendent of the *whole* railroad! Carnegie had made his name by continually finding ways to use resources more productively to reduce costs and increase profitability. Under his oversight of the western division, his company's stock price had shot up–which explains why he was offered the railroad's top job. He had also invested cleverly in railroad stock and was now a wealthy man with an income of $48,000 a year, of which only $2,800 came from his railroad salary.

Carnegie had ambitions other than remaining in his top railroad job, however. He had noticed U.S. railroads' growing demand for steel rails as they expanded rapidly across the country. At that time steel was made by the method of small-batch production, a labor-intensive process in which groups of employees worked together to produce small quantities of steel. This method was expensive, and the steel produced cost $135 a ton. As he searched for ways to reduce the cost of steelmaking, Carnegie was struck by the fact that many different companies performed each of the different operations necessary to convert iron ore into finished steel products. One company smelted iron ore into "pig iron." Another company transported the pig iron to other companies that rolled the pig iron into bars or slabs. Many other companies then bought these bars and slabs and made them into finished products such as steel rails, nails, wire, and so on. Intermediaries that bought the products of one company and then sold them to another connected the activities of these different companies. The many exchanges involved in converting iron ore into finished products greatly increased operating costs. At each stage of the production process, iron and steel had to be shipped to the next company and reheated until they became soft enough to work on. Moreover, these intermediaries were earning large profits for providing this service, which raised the cost of the finished products.

The second thing Carnegie noticed was that the steel produced by British steel mills was of a higher quality than that made in U.S. mills. The British had made major advances in steelmaking technology, and U.S. railroads preferred to buy their steel rails. On one of his frequent trips to Britain Carnegie saw a demonstration of Sir Henry Bessemer's new "hot blasting" method for making steel. Bessemer's famous process made it possible to produce great quantities of higher-quality steel *continuously*–as a process, not in small batches. Carnegie instantly realized the enormous cost-saving potential of the new technology. He rushed to become the first steelmaker in the United States to adopt it.

Carnegie subsequently sold all his railroad stock and used the proceeds to create the Carnegie Steel Company, the first low-cost Bessemer steelmaking plant in the United States. Determined to retain the profit that intermediaries were making in his business, he decided his company would perform *all* the steelmaking operations necessary to convert iron ore into finished products. For

example, he constructed rolling mills to make steel rails next to his blast furnace so iron ore could be converted into finished steel products in one continuous process. Carnegie's innovations led to a dramatic fall in steelmaking costs and revolutionized the U.S. steel industry. His new production methods reduced the price of U.S. steel from $135 a ton to $12 a ton! Despite the cheaper price, his company was still enormously profitable, and he plowed back all his profits into building his steel business and constructed many new low-cost steel plants. By 1900 most of his competitors had been driven out of business because of his low prices; his company was the leading U.S. steelmaker, and he was one of the richest men in the world.

Although the story of Carnegie's new approach to management might seem like "business as usual," there is another side to Carnegie's management style. Critics say he increased profitability "on the backs" of his workers. Despite the enormous increase in productivity he achieved by using the new mass-production steelmaking technology, he was continually driven by the need to find every way possible to reduce operating costs. To increase productivity, Carnegie gradually increased the normal workday from an already long 10 hours to 12 hours, six days a week. He also paid his workers the lowest wage rate possible even though their increasing skills in mastering the new technology were contributing to the huge increase in productivity. He paid no attention to improving the safety of his mills, where workers toiled in dangerous conditions and thousands of workers were injured each year by spills of molten steel. Any attempts by workers to improve their work conditions were rejected, and Carnegie routinely crushed any of the workers' attempts to unionize. In implementing new management techniques and creating the modern industrial company, Carnegie also created the need for new administrative management theory–theory that could help managers find better ways of organizing and controlling resources to increase performance, as well as find new strategies for negotiating with and managing the increasingly unionized workforce that modern production methods had brought into being.

LO2-3 Identify the principles of administration and organization that underlie effective organizations.

Administrative Management Theory

Side by side with scientific managers like Carnegie studying the person–technology mix to increase efficiency, other managers and researchers were focusing on **administrative management,** the study of how to create an organizational structure and control system that leads to high efficiency and effectiveness. *Organizational structure* is the system of task and authority relationships that controls how employees use resources to achieve the organization's goals. Two of the most influential early views regarding the creation of efficient systems of organizational administration were developed in Europe: Max Weber, a German sociology professor, developed one theory; and Henri Fayol, the French manager who developed the model of management introduced in Chapter 1, developed the other.

administrative management The study of how to create an organizational structure and control system that leads to high efficiency and effectiveness.

The Theory of Bureaucracy

Max Weber (1864–1920) wrote at the turn of the 20th century, when Germany was undergoing its industrial revolution.[18] To help Germany manage its growing industrial enterprises while it was striving to become a world power, Weber developed the principles of **bureaucracy**–a formal system of organization and administration designed to ensure efficiency and effectiveness. A bureaucratic system of administration is based on the five principles summarized in Figure 2.2:

bureaucracy A formal system of organization and administration designed to ensure efficiency and effectiveness.

- Principle 1: *In a bureaucracy, a manager's formal authority derives from the position he or she holds in the organization.*

Figure 2.2
Weber's Principles of Bureaucracy

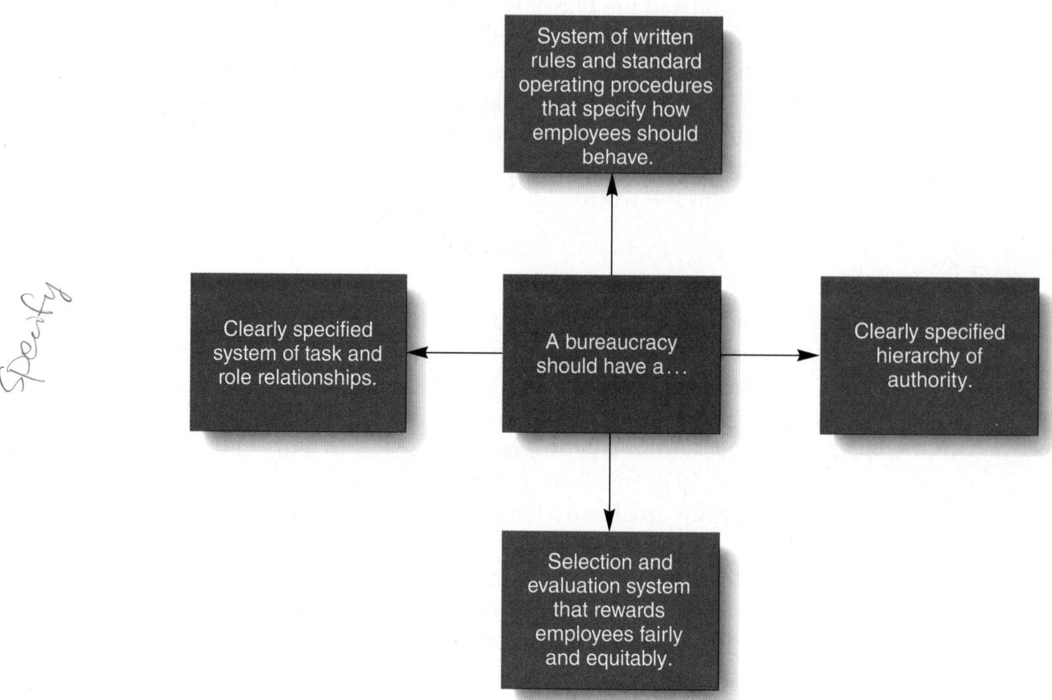

authority The power to hold people accountable for their actions and to make decisions concerning the use of organizational resources.

Authority is the power to hold people accountable for their actions and to make decisions concerning the use of organizational resources. Authority gives managers the right to direct and control their subordinates' behavior to achieve organizational goals. In a bureaucratic system of administration, obedience is owed to a manager not because of any personal qualities–such as personality, wealth, or social status–but because the manager occupies a position that is associated with a certain level of authority and responsibility.[19]

- Principle 2: *In a bureaucracy, people should occupy positions because of their performance, not because of their social standing or personal contacts.*

This principle was not always followed in Weber's time and is often ignored today. Some organizations and industries are still affected by social networks in which personal contacts and relations, not job-related skills, influence hiring and promotional decisions.

- Principle 3: *The extent of each position's formal authority and task responsibilities, and its relationship to other positions in an organization, should be clearly specified.*

When the tasks and authority associated with various positions in the organization are clearly specified, managers and workers know what is expected of them and what to expect from each other. Moreover, an organization can hold all its employees strictly accountable for their actions when they know their exact responsibilities.

- Principle 4: *Authority can be exercised effectively in an organization when positions are arranged hierarchically, so employees know whom to report to and who reports to them.*[20]

Managers must create an organizational hierarchy of authority that makes it clear who reports to whom and to whom managers and workers should go if conflicts or problems arise. This principle is especially important in the armed forces, FBI, CIA, and other organizations that deal with sensitive issues involving possible major repercussions. It is vital that managers at high levels of the hierarchy be able to hold subordinates accountable for their actions.

- Principle 5: *Managers must create a well-defined system of rules, standard operating procedures, and norms so they can effectively control behavior within an organization.*

Max Weber developed the principles of bureaucracy during Germany's burgeoning industrial revolution to help organizations increase their efficiency and effectiveness.

Rules are formal written instructions that specify actions to be taken under different circumstances to achieve specific goals (for example, if A happens, do B). **Standard operating procedures (SOPs)** are specific sets of written instructions about how to perform a certain aspect of a task. A rule might state that at the end of the workday employees are to leave their machines in good order, and a set of SOPs would specify exactly how they should do so, itemizing which machine parts must be oiled or replaced. **Norms** are unwritten, informal codes of conduct that prescribe how people should act in particular situations and are considered important by most members of a group or organization. For example, an organizational norm in a restaurant might be that waiters should help each other if time permits.

Rules, SOPs, and norms provide behavioral guidelines that increase the performance of a bureaucratic system because they specify the best ways to accomplish organizational tasks. Companies such as McDonald's and Walmart have developed extensive rules and procedures to specify the behaviors required of their employees, such as "Always greet the customer with a smile."

Weber believed organizations that implement all five principles establish a bureaucratic system that improves organizational performance. The specification of positions and the use of rules and SOPs to regulate how tasks are performed make it easier for managers to organize and control the work of subordinates. Similarly, fair and equitable selection and promotion systems improve managers' feelings of security, reduce stress, and encourage organizational members to act ethically and further promote the interests of the organization.[21]

If bureaucracies are not managed well, however, many problems can result. Sometimes managers allow rules and SOPs, "bureaucratic red tape," to become so cumbersome that decision making is slow and inefficient and organizations cannot change. When managers rely too much on rules to solve problems and not enough on their own skills and judgment, their behavior becomes inflexible. A key challenge for managers is to use bureaucratic principles to benefit, rather than harm, an organization.

rules Formal written instructions that specify actions to be taken under different circumstances to achieve specific goals.

standard operating procedures (SOPs) Specific sets of written instructions about how to perform a certain aspect of a task.

norms Unwritten, informal codes of conduct that prescribe how people should act in particular situations and are considered important by most members of a group or organization.

Fayol's Principles of Management

Henri Fayol (1841–1925) was the CEO of Comambault Mining. Working at the same time as Weber, but independently, Fayol identified 14 principles (summarized in Table 2.1) that he believed essential to increase the efficiency of the management process.[22] We discuss these principles in detail here because, although they were developed at the turn of the 20th century, they remain the bedrock on which much of recent management theory and research is based. In fact, as the "Management Insight" box following this discussion suggests, modern writers such as well-known management guru Tom Peters continue to extol these principles.

DIVISION OF LABOR A champion of job specialization and the division of labor for reasons already mentioned, Fayol was nevertheless among the first to point out the downside of too much specialization: boredom–a state of mind likely to diminish product quality, worker initiative, and flexibility. As a result, Fayol advocated that workers be given more job duties to perform or be encouraged to assume more responsibility for work outcomes–a principle increasingly applied today in organizations that empower their workers.

Table 2.1
Fayol's 14 Principles of Management

Division of labor Job specialization and the division of labor should increase efficiency, especially if managers take steps to lessen workers' boredom.

Authority and responsibility Managers have the right to give orders and the power to exhort subordinates for obedience.

Unity of command An employee should receive orders from only one superior.

Line of authority The length of the chain of command that extends from the top to the bottom of an organization should be limited.

Centralization Authority should not be concentrated at the top of the chain of command.

Unity of direction The organization should have a single plan of action to guide managers and workers.

Equity All organizational members are entitled to be treated with justice and respect.

Order The arrangement of organizational positions should maximize organizational efficiency and provide employees with satisfying career opportunities.

Initiative Managers should allow employees to be innovative and creative.

Discipline Managers need to create a workforce that strives to achieve organizational goals.

Remuneration of personnel The system that managers use to reward employees should be equitable for both employees and the organization.

Stability of tenure of personnel Long-term employees develop skills that can improve organizational efficiency.

Subordination of individual interests to the common interest Employees should understand how their performance affects the performance of the whole organization.

Esprit de corps Managers should encourage the development of shared feelings of comradeship, enthusiasm, or devotion to a common cause.

AUTHORITY AND RESPONSIBILITY Like Weber, Fayol emphasized the importance of authority and responsibility. Fayol, however, went beyond Weber's formal authority, which derives from a manager's position in the hierarchy, to recognize the *informal* authority that derives from personal expertise, technical knowledge, moral worth, and the ability to lead and to generate commitment from subordinates. (The study of authority is the subject of recent research into leadership, discussed in Chapter 14.)

unity of command A reporting relationship in which an employee receives orders from, and reports to, only one superior.

UNITY OF COMMAND The principle of **unity of command** specifies that an employee should receive orders from, and report to, only one superior. Fayol believed that *dual command,* the reporting relationship that exists when two supervisors give orders to the same subordinate, should be avoided except in exceptional circumstances. Dual command confuses subordinates, undermines order and discipline, and creates havoc within the formal hierarchy of authority. Assessing any manager's authority and responsibility in a system of dual command is difficult, and the manager who is bypassed feels slighted and angry and may be uncooperative in the future.

Scalar chain

line of authority The chain of command extending from the top to the bottom of an organization.

LINE OF AUTHORITY The **line of authority** is the chain of command extending from the top to the bottom of an organization. Fayol was one of the first management theorists to point out the importance of limiting the length of the chain of command by controlling the number of levels in the managerial hierarchy. The more levels in

Henri Fayol, who maintained Weber's principles of formal organization but added recognition of the pivotal role played by informal authority.

the hierarchy, the longer communication takes between managers at the top and bottom and the slower the pace of planning and organizing. Restricting the number of hierarchical levels to lessen these communication problems lets an organization act quickly and flexibly; this is one reason for the recent trend toward restructuring (discussed in Chapter 1).

Fayol also pointed out that when organizations are split into different departments or functions, each with its own hierarchy, it is important to allow middle and first-line managers in each department to interact with managers at similar levels in other departments. This interaction helps speed decision making because managers know each other and know whom to go to when problems arise. For cross-departmental integration to work, Fayol noted the importance of keeping one's superiors informed about what is taking place so that lower-level decisions do not harm activities taking place in other parts of the organization. One alternative to cross-departmental integration is to create cross-departmental teams controlled by a team leader (see Chapter 1).

CENTRALIZATION Fayol also was one of the first management writers to focus on **centralization,** the concentration of authority at the top of the managerial hierarchy. Fayol believed authority should not be concentrated at the top of the chain of command. One of the most significant issues that top managers face is how much authority to centralize at the top of the organization and what authority to decentralize to managers and workers at lower hierarchical levels. This important issue affects the behavior of people at all levels in the organization.

centralization The concentration of authority at the top of the managerial hierarchy.

If authority is very centralized, only managers at the top make important decisions, and subordinates simply follow orders. This arrangement gives top managers great control over organizational activities and helps ensure that the organization is pursuing its strategy, but it makes it difficult for the people who are closest to problems and issues to respond to them in a timely manner. It also can reduce the motivation of middle and first-line managers and make them less flexible and adaptable because they become reluctant to make decisions on their own, even when doing so is necessary. They get used to passing the buck. As we saw in Chapter 1, the pendulum is now swinging toward decentralization as organizations seek to empower middle managers and create self-managed teams that monitor and control their own activities both to increase organizational flexibility and to reduce operating costs and increase efficiency.

UNITY OF DIRECTION Just as there is a need for unity of command, there is also a need for **unity of direction,** the singleness of purpose that makes possible the creation of one plan of action to guide managers and workers as they use organizational resources. An organization without a single guiding plan becomes inefficient and ineffective; its activities become unfocused, and individuals and groups work at cross-purposes. Successful planning starts with top managers working as a team to craft the organization's strategy, which they communicate to middle managers, who decide how to use organizational resources to implement the strategy.

unity of direction The singleness of purpose that makes possible the creation of one plan of action to guide managers and workers as they use organizational resources.

EQUITY As Fayol wrote, "For personnel to be encouraged to carry out their duties with all the devotion and loyalty of which they are capable, they must be treated with respect for their own sense of integrity, and equity results from the combination of respect and justice."[23] **Equity**–the justice, impartiality, and fairness to which all organizational members are entitled–is receiving much attention today; the desire to treat employees fairly is a primary concern of managers. (Equity theory is discussed in Chapter 13.)

equity The justice, impartiality, and fairness to which all organizational members are entitled.

ORDER Like Taylor and the Gilbreths, Fayol was interested in analyzing jobs, positions, and individuals to ensure that the organization was using resources as efficiently as possible. To Fayol, **order** meant the methodical arrangement of positions

order The methodical arrangement of positions to provide the organization with the greatest benefit and to provide employees with career opportunities.

to provide the organization with the greatest benefit and to provide employees with career opportunities that satisfy their needs. Thus Fayol recommended the use of organizational charts to show the position and duties of each employee and to indicate which positions an employee might move to or be promoted into in the future. He also advocated that managers engage in extensive career planning to help ensure orderly career paths. Career planning is of primary interest today as organizations increase the resources they are willing to devote to training and developing their workforces.

initiative The ability to act on one's own without direction from a superior.

INITIATIVE Although order and equity are important means to fostering commitment and loyalty among employees, Fayol believed managers must also encourage employees to exercise **initiative,** the ability to act on their own without direction from a superior. Used properly, initiative can be a major source of strength for an organization because it leads to creativity and innovation. Managers need skill and tact to achieve the difficult balance between the organization's need for order and employees' desire for initiative. Fayol believed the ability to strike this balance was a key indicator of a superior manager.

discipline Obedience, energy, application, and other outward marks of respect for a superior's authority.

DISCIPLINE In focusing on the importance of **discipline**–obedience, energy, application, and other outward marks of respect for a superior's authority–Fayol was addressing the concern of many early managers: how to create a workforce that was reliable and hardworking and would strive to achieve organizational goals. According to Fayol, discipline results in respectful relations between organizational members and reflects the quality of an organization's leadership and a manager's ability to act fairly and equitably.

REMUNERATION OF PERSONNEL Fayol proposed reward systems including bonuses and profit-sharing plans, which are increasingly used today as organizations seek improved ways to motivate employees. Convinced from his own experience that an organization's payment system has important implications for organizational success, Fayol believed effective reward systems should be equitable for both employees and the organization, encourage productivity by rewarding well-directed effort, not be subject to abuse, and be uniformly applied to employees.

STABILITY OF TENURE OF PERSONNEL Fayol also recognized the importance of long-term employment, and this idea has been echoed by contemporary management gurus such as Tom Peters, Jeff Pfeffer, and William Ouchi. When employees stay with an organization for extended periods, they develop skills that improve the organization's ability to use its resources.

SUBORDINATION OF INDIVIDUAL INTERESTS TO THE COMMON INTEREST The interests of the organization as a whole must take precedence over the interests of any individual or group if the organization is to survive. Equitable agreements must be established between the organization and its members to ensure that employees are treated fairly and rewarded for their performance and to maintain the disciplined organizational relationships so vital to an efficient system of administration.

esprit de corps Shared feelings of comradeship, enthusiasm, or devotion to a common cause among members of a group.

ESPRIT DE CORPS As this discussion of Fayol's ideas suggests, the appropriate design of an organization's hierarchy of authority and the right mix of order and discipline foster cooperation and commitment. Likewise, a key element in a successful organization is the development of **esprit de corps,** a French expression that refers to shared feelings of comradeship, enthusiasm, or devotion to a common cause among members of a group. Esprit de corps can result when managers encourage personal, verbal contact between managers and workers and encourage communication to solve problems and implement solutions. (Today the term *organizational culture* is used to refer to these shared feelings; this concept is discussed at length in Chapter 3.)

Some of the principles that Fayol outlined have faded from contemporary management practices, but most have endured. The characteristics of organizations that Tom Peters and Robert Waterman identified as being "excellently managed" in their best-selling book *In Search of Excellence* (1982) are discussed in the following "Management Insight."[24]

Management Insight

Peters and Waterman's Excellent Companies

In the early 1980s Tom Peters and Robert Waterman identified 62 organizations that they considered to be the best-performing organizations in the United States. They asked, "Why do these companies perform better than their rivals?" and discovered that successful organizations are managed according to three sets of related principles. Those principles have a great deal in common with Fayol's principles.

First, Peters and Waterman argued, top managers of successful companies create principles and guidelines that emphasize managerial autonomy and entrepreneurship and encourage risk taking and *initiative.* For example, they allow middle managers to develop new products even though there is no assurance that these products will be winners. In high-performing organizations, top managers are closely involved in the day-to-day operations of the company, provide *unity of command* and *unity of direction,* and do not simply make isolated decisions. Top managers *decentralize authority* to lower-level managers and nonmanagerial employees and give them the freedom to get involved and the motivation to get things done.

The second approach that managers of excellent organizations use to increase performance is to create one central plan that puts organizational goals at center stage. In high-performing organizations, managers focus attention on what the organization does best, and the emphasis is on continuously improving the goods and services the organization provides to its customers. Managers of top-performing companies resist the temptation to get sidetracked into pursuing ventures outside their area of expertise just because they seem to promise a quick return. These managers also focus on customers and establish close relationships with them to learn their needs; responsiveness to customers increases competitive advantage.

The third set of management principles pertains to organizing and controlling the organization. Excellent companies establish a *division of work* and a *division of authority and responsibility* that will motivate employees to *subordinate their individual interests to the common interest.* Inherent in this approach is the belief that high performance derives from individual skills and abilities and that *equity, order, initiative,* and other indications of respect for the individual create the *esprit de corps* that fosters productive behavior. An emphasis on entrepreneurship and respect for every employee leads the best managers to create a structure that gives employees room to exercise *initiative* and motivates them to succeed. Because a simple, streamlined managerial hierarchy is best suited to achieving this outcome, top managers keep the line of *authority* as short as possible. They also decentralize authority to permit employee participation, but they keep enough control to maintain *unity of direction.*

As this insight into contemporary management suggests, the basic concerns that motivated Fayol continue to inspire management theorists.[25] The principles that Fayol and Weber set forth still provide clear and appropriate guidelines that managers can use to create a work setting that efficiently and effectively uses organizational resources. These principles remain the bedrock of modern management theory; recent researchers have refined or developed them to suit modern conditions. For example, Weber's and Fayol's concerns for equity and for establishing appropriate links between performance and reward are central themes in contemporary theories of motivation and leadership.

Behavioral Management Theory

LO2-4 Trace the changes in theories about how managers should behave to motivate and control employees.

Because the writings of Weber and Fayol were not translated into English and published in the United States until the late 1940s, American management theorists in the first half of the 20th century were unaware of the contributions of these European pioneers. American management theorists began where Taylor and his followers left off. Although their writings were different, these theorists all espoused a theme that focused on **behavioral management,** the study of how managers should personally behave to motivate employees and encourage them to perform at high levels and be committed to achieving organizational goals.

behavioral management The study of how managers should behave to motivate employees and encourage them to perform at high levels and be committed to the achievement of organizational goals.

The Work of Mary Parker Follett

If F. W. Taylor is considered the father of management thought, Mary Parker Follett (1868–1933) serves as its mother.[26] Much of her writing about management and about the way managers should behave toward workers was a response to her concern that Taylor was ignoring the human side of the organization. She pointed out that management often overlooks the multitude of ways in which employees can contribute to the organization when managers allow them to participate and exercise initiative in their everyday work lives.[27] Taylor, for example, never proposed that managers should involve workers in analyzing their jobs to identify better ways to perform tasks or should even ask workers how they felt about their jobs. Instead he used time-and-motion experts to analyze workers' jobs for them. Follett, in contrast, argued that because workers know the most about their jobs, they should be involved in job analysis and managers should allow them to participate in the work development process.

Mary Parker Follett, an early management thinker who advocated, "Authority should go with knowledge . . . whether it is up the line or down."

Follett proposed that "authority should go with knowledge . . . whether it is up the line or down." In other words, if workers have the relevant knowledge, then workers, rather than managers, should be in control of the work process itself, and managers should behave as coaches and facilitators–not as monitors and supervisors. In making this statement, Follett anticipated the current interest in self-managed teams and empowerment. She also recognized the importance of having managers in different departments communicate directly with each other to speed decision making. She advocated what she called "cross-functioning": members of different departments working together in cross-departmental teams to accomplish projects–an approach that is increasingly used today.[28]

Fayol also mentioned expertise and knowledge as important sources of managers' authority, but Follett went further. She proposed that knowledge and expertise, and not managers' formal authority deriving from their position in the hierarchy, should decide who will lead at any particular moment. She believed, as do many management theorists today, that power is fluid and should flow to the person who can best help the organization achieve its goals. Follett took a horizontal view of power and authority, in contrast to Fayol, who saw the formal line of authority and vertical chain of command as being most essential to effective management. Follett's behavioral approach to management was very radical for its time.

Workers in a telephone manufacturing plant in 1931. Around this time, researchers at the Hawthorne Works of the Western Electric Company began to study the effects of work setting characteristics—such as lighting and rest periods—on productivity. To their surprise, they discovered that workers' productivity was affected more by the attention they received from researchers than by the characteristics of the work setting—a phenomenon that became known as the Hawthorne effect.

The Hawthorne Studies and Human Relations

Probably because of its radical nature, Follett's work was unappreciated by managers and researchers until quite recently. Most continued to follow in the footsteps of Taylor and the Gilbreths. To increase efficiency, they studied ways to improve various characteristics of the work setting, such as job specialization or the kinds of tools workers used. One series of studies was conducted from 1924 to 1932 at the Hawthorne Works of the Western Electric Company.[29] This research, now known as the *Hawthorne studies,* began as an attempt to investigate how characteristics of the work setting–specifically the level of lighting or illumination–affect worker fatigue and performance. The researchers conducted an experiment in which they systematically measured worker productivity at various levels of illumination.

The experiment produced some unexpected results. The researchers found that regardless of whether they raised or lowered the level of illumination, productivity increased. In fact, productivity began to fall only when the level of illumination dropped to the level of moonlight–a level at which workers could presumably no longer see well enough to do their work efficiently.

The researchers found these results puzzling and invited a noted Harvard psychologist, Elton Mayo, to help them. Mayo proposed another series of experiments to solve the mystery. These experiments, known as the *relay assembly test experiments,* were designed to investigate the effects of other aspects of the work context on job performance, such as the effect of the number and length of rest periods and hours of work on fatigue and monotony.[30] The goal was to raise productivity.

During a two-year study of a small group of female workers, the researchers again observed that productivity increased over time, but the increases could not be solely attributed to the effects of changes in the work setting. Gradually the researchers discovered that, to some degree, the results they were obtaining were influenced by the fact that the researchers themselves had become part of the experiment. In other words, the presence of the researchers was affecting the results because the workers enjoyed receiving attention and being the subject of study and were willing to cooperate with the researchers to produce the results they believed the researchers desired.

Subsequently it was found that many other factors also influence worker behavior, and it was not clear what was actually influencing the Hawthorne workers' behavior. However, this particular effect–which became known as the **Hawthorne effect**–seemed to suggest that workers' attitudes toward their managers affect the level of workers' performance. In particular, the significant finding was that each manager's personal behavior or leadership approach can affect performance. This finding led many researchers to turn their attention to managerial behavior and leadership. If supervisors could be trained to behave in ways that would elicit cooperative behavior from their subordinates, productivity could be increased. From this view emerged the **human relations movement,** which advocates that supervisors be behaviorally trained to manage subordinates in ways that elicit their cooperation and increase their productivity.

Hawthorne effect The finding that a manager's behavior or leadership approach can affect workers' level of performance.

human relations movement A management approach that advocates the idea that supervisors should receive behavioral training to manage subordinates in ways that elicit their cooperation and increase their productivity.

The importance of behavioral or human relations training became even clearer to its supporters after another series of experiments–the *bank wiring room experiments.* In a study of workers making telephone switching equipment, researchers Elton Mayo and F. J. Roethlisberger discovered that the workers, as a group, had deliberately adopted a norm of output restriction to protect their jobs. Workers who violated this informal production norm were subjected to sanctions by other group members. Those who violated group performance norms and performed above the norm were called "ratebusters"; those who performed below the norm were called "chiselers."

The experimenters concluded that both types of workers threatened the group as a whole. Ratebusters threatened group members because they revealed to managers how fast the work could be done. Chiselers were looked down on because they were not doing their share of the work. Work group members disciplined both ratebusters and chiselers to create a pace of work that the workers (not the managers) thought was fair. Thus a work group's influence over output can be as great as the supervisors' influence. Because the work group can influence the behavior of its members, some management theorists argue that supervisors should be trained to behave in ways that gain the goodwill and cooperation of workers so that supervisors, not workers, control the level of work group performance.

informal organization The system of behavioral rules and norms that emerge in a group.

One implication of the Hawthorne studies was that the behavior of managers and workers in the work setting is as important in explaining the level of performance as the technical aspects of the task. Managers must understand the workings of the **informal organization,** the system of behavioral rules and norms that emerge in a group, when they try to manage or change behavior in organizations. Many studies have found that as time passes, groups often develop elaborate procedures and norms that bond members together, allowing unified action either to cooperate with management to raise performance or to restrict output and thwart the attainment of organizational goals.[31] The Hawthorne studies demonstrated the importance of understanding how the feelings, thoughts, and behavior of work group members and managers affect performance. It was becoming increasingly clear to researchers that understanding behavior in organizations is a complex process that is critical to increasing performance.[32] Indeed, the increasing interest in the area of management known as **organizational behavior,** the study of the factors that have an impact on how individuals and groups respond to and act in organizations, dates from these early studies.

organizational behavior The study of the factors that have an impact on how individuals and groups respond to and act in organizations.

Theory X and Theory Y

Several studies after World War II revealed how assumptions about workers' attitudes and behavior affect managers' behavior. Perhaps the most influential approach was developed by Douglas McGregor. He proposed two sets of assumptions about how work attitudes and behaviors not only dominate the way managers think but also affect how they behave in organizations. McGregor named these two contrasting sets of assumptions *Theory X* and *Theory Y* (see Figure 2.3).[33]

Figure 2.3
Theory X versus Theory Y

THEORY X	THEORY Y
The average employee is lazy, dislikes work, and will try to do as little as possible.	Employees are not inherently lazy. Given the chance, employees will do what is good for the organization.
To ensure that employees work hard, managers should closely supervise employees.	To allow employees to work in the organization's interest, managers must create a work setting that provides opportunities for workers to exercise initiative and self-direction.
Managers should create strict work rules and implement a well-defined system of rewards and punishments to control employees.	Managers should decentralize authority to employees and make sure employees have the resources necessary to achieve organizational goals.

Source: D. McGregor, *The Human Side of Enterprise,* © 1960 by The McGraw-Hill Companies, Inc. Used with permission.

Theory X A set of negative assumptions about workers that leads to the conclusion that a manager's task is to supervise workers closely and control their behavior.

THEORY X According to the assumptions of **Theory X,** the average worker is lazy, dislikes work, and will try to do as little as possible. Moreover, workers have little ambition and wish to avoid responsibility. Thus the manager's task is to counteract workers' natural tendencies to avoid work. To keep workers' performance at a high level, the manager must supervise workers closely and control their behavior by means of "the carrot and stick"–rewards and punishments.

Managers who accept the assumptions of Theory X design and shape the work setting to maximize their control over workers' behaviors and minimize workers' control over the pace of work. These managers believe workers must be made to do what is necessary for the success of the organization, and they focus on developing rules, SOPs, and a well-defined system of rewards and punishments to control behavior. They see little point in giving workers autonomy to solve their own problems because they think the workforce neither expects nor desires cooperation. Theory X managers see their role as closely monitoring workers to ensure that they contribute to the production process and do not threaten product quality. Henry Ford, who closely supervised and managed his workforce, fits McGregor's description of a manager who holds Theory X assumptions.

Theory Y A set of positive assumptions about workers that leads to the conclusion that a manager's task is to create a work setting that encourages commitment to organizational goals and provides opportunities for workers to be imaginative and to exercise initiative and self-direction.

THEORY Y In contrast, **Theory Y** assumes that workers are not inherently lazy, do not naturally dislike work, and, if given the opportunity, will do what is good for the organization. According to Theory Y, the characteristics of the work setting determine whether workers consider work to be a source of satisfaction or punishment, and managers do not need to closely control workers' behavior to make them perform at a high level because workers exercise self-control when they are committed to organizational goals. The implication of Theory Y, according to McGregor, is that "the limits of collaboration in the organizational setting are not limits of human nature but of management's ingenuity in discovering how to realize the potential represented by its human resources."[34] It is the manager's task to create a work setting that encourages commitment to organizational goals and provides opportunities for workers to be imaginative and to exercise initiative and self-direction.

When managers design the organizational setting to reflect the assumptions about attitudes and behavior suggested by Theory Y, the characteristics of the organization are quite different from those of an organizational setting based on Theory X. Managers who believe workers are motivated to help the organization reach its goals can decentralize authority and give more control over the job to workers, both as individuals and in groups. In this setting, individuals and groups are still accountable for their activities; but the manager's role is not to control employees but to provide support and advice, to make sure employees have the resources they need to perform their jobs, and to evaluate them on their ability to help the organization meet its goals. Henri Fayol's approach to administration more closely reflects the assumptions of Theory Y rather than Theory X.

From the time that Dave Packard and Bill Hewlett first set up shop in a garage in 1938, they established a new people-oriented approach to management, known as the "HP Way."

One company that was founded on the type of management philosophy inherent in Theory Y is the electronics company Hewlett-Packard (HP), which from its founding consistently put into practice principles derived from Theory Y. (Go to the company's Web site at www.hp.com for additional information.) Founders William Hewlett and David Packard–Bill and Dave, as they are still known throughout the organization–established a philosophy of management known as the "HP Way" that is people-oriented, stresses the importance of treating every person with consideration and respect, and offers recognition for achievements.[35]

The HP Way was based on several guiding principles. One was a policy of long-term employment, and in the past HP went to great lengths not to lay off workers. At times when fewer people were needed, rather than lay off workers, management would cut pay and shorten the workday until demand for HP products picked up. This policy strengthened employees' loyalty to the organization. Another guiding principle in the HP Way concerned how to treat members of the organization so they would feel free to be innovative and creative. HP managers believed that every employee of the company was a member of the HP team. They emphasized the need to increase communication among employees, believing that horizontal communication between peers, not just vertical communication up and down the hierarchy, is essential for creating a positive climate for innovation. So to promote communication between employees at different levels of the hierarchy, HP encouraged informality. Managers and workers were on a first-name basis with each other and with the founders, Bill and Dave. In addition, Bill and Dave pioneered the technique known as "managing by wandering around": People were expected to wander around learning what others were doing so they could tap into opportunities to develop new products or find new avenues for cooperation. Bill and Dave also pioneered the principle that employees should spend 15% of their time working on projects of their own choosing, and HP's product design engineers were told to leave their current work out in the open on their desks so anybody could see what they were doing, learn from it, or suggest ways to improve it. Bill and Dave promoted managers because of their ability to engender excitement and enthusiasm for innovation in their subordinates.[36]

HP's practices helped it become one of the leading electronics companies in the world. In 2001, however, HP, like most other high-tech companies, was experiencing major problems because of the collapse of the telecommunications industry, and the company announced that it was searching for ways to reduce costs. At first its new CEO, Carly Fiorina, did not lay off employees but asked them to accept lower salaries to help the company through this rough spot.[37] It soon became clear, however, that HP's survival was at stake as it battled with efficient global competitors such as Dell and Canon. Fiorina was forced to begin layoffs, and by 2004 HP had laid off over 40% of its employees and outsourced thousands of jobs abroad to remain competitive. In 2005 Fiorina lost her job after investors became concerned that she was pursuing the wrong strategies and that the HP Way seemed to have disappeared. She was replaced as CEO by Mark Hurd, a manager known for his cost-cutting skills; but by 2006 HP had turned the corner, and Fiorina's efforts were shown to be the right ones for meeting the challenges HP had faced. By 2008 HP was profitable once again, and it overtook Dell to become the largest global PC maker, perhaps because of Fiorina's strategies and Hurd's prudence. Whether the company will once again choose to pursue the HP Way is open to question, however. Today Google exemplifies a company that follows Theory Y and the HP Way, but so is Trader Joe's, established by Joe Coulombe (see the accompanying "Manager as a Person" box).

Manager as a Person

Joe Coulombe Knows How to Make an Organization Work

Trader Joe's, an upscale specialty supermarket chain, was started in 1967 by Joe Coulombe, who owned a few convenience stores that were fighting an uphill battle against the growing 7-11 chain. 7-11 offered customers a wider selection of lower-priced products, and Coulombe had to find a new way to manage his small business if it was going to survive. As he began planning new strategies to

Pictured is Trader Joe's first New York City store that opened in 2006. Founder Joe Coulombe's approach to motivating and rewarding his employees to provide excellent customer service paid off in a city where the prices of food and drink are so high that customers were delighted to shop in stores with a great ambiance and friendly customer service.

help his small business grow, he was struck by the fact that there might be a niche for supplying specialty products, such as wine, drinks, and gourmet foods, which were more profitable to sell; moreover, he would no longer be competing against giant 7-11. Coulombe changed the name of his stores to Trader Joe's and stocked them with every variety and brand of California wine produced at the time. He also began to offer fine foods like bread, crackers, cheese, fruits, and vegetables to complement and encourage wine sales.

From the beginning Coulombe realized that good planning was only the first step in successfully managing his small, growing company. He knew that to encourage customers to visit his stores and buy high-priced gourmet products, he needed to give them excellent customer service. So he had to motivate his salespeople to perform at a high level. His approach was to decentralize authority, empowering salespeople to take responsibility for meeting customer needs. Rather than forcing employees to follow strict operating rules and to obtain the consent of their superiors in the hierarchy of authority, employees were given autonomy to make decisions and provide personalized customer service. Coulombe's approach led employees to feel they "owned" their supermarkets, and he worked to develop a store culture based on values and norms about providing excellent customer service and developing personalized relationships with customers. Today many employees and customers are on first-name terms.

Coulombe led by example and created a store environment in which employees were treated as individuals and felt valued as people. For example, the theme behind the design of his stores was to create the feeling of a Hawaiian resort: He and his employees wear loud Hawaiian shirts, store managers are called captains, and the store decor uses lots of wood and contains tiki huts where employees give customers food and drink samples and interact with them. Once again, this helped create strong values and norms that emphasize personalized customer service.

Finally, Joe Coulombe's approach from the beginning was to create a policy of promotion from within the company so that the highest-performing salespeople could rise to become store captains and beyond in the organization. He had always recognized the need to treat employees (people) in a fair and equitable way to encourage them to develop the customer-oriented values and norms needed to provide personalized customer service. He decided that full-time employees should earn at least the median household income for their communities, which averaged $7,000 a year in the 1960s and is $48,000 today–an astonishingly high amount compared to the pay of employees of regular supermarkets such as Kroger's and Safeway. Moreover, store captains, who are vital in helping create and reinforce Trader Joe's store culture, are rewarded with salaries and bonuses that can exceed $100,000 a year. And all salespeople know that as the store chain expands, they may also be promoted to this level. Today Trader Joe's has over 300 stores in 23 states and is still expanding because Coulombe's approach to managing his small business created the right foundation for an upscale specialty supermarket to grow and prosper.

Management Science Theory

Management science theory is a contemporary approach to management that focuses on the use of rigorous quantitative techniques to help managers make maximum use of organizational resources to produce goods and services. In essence, management science theory is a contemporary extension of scientific management, which, as developed by Taylor, also took a quantitative approach to measuring the worker–task mix to raise efficiency. There are many branches of management science; and IT, which is having a significant impact on all kinds of management practices, is affecting the tools managers use to make decisions.[38] Each branch of management science deals with a specific set of concerns:

LO2-5 Explain the contributions of management science to the efficient use of organizational resources.

management science theory An approach to management that uses rigorous quantitative techniques to help managers make maximum use of organizational resources.

- *Quantitative management* uses mathematical techniques–such as linear and nonlinear programming, modeling, simulation, queuing theory, and chaos theory–to help managers decide, for example, how much inventory to hold at different times of the year, where to locate a new factory, and how best to invest an organization's financial capital. IT offers managers new and improved ways of handling information so they can make more accurate assessments of the situation and better decisions.
- *Operations management* gives managers a set of techniques they can use to analyze any aspect of an organization's production system to increase efficiency. IT, through the Internet and through growing B2B networks, is transforming how managers acquire inputs and dispose of finished products.
- *Total quality management (TQM)* focuses on analyzing an organization's input, conversion, and output activities to increase product quality.[39] Once again, through sophisticated software packages and computer-controlled production, IT is changing how managers and employees think about the work process and ways of improving it.
- *Management information systems (MISs)* give managers information about events occurring inside the organization as well as in its external environment–information that is vital for effective decision making. Once again, IT gives managers access to more and better information and allows more managers at all levels to participate in the decision-making process.

All these subfields of management science, enhanced by sophisticated IT, provide tools and techniques that managers can use to help improve the quality of their decision making and increase efficiency and effectiveness. We discuss many important developments in management science theory thoroughly in this book. In particular, Chapter 9, "Value Chain Management: Functional Strategies for Competitive Advantage," focuses on how to use operations management and TQM to improve quality, efficiency, and responsiveness to customers. And Chapter 18, "Using Advanced Information Technology to Increase Performance," describes the many ways managers use information systems and technologies to improve their planning, organizing, and controlling functions.

organizational environment The set of forces and conditions that operate beyond an organization's boundaries but affect a manager's ability to acquire and utilize resources.

Organizational Environment Theory

An important milestone in the history of management thought occurred when researchers went beyond the study of how managers can influence behavior within organizations to consider how managers control the organization's relationship with its external environment, or **organizational environment**–the set of forces and conditions that operate beyond an organization's boundaries but affect a manager's ability to acquire and utilize resources. Resources in the organizational environment include the raw materials and skilled people that an organization requires to produce goods and services, as well as the support of groups, including customers who buy these goods and services and

LO2-6 Explain why the study of the external environment and its impact on an organization has become a central issue in management thought.

provide the organization with financial resources. One way of determining the relative success of an organization is to consider how effective its managers are at obtaining scarce and valuable resources.[40] The importance of studying the environment became clear after the development of open-systems theory and contingency theory during the 1960s.

The Open-Systems View

open system A system that takes in resources from its external environment and converts them into goods and services that are then sent back to that environment for purchase by customers.

One of the most influential views of how an organization is affected by its external environment was developed by Daniel Katz, Robert Kahn, and James Thompson in the 1960s.[41] These theorists viewed the organization as an **open system**–a system that takes in resources from its external environment and converts or transforms them into goods and services that are sent back to that environment, where they are bought by customers (see Figure 2.4).

At the *input stage* an organization acquires resources such as raw materials, money, and skilled workers to produce goods and services. Once the organization has gathered the necessary resources, conversion begins. At the *conversion stage* the organization's workforce, using appropriate tools, techniques, and machinery, transforms the inputs into outputs of finished goods and services such as cars, hamburgers, or flights to Hawaii. At the *output stage* the organization releases finished goods and services to its external environment, where customers purchase and use them to satisfy their needs. The money the organization obtains from the sales of its outputs allows the organization to acquire more resources so the cycle can begin again.

closed system A system that is self-contained and thus not affected by changes occurring in its external environment.

entropy The tendency of a closed system to lose its ability to control itself and thus to dissolve and disintegrate.

The system just described is said to be open because the organization draws from and interacts with the external environment in order to survive; in other words, the organization is open to its environment. A **closed system,** in contrast, is a self-contained system that is not affected by changes in its external environment. Organizations that operate as closed systems, that ignore the external environment, and that fail to acquire inputs are likely to experience **entropy,** which is the tendency of a closed system to lose its ability to control itself and thus to dissolve and disintegrate.

Management theorists can model the activities of most organizations by using the open-systems view. Manufacturing companies like Ford and General Electric, for

Figure 2.4
The Organization as an Open System

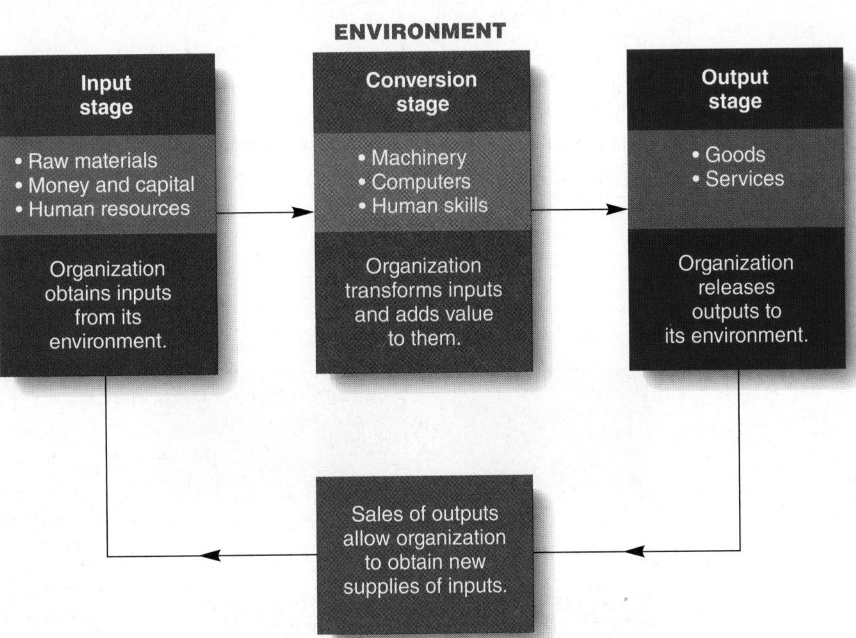

example, buy inputs such as component parts, skilled and semiskilled labor, and robots and computer-controlled manufacturing equipment; then at the conversion stage they use their manufacturing skills to assemble inputs into outputs of cars and appliances. As we discuss in later chapters, competition between organizations for resources is one of several major challenges to managing the organizational environment.

Researchers using the open-systems view are also interested in how the various parts of a system work together to promote efficiency and effectiveness. Systems theorists like to argue that the whole is greater than the sum of its parts; they mean that an organization performs at a higher level when its departments work together rather than separately. **Synergy,** the performance gains that result from the *combined* actions of individuals and departments, is possible only in an organized system. The recent interest in using teams combined or composed of people from different departments reflects systems theorists' interest in designing organizational systems to create synergy and thus increase efficiency and effectiveness.

synergy Performance gains that result when individuals and departments coordinate their actions.

Contingency Theory

Another milestone in management theory was the development of **contingency theory** in the 1960s by Tom Burns and G. M. Stalker in Britain and Paul Lawrence and Jay Lorsch in the United States.[42] The crucial message of contingency theory is that *there is no one best way to organize:* The organizational structures and the control systems that managers choose depend on (are contingent on) characteristics of the external environment in which the organization operates. According to contingency theory, the characteristics of the environment affect an organization's ability to obtain resources; and to maximize the likelihood of gaining access to resources, managers must allow an organization's departments to organize and control their activities in ways most likely to allow them to obtain resources, given the constraints of the particular environment they face. In other words, how managers design the organizational hierarchy, choose a control system, and lead and motivate their employees is contingent on the characteristics of the organizational environment (see Figure 2.5).

contingency theory The idea that the organizational structures and control systems managers choose depend on (are contingent on) characteristics of the external environment in which the organization operates.

An important characteristic of the external environment that affects an organization's ability to obtain resources is the degree to which the environment is changing. Changes in the organizational environment include changes in technology, which can lead to the creation of new products (such as compact discs) and result in the obsolescence of existing products (eight-track tapes); the entry of new competitors (such as foreign organizations that compete for available resources); and unstable economic conditions. In general, the more quickly the organizational environment is changing,

Figure 2.5
Contingency Theory of Organizational Design

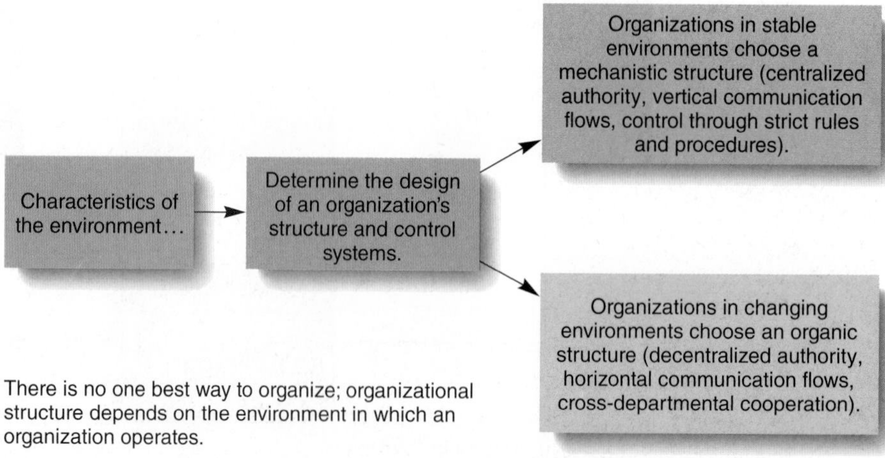

Characteristics of the environment...
Determine the design of an organization's structure and control systems.
Organizations in stable environments choose a mechanistic structure (centralized authority, vertical communication flows, control through strict rules and procedures).
Organizations in changing environments choose an organic structure (decentralized authority, horizontal communication flows, cross-departmental cooperation).

There is no one best way to organize; organizational structure depends on the environment in which an organization operates.

the greater are the problems associated with gaining access to resources, and the greater is managers' need to find ways to coordinate the activities of people in different departments to respond to the environment quickly and effectively.

MECHANISTIC AND ORGANIC STRUCTURES Drawing on Weber's and Fayol's principles of organization and management, Burns and Stalker proposed two basic ways in which managers can organize and control an organization's activities to respond to characteristics of its external environment: They can use a *mechanistic structure* or an *organic structure*.[43] As you will see, a mechanistic structure typically rests on Theory X assumptions, and an organic structure typically rests on Theory Y assumptions.

When the environment surrounding an organization is stable, managers tend to choose a mechanistic structure to organize and control activities and make employee behavior predictable. In a **mechanistic structure,** authority is centralized at the top of the managerial hierarchy, and the vertical hierarchy of authority is the main means used to control subordinates' behavior. Tasks and roles are clearly specified, subordinates are closely supervised, and the emphasis is on strict discipline and order. Everyone knows his or her place, and there is a place for everyone. A mechanistic structure provides the most efficient way to operate in a stable environment because it allows managers to obtain inputs at the lowest cost, giving an organization the most control over its conversion processes and enabling the most efficient production of goods and services with the smallest expenditure of resources. McDonald's restaurants operate with a mechanistic structure. Supervisors make all important decisions; employees are closely supervised and follow well-defined rules and standard operating procedures.

mechanistic structure An organizational structure in which authority is centralized, tasks and rules are clearly specified, and employees are closely supervised.

In contrast, when the environment is changing rapidly, it is difficult to obtain access to resources, and managers need to organize their activities in a way that allows them to cooperate, to act quickly to acquire resources (such as new types of inputs to produce new kinds of products), and to respond effectively to the unexpected. In an **organic structure,** authority is decentralized to middle and first-line managers to encourage them to take responsibility and act quickly to pursue scarce resources. Departments are encouraged to take a cross-departmental or functional perspective, and cross-functional teams composed of people from different departments are formed. As in Mary Parker Follett's model, the organization operates in an organic way because authority rests with the individuals, departments, and teams best positioned to control the current problems the organization is facing. As a result, managers in an organic structure can react more quickly to a changing environment than can managers in a mechanistic structure. However, an organic structure is generally more expensive to operate because it requires that more managerial time, money, and effort be spent on coordination. So it is used only when needed–when the organizational environment is unstable and rapidly changing.[44] Google, Apple, Xerox, and other companies discussed in this book are examples of companies that operate with organic structures.

organic structure An organizational structure in which authority is decentralized to middle and first-line managers and tasks and roles are left ambiguous to encourage employees to cooperate and respond quickly to the unexpected.

Summary and Review

In this chapter we examined the evolution of management theory and research over the last century. Much of the material in the rest of this book stems from developments and refinements of this work. Indeed, the rest of this book incorporates the results of the extensive research in management that has been conducted since the development of the theories discussed here.

LO2-1, 2-2 **SCIENTIFIC MANAGEMENT THEORY** The search for efficiency started with the study of how managers could improve person–task relationships to increase efficiency. The concept of job specialization and division of labor remains the basis for the design of work settings in modern organizations. New developments such as lean production and total quality management are often viewed as advances on the early scientific management principles developed by Taylor and the Gilbreths.

LO2-3 **ADMINISTRATIVE MANAGEMENT THEORY** Max Weber and Henri Fayol outlined principles of bureaucracy and administration that are as relevant to managers today as they were when developed at the turn of the 20th century. Much of modern management research refines these principles to suit contemporary conditions. For example, the increasing interest in the use of cross-departmental teams and the empowerment of workers are issues that managers also faced a century ago.

LO2-4 **BEHAVIORAL MANAGEMENT THEORY** Researchers have described many different approaches to managerial behavior, including Theories X and Y. Often the managerial behavior that researchers suggest reflects the context of their own historical eras and cultures. Mary Parker Follett advocated managerial behaviors that did not reflect accepted modes of managerial behavior at the time, and her work was largely ignored until conditions changed.

LO2-5 **MANAGEMENT SCIENCE THEORY** The various branches of management science theory provide rigorous quantitative techniques that give managers more control over each organization's use of resources to produce goods and services.

LO2-6 **ORGANIZATIONAL ENVIRONMENT THEORY** The importance of studying the organization's external environment became clear after the development of open-systems theory and contingency theory during the 1960s. A main focus of contemporary management research is to find methods to help managers improve how they use organizational resources and compete in the global environment. Strategic management and total quality management are two important approaches intended to help managers make better use of organizational resources.

Management in Action

Topics for Discussion and Action

Discussion

1. Choose a fast-food restaurant, a department store, or some other organization with which you are familiar, and describe the division of labor and job specialization it uses to produce goods and services. How might this division of labor be improved? [LO2-1, 2-2]
2. Apply Taylor's principles of scientific management to improve the performance of the organization you chose in topic 1. [LO2-2]
3. In what ways are Weber's and Fayol's ideas about bureaucracy and administration similar? How do they differ? [LO2-3]
4. Which of Weber's and Fayol's principles seem most relevant to the creation of an ethical organization? [LO2-4, 2-6]
5. Why was the work of Mary Parker Follett ahead of its time? To what degree do you think it is appropriate today? [LO2-4, 2-5]
6. What is contingency theory? What kinds of organizations familiar to you have been successful or unsuccessful in dealing with contingencies from the external environment? [LO2-6]
7. Why are mechanistic and organic structures suited to different organizational environments? [LO2-4, 2-6]

Action

8. Question a manager about his or her views of the relative importance of Fayol's 14 principles of management. [LO2-3, 2-4]
9. Visit at least two organizations in your community, and identify those that seem to operate with a Theory X or a Theory Y approach to management. [LO2-4]

Building Management Skills

Managing Your Own Business [LO2-2, 2-4]

Now that you understand the concerns addressed by management thinkers over the last century, use this exercise to apply your knowledge to developing your management skills.

Imagine that you are the founding entrepreneur of a software company that specializes in developing games for home computers. Customer demand for your games has increased so much that over the last year your company has grown from a busy one-person operation to one with 16 employees. In addition to yourself, you employ six software developers to produce the software, three graphic artists, two computer technicians, two marketing and sales personnel, and two secretaries. In the next year you expect to hire 30 new employees, and you are wondering how best to manage your growing company.

1. Use the principles of Weber and Fayol to decide on the system of organization and management that you think will be most effective for your growing organization. How many levels will the managerial hierarchy of your organization have? How much authority will you decentralize to your subordinates? How will you establish the division of labor between subordinates? Will your subordinates work alone and report to you or work in teams?
2. Which management approach (for example, Theory X or Y) do you propose to use to run your organization? In 50 or fewer words write a statement describing the management approach you believe will motivate and coordinate your subordinates, and tell why you think this style will be best.

Managing Ethically [LO2-3, 2-4]

Ethics in Action: How to Manage Ethical Problems Ethics in the Global Flower-Growing Business

Every year on Valentine's Day tens of millions of roses are delivered to loved ones in the United States, and anyone who has bought roses knows that their price has been dropping. One of the main reasons for this is that global rose growing is now concentrated in poorer countries in Central and South America. Rose growing has been a boon to poor countries because the extra income women earn can mean the difference between starving or eating for their families. The hidden side of the global rose-growing business is that poorer countries tend to have lax or unenforced health and safety laws—a major reason why they have lower rose-growing costs. And, many rose-growing companies are *not* considering the well-being of their workers; neither are the companies around the world that distribute and sell roses to customers. For example, almost 60% of workers of Rosas del Ecuador, a major U.S. importer have experienced blurred vision, nausea, headaches, asthma, and other symptoms of pesticide poisoning.[45] Workers labor in hot, poorly ventilated greenhouses in which roses have been sprayed with pesticides and herbicides for long hours and safety equipment such as masks and ventilators is scarce. If workers complain, they may be fired and blacklisted, so to protect their families' well-being, workers rarely complain and thus their health remains at risk. Given this lack of protest, U.S. companies that buy its roses are often unaware of the conditions under which they are produced.

Questions

1. Use the theories discussed in the chapter to debate the ethical issues involved in the global flower-growing business.
2. In what ways do the way cars were made in the past reflect the way in which the rose-growing business is being conducted today?
3. Search the Web for changes occurring in the global flower-growing business.

Small Group Breakout Exercise [LO2-6]

Modeling an Open System

Form groups of three to five people, and appoint one group member as the spokesperson who will communicate your findings to the class when called on by the instructor. Then discuss the following scenario:

Think of an organization with which you are all familiar, such as a local restaurant, store, or bank. After choosing an organization, model it from an open-systems perspective. Identify its input, conversion, and output processes; and identify forces in the external environment that help or hurt the organization's ability to obtain resources and dispose of its goods or services.

Exploring the World Wide Web [LO2-3, 2-6]

Research Ford's Web site (www.ford.com), and locate and read the material about Ford's history and evolution over time. What have been the significant stages in the company's development? What problems and issues confronted managers at these stages? What challenges face Ford's managers now?

Be the Manager [LO 2-2, 2-4]

How to Manage a Hotel

You have been called in to advise the owners of an exclusive new luxury hotel. For the venture to succeed, hotel employees must focus on providing customers with the highest-quality customer service possible. The challenge is to devise a way of organizing and controlling employees that will promote high-quality service, that will encourage employees to be committed to the hotel, and that will reduce the level of employee turnover and absenteeism—which are typically high in the hotel business.

Questions

1. How do the various management theories discussed in this chapter offer clues for organizing and controlling hotel employees?
2. Which parts would be the most important for an effective system to organize and control employees?

Case in the News [LO2-3, 2-4]

Mr. Edens Profits from Watching His Workers' Every Move

Control is one of Ron Edens's favorite words. "This is a controlled environment," he says of the blank brick building that houses his company, Electronic Banking System Inc.

Inside, long lines of women sit at spartan desks, slitting envelopes, sorting contents, and filling out "control cards" that record how many letters they have opened and how long it has taken them. Workers here, in "the cage," must process three envelopes a minute. Nearby, other women tap keyboards, keeping pace with a quota that demands 8,500 strokes an hour.

The room is silent. Talking is forbidden. The windows are covered. Coffee mugs, religious pictures, and other adornments are barred from workers' desks.

In his office upstairs, Mr. Edens sits before a TV monitor that flashes images from eight cameras posted throughout the plant. "There's a little bit of Sneaky Pete to it," he says, using a remote control to zoom in on a document atop a worker's desk. "I can basically read that and figure out how someone's day is going."

This day, like most others, is going smoothly, and Mr. Edens's business has boomed as a result. "We maintain a lot of control," he says. "Order and control are everything in this business."

Mr. Edens's business belongs to a small but expanding financial service known as "lockbox processing." Many companies and charities that once did their paperwork in-house now outsource clerical tasks to firms like EBS, which processes donations to groups such as Mothers Against Drunk Driving, the Doris Day Animal League, Greenpeace, and the National Organization for Women.

More broadly, EBS reflects the explosive growth of jobs in which workers perform low-wage and limited tasks in white-collar settings. This has transformed towns like Hagerstown—a blue-collar community hit hard by industrial layoffs in the 1970s—into sites for thousands of jobs in factory-sized offices.

Many of these jobs, though, are part-time, and most pay far less than the manufacturing occupations they replaced. Some workers at EBS start at the minimum wage of $4.25 an hour, and most earn about $6 an hour. The growth of such jobs—which often cluster outside major cities—also completes a curious historic circle. During the industrial revolution, farmers' daughters went to work in textile towns like Lowell, Massachusetts. In postindustrial America, many women of modest means and skills are entering clerical mills where they process paper instead of cloth (coincidentally, EBS occupies a former garment factory).

"The office of the future can look a lot like the factory of the past," says Barbara Garson, author of *The Electronic Sweatshop* and other books on the modern workplace. "Modern tools are being used to bring 19th-century working conditions into the white-collar world."

The time-and-motion philosophies of Frederick Taylor, for instance, have found a 1990s correlate in the phone, computer, and camera, which can be used to monitor workers more closely than a foreman with a stopwatch ever could. Also, the nature of the work often justifies a vigilant eye. In EBS workers handle thousands of dollars in checks and cash, and Mr. Edens says cameras help deter would-be thieves. Tight security also reassures visiting clients. "If you're disorderly, they'll think we're out of control and that things could get lost," says Mr. Edens, who worked as a financial controller for the National Rifle Association before founding EBS in 1983.

But tight observation also helps EBS monitor productivity and weed out workers who don't keep up. "There's multiple uses," Mr. Edens says of surveillance. His desk is covered with computer printouts recording the precise toll of keystrokes tapped by each data entry worker. He also keeps a day-to-day tally of errors. The work floor itself resembles an enormous classroom in the throes of exam period. Desks point toward the front, where a manager keeps watch from a raised platform that workers call "the pedestal" or "the birdhouse." Other supervisors are positioned toward the back of the room. "If you want to watch someone," Mr. Edens explains, "it's easier from behind because they don't know you're watching." There also is a black globe hanging from the ceiling, in which cameras are positioned.

Mr. Edens sees nothing Orwellian about this omniscience. "It's not a Big Brother attitude," he says. "It's more of a calming attitude."

But studies of workplace monitoring suggest otherwise. Experts say that surveillance can create a hostile environment in which workers feel pressured, paranoid, and prone to stress-related illness. Surveillance also can be used punitively, to intimidate workers or to justify their firing.

Following a failed union drive at EBS, the National Labor Relations Board filed a series of complaints against the company, including charges that EBS threatened, interrogated, and spied on workers. As part of an out-of-court settlement, EBS reinstated a fired worker and posted a notice that it would refrain from illegal practices during a second union vote, which also failed.

"It's all noise," Mr. Edens says of the unfair labor charges. As for the pressure that surveillance creates, Mr. Edens sees that simply as "the nature of the beast." He adds, "It's got to add stress when everyone knows their production is being monitored. I don't apologize for that."

Mr. Edens also is unapologetic about the draconian work rules he maintains, including one that forbids all talk unrelated to the completion of each task. "I'm not paying people to chat. I'm paying them to open envelopes," he says. Of the blocked windows, Mr. Edens adds, "I don't want them looking out—it's distracting. They'll make mistakes."

This total focus boosts productivity, but it makes many workers feel lonely and trapped. Some try to circumvent the silence rule, like kids in a school library. "If you don't turn your head and sort of mumble out of the side of your mouth, supervisors won't hear you most of the time," Cindy Kesselring explains during her lunch break. Even so, she feels isolated and often longs for her former job as a waitress. "Work is your social life, particularly if you've got kids," says the 27-year-old mother. "Here it's hard to get to know people because you can't talk."

During lunch, workers crowd in the parking lot outside, chatting nonstop. "Some of us don't eat much because the more you chew the less you can talk," Ms. Kesselring says. There aren't other breaks, and workers aren't allowed to sip coffee or eat at their desks during the long stretches before and after lunch. Hard candy is the only permitted desk snack.

New technology and the breaking down of labor into discrete, repetitive tasks also have effectively stripped jobs such as those at EBS of whatever variety and skills clerical work once possessed. Workers in the cage (an antiquated banking term for a money-handling area) only open envelopes and sort contents; those in the audit department compute figures; and data entry clerks punch in the information that the others have collected. If they make a mistake, the computer buzzes, and a message such as "check digit error" flashes on the screen.

"We don't ask these people to think—the machines think for them," Mr. Edens says. "They don't have to make any decisions." This makes the work simpler but also deepens its monotony. In the cage, Carol Smith says she looks forward to envelopes that contain anything out of the ordinary, such as letters reporting that the donor is deceased. Or she plays mental games. "I think to myself, A goes in this pile, B goes here, and C goes there—sort of like Bingo." She says she sometimes feels "like a machine," particularly when she fills out the "control card" on which she lists "time in" and "time out" for each tray of envelopes. In a slot marked "cage operator" Ms. Smith writes her code number, 3173. "That's me," she says.

Barbara Ann Wiles, a keyboard operator, also plays mind games to break up the boredom. Tapping in the names and addresses of new donors, she tries to imagine the faces behind the names, particularly the odd ones. "Like this one, Mrs. Fittizzi," she chuckles. "I can picture her as a very stout lady with a strong accent, hollering on a street corner." She picks out another: "Doris Angelroth—she's very sophisticated, a monocle maybe, drinking tea on an overstuffed mohair couch."

It is a world remote from the one Ms. Wiles inhabits. Like most EBS employees, she must juggle her low-paying job with child care. On this Friday, for instance, Ms. Wiles will finish her eight-hour shift at about 4 p.m., go home for a few hours, then return for a second shift from midnight to 8 a.m. Otherwise she would have to come in on Saturday to finish the week's work. "This way I can be home on the weekend to look after my kids," she says.

Others find the work harder to leave behind at the end of the day. In the cage, Ms. Smith says her husband used to complain because she often woke him in the middle of the night. "I'd be shuffling my hands in my sleep," she says, mimicking the motion of opening envelopes.

Her cage colleague, Ms. Kesselring, says her fiancé has a different gripe. "He dodges me for a couple of hours after work because I don't shut up—I need to talk, talk, talk," she says. And there is one household task she can no longer abide.

"I won't pay bills because I can't stand to open another envelope," she says. "I'll leave letters sitting in the mailbox for days."

Questions for Discussion

1. Which of the management theories described in the chapter does Ron Edens make most use of?
2. What do you think are the effects of this approach on (a) workers and (b) supervisors?
3. Do you regard Ron Edens's approach to management as ethical and acceptable or unethical and unacceptable in the 2000s? Why?

Source: T. Horwitz, "Mr. Edens Profits from Watching His Workers' Every Move," *The Wall Street Journal*, December 1, 1994. Reproduced with permission of Dow Jones & Company Inc.

CHAPTER 3

Values, Attitudes, Emotions, and Culture: The Manager as a Person

Learning Objectives

After studying this chapter, you should be able to:

LO3-1 Describe the various personality traits that affect how managers think, feel, and behave.

LO3-2 Explain what values and attitudes are and describe their impact on managerial action.

LO3-3 Appreciate how moods and emotions influence all members of an organization.

LO3-4 Describe the nature of emotional intelligence and its role in management.

LO3-5 Define organizational culture and explain how managers both create and are influenced by organizational culture.

A MANAGER'S CHALLENGE

Values of a Founder Live On at PAETEC

How can managers create and sustain a caring culture while ensuring their organization's growth and effectiveness? PAETEC Communications is a broadband telecommunications company that provides local and long distance voice, data, and broadband Internet services to businesses in 84 markets across the United States.[1] When PAETEC was founded in 1998, it had fewer than 20 employees and revenues of only $150,000; today it has over 3,600 employees and over $1 billion in revenues.[2] Moreover, this phenomenal rate of growth occurred while the telecommunications industry lost hundreds of thousands of jobs.[3] PAETEC's amazing growth trajectory has not gone without notice; the company recently was included on Deloitte's 2009 Fast 500™ Ranking, which ranks the technology industry's top 500 fastest-growing companies in North America.[4]

PAETEC's growth and ongoing success are a tribute to the values of its five founders and the culture they created.[5] In particular, Arunas Chesonis, one of the founders and its current chairman and CEO, ensures that PAETEC's values are upheld by using them to guide the way he manages every day. The four core values of PAETEC are "a caring culture, open communication, unmatched service, and personalized solutions."[6] The ways in which these values are enacted daily result in a satisfied, motivated, and loyal workforce whose members have developed a unique and distinct approach to the way they perform their jobs.[7]

An overarching principle at PAETEC is that people—employees and customers—come first.[8] Chesonis believes that when a company takes good care of its employees, they

PAETEC founder and current CEO Arunas Chesonis believes that when a company takes good care of its employees, they will take good care of their customers.

will take good care of their customers.[9] Chesonis believes in helping employees attain a well-balanced and prosperous work and family life, providing them with deserved recognition and admiration, and fostering open communication and helping behavior.[10] Chesonis also believes that all employees should be treated with respect and as equals. Managers at PAETEC do not receive special perks, and pay differentials between managers and nonmanagers are deliberately kept relatively low. In recognition of its commitment to its employees and ethical action, PAETEC received the American Business Ethics Award for midsize companies in 2005.[11] In both 2009 and 2010, PAETEC was named a Best Large Company to Work For in New York State by the New York State Society for Human Resource Management.[12]

Chesonis takes walks around PAETEC's headquarters in Fairport, New York, talking with employees, answering questions, and recognizing accomplishments. Accomplishments are also recognized through two kinds of special awards: Maestro Awards and John Budney Awards. Maestro Awards can range from dinner for two to stock options and are given to recognize outstanding employee accomplishments. Employees who have sustained levels of exceptional performance receive the John Budney Award, a $5,000 award that might include a Rolex watch or a luxury vacation.[13] Employee contributions are recognized with an annual bonus based on individual and firm performance.[14]

Chesonis nurtures a culture of care, cooperation, and open communication in which every employee voluntarily offers help when it is needed.[15] Employees are expected to share their knowledge, and Chesonis strives to eliminate boundaries between departments and units. True to this culture, Chesonis has a companywide conference call every two weeks in which he shares up-to-date information with employees and solicits and answers their questions. More often than not, the information he conveys is the kind that managers in other companies rarely, if ever, would share with their employees.[16]

He also recognizes that employees at the front line are often in the best position to make suggestions for improvements and develop new services and ways to deliver them. For example, Mike Meath, an employee in the Network Operations Center, came up with the idea of a managed router service whereby companies (that is, PAETEC's customers) could remotely maintain their customers' voice and data services. Meath presented his idea to his team, the team implemented the idea, and the new service increased revenues by $50,000 in its first six months.[17]

While Chesonis is driven to succeed and motivates those around him to have equally high aspirations, he also values family life and the need for play. Chesonis has been described as a "fanatical family man," and he named the company with the initials of his family members (*P* for his wife Pam; *A, E, T,* and *E* for his children Adam, Erik, Tessa, and Emma; and *C* for Chesonis). Employees can take as much time off as they need, with pay, to deal with family emergencies and illnesses.[18] PAETEC also celebrates holidays with parties that include employees, their families, and customers. For example, employees dress up for Halloween, and their children trick-or-treat from office to office. Outings are planned, such as a scavenger hunt around Rochester culminating in dinner and an open bar, so that employees can spend a day socializing with one another.[19]

Chesonis's values and PAETEC's culture emphasize putting employees first; this employee-centered approach makes good business sense. Employees at PAETEC really want the company to continue to grow and succeed; they are highly motivated and committed to providing the best service they can to their customers.[20] As Chesonis puts it, "Since our inception, we've believed that a strong focus on the needs of our employees and their families will ultimately translate into superior service and performance for our customers."[21]

Overview

Like people everywhere, Arunas Chesonis has his own distinctive personality, values, ways of viewing things, and personal challenges and disappointments. In this chapter we focus on the manager as a feeling, thinking human being. We start by describing enduring characteristics that influence how managers manage, as well as how they view other people, their organizations, and the world around them. We also discuss how managers' values, attitudes, and moods play out in organizations, shaping organizational culture. By the end of this chapter, you will appreciate how the personal characteristics of managers influence the process of management in general–and organizational culture in particular.

LO3-1 Describe the various personality traits that affect how managers think, feel, and behave.

Enduring Characteristics: Personality Traits

All people, including managers, have certain enduring characteristics that influence how they think, feel, and behave both on and off the job. These characteristics are **personality traits:** particular tendencies to feel, think, and act in certain ways that can be used to describe the personality of every individual. It is important to understand the personalities of managers because their personalities influence their behavior and their approach to managing people and resources.

personality traits Enduring tendencies to feel, think, and act in certain ways.

Some managers are demanding, difficult to get along with, and highly critical of other people. Other managers may be as concerned about effectiveness and efficiency as highly critical managers but are easier to get along with, are likable, and frequently praise the people around them. Both management styles may produce excellent results, but their effects on employees are quite different. Do managers deliberately decide to adopt one or the other of these approaches to management? Although they may do so part of the time, in all likelihood their personalities account for their different approaches. Indeed, research suggests that the way people react to different conditions depends, in part, on their personalities.[22]

The Big Five Personality Traits

We can think of an individual's personality as being composed of five general traits or characteristics: extraversion, negative affectivity, agreeableness, conscientiousness, and openness to experience.[23] Researchers often consider these the Big Five personality traits.[24] Each of them can be viewed as a continuum along which every individual or, more specifically, every manager falls (see Figure 3.1).

Some managers may be at the high end of one trait continuum, others at the low end, and still others somewhere in between. An easy way to understand how these traits can affect a person's approach to management is to describe what people are

Figure 3.1

The Big Five Personality Traits

Manager's personalities can be described by determining which point on each of the following dimensions best characterizes the manager in question:

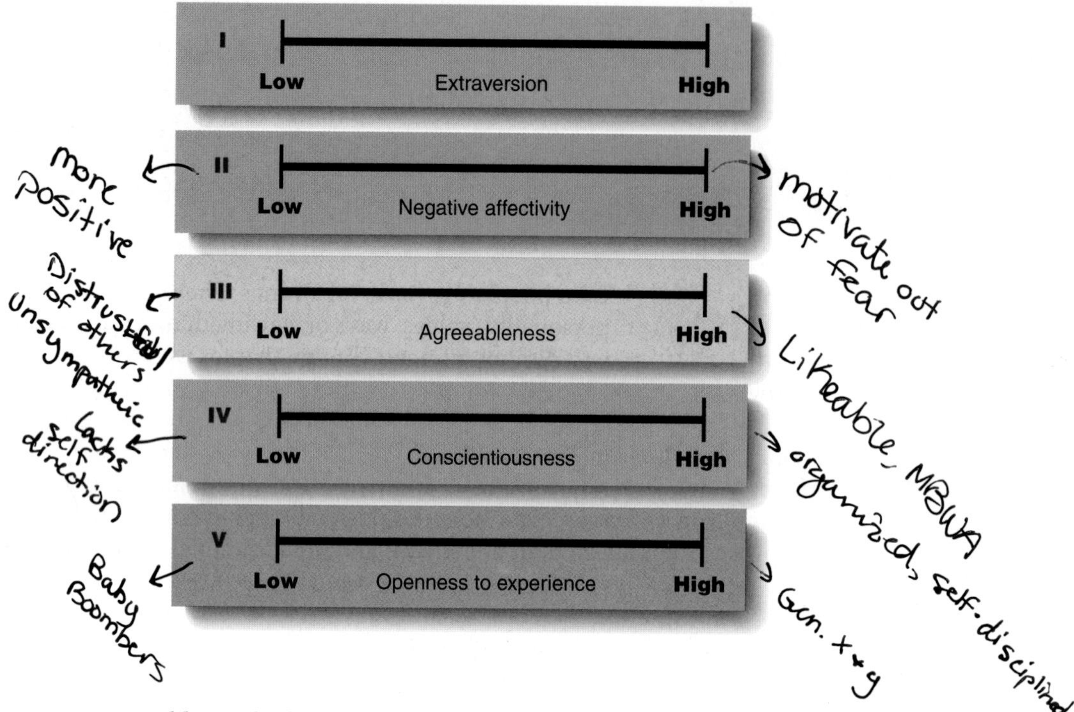

like at the high and low ends of each trait continuum. As will become evident as you read about each trait, no single trait is right or wrong for being an effective manager. Rather, effectiveness is determined by a complex interaction between the characteristics of managers (including personality traits) and the nature of the job and organization in which they are working. Moreover, personality traits that enhance managerial effectiveness in one situation may impair it in another.

extraversion The tendency to experience positive emotions and moods and to feel good about oneself and the rest of the world.

EXTRAVERSION **Extraversion** is the tendency to experience positive emotions and moods and feel good about oneself and the rest of the world. Managers who are high on extraversion (often called *extraverts*) tend to be sociable, affectionate, outgoing, and friendly. Managers who are low on extraversion (often called *introverts*) tend to be less inclined toward social interactions and to have a less positive outlook. Being high on extraversion may be an asset for managers whose jobs entail especially high levels of social interaction. Managers who are low on extraversion may nevertheless be highly effective and efficient, especially when their jobs do not require much social interaction. Their quieter approach may enable them to accomplish quite a bit of work in limited time. See Figure 3.2 for an example of a scale that can be used to measure a person's level of extraversion.

negative affectivity The tendency to experience negative emotions and moods, to feel distressed, and to be critical of oneself and others.

NEGATIVE AFFECTIVITY **Negative affectivity** is the tendency to experience negative emotions and moods, feel distressed, and be critical of oneself and others. Managers high on this trait may often feel angry and dissatisfied and complain about their own and others' lack of progress. Managers who are low on negative affectivity do not tend to experience many negative emotions and moods and are less pessimistic and critical of themselves and others. On the plus side, the critical approach of a manager high on negative affectivity may sometimes spur both the manager and others to improve their performance. Nevertheless, it is probably more pleasant to work with a manager who is low on negative affectivity; the better working relationships that such a manager is likely to cultivate also can be an important asset.

Figure 3.2

Measures of Extraversion, Agreeableness, Conscientiousness, and Openness to Experience

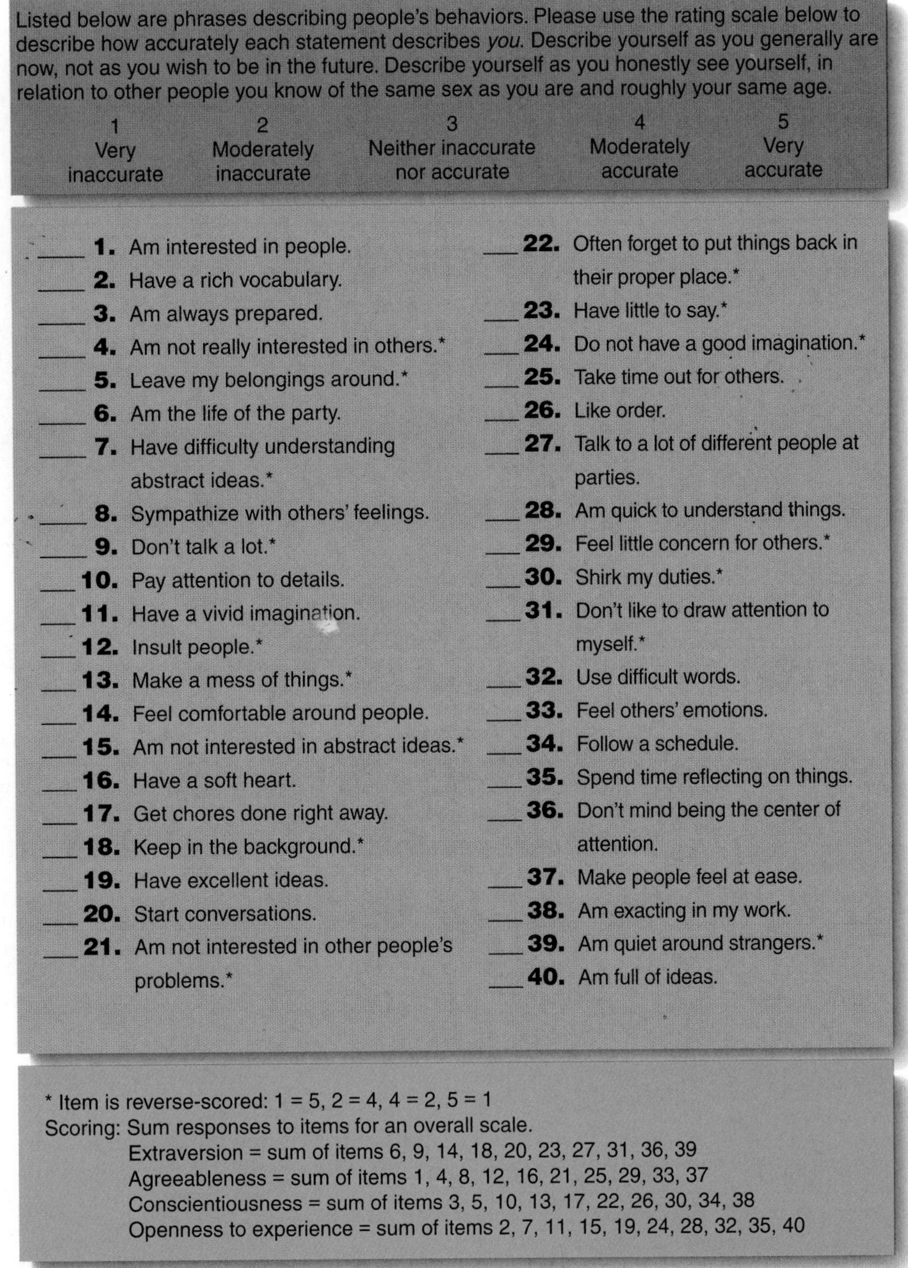

Listed below are phrases describing people's behaviors. Please use the rating scale below to describe how accurately each statement describes *you.* Describe yourself as you generally are now, not as you wish to be in the future. Describe yourself as you honestly see yourself, in relation to other people you know of the same sex as you are and roughly your same age.

1	2	3	4	5
Very inaccurate	Moderately inaccurate	Neither inaccurate nor accurate	Moderately accurate	Very accurate

____ **1.** Am interested in people.
____ **2.** Have a rich vocabulary.
____ **3.** Am always prepared.
____ **4.** Am not really interested in others.*
____ **5.** Leave my belongings around.*
____ **6.** Am the life of the party.
____ **7.** Have difficulty understanding abstract ideas.*
____ **8.** Sympathize with others' feelings.
____ **9.** Don't talk a lot.*
____ **10.** Pay attention to details.
____ **11.** Have a vivid imagination.
____ **12.** Insult people.*
____ **13.** Make a mess of things.*
____ **14.** Feel comfortable around people.
____ **15.** Am not interested in abstract ideas.*
____ **16.** Have a soft heart.
____ **17.** Get chores done right away.
____ **18.** Keep in the background.*
____ **19.** Have excellent ideas.
____ **20.** Start conversations.
____ **21.** Am not interested in other people's problems.*
____ **22.** Often forget to put things back in their proper place.*
____ **23.** Have little to say.*
____ **24.** Do not have a good imagination.*
____ **25.** Take time out for others.
____ **26.** Like order.
____ **27.** Talk to a lot of different people at parties.
____ **28.** Am quick to understand things.
____ **29.** Feel little concern for others.*
____ **30.** Shirk my duties.*
____ **31.** Don't like to draw attention to myself.*
____ **32.** Use difficult words.
____ **33.** Feel others' emotions.
____ **34.** Follow a schedule.
____ **35.** Spend time reflecting on things.
____ **36.** Don't mind being the center of attention.
____ **37.** Make people feel at ease.
____ **38.** Am exacting in my work.
____ **39.** Am quiet around strangers.*
____ **40.** Am full of ideas.

* Item is reverse-scored: 1 = 5, 2 = 4, 4 = 2, 5 = 1
Scoring: Sum responses to items for an overall scale.
Extraversion = sum of items 6, 9, 14, 18, 20, 23, 27, 31, 36, 39
Agreeableness = sum of items 1, 4, 8, 12, 16, 21, 25, 29, 33, 37
Conscientiousness = sum of items 3, 5, 10, 13, 17, 22, 26, 30, 34, 38
Openness to experience = sum of items 2, 7, 11, 15, 19, 24, 28, 32, 35, 40

Source: Lewis R. Goldberg, Oregon Research Institute, http://ipip.ori.org/ipip/. Reprinted with permission.

Figure 3.3 is an example of a scale developed to measure a person's level of negative affectivity.

agreeableness The tendency to get along well with other people.

AGREEABLENESS **Agreeableness** is the tendency to get along well with others. Managers who are high on the agreeableness continuum are likable, tend to be affectionate, and care about other people. Managers who are low on agreeableness may be somewhat distrustful of others, unsympathetic, uncooperative, and even at times antagonistic. Being high on agreeableness may be especially important for managers whose responsibilities require that they develop good, close relationships with others.

Figure 3.3

A Measure of Negative Affectivity

Instructions: Listed below are a series of statements a person might use to describe her/his attitudes, opinions, interests, and other characteristics. If a statement is true or largely true, put a "T" in the space next to the item. Or if the statement is false or largely false, mark an "F" in the space.

Please answer every statement, even if you are not completely sure of the answer. Read each statement carefully, but don't spend too much time deciding on the answer.

___ **1.** I worry about things a lot.

___ **2.** My feelings are often hurt.

___ **3.** Small problems often irritate me.

___ **4.** I am often nervous.

___ **5.** My moods often change.

___ **6.** Sometimes I feel bad for no apparent reason.

___ **7.** I often have very strong emotions such as anger or anxiety without really knowing why.

___ **8.** The unexpected can easily startle me.

___ **9.** Sometimes, when I am thinking about the day ahead of me, I feel anxious and tense.

___ **10.** Small setbacks sometimes bother me too much.

___ **11.** My worries often cause me to lose sleep.

___ **12.** Some days I seem to be always "on edge."

___ **13.** I am more sensitive than I should be.

___ **14.** Sometimes I go from feeling happy to sad, and vice versa, for no good reason.

Scoring: Level of negative affectivity is equal to the number of items answered "True."

Source: Auke Tellegen, *Brief Manual for the Differential Personality Questionnaire,* Copyright © 1982. Paraphrased version reproduced by permission of University of Minnesota Press.

Nevertheless, a low level of agreeableness may be an asset in managerial jobs that actually require that managers be antagonistic, such as drill sergeants and some other kinds of military managers. See Figure 3.2 for an example of a scale that measures a person's level of agreeableness.

conscientiousness The tendency to be careful, scrupulous, and persevering.

CONSCIENTIOUSNESS **Conscientiousness** is the tendency to be careful, scrupulous, and persevering.[25] Managers who are high on the conscientiousness continuum are organized and self-disciplined; those who are low on this trait might sometimes appear to lack direction and self-discipline. Conscientiousness has been found to be a good predictor of performance in many kinds of jobs, including managerial jobs in a variety of organizations.[26] Entrepreneurs who found their own companies, like Arunas Chesonis profiled in "A Manager's Challenge," often are high on conscientiousness, and their persistence and determination help them to overcome obstacles and turn their ideas into successful new ventures. Figure 3.2 provides an example of a scale that measures conscientiousness.

openness to experience The tendency to be original, have broad interests, be open to a wide range of stimuli, be daring, and take risks.

OPENNESS TO EXPERIENCE **Openness to experience** is the tendency to be original, have broad interests, be open to a wide range of stimuli, be daring, and take risks.[27] Managers who are high on this trait continuum may be especially likely to take risks and be innovative in their planning and decision making. Entrepreneurs who start their own businesses–like Bill Gates of Microsoft, Jeff Bezos of Amazon .com, and Anita Roddick of The Body Shop–are, in all likelihood, high on openness to experience, which has contributed to their success as entrepreneurs and managers. Arunas Chesonis, discussed in this chapter's "A Manager's Challenge," founded his own company and continues to explore new ways for it to grow–a testament to his high level of openness to experience. Managers who are low on openness to experience may be less prone to take risks and more conservative in their planning and decision making. In certain organizations and positions, this tendency might be an asset. The manager of the fiscal office in a public university, for example, must ensure that all university departments and units follow the university's rules and regulations pertaining to budgets, spending accounts, and reimbursements of expenses. Figure 3.2 provides an example of a measure of openness to experience.

Managers who come up with and implement radically new ideas are often high on openness to experience, as is true of Mike Rowe, creator of the hit Discovery Channel TV show *Dirty Jobs.*

Manager as a Person

Who Would Have Thought *Dirty Jobs* Would Be a Hit?

Mike Rowe is hardly the person you would have thought could have created a hit TV show like the Discovery Channel's *Dirty Jobs.*[28] Not the most ambitious of types, and as an actor for over two decades who never made it big, his work experiences have ranged from performing with the Baltimore Opera to selling fake simulated diamonds on QVC to appearing in Tylenol commercials.[29] While cohosting a local TV show on CBS-5 in San Francisco, Rowe hit on the idea behind *Dirty Jobs.* Rowe did a segment on the show called "Somebody's Gotta Do It," viewers liked it, and it really struck a chord with him personally.[30]

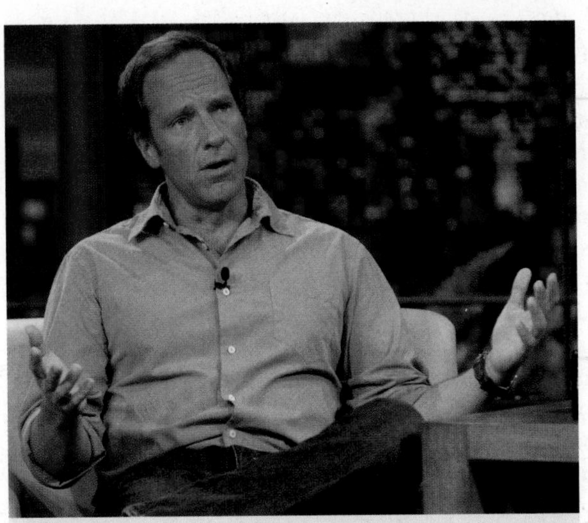

Mike Rowe's openness to experience has given him a real appreciation of all kinds of work and jobs.

His openness to experience led him to develop a TV show featuring him working as an apprentice to men and women performing the kinds of hard, dirty work we all depend on and no one wants to do (think bat cave scavenger, worm dung farmer, roadkill cleaner, sewer inspector, pig farmer . . .).[31] As he puts it, his show features "men and women who do the kinds of jobs that make civilized life possible for the rest of us."[32] While he originally had a hard time finding a home for *Dirty Jobs* (the Discovery Channel turned him down twice before agreeing to air a pilot series in 2003), the show has become a hit.[33]

Rowe's openness to experience enables him to get down and dirty with the best of them, try his hand at all sorts of dirty jobs, and thoroughly enjoy it. As would be expected, all sorts of mishaps occur–and that is part of the fun. Rowe has come to appreciate the earnestness of the workers he profiles–"the celebration of work, and the mixing of pain and fun."[34] Interestingly enough, as one who never had embraced the value of too much hard work in the past, Rowe has gleaned from *Dirty Jobs* a healthy respect and admiration for the people who perform all sorts of dirty jobs, work hard at them, and are happy when the work is done.[35]

Successful managers occupy a variety of positions on the Big Five personality trait continua. One highly effective manager may be high on extraversion and negative affectivity; another equally effective manager may be low on both these traits; and still another may be somewhere in between. Members of an organization must understand these differences among managers because they can shed light on how managers behave and on their approach to planning, leading, organizing, or controlling. If subordinates realize, for example, that their manager is low on extraversion, they will not feel slighted when their manager seems to be aloof because they will realize that by nature he or she is simply not outgoing.

Managers themselves also need to be aware of their own personality traits and the traits of others, including their subordinates and fellow managers. A manager who knows that he has a tendency to be highly critical of other people might try to tone down his negative approach. Similarly, a manager who realizes that her chronically complaining subordinate tends to be so negative because of his personality may take all his complaints with a grain of salt and realize that things probably are not as bad as this subordinate says they are.

In order for all members of an organization to work well together and with people outside the organization, such as customers and suppliers, they must understand each other. Such understanding comes, in part, from an appreciation of some fundamental ways in which people differ from one another–that is, an appreciation of personality traits.

Other Personality Traits That Affect Managerial Behavior

Many other specific traits in addition to the Big Five describe people's personalities. Here we look at traits that are particularly important for understanding managerial effectiveness: locus of control; self-esteem; and the needs for achievement, affiliation, and power.

internal locus of control The tendency to locate responsibility for one's fate within oneself.

external locus of control The tendency to locate responsibility for one's fate in outside forces and to believe one's own behavior has little impact on outcomes.

LOCUS OF CONTROL People differ in their views about how much control they have over what happens to and around them. The locus of control trait captures these beliefs.[36] People with an **internal locus of control** believe they themselves are responsible for their own fate; they see their own actions and behaviors as being major and decisive determinants of important outcomes such as attaining levels of job performance, being promoted, or being turned down for a choice job assignment. Some managers with an internal locus of control see the success of a whole organization resting on their shoulders. One example is Arunas Chesonis in "A Manager's Challenge." An internal locus of control also helps to ensure ethical behavior and decision making in an organization because people feel accountable and responsible for their own actions.

People with an **external locus of control** believe that outside forces are responsible for what happens to and around them; they do not think their own actions make much of a difference. As such, they tend not to intervene to try to change a situation or solve a problem, leaving it to someone else.

Managers need an internal locus of control because they *are* responsible for what happens in organizations; they need to believe they can and do make a difference, as does Arunas Chesonis at PAETEC. Moreover, managers are responsible for ensuring that organizations and their members behave in an ethical fashion, and for this as well they need an internal locus of control–they need to know and feel they can make a difference.

self-esteem The degree to which individuals feel good about themselves and their capabilities.

SELF-ESTEEM **Self-esteem** is the degree to which individuals feel good about themselves and their capabilities. People with high self-esteem believe they are competent, deserving, and capable of handling most situations, as does Arunas Chesonis. People with low self-esteem have poor opinions of themselves, are unsure about their capabilities, and question their ability to succeed at different endeavors.[37] Research suggests that people tend to choose activities and goals consistent with their levels of self-esteem. High self-esteem is desirable for managers because it facilitates their setting and keeping high standards for themselves, pushes them ahead on difficult projects, and gives them the confidence they need to make and carry out important decisions.

need for achievement The extent to which an individual has a strong desire to perform challenging tasks well and to meet personal standards for excellence.

need for affiliation The extent to which an individual is concerned about establishing and maintaining good interpersonal relations, being liked, and having other people get along.

need for power The extent to which an individual desires to control or influence others.

NEEDS FOR ACHIEVEMENT, AFFILIATION, AND POWER Psychologist David McClelland has extensively researched the needs for achievement, affiliation, and power.[38] The **need for achievement** is the extent to which an individual has a strong desire to perform challenging tasks well and to meet personal standards for excellence. People with a high need for achievement often set clear goals for themselves and like to receive performance feedback. The **need for affiliation** is the extent to which an individual is concerned about establishing and maintaining good interpersonal relations, being liked, and having the people around him or her get along with one another. The **need for power** is the extent to which an individual desires to control or influence others.[39]

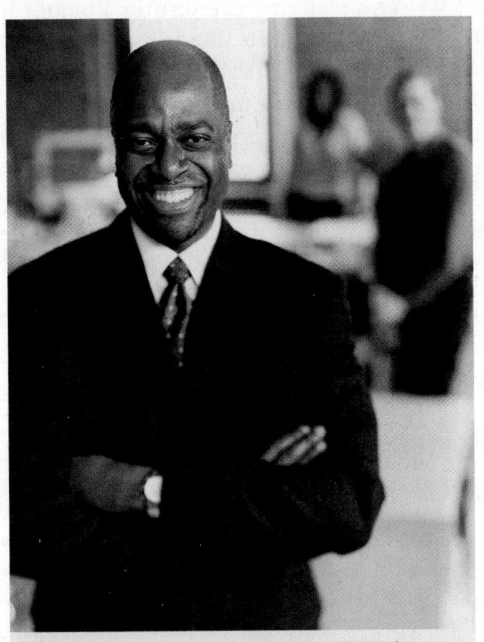

Confidence matters: a manager who takes difficulties in stride and can effectively lead is able to inspire subordinates while getting the job done.

Research suggests that high needs for achievement and for power are assets for first-line and middle managers and that a high need for power is especially important for upper-level managers.[40] One study found that U.S. presidents with a relatively high need for power tended to be especially effective during their terms of office.[41] A high need for affiliation may not always be desirable in managers because it might lead them to try too hard to be liked by others (including subordinates) rather than doing all they can to ensure that performance is as high as it can and should be. Although most research on these needs has been done in the United States, some studies suggest that these findings may also apply to people in other countries such as India and New Zealand.[42]

Taken together, these desirable personality traits for managers–an internal locus of control, high self-esteem, and high needs for achievement and power–suggest that managers need to be take-charge people who not only believe their own actions are decisive in determining their own and their organizations' fates but also believe in their own capabilities. Such managers have a personal desire for accomplishment and influence over others.

Values, Attitudes, and Moods and Emotions

LO3-2 Explain what values and attitudes are and describe their impact on managerial action.

What are managers striving to achieve? How do they think they should behave? What do they think about their jobs and organizations? And how do they actually feel at work? We can find some answers to these questions by exploring managers' values, attitudes, and moods.

Values, attitudes, and moods and emotions capture how managers experience their jobs as individuals. *Values* describe what managers are trying to achieve through work and how they think they should behave. *Attitudes* capture their thoughts and feelings about their specific jobs and organizations. *Moods and emotions* encompass how managers actually feel when they are managing. Although these three aspects of managers' work experience are highly personal, they also have important implications for understanding how managers behave, how they treat and respond to others, and how, through their efforts, they help contribute to organizational effectiveness through planning, leading, organizing, and controlling.

Values: Terminal and Instrumental

terminal value A lifelong goal or objective that an individual seeks to achieve.

instrumental value A mode of conduct that an individual seeks to follow.

norms Unwritten, informal codes of conduct that prescribe how people should act in particular situations and are considered important by most members of a group or organization.

value system The terminal and instrumental values that are guiding principles in an individual's life.

The two kinds of personal values are *terminal* and *instrumental*. A **terminal value** is a personal conviction about lifelong goals or objectives; an **instrumental value** is a personal conviction about desired modes of conduct or ways of behaving.[43] Terminal values often lead to the formation of **norms,** which are unwritten, informal codes of conduct, such as behaving honestly or courteously, that prescribe how people should act in particular situations and are considered important by most members of a group or organization.

Milton Rokeach, a leading researcher in the area of human values, identified 18 terminal values and 18 instrumental values that describe each person's value system (see Figure 3.4).[44] By rank ordering the terminal values from 1 (most important as a guiding principle in one's life) to 18 (least important as a guiding principle in one's life) and then rank ordering the instrumental values from 1 to 18, people can give good pictures of their **value systems**–what they are striving to achieve in life and how they want to behave.[45] (You can gain a good understanding of your own values by rank ordering first the terminal values and then the instrumental values listed in Figure 3.4.)

Several of the terminal values listed in Figure 3.4 seem to be especially important for managers–such as *a sense of accomplishment (a lasting contribution), equality*

Figure 3.4
Terminal and Instrumental Values

Terminal Values	Instrumental Values
A comfortable life (a prosperous life)	Ambitious (hardworking, aspiring)
An exciting life (a stimulating, active life)	Broad-minded (open-minded)
A sense of accomplishment (lasting contribution)	Capable (competent, effective)
A world at peace (free of war and conflict)	Cheerful (lighthearted, joyful)
A world of beauty (beauty of nature and the arts)	Clean (neat, tidy)
Equality (brotherhood, equal opportunity for all)	Courageous (standing up for your beliefs)
Family security (taking care of loved ones)	Forgiving (willlng to pardon others)
Freedom (independence, free choice)	Helpful (working for the welfare of others)
Happiness (contentedness)	Honest (sincere, truthful)
Inner harmony (freedom from inner conflict)	Imaginative (daring, creative)
Mature love (sexual and spiritual intimacy)	Independent (self-reliant, self-sufficient)
National security (protection from attack)	Intellectual (intelligent, reflective)
Pleasure (an enjoyable, leisurely life)	Logical (consistent, rational)
Salvation (saved, eternal life)	Loving (affectionate, tender)
Self-respect (self-esteem)	Obedient (dutiful, respectful)
Social recognition (respect, admiration)	Polite (courteous, well-mannered)
True friendship (close companionship)	Responsible (dependable, reliable)
Wisdom (a mature understanding of life)	Self-controlled (restrained, self-disciplined)

Source: Adapted with the permission of The Free Press, a Division of Simon & Schuster, Inc., from *The Nature of Human Values* by Milton Rokeach. Copyright © 1973 by The Free Press. Copyright renewed © 2001 by Sandra Ball-Rokeach. All rights reserved.

(brotherhood, equal opportunity for all), and *self-respect (self-esteem).* A manager who thinks a sense of accomplishment is of paramount importance might focus on making a lasting contribution to an organization by developing a new product that can save or prolong lives, as is true of managers at Medtronic (a company that makes medical devices such as cardiac pacemakers), or by opening a new foreign subsidiary. A manager who places equality at the top of his or her list of terminal values may be at the forefront of an organization's efforts to support, provide equal opportunities to, and capitalize on the many talents of an increasingly diverse workforce.

Other values are likely to be considered important by many managers, such *as a comfortable life (a prosperous life), an exciting life (a stimulating, active life), freedom (independence, free choice),* and *social recognition (respect, admiration).* The relative importance that managers place on each terminal value helps explain what they are striving to achieve in their organizations and what they will focus their efforts on.

Several of the instrumental values listed in Figure 3.4 seem to be important modes of conduct for managers, such as being *ambitious (hardworking, aspiring), broad-minded (open-minded), capable (competent, effective), responsible (dependable, reliable),* and *self-controlled (restrained, self-disciplined).* Moreover, the relative importance a manager places on these and other instrumental values may be a significant determinant of actual behaviors on the job. A manager who considers being *imaginative (daring, creative)* to be highly important, for example, is more likely to be innovative and take risks than is a manager who considers this to be less important (all else being equal). A manager who considers being *honest (sincere, truthful)* to be

Ethics in Action

Telling the Truth at Gentle Giant Moving

Gentle Giant Moving Company, based in Somerville, Massachusetts, was founded by Larry O'Toole in 1980 and now has over $28 million in revenues and offices in multiple states.[46] Although moving is undoubtedly hard work and many people would never think about having a career in this industry, Gentle Giant's unique culture and approach to managing people have not only contributed to the company's success but also provided its employees with satisfying careers. For example, when Ryan Libby was in college, he worked for Gentle Giant during one of his summer vacations to make some extra money. Now the assistant manager for the Providence, Rhode Island, Gentle Giant Office, Libby is contemplating opening an office of his own. As he puts it, "First it was just a paycheck, and it kind of turned into a long-term career."[47]

At Gentle Giant Moving Company, employees are given leadership training, access to company outings, and the opportunity to advance to management positions.

Libby is just the kind of employee O'Toole seeks to hire–employees who start out driving moving trucks and eventually move into management positions running offices. Whereas some moving companies hire a lot of temporary help in the summer to meet seasonal demand, 60% of Gentle Giant employees are employed full-time.[48]

Because the demand for moving services is lower in the winter, Gentle Giant uses this time to give employees training and leadership development activities. Of course new employees receive training in the basics of moving: packing, lifting, and carrying household goods in a safe manner. However, employees looking to advance in the company receive training in a host of other areas ranging from project management, communication, problem solving, and customer relations to leadership. An overarching goal of Gentle Giant's training efforts is inculcating in employees the importance of honesty. According to O'Toole, "We really emphasize that what matters most to us is telling the truth."[49]

Training benefits Gentle Giant's employees, customers, and the company as a whole. About one-third of the company's office and management employees started out driving moving trucks. Customers are satisfied because employees are capable, honest, and professional. And the company has continued to grow, prosper, and receive recognition in the business press as well as awards. For example, Gentle Giant was named one of the 15 Top Small Workplaces by *The Wall Street Journal* in collaboration with Winning Workplaces (a nonprofit organization that focuses on helping small and medium-size companies improve their work environments).[50]

Having fun and getting to know each other as people is also important at Gentle Giant.[51] The company holds parties and arranges outings for employees to sporting events, amusement parks, and other local attractions. Most workdays, O'Toole takes an employee out to lunch. Some college athletes are attracted to work for Gentle Giant because they see moving as a way to keep fit while at the same time having the opportunity to grow and develop on the job and move into a managerial position if they desire.[52]

of paramount importance may be a driving force for taking steps to ensure that all members of a unit or organization behave ethically, as indicated in the following "Ethics in Action" box.

All in all, managers' value systems signify what managers as individuals are trying to accomplish and become in their personal lives and at work. Thus managers' value systems are fundamental guides to their behavior and efforts at planning, leading, organizing, and controlling.

Attitudes

attitude A collection of feelings and beliefs.

An **attitude** is a collection of feelings and beliefs. Like everyone else, managers have attitudes about their jobs and organizations, and these attitudes affect how they approach their jobs. Two of the most important attitudes in this context are job satisfaction and organizational commitment.

job satisfaction The collection of feelings and beliefs that managers have about their current jobs.

JOB SATISFACTION **Job satisfaction** is the collection of feelings and beliefs that managers have about their current jobs.[53] Managers who have high levels of job satisfaction generally like their jobs, feel they are fairly treated, and believe their jobs have many desirable features or characteristics (such as interesting work, good pay and job security, autonomy, or nice coworkers). Figure 3.5 shows sample items from two scales that managers can use to measure job satisfaction. Levels of job satisfaction tend to increase as one moves up the hierarchy in an organization. Upper managers, in general, tend to be more satisfied with their jobs than entry-level employees. Managers' levels of job satisfaction can range from very low to very high. As profiled in the following "Management Insight" box, levels of job satisfaction have hit all-time lows in the United States.

Figure 3.5
Sample Items from Two Measures of Job Satisfaction

Sample items from the Minnesota Satisfaction Questionnaire:
People respond to each of the items in the scale by checking whether they are:

[ ] Very dissatisfied
[ ] Dissatisfied
[ ] Can't decide whether satisfied or not
[ ] Satisfied
[ ] Very satisfied

On my present job, this is how I feel about . . .

____ **1.** Being able to do things that don't go against my conscience.
____ **2.** The way my job provides for steady employment.
____ **3.** The chance to do things for other people.
____ **4.** The chance to do something that makes use of my abilities.
____ **5.** The way company policies are put into practice.
____ **6.** My pay and the amount of work I do.
____ **7.** The chances for advancement on this job.
____ **8.** The freedom to use my own judgment.
____ **9.** The working conditions.
____ **10.** The way my coworkers get along with each other.
____ **11.** The praise I get for doing a good job.
____ **12.** The feeling of accomplishment I get from the job.

The Faces Scale
Workers select the face which best expresses how they feel about their job in general.

11 10 9 8 7 6 5 4 3 2 1

Source: D. J. Weiss et al., *Manual for the Minnesota Satisfaction Questionnaire,* 1967, Minnesota Studies in Vocational Rehabilitation: XXII. Copyright © 1967 University of Minnesota. Copyright © 1975 by the American Psychological Association. Adapted by permission of Randall B. Dunham and J. B. Brett.

Management Insight

Job Satisfaction at Record Low in the United States

In December 2009 the U.S. unemployment rate was 10%, 85,000 jobs were lost from the economy, and the underemployment rate (which includes people who have given up looking for jobs and those who are working part-time because they can't find a full-time position) was 17.3%.[54] Under recessionary conditions like these, one might think people who have jobs would be satisfied with them. But in fact job satisfaction levels in the United States have fallen to record lows.[55]

The Conference Board has been tracking levels of U.S. job satisfaction since 1987, when 61.1% of workers surveyed indicated that they were satisfied with their jobs.[56] In 2009 only 45% of workers surveyed indicated that they were satisfied with their jobs, an all-time low for the survey.[57] Some sources of job dissatisfaction include uninteresting work, lack of job security, incomes that have not kept pace with inflation, and having to spend more money on health insurance. For example, three times as many workers in 2009 had to contribute to paying for their health insurance and had rising levels of contributions compared to 1980. Only 43% of workers thought their jobs were secure in 2009 compared to 59% in 1987. In the 2000s, average household incomes adjusted for inflation declined.[58]

Of all age groups, workers under 25 were the most dissatisfied with their jobs. More specifically, approximately 64% of workers in this age group were dissatisfied with their jobs, perhaps due to declining opportunities and relatively low earnings. Around 22% of all respondents didn't think they would still have the same job in a year.[59]

The Conference Board study, conducted by TNS, a global market research firm, surveyed 5,000 households in the United States.[60] Lynn Franco, who directs the Consumer Research Center at the Conference Board, summarized the survey results this way: "While 1 in 10 Americans is now unemployed, their working compatriots of all ages and incomes continue to grown increasingly unhappy."[61]

organizational citizenship behaviors (OCBs) Behaviors that are not required of organizational members but that contribute to and are necessary for organizational efficiency, effectiveness, and competitive advantage.

In general, it is desirable for managers to be satisfied with their jobs, for at least two reasons. First, satisfied managers may be more likely to go the extra mile for their organization or perform **organizational citizenship behaviors (OCBs)**–behaviors that are not required of organizational members but that contribute to and are necessary for organizational efficiency, effectiveness, and competitive advantage.[62] Managers who are satisfied with their jobs are more likely to perform these "above and beyond the call of duty" behaviors, which can range from putting in long hours when needed to coming up with truly creative ideas and overcoming obstacles to implement them (even when doing so is not part of the manager's job), or to going out of one's way to help a coworker, subordinate, or superior (even when doing so entails considerable personal sacrifice).[63]

Staying late to double-check the numbers and look ahead to tomorrow? Not a drag for a motivated, satisfied employee.

A second reason why it is desirable for managers to be satisfied with their jobs is that satisfied managers may be less likely to quit.[64] A manager who is highly satisfied may never even think about looking for another position; a dissatisfied manager may always be on the lookout for new opportunities. Turnover can hurt an organization because it results in the loss of the experience and knowledge that managers have gained about the company, industry, and business environment.

A growing source of dissatisfaction for many lower- and middle-level managers, as well as for nonmanagerial employees, is the threat of unemployment and increased workloads from organizational downsizings and layoffs. Organizations that try to improve their efficiency through restructuring and layoffs often eliminate a sizable number of first-line and middle management positions. This decision obviously hurts the managers who are laid off, and it also can reduce the job satisfaction levels of managers who remain. They might fear being the next to be let go. In addition, the workloads of remaining employees often are dramatically increased as a result of restructuring, and this can contribute to dissatisfaction.

How managers and organizations handle layoffs is of paramount importance, not only for the layoff victims but also for employees who survive the layoff and keep their jobs.[65] Showing compassion and empathy for layoff victims, giving them as much advance notice as possible about the layoff, providing clear information about severance benefits, and helping layoff victims in their job search efforts are a few of the ways in which managers can humanely manage a layoff.[66] For example, when Ron Thomas, vice president of organizational development for Martha Stewart Living Omnimedia, had to lay off employees as a result of closing the organization's catalog business, he personally called all the catalog businesses he knew to find out about potential positions for laid-off employees.[67] Efforts such as Thomas's to help layoff victims find new jobs can contribute to the job satisfaction of those who survive the layoff. As Thomas puts it, "If you handle a restructuring well, the word gets out that you're a good place to work . . . if we post a job opening today, we'll get 1,500 résumés tomorrow."[68]

Unfortunately, when the unemployment rate is high, laid-off employees sometimes find it difficult to find new jobs and can remain jobless for months.[69] For small businesses, the decision to lay off employees and communicating that decision can be especially painful because managers often have developed close personal relationships with the people they have to let go, know their families, and fear what will happen to them with the loss of a steady income.[70] Shelly Polum, vice president for administration at Ram Tool, a small family-owned manufacturing company in Grafton, Wisconsin, broke down in tears in her office after she had to let employees know they were being laid off.[71] When Charlie Thomas, vice president of Shuqualak Lumber in Shuqualak, Mississippi, had to announce layoffs of close to a quarter of his employees, he wrote a speech that he could not get through without stopping and retreating to his office to pull himself together. As he put it, "I couldn't get it out . . . It just killed my soul."[72] As these managers realize, getting laid off during a recession can be devastating for employees and their families because jobs are few and far between.

organizational commitment The collection of feelings and beliefs that managers have about their organization as a whole.

ORGANIZATIONAL COMMITMENT **Organizational commitment** is the collection of feelings and beliefs that managers have about their organization as a whole.[73] Managers who are committed to their organizations believe in what their organizations are doing, are proud of what these organizations stand for, and feel a high degree of loyalty toward their organizations. Committed managers are more likely to go above and beyond the call of duty to help their company and are less likely to quit.[74] Organizational commitment can be especially strong when employees and managers truly believe in organizational values; it also leads to a strong organizational culture, as found in PAETEC.

Organizational commitment is likely to help managers perform some of their figurehead and spokesperson roles (see Chapter 1). It is much easier for a manager to persuade others both inside and outside the organization of the merits of what the organization has done and is seeking to accomplish if the manager truly believes in and is committed to the organization. Figure 3.6 is an example of a scale that can measure a person's level of organizational commitment.

Do managers in different countries have similar or different attitudes? Differences in the levels of job satisfaction and organizational commitment among managers in different countries are likely because these managers have different kinds of opportunities and rewards and because they face different economic, political, and sociocultural forces in their organizations' general environments. Levels of organizational commitment from one country to another may depend on the extent to which countries have legislation affecting firings and layoffs and the extent to which citizens of a country are geographically mobile.

LO3-3 Appreciate how moods and emotions influence all members of an organization.

Moods and Emotions

mood A feeling or state of mind.

Just as you sometimes are in a bad mood and at other times are in a good mood, so too are managers. A **mood** is a feeling or state of mind. When people are in a positive mood, they feel excited, enthusiastic, active, or elated.[75] When people are in a negative mood, they feel distressed, fearful, scornful, hostile, jittery, or nervous.[76] People who are high on extraversion are especially likely to experience positive moods; people who are high on negative affectivity are especially likely to experience negative moods. People's situations or circumstances also determine their moods; however, receiving a raise is likely to put most people in a good mood regardless of their personality traits. People who are high on negative affectivity are not always in a bad mood, and people who are low on extraversion still experience positive moods.[77]

emotions Intense, relatively short-lived feelings.

Emotions are more intense feelings than moods, are often directly linked to whatever caused the emotion, and are more short-lived.[78] However, once whatever has triggered the emotion has been dealt with, the feelings may linger in the form of a less intense mood.[79] For example, a manager who gets very angry when a subordinate has

Figure 3.6

A Measure of Organizational Commitment

People respond to each of the items in the scale by checking whether they:

[ ] Strongly disagree
[ ] Moderately disagree
[ ] Slightly disagree
[ ] Neither disagree nor agree
[ ] Slightly agree
[ ] Moderately agree
[ ] Strongly agree

____ **1.** I am willing to put in a great deal of effort beyond that normally expected in order to help this organization be successful.

____ **2.** I talk up this organization to my friends as a great organization to work for.

____ **3.** I feel very little loyalty to this organization.*

____ **4.** I would accept almost any type of job assignment in order to keep working for this organization.

____ **5.** I find that my values and the organization's values are very similar.

____ **6.** I am proud to tell others that I am part of this organization.

____ **7.** I could just as well be working for a different organization as long as the type of work was similar.*

____ **8.** This organization really inspires the very best in me in the way of job performance.

____ **9.** It would take very little change in my present circumstances to cause me to leave this organization.*

____ **10.** I am extremely glad that I chose this organization to work for over others I was considering at the time I joined.

____ **11.** There's not too much to be gained by sticking with this organization indefinitely.*

____ **12.** Often, I find it difficult to agree with this organization's policies on important matters relating to its employees.*

____ **13.** I really care about the fate of this organization.

____ **14.** For me this is the best of all possible organizations for which to work.

____ **15.** Deciding to work for this organization was a definite mistake on my part.*

Scoring: Responses to items 1, 2, 4, 5, 6, 8, 10, 13, and 14 are scored such that 1 = strongly disagree; 2 = moderately disagree; 3 = slightly disagree; 4 = neither disagree nor agree; 5 = slightly agree; 6 = moderately agree; and 7 = strongly agree. Responses to "*" items 3, 7, 9, 11, 12, and 15 are scored 7 = strongly disagree; 6 = moderately disagree; 5 = slightly disagree; 4 = neither disagree nor agree; 3 = slightly agree; 2 = moderately agree; and 1 = strongly agree. Responses to the 15 items are averaged for an overall score from 1 to 7; the higher the score, the higher the level of organizational commitment.

Source: L. W. Porter and F. J. Smith, "Organizational Commitment Questionnaire," in J. D. Cook, S. J. Hepworth, T. D. Wall, and P. B. Warr, eds., *The Experience of Work: A Compendium and Review of 249 Measures and Their Use* (New York: Academic Press, 1981), 84–86.

engaged in an unethical behavior may find his anger decreasing in intensity once he has decided how to address the problem. Yet he continues to be in a bad mood the rest of the day, even though he is not directly thinking about the unfortunate incident.[80]

Research has found that moods and emotions affect the behavior of managers and all members of an organization. For example, research suggests that the subordinates of managers who experience positive moods at work may perform at somewhat higher levels and be less likely to resign and leave the organization than the subordinates of managers who do not tend to be in a positive mood at work.[81] Other research suggests that under certain conditions creativity might be enhanced by positive moods, whereas under other conditions negative moods might push people to work harder to come up with truly creative ideas.[82] Recognizing that both mood states have the

Laugh it up: seeing the silly side can help get your brain in gear for making tougher decisions.

potential to contribute to creativity in different ways, recent research suggests that employees may be especially likely to be creative to the extent that they experience both mood states (at different times) on the job and to the extent that the work environment is supportive of creativity.[83]

Other research suggests that moods and emotions may play an important role in ethical decision making. For example, researchers at Princeton University found that when people are trying to solve difficult personal moral dilemmas, the parts of their brains that are responsible for emotions and moods are especially active.[84]

More generally, emotions and moods give managers and all employees important information and signals about what is going on in the workplace.[85] Positive emotions and moods signal that things are going well and thus can lead to more expansive, and even playful, thinking. Negative emotions and moods signal that there are problems in need of attention and areas for improvement. So when people are in negative moods, they tend to be more detail-oriented and focused on the facts at hand.[86] Some studies suggest that critical thinking and devil's advocacy may be promoted by a negative mood, and sometimes especially accurate judgments may be made by managers in negative moods.[87]

Managers and other members of an organization need to realize that how they feel affects how they treat others and how others respond to them, including their subordinates. For example, a subordinate may be more likely to approach a manager with a somewhat unusual but potentially useful idea if the subordinate thinks the manager is in a good mood. Likewise, when managers are in very bad moods, their subordinates might try to avoid them at all costs. Figure 3.7 is an example of a scale that can measure the extent to which a person experiences positive and negative moods at work.

Figure 3.7

A Measure of Positive and Negative Mood at Work

People respond to each item by indicating the extent to which the item describes how they felt at work during the past week on the following scale:

1 = Very slightly or not at all
2 = A little
3 = Moderately
4 = Quite a bit
5 = Very much

____ **1.** Active	____ **7.** Enthusiastic
____ **2.** Distressed	____ **8.** Fearful
____ **3.** Strong	____ **9.** Peppy
____ **4.** Excited	____ **10.** Nervous
____ **5.** Scornful	____ **11.** Elated
____ **6.** Hostile	____ **12.** Jittery

Scoring: Responses to items 1, 3, 4, 7, 9, and 11 are summed for a positive mood score; the higher the score, the more positive mood is experienced at work. Responses to items 2, 5, 6, 8, 10, and 12 are summed for a negative mood score; the higher the score, the more negative mood is experienced at work.

Source: A. P. Brief, M. J. Burke, J. M. George, B. Robinson, and J. Webster, "Should Negative Affectivity Remain an Unmeasured Variable in the Study of Job Stress?" *Journal of Applied Psychology* 73 (1988), 193–98; M. J. Burke, A. P. Brief, J. M. George, L. Robinson, and J. Webster, "Measuring Affect at Work: Confirmatory Analyses of Competing Mood Structures with Conceptual Linkage in Cortical Regulatory Systems," *Journal of Personality and Social Psychology* 57 (1989), 1091–102.

Emotional Intelligence

LO3-4 Describe the nature of emotional intelligence and its role in management.

emotional intelligence The ability to understand and manage one's own moods and emotions and the moods and emotions of other people.

In understanding the effects of managers' and all employees' moods and emotions, it is important to take into account their levels of emotional intelligence. **Emotional intelligence** is the ability to understand and manage one's own moods and emotions and the moods and emotions of other people.[88] Managers with a high level of emotional intelligence are more likely to understand how they are feeling and why, and they are more able to effectively manage their feelings. When managers are experiencing stressful feelings and emotions such as fear or anxiety, emotional intelligence lets them understand why and manage these feelings so they do not get in the way of effective decision making.[89]

Emotional intelligence also can help managers perform their important roles such as their interpersonal roles (figurehead, leader, and liaison).[90] Understanding how your subordinates feel, why they feel that way, and how to manage these feelings is central to developing strong interpersonal bonds with them.[91] Moreover, emotional intelligence has the potential to contribute to effective leadership in multiple ways[92] and can help managers make lasting contributions to society. For example, Bernard (Bernie) Goldhirsh founded *INC.* magazine back in 1979, when entrepreneurs received more notoriety than respect, if they were paid attention at all.[93] Goldhirsh was an entrepreneur himself at the time, with his own publishing company. He recognized the vast contributions entrepreneurs could make to society, creating something out of nothing, and also realized firsthand what a tough task entrepreneurs faced.[94] His emotional intelligence helped him understand the challenges and frustrations entrepreneurs like himself faced and their need for support.

When Goldhirsh founded *INC.*, entrepreneurs had few sources to which they could turn for advice, guidance, and solutions to management problems. *INC.* was born to fill this gap and give entrepreneurs information and support by profiling successful and unsuccessful entrepreneurial ventures, highlighting management techniques that work, and providing firsthand accounts of how successful entrepreneurs developed and managed their businesses.[95]

Goldhirsh's emotional intelligence helped him recognize the many barriers entrepreneurs face and the emotional roller coaster of staking all one has on an idea that may or may not work. Goldhirsh believed that helping society understand the entrepreneurial process through *INC.* magazine not only helped entrepreneurs but also enlightened bankers, lawmakers, and the public at large about the role these visionaries play, the challenges they face, and the support their ventures depend on.[96]

Emotional intelligence helps managers understand and relate well to other people.[97] It also helps managers maintain their enthusiasm and confidence and energize subordinates to help the organization attain its goals.[98] Recent theorizing and research suggest that emotional intelligence may be especially important in awakening employee creativity.[99] Managers themselves are increasingly recognizing the importance of emotional intelligence. As Andrea Jung, CEO of Avon Products, has indicated, "Emotional intelligence is in our DNA here at Avon because relationships are critical at every stage of our business."[100] An example of a scale that measures emotional intelligence is provided in Figure 3.8.

LO3-5 Define organizational culture and explain how managers both create and are influenced by organizational culture.

Organizational Culture

Personality is a way of understanding why all managers and employees, as individuals, characteristically think and behave in different ways. However, when people belong to the same organization, they tend to share certain beliefs and values that lead them to act in similar ways.[101] **Organizational culture** comprises the shared set of beliefs, expectations, values, norms, and work routines that influence how members of an organization relate to one another and work together to achieve organizational goals. In essence, organizational culture reflects the distinctive ways in which organizational members perform their jobs and relate to others inside and outside the organization. It may, for example, be how customers in a particular hotel chain are treated

Figure 3.8
A Measure of Emotional Intelligence

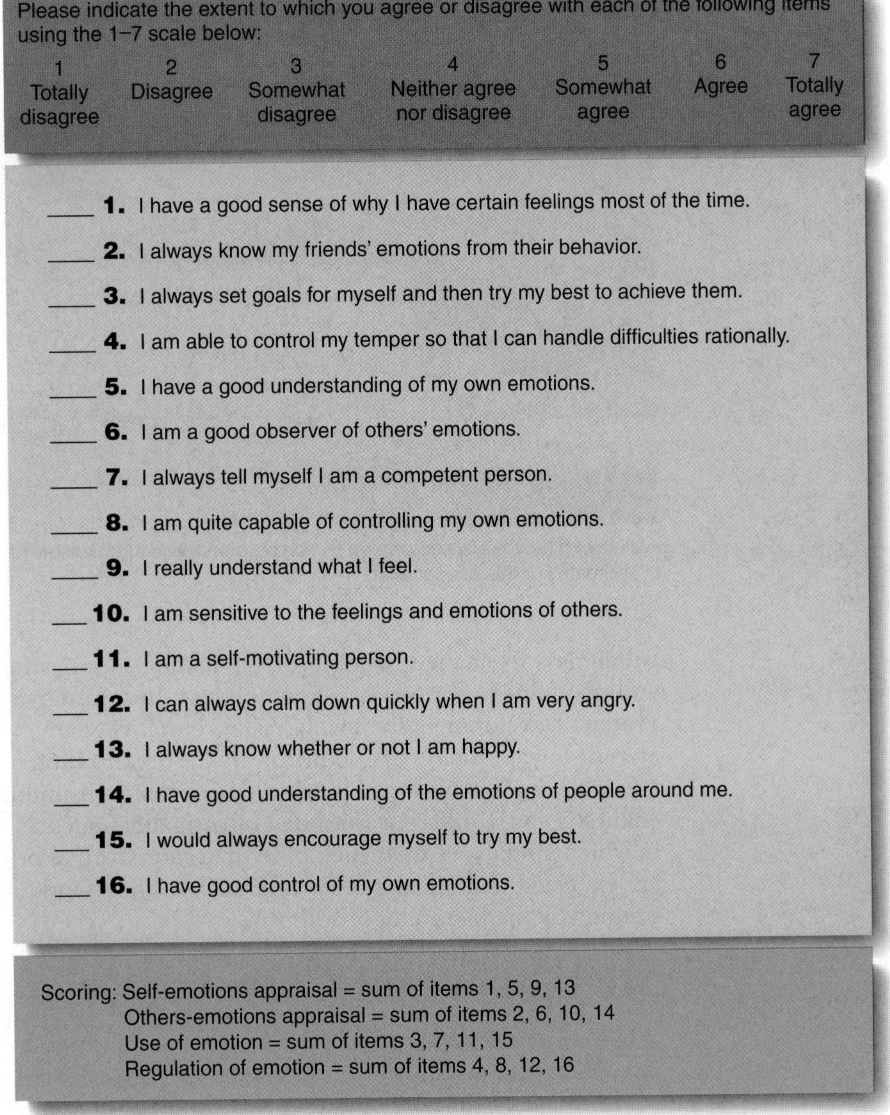
Please indicate the extent to which you agree or disagree with each of the following items using the 1–7 scale below:

1	2	3	4	5	6	7
Totally disagree	Disagree	Somewhat disagree	Neither agree nor disagree	Somewhat agree	Agree	Totally agree

____ **1.** I have a good sense of why I have certain feelings most of the time.
____ **2.** I always know my friends' emotions from their behavior.
____ **3.** I always set goals for myself and then try my best to achieve them.
____ **4.** I am able to control my temper so that I can handle difficulties rationally.
____ **5.** I have a good understanding of my own emotions.
____ **6.** I am a good observer of others' emotions.
____ **7.** I always tell myself I am a competent person.
____ **8.** I am quite capable of controlling my own emotions.
____ **9.** I really understand what I feel.
____ **10.** I am sensitive to the feelings and emotions of others.
____ **11.** I am a self-motivating person.
____ **12.** I can always calm down quickly when I am very angry.
____ **13.** I always know whether or not I am happy.
____ **14.** I have good understanding of the emotions of people around me.
____ **15.** I would always encourage myself to try my best.
____ **16.** I have good control of my own emotions.

Scoring: Self-emotions appraisal = sum of items 1, 5, 9, 13
Others-emotions appraisal = sum of items 2, 6, 10, 14
Use of emotion = sum of items 3, 7, 11, 15
Regulation of emotion = sum of items 4, 8, 12, 16

Source: K. Law, C. Wong, and L. Song, "The Construct and Criterion Validity of Emotional Intelligence and Its Potential Utility for Management Studies," *Journal of Applied Psychology* 89, no. 3 (June 2004), 496; C. S. Wong and K. S. Law, "The Effects of Leader and Follower Emotional Intelligence on Performance and Attitude: An Exploratory Study," *Leadership Quarterly* 13 (2002), 243–74.

organizational culture The shared set of beliefs, expectations, values, norms, and work routines that influence how individuals, groups, and teams interact with one another and cooperate to achieve organizational goals.

from the time they are greeted at check-in until they leave; or it may be the shared work routines that research teams use to guide new product development. When organizational members share an intense commitment to cultural values, beliefs, and routines and use them to achieve their goals, a *strong* organizational culture exists.[102] When organizational members are not strongly committed to a shared system of values, beliefs, and routines, organizational culture is weak.

The stronger the culture of an organization, the more one can think about it as being the "personality" of an organization because it influences the way its members behave.[103] Organizations that possess strong cultures may differ on a wide variety of dimensions that determine how their members behave toward one another and perform their jobs. For example, organizations differ in how members relate to each other (formally or informally), how important decisions are made (top-down or bottom-up),

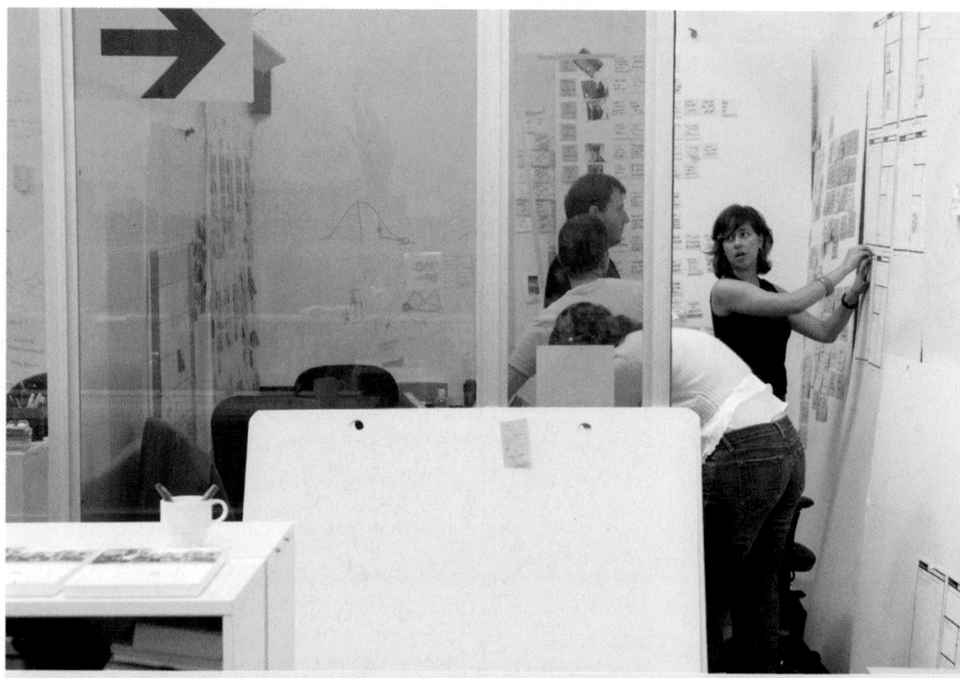

IDEO employees brainstorming—informal communication, casual attire, and flexibility are all hallmarks of this organization.

willingness to change (flexible or unyielding), innovation (creative or predictable), and playfulness (serious or serendipitous). In an innovative design firm like IDEO Product Development in Silicon Valley, employees are encouraged to adopt a playful attitude toward their work, look outside the organization to find inspiration, and adopt a flexible approach toward product design that uses multiple perspectives.[104] IDEO's culture is vastly different from that of companies such as Citibank and ExxonMobil, in which employees treat each other in a more formal or deferential way, employees are expected to adopt a serious approach to their work, and decision making is constrained by the hierarchy of authority.

Managers and Organizational Culture

While all members of an organization can contribute to developing and maintaining organizational culture, managers play a particularly important part in influencing organizational culture[105] because of their multiple and important roles (see Chapter 1). How managers create culture is most vividly evident in start-ups of new companies. Entrepreneurs who start their own companies are typically also the startups' top managers until the companies grow and become profitable. Often referred to as the firms' founders, these managers literally create their organizations' cultures.

The founders' personal characteristics play an important role in the creation of organizational culture. Benjamin Schneider, a well-known management researcher, developed a model that helps to explain the role that founders' personal characteristics play in determining organizational culture.[106] His model, called the **attraction–selection–attrition (ASA) framework,** posits that when founders hire employees for their new ventures, they tend to be attracted to and choose employees whose personalities are similar to their own.[107] These similar employees are more likely to stay with the organization. Although employees who are dissimilar in personality might be hired, they are more likely to leave the organization over time.[108] As a result of these attraction, selection, and attrition processes, people in the organization tend to have similar personalities, and the typical or dominant personality profile of organizational members determines and shapes organizational culture.[109]

attraction–selection–attrition (ASA) framework A model that explains how personality may influence organizational culture.

For example, when David Kelley became interested in engineering and product design challenges in the late 1970s, he realized that who he was as a person meant he would not be happy working in a typical corporate environment. Kelley is high on openness to experience, driven to go where his interests take him, and not content to follow others' directives. Kelley recognized that he needed to start his own business, and with the help of other Stanford-schooled engineers and design experts, IDEO was born.[110]

From the start, IDEO's culture has embodied Kelley's spirited, freewheeling approach to work and design–from colorful and informal work spaces to an emphasis on networking and communicating with as many people as possible to understand a design problem. No project or problem is too big or too small for IDEO; the company designed the Apple Lisa computer and mouse (the precursor of the Mac) and the Palm as well as the Crest Neat Squeeze toothpaste dispenser and the Racer's Edge water bottle.[111] Kelley hates rules, job titles, big corner offices, and all the other trappings of large traditional organizations that stifle creativity. Employees who are attracted to, selected by, and remain with IDEO value creativity and innovation and embrace one of IDEO's mottos: "Fail often to succeed sooner."[112]

Although ASA processes are most evident in small firms such as IDEO, they also can operate in large companies.[113] According to the ASA model, this is a naturally occurring phenomenon to the extent that managers and new hires are free to make the kinds of choices the model specifies. However, while people tend to get along well with others who are similar to themselves, too much similarity in an organization can impair organizational effectiveness. That is, similar people tend to view conditions and events in similar ways and thus can be resistant to change. Moreover, organizations benefit from a diversity of perspectives rather than similarity in perspectives (see Chapter 5). At IDEO Kelley recognized early on how important it is to take advantage of the diverse talents and perspectives that people with different personalities, backgrounds, experiences, and education can bring to a design team. Hence IDEO's design teams include not only engineers but others who might have a unique insight into a problem, such as anthropologists, communications experts, doctors, and users of a product. When new employees are hired at IDEO, they meet many employees who have different backgrounds and characteristics; the focus is not on hiring someone who will fit in but, rather, on hiring someone who has something to offer and can "wow" different kinds of people with his or her insights.[114]

In addition to personality, other personal characteristics of managers shape organizational culture; these include managers' values, attitudes, moods and emotions, and emotional intelligence.[115] For example, both terminal and instrumental values of managers play a role in determining organizational culture. Managers who highly value freedom and equality, for example, might be likely to stress the importance of autonomy and empowerment in their organizations, as well as fair treatment for all. As another example, managers who highly value being helpful and forgiving might not only tolerate mistakes but also emphasize the importance of organizational members' being kind and helpful to one another.

Managers who are satisfied with their jobs, are committed to their organizations, and experience positive moods and emotions might also encourage these attitudes and feelings in others. The result would be an organizational culture emphasizing positive attitudes and feelings. Research suggests that attitudes like job satisfaction and organizational commitment can be affected by the influence of others. Managers are in a particularly strong position to engage in social influence given their multiple roles. Moreover, research suggests that moods and emotions can be contagious and that spending time with people who are excited and enthusiastic can increase one's own levels of excitement and enthusiasm.

The Role of Values and Norms in Organizational Culture

Shared terminal and instrumental values play a particularly important role in organizational culture. *Terminal values* signify what an organization and its employees are trying to accomplish, and *instrumental values* guide how the organization and its members achieve organizational goals. In addition to values, shared norms also are a key aspect of organizational culture. Recall that norms are unwritten, informal rules or guidelines that prescribe appropriate behavior in particular situations. For example, norms at IDEO include not being critical of others' ideas, coming up with multiple ideas before settling on one, and developing prototypes of new products.[116]

Managers determine and shape organizational culture through the kinds of values and norms they promote in an organization. Some managers, like David Kelley of IDEO, cultivate values and norms that encourage risk taking, creative responses to problems and opportunities, experimentation, tolerance of failure in order to succeed, and autonomy.[117] Top managers at organizations such as Microsoft and Google encourage employees to adopt such values to support their commitment to innovation as a source of competitive advantage.

Other managers, however, might cultivate values and norms that tell employees they should be conservative and cautious in their dealings with others and should consult their superiors before making important decisions or any changes to the status quo. Accountability for actions and decisions is stressed, and detailed records are kept to ensure that policies and procedures are followed. In settings where caution is needed–nuclear power stations, oil refineries, chemical plants, financial institutions, insurance companies–a conservative, cautious approach to making decisions might be appropriate.[118] In a nuclear power plant, for example, the catastrophic consequences of a mistake make a high level of supervision vital. Similarly, in a bank or mutual fund company, the risk of losing investors' money makes a cautious approach to investing appropriate.

Managers of different kinds of organizations deliberately cultivate and develop the organizational values and norms that are best suited to their task and general environments, strategy, or technology. Organizational culture is maintained and transmitted to organizational members through the values of the founder, the process of socialization, ceremonies and rites, and stories and language (see Figure 3.9).

VALUES OF THE FOUNDER From the ASA model just discussed, it is clear that founders of an organization can have profound and long-lasting effects on organizational culture. Founders' values inspire the founders to start their own companies and, in turn, drive the nature of these new companies and their defining characteristics. Thus an organization's founder and his or her terminal and instrumental values have a substantial influence on the values, norms, and standards of behavior that develop over time within the organization.[119] Founders set the scene for the way cultural values and norms develop because their own values guide the building of the company and they hire other managers and employees who they believe will share these values and help the organization to attain them. Moreover, new managers quickly learn from the founder what values and norms are appropriate in the organization and thus what

Figure 3.9
Factors That Maintain and Transmit Organizational Culture

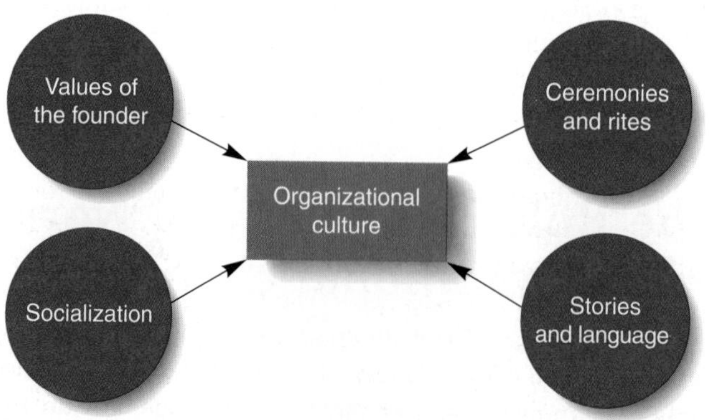

is desired of them. Subordinates imitate the style of the founder and, in turn, transmit their values and norms to their subordinates. Gradually, over time, the founder's values and norms permeate the organization, as has been the case at Ryla, profiled in the following "Manager as a Person" box.[120]

Manager as a Person

A Caring Culture at Ryla

Ryla Inc., founded by Mark Wilson in 2001, is a customer contact and business process outsourcing firm headquartered in Kennesaw, Georgia.[121] Telemarketing and customer contact organizations are notorious for high levels of turnover, dismal working conditions, and employees who are eager to abandon what they see as dead-end jobs as soon as a better opportunity comes along. Wilson imagined a different kind of customer contact business, one in which his employees would feel "like it's the best job they've ever had."[122]

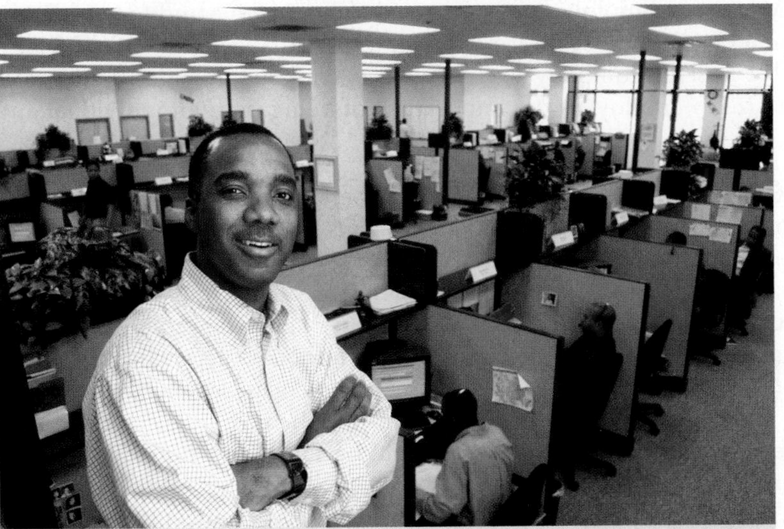

Mark Wilson, shown here at Ryla's call center headquarters, demonstrates that managing for a productive work environment can also include managing for employees' well-being.

From the start, Wilson has strived to create and sustain a work environment and company culture that are true to his personal values. Treating employees with respect, fostering open communication, providing opportunities for training, growth, and development, and demonstrating commitment to the well-being of employees as well as the local community have helped Ryla to grow and prosper. Today Ryla has nearly 400 full-time employees, less than 30% annual turnover in an industry with average turnover rates over 75%, high client retention rates, and revenue growth of at least 10% per year.[123] Ryla has over a 1,500 telemarketing seat capacity and thus hires many people who are not full-time employees, as is common in this industry.[124]

Although call center work tends to be relatively routine and boring, Wilson's emphasis on both creating a caring culture and giving employees opportunities for training and advancement go a long way toward building employee loyalty.[125] Wilson maintains an open-door policy and keeps employees informed about how the business is doing.[126] He not only solicits employee suggestions for improvements but also acts on them.[127]

Ryla employees have access to a variety of benefits ranging from medical and life insurance to 401(k) plans, employee assistance programs, and aerobics classes.[128] Employees who remain with Ryla for three years and attain performance and attendance goals become eligible for stock options in the company.[129] Based on employee feedback about areas in which employees would like to develop and improve their skills, Ryla provides training and development seminars on both professional and personal topics (such as financial planning). Ryla also allows employees to advance within the company by promoting from within, so telemarketing is no longer viewed as a dead-end job with no opportunities for advancement. Eighty percent of the managers in Ryla once staffed the telephones.[130] During "Ryla Huddles," employees celebrate team accomplishments as well as individual achievements.[131]

Wilson's efforts to create a new and different kind of call center that provides excellent service to clients and a caring and supportive environment for employees have not gone unnoticed in the business community. For example, Ryla was one of 35 finalists in *The Wall Street Journal*–Winning Workplace's Top Small Workplaces competition.[132] And it is not surprising that loyal employees like Denise Burdick, who never imagined working in telemarketing, are satisfied with their jobs and committed to Ryla.[133]

A founder who requires a great display of respect from subordinates and insists on proprieties such as formal job titles and formal dress encourages subordinates to act in this way toward their subordinates. Often a founder's personal values affect an organization's competitive advantage. For example, McDonald's founder Ray Kroc insisted from the beginning on high standards of customer service and cleanliness at McDonald's restaurants; these became core sources of McDonald's competitive advantage. Similarly, Bill Gates, the founder of Microsoft, pioneered certain cultural values in Microsoft. Employees are expected to be creative and to work hard, but they are encouraged to dress informally and to personalize their offices. Gates also established a host of company events such as cookouts, picnics, and sports events to emphasize to employees the importance of being both an individual and a team player.

SOCIALIZATION Over time, organizational members learn from each other which values are important in an organization and the norms that specify appropriate and inappropriate behaviors. Eventually organizational members behave in accordance with the organization's values and norms–often without realizing they are doing so.

organizational socialization The process by which newcomers learn an organization's values and norms and acquire the work behaviors necessary to perform jobs effectively.

Organizational socialization is the process by which newcomers learn an organization's values and norms and acquire the work behaviors necessary to perform jobs effectively.[134] As a result of their socialization experiences, organizational members internalize an organization's values and norms and behave in accordance with them not only because they think they have to but because they think these values and norms describe the right and proper way to behave.[135]

At Texas A&M University, for example, all new students are encouraged to go to "Fish Camp" to learn how to be an "Aggie" (the traditional nickname of students at the university). They learn about the ceremonies that have developed over time to commemorate significant events or people in A&M's history. In addition, they learn how to behave at football games and in class and what it means to be an Aggie. As a result of this highly organized socialization program, by the time new students arrive on campus and start their first semester, they have been socialized into what a Texas A&M student is supposed to do, and they have relatively few problems adjusting to the college environment.

Most organizations have some kind of socialization program to help new employees learn the ropes–the values, norms, and culture of the organization. The military, for example, is well known for the rigorous socialization process it uses to turn raw recruits into trained soldiers. Organizations such as the Walt Disney Company also put new recruits through a rigorous training program to teach them to perform well in their jobs and play their parts in helping Disneyland visitors have fun in a wholesome theme park. New recruits at Disney are called "cast members" and attend Disney University to learn the Disney culture and their parts in it. Disney's culture emphasizes the values of safety, courtesy, entertainment, and efficiency, and these values are brought to life for newcomers at Disney University. Newcomers also learn about the attraction area they will be joining (such as Adventureland or Fantasyland) at Disney University and then receive on-the-job socialization in the area itself from experienced cast members.[136] Through organizational socialization, founders and managers

Service with a smile: Disney prides itself on training its employees to carry on Walt's vision, right down to how they sell Mickey ice-cream bars.

of an organization transmit to employees the cultural values and norms that shape the behavior of organizational members. Thus the values and norms of founder Walt Disney live on today at Disneyland as newcomers are socialized into the Disney way.

CEREMONIES AND RITES Another way in which managers can create or influence organizational culture is by developing organizational ceremonies and rites–formal events that recognize incidents of importance to the organization as a whole and to specific employees.[137] The most common rites that organizations use to transmit cultural norms and values to their members are rites of passage, of integration, and of enhancement (see Table 3.1).[138]

Rites of passage determine how individuals enter, advance within, and leave the organization. The socialization programs developed by military organizations (such as the U.S. Army) or by large accountancy and law firms are rites of passage. Likewise, the ways in which an organization prepares people for promotion or retirement are rites of passage.

Rites of integration, such as shared announcements of organizational successes, office parties, and company cookouts, build and reinforce common bonds among organizational members. IDEO uses many rites of integration to make its employees feel connected to one another and special. In addition to having wild "end-of-year" celebratory bashes, groups of IDEO employees periodically take time off to go to a sporting event, movie, or meal, or sometimes on a long bike ride or for a sail. These kinds of shared activities not only reinforce IDEO's culture but also can be a source of inspiration on the job (for example, IDEO has been involved in making movies such as *The Abyss* and *Free Willy*). One 35-member design studio at IDEO led by Dennis Boyle has bimonthly lunch fests with no set agenda–anything goes. While enjoying great food, jokes, and camaraderie, studio members often end up sharing ideas for their latest great products, and the freely flowing conversation that results often leads to creative insights.[139]

A company's annual meeting also may be used as a ritual of integration, offering an opportunity to communicate organizational values to managers, other employees, and shareholders. Walmart, for example, makes its annual stockholders' meeting an extravagant ceremony that celebrates the company's success. The company often flies thousands of its highest-performing employees to its annual meeting at its Bentonville, Arkansas, headquarters for a huge weekend entertainment festival complete with star musical performances. Walmart believes that rewarding its supporters with entertainment reinforces the company's high-performance values and culture. The proceedings are shown live over closed-circuit television in all Walmart stores so all employees can join in the rites celebrating the company's achievements.[140]

Rites of enhancement, such as awards dinners, newspaper releases, and employee promotions, let organizations publicly recognize and reward employees' contributions and thus strengthen their commitment to organizational values. By bonding

Table 3.1
Organizational Rites

Type of Rite	Example of Rite	Purpose of Rite
Rite of passage	Induction and basic training	Learn and internalize norms and values
Rite of integration	Office Christmas party	Build common norms and values
Rite of enhancement	Presentation of annual award	Motivate commitment to norms and values

members within the organization, rites of enhancement reinforce an organization's values and norms.

Stories and language also communicate organizational culture. Stories (whether fact or fiction) about organizational heroes and villains and their actions provide important clues about values and norms. Such stories can reveal the kinds of behaviors that are valued by the organization and the kinds of practices that are frowned on.[141] At the heart of McDonald's rich culture are hundreds of stories that organizational members tell about founder Ray Kroc. Most of these stories focus on how Kroc established the strict operating values and norms that are at the heart of McDonald's culture. Kroc was dedicated to achieving perfection in McDonald's quality, service, cleanliness, and value for money (QSC&V), and these four central values permeate McDonald's culture. For example, an often retold story describes what happened when Kroc and a group of managers from the Houston region were touring various restaurants. One of the restaurants was having a bad day operationally. Kroc was incensed about the long lines of customers, and he was furious when he realized that the products customers were receiving that day were not up to his high standards. To address the problem, he jumped up and stood on the front counter to get the attention of all customers and operating crew personnel. He introduced himself, apologized for the long wait and cold food, and told the customers they could have freshly cooked food or their money back–whichever they wanted. As a result, the customers left happy; and when Kroc checked on the restaurant later, he found that his message had gotten through to its managers and crew–performance had improved. Other stories describe Kroc scrubbing dirty toilets and picking up litter inside or outside a restaurant. These and similar stories are spread around the organization by McDonald's employees. They are the stories that have helped establish Kroc as McDonald's "hero."

Because spoken language is a principal medium of communication in organizations, the characteristic slang or jargon–that is, organization-specific words or phrases–that people use to frame and describe events provides important clues about norms and values. "McLanguage," for example, is prevalent at all levels of McDonald's. A McDonald's employee described as having "ketchup in his or her blood" is someone who is truly dedicated to the McDonald's way–someone who has been completely socialized to its culture. McDonald's has an extensive training program that teaches new employees "McDonald's speak," and new employees are welcomed into the family with a formal orientation that illustrates Kroc's dedication to QSC&V.

The concept of organizational language encompasses not only spoken language but how people dress, the offices they occupy, the cars they drive, and the degree of formality they use when they address one another. For example, casual dress reflects and reinforces Microsoft's entrepreneurial culture and values. Formal business attire supports the conservative culture found in many banks, which emphasize the importance of conforming to organizational norms such as respect for authority and staying within one's prescribed role. When employees speak and understand the language of their organization's culture, they know how to behave in the organization and what is expected of them.

At IDEO, language, dress, the physical work environment, and extreme informality all underscore a culture that is adventuresome, playful, risk taking, egalitarian, and innovative. For example, at IDEO, employees refer to taking the consumers' perspective when designing products as "being left-handed." Employees dress in T-shirts and jeans, the physical work environment continually evolves and changes depending on how employees wish to personalize their workspace, no one "owns" a fancy office with a window, and rules are nonexistent.[142]

Culture and Managerial Action

While founders and managers play a critical role in developing, maintaining, and communicating organizational culture, this same culture shapes and controls the behavior of all employees, including managers themselves. For example, culture influences how managers perform their four main functions: planning, organizing, leading, and controlling. As we consider these functions, we continue to distinguish between top managers who create organizational values and norms that encourage creative, innovative behavior and top managers who encourage a conservative, cautious approach by their subordinates. We noted earlier that both kinds of values and norms can be appropriate depending on the situation and type of organization.

PLANNING Top managers in an organization with an innovative culture are likely to encourage lower-level managers to participate in the planning process and develop a flexible approach to planning. They are likely to be willing to listen to new ideas and to take risks involving the development of new products. In contrast, top managers in an organization with conservative values are likely to emphasize formal top-down planning. Suggestions from lower-level managers are likely to be subjected to a formal review process, which can significantly slow decision making. Although this deliberate approach may improve the quality of decision making in a nuclear power plant, it can have unintended consequences. In the past, at conservative IBM, the planning process became so formalized that managers spent most of their time assembling complex slide shows and overheads to defend their current positions rather than thinking about what they should do to keep IBM abreast of the changes taking place in the computer industry. When former CEO Lou Gerstner took over, he used every means at his disposal to abolish this culture, even building a brand-new campus-style headquarters to change managers' mind-sets. IBM's culture is undergoing further changes initiated by its current CEO, Samuel Palmisano.[143]

ORGANIZING What kinds of organizing will managers in innovative and in conservative cultures encourage? Valuing creativity, managers in innovative cultures are likely to try to create an organic structure–one that is flat, with few levels in the hierarchy, and one in which authority is decentralized so employees are encouraged to work together to solve ongoing problems. A product team structure may be suitable for an organization with an innovative culture. In contrast, managers in a conservative culture are likely to create a well-defined hierarchy of authority and establish clear reporting relationships so employees know exactly whom to report to and how to react to any problems that arise.

LEADING In an innovative culture, managers are likely to lead by example, encouraging employees to take risks and experiment. They are supportive regardless of whether employees succeed or fail. In contrast, managers in a conservative culture are likely to use management by objectives and to constantly monitor subordinates' progress toward goals, overseeing their every move. We examine leadership in detail in Chapter 14 when we consider the leadership styles that managers can adopt to influence and shape employee behavior.

CONTROLLING The ways in which managers evaluate, and take actions to improve, performance differ depending on whether the organizational culture emphasizes formality and caution or innovation and change. Managers who want to encourage risk taking, creativity, and innovation recognize that there are multiple potential paths to success and that failure must be accepted for creativity to thrive. Thus they are less concerned about employees' performing their jobs in a specific, predetermined manner and in strict adherence to preset goals and more concerned about employees' being flexible and taking the initiative to come up with ideas for improving performance. Managers in innovative cultures are also more concerned about long-term performance than short-term targets because they recognize that real innovation entails much uncertainty that necessitates flexibility. In contrast, managers in cultures that emphasize caution and maintenance of the status quo often set specific, difficult goals for employees, frequently monitor progress toward these goals, and develop a clear set of rules that employees are expected to adhere to.

The values and norms of an organization's culture strongly affect the way managers perform their management functions. The extent to which managers buy into the values and norms of their organization shapes their view of the world and their actions and decisions in particular circumstances. In turn, the actions that managers take can have an impact on the performance of the organization. Thus organizational culture, managerial action, and organizational performance are all linked together.

This linkage is apparent at Hewlett-Packard (HP), a leader in the electronic instrumentation and computer industries. Established in the 1940s, HP developed a culture that is an outgrowth of the strong personal beliefs of the company's founders, William Hewlett and David Packard. As discussed in Chapter 2, Bill and Dave, as they are known within the company, formalized HP's culture in 1957 in a statement of corporate objectives known as the "HP Way." The basic values informing the HP Way stress serving everyone who has a stake in the company with integrity and fairness, including customers, suppliers, employees, stockholders, and society in general. Bill and Dave helped build this culture within HP by hiring like-minded people and by letting the HP Way guide their own actions as managers.

Although the Hewlett-Packard example and our earlier example of IDEO illustrate how organizational culture can give rise to managerial actions that ultimately benefit the organization, this is not always the case. The cultures of some organizations become dysfunctional, encouraging managerial actions that harm the organization and discouraging actions that might improve performance.[144] Recent corporate scandals at large companies like Enron, Tyco, and WorldCom show how damaging a dysfunctional culture can be to an organization and its members. For example, Enron's arrogant, "success at all costs" culture led to fraudulent behavior on the part of its top managers.[145] Unfortunately hundreds of Enron employees paid a heavy price for the unethical behavior of these top managers and the dysfunctional organizational culture. Not only did these employees lose their jobs, but many also lost their life savings in Enron stock and pension funds, which became worth just a fraction of their former value before the wrongdoing at Enron came to light. We discuss ethics and ethical cultures in depth in the next chapter.

Summary and Review

ENDURING CHARACTERISTICS: PERSONALITY TRAITS Personality traits are enduring tendencies to feel, think, and act in certain ways. The Big Five general traits are extraversion, negative affectivity, agreeableness, conscientiousness, and openness to experience. Other personality traits that affect managerial behavior are
LO3-1 locus of control, self-esteem, and the needs for achievement, affiliation, and power.

LO3-2, 3-3, 3-4 **VALUES, ATTITUDES, AND MOODS AND EMOTIONS** A terminal value is a personal conviction about lifelong goals or objectives; an instrumental value is a personal conviction about modes of conduct. Terminal and instrumental values have an impact on what managers try to achieve in their organizations and the kinds of behaviors they engage in. An attitude is a collection of feelings and beliefs. Two attitudes important for understanding managerial behaviors include job satisfaction (the collection of feelings and beliefs that managers have about their jobs) and organizational commitment (the collection of feelings and beliefs that managers have about their organizations). A mood is a feeling or state of mind; emotions are intense feelings that are short-lived and directly linked to their causes. Managers' moods and emotions, or how they feel at work on a day-to-day basis, have the potential to impact not only their own behavior and effectiveness but also those of their subordinates. Emotional intelligence is the ability to understand and manage one's own and other people's moods and emotions.

LO3-5 **ORGANIZATIONAL CULTURE** Organizational culture is the shared set of beliefs, expectations, values, norms, and work routines that influence how members of an organization relate to one another and work together to achieve organizational goals. Founders of new organizations and managers play an important role in creating and maintaining organizational culture. Organizational socialization is the process by which newcomers learn an organization's values and norms and acquire the work behaviors necessary to perform jobs effectively.

Management in Action

Topics for Discussion and Action

Discussion

1. Discuss why managers who have different types of personalities can be equally effective and successful. [LO3-1]
2. Can managers be too satisfied with their jobs? Can they be too committed to their organizations? Why or why not? [LO3-2]
3. Assume that you are a manager of a restaurant. Describe what it is like to work for you when you are in a negative mood. [LO3-3]
4. Why might managers be disadvantaged by low levels of emotional intelligence? [LO3-4]

Action

5. Interview a manager in a local organization. Ask the manager to describe situations in which he or she is especially likely to act in accordance with his or her values. Ask the manager to describe situations in which he or she is less likely to act in accordance with his or her values. [LO3-2]
6. Watch a popular television show, and as you watch it, try to determine the emotional intelligence levels of the characters the actors in the show portray. Rank the characters from highest to lowest in terms of emotional intelligence. As you watched the show, what factors influenced your assessments of emotional intelligence levels? [LO3-4]
7. Go to an upscale clothing store in your neighborhood, and go to a clothing store that is definitely not upscale. Observe the behavior of employees in each store as well as the store's environment. In what ways are the organizational cultures in each store similar? In what ways are they different? [LO3-5]

Building Management Skills [LO3-5]

Diagnosing Culture

Think about the culture of the last organization you worked for, your current university, or another organization or club to which you belong. Then answer the following questions:

1. What values are emphasized in this culture?
2. What norms do members of this organization follow?
3. Who seems to have played an important role in creating the culture?
4. In what ways is the organizational culture communicated to organizational members?

Managing Ethically [LO3-1, 3-2]

Some organizations rely on personality and interest inventories to screen potential employees. Other organizations attempt to screen employees by using paper-and-pencil honesty tests.

Questions

1. Either individually or in a group, think about the ethical implications of using personality and interest inventories to screen potential employees. How might this practice be unfair to potential applicants? How might organizational members who are in charge of hiring misuse it?
2. Because of measurement error and validity problems, some relatively trustworthy people may "fail" an honesty test given by an employer. What are the ethical implications of trustworthy people "failing" honesty tests, and what obligations do you think employers should have when relying on honesty tests for screening?

Small Group Breakout Exercise [LO3-2, 3-3, 3-4, 3-5]

Making Difficult Decisions in Hard Times

Form groups of three or four people, and appoint one member as the spokesperson who will communicate your findings to the whole class when called on by the instructor. Then discuss the following scenario:

You are on the top management team of a medium-size company that manufactures cardboard boxes, containers, and other cardboard packaging materials. Your company is facing increasing levels of competition for major corporate customer accounts, and profits have declined significantly. You have tried everything you can to cut costs and remain competitive, with the exception of laying off employees. Your company has had a no-layoff policy for the past 20 years, and you believe it is an important part of the organization's culture. However, you are experiencing mounting pressure to increase your firm's performance, and your no-layoff policy has been questioned by shareholders. Even though you haven't decided whether to lay off employees and thus break with a 20-year tradition for your company, rumors are rampant in your organization that something is afoot, and employees are worried. You are meeting today to address this problem.

1. Develop a list of options and potential courses of action to address the heightened competition and decline in profitability that your company has been experiencing.
2. Choose your preferred course of action, and justify why you will take this route.
3. Describe how you will communicate your decision to employees.
4. If your preferred option involves a layoff, justify why. If it doesn't involve a layoff, explain why.

Exploring the World Wide Web [LO3-1, 3-2, 3-5]

Go to IDEO's Web site (www.ideo.com) and read about this company. Try to find indicators of IDEO's culture that are provided on the Web site. How does the design of the Web site itself, and the pictures and words it contains, communicate the nature of IDEO's organizational culture? What kinds of people do you think would be attracted to IDEO? What kinds of people do you think would be likely to be dissatisfied with a job at IDEO?

Be the Manager [LO3-1, 3-2, 3-3, 3-4, 3-5]

You have recently been hired as the vice president for human resources in an advertising agency. One problem that has been brought to your attention is the fact that the creative departments at the agency have dysfunctionally high levels of conflict. You have spoken with members of each of these departments, and in each one it seems that a few members of the department are creating all the problems. All these individuals are valued contributors who have many creative ad campaigns to their credit. The high levels of conflict are creating problems in the departments, and negative moods and emotions are much more prevalent than positive feelings. What are you going to do to both retain valued employees and alleviate the excessive conflict and negative feelings in these departments?

Case in the News [LO3-2, 3-4, 3-5]

A Steely Resolve

Sitting on John J. Ferriola's desk at Nucor's headquarters in Charlotte is a greeting card. Yellow, with bright green, pink, and blue flowers, it's from Diane Williamson, a line worker at Nucor's plant in Darlington, South Carolina. Inside it says, "Thank you for caring about me and my family." In the past few months, Ferriola, Nucor's chief operating officer, and his boss, CEO Daniel R. DiMicco, have received hundreds of similar cards and e-mail messages from their staff of 22,000.

It's hard to imagine too many other C-suite types getting thank-you notes by the basketload these days. But while rivals have laid off thousands, Nucor has shown remarkable loyalty to its people, eschewing layoffs altogether. Despite a dismal fourth quarter, the company paid out a special one-time bonus in January 2009 of $1,000 or $2,000 per worker, reward for a record 2008. Total cost to Nucor: $40 million. In March 2009 the company paid an additional $270 million in 2008 profit sharing. "We're making money. We've got jobs," says Michael May, a seven-year veteran of Nucor's Crawfordsville (Indiana) plant. "Financially, Nucor employees are still better off than most."

But not as well off as they once were. After years of record-setting profits, Nucor is struggling just like the automakers, appliance manufacturers, and builders that buy its steel. In the fourth quarter of 2008, its mills went from running at 95% of capacity to 50% practically overnight, as credit-squeezed customers slashed orders. "It was something none of us had ever seen before," says DiMicco.

The pain of the downturn has quickly gone all the way to the shop floor as the drop in output has hit workers' paychecks. Unlike other steelmakers, Nucor pushes as much responsibility for production and efficiency as possible to frontline workers and ties most of their pay to production. The company, which melts scrap metal and reshapes it into beams and sheets of steel using electric arc furnaces, can ramp up or slow down production more quickly than traditional steelmakers, which need weeks to get a cold mill hot again. So customers are quick to cancel orders, knowing they can get what they need fast enough.

Boosting Morale, Keeping Busy

For many years, Nucor's model has led to superior productivity and growth. That's one reason the company has appeared four times on *BusinessWeek*'s list of top performers. But for workers there's a downside to the model, particularly in tough times. With the line down half the time, bonuses have dwindled, and total pay is down as much as 40%. To keep up morale, management has put a big focus on communication. Ferriola has doubled the time he spends in the plants. Ron Dickerson, general manager of Nucor's Crawfordsville plant, sends weekly notes updating his 750-person staff on order volumes. But the question all managers hear the most is the one they can't answer: "When is this going to end?"

For now, Dickerson is keeping his crews busy rewriting safety manuals, looking for cost savings, and getting ahead on maintenance. Work that used to be done by contractors, such as making special parts, mowing the lawns, and even cleaning the bathrooms, is now handled by Nucor staff. The bathrooms, managers say, were an employee suggestion.

For Nucor's management team, there have been trade-offs. Growth plans are on hold. The company has put off exploring acquisitions. A just-finished galvanizing line is idle. Still, Wall Street is betting the company will take advantage of the turnaround quickly when it comes. It probably won't be this year. But with all the extra efforts in the mills now, DiMicco says he hopes Nucor will be "first out of the box."

Questions for Discussion

1. What factors likely contribute to employees' job satisfaction and organizational commitment at Nucor?
2. How would you describe Nucor's organizational culture?
3. What terminal and instrumental values do you think are important in Nucor's culture?
4. How might managers' levels of emotional intelligence influence how they treat employees at Nucor?

Source: N. Byrnes, "A Steely Resolve." Reprinted from April 6, 2009 issue of *Bloomberg Businessweek* by special permission, copyright © 2009 by Bloomberg L.P.

CHAPTER 4

Ethics and Social Responsibility

Learning Objectives

After studying this chapter, you should be able to:

LO4-1 Explain the relationship between ethics and the law.

LO4-2 Differentiate between the claims of the different stakeholder groups that are affected by managers and their companies' actions.

LO4-3 Describe four rules that can help companies and their managers act in ethical ways.

LO4-4 Discuss why it is important for managers to behave ethically.

LO4-5 Identify the four main sources of managerial ethics.

LO4-6 Distinguish among the four main approaches toward social responsibility that a company can take.

A MANAGER'S CHALLENGE

Unethical Managers and the Perils of Peanut Butter

Why should ethics guide managers' decisions? Peanut Corporation of America's (PCA) president, Stewart Parnell, was fond of telling his friends and clients in his hometown of Lynchburg, Virginia, just how good things were in his commercial peanut butter processing business, which operated three plants in Virginia, Georgia, and Texas. The company produced industrial-sized containers of peanut butter that were included as an ingredient in more than 3,900 products: cakes, candies, cookies, peanut crackers, ice cream, snack mixes, and pet food made by over 200 different companies, including Kellogg's and Nestlé. Also, the peanut butter was shipped to school systems and food outlets around the United States, where it was used to make millions of peanut butter and jelly sandwiches.

Parnell had a reputation as an upstanding businessman and a generous donor to many worthy causes, so it came as a shock to his friends and customers when in 2009 a major nationwide outbreak of salmonella poisoning was traced by the Food and Drug Administration (FDA) to the peanut butter produced at his plant in Blakely, Georgia. PCA's contaminated peanut butter had caused over 600 illnesses and nine deaths across the United States. The 200 food makers who used or sold Parnell's products were forced to recall more than 1,900 different peanut butter products. This was one of the nation's largest food recalls even though PCA accounted for only 2% of the nation's supply of peanut butter. In the immediate aftermath of the nationwide outbreak, peanut butter sales plummeted 24% across the board, and total industry losses amounted to over $1 billion. How could this tragedy and disaster have occurred?[1]

Apparently the major cause of the disaster was the unethical and illegal actions of owner and manager Parnell. The FDA investigation that took place at the PCA Georgia plant in

Stewart Parnell, the erstwhile owner of PCA, was called before Congress to answer for poor safety standards at PCA plants. A full year later, more problems having come to light, PCA's doors are closed for good.

2009 revealed serious problems with food safety at that plant and inadequate cleaning and sanitary procedures. The investigation also revealed internal company documents that showed at least 12 instances in which the company's own tests of its products in 2007 and 2008 found they were contaminated by salmonella. Previous inspections of the plant had found dirty surfaces, grease residue, dirt buildup throughout the plant, gaps in warehouse doors large enough for rodents to enter, and major problems with the plant's routine cleaning procedures that still existed in 2009. But PCA managers had taken no steps to clean up operations or protect food safety. In fact, Parnell's poor attention to food safety was traced back to 1990, when inspectors found toxic mold in products produced in PCA's Virginia plant; the mold forced food recalls, and Parnell settled privately with the two companies whose products were affected.[2]

After interviewing employees, FDA investigators found that this long-term inattention to food safety had arisen inside PCA's processing plants because Parnell was worried about maximizing his profits, especially when prices of peanut products had started to fall. To reduce operating costs, Parnell ordered a plant manager to ship products that had already been identified as contaminated and had pleaded with health inspectors to let him "turn the raw peanuts on our floor into money." Parnell complained to his managers that the salmonella tests were costing him business, and somehow the Georgia plant received information about the dates on which the plant would be inspected—so on those days the plant was scrubbed clean.[3]

After the problems with the Georgia plant were discovered, it was shut down and the other PCA plants were inspected closely. In May 2009 Texas health officials told Parnell to close his plant there and ordered a recall of all its products after salmonella was discovered, along with "dead rodents, rodent excrement, and bird feathers." The PCA Virginia plant was also shut down. After hundreds of lawsuits were filed against the company because of the deaths and illnesses caused by its contaminated products, PCA was forced to seek protection under the U.S. bankruptcy code. The company is now defunct; its unethical and illegal management practices put it out of business. In spring 2010 criminal charges had still not been filed against Stewart Parnell, although a federal investigation was under way. Also in 2010, 123 victims and surviving relatives and the bankruptcy court in charge of PCA agreed to a $12 million settlement—the money coming from PCA's insurance policies because the Parnell family lost nearly everything it owned.

In March 2010 another crisis occurred in the food industry when salmonella was found in a flavoring agent called hydrolyzed vegetable protein, an additive made by Basic Food Flavors Inc. of Las Vegas and used in many food products to bring out flavor. Problems with the contaminated flavoring, which is sold only to food processing companies, were revealed by one of these companies, which notified the FDA that its own tests had found salmonella.

After being criticized for the length of time it took the FDA to finally close down PCA's operations, FDA officials responded that the agency doesn't have the personnel or funding to regulate the millions of shipments made within the food industry every week. In large part, the FDA and the U.S. public must rely on the basic integrity, ethics, and honesty of food industry managers to make food that is safe to eat.

Overview

As the story of PCA and Parnell suggests, an ethical dimension is always present in management decision making that involves the production and sale of products–be they food products, cars, computers, or clothing–because managers' decisions affect people's well-being. But globally, nations, companies, and managers differ enormously in their commitment to these people, or *stakeholders*–various groups of people who may benefit or be harmed by how managers make decisions that affect them. Managers of some companies make the need to behave ethically toward stakeholders their main priority. Managers of other companies pursue their own self-interest at the expense of their stakeholders and do harm to them–such as the harm done to the millions of people around the world who work in dangerous, unsanitary conditions or who work for a pittance.

In this chapter we examine the obligations and responsibilities of managers and the companies they work for toward the people and society that are affected by their actions. First we examine the nature of ethics and the sources of ethical problems. Next we discuss the major stakeholder groups that are affected by how companies operate. We also look at four rules or guidelines managers can use to decide whether a specific business decision is ethical or unethical. Finally we consider the sources of managerial ethics and the reasons why it is important for a company to behave in a socially responsible manner. By the end of this chapter you will understand the central role of ethics in shaping the practice of management and the life of a people, society, and nation.

The Nature of Ethics

Suppose you see a person being mugged. Will you act in some way to help, even though you risk being hurt? Will you walk away? Perhaps you might not intervene but call the police? Does how you act depend on whether the person being mugged is a fit male, an elderly person, or a street person? Does it depend on whether other people are around so you can tell yourself, "Oh well, someone else will help or call the police. I don't need to"?

Ethical Dilemmas

ethical dilemma The quandary people find themselves in when they have to decide if they should act in a way that might help another person or group even though doing so might go against their own self-interest.

The situation just described is an example of an **ethical dilemma,** the quandary people find themselves in when they have to decide if they should act in a way that might help another person or group and is the right thing to do, even though doing so might go against their own self-interest.[4] A dilemma may also arise when a person has to choose between two different courses of action, knowing that whichever course he or she selects will harm one person or group even while it may benefit another. The ethical dilemma here is to decide which course of action is the lesser of two evils.

ethics The inner guiding moral principles, values, and beliefs that people use to analyze or interpret a situation and then decide what is the right or appropriate way to behave.

People often know they are confronting an ethical dilemma when their moral scruples come into play and cause them to hesitate, debate, and reflect upon the rightness or goodness of a course of action. Moral scruples are thoughts and feelings that tell a person what is right or wrong; they are a part of a person's ethics. **Ethics** are the inner guiding moral principles, values, and beliefs that people use to analyze or interpret a situation and then decide what is the right or appropriate way to behave. Ethics also indicate what is inappropriate behavior and how a person should behave to avoid harming another person.

The essential problem in dealing with ethical issues, and thus solving moral dilemmas, is no absolute or indisputable rules or principles can be developed to decide whether an action is ethical or unethical. Put simply, different people or groups may dispute which actions are ethical or unethical depending on their personal self-interest and specific attitudes, beliefs, and values–concepts we discussed in Chapter 3. How, therefore, are we and companies and their managers and employees to decide what is ethical and so act appropriately toward other people and groups?

LO4-1 Explain the relationship between ethics and the law.

Ethics and the Law

The first answer to this question is that society as a whole, using the political and legal process, can lobby for and pass laws that specify what people can and cannot do. Many different kinds of laws govern business–for example, laws against fraud and deception and laws governing how companies can treat their employees and customers. Laws also specify what sanctions or punishments will follow if those laws are broken. Different groups in society lobby for which laws should be passed based on their own personal interests and beliefs about right and wrong. The group that can summon the most support can pass laws that align with its interests and beliefs. Once a law is passed, a decision about what the appropriate behavior is with regard to a person or situation is taken from the personally determined ethical realm to the societally determined legal realm. If you do not conform to the law, you can be prosecuted; and if you are found guilty of breaking the law, you can be punished. You have little say in the matter; your fate is in the hands of the court and its lawyers.

In studying the relationship between ethics and law, it is important to understand that *neither laws nor ethics are fixed principles* that do not change over time. Ethical beliefs change as time passes; and as they do so, laws change to reflect the changing ethical beliefs of a society. It was seen as ethical, and it was legal, for example, to acquire and possess slaves in ancient Rome and Greece and in the United States until the late 19th century. Ethical views regarding whether slavery was morally right or appropriate changed, however. Slavery was made illegal in the United States when those in power decided that slavery degraded the meaning of being human. Slavery makes a statement about the value or worth of human beings and about their right to life, liberty, and the pursuit of happiness. And if we deny these rights to other people, how can we claim to have any natural rights to these things?

Moreover, what is to stop any person or group that becomes powerful enough to take control of the political and legal process from enslaving us and denying us the right to be free and to own property? In denying freedom to others, one risks losing it oneself, just as stealing from others opens the door for them to steal from us in return. "Do unto others as you would have them do unto you" is a common ethical or moral rule that people apply in such situations to decide what is the right thing to do.

Changes in Ethics over Time

There are many types of behavior–such as murder, theft, slavery, rape, and driving while intoxicated–that most people currently believe are unacceptable and unethical and should therefore be illegal. However, the ethics of many other actions and behaviors are open to dispute. Some people might believe a particular behavior–for example, smoking tobacco or possessing guns–is unethical and so should be made illegal. Others might argue that it is up to the individual or group to decide if such behaviors are ethical and thus whether a particular behavior should remain legal.

As ethical beliefs change over time, some people may begin to question whether existing laws that make specific behaviors illegal are still appropriate. They might argue that although a specific behavior is deemed illegal, this does not make it unethical and thus the law should be changed. In the United States, for example, it is illegal to possess or use marijuana (cannabis). To justify this law, it is commonly argued that smoking marijuana leads people to try more dangerous drugs. Once the habit of taking drugs has been acquired, people can get hooked on them. More powerful drugs such as the murderous heroin, and other narcotics, are fearfully addictive, and most people cannot stop using them without help. Thus the use of marijuana, because it might lead to further harm, is an unethical practice.

It has been documented medically, however, that marijuana use can help people with certain illnesses. For example, for cancer sufferers who are undergoing chemotherapy and for those with AIDS who are on potent medications, marijuana offers relief from many treatment side effects, such as nausea and lack of appetite. Yet in the United States it is illegal in many states for doctors to prescribe marijuana for these patients, so their suffering continues. Since 1996, however, 15 states have made it legal to prescribe marijuana for medical purposes; nevertheless, the federal government has sought to

Coldbath Fields Prison, London, circa 1810. The British criminal justice system around this time was severe: there were over 350 different crimes for which a person could be executed, including sheep stealing. As ethical beliefs change over time, so do laws.

stop such state legislation. The U.S. Supreme Court ruled in 2005 that only Congress or the states could decide whether medical marijuana use should be made legal, and people in many states are currently lobbying for a relaxation of state laws against its use for medical purposes.[5] In Canada there has been a widespread movement to decriminalize marijuana. While not making the drug legal, decriminalization removes the threat of prosecution even for uses that are not medically related and allows the drug to be taxed. In 2010, for example, an initiative was under way in California to legalize possession of marijuana for personal use and then to heavily tax it to raise an expected $5 billion to help reduce the state's crushing budget deficit that has led to a 32% increase in college tuition costs since 2009. A major ethical debate is currently raging over this issue in many states and countries.

The important point to note is that while ethical beliefs lead to the development of laws and regulations to prevent certain behaviors or encourage others, laws themselves change or even disappear as ethical beliefs change. In Britain in 1830 a person could be executed for over 350 different crimes, including sheep stealing. Today the death penalty is no longer legal in Britain. Thus both ethical and legal rules are *relative:* No absolute or unvarying standards exist to determine how we should behave, and people are caught up in moral dilemmas all the time. Because of this we have to make ethical choices.

The previous discussion highlights an important issue in understanding the relationship between ethics, law, and business. Throughout the 2000s many scandals plagued major companies such as Enron, WorldCom, Tyco, Lehman Brothers, and others. Managers in some of these companies clearly broke the law and used illegal means to defraud investors. At Enron former chief financial officer Andrew Fastow and his wife pleaded guilty to falsifying the company's books so they could siphon off tens of millions of dollars of Enron's money for their own use.

In other cases managers took advantage of loopholes in the law to divert hundreds of millions of dollars of company capital into their own personal fortunes. At WorldCom, for example, former CEO Bernie Ebbers used his position to place six personal friends on the 13-member board of directors. Although this is not illegal, obviously these people would vote in his favor at board meetings. As a result of their support Ebbers received huge stock options and a personal loan of over $150 million from WorldCom. In return, his supporters were well rewarded for being directors; for example, Ebbers allowed them to use WorldCom's corporate jets for a minimal cost, saving them hundreds of thousands of dollars a year.[6]

In the light of these events some people said, "Well, what these people did was not illegal," implying that because such behavior was not illegal it was also not unethical. However, not being illegal does *not* make behavior ethical; such behavior is clearly unethical.[7] In many cases laws are passed *later* to close loopholes and prevent unethical people, such as Fastow and Ebbers, from taking advantage of them to pursue their own self-interest at the expense of others. Like ordinary people, managers must decide what is appropriate and inappropriate as they use a company's resources to produce goods and services for customers.[8]

Stakeholders and Ethics

Just as people have to work out the right and wrong ways to act, so do companies. When the law does not specify how companies should behave, their managers must decide the right or ethical way to behave toward the people and groups affected by their actions. Who are the people or groups that are affected by a company's business decisions? If a company behaves in an ethical way, how does this benefit people and society? Conversely, how are people harmed by a company's unethical actions?

stakeholders The people and groups that supply a company with its productive resources and so have a claim on and stake in the company.

The people and groups affected by how a company and its managers behave are called its stakeholders. **Stakeholders** supply a company with its productive resources; as a result, they have a claim on and stake in the company.[9] Because stakeholders can directly benefit or be harmed by its actions, the ethics of a company and its managers are important to them. Who are a company's major stakeholders? What do they contribute to a company, and what do they claim in return? Here we examine the claims of these stakeholders–stockholders; managers; employees; suppliers and distributors; customers; and community, society, and nation-state (Figure 4.1).

LO4-2 Differentiate between the claims of the different stakeholder groups that are affected by managers and their companies' actions.

Stockholders

Stockholders have a claim on a company because when they buy its stock or shares they become its owners. When the founder of a company decides to publicly incorporate the business to raise capital, shares of the stock of that company are issued. This stock grants its buyers ownership of a certain percentage of the company and the right to receive any future stock dividends. For example, in 2005 Microsoft decided to pay the owners of its 5 billion shares a record dividend payout of $32 billion. Bill Gates received $3.3 billion in dividends based on his stockholding, and he donated this money to the Bill and Melinda Gates Foundation, to which he has reportedly donated over $30 billion to date, with the promise of much more to come; and Warren Buffet committed in 2006 to donate at least $30 billion to the Gates Foundation over the next decade. The two richest people in the world have decided to give away a large part of their wealth to serve global ethical causes–in particular to address global health concerns such as malnutrition, malaria, tuberculosis, and AIDS.

Stockholders are interested in how a company operates because they want to maximize the return on their investment. Thus they watch the company and its managers closely to ensure that management is working diligently to increase the company's profitability.[10] Stockholders also want to ensure that managers are behaving ethically and not risking investors' capital by engaging in actions that could hurt the company's reputation. Managers of companies such as WorldCom, Brocade Communications, and Enron pursued their own self-interest at the expense of their stakeholders. As a result of these managers' unethical actions, in 2006 WorldCom's ex-CEO Bernie Ebbers was sentenced to a long jail term, as was Enron's former top manager Jeffrey Skilling (who launched an appeal against his conviction and 24-year prison sentence that will be heard by the Supreme Court in 2010). And in 2008 ex-CEO of Brocade Communications Gregory

Figure 4.1
Types of Company Stakeholders

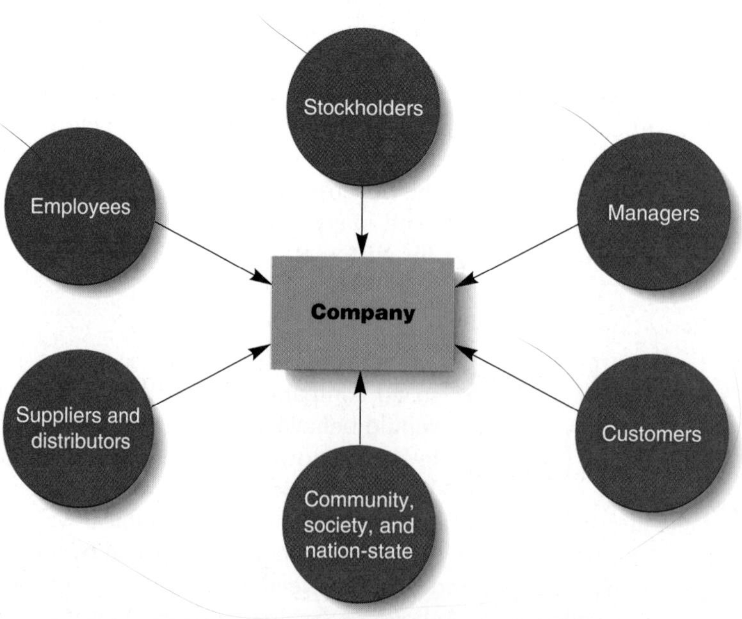

Reyes was the first to be convicted of a long line of top managers from many companies who have been accused of backdating stock options to inflate their personal wealth at the expense of stockholders. He was sentenced to 21 months in jail and fined $15 million.[11]

Managers

Managers are a vital stakeholder group because they are responsible for using a company's financial, capital, and human resources to increase its performance and thus its stock price.[12] Managers have a claim on an organization because they bring to it their skills, expertise, and experience. They have the right to expect a good return or reward by investing their human capital to improve a company's performance. Such rewards include good salaries and benefits, the prospect of promotion and a career, and stock options and bonuses tied to company performance.

Managers are the stakeholder group that bears the responsibility to decide which goals an organization should pursue to most benefit stakeholders and how to make the most efficient use of resources to achieve those goals. In making such decisions, managers are frequently in the position of having to juggle the interests of different stakeholders, including themselves.[13] These sometimes difficult decisions challenge managers to uphold ethical values because some decisions that benefit certain stakeholder groups (managers and stockholders) harm other groups (individual workers and local communities). For example, in economic downturns or when a company experiences performance shortfalls, layoffs may help cut costs (thus benefiting shareholders) at the expense of the employees laid off. Many U.S. managers have recently faced this difficult decision. Until the 2009 financial crisis sent unemployment soaring over 10%, on average about 1.6 million U.S. employees out of a total labor force of 140 million were affected by mass layoffs each year; and over 3 million jobs from the United States, Europe, and Japan have been outsourced to Asia since 2005. Layoff decisions are always difficult: They not only take a heavy toll on workers, their families, and local communities but also mean the loss of the contributions of valued employees to an organization. In 2010, after GM pulled out, Toyota announced it would close down its NUMMI plant in Fremont, California; the resulting loss of jobs would raise total unemployment to 25% in this community. Whenever decisions such as these are made–benefiting some groups at the expense of others–ethics come into play.

As we discussed in Chapter 1, managers must be motivated and given incentives to work hard in the interests of stockholders. Their behavior must also be scrutinized to

Top executives, including Angelo Mozilo of Countryside Mortgage and Stanley O'Neal of Merrill Lynch, testify before Senator Henry Waxman about the issue of exorbitant CEO compensation packages that remained in full effect even though these companies lost billions of dollars. In 2010 Goldman Sachs executives came under similar scrutiny.

ensure they do not behave illegally or unethically, pursuing goals that threaten stockholders and the company's interests.[14] Unfortunately we have seen in the 2000s how easy it is for top managers to find ways to ruthlessly pursue their self-interest at the expense of stockholders and employees because laws and regulations are not strong enough to force them to behave ethically.

In a nutshell, the problem has been that in many companies corrupt managers focus not on building the company's capital and stockholders' wealth but on maximizing their own personal capital and wealth. In an effort to prevent future scandals, the Securities and Exchange Commission (SEC), the government's top business watchdog, has begun to rework the rules governing a company's relationship with its auditor, as well as regulations concerning stock options, and to increase the power of outside directors to scrutinize a CEO. The SEC's goal is to outlaw many actions that were previously classified as merely unethical. For example, companies are now forced to reveal to stockholders the value of the stock options they give their top executives and directors, and when they give them these options, and this shows how much such payments reduce company profits. Managers and directors can now be prosecuted if they disguise or try to hide these payments. In 2007 the SEC announced new rules requiring that companies disclose myriad details of executive compensation packages to investors; already the boards of directors of many companies have stopped giving CEOs perks such as free personal jet travel, membership in exclusive country clubs, and luxury accommodations on "business trips." In 2010 Congress considered a major new set of financial regulations that would prevent the many unethical and illegal actions of managers of banks and other financial institutions that had led to the 2008–2009 financial crisis.

Indeed, many experts argue that the rewards given to top managers, particularly the CEO and COO, grew out of control in the 2000s. Top managers are today's "aristocrats," and through their ability to influence the board of directors and raise their own pay, they have amassed personal fortunes worth hundreds of millions of dollars. For example, according to a study by the Federal Reserve, U.S. CEOs now get paid about 600 times what the average worker earns, compared to about 40 times in 1980–a staggering increase. We noted in Chapter 1 that besides their salaries, top managers often receive tens of millions in stock bonuses and options–even when their companies perform poorly.

Is it ethical for top managers to receive such vast amounts of money from their companies? Do they really earn it? Remember, this money could have gone to shareholders in the form of dividends. It could also have reduced the huge salary gap between those at the top and those at the bottom of the hierarchy. Many people argue that the growing disparity between the rewards given to CEOs and to other employees is unethical and should be regulated. CEO pay has skyrocketed because CEOs are the people who set and control one another's salaries and bonuses; they can do this because they sit on the boards of other companies as outside directors. Others argue that because top managers play an important role in building a company's capital and wealth, they deserve a significant share of its profits. Some recent research has suggested that the companies whose CEO compensation includes a large percentage of stock options tend to experience big share losses more often than big gains, and that on average, company performance improves as stock option use declines.[15] The debate over how much money CEOs and other top managers should be paid is still raging, particularly because the subprime mortgage crisis that began in 2007 and caused the 2008–2009 financial crisis showed how much money the CEOs of troubled financial companies earned even as their companies' performance and stock prices collapsed. For example, Countrywide Mortgage, which pioneered the subprime business, suffered losses of over $1.7 billion in 2007, and its stock fell 80%; yet its CEO Angelo Mozilo still received a $1.9 million salary and $20 million more in stock awards, and sold stock worth $121 million that he had already been given before the company's price collapsed.

Ethics and Nonprofit Organizations

The issue of what is fair compensation for top managers is not limited to for-profit companies; it is one of many issues facing nonprofits. The many ethics scandals that have plagued companies in the 2000s might suggest that the issue of ethics is important only for profit-seeking companies, but this would be untrue. There are almost two million private nonprofit charitable and philanthropic organizations in the United States, and charges that their managers have acted in unethical and even illegal ways have grown in the 2000s. For example, many states and the federal government are investigating the huge salaries that the top executives of charitable institutions earn.

One impetus for this was the revelation that the NYSE, which is classified as a charitable organization, paid its disgraced top executive Richard A. Grasso over $187 million in pension benefits. It turns out that over 200 nonprofits pay their top executives more than $1 million a year in salary, and the boards of trustees or directors of many of these organizations also enjoy lavish perks and compensation for attendance at board meetings. And unlike for-profit companies, which are required by law to provide detailed reports of their operations to their shareholders, nonprofits do not have shareholders, so the laws governing disclosure are far weaker. As a result, the board and its top managers have considerable latitude to decide how they will spend a nonprofit's resources, and little oversight exists.

To remedy this situation, many states and the federal government are considering new laws that would subject nonprofits to strict Sarbanes-Oxley-type regulations that force the disclosure of issues related to managerial compensation and financial integrity. There are also efforts in progress to strengthen the legal power of the IRS to oversee nonprofits' expenditures so that it has more scope to examine how these organizations spend their resources on managerial and director compensation and perks.

Experts hope that the introduction of new rules and regulations to monitor and oversee how nonprofits spend their funds will result in much more value being created from the funds given by donors. After all, every cent that is spent administering a nonprofit is a cent not being used to help the people or cause for which the money was intended. Major ethical issues are involved because some badly run charities spend 70 cents of every dollar on administration costs. And charges have been leveled against charities such as the Red Cross for mishandling the hundreds of millions of dollars they received in donations after Hurricane Katrina struck. Major changes have been made in the Red Cross to address these issues. Clearly the directors and managers of all organizations need to carefully consider the ethical issues involved in their decision making.

Employees

A company's employees are the hundreds of thousands of people who work in its various departments and functions, such as research, sales, and manufacturing. Employees expect to receive rewards consistent with their performance. One principal way that a company can act ethically toward employees and meet their expectations is by creating an occupational structure that fairly and equitably rewards employees for their contributions. Companies, for example, need to develop recruitment, training, performance appraisal, and reward systems that do not discriminate against employees and that employees believe are fair.

Suppliers and Distributors

No company operates alone. Every company is in a network of relationships with other companies that supply it with the inputs (such as raw materials, components, contract labor, and clients) that it needs to operate. It also depends on intermediaries such as wholesalers and retailers to distribute its products to the final customers. Suppliers expect to be paid fairly and promptly for their inputs; distributors expect to receive quality products at agreed-upon prices. Once again, many ethical issues arise in how companies contract and interact with their suppliers and distributors. Important issues concerning how and when payments are made or product quality and safety specifications are governed by the contracts a company signs with its suppliers and distributors.

It is instructive to see how two major firms, Nestlé and Kellogg's, manage their relationships with suppliers to ensure that they act in an ethical way and make safe products. During 2008 Nestlé was deciding whether to continue to purchase from the now bankrupt Peanut Corporation of America (discussed at the beginning of the chapter); it has a policy of using its own inspectors to investigate potential suppliers' operating facilities. Nestlé's inspectors found rodent feces and live beetles on two separate occasions when touring PCA's plants, and the company decided to find a new peanut supplier–which saved it millions of dollars because it did not suffer from product recalls. On the other hand, Kellogg's does not use its own inspectors but relies on third parties, such as FDA inspectors, to investigate suppliers. As a result, Kellogg's continued to buy PCA's products and lost more than $70 million because it had to recall its peanut products.

Many other issues depend on business ethics. For example, numerous products sold in U.S. stores have been outsourced to countries that do not have U.S.-style regulations and laws to protect the workers who make these products. All companies must take an ethical position on the way they obtain and make the products they sell. Commonly this stance is published on a company's Web site. Table 4.1 presents part of the Gap's statement about its approach to global ethics (www.gapinc.com).

Table 4.1

Some Principles from the Gap's Code of Vendor Conduct

As a condition of doing business with Gap Inc., each and every factory must comply with this Code of Vendor Conduct. Gap Inc. will continue to develop monitoring systems to assess and ensure compliance. If Gap Inc. determines that any factory has violated this Code, Gap Inc. may either terminate its business relationship or require the factory to implement a corrective action plan. If corrective action is advised but not taken, Gap Inc. will suspend placement of future orders and may terminate current production.

I. General Principles

Factories that produce goods for Gap Inc. shall operate in full compliance with the laws of their respective countries and with all other applicable laws, rules, and regulations.

II. Environment

Factories must comply with all applicable environmental laws and regulations. Where such requirements are less stringent than Gap Inc.'s own, factories are encouraged to meet the standards outlined in Gap Inc.'s statement of environmental principles.

III. Discrimination

Factories shall employ workers on the basis of their ability to do the job, without regard to race, color, gender, nationality, religion, age, maternity, or marital status.

IV. Forced Labor

Factories shall not use any prison, indentured, or forced labor.

V. Child Labor

Factories shall employ only workers who meet the applicable minimum legal age requirement or are at least 14 years of age, whichever is greater. Factories must also comply with all other applicable child labor laws. Factories are encouraged to develop lawful workplace apprenticeship programs for the educational benefit of their workers, provided that all participants meet both Gap Inc.'s minimum age standard of 14 and the minimum legal age requirement.

VI. Wages & Hours

Factories shall set working hours, wages, and overtime pay in compliance with all applicable laws. Workers shall be paid at least the minimum legal wage or a wage that meets local industry standards, whichever is greater. While it is understood that overtime is often required in garment production, factories shall carry out operations in ways that limit overtime to a level that ensures humane and productive working conditions.

Customers

Customers are often regarded as the most critical stakeholder group because if a company cannot attract them to buy its products, it cannot stay in business. Thus managers and employees must work to increase efficiency and effectiveness in order to create loyal customers and attract new ones. They do so by selling customers quality products at a fair price and providing good after-sales service. They can also strive to improve their products over time and provide guarantees to customers about the integrity of their products like Whole Foods Market, profiled in the following "Ethics in Action" box.

Ethics in Action

Whole Foods Market Practices What It Preaches

The Whole Foods Market supermarket chain was founded by two hippies in Austin, Texas, in 1978 as a natural counterculture food store. Today it is the world's leading retailer of natural and organic foods, with over 285 stores in North America and the United Kingdom. Whole Foods specializes in selling chemical- and drug-free meat, poultry, and produce; its products are the "purest" possible, meaning it selects the ones least adulterated by artificial additives, sweeteners, colorings, and preservatives.[16] Despite the high prices it charges for its pure produce, sales per store are growing, and its revenues had grown to over $8 billion by 2010.[17]

Where do your grocery dollars go? Whole Foods Market's goal is to make shopping fun and socially responsible. Customers' money supports an organization that monitors its suppliers, rewards its employees, and seeks to reduce its impact on the environment.

Why has Whole Foods been so successful? Because, says founder and CEO John Mackey, of the principles he established to manage his company since its beginning–principles founded on the need to behave in an ethical and socially responsible way toward everybody affected by its business. How Whole Foods views its responsibilities to stakeholders and its approach to ethical business are depicted in Figure 4.2.

Mackey says he started his business for three reasons–to have fun, to make money, and to contribute to the well-being of other people.[18] The company's mission is based on its members' collective responsibility to the well-being of the people and groups it affects, its *stakeholders;* in order of priority, at Whole Foods these are customers, team members, investors, suppliers, the community, and the natural environment. Mackey measures his company's success by how well it satisfies the needs of these stakeholders. His ethical stance toward customers is that they are guaranteed that Whole Foods products are 100% organic, hormone-free, or as represented. To help achieve this promise, Whole Foods insists that its suppliers also behave in an ethical way so it knows, for example, that the beef it sells comes from cows pastured on grass, not corn-fed in feed lots, and the chicken it sells is from free-range hens and not from hens that have been confined in tiny cages that prevent movement.

Mackey's management approach toward "team members," as Whole Foods employees are called, is also based on a well-defined ethical position. He says, "We put great emphasis at Whole Foods on the 'Whole People' part of the company mission. We believe in helping support our team members to grow as individuals–to become 'Whole People.' We allow tremendous individual initiative at Whole Foods, and that's why our company is so innovative and creative."[19] Mackey claims that each supermarket in the chain is unique because in each one team members are constantly experimenting with new and better ways to serve customers and improve their well-being. As team members learn, they become "self-actualized" or self-fulfilled, and this increase in their well-being translates into a desire to increase the well-being of other stakeholders.

Finally, Mackey's strong views on ethics and social responsibility also serve shareholders. Mackey does not believe the object of being in business is to primarily maximize profits for shareholders; he puts customers first. He believes, however, that companies that behave ethically, and strive to satisfy the needs of customers and employees, simultaneously satisfy the needs of investors because high profits are the result of loyal customers and committed employees. Indeed, since Whole Foods issued shares to the public in 1992, the value of those shares has increased 25 times in value. Clearly, taking a strong position on ethics and social responsibility has worked so far at Whole Foods.

Many laws protect customers from companies that attempt to provide dangerous or shoddy products. Laws allow customers to sue a company whose product causes them injury or harm, such as a defective tire or vehicle. Other laws force companies to clearly disclose the interest rates they charge on purchases–an important hidden cost that customers frequently do not factor into their purchase decisions. Every year thousands of companies are prosecuted for breaking these laws, so "buyer beware" is an important rule customers must follow when buying goods and services.

Figure 4.2
Whole Foods Market's Stakeholder Approach to Ethical Business

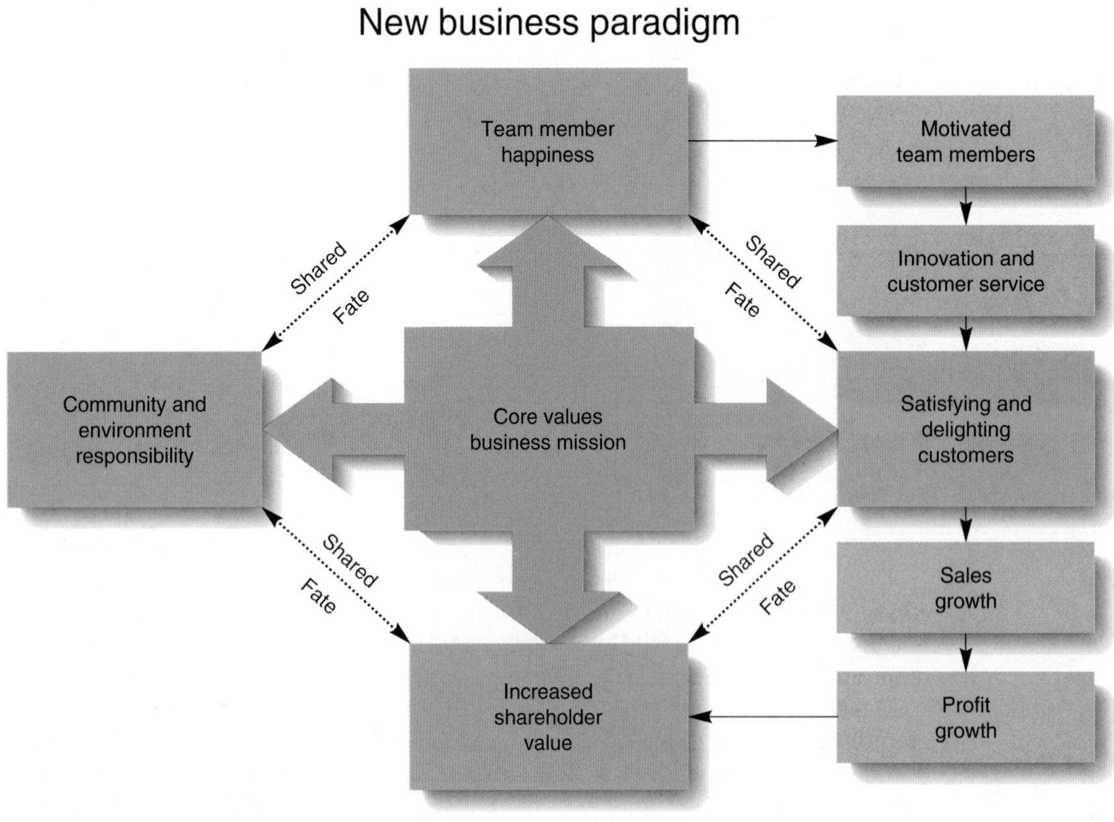

Source: www.wholefoodsmarket.com.

Community, Society, and Nation

The effects of the decisions made by companies and their managers permeate all aspects of the communities, societies, and nations in which they operate. *Community* refers to physical locations like towns or cities or to social milieus like ethnic neighborhoods in which companies are located. A community provides a company with the physical and social infrastructure that allows it to operate; its utilities and labor force; the homes in which its managers and employees live; the schools, colleges, and hospitals that serve their needs; and so on.

Through the salaries, wages, and taxes it pays, a company contributes to the economy of its town or region and often determines whether the community prospers or declines. Similarly, a company affects the prosperity of a society and a nation and, to the degree that a company is involved in global trade, all the countries it operates in and thus the prosperity of the global economy. We have already discussed the many issues surrounding global outsourcing and the loss of jobs in the United States, for example.

Although the individual effects of the way each McDonald's restaurant operates might be small, for instance, the combined effects of how all McDonald's and other fast-food companies do business are enormous. In the United States alone, over 500,000 people work in the fast-food industry, and many thousands of suppliers like farmers, paper cup manufacturers, builders, and so on depend on it for their livelihood. Small wonder then that the ethics of the fast-food business are scrutinized closely. This industry was the major lobbyer against attempts to raise the national minimum wage (which was raised to $7.25 an hour in 2009, up from $5.15–a figure that had not changed since 1997), for example, because a higher minimum wage would substantially increase its operating costs. However, responding to protests about chickens raised in cages where they cannot move, McDonald's–the largest egg buyer in the United States–issued new ethical guidelines concerning cage size and related matters that its egg suppliers must abide by if they are to retain its business. What ethical rules does McDonald's use to decide its stance toward minimum pay or minimum cage size?

Business ethics are also important because the failure of a company can have catastrophic effects on a community; a general decline in business activity affects a whole nation. The decision of a large company to pull out of a community, for example, can seriously threaten the community's future. Some companies may attempt to improve their profits by engaging in actions that, although not illegal, can hurt communities and nations. One of these actions is pollution. For example, many U.S. companies reduce costs by trucking their waste to Mexico, where it is legal to dump waste in the Rio Grande. The dumping pollutes the river from the Mexican side, but the U.S. side of the river is increasingly experiencing pollution's negative effects.

Rules for Ethical Decision Making

When a stakeholder perspective is taken, questions on company ethics abound.[20] What is the appropriate way to manage the claims of all stakeholders? Company decisions that favor one group of stakeholders, for example, are likely to harm the interests of others.[21] High prices charged to customers may bring high returns to shareholders and high salaries to managers in the short run. If in the long run customers turn to companies that offer lower-cost products, however, the result may be declining sales, laid-off employees, and the decline of the communities that support the high-priced company's business activity.

When companies act ethically, their stakeholders support them. For example, banks are willing to supply them with new capital, they attract highly qualified job applicants, and new customers are drawn to their products. Thus ethical companies grow and expand over time, and all their stakeholders benefit. The results of unethical behavior are loss of reputation and resources, shareholders selling their shares, skilled managers and employees leaving the company, and customers turning to the products of more reputable companies.

When making business decisions, managers must consider the claims of all stakeholders.[22] To help themselves and employees make ethical decisions and behave in ways that benefit their stakeholders, managers can use four ethical rules or principles to analyze the effects of their business decisions on stakeholders: the *utilitarian, moral rights, justice,* and *practical* rules (Figure 4.3).[23] These rules are useful guidelines that help managers decide on the appropriate way to behave in situations where it is necessary to balance a company's self-interest and the interests of its stakeholders. Remember, the right choices will lead resources to be used where they can create the most value. If all companies make the right choices, all stakeholders will benefit in the long run.[24]

utilitarian rule An ethical decision is a decision that produces the greatest good for the greatest number of people.

UTILITARIAN RULE The **utilitarian rule** is that an ethical decision is a decision that produces the greatest good for the greatest number of people. To decide which is the most ethical course of business action, managers should first consider how different possible courses of business action would benefit or harm different stakeholders. They should then choose the course of action that provides the most benefits, or conversely the one that does the least harm, to stakeholders.[25]

The ethical dilemma for managers is this: How do you measure the benefit and harm that will be done to each stakeholder group? Moreover, how do you evaluate the rights of different stakeholder groups, and the relative importance of each group, in coming to a decision? Because stockholders own the company, shouldn't their claims be held above those of employees? For example, managers might face a choice of using global outsourcing to reduce costs and lower prices or continuing with high-cost production at home. A decision to use global outsourcing benefits shareholders and customers but will result in major layoffs that will harm employees and the communities in which they live. Typically, in a capitalist society such as the United States, the interests of shareholders are put above those of employees, so production will move abroad. This is commonly regarded as being an ethical choice because in the long run the alternative, home production, might cause the business to collapse and go bankrupt, in which case greater harm will be done to all stakeholders.

Figure 4.3
Four Ethical Rules

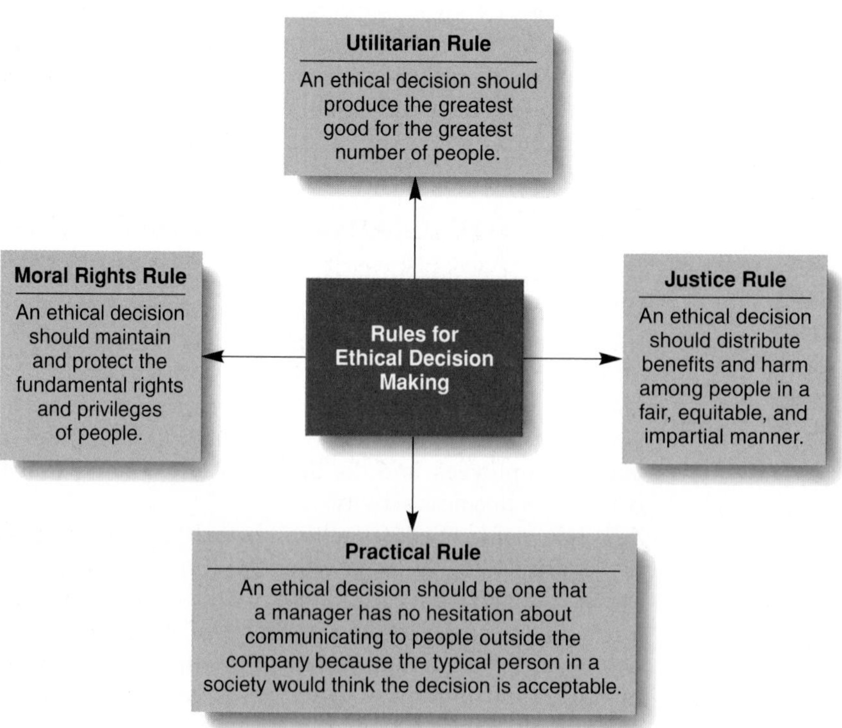
Utilitarian Rule
An ethical decision should produce the greatest good for the greatest number of people.
Moral Rights Rule
An ethical decision should maintain and protect the fundamental rights and privileges of people.
Rules for Ethical Decision Making
Justice Rule
An ethical decision should distribute benefits and harm among people in a fair, equitable, and impartial manner.
Practical Rule
An ethical decision should be one that a manager has no hesitation about communicating to people outside the company because the typical person in a society would think the decision is acceptable.

LO4-3 Describe four rules that can help companies and their managers act in ethical ways.

MORAL RIGHTS RULE Under the **moral rights rule,** an ethical decision is one that best maintains and protects the fundamental or inalienable rights and privileges of the people affected by it. For example, ethical decisions protect people's rights to freedom, life and safety, property, privacy, free speech, and freedom of conscience. The adage "Do unto others as you would have them do unto you" is a moral rights principle that managers should use to decide which rights to uphold. Customers must also consider the rights of the companies and people who create the products they wish to consume (see the "Ethics in Action" box "Digital Piracy, Ethics, and Napster").

moral rights rule An ethical decision is one that best maintains and protects the fundamental or inalienable rights and privileges of the people affected by it.

From a moral rights perspective, managers should compare and contrast different courses of business action on the basis of how each course will affect the rights of the company's different stakeholders. Managers should then choose the course of action that best protects and upholds the rights of *all* stakeholders. For example, decisions that might significantly harm the safety or health of employees or customers would clearly be unethical choices.

The ethical dilemma for managers is that decisions that will protect the rights of some stakeholders often will hurt the rights of others. How should they choose which group to protect? For example, in deciding whether it is ethical to snoop on employees, or search them when they leave work to prevent theft, does an employee's right to privacy outweigh an organization's right to protect its property? Suppose a coworker is having personal problems and is coming in late and leaving early, forcing you to pick up the person's workload. Do you tell your boss even though you know this will probably get that person fired?

justice rule An ethical decision distributes benefits and harms among people and groups in a fair, equitable, or impartial way.

JUSTICE RULE The **justice rule** is that an ethical decision distributes benefits and harms among people and groups in a fair, equitable, or impartial way. Managers should compare and contrast alternative courses of action based on the degree to which they will fairly or equitably distribute outcomes to stakeholders. For example, employees who are similar in their level of skill, performance, or responsibility should receive similar pay; allocation of outcomes should not be based on differences such as gender, race, or religion.

The ethical dilemma for managers is to determine the fair rules and procedures for distributing outcomes to stakeholders. Managers must not give people they like bigger raises than they give to people they do not like, for example, or bend the rules to help their favorites. On the other hand, if employees want managers to act fairly toward them, then employees need to act fairly toward their companies by working hard and being loyal. Similarly, customers need to act fairly toward a company if they expect it to be fair to them–something people who illegally copy digital media should consider.

PRACTICAL RULE Each of these rules offers a different and complementary way of determining whether a decision or behavior is ethical, and all three rules should be used to sort out the ethics of a particular course of action. Ethical issues, as we just discussed, are seldom clear-cut, however, because the rights, interests, goals, and incentives of different stakeholders often conflict. For this reason many experts on ethics add a fourth rule to determine whether a business decision is ethical: The **practical rule** is that an ethical decision is one that a manager has no hesitation or reluctance about communicating to people outside the company because the typical person in a society would think it is acceptable. A business decision is probably acceptable on ethical grounds if a manager can answer yes to each of these questions:

practical rule An ethical decision is one that a manager has no reluctance about communicating to people outside the company because the typical person in a society would think it is acceptable.

1. Does my decision fall within the accepted values or standards that typically apply in business activity today?
2. Am I willing to see the decision communicated to all people and groups affected by it–for example, by having it reported in newspapers or on television?
3. Would the people with whom I have a significant personal relationship, such as family members, friends, or even managers in other organizations, approve of the decision?

Applying the practical rule to analyze a business decision ensures that managers are taking into account the interests of all stakeholders.[26] After applying this rule managers can judge if they have chosen to act in an ethical or unethical way, and they must abide by the consequences. The following "Ethics in Action" box, which describes the issues surrounding individuals copying digital content from the Internet, provides a good example to test these different ethical issues. What is the right or ethical thing to do in this situation?

Ethics in Action

Digital Piracy, Ethics, and Napster

Today almost all written text, music, movies, and software are recorded in digital form and can be easily copied electronically and sent between personal computers through the Internet. Many sites on the Internet contain illegal copies of music, movies, and so on that can be easily accessed and downloaded. Millions of people and companies have taken advantage of this to make illegal copies of music CDs, software programs, and DVDs. As a result, it has been estimated that over one-third of all CDs and cassettes recorded around the world were illegally produced and sold in the 2000s, and the music industry has lost tens of billions in sales revenues.[27]

As you can imagine, the managers of music and movie companies have been doing all they can to reduce illegal recording because it decreases their sales and profits. One enterprise that music company CEOs went after with a vengeance was Napster.[28] Shawn Fanning created Napster while he was an undergraduate student at Northeastern University. His roommate downloaded music from Internet sites using the MP3 format, which compresses digital files, making them faster to transmit and easier to store. As Fanning watched his roommate search the Internet for new material, he realized that it would be easy to create a software platform to help people easily locate and download digital music files stored in any PC that was logged into this platform. Fanning created the necessary software, and word of mouth did the rest; soon Napster was a phenomenon, and millions of people were swapping and downloading music.[29]

Shawn Fanning created a company and an ethical controversy when he took Napster's copying platform public. Was it a work of genius or just promotion of selfishness? What about Google's similar book-scanning operations today?

Managers in the music industry became desperate to stop this practice. The value of their companies' copyrights to songs and contracts with artists was being destroyed by this new technology that allowed pirating of their products. They sought legal injunctions against Napster to shut the company down; and because it was clearly violating copyright laws, the courts stopped Napster's operations. However, many other Internet sites sprang up from which people can still download music and other digital media, and Napster eventually became one of these sites when it was bought by Best Buy in 2008.

Copying digital material is illegal because it infringes on copyright laws that protect the rights of artists, authors, composers, and the companies that produce and distribute their work. Is this copying unethical? Is it an unacceptable or acceptable way to behave? Why are so many people doing it if it is illegal? The obvious answer is that people are doing it to pursue their self-interest. Paying nothing for valuable digital media is attractive, and who, goes the argument, suffers anyway? Music companies have been making billions of dollars of profit from music sales for decades. Songs may be the property of music stars like the Rolling Stones and Eminem, but these people are fabulously wealthy. Why shouldn't the average person benefit from digital technology? After all, the pleasure gained by hundreds of millions of people is more important than the harm done to only a few thousand musicians and a handful of music companies, so copying is not really unethical. It may be illegal, but it's not actually such a bad thing to do, is it?

Arguments like these may make people feel that their copying does no real harm to others. But what about the rights of artists and companies to profit from their property–the songs, books, and movies that result from their creative endeavors? The average person would not like it if someone came along and said, "You don't need all those appliances, cars, and jewelry. I'll just help myself; you'll never miss it." Those who steal digital media not only weaken the rights of musicians and writers to own property but also weaken *their* rights to own property. Digital piracy is not a fair or equitable practice. And although each person may argue that engaging in it doesn't have much of an effect because he or she is only one person, if many people do it, a major problem emerges.

To illustrate the problem, by 2010 over 85% of all music and movies were illegally copied rather than bought. What will musicians, music companies, movie stars, and movie studios do as a result? If people and companies cannot protect their property and profit from it, they are not going to make or sell digital products. Over time, music and movie companies will cease to operate. Creative people will find new ways to make money, or musicians will perform music only for their own pleasure or in live concerts (where recording devices are not permitted). The result will be a loss to everyone because no new music or movies will be made, and the world will become a less interesting place to live in.

It is no easy matter to determine a fair or equitable division of the value and profit in a particular business activity. Music companies have no desire to see their revenues fall because potential customers profit from their ability to illegally copy CDs. Music companies have a responsibility to make profits so they can reward their stockholders, pay the musicians royalties on their record sales, and pay their employees' salaries. Of course they also have a responsibility toward customers–they should charge only a fair price for their CDs. In fact, since Apple opened its iTunes store in 2001 and other online music stores followed suit, billions of songs have been legally downloaded and paid for (over 10 billion from iTunes alone), which indicates that millions of customers accept their obligation to pay a fair price for the products they receive. At the same time artists and companies recognize that they must provide first-class content if customers are going to continue to purchase, rather than copy, digital content.

LO4-4 Discuss why it is important for managers to behave ethically.

Why Should Managers Behave Ethically?

Why is it so important that managers, and people in general, should act ethically and temper their pursuit of self-interest by considering the effects of their actions on others? The answer is that the relentless pursuit of self-interest can lead to a collective disaster when one or more people start to profit from being unethical because this encourages other people to act in the same way.[30] More and more people jump onto the bandwagon, and soon everybody is trying to manipulate the situation to serve their personal ends with no regard for the effects of their action on others. The situation brought about by Napster is an example of what is called the "tragedy of the commons."

Suppose that in an agricultural community there is common land that everybody has an equal right to use. Pursuing self-interest, each farmer acts to make the maximum use of the free resource by grazing his or her own cattle and sheep. Collectively all the farmers overgraze the land, which quickly becomes worn out. Then a strong wind blows away the exposed topsoil, so the common land is destroyed. The pursuit of individual self-interest with no consideration of societal interests leads to disaster for each individual and for the whole society because scarce resources are destroyed.[31] In the Napster case the tragedy that would result if all people were to steal digital media would be the disappearance of music, movie, and book companies as creative people decided there was no point in working hard to produce original songs, stories, and so on.

We can look at the effects of unethical behavior on business activity in another way. Suppose companies and their managers operate in an unethical society, meaning one in which stakeholders routinely try to cheat and defraud one another. If stakeholders expect each other to cheat, how long will it take them to negotiate the purchase and shipment of products? When they do not trust each other, stakeholders will probably spend hours bargaining over fair prices, and this is a largely unproductive activity that reduces efficiency and effectiveness.[32] The time and effort that could be spent improving product quality or customer service are lost to negotiating and bargaining. Thus unethical behavior ruins business commerce, and society has a lower standard of living because fewer goods and services are produced, as Figure 4.4 illustrates.

trust The willingness of one person or group to have faith or confidence in the goodwill of another person, even though this puts them at risk.

On the other hand, suppose companies and their managers operate in an ethical society, meaning stakeholders believe they are dealing with others who are basically moral and honest. In this society stakeholders have a greater reason to trust others. **Trust** is the willingness of one person or group to have faith or confidence in the goodwill of another person, even though this puts them at risk (because the other might act in a deceitful way). When trust exists, stakeholders are likely to signal their

Figure 4.4
Some Effects of Ethical and Unethical Behavior

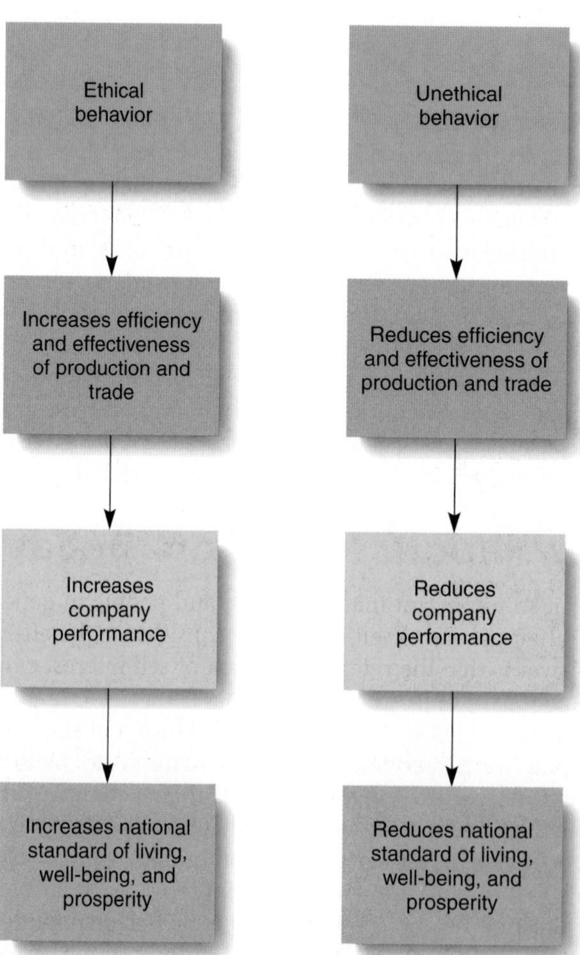

good intentions by cooperating and providing information that makes it easier to exchange and price goods and services. When one person acts in a trustworthy way, this encourages others to act in the same way. Over time, as greater trust between stakeholders develops, they can work together more efficiently and effectively, which raises company performance (see Figure 4.4). As people see the positive results of acting in an honest way, ethical behavior becomes a valued social norm, and society in general becomes increasingly ethical.

As noted in Chapter 1, a major responsibility of managers is to protect and nurture the resources under their control. Any organizational stakeholders–managers, workers, stockholders, suppliers–who advance their own interests by behaving unethically toward other stakeholders, either by taking resources or by denying resources to others, waste collective resources. If other individuals or groups copy the behavior of the unethical stakeholder, the rate at which collective resources are misused increases, and eventually few resources are available to produce goods and services. Unethical behavior that goes unpunished creates incentives for people to put their unbridled self-interests above the rights of others.[33] When this happens, the benefits that people reap from joining together in organizations disappear quickly.

reputation The esteem or high repute that individuals or organizations gain when they behave ethically.

An important safeguard against unethical behavior is the potential for loss of reputation.[34] **Reputation,** the esteem or high repute that people or organizations gain when they behave ethically, is an important asset. Stakeholders have valuable reputations that they must protect because their ability to earn a living and obtain resources in the long run depends on how they behave.

If a manager misuses resources and other parties regard that behavior as being at odds with acceptable standards, the manager's reputation will suffer. Behaving unethically in the short run can have serious long-term consequences. A manager who has a poor reputation will have difficulty finding employment with other companies. Stockholders who see managers behaving unethically may refuse to invest in their companies, and this will decrease the stock price, undermine the companies' reputations, and ultimately put the managers' jobs at risk.[35]

All stakeholders have reputations to lose. Suppliers who provide shoddy inputs find that organizations learn over time not to deal with them, and eventually, like PCA, they go out of business. Powerful customers who demand ridiculously low prices find that their suppliers become less willing to deal with them, and resources ultimately become harder for them to obtain. Workers who shirk responsibilities on the job find it hard to get new jobs when they are fired. In general, if a manager or company is known for being unethical, other stakeholders are likely to view that individual or organization with suspicion and hostility, creating a poor reputation. But a manager or company known for ethical business practices will develop a good reputation.[36]

In summary, in a complex, diverse society, stakeholders, and people in general, need to recognize they are part of a larger social group. How they make decisions and act not only affects them personally but also affects the lives of many other people. Unfortunately, for some people, the daily struggle to survive and succeed or their total disregard for others' rights can lead them to lose that bigger connection to other people. We can see our relationships to our families and friends, to our school, church, and so on. But we must go further and keep in mind the effects of our actions on other people–people who will be judging our actions and whom we might harm by acting unethically. Our moral scruples are like those "other people" but are inside our heads.

Ethics and Social Responsibility

Some companies, like GlaxoSmithKline, Bristol Myers Squib, Prudential Insurance, Whole Foods, and Blue Cross–Blue Shield, are known for their ethical business practices.[37] Other companies, such as PAC, Arthur Andersen, and Enron, which are now out of business, or WorldCom, Tyco, Qwest, and Adelphia, which have been totally restructured, repeatedly engaged in unethical and illegal business activities. What explains such differences between the ethics of these companies and their managers?

LO4-5 Identify the four main sources of managerial ethics.

There are four main determinants of differences in ethics between people, employees, companies, and countries: *societal* ethics, *occupational* ethics, *individual* ethics, and *organizational* ethics–especially the ethics of a company's top managers.[38] (See Figure 4.5.)

Societal Ethics

societal ethics Standards that govern how members of a society should deal with one another in matters involving issues such as fairness, justice, poverty, and the rights of the individual.

Societal ethics are standards that govern how members of a society should deal with one another in matters involving issues such as fairness, justice, poverty, and the rights of the individual. Societal ethics emanate from a society's laws, customs, and practices and from the unwritten values and norms that influence how people interact with each other. People in a particular country may automatically behave ethically because they have *internalized* (made a part of their morals) certain values, beliefs, and norms that specify how they should behave when confronted with an ethical dilemma.

Societal ethics vary among societies. Countries like Germany, Japan, Sweden, and Switzerland are known as being some of the most ethical countries in the world, with strong values about social order and the need to create a society that protects the welfare of all their citizens. In other countries the situation is different. In many economically poor countries bribery is standard practice to get things done–such as getting a telephone installed or a contract awarded. In the United States and other economically advanced countries, bribery is considered unethical and has been made illegal.

IBM experienced the problem of different ethical standards in its Argentine division. Managers there became involved in an unethical scheme to secure a $250 million contract for IBM to provide and service the computers of one of Argentina's largest state-owned banks. After $6 million was paid to bribe the bank executives who agreed to give IBM the contract, IBM announced that it had fired the three top managers of its Argentine division. According to IBM, transactions like this, though unethical by IBM's standards, are not necessarily illegal under Argentine law. The Argentine managers were fired, however, for failing to follow IBM's organizational rules, which preclude bribery to obtain contracts in foreign countries. Moreover, bribery violates

Figure 4.5
Sources of Ethics

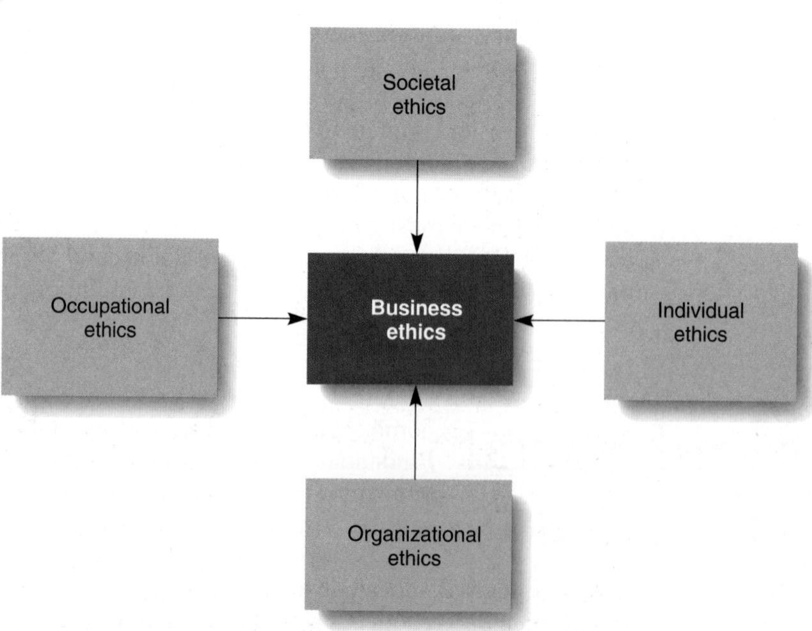

the U.S. Foreign Corrupt Practices Act, which forbids payment of bribes by U.S. companies to secure contracts abroad, makes companies liable for the actions of their foreign managers, and allows companies found in violation to be prosecuted in the United States. By firing the managers, IBM signaled that it would not tolerate unethical behavior by any of its employees, and it continues today to take a rigorous stance toward ethical issues.

Countries also differ widely in their beliefs about appropriate treatment for their employees. In general, the poorer a country is, the more likely employees are to be treated with little regard. One issue of particular concern on a global level is whether it is ethical to use child labor, as discussed in the following "Ethics in Action" box.

Ethics in Action

Is It Right to Use Child Labor?

In recent years, the number of U.S. companies that buy their products from low-cost foreign suppliers has been growing, and concern about the ethics associated with employing young children in factories has been increasing. In Pakistan, children as young as 6 years old work long hours in deplorable conditions to make rugs and carpets for export to Western countries. Children in poor countries throughout Africa, Asia, and South America work in similar conditions. Is it ethical to employ children in factories, and should U.S. companies buy and sell products made by these children?

Opinions about the ethics of child labor vary widely. Robert Reich, an economist and secretary of labor in the first Clinton administration, believed that the practice is totally reprehensible and should be outlawed on a global level. Another view, championed by *The Economist* magazine, is that while nobody wants to see children employed in factories, citizens of rich countries need to recognize that in poor countries children are often a family's breadwinners. Thus denying children employment would cause whole families to suffer, and one wrong (child labor) might produce a greater wrong (poverty). Instead *The Economist* favors regulating the conditions under which children are employed and hopes that over time, as poor countries become richer, the need for child employment will disappear.

Afghan boys weave a rug while their father stands nearby inside their home in Kabul, Afghanistan. Afghan rug makers contract children to make rugs, paying their families roughly $8 per yard. Making one 18-foot rug takes approximately a month, and the children often work in shifts around their schooling or other household duties.

Many U.S. retailers buy clothing from low-cost foreign suppliers, and managers in these companies have had to take their own ethical stance on child labor. Managers in Walmart, Target, JCPenney, and Gap Inc. (see Table 4.1) have followed U.S. standards and rules and have policies dictating that their foreign suppliers not employ child labor. They have also vowed to sever ties with any foreign supplier found violating this standard.

Apparently, however, retailers differ widely in how they enforce such policies. It has been estimated that more than 300,000 children under age 14 are employed in garment factories in Guatemala, a popular low-cost location for clothing manufacturers that supply the U.S. market. These children frequently work more than 60 hours a week and often are paid less than $3 a day—close to the minimum wage in Guatemala. Many U.S. retailers do not check up on their foreign suppliers. Clearly, if U.S. retailers are to be true to their ethical stance on this troubling issue, they cannot ignore the fact that they are buying clothing made by children, and they must do more to regulate the conditions under which these children work.

One recent attempt to do this is through the Fair Factories Clearinghouse, a joint effort launched by companies such as L.L. Bean, Reebok, and Timberland to pool the information they collect about the work practices of the factories with which they have contracted to make their products. The aim is to create a single set of labor code standards that plants the world over must comply with if they are to be certified as ethical suppliers–or else they will be axed by all reputable companies.[39]

Occupational Ethics

occupational ethics Standards that govern how members of a profession, trade, or craft should conduct themselves when performing work-related activities.

Occupational ethics are standards that govern how members of a profession, trade, or craft should conduct themselves when performing work-related activities.[40] For example, medical ethics govern how doctors and nurses should treat their patients. Doctors are expected to perform only necessary medical procedures and to act in the patient's interest, not their own self-interest. The ethics of scientific research require that scientists conduct their experiments and present their findings in ways that ensure the validity of their conclusions. Like society at large, most professional groups can impose punishments for violations of ethical standards.[41] Doctors and lawyers can be prevented from practicing their professions if they disregard professional ethics and put their own interests first.

Former Enron Chief Financial Officer Andrew Fastow (center) is escorted by U.S. marshals as Fastow leaves court in Houston March 7, 2006, after testifying against former bosses Ken Lay and Jeff Skilling. In 2010 he is appealing his sentence to reduce his jail term by 10 years.

Within an organization, occupational rules and norms often govern how employees such as lawyers, researchers, and accountants should make decisions to further stakeholder interests. Employees internalize the rules and norms of their occupational group (just as they do those of society) and often follow them automatically when deciding how to behave. Because most people tend to follow established rules of behavior, people frequently take ethics for granted. However, when occupational ethics are violated, such as when scientists fabricate data to disguise the harmful effects of products, ethical issues come to the forefront. For example, Merck scientists were accused of playing down evidence that Vioxx, a best-selling drug, increased the risk of heart attacks; the drug was pulled from the market. Top researchers in pharmaceutical companies have been accused of deliberately hiding research evidence that revealed the harmful effects of products such as Merck's Vioxx painkilling drug and Guidant's heart pacemaker, so doctors and patients could not make informed medical treatment decisions. Table 4.2 lists some failures or lapses in professional ethics according to type of functional manager.

Individual Ethics

individual ethics Personal standards and values that determine how people view their responsibilities to others and how they should act in situations when their own self-interests are at stake.

Individual ethics are personal standards and values that determine how people view their responsibilities to other people and groups and thus how they should act in situations when their own self-interests are at stake.[42] Sources of individual ethics include the influence of one's family, peers, and upbringing in general. The experiences gained over a lifetime–through membership in social institutions such as schools and religions, for example–also contribute to the development of the personal standards and values that a person uses to evaluate a situation and decide what is the

Table 4.2
Some Failures in Professional Ethics

For manufacturing and materials management managers:

- Releasing products that are not of a consistent quality because of defective inputs.
- Producing product batches that may be dangerous or defective and harm customers.
- Compromising workplace health and safety to reduce costs (for example, to maximize output, employees are not given adequate training to maintain and service machinery and equipment).

For sales and marketing managers:

- Knowingly making unsubstantiated product claims.
- Engaging in sales campaigns that use covert persuasive or subliminal advertising to create customer need for the product.
- Marketing to target groups such as the elderly, minorities, or children to build demand for a product.
- Having ongoing campaigns of unsolicited junk mail, spam, door-to-door, or telephone selling.

For accounting and finance managers:

- Engaging in misleading financial analysis involving creative accounting or "cooking the books" to hide salient facts.
- Authorizing excessive expenses and perks to managers, customers, and suppliers.
- Hiding the level and amount of top management and director compensation.

For human resource managers:

- Failing to act fairly, objectively, and in a uniform way toward different employees or kinds of employees because of personal factors such as personality and beliefs.
- Excessively encroaching on employee privacy through non-job-related surveillance or personality, ability, and drug testing.
- Failing to respond to employee observations and concerns surrounding health and safety violations, hostile workplace issues, or inappropriate or even illegal behavior by managers or employees.

morally right or wrong way to behave. However, suppose you are the son or daughter of a mobster, and your upbringing and education take place in an organized crime context; this affects how you evaluate a situation. You may come to believe that it is ethical to do anything and perform any act, up to and including murder, if it benefits your family or friends. These are your ethics. They are obviously not the ethics of the wider society and so are subject to sanction. In a similar way, managers and employees in an organization may come to believe that actions they take to promote or protect their organization are more important than any harm these actions may cause other stakeholders. So they behave unethically or illegally, and when this is discovered, they also are sanctioned–as happened to New York's cab drivers, discussed in the following "Ethics in Action" box.

Consider the unethical way in which Jim McCormick, director of a "bomb detecting device" company based in rural Somerset, England, set out to make money by developing a bomb detector, the ADE-51, that he sold to 20 countries, including Iraq, for $40,000 each. The Iraqi government alone spent $85 million on the handheld detectors that were used at checkpoints in Baghdad. The device used a "special electronic card" to detect bombs and was powered by the users' own "kinetic energy." However, in 2010 after a tipoff, an independent computer laboratory that tested the device said the card contained only a common tag used by stores to prevent theft.[43] The ADE-51 could not possibly detect the bombs that have killed hundreds of Iraqis; as

Ethics in Action

How Unethical New York City Taxi Drivers Made a Fast Buck

In 2009 the New York City taxi commission, which regulates cab fares, began an investigation after it found that one cab driver from Brooklyn, Wasim Khalid Cheema, overcharged 574 passengers in just one month. The taxi drivers' scheme, the commission said, involved 1.8 million rides and cost passengers an average of $4 to $5 extra per trip. The drivers pressed a button on the taxi's payment meter that categorized the fare as a Code No. 4, which is charged for trips outside the city to Nassau or Westchester and is twice the rate of Code No. 1, which is charged for rides within New York City limits. Passengers can see which rate is being charged by looking at the meter, but few bother to do so; they rely on the cab driver's honesty.

Check that meter before you pay! Relying on cab driver honesty failed in NYC, finally resulting in tighter regulation of the industry.

After the commission discovered the fraud, it used GPS data, collected in every cab, to review millions of trips within New York City and found that in 36,000 cabs the higher rates were improperly activated at least once; in each of about 3,000 cabs it was done more than 100 times; and 35,558 of the city's roughly 48,000 drivers had applied the higher rate. This scheme cost New York City riders more than $8 million plus all the higher tips they paid as a result of the higher charges. The fraud ranks as one of the biggest in the taxi industry's history, and New York City Mayor Michael R. Bloomberg said criminal charges could be brought against cab drivers.

The commission also demanded that in the future a new digital metering system be introduced to alert passengers, who would have to acknowledge that they accepted the higher rate charge. Also, officials said taxi companies would eventually be forced to use meters based on a GPS system that would automatically set the charge based on the location of the cab, and drivers would no longer be able to manually activate the higher rate–and cheat their customers. In May 2010, 630 taxi drivers were told their licenses would be revoked.

you might expect, McCormick is now being prosecuted for misrepresentation and fraud, and his device has been banned.

In general, many decisions or behaviors that one person finds unethical, such as using animals for cosmetics testing, may be acceptable to another person. If decisions or behaviors are not illegal, individuals may agree to disagree about their ethical beliefs, or they may try to impose their own beliefs on other people and make those ethical beliefs the law. In all cases, however, people should develop and follow the ethical criteria described earlier to balance their self-interests against those of others when determining how they should behave in a particular situation.

Organizational Ethics

organizational ethics The guiding practices and beliefs through which a particular company and its managers view their responsibility toward their stakeholders.

Organizational ethics are the guiding practices and beliefs through which a particular company and its managers view their responsibility toward their stakeholders. The individual ethics of a company's founders and top managers are especially important in shaping the organization's code of ethics. Organizations whose founders had a vital role in creating a highly ethical code of organizational behavior include UPS, Procter & Gamble, Johnson & Johnson, and the Prudential Insurance Company.

Johnson & Johnson's code of ethics–its credo–reflects a well-developed concern for its stakeholders (see Figure 4.7). Company credos, such as that of Johnson & Johnson, are meant to deter self-interested, unethical behavior; to demonstrate to managers and employees that a company will not tolerate people who, because of their own poor ethics, put their personal interests above the interests of other organizational stakeholders and ignore the harm they are inflicting on others; and to demonstrate that those who act unethically will be punished.

Managers or workers may behave unethically if they feel pressured to do so by the situation they are in and by unethical top managers. People typically confront ethical issues when weighing their personal interests against the effects of their actions on others. Suppose a manager knows that promotion to vice president is likely if she can secure a $100 million contract, but getting the contract requires bribing the contract giver with $1 million. The manager reasons that performing this act will ensure her career and future, and what harm would it do anyway? Bribery is common, and she knows that even if she decides not to pay the bribe, someone else surely will. So what to do? Research seems to suggest that people who realize they have the most at stake in a career sense or a monetary sense are the ones most likely to act unethically. And it is exactly in this situation that a strong code of organizational ethics can help people behave in the right or appropriate way. *The New York Times* detailed code of ethics (see nytco.com/corporate_governance/code_of_ethics/business_ethics.html), for example, was crafted by its editors to ensure the integrity and honesty of its journalists as they report sensitive information.

If a company's top managers consistently endorse the ethical principles in its corporate credo, they can prevent employees from going astray. Employees are much more likely to act unethically when a credo does not exist or is disregarded. Arthur Andersen, for example, did not follow its credo at all; its unscrupulous partners ordered middle managers to shred records that showed evidence of their wrongdoing. Although the middle managers knew this was wrong, they followed the orders because they responded to the personal power and status of the partners and not the company's code of ethics. They were afraid they would lose their jobs if they did not behave unethically, but their actions cost them their jobs anyway.

Top managers play a crucial role in determining a company's ethics. It is clearly important, then, that when making appointment decisions, the board of directors should scrutinize the reputations and ethical records of top managers. It is the responsibility of the board to decide whether a prospective CEO has the maturity, experience, and integrity needed to head a company and be entrusted with the capital and wealth of the organization, on which the fate of all its stakeholders depends. Clearly a track record of success is not enough to decide whether a top manager is capable of moral decision making; a manager might have achieved this success through unethical or illegal means. It is important to investigate prospective top managers and examine their credentials. Although the best predictor of future behavior is often past behavior, the board of directors needs to be on guard against unprincipled executives who use unethical means to rise to the top of the organizational hierarchy. For this reason it is necessary that a company's directors continuously monitor the behavior of top executives. In the 2000s this increased scrutiny has led to the dismissal of many top executives for breaking ethical rules concerning issues such as excessive personal loans, stock options, inflated expense accounts, and even sexual misconduct–as the "Ethics in Action" box on the next page discusses.

social responsibility The way a company's managers and employees view their duty or obligation to make decisions that protect, enhance, and promote the welfare and well-being of stakeholders and society as a whole.

Approaches to Social Responsibility

A company's ethics are the result of differences in societal, organizational, occupational, and individual ethics. In turn, a company's ethics determine its stance or position on social responsibility. A company's stance on **social responsibility** is the way its managers and employees view their duty or obligation to make decisions that protect, enhance, and promote the welfare

Ethics in Action

Jonathan Reckford Rebuilds Goodwill at Habitat for Humanity

Habitat for Humanity is the 17th largest U.S. nonprofit, and its mission is to build or renovate cost-effective, modest homes in partnership with families in need, who repay the organization by helping to build their own homes or the homes of others and by repaying a no-profit mortgage. Founded decades ago by Millard and Linda Fuller, it receives more than $1 billion in donations a year for its work in more than 90 countries around the world. In 2004 a scandal struck the nonprofit when Millard Fuller was accused of sexually harassing a female employee. The board brought in an investigator to review the complaint. As the investigation unfolded, the Fullers' behavior and ongoing comments about the matter were deemed divisive to the organization's work and led to their dismissal.

When Habitat for Humanity needed a new CEO, they looked to Jonathan Reckford, a Presbyterian pastor and former executive at Walt Disney and Best Buy. Reckford, pictured here with Habitat spokesperson Jimmy Carter, quickly implemented best-practice techniques in order to help Habitat perform more effectively.

In the 2000s the efficiency and effectiveness of nonprofits have been questioned, and many analysts believe that nonprofits need to introduce new management techniques to improve their level of performance. Indeed, one study estimated that nonprofits could save $100 billion by using such techniques as total quality management and benchmarking, which involve an organization's imitating a company that excels in performing some functional activity.

So Habitat's board of directors searched for a new CEO who could simultaneously help the organization continue its work and improve its performance. The person they chose was Jonathan Reckford, an ex-Walt Disney, Best Buy executive and Presbyterian pastor. Reckford relished the challenge of using his management skills to find better ways to use Habitat's $1 billion in donations and to attract more donors. Quickly Reckford began to introduce best practice techniques. For example, modeling companies like Dell and Walmart that use their huge buying power to lower their input costs, he emphasized the need for volume purchasing of building products. He introduced new kinds of output controls to provide detailed feedback on vital aspects of Habitat's performance, such as the number of new houses it built in different regions and countries and the time and cost of construction involved per house. He also introduced better human resource management practices, including creating a promotion ladder in Habitat and raising salaries to competitive levels found in other nonprofits. He decided to move a portion of Habitat's headquarters from the small city in which it had been founded to Atlanta, Georgia, to make it easier to hire skilled functional managers. Finally, he established a new set of goals and priorities for the company; and given that Reckford took over only a month after Hurricane Katrina struck, one obvious priority was to rebuild homes along the Gulf Coast. Habitat's goal was to begin construction or complete 1,000 permanent homes by the end of 2007–a feat it achieved by May 2007, upon which Reckford announced that its new goal was to build 1,000 more.[44]

Habitat for Humanity has steadily increased its international focus; for example, it already had 50 employees in place in Haiti in 2010 when the earthquake struck. Reckford, traveling with singer Ricky Martin, toured the earthquake's devastation and announced, "With more than 200,000 houses severely damaged or destroyed and 1.2 million people homeless or displaced, there is a critical need for shelter in Haiti. Based on our responses to the Asian tsunami and

Hurricanes Katrina and Rita in the U.S. Gulf Coast, we are confident that we can empower families to improve their housing conditions by giving them the tools and then working alongside them. But Habitat for Humanity is in need of significant financial support so that we can help 50,000 families improve their lives."[45] In total, since its founding in 1976, Habitat has built, rehabilitated, repaired, or improved more than 350,000 houses worldwide that provide simple and affordable shelter to over 1.75 million people.

LO4-6 Distinguish among the four main approaches toward social responsibility that a company can take.

and well-being of stakeholders and society as a whole.[46] As we noted earlier, when no laws specify how a company should act toward stakeholders, managers must decide the right, ethical, and socially responsible thing to do. Differences in business ethics can lead companies to diverse positions or views on their responsibility toward stakeholders.

Many kinds of decisions signal a company's beliefs about its obligations to make socially responsible business decisions (see Table 4.3). The decision to spend money on training and educating employees–investing in them–is one such decision; so is the decision to minimize or avoid layoffs whenever possible. The decision to act promptly and warn customers when a batch of defective merchandise has been accidentally sold is another one. Companies that try to hide such problems show little regard for social responsibility. In the past both GM and Ford tried to hide the fact that several of their vehicles had defects that made them dangerous to drive; the companies were penalized with hundreds of millions of dollars in damages for their unethical behavior, and today they move more quickly to recall vehicles to fix problems. In 2010 quality leader Toyota apologized for being slow to announce recalls to fix brake system problems on some of its vehicles, which had caused uncontrolled

Table 4.3
Forms of Socially Responsible Behavior

Managers are being socially responsible and showing their support for their stakeholders when they

- Provide severance payments to help laid-off workers make ends meet until they can find another job.
- Give workers opportunities to enhance their skills and acquire additional education so they can remain productive and do not become obsolete because of changes in technology.
- Allow employees to take time off when they need to and provide health care and pension benefits for employees.
- Contribute to charities or support various civic-minded activities in the cities or towns in which they are located. (Target and Levi Strauss both contribute 5% of their profits to support schools, charities, the arts, and other good works.)
- Decide to keep open a factory whose closure would devastate the local community.
- Decide to keep a company's operations in the United States to protect the jobs of American workers rather than move abroad.
- Decide to spend money to improve a new factory so it will not pollute the environment.
- Decline to invest in countries that have poor human rights records.
- Choose to help poor countries develop an economic base to improve living standards.

acceleration; Toyota had to deal with a public relations nightmare as a result. On the other hand, after HP discovered one of its most popular cameras could catch fire if users attempted to recharge ordinary batteries, it quickly announced a software fix for the problem; informing the public was the right thing to do.[47] The way a company announces business problems or admits its mistakes provides strong clues about its stance on social responsibility.

Four Different Approaches

obstructionist approach Companies and their managers choose *not* to behave in a socially responsible way and instead behave unethically and illegally.

The strength of companies' commitment to social responsibility can range from low to high (see Figure 4.6). At the low end of the range is an **obstructionist approach,** in which companies and their managers choose *not* to behave in a socially responsible way. Instead they behave unethically and often illegally and do all they can to prevent knowledge of their behavior from reaching other organizational stakeholders and society at large. Managers at the Manville Corporation adopted this approach when they sought to hide evidence that asbestos causes lung damage; so too did tobacco companies when they sought to hide evidence that cigarette smoking causes lung cancer. In 2010 it was revealed that the managers of Lehman Brothers, whose bankruptcy helped propel the 2008–2009 financial crisis, used loopholes in U.K. law to hide billions of dollars of worthless assets on its balance sheet to disguise its poor financial condition.

Top managers at Enron also acted in an obstructionist way when they prevented employees from selling Enron shares in their pension funds while they sold hundreds of millions of dollars' worth of their own Enron stock. Most employees lost all their retirement savings. Senior partners at Arthur Andersen who instructed their subordinates to shred files chose an obstructionist approach that caused not only a loss of reputation but devastation for the organization and for all stakeholders involved. These companies are no longer in business. The unethical behavior characteristic of the obstructionist approach is exemplified by how PCA's president put his personal interests before customers' health and above the law.

defensive approach Companies and their managers behave ethically to the degree that they stay within the law and strictly abide by legal requirements.

A **defensive approach** indicates at least some commitment to ethical behavior.[48] Defensive companies and managers stay within the law and abide strictly by legal requirements but make no attempt to exercise social responsibility beyond what the law dictates; thus they can and often do act unethically. These are the kinds of companies, like Computer Associates, WorldCom, and Merrill Lynch, that gave their managers large stock options and bonuses even as company performance was declining rapidly. The managers are the kind who sell their stock in advance of other stockholders because they know their company's performance is about to fall. Although acting on inside information is illegal, it is often hard to prove because top managers have wide latitude in when they sell their shares. The founders of most dot-com companies took advantage of this legal loophole to sell billions of dollars of their dot-com shares before their stock prices collapsed. When

Figure 4.6
Four Approaches to Social Responsibility

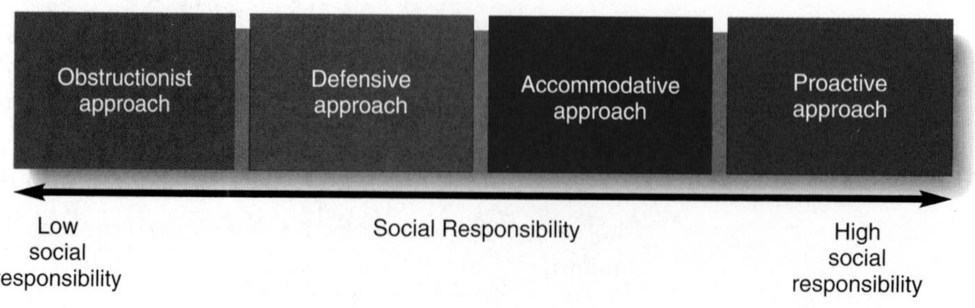

making ethical decisions, such managers put their own interests first and commonly harm other stakeholders.

accommodative approach Companies and their managers behave legally and ethically and try to balance the interests of different stakeholders as the need arises.

An **accommodative approach** acknowledges the need to support social responsibility. Accommodative companies and managers agree that organizational members ought to behave legally and ethically, and they try to balance the interests of different stakeholders so the claims of stockholders are seen in relation to the claims of other stakeholders. Managers adopting this approach want to make choices that are reasonable in the eyes of society and want to do the right thing.

This approach is the one taken by the typical large U.S. company, which has the most to lose from unethical or illegal behavior. Generally, the older and more reputable a company, the more likely its managers are to curb attempts by their subordinates to act unethically. Large companies like GM, Intel, DuPont, and Dell seek every way to build their companies' competitive advantage. Nevertheless, they rein in attempts by their managers to behave unethically or illegally, knowing the grave consequences such behavior can have on future profitability. Sometimes they fail, however, such as when it was revealed in 2009 that senior executives at Intel and AMD gave inside information to a hedge fund manager and received millions in kickbacks.

proactive approach Companies and their managers actively embrace socially responsible behavior, going out of their way to learn about the needs of different stakeholder groups and using organizational resources to promote the interests of all stakeholders.

Companies and managers taking a **proactive approach** actively embrace the need to behave in socially responsible ways. They go out of their way to learn about the needs of different stakeholder groups and are willing to use organizational resources to promote the interests not only of stockholders but also of the other stakeholders such as their employees and communities. U.S. steelmaker Nucor is one such company. In 1977 its visionary CEO Ken Iverson announced that throughout its history Nucor had never laid off one employee, and even though a major recession was raging, it did not plan to start now. In 2009 Nucor CEO Daniel R. DiMicco announced that Nucor again would not start layoffs despite the fact its steel mills were operating at only 50% of capacity (compared to 95% just months earlier) because customers had slashed orders due to the recession. While rivals laid off thousands of employees, Nucor remained loyal to its employees. However, even though there were no layoffs, both managers and employees took major cuts in pay and bonuses to weather the storm together, as they always had, and they searched for ways to reduce operating costs so they would all benefit when the economy recovered.

Proactive companies are often at the forefront of campaigns for causes such as a pollution-free environment; recycling and conservation of resources; the minimization or elimination of the use of animals in drug and cosmetics testing; and the reduction of crime, illiteracy, and poverty. For example, companies like McDonald's, Google, Green Mountain Coffee, Whole Foods, and Target all have reputations for being proactive in the support of stakeholders such as their suppliers or the communities in which they operate.

Why Be Socially Responsible?

Several advantages result when companies and their managers behave in a socially responsible manner. First, demonstrating its social responsibility helps a company build a good reputation. Reputation is the trust, goodwill, and confidence others have in a company that lead them to want to do business with it. The rewards for a good company reputation are increased business and improved ability to obtain resources from stakeholders.[49] Reputation thus can enhance profitability and build stockholder wealth; and behaving responsibly socially is the economically right thing to do because companies that do so benefit from increasing business and rising profits.

A second major reason for companies to act responsibly toward employees, customers, and society is that in a capitalist system companies, as well as the government, have to bear the costs of protecting their stakeholders, providing health care and income, paying taxes, and so on. So if all companies in a society act responsibly, the quality of life as a whole increases.

Wanna bike around the office complex in your blue jeans? Google's model of employee social responsibility lets you do whatever floats your boat—so the company's boat floats higher.

Moreover, how companies behave toward their employees determines many of a society's values and norms and the ethics of its citizens, as already noted. It has been suggested that if all organizations adopted a caring approach and agreed that their responsibility is to promote the interests of their employees, a climate of caring would pervade the wider society. Experts point to Japan, Sweden, Germany, the Netherlands, and Switzerland as countries where organizations are highly socially responsible and where, as a result, crime, poverty, and unemployment rates are relatively low, literacy rates are relatively high, and sociocultural values promote harmony between different groups of people. Business activity affects all aspects of people's lives, so how business behaves toward stakeholders affects how stakeholders behave toward business. You "reap what you sow," as the adage goes.

The Role of Organizational Culture

Although an organization's code of ethics guides decision making when ethical questions arise, managers can go one step further by ensuring that important ethical values and norms are key features of an organization's culture. For example, Herb Kelleher and Coleen Barrett created Southwest Airlines' culture in which promoting employee well-being is a main company priority; this translates into organizational values and norms dictating that layoffs should be avoided and employees should share in the profits the company makes.[50] Google, UPS, and Toyota are among the many companies that espouse similar values. When ethical values and norms such as these are part of an organization's culture, they help organizational members resist self-interested action because they recognize that they are part of something bigger than themselves.[51]

Managers' roles in developing ethical values and standards in other employees are important. Employees naturally look to those in authority to provide leadership, just as a country's citizens look to its political leaders, and managers become ethical role models whose behavior is scrutinized by subordinates. If top managers are perceived as being self-interested and not ethical, their subordinates are not likely to behave in an ethical manner. Employees may think that if it's all right for a top manager to engage in dubious behavior, it's all right for them too, and for employees this might mean slacking off, reducing customer support, and not taking supportive kinds of actions to help their company. The actions of top managers such as CEOs and the president of the United States are scrutinized so closely for ethical improprieties because their actions represent the values of their organizations and, in the case of the president, the values of the nation.

ethics ombudsperson A manager responsible for communicating and teaching ethical standards to all employees and monitoring their conformity to those standards.

Managers can also provide a visible means of support to develop an ethical culture. Increasingly, organizations are creating the role of ethics officer, or **ethics ombudsperson,** to monitor their ethical practices and procedures. The ethics ombudsperson is responsible for communicating ethical standards to all employees, designing systems to monitor employees' conformity to those standards, and teaching managers and employees at all levels of the organization how to respond to ethical dilemmas appropriately.[52] Because the ethics ombudsperson has organizationwide authority, organizational members in any department can communicate instances of unethical behavior by their managers or coworkers without fear of retribution. This arrangement makes it easier for everyone to behave ethically. In addition, ethics ombudspeople can provide guidance when organizational members are uncertain about whether an action is ethical. Some organizations have an organizationwide ethics committee to provide guidance on ethical issues and help write and update the company code of ethics.

Ethical organizational cultures encourage organizational members to behave in a socially responsible manner. In fact, managers at Johnson & Johnson take social responsibility so seriously that their organization is often held up as an example of a socially responsible firm. The Johnson & Johnson Credo (see Figure 4.7) is one of many ways in which social responsibility is emphasized at the company. As discussed in the following "Ethics in Action" box, Johnson & Johnson's ethical organizational culture gives the company and its various stakeholder groups numerous benefits.

Figure 4.7
Johnson & Johnson's Credo

Our Credo

We believe our first responsibility is to the doctors, nurses and patients,
to mothers and fathers and all others who use our products and services.
In meeting their needs everything we do must be of high quality.
We must constantly strive to reduce our costs
in order to maintain reasonable prices.
Customers' orders must be serviced promptly and accurately.
Our suppliers and distributors must have an opportunity
to make a fair profit.

We are responsible to our employees,
the men and women who work with us throughout the world.
Everyone must be considered as an individual.
We must respect their dignity and recognize their merit.
They must have a sense of security in their jobs.
Compensation must be fair and adequate,
and working conditions clean, orderly and safe.
We must be mindful of ways to help our employees fulfill
their family responsibilities.
Employees must feel free to make suggestions and complaints.
There must be equal opportunity for employment, development
and advancement for those qualified.
We must provide competent management,
and their actions must be just and ethical.

We are responsible to the communities in which we live and work
and to the world community as well.
We must be good citizens—support good works and charities
and bear our fair share of taxes.
We must encourage civic improvements and better health and education.
We must maintain in good order
the property we are privileged to use,
protecting the environment and natural resources.

Our final responsibility is to our stockholders.
Business must make a sound profit.
We must experiment with new ideas.
Research must be carried on, innovative programs developed
and mistakes paid for.
New equipment must be purchased, new facilities provided
and new products launched.
Reserves must be created to provide for adverse times.
When we operate according to these principles,
the stockholders should realize a fair return.

Johnson & Johnson

Source: © Johnson & Johnson. Used with permission.

Ethics in Action

Johnson & Johnson's Ethical Culture

Johnson & Johnson (J&J) is so well known for its ethical culture that it has been judged as having the best corporate reputation for two years in a row, based on a survey of over 26,000 consumers conducted by Harris Interactive and the Reputation Institute at New York University.[53] J&J grew from a family business led by General Robert Wood Johnson in the 1930s to a major maker of pharmaceutical and medical products. Attesting to the role of managers in creating ethical organizational cultures, Johnson emphasized the importance of ethics and responsibility to stakeholders and wrote the first J&J Credo in 1943.[54]

The credo continues to guide employees at J&J today and outlines the company's commitments to its different stakeholder groups. It emphasizes that the organization's first responsibility is to doctors, nurses, patients, and consumers. Following this group are suppliers and distributors, employees, communities, and finally stockholders.[55] This credo has served managers and employees at Johnson & Johnson well and has guided some difficult decision making, such as the decision to recall all Tylenol capsules in the U.S. market after cyanide-laced capsules killed seven people in Chicago.

True to its ethical culture and outstanding reputation, Johnson & Johnson always puts consumer well-being before profit considerations. For example, around 20 years ago J&J's baby oil was used as a tanning product when the harmful effects of sun exposure were not well known by the public.[56] The product manager for baby oil at the time, Carl Spalding, was making a presentation to top management about marketing plans when the company's president, David Clare, mentioned that tanning might not be healthful.[57] Before launching his planned marketing campaign, Spalding looked into the health-related concerns connected with tanning and discovered some evidence suggesting that health problems could arise from too much exposure to the sun. Even though the evidence was not definitive, Spalding recommended that baby oil should no longer be marketed as a tanning aid–a decision that cut sales by 50% and cost the company over $5 million.[58]

The ethical values and norms in Johnson & Johnson's culture, along with its credo, guide managers such as Spalding to make the right decision in difficult situations. Hence it is understandable why J&J is renowned for its corporate reputation. An ethical culture and outstanding reputation have other benefits, too. Jeanne Hamway, vice president for recruiting, finds that Johnson & Johnson's reputation helps the company recruit and attract a diverse workforce.[59] Moreover, when organizations develop an outstanding reputation, their employees often are less tempted to act in a self-interested or unethical manner. For example, managers at Johnson & Johnson suggest that because employees in the company never accept bribes, the company is known as one in which bribes should not be offered in the first place.[60] All in all, ethical cultures such as J&J's benefit various stakeholder groups in multiple ways.

Summary and Review

THE NATURE OF ETHICS Ethical issues are central to how companies and their managers make decisions, and they affect not only the efficiency and effectiveness of company operations but also the prosperity of the nation. The result of ethical behavior is a general increase in company performance and in a nation's standard of living, well-being, and wealth.

LO4-1

An ethical dilemma is the quandary people find themselves in when they have to decide if they should act in a way that might help another person or group and is the right thing to do, even though it might go against their own self-interest. Ethics are the inner guiding moral principles, values, and beliefs that people use to analyze or interpret a situation and then decide what is the right or appropriate way to behave.

Ethical beliefs alter and change as time passes, and as they do so laws change to reflect the changing ethical beliefs of a society.

LO4-2, 4-4 **STAKEHOLDERS AND ETHICS** Stakeholders are people and groups who have a claim on and a stake in a company. The main stakeholder groups are stockholders, managers, employees, suppliers and distributors, customers, and the community, society, and nation. Companies and their managers need to make ethical business decisions that promote the well-being of their stakeholders and avoid doing them harm.

LO4-3, 4-5 To determine whether a business decision is ethical, managers can use four ethical rules to analyze it: the utilitarian, moral rights, justice, and practical rules. Managers should behave ethically because this avoids the tragedy of the commons and results in a general increase in efficiency, effectiveness, and company performance. The main determinants of differences in a manager's, company's, and country's business ethics are societal, occupational, individual, and organizational.

LO4-6 **ETHICS AND SOCIAL RESPONSIBILITY** A company's stance on social responsibility is the way its managers and employees view their duty or obligation to make decisions that protect, enhance, and promote the welfare and well-being of stakeholders and society as a whole.

There are four main approaches to social responsibility: obstructionist, defensive, accommodative, and proactive. The rewards from behaving in a socially responsible way are a good reputation, the support of all organizational stakeholders, and thus superior company performance.

Management in Action

Topics for Discussion and Action

Discussion

1. What is the relationship between ethics and the law? [LO4-1]
2. Why do the claims and interests of stakeholders sometimes conflict? [LO4-2]
3. Why should managers use ethical criteria to guide their decision making? [LO4-3]
4. As an employee of a company, what are some of the most unethical business practices that you have encountered in its dealings with stakeholders? [LO4-4]
5. What are the main determinants of business ethics? [LO4-5]

Action

6. Find a manager and ask about the most important ethical rules he or she uses to make the right decisions. [LO4-3]
7. Find an example of (a) a company that has an obstructionist approach to social responsibility and (b) one that has an accommodative approach. [LO4-6]

Building Management Skills

Dealing with Ethical Dilemmas [LO4-1, 4-4]

Use the chapter material to decide how you, as a manager, should respond to each of the following ethical dilemmas:

1. You are planning to leave your job to go work for a competitor; your boss invites you to an important meeting where you will learn about new products your company will be bringing out next year. Do you go to the meeting?
2. You're the manager of sales in an expensive sports car dealership. A young executive who has just received a promotion comes in and wants to buy a car that you know is out of her price range. Do you encourage the executive to buy it so you can receive a big commission on the sale?
3. You sign a contract to manage a young rock band, and that group agrees to let you produce their next seven records, for which they will receive royalties of 5%. Their first record is a smash hit and sells millions. Do you increase their royalty rate on future records?

Managing Ethically [LO4-3, 4-5]

Apple Juice or Sugar Water?

In the early 1980s Beech-Nut, a maker of baby foods, was in grave financial trouble as it strove to compete with Gerber Products, the market leader. Threatened with bankruptcy if it could not lower its operating costs, Beech-Nut entered an agreement with a low-cost supplier of apple juice concentrate. The agreement would save the company over $250,000 annually when every dollar counted. Soon one of Beech-Nut's food scientists became concerned about the quality of the concentrate. He believed it was not made from apples alone but contained large quantities of corn syrup and cane sugar. He brought this information to the attention of top managers at Beech-Nut, but they were obsessed with the need to keep costs down and chose to ignore his concerns. The company continued to produce and sell its product as pure apple juice.[61]

Eventually investigators from the U.S. Food and Drug Administration (FDA) confronted Beech-Nut with evidence that the concentrate was adulterated. The top managers issued denials and quickly shipped the remaining stock of apple juice to the market before their inventory could be seized. The scientist who had questioned the purity of the apple juice had resigned from Beech-Nut, but he decided to blow the whistle on the company. He told the FDA that Beech-Nut's top management had known of the problem with the concentrate and had acted to maximize company profits rather than to inform customers about the additives in the apple juice. In 1987 the company pleaded guilty to charges that it had deliberately sold adulterated juice and was fined over $2 million. Its top managers were also found guilty and were sentenced to prison terms. The company's reputation was ruined, and it was eventually sold to Ralston Purina, now owned by Nestlé, which installed a new management team and a new ethical code of values to guide future business decisions.

Questions

1. Why is it that an organization's values and norms can become too strong and lead to unethical behavior?
2. What steps can a company take to prevent this problem—to stop its values and norms from becoming so inwardly focused that managers and employees lose sight of their responsibility to their stakeholders?

Small Group Breakout Exercise

Is Chewing Gum the "Right" Thing to Do? [LO4-1, 4-3]

Form groups of three or four people, and appoint one member as the spokesperson who will communicate your findings to the class when called on by the instructor. Then discuss the following scenario:

In the United States the right to chew gum is taken for granted. Although it is often against the rules to chew gum in a high school classroom, church, and so on, it is legal to do so on the street. If you possess or chew gum on a street in Singapore, you can be arrested. Chewing gum has been made illegal in Singapore because those in power believe it creates a mess on pavements and feel that people cannot be trusted to dispose of their gum properly and thus should have no right to use it.

1. What makes chewing gum acceptable in the United States and unacceptable in Singapore?
2. Why can you chew gum on the street but not in a church?
3. How can you use ethical principles to decide when gum chewing is ethical or unethical and if and when it should be made illegal?

Exploring the World Wide Web [LO4-2, 4-5]

Go to Walmart's Web site (www.walmart.com) and read the information there about the company's stance on the ethics of global outsourcing and the treatment of workers in countries abroad. Then search the Web for some recent stories about Walmart's global purchasing practices and reports on the enforcement of its code of conduct.

1. What ethical principles guide Walmart's approach to global purchasing?
2. Does Walmart appear to be doing a good job of enforcing its global code of conduct?

Be the Manager [LO4-3]

Creating an Ethical Code

You are an entrepreneur who has decided to go into business and open a steak and chicken restaurant. Your business plan requires that you hire at least 20 people as chefs, waiters, and so on. As the owner, you are drawing up a list of ethical principles that each of these people will receive and must agree to when he or she accepts a job offer. These principles outline your view of what is right or acceptable behavior and what will be expected both from you and from your employees.

Create a list of the five main ethical rules or principles you will use to govern how your business operates. Be sure to spell out how these principles relate to your stakeholders; for example, state the rules you intend to follow in dealing with your employees and customers.

Case in the News [LO4-1, 4-3, 4-5]

America's High-Tech Sweatshops

Vimal Patel was studying for a master's in business administration in London when he saw an advertisement for work in the United States. The ad offered a job in the tech industry, as well as sponsorship for the kind of work visa that allows foreign nationals to take professional-level jobs in the country. So Patel applied and paid his prospective employer, Cygate Software & Consulting, in Edison, New Jersey, thousands of dollars in up-front fees. But when Patel arrived, Cygate had no tech job for him. He ended up working at a gas station, and Cygate nevertheless took a chunk of his wages for years, according to documents in a criminal case against Cygate. After a federal investigation into Cygate, Patel and five other natives of India recruited by the company pled guilty to visa violations in June. They were sentenced to 12 to 18 months of probation, assessed fines of $2,000 each, and now face deportation. But at Patel's sentencing in the federal courthouse in Newark, New Jersey, his lawyer said the slim 36-year-old, with a mop of brown hair spilling over his forehead, was more victim than villain. Like many ambitious workers from abroad, he came to the country seeking his fortune, and he suffered for the effort. "It's a sad day," said Anthony Thomas, the public defender assigned to represent Patel. "He always dreamed of coming to the United States."

Cygate, which changed its name to Sterling System after the lawsuit, is one of thousands of low-profile companies that have come to play a central role in the U.S. tech industry in recent years. These companies, many with just 10 to 50 employees, recruit workers from abroad and, when possible, place them at U.S. corporations to provide tech support, software programming, and other services. While many outfits operate legally and provide high-quality talent, there is growing evidence that others violate U.S. laws and mistreat their recruits.

Several types of fraud have become common, according to documents from recent lawsuits and interviews with foreign workers, employers, lawyers, and consultants. In some cases companies target young men and women hungry to get well-paid tech jobs in the United States and charge them exorbitant fees for visas, which is not allowed under American immigration laws. Even after paying, some workers never get a visa; those who do may find the company they paid has no job for them, as Patel did. This violates U.S. law because companies are supposed to have an open position before they apply for a work visa. Workers who land tech jobs may face other kinds of trouble. Some companies place foreign workers at client sites and then siphon off part of their pay or charge ongoing fees, which violates U.S. law. Many workers allege they're not paid in between jobs at client sites, though such "benching" without pay isn't allowed either. In other cases, companies claim they're employing people in low-salary regions when they're actually working in high-wage areas, in violation of rules requiring payment of the region's prevailing wage.

Sterling President Nilesh Dasondi was charged with multiple counts of visa violations in the case filed by the U.S. attorney in New Jersey. The government says he collected fees of up to $15,000 from the six workers, left them to find jobs on their own, and extracted more fees to launder their pay through his company. The workers acquiesced because Dasondi, like all employers of visa recipients, held their H1-B temporary work visa documents and could have revoked the papers if they objected. "This is a microcosm of a big issue that's facing our country—visa fraud," said Sandra L. Moser, the assistant U.S. attorney prosecuting the case in an interview after Patel's sentencing.

"Body Shops"

Tech service outfits such as Sterling have thrived in recent years because of shifts in the U.S. economy. As cost-cutting pressures have increased, companies turned over management of tech systems and other back-office operations to outsourcing firms, including many that bring workers from India and other countries into the United States on temporary visas such as the H-1B. One important way outsourcers hold down costs is by keeping a lean workforce at each client site—then turning to smaller companies, such as Sterling, when they need to increase staff for specific projects, such as installing new software or building a new Web site. These companies are known as "body shops" because of their role, and often rely heavily on foreign workers who come into the country on H-1Bs and other visas. A study by the federal government last year estimated that 54% of visa rule violations were committed by companies with fewer than 25 employees. U.S. companies usually don't know—and don't press to find out—which body shops are tapped to support their tech operations. The result is that prominent American companies can easily end up doing business with tech service outfits that violate visa laws.

In recent months workers have alleged mistreatment while working for body shops in the offices of Computer Associates, Qualcomm, and JPMorgan Chase. In a civil suit filed in May and a complaint to the U.S. Labor Dept., for example, Prasad Nair charged that Unified Business Technologies got him an H-1B visa in 2007 by saying he would work in the company's Troy (Michigan) offices and receive $60,000 a year as a programmer and analyst. Instead UBT sent him to work at chipmaker Qualcomm's offices in San Diego, where the cost of living and prevailing wage for such a position are much higher. The 32-year-old alleged UBT made unlawful pay deductions, delayed payments, failed to pay overtime, and postponed health benefits for his family. David Blanchard, Nair's attorney, says he struggled "paycheck to paycheck" to take care of his wife and 9-month-old daughter and to save money. UBT's lawyer, John G. Coutilish, says Nair's charges are "baseless." Coutilish says UBT agreed to make a "nuisance" payment of $2,500 to end the civil suit, though the Labor Department investigation is continuing. Qualcomm declined to comment on the case, but a spokeswoman says the company requires vendors it works with to "explicitly acknowledge that they must comply with all applicable laws and regulations, including employment and immigration laws."

U.S. executives often have little visibility into the treatment of contract employees because several layers of companies are involved. One recruiter for a major U.S. outsourcing firm says there's no way his clients know how body shop workers are treated because, until recently, even he didn't know. He discovered that some of the firms he was hiring for short-term projects weren't using their own people but instead were bringing in subcontractors, which often were underpaid workers. He just put in place new policies so he knows when a firm he hires is using a subcontractor, but he still can't find out how much workers are paid or in which state they're supposed to be working. "We don't like it," he says. "The agreements seem almost criminal."

Ron Hira, an assistant professor of public policy at the Rochester Institute of Technology, says the situation is similar to what happened years ago when Western companies began using sweatshops in China for manufacturing. Companies such as Nike sought to lower costs by using overseas manufacturers, which in turn squeezed workers with low pay and poor working conditions. After a public outcry, Nike, Disney, and others started to monitor labor standards abroad. American companies may know little about the tech contractors who work for them in the United States now, but Hira says companies should take steps to track the situation more closely. "I don't know of any [top executives] who have made an issue of this," he says. "We haven't had a public discussion of what the clients' responsibility is." Foreign workers aren't waiting for American companies or the U.S. government to address the issue of high-tech sweatshops. They've set up Web sites to discuss their experiences with different companies; they talk anonymously and steer one another away from the worst employers, which are like "an H-1B prison camp."

Questions for Discussion

1. What kinds of unethical and illegal kinds of behaviors do high-tech sweatshop companies engage in? What criteria should these companies use to decide if they are treating their overseas employees fairly?
2. How would you characterize the stance on social responsibility of companies that function as body shops?
3. In what ways can developing an ethical approach to managing outsourcing—whether inside the United States or in countries abroad—affect the well-being and performance of both employees and the companies they work for?

Source: S. Hamm and M. Herbst, "America's High-Tech Sweatshops," *BusinessWeek*, October 1, 2009. Reprinted from October 1, 2009 issue of *Bloomberg Businessweek* by special permission, copyright © 2009 by Bloomberg L.P.

CHAPTER 5

Managing Diverse Employees in a Multicultural Environment

Learning Objectives

After studying this chapter, you should be able to:

LO5-1 Discuss the increasing diversity of the workforce and the organizational environment.

LO5-2 Explain the central role that managers play in the effective management of diversity.

LO5-3 Explain why the effective management of diversity is both an ethical and a business imperative.

LO5-4 Discuss how perception and the use of schemas can result in unfair treatment.

LO5-5 List the steps managers can take to effectively manage diversity.

LO5-6 Identify the two major forms of sexual harassment and how they can be eliminated.

A MANAGER'S CHALLENGE

Effectively Managing Diversity at Sodexo and Principal Financial Group

How can managers reap the benefits of an increasingly diverse workforce? By all counts, the diversity of the workforce is increasing. Effectively managing diversity is more than just ensuring that diverse members of organizations are treated fairly (itself a challenging task). When diversity is effectively managed, organizations can benefit from the diverse perspectives, points of view, experiences, and knowledge bases of their diverse members to produce better goods and services and be responsive to their increasingly diverse customer bases.

Extolling the benefits of effectively managing diversity is one thing; taking real and tangible steps to ensure that an organization continuously improves in this regard is another. Both organizationwide initiatives and the steps that each individual manager takes to effectively manage diversity have the potential for substantial payoffs in terms of both improved organizational effectiveness and maintaining a satisfied, committed, and motivated workforce.

Consider the steps that Sodexo, Inc., a major food and facilities management company serving over 10 million customers per day in businesses, health care facilities, schools and universities, and government agencies, takes to ensure that diversity is effectively managed.[1] Sodexo encourages managers like Ron Bond, in his late 50s, to interact with diverse groups to gain a better appreciation and understanding of their experiences. When Bond attended a meeting of the Women's Food Service Forum with some of his female coworkers, he stood out as one of the few men in attendance among 1,500 women. Thinking back on his own experiences when, for example, he started out his career and women were rare in the management ranks, Bond gained a deeper appreciation of what it means to be different in a group

Managers at Sodexo, which supplies and manages cafeterias like this one, have taken numerous steps to effectively manage diversity.

or organization. As he suggests, "That's a profound experience . . . I can begin to feel what it must have felt like to be different."[2]

Sodexo provides employees and managers with extensive diversity training, encourages managers to mentor and coach employees who are different from themselves, and bases 25% of top managers' bonuses on their performance on diversity initiatives, including hiring and training diverse employees.[3] Managers are encouraged to sponsor affinity groups for employees that differ from themselves. For example, Bond sponsored the women's affinity group, which provides a forum for female employees to connect with each other and address their mutual concerns (such as a lactation room so new mothers can pump breast milk). Sponsoring such groups helps managers become aware of and address concerns of some employee groups they might never have thought of otherwise. Bond realized that having a lactation room was "just one of those things I'd never thought about."[4]

Lorna Donatone manages a unit of Sodexo that provides food services for cruise companies. Of Swedish and German ancestry and raised in Nebraska, she sponsored Sodexo's Latino affinity group and discovered a better way to serve her unit's customers. Donatone now relies on more bilingual materials to promote the services she provides to cruise companies and their customers. As senior vice president and global chief diversity officer for Sodexo, Dr. Rohini Anand indicates, "To really engage people, you have to create a series of epiphanies and take leaders through those epiphanies."[5]

Sodexo's effective management of diversity has not gone unnoticed in the business community, and the company and its diverse employees have received numerous awards and recognition for their diversity initiatives.[6] Frequently ranked as a best place to work for diverse employees by magazines such as *DiversityInc.*, *Working Mother,* and *Latina Style,* Sodexo recently received the DiversityFirst Leadership Award from the Texas Diversity Council.[7] Dr. Anand recently was named one of the Top 20 Diversity Champions by *Diversity Edge* magazine, and Ivan Gutierrez, who heads up Sodexo's supply management unit, was recently named one of 28 Young Hispanic Corporate Achievers by the Hispanic Association on Corporate Responsibility.[8]

Principal Financial Group, headquartered in Des Moines, Iowa, operates in a vastly different industry: financial products, services, and insurance.[9] Yet Principal Financial also has been recognized for its effective management of diversity by *Fortune* magazine; Principal earned the second highest rating in 2010 Corporate Equality Index of the Human Rights Campaign.[10] To ensure that opportunities are open for diverse employees, Principal has offered its employees flexible work schedules since 1974—decades before many other companies provided this option. And employees who take advantage of this and other benefits, such as having 12 weeks off work after the birth of a child, do not find their career progress hampered as is sometimes the case at other companies.[11]

Valarie Vest, a regional client service director at Principal, was on her second maternity leave when her supervisors called to offer her a promotion to a position that included more responsibility, more travel, and relocation to a different city. They thought she was the best candidate for the position and let her decide if she wanted to take it. She was delighted to accept the position, which includes managing 10 employees.[12]

Principal seeks to hire diverse employees and then gives them the resources and opportunities to help them reach their potential while helping Principal achieve its goals. These resources and opportunities include, but are not limited to, mentoring programs, multicultural celebrations, on-site child care, development programs, and domestic partner benefits.[13] Additionally, there are a variety of employee resource groups that all employees can join to network, engage in career development activities, and become involved in the community.[14]

All in all, Sodexo and Principal Financial Group are among the growing numbers of companies that are reaping the benefits of an increasingly diverse workforce.

Overview

As indicated in "A Manager's Challenge," effective management of diversity means much more than hiring diverse employees. It means learning to appreciate and respond appropriately to the needs, attitudes, beliefs, and values that diverse people bring to an organization. It also means correcting misconceptions about why and how various kinds of employee groups differ from one another and finding the most effective way to use the skills and talents of diverse employees.

In this chapter we focus on the effective management of diversity in an environment that is becoming increasingly diverse in all respects. Not only is the diversity of the global workforce increasing, but suppliers and customers are also becoming increasingly diverse. Managers need to proactively manage diversity to attract and retain the best employees and effectively compete in a diverse global environment. For example, managers at the audit and consulting firm Deloitte & Touche have instituted a program to encourage minority suppliers to compete for its business, and the firm sponsors schools and colleges that supply a stream of well-trained recruits.[15]

LO5-1 Discuss the increasing diversity of the workforce and the organizational environment.

Sometimes well-intentioned managers inadvertently treat one group of employees differently from another group, even though there are no performance-based differences between the two groups. This chapter explores why differential treatment occurs and the steps managers and organizations can take to ensure that diversity, in all respects, is effectively managed for the good of all organizational stakeholders.

The Increasing Diversity of the Workforce and the Environment

One of the most important management issues to emerge over the last 30 years has been the increasing diversity of the workforce. **Diversity** is dissimilarities–differences–among people due to age, gender, race, ethnicity, religion, sexual orientation, socioeconomic background, education, experience, physical appearance, capabilities/disabilities, and any other characteristic that is used to distinguish between people (see Figure 5.1).

Diversity raises important ethical issues and social responsibility issues (see Chapter 4). It is also a critical issue for organizations, one that if not handled well can bring an organization to its knees, especially in our increasingly global environment. There are several reasons why diversity is such a pressing concern and issue both in the popular press and for managers and organizations:

diversity Differences among people in age, gender, race, ethnicity, religion, sexual orientation, socioeconomic background, and capabilities/disabilities.

- There is a strong ethical imperative in many societies that diverse people must receive equal opportunities and be treated fairly and justly. Unfair treatment is also illegal.

Figure 5.1
Sources of Diversity in the Workplace

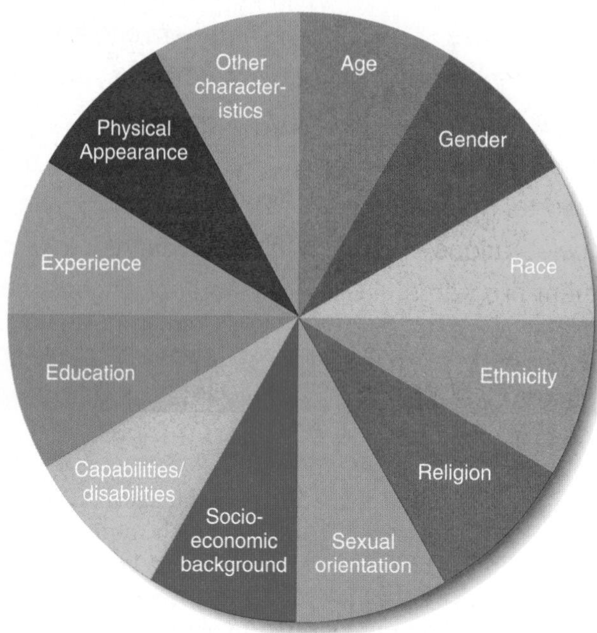

- Effectively managing diversity can improve organizational effectiveness.[16] When managers effectively manage diversity, they not only encourage other managers to treat diverse members of an organization fairly and justly but also realize that diversity is an important organizational resource that can help an organization gain a competitive advantage.
- There is substantial evidence that diverse individuals continue to experience unfair treatment in the workplace as a result of biases, stereotypes, and overt discrimination.[17] In one study, résumés of equally qualified men and women were sent to high-priced Philadelphia restaurants (where potential earnings are high). Though equally qualified, men were more than twice as likely as women to be called for a job interview and more than five times as likely to receive a job offer.[18] Findings from another study suggest that both women and men tend to believe that women will accept lower pay than men; this is a possible explanation for the continuing gap in pay between men and women.[19]

Other kinds of diverse employees may face even greater barriers. For example, the federal Glass Ceiling Commission Report indicated that African-Americans have the hardest time being promoted and climbing the corporate ladder, that Asians are often stereotyped into technical jobs, and that Hispanics are assumed to be less well educated than other minority groups.[20] (The term **glass ceiling** alludes to the invisible barriers that prevent minorities and women from being promoted to top corporate positions.)[21]

glass ceiling A metaphor alluding to the invisible barriers that prevent minorities and women from being promoted to top corporate positions.

Before we can discuss the multitude of issues surrounding the effective management of diversity, we must document just how diverse the U.S. workforce is becoming.

Age

According to data from the U.S. Census Bureau, the median age of a person in the United States is the highest it has ever been, 36.2 years.[22] Moreover, by 2030 it is projected that 20% of the population will be over 65.[23] The Age Discrimination in Employment Act of 1967 prohibits age discrimination.[24] Although we discuss federal

Table 5.1
Major Equal Employment Opportunity Laws Affecting Human Resources Management

Year	Law	Description
1963	Equal Pay Act	Requires that men and women be paid equally if they are performing equal work.
1964	Title VII of the Civil Rights Act	Prohibits discrimination in employment decisions on the basis of race, religion, sex, color, or national origin; covers a wide range of employment decisions, including hiring, firing, pay, promotion, and working conditions.
1967	Age Discrimination in Employment Act	Prohibits discrimination against workers over the age of 40 and restricts mandatory retirement.
1978	Pregnancy Discrimination Act	Prohibits discrimination against women in employment decisions on the basis of pregnancy, childbirth, and related medical decisions.
1990	Americans with Disabilities Act	Prohibits discrimination against disabled individuals in employment decisions and requires that employers make accommodations for disabled workers to enable them to perform their jobs.
1991	Civil Rights Act	Prohibits discrimination (as does Title VII) and allows for the awarding of punitive and compensatory damages, in addition to back pay, in cases of intentional discrimination.
1993	Family and Medical Leave Act	Requires that employers provide 12 weeks of unpaid leave for medical and family reasons, including paternity and illness of a family member.

employment legislation in more depth in Chapter 12, major equal employment opportunity legislation that prohibits discrimination among diverse groups is summarized in Table 5.1.

The aging of the population suggests managers need to be vigilant to ensure that employees are not discriminated against because of age. Moreover, managers need to ensure that the policies and procedures they have in place treat all workers fairly, regardless of their ages. Additionally, effectively managing diversity means employees of diverse ages are able to learn from each other, work well together, and take advantage of the different perspectives each has to offer.

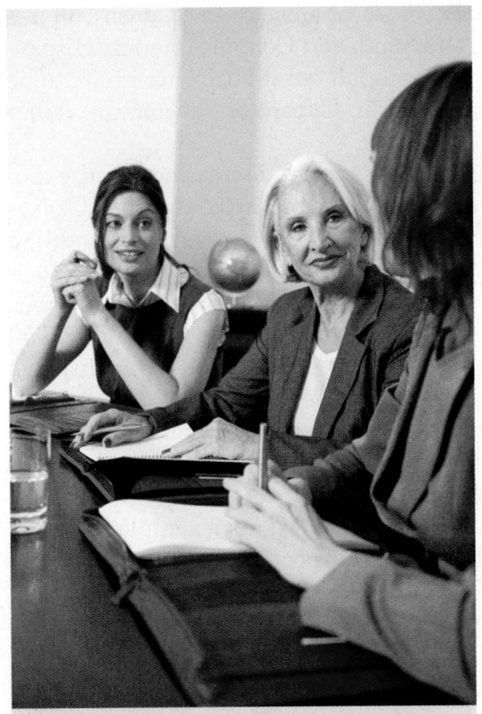

Age and gender discrimination on the job are both alive and well, despite burgeoning legislation against them. Managing for diversity includes not just avoiding bad behavior but also learning how to respect and value others' differences.

Gender

Women and men are almost equally represented in the U.S. workforce (approximately 53.5% of the U.S. workforce is male and 46.5% female),[25] yet women's median weekly earnings are estimated to be $638 compared to $798 for men.[26] Thus the gender pay gap appears to be as alive and well as the glass ceiling. According to the nonprofit organization Catalyst, which studies women in business, while women compose about 50.5% of the employees in managerial and professional positions, only around 15.4% of corporate officers in the 500 largest U.S. companies (that is, the *Fortune* 500) are women, and only 6.7% of the top earners are women.[27] These women, such as Andrea Jung, CEO of Avon Products, and Indra Nooyi, CEO of Pepsico, stand out among their male peers and often receive a disparate amount of attention in the media. (We address this issue later, when we discuss the effects of being salient.) Women are also very underrepresented on boards of directors–they currently hold 14.8% of the board seats of *Fortune* 500 companies.[28] However, as Sheila Wellington, president of Catalyst, indicates, "Women either control or influence nearly all consumer purchases, so it's important to have their perspective represented on boards."[29]

Additionally, research conducted by consulting firms suggests that female executives outperform their male colleagues in skills such as motivating others, promoting good communication, turning out high-quality work, and being a good listener.[30] For example, the Hagberg Group performed in-depth evaluations of 425 top executives in a variety of industries, with each executive rated by approximately 25 people. Of the 52 skills assessed, women received higher ratings than men on 42 skills, although at times the differences were small.[31] Results of a recent study conducted by Catalyst found that organizations with higher proportions of women in top management positions had significantly better financial performance than organizations with lower proportions of female top managers.[32] Another study conducted by Catalyst found that companies with three or more women on their boards of directors performed better in terms of returns on equity, sales, and invested capital than companies with fewer women on their boards or no women.[33] All in all, studies such as these make one wonder why the glass ceiling continues to hamper the progress of women in business (a topic we address later in the chapter).

Race and Ethnicity

The U.S. Census Bureau distinguished between the following races in the 2010 Census: American Indian or Alaska Native, Asian Indian, Black, African American, or Negro, Chinese, Filipino, Japanese, Korean, Vietnamese, Other Asian, Native Hawaiian, Guamanian or Chamorro, Samoan, Other Pacific Islander, White, and other races.[34] Although *ethnicity* refers to a grouping of people based on some shared characteristic such as national origin, language, or culture, the U.S. Census Bureau treats ethnicity in terms of whether a person is Hispanic, Latino, or of Spanish origin or not.[35] Hispanics, also referred to as Latinos, are people whose origins are in Spanish cultures such as those of Cuba, Mexico, Puerto Rico, and South and Central America. Hispanics can be of different races.[36] According to a recent poll, most Hispanics prefer to be identified by their country of origin (such as Mexican, Cuban, or Salvadoran) rather than by the overarching term *Hispanic*.[37]

The racial and ethnic diversity of the U.S. population is increasing at an exponential rate, as is the composition of the workforce.[38] According to the U.S. Census Bureau, approximately one of every three U.S. residents belongs to a minority group (is not a non-Hispanic white); approximately 67% of the population is white, 13.4% is African-American, 14.4% is Hispanic, and 4.8% is Asian.[39] According to projections released by the U.S. Census Bureau, the composition of the U.S. population in 2050 will be quite different from its composition in 2000. It is estimated that the Hispanic and Asian populations will triple during this 50-year period.[40]

The increasing racial and ethnic diversity of the workforce and the population as a whole underscores the importance of effectively managing diversity. Statistics compiled by the National Urban League suggest that much needs to be done in terms of ensuring that diverse employees have equal opportunities. For example, African-Americans' earnings are approximately 73% of the earnings of whites;[41] and of 10,092 corporate officers in *Fortune* 500 companies, only 106 are African-American women.[42] In the remainder of this chapter, we focus on the fair treatment of diverse employees and explore why this is such an important challenge and what managers can do to meet it. We begin by taking a broader perspective and considering how increasing racial and ethnic diversity in an organization's environment (such as customers and suppliers) affects decision making and organizational effectiveness.

At a general level, managers and organizations are increasingly being reminded that stakeholders in the environment are diverse and expect organizational decisions and actions to reflect this diversity. For example, the NAACP (National Association for the Advancement of Colored People) and Children Now (an advocacy group) have lobbied the entertainment industry to increase the diversity in television programming, writing, and producing.[43] The need for such increased diversity is more than apparent. For example, while Hispanics make up 12.5% of the U.S. population (or 35 million potential TV viewers), only about 2% of the characters in prime-time TV shows are Hispanics (of the 2,251 characters in prime-time shows, only 47 are Hispanic), according to a study conducted by Children Now.[44] Moreover, only about 1.3% of the evening network TV news stories are reported by Hispanic correspondents, according to the Center for Media and Public Affairs.[45]

Pressure is mounting on networks to increase diversity for a variety of reasons revolving around the diversity of the population as a whole, TV viewers, and consumers. For example, home and automobile buyers are increasingly diverse, reflecting the increasing diversity of the population as a whole.[46] Moreover, managers have to be especially sensitive to avoid stereotyping different groups when they communicate with potential customers. For example, Toyota Motor Sales USA made a public apology to the Reverend Jesse Jackson and his Rainbow Coalition for using a print advertisement depicting an African-American man with a Toyota RAV4 sport utility image embossed on his gold front tooth.[47]

Religion

Title VII of the Civil Rights Act prohibits discrimination based on religion (as well as based on race/ethnicity, country of origin, and sex; see Table 5.1 and Chapter 12). In addition to enacting Title VII, in 1997 the federal government issued "The White House Guidelines on Religious Exercise and Expression in the Federal Workplace."[48] These guidelines, while technically applicable only in federal offices, also are frequently relied on by large corporations. The guidelines require that employers make reasonable accommodations for religious practices, such as observances of holidays, as long as doing so does not entail major costs or hardships.[49]

A key issue for managers when it comes to religious diversity is recognizing and being aware of different religions and their beliefs, with particular attention being paid to when religious holidays fall. For example, critical meetings should not be scheduled during a holy day for members of a certain faith, and managers should be flexible in allowing people to have time off for religious observances. According to Lobna Ismail, director of a diversity training company in Silver Spring, Maryland, when managers acknowledge, respect, and make even small accommodations for religious diversity, employee loyalty is often enhanced. For example, allowing employees to leave work early on certain days instead of taking a lunch break or posting holidays for different religions on the company calendar can go a long way toward making individuals of diverse religions feel respected and valued as well as enabling them to practice their faith.[50] According to research conducted by the Tanenbaum Center for Interreligious Understanding in New York, while only about 23% of employees who feel they are victims of religious discrimination actually file complaints, about 45% of these employees start looking for other jobs.[51]

Capabilities/Disabilities

The Americans with Disabilities Act (ADA) of 1990 prohibits discrimination against persons with disabilities and also requires that employers make reasonable accommodations to enable these people to effectively perform their jobs. On the surface, few would argue with the intent of this legislation. However, as managers attempt to implement policies and procedures to comply with the ADA, they face a number of interpretation and fairness challenges.

On one hand, some people with real disabilities warranting workplace accommodations are hesitant to reveal their disabilities to their employers and claim the accommodations they deserve.[52] On the other hand, some employees abuse the ADA by seeking unnecessary accommodations for disabilities that may or may not exist.[53] Thus it is perhaps not surprising that the passage of the ADA does not appear to have increased employment rates significantly for those with disabilities.[54] A key challenge for managers is to promote an environment in which employees needing accommodations feel comfortable disclosing their need and, at the same time, to ensure that the accommodations not only enable those with disabilities to effectively perform their jobs but also are perceived to be fair by those not disabled.[55]

In addressing this challenge, often managers must educate both themselves and their employees about the disabilities, as well as the real capabilities, of those who are disabled. For example, during Disability Awareness Week, administrators at the University of Notre Dame sought to increase the public's knowledge of disabilities while also heightening awareness of the abilities of persons who are disabled.[56] The University of Houston conducted a similar program called "Think Ability."[57] According to Cheryl Amoruso, director of the University of Houston's Center for Students with Disabilities, many people are unaware of the prevalence of disabilities as well as misinformed about their consequences. She suggests, for example, that although students may not be able to see, they can still excel in their coursework and have successful careers.[58] Accommodations enabling such students to perform up to their capabilities are covered under the ADA.

The ADA also protects employees with acquired immune deficiency syndrome (AIDS) from being discriminated against in the workplace. AIDS is caused by the human immunodeficiency virus (HIV) and is transmitted through sexual contact, infected needles, and contaminated blood products. HIV is not spread through casual, nonsexual contact. Yet out of ignorance, fear, or prejudice, some people wish to avoid all contact with anyone infected with HIV. Infected individuals may not necessarily develop AIDS, and some individuals with HIV are able to remain effective performers of their jobs while not putting others at risk.[59]

AIDS awareness training can help people overcome their fears and also give managers a tool to prevent illegal discrimination against HIV-infected employees. Such training focuses on educating employees about HIV and AIDS, dispelling myths, communicating relevant organizational policies, and emphasizing the rights of HIV-positive employees to privacy and an environment that allows them to be productive.[60] The need for AIDS awareness training is underscored by some of the problems HIV-positive employees experience once others in their workplace become aware of their condition.[61] Moreover, organizations are required to make reasonable accommodations to enable people with AIDS to effectively perform their jobs.

Thus managers have an obligation to educate employees about HIV and AIDS, dispel myths and the stigma of AIDS, and ensure that HIV-related discrimination is not occurring in the workplace. For example, Home Depot has provided HIV training and education to its store managers; such training was sorely needed given that over half of the managers indicated it was the first time they had the opportunity to talk about AIDS.[62] Moreover, advances in medication and treatment mean that more infected individuals are able to continue working or are able to return to work after their condition improves. Thus managers need to ensure that these employees are fairly treated by all members of their organizations.[63] And managers and organizations that do not treat HIV-positive employees in a fair manner, as well as provide reasonable accommodations (such as allowing time off for doctor visits or to take medicine), risk costly lawsuits.

Socioeconomic Background

The term *socioeconomic background* typically refers to a combination of social class and income-related factors. From a management perspective, socioeconomic diversity (and in particular diversity in income levels) requires that managers be sensitive and responsive to the needs and concerns of individuals who might not be as well off as others. U.S. welfare reform in the middle to late 1990s emphasized the need for single mothers and others receiving public assistance to join or return to the workforce. In conjunction with a strong economy, this led to record declines in the number of families, households, and children living below the poverty level, according to the 2000 U.S. census.[64] However, the economic downturns in the early and late 2000s suggest that some past gains, which lifted families out of poverty, have been reversed. In a strong economy, it is much easier for poor people with few skills to find jobs; in a weak economy, when companies lay off employees in hard times, people who need their incomes the most are unfortunately often the first to lose their jobs.[65] And in recessionary times, it is difficult for laid-off employees to find new positions. For example, in December 2009 there was an average of 6.1 unemployed workers for every open position.[66]

In particular, coinciding with the recession that started in December 2007, the official poverty rate in the United States in 2008 increased to 13.2% or 39.8 million people; 10.3% of families (8.1 million families) had incomes below the poverty level in 2008.[67] The Census Bureau relies on predetermined threshold income figures, based on family size and composition, adjusted annually for inflation, to determine the poverty level. Families whose income falls below the threshold level are considered poor.[68] For example, in 2008 a family of four was considered poor if their annual income fell below $22,025.[69] When workers earn less than $10 or $15 per hour, it is often difficult, if not impossible, for them to meet their families' needs.[70] Moreover, increasing numbers of families are facing the challenge of finding suitable child care arrangements that enable the adults to work long hours and/or through the night to maintain an adequate income level. New information technology has led to more businesses operating 24 hours a day, creating real challenges for workers on the night shift, especially those with children.[71]

Hundreds of thousands of parents across the country are scrambling to find someone to care for their children while they are working the night shift, commuting several hours a day, working weekends and holidays, or putting in long hours on one or more jobs. This has led to the opening of day care facilities that operate around the clock as well as to managers seeking ways to provide such care for children of their employees. For example, the Children's Choice Learning Center in Las Vegas, Nevada, operates around the clock to accommodate employees working nights in neighboring casinos, hospitals, and call centers. Randy Donahue, a security guard who works until midnight, picks his children up from the center when he gets off work; his wife is a nurse on the night shift.[72]

Judy Harden, who focuses on families and child care issues for the United Workers Union, indicates that the demands families are facing necessitate around-the-clock and odd-hour child care options. Many parents simply do not have the choice of working at hours that allow them to take care of their children at night and/or on weekends, never mind when the children are sick.[73] Some parents and psychologists feel uneasy having children separated from their families for so much time and particularly at night. Most agree that, unfortunately for many families, this is not a choice but a necessity.[74]

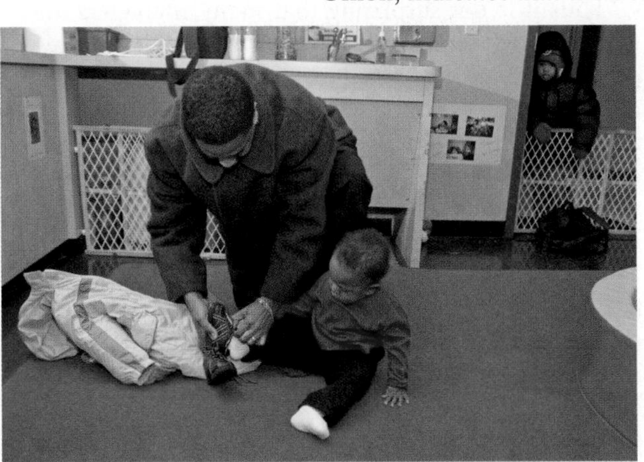

A father drops his children off at a day care facility before going to work. Managers need to be aware that many employees deal with challenging socioeconomic factors such as long commutes and finding suitable child care arrangements.

Socioeconomic diversity suggests that managers need to be sensitive and responsive to the needs and concerns of workers who may be less fortunate than themselves in terms of income and financial resources, child care and elder care options, housing opportunities, and existence of sources of social and family support. Moreover–and equally important–managers should try to give such individuals opportunities to learn, advance, and make meaningful contributions to their organizations while improving their economic well-being.

Sexual Orientation

Approximately 2% to 10% of the U.S. population is gay or lesbian.[75] Although no federal law prohibits discrimination based on sexual orientation, 20 states have such laws, and a 1998 executive order prohibits sexual orientation discrimination in civilian federal offices.[76] Moreover, an increasing number of organizations recognize the minority status of gay and lesbian employees, affirm their rights to fair and equal treatment, and provide benefits to same-sex partners of gay and lesbian employees.[77] For example, 95% of *Fortune* 500 companies prohibit discrimination based on sexual orientation, and 70% of the *Fortune* 500 provide domestic partner benefits.[78] As indicated in the following "Focus on Diversity" box, managers can take many steps to ensure that sexual orientation is not used to unfairly discriminate among employees.

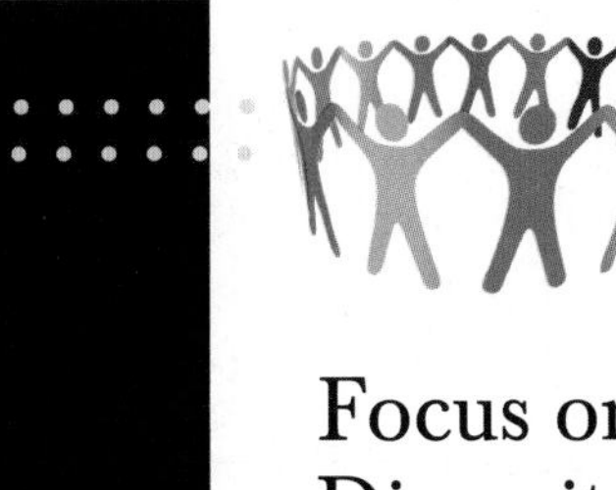

Focus on Diversity

Preventing Discrimination Based on Sexual Orientation

Although gays and lesbians have made great strides in attaining fair treatment in the workplace, much more needs to be done. In a recent study conducted by Harris Interactive Inc. (a research firm) and Witeck Communications Inc. (a marketing firm), over 40% of gay and lesbian employees indicated that they had been unfairly treated, denied a promotion, or pushed to quit their jobs because of their sexual orientation.[79] Given continued harassment and discrimination despite the progress that has been made,[80] many gay and lesbian employees fear disclosing their sexual orientation in the workplace and thus live a life of secrecy. While there are a few openly gay top managers, such as David Geffen, cofounder of DreamWorks SKG, and Allan Gilmour, former vice chairman and CFO of Ford and currently a member of the board of directors of Whirlpool and DTE Energy Company, many others choose not to disclose or discuss their personal lives, including long-term partners.[81]

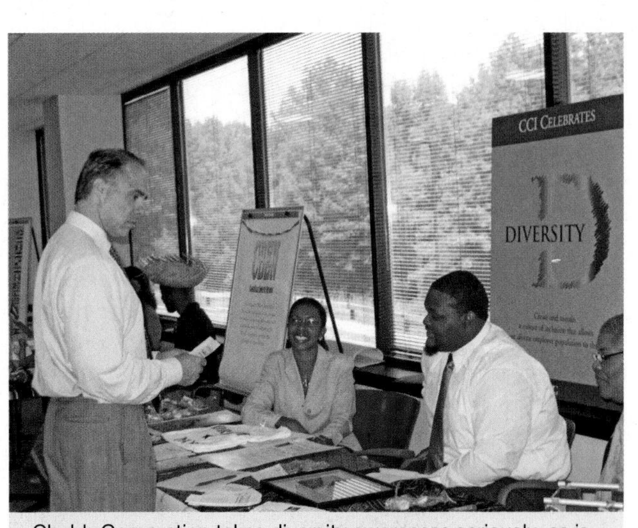

Chubb Corporation takes diversity awareness seriously, as is evidenced by this LGBT sensitivity training session.

Thus it is not surprising that many managers are taking active steps to educate and train their employees about issues of sexual orientation. S. C. Johnson & Sons, Inc., maker of Raid insecticide and Glade air fresheners in Racine, Wisconsin, provides mandatory training to its plant managers to overturn stereotypes; and Eastman Kodak, Lehman Brothers Holdings Inc., Merck & Co., Ernst & Young, and Toronto-Dominion Bank all train managers in how to prevent sexual orientation discrimination.[82] Other organizations such as Lucent Technologies, Microsoft, and Southern California Edison send employees to seminars conducted at prominent business schools. And many companies such as Raytheon, IBM, Eastman Kodak, and Lockheed Martin provide assistance to their gay and lesbian employees through gay and lesbian support groups.[83]

The Chubb Group of Insurance Companies, a property and casualty insurance company, provides its managers with a two-hour training session to help create work environments that are safe and welcoming for lesbian, gay, bisexual, and transgender (LGBT) people.[84] The sessions are conducted by two Chubb employees; usually one of the trainers is straight and the other is gay. The sessions focus on issues that affect a manager's ability to lead diverse teams, such as assessing how safe and welcoming the workplace is for LGBT people, how to refer to gay employees' significant others, and how to respond if employees or customers use inappropriate language or behavior. The idea for the program originated from one of Chubb's employee resource groups. Managers rate the program highly and say they are better able to respond to the concerns of their LGBT employees while creating a safe and productive work environment for all.[85]

Other Kinds of Diversity

Other kinds of diversity are important in organizations, are critical for managers to deal with effectively, and also are potential sources of unfair treatment. For example, organizations and teams need members with diverse backgrounds and experiences. This is clearly illustrated by the prevalence of cross-functional teams in organizations whose members might come from various departments such as marketing, production, finance, and sales (teams are covered in depth in Chapter 15). A team responsible for developing and introducing a new product, for example, often needs the expertise of employees not only from R&D and engineering but also from marketing, sales, production, and finance.

Other types of diversity can affect how employees are treated in the workplace. For example, employees differ from each other in how attractive they are (based on the standards of the cultures in which an organization operates) and in body weight. Whether individuals are attractive or unattractive, thin or overweight, in most cases has no bearing on their job performance unless they have jobs in which physical appearance plays a role, such as modeling. Yet sometimes these physical sources of diversity end up influencing advancement rates and salaries. A recent study published in the *American Journal of Public Health* found that highly educated obese women earned approximately 30% less per year than women who were not obese and men (regardless of whether or not the men were obese).[86] Clearly managers need to ensure that all employees are treated fairly, regardless of their physical appearance.

LO5-2 Explain the central role that managers play in the effective management of diversity.

Managers and the Effective Management of Diversity

The increasing diversity of the environment–which, in turn, increases the diversity of an organization's workforce–increases the challenges managers face in effectively managing diversity. Each of the kinds of diversity just discussed presents a particular set of issues managers need to appreciate before they can respond to them effectively. Understanding these issues is not always a simple matter, as many informed managers have discovered. Research on how different groups are currently treated and the unconscious biases that might adversely affect them is vital because it helps managers become aware of the many subtle and unobtrusive ways in which diverse employee groups can come to be treated unfairly over time. Managers can take many more steps to become sensitive to the ongoing effects of diversity in their organizations, take advantage of all the contributions diverse employees can make, and prevent diverse employees from being unfairly treated.

Critical Managerial Roles

In each of their managerial roles (see Chapter 1), managers can either promote the effective management of diversity or derail such efforts; thus they are critical to this process. For example, in their interpersonal roles, managers can convey that the effective management of diversity is a valued goal and objective (figurehead role), can serve as a role model and institute policies and procedures to ensure that diverse organizational members are treated fairly (leader role), and can enable diverse individuals and groups to coordinate their efforts and cooperate with each other both inside the organization and at the organization's boundaries (liaison role). In Table 5.2 we summarize some ways managers can ensure that diversity is effectively managed as they perform their different roles.

Given the formal authority that managers have in organizations, they typically have more influence than rank-and-file employees. When managers commit to supporting diversity, as was discussed for managers at Sodexo and Principal Financial Group in "A Manager's Challenge," their authority and positions of power and status influence other members of an organization to make a similar commitment.[87] Research on social influence supports such a link: People are likely to be influenced and persuaded by others who have high status.[88]

Moreover, when managers commit to diversity, their commitment legitimizes the diversity management efforts of others.[89] In addition, resources are devoted to such efforts, and all members of an organization believe that their diversity-related efforts are supported and valued. Consistent with this reasoning, top management commitment and rewards for the support of diversity are often cited as critical ingredients in the success of diversity management initiatives.[90] Additionally, seeing managers express confidence in the abilities and talents of diverse employees causes other organizational members to be similarly confident and helps reduce any misconceived misgivings they may have as a result of ignorance or stereotypes.[91]

Two other important factors emphasize why managers are so central to the effective management of diversity. The first factor is that women, African-Americans, Hispanics, and other minorities often start out at a slight disadvantage due to how they are perceived by others in organizations, particularly in work settings where they are a numerical minority. As Virginia Valian, a psychologist at Hunter College who studies gender, indicates, "In most organizations women begin at a slight disadvantage. A woman does not walk into the room with the same status as an equivalent man, because she is less likely than a man to be viewed as a serious professional."[92]

Table 5.2
Managerial Roles and the Effective Management of Diversity

Type of Role	Specific Role	Example
Interpersonal	Figurehead	Convey that the effective management of diversity is a valued goal and objective.
	Leader	Serve as a role model and institute policies and procedures to ensure that diverse members are treated fairly.
	Liaison	Enable diverse individuals to coordinate their efforts and cooperate with one another.
Informational	Monitor	Evaluate the extent to which diverse employees are being treated fairly.
	Disseminator	Inform employees about diversity policies and initiatives and the intolerance of discrimination.
	Spokesperson	Support diversity initiatives in the wider community and speak to diverse groups to interest them in career opportunities.
Decisional	Entrepreneur	Commit resources to develop new ways to effectively manage diversity and eliminate biases and discrimination.
	Disturbance handler	Take quick action to correct inequalities and curtail discriminatory behavior.
	Resource allocator	Allocate resources to support and encourage the effective management of diversity.
	Negotiator	Work with organizations (e.g., suppliers) and groups (e.g., labor unions) to support and encourage the effective management of diversity.

The second factor is that research suggests that slight differences in treatment can accumulate and result in major disparities over time. Even small differences–such as a very slight favorable bias toward men for promotions–can lead to major differences in the number of male and female managers over time.[93] Thus while women and other minorities are sometimes advised not to make "a mountain out of a molehill" when they perceive they have been unfairly treated, research conducted by Valian and others suggests that molehills (slight differences in treatment based on irrelevant distinctions such as race, gender, or ethnicity) can turn into mountains over time (major disparities in important outcomes such as promotions) if they are ignored.[94] Once again, managers have the obligation, from both an ethical and a business perspective, to prevent any disparities in treatment and outcomes due to irrelevant distinctions such as race or ethnicity.

LO5-3 Explain why the effective management of diversity is both an ethical and a business imperative.

The Ethical Imperative to Manage Diversity Effectively

Effectively managing diversity not only makes good business sense (which is discussed in the next section) but also is an ethical imperative in U.S. society. Two moral principles guide managers in their efforts to meet this imperative: distributive justice and procedural justice.

distributive justice A moral principle calling for fair distribution of pay, promotions, and other organizational resources based on meaningful contributions that individuals have made and not personal characteristics over which they have no control.

DISTRIBUTIVE JUSTICE The principle of **distributive justice** dictates fair distribution of pay, promotions, job titles, interesting job assignments, office space, and other organizational resources among members of an organization. These outcomes should be distributed according to the meaningful contributions that individuals have made to the organization (such as time, effort, education, skills, abilities, and performance levels) and not irrelevant personal characteristics over which individuals have no control (such as gender, race, or age).[95] Managers have an obligation to ensure that distributive justice exists in their organizations. This does not mean that all members of an organization receive identical or similar outcomes; rather, it means that members who receive more favorable outcomes than others have made substantially higher or more significant contributions to the organization.

Is distributive justice common in organizations in corporate America? Probably the best way to answer this question is to say things are getting better. Fifty years ago, overt discrimination against women and minorities was common; today organizations are inching closer toward the ideal of distributive justice. Statistics comparing the treatment of women and minorities with the treatment of other employees suggest that most managers would need to take a proactive approach to achieve distributive justice in their organizations.[96] For example, across occupations, women consistently earn less than men (see Table 5.3) according to data collected by the U.S. Bureau of Labor Statistics.[97] Even in occupations dominated by women, such as sales and office occupations, men tend to earn more than women.[98]

In many countries, managers have not only an ethical obligation to strive to achieve distributive justice in their organizations but also a legal obligation to treat all employees fairly. They risk being sued by employees who believe they are not being fairly treated. That is precisely what six African-American Texaco employees did when they experienced racial bias and discrimination.[99]

procedural justice A moral principle calling for the use of fair procedures to determine how to distribute outcomes to organizational members.

PROCEDURAL JUSTICE The principle of **procedural justice** requires that managers use fair procedures to determine how to distribute outcomes to organizational members.[100] This principle applies to typical procedures such as appraising subordinates' performance, deciding who should receive a raise or a promotion, and deciding whom to lay off when an organization is forced to downsize. Procedural justice exists, for example, when managers (1) carefully appraise a subordinate's performance, (2) take into account any environmental obstacles to high performance beyond the subordinate's control, such as lack of supplies, machine breakdowns, or

Table 5.3
Weekly Earnings by Sex and Occupation in 2009

Median Weekly Earning for Full-Time Workers in 2009

Occupation	Men	Women	Women's Earnings as a Percentage of Men's
Management, professional, and related	$1,248	$907	73
Service	524	418	80
Sales and office	737	590	80
Natural resources, construction, and maintenance	727	542	75
Production, transportation, and material moving	648	472	73

Source: "Table 7. Median Usual Weekly Earnings of Full-Time Wage and Salary Workers by Occupation and Sex, Annual Wages," http://data.bls.gov/cgi-bin/print.pl/news.release/wkyeng.t07.htm, February 9, 2010.

dwindling customer demand for a product, and (3) ignore irrelevant personal characteristics such as the subordinate's age or ethnicity. Like distributive justice, procedural justice is necessary not only to ensure ethical conduct but also to avoid costly lawsuits.

Effectively Managing Diversity Makes Good Business Sense

Diverse organizational members can be a source of competitive advantage, helping an organization provide customers with better goods and services.[101] The variety of points of view and approaches to problems and opportunities that diverse employees provide can improve managerial decision making. Suppose the Budget Gourmet frozen food company is trying to come up with creative ideas for new frozen meals that will appeal to health-conscious, time-conscious customers tired of the same old frozen fare. Which group do you think is likely to come up with the most creative ideas: a group of white women with marketing degrees from Yale University who grew up in upper-middle-class families in the Northeast or a racially mixed group of men and women who grew up in families with varying income levels in different parts of the country and attended a mix of business schools (New York University, Oklahoma State, University of Michigan, UCLA, Cornell University, Texas A&M University, and Iowa State)? Most people would agree that the diverse group is likely to have a wider range of creative ideas. Although this example is simplistic, it underscores one way in which diversity can lead to a competitive advantage.

Just as the workforce is becoming increasingly diverse, so too are the customers who buy an organization's goods or services. In an attempt to suit local customers' needs and tastes, organizations like Target often vary the selection of products available in stores in different cities and regions.[102]

Diverse members of an organization are likely to be attuned to what goods and services diverse segments of the market want and do not want. Automakers, for example, are increasingly assigning women to their design teams to ensure that the needs and desires of female customers are taken into account in new car design.

For Darden Restaurants, the business case for diversity rests on market share and growth. Darden seeks to satisfy the needs and tastes of diverse customers by providing menus in Spanish in communities with large Hispanic populations.[103] Similarly, market share and growth and the identification of niche markets led Tracey Campbell to cater to travelers with disabilities.[104] She heads InnSeekers, a telephone and online listing resource for bed and breakfasts. Nikki Daruwala works for the Calvert Group in Bethesda, Maryland, a mutual fund that emphasizes social responsibility and diversity. She indicates that profit alone is more than enough of an incentive to effectively manage diversity. As she puts it, "You can look at an automaker. There are more women making decisions about car buying or home buying . . . $3.72 trillion per year are spent by women."[105]

Another way that effective management of diversity can improve profitability is by increasing retention of valued employees, which decreases the costs of hiring replacements for those who quit as well as ensures that all employees are highly motivated. In terms of retention, given the current legal environment, more and more organizations are attuned to the need to emphasize the importance of diversity in hiring. Once hired, if diverse employees think they are being unfairly treated, however, they will be likely to seek opportunities elsewhere. Thus recruiting diverse employees has to be followed up by ongoing effective management of diversity to retain valued organizational members.

If diversity is not effectively managed and turnover rates are higher for members of groups who are not treated fairly, profitability will suffer on several counts. Not only are the future contributions of diverse employees lost when they quit, but the organization also has to bear the costs of hiring replacement workers. According to the Employment Management Association, on average it costs more than $10,000 to hire a new employee; other estimates are significantly higher. For example, Ernst & Young estimates it costs about $1,200,000 to replace 10 professionals, and the diversity consulting firm Hubbard & Hubbard estimates replacement costs average one-and-a-half times an employee's annual salary.[106] Moreover, additional costs from failing to effectively manage diversity stem from time lost due to the barriers diverse members of an organization perceive as thwarting their progress and advancement.[107]

Effectively managing diversity makes good business sense for another reason. More and more, managers and organizations concerned about diversity are insisting that their suppliers also support diversity.[108]

Finally, from both business and ethical perspectives, effective management of diversity is necessary to avoid costly lawsuits such as those settled by Advantica (owner of the Denny's chain) and the Coca-Cola Company. In 2000 Coca-Cola settled a class action suit brought by African-American employees, at a cost of $192 million. The damage such lawsuits cause goes beyond the monetary awards to the injured parties; it can tarnish a company's image. One positive outcome of Coca-Cola's 2000 settlement is the company's recognition of the need to commit additional resources to diversity management initiatives. Coca-Cola is increasing its use of minority suppliers, instituting a formal mentoring program, and instituting days to celebrate diversity with its workforce.[109]

LO5-4 Discuss how perception and the use of schemas can result in unfair treatment.

By now it should be clear that effectively managing diversity is a necessity on both ethical and business grounds. This brings us to the question of why diversity presents managers and all of us with so many challenges–a question we address in the next section on perception.

Perception

Most people tend to think that the decisions managers make in organizations and the actions they take are the result of objective determination of the issues involved and the surrounding situation. However, each manager's interpretation of a situation or even of another person is precisely that–an interpretation. Nowhere are the effects of perception more likely to lead to different interpretations than in the area of diversity. This is because each person's interpretation of a situation, and subsequent response to it, is affected by his or her own age, race, gender, religion, socioeconomic status, capabilities, and sexual orientation. For example, different managers may see the same 21-year-old, black, male, gay, gifted, and talented subordinate in different ways: One may see a creative maverick with a great future in the organization, while another may see a potential troublemaker who needs to be watched closely.

perception The process through which people select, organize, and interpret what they see, hear, touch, smell, and taste to give meaning and order to the world around them.

Perception is the process through which people select, organize, and interpret sensory input–what they see, hear, touch, smell, and taste–to give meaning and order to the world around them.[110] All decisions and actions of managers are based on their subjective perceptions. When these perceptions are relatively accurate–close to the true nature of what is actually being perceived–good decisions are likely to be made and appropriate actions taken. Managers of fast-food restaurant chains such as McDonald's, Pizza Hut, and Wendy's accurately perceived that their customers were becoming more health-conscious in the 1980s and 1990s and added salad bars and low-fat entries to their menus. Managers at Kentucky Fried Chicken, Jack-in-the-Box, and Burger King took much longer to perceive this change in what customers wanted.

One reason why McDonald's is so successful is that its managers go to great lengths to make sure their perceptions of what customers want are accurate. McDonald's has over 14,880 restaurants outside the United States that generate over $14.1 billion in annual revenues.[111] Key to McDonald's success in these diverse markets are managers' efforts to perceive accurately a country's culture and taste in food and then to act on these perceptions. For instance, McDonald's serves veggie burgers in Holland and black currant shakes in Poland.[112]

When managers' perceptions are relatively inaccurate, managers are likely to make bad decisions and take inappropriate actions, which hurt organizational effectiveness. Bad decisions concerning diversity for reasons of age, ethnicity, or sexual orientation include (1) not hiring qualified people, (2) failing to promote top-performing subordinates, who subsequently may take their skills to competing organizations, and (3) promoting poorly performing managers because they have the same "diversity profile" as the manager or managers making the decision.

Factors That Influence Managerial Perception

Several managers' perceptions of the same person, event, or situation are likely to differ because managers differ in personality, values, attitudes, and moods (see Chapter 3). Each of these factors can influence how someone perceives a person or situation. An older middle manager who is high on openness to experience is likely to perceive the recruitment of able young managers as a positive learning opportunity; a similar middle manager who is low on openness to experience may perceive able younger subordinates as a threat. A manager who has high levels of job satisfaction and organizational commitment may perceive a job transfer to another department or geographic location that has very different employees (age, ethnicity, and so on) as an opportunity to learn and develop new skills. A dissatisfied, uncommitted manager may perceive the same transfer as a demotion.

Managers' and all organizational members' perceptions of one another also are affected by their past experiences with and acquired knowledge about people, events, and situations–information that is organized into preexisting schemas.

schema An abstract knowledge structure that is stored in memory and makes possible the interpretation and organization of information about a person, event, or situation.

Schemas are abstract knowledge structures stored in memory that allow people to organize and interpret information about a person, an event, or a situation.[113] Once a person develops a schema for a kind of person or event, any newly encountered person or situation that is related to the schema activates it, and information is processed in ways consistent with the information stored in the schema. Thus people tend to perceive others by using the expectations or preconceived notions contained in their schemas.[114] Once again, these expectations are derived from past experience and knowledge.

People tend to pay attention to information that is consistent with their schemas and to ignore or discount inconsistent information. Thus schemas tend to be reinforced and strengthened over time because the information attended to is seen as confirming the schemas. This also results in schemas being resistant to change.[115] This does not mean schemas never change; if that were the case, people could never adapt to changing conditions and learn from their mistakes. Rather, it suggests that schemas are slow to change and that a considerable amount of contradictory information needs to be encountered for people to change their schemas.

Schemas that accurately depict the true nature of a person or situation are functional because they help people make sense of the world around them. People typically confront so much information that it is not possible to make sense of it without relying on schemas. Schemas are dysfunctional when they are inaccurate because they cause managers and all members of an organization to perceive people and situations inaccurately and assume certain things that are not necessarily true.

gender schemas Preconceived beliefs or ideas about the nature of men and women and their traits, attitudes, behaviors, and preferences.

Psychologist Virginia Valian refers to inaccurate preconceived notions of men and women as gender schemas. **Gender schemas** are a person's preconceived notions about the nature of men and women and their traits, attitudes, behaviors, and preferences.[116] Research suggests that among white, middle-class Americans, the following gender schemas are prevalent: Men are action-oriented, assertive, independent, and task-focused; women are expressive, nurturing, and oriented toward and caring of other people.[117] Any schemas such as these–which assume a single visible characteristic such as gender causes a person to possess specific traits and tendencies–are bound to be inaccurate. For example, not all women are alike and not all men are alike, and many women are more independent and task-focused than men. Gender schemas can be learned in childhood and are reinforced in a number of ways in society. For instance, while young girls may be encouraged by their parents to play with toy trucks and tools (stereotypically masculine toys), boys generally are not encouraged, and sometimes are actively discouraged, from playing with dolls (stereotypically feminine toys).[118] As children grow up, they learn that occupations dominated by men have higher status than occupations dominated by women.

Perception as a Determinant of Unfair Treatment

Even though most people would agree that distributive justice and procedural justice are desirable goals, diverse organizational members are sometimes treated unfairly, as previous examples illustrate. Why is this problem occurring? One important overarching reason is inaccurate perceptions. To the extent that managers and other members of an organization rely on inaccurate schemas such as gender schemas to guide their perceptions of each other, unfair treatment is likely to occur.

stereotype Simplistic and often inaccurate beliefs about the typical characteristics of particular groups of people.

Gender schemas are a kind of **stereotype,** which is composed of simplistic and often inaccurate beliefs about the typical characteristics of particular groups of people. Stereotypes are usually based on a visible characteristic such as a person's age, gender, or race.[119] Managers who allow stereotypes to influence their perceptions assume erroneously that a person possesses a whole host of characteristics simply because the person happens to be an Asian woman, a white man, or a lesbian, for example. African-American men are often stereotyped as good athletes, Hispanic women as subservient.[120] Obviously there is no reason to assume that every African-American man is a good athlete or that every Hispanic woman is subservient. Stereotypes, however, lead people to make such erroneous assumptions. A manager who accepts stereotypes might, for example, decide not to promote a highly capable Hispanic woman into a management position because the manager is certain that she will not be assertive enough to supervise others.

A recent study suggests that stereotypes might hamper the progress of mothers in their organizations when they are seeking to advance in positions that are traditionally held by men. According to the study, based on gender stereotypes, people tend to view mothers as less competent in terms of skills and capabilities related to advancing in such positions.[121]

People with disabilities might also be unfairly treated due to stereotypes.[122] Although the ADA requires (as mentioned previously) that organizations provide disabled employees with accommodations, employment rates of people with disabilities have declined in recent years. As profiled in the following "Ethics in Action" box, a number of organizations have not only provided employment opportunities for disabled adults but also have benefited from their valuable contributions.[123]

Ethics in Action

Disabled Employees Make Valuable Contributions

Some large organizations like McDonald's, Walmart, Home Depot, and Walgreens actively recruit disabled employees to work in positions such as cashiers, maintenance workers, greeters, shelf stockers, and floor workers that help customers find items. Home Depot, for example, works with a nonprofit agency called Ken's Kids, founded by parents of disabled adults, to recruit and place disabled employees in its stores. Thus far, working with Ken's Kids has enabled Home Depot to recruit and place around 100 disabled adults in over 50 of its stores.[124]

Often, when given the opportunity, disabled employees make valuable contributions to their organizations. Walgreens recently opened an automated distribution center in Anderson, South Carolina, in which more than 40% of its 264 employees are disabled.[125] For disabled employees like 18-year-old Harrison Mullinax, who has autism and checks in merchandise to be distributed to drugstores with a bar code scanner, having a regular job is a godsend. Randy Lewis, senior vice president of distribution and logistics at Walgreens, thought about hiring workers with disabilities when Walgreens was considering using technology to increase automation levels in a distribution center. Lewis, the father of a young adult son who has autism, was aware of how difficult it can be for young adults like his son to find employment. Various accommodations were made, like redesigning workstations and computer displays to suit employees' needs, and employees received appropriate training in how to do their jobs. Some days, disabled employees are actually the most productive in the center. As Lewis puts it, "One thing we found is they can all do the job. . . . What surprised us is the environment that it's created. It's a building where everybody helps each other out."[126]

Walgreens is a large organization, but small organizations also have benefited from the valuable contributions of disabled employees. Habitat International, founded by current CEO David Morris and his father Saul over 20 years ago, is a manufacturer and contractor of indoor–outdoor carpet and artificial grass and a supplier to home improvement companies like Lowe's and Home Depot.[127] Habitat's profits have steadily increased over the years, and the factory's defect rate is less than 0.5%.[128]

Morris attributes Habitat's success to its employees, 75% of whom have either a physical or a mental disability or both.[129] Habitat has consistently provided employment opportunities to people with disabilities such as Down syndrome, schizophrenia, or cerebral palsy.[130] The company has also hired the homeless, recovering alcoholics, and non-English-speaking refugees from other countries. And these employees were relied on by plant manager Connie Presnell when she needed to fill a rush order by assigning it to a team of her fastest workers.[131] Habitat pays its employees regionally competitive wages and has low absence

The first clue that Habitat isn't your run-of-the mill factory may be the gigantic animal sculptures at the plant entrance in Chattanooga, Tennessee. The Habitat team produces the sculptures, which can also be seen at restaurants, parks, garden centers, medical centers, museums, and other sites.

and turnover rates. Employees who need accommodations to perform their jobs are provided them, and Habitat has a highly motivated, satisfied, and committed workforce.[132]

While Habitat has actually gained some business from clients who applaud its commitment to diversity, Habitat's ethical values and social responsibility have also led the company to forgo a major account when stereotypes reared their ugly heads. A few years ago CEO Morris dropped the account of a distribution company because its representatives had made derogatory comments about his employees. Although it took Habitat two years to regain the lost revenues from this major account, Morris had no regrets.[133] Habitat's commitment to diversity and fair treatment is a win–win situation; the company is thriving, and so are its employees.[134]

bias The systematic tendency to use information about others in ways that result in inaccurate perceptions.

Inaccurate perceptions leading to unfair treatment of diverse members of an organization also can be due to biases. **Biases** are systematic tendencies to use information about others in ways that result in inaccurate perceptions. Because of the way biases operate, people often are unaware that their perceptions of others are inaccurate. There are several types of biases.

The *similar-to-me effect* is the tendency to perceive others who are similar to ourselves more positively than we perceive people who are different.[135] The similar-to-me effect is summed up by the saying, "Birds of a feather flock together." It can lead to unfair treatment of diverse employees simply because they are different from the managers who are perceiving them, evaluating them, and making decisions that affect their future in the organization.

Managers (particularly top managers) are likely to be white men. Although these managers may endorse the principles of distributive and procedural justice, they may unintentionally fall into the trap of perceiving other white men more positively than they perceive women and minorities. This is the similar-to-me effect. Being aware of this bias as well as using objective information about employees' capabilities and performance as much as possible in decision making about job assignments, pay raises, promotions, and other outcomes can help managers avoid the similar-to-me effect.

The salience effect focuses extra attention on a person who stands out from the group mold. Part of being a good manager includes being aware of these sorts of tendencies and actively working against them.

Social status–a person's real or perceived position in a society or an organization–can be the source of another bias. The *social status effect* is the tendency to perceive individuals with high social status more positively than we perceive those with low social status. A high-status person may be perceived as smarter and more believable, capable, knowledgeable, and responsible than a low-status person, even in the absence of objective information about either person.

Imagine being introduced to two people at a company Christmas party. Both are white men in their late 30s, and you learn that one is a member of the company's top management team and the other is a supervisor in the mailroom. From this information alone, you might assume that the top manager is smarter, more capable, more responsible, and even more interesting than the mailroom supervisor. Because women and minorities have traditionally had lower social status than white men, the social status effect may lead some people to perceive women and minorities less positively than they perceive white men.

Have you ever stood out in a crowd? Maybe you were the only man in a group of women; or maybe you were dressed formally for a social gathering, and everyone else was in jeans. Salience (that is, conspicuousness) is another source of bias. The *salience effect* is the tendency to focus attention on individuals who are conspicuously different from us. When people are salient, they often feel as though all eyes are watching them, and this perception is not far from the mark. Salient individuals are more often the object of attention than are other members of a work group, for example. A manager who has six white subordinates and one Hispanic subordinate reporting to her may inadvertently pay more attention to the Hispanic in group meetings because of the salience effect. In "A Manager's Challenge," Rod Bond of Sodexo experienced salience firsthand when he attended the Women's Food Service Forum.

Individuals who are salient are often perceived to be primarily responsible for outcomes and operations and are evaluated more extremely in either a positive or a negative direction.[136] Thus when the Hispanic subordinate does a good job on a project, she receives excessive praise, and when she misses a deadline, she is excessively chastised.

Overt Discrimination

overt discrimination Knowingly and willingly denying diverse individuals access to opportunities and outcomes in an organization.

Inaccurate schemas and perceptual biases can lead well-meaning managers and organizational members to unintentionally discriminate against others. On the other hand, **overt discrimination,** or knowingly and willingly denying diverse individuals access to opportunities and outcomes in an organization, is intentional and deliberate. Overt discrimination is both unethical and illegal. Unfortunately, just as some managers steal from their organizations, others engage in overt discrimination.

Overt discrimination is a clear violation of the principles of distributive and procedural justice. Moreover, when managers are charged with overt discrimination, costly lawsuits can ensue. Organizations ranging from the Adam's Mark chain of luxury hotels, Texaco, and Ford Motor Company to Johnson & Johnson, BellSouth, the National Football League, General Electric, Walmart, and Nike either have settled or face pending lawsuits alleging overt workplace discrimination.[137] Whereas in the past, lawsuits due to overt workplace discrimination focused on unfair treatment of women and minority group members, given the aging of the U.S. workforce, increasing numbers of discrimination cases are being brought by older workers who believe they were unfairly dismissed from their jobs due to their age.[138]

Despite all the advances that have been made, allegations of overt discrimination based on gender, race, age, and other forms of diversity continue to occur in the United States. For example, Nike recently settled a class action lawsuit filed on behalf of 400 African-American employees of its Chicago Niketown store.[139] Employees claimed that managers used racial slurs when referring to African-American employees and customers, gave African-American employees lower-paying jobs, made unwarranted accusations of theft, and had security personnel monitor employees and customers based on race.[140] Although Nike denied the allegations, as part of the settlement, Nike agreed to pay current and former employees $7.6 million and also agreed to promote effective management of diversity, partly by providing diversity training to all managers and supervisors in the store.[141]

Overt discrimination continues to be a problem in other countries as well. For example, although Japan passed its first Equal Employment Opportunity Law in 1985 and Japanese women are increasingly working in jobs once dominated by men, professional Japanese women have continued to find it difficult to advance in their careers and assume managerial positions.[142] Women make up almost half of the Japanese workforce, but only around 10% of managerial positions in business and government are occupied by women, according to the International Labor Organization agency of the United Nations.[143]

According to the United Nations Development Program's gender empowerment measure, which assesses the participation of women in a country's politics and economy, Japan is the most unequal of the world's wealthy nations when it comes to women.[144] Takako Ariishi has witnessed women's struggle in Japan firsthand. As an employee of a family-owned manufacturing business that supplies parts to Nissan,[145] Ariishi was fired by her own father (who was then president of the company) when she had a son (her father claimed that her son would be his successor as president). Nonetheless, when Ariishi's father died, she took over as company president. Her company is one of 160 Nissan suppliers in Japan, and the heads of these companies meet twice a year; Arrishi is the only woman among the 160 presidents, and the first time the group met, she was asked to wait in a separate room with the secretaries. Miiko Tsuda, an employee of a tutoring company, indicates that she is paid less than her male coworkers, and she is often asked to push elevator buttons and make tea for male coworkers. Only 5 of the company's 300 management employees are women.[146]

Overt discrimination also can be a potential problem when in comes to layoff decisions, as profiled in the following "Focus on Diversity" box.

Focus on Diversity

Layoff Discrimination?

Organizational restructurings, a weak economy, and the recession that began in December 2007[147] led to record numbers of U.S. employees being laid off from 2007 to 2010. Although it is always a challenge for managers to decide whom should be let go when layoffs take place, some laid-off employees feel that factors that should be irrelevant to this tough decision played a role in the layoffs at their former employers. And while many workers who believe they were unfairly discriminated against do not pursue legal remedies, some are filing lawsuits alleging discrimination in layoff decisions.

Age-related discrimination complaints were at a record high during this period.[148] Although this might be due to the fact that there were more older employees in the workforce than in previous years, David Grinberg, speaking on behalf of the EEOC, suggests that the rise in age discrimination allegations could also be due to the fact that older workers tend to be paid more and have better benefits.[149] For example, Joan Zawacki, in her late 50s, was laid off from her position as a vice president at the Cartus division of Realogy Corp. after having worked at the company for over 30 years. According to Zawacki, senior managers such as herself were told to discreetly talk with older workers in a friendly manner and suggest that they inquire with human resources about early retirement packages while protecting the jobs of younger workers. Zawacki indicates that she was laid off after not having convinced an older employee in her department to retire. A company spokesperson disputed the allegations in Zawacki's age discrimination lawsuit. In addition, over 90 employees at the Lawrence Livermore National Laboratory have filed complaints alleging age discrimination in layoffs. Eddy Stappaerts, a 62-year-old senior scientist who had worked at the lab for 11 years and has a Ph.D. from Stanford University, says, "A week before I was laid off, my boss said my contributions were essential."[150] He alleges that some of the work he did was given to a younger employee.[151]

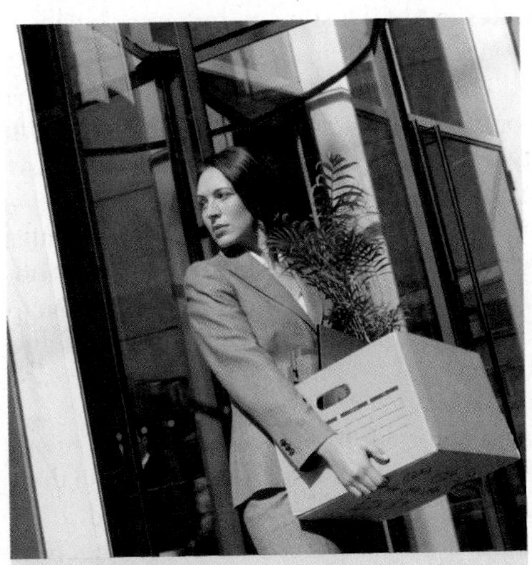

Who gets laid off and why? Discrimination runs across the board of business practices, including the arena of layoffs.

Some women laid off from their jobs in the financial industry are filing lawsuits alleging gender discrimination. Laid-off female executives at Citigroup, Merrill Lynch, Bank of America, and Bank of Toyko have claimed that gender played a role in their firings.[152] In some cases the women had done very well in their early years with the firms, were transferred to less desirable positions after becoming pregnant and taking maternity leaves, and ultimately were let go. Some of these women suggest that they were laid off even though they were just as (or more) qualified as men who were able to keep their jobs.[153]

Four former human resource managers at Dell filed a class action lawsuit alleging that Dell's massive layoffs discriminated against women and employees over age 40 and that women were unfairly treated in pay and promotions.[154] Although in many of these cases the companies involved allege that no discrimination took place, clearly these are matters for the courts to decide.[155]

How to Manage Diversity Effectively

Various kinds of barriers arise to managing diversity effectively in organizations. Some barriers originate in the person doing the perceiving; others are based on the information and schemas that have built up over time concerning the person being perceived. To overcome these barriers and effectively manage diversity, managers (and other organizational members) must possess or develop certain attitudes and values and the skills needed to change other people's attitudes and values.

LO5-5 List the steps managers can take to effectively manage diversity.

Steps in Managing Diversity Effectively

Managers can take a number of steps to change attitudes and values and promote the effective management of diversity. Here we describe these steps, some of which we have referred to previously (see Table 5.4).

SECURE TOP MANAGEMENT COMMITMENT As we mentioned earlier in the chapter, top management's commitment to diversity is crucial for the success of any diversity-related initiatives. Top managers need to develop the correct ethical values and performance- or business-oriented attitudes that allow them to make appropriate use of their human resources.

STRIVE TO INCREASE THE ACCURACY OF PERCEPTIONS One aspect of developing the appropriate values and attitudes is to take steps to increase the accuracy of perceptions. Managers should consciously attempt to be open to other points of view and perspectives, seek them out, and encourage their subordinates to do the same.[156] Organizational members who are open to other perspectives put their own beliefs and knowledge to an important reality test and will be more inclined to modify or change them when necessary. Managers should not be afraid to change their views about a person, issue, or event; moreover, they should encourage their subordinates to be open to changing their views in the light of disconfirming evidence. Additionally, managers and all members of an organization should strive to avoid making snap judgments about people; rather, judgments should be made only when sufficient and relevant information has been gathered.[157]

INCREASE DIVERSITY AWARENESS It is natural for managers and other members of an organization to view other people from their own perspective because their own feelings, thoughts, attitudes, and experiences guide their perceptions and interactions. The ability to appreciate diversity, however, requires that people become aware of other perspectives and the various attitudes and experiences of others. Many diversity awareness programs in organizations strive to increase managers' and workers' awareness of (1) their own attitudes, biases, and stereotypes and (2) the differing

Table 5.4
Promoting the Effective Management of Diversity

- Secure top management commitment.
- Increase the accuracy of perceptions.
- Increase diversity awareness.
- Increase diversity skills.
- Encourage flexibility.
- Pay close attention to how employees are evaluated.
- Consider the numbers.
- Empower employees to challenge discriminatory behaviors, actions, and remarks.
- Reward employees for effectively managing diversity.
- Provide training utilizing a multipronged, ongoing approach.
- Encourage mentoring of diverse employees.

perspectives of diverse managers, subordinates, coworkers, and customers. Diversity awareness programs often have these goals:[158]

- Providing organizational members with accurate information about diversity.
- Uncovering personal biases and stereotypes.
- Assessing personal beliefs, attitudes, and values and learning about other points of view.
- Overturning inaccurate stereotypes and beliefs about different groups.
- Developing an atmosphere in which people feel free to share their differing perspectives and points of view.
- Improving understanding of others who are different from oneself.

Sometimes simply taking the time to interact with someone who is different in some way can increase awareness. When employees and managers are at social functions or just having lunch with a coworker, often the people they interact with are those they feel most comfortable with. If all members of an organization make an effort to interact with people they ordinarily would not, mutual understanding is likely to be enhanced.[159]

In large organizations, top managers are often far removed from entry-level employees– they may lack a real understanding and appreciation for what these employees do day in and day out, the challenges and obstacles they face, and the steps that can be taken to improve effectiveness. Recognizing this fact, some managers have taken concrete steps to improve their understanding of the experiences, attitudes, and perspectives of frontline employees, as indicated in the following "Management Insight" box.

Management Insight

Top Execs Improve Their Understanding of the Front Line

A growing number of organizations are implementing programs whereby top managers spend time performing the jobs of frontline employees to improve their understanding of the challenges these employees face and ways to improve their working conditions.[160] For example, DaVita Inc.,[161] a major provider of kidney dialysis services in the United States, has a program called "Reality 101"

"Now how did I do that, again?" Spending time doing frontline work can be immensely beneficial for executives to understand the nuts and bolts of their subordinates' days.

through which senior executives who have never worked in a dialysis clinic spend three days working as clinic technicians. Dialysis helps patients whose kidneys are not working properly to eliminate waste from their bloodstream. Treatments last around four hours, and patients often require multiple treatments per week.[162]

Carolyn Kibler, a senior executive at DaVita who oversees 48 clinics and around 750 employees, gained a much better understanding of the challenges technicians face, the nature of their jobs, and how best to manage them as a result of her participation in Reality 101. A former nurse, Kibler was surprised at how physically and emotionally demanding the job was and the high levels of stress it entailed. She also gained a real appreciation of the high levels of empathy technicians have for their patients–trying to make them as comfortable as possible, helping them deal with their frustrations, and mourning the loss of those who die as a result of their often multiple medical problems.[163]

Realizing how hard technicians work and how hectic and stressful the clinics can be, Kibler is now more understanding when paperwork is submitted late due to staff shortages, gives positive feedback to those who might have to miss meetings or conference calls to treat patients, tries to avoid giving clinics last-minute requests and deadlines for reports, and is more forthcoming with praise for clinic staff. More fully appreciating how patient care is the top priority and the nature of work on the clinic floor, Kibler is also more sensitive to how her own initiatives might affect these frontline employees and the patients they serve. As she indicates, "I am more conscious of the power of my words and my actions and the impact they have down in the organization."[164]

As part of its "Now Who's Boss Day," senior executives at Loews Hotels perform entry-level jobs one day per year to appreciate and understand the challenges in these jobs and ways to make performing them easier while improving customer service.[165] This program originated when Loews CEO Jonathan Tisch took part in a reality TV show called *Now Who's Boss?* and performed the jobs of pool attendant, housekeeper, and bellman at a Florida hotel. He perspired so much in the polyester uniform people in these jobs were required to wear that he changed the uniform. As a result of another manager's experience in the trenches, handlebars were installed on room service carts so they weren't as difficult to push.[166]

Clearly the jobs frontline employees perform are essential for organizational functioning. When top managers, who are far removed from these jobs, gain a better understanding of these jobs and the employees who perform them, they are in a better position to manage them effectively.

INCREASE DIVERSITY SKILLS Efforts to increase diversity skills focus on improving how managers and their subordinates interact with each other and improving their ability to work with different kinds of people.[167] An important issue here is being able to communicate with diverse employees. Diverse organizational members may have different communication styles, may differ in their language fluency, may use words differently, may differ in the nonverbal signals they send through facial expressions and body language, and may differ in how they perceive and interpret information. Managers and their subordinates must learn to communicate effectively with one another if an organization is to take advantage of the skills and abilities of its diverse workforce. Educating organizational members about differences in ways of communicating is often a good starting point.

Diversity education can help managers and subordinates gain a better understanding of how people may interpret certain kinds of comments. Diversity education also can help employees learn how to resolve misunderstandings. Organizational members should feel comfortable enough to "clear the air" and solve communication difficulties and misunderstandings as they occur rather than letting problems grow and fester without acknowledgment.

ENCOURAGE FLEXIBILITY Managers and their subordinates must learn how to be open to different approaches and ways of doing things. This does not mean organizational members have to suppress their personal styles. Rather, it means they must be open to, and not feel threatened by, different approaches and perspectives and must have the patience and flexibility needed to understand and appreciate diverse perspectives.[168]

To the extent feasible, managers should also be flexible enough to incorporate the differing needs of diverse employees. Earlier we mentioned that religious diversity suggests that people of certain religions might need time off for holidays that are traditionally workdays in the United States; managers need to anticipate and respond to such needs with flexibility (perhaps letting people skip the lunch hour so they can leave work early). Moreover, flexible work hours, the option to work from home, and cafeteria-style benefit plans (see Chapter 12) are just a few of the many ways in which managers can respond to the differing needs of diverse employees while enabling those employees to be effective contributors to an organization.

PAY CLOSE ATTENTION TO HOW ORGANIZATIONAL MEMBERS ARE EVALUATED Whenever feasible, it is desirable to rely on objective performance indicators (see Chapter 12) because they are less subject to bias. When objective indicators are not available or are inappropriate, managers should ensure that adequate time and attention are focused on the evaluation of employees' performance and that evaluators are held accountable for their evaluations.[169] Vague performance standards should be avoided.[170]

CONSIDER THE NUMBERS Looking at the numbers of members of different minority groups and women in various positions, at various levels in the hierarchy, in locations that differ in their desirability, and in any other relevant categorizations in an organization can tell managers important information about potential problems and ways to rectify them.[171] If members of certain groups are underrepresented in particular kinds of jobs or units, managers need to understand why this is the case and resolve any problems they might uncover.

EMPOWER EMPLOYEES TO CHALLENGE DISCRIMINATORY BEHAVIORS, ACTIONS, AND REMARKS When managers or employees witness another organizational member being unfairly treated, they should be encouraged to speak up and rectify the situation. Top managers can make this happen by creating an organizational culture (see Chapter 3) that has zero tolerance for discrimination. As part of such a culture, organizational members should feel empowered to challenge discriminatory behavior, whether the behavior is directed at them or they witness it being directed at another employee.[172]

REWARD EMPLOYEES FOR EFFECTIVELY MANAGING DIVERSITY If effective management of diversity is a valued organizational objective, then employees should be rewarded for their contributions to this objective, as is true at Sodexo in "A Manager's Challenge."[173] For example, after settling a major race discrimination lawsuit, Coca-Cola Company now ties managers' pay to their achievement of diversity goals. Examples of other organizations that do so include American Express and Bayer Corporation.[174]

PROVIDE TRAINING UTILIZING A MULTIPRONGED, ONGOING APPROACH Many managers use a multipronged approach to increase diversity awareness and skills in their organizations; they use films and printed materials supplemented by experiential exercises to uncover hidden biases and stereotypes. Sometimes simply providing a forum for people to learn about and discuss their differing attitudes, values, and experiences can be a powerful means of increasing awareness. Also useful are role-plays that enact problems resulting from lack of awareness and show the increased understanding that comes from appreciating others' viewpoints. Accurate information and training experiences can debunk stereotypes. Group exercises, role-plays, and diversity-related experiences can help organizational members develop the skills they need to work effectively with a variety of people. Many organizations hire outside consultants to provide diversity training, in addition to utilizing their own in-house diversity experts.[175]

United Parcel Service (UPS), a package delivery company, developed an innovative community internship program to increase the diversity awareness and skills of its managers and, at the same time, benefit the wider community. Upper and middle managers participating in the program take one month off the job to be community interns.[176] They work in community organizations helping people who in many instances are very different from themselves–such organizations include a detention center in McAllen, Texas, for Mexican immigrants; homeless shelters; AIDS centers; Head Start programs; migrant farmworker assistance groups; and groups aiming to halt the spread of drug abuse in inner cities.

Interacting with and helping diverse people enhances the interns' awareness of diversity because they experience it firsthand. Bill Cox, a UPS division manager who spent a month in the McAllen detention center, summed up his experience of diversity: "You've got these [thousands of] migrant workers down in McAllen . . . and they don't want what you have. All they want is an opportunity to earn what you have. That's a fundamental change in understanding that only comes from spending time with these people." [177]

mentoring A process by which an experienced member of an organization (the mentor) provides advice and guidance to a less experienced member (the protégé) and helps the less experienced member learn how to advance in the organization and in his or her career.

Many managers who complete the UPS community internship program have superior diversity skills as a result of their experiences. During their internships, they learn about different cultures and approaches to work and life; they learn to interact effectively with people whom they ordinarily do not come into contact with; and they are forced to learn flexibility because of the dramatic differences between their roles at the internship sites and their roles as managers at UPS.

ENCOURAGE MENTORING OF DIVERSE EMPLOYEES Unfortunately African-Americans and other minorities continue to be less likely to attain high-level positions in their organizations; and for those who do attain them, the climb up the corporate ladder typically takes longer than it does for white men. David Thomas, a professor at the Harvard Business School, has studied the careers of minorities in corporate America. One of his major conclusions is that mentoring is very important for minorities, most of whom have reached high levels in their organizations by having a solid network of mentors and contacts.[178] **Mentoring** is a process by which an experienced member of an organization (the mentor) provides advice and guidance to a less experienced member (the protégé) and helps the less experienced member learn how to advance in the organization and in his or her career.

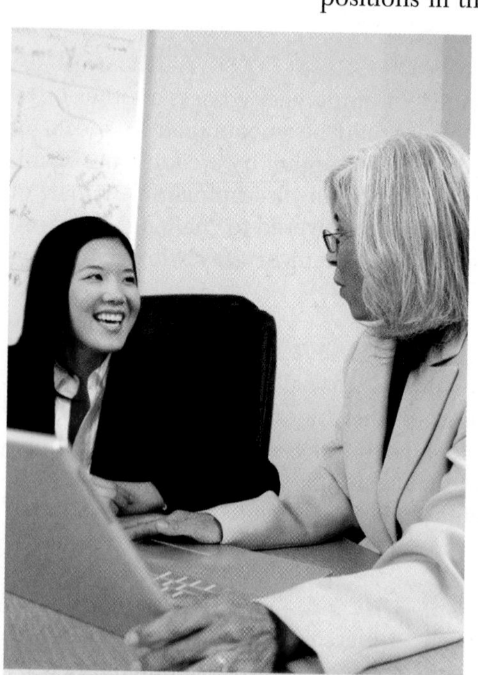

Ah, the power of a listening ear. The mentoring process allows a newer employee the chance to gain an edge through informal conversation.

According to Thomas, effective mentoring is more than providing instruction, offering advice, helping build skills, and sharing technical expertise. Of course these aspects of mentoring are important and necessary. However, equally important is developing a high-quality, close, and supportive relationship with the protégé. Emotional bonds between a mentor and a protégé can enable a protégé, for example, to express fears and concerns, and sometimes even reluctance to follow a mentor's advice. The mentor can help the protégé build his or her confidence and feel comfortable engaging in unfamiliar work behaviors.[179]

Pat Carmichael, a senior vice president at JPMorgan Chase, has mentored hundreds of protégés throughout her career and exemplifies effective mentoring.[180] She encourages her protégés to seek difficult assignments and feedback from their supervisors. She also helps her protégés build networks of contacts and has an extensive network herself. She serves as both a coach and a counselor to her protégés and encourages them to seek opportunities to address their weaknesses and broaden their horizons.[181]

Sexual Harassment

Sexual harassment seriously damages both the people who are harassed and the reputation of the organization in which it occurs. It also can cost organizations large amounts of money. In 1995, for example, Chevron Corporation agreed to pay $2.2 million to settle a sexual harassment lawsuit filed by four women who worked at the Chevron Information Technology Company in San Ramon, California. One woman involved in the suit said she had received violent pornographic material through the company mail. Another, an electrical engineer, said she had been asked to bring pornographic videos to Chevron workers at an Alaska drill site.[182] More recently, in 2001 TWA settled a lawsuit to the tune of $2.6 million that alleged that female employees were sexually harassed at JFK International Airport in New York. According to the EEOC, not only was sexual harassment tolerated at TWA, but company officials did little to curtail it when it was brought to their attention.[183]

Unfortunately the events at Chevron and TWA are not isolated incidents.[184] Of the 607 women surveyed by the National Association for Female Executives, 60% indicated that they had experienced some form of sexual harassment.[185] Sexual harassment victims can be women or men, and their harassers do not necessarily have to be of the opposite sex.[186] However, women are the most frequent victims of sexual harassment, particularly those in male-dominated occupations or those who occupy positions stereotypically associated with certain gender relationships, such as a female secretary reporting to a male boss. Though it occurs less frequently, men can also be victims of sexual harassment. For instance, several male employees at Jenny Craig filed a lawsuit claiming they were subject to lewd and inappropriate comments from female coworkers and managers.[187] Sexual harassment is not only unethical; it is also illegal. Managers have an ethical obligation to ensure that they, their coworkers, and their subordinates never engage in sexual harassment, even unintentionally.

LO5-6 Identify the two major forms of sexual harassment and how they can be eliminated.

Forms of Sexual Harassment

There are two basic forms of sexual harassment: quid pro quo sexual harassment and hostile work environment sexual harassment. **Quid pro quo sexual harassment** occurs when a harasser asks or forces an employee to perform sexual favors to keep a job, receive a promotion, receive a raise, obtain some other work-related opportunity, or avoid receiving negative consequences such as demotion or dismissal.[188] This "Sleep with me, honey, or you're fired" form of harassment is the more extreme type and leaves no doubt in anyone's mind that sexual harassment has taken place.[189]

quid pro quo sexual harassment Asking for or forcing an employee to perform sexual favors in exchange for receiving some reward or avoiding negative consequences.

hostile work environment sexual harassment Telling lewd jokes, displaying pornography, making sexually oriented remarks about someone's personal appearance, and other sex-related actions that make the work environment unpleasant.

Hostile work environment sexual harassment is more subtle. It occurs when organizational members face an intimidating, hostile, or offensive work environment because of their sex.[190] Lewd jokes, sexually oriented comments or innuendos, vulgar language, displays of pornography, displays or distribution of sexually oriented objects, and sexually oriented remarks about one's physical appearance are examples of hostile work environment sexual harassment.[191] A hostile work environment interferes with organizational members' ability to perform their jobs effectively and has been deemed illegal by the courts. Managers who engage in hostile work environment harassment or allow others to do so risk costly lawsuits for their organizations. For example, in February 2004 a federal jury awarded Marion Schwab $3.24 million after deliberating on her sexual harassment case against FedEx.[192] Schwab was the only female tractor-trailer driver at the FedEx facility serving the Harrisburg International Airport vicinity in Middletown, Pennsylvania, from 1997 to 2000. During that period she was the target of sexual innuendos, was given inferior work assignments, and was the brunt of derogatory comments about her appearance and the role of women in society. On five occasions the brakes on her truck were tampered with. The federal EEOC sued FedEx, and Schwab was part of the suit.[193]

The courts have recently recognized other forms of hostile work environment harassment, in addition to sexual harassment. For example, in June 2006 a California jury awarded $61 million in punitive and compensatory damages to two FedEx Ground drivers. The drivers, who are of Lebanese descent, indicated that they faced a hostile work environment and high levels of stress because a manager harassed them with racial slurs for two years.[194] FedEx plans to appeal the decision.[195]

Steps Managers Can Take to Eradicate Sexual Harassment

Managers have an ethical obligation to eradicate sexual harassment in their organizations. There are many ways to accomplish this objective. Here are four initial steps managers can take to deal with the problem:[196]

- *Develop and clearly communicate a sexual harassment policy endorsed by top management.* This policy should include prohibitions against both quid pro quo and hostile work environment sexual harassment. It should contain (1) examples of types of behavior that are unacceptable, (2) a procedure for employees to use to report instances of harassment, (3) a discussion of the disciplinary actions that will be taken when harassment has taken place, and (4) a commitment to educate and train organizational members about sexual harassment.
- *Use a fair complaint procedure to investigate charges of sexual harassment.* Such a procedure should (1) be managed by a neutral third party, (2) ensure that complaints are dealt with promptly and thoroughly, (3) protect and fairly treat victims, and (4) ensure that alleged harassers are fairly treated.
- *When it has been determined that sexual harassment has taken place, take corrective actions as soon as possible.* These actions can vary depending on the severity of the harassment. When harassment is extensive, prolonged, of a quid pro quo nature, or severely objectionable in some other manner, corrective action may include firing the harasser.
- *Provide sexual harassment education and training to all organizational members, including managers.* The majority of *Fortune* 500 firms currently provide this education and training for their employees. Managers at DuPont, for example, developed DuPont's "A Matter of Respect" program to help educate employees about sexual harassment and eliminate its occurrence. The program includes a four-hour workshop in which participants are given information that defines sexual harassment, sets forth the company's policy against it, and explains how to report complaints and access a 24-hour hotline. Participants watch video clips showing actual instances of harassment. One clip shows a saleswoman having dinner with a male client who, after much negotiating, seems about to give her company his business when he suddenly suggests that they continue their conversation in his hotel room. The saleswoman is confused about what to do. Will she be reprimanded if she says no and the deal is lost? After watching a video, participants discuss what they have seen, why the behavior is inappropriate, and what organizations can do to alleviate the problem.[197] Throughout the program, managers stress to employees that they do not have to tolerate sexual harassment or get involved in situations in which harassment is likely to occur.

Barry S. Roberts and Richard A. Mann, experts on business law and authors of several books on the topic, suggest a number of additional factors that managers and all members of an organization need to keep in mind about sexual harassment:[198]

- Every sexual harassment charge should be taken seriously.
- Employees who go along with unwanted sexual attention in the workplace can be sexual harassment victims.

- Employees sometimes wait before they file complaints of sexual harassment.
- An organization's sexual harassment policy should be communicated to each new employee and reviewed with current employees periodically.
- Suppliers and customers need to be familiar with an organization's sexual harassment policy.
- Managers should give employees alternative ways to report incidents of sexual harassment.
- Employees who report sexual harassment must have their rights protected; this includes being protected from any potential retaliation.
- Allegations of sexual harassment should be kept confidential; those accused of harassment should have their rights protected.
- Investigations of harassment charges and any resultant disciplinary actions need to proceed in a timely manner.
- Managers must protect employees from sexual harassment from third parties they may interact with while performing their jobs, such as suppliers or customers.[199]

Summary and Review

LO5-1 **THE INCREASING DIVERSITY OF THE WORKFORCE AND THE ENVIRONMENT** Diversity is dissimilarity or differences among people. Diversity is a pressing concern for managers and organizations for business and ethical reasons. There are multiple forms of diversity such as age, gender, race and ethnicity, religion, capabilities/disabilities, socioeconomic background, sexual orientation, and physical appearance.

LO5-2, 5-3 **MANAGERS AND THE EFFECTIVE MANAGEMENT OF DIVERSITY** Both the workforce and the organizational environment are increasingly diverse, and effectively managing this diversity is an essential component of management. In each of their managerial roles, managers can encourage the effective management of diversity, which is both an ethical and a business imperative.

LO5-4 **PERCEPTION** Perception is the process through which people select, organize, and interpret sensory input to give meaning and order to the world around them. It is inherently subjective. Schemas guide perception; when schemas are based on a single visible characteristic such as race or gender, they are stereotypes and highly inaccurate, leading to unfair treatment. Unfair treatment also can result from biases and overt discrimination.

LO5-5 **HOW TO MANAGE DIVERSITY EFFECTIVELY** Managers can take many steps to effectively manage diversity. Effective management of diversity is an ongoing process that requires frequent monitoring.

LO5-6 **SEXUAL HARASSMENT** Two forms of sexual harassment are quid pro quo sexual harassment and hostile work environment sexual harassment. Steps that managers can take to eradicate sexual harassment include development and communication of a sexual harassment policy endorsed by top management, use of fair complaint procedures, prompt corrective action when harassment occurs, and sexual harassment training and education.

Management in Action

Topics for Discussion and Action

Discussion

1. Discuss why violations of the principles of distributive and procedural justice continue to occur in modern organizations. What can managers do to uphold these principles in their organizations? [LO5-2, 5-3, 5-4, 5-5]
2. Why do workers who test positive for HIV sometimes get discriminated against? [LO5-1, 5-4]
3. Why would some employees resent accommodations made for employees with disabilities that are dictated by the Americans with Disabilities Act? [LO5-1, 5-4]
4. Discuss the ways in which schemas can be functional and dysfunctional. [LO5-4]
5. Discuss an occasion when you may have been treated unfairly because of stereotypical thinking. What stereotypes were applied to you? How did they result in your being treated unfairly? [LO5-4]
6. How does the similar-to-me effect influence your own behavior and decisions? [LO5-4]
7. Why is mentoring particularly important for minorities? [LO5-5]
8. Why is it important to consider the numbers of different groups of employees at various levels in an organization's hierarchy? [LO5-5]
9. Think about a situation in which you would have benefited from mentoring but a mentor was not available. What could you have done to try to get the help of a mentor in this situation? [LO5-5]

Action

10. Choose a *Fortune* 500 company not mentioned in the chapter. Conduct research to determine what steps this organization has taken to effectively manage diversity and eliminate sexual harassment. [LO5-2, 5-5, 5-6]

Building Management Skills [LO5-1, 5-2, 5-3, 5-4, 5-5, 5-6]

Solving Diversity-Related Problems

Think about the last time that you (1) were treated unfairly because you differed from a decision maker on a particular dimension of diversity or (2) observed someone else being treated unfairly because that person differed from a decision maker on a particular dimension of diversity. Then answer these questions:

1. Why do you think the decision maker acted unfairly in this situation?
2. In what ways, if any, were biases, stereotypes, or overt discrimination involved in this situation?
3. Was the decision maker aware that he or she was acting unfairly?
4. What could you or the person who was treated unfairly have done to improve matters and rectify the injustice on the spot?
5. Was any sexual harassment involved in this situation? If so, what kind was it?
6. If you had authority over the decision maker (that is, if you were his or her manager or supervisor), what steps would you take to ensure that the decision maker no longer treated diverse individuals unfairly?

Managing Ethically [LO5-1, 5-2, 5-3, 5-5]

Some companies require that their employees work long hours and travel extensively. Employees with young children, employees taking care of elderly relatives, and employees who have interests outside the workplace sometimes find that their careers are jeopardized if they try to work more reasonable hours or limit their work-related travel. Some of these employees feel that it is unethical for their managers to expect so much of them in the workplace and not understand their needs as parents and caregivers.

Questions

1. Either individually or in a group, think about the ethical implications of requiring long hours and extensive amounts of travel for some jobs.
2. What obligations do you think managers and companies have to enable employees to have balanced lives and meet nonwork needs and demands?

Small Group Breakout Exercise [LO5-1, 5-2, 5-3, 5-4, 5-5]

Determining If a Problem Exists

Form groups of three or four people, and appoint one member as the spokesperson who will communicate your findings to the whole class when called on by the instructor. Then discuss the following scenario:

You and your partners own and manage a local chain of restaurants, with moderate to expensive prices, that are open for lunch and dinner during the week and for dinner on weekends. Your staff is diverse, and you believe that you are effectively managing diversity. Yet on visits to the different restaurants you have noticed that your African-American employees tend to congregate together and communicate mainly with each other. The same is true for your Hispanic employees and your white employees. You are meeting with your partners today to discuss this observation.

1. Discuss why the patterns of communication that you observed might be occurring in your restaurants.
2. Discuss whether your observation reflects an underlying problem. If so, why? If not, why not?
3. Discuss whether you should address this issue with your staff and in your restaurants. If so, how and why? If not, why not?

Exploring the World Wide Web [LO5-1, 5-2, 5-3, 5-5, 5-6]

Go to the U.S. government Web sites that deal with employment issues, diversity, and sexual harassment, such as the Web sites of the Equal Employment Opportunity Commission (EEOC) and the Bureau of Labor Statistics. After reviewing these Web sites, develop a list of tips to help managers effectively manage diversity and avoid costly lawsuits.

Be the Manager [LO5-1, 5-2, 5-3, 5-4, 5-5]

You are Maria Herrera and have been recently promoted to the position of director of financial analysis for a medium-sized consumer goods firm. During your first few weeks on the job, you took the time to have lunch with each of your subordinates to try to get to know them better. You have 12 direct reports who are junior and senior financial analysts who support different product lines. Susan Epstein, one of the female financial analysts you had lunch with, made the following statement: "I'm so glad we finally have a woman in charge. Now, hopefully things will get better around here." You pressed Epstein to elaborate, but she clammed up. She indicated that she didn't want to unnecessarily bias you and that the problems were pretty self-evident. In fact, Epstein was surprised that you didn't know what she was talking about and jokingly mentioned that perhaps you should spend some time undercover, observing her group and their interactions with others.

You spoke with your supervisor and the former director, who had been promoted and had volunteered to be on call if you had any questions. Neither man knew of any diversity-related issues in your group. In fact, your supervisor's response was, "We've got a lot of problems, but fortunately that's not one of them."

What are you going to do to address this issue?

Case in the News [LO5-1, 5-2, 5-3, 5-4, 5-5]

A Historic Succession at Xerox

Ursula M. Burns isn't one to savor victory—even if it's being the first African-American woman to lead a major U.S. corporation and the first female CEO to take the reins from another woman. Within days of being named chief executive of Xerox she was on a plane to Europe. The mission: a 30-day tour to meet with staff outside the United States, where Xerox has almost half its sales, and discuss ways to get customers buying again. "I think the celebration of her announcement ended about 60 seconds after the e-mail went out," says Clarke Murphy, a recruiter at Russell Reynolds.

Burns, 50, has a war to fight. Xerox, a brand so synonymous with copying that its name long ago became a verb, faces a brutal business outlook. Customers are buying less equipment. Prices keep dropping. Managers are curbing paper use for cost-saving and environmental reasons. While departing CEO Anne M. Mulcahy, 56, pulled the $17.6 billion-a-year copier giant from the brink of bankruptcy and restored profitability, her successor has much to do. Burns will find herself battling competitors with stronger balance sheets and more heft as the industry consolidates. The Norwalk (Connecticut) company's sales dropped 18% in the first quarter, to $3.6 billion, producing a profit of only $49 million. The stock, trading at more than $14 a share in September, is now less than half that.

And yet expectations are high as Burns ascends to the CEO post. Executives inside and outside the company speak of her deep industry knowledge and technical prowess, as well as her frankness, sharp humor, and willingness to take risks. For many working mothers, it's inspiring to see Mulcahy, a mother of two grown sons, step down in favor of a woman who has a 16-year-old daughter and 20-year-old stepson—and was herself raised by a single mother in a New York City housing project. "This is a bases-loaded home run," says Noel M. Tichy, a professor at the University of Michigan Ross School of Business. "We now have something to share with our MBA females that we've never had." Adds Robert A. McDonald, chief operating officer of Procter & Gamble and a Xerox board member since 2005, "Ursula is a strong leader who has an unusual ability to understand the power of technology and innovation."

The excitement is understandable. Three decades after women flooded into professional jobs, the C-suite continues to be dominated by men. While women now make up 59.6% of the U.S. labor force, fewer than 16% of top corporate officers are female, according to Catalyst, an advocacy group that tracks women's advancement in the workplace. For minorities, the figures are even worse. Avon CEO Andrea Jung became the first nonwhite woman to lead a major company in 1999. Frank D. Raines, former chief of Fannie Mae, became the first African-American CEO of a top company the same year, though he later left amid an accounting scandal. By 2007, there were seven black men running major corporations. Since then, three have left. While other black women have run major divisions, Burns is the first to lead a large public company.

"Classic New Yorker"

A mechanical engineer by training, Burns has a strong understanding of the business and its challenges. Like Mulcahy, she's a Xerox veteran. She came to the company as a summer intern in 1980, joining full-time a year later after completing her master's degree in engineering at Columbia University. Xerox was drifting at the time, having largely ignored the threat posed by Japanese copiers and new office printers, while failing to get innovative products to market. She took on roles of increasing responsibility, distinguishing herself as a quick study who could handle multiple tasks at once and wasn't afraid to flag a problem. "Ursula is your classic New Yorker," says Christa Carone, Xerox's vice president for marketing and communications. "She's known for being very frank."

Reginald L. Brown Jr., CEO of consultancy Brown Technology Group, says many colleagues saw her as CEO material almost two decades ago. Brown began working with Burns in the late 1980s in Xerox's custom systems division, which helped clients switch from standard copier machines to ones that could be integrated with computer networks. When Burns was appointed special assistant to Wayland Hicks, then president of marketing and customer operations, in 1990, everyone knew she was on the fast track. "These were jobs in the company that division presidents put their best people in," says Brown. "Most of them were white males, so to have an African-American female in such a position of power, you knew early on she had great potential." She later took on a similar role with then-CEO Paul A. Allaire. Appointed general manager in 1997 and vice president for worldwide manufacturing two years later, Burns helped lead a push into color copying.

But the overall business continued to struggle. By the time Mulcahy took over as CEO in 2001, Xerox was in deep trouble. Customers had migrated from Xerox's stand-alone copiers to using cheaper desktop printers to get multiple copies of documents. Rivals such as Canon and Hewlett-Packard had stolen the lead in key product areas, and the company had pulled down almost its entire credit line as the business hemorrhaged money.

Early in Mulcahy's tenure, she forged a partnership with Burns. Over time, she entrusted her lieutenant with much of the day-to-day operations while she focused on improving customer service and Xerox's financial health. Mulcahy oversaw major moves such as shedding the desktop printer business while trying to get the balance sheet in shape.

All the while, Tichy observes, Burns was the one who was "clearly running the majority of the business." With the company in crisis, she helped downsize the workforce by close to 40%, to 57,100 from 94,600. She spearheaded Xerox's move out of manufacturing, with Flextronics now making most of the actual copiers. Burns, who was named president in 2007, also identified some gaps in its offerings, filling them with lower-end products from Xerox or partners. That has given the company its largest product portfolio in history and allowed it to be more competitive in selling to small and midsize businesses. And she has proven adept at garnering the support of the board. "She understands the technology and can communicate it in a way that a director can understand it," says P&G's McDonald.

Another factor in Burns's rise has been the strength and depth of Xerox's commitment to diversity. One-third of Xerox's 3,819 executives are women, and 22% are minorities. Employee affinity networks first sprang up in the late 1960s, and senior executives have long had responsibility for sponsoring them. Burns was a liaison to the Hispanic employees' caucus. "It was a system that allowed you to be recognized" at a time when women and minorities often weren't, notes Nina Smith, who moved up the ranks at Xerox at much the same time as Burns, eventually becoming chief marketing officer. She's now a senior vice president at IT consultant Mitchell International.

Much of what Xerox does is now replicated in other companies: an Executive Diversity Council, leadership programs, and performance reviews that rate managers on their ability to recruit, mentor, and promote underrepresented groups. (If they don't hit the mark, their review, pay, and chances at promotion get dinged.) What has distinguished Xerox is less the outline of its programs than the actual makeup of its senior ranks. As Harvard Business School professor David A. Thomas observes, "You have a culture where having women and people of color as candidates for powerful jobs has been going on for two decades."

Now Burns's toughest job will be restoring the company's top-line growth. Equipment sales were down 30% in the first quarter. And once fast-growing developing markets, which make up 15% of sales, have slowed to a crawl with demand in countries such as Russia off 33%. While analyst Richard Gardner of Citigroup Global Markets argues that the company's strength in color printing and recent acquisitions should help it rebuild, he expects a steep dip in sales this year, to $14.7 billion.

Xerox says its investment in innovative products will help it emerge from the recession stronger. But Gartner Group says it expects corporate purchases of copiers, printers, and other hardware to remain flat through 2012 while prices will continue to slide. And Fitch Ratings put Xerox's $9 billion in BBB-rated debt on a negative outlook after the first-quarter numbers came in. "Will they be able to make acquisitions?" asks Fitch analyst Nick N. Nilarp. "Or will they just continue very slow growth, if at all?"

In the short term, analysts hope Burns will focus on reviving sales in emerging markets while continuing to expand into higher-margin services at home. And Xerox needs to be more efficient to compete against aggressive and deep-pocketed competitors.

While Burns has much to do to rebuild Xerox's strength, she's aware of the significance of what she has already achieved. As president, she once told an audience at the YWCA in Cleveland, "I'm in this job because I believe I earned it through hard work and high performance. Did I get some opportunities early in my career because of my race and gender? Probably. . . . I went to work for a company that was openly seeking to diversify its workforce. So, I imagine race and gender got the hiring guys' attention. And then the rest was really up to me."

Questions for Discussion

1. Why was the succession of Ursula Burns to the top position at Xerox considered historic?
2. Why are there so few women and minority CEOs of large corporations?
3. What steps have managers at Xerox taken to effectively manage diversity? What are the consequences of these initiatives?
4. Why does the effective management of diversity make good business sense?

Source: N. Byrnes and R. O. Crockett, "An Historic Succession at Xerox," *BusinessWeek*, June 8, 2009, 18–22. Reprinted from June 8, 2009 issue of *Bloomberg Businessweek* by special permission, copyright © 2009 by Bloomberg L.P.

CHAPTER 6

Managing in the Global Environment

Learning Objectives

After studying this chapter, you should be able to:

LO6-1 Explain why the ability to perceive, interpret, and respond appropriately to the global environment is crucial for managerial success.

LO6-2 Differentiate between the global task and global general environments.

LO6-3 Identify the main forces in the global task and general environments, and describe the challenges that each force presents to managers.

LO6-4 Explain why the global environment is becoming more open and competitive, and identify the forces behind the process of globalization that increase the opportunities, complexities, challenges, and threats managers face.

LO6-5 Discuss why national cultures differ and why it is important that managers be sensitive to the effects of falling trade barriers and regional trade associations on the political and social systems of nations around the world.

A MANAGER'S CHALLENGE

A Turnaround at Sony Is in the Works

Why is managing the global environment so complex today? Sony, the Japanese electronics maker, was renowned in the 1990s for using its engineering prowess to develop blockbuster new products such as the Walkman, Trinitron TV, and PlayStation. Its engineers churned out an average of four new product ideas every day—something attributed to its culture, called the "Sony Way," which emphasized communication, cooperation, and harmony between its product engineering teams across the company.[1] Sony's engineers were given the freedom to pursue their own ideas, and its different product teams pursued their own innovations; but problems arose with this approach in the 2000s.

Companies in Korea and Taiwan such as LG and Samsung made major innovations in technologies such as the development of advanced LCD screen displays and flash memory that made Sony's technologies obsolete. On the product front, companies such as Apple, Nokia, and Nintendo came out with digital devices such as the iPod, smartphones, and the Wii game console that better met customer needs than Sony's old-fashioned and expensive products. Finally, all these companies were working to reduce manufacturing costs, and Sony lagged behind because its bloated cost structure had made its products expensive and uncompetitive. Why did Sony lose its competitive advantage in both style and price?

One reason was that Sony's culture no longer worked in its favor. The top managers of its most successful divisions worked to protect their own divisions' interests—not Sony's—and they had been slow to recognize the major changes taking place in the technological and global environment. As Sony's performance fell, competition between managers increased, slowing strategic decision

Sir Howard Stringer, flanked by two younger executives, shows off new Sony products. Stringer's embrace of those outside Japan may help turn the flagging multinational around.

making, making it harder for the company to take advantage of its extensive pipeline of new product innovations, and increasing operating costs because each division fought to obtain the funding necessary to develop and promote new products.

By 2005 Sony was in big trouble; and at this crucial point in their company's history, Sony's Japanese top managers turned to a *gaijin,* or non-Japanese, executive to lead their company. Their choice was Sir Howard Stringer, a Welshman, the previous head of Sony's North American operations who had been instrumental in cutting costs and increasing the profits of Sony's U.S. division. Once he became CEO in 2005, Stringer faced the immediate problem of reducing Sony's operating costs, which were double those of its competitors even as it was losing its technological leadership. Stringer had to make many radical strategic decisions.

Japan is a country where large companies traditionally had a policy of lifetime employment, but Stringer made it clear that layoffs were inevitable. Within five years he cut Sony's Japanese workforce by over 25,000 employees and closed 12 factories to reduce costs. Stringer also recognized how the extensive power struggles among the top managers of Sony's different product divisions were hurting the company, and he made it clear that these problems had to stop. Many top divisional managers, including the manager of Sony's successful PlayStation division, ignored Stringer; they were replaced, and he worked steadily to downsize Sony's bloated corporate headquarters staff and to change its culture. In Stringer's own words, the culture or "business of Sony has been management, not making products." In 2009 Stringer announced he would take charge of the Japanese company's struggling core electronics group and would add the title of president to his existing roles as chairman and CEO as he reorganized Sony's divisions. He also replaced four more top executives with young managers who had held positions outside Japan and were "familiar with the digital world." In the future, according to Stringer, managers must prioritize new products and invest in only those with the greatest chance of success so Sony could reduce its out-of-control R&D costs.

Stringer worked hard to bring the realities of global competition to the forefront at Sony—along with the need to deal with them quickly. Beyond his internal problems, he also pushed for major changes in how Sony picked its suppliers. Stringer's goal was to reduce the number of Sony's parts suppliers from 2,500 to 1,200 to cut purchasing costs by over $5 billion or 20 percent. This would require cooperation between divisions because in the past each division made its own purchasing decisions. In the future Sony will centralize purchasing to negotiate cheaper prices by increasing the amount of business it does with its remaining suppliers.

By 2010 Sony's financial results suggested that Stringer's initiatives were finally paying off; he had stemmed Sony's huge losses, and its products were selling better. For example, PlayStation 3 sales jumped more than 40% after a 25% price cut and continued to outperform Nintendo's Wii. Although Sony still expected to lose money in 2010, Stringer expected Sony to become profitable by 2011. To help ensure this Stringer also took charge of a newly created networked products and services group that included its Vaio computers, Walkman media players, Sony's PlayStation gaming console, and the software and online services to support these products. Stringer's goal was for Sony to regain its global leadership in making the premium, differentiated digital products that command high prices and result in good profit margins. In 2010 Sony announced a major initiative to push into new technologies such as 3D LCD TVs, tablet computers, digital viewers, and action gaming and introduced a new motion controller for its PlayStation.[2] But competitors such as Apple, Samsung, and Panasonic were also competing in these markets, so global rivalry was likely to remain intense.

Overview

LO6-1 Explain why the ability to perceive, interpret, and respond appropriately to the global environment is crucial for managerial success.

LO6-2 Differentiate between the global task and global general environments.

global organization An organization that operates and competes in more than one country.

Top managers of a global company like Sony operate in an environment where they compete with other companies for scarce and valuable resources. Managers of companies large and small have found that to survive and prosper in the 21st century, most organizations must become **global organizations** that operate and compete not only domestically, at home, but also globally, in countries around the world. Operating in the global environment is uncertain and unpredictable because it is complex and changes constantly.

If organizations are to adapt successfully to this changing environment, their managers must learn to understand the forces that operate in it and how these forces give rise to opportunities and threats. In this chapter we examine why the environment, both domestically and globally, has become more open, vibrant, and competitive. We examine how forces in the task and general environments affect global organizations and their managers. By the end of this chapter, you will appreciate the changes that are taking place in the environment and understand why it is important for managers to develop a global perspective as they strive to increase organizational efficiency and effectiveness.

What Is the Global Environment?

global environment The set of global forces and conditions that operate beyond an organization's boundaries but affect a manager's ability to acquire and utilize resources.

The **global environment** is a set of forces and conditions in the world outside an organization's boundary that affect how it operates and shape its behavior.[3] These forces change over time and thus present managers with *opportunities* and *threats.* Some changes in the global environment, such as the development of efficient new production technology, the availability of lower-cost components, or the opening of new global markets, create opportunities for managers to make and sell more products, obtain more resources and capital, and thereby strengthen their organization. In contrast, the rise of new global competitors, a global economic recession, or an oil shortage poses threats that can devastate an organization if managers are unable to sell its products so that revenues and profits plunge. The quality of managers' understanding of forces in the global environment and their ability to respond appropriately to those forces, such as Sony's managers' ability to make and sell the electronic products customers around the world want to buy, are critical factors affecting organizational performance.

In this chapter we explore the nature of these forces and consider how managers can respond to them. To identify opportunities and threats caused by forces in the environment, it is helpful for managers to distinguish between the *task environment* and the more encompassing *general environment* (see Figure 6.1).

Figure 6.1
Forces in the Global Environment

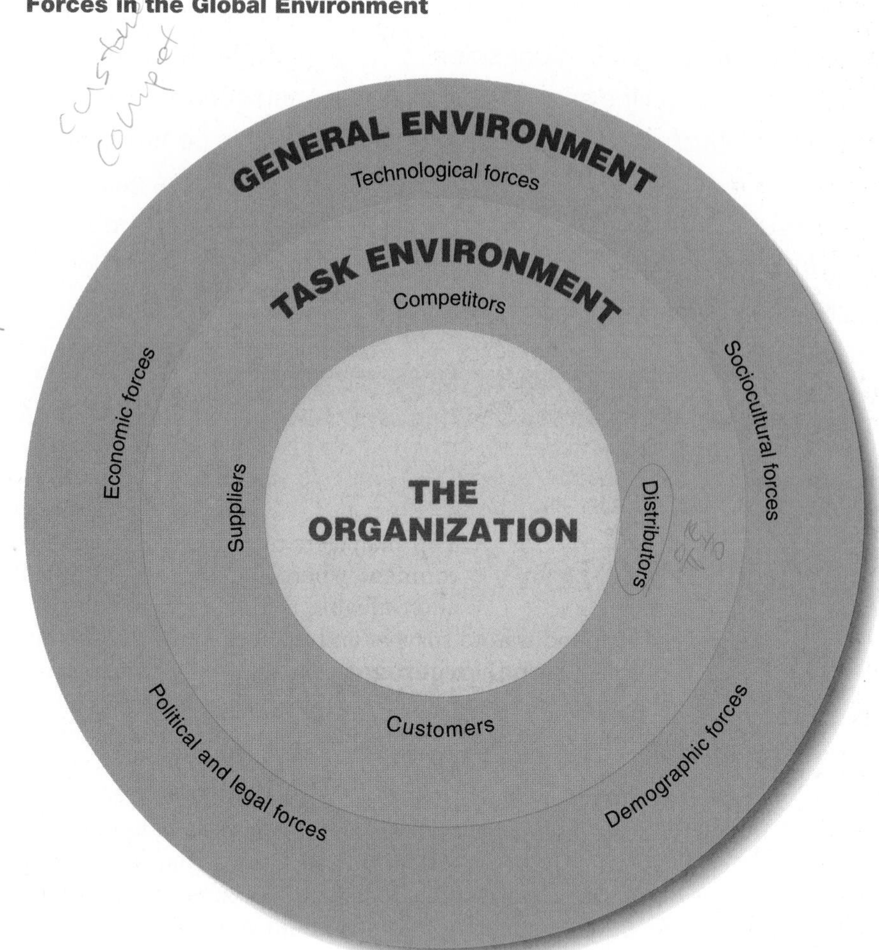

task environment The set of forces and conditions that originate with suppliers, distributors, customers, and competitors and affect an organization's ability to obtain inputs and dispose of its outputs because they influence managers daily.

general environment The wide-ranging global, economic, technological, sociocultural, demographic, political, and legal forces that affect an organization and its task environment.

The **task environment** is the set of forces and conditions that originate with global suppliers, distributors, customers, and competitors; these forces and conditions affect an organization's ability to obtain inputs and dispose of its outputs. The task environment contains the forces that have the most *immediate* and *direct* effect on managers because they pressure and influence managers daily. When managers turn on the radio or television, arrive at their offices in the morning, open their mail, or look at their computer screens, they are likely to learn about problems facing them because of changing conditions in their organization's task environment.

The **general environment** includes the wide-ranging global, economic, technological, sociocultural, demographic, political, and legal forces that affect the organization and its task environment. For the individual manager, opportunities and threats resulting from changes in the general environment are often more difficult to identify and respond to than are events in the task environment. However, changes in these forces can have major impacts on managers and their organizations.

The Task Environment

Forces in the task environment result from the actions of suppliers, distributors, customers, and competitors both at home and abroad (see Figure 6.1). These four groups affect a manager's ability to obtain resources and dispose of outputs daily, weekly, and monthly and thus have a significant impact on short-term decision making.

LO6-3 Identify the main forces in the global task and general environments, and describe the challenges that each force presents to managers.

suppliers Individuals and organizations that provide an organization with the input resources it needs to produce goods and services.

rev. increase during war

Suppliers

Suppliers are the individuals and companies that provide an organization with the input resources (such as raw materials, component parts, or employees) it needs to produce goods and services. In return, the suppliers receive payment for those goods and services. An important aspect of a manager's job is to ensure a reliable supply of input resources.

Take Dell Computer, for example, the company we focused on in Chapter 1. Dell has many suppliers of component parts such as microprocessors (Intel and AMD) and disk drives (Quantum and Seagate Technologies). It also has suppliers of preinstalled software, including the operating system and specific applications software (Microsoft and Google). Dell's providers of capital, such as banks and financial institutions, are also important suppliers. Cisco Systems and Oracle are important providers of Internet hardware and software for dot-coms.

Dell has several suppliers of labor. One source is the educational institutions that train future Dell employees and therefore provide the company with skilled workers. Another is trade unions, organizations that represent employee interests and can control the supply of labor by exercising the right of unionized workers to strike. Unions also can influence the terms and conditions under which labor is employed. Dell's workers are not unionized; when layoffs became necessary after the financial crisis of 2008–2009, Dell had few problems in laying off workers to reduce costs. In organizations and industries where unions are strong, however, such as the transportation industry, an important part of a manager's job is negotiating and administering agreements with unions and their representatives.

Changes in the nature, number, or type of suppliers produce opportunities and threats to which managers must respond if their organizations are to prosper. For example, a major supplier-related threat that confronts managers arises when suppliers' bargaining position is so strong that they can raise the prices of the inputs they supply to the organization. A supplier's bargaining position is especially strong when (1) the supplier is the sole source of an input and (2) the input is vital to the organization.[4] For example, for 17 years G. D. Searle was the sole supplier of NutraSweet, the artificial sweetener used in most diet soft drinks. Not only was NutraSweet an important ingredient in diet soft drinks, but it also was one for which there was no acceptable substitute (saccharin and other artificial sweeteners raised health concerns). Searle earned its privileged position because it invented and held the patent for NutraSweet, and patents prohibit other organizations from introducing competing products for 17 years. As a result Searle was able to demand a high price for NutraSweet, charging twice the price of an equivalent amount of sugar; and paying that price raised the costs of soft drink manufacturers such as Coca-Cola and PepsiCo. When Searle's patent expired many other companies introduced products similar to NutraSweet, and prices fell.[5] In the 2000s Splenda, which was made by McNeil Nutritionals, owned by Tate & Lyle, a British company, replaced NutraSweet as the artificial sweetener of choice, and NutraSweet's price fell further; Splenda began to command a high price from soft drink companies.[6]

In contrast, when an organization has many suppliers for a particular input, it is in a relatively strong bargaining position with those suppliers and can demand low-cost, high-quality inputs from them. Often an organization can use its power with suppliers to force them to reduce their prices, as Dell frequently does. Dell, for example, is constantly searching for low-cost suppliers abroad to keep its PC prices competitive. At a global level, organizations can buy products from suppliers overseas or become their own suppliers by manufacturing their products abroad.

It is important that managers recognize the opportunities and threats associated with managing the global supply chain. On one hand, gaining access to low-cost products made abroad represents an opportunity for U.S. companies to lower their input costs. On the other hand, managers who fail to use low-cost overseas suppliers create a threat and put their organizations at a competitive disadvantage.[7] Levi Strauss, for example, was slow to realize that it could not compete with the low-priced jeans sold

The purchasing activities of global companies have become increasingly complicated in recent years. More than 700 suppliers around the world produce parts for Boeing's new Dreamliner.

by Walmart and other retailers, and it was eventually forced to close all its U.S. jean factories and outsource manufacturing to low-cost overseas suppliers to cut the price of its jeans to a competitive level. Now it sells its low-priced jeans in Walmart. The downside to global outsourcing is, of course, the loss of millions of U.S. jobs, an issue we have discussed in previous chapters.

A common problem facing managers of large global companies such as Ford, Sony, and Dell is managing the development of a global supplier network that will allow their companies to keep costs down and quality high. For example, Boeing's 777 jet was originally built using 132,500 engineered components made by 545 global suppliers.[8] Although Boeing made the majority of these parts, eight Japanese suppliers made parts for the 777 fuselage, doors, and wings; a Singapore supplier made the doors for the plane's forward landing gear; and three Italian suppliers produced its wing flaps. Boeing decided to buy so many inputs from overseas suppliers because these suppliers were the best in the world at performing their particular activities, and Boeing's goal was to produce a high-quality final product–a vital requirement for aircraft safety and reliability.[9]

The purchasing activities of global companies have become increasingly complicated as a result of the development of a whole range of skills and competencies in different countries around the world. It is clearly in companies' interests to search out the lowest-cost, best-quality suppliers. IT and the Internet are continually making it easier for companies to coordinate complicated, long-distance exchanges involving the purchasing of inputs and the disposal of outputs–something Sony has taken advantage of as it trims the number of its suppliers to reduce costs.

global outsourcing The purchase or production of inputs or final products from overseas suppliers to lower costs and improve product quality or design.

Global outsourcing occurs when a company contracts with suppliers in other countries to make the various inputs or components that go into its products or to assemble the final products to reduce costs. For example, Apple contracts with companies in Taiwan to make inputs such as the chips, batteries, and LCD displays that power its digital devices; then it contracts with Chinese outsourcing companies such as Foxcom to assemble its final products–such as iPods, iPhones, and iPads. Apple outsources the distribution of its products around the world by contracting with companies such as FedEx or DHL.

Global outsourcing has grown enormously to take advantage of national differences in the cost and quality of resources such as labor or raw materials that can significantly reduce manufacturing costs or increase product quality or reliability. Today such global exchanges are becoming so complex that some companies specialize in managing other companies' global supply chains. Global companies use the services of overseas intermediaries or brokers, which are located close to potential suppliers, to find the suppliers that can best meet the needs of a particular company. They can design the most efficient supply chain for a company to outsource the component and assembly operations required to produce its final products. Because these suppliers are located in thousands of cities in many countries, finding them is difficult. Li & Fung, based in Hong Kong, is one broker that has helped hundreds of global companies to outsource their component or assembly operations to suitable overseas suppliers, especially suppliers in mainland China.[10]

Although outsourcing to take advantage of low labor costs has helped many companies perform better, in the late 2000s its risks have also become apparent, especially when issues such as reliability, quality, and speed are important. For example, the introduction of Boeing's 787 Dreamliner plane was delayed for over two years because the company, encouraged by the success of its 777 outsourcing program, increased its reliance on companies abroad. To design and make the 787, Boeing turned to its suppliers early in the development process to gain access to foreign ingenuity and cut costs. Boeing uses 50 U.S. suppliers but also 23 suppliers abroad, many of whom had problems in meeting Boeing's delivery requirements.

Design and quality issues arose, such as in 2008 when Boeing announced that an Italian supplier had stopped production of two sections of the fuselage because of structural design problems. The Dreamliner finally took its inaugural flight in 2010.[11] By contrast, in 2010 Hanes Brands (HBI), the underwear maker, announced an agreement to sell its yarn and thread operations to Parkdale, a large-scale yarn manufacturer based in Gastonia, North Carolina. In the future Parkdale will be HBI's yarn supplier in North America; because yarn is a simple product to make, HBI did not need to look outside the United States. Clearly outsourcing decisions need to be carefully considered given the nature of a company's products.[12] For example, in spring 2010 Caterpillar was deciding whether to "insource" production of excavators back to the United States because lower labor costs and increasing global shipping costs were making this the most efficient way to do business. On the other hand, some companies do not outsource production; they prefer to establish their own factories in countries around the world, as the example of Nokia in the following "Managing Globally" box suggests.

Managing Globally

Why Nokia Makes Cell Phones in Romania

Nokia is still the world's largest cell phone maker, although it has been fighting hard to maintain its lead as the popularity of smartphones has soared and companies like Apple, BlackBerry, Samsung, and now Google and Microsoft are competing for the lucrative smartphone segment of the market. While these other companies outsource their cell phone production to Asian companies, Nokia does not. Indeed, one reason for Nokia's continuing dominance in cell phones is its skills in global supply chain management, which allow it to provide low-cost phones that are customized to the needs of customers in different world regions. To achieve this, Nokia's global strategy is to make its phones in the world region where they are to be sold; so Nokia has built state-of-the-art factories in Germany, Brazil, China, and India, and in 2008 it opened a new plant in Romania to make phones for the expanding eastern European and Russian market.

A major reason for beginning operations in Romania is low labor costs. Skilled Romanian engineers can be hired for a quarter of what they would earn in Finland or Germany, and production line employees can expect to earn about $450 a month–a fraction of what Nokia's German employees earn. In fact, once Nokia's Romanian factory was running, Nokia closed its factory in Bochum, Germany, in 2008 because it was too expensive to operate in a highly competitive global environment.

Opening a new factory in a new country is a complex process; and to increase the chances its new factory would operate efficiently, Nokia's managers adopted several strategies. First they worked to create a culture in the factory that is attractive to its new Romanian employees so they will stay with the company and learn the skills required to make it operate more efficiently over time. For example, the factory's cafeteria offer free food, and there are gyms, sports facilities, and (of course) a Finnish sauna. In addition, although managers from other countries run the plant at present, Nokia hopes that within a few years most of the factory's managers and supervisors will be Romanian. Its goal is to create a career ladder that will motivate employees to perform at a high level and so be promoted.

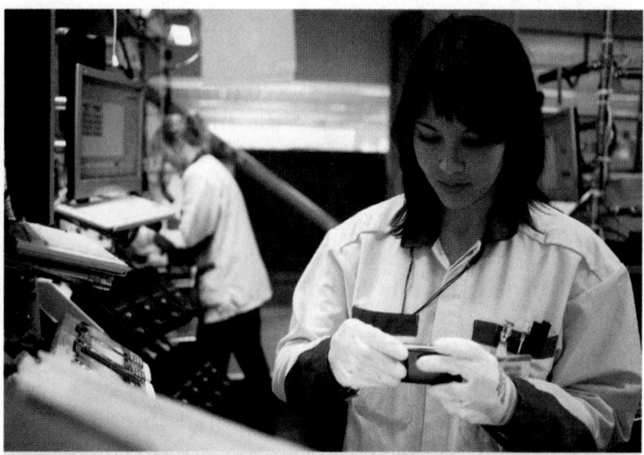

Nokia goes global by establishing operations in Romania. The plant has already performed beyond management's expectations, resulting in pay raises and more jobs for the area.

At the same time Nokia is hardheaded about how efficiently it expects its Romanian factory to operate because all its factories are required to operate at the same level of efficiency that its *most* efficient global factory has achieved. Thus Nokia has created a compensation plan for factory managers based on the *collective* performance of all its factories. This means managers in all its factories will see their bonuses reduced if just one factory in any country performs below expectations. This is a tough approach, but its purpose is to encourage all managers to develop more efficient manufacturing techniques, which, when learned in one factory, must be shared with all other factories around the world for managers to obtain their bonuses. Nokia's goal is that efficiency will improve constantly over time as managers are encouraged to find better ways to operate and then share this knowledge across the company.

Just six months after it opened in June 2008 the Romanian plant reached the 1 million handset produced milestone. The plant's efficiency has exceeded Nokia's expectations–so much so that Nokia opened a new cell phone accessory factory next to the plant and has hired hundreds of new workers who received a 9% salary increase in 2010 because of their high productivity. In 2010 Nokia was contemplating opening a plant in Argentina to serve the booming South American market.[13]

Distributors

distributors Organizations that help other organizations sell their goods or services to customers.

Distributors are organizations that help other organizations sell their goods or services to customers. The decisions managers make about how to distribute products to customers can have important effects on organizational performance. For example, package delivery companies such as Federal Express, UPS, and the U.S. Postal Service have become vital distributors for the millions of items bought online and shipped to customers by dot-com companies both at home and abroad.

The changing nature of distributors and distribution methods can bring opportunities and threats for managers. If distributors become so large and powerful that they can control customers' access to a particular organization's goods and services, they can threaten the organization by demanding that it reduce the prices of its goods and services.[14] For example, the huge retail distributor Walmart controls its suppliers' access to millions of customers and thus can demand that its suppliers reduce their prices to keep its business. If an organization such as Procter & Gamble refuses to reduce its prices, Walmart might respond by buying products only from Procter & Gamble's competitors–companies such as Unilever and Colgate. To reduce costs, Walmart also has used its power as a distributor to demand that all its suppliers adopt a new wireless radio frequency scanning technology to reduce the cost of shipping and stocking products in its stores; otherwise it would stop doing business with them.[15]

It is illegal for distributors to collaborate or collude to keep prices high and thus maintain their power over buyers; however, this frequently happens. In the early 2000s several European drug companies conspired to keep the price of vitamins artificially high. In 2005 the three largest global makers of flash memory, including Samsung, were found guilty of price fixing (they collaborated to keep prices high). All these companies paid hundreds of millions of dollars in fines, and many of their top executives were sentenced to jail terms. And sometimes government regulation can hurt customers because it confers monopoly power on distributors, as the following "Ethics in Action" box suggests.

Ethics in Action

Why Beer and Wine Are So Expensive: Powerful Distributors

One of the reasons Prohibition came into being in the United States was that many bars were owned by brewers of alcoholic beverages, and it was thought that this could lead to abuse. To separate the makers of alcoholic drinks such as beer and wine from alcohol sellers, most states adopted a three-tier distribution system that required manufacturers to sell to large distributors or wholesalers, which would sell to retailers–bars, liquor stores, and increasingly supermarkets and chain stores. It is estimated that this three-tier distribution system results in wholesalers adding a markup of about 25%, which means customers pay 25% more than they need to pay and wholesalers are making huge profits.

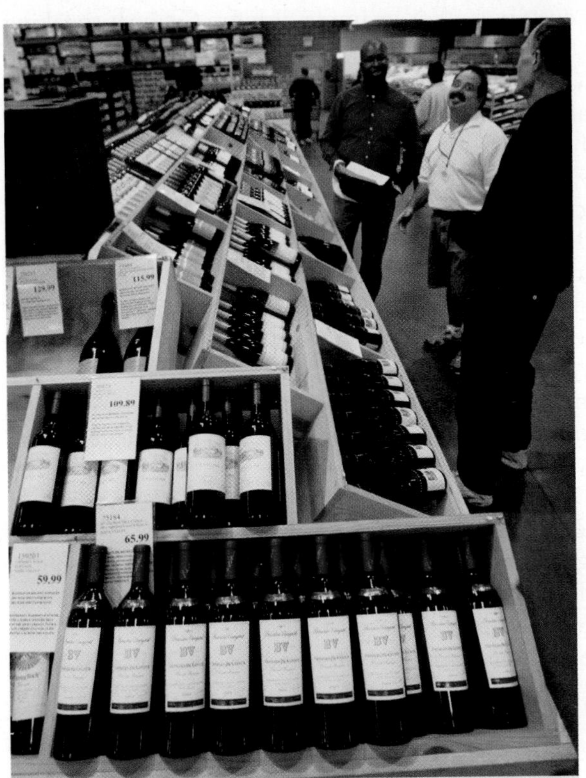

Costco's recent lawsuit means that U.S. lawmakers will be rethinking the regulation of alcohol sales in order to recoup the greatest profit for the states and to avoid wholesalers gobbling it up.

In 2006 Costco, the large warehouse store chain, won an antitrust lawsuit challenging its home state's three-tier system. As its CEO James Sinegal said of alcohol wholesalers, "I would like to have a business where everybody had to buy from me," and he estimated Costco could sell beer and wine for at least 10–20% less if retailers like Costco–or Walmart or Kroger's– could buy directly from the makers of alcoholic products.[16] Their great buying power would allow them to demand large price discounts from sellers, as has happened for other products such as soap and detergent.

The state of Washington appealed, however, arguing that the 21st Amendment ending prohibition gave states the authority to control alcohol regulation, including distribution. Washington was supported by 30 other states for an important reason: Sales of alcohol generate billions of dollars in state revenues, and it is much easier for states to collect that money when wholesalers distribute alcohol. In 2008 the U.S. Ninth Circuit Court of Appeals ruled largely in favor of Washington State, agreeing it had the right to decide if the three-tier system was appropriate. However, it also agreed with Costco that an important distribution rule, called a post-and-hold requirement, requiring every beer or wine distributor to file with the Liquor Control Board its wholesale prices and then maintain those prices for at least 30 days, was illegal and anticompetitive because it gave large wholesalers the information they needed to keep prices high.[17]

Despite the fact that Costco lost the appeal, the lawsuit showed how much profit goes to wholesalers, and it has led many lawmakers to think about how to change the whole distribution system so that each state–not the wholesalers–receives the high profits or taxes from the sale of alcohol. Thus while consumers might gain some relief if prices were lowered, each state would receive billions of dollars more in revenue and, moreover, could decide how high to set the sales taxes on alcohol to discourage its use. In Sweden, for example, taxes on alcohol are 300–400%; the cheapest bottle of liquor costs over $100 because that country wishes to reduce the amount of alcohol its citizens consume.

Customers

customers Individuals and groups that buy the goods and services an organization produces.

Customers are the individuals and groups that buy the goods and services an organization produces. For example, Dell's customers can be segmented into several distinct groups: (1) individuals who purchase PCs for home use, (2) small companies, (3) large companies, and (4) government agencies and educational institutions. Changes in the number and types of customers or in customers' tastes and needs create opportunities and threats. An organization's success depends on its responsiveness to customers–whether it can satisfy their needs. In the PC industry, customers are demanding thinner computers, better graphics and speed, and increased wireless and Internet connections–and lower prices–and PC makers must respond to the changing types and needs of customers, such as by introducing tablet computers. A school, too, must adapt to the changing needs of its customers. For example, if more Spanish-speaking students enroll, additional classes in English as a second language may need to be scheduled. A manager's ability to identify an organization's main customer groups, and make the products that best satisfy their particular needs, is a crucial factor affecting organizational and managerial success.

The most obvious opportunity associated with expanding into the global environment is the prospect of selling goods and services to millions or billions of new customers, as Amazon.com's CEO Jeff Bezos discovered when he expanded his company's operations in many countries.[18] Similarly, Accenture and Cap Gemini, two large consulting companies, established regional operating centers around the globe, and they recruit and train thousands of overseas consultants to serve the needs of customers in their respective world regions.

Today many products have gained global customer acceptance. This consolidation is occurring both for consumer goods and for business products and has created enormous opportunities for managers. The worldwide acceptance of Coca-Cola, Apple iPods, McDonald's hamburgers, Doc Martin boots, and Nokia cell phones is a sign that the tastes and preferences of customers in different countries may not be so different after all.[19] Likewise, large global markets exist for business products such as telecommunications equipment, electronic components, and computer and financial services. Thus Cisco and Motorola sell their telecommunications equipment, Intel its microprocessors, and Oracle and SAP their business systems management software to customers all over the world.

Competitors

competitors Organizations that produce goods and services that are similar to a particular organization's goods and services.

One of the most important forces an organization confronts in its task environment is competitors. **Competitors** are organizations that produce goods and services that are similar and comparable to a particular organization's goods and services. In other words, competitors are organizations trying to attract the same customers. Dell's competitors include other domestic PC makers (such as Apple and HP) as well as overseas competitors (such as Sony and Toshiba in Japan, Lenovo, the Chinese company that bought IBM's PC division, and Acer, the Taiwanese company that bought Gateway). Similarly, dot-com stockbroker E*Trade has other competitors such as Ameritrade, Scottrade, and Charles Schwab.

Rivalry between competitors is potentially the most threatening force managers must deal with. A high level of rivalry typically results in price competition, and falling prices reduce customer revenues and profits. In the early 2000s competition in the PC industry became intense because Dell was aggressively cutting costs and prices to increase its global market share.[20] IBM had to exit the PC business after it lost billions in its battle against low-cost rivals, and Gateway and HP also suffered losses while Dell's profits soared. By 2006, however, HP's fortunes had recovered because it had found ways to lower its costs and offer stylish new PCs, and Apple was growing rapidly, so Dell's profit margins shrunk. In 2009 HP overtook Dell to become the largest global PC maker, and in 2010 Apple and Acer's sales were also expanding rapidly. Dell's managers had failed to appreciate how fast its global competitors were catching up and had not developed the right strategies to keep the company at the top.

Although extensive rivalry between existing competitors is a major threat to profitability, so is the potential for new competitors to enter the task environment. **Potential competitors** are organizations that are not presently in a task environment but have the resources to enter if they so choose. In 2010 Amazon.com, for example, was not in the retail furniture or large appliance business, but it could enter these businesses if its managers decided it could profitably sell such products online. When new competitors enter an industry, competition increases, and prices and profits decrease.

potential competitors Organizations that presently are not in a task environment but could enter if they so choose.

BARRIERS TO ENTRY In general, the potential for new competitors to enter a task environment (and thus increase competition) is a function of barriers to entry.[21] **Barriers to entry** are factors that make it difficult and costly for a company to enter a particular task environment or industry.[22] In other words, the more difficult and costly it is to enter the task environment, the higher are the barriers to entry. The higher the barriers to entry, the fewer the competitors in an organization's task environment and thus the lower the threat of competition. With fewer competitors, it is easier to obtain customers and keep prices high.

barriers to entry Factors that make it difficult and costly for an organization to enter a particular task environment or industry.

Barriers to entry result from three main sources: economies of scale, brand loyalty, and government regulations that impede entry (see Figure 6.2). **Economies of scale** are the cost advantages associated with large operations. Economies of scale result from factors such as manufacturing products in very large quantities, buying inputs in bulk, or making more effective use of organizational resources than do competitors by fully utilizing employees' skills and knowledge. If organizations already in the task environment are large and enjoy significant economies of scale, their costs are lower than the costs that potential entrants will face, and newcomers will find it expensive to enter the industry. Amazon.com, for example, enjoys significant economies of scale relative to most other dot-com companies because of its highly efficient distribution system.[23]

economies of scale Cost advantages associated with large operations.

Brand loyalty is customers' preference for the products of organizations currently in the task environment. If established organizations enjoy significant brand loyalty, a new entrant will find it difficult and costly to obtain a share of the market. Newcomers must bear huge advertising costs to build customer awareness of the goods or services they intend to provide.[24] Today Google, Amazon.com, and eBay enjoy a high level of brand loyalty and have some of the highest Web site hit rates, which allows them to increase their marketing revenues.

brand loyalty Customers' preference for the products of organizations currently existing in the task environment.

In some cases, *government regulations* function as a barrier to entry at both the industry and the country levels. Many industries that were deregulated, such as air transport, trucking, utilities, and telecommunications, experienced a high level of new

Figure 6.2
Barriers to Entry and Competition

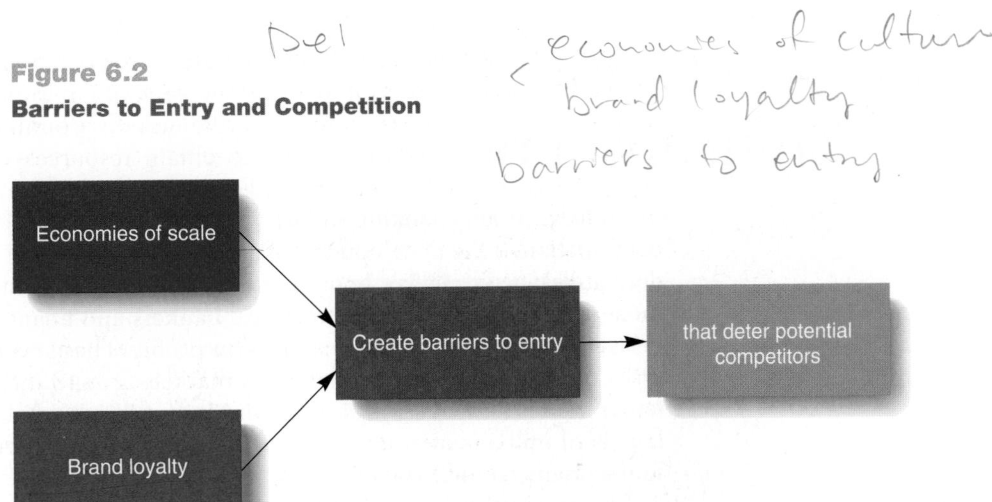

The tyranny of the lower price. A Japanese businessman purchases a frozen, U.S.-sourced rice O-bento lunch at a Nippon Tokyo store. Nippon's importing practices have angered Japanese rice farmers.

entry after deregulation; this forced existing companies in those industries to operate more efficiently or risk being put out of business. At the national and global levels, administrative barriers are government policies that create barriers to entry and limit imports of goods by overseas companies. Japan is well known for the many ways in which it attempts to restrict the entry of overseas competitors or lessen their impact on Japanese firms. Japan has come under intense pressure to relax and abolish regulations such as those governing the import of rice, for example.

The Japanese rice market, like many other Japanese markets, was closed to overseas competitors until 1993 to protect Japan's thousands of high-cost, low-output rice farmers. Rice cultivation is expensive in Japan because of the country's mountainous terrain, and Japanese consumers have always paid high prices for rice. Under overseas pressure, the Japanese government opened the market; but overseas competitors are allowed to export to Japan only 8% of its annual rice consumption to protect its farmers.

In the 2000s, however, an alliance between organic rice grower Lundberg Family Farms of California and the Nippon Restaurant Enterprise Co. found a new way to break into the Japanese rice market. Because there is no tariff on rice used in processed foods, Nippon converts the U.S. organic rice into "O-bento," an organic hot boxed lunch packed with rice, vegetables, chicken, beef, and salmon, all imported from the United States. The lunches, which cost about $4 compared to a Japanese rice bento that costs about $9, are sold at railway stations and other outlets throughout Japan and have become very popular. A storm of protest from Japanese rice farmers arose because the entry of U.S. rice growers forced them to leave their rice fields idle or grow less profitable crops. Other overseas companies are increasingly forming alliances with Japanese companies to find new ways to break into the high-priced Japanese market, and little by little, Japan's restrictive trade practices are being whittled away.

In summary, intense rivalry among competitors creates a task environment that is highly threatening and makes it increasingly difficult for managers to gain access to the resources an organization needs to make goods and services. Conversely, low rivalry results in a task environment where competitive pressures are more moderate and managers have greater opportunities to acquire the resources they need to make their organizations effective.

The General Environment

Economic, technological, sociocultural, demographic, political, and legal forces in the general environment often have important effects on forces in the task environment that determine an organization's ability to obtain resources–effects that managers may not be aware of. For example, the sudden, dramatic upheavals in the mortgage and banking industry that started in 2007 were brought about by a combination of the development of complex new financial lending instruments called derivatives; a speculative boom in commodities and housing prices; and lax government regulation that allowed unethical bankers and financial managers to exploit the derivatives to make immense short-term profits. These events triggered the economic crisis of 2008–2009 that caused stock markets around the world to plummet, devastating the retirement savings of hundreds of millions of ordinary people, and caused layoffs of millions of employees as companies slashed their workforces because customers reduced their spending.

The implication is clear: Managers must continuously analyze forces in the general environment because these forces affect ongoing decision making and planning. How well managers can perform this task determines how quickly an organization can respond to the changes taking place. Next we discuss the major forces in the general environment and examine their impact on an organization's task environment.

Economic Forces

economic forces Interest rates, inflation, unemployment, economic growth, and other factors that affect the general health and well-being of a nation or the regional economy of an organization.

Economic forces affect the general health and well-being of a country or world region. They include interest rates, inflation, unemployment, and economic growth. Economic forces produce many opportunities and threats for managers. Low levels of unemployment and falling interest rates give people more money to spend, and as a result organizations can sell more goods and services. Good economic times affect the supply of resources that become easier or more inexpensive to acquire, and organizations have an opportunity to flourish. High-tech companies enjoyed this throughout the 1990s as computer and electronics companies like Sony made record profits as the global economy boomed because of advances in IT and growing global trade.

In contrast, worsening macroeconomic conditions, like those in the late 2000s, pose a major threat because they reduce managers' ability to gain access to the resources their organizations need to survive and prosper. Profit-seeking organizations such as hotels and retail stores have fewer customers during economic downturns; hotel rates dropped by 14% in 2009 compared to 2008, for example, just as retail sales plunged. Nonprofits such as charities and colleges also saw donations decline by more than 20% because of the economic downturn.

Poor economic conditions make the environment more complex and managers' jobs more difficult and demanding. Companies often need to reduce the number of their managers and employees, streamline their operations, and identify ways to acquire and use resources more efficiently and effectively. Successful managers realize the important effects that economic forces have on their organizations, and they pay close attention to what is occurring in the economy at the national and regional levels to respond appropriately.

Technological Forces

technology The combination of skills and equipment that managers use in designing, producing, and distributing goods and services.

technological forces Outcomes of changes in the technology managers use to design, produce, or distribute goods and services.

Technology is the combination of tools, machines, computers, skills, information, and knowledge that managers use to design, produce, and distribute goods and services; **technological forces** are outcomes of changes in that technology. The overall pace of technological change has accelerated greatly in the last decades because technological advances in microprocessors and computer hardware and software have spurred technological advances in most businesses and industries. The effects of changing technological forces are still increasing in magnitude.[25]

Technological forces can have profound implications for managers and organizations. Technological change can make established products obsolete–for example, cathode-ray tube (CRT) computer monitors and televisions (such as Sony's Trinitron), bound sets of encyclopedias, and even newspapers–forcing managers to find new ways to satisfy customer needs. Although technological change can threaten an organization, it also can create a host of new opportunities for designing, making, or distributing new and better kinds of goods and services. Ever more powerful microprocessors developed by Intel and AMD, which now have 8 or 12 processing cores on each chip, are continuing the IT revolution that has spurred demand for all kinds of new digital computing devices and services and has affected the competitive position of all high-tech companies. Will Google devastate Microsoft, for example, just as Microsoft devastated IBM in the 1990s? Managers must move quickly to respond to such changes if their organizations are to survive and prosper.

Changes in IT are altering the nature of work itself within organizations, including that of the manager's job. Today telecommuting, videoconferencing, and text messaging are everyday activities that let managers supervise and coordinate geographically dispersed employees. Salespeople in many companies work from home offices and commute electronically to work. They communicate with other employees through companywide electronic communication networks using PCs and webcams to orchestrate "face-to-face" meetings with coworkers across the country or globe.

Sociocultural Forces

sociocultural forces Pressures emanating from the social structure of a country or society or from the national culture.

social structure The traditional system of relationships established between people and groups in a society.

Sociocultural forces are pressures emanating from the social structure of a country or society or from the national culture, such the concern for diversity, discussed in the previous chapter. Pressures from both sources can either constrain or facilitate the way organizations operate and managers behave. **Social structure** is the traditional system of relationships established between people and groups in a society. Societies differ substantially in social structure. In societies that have a high degree of social stratification, there are many distinctions among individuals and groups. Caste systems in India and Tibet and the recognition of numerous social classes in Great Britain and France produce a multilayered social structure in each of those countries. In contrast, social stratification is lower in relatively egalitarian New Zealand and in the United States, where the social structure reveals few distinctions among people. Most top managers in France come from the upper classes of French society, but top managers in the United States come from all strata of American society.

national culture The set of values that a society considers important and the norms of behavior that are approved or sanctioned in that society.

Societies also differ in the extent to which they emphasize the individual over the group. Such differences may dictate how managers need to motivate and lead employees. **National culture** is the set of values that a society considers important and the norms of behavior that are approved or sanctioned in that society. Societies differ substantially in the values and norms they emphasize. For example, in the United States individualism is highly valued, and in Korea and Japan individuals are expected to conform to group expectations.[26] National culture, discussed at length later in this chapter, also affects how managers motivate and coordinate employees and how organizations do business. Ethics, an important aspect of national culture, were discussed in detail in Chapter 4.

Social structure and national culture not only differ across societies but also change within societies over time. In the United States, attitudes toward the roles of women, sex, marriage, and gays and lesbians changed in each past decade. Many people in Asian countries such as Hong Kong, Singapore, Korea, and even China think the younger generation is far more individualistic and "American-like" than previous generations. Currently, throughout much of eastern Europe, new values that emphasize individualism and entrepreneurship are replacing communist values based on collectivism and obedience to the state. The pace of change is accelerating.

Pick your poison. The American trend towards fitness has prompted traditional soft drink manufacturers to expand their offerings into a staggering array of energy drinks.

Individual managers and organizations must be responsive to changes in, and differences among, the social structures and national cultures of all the countries in which they operate. In today's increasingly integrated global economy, managers are likely to interact with people from several countries, and many managers live and work abroad. Effective managers are sensitive to differences between societies and adjust their behavior accordingly.

Managers and organizations also must respond to social changes within a society. In the last decades, for example, Americans have become increasingly interested in their personal health and fitness. Managers who recognized this trend early and took advantage of the opportunities that resulted from it were able to reap significant gains for their organizations such as chains of health clubs. PepsiCo used the opportunity presented by the fitness trend and took market share from archrival Coca-Cola by being the first to introduce diet colas and fruit-based soft drinks. Then Quaker Oats made Gatorade the most popular energy drink, and now others like Red Bull, Monster, and Rockstar are increasing in popularity. The health trend, however, did not offer opportunities to all companies; to some it posed a threat. Tobacco companies came under intense pressure due to consumers' greater awareness of negative health impacts from smoking. The rage for "low-carb" foods in the 2000s increased demand

for meat and protein, and bread and doughnut companies such as Kraft and Krispy Kreme suffered–until the 2008 recession boosted the sale of inexpensive products such as macaroni and cheese and hamburger helper.

Demographic Forces

demographic forces Outcomes of changes in, or changing attitudes toward, the characteristics of a population, such as age, gender, ethnic origin, race, sexual orientation, and social class.

Demographic forces are outcomes of changes in, or changing attitudes toward, the characteristics of a population, such as age, gender, ethnic origin, race, sexual orientation, and social class. Like the other forces in the general environment, demographic forces present managers with opportunities and threats and can have major implications for organizations. We examined the nature of these challenges in depth in our discussion of diversity in Chapter 5.

Today most industrialized nations are experiencing the aging of their populations as a consequence of falling birth and death rates and the aging of the baby boom generation. Consequently, the absolute number of older people has increased substantially, which has generated opportunities for organizations that cater to older people such as the home health care, recreation, and medical industries, which have seen an upswing in demand for their services. The aging of the population also has several implications for the workplace. Most significant are a relative decline in the number of young people joining the workforce and an increase in the number of active employees who are postponing retirement beyond the traditional age of 65. Indeed, the financial crisis of 2008–2009 has made it impossible for millions of older people to retire because their savings have been decimated. These changes suggest that organizations need to find ways to motivate older employees and use their skills and knowledge–an issue that many Western societies have yet to tackle.

Political and Legal Forces

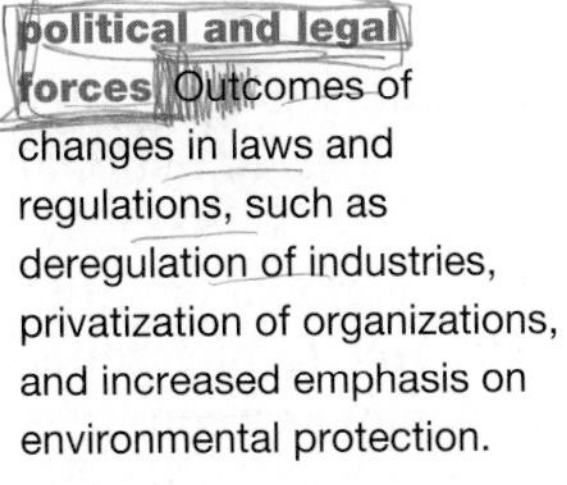

political and legal forces Outcomes of changes in laws and regulations, such as deregulation of industries, privatization of organizations, and increased emphasis on environmental protection.

Political and legal forces are outcomes of changes in laws and regulations. They result from political and legal developments that take place within a nation, within a world region, or across the world and significantly affect managers and organizations everywhere. Political processes shape a nation's laws and the international laws that govern the relationships between nations. Laws constrain the operations of organizations and managers and thus create both opportunities and threats.[27] For example, throughout much of the industrialized world there has been a strong trend toward deregulation of industries previously controlled by the state and privatization of organizations once owned by the state.

Another important political and legal force affecting managers and organizations is the political integration of countries that has been taking place during the past decades.[28] Increasingly, nations are forming political unions that allow free exchange of resources and capital. The growth of the European Union (EU) is one example: Common laws govern trade and commerce between EU member countries, and the European Court has the right to examine the business of any global organization and to approve any proposed mergers between overseas companies that operate inside the EU. For example, Microsoft's anticompetitive business practices came under scrutiny, and it was fined hundreds of millions for its uncompetitive practice of bundling its Internet Explorer Web browser with its software. As part of its agreement with the European Court, Microsoft agreed that from spring 2010 forward it would ship its Windows 7 software with a choice of 10 Web browsers (such as Chrome, Safari, and Mozilla). Also in 2010, after months of delay, the court allowed the merger between Oracle and Sun to proceed providing the companies followed some strict competitive guidelines. The North American Free Trade Agreement (NAFTA), discussed later in the chapter, has more modest political goals; but like the EU, it has changed the laws that affect international commerce by lowering barriers to the free flow of goods and services between member nations.[29]

Indeed, international agreements to abolish laws and regulations that restrict and reduce trade between countries have been having profound effects on global organizations. The falling legal trade barriers create enormous opportunities for companies to sell goods and services internationally. But by allowing overseas companies to compete in a nation's domestic market for customers, falling trade barriers also pose a serious threat because they increase competition in the task environment. Between 1980 and 2010, for example, Japanese companies increased their share of the U.S. car market from around 20% to 40%; Taiwanese companies' share grew from 2% to 7%. In essence, removing legal restrictions on global trade has the same effect as deregulating industries and removing restrictions against competition: It increases the intensity of competition in the task environment and forces conservative, slow-moving companies–such as GM and Chrysler–to become more efficient, improve product quality, and learn new values and norms to compete in the global environment. To help turn around their performance, GM was forced to declare bankruptcy in 2009 and Chrysler was bought by Fiat; but will these companies prosper in the new global environment?

Deregulation, privatization, and the removal of legal barriers to trade are just a few of the many ways in which changing political and legal forces can challenge organizations and managers. Others include increased emphasis on environmental protection and the preservation of endangered species, increased emphasis on workplace safety, and legal constraints against discrimination on the basis of race, gender, or age. Managers face major challenges when they seek to take advantage of the opportunities created by changing political, legal, and economic forces.

The Changing Global Environment

The 21st century has banished the idea that the world is composed of distinct national countries and markets that are separated physically, economically, and culturally. Managers need to recognize that companies compete in a truly global marketplace, which is the source of the opportunities and threats they must respond to. Managers continually confront the challenges of global competition such as establishing operations in a country abroad, obtaining inputs from suppliers abroad, or managing in a different national culture.[30] (See Figure 6.3.)

LO6-4 Explain why the global environment is becoming more open and competitive, and identify the forces behind the process of globalization that increase the opportunities, complexities, challenges, and threats managers face.

In essence, as a result of falling trade barriers, managers view the global environment as open–that is, as an environment in which companies are free to buy goods and services from, and sell goods and services to, whichever companies and countries they choose. They also are free to compete against each other to attract customers around the world. All large companies must establish an international network of operations and subsidiaries to build global competitive advantage. Coca-Cola and PepsiCo, for example, have competed aggressively for decades to develop the strongest global soft drink empire, just as Toyota and Honda have built hundreds of car plants around the world to provide the vehicles that global customers like. This is also true in the food processing industry, as the following "Managing Globally" box suggests.

Managing Globally

Nestlé's Global Food Empire

Nestlé is the world's largest food company. In 2009 its sales increased by 4%, and it enjoyed record profits of over $100 billion; globally it had over 190,000 employees and 500 factories in 80 countries. It makes and sells over 8,000 food products, including such popular brands as Kit-Kat chocolate bars, Taster's Choice coffee, Carnation Instant milk, and Stouffer's Foods. At its corporate headquarters in Vevey, Switzerland, CEO Peter Brabeck-Latmathe, who has

Nescafé anywhere, anytime. Nestlé's expanded operations and benchmarked processes make it a force to be reckoned with.

been in charge since 1997, is responsible for Nestlé's improving global performance and has faced and managed many global challenges.[31]

From the beginning Brabeck worked to increase Nestlé's revenues and profits by entering new attractive national markets in both developed and emerging nations as trade barriers fell. He continued the ambitious global expansion that Nestlé began in the 1990s, when, for example, it bought the U.S. food companies Carnation and Buitoni Pasta, the British chocolate maker Rowntree, the French bottled water company Perrier, and the Mexican food maker Ortega. Under Brabeck, Nestlé spent $18 billion to acquire U.S. companies Ralston Purina, Dreyer's Ice Cream, and Chef America. Brabeck's intention was not only to develop these food brands in the United States but also to customize their products to suit the tastes of customers in countries around the world. He was particularly anxious to enter emerging markets such as those in eastern Europe, India, and Asia to take advantage of the enormous numbers of potential new customers in these regions. In this way Nestlé could leverage its well-known brand image and products around the world to drive up its performance.

Increasing global product sale revenues was only the first part of Brabeck's global business model, however. He was also anxious to increase Nestlé's operating efficiency and reduce the cost of managing its global operations. As you can imagine, with over 500 factories the costs of organizing Nestlé's global activities were enormous. Brabeck benchmarked its operating costs to those of competitors such as Kraft Foods and Unilever and found that Nestlé's costs were significantly higher than theirs. Brabeck cut the workforce by 20%, closed 150 factories, and reduced operating costs by over 12%. Nestlé was also using advanced IT both to reduce the number of its global suppliers and to negotiate more favorable supply contracts with them–moves that significantly cut purchasing costs. Brabeck also designed Nestlé's new streamlined operating structure and IT to increase the flow of information between its food products units and all the countries in which it sells its products. His goal was to capitalize on a prime source of its competitive advantage: superior innovation.

Thus Brabeck's global strategy for Nestlé was driven by three main goals: (1) Expand Nestlé's range of products, and offer them to new and existing customers in countries throughout the world; (2) find lower-cost ways to make and sell these products; and (3) speed up Nestlé's product innovation by leveraging its expertise across its food businesses to create more attractive food products that would increase its global market share. In addition, many customers around the world have been demanding more nutritious food products. So Brabeck adopted what he called an "organic approach" to developing Nestlé's products. Brabeck claimed his company was engaged in a "transformation" that would lead it to become the "world's leading nutrition, health, and wellness" food company that made consumer health and safety its prime concern.[32]

In this section we first explain how this open global environment is the result of globalization and the flow of capital around the world. Next we examine how specific economic, political, and legal changes, such as the lowering of barriers to trade and investment, have increased globalization and led to greater interaction and exchanges between organizations and countries. Then we discuss how declining barriers of distance and culture have also increased the pace of globalization, and we consider the

Figure 6.3
The Global Environment

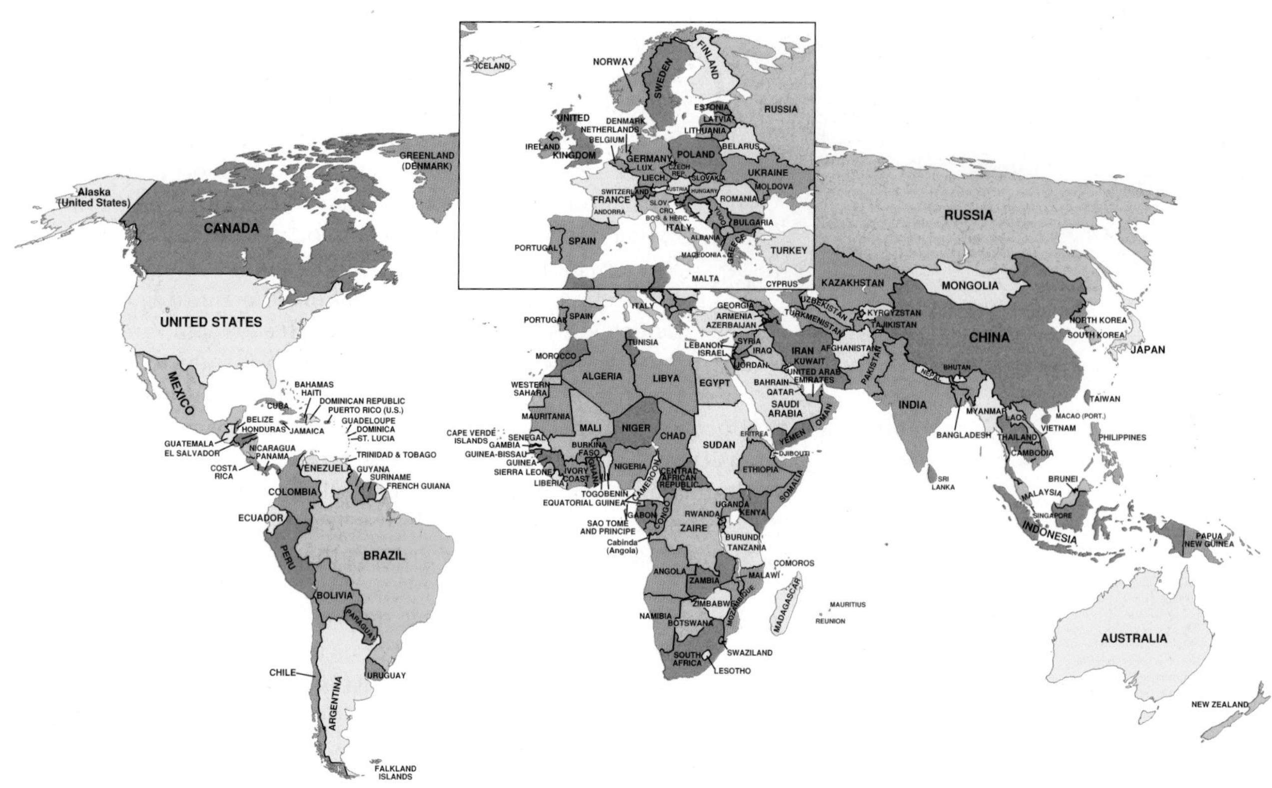

specific implications of these changes for managers and organizations. Finally we note that nations still differ widely from each other because they have distinct cultural values and norms and that managers must appreciate these differences to compete successfully across countries.

The Process of Globalization

globalization The set of specific and general forces that work together to integrate and connect economic, political, and social systems *across* countries, cultures, or geographical regions so that nations become increasingly interdependent and similar.

Perhaps the most important reason why the global environment has become more open and competitive is the increase in globalization. **Globalization** is the set of specific and general forces that work together to integrate and connect economic, political, and social systems *across* countries, cultures, or geographic regions. The result of globalization is that nations and peoples become increasingly *interdependent* because the same forces affect them in similar ways. The fates of peoples in different countries become interlinked as the world's markets and businesses become increasingly interconnected. And as nations become more interdependent, they become more similar to one another in the sense that people develop a similar liking for products as diverse as cell phones, iPods, blue jeans, soft drinks, sports teams, Japanese cars, and foods such as curry, green tea, and Colombian coffee. One outcome of globalization is that the world is becoming a "global village": Products, services, or people can become well known throughout the world–something IKEA, with its range of furniture designed to appeal to customers around the world, is taking advantage of, as the following "Managing Globally" box describes.

But what drives or spurs globalization? What makes companies like IKEA, Toyota, or Microsoft want to venture into an uncertain global environment? The answer is that the path of globalization is shaped by the ebb and flow of *capital*–valuable wealth-generating assets or resources that people move through companies, countries, and world regions to seek their greatest returns or profits. Managers, employees, and

Managing Globally

IKEA Is on Top of the Furniture World

IKEA is the largest furniture chain in the world, and in 2010 the Swedish company operated over 267 stores in 25 countries. In 2009 IKEA sales soared to over $33 billion, or over 20% of the global furniture market; but to its managers and employees this was just the tip of the iceberg. They believed IKEA was poised for massive growth throughout the world in the coming decade because it could provide what the average customer wanted: well-designed and well-made contemporary furniture at an affordable price. IKEA's ability to provide customers with affordable furniture is the result of its approach to globalization, to how it treats its global employees and operates its global store empire. In a nutshell, IKEA's global approach focuses on simplicity, attention to detail, cost consciousness, and responsiveness in every aspect of its operations and behavior.

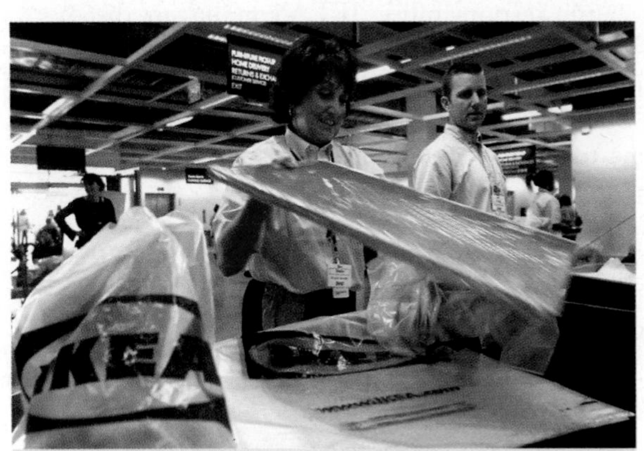

Need a new kitchen table? How about a cute rug to go with it, and while you're at it, a cookie sheet, too? Options await you at any one of the thousands of IKEA stores worldwide.

IKEA's global approach derives from the personal values and beliefs of its founder, Ingvar Kamprad, about how companies should treat their employees and customers. Kamprad, who is in his early 80s (and in 2010 ranked as the 11th richest person in the world), was born in Smaland, a poor Swedish province whose citizens are known for being entrepreneurial, frugal, and hardworking. Kamprad definitely absorbed these values–when he entered the furniture business, he made them the core of his management approach. He teaches store managers and employees his values; his beliefs about the need to operate in a no-frills, cost-conscious way; and his view that they are all in business "together," by which he means that every person who works in his global empire plays an essential role and has an obligation to everyone else.

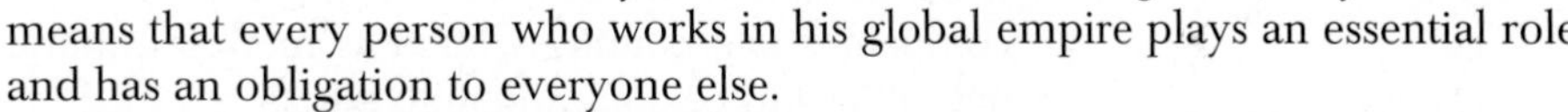

What does Kamprad's approach mean in practice? All IKEA employees fly coach class on business trips, stay in inexpensive hotels, and keep traveling expenses to a minimum. And IKEA stores operate on the simplest rules and procedures possible, with employees expected to cooperate to solve problems and get the job done. Many famous stories circulate about the frugal Kamprad, such as that even he always flies coach class and that when he takes a soda can from the minibar in a hotel room, he replaces it with one bought in a store–despite the fact that he is a multibillionaire.

IKEA's employees see what Kamprad's global approach means as soon as they are recruited to work in a store in one of the many countries in which the company operates. They start learning about IKEA's global corporate culture by performing jobs at the bottom of the ladder, and they are quickly trained to perform all the various jobs involved in store operations. During this process they internalize IKEA's global values and norms, which center on the importance the company attaches to their taking the initiative and responsibility for solving problems and for focusing on customers. Employees are rotated between departments and sometimes stores, and rapid promotion is possible for those who demonstrate the enthusiasm and togetherness that show they have bought into IKEA's global culture.

Most of IKEA's top managers rose from its ranks, and the company holds "breaking the bureaucracy weeks" in which managers are required to work in stores and warehouses for a week each year to make sure they and all employees stay committed to IKEA's global values. No matter which country they operate in, all employees wear informal clothes to work at IKEA–Kamprad has always worn an open-neck shirt–and there are no marks of status such as executive dining rooms or private parking places. Employees believe that if they buy into IKEA's work values, behave in ways that keep its growing global operations streamlined and efficient, and focus on being one step ahead of potential problems, they will share in its success. Promotion, training, above-average pay, a generous store bonus system, and the personal well-being that comes from working in a company where people feel valued are some of the rewards that Kamprad pioneered to build and strengthen IKEA's global approach.

Whenever IKEA enters a new country, it sends its most experienced store managers to establish its global approach in its new stores. When IKEA first entered the United States, the attitude of U.S. employees puzzled its managers. Despite their obvious drive to succeed and good education, employees seemed reluctant to take initiative and assume responsibility. IKEA's managers discovered that their U.S. employees were afraid mistakes would result in the loss of their jobs, so the managers strove to teach employees the "IKEA way." The approach paid off: The United States has become the company's second best country market, and IKEA plans to open many more U.S. stores, as well as stores around the world, over the next decade.[33]

companies like IKEA and Sony are motivated to try to profit or benefit by using their skills to make products customers around the world want to buy. The four principal forms of capital that flow between countries are these:

- *Human capital:* the flow of people around the world through immigration, migration, and emigration.
- *Financial capital:* the flow of money capital across world markets through overseas investment, credit, lending, and aid.
- *Resource capital:* the flow of natural resources, parts, and components between companies and countries, such as metals, minerals, lumber, energy, food products, microprocessors, and auto parts.
- *Political capital:* the flow of power and influence around the world using diplomacy, persuasion, aggression, and force of arms to protect the right or access of a country, world region, or political bloc to the other forms of capital.

Most of the economic advances associated with globalization are the result of these four capital flows and the interactions between them, as nations compete on the world stage to protect and increase their standards of living and to further the political goals and social causes that are espoused by their societies' cultures. The next sections look at the factors that have increased the rate at which capital flows between companies and countries. In a positive sense the faster the flow, the more capital is being utilized where it can create the most value, in the sense of people moving to where their skills earn them more money, or investors switching to the stocks or bonds that give them higher dividends or interest, or companies finding lower-cost sources of inputs. In a negative sense, however, a fast flow of capital also means that individual countries or world regions can find themselves in trouble when companies and investors move their capital to invest it in more productive ways in other countries or world regions–often those with lower labor costs or rapidly expanding markets. When capital leaves a country, the results are higher unemployment, recession, and a lower standard of living for its people.

Declining Barriers to Trade and Investment

One of the main factors that has speeded globalization by freeing the movement of capital has been the decline in barriers to trade and investment, discussed earlier. During the 1920s and 1930s many countries erected formidable barriers to international trade and investment in the belief that this was the best way to promote their economic well-being. Many of these barriers were high tariffs on imports of manufactured goods. A **tariff** is a tax that a government imposes on goods imported into one country from another. The aim of import tariffs is to protect domestic industries and jobs, such as those in the auto or steel industry, from overseas competition by raising the price of these products from abroad. In 2009, for example, the U.S. government increased the tariffs on vehicle tires imported from China to protect U.S. tire makers from unfair competition; China vigorously protested that the price of its tires was fair and it would retaliate by increasing tariffs on U.S. imports of chicken and other products.

tariff A tax that a government imposes on imported or, occasionally, exported goods.

The reason for removing tariffs is that, very often, when one country imposes an import tariff, others follow suit and the result is a series of retaliatory moves as countries progressively raise tariff barriers against each other. In the 1920s this behavior depressed world demand and helped usher in the Great Depression of the 1930s and massive unemployment. During the 2008–2009 economic crisis, the governments of most countries worked hard not to fall into the trap of raising tariffs to protect jobs and industries in the short run because they knew the long-term consequences of this would be the loss of even more jobs. Governments of countries that resort to raising tariff barriers ultimately reduce employment and undermine the economic growth of their countries because capital and resources will always move to their most highly valued use–wherever that is in the world.[34]

GATT AND THE RISE OF FREE TRADE After World War II, advanced Western industrial countries, having learned from the Great Depression, committed themselves to the goal of removing barriers to the free flow of resources and capital between countries. This commitment was reinforced by acceptance of the principle that free trade, rather than tariff barriers, was the best way to foster a healthy domestic economy and low unemployment.[35]

The **free-trade doctrine** predicts that if each country agrees to specialize in the production of the goods and services that it can produce most efficiently, this will make the best use of global capital resources and will result in lower prices.[36] For example, if Indian companies are highly efficient in the production of textiles and U.S. companies are highly efficient in the production of computer software, then under a free-trade agreement capital would move to India and be invested there to produce textiles, while capital from around the world would flow to the United States and be invested in its innovative computer software companies. Consequently, prices of both textiles and software should fall because each product is being produced where it can be made at the lowest cost, benefiting consumers and making the best use of scarce capital. This doctrine is also responsible for the increase in global outsourcing and the loss of millions of U.S. jobs in textiles and manufacturing as capital has been invested in factories in Asian countries such as China and Malaysia. However, millions of U.S. jobs have also been created because of new capital investments in the high-tech, IT, and service sectors, which in theory should offset manufacturing job losses in the long run.

free-trade doctrine The idea that if each country specializes in the production of the goods and services that it can produce most efficiently, this will make the best use of global resources.

Historically countries that accepted this free-trade doctrine set as their goal the removal of barriers to the free flow of goods, services, and capital between countries. They attempted to achieve this through an international treaty known as the General Agreement on Tariffs and Trade (GATT). In the half-century since World War II, there have been eight rounds of GATT negotiations aimed at lowering tariff barriers. The last round, the Uruguay Round, involved 117 countries and was completed in December 1993. This round succeeded in lowering tariffs by over 30% from the previous level. It also led to the dissolving of GATT and its replacement by the World Trade Organization (WTO), which continues the struggle to reduce tariffs and has more power to sanction countries that break global agreements.[37] On average, the tariff barriers among the governments of developed countries declined from over 40% in 1948 to about 3% today, causing a dramatic increase in world trade.[38]

Declining Barriers of Distance and Culture

Historically, barriers of distance and culture also closed the global environment and kept managers focused on their domestic market. The management problems Unilever, the huge British-based soap and detergent maker, experienced at the turn of the 20th century illustrate the effect of these barriers.

Founded in London during the 1880s by William Lever, a Quaker, Unilever had a worldwide reach by the early 1900s and operated subsidiaries in most major countries of the British Empire, including India, Canada, and Australia. Lever had a very hands-on, autocratic management style and found his far-flung business empire difficult to control. The reason for Lever's control problems was that communication over great distances was difficult. It took six weeks to reach India by ship from England, and international telephone and telegraph services were unreliable.

Another problem Unilever encountered was the difficulty of doing business in societies that were separated from Britain by barriers of language and culture. Different countries have different sets of national beliefs, values, and norms, and Lever found that a management approach that worked in Britain did not necessarily work in India or Persia (now Iran). As a result, management practices had to be tailored to suit each unique national culture. After Lever's death in 1925, top management at Unilever lowered or *decentralized* (see Chapter 10) decision-making authority to the managers of the various national subsidiaries so they could develop a management approach that suited the country in which they were operating. One result of this strategy was that the subsidiaries grew distant and remote from one another, which reduced Unilever's performance.[39]

Since the end of World War II, a continuing stream of advances in communications and transportation technology has worked to reduce the barriers of distance and culture that affected Unilever and all global organizations. Over the last decades, global communication has been revolutionized by developments in satellites, digital technology, the Internet and global computer networks, and video teleconferencing that allow transmission of vast amounts of information and make reliable, secure, and instantaneous communication possible between people and companies anywhere in the world.[40] This revolution has made it possible for a global organization–a tiny garment factory in Li & Fung's network or a huge company such as Sony or Unilever–to do business anywhere, anytime, and to search for customers and suppliers around the world.

One of the most important innovations in transportation technology that has opened the global environment has been the growth of commercial jet travel. New York is now closer in travel time to Tokyo than it was to Philadelphia in the days of the 13 colonies–a fact that makes control of far-flung international businesses much easier today than in William Lever's era. In addition to speeding travel, modern communications and transportation technologies have also helped reduce the cultural distance between countries. The Internet and its millions of Web sites facilitate the development of global communications networks and media that are helping to create a worldwide culture above and beyond unique national cultures. Moreover, television networks such as CNN, MTV, ESPN, BBC, and HBO can now be received in many countries, and Hollywood films are shown throughout the world.

Effects of Free Trade on Managers

The lowering of barriers to trade and investment and the decline of distance and culture barriers has created enormous opportunities for companies to expand the market for their goods and services through exports and investments in overseas countries. The shift toward a more open global economy has created not only more opportunities to sell goods and services in markets abroad but also the opportunity to buy more from other countries. For example, the success of clothing companies such as Lands' End has been based on its managers' willingness to import low-cost clothing and bedding from overseas manufacturers. Lands' End works closely with manufacturers in Hong Kong, Malaysia, Taiwan, and China to make the clothing that its managers decide has the quality and styling its customers want at a price they will pay.[41] A manager's job is more challenging in a dynamic global environment because of the increased intensity of competition that goes hand in hand with the lowering of barriers to trade and investment.

REGIONAL TRADE AGREEMENTS The growth of regional trade agreements such as the North American Free Trade Agreement (NAFTA), and more recently the Central American Free Trade Agreement (CAFTA), also presents opportunities and threats for managers and their organizations. In North America, NAFTA, which became effective in 1994, had the aim of abolishing the tariffs on 99% of the goods traded between Mexico, Canada, and the United States by 2004. Although it did not achieve this lofty goal, NAFTA has removed most barriers on the cross-border flow of resources, giving, for example, financial institutions and retail businesses in Canada and the United States unrestricted access to the Mexican marketplace. After NAFTA was signed, there was a flood of investment into Mexico from the United States, as well as many other countries such as Japan. Walmart, Costco, Radio Shack, and other major U.S. retail chains have expanded their operations in Mexico; Walmart, for example, is stocking many more products from Mexico in its U.S. stores, and its Mexican store chain is also expanding rapidly.

The establishment of free-trade areas creates an opportunity for manufacturing organizations because it lets them reduce their costs. They can do this either by shifting production to the lowest-cost location within the free-trade area (for example, U.S. auto and textile companies shifting production to Mexico) or by serving the whole region from one location rather than establishing separate operations in each country. Some managers, however, view regional free-trade agreements as a threat because they expose a company based in one member country to increased competition from companies based in the other member countries. NAFTA has had this effect; today Mexican managers in some industries face the threat of head-to-head competition against efficient U.S. and Canadian companies. But the opposite is true as well: U.S. and Canadian managers are experiencing threats in labor-intensive industries, such as the flooring tile and textile industries, where Mexican businesses have a cost advantage.

In July 2005 the U.S. House of Representatives approved the formation of CAFTA, a regional trade agreement designed to eliminate tariffs on products moving between the United States and all countries in Central America. By 2006 the Dominican Republic, El Salvador, Guatemala, Nicaragua, and Honduras had also approved and implemented the agreement, but Costa Rica still has not. CAFTA is seen as a stepping-stone toward establishing the Free Trade Area of the Americas (FTAA), which is an ambitious attempt to establish a free-trade agreement that would increase economic prosperity throughout the Americas. FTAA would include all South American and Caribbean nations except Cuba, as well as those of North and Central America. However, the economic problems many countries have been experiencing, together with major political and ideological differences–such as the political resistance within the United States because of jobs lost to Mexico and Canada–have slowed the process of integration and globalization. The more competitive environment NAFTA has brought about has increased both the opportunities that managers can take advantage of and the threats they must respond to in performing their jobs effectively.

The Role of National Culture

Despite evidence that countries are becoming more similar because of globalization, and that the world may become "a global village," the cultures of different countries still vary widely because of vital differences in their values, norms, and attitudes. As noted earlier, national culture includes the values, norms, knowledge, beliefs, moral principles, laws, customs, and other practices that unite the citizens of a country.[42] National culture shapes individual behavior by specifying appropriate and inappropriate behavior and interaction with others. People learn national culture in their everyday lives by interacting with those around them. This learning starts at an early age and continues throughout their lives.

Cultural Values and Norms

values Ideas about what a society believes to be good, right, desirable, or beautiful.

The basic building blocks of national culture are values and norms. **Values** are beliefs about what a society considers to be good, right, desirable, or beautiful–or their opposites. They provide the basic underpinnings for notions of individual freedom, democracy, truth, justice, honesty, loyalty, social obligation, collective responsibility, the appropriate roles for men and women, love, sex, marriage, and so on. Values are more than merely abstract concepts; they are invested with considerable emotional significance. People argue, fight, and even die over values such as freedom or dignity.

Although deeply embedded in society, values are not static and change over time; but change is often the result of a slow and painful process. For example, the value systems of many formerly communist states such as Russia and Romania are undergoing significant changes as those countries move away from a value system that emphasizes the state and toward one that emphasizes individual freedom. Social turmoil often results when countries undergo major changes in their values.

norms Unwritten, informal codes of conduct that prescribe how people should act in particular situations and are considered important by most members of a group or organization.

mores Norms that are considered to be central to the functioning of society and to social life.

Norms are unwritten, informal codes of conduct that prescribe appropriate behavior in particular situations and are considered important by most members of a group or organization. They shape the behavior of people toward one another. Two types of norms play a major role in national culture: mores and folkways. **Mores** are norms that are considered to be of central importance to the functioning of society and to social life. Accordingly, the violation of mores brings serious retribution. Mores include proscriptions against murder, theft, adultery, and incest. In many societies mores have been enacted into law. Thus all advanced societies have laws against murder and theft. However, there are many differences in mores from one society to another.[43] In the United States, for example, drinking alcohol is widely accepted; but in Saudi Arabia consumption of alcohol is viewed as a serious violation of social mores and is punishable by imprisonment.

folkways The routine social conventions of everyday life.

Folkways are the routine social conventions of everyday life. They concern customs and practices such as dressing appropriately for particular situations, good social manners, eating with the correct utensils, and neighborly behavior. Although folkways define how people are expected to behave, violation of folkways is not a serious or moral matter. People who violate folkways are often thought to be eccentric or ill-mannered, but they are not usually considered immoral or wicked. In many countries, strangers are usually excused for violating folkways because they are unaccustomed to local behavior; but if they repeat the violation they are censured because they are expected to learn appropriate behavior. Hence the importance of managers working in countries abroad to gain wide experience.

LO6-5 Discuss why national cultures differ and why it is important that managers be sensitive to the effects of falling trade barriers and regional trade associations on the political and social systems of nations around the world.

Hofstede's Model of National Culture

Researchers have spent considerable time and effort identifying similarities and differences in the values and norms of different countries. One model of national culture was developed by Geert Hofstede.[44] As a psychologist for IBM, Hofstede collected data on employee values and norms from more than 100,000 IBM employees in 64 countries. Based on his research, Hofstede developed five dimensions along which national cultures can be placed (see Figure 6.4).[45]

individualism A worldview that values individual freedom and self-expression and adherence to the principle that people should be judged by their individual achievements rather than by their social background.

INDIVIDUALISM VERSUS COLLECTIVISM The first dimension, which Hofstede labeled "individualism versus collectivism," has a long history in human thought. **Individualism** is a worldview that values individual freedom and self-expression and adherence to the principle that people should be judged by their individual achievements rather than by their social background. In Western countries, individualism usually includes admiration for personal success, a strong belief in individual rights, and high regard for individual entrepreneurs.[46]

Figure 6.4
Hofstede's Model of National Culture

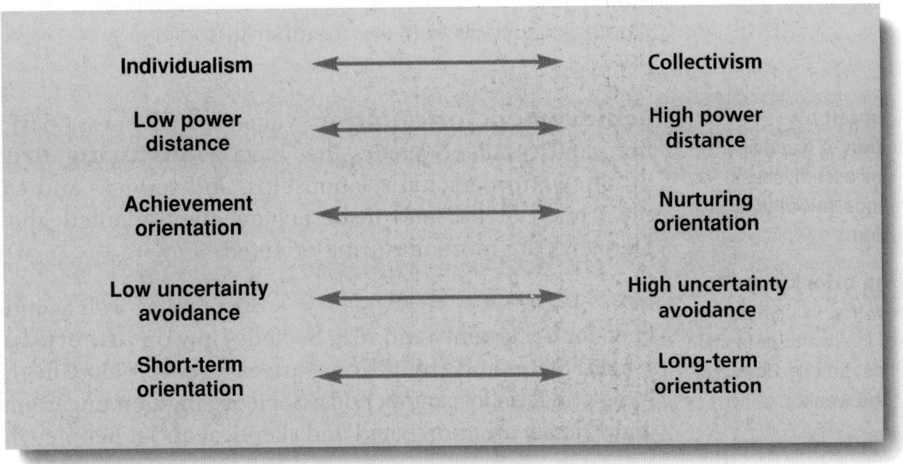

Source: G. Hofstede, B. Nevijen, D. D. Ohayv, and G. Sanders, "Measuring Organizational Cultures: A Qualitative and Quantitative Study across Twenty Cases," *Administrative Science Quarterly* 35, no. 2 (June 1990), pp. 286–316. Approval of request for permission to reprint. © Johnson Graduate School of Management, Cornell University.

collectivism A worldview that values subordination of the individual to the goals of the group and adherence to the principle that people should be judged by their contribution to the group.

In contrast, **collectivism** is a worldview that values subordination of the individual to the goals of the group and adherence to the principle that people should be judged by their contribution to the group. Collectivism was widespread in communist countries but has become less prevalent since the collapse of communism in most of those countries. Japan is a noncommunist country where collectivism is highly valued.

Collectivism in Japan traces its roots to the fusion of Confucian, Buddhist, and Shinto thought that occurred during the Tokugawa period in Japanese history (1600–1870s).[47] A central value that emerged during this period was strong attachment to the group–whether a village, a work group, or a company. Strong identification with the group is said to create pressures for collective action in Japan, as well as strong pressure for conformity to group norms and a relative lack of individualism.[48]

Managers must realize that organizations and organizational members reflect their national culture's emphasis on individualism or collectivism. Indeed, one of the major reasons why Japanese and American management practices differ is that Japanese culture values collectivism and U.S. culture values individualism.[49]

power distance The degree to which societies accept the idea that inequalities in the power and well-being of their citizens are due to differences in individuals' physical and intellectual capabilities and heritage.

POWER DISTANCE By **power distance** Hofstede meant the degree to which societies accept the idea that inequalities in the power and well-being of their citizens are due to differences in individuals' physical and intellectual capabilities and heritage. This concept also encompasses the degree to which societies accept the economic and social differences in wealth, status, and well-being that result from differences in individual capabilities.

Societies in which inequalities are allowed to persist or grow over time have *high power distance.* In high-power-distance societies, workers who are professionally successful amass wealth and pass it on to their children, and, as a result, inequalities may grow over time. In such societies, the gap between rich and poor, with all the attendant political and social consequences, grows very large. In contrast, in societies with *low power distance,* large inequalities between citizens are not allowed to develop. In low-power-distance countries, the government uses taxation and social welfare programs to reduce inequality and improve the welfare of the least fortunate. These societies are more attuned to preventing a large gap between rich and poor and minimizing discord between different classes of citizens.

Advanced Western countries such as the United States, Germany, the Netherlands, and the United Kingdom have relatively low power distance and high individualism.

Economically poor Latin American countries such as Guatemala and Panama, and Asian countries such as Malaysia and the Philippines, have high power distance and low individualism.[50] These findings suggest that the cultural values of richer countries emphasize protecting the rights of individuals and, at the same time, provide a fair chance of success to every member of society.

achievement orientation A worldview that values assertiveness, performance, success, and competition.

nurturing orientation A worldview that values the quality of life, warm personal friendships, and services and care for the weak.

ACHIEVEMENT VERSUS NURTURING ORIENTATION Societies that have an **achievement orientation** value assertiveness, performance, success, competition, and results. Societies that have a **nurturing orientation** value the quality of life, warm personal relationships, and services and care for the weak. Japan and the United States tend to be achievement-oriented; the Netherlands, Sweden, and Denmark are more nurturing-oriented.

uncertainty avoidance The degree to which societies are willing to tolerate uncertainty and risk.

UNCERTAINTY AVOIDANCE Societies as well as individuals differ in their tolerance for uncertainty and risk. Societies low on **uncertainty avoidance** (such as the United States and Hong Kong) are easygoing, value diversity, and tolerate differences in personal beliefs and actions. Societies high on uncertainty avoidance (such as Japan and France) are more rigid and skeptical about people whose behaviors or beliefs differ from the norm. In these societies, conformity to the values of the social and work groups to which a person belongs is the norm, and structured situations are preferred because they provide a sense of security.

long-term orientation A worldview that values thrift and persistence in achieving goals.

short-term orientation A worldview that values personal stability or happiness and living for the present.

LONG-TERM VERSUS SHORT-TERM ORIENTATION The last dimension that Hofstede described is orientation toward life and work.[51] A national culture with a **long-term orientation** rests on values such as thrift (saving) and persistence in achieving goals. A national culture with a **short-term orientation** is concerned with maintaining personal stability or happiness and living for the present. Societies with a long-term orientation include Taiwan and Hong Kong, well known for their high rate of per capita savings. The United States and France have a short-term orientation, and their citizens tend to spend more and save less.

National Culture and Global Management

Differences among national cultures have important implications for managers. First, because of cultural differences, management practices that are effective in one country might be troublesome in another. General Electric's managers learned this while trying to manage Tungsram, a Hungarian lighting products company GE acquired for $150 million. GE was attracted to Tungsram, widely regarded as one of Hungary's best companies, because of Hungary's low wage rates and the possibility of using the company as a base from which to export lighting products to western Europe. GE transferred some of its best managers to Tungsram and hoped it would soon become a leader in Europe. Unfortunately many problems arose.

One problem resulted from major misunderstandings between the American managers and the Hungarian workers. The Americans complained that the Hungarians were lazy; the Hungarians thought the Americans were pushy. The Americans wanted strong sales and marketing functions that would pamper customers. In the prior command economy, sales and marketing activities were unnecessary. In addition, Hungarians expected GE to deliver Western-style wages, but GE came to Hungary to take advantage of the country's low-wage structure.[52] As Tungsram's losses mounted, GE managers had to admit that, because of differences in basic attitudes between countries, they had underestimated the difficulties they would face in turning Tungsram around. Nevertheless, by 2001 these problems had been solved, and the increased efficiency of GE's Hungarian operations made General Electric a major player in the European lighting market, causing it to invest another $1 billion.[53]

Often management practices must be tailored to suit the cultural contexts within which an organization operates. An approach effective in the United States might not work in Japan, Hungary, or Mexico because of differences in national culture. For example, U.S.-style pay-for-performance systems that emphasize the performance of individuals might not work well in Japan, where individual performance in pursuit of group goals is the value that receives emphasis.

Managers doing business with individuals from another country must be sensitive to the value systems and norms of that country and behave accordingly. For example, Friday is the Islamic Sabbath. Thus it would be impolite and inappropriate for a U.S. manager to schedule a busy day of activities for Saudi Arabian managers on a Friday.

A culturally diverse management team can be a source of strength for an organization participating in the global marketplace. Compared to organizations with culturally homogeneous management teams, organizations that employ managers from a variety of cultures have a better appreciation of how national cultures differ, and they tailor their management systems and behaviors to the differences.[54] Indeed, one advantage that many Western companies have over their Japanese competitors is greater willingness to create global teams composed of employees from different countries around the world who can draw on and share their different cultural experiences and knowledge to provide service that is customized to the needs of companies in different countries, as the following "Information Technology Byte" box suggests.

Information Technology Byte

Global Self-Managed Teams Give IBM a Competitive Advantage

IBM has been experiencing tough competition in the 2000s from IT service companies around the world that can undercut IBM's prices because they have lower labor costs (for example, programmers in India earn one-third as much as U.S. programmers). Because IT services account for more than half of IBM's $90 billion annual revenues, it has been searching for ways to better use its talented workforce to both lower costs and offer customers unique, specialized kinds of services that its competitors cannot (and that it can charge a high price for). IBM has developed several kinds of techniques to accomplish this.[55]

IT services with an edge: IBM's new competency centers customize teams of workers who can manage their own tasks.

In the 2000s IBM created "competency centers" around the world that are staffed by employees who share the same specific IT skill. In India, for example, IBM employs over 10,000 IT personnel who specialize in providing technical customer support for large U.S. companies. These employees work in self-managed teams and are responsible for managing all aspects of a particular client's specific needs. By using teams, IBM can offer high-quality personalized service at a low price and compete effectively in the global marketplace.

Most of IBM's employees are concentrated in competency centers located in the countries in which IBM has the most clients and does the most business. These employees have a wide variety of skills, developed from their previous work experience, and the challenge facing IBM is to use these experts efficiently. To accomplish this, IBM used its own IT expertise to develop sophisticated software that allows it to create self-managed teams composed of IBM experts who have the optimum mix of skills to solve a client's particular problems. First IBM programmers analyzed the skills and experience of its 70,000 global employees and entered the results into the software program. Then they analyze and code the nature of a client's specific problem and input that information. IBM's program matches each specific client problem to the skills of IBM's experts and identifies a list of "best fit" employees. One of IBM's senior managers narrows this list and decides on the actual composition of the self-managed team. Once selected, team members, from wherever they happen to be in the world, assemble as quickly as possible and go to work analyzing the client's problem. Together, team members use their authority to develop the software and service package necessary to solve and manage the client's problem.

This new IT lets IBM create an ever-changing set of global self-managed teams that form to solve the problems of IBM's global clients. At the same time, IBM's IT also optimizes the use of its whole talented workforce because each employee is placed in his or her "most highly valued use"–that is, in the team where the employee's skills can best increase efficiency and effectiveness. In addition, because each team inputs knowledge about its activities into IBM's internal information system, teams can watch and learn from one another–so their skills increase over time.

Summary and Review

LO6-1 **WHAT IS THE GLOBAL ENVIRONMENT?** The global environment is the set of forces and conditions that operate beyond an organization's boundaries but affect a manager's ability to acquire and use resources. The global environment has two components: the task environment and the general environment.

LO6-2, 6-3 **THE TASK ENVIRONMENT** The task environment is the set of forces and conditions that originate with global suppliers, distributors, customers, and competitors and influence managers daily. The opportunities and threats associated with forces in the task environment become more complex as a company expands globally.

LO6-2, 6-3 **THE GENERAL ENVIRONMENT** The general environment comprises wide-ranging global economic, technological, sociocultural, demographic, political, and legal forces that affect an organization and its task environment.

LO6-4, 6-5 **THE CHANGING GLOBAL ENVIRONMENT** In recent years there has been a marked shift toward a more open global environment in which capital flows more freely as people and companies search for new opportunities to create profit and wealth. This has hastened the process of globalization. Globalization is the set of specific and general forces that work together to integrate and connect economic, political, and social systems across countries, cultures, or geographic regions so that nations become increasingly interdependent and similar. The process of globalization has been furthered by declining barriers to international trade and investment and declining barriers of distance and culture.

Management in Action

Topics for Discussion and Action

Discussion

1. Why is it important for managers to understand the forces in the global environment that are acting on them and their organizations? [LO6-1]
2. Which organization is likely to face the most complex task environment—a biotechnology company trying to develop a cure for cancer or a large retailer like The Gap or Macy's? Why? [LO6-2, 6-3]
3. The population is aging because of declining birth rates, declining death rates, and the aging of the baby boom generation. What might some of the implications of this demographic trend be for (a) a pharmaceutical company and (b) the home construction industry? [LO6-1, 6-2, 6-3]
4. How do political, legal, and economic forces shape national culture? What characteristics of national culture do you think have the most important effect on how successful a country is in doing business abroad? [LO6-3, 6-5]
5. After the passage of NAFTA, many U.S. companies shifted production operations to Mexico to take advantage of lower labor costs and lower standards for environmental and worker protection. As a result, they cut their costs and were better able to survive in an increasingly competitive global environment. Was their behavior ethical—that is, did the ends justify the means? [LO6-4]

Action

6. Choose an organization, and ask a manager in that organization to list the number and strengths of forces in the organization's task environment. Ask the manager to pay particular attention to identifying opportunities and threats that result from pressures and changes in customers, competitors, and suppliers. [LO6-1, 6-2, 6-3]

Building Management Skills

Analyzing an Organization's Environment [LO6-1, 6-2, 6-3]

Pick an organization with which you are familiar. It can be an organization in which you have worked or currently work or one that you interact with regularly as a customer (such as the college you are attending). For this organization do the following:

1. Describe the main forces in the global task environment that are affecting the organization.
2. Describe the main forces in the global general environment that are affecting the organization.
3. Explain how environmental forces affect the job of an individual manager within this organization. How do they determine the opportunities and threats that its managers must confront?

Managing Ethically [LO6-4, 6-5]

In recent years the number of U.S. companies that buy their inputs from low-cost overseas suppliers has been growing, and concern about the ethics associated with employing young children in factories has been increasing. In Pakistan and India, children as young as six years old work long hours to make rugs and carpets for export to Western countries or clay bricks for local use. In countries like Malaysia and in Central America, children and teenagers routinely work long hours in factories and sweatshops to produce the clothing that is found in most U.S. discount and department stores.

Questions

1. Either by yourself or in a group, discuss whether it is ethical to employ children in factories and whether U.S. companies should buy and sell products made by these children. What are some arguments for and against child labor?
2. If child labor is an economic necessity, what methods could be employed to make it as ethical a practice as possible? Or is it simply unethical?

Small Group Breakout Exercise

How to Enter the Copying Business [LO6-1, 6-2]

Form groups of three to five people, and appoint one group member as the spokesperson who will communicate your findings to the whole class when called on by the instructor. Then discuss the following scenario:

You and your partners have decided to open a small printing and copying business in a college town of 100,000 people. Your business will compete with companies like FedEx Kinko's. You know that over 50% of small businesses fail in their first year, so to increase your chances of success, you have decided to perform a detailed analysis of the task environment of the copying business to discover what opportunities and threats you will encounter.

1. Decide what you must know about (a) your future customers, (b) your future competitors, and (c) other critical forces in the task environment if you are to be successful.
2. Evaluate the main barriers to entry into the copying business.
3. Based on this analysis, list some steps you would take to help your new copying business succeed.

Exploring the World Wide Web [LO6-2, 6-3, 6-4]

Go to Fuji Films' Web site (www.fujifilm.com), click on "About Us," "History," and then "Corporate History," and consider how Fuji's global activities have expanded over time.

1. How would you characterize the way Fuji manages the global environment? For example, how has Fuji responded to the needs of customers in different countries?
2. How have increasing global competition and declining barriers of distance and culture affected Fuji's global operations?

Be the Manager [LO6-1, 6-2]

The Changing Environment of Retailing

You are the new manager of a major clothing store that is facing a crisis. This clothing store has been the leader in its market for the last 15 years. In the last three years, however, two other major clothing store chains have opened, and they have steadily been attracting customers away from your store—your sales are down 30%. To find out why, your store surveyed former customers and learned that they perceive your store as not keeping up with changing fashion trends and new forms of customer service. In examining how the store operates, you found out that the 10 purchasing managers who buy the clothing and accessories for the store have been buying from the same clothing suppliers and have become reluctant to try new ones. Moreover, salespeople rarely, if ever, make suggestions for changing how the store operates, and they don't respond to customer requests; the culture of the store has become conservative and risk-averse.

Questions

1. Analyze the major forces in the task environment of a retail clothing store.
2. Devise a program that will help other managers and employees to better understand and respond to their store's task environment.

Case in the News [LO6-1, 6-4, 6-5]

The Transformer: Why VW Is the Car Giant to Watch

When Volkswagen CEO Martin Winterkorn said two years ago that he was determined to zoom past Toyota to become the world's biggest automaker, the notion seemed laughable. At the time, the German automaker sold 3 million fewer vehicles than Toyota, was losing ground in the United States, and had a reputation for iffy quality. Toyota, then set to pass General Motors as the best-selling carmaker on the planet, seemed unassailable. Today Toyota is vulnerable, and Winterkorn's ambitions seem a lot less outlandish. In November, for the first time, VW built more cars than its Japanese rival. Toyota still sells more each year, but VW has closed the gap to fewer than 1.5 million cars. Quality continues to be an issue for VW in the United States, but Toyota is the one suffering negative headlines after a series of embarrassing recalls. Toyota's CEO—in an act of extreme self-flagellation—has even said his company's best days may be behind it.

Winterkorn sees an historic opportunity. And with the backing of his formidable boss and mentor, VW Chairman Ferdinand Piëch, he's seizing it. By 2018, Winterkorn vows, VW will pass Toyota. "VW saw a chink in Toyota's armor and realized they could act on their ambitions," says Stephen Pope, who follows the industry for Cantor Fitzgerald in London. "They went for it straightaway." All over the globe, Winterkorn, 62, is punching the accelerator. VW has agreed to buy a 20% stake in Suzuki Motors to gear up for an assault on the rapidly growing markets of Southeast Asia and India. Winterkorn is going after BMW and Mercedes, committing $11 billion over the next three years to Audi, VW's luxury brand. Peter Schwarzenbauer, a board member who oversees Audi's sales and marketing, says the brand plans 10 new models, including the A1, the world's first "premium subcompact."

Aiming Downmarket

Winterkorn's most ambitious plans are in the United States, where he aims to double sales by 2012. It was only five years ago that VW tried and failed to move upmarket in the United States. Remember the Phaeton, the VW with a sticker price of $85,000? Now Winterkorn is reversing course. He's betting that Volkswagen can steal customers from Toyota, Honda, Ford, and others by selling Americans on German engineering and style at affordable prices. This year, VW will introduce a compact priced to compete with cars like the $16,000 Toyota Corolla. "We have to bring the masses to VW," says Mark Barnes, VW's U.S. chief operating officer. Beating Toyota won't be easy. For starters, VW sells fewer vehicles in the United States than Subaru or Kia and still has a reputation for making unreliable, overpriced cars. In Southeast Asia—a Toyota stronghold—the VW brand is practically unknown. Ditto for India. Winterkorn's plan to double Audi's sales in the United States by 2018, meanwhile, isn't exactly scaring BMW. "They have been saying that for years," says Jim O'Donnell, president of BMW of North America.

Still, VW is a formidable competitor; it earned $975 million in the first three quarters of 2009, despite the global collapse of car sales, and it has $33.3 billion in cash. "We want to make [VW] the economic, ecological, and technological leader by 2018," Winterkorn wrote in an e-mail. "Our goal is not just about size—we are aiming for quality-driven growth." Piëch has long wanted to move beyond VW's bases in Europe, China, and Brazil. In the 1990s, as Audi chairman and later VW CEO, Piëch acquired lower-end brands, including Spain's SEAT and the Czech Republic's Skoda. Later he added ritzy names like Bentley, Lamborghini, and Bugatti. "He used to privately talk about selling a car for every purse and purpose as Alfred Sloan did at GM," says Garel Rhys, president of the Center for Auto Industry Studies at Cardiff University in Wales.

Fixing VW's America Problem

By the end of 2006 it was clear that VW's move upmarket wasn't working, and in January 2007 Piëch installed Winterkorn as CEO. Before his elevation, Winterkorn ran Audi, where he boosted quality and supercharged growth with new models that rivaled BMW's cars. Winterkorn rewarded employees for speaking their minds and bringing ideas to his attention. In the summer of 2007, Winterkorn and the board met to brainstorm ways to become the world's biggest automaker, says VW's U.S. chief, Stefan Jacoby. High on the agenda was fixing VW's America problem. That year, VW expected to sell 200,000 cars in the United States, a 40% drop from 2000 and a third of what VW sold in 1970 when the Bug and Bus were hippie icons. Jacoby says executives at the meeting saw three choices: They could continue to lose buckets of money selling cars that were too small and too expensive; they could wave the white flag; or they could go on the offensive. They chose door number 3.

Jacoby says he persuaded the board to build VW's first U.S. plant since closing a Pennsylvania factory in 1988. He recalls arguing that doing so would help VW overcome resistance in the American heartland to imported vehicles. If VW built the plant, Jacoby recalls saying, he would sell 150,000 cars from that factory alone each year. The board approved the plan and allocated $1 billion for the facility, which is scheduled to open next year in Chattanooga, Tennessee. VW's decision to build cars in the United States has not gone unnoticed by its main rival. "The fact that they are producing in the United States gives them a leg up," says Donald V. Esmond, senior vice president for automotive operations at Toyota Motor Sales USA. "But we'll just keep focusing on our customers."

Jacoby's most pressing challenge is devising a roomy family sedan at a price Americans will pay. Today's Passat, despite being smaller than most midsize sedans, sells for $28,000, or $8,000 more than a Toyota Camry. That's largely why VW sold only 11,000 Passats in the United States last year, compared with some 350,000 Camrys. VW plans to stretch the Passat's successor four inches, add three inches of legroom, and sell it for a starting price of about $20,000. Timothy Ellis, VW's U.S. marketing chief, says he expects to move more than 135,000 midsize sedans a year starting in 2011. James N. Hall, principal of the auto consulting firm 2953 Analytics, is skeptical. Typically, Hall says, it takes two generations for a new midsize sedan to get traction in the United States. "The first-generation car is going to have to hit it out of the park," he says.

Expansion Plans for U.S. Lineup

Industry analysts say Winterkorn's mass market approach could work in the United States. VW will be the only company offering affordable European cars. BMW and Mercedes sell German engineering, but their cheapest models start at $30,000. According to a source briefed on VW's plans for the United States, the company plans to expand its lineup from 10 cars today to 14 in five years. VW will have new compact and midsize sedans priced for the American market, plus a small SUV. VW also may introduce its Polo compact—now available in Europe, China, and other markets—to the United States. VW will have to convince Americans its cars are worth buying. In J.D. Power & Associates' Initial Quality Study, which ranks cars in the first three months of ownership, VW came in 15th out of 37 last year. The company's ranking improved from 24th in 2008. But VW still trails Toyota, Honda, and Nissan, as well as the Chevrolet and Ford brands. What's more, though 78% of Americans know the VW brand, only 2% buy the cars. Most Americans recognize the Beetle and Jetta, says Ellis, but draw a blank on VW's other eight U.S. models. "Volkswagen has a bigger brand than it deserves," he says. "But we have a low sense of awareness for our products."

Asia Push

If VW is playing catch-up in the United States, it is many laps behind its rivals in India and Southeast Asia. Indians now buy about 2 million cars a year; Southeast Asians buy about 1 million. VW is lucky to sell 20,000 cars a year in each region. It will have to steal customers from Honda and Toyota, which have dominated Southeast Asia for many years. That's where Suzuki comes in. By buying a stake in the Japanese company, VW gets access to Suzuki's small-car technology. Suzuki's Indian joint venture already does well with its Alto and Swift subcompacts. "India has a massive road-building program," says Cantor Fitzgerald's Pope. "With Suzuki, VW will be able to put out very efficient vehicles."

VW has tapped Weiming Soh to oversee its Asia push. A U.S.-educated Singaporean, Soh most recently helped orchestrate a turnaround of VW's operations in China. Soh says VW Group, which includes VW, Audi, and Skoda, will add or freshen 20 models in China by late 2011. His goal is to double VW's Chinese retail network to 1,600 dealers in five years and sell 2 million cars. As part of his Southeast Asia strategy, Soh plans beachheads in Hong Kong and Singapore. Those markets are tiny, selling 30,000 and 100,000 cars a year, respectively. But Soh says Singapore sets trends for Southeast Asia, and Hong Kong is influential in southern China. "My aim is to make these two markets VW states," Soh says.

Winterkorn and Piëch have put in place the pieces of their global strategy. Now that VW's two main rivals, Toyota and GM, are retrenching, they're speeding up their plans. The big question is whether size for size's sake generates real benefits for a car company. Automakers like to get big so they can spread the huge costs of developing new models over mass volumes. Of course, car companies have a tendency to get so big that they become unmanageable. Winterkorn and his executives argue that they can retain management control of their sprawling enterprise because VW is more decentralized than many automakers. "The critical factor is that each brand has its independence, a clear positioning, and autonomous management." Winterkorn wrote in his e-mail to *Bloomberg Businessweek*.

Questions for Discussion

1. Use the chapter material to decide which strategies Volkswagen has been using to expand globally.
2. In what ways will the different specific and general forces in the environment affect the success of its strategies?
3. Search the Web: How have Volkswagen's new global initiatives been working? Has its performance improved?

Source: D. Welch, "The Transformer: Why VW Is the Car Giant to Watch," *BusinessWeek*, January 13, 2010. Reprinted from January 13, 2010 issue of *Bloomberg Businessweek* by special permission, copyright © 2010 by Bloomberg L.P.

CHAPTER 7

Decision Making, Learning, Creativity, and Entrepreneurship

Learning Objectives

After studying this chapter, you should be able to:

LO7-1 Understand the nature of managerial decision making, differentiate between programmed and nonprogrammed decisions, and explain why nonprogrammed decision making is a complex, uncertain process.

LO7-2 Describe the six steps managers should take to make the best decisions, and explain how cognitive biases can lead managers to make poor decisions.

LO7-3 Identify the advantages and disadvantages of group decision making, and describe techniques that can improve it.

LO7-4 Explain the role that organizational learning and creativity play in helping managers to improve their decisions.

LO7-5 Describe how managers can encourage and promote entrepreneurship to create a learning organization, and differentiate between entrepreneurs and intrapreneurs.

A MANAGER'S CHALLENGE

Decision Making in Response to Threats and Opportunities at PUMA

Why is decision making of paramount importance in organizations? When Jochen Zeitz took over as CEO of PUMA AG in 1993 at the age of 30, the company was facing major threats.[1] PUMA AG, based in the small German sneaker-producing town of Herzogenaurach,[2] had lost money for the past eight years, and PUMA North America was facing imminent bankruptcy. The company's cash levels were low, and it was no match for major industry leaders like Adidas (Adidas and PUMA were both founded in Herzogenaurach by two brothers who have long competed with each other), Reebok, and Nike.[3]

Facing tough decisions about how to turn around the company's fortunes, Zeitz decided that rather than trying to compete based on the performance capabilities of its athletic shoes and equipment, PUMA would focus more on style, colors, and lines of shoes. Essentially Zeitz saw a potential opportunity in trying to start up a new division focus on experimental fashion and sport as lifestyle. Of course Zeitz also made difficult decisions to respond to the threats the company was facing by, for example, dramatically reducing production costs and taking back control over U.S. distribution of PUMA products.[4] And PUMA continued to produce high-performance

The decisions CEO Jochen Zeitz has made at PUMA and the daily decisions he and other managers continue to make are key contributors to PUMA's success today.

athletic shoes and gear for serious sport. In 2008, for example, PUMA sponsored 9 teams participating in the African Nations Cup soccer tournament and 5 teams in the European soccer championships; 17 teams competing in the summer Olympics in Beijing were outfitted with PUMA products.[5] In 2009 PUMA sponsored the Jamaican track and field team and Usain "Lightning" Bolt at the World Athletics Championships in Berlin, during which Bolt, a three-time winner of Olympic gold medals, broke his own 100- and 200-meter world records.[6]

Nonetheless, Zeitz's bold decision to pursue the world of fashion and style contributed to PUMA becoming the major athletic apparel company it is today.[7] Recognizing the importance of creative designs and products, he decided to start a new division called "sport lifestyle" led by Antonio Bertone, a then 21-year-old skateboarder.[8] The division was asked to create experimental fashion products. In 1998 Bertone partnered with German fashion designer Jil Sander to turn PUMA's traditional 1960s-style cleated soccer shoe into a trendy fashion sneaker using funky colors and suede. At first this experimental product line received a lot of skepticism from industry experts and retailers alike; famed soccer player Pelé had worn PUMA cleats, and it was unthinkable to many that PUMA would succeed in the world of fashion. As Zeitz indicates, "It took a while—and from my perspective, a lot of energy—to protect this new little child [the lifestyle group] of PUMA from getting killed. . . . Eventually, it became the entire company."[9]

Customers loved the retro look and edgy colors of the new sneakers, which are now sold in a variety of venues ranging from the Foot Locker to high-end stores like Barneys to upscale department stores. PUMA has its own showcase boutique in the meatpacking district of Manhattan and over 70 stores around the world.[10]

Zeitz continues to pursue new opportunities at PUMA—reinventing traditional products to combine performance with style—and continues to partner with creative thinkers such as Xuly Bet, born in Mali and now a Paris fashion designer, and Yasuhiro Mihara of Japan to create new products.[11] Designers Philippe Starck and Alexander McQueen both created product lines for PUMA. PUMA partnered with the BMW Mini to make a new driving shoe; and PUMA's Mostro shoe continues to be a top seller.[12]

Former skateboarder Bertone is now based in Boston as PUMA's global director of brand management. Now a top manager, Bertone continues to make decisions to seize opportunities for creative and innovative product lines such as the limited-edition line called Thrift (products made from vintage clothing) and Mongolian Shoe BBQ (shoes that can be customized online).

Zeitz continues to make decisions in response to opportunities and, in the process, has expanded PUMA's range of products in far-reaching directions. The company's 24 Hour Tubism is an aluminum-covered wardrobe carrier designed for business travelers. Teaming up with Danish bicycle maker Biomega and the London design group Vexed Generation, PUMA created a foldable "unstealable" bicycle that retails for around $775. When they first started working on the project, the team decided that they wanted to develop a truly creative bike—one that had never been built before. The "unstealable" bicycle met the bill—its lock is integrated into the frame of the bike and, if broken, renders the bike unusable.[13]

Clearly the decisions Zeitz and other managers made at PUMA, and continue to make daily, are key contributors to the success of PUMA today.[14] And although much uncertainty and ambiguity surrounds these decisions when they are made, and they are sometimes greeted with skepticism, they have propelled PUMA to be a powerhouse of innovation.[15]

Overview

The "Manager's Challenge" illustrates how decision making can have a profound influence on organizational effectiveness. The decisions managers make at all levels in companies large and small can have a dramatic impact on the growth and prosperity of these companies and the well-being of their employees, customers, and other stakeholders. Yet such decisions can be difficult to make because they are fraught with uncertainty.

LO7-1 Understand the nature of managerial decision making, differentiate between programmed and nonprogrammed decisions, and explain why nonprogrammed decision making is a complex, uncertain process.

In this chapter we examine how managers make decisions, and we explore how individual, group, and organizational factors affect the quality of the decisions they make and ultimately determine organizational performance. We discuss the nature of managerial decision making and examine some models of the decision-making process that help reveal the complexities of successful decision making. Then we outline the main steps of the decision-making process; in addition, we explore the biases that may cause capable managers to make poor decisions both as individuals and as members of a group. Next we examine how managers can promote organizational learning and creativity and improve the quality of decision making throughout an organization. Finally we discuss the important role of entrepreneurship in promoting organizational creativity, and we differentiate between entrepreneurs and intrapreneurs. By the end of this chapter you will appreciate the critical role of management decision making in creating a high-performing organization.

The Nature of Managerial Decision Making

Every time managers act to plan, organize, direct, or control organizational activities, they make a stream of decisions. In opening a new restaurant, for example, managers have to decide where to locate it, what kinds of food to provide, which people to employ, and so on. Decision making is a basic part of every task managers perform. In this chapter we study how these decisions are made.

As we discussed in the last three chapters, one of the main tasks facing a manager is to manage the organizational environment. Forces in the external environment give rise to many opportunities and threats for managers and their organizations. In addition, inside an organization managers must address many opportunities and threats that may arise as organizational resources are used. To deal with these opportunities and threats, managers must make decisions–that is, they must select one solution from a set of alternatives. **Decision making** is the process by which managers respond to opportunities and threats by analyzing the options and making determinations, or *decisions,* about specific organizational goals and courses of action. Good decisions result in the selection of appropriate goals and courses of action that increase organizational performance; bad decisions lower performance.

decision making The process by which managers respond to opportunities and threats by analyzing options and making determinations about specific organizational goals and courses of action.

Decision making in response to opportunities occurs when managers search for ways to improve organizational performance to benefit customers, employees, and other stakeholder groups. In "A Manager's Challenge," Jochen Zeitz turned around PUMA's fortunes by the decisions he made in response to opportunities. *Decision making in response to threats* occurs when events inside or outside the organization adversely affect organizational performance and managers search for ways to increase performance.[16] When Zeitz become CEO of PUMA, high production costs and an ineffective distribution system were threats that prompted Zeitz to make a number of decisions to improve the performance and viability of the company.[17] Decision making is central to being a manager, and whenever managers engage in planning, organizing, leading, and controlling–their four principal tasks–they are constantly making decisions.

Managers are always searching for ways to make better decisions to improve organizational performance. At the same time they do their best to avoid costly mistakes that will hurt organizational performance. Examples of spectacularly good decisions include Martin Cooper's decision to develop the first cell phone at Motorola and Apple's decision to develop the iPod.[18] Examples of spectacularly bad decisions include the decision by managers at NASA and Morton Thiokol to launch the *Challenger* space shuttle–a decision that killed six astronauts in 1986–and the decision by NASA to launch the *Columbia* space shuttle in 2003, which killed seven astronauts.

Programmed and Nonprogrammed Decision Making

Regardless of the specific decisions a manager makes, the decision-making process is either programmed or nonprogrammed.[19]

programmed decision making Routine, virtually automatic decision making that follows established rules or guidelines.

PROGRAMMED DECISION MAKING **Programmed decision making** is a *routine*, virtually automatic process. Programmed decisions are decisions that have been made so many times in the past that managers have developed rules or guidelines to be applied when certain situations inevitably occur. Programmed decision making takes place when a school principal asks the school board to hire a new teacher whenever student enrollment increases by 40 students; when a manufacturing supervisor hires new workers whenever existing workers' overtime increases by more than 10%; and when an office manager orders basic office supplies, such as paper and pens, whenever the inventory of supplies drops below a certain level. Furthermore, in the last example, the office manager probably orders the same amount of supplies each time.

This decision making is called *programmed* because office managers, for example, do not need to repeatedly make new judgments about what should be done. They can rely on long-established decision rules such as these:

- *Rule 1:* When the storage shelves are three-quarters empty, order more copy paper.
- *Rule 2:* When ordering paper, order enough to fill the shelves.

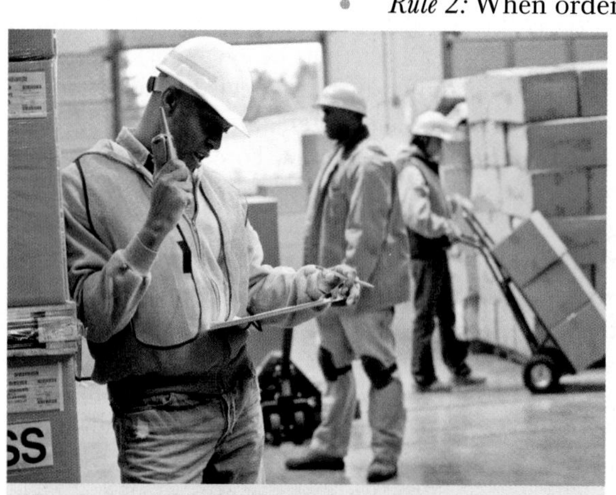
Programmed decisions allow warehouse supervisors such as this one to develop simple rubrics so the job is done consistently and with less error.

Managers can develop rules and guidelines to regulate all routine organizational activities. For example, rules can specify how a worker should perform a certain task, and rules can specify the quality standards that raw materials must meet to be acceptable. Most decision making that relates to the day-to-day running of an organization is programmed decision making. Examples include deciding how much inventory to hold, when to pay bills, when to bill customers, and when to order materials and supplies. Programmed decision making occurs when managers have the information they need to create rules that will guide decision making. There is little ambiguity involved in assessing when the stockroom is empty or counting the number of new students in class.

As profiled in the following "Focus on Diversity" box, effectively training new employees is essential to reap the benefits of programmed decision making.

Focus on Diversity

Programmed Decision Making at UPS

UPS is unrivaled in its use of programmed decision making. Practically all the motions, behaviors, and actions that its drivers perform each day have been carefully honed to maximize efficiency and minimize strain and injuries while delivering high-quality customer service. For example, a 12-step process prescribes how drivers should park their trucks, locate the package they are about to deliver, and step off the truck in 15.5 seconds (a process called "selection" at UPS).[20] Rules and routines such as these are carefully detailed in UPS's "340 Methods" manual (UPS actually has far more than 340 methods). Programmed decision making dictates where drivers should stop to get gas, how they should hold their keys in their hands, and how to lift and lower packages.[21]

Did he make it in 15.5 seconds? UPS driver training enforces productivity and safety by teaching new employees a variety of programmed decisions.

When programmed decision making is so heavily relied on, ensuring that new employees learn tried-and-true routines is essential. UPS has traditionally taught new employees with a two-week period of lectures followed by practice.[22] In the 2000s, however, managers began to wonder if they needed to alter their training methods to suit their new Generation Y trainees (Generation Y typically refers to people born after 1980), who were not so keen on memorization and drills.[23] Generation Y trainees seemed to require more training time to become effective drivers (90–180 days compared to a typical average of 30–45 days), and quit rates for new drivers had increased.[24]

Given the fundamental importance of performance programs for UPS operations, managers decided to try to alter the training new hires receive so it would be better received by Generation Y trainees. In September 2007 UPS opened a new Landover, Maryland, pilot training center called UPS Integrad, which is over 11,000 square feet and cost over $30 million to build and equip. Integrad was developed over a three-year period through a collaborative effort of over 170 people, including UPS top managers (many of whom started their careers with UPS as drivers), teams from Virginia Tech and MIT, animators from the Indian company Brainvisa, and forecasters from the Institute for the Future with the support of a grant from the Department of Labor for $1.8 million.[25] Results thus far suggest that Integrad training results in greater driver proficiency and fewer first-year accidents and injuries.[26]

Training at Integrad emphasizes hands-on learning.[27] For example, at Integrad a UPS truck with transparent sides is used to teach trainees selection so they can actually see the instructor performing the steps and then practice the steps themselves rather than trying to absorb the material in a lecture. Trainees can try different movements and see, with the help of computer diagrams and simulations, how following UPS routines will help protect them from injury and how debilitating work as a driver can be if they do not follow routines. Video recorders track and document what trainees do correctly and incorrectly so they can see it for themselves rather relying on feedback from an instructor, which they might question. As Stephen Jones, who is in charge of training for UPS and manages Integrad, indicates, "Tell them what they did incorrectly, and they'll tell you, 'I didn't do that. You saw wrong.' This way we've got it on tape and they can see it for themselves."[28]

At Integrad, trainees get practice driving in a pseudo town that has been constructed in a parking lot.[29] They also watch animated demonstrations on computer screens, participate in simulations, take electronic quizzes, and receive scores on various components that are retained in a database to track learning and performance. Recognizing that Generation Y trainees have a lot of respect for expertise and reputation, older employees also are brought in to facilitate learning at Integrad. For example, long-time UPS employee Don Petersik, who is about to retire, trains facilitators at Integrad and shares stories with them to reinforce the UPS culture–such as the time he was just starting out as a preloader and, unknown to him, the founder of UPS, Jim Casey, approached him and said, "Hi, I'm Jim. I work for UPS."[30] As Petersik indicates, "What's new about the company now is that our teaching style matches your learning styles."[31] Clearly, when learning programmed decision making is of utmost importance, as it is at UPS, it is essential to take into account diversity in learning styles and approaches.

NONPROGRAMMED DECISION MAKING Suppose, however, managers are not certain that a course of action will lead to a desired outcome. Or in even more ambiguous terms, suppose managers are not even sure what they are trying to achieve. Obviously rules cannot be developed to predict uncertain events.

nonprogrammed decision making Nonroutine decision making that occurs in response to unusual, unpredictable opportunities and threats.

Nonprogrammed decision making is required for these *nonroutine* decisions. Nonprogrammed decisions are made in response to unusual or novel opportunities and threats. Nonprogrammed decision making occurs when there are no ready-made decision rules that managers can apply to a situation. Rules do not exist because the situation is unexpected or uncertain and managers lack the information they would need to develop rules to cover it. Examples of nonprogrammed decision making include decisions to invest in a new technology, develop a new kind of product, as Jochen Zeitz did in "A Manager's Challenge," launch a new promotional campaign, enter a new market, expand internationally, or start a new business.

intuition Feelings, beliefs, and hunches that come readily to mind, require little effort and information gathering, and result in on-the-spot decisions.

reasoned judgment A decision that requires time and effort and results from careful information gathering, generation of alternatives, and evaluation of alternatives.

How do managers make decisions in the absence of decision rules? They may rely on their **intuition**–feelings, beliefs, and hunches that come readily to mind, require little effort and information gathering, and result in on-the-spot decisions.[32] Or they may make **reasoned judgments**–decisions that require time and effort and result from careful information gathering, generation of alternatives, and evaluation of alternatives. "Exercising" one's judgment is a more rational process than "going with" one's intuition. For reasons that we examine later in this chapter, both intuition and judgment often are flawed and can result in poor decision making. Thus the likelihood of error is much greater in nonprogrammed decision making than in programmed decision making.[33] In the remainder of this chapter, when we talk about decision making, we are referring to *nonprogrammed* decision making because it causes the most problems for managers and is inherently challenging.

Sometimes managers have to make rapid decisions and don't have time to carefully consider the issues involved. They must rely on their intuition to quickly respond to a pressing concern. For example, when fire chiefs, captains, and lieutenants manage firefighters battling dangerous, out-of-control fires, they often need to rely on their expert intuition to make on-the-spot decisions that will protect the lives of the firefighters and save the lives of others, contain the fires, and preserve property–decisions made in emergency situations entailing high uncertainty, high risk, and rapidly changing conditions.[34] In other cases managers do have time to make reasoned judgments, but there are no established rules to guide their decisions, such as when deciding whether to proceed with a proposed merger.

Regardless of the circumstances, making nonprogrammed decisions can result in effective or ineffective decision making. As indicated in the "Manager as a Person" box on the next page, managers have to be on their guard to avoid being overconfident in decisions that result from either intuition or reasoned judgment.

The classical and administrative decision-making models reveal many of the assumptions, complexities, and pitfalls that affect decision making. These models help reveal the factors that managers and other decision makers must be aware of to

Manager as a Person

Curbing Overconfidence

Should managers be confident in their intuition and reasoned judgments?[35] Decades of research by Nobel Prize winner Daniel Kahneman, his longtime collaborator the late Amos Tversy, and other researchers suggests that managers (like all people) tend to be overconfident in the decisions they make, whether based on intuition or reasoned judgment. And with overconfidence comes failure to evaluate and rethink the wisdom of the decisions one makes and failure to learn from mistakes.[36]

Kahneman distinguishes between the intuition of managers who are truly expert in the content domain of a decision and the intuition of managers who have some knowledge and experience but are not true experts.[37] Although the intuition of both types can be faulty, that of experts is less likely to be flawed. This is why fire captains can make good decisions and why expert chess players can make good moves, in both cases without spending much time or deliberating carefully on what, for nonexperts, is a complicated set of circumstances. What distinguishes expert managers from those with limited expertise is that the experts have extensive experience under conditions in which they receive quick and clear feedback about the outcomes of their decisions.[38]

Unfortunately managers who have some experience in a content area but are not true experts tend to be overly confident in their intuition and their judgments.[39] As Kahneman puts it, "People jump to statistical conclusions on the basis of very weak evidence. We form powerful intuitions about trends and about the replicability of results on the basis of information that is truly inadequate."[40] Not only do managers, and all people, tend to be overconfident about their intuition and judgments, but they also tend not to learn from mistakes. Compounding this undue optimism is the human tendency to be overconfident in one's own abilities and influence over unpredictable events. Surveys have found that the majority of people think they are above average, make better decisions, and are less prone to making bad decisions than others (of course it is impossible for most people to be above average on any dimension).[41]

Examples of managerial overconfidence abound. Research has consistently found that mergers tend to turn out poorly–postmerger profitability declines, stock prices drop, and so forth. For example, Chrysler had the biggest profits of the three largest automakers in the United States when it merged with Daimler; the merger was a failure, and both Chrysler and Daimler would have been better off if it never had happened.[42] So one would imagine that top executives and boards of directors would learn from this research and from articles in the business press about the woes of merged companies (such as the AOL–Time Warner merger and the Hewlett-Packard–Compaq merger).[43] Evidently not. According to a recent study by Hewitt Associates, top executives and board members are, if anything, planning to increase their involvement in mergers over the next few years. These top managers seem to overconfidently believe that they can succeed where others have failed.[44]

Jeffrey Pfeffer, a professor at Stanford University's Graduate School of Business, suggests that managers can avoid the perils of overconfidence by critically evaluating the decisions they have made and the outcomes of those decisions. They should admit to themselves when they have made a mistake and really learn from their mistakes (rather than dismissing them as flukes or situations out of their control). In addition, managers should be leery of too much agreement at the top. As Pfeffer puts it, "If two people agree all the time, one of them is redundant."[45]

improve the quality of their decision making. Keep in mind, however, that the classical and administrative models are just guides that can help managers understand the decision-making process. In real life the process is typically not cut-and-dried, but these models can help guide a manager through it.

The Classical Model

classical decision-making model A prescriptive approach to decision making based on the assumption that the decision maker can identify and evaluate all possible alternatives and their consequences and rationally choose the most appropriate course of action.

optimum decision The most appropriate decision in light of what managers believe to be the most desirable consequences for the organization.

One of the earliest models of decision making, the **classical model,** is *prescriptive,* which means it specifies how decisions *should* be made. Managers using the classical model make a series of simplifying assumptions about the nature of the decision-making process (see Figure 7.1). The premise of the classical model is that once managers recognize the need to make a decision, they should be able to generate a complete list of *all* alternatives and consequences and make the best choice. In other words, the classical model assumes managers have access to *all* the information they need to make the **optimum decision,** which is the most appropriate decision possible in light of what they believe to be the most desirable consequences for the organization. Furthermore, the classical model assumes managers can easily list their own preferences for each alternative and rank them from least to most preferred to make the optimum decision.

The Administrative Model

administrative model An approach to decision making that explains why decision making is inherently uncertain and risky and why managers usually make satisfactory rather than optimum decisions.

James March and Herbert Simon disagreed with the underlying assumptions of the classical model of decision making. In contrast, they proposed that managers in the real world do *not* have access to all the information they need to make a decision. Moreover, they pointed out that even if all information were readily available, many managers would lack the mental or psychological ability to absorb and evaluate it correctly. As a result, March and Simon developed the **administrative model** of decision making to explain why decision making is always an inherently uncertain and risky process–and why managers can rarely make decisions in the manner prescribed by the classical model. The administrative model is based on three important concepts: *bounded rationality, incomplete information,* and *satisficing.*

BOUNDED RATIONALITY March and Simon pointed out that human decision-making capabilities are bounded by people's cognitive limitations–that is, limitations in their ability to interpret, process, and act on information.[46] They argued that the limitations of human intelligence constrain the ability of decision makers to determine

Figure 7.1
The Classical Model of Decision Making

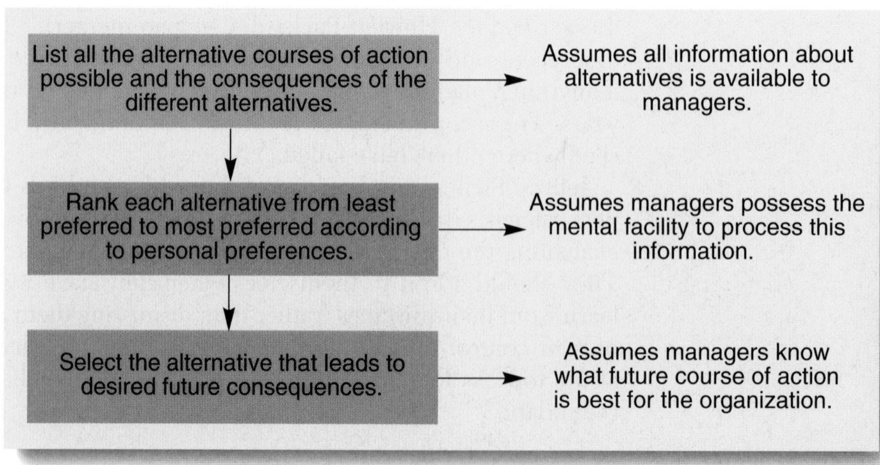

bounded rationality Cognitive limitations that constrain one's ability to interpret, process, and act on information.

the optimum decision. March and Simon coined the term **bounded rationality** to describe the situation in which the number of alternatives a manager must identify is so great and the amount of information so vast that it is difficult for the manager to even come close to evaluating it all before making a decision.[47]

INCOMPLETE INFORMATION Even if managers had unlimited ability to evaluate information, they still would not be able to arrive at the optimum decision because they would have incomplete information. Information is incomplete because the full range of decision-making alternatives is unknowable in most situations, and the consequences associated with known alternatives are uncertain.[48] In other words, information is incomplete because of risk and uncertainty, ambiguity, and time constraints (see Figure 7.2).

risk The degree of probability that the possible outcomes of a particular course of action will occur.

RISK AND UNCERTAINTY As we saw in Chapter 6, forces in the organizational environment are constantly changing. **Risk** is present when managers know the possible outcomes of a particular course of action and can assign probabilities to them. For example, managers in the biotechnology industry know that new drugs have a 10% probability of successfully passing advanced clinical trials and a 90% probability of failing. These probabilities reflect the experiences of thousands of drugs that have gone through advanced clinical trials. Thus when managers in the biotechnology industry decide to submit a drug for testing, they know that there is only a 10% chance that the drug will succeed, but at least they have some information on which to base their decision.

uncertainty Unpredictability.

When **uncertainty** exists, the probabilities of alternative outcomes *cannot* be determined and future outcomes are *unknown*. Managers are working blind. Because the probability of a given outcome occurring is not known, managers have little information to use in making a decision. For example, in 1993, when Apple Computer introduced the Newton, its personal digital assistant (PDA), managers had no idea what the probability of a successful product launch for a PDA might be. Because Apple was the first to market this totally new product, there was no body of well-known data that Apple's managers could draw on to calculate the probability of a successful launch. Uncertainty plagues most managerial decision making.[49] Although Apple's initial launch of its PDA was a disaster due to technical problems, an improved version was more successful. In fact, Apple created the PDA market that has boomed during the 2000s as new and different wireless products have been introduced.

As indicated in the following "Information Technology Byte" box, a major source of uncertainty for top managers is being unable to accurately predict future demand for products and services.

Figure 7.2
Why Information Is Incomplete

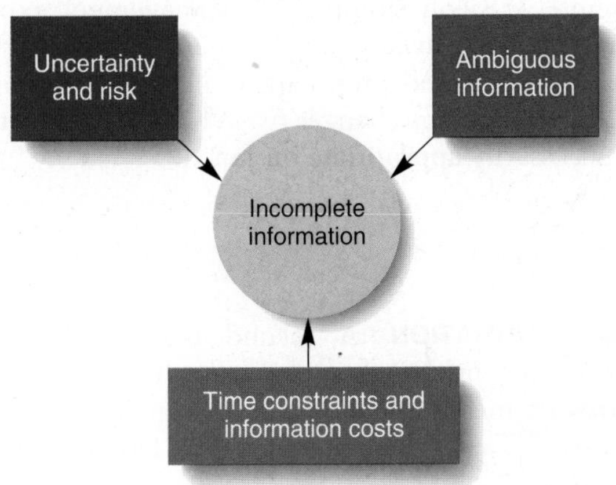

Information Technology Byte

Revising Plans at Associated Business Systems

Having a good business plan is essential for entrepreneurs to obtain funding from banks, venture capitalists, and other sources of funds. Once entrepreneurs have secured funding and their businesses are up and running, their business plans are typically reviewed only once a year as part of an annual planning process–unless, of course, the entrepreneurs are seeking additional funds. These business plans are inherently fraught with uncertainty, as is starting a new business and having it actually succeed. However, viewing a business plan as a work in progress that should be evolving almost continuously has turned out to be a blessing for Craig Knouf, founder, CEO, and majority owner of Associated Business Systems (ABS), a Portland, Oregon, supplier of office equipment.[50]

Craig Knouf appreciates the inherent uncertainty of the best-made plans and decisions.

Knouf estimates that he has revised his business plan over 120 times since founding ABS in 1997; he makes a point of reviewing and, if necessary, revising ABS's business plan monthly after consulting with the firm's seven vice presidents. As Knouf puts it, "If you only looked at the plan every quarter, by the time you realize the mistake, you're five months off. . . . You're done. You're not going to get back on track."[51] Of course the reason why managers like Knouf have to continually rethink their decisions is the inherent uncertainty in all that they do. As a case in point, in the early years Knouf never anticipated that scanners would be a significant part of his business. But during his monthly reviews of the business, he noticed that sales of office equipment with scanning capabilities were steadily increasing. Acting on what his sales data were telling him, Knouf quickly added products with scanning capabilities to his company's offerings.[52]

Knouf's ability to appreciate the inherent uncertainty of plans and decisions, and the benefit of frequently changing courses of action in response to feedback from customers and the market, has paid off handsomely for his company. Since its founding in 1997, ABS's revenues have grown exponentially.[53] ABS appeared on *Inc.* magazine's list of fastest-growing private companies, was on the *Portland Business Journal*'s list of fastest-growing companies in Oregon, and has been one of the 100 fastest-growing companies in Oregon for six consecutive years.[54] In 2008 ABS merged with Ricoh Americas Corporation, a major supplier of office automation equipment and electronics.[55] Knouf manages the partnership, called Associated Business Systems, A Ricoh Company.[56] Management experts agree that Knouf's approach to planning makes good business sense. As Eric Siegel, Wharton Business School lecturer and president of Siegel Management Consultants, put it, "The world turns; things change. . . . What you commit to a document on Dec. 19 is not necessarily appropriate on Jan. 19."[57]

ambiguous information Information that can be interpreted in multiple and often conflicting ways.

AMBIGUOUS INFORMATION A second reason why information is incomplete is that much of the information managers have at their disposal is **ambiguous information.** Its meaning is not clear–it can be interpreted in multiple and often conflicting ways.[58] Take a look at Figure 7.3. Do you see a young woman or an old

Figure 7.3
Ambiguous Information: Young Woman or Old Woman?

woman? In a similar fashion, managers often interpret the same piece of information differently and make decisions based on their own interpretations.

TIME CONSTRAINTS AND INFORMATION COSTS The third reason why information is incomplete is that managers have neither the time nor the money to search for all possible alternative solutions and evaluate all the potential consequences of those alternatives. Consider the situation confronting a Ford Motor Company purchasing manager who has one month to choose a supplier for a small engine part. There are 20,000 potential suppliers for this part in the United States alone. Given the time available, the purchasing manager cannot contact all potential suppliers and ask each for its terms (price, delivery schedules, and so on). Moreover, even if the time were available, the costs of obtaining the information, including the manager's own time, would be prohibitive.

SATISFICING March and Simon argued that managers do not attempt to discover every alternative when faced with bounded rationality, an uncertain future, unquantifiable risks, considerable ambiguity, time constraints, and high information costs. Rather, they use a strategy known as **satisficing,** which is exploring a limited sample of all potential alternatives.[59] When managers satisfice, they search for and choose acceptable, or satisfactory, ways to respond to problems and opportunities rather than trying to make the optimal decision.[60] In the case of the Ford purchasing manager's search, for example, satisficing may involve asking a limited number of suppliers for their terms, trusting that they are representative of suppliers in general, and making a choice from that set. Although this course of action is reasonable from the perspective of the purchasing manager, it may mean that a potentially superior supplier is overlooked.

satisficing Searching for and choosing an acceptable, or satisfactory, response to problems and opportunities, rather than trying to make the best decision.

March and Simon pointed out that managerial decision making is often more art than science. In the real world, managers must rely on their intuition and judgment to make what seems to them to be the best decision in the face of uncertainty and ambiguity.[61] Moreover, managerial decision making is often fast-paced; managers use their experience and judgment to make crucial decisions under conditions of incomplete information. Although there is nothing wrong with this approach, decision makers should be aware that human judgment is often flawed. As a result, even the best managers sometimes make poor decisions.[62]

Steps in the Decision-Making Process

LO7-2 Describe the six steps managers should take to make the best decisions, and explain how cognitive biases can lead managers to make poor decisions.

Using the work of March and Simon as a basis, researchers have developed a step-by-step model of the decision-making process and the issues and problems that managers confront at each step. Perhaps the best way to introduce this model is to examine the real-world nonprogrammed decision making of Scott McNealy at a crucial point in Sun Microsystems' history. McNealy was a founder of Sun Microsystems and was the chairman of the board of directors until Sun was acquired by Oracle in 2010.[63]

In early August 1985, Scott McNealy, then CEO of Sun Microsystems[64] (a hardware and software computer workstation manufacturer focused on network solutions), had to decide whether to go ahead with the launch of the new Carrera workstation computer, scheduled for September 10. Sun's managers had chosen the date nine months earlier when the development plan for the Carrera was first proposed. McNealy knew it would take at least a month to prepare for the September 10 launch, and the decision could not be put off.

Customers were waiting for the new machine, and McNealy wanted to be the first to provide a workstation that took advantage of Motorola's powerful 16-megahertz 68020 microprocessor. Capitalizing on this opportunity would give Sun a significant edge over Apollo, its main competitor in the workstation market. McNealy knew, however, that committing to the September 10 launch date was risky. Motorola was having production problems with the 16-megahertz 68020 microprocessor and could not guarantee Sun a steady supply of these chips. Moreover, the operating system software was not completely free of bugs.

If Sun launched the Carrera on September 10, the company might have to ship some machines with software that was not fully operational, was likely to crash the system, and utilized Motorola's less powerful 12-megahertz 68020 microprocessor instead of the 16-megahertz version.[65] Of course Sun could later upgrade the microprocessor and operating system software in any machines purchased by early customers, but the company's reputation would suffer. If Sun did not go ahead with the September launch, the company would miss an important opportunity.[66] Rumors were circulating in the industry that Apollo would be launching a new machine of its own in December.

McNealy clearly had a difficult decision to make. He had to decide quickly whether to launch the Carrera, but he did not have all the facts. He did not know, for example, whether the microprocessor or operating system problems could be resolved by September 10; nor did he know whether Apollo was going to launch a competing machine in December. But he could not wait to find these things out–he had to make a decision. We'll see what he decided later in the chapter.

Many managers who must make important decisions with incomplete information face dilemmas similar to McNealy's. Managers should consciously follow six steps to make a good decision (see Figure 7.4).[67] We review these steps in the remainder of this section.

Recognize the Need for a Decision

The first step in the decision-making process is to recognize the need for a decision. Scott McNealy recognized this need, and he realized a decision had to be made quickly.

Some stimuli usually spark the realization that a decision must be made. These stimuli often become apparent because changes in the organizational environment result in new kinds of opportunities and threats. This happened at Sun Microsystems. The September 10 launch date had been set when it seemed that Motorola chips would be readily available. Later, with the supply of chips in doubt and bugs remaining in the system software, Sun was in danger of failing to meet its launch date.

The stimuli that spark decision making are as likely to result from the actions of managers inside an organization as they are from changes in the external environment.[68] An organization possesses a set of skills, competencies, and resources in its employees and in departments such as marketing, manufacturing, and research and

Figure 7.4
Six Steps in Decision Making

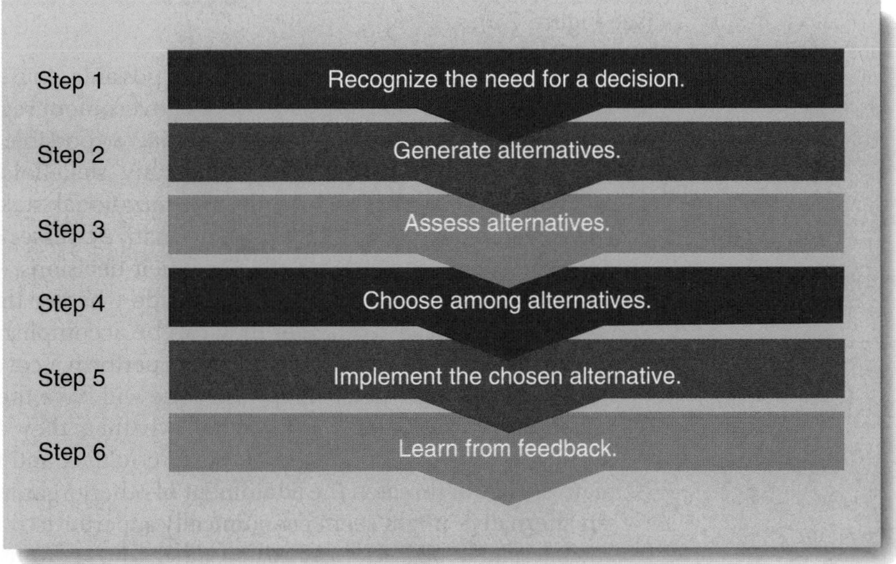
Step 1
Recognize the need for a decision.
Step 2
Generate alternatives.
Step 3
Assess alternatives.
Step 4
Choose among alternatives.
Step 5
Implement the chosen alternative.
Step 6
Learn from feedback.

development. Managers who actively pursue opportunities to use these competencies create the need to make decisions. Managers thus can be proactive or reactive in recognizing the need to make a decision, but the important issue is that they must recognize this need and respond in a timely and appropriate way.[69]

Generate Alternatives

Having recognized the need to make a decision, a manager must generate a set of feasible alternative courses of action to take in response to the opportunity or threat. Management experts cite failure to properly generate and consider different alternatives as one reason why managers sometimes make bad decisions.[70] In the Sun Microsystems decision, the alternatives seemed clear: to go ahead with the September 10 launch or to delay the launch until the Carrera was 100% ready for market introduction. Often, however, the alternatives are not so obvious or so clearly specified.

One major problem is that managers may find it difficult to come up with creative alternative solutions to specific problems. Perhaps some of them are used to seeing the world from a single perspective–they have a certain "managerial mind-set." Many managers find it difficult to view problems from a fresh perspective. According to best-selling management author Peter Senge, we all are trapped within our personal mental models of the world–our ideas about what is important and how the world works.[71] Generating creative alternatives to solve problems and take advantage of opportunities may require that we abandon our existing mind-sets and develop new ones–something that usually is difficult to do.

The importance of getting managers to set aside their mental models of the world and generate creative alternatives is reflected in the growth of interest in the work of authors such as Peter Senge and Edward de Bono, who have popularized techniques for stimulating problem solving and creative thinking among managers.[72] Later in this chapter, we discuss the important issues of organizational learning and creativity in detail.

Assess Alternatives

Once managers have generated a set of alternatives, they must evaluate the advantages and disadvantages of each one.[73] The key to a good assessment of the alternatives is to define the opportunity or threat exactly and then specify the criteria that *should* influence the selection of alternatives for responding to the problem or opportunity. One reason for bad decisions is that managers often fail to specify the criteria that are important in reaching a decision.[74] In general, successful managers use four criteria to evaluate the pros and cons of alternative courses of action (see Figure 7.5):

1. *Legality:* Managers must ensure that a possible course of action will not violate any domestic or international laws or government regulations.
2. *Ethicalness:* Managers must ensure that a possible course of action is ethical and will not unnecessarily harm any stakeholder group. Many decisions managers make may help some organizational stakeholders and harm others (see Chapter 4). When examining alternative courses of action, managers need to be clear about the potential effects of their decisions.
3. *Economic feasibility:* Managers must decide whether the alternatives are economically feasible–that is, whether they can be accomplished given the organization's performance goals. Typically managers perform a cost–benefit analysis of the various alternatives to determine which one will have the best net financial payoff.
4. *Practicality:* Managers must decide whether they have the capabilities and resources required to implement the alternative, and they must be sure the alternative will not threaten the attainment of other organizational goals. At first glance an alternative might seem economically superior to other alternatives; but if managers realize it is likely to threaten other important projects, they might decide it is not practical after all.

Often a manager must consider these four criteria simultaneously. Scott McNealy framed the problem at hand at Sun Microsystems quite well. The key question was whether to go ahead with the September 10 launch date. Two main criteria were influencing McNealy's choice: the need to ship a machine that was as "complete" as possible (the *practicality* criterion) and the need to beat Apollo to market with a new workstation (the *economic feasibility* criterion). These two criteria conflicted. The first suggested that the launch should be delayed; the second, that the launch should go ahead. McNealy's actual choice was based on the relative importance that he assigned

Figure 7.5
General Criteria for Evaluating Possible Courses of Action

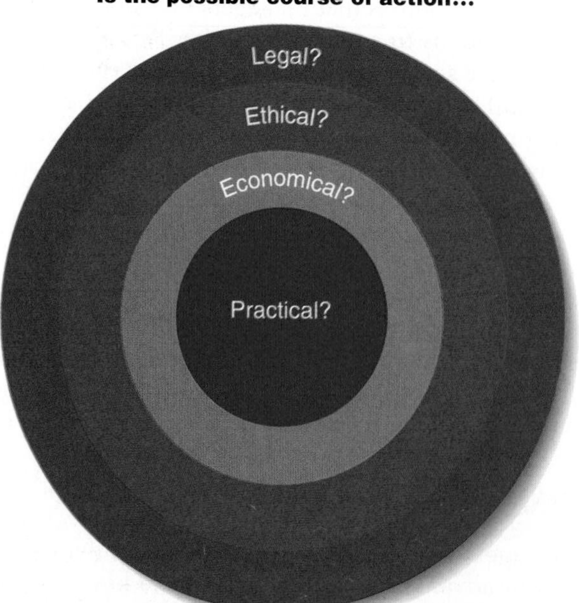

to these two criteria. In fact, Sun Microsystems went ahead with the September 10 launch, which suggests that McNealy thought the need to beat Apollo to market was the more important criterion.

Some of the worst managerial decisions can be traced to poor assessment of the alternatives, such as the decision to launch the *Challenger* space shuttle, mentioned earlier. In that case, the desire of NASA and Morton Thiokol managers to demonstrate to the public the success of the U.S. space program in order to ensure future funding (*economic feasibility*) conflicted with the need to ensure the safety of the astronauts (*ethicalness*). Managers deemed the economic criterion more important and decided to launch the space shuttle even though there were unanswered questions about safety. Tragically, some of the same decision-making problems that resulted in the *Challenger* tragedy led to the demise of the *Columbia* space shuttle 17 years later, killing all seven astronauts on board.[75] In both the *Challenger* and the *Columbia* disasters, safety questions were raised before the shuttles were launched; safety concerns took second place to budgets, economic feasibility, and schedules; top decision makers seemed to ignore or downplay the inputs of those with relevant technical expertise; and speaking up was discouraged.[76] Rather than making safety a top priority, decision makers seemed overly concerned with keeping on schedule and within budget.[77]

Choose among Alternatives

Once the set of alternative solutions has been carefully evaluated, the next task is to rank the various alternatives (using the criteria discussed in the previous section) and make a decision. When ranking alternatives, managers must be sure *all* the information available is brought to bear on the problem or issue at hand. As the Sun Microsystems case indicates, however, identifying all *relevant* information for a decision does not mean the manager has *complete* information; in most instances, information is incomplete.

Perhaps more serious than the existence of incomplete information is the often-documented tendency of managers to ignore critical information, even when it is available. We discuss this tendency in detail later when we examine the operation of cognitive biases and groupthink.

Implement the Chosen Alternative

Once a decision has been made and an alternative has been selected, it must be implemented, and many subsequent and related decisions must be made. After a course of action has been decided–say, to develop a new line of women's clothing–thousands of subsequent decisions are necessary to implement it. These decisions would involve recruiting dress designers, obtaining fabrics, finding high-quality manufacturers, and signing contracts with clothing stores to sell the new line.

Although the need to make subsequent decisions to implement the chosen course of action may seem obvious, many managers make a decision and then fail to act on it. This is the same as not making a decision at all. To ensure that a decision is implemented, top managers must assign to middle managers the responsibility for making the follow-up decisions necessary to achieve the goal. They must give middle managers sufficient resources to achieve the goal, and they must hold the middle managers accountable for their performance. If the middle managers succeed in implementing the decision, they should be rewarded; if they fail, they should be subject to sanctions.

Learn from Feedback

The final step in the decision-making process is learning from feedback. Effective managers always conduct a retrospective analysis to see what they can learn from past successes or failures. Managers who do not evaluate the results of their decisions do not learn from experience; instead they stagnate and are likely to make the same mistakes again and again.[78] To avoid this problem, managers must establish a formal procedure with which they can learn from the results of past decisions. The procedure should include these steps:

1. Compare what actually happened to what was expected to happen as a result of the decision.
2. Explore why any expectations for the decision were not met.
3. Derive guidelines that will help in future decision making.

Managers who always strive to learn from past mistakes and successes are likely to continuously improve the decisions they make. A significant amount of learning can take place when the outcomes of decisions are evaluated, and this assessment can produce enormous benefits. Learning from feedback is particularly important for entrepreneurs who start their own businesses, as profiled in the following "Management Insight" box.

Management Insight

Decision Making and Learning from Feedback at GarageTek

Decision making has been an ongoing challenge for Marc Shuman, founder and president of GarageTek, headquartered in Syosset, New York.[79] Since founding his company less than 12 years ago, he has met this challenge time and time again, recognizing when decisions need to be made and learning from feedback about prior decisions.

Shuman was working with his father in a small business, designing and building interiors of department stores, when he created and installed a series of wall panels with flexible shelving for a store to display its merchandise. When he realized that some of his employees were using the same concept in their own homes to organize the clutter in their basements and garages, he recognized that he had a potential opportunity to start a new business, GarageTek, designing and installing custom garage systems to organize and maximize storage capacities and uses for home garage space.[80]

Marc Shuman, founder of GarageTek, recognizes when decisions need to be made and learns from feedback about prior decisions.

Schuman decided to franchise his idea because he feared that other entrepreneurs were probably having similar thoughts and competition could be around the corner.[81] Within three years GarageTek had 57 franchises in 33 states, contributing revenues to the home office of around $12 million. While this would seem to be an enviable track record of success, Shuman recognized that although many of the franchises were succeeding, some were having serious problems. With the help of a consulting company, Shuman and home office managers set about trying to figure out why some franchises were failing. They gathered detailed information about each franchise: the market served, pricing strategies, costs, managerial talent, and franchisee investment. From this information, Shuman learned that the struggling franchises tended either to have lower levels of capital investment behind them or to be managed by nonowners.[82]

Shuman learned from this experience. He now has improved decision criteria for accepting new franchisees to help ensure that their investments of time and money lead to a successful franchise.[83] Shuman also decided to give new franchisees much more training and support than he had in the past. New franchisees now receive two weeks of training at the home office; on-site assistance in sales, marketing, and operations; a multivolume training manual; a sales and marketing kit; and access to databases and GarageTek's intranet. Franchisees learn from each other through monthly conference calls and regional and national meetings. For Shuman, however, making good decisions and learning from prior ones are still an ongoing challenge; in his words, "We're not, by any stretch, done."[84]

Cognitive Biases and Decision Making

In the 1970s psychologists Daniel Kahneman and Amos Tversky suggested that because all decision makers are subject to bounded rationality, they tend to use **heuristics,** which are rules of thumb that simplify the process of making decisions.[85] Kahneman and Tversky argued that rules of thumb are often useful because they help decision makers make sense of complex, uncertain, and ambiguous information. Sometimes, however, the use of heuristics can lead to systematic errors in the way decision makers process information about alternatives and make decisions. **Systematic errors** are errors that people make over and over and that result in poor decision making. Because of cognitive biases, which are caused by systematic errors, otherwise capable managers may end up making bad decisions.[86] Four sources of bias that can adversely affect the way managers make decisions are prior hypotheses, representativeness, the illusion of control, and escalating commitment (see Figure 7.6).

heuristics Rules of thumb that simplify decision making.

systematic errors Errors that people make over and over and that result in poor decision making.

Prior-Hypothesis Bias

Decision makers who have strong prior beliefs about the relationship between two variables tend to make decisions based on those beliefs *even when presented with evidence that their beliefs are wrong.* In doing so, they fall victim to **prior-hypothesis bias.** Moreover, decision makers tend to seek and use information that is consistent with their prior beliefs and to ignore information that contradicts those beliefs.

prior-hypothesis bias A cognitive bias resulting from the tendency to base decisions on strong prior beliefs even if evidence shows that those beliefs are wrong.

Representativeness Bias

Many decision makers inappropriately generalize from a small sample or even from a single vivid case or episode; these are instances of the **representativeness bias.** Consider the case of a bookstore manager in the southeast United States who decided to partner with a local independent school for a "Book Day": Students and parents from the school would be encouraged to buy books at the bookstore as a fund-raiser for the school, and the bookstore would share a small portion of proceeds from these sales with the school. After quite a bit of planning, the Book Day generated lackluster sales and publicity for the store. When other public and independent schools approached the manager with similar proposals for fund-raising and Book Days, the manager declined based on her initial bad experience. As a result, she lost real opportunities to expand sales and gain word-of-mouth advertising and publicity

representativeness bias A cognitive bias resulting from the tendency to generalize inappropriately from a small sample or from a single vivid event or episode.

Figure 7.6
Sources of Cognitive Bias at the Individual and Group Levels

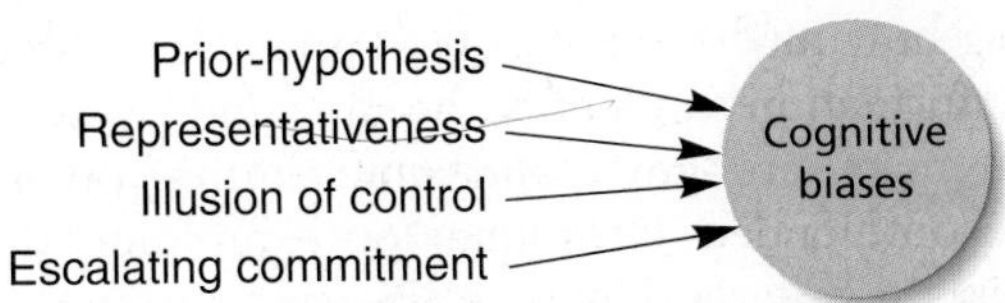

for her store; her initial bad experience was the result of an inadvertent scheduling snafu at the school, whereby a key lacrosse game was scheduled the same day as the Book Day.

Illusion of Control

illusion of control A source of cognitive bias resulting from the tendency to overestimate one's own ability to control activities and events.

Other errors in decision making result from the **illusion of control,** which is the tendency of decision makers to overestimate their ability to control activities and events. Top managers seem particularly prone to this bias. Having worked their way to the top of an organization, they tend to have an exaggerated sense of their own worth and are overconfident about their ability to succeed and to control events.[87] The illusion of control causes managers to overestimate the odds of a favorable outcome and, consequently, to make inappropriate decisions. As mentioned earlier, most mergers turn out unfavorably; yet time and time again, top managers overestimate their abilities to combine companies with vastly different cultures in a successful merger.[88]

Escalating Commitment

escalating commitment A source of cognitive bias resulting from the tendency to commit additional resources to a project even if evidence shows that the project is failing.

Having already committed significant resources to a course of action, some managers commit more resources to the project *even if they receive feedback that the project is failing.*[89] Feelings of personal responsibility for a project apparently bias the analysis of decision makers and lead to this **escalating commitment.** The managers decide to increase their investment of time and money in a course of action and even ignore evidence that it is illegal, unethical, uneconomical, or impractical (see Figure 7.5). Often the more appropriate decision would be to cut their losses and run.

Consider the case of Mark Gracin, who owns a landscape company in the southwest United States. Gracin had a profitable business doing general landscape work (such as mowing grass, picking up leaves, and fertilizing) for homeowners in a large city. To expand his business into landscape design, he hired a landscape designer, advertised landscape design services in local newspapers, and gave his existing customers free design proposals for their front and back yards. After a few months, Gracin had no landscape design customers. Still convinced that landscape design was a great way to expand his business despite this negative feedback, he decided he needed to do more. He rented a small office for his landscape designer (who used to work from her own home office) to work from and meet with clients, hired an assistant for the designer, had a public relations firm create promotional materials, and started advertising on local TV. These efforts also did not generate sufficient interest in his landscape design services to offset their costs. Yet Gracin's escalating commitment caused him to continue to pour money into trying to drum up business in landscape design. In fact, Gracin reluctantly decided to abandon his landscape design services only when he realized he could no longer afford their mounting costs.

Be Aware of Your Biases

How can managers avoid the negative effects of cognitive biases and improve their decision-making and problem-solving abilities? Managers must become aware of biases and their effects, and they must identify their own personal style of making decisions.[90] One useful way for managers to analyze their decision-making style is to review two decisions that they made recently–one decision that turned out well and one that turned out poorly. Problem-solving experts recommend that managers start by determining how much time to spend on each of the decision-making steps, such as gathering information to identify the pros and cons of alternatives or ranking the alternatives, to make sure they spend sufficient time on each step.[91]

Another recommended technique for examining decision-making style is for managers to list the criteria they typically use to assess and evaluate alternatives–the heuristics (rules of thumb) they typically employ, their personal biases, and so on–and then critically evaluate the appropriateness of these different factors.

Many individual managers are likely to have difficulty identifying their own biases, so it is often advisable for managers to scrutinize their own assumptions by working with other managers to help expose weaknesses in their decision-making style. In this context, the issue of group decision making becomes important.

Group Decision Making

LO7-3 Identify the advantages and disadvantages of group decision making, and describe techniques that can improve it.

Many (or perhaps most) important organizational decisions are made by groups or teams of managers rather than by individuals. Group decision making is superior to individual decision making in several respects. When managers work as a team to make decisions and solve problems, their choices of alternatives are less likely to fall victim to the biases and errors discussed previously. They are able to draw on the combined skills, competencies, and accumulated knowledge of group members and thereby improve their ability to generate feasible alternatives and make good decisions. Group decision making also allows managers to process more information and to correct one another's errors. And in the implementation phase, all managers affected by the decisions agree to cooperate. When a group of managers makes a decision (as opposed to one top manager making a decision and imposing it on subordinate managers), the probability that the decision will be implemented successfully increases. (We discuss how to encourage employee participation in decision making in Chapter 14.)

When everyone agrees right off the bat, chances are high that the lack of conflict is in fact groupthink and more critical evaluation is needed.

Some potential disadvantages are associated with group decision making. Groups often take much longer than individuals to make decisions. Getting two or more managers to agree to the same solution can be difficult because managers' interests and preferences are often different. In addition, just like decision making by individual managers, group decision making can be undermined by biases. A major source of group bias is *groupthink.*

The Perils of Groupthink

groupthink A pattern of faulty and biased decision making that occurs in groups whose members strive for agreement among themselves at the expense of accurately assessing information relevant to a decision.

Groupthink is a pattern of faulty and biased decision making that occurs in groups whose members strive for agreement among themselves at the expense of accurately assessing information relevant to a decision.[92] When managers are subject to groupthink, they collectively embark on a course of action without developing appropriate criteria to evaluate alternatives. Typically a group rallies around one central manager, such as the CEO, and the course of action that manager supports. Group members become blindly committed to that course of action without evaluating its merits. Commitment is often based on an emotional, rather than an objective, assessment of the optimal course of action.

The decision President Kennedy and his advisers made to launch the unfortunate Bay of Pigs invasion in Cuba in 1962, the decisions made by President Johnson and his advisers from 1964 to 1967 to escalate the war in Vietnam, the decision made by President Nixon and his advisers in 1972 to cover up the Watergate break-in, and the decision made by NASA and Morton Thiokol in 1986 to launch the ill-fated *Challenger* shuttle–all were likely influenced by groupthink. After the fact, decision makers such as these who may fall victim to groupthink are often surprised that their decision-making process and outcomes were so flawed.

When groupthink occurs, pressures for agreement and harmony within a group have the unintended effect of discouraging individuals from raising issues that run counter to majority opinion. For example, when managers at NASA and Morton

Thiokol fell victim to groupthink, they convinced each other that all was well and that there was no need to delay the launch of the *Challenger* space shuttle.

Devil's Advocacy and Dialectical Inquiry

The existence of cognitive biases and groupthink raises the question of how to improve the quality of group and individual decision making so managers make decisions that are realistic and are based on thorough evaluation of alternatives. Two techniques known to counteract groupthink and cognitive biases are devil's advocacy and dialectic inquiry (see Figure 7.7).[93]

devil's advocacy Critical analysis of a preferred alternative, made in response to challenges raised by a group member who, playing the role of devil's advocate, defends unpopular or opposing alternatives for the sake of argument.

dialectical inquiry Critical analysis of two preferred alternatives in order to find an even better alternative for the organization to adopt.

Devil's advocacy is a critical analysis of a preferred alternative to ascertain its strengths and weaknesses before it is implemented.[94] Typically one member of the decision-making group plays the role of devil's advocate. The devil's advocate critiques and challenges the way the group evaluated alternatives and chose one over the others. The purpose of devil's advocacy is to identify all the reasons that might make the preferred alternative unacceptable after all. In this way, decision makers can be made aware of the possible perils of recommended courses of action.

Dialectical inquiry goes one step further. Two groups of managers are assigned to a problem, and each group is responsible for evaluating alternatives and selecting one of them.[95] Top managers hear each group present its preferred alternative, and then each group critiques the other's position. During this debate, top managers challenge both groups' positions to uncover potential problems and perils associated with their solutions. The goal is to find an even better alternative course of action for the organization to adopt.

Both devil's advocacy and dialectical inquiry can help counter the effects of cognitive biases and groupthink.[96] In practice, devil's advocacy is probably easier to implement because it involves less managerial time and effort than does dialectical inquiry.

Diversity among Decision Makers

Another way to improve group decision making is to promote diversity in decision-making groups (see Chapter 5).[97] Bringing together managers of both genders from various ethnic, national, and functional backgrounds broadens the range of life experiences and opinions that group members can draw on as they generate, assess, and choose among alternatives. Moreover, diverse groups are sometimes less prone to groupthink because group members already differ from each other and thus are less subject to pressures for uniformity.

Figure 7.7
Devil's Advocacy and Dialectical Inquiry

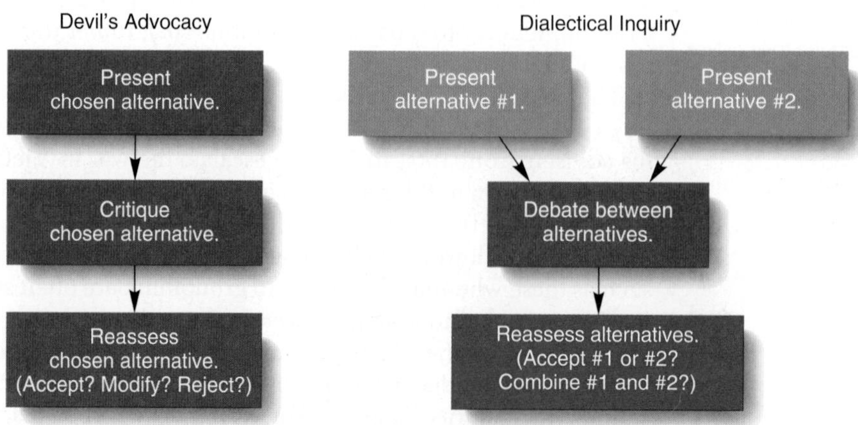

Organizational Learning and Creativity

The quality of managerial decision making ultimately depends on innovative responses to opportunities and threats. How can managers increase their ability to make nonprogrammed decisions that will allow them to adapt to, modify, and even drastically alter their task environments so they can continually increase organizational performance? The answer is by encouraging organizational learning.[98]

LO7-4 Explain the role that organizational learning and creativity play in helping managers to improve their decisions.

Organizational learning is the process through which managers seek to improve employees' desire and ability to understand and manage the organization and its task environment so employees can make decisions that continuously raise organizational effectiveness.[99] A **learning organization** is one in which managers do everything possible to maximize the ability of individuals and groups to think and behave creatively and thus maximize the potential for organizational learning to take place. At the heart of organizational learning is **creativity,** which is the ability of a decision maker to discover original and novel ideas that lead to feasible alternative courses of action. Encouraging creativity among managers is such a pressing organizational concern that many organizations hire outside experts to help them develop programs to train their managers in the art of creative thinking and problem solving.

organizational learning The process through which managers seek to improve employees' desire and ability to understand and manage the organization and its task environment.

learning organization An organization in which managers try to maximize the ability of individuals and groups to think and behave creatively and thus maximize the potential for organizational learning to take place.

creativity A decision maker's ability to discover original and novel ideas that lead to feasible alternative courses of action.

Creating a Learning Organization

How do managers go about creating a learning organization? Learning theorist Peter Senge identified five principles for creating a learning organization (see Figure 7.8):[100]

1. For organizational learning to occur, top managers must allow every person in the organization to develop a sense of *personal mastery.* Managers must empower employees and allow them to experiment, create, and explore what they want.
2. As part of attaining personal mastery, organizations need to encourage employees to develop and use *complex mental models*–sophisticated ways of thinking that challenge them to find new or better ways of performing a task–to deepen their understanding of what is involved in a particular activity. Here Senge argued that managers must encourage employees to develop a taste for experimenting and risk taking.[101]
3. Managers must do everything they can to promote group creativity. Senge thought that *team learning* (learning that takes place in a group or team) is more important than individual learning in increasing organizational learning. He pointed out that most important decisions are made in subunits such as groups, functions, and divisions.

Figure 7.8
Senge's Principles for Creating a Learning Organization

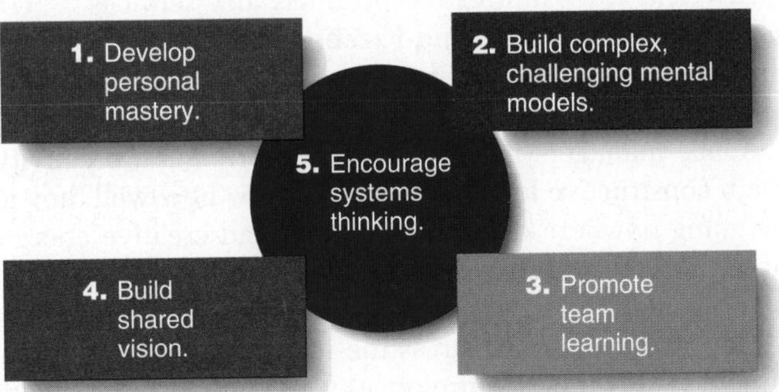

4. Managers must emphasize the importance of *building a shared vision*—a common mental model that all organizational members use to frame problems or opportunities.
5. Managers must encourage *systems thinking* (a concept drawn from systems theory, discussed in Chapter 2). Senge emphasized that to create a learning organization, managers must recognize the effects of one level of learning on another. Thus, for example, there is little point in creating teams to facilitate team learning if managers do not also take steps to give employees the freedom to develop a sense of personal mastery.

Building a learning organization requires that managers change their management assumptions radically. Developing a learning organization is neither a quick nor an easy process. Senge worked with Ford Motor Company to help managers make Ford a learning organization. Why would Ford want this? Top management believed that to compete successfully, Ford must improve its members' ability to be creative and make the right decisions.

Increasingly, managers are being called on to promote global organizational learning. For example, managers at Walmart have used the lessons derived from its failures and successes in one country to promote global organizational learning across the many countries in which it now operates. For instance, when Walmart entered Malaysia, it was convinced customers there would respond to its one-stop shopping format. It found, however, that Malaysians enjoy the social experience of shopping in a lively market or bazaar and thus did not like the impersonal efficiency of the typical Walmart store. As a result, Walmart learned the importance of designing store layouts to appeal specifically to the customers of each country in which it operates.

When purchasing and operating a chain of stores in another country, such as the British ASDA chain, Walmart now strives to retain what customers value in the local market while taking advantage of its own accumulated organizational learning. For example, Walmart improved ASDA's information technology used for inventory and sales tracking in stores and enrolled ASDA in Walmart's global purchasing operations, which has enabled the chain to pay less for certain products, sell them for less, and, overall, significantly increase sales. At the same time Walmart empowered local ASDA managers to run the stores; as the president of ASDA indicates, "This is still essentially a British business in the way it's run day to day."[102] Clearly global organizational learning is essential for companies such as Walmart that have significant operations in multiple countries.

Promoting Individual Creativity

Research suggests that when certain conditions are met, managers are more likely to be creative. People must be given the opportunity and freedom to generate new ideas.[103] Creativity declines when managers look over the shoulders of talented employees and try to "hurry up" a creative solution. How would you feel if your boss said you had one week to come up with a new product idea to beat the competition? Creativity results when employees have an opportunity to experiment, to take risks, and to make mistakes and learn from them. And employees must not fear that they will be looked down on or penalized for ideas that might at first seem outlandish; sometimes those ideas yield truly innovative products and services.[104] Highly innovative companies such as Google, Apple, and Facebook are well known for the wide degree of freedom they give their managers and employees to experiment and develop innovative goods and services.[105]

Once managers have generated alternatives, creativity can be fostered by giving them constructive feedback so they know how well they are doing. Ideas that seem to be going nowhere can be eliminated and creative energies refocused in other directions. Ideas that seem promising can be promoted, and help from other managers can be obtained.[106]

Top managers must stress the importance of looking for alternative solutions and should visibly reward employees who come up with creative ideas. Being creative can be demanding and stressful. Employees who believe they are working on important, vital issues are motivated to put forth the high levels of effort that creativity demands. Creative people like to receive the acclaim of others, and innovative organizations have many kinds of ceremonies and rewards to recognize creative employees.

Employees on the front line are often in a good position to come up with creative ideas for improvements but may be reluctant to speak up or share their ideas. In order to encourage frontline employees to come up with creative ideas and share them, some managers have used contests and rewards.[107] Contests and rewards both signal the importance of coming up with creative ideas and encourage employees to share them. Examples of companies that have benefited from contests and rewards for creativity include Hammond's Candies in Denver, Colorado, Borrego Solar Systems in San Diego, California, and Infosurv in Atlanta, Georgia.

Promoting Group Creativity

To encourage creativity at the group level, organizations can use group problem-solving techniques that promote creative ideas and innovative solutions. These techniques can also prevent groupthink and help managers uncover biases. Here we look at three group decision-making techniques: *brainstorming,* the *nominal group technique,* and the *Delphi technique.*

BRAINSTORMING *Brainstorming* is a group problem-solving technique in which managers meet face-to-face to generate and debate a wide variety of alternatives from which to make a decision.[108] Generally from 5 to 15 managers meet in a closed-door session and proceed like this:

These ad agency employees are conducting a brainstorming session. Brainstorming can be used to generate multiple ideas and solutions for problems.

- One manager describes in broad outline the problem the group is to address.
- Group members share their ideas and generate alternative courses of action.
- As each alternative is described, group members are not allowed to criticize it; everyone withholds judgment until all alternatives have been heard. One member of the group records the alternatives on a flip chart.
- Group members are encouraged to be as innovative and radical as possible. Anything goes; and the greater the number of ideas put forth, the better. Moreover, group members are encouraged to "piggyback" or build on each other's suggestions.
- When all alternatives have been generated, group members debate the pros and cons of each and develop a short list of the best alternatives.

production blocking A loss of productivity in brainstorming sessions due to the unstructured nature of brainstorming.

Brainstorming is very useful in some problem-solving situations–for example, when managers are trying to find a name for a new perfume or car model. But sometimes individuals working alone can generate more alternatives. The main reason for the loss of productivity in brainstorming appears to be **production blocking,** which occurs because group members cannot always simultaneously make sense of all the alternatives being generated, think up additional alternatives, and remember what they were thinking.[109]

nominal group technique A decision-making technique in which group members write down ideas and solutions, read their suggestions to the whole group, and discuss and then rank the alternatives.

NOMINAL GROUP TECHNIQUE To avoid production blocking, the **nominal group technique** is often used. It provides a more structured way of generating alternatives in writing and gives each manager more time and opportunity to come up with potential solutions. The nominal group technique is especially useful when an issue is controversial and when different managers might be expected to champion different courses of action. Generally a small group of managers meets in a closed-door session and adopts the following procedures:

- One manager outlines the problem to be addressed, and 30 or 40 minutes are allocated for group members, working individually, to write down their ideas and solutions. Group members are encouraged to be innovative.
- Managers take turns reading their suggestions to the group. One manager writes all the alternatives on a flip chart. No criticism or evaluation of alternatives is allowed until all alternatives have been read.
- The alternatives are then discussed, one by one, in the sequence in which they were proposed. Group members can ask for clarifying information and critique each alternative to identify its pros and cons.
- When all alternatives have been discussed, each group member ranks all the alternatives from most preferred to least preferred, and the alternative that receives the highest ranking is chosen.[110]

delphi technique A decision-making technique in which group members do not meet face-to-face but respond in writing to questions posed by the group leader.

entrepreneur An individual who notices opportunities and decides how to mobilize the resources necessary to produce new and improved goods and services.

DELPHI TECHNIQUE Both the nominal group technique and brainstorming require that managers meet to generate creative ideas and engage in joint problem solving. What happens if managers are in different cities or in different parts of the world and cannot meet face-to-face? Videoconferencing is one way to bring distant managers together to brainstorm. Another way is to use the **Delphi technique,** which is a written approach to creative problem solving.[111] The Delphi technique works like this:

- The group leader writes a statement of the problem and a series of questions to which participating managers are to respond.
- The questionnaire is sent to the managers and departmental experts who are most knowledgeable about the problem. They are asked to generate solutions and mail the questionnaire back to the group leader.
- A team of top managers records and summarizes the responses. The results are then sent back to the participants, with additional questions to be answered before a decision can be made.
- The process is repeated until a consensus is reached and the most suitable course of action is apparent.

LO7-5 Describe how managers can encourage and promote entrepreneurship to create a learning organization, and differentiate between entrepreneurs and intrapreneurs.

Entrepreneurship and Creativity

Entrepreneurs are individuals who notice opportunities and decide how to mobilize the resources necessary to produce new and improved goods and services. Entrepreneurs make all of the planning, organizing, leading, and controlling decisions necessary to start new business ventures. Thus entrepreneurs are an important source of creativity in the organizational world. These people, such as David Filo and Jerry Yang (founders of Yahoo!), make vast fortunes when their businesses succeed. Or they are among the millions of people who start new business ventures only to lose their money when they fail. Despite the fact that an estimated 80% of small businesses fail in the first three to five years, by some estimates 38% of men and 50% of women in today's workforce want to start their own companies.[112]

social entrepreneur An individual who pursues initiatives and opportunities and mobilizes resources to address social problems and needs in order to improve society and well-being through creative solutions.

Social entrepreneurs are individuals who pursue initiatives and opportunities to address social problems and needs in order to improve society and well-being, such as reducing poverty, increasing literacy, protecting the natural environment, or reducing substance abuse.[113] Social entrepreneurs seek to mobilize resources to solve social problems through creative solutions.[114]

As indicated in the following "Ethics in Action" box, although social entrepreneurs often face challenges in raising funds to support their initiatives, their options are increasing.

Ethics in Action

Finding Funding to Do Good

Typically venture capitalists who provide funding for entrepreneurs to start their businesses are concerned with getting a good return on their investment and not having to wait a long time to do so; and banks expect entrepreneurs to have a prior track record of success. For social entrepreneurs, this can make raising funds to support their new ventures a real challenge. Fortunately an increasing number of social venture funds seek to invest in companies that are focused on social goals.[115]

World of Good is a San Francisco Bay Area start-up that creates opportunities for thousands of producers in the developing world by bringing their products to the mainstream consumer market. This organization seeks to create a global network of entrepreneurs in the informal sector, uplifted by their direct access to large-scale markets and empowered through the use of ethical wage standards. World of Good has helped more than 25,000 women in 34 countries receive fair wages for their artisan work.[116]

Priya Haji, founder of World of Good, Inc.

When Priya Haji, the company's cofounder and CEO, initially sought funding for her venture, she had to look beyond traditional banks, which weren't interested because she didn't have a three-year track record.[117] "For them, it didn't make sense," Haji says. "There is a consumer driven demand for this kind of ethical consumption, but the debt markets don't understand that." Instead Haji turned to social lenders, and in 2006 she reached a deal with three of them: RSF Social Finance, Root Capital, and Shared Interest, each of which insists that portfolio companies maintain their social missions as they grow.[118] Their investment paid off: The company has doubled revenues every year since.

When Charlie Crystle sought funding for Mission Research, the new social enterprise he cofounded to provide nonprofits with fund-raising software, traditional investors questioned some of Mission's practices–such as giving the software away to nonprofits with annual budgets of less than $25,000–and even the fact that he was starting a business focused on selling to nonprofits.[119] Crystle was able to secure $300,000 in funding from Underdog Ventures in return for a 5% share in the company. Unlike other venture capital firms that aim to sell their stake in new ventures within five to seven years, Underdog is willing to wait seven to eight years and also requires that companies it invests in get prior approval from Underdog if they want to change their social mission.[120]

World of Good and Mission Research have both experienced substantial revenue growth since receiving funding from social investors.[121] Of equal importance, they also are achieving their social goals, which is a prime reason they were founded. As Crystle indicates, "I focus on building my business and building revenues. . . . But it's not the reason I get up every morning and go to work."[122]

Many managers, scientists, and researchers employed by companies engage in entrepreneurial activity, and they are an important source of organizational creativity. They are involved in innovation, developing new and improved products and ways to make them, which we describe in detail in Chapter 9. Such employees notice opportunities for either quantum or incremental product improvements and are responsible for managing the product development process. These individuals are known

intrapreneur A manager, scientist, or researcher who works inside an organization and notices opportunities to develop new or improved products and better ways to make them.

as **intrapreneurs** to distinguish them from entrepreneurs who start their own businesses. But in general, entrepreneurship involves creative decision making that gives customers new or improved goods and services.

There is an interesting relationship between entrepreneurs and intrapreneurs. Many managers with intrapreneurial talents become dissatisfied if their superiors decide neither to support nor to fund new product ideas and development efforts that the managers think will succeed. What do intrapreneurial managers who feel they are getting nowhere do? Often they decide to leave their current organizations and start their own companies to take advantage of their new product ideas! In other words, intrapreneurs become entrepreneurs and found companies that often compete with the companies they left. To avoid losing these individuals, top managers must find ways to facilitate the entrepreneurial spirit of their most creative employees. In the remainder of this section we consider issues involved in promoting successful entrepreneurship in both new and existing organizations.

Entrepreneurship and New Ventures

The fact that a significant number of entrepreneurs were frustrated intrapreneurs provides a clue about the personal characteristics of people who are likely to start a new venture and bear all the uncertainty and risk associated with being an entrepreneur.

CHARACTERISTICS OF ENTREPRENEURS Entrepreneurs are likely to possess a particular set of the personality characteristics we discussed in Chapter 3. First, they are likely to be high on the personality trait of *openness to experience,* meaning they are predisposed to be original, to be open to a wide range of stimuli, to be daring, and to take risks. Entrepreneurs also are likely to have an *internal locus of control,* believing that they are responsible for what happens to them and that their own actions determine important outcomes such as the success or failure of a new business. People with an external locus of control, in contrast, would be unlikely to leave a secure job in an organization and assume the risk associated with a new venture.

Intrapreneurs face unique challenges in balancing their championing of new ideas with the company's overall need for stability.

Entrepreneurs are likely to have a high level of *self-esteem* and feel competent and capable of handling most situations–including the stress and uncertainty surrounding a plunge into a risky new venture. Entrepreneurs are also likely to have a high *need for achievement* and have a strong desire to perform challenging tasks and meet high personal standards of excellence.

ENTREPRENEURSHIP AND MANAGEMENT Given that entrepreneurs are predisposed to activities that are somewhat adventurous and risky, in what ways can people become involved in entrepreneurial ventures? One way is to start a business from scratch. Taking advantage of modern IT, many people are starting solo ventures. The total number of small-office and home-office workers is more than 40 million, and each year more than a million new solo entrepreneurs join the ranks of the more than 29 million self-employed.

When people who go it alone succeed, they frequently need to hire other people to help them run the business. Michael Dell, for example, began his computer business as a college student and within weeks had hired several people to help him assemble computers from the components he bought from suppliers. From his solo venture grew Dell Computer.

entrepreneurship The mobilization of resources to take advantage of an opportunity to provide customers with new or improved goods and services.

Some entrepreneurs who start a new business have difficulty deciding how to manage the organization as it grows; **entrepreneurship** is *not* the same as management. Management encompasses all the decisions involved in planning, organizing, leading, and controlling resources. Entrepreneurship is noticing an opportunity to satisfy a customer need and then deciding how to find and use resources to make a product that satisfies that need. When an entrepreneur has produced something customers want, entrepreneurship gives way to management because the pressing need becomes providing the product both efficiently and effectively. Frequently a founding entrepreneur lacks the skills, patience, and experience to engage in the difficult and challenging work of management. Some entrepreneurs find it hard to delegate authority because they are afraid to risk their company by letting others manage it. As a result they become overloaded, and the quality of their decision making declines. Other entrepreneurs lack the detailed knowledge necessary to establish state-of-the-art information systems and technology or to create the operations management procedures that are vital to increase the efficiency of their organizations' production systems. Thus, to succeed, it is necessary to do more than create a new product; an entrepreneur must hire managers who can create an operating system that will let a new venture survive and prosper.

Intrapreneurship and Organizational Learning

The intensity of competition today, particularly from agile, small companies, has made it increasingly important for large, established organizations to promote and encourage intrapreneurship to raise their level of innovation and organizational learning. As we discussed earlier, a learning organization encourages all employees to identify opportunities and solve problems, thus enabling the organization to continuously experiment, improve, and increase its ability to provide customers with new and improved goods and services. The higher the level of intrapreneurship, the higher will be the level of learning and innovation. How can organizations promote organizational learning and intrapreneurship?

product champion A manager who takes "ownership" of a project and provides the leadership and vision that take a product from the idea stage to the final customer.

PRODUCT CHAMPIONS One way to promote intrapreneurship is to encourage individuals to assume the role of **product champion,** a manager who takes "ownership" of a project and provides the leadership and vision that take a product from the idea stage to the final customer. 3M, a company well known for its attempts to promote intrapreneurship, encourages all its managers to become product champions and identify new product ideas. A product champion becomes responsible for developing a business plan for the product. Armed with this business plan, the champion appears before 3M's product development committee, a team of senior 3M managers who probe the strengths and weaknesses of the plan to decide whether it should be funded. If the plan is accepted, the product champion assumes responsibility for product development.

skunkworks A group of intrapreneurs who are deliberately separated from the normal operation of an organization to encourage them to devote all their attention to developing new products.

SKUNKWORKS The idea behind the product champion role is that employees who feel ownership for a project are inclined to act like outside entrepreneurs and go to great lengths to make the project succeed. Using skunkworks and new venture divisions can also strengthen this feeling of ownership. A **skunkworks** is a group of intrapreneurs who are deliberately separated from the normal operation of an organization–for example, from the normal chain of command–to encourage them to devote all their attention to developing new products. The idea is that if these people are isolated, they will become so intensely involved in a project that development time will be relatively brief and the quality of the final product will be enhanced. The term *skunkworks* was coined at the Lockheed Corporation, which formed a team of design engineers to develop special aircraft such as the U2 spy plane. The secrecy with which this unit functioned and speculation about its goals led others to refer to it as "the skunkworks."

REWARDS FOR INNOVATION To encourage managers to bear the uncertainty and risk associated with the hard work of entrepreneurship, it is necessary to link performance to rewards. Increasingly companies are rewarding intrapreneurs on the basis of the outcome of the product development process. Intrapreneurs are paid large bonuses if their projects succeed, or they are granted stock options that can make them millionaires if their products sell well. Both Microsoft and Google, for example, have made hundreds of their employees multimillionaires as a result of the stock options they were granted as part of their reward packages. In addition to receiving money, successful intrapreneurs can expect to receive promotion to the ranks of top management. Most of 3M's top managers, for example, reached the executive suite because they had a track record of successful entrepreneurship. Organizations must reward intrapreneurs equitably if they wish to prevent them from leaving and becoming outside entrepreneurs who might form a competitive new venture. Nevertheless, intrapreneurs frequently do so.

Summary and Review

LO7-1 **THE NATURE OF MANAGERIAL DECISION MAKING** Programmed decisions are routine decisions made so often that managers have developed decision rules to be followed automatically. Nonprogrammed decisions are made in response to situations that are unusual or novel; they are nonroutine decisions. The classical model of decision making assumes that decision makers have complete information, are able to process that information in an objective, rational manner, and make optimum decisions. March and Simon argued that managers exhibit bounded rationality, rarely have access to all the information they need to make optimum decisions, and consequently satisfice and rely on their intuition and judgment when making decisions.

LO7-2 **STEPS IN THE DECISION-MAKING PROCESS** When making decisions, managers should take these six steps: recognize the need for a decision, generate alternatives, assess alternatives, choose among alternatives, implement the chosen alternative, and learn from feedback.

LO7-2 **COGNITIVE BIASES AND DECISION MAKING** Most of the time managers are fairly good decision makers. On occasion, however, problems can result because human judgment can be adversely affected by the operation of cognitive biases that result in poor decisions. Cognitive biases are caused by systematic errors in the way decision makers process information and make decisions. Sources of these errors include prior hypotheses, representativeness, the illusion of control, and escalating commitment. Managers should undertake a personal decision audit to become aware of their biases and thus improve their decision making.

LO7-3 **GROUP DECISION MAKING** Many advantages are associated with group decision making, but there are also several disadvantages. One major source of poor decision making is groupthink. Afflicted decision makers collectively embark on a dubious course of action without questioning the assumptions that underlie their decision. Managers can improve the quality of group decision making by using techniques such as devil's advocacy and dialectical inquiry and by increasing diversity in the decision-making group.

LO7-4 **ORGANIZATIONAL LEARNING AND CREATIVITY** Organizational learning is the process through which managers seek to improve employees' desire and ability to understand and manage the organization and its task environment so employees can make decisions that continuously raise organizational effectiveness. Managers must take steps to promote organizational learning and creativity at the individual and group levels to improve the quality of decision making.

LO7-5 **ENTREPRENEURSHIP** Entrepreneurship is the mobilization of resources to take advantage of an opportunity to provide customers with new or improved goods and services. Entrepreneurs find new ventures of their own. Intrapreneurs work inside organizations and manage the product development process. Organizations need to encourage intrapreneurship because it leads to organizational learning and innovation.

Management in Action

Topics for Discussion and Action

Discussion

1. What are the main differences between programmed decision making and nonprogrammed decision making? [LO7-1]
2. In what ways do the classical and administrative models of decision making help managers appreciate the complexities of real-world decision making? [LO7-1]
3. Why do capable managers sometimes make bad decisions? What can individual managers do to improve their decision-making skills? [LO7-1, 7-2]
4. In what kinds of groups is groupthink most likely to be a problem? When is it least likely to be a problem? What steps can group members take to ward off groupthink? [LO7-3]
5. What is organizational learning, and how can managers promote it? [LO7-4]
6. What is the difference between entrepreneurship and intrapreneurship? [LO7-5]

Action

7. Ask a manager to recall the best and the worst decisions he or she ever made. Try to determine why these decisions were so good or so bad. [LO7-1, 7-2, 7-3]
8. Think about an organization in your local community or your university, or an organization that you are familiar with, that is doing poorly. Now think of questions managers in the organization should ask stakeholders to elicit creative ideas for turning around the organization's fortunes. [LO7-4]

Building Management Skills [LO7-1, 7-2, 7-4]

How Do You Make Decisions?

Pick a decision you made recently that has had important consequences for you. It may be your decision about which college to attend, which major to select, whether to take a part-time job, or which part-time job to take. Using the material in this chapter, analyze how you made the decision:

1. Identify the criteria you used, either consciously or unconsciously, to guide your decision making.
2. List the alternatives you considered. Were they all possible alternatives? Did you unconsciously (or consciously) ignore some important alternatives?
3. How much information did you have about each alternative? Were you making the decision on the basis of complete or incomplete information?
4. Try to remember how you reached the decision. Did you sit down and consciously think through the implications of each alternative, or did you make the decision on the basis of intuition? Did you use any rules of thumb to help you make the decision?
5. In retrospect, do you think your choice of alternative was shaped by any of the cognitive biases discussed in this chapter?
6. Having answered the previous five questions, do you think in retrospect that you made a reasonable decision? What, if anything, might you do to improve your ability to make good decisions in the future?

Managing Ethically [LO7-3]

Sometimes groups make extreme decisions—decisions that are either more risky or more conservative than they would have been if individuals acting alone had made them. One explanation for the tendency of groups to make extreme decisions is diffusion of responsibility. In a group, responsibility for the outcomes of a decision is spread among group members, so each person feels less than fully accountable. The group's decision is extreme because no individual has taken full responsibility for it.

Questions

1. Either alone or in a group, think about the ethical implications of extreme decision making by groups.
2. When group decision making takes place, should members of a group each feel fully accountable for outcomes of the decision? Why or why not?

Small Group Breakout Exercise [LO7-3, 7-4]

Brainstorming

Form groups of three or four people, and appoint one member as the spokesperson who will communicate your findings to the class when called on by the instructor. Then discuss the following scenario:

You and your partners are trying to decide which kind of restaurant to open in a centrally located shopping center that has just been built in your city. The problem confronting you is that the city already has many restaurants that provide different kinds of food at all price ranges. You have the resources to open any type of restaurant. Your challenge is to decide which type is most likely to succeed.

Use brainstorming to decide which type of restaurant to open. Follow these steps:

1. As a group, spend 5 or 10 minutes generating ideas about the alternative restaurants that the members think will be most likely to succeed. Each group member should be as innovative and creative as possible, and no suggestions should be criticized.
2. Appoint one group member to write down the alternatives as they are identified.
3. Spend the next 10 or 15 minutes debating the pros and cons of the alternatives. As a group, try to reach a consensus on which alternative is most likely to succeed.

After making your decision, discuss the pros and cons of the brainstorming method, and decide whether any production blocking occurred.

When called on by the instructor, the spokesperson should be prepared to share your group's decision with the class, as well as the reasons for the group's decision.

Exploring the World Wide Web [LO7-4]

Go to www.brainstorming.co.uk. This Web site contains "Training on Creativity Techniques" and "Creativity Puzzles." Spend at least 30 minutes on the training and/or puzzles. Think about what you have learned. Come up with specific ways in which you can be more creative in your thinking and decision making based on what you have learned.

Be the Manager [LO7-1, 7-2, 7-3, 7-4, 7-5]

You are a top manager who was recently hired by an oil field services company in Oklahoma to help it respond more quickly and proactively to potential opportunities in its market. You report to the chief operating officer (COO), who reports to the CEO, and you have been on the job for eight months. Thus far you have come up with three initiatives you carefully studied, thought were noteworthy, and proposed and justified to the COO. The COO seemed cautiously interested when you presented the proposals, and each time he indicated he would think about them and discuss them with the CEO because considerable resources were involved. Each time you never heard back from the COO, and after a few weeks elapsed, you casually asked the COO if there was any news on the proposal in question. For the first proposal, the COO said, "We think it's a good idea, but the timing is off. Let's shelve it for the time being and reconsider it next year." For the second proposal, the COO said, "Mike [the CEO] reminded me that we tried that two years ago and it wasn't well received in the market. I am surprised I didn't remember it myself when you first described the proposal, but it came right back to me once Mike mentioned it." For the third proposal, the COO simply said, "We're not convinced it will work."

You believe your three proposed initiatives are viable ways to seize opportunities in the marketplace, yet you cannot proceed with any of them. Moreover, for each proposal, you invested considerable time and even worked to bring others on board to support the proposal, only to have it shot down by the CEO. When you interviewed for the position, both the COO and the CEO claimed they wanted "an outsider to help them step out of the box and innovate." Yet your experience to date has been just the opposite. What are you going to do?

Case in the News [LO7- 1, 7-2, 7-4]

Dell's Do-Over

When a wave of mergers swept the tech industry in 2004, Michael S. Dell promised investors they wouldn't see his computer company anywhere near a negotiating table. "When was the last time you saw a successful acquisition or merger in the computer industry?" he asked at the time. Five years later, it's a different story. Round Rock (Texas)–based Dell is weeks away from closing its largest acquisition ever, a $3.9 billion deal for tech services provider Perot Systems. The chief executive says more deals are likely, and this won't be the end of his changes in strategy. "Everything's on the table," he says.

And with good reason. The company Michael Dell started in his college dorm and built into the preeminent personal computer maker has fallen on hard times. As the center of the tech industry has shifted from the PC to the Internet, Dell has struggled mightily to find its place. While Hewlett-Packard, IBM, and other rivals transformed themselves in recent years by acquiring new companies and capabilities, Dell long stuck with its old playbook of cranking out PCs as efficiently as possible. It's hard to remember that in 2005 Dell was valued at $100 billion, or more than HP and Apple combined. Today it's worth $30 billion, less than a third of its rivals' market values.

While such signs of struggle are clear to the public, what isn't apparent is the steady overhaul Michael Dell has been working on since he returned to the chief executive role in 2007. The 44-year-old has been making sweeping changes in everything from personnel and partnerships to acquisitions and distribution. He hasn't talked publicly about his comeback strategy before. But in interviews with *BusinessWeek,* the CEO made it clear he is determined to change almost everything about the company he started 25 years ago. "There's been a pretty ginormous shift in our business over the last several years," says Dell, dressed in a black suit and tieless white shirt in the sprawling conference room next to his office. "We can do, and must do, more."

He has installed an almost completely new management team to help with the turnaround. Seven of his ten direct reports are new to their posts, including veterans from General Electric, IBM, and Motorola. The company has been restructured to sharpen the focus on customers. And it is branching out into services, software, and new hardware categories, including smartphones and tablet-like devices. Sources say Dell is even preparing to add social networking features and music and video services to Dell.com. The old Dell is history, the CEO vows, and a new one is just beginning. "We're not trying to become like our competitors," he says. "We're digging our own path."

It's not at all clear Dell can pull this off. The old Dell succeeded because of its mastery of logistics and the supply chain, allowing it to sell computers directly to customers at prices no rival could match. The new Dell requires completely different skills—flexibility, customer focus, and innovation. Leadership experts say changing a management approach is one of the toughest undertakings in business, particularly for a founder who has had early success. "He's got tremendous challenges ahead of him, because he's in an industry that itself is undergoing rapid, sweeping change," says Warren Bennis, chairman of the Leadership Institute at the University of Southern California Marshall School of Business.

A Slow Restart

Investors have given Dell virtually no credit for his work so far. The company's stock is off about 40% since the start of 2007, while Apple shares have more than doubled and HP's have risen about 10%. David Eiswert, manager of T. Rowe Price's Global Technology Fund, sold his last 140,000 Dell shares last fall because he thinks Dell has too many rivals in its PC business and doesn't spend enough on research and development to create stand-out technology. Dell is "saying, 'Don't worry, we have a lot of ammo,' " says Eiswert. "The problem is the invading armies have a lot more troops and a lot more ammo."

Dell is convinced he can prove the skeptics wrong. He understands that only a handful of former chiefs have returned to lead their companies to brighter futures. For every Steve Jobs there's a Jerry Yang, the Yahoo! cofounder who struggled after retaking the helm. Yet for Dell, this is an opportunity to prove himself, to show he not only can launch a great business but revive a struggling one. "What you do is walk outside the building, you pretend you're the new guy, and walk back in," he says. "You force yourself to do what you need to do."

He has already pulled off a more extensive overhaul than most outsiders realize. He still has a long way to go, but insiders say the CEO is as driven as ever, back to working the kind of hours he did when he started the company. Ronald G. Garriques, head of Dell's consumer division, fields questions from his boss after midnight these days. "I get these e-mails from him saying, 'Hey, Ron, I was on this Web site, and wouldn't it be really cool if our product does this or does that?' " he says. Roger L. Kay, founder of researcher Endpoint Technologies Associates, got a call from Dell one weekend late last year. "He wanted to know if I knew any people who might be good as head of marketing," says Kay. "On a Saturday when I'm repairing my garage door, he's making calls to analysts."

Dell hasn't had any time to waste since beginning his second stint as chief executive. It was January 2007 when Dell told his board he thought it was time to replace Kevin B. Rollins, his handpicked successor. With the company losing share in the PC market and struggling with an investigation into its accounting practices, the directors agreed. Dell told them he was ready to step into his old job, but before they accepted, Donald J. Carty, the longest-serving director, stopped into Dell's office for a frank, one-on-one talk. "This is not going to be a stopgap thing," he cautioned the founder. "You're going to have to take the reins for a very long time." Dell pledged his commitment. "I'm going to care about this company when I'm dead," he told Carty. Dell's return was announced January 31.

The business Dell took over was floundering. Corporate PC sales were slowing, while HP under the direction of CEO Mark V. Hurd was pulling consumers into stores—and away from Dell—with its stylish notebook PC designs. Dell suffered the consequences. It lost its position as the largest PC maker in the world to HP, and profits tumbled. Dell's net income dropped 28%, to $2.6 billion, for the fiscal year ending February 2, 2007, while revenue inched up 3%, to $57.4 billion.

Dell's first move was to try to stop the bleeding in the consumer business. The head of the division left in February, and Dell started looking for a replacement by working his jam-packed Rolodex. He wanted someone who could cut costs and also guide the company's foray into retail chains around the world.

One name stood out: Garriques, head of Motorola's mobile devices business. When he and Dell had met years earlier, Dell had been impressed with how Garriques had guided development of the hit Razr phone. His broad experience dealing with top executives at retailers and wireless carriers would be invaluable as Dell tried to build a distribution network from scratch. Dell picked up the phone to call Garriques—no headhunters got involved—and quickly persuaded him to take the job. Dell's marching orders were simple: Create a profitable consumer business with designs that rival Apple's or HP's.

Garriques took a step back before moving forward. He killed a line of less-than-flashy consumer PCs Dell planned to introduce, called Mantra, and halted plans to copy Apple by opening more than a dozen Dell-owned stores. "The first order of business was to slow Dell's go, go, go mind-set and stop to think about what we were trying to do," he says.

Then Garriques went hunting for a heavy hitter to go up against Apple and HP. In March 2007 he approached Ed Boyd, a 42-year-old designer at Nike. Boyd had worked on sunglasses and running shoes but didn't have experience in computers. Garriques told Boyd he would have the opportunity to make design matter at Dell; Boyd jumped at the chance. "Here was a great company founded on the notion of customizing products and shipping them to people, yet it was missing the fact that people want to convey a sense of personal style with their products, too," Boyd says.

The changes sent a clear signal to Dell employees. The consumer business, long considered a professional dead end, was going to be a priority. What's more, Boyd launched experiments that showed it could be an exciting place to work. At one point, Boyd hatched a plan for customers to pay an extra $75 to get certain designs on laptops, which so unsettled Dell's manufacturing team that they balked. Boyd appealed directly to Dell, who green-lighted the move.

Later that year, Dell broke for good with its tradition of selling only directly to customers. It announced plans to sell its machines at Walmart in what the CEO called a "first step" in using retail stores to reach customers.

Complete Restructuring

Even more far-reaching changes were in store for 2008. Dell knew he wanted to change the company's management culture, to get executives to jump on new business opportunities and take more risks, but he wasn't sure how to go about it. He turned to Brian Gladden, a 20-year veteran of GE, the bastion of modern management. In March that year, he asked Gladden to fly to Texas to talk about a job as chief financial officer overseeing day-to-day operations. Dell was in such a rush he didn't even tell Gladden he had the job before slapping an inch-thick sheaf of confidential documents on the table. "I said to myself, there's a lot of inside information here that I really shouldn't see," Gladden says. "But he was like this mad scientist saying, 'Brian, you can help with this, and you can help with this.' "

Gladden quickly slipped into an easy rapport with Dell. But the lack of structure at the massive company surprised him. "The processes, the tools, the culture here didn't support a $60 billion business," Gladden says.

He dove into figuring out how to change that, in consultation with Dell. After months of study, they became convinced the company had to be restructured around customers. It was a radical move: Most tech companies organize around the products they sell, such as computers or software. But Gladden and Dell thought that by focusing outward they could give top managers more responsibility and more flexibility to respond to clients. On December 31 Dell said it would restructure into four customer groupings: consumers, corporations, small and midsize businesses, and governments and educational buyers.

With the global economy in crisis, almost no one took notice. Dell's stock, which had topped $25 the previous August, closed the year at $10.24. It kept falling with the market, and dropped below $8 in February, off 70% in five months.

Still, in those dark days, Dell began to gain confidence his company finally had a solid foundation for the future. He saw his executive team quickly take to the new management approach, which was modeled after GE's. Leaders of each division are responsible for meeting financial targets and have broad authority to figure out how to reach them. The main beneficiaries have been the consumer, government, and small and medium-size business units, which in the past often received less attention as Dell focused on large corporations. "[It's] a different dynamic than [Dell] is used to," says Gladden.

In the small and midsize business group, led by Steve Felice, salespeople have been given incentives to offer a broad range of solutions, instead of just hardware. It seems to be working. Mark Konik, vice president for technology at the marketing and ad shop GA Communications in Georgia, says Dell's regional sales manager showed up at his door six hours after he made an inquiry. Though the deal was for only $1 million, Dell offered to help integrate the company's Macs into the package and volunteered to talk to software providers VMware and Microsoft about including their products in the purchase. "The speed and competence Dell brought to the table in such a short period of time was really quite different," says Konik.

Garriques's consumer group has been making some dramatic changes. In October, to coincide with the launch of Microsoft's Windows 7 operating system, Dell began selling the world's thinnest notebook, at 0.39 inches thick. The Adamo XPS has a heat-sensing strip on the lip that, when swiped with a finger, glows white and automatically opens the aluminum lid. Garriques says the $2,000 computer will serve as a statement about Dell. "This isn't going to be a high-volume product for us, but it's going to be a product that says, 'Wow! Dell did that. What else does Dell have?' " he says.

With Garriques and the other division heads taking more control over operations, Michael Dell has been freed up to explore new opportunities. Over the summer, he had dinner at the Four Seasons in Washington's Georgetown neighborhood with James W. Breyer, a Dell board member and founding partner of the venture capital firm Accel Partners. Over steaks and red wine, Dell talked about prospects in mobile phones and other products. He then pulled out a half-dozen smartphone prototypes. "The way he laid it out, his thinking, led me to believe that in many ways the journey at Dell is just in the first or second inning," Breyer says. The company is expected to introduce its first smartphones early next year.

Dell is beginning to show improvement in its financial results. In its most recent earnings report, the company handily beat Wall Street's expectations. Dell shares have doubled since their low in February, to $16, as hopes mount that the company will benefit from a surge in PC purchases tied to Windows 7.

But Michael Dell is clearly looking for more than incremental improvements. He wants his namesake company to be the kind of force it was in the past, when it drove IBM out of the PC business and humbled industry giants like HP. "He's thinking, 'I'm going to make this company what it should be again,'" says Alex Mandl, a longtime Dell board member.

Rivals contend that Dell has waited too long to take the initiative. In an industry undergoing rapid consolidation, companies that haven't already positioned themselves to withstand the cyclical nature of technology will have a hard time thriving over the long term. That means Dell itself may be forced to merge with another company or become takeover bait. "Being a fast follower doesn't work in an industry that is moving faster every day," says Shane Robison, chief technology officer at HP.

Dell is more reflective than usual these days. During the interview in his conference room, he acknowledges he stuck with the one innovative idea of selling computers directly for too long. "Mea culpa," he says. But he says talk that he and his company aren't moving fast enough now is nonsense. "We're going to be stronger, faster, and more hyper than we've ever been," he says. "If you don't believe, then just sit back and watch."

Questions for Discussion

1. Are most decisions Michael Dell makes programmed decisions or nonprogrammed decisions?
2. To what extent are the decisions Michael Dell makes characterized by risk and uncertainty?
3. What are some of the ways in which Michael Dell and other top managers at Dell recognize the need to make a decision? To what extent do they learn from feedback?
4. To what extent do you think Michael Dell and other Dell top managers satisfice when they make decisions? Why do you think this is the case?

Source: C. Edwards, "Dell's Do-Over," *BusinessWeek,* October 26, 2009, 37–40. Reprinted from October 26, 2010 issue of *Bloomberg Businessweek* by special permission,

CHAPTER 8

The Manager as a Planner and Strategist

Learning Objectives

After studying this chapter, you should be able to:

LO8-1 Identify the three main steps of the planning process and explain the relationship between planning and strategy.

LO8-2 Describe some techniques managers can use to improve the planning process so they can better predict the future and mobilize organizational resources to meet future contingencies.

LO8-3 Differentiate between the main types of business-level strategies and explain how they give an organization a competitive advantage that may lead to superior performance.

LO8-4 Differentiate between the main types of corporate-level strategies and explain how they are used to strengthen a company's business-level strategy and competitive advantage.

LO8-5 Describe the vital role managers play in implementing strategies to achieve an organization's mission and goals.

A MANAGER'S CHALLENGE

Cisco Systems' Strategy? New Products and New Customers

What makes it hard to compete in an industry? Cisco Systems is famous for developing the Internet routers and switches on which the World Wide Web (WWW) is built. In 2010 Cisco still made most of its $10 billion yearly revenue by selling its Internet routers and switches to large companies and Internet service providers (ISPs)—and increasingly to data center storage companies, such as IBM and Silicon Graphics, which have entered the "cloud computing" outsourcing market to satisfy the growing need for low-cost online or remote data storage. But the boom years of Internet building in the 1990s that allowed Cisco to make enormous profits are over; like all high-tech companies, Cisco was hit hard by the drop in demand for Internet hardware that followed the dot-com bust and the recession that began in 2008. However, CEO John Chambers, who has led the company from the beginning, has a reputation for acquiring high-tech companies when their stock price is low because of hard economic times and then using their competencies to spur its future growth. And Cisco has billions in cash available to make whatever acquisitions Chambers decides will increase its future profitability.[1]

Realizing that the Internet router market by itself would not generate the huge profits necessary to drive up the company's profits, Chambers has embarked on a major planning initiative to enter new markets and industries. One strategy has been to expand rapidly into the consumer electronics industry from its core Internet hardware and software business by acquiring companies whose products are related to the Internet in some way. Specifically, Chambers has sought to acquire companies that make products in the industries that facilitate and drive up customer demand for Internet bandwidth or usage because this

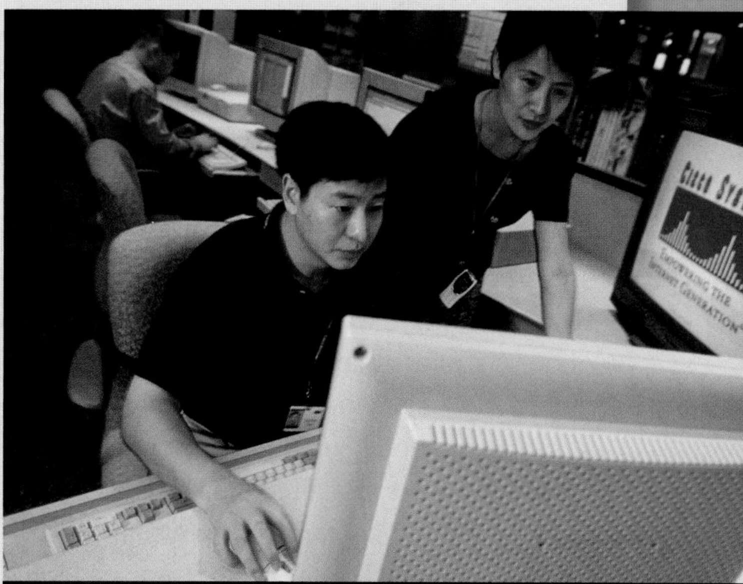

From its groundbreaking role in the Internet phenomenon to its current diversification, Cisco continues to innovate its way into all corners of the market.

increases the demand for Cisco's core products: the Internet routers and switches that provide the extra bandwidth needed by ISPs and data centers to satisfy their business customers' growing demand for fast Internet service. For example, the products made by Cisco's new acquisitions encourage companies and individuals to engage in activities such as sharing personal videos online or teleconferencing. These activities cause a huge increase in demand for Internet bandwidth. So to increase the speed and capacity of their Internet service, online companies such as YouTube and Facebook, ISPs, telecommunications companies such as AT&T and Verizon, and cable companies such as Comcast have had to spend billions of dollars on Cisco's routers to keep up with ever-increasing customer demand for fast Internet service.

While driving up demand for Internet use is one part of Chamber's strategic plan, from its founding Cisco has also focused on pioneering new products. Its strategy is to transfer its R&D competencies to make a wider range of products, and to use them to make new products to enter new industries. For example, to help customers get online more easily, Cisco bought home networking equipment maker Linksys for $500 million and implanted its technology in the company. By 2009 Linksys was the major supplier of home routers that customers use to create wireless home networks that give all family members instant access to the Web—which also drives up the need for bandwidth. The home routers share Cisco's Internet technology and work flawlessly with its routers and switches to make the Internet easier to access and use. In addition, to increase TV viewers' ability to take advantage of the Internet to download TV shows and movies (and thus increase Internet usage), Chambers acquired Scientific Atlanta, which made the set-top boxes bought by subscription TV providers, for $7 billion. Today Cisco supplies all the set-top boxes to companies such as Comcast and Time Warner; of course the boxes also work with its other Internet products.

In 2009 Cisco announced that it would pay $590 million to purchase Pure Digital, the company that makes the colorful, pocket-sized flip video camcorders that allow people to quickly make and share their videos on the Web. Over 2 million have been sold so far. Chambers claims this acquisition will help drive up demand for the next generation of entertainment and communication products such as Wiis, iPhones, iPads, and laptops, all designed to make it easier and faster for people to use the Internet. Cisco's goal once again is to increase customer demand for fast Internet service and force Internet-related companies to increase their bandwidth capacity and buy the networking giant's hardware and software.

By 2010 Cisco's strategy of creating synergies and sharing its competencies among all its Internet-related products led it to enter 28 different industries, including smaller ventures into home digital music and public surveillance systems, all of which generate demand for bandwidth. Chambers announced that his plan was to emerge from the recession with the products in place to make Cisco the global leader in both communications technology and Internet-linked IT hardware for business and individual customers.

Overview

As the opening case suggests, in a fast-changing competitive environment such as Internet network and communications equipment, managers must continually evaluate how well products are meeting customer needs, and they must engage in thorough, systematic planning to find new strategies to better meet those needs. This chapter explores the manager's role both as planner and as strategist. First, we discuss the nature and importance of planning, the kinds of plans managers develop, and the levels at which planning takes place. Second, we discuss the three major steps in the planning process: (1) determining an organization's mission and major goals, (2) choosing or formulating strategies to realize the mission and goals, and (3) selecting the most effective ways to implement and put these strategies into action. We also examine several techniques, such as scenario planning and SWOT analysis, that can help managers improve the quality of their planning; and we discuss a range of strategies managers can use to give their companies a competitive advantage over their rivals. By the end of this chapter, you will understand the vital role managers carry out when they plan, develop, and implement strategies to create a high-performing organization.

planning Identifying and selecting appropriate goals and courses of action; one of the four principal tasks of management.

strategy A cluster of decisions about what goals to pursue, what actions to take, and how to use resources to achieve goals.

Planning and Strategy

LO8-1 Identify the three main steps of the planning process and explain the relationship between planning and strategy.

Planning, as we noted in Chapter 1, is a process managers use to identify and select appropriate goals and courses of action for an organization.[2] The organizational plan that results from the planning process details the goals of the organization and the specific strategies managers will implement to attain those goals. Recall from Chapter 1 that a **strategy** is a cluster of related managerial decisions and actions to help an organization attain one of its goals. Thus planning is both a goal-making and a strategy-making process.

In most organizations, planning is a three-step activity (see Figure 8.1). The first step is determining the organization's mission and goals. A **mission statement** is a broad declaration of an organization's overriding purpose, what it is seeking to achieve from its activities; this statement also identifies what is *unique or important* about its products to its employees and customers; finally it *distinguishes or differentiates* the organization in some ways from its competitors. (Three examples of mission statements, those created by Cisco Systems, Walmart, and AT&T, are illustrated later in Figure 8.4.)

mission statement A broad declaration of an organization's purpose that identifies the organization's products and customers and distinguishes the organization from its competitors.

The second step is formulating strategy. Managers analyze the organization's current situation and then conceive and develop the strategies necessary to attain the organization's mission and goals. The third step is implementing strategy. Managers

Figure 8.1
Three Steps in Planning

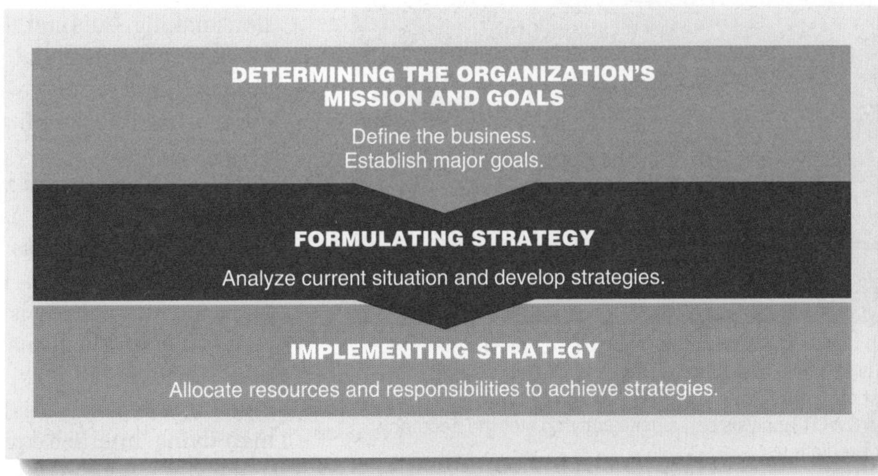
DETERMINING THE ORGANIZATION'S MISSION AND GOALS
Define the business.
Establish major goals.
FORMULATING STRATEGY
Analyze current situation and develop strategies.
IMPLEMENTING STRATEGY
Allocate resources and responsibilities to achieve strategies.

decide how to allocate the resources and responsibilities required to implement the strategies among people and groups within the organization.[3] In subsequent sections of this chapter we look in detail at the specifics of these steps. But first we examine the general nature and purpose of planning.

The Nature of the Planning Process

Essentially, to perform the planning task, managers (1) establish and discover where an organization is at the *present time;* (2) determine where it should be in the future, its *desired future state;* and (3) decide how to *move it forward* to reach that future state. When managers plan, they must forecast what may happen in the future to decide what to do in the present. The better their predictions, the more effective will be the strategies they formulate to take advantage of future opportunities and counter emerging competitive threats in the environment. As previous chapters noted, however, the external environment is uncertain and complex, and managers typically must deal with incomplete information and bounded rationality. This is why planning and strategy making are so difficult and risky; and if managers' predictions are wrong and strategies fail, organizational performance falls.

Why Planning Is Important

Almost all managers participate in some kind of planning because they must try to predict future opportunities and threats and develop a plan and strategies that will result in a high-performing organization. Moreover, the absence of a plan often results in hesitations, false steps, and mistaken changes of direction that can hurt an organization or even lead to disaster. Planning is important for four main reasons:

1. *Planning is necessary to give the organization a sense of direction and purpose.*[4] A plan states what goals an organization is trying to achieve and what strategies it intends to use to achieve them. Without the sense of direction and purpose that a formal plan provides, managers may interpret their own specific tasks and jobs in ways that best suit themselves. The result will be an organization that is pursuing multiple and often conflicting goals and a set of managers who do not cooperate and work well together. By stating which organizational goals and strategies are important, a plan keeps managers on track so they use the resources under their control efficiently and effectively.
2. *Planning is a useful way of getting managers to participate in decision making about the appropriate goals and strategies for an organization.* Effective planning gives all managers the opportunity to participate in decision making. At Intel, for example, top managers, as part of their annual planning process, regularly request input from lower-level managers to determine what the organization's goals and strategies should be.
3. *A plan helps coordinate managers of the different functions and divisions of an organization to ensure that they all pull in the same direction and work to achieve its desired future state.* Without a well-thought-out plan, for example, it is possible that the manufacturing function will make more products than the sales function can sell, resulting in a mass of unsold inventory. In fact, this happened to the currently high-flying Internet equipment supplier Cisco Systems, discussed in "A Manager's Challenge." In

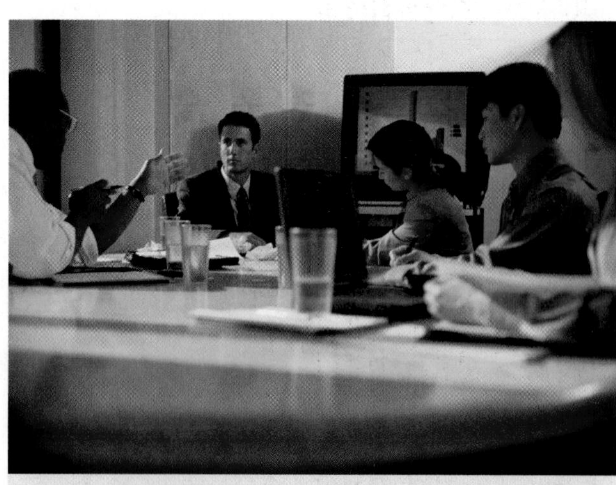

A group of managers meets to plot their company's strategy. Their ability to assess opportunities and challenges and to forecast the future doesn't just depend on brilliance. Such tools as SWOT analysis can significantly bolster the accuracy of their predictions.

the early 2000s it was able to sell all the routers it produced; but in 2003 Cisco found it had over $2 billion of inventory that its sales force could not sell because customers now wanted new kinds of optical routers that Cisco had not planned to develop–even though sales had told manufacturing that customer needs were changing.

4. *A plan can be used as a device for controlling managers within an organization.* A good plan specifies not only which goals and strategies the organization is committed to but also *who* bears the responsibility for putting the strategies into action to attain the goals. When managers know they will be held accountable for attaining a goal, they are motivated to do their best to make sure the goal is achieved.

Henri Fayol, the originator of the model of management we discussed in Chapter 1, said that effective plans should have four qualities: unity, continuity, accuracy, and flexibility.[5] *Unity* means that at any time only one central, guiding plan is put into operation to achieve an organizational goal; more than one plan to achieve a goal would cause confusion and disorder. *Continuity* means that planning is an ongoing process in which managers build and refine previous plans and continually modify plans at all levels–corporate, business, and functional–so they fit together into one broad framework. *Accuracy* means that managers need to make every attempt to collect and use all available information in the planning process. Of course managers must recognize that uncertainty exists and that information is almost always incomplete (for reasons we discussed in Chapter 7). Despite the need for continuity and accuracy, however, Fayol emphasized that the planning process should be *flexible* enough so plans can be altered and changed if the situation changes; managers must not be bound to a static plan.

Levels of Planning

In large organizations planning usually takes place at three levels of management: corporate, business or division, and department or functional. Consider how General Electric (GE) operates. One of the world's largest global organizations, GE competes in over 150 different businesses or industries.[6] GE has three main levels of management: corporate level, business or divisional level, and functional level (see Figure 8.2). At the corporate level are CEO and Chairman Jeffrey Immelt, his top management team, and their corporate support staff. Together they are responsible for planning and strategy making for the organization as a whole.

Below the corporate level is the business level. At the business level are the different *divisions* or *business units* of the company that compete in distinct industries; GE has over 150 divisions, including GE Aircraft Engines, GE Financial Services, GE Lighting, GE Motors, and GE Plastics. Each division or business unit has its own set of *divisional managers* who control planning and strategy for their particular division or unit. So, for example, GE Lighting's divisional managers plan how to operate globally to reduce costs while meeting the needs of customers in different countries.

Going down one more level, each division has its own set of *functions* or *departments,* such as manufacturing, marketing, human resource management (HRM), and research and development (R&D). For example, GE Aircraft has its own marketing function, as do GE Lighting and GE Motors. Each division's *functional managers* are responsible for the planning and strategy making necessary to increase the efficiency and effectiveness of their particular function. So, for example, GE Lighting's marketing managers are responsible for increasing the effectiveness of its advertising and sales campaigns in different countries to improve lightbulb sales.

Levels and Types of Planning

As just discussed, planning at GE, as at all other large organizations, takes place at each level. Figure 8.3 shows the link between these three levels and the three steps in the planning and strategy-making process illustrated in Figure 8.1.

Figure 8.2
Levels of Planning at General Electric

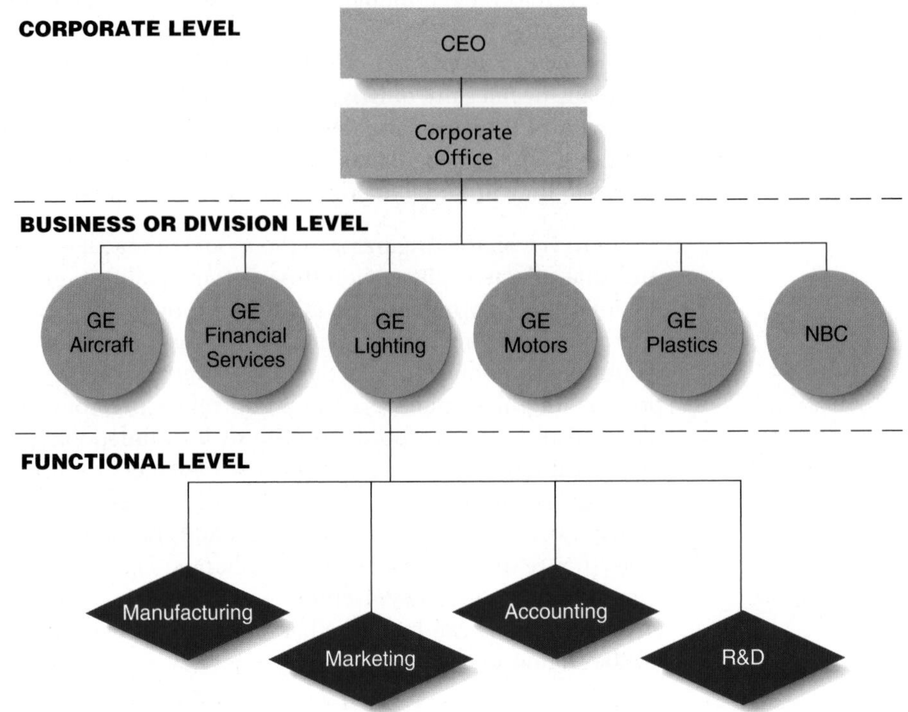

Figure 8.3
Levels and Types of Planning

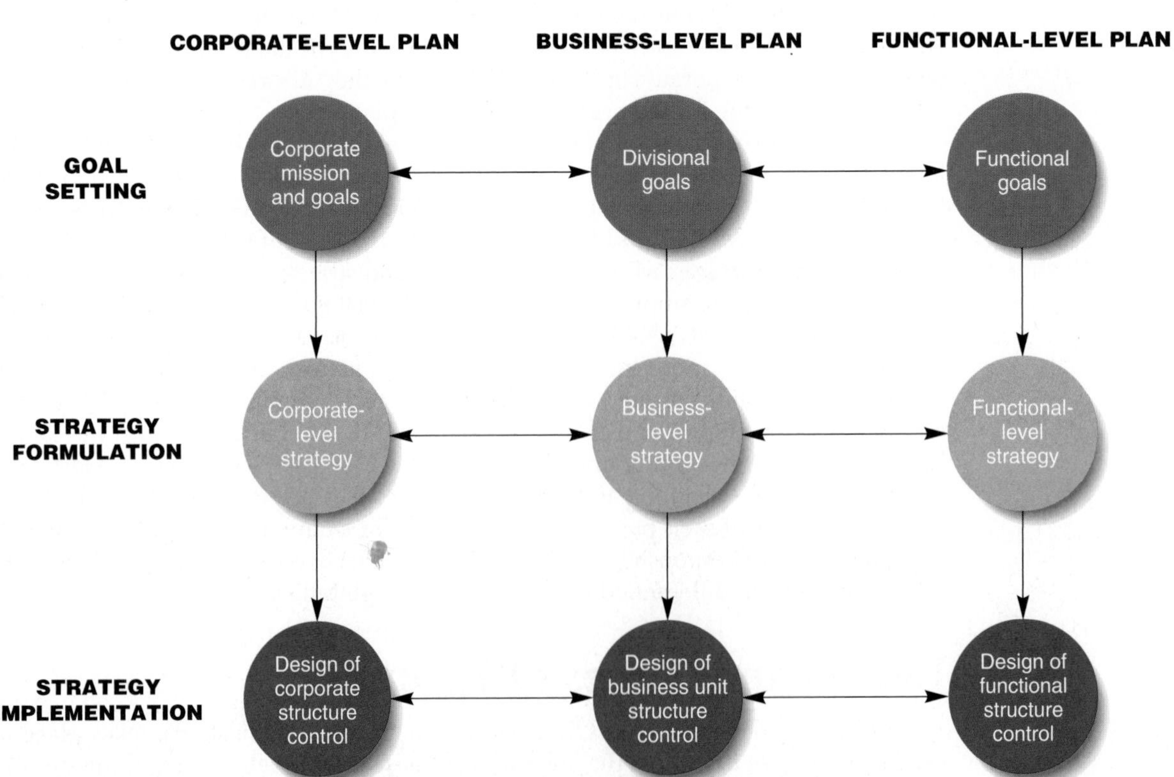

corporate-level plan Top management's decisions pertaining to the organization's mission, overall strategy, and structure.

corporate-level strategy A plan that indicates in which industries and national markets an organization intends to compete.

The **corporate-level plan** contains top management's decisions concerning the organization's mission and goals, overall (corporate-level) strategy, and structure (see Figure 8.3). **Corporate-level strategy** specifies in which industries and national markets an organization intends to compete and why. One of the goals stated in GE's corporate-level plan is that GE should be first or second in market share in every industry in which it competes. A division that cannot attain this goal may be sold to another company. GE Medical Systems was sold to Thompson of France for this reason. Another GE goal is to acquire other companies that can help a division build its market share to reach its corporate goal of being first or second in an industry.

In general, corporate-level planning and strategy are the primary responsibility of top or corporate managers.[7] The corporate-level goal of GE is to be the first or second leading company in every industry in which it competes. Jeffrey Immelt and his top management team decide which industries GE should compete in to achieve this goal. The corporate-level plan provides the framework within which divisional managers create their business-level plans. At the business level, the managers of each division create a **business-level plan** that details (1) the long-term divisional goals that will allow the division to meet corporate goals and (2) the division's business-level strategy and structure necessary to achieve divisional goals. **Business-level strategy** outlines the specific methods a division, business unit, or organization will use to compete effectively against its rivals in an industry. Managers at GE's lighting division (currently number two in the global lighting industry, behind the Dutch company Philips NV) develop strategies designed to help their division take over the number one spot and better contribute to GE's corporate goals. The lighting division's specific strategies might focus on ways to reduce costs in all departments to lower prices and so gain market share from Philips. For example, GE has expanded its European lighting operations in Hungary, which is a low-cost location.[8]

business-level plan Divisional managers' decisions pertaining to divisions' long-term goals, overall strategy, and structure.

business-level strategy A plan that indicates how a division intends to compete against its rivals in an industry.

At the functional level, the business-level plan provides the framework within which functional managers devise their plans. A **functional-level plan** states the goals that the managers of each function will pursue to help their division attain its business-level goals, which, in turn, will allow the entire company to achieve its corporate goals. **Functional-level strategy** is a plan of action that managers of individual functions (such as manufacturing or marketing) can follow to improve the ability of each function to perform its task-specific activities in ways that add value to an organization's goods and services and thereby increase the value customers receive. Thus, for example, consistent with the lighting division's strategy of driving down costs, its manufacturing function might adopt the goal "To reduce production costs by 20% over the next three years," and functional strategies to achieve this goal might include (1) investing in state-of-the-art European production facilities and (2) developing an electronic global business-to-business network to reduce the costs of inputs and inventory holding. The many ways in which managers can use functional-level strategy to strengthen business-level strategy are discussed in detail in Chapter 9.

functional-level plan Functional managers' decisions pertaining to the goals that they propose to pursue to help the division attain its business-level goals.

functional-level strategy A plan of action to improve the ability of each of an organization's functions to perform its task-specific activities in ways that add value to an organization's goods and services.

In the planning process, it is important to ensure that planning across the three different levels is *consistent*–functional goals and strategies should be consistent with divisional goals and strategies, which, in turn, should be consistent with corporate goals and strategies, and vice versa. When consistency is achieved, the whole company operates in harmony; activities at one level reinforce and strengthen those at the other levels, increasing efficiency and effectiveness. To help accomplish this, each function's plan is linked to its division's business-level plan, which, in turn, is linked to the corporate plan. Although few organizations are as large and complex as GE, most plan in the same way as GE and have written plans, which are frequently updated, to guide managerial decision making.

Time Horizons of Plans

time horizon The intended duration of a plan.

Plans differ in their **time horizons,** the periods of time over which they are intended to apply or endure. Managers usually distinguish among *long-term plans,* with a time horizon of five years or more; *intermediate-term plans,* with a horizon between one and five years; and *short-term plans,* with a horizon of one year or less.[9] Typically corporate- and business-level goals and strategies require long- and intermediate-term plans, and functional-level goals and strategies require intermediate- and short-term plans.

Although most companies operate with planning horizons of five years or more, this does not mean that managers undertake major planning exercises only once every five years and then "lock in" a specific set of goals and strategies for that period. Most organizations have an annual planning cycle that is usually linked to the annual financial budget (although a major planning effort may be undertaken only every few years). So a corporate- or business-level plan that extends over several years is typically treated as a *rolling plan*–a plan that is updated and amended every year to take account of changing conditions in the external environment. Thus the time horizon for an organization's 2009 corporate-level plan might be 2014; for the 2010 plan it might be 2015; and so on. The use of rolling plans is essential because of the high rate of change in the environment and the difficulty of predicting competitive conditions five years in the future. Rolling plans enable managers to make midcourse corrections if environmental changes warrant or to change the thrust of the plan altogether if it no longer seems appropriate. The use of rolling plans allows managers to plan flexibly without losing sight of the need to plan for the long term.

Standing Plans and Single-Use Plans

Another distinction often made between plans is whether they are standing plans or single-use plans. Managers create standing and single-use plans to help achieve an organization's specific goals. *Standing plans* are used in situations in which programmed decision making is appropriate. When the same situations occur repeatedly, managers develop policies, rules, and standard operating procedures (SOPs) to control the way employees perform their tasks. A policy is a general guide to action; a rule is a formal, written guide to action; and a standing operating procedure is a written instruction describing the exact series of actions that should be followed in a specific situation. For example, an organization may have a standing plan about ethical behavior by employees. This plan includes a policy that all employees are expected to behave ethically in their dealings with suppliers and customers; a rule that requires any employee who receives from a supplier or customer a gift worth more than $20 to report the gift; and an SOP that obliges the recipient of the gift to make the disclosure in writing within 30 days.

In contrast, *single-use plans* are developed to handle nonprogrammed decision making in unusual or one-of-a-kind situations. Examples of single-use plans include *programs,* which are integrated sets of plans for achieving certain goals, and *projects,* which are specific action plans created to complete various aspects of a program. One of NASA's major programs was to reach the moon, and one project in this program was to develop a lunar module capable of landing on the moon and returning to the earth.

LO8-2 Describe some techniques managers can use to improve the planning process so they can better predict the future and mobilize organizational resources to meet future contingencies.

Scenario Planning

Earlier we noted that effective plans have four qualities: unity, continuity, accuracy, and flexibility. One of the most widely used planning methods or techniques that can help managers create plans that have these qualities is scenario planning. **Scenario planning** (also known as *contingency planning*) is the generation of multiple forecasts of future conditions followed by an analysis of how to respond effectively to each of those conditions.

scenario planning The generation of multiple forecasts of future conditions followed by an analysis of how to respond effectively to each of those conditions.

As noted previously, planning is about trying to forecast and predict the future in order to be able to anticipate future opportunities and threats. The future, however, is inherently unpredictable. How can managers best deal with this unpredictability? This question preoccupied managers at Royal Dutch Shell, the third largest global oil company, in the 1980s. In 1984 oil was $30 a barrel, and most analysts and managers, including Shell's, believed it would hit $50 per barrel by 1990. Although these high prices guaranteed high profits, Shell's top managers decided to conduct a scenario-planning exercise. Shell's corporate and divisional managers were told to use scenario planning to generate different future scenarios of conditions in the oil market and then to develop

As we know all too well, oil and gas prices are unpredictable. Oil industry managers therefore sometimes use scenario planning to deal with this chaotic market.

a set of plans that detailed how they would respond to these opportunities and threats if any such scenario occurred.

One scenario assumed that oil prices would fall to $15 per barrel, and managers had to decide what they should do in such a case. Managers went to work with the goal of creating a plan consisting of a series of recommendations. The final plan included proposals to cut oil exploration costs by investing in new technologies, to accelerate investments in cost-efficient oil-refining facilities, and to weed out unprofitable gas stations.[10] In reviewing these proposals, top management came to the conclusion that even if oil prices continued to rise, all of these actions would benefit Shell and increase its profit margin. So they decided to put the cost-cutting plan into action. As it happened, in the mid-1980s oil prices did not rise; they collapsed to $15 a barrel, but Shell, unlike its competitors, had already taken steps to be profitable in a low-oil-price world. Consequently, by 1990 the company was twice as profitable as its major competitors.

As this example suggests, because the future is unpredictable–the $30-a-barrel oil level was not reached again until the early 2000s, for example–the best way to improve planning is first to generate "multiple futures," or scenarios of the future, based on different assumptions about conditions that *might prevail* in the future and then to develop different plans that detail what a company should do if one of these scenarios occurs. Scenario planning is a learning tool that raises the quality of the planning process and can bring real benefits to an organization.[11] Shell's success with scenario planning influenced many other companies to adopt similar systems. By 1990 more than 50% of *Fortune* 500 companies were using some version of scenario planning, and the number has increased since then. A major advantage of scenario planning is its ability not only to anticipate the challenges of an uncertain future but also to educate managers to think about the future–*to think strategically*.[12]

Determining the Organization's Mission and Goals

As we discussed earlier, determining the organization's mission and goals is the first step of the planning process. Once the mission and goals are agreed upon and formally stated in the corporate plan, they guide the next steps by defining which strategies are appropriate.[13] Figure 8.4 presents the missions and goals of three companies: Cisco, Walmart, and AT&T.

Defining the Business

To determine an organization's *mission*–the overriding reason it exists to provide customers with goods or services they value–managers must first *define its business* so they can identify what kind of value customers are receiving. To define the business, managers must ask three related questions about a company's products: (1) *Who* are our customers? (2) *What* customer needs are being satisfied? (3) *How* are we satisfying customer needs?[14] Managers ask these questions to identify the customer needs that the organization satisfies and how the organization satisfies those needs. Answering these questions helps managers identify not only the customer needs they are satisfying now but also the needs they should try to satisfy in the future and who their true competitors are. All this information helps managers plan and establish appropriate goals. In the following "Management Insight" box, the case of Mattel shows the important role that defining the business has in the planning process.

Figure 8.4
Three Mission Statements

COMPANY	MISSION STATEMENT
Cisco	Cisco solutions provide competitive advantage to our customers through more efficient and timely exchange of information, which in turn leads to cost savings, process efficiencies, and closer relationships with our customers, prospects, business partners, suppliers, and employees.
Walmart	We work for you. We think of ourselves as buyers for our customers, and we apply our considerable strengths to get the best value for you. We've built Walmart by acting on behalf of our customers, and that concept continues to propel us. We're working hard to make our customers' shopping easy.
AT&T	We are dedicated to being the world's best at bringing people together–giving them easy access to each other and to the information and services they want and need–anytime, anywhere.

Management Insight

Has Mattel's Barbie Won the War Against the Bratz Doll?

The rapid pace at which the world is changing is forcing strategic managers at all kinds of companies to speed up their decision making; otherwise they get left behind by agile competitors who respond faster to changing customer fads and fashions. Nowhere is this truer than in the global toy industry, in which vicious combat rages in the doll business, worth over $10 billion a year in sales. The largest global toy company, Mattel, has earned tens of billions of dollars from the world's best-selling doll, Barbie, since it introduced her over 50 years ago.[15] Mothers who played with the original dolls bought them for their daughters and granddaughters, and Barbie became an American icon. However, Barbie's advantage as a best-selling global doll led Mattel's managers to make major strategic errors in the 2000s.

Barbie and all Barbie accessories have accounted for about 50% of Mattel's toy sales since the 1990s, so protecting this star product was crucial. The Barbie doll was created in the 1960s when most women were homemakers; her voluptuous shape was a response to a dated view of what the "ideal" woman should look like. Barbie's continuing success, however, led Mattel's CEO Bob Eckert and his top managers to underestimate how much the world had altered. Changing cultural views about the role of girls, women, sex, marriage, and women working in the last decades shifted the tastes of doll buyers. But Mattel's managers continued to bet on Barbie's eternal appeal and collectively bought into an "If it's not broken don't fix it" approach. In fact, given that Barbie was the best-selling doll, they thought it might be dangerous to change her appearance; customers might not like the product development changes and stop buying the doll. Mattel's top managers decided not to rock the boat; they left the brand and business model unchanged and focused their efforts on developing new digital toys.

As a result, Mattel was unprepared when a challenge came along in the form of a new kind of doll, the Bratz doll, introduced by MGA Entertainment. Many competitors to Barbie had emerged over the years because the doll business is so profitable, but no other doll had matched Barbie's appeal to young girls (or their mothers). The marketers and designers behind the Bratz line of dolls had spent a lot of time to discover what the new generation of girls, especially those aged 7–11, wanted from a doll, however. It turned out that the Bratz dolls they designed met the desires of these girls. Bratz dolls have larger heads and oversized eyes, wear lots of makeup and short dresses, and are multicultural to give each doll "personality and attitude."[16] The dolls were designed to appeal to a new generation of girls brought up in a fast-changing fashion, music, and television market. The Bratz dolls met the untapped needs of "tween" girls, and the new line took off. MGA quickly licensed the rights to make and sell the dolls to toy companies overseas, and Bratz became a serious competitor to Barbie.

Mattel was in trouble. Its strategic managers had to change its business model and strategies and bring Barbie up to date; Mattel's designers must have been wishing they had been adventurous and made more radical changes earlier when they did not need to change. However, they decided to change Barbie's extreme shape; they killed off her old-time boyfriend Ken and replaced him with Blaine, an Aussie surfer.[17] They also recognized they had waited much too long to introduce new lines of dolls to meet the changed needs of tweens and older girls in the 2000s. They rushed out the "My Scene" and "Flava" lines of dolls that were obvious imitations of Bratz dolls, but they both flopped. And the decisions they made to change Barbie–her figure, looks, clothing, and boyfriends–came too late, and sales of Barbie dolls continued to fall.

By 2006 sales of the Barbie collection had dropped by 30%, which was critical to Mattel because its profits and stock price hinged on Barbie's success–and they both plunged. Analysts argued that Mattel had not paid enough attention to its customers' changing needs or moved quickly to introduce the new and improved products necessary to keep a company on top of its market. Mattel brought back Ken, but then in a sign of its mounting problems Mattel's lawyers sued MGA Entertainment, arguing that the Bratz dolls' copyright rightfully belonged to them. Mattel complained that the head designer of Bratz was a Mattel employee when he made the initial drawings for the dolls and that Mattel had applied for copyright protection on a number of early Bratz drawings. Mattel claimed that MGA hired key Mattel employees away from the firm and these employees stole sensitive sales information and transferred it to MGA.

In 2008 a judge ruled in Mattel's favor and ordered MGA to stop using the Bratz name, and a jury awarded Mattel $100 million in damages. After an appeal, in 2009 a federal judge upheld the verdict and ruled that the Bratz doll is Mattel property and that MGA could sell the doll only until the end of 2009. In 2010 the companies were locked in a bitter dispute: Mattel wanted the rights to produce and sell the Bratz doll line, but MGA's founder was still trying to protect the profits made from the Bratz dolls' success. Meanwhile stores stopped selling the Bratz doll, Mattel revitalized its line of Barbie dolls, and its CEO exultantly declared that "Barbie is back" as increased doll sales helped raise the company's profits by 86% in the spring of 2010.[18]

Planning in and of itself does not always pay off—it must be realistic. With its diversion into buying a game company, Mattel failed to anticipate the rise of such competitors as these Bratz dolls, which have taken a big chunk out of Barbie's profitability.

Imagine then, how Mattel's managers reacted to the decision of the federal appeals court in July 2010 that threw out the previous court decision and ruled that MGA Entertainment did have the right to make and sell the Bratz doll because their looks and image were not subject to existing copyright law! A new trial seems inevitable and the doll war will go on as both companies battle for the billions of dollars in future doll sales.

Establishing Major Goals

Once the business is defined, managers must establish a set of primary goals to which the organization is committed. Developing these goals gives the organization a sense of direction or purpose. In most organizations, articulating major goals is the job of the CEO, although other managers have input into the process. Thus, at Mattel, CEO Eckert's primary goal is still to be the leader in every segment of the toy market in which the company competes, even though this is highly challenging. However, the best statements of organizational goals are ambitious–that is, they *stretch* the organization and require that each of its members work to improve company performance.[19] The role of **strategic leadership,** the ability of the CEO and top managers to convey a compelling vision of what they want to achieve to their subordinates, is important here. If subordinates buy into the vision and model their behaviors on their leaders, they develop a willingness to undertake the hard, stressful work that is necessary for creative, risk-taking strategy making.[20] Many popular books such as *Built to Last* provide lucid accounts of strategic leaders establishing "big, hairy, audacious goals (BHAGs)" that serve as rallying points to unite their subordinates.[21]

strategic leadership The ability of the CEO and top managers to convey a compelling vision of what they want the organization to achieve to their subordinates.

Although goals should be challenging, they should also be realistic. Challenging goals give managers at all levels an incentive to look for ways to improve organizational performance, but a goal that is clearly unrealistic and impossible to attain may prompt managers to give up.[22] Bob Eckert had to be careful not to discourage Mattel's Barbie doll designers by setting unrealistic sales targets when the Bratz dolls threatened it, for example.

Finally, the time period in which a goal is expected to be achieved should be stated. Time constraints are important because they emphasize that a goal must be attained within a reasonable period; they inject a sense of urgency into goal attainment and act as a motivator. Mattel's managers committed themselves to reviving the Barbie line and to significantly increasing sales by 2008, but only in 2010 were they able to achieve this–and of course they were aided by their legal victory over MGA's Bratz dolls.[23]

Formulating Strategy

In **strategy formulation** managers work to develop the set of strategies (corporate, divisional, and functional) that will allow an organization to accomplish its mission and achieve its goals.[24] Strategy formulation begins with managers' systematically analyzing the factors or forces inside an organization, and outside in the global environment, that affect the organization's ability to meet its goals now and in the future. SWOT analysis and the five forces model are two handy techniques managers can use to analyze these factors.

strategy formulation The development of a set of corporate, business, and functional strategies that allow an organization to accomplish its mission and achieve its goals.

SWOT Analysis

SWOT analysis is a planning exercise in which managers identify *internal* organizational strengths (S) and weaknesses (W) and *external* environmental opportunities (O) and threats (T). Based on a SWOT analysis, managers at the different levels of the organization select the corporate, business, and functional strategies to best position the organization to achieve its mission and goals (see Figure 8.5). In Chapter 6 we discussed forces in the task and general environments that have the potential to affect an organization. We noted that changes in these forces can produce opportunities that an organization might take advantage of and threats that may harm its current situation.

SWOT analysis A planning exercise in which managers identify organizational strengths (S) and weaknesses (W) and environmental opportunities (O) and threats (T).

The first step in SWOT analysis is to identify an organization's strengths and weaknesses. Table 8.1 lists many important strengths (such as high-quality skills in marketing and in research and development) and weaknesses (such as rising manufacturing costs and outdated technology). The task facing managers is to identify the strengths and weaknesses that characterize the present state of their organization.

The second step in SWOT analysis begins when managers embark on a full-scale SWOT planning exercise to identify potential opportunities and threats in the environment that affect the organization now or may affect it in the future. Examples of possible opportunities and threats that must be anticipated (many of which were discussed in Chapter 6) are listed in Table 8.1. Scenario planning is often used to strengthen this analysis.

With the SWOT analysis completed, and strengths, weaknesses, opportunities, and threats identified, managers can continue the planning process and determine specific strategies for achieving the organization's mission and goals. The resulting strategies should enable the organization to attain its goals by taking advantage of opportunities,

Figure 8.5
Planning and Strategy Formulation

SWOT Analysis
A planning exercise to identify strengths and weaknesses inside an organization and opportunities and threats in the environment
Corporate-Level Strategy
A plan of action to manage the growth and development of an organization so as to maximize its long-run ability to create value
Business-Level Strategy
A plan of action to take advantage of favorable opportunities and find ways to counter threats so as to compete effectively in an industry
Functional-Level Strategy
A plan of action to improve the ability of an organization's departments to create value

countering threats, building strengths, and correcting organizational weaknesses. To appreciate how managers use SWOT analysis to formulate strategy, consider how Douglas Conant, CEO of Campbell Soup since 2001, has used it to find strategies to turn around the performance of the troubled food products maker in the 2000s. In fact, his self-described mission was to take a "bad" company and lift its performance to "extraordinary" by the end of 2011.[25]

Table 8.1
Questions for SWOT Analysis

Potential Strengths	Potential Opportunities	Potential Weaknesses	Potential Threats
Well-developed strategy? Strong product lines? Broad market coverage? Manufacturing competence? Good marketing skills? Good materials management systems? R&D skills and leadership? Human resource competencies? Brand-name reputation? Cost of differentiation advantage? Appropriate management style? Appropriate organizational structure? Appropriate control systems? Ability to manage strategic change? Others?	Expand core business(es)? Exploit new market segments? Widen product range? Extend cost or differentiation advantage? Diversify into new growth businesses? Expand into foreign markets? Apply R&D skills in new areas? Enter new related businesses? Vertically integrate forward? Vertically integrate backward? Overcome barriers to entry? Reduce rivalry among competitors? Apply brand-name capital in new areas? Seek fast market growth? Others?	Poorly developed strategy? Obsolete, narrow product lines? Rising manufacturing costs? Decline in R&D innovations? Poor marketing plan? Poor materials management systems? Loss of customer goodwill? Inadequate human resources? Loss of brand name? Growth without direction? Loss of corporate direction? Infighting among divisions? Loss of corporate control? Inappropriate organizational structure and control systems? High conflict and politics? Others?	Attacks on core business(es)? Increase in domestic competition? Increase in foreign competition? Change in consumer tastes? Fall in barriers to entry? Rise in new or substitute products? Increase in industry rivalry? New forms of industry competition? Potential for takeover? Changes in demographic factors? Changes in economic factors? Downturn in economy? Rising labor costs? Slower market growth? Others?

Manager as a Person

Douglas Conant Keeps Stirring Up Campbell Soup

Campbell Soup Co., one of the oldest and best-known global food companies, saw demand for its major product, condensed soup, plummet by 30% between 1998 and 2004 as customers switched from high-salt, processed soups to more healthful low-fat, low-salt varieties. Campbell's profits and stock price plunged as its condensed soup business collapsed, and in 2001 its directors brought in a new CEO, Douglas Conant, to help the troubled company. Conant decided it was necessary to develop a three-year turnaround plan to help the company strengthen its market position against aggressive competitors such as General Mills, whose Progresso Soup division had attracted away many Campbell customers with its innovative new lines of healthful soup.

One of Conant's first actions was to initiate a thorough SWOT planning exercise. *External analysis* of the environment identified the growth of the organic and health food segment of the food market and the increasing number of other kinds of convenience foods as a threat to Campbell's core soup business. It also revealed three growth opportunities: (1) the growing market for health and sports drinks, in which Campbell already was a competitor with its V8 juice; (2) the growing market for quality bread and cookies, in which Campbell competed with its Pepperidge Farm brand; and (3) chocolate products, where Campbell's Godiva brand had enjoyed increasing sales throughout the 1990s.

With the analysis of the environment complete, Conant turned his attention to his organization's resources and capabilities. His *internal analysis* of Campbell identified a number of major weaknesses. These included staffing levels that were too high relative to its competitors and high costs associated with manufacturing its soups because of the use of outdated machinery.

Douglas Conant, CEO of Campbell's, has revitalized the company through SWOT analysis. From SWOT analysis he has learned how to innovate successful new food products, and Campbell's has emerged as a leader in the low-carb, health-conscious, and luxury-food market segments.

Also, Conant noted that Campbell had a conservative culture in which people seemed to be afraid to take risks–something that was a real problem in an industry where customer tastes are always changing and new products must be developed constantly. At the same time, the SWOT analysis identified an enormous strength: Campbell enjoyed huge economies of scale because of the enormous quantity of food products that it makes, and it also had a first-rate R&D division capable of developing exciting new food products.

Using the information from this SWOT analysis, Conant and his managers decided that Campbell needed to use its product development skills to revitalize its core products and modify or reinvent them in ways that would appeal to increasingly health-conscious and busy consumers. Conant stressed convenience with microwaveable soups and cans that open with a pull. The recipes became more healthful for its soups, V8 drinks, and Pepperidge Farm snacks because Conant needed to expand Campbell's share of the health, sports, snack, and luxury food market segments. Also, to increase sales, Campbell needed to tap into new food outlets, such as corporate cafeterias, college dining halls, and other mass eateries, to expand consumers' access to its foods. Finally, Conant decided to decentralize authority to managers at lower levels in the organization and make them responsible for developing new soup, bread, and chocolate products that met customers' changing needs. In this way he hoped to revitalize Campbell's slow-moving culture and speed the flow of improved and new products to the market.

Conant put his new plan into action, sales of new soup products increased, and he began to put more emphasis on sales of soup at outlets such as 7-11 and Subway and less on supermarket sales.[26] By 2005 analysts felt that he had made a significant difference in Campbell's performance but that there was still a lot to do–Campbell's operating margins were still shrinking. Carrying on the SWOT analysis, Conant decided Campbell should produce more products to meet the needs of the "low-carb diet," such as new kinds of low-carb bread and cookies. He also decided to shrink the company's operations to lower costs. His goal was to raise profit margins to the level of his major competitors Kraft and General Mills by 2007 using a new three-year plan based on this SWOT analysis.[27]

By 2007 Conant had substantially achieved his goals: Sales of soup had recovered, and the Pepperidge Farm and Godiva divisions were earning record sales and profits.[28] (Sales of Goldfish crackers had increased by 100%!) Campbell's stock price soared, and Conant and employees at all levels received bonuses that rewarded their intense efforts to turn around the company. However, Conant immediately set in motion a new round of SWOT analysis to find fresh opportunities for developing new products.[29]

On the threat side, it was clear that customers wanted more nutritious food and snack products; so Conant set into motion research to make Campbell's food products more appealing to health-conscious customers. One major opportunity was to reformulate a number of its soups to reduce sodium content, and it introduced new kinds of low-salt soup in 2007. Another opportunity was to develop nutritious luxury soups that would command premium prices.[30] Both these initiatives worked well. On the other hand, pursuing his new goal of making Campbell's foods more nutritious led Conant to question if its highly profitable Godiva chocolate brand was still a good fit for the company. He decided it had become a weakness, and in 2008 he sold it for $850 million.[31] He used some of the proceeds of this sale to build new company strengths. For example, he invested in R&D to develop the skills needed to customize Campbell's brands to the needs of customers in countries such as India and China–a move that spearheaded global expansion into major soup-eating nations.

Under Conant, Campbell's profits and stock price have increased each year during the 2000s; and with a culture of innovation permeating the organization, in 2010 its future looks even brighter. Thanks to his leadership employees are more engaged and involved, sales are up, and many new leaders and managers have been promoted to change the company's culture and stretch its employees. How does Conant himself encourage employees to perform at a high level? Obviously he rewards good performance, but he also sends around 20 daily "thank-you" e-mail messages to employees at every level of the organization to show he understands how everyone can contribute to help the company meet its goals and mission over the next three years.

The Five Forces Model

A well-known model that helps managers focus on the five most important competitive forces, or potential threats, in the external environment is Michael Porter's five forces model. We discussed the first four forces in the following list in Chapter 6. Porter identified these five factors as major threats because they affect how much profit organizations competing within the same industry can expect to make:

- *The level of rivalry among organizations in an industry:* The more that companies compete against one another for customers–for example, by lowering the prices of their products or by increasing advertising–the lower is the level of industry profits (low prices mean less profit).

- *The potential for entry into an industry:* The easier it is for companies to enter an industry–because, for example, barriers to entry, such as brand loyalty, are low–the more likely it is for industry prices and therefore industry profits to be low.
- *The power of large suppliers:* If there are only a few large suppliers of an important input, then suppliers can drive up the price of that input, and expensive inputs result in lower profits for companies in an industry.
- *The power of large customers:* If only a few large customers are available to buy an industry's output, they can bargain to drive down the price of that output. As a result, industry producers make lower profits.
- *The threat of substitute products:* Often the output of one industry is a substitute for the output of another industry (plastic may be a substitute for steel in some applications, for example; similarly, bottled water is a substitute for cola). When a substitute for their product exists, companies cannot demand high prices for it or customers will switch to the substitute, and this constraint keeps their profits low.

Porter argued that when managers analyze opportunities and threats, they should pay particular attention to these five forces because they are the major threats an organization will encounter. It is the job of managers at the corporate, business, and functional levels to formulate strategies to counter these threats so an organization can manage its task and general environments, perform at a high level, and generate high profits. At Campbell, Conant performed such analysis to identify the opportunities and threats stemming from the actions of food industry rivals. For example, as noted earlier, General Mill's Progresso Soups division developed more healthful kinds of soups, and this increased rivalry and lowered Campbell's sales and profits until it successfully developed new lines of healthful soups. Both companies have been affected by the threat of rising global food prices as the costs of wheat, corn, rice, and dairy products have increased. Both companies are striving to reduce operating costs to limit food price increases because the company with the lowest prices will attract the most customers and gain a competitive advantage–especially during the recent recession.

hypercompetition Permanent, ongoing, intense competition brought about in an industry by advancing technology or changing customer tastes.

Today competition is tough in most industries, whether companies make cars, soup, computers, or dolls. The term **hypercompetition** applies to industries that are characterized by permanent, ongoing, intense competition brought about by advancing technology or changing customer tastes and fads and fashions.[32] Clearly, planning and strategy formulation are much more difficult and risky when hypercompetition prevails in an industry.

Formulating Business-Level Strategies

Michael Porter, the researcher who developed the five forces model, also developed a theory of how managers can select a business-level strategy–a plan to gain a competitive advantage in a particular market or industry.[33] Porter argued that business-level strategy creates a competitive advantage because it allows an organization (or a division of a company) to *counter and reduce* the threat of the five industry forces. That is, successful business-level strategy reduces rivalry, prevents new competitors from entering the industry, reduces the power of suppliers or buyers, and lowers the threat of substitutes–and this raises prices and profits.

LO8-3 Differentiate between the main types of business-level strategies and explain how they give an organization a competitive advantage that may lead to superior performance.

According to Porter, to obtain these higher profits managers must choose between two basic ways of increasing the value of an organization's products: *differentiating the product* to increase its value to customers or *lowering the costs* of making the product. Porter also argues that managers must choose between serving the whole market or serving just one segment or part of a market. Based on those choices, managers choose to pursue one of four business-level strategies: low cost, differentiation, focused low cost, or focused differentiation (see Table 8.2).

Table 8.2
Porter's Business-Level Strategies

	Number of Market Segments Served	
Strategy	**Many**	**Few**
Low cost	✓	
Focused low cost		✓
Differentiation	✓	
Focused differentiation		✓

Low-Cost Strategy

low-cost strategy Driving the organization's costs down below the costs of its rivals.

With a **low-cost strategy,** managers try to gain a competitive advantage by focusing the energy of all the organization's departments or functions on driving the company's costs down below the costs of its industry rivals. This strategy, for example, would require that manufacturing managers search for new ways to reduce production costs, R&D managers focus on developing new products that can be manufactured more cheaply, and marketing managers find ways to lower the costs of attracting customers. According to Porter, companies pursuing a low-cost strategy can sell a product for less than their rivals sell it and yet still make a good profit because of their lower costs. Thus such organizations enjoy a competitive advantage based on their low prices. For example, BIC pursues a low-cost strategy: It offers customers razor blades priced lower than Gillette's and ballpoint pens less expensive than those offered by Cross or Waterman. Also, when existing companies have low costs and can charge low prices, it is difficult for new companies to enter the industry because entering is always an expensive process.

Differentiation Strategy

differentiation strategy Distinguishing an organization's products from the products of competitors on dimensions such as product design, quality, or after-sales service.

With a **differentiation strategy,** managers try to gain a competitive advantage by focusing all the energies of the organization's departments or functions on *distinguishing* the organization's products from those of competitors on one or more important dimensions, such as product design, quality, or after-sales service and support. Often the process of making products unique and different is expensive. This strategy, for example, frequently requires that managers increase spending on product design or R&D to differentiate products, and costs rise as a result. Organizations that successfully pursue a differentiation strategy may be able to charge a *premium price* for their products; the premium price lets organizations pursuing a differentiation strategy recoup their higher costs. Coca-Cola, PepsiCo, and Procter & Gamble are some of the many well-known companies that pursue a strategy of differentiation. They spend enormous amounts of money on advertising to differentiate, and create a unique image for, their products. Also, differentiation makes industry entry difficult because new companies have no brand name to help them compete and customers don't perceive other products to be close substitutes, so this also allows premium pricing and results in high profits.

"Stuck in the Middle"

According to Porter's theory, managers cannot simultaneously pursue both a low-cost strategy and a differentiation strategy. Porter identified a simple correlation: Differentiation raises costs and thus necessitates premium pricing to recoup those high costs. For example, if BIC suddenly began to advertise heavily to try to build a strong global brand image for its products, BIC's costs would rise. BIC then could no longer make a profit simply by pricing its blades or pens lower than Gillette or Cross. According to Porter, managers must choose between a low-cost strategy and a differentiation strategy. He refers to managers and organizations that have not made this choice as being "stuck in the middle."

Organizations stuck in the middle tend to have lower levels of performance than do those that pursue a low-cost or a differentiation strategy. To avoid being stuck in the middle, top managers must instruct departmental managers to take actions that will result in either low cost or differentiation.

However, exceptions to this rule can be found. In many organizations managers have been able to drive costs below those of rivals and simultaneously differentiate their products from those offered by rivals.[34] For example, Toyota's production system is the most efficient–and still one of the most reliable–of any global carmaker, as we discuss in the next chapter. This efficiency gives Toyota a low-cost advantage over its rivals in the global car industry. At the same time, Toyota has differentiated its cars from those of rivals on the basis of superior design and quality. This superiority allows the company to charge a premium price for many of its popular models.[35] Thus Toyota seems to be simultaneously pursuing both a low-cost and a differentiated business-level strategy. This example suggests that although Porter's ideas may be valid in most cases, very well managed companies such as Cisco, Campbell, Toyota, and McDonald's may have both low costs and differentiated products–and so make the highest profits of any company in an industry.

Focused Low-Cost and Focused Differentiation Strategies

Both the differentiation strategy and the low-cost strategy are aimed at serving many or most segments of a particular market, such as for cars, toys, foods, or computers. Porter identified two other business-level strategies that aim to serve the needs of customers in only one or a few market segments.[36] Managers pursuing a **focused low-cost strategy** serve one or a few segments of the overall market and aim to make their organization the lowest-cost company serving that segment. By contrast, managers pursuing a **focused differentiation strategy** serve just one or a few segments of the market and aim to make their organization the most differentiated company serving that segment.

focused low-cost strategy Serving only one segment of the overall market and trying to be the lowest-cost organization serving that segment.

focused differentiation strategy Serving only one segment of the overall market and trying to be the most differentiated organization serving that segment.

Companies pursuing either of these strategies have chosen to *specialize* in some way by directing their efforts at a particular kind of customer (such as serving the needs of babies or affluent customers) or even the needs of customers in a specific geographic region (customers on the East or West Coast). BMW, for example, pursues a focused differentiation strategy, producing cars exclusively for higher-income customers. By contrast, Toyota pursues a differentiation strategy and produces cars that appeal to consumers in almost all segments of the car market, from basic transportation (Toyota Corolla) through the middle of the market (Toyota Camry) to the high-income end of the market (Lexus). An interesting example of how a company pursuing a focused low-cost strategy, by specializing in one market segment, can compete with powerful differentiators is profiled in the following "Management Insight" box.

Management Insight

Different Ways to Compete in the Soft Drink Business

"Coke" and "Pepsi" are household names worldwide. Together Coca-Cola and PepsiCo control over 70% of the global soft drink market and over 75% of the U.S. soft drink market. Their success can be attributed to the differentiation strategies they developed to produce and promote their products–strategies that have made them two of the most profitable global organizations. There are several parts to their differentiation strategies. First, both companies built global brands by manufacturing the soft drink concentrate that gives cola its flavor but then selling the concentrate in a syrup form to bottlers throughout the world. The bottlers are responsible for producing and distributing the actual cola. They add carbonated water to the syrup, package the resulting drinks, and distribute them to vending machines, supermarkets, restaurants, and other retail outlets. The bottlers must also sign an exclusive agreement that prohibits them from bottling or distributing the products of competing soft drink companies. This creates a barrier to entry that helps prevent new companies from entering the industry.

Second, Coca-Cola and PepsiCo charge the bottlers a premium price for the syrup; they then invest a large part of the profits in advertising to build and maintain brand awareness. The hundreds of millions they spend on advertising to develop a global brand name help Coca-Cola and PepsiCo differentiate their products so consumers are more likely to buy a Coke or a Pepsi than a less well-known cola. Moreover, brand loyalty allows both companies to charge a premium or comparatively high price for what is, after all, merely colored water and flavoring.

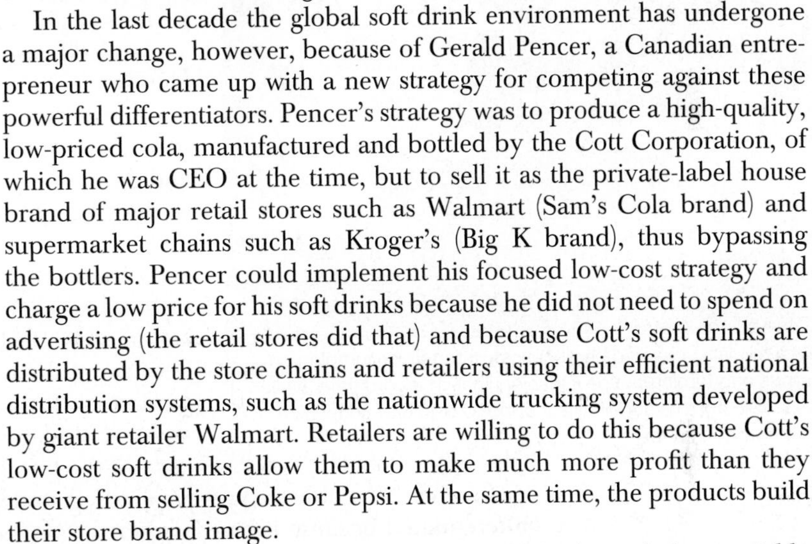

In the last decade the global soft drink environment has undergone a major change, however, because of Gerald Pencer, a Canadian entrepreneur who came up with a new strategy for competing against these powerful differentiators. Pencer's strategy was to produce a high-quality, low-priced cola, manufactured and bottled by the Cott Corporation, of which he was CEO at the time, but to sell it as the private-label house brand of major retail stores such as Walmart (Sam's Cola brand) and supermarket chains such as Kroger's (Big K brand), thus bypassing the bottlers. Pencer could implement his focused low-cost strategy and charge a low price for his soft drinks because he did not need to spend on advertising (the retail stores did that) and because Cott's soft drinks are distributed by the store chains and retailers using their efficient national distribution systems, such as the nationwide trucking system developed by giant retailer Walmart. Retailers are willing to do this because Cott's low-cost soft drinks allow them to make much more profit than they receive from selling Coke or Pepsi. At the same time, the products build their store brand image.

"I'll have a Coke" may not be as easy a decision for much longer, as Cott's and other competitors wedge lower-cost sodas into the big retail chains.

Pencer implemented this plan first in Canada and then quickly expanded into the United States as retailers' demand for his products grew. He went on to supply the international market by offering to sell soft drink concentrate to global retailers at prices lower than Coca-Cola and PepsiCo. By 2004 Cott was the world's largest supplier of retailer-branded carbonated soft drinks.[37] It has manufacturing facilities in Canada, the United States, and the United Kingdom, and a syrup concentrate production plant in Columbus, Georgia, that supply most of the private-label grocery store, drugstore, mass merchandising, and convenience store chains in these countries. However, note that while Cott is the leading supplier of retailer-branded sodas, it is still focusing on its low-cost strategy. It makes no attempt to compete with Coke and Pepsi, which pursue differentiation strategies and whose brand-name sodas dominate the global soda market. Indeed, in 2010 both these companies announced plans to buy back their bottlers at a cost of billions of dollars because this would increase their long-term profits–a strategy known as vertical integration, discussed later in the chapter.[38] But Cott is its own bottler; it knows the value of this strategy.

Increasingly, smaller companies are finding it easier to pursue a focused strategy and compete successfully against large, powerful, low-cost and differentiated companies because of advances in IT that lower costs and enable them to reach and attract customers. By establishing a storefront on the Web, thousands of small, specialized companies have been able to carve out a profitable niche against large bricks-and-mortar competitors. Zara, a Spanish manufacturer of fashionable clothing whose sales have soared in recent years, provides an excellent example of the way even a small bricks-and mortar company can use IT to pursue a focused strategy and compete globally.[39] Zara has managed to position itself as the low-price, low-cost leader in the fashion segment of the clothing market, against differentiators like Gucci, Dior, and Armani, because it has applied IT to its specific needs. Zara has created IT that allows it to manage its design and manufacturing process in a way that minimizes the inventory it has to carry–the major cost borne by a clothing retailer. However, its IT also gives its designers instantaneous feedback on which clothes are selling well and in which countries, and this gives Zara a competitive advantage from differentiation. Specifically, Zara can manufacture more of a particular kind of dress or suit to meet high customer demand, decide which clothing should be sold in its rapidly expanding network of global stores, and constantly change the mix of clothes it offers customers to keep up with fashion–at low cost.

Zara models an incredibly successful strategy in jumping on trends and turning out new fashion lines in record time, while its smart store layout allows shoppers to quickly find which styles appeal to them.

Zara's IT also lets it efficiently manage the interface between its design and manufacturing operations. Zara takes only five weeks to design a new collection and then a week to make it. Fashion houses like Chanel and Armani, by contrast, can take six or more months to design a collection and then three more months to make it available in stores.[40] This short time to market gives Zara great flexibility and allows the company to respond quickly to the rapidly changing fashion market, in which fashions can change several times a year. Because of the quick manufacturing-to-sales cycle and just-in-time fashion, Zara offers its clothes collections at relatively low prices and still makes profits that are the envy of the fashion clothing industry.[41]

Zara has been able to pursue a focused strategy that is simultaneously low-cost and differentiated because it has developed many strengths in functions such as clothing design, marketing, and IT that have given it a competitive advantage. Developing functional-level strategies that strengthen business-level strategy and increase competitive advantage is a vital managerial task. Discussion of this important issue is left until the next chapter. First, we need to go up one planning level and examine how corporate strategy helps an organization achieve its mission and goals.

Formulating Corporate-Level Strategies

Once managers have formulated the business-level strategies that will best position a company, or a division of a company, to compete in an industry and outperform its rivals, they must look to the future. If their planning has been successful the company will be generating high profits, and their task now is to plan how to invest these profits to increase performance over time.

Recall that *corporate-level strategy* is a plan of action that involves choosing in which industries and countries a company should invest its resources to achieve its mission and goals. In choosing a corporate-level strategy, managers ask, How should the growth and development of our company be managed to increase its ability to create value for customers (and thus increase its performance) over the long run? Managers of effective organizations actively seek new opportunities to use a company's resources to create new and improved

LO8-4 Differentiate between the main types of corporate-level strategies and explain how they are used to strengthen a company's business-level strategy and competitive advantage.

goods and services for customers. Examples of organizations whose product lines are growing rapidly are Google, Intel, Apple, and Toyota, whose managers pursue any feasible opportunity to use their companies' skills to provide customers with new products.

In addition, some managers must help their organizations respond to threats due to changing forces in the task or general environment that have made their business-level strategies less effective and reduced profits. For example, customers may no longer be buying the kinds of goods and services a company is producing (high-salt soup, bulky CRTtelevisions, or gas-guzzling SUVs), or other organizations may have entered the market and attracted away customers (this happened to Sony in the 2000s after Apple and Samsung began to produce better portable music players, laptops, and flat-screen LCD televisions). Top managers aim to find corporate strategies that can help the organization strengthen its business-level strategies and thus respond to these changes and improve performance.

The principal corporate-level strategies that managers use to help a company grow and keep it at the top of its industry, or to help it retrench and reorganize to stop its decline, are (1) concentration on a single industry, (2) vertical integration, (3) diversification, and (4) international expansion. An organization will benefit from pursuing any of these strategies only when the strategy helps further increase the value of the organization's goods and services so more customers buy them. Specifically, to increase the value of goods and services, a corporate-level strategy must help a company, or one of its divisions, either (1) lower the costs of developing and making products or (2) increase product differentiation so more customers want to buy the products even at high or premium prices. Both of these outcomes strengthen a company's competitive advantage and increase its performance.

Concentration on a Single Industry

concentration on a single industry Reinvesting a company's profits to strengthen its competitive position in its current industry.

Most growing companies reinvest their profits to strengthen their competitive position in the industry in which they are currently operating; in doing so, they pursue the corporate-level strategy of **concentration on a single industry.** Most commonly, an organization uses its functional skills to develop new kinds of products, or it expands the number of locations in which it uses those skills. For example, Apple continuously introduces improved iPods and mobile wireless devices such as the iPhone and iPad, whereas McDonald's, which began as one restaurant in California, focused all its efforts on using its resources to quickly expand across the globe to become the biggest and most profitable U.S. fast-food company. On the other hand, concentration on a single industry becomes an appropriate corporate-level strategy when managers see the need to *reduce* the size of their organizations to increase performance. Managers may decide to get out of certain industries when, for example, the business-level strategy pursued by a particular division no longer works and the division has lost its competitive advantage. To improve performance, managers can sell off low-performing divisions, concentrate remaining organizational resources in one industry, and try to develop new products customers want to buy. For example, Campbell sold its Godiva chocolate division and invested the proceeds in its core food and snack divisions.

By contrast, when organizations are performing effectively, they often decide to enter new industries in which they can use their resources to create more valuable products. Thus they begin to pursue vertical integration or diversification–such as Coca-Cola, PepsiCo, and Cisco Systems, discussed earlier.

Vertical Integration

When an organization is performing well in its industry, managers often see new opportunities to create value either by producing the inputs it uses to make its products or by distributing and selling its products to customers. Managers at E. & J. Gallo Winery, for example, realized they could lower Gallo's costs if the company produced

Figure 8.6
Stages in a Vertical Value Chain

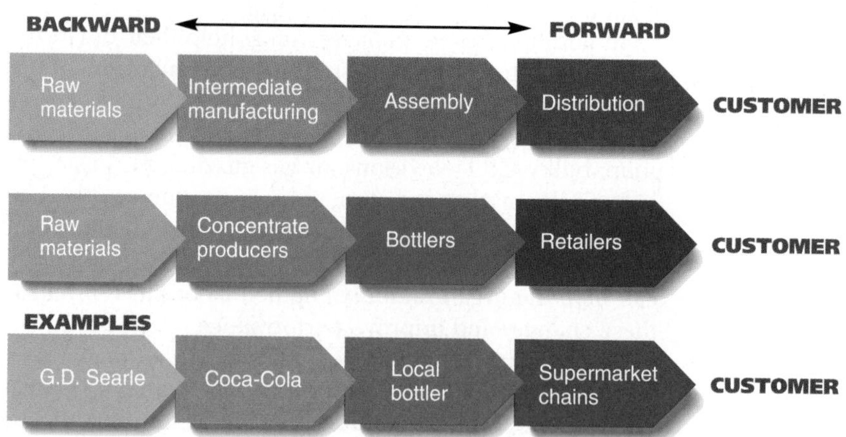

its own wine bottles rather than buying bottles from a glass company that was earning good profits from its bottle sales to Gallo. So Gallo established a new division to produce glass bottles more cheaply than buying them; it quickly found it could also produce bottles in new shapes to help differentiate its wines. **Vertical integration** is a corporate-level strategy in which a company expands its business operations either backward into a new industry that produces inputs for the company's products (*backward vertical integration*) or forward into a new industry that uses, distributes, or sells the company's products (*forward vertical integration*).[42] A steel company that buys iron ore mines and enters the raw materials industry to supply the ore needed to make steel is engaging in backward vertical integration. A PC maker that decides to enter the retail industry and open a chain of company-owned retail outlets to sell its PCs is engaging in forward integration. For example, Apple entered the retail industry when it set up a chain of Apple stores to sell its computers and other electronic devices.

vertical integration
Expanding a company's operations either backward into an industry that produces inputs for its products or forward into an industry that uses, distributes, or sells its products.

Figure 8.6 illustrates the four main stages in a typical raw material to customer value chain; value is added to the product at each stage by the activities involved in each industry. For a company based in the assembly stage, backward integration would involve establishing a new division in the intermediate manufacturing or raw material production industries; and forward integration would involve establishing a new division to distribute its products to wholesalers or a retail division to sell directly to customers. A division at one stage or one industry receives the product produced by the division in the previous stage or industry, transforms it in some way–adding value–and then transfers the output at a higher price to the division at the next stage in the chain.

As an example of how this industry value chain works, consider the cola segment of the soft drink industry. In the raw material industry, suppliers include sugar companies and manufacturers of artificial sweeteners such as NutraSweet and Splenda, which are used in diet colas. These companies sell their products to companies in the soft drink industry that make concentrate–such as Coca-Cola and PepsiCo, which mix these inputs with others to produce the cola concentrate. In the process, they add value to these inputs. The concentrate producers then sell the concentrate to companies in the bottling and distribution industry, which add carbonated water to the concentrate and package the resulting drinks–again adding value to the concentrate. Next the bottlers distribute and sell the soft drinks to retailers, including stores such as Costco and Walmart and fast-food chains such as McDonald's. Companies in the retail industry add value by making the product accessible to customers, and they profit from direct sales to customers. Thus value is added by companies at each stage in the raw material to consumer chain.

The reason managers pursue vertical integration is that it allows them either to add value to their products by making them special or unique or to lower the costs of making and selling them. An example of using forward vertical integration to increase differentiation is Apple's decision to open its own stores to make its unique products more accessible to customers who could try them out before they bought them. An example of using forward vertical integration to lower costs is Matsushita's decision to open company-owned stores to sell its Panasonic and JVC products and thus keep the profit that otherwise would be earned by independent retailers.[43] So too is Coca-Cola and PepsiCo's decision to buy their bottlers so they can better differentiate their products and lower costs in the future.

Although vertical integration can strengthen an organization's competitive advantage and increase its performance, it can also reduce an organization's flexibility to respond to changing environmental conditions and create threats that must be countered by changing the organization's strategy. For example, IBM used to produce most of the components of its mainframe computers. Although this made sense in the past when IBM enjoyed a major competitive advantage, it became a major handicap for the company in the 1990s when the increasing use of organizationwide networks of PCs cut demand for mainframes. IBM had lost its competitive advantage and found itself with an excess capacity problem in its component operations. Closing down this capacity by exiting the computer components industry cost IBM over $5 billion.[44]

Thus, when considering vertical integration as a strategy to add value, managers must be careful because sometimes it may *reduce* a company's ability to create value when the environment changes. This is why so many companies now outsource the production of component parts to other companies and, like IBM, have exited the components industry–by vertically *disintegrating* backward. IBM, however, found a profitable new opportunity for forward vertical integration in the 2000s: It entered the IT consulting services industry to provide advice to large companies about how to install and manage their computer hardware and software, which has become the major source of IBM's profitability in the 2000s.[45]

Diversification

diversification Expanding a company's business operations into a new industry in order to produce new kinds of valuable goods or services.

Diversification is the corporate-level strategy of expanding a company's business operations into a new industry in order to produce new kinds of valuable goods or services.[46] Examples include PepsiCo's diversification into the snack food business with the purchase of Frito Lay, and Cisco's diversification into consumer electronics when it purchased Linksys. There are two main kinds of diversification: related and unrelated.

related diversification Entering a new business or industry to create a competitive advantage in one or more of an organization's existing divisions or businesses.

synergy Performance gains that result when individuals and departments coordinate their actions.

RELATED DIVERSIFICATION **Related diversification** is the strategy of entering a new business or industry to create a competitive advantage in one or more of an organization's existing divisions or businesses. Related diversification can add value to an organization's products if managers can find ways for its various divisions or business units to share their valuable skills or resources so that synergy is created.[47] **Synergy** is obtained when the value created by two divisions cooperating is greater than the value that would be created if the two divisions operated separately and independently. For example, suppose two or more divisions of a diversified company can use the same manufacturing facilities, distribution channels, or advertising campaigns–that is, share functional activities. Each division has to invest fewer resources in a shared functional activity than it would have to invest if it performed the functional activity by itself. Related diversification can be a major source of cost savings when divisions share the costs of performing a functional activity.[48] Similarly, if one division's R&D skills can improve another division's products and increase their differentiated appeal, this synergy can give the second division an important competitive advantage over its industry rivals–so the company as a whole benefits from diversification.

The way Procter & Gamble's disposable diaper and paper towel divisions cooperate is a good example of the successful production of synergies. These divisions share the costs of procuring inputs such as paper and packaging; a joint sales force sells both products to retail outlets; and both products are shipped using the same distribution system. This resource sharing has enabled both divisions to reduce their costs, and as a result, they can charge lower prices than their competitors and so attract more customers.[49] In addition, the divisions can share the research costs of developing new and improved products, such as finding more absorbent material, that increase both products' differentiated appeal. This is something that is also at the heart of 3M's corporate strategy, which is discussed in the following "Management Insight" box.

Management Insight

How to Make Related Diversification Work

3M is a 100-year-old industrial giant that in 2009 generated over $23 billion in revenues and over $6 billion in profits from its more than 50,000 individual products, ranging from sandpaper and adhesive tape to medical devices, office supplies, and electronic components.[50] From the beginning, 3M has pursued related diversification and created new businesses by leveraging its skills in research and development. Today the company is composed of more than 40 separate divisions positioned in six major business groups: transportation, health care, industrial, consumer and office, electronics and communications, and specialty materials. The company currently operates with the goal of producing 40% of sales revenues from products introduced within the previous four years. Its CEO George Buckley's mission was to "kick-start growth," and he has achieved this by increasing spending on R&D to almost $1 billion or about 6% of sales.[51]

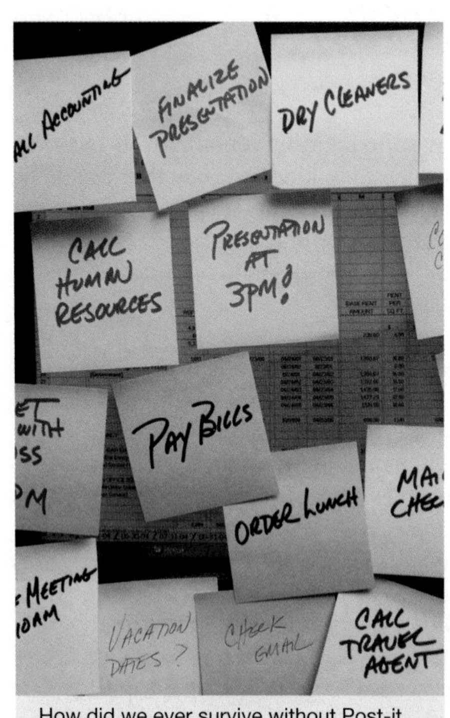

How did we ever survive without Post-it Notes? 3M's intense focus on solving customer problems results in new products that sell well, including countless variations of the original sticky note.

How does 3M do it? First, the company is a science-based enterprise with a strong tradition of innovation and risk taking. Risk taking is encouraged, and failure is not punished but is seen as a natural part of the process of creating new products and business.[52] Second, 3M's management is relentlessly focused on the company's customers and the problems they face. Many of 3M's products have come from helping customers to solve difficult problems. Third, managers set stretch goals that require the company to create new products and businesses at a rapid rate. Fourth, employees are given considerable autonomy to pursue their own ideas; indeed, 15% of employees' time can be spent working on projects of their own choosing without management approval. Many products have resulted from this autonomy, including the ubiquitous Post-it Notes. Fifth, while products belong to business units and business units are responsible for generating profits, the technologies belong to every unit within the company. Anyone at 3M is free to try to develop new applications for a technology developed by its business units. Finally, 3M organizes many companywide meetings where researchers from its different divisions are brought together to share the results of their work. It also implemented an IT system that promotes the sharing of technological knowledge between researchers so new opportunities can be identified.

In sum, to pursue related diversification successfully, managers search for new businesses where they can use the existing skills and resources in their departments and divisions to create synergies, add value to new products and businesses, and improve their competitive position and that of the entire company. In addition, managers may try to acquire a company in a new industry because they believe it possesses skills and resources that will improve the performance of one or more of their existing divisions–this is Cisco's strategy that was discussed at the beginning of the chapter. If successful, such skill transfers can help an organization to lower its costs or better differentiate its products because they create synergies between divisions.

unrelated diversification Entering a new industry or buying a company in a new industry that is not related in any way to an organization's current businesses or industries.

UNRELATED DIVERSIFICATION Managers pursue **unrelated diversification** when they establish divisions or buy companies in new industries that are *not* linked in any way to their current businesses or industries. One main reason for pursuing unrelated diversification is that sometimes managers can buy a poorly performing company, transfer their management skills to that company, turn around its business, and increase its performance–all of which create value.

Another reason for pursuing unrelated diversification is that purchasing businesses in different industries lets managers engage in *portfolio strategy,* which is apportioning financial resources among divisions to increase financial returns or spread risks among different businesses, much as individual investors do with their own portfolios. For example, managers may transfer funds from a rich division (a "cash cow") to a new and promising division (a "star") and, by appropriately allocating money between divisions, create value. Though used as a popular explanation in the 1980s for unrelated diversification, portfolio strategy ran into increasing criticism in the 1990s because it simply does not work.[53] Why? As managers expand the scope of their organization's operations and enter more and more industries, it becomes increasingly difficult for top managers to be knowledgeable about all of the organization's diverse businesses. Managers do not have the time to process all of the information required to adequately assess the strategy and performance of each division, and so the performance of the entire company often falls.

This problem has occurred at GE, as its then CEO Reg Jones commented: "I tried to review each business unit plan in great detail. This effort took untold hours and placed a tremendous burden on the corporate executive office. After a while I began to realize that no matter how hard we would work, we could not achieve the necessary in-depth understanding of the 40-odd business unit plans."[54] Unable to handle so much information, top managers are overwhelmed and eventually make important resource allocation decisions on the basis of only a superficial analysis of the competitive position of each division. This usually results in value being lost rather than created.[55]

Thus, although unrelated diversification can potentially create value for a company, research evidence suggests that *too much* diversification can cause managers to lose control of their organization's core business. As a result, diversification can reduce value rather than create it.[56] Because of this, during the last decade there has been an increasing trend for diversified companies to divest many of their unrelated, and sometimes related, divisions. Managers in companies like Tyco, Dial, and Textron have sold off many or most of their divisions and focused on increasing the performance of the core division that remained–in other words, they went back to a strategy of concentrating on a single industry.[57] For example, in 2007 Tyco split into three different companies when it spun off its health care and electronics businesses and focused its activities on engineered and fire and security products, such as its ADT home security business.[58] By 2008 each of the different companies was performing at a higher level under its own team of top managers, by 2010 each division's performance had improved even further.[59]

International Expansion

As if planning whether to vertically integrate, diversify, or concentrate on the core business were not a difficult enough task, corporate-level managers also must decide on the appropriate way to compete internationally. A basic question confronts the managers of any organization that needs to sell its products abroad and compete in more than one national market: To what extent should the organization customize features of its products and marketing campaign to different national conditions?[60]

global strategy Selling the same standardized product and using the same basic marketing approach in each national market.

multidomestic strategy Customizing products and marketing strategies to specific national conditions.

If managers decide that their organization should sell the same standardized product in each national market in which it competes, and use the same basic marketing approach, they adopt a **global strategy.**[61] Such companies undertake little, if any, customization to suit the specific needs of customers in different countries. But if managers decide to customize products and marketing strategies to specific national conditions, they adopt a **multidomestic strategy.** Matsushita, with its Panasonic and JVC brands, has traditionally pursued a global strategy, selling the same basic TVs, camcorders, and DVD and MP3 players in every country in which it does business and often using the same basic marketing approach. Unilever, the European food and household products company, has pursued a multidomestic strategy. Thus, to appeal to German customers, Unilever's German division sells a different range of food products and uses a different marketing approach than its North American division.

Both global and multidomestic strategies have advantages and disadvantages. The major advantage of a global strategy is the significant cost savings associated with not having to customize products and marketing approaches to different national conditions. For example, Rolex watches, Ralph Lauren or Tommy Hilfiger clothing, Chanel or Armani clothing or accessories or perfume, Dell computers, Chinese-made plastic toys and buckets, and U.S.-grown rice and wheat are all products that can be sold using the same marketing across many countries by simply changing the language. Thus companies can save a significant amount of money. The major disadvantage of pursuing a global strategy is that by ignoring national differences, managers may leave themselves vulnerable to local competitors that differentiate their products to suit local tastes.

Global food makers Kellogg's and Nestlé learned this when they entered the Indian processed food market, which is worth over $100 billion a year. These companies did not understand how to customize their products to the tastes of the Indian market and initially suffered large losses. When Kellogg's launched its breakfast cereals in India, for example, it failed to understand that most Indians eat cooked breakfasts because milk is normally not pasteurized. Today, with the growing availability of pasteurized or canned milk, it offers exotic cereals made from basmati rice and flavored with mango to appeal to customers. Similarly, Nestlé's Maggi noodles failed to please Indian customers until it gave them a "marsala" or mixed curry spice flavor; today its noodles have became a staple in Indian school lunches.

The advantages and disadvantages of a multidomestic strategy are the opposite of those of a global strategy. The major advantage of a multidomestic strategy is that by customizing product offerings and marketing approaches to local conditions, managers may be able to gain market share or charge higher prices for their products. The major disadvantage is that customization raises production costs and puts the multidomestic company at a price disadvantage because it often has to charge prices higher than the prices charged by competitors pursuing a global strategy. Obviously the choice between these two strategies calls for trade-offs.

Managers at Gillette, the well-known razor blade maker that is now part of Procter & Gamble (P&G), created a strategy that combined the best features of both international strategies. Like P&G, Gillette has always been a global organization because its managers quickly saw the advantages of selling its core product, razor blades, in as many countries as possible. Gillette's strategy over the years has been pretty constant: Find a new country with a growing market for razor blades, form a strategic alliance with a local razor blade company and take a majority stake in it, invest in a large marketing campaign, and then build a modern factory to make razor blades and other products for the local market. For example, when Gillette entered Russia after the breakup of the Soviet Union, it saw a huge opportunity to increase sales. It formed a joint venture with a local company called Leninets Concern, which made a razor known as the Sputnik, and then with this base began to import its own brands into Russia. When sales grew sharply, Gillette decided to offer more products in the market and built a new plant in St. Petersburg.[62]

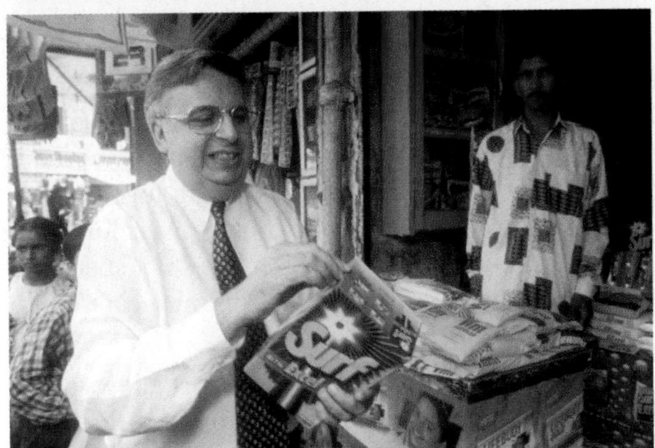

A study in contrasts. Matsushita, with its Panasonic brand (shown on the top), has largely pursued a global strategy, selling the same basic TVs and DVD players in every market and using a similar marketing message. Unilever, on the other hand, has pursued a multidomestic strategy, tailoring its product line and marketing approach to specific locations. On the bottom, the CEO of Hindustan Unilever, Keki Dadiseth, holds a box of Surf detergent designed for local customers.

In establishing factories in countries where labor and other costs are low and then distributing and marketing its products to countries in that region of the world, Gillette pursued a global strategy. However, all of Gillette's research and development and design activities are located in the United States. As it develops new kinds of razors, it equips its foreign factories to manufacture them when it decides that local customers are ready to trade up to the new product. So, for example, Gillette's latest razor may be introduced in a country abroad years later than in the United States. Thus Gillette is customizing its products to the needs of different countries and so also pursues a multidomestic strategy.

By pursuing this kind of international strategy, Gillette achieves low costs and still differentiates and customizes its product range to suit the needs of each country or world region.[63] P&G pursues a similar international strategy, and the merger between them to create the world's largest consumer products company came about because of the value that could be realized by pursuing related diversification at a global level. For example, P&G's corporate managers realized that substantial global synergies could be obtained by combining their global manufacturing, distribution, and sales operations across countries and world regions. These synergies have saved billions of dollars.[64] At the same time, by pooling their knowledge of the needs of customers in different countries, the combined companies can better differentiate and position products throughout the world. P&G's strategy is working; its principal competitors Colgate and Unilever have not performed well in the 2000s, and P&G has developed a commanding global position.

CHOOSING A WAY TO EXPAND INTERNATIONALLY

As we have discussed, a more competitive global environment has proved to be both an opportunity and a threat for organizations and managers. The opportunity is that organizations that expand globally can open new markets, reach more customers, and gain access to new sources of raw materials and to low-cost suppliers of inputs. The threat is that organizations that expand globally are likely to encounter new competitors in the foreign countries they enter and must respond to new political, economic, and cultural conditions.

Before setting up foreign operations, managers of companies such as Amazon.com, Lands' End, GE, P&G, and Boeing needed to analyze the forces in the environment of a particular country (such as Korea or Brazil) to choose the right method to expand and respond to those forces in the most appropriate way. In general, four basic ways to operate in the global environment are importing and exporting, licensing and franchising, strategic alliances, and wholly owned foreign subsidiaries, Gillette's preferred approach. We briefly discuss each one, moving from the lowest level of foreign involvement and investment required of a global organization and its managers, and the least amount of risk, to the high end of the spectrum (see Figure 8.7).[65]

exporting Making products at home and selling them abroad.

IMPORTING AND EXPORTING The least complex global operations are exporting and importing. A company engaged in **exporting** makes products at home and sells them abroad. An organization might sell its own products abroad or allow a local organization in the foreign country to distribute its products. Few risks are associated with exporting because a company does not have to invest in developing manufacturing facilities abroad. It can further reduce its investment abroad if it allows a local company to distribute its products.

Figure 8.7

Four Ways to Expand Internationally

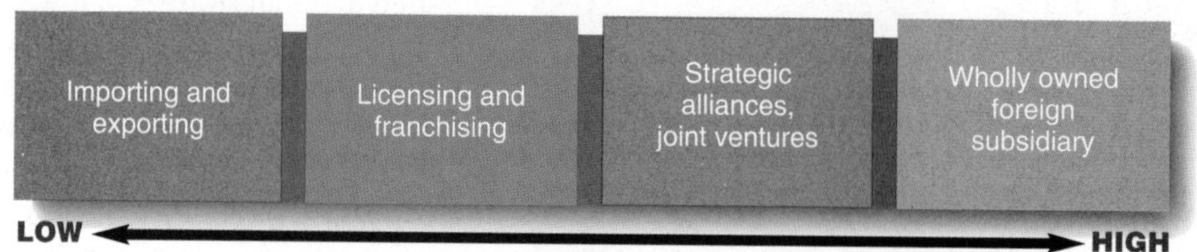

importing Selling products at home that are made abroad.

A company engaged in **importing** sells products at home that are made abroad (products it makes itself or buys from other companies). For example, most of the products that Pier 1 Imports and The Limited sell to their customers are made abroad. In many cases the appeal of a product–Irish crystal, French wine, Italian furniture, or Indian silk–is that it is made abroad. The Internet has made it much easier for companies to tell potential foreign buyers about their products; detailed product specifications and features are available online, and informed buyers can communicate easily with prospective sellers.

licensing Allowing a foreign organization to take charge of manufacturing and distributing a product in its country or world region in return for a negotiated fee.

LICENSING AND FRANCHISING In **licensing,** a company (the licenser) allows a foreign organization (the licensee) to take charge of both manufacturing and distributing one or more of its products in the licensee's country or world region in return for a negotiated fee. Chemical maker DuPont might license a local factory in India to produce nylon or Teflon. The advantage of licensing is that the licenser does not have to bear the development costs associated with opening up in a foreign country; the licensee bears the costs. The risks associated with this strategy are that the company granting the license has to give its foreign partner access to its technological know-how and so risks losing control of its secrets.

franchising Selling to a foreign organization the rights to use a brand name and operating know-how in return for a lump-sum payment and a share of the profits.

Whereas licensing is pursued primarily by manufacturing companies, franchising is pursued primarily by service organizations. In **franchising,** a company (the franchiser) sells to a foreign organization (the franchisee) the rights to use its brand name and operating know-how in return for a lump-sum payment and share of the franchiser's profits. Hilton Hotels might sell a franchise to a local company in Chile to operate hotels under the Hilton name in return for a franchise payment. The advantage of franchising is that the franchiser does not have to bear the development costs of overseas expansion and avoids the many problems associated with setting up foreign operations. The downside is that the organization that grants the franchise may lose control over how the franchisee operates, and product quality may fall. In this way franchisers, such as Hilton, Avis, and McDonald's, risk losing their good names. American customers who buy McDonald's hamburgers in Korea may reasonably expect those burgers to be as good as the ones they get at home. If they are not, McDonald's reputation will suffer over time. Once again, the Internet facilitates communication between partners and allows them to better meet each other's expectations.

strategic alliance An agreement in which managers pool or share their organization's resources and know-how with a foreign company, and the two organizations share the rewards and risks of starting a new venture.

STRATEGIC ALLIANCES One way to overcome the loss-of-control problems associated with exporting, licensing, and franchising is to expand globally by means of a strategic alliance. In a **strategic alliance,** managers pool or share their organization's resources and know-how with those of a foreign company, and the two organizations share the rewards or risks of starting a new venture in a foreign country. Sharing resources allows a U.S. company, for example, to take advantage of the high-quality skills of foreign manufacturers and the specialized knowledge of foreign managers about the needs of local customers and to reduce the risks involved in a venture.

At the same time, the terms of the alliance give the U.S. company more control over how the good or service is produced or sold in the foreign country than it would have as a franchiser or licenser.

A strategic alliance can take the form of a written contract between two or more companies to exchange resources, or it can result in the creation of a new organization. A **joint venture** is a strategic alliance among two or more companies that agree to jointly establish and share the ownership of a new business.[66] An organization's level of involvement abroad increases in a joint venture because the alliance normally involves a capital investment in production facilities abroad in order to produce goods or services outside the home country. Risk, however, is reduced. The Internet and global teleconferencing provide the increased communication and coordination necessary for global partners to work together. For example, Coca-Cola and Nestlé formed a joint venture to market their teas, coffees, and health-oriented beverages in more than 50 countries.[67] Similarly, BP Amoco and Italy's ENI formed a joint venture to build a $2.5 billion gas liquefaction plant in Egypt.[68]

joint venture A strategic alliance among two or more companies that agree to jointly establish and share the ownership of a new business.

WHOLLY OWNED FOREIGN SUBSIDIARIES When managers decide to establish a **wholly owned foreign subsidiary,** they invest in establishing production operations in a foreign country independent of any local direct involvement. Many Japanese car component companies, for example, have established their own operations in the United States to supply U.S.-based Japanese carmakers such as Toyota and Honda with high-quality car components.

wholly owned foreign subsidiary Production operations established in a foreign country independent of any local direct involvement.

Operating alone, without any direct involvement from foreign companies, an organization receives all of the rewards and bears all of the risks associated with operating abroad.[69] This method of international expansion is much more expensive than the others because it requires a higher level of foreign investment and presents managers with many more threats. However, investment in a foreign subsidiary or division offers significant advantages: It gives an organization high potential returns because the organization does not have to share its profits with a foreign organization, and it reduces the level of risk because the organization's managers have full control over all aspects of their foreign subsidiary's operations. Moreover, this type of investment allows managers to protect their technology and know-how from foreign organizations. Large, well-known companies like DuPont, General Motors, and P&G, which have plenty of resources, make extensive use of wholly owned subsidiaries. Recall from Chapter 6 that Nokia establishes a wholly owned manufacturing subsidiary in each world region to make the mobile phones it sells in that region.

Obviously, global companies can use many of these different corporate strategies simultaneously to create the most value and strengthen their competitive position. We discussed earlier how P&G pursues related diversification at the global level while it pursues an international strategy that is a mixture of global and multidomestic. P&G also pursues vertical integration: It operates factories that make many of the specialized chemicals used in its products; it operates in the container industry and makes the thousands of different glass and plastic bottles and jars that contain its products; it prints its own product labels; and it distributes its products using its own fleet of trucks. Although P&G is highly diversified, it still puts the focus on its core individual product lines because it is famous for pursuing brand management–it concentrates resources around each brand, which in effect is managed as a "separate company." So P&G is trying to add value in every way it can from its corporate and business strategies. At the business level, for example, P&G aggressively pursues differentiation and charges premium prices for its products. However, it also strives to lower its costs and pursues the corporate-level strategies just discussed to achieve this. The way in which Samsung, the second largest global electronics company (discussed in the following "Managing Globally" box), chose to expand globally also illustrates the complex issues surrounding developing the right strategies to expand globally.

Managing Globally

How Samsung Became a Global Technology Leader

In the 2000s Samsung Electronics, based in Seoul, Korea, became the second most profitable global technology company after Microsoft. Samsung accomplished this when its CEO Lee Kun Hee decided to develop and build competencies first in low-cost manufacturing, and second in R&D, and then use them to make new and improved products for customers the world over.

Samsung's core industry is the consumer electronics industry; in the 1990s its engineers studied how companies such as Sony, Panasonic, Motorola, and Nokia had innovated products such as the Walkman, home video recorders, high-quality televisions, and cell phones. Then they imitated this technology but used Samsung's low-cost advantage to make lower-priced versions of these products that they could sell at lower prices. For example, Samsung decided to enter the cell phone industry and to make lower-cost phones than companies such as Nokia and Motorola. Samsung also entered the semiconductor industry in which it worked to make the lowest-cost memory chips; soon it became the global cost leader. It also entered markets for other digital products such as cameras, printers, and storage devices.

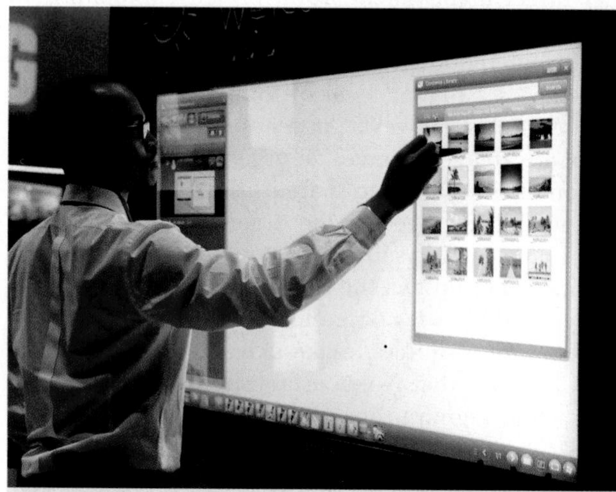

As this Samsung employee demonstrates, the invention of color screens hit a sweet spot in the digital phone market; now we can't live without carrying around detailed photos of our dogs, friends, and workplaces.

Samsung was pursuing the corporate-level strategy of related diversification; its goal was to increase its profitability by using and developing its core competencies in product development and manufacturing to enter new industries and produce attractive new products for global customers. Samsung's strategy was successful and profitable, but it was not playing in the same league as Sony or Nokia, for example. CEO Hee decided to adopt new strategies that would allow his company to compete head-to-head with leading global electronics companies to make it a global technology leader. Now Samsung's goal was not to imitate technology innovated by Sony, Nokia, and so on, but for its engineers to develop the R&D skills necessary to develop leading-edge technologies, such as LCD displays, to create products more advanced than those of its competitors.[70]

Within a decade, SE became the leading supplier of advanced flash memory chips and LCD screens—premium-priced products that it sold to other global electronics makers, including Japanese flat screen TV makers such as Sony. Samsung also developed a new core competence in global marketing. For example, in the early 2000s Samsung was first to realize customers wanted color screens for their cell phones to play games and built-in cameras to send photographs to their friends. Both of these incremental advances allowed Samsung to increase its share of the cell phone market; it has become the second largest cell phone maker after Nokia.[71]

Today Samsung has become one of the most innovative global electronics makers; however, like most other electronics companies it has been forced to find ways to reduce costs because of the global recession. In 2009 Samsung's new CEO Lee Yoon Woo announced a major restructuring that would consolidate its four global divisions into two to reduce costs but still speed product development. Samsung's semiconductor and LCD display businesses are now combined into a new Device Solutions Division, and its television, mobile phone, and consumer electronics products such as printers and computers are in the Digital Media and Communications Division. Because all of Samsung's products use in-house chips and LCD displays, this means that while SE is pursuing related diversification, it is also using its low-cost skills to benefit from vertical integration as it continues its rapid global expansion.

Planning and Implementing Strategy

After identifying appropriate business and corporate strategies to attain an organization's mission and goals, managers confront the challenge of putting those strategies into action. Strategy implementation is a five-step process:

LO8-5 Describe the vital role managers play in implementing strategies to achieve an organization's mission and goals.

1. Allocating responsibility for implementation to the appropriate individuals or groups.
2. Drafting detailed action plans that specify how a strategy is to be implemented.
3. Establishing a timetable for implementation that includes precise, measurable goals linked to the attainment of the action plan.
4. Allocating appropriate resources to the responsible individuals or groups.
5. Holding specific individuals or groups responsible for the attainment of corporate, divisional, and functional goals.

The planning process goes beyond just identifying effective strategies; it also includes plans to ensure that these strategies are put into action. Normally the plan for implementing a new strategy requires the development of new functional strategies, the redesign of an organization's structure, and the development of new control systems; it might also require a new program to change an organization's culture. These are issues we address in the next three chapters.

Summary and Review

LO8-1, 8-2

PLANNING Planning is a three-step process: (1) determining an organization's mission and goals; (2) formulating strategy; and (3) implementing strategy. Managers use planning to identify and select appropriate goals and courses of action for an organization and to decide how to allocate the resources they need to attain those goals and carry out those actions. A good plan builds commitment for the organization's goals, gives the organization a sense of direction and purpose, coordinates the different functions and divisions of the organization, and controls managers by making them accountable for specific goals. In large organizations planning takes place at three levels: corporate, business or divisional, and functional or departmental. Long-term plans have a time horizon of five years or more; intermediate-term plans, between one and five years; and short-term plans, one year or less.

LO8-1, 8-2, 8-3, 8-4

DETERMINING MISSION AND GOALS AND FORMULATING STRATEGY Determining the organization's mission requires that managers define the business of the organization and establish major goals. Strategy formulation requires that managers perform a SWOT analysis and then choose appropriate strategies at the corporate, business, and functional levels. At the business level, managers are responsible for developing a successful low-cost and/or differentiation strategy, either for the whole market or a particular segment of it. At the functional level, departmental managers develop strategies to help the organization either add value to its products by differentiating them or lower the costs of value creation. At the corporate level, organizations use strategies such as concentration on a single industry, vertical integration, related and unrelated diversification, and international expansion to strengthen their competitive advantage by increasing the value of the goods and services provided to customers.

LO8-5 **IMPLEMENTING STRATEGY** Strategy implementation requires that managers allocate responsibilities to appropriate individuals or groups; draft detailed action plans that specify how a strategy is to be implemented; establish a timetable for implementation that includes precise, measurable goals linked to the attainment of the action plan; allocate appropriate resources to the responsible individuals or groups; and hold individuals or groups accountable for the attainment of goals.

Management in Action

Topics for Discussion and Action

Discussion

1. Describe the three steps of planning. Explain how they are related. [LO8-1]
2. How can scenario planning help managers predict the future? [LO8-2]
3. What is the relationship among corporate-, business-, and functional-level strategies, and how do they create value for an organization? [LO8-3, 8-4]
4. Pick an industry and identify four companies in the industry that pursue one of the four main business-level strategies (low-cost, focused low-cost, and so on). [LO8-2, 8-3]
5. What is the difference between vertical integration and related diversification? [LO8-4]

Action

6. Ask a manager about the kinds of planning exercises he or she regularly uses. What are the purposes of these exercises, and what are their advantages or disadvantages? [LO8-1, 8-2]
7. Ask a manager to identify the corporate- and business-level strategies used by his or her organization. [LO8-3, 8-4]

Building Management Skills

How to Analyze a Company's Strategy [LO8-3, 8-4]

Pick a well-known business organization that has received recent press coverage and that provides annual reports at its Web site. From the information in the articles and annual reports, answer these questions:

1. What is (are) the main industry(ies) in which the company competes?
2. What business-level strategy does the company seem to be pursuing in this industry? Why?
3. What corporate-level strategies is the company pursuing? Why?
4. Have there been any major changes in its strategy recently? Why?

Managing Ethically [LO8-2, 8-5]

A few years ago, IBM announced that it had fired the three top managers of its Argentine division because of their involvement in a scheme to secure a $250 million contract for IBM to provide and service the computers of one of Argentina's largest state-owned banks. The three executives paid $14 million of the contract money to a third company, CCR, which paid nearly $6 million to phantom companies. This $6 million was then used to bribe the bank executives who agreed to give IBM the contract.

These bribes are not necessarily illegal under Argentine law. Moreover, the three managers argued that all companies have to pay bribes to get new business contracts, and they were not doing anything that managers in other companies were not.

Questions

1. Either by yourself or in a group decide if the business practice of paying bribes is ethical or unethical.
2. Should IBM allow its foreign divisions to pay bribes if all other companies are doing so?
3. If bribery is common in a particular country, what effect would this likely have on the nation's economy and culture?

Small Group Breakout Exercise

Low Cost or Differentiation? [LO8-2, 8-3]

Form groups of three or four people, and appoint one member as the spokesperson who will communicate your findings to the class when called on by the instructor. Then discuss the following scenario:

You are a team of managers of a major national clothing chain, and you have been charged with finding a way to restore your organization's competitive advantage. Recently your organization has been experiencing increasing competition from two sources. First, discount stores such as Walmart and Target have been undercutting your prices because they buy their clothes from low-cost foreign manufacturers whereas you buy most of yours from high-quality domestic suppliers. Discount stores have been attracting your customers who buy at the low end of the price range. Second, small boutiques opening in malls provide high-price designer clothing and are attracting your customers at the high end of the market. Your company has become stuck in the middle, and you have to decide what to do: Should you start to buy abroad so you can lower your prices and pursue a low-cost strategy? Should you focus on the high end of the market and become more of a differentiator? Or should you try to pursue both a low-cost strategy and a differentiation strategy?

1. Using scenario planning, analyze the pros and cons of each alternative.
2. Think about the various clothing retailers in your local malls and city, and analyze the choices they have made about how to compete along the low-cost and differentiation dimensions.

Exploring the World Wide Web [LO8-1, 8-3, 8-4]

Go to Google (www.google.com) and click on About Google; then click on Corporate Info and explore this Web page. For example, click on Technology, Business, Culture, Milestones, and the Ten Things that guide Google's corporate philosophy.

1. How would you describe Google's mission and goals?
2. What business-level strategies is Google pursuing? Why?
3. What corporate-level strategies is Google pursuing? Why?

Be the Manager [LO8-2, 8-3]

A group of investors in your city is considering opening a new upscale supermarket to compete with the major supermarket chains that are currently dominating the city's marketplace. They have called you in to help them determine what kind of upscale supermarket they should open. In other words, how can they best develop a competitive advantage against existing supermarket chains?

Questions

1. List the supermarket chains in your city, and identify their strengths and weaknesses.
2. What business-level strategies are these supermarkets currently pursuing?
3. What kind of supermarket would do best against the competition? What kind of business-level strategy should it pursue?

Case in the News [LO8-1, 8-2, 8-3]

How Procter & Gamble Plans to Clean Up

Since becoming chief executive of Procter & Gamble in 2000, A.G. Lafley has never had it tougher. Shares of the world's biggest consumer products company have lost a third of their value since last fall. U.S. shoppers are trading down to private-label products from premium-priced brands such as P&G's Tide, Gillette, and Pampers. And the economic downturn is spilling into developing nations where P&G has notched its best growth. Lafley, nonetheless, seems undaunted. The 61-year-old sat down in his Cincinnati office with *BusinessWeek*'s Roger O. Crockett to talk about managing through the recession. Here are edited excerpts:

On Spending Priorities

We continue to invest in our core strengths. First, we don't skimp in understanding the consumer. Second is innovation. Our capital spending will go up in 2009 for new engineering and manufacturing technology. And third is branding. Although we actually are spending fewer dollars on advertising because the price of media has gone down, we're delivering more messages to our consumers.

On Product Failures

In our industry only 15% to 20% of new products succeed. P&G's success rate is a little over 50%. But we were at that industry average in the 1990s. We improved our batting average by clarifying and simplifying the innovation process. We set checkpoints with clear measures for each phase of the process from ideation through development and commercialization. If a project looks like it will not make it, we drop it. You learn more from failure than you do from success but the key is to fail early, fail cheaply, and don't make the same mistake twice.

On Premium Pricing

The key thing to understand is that we're not in the commodity business. We're not selling items that fluctuate based on the price of the input materials. We're selling a brand. We can create better value for $1 with a new Downy dishwashing product in Mexico. Or we can do it for $5 or $10 with a household cleaning product like Tide, or for $40 to $50 with a personal care product like some Olay facial creams. It's all about who is the consumer and what represents value for her.

On Innovation

You need creativity and invention, but until you can connect that creativity to the customer in the form of a product or a service that meaningfully changes their lives, I would argue you don't yet have innovation. We invented a material back in the 1960s that would absorb a lot of water. Until we converted it into a Pampers disposable baby diaper, it was just a new kind of material. We created this entirely new product category, and that created an industry. We'd like to have these kinds of discontinuous innovations be 20% to 25% of what we do. For us to sustain sales and profit growth, we have to innovate.

On P&G's Relationship with Retailers

Virtually every retailer we work with likes the fact that we lead innovation. It creates sales growth in existing categories. It creates new categories that are a source of sales and profit growth in the future. It brings consumers into their stores to try new products, and it brings consumers back to their stores, where they can get products they trust.

On the Rise of Private Labels

Private label is less than 1% of the U.S. retail market, and where it gains traction is in segments that lack innovation. It is difficult to innovate in commodity food categories, which is where private label is winning the most. Private labels are imitators. P&G brands and products are innovators.

On Growth Opportunities

Today we reach a little more than half of the world's 6.7 billion consumers. We want to reach another billion in the next several years, and much of that growth is going to be in the emerging markets, where most babies are being born and where most families are being formed. We see growth across our entire portfolio.

On Acquisitions

Our focus is on long-term, sustainable growth. Acquisitions and divestitures have always been part of that strategy and will continue to be in the future.

On Business Partnerships

Back in 2000 we set a goal of having partners for half of all new products. We hit that goal in 2007–2008. That obviously saves us a lot of money. We can take a P&G dollar and turn it into a dollar and a half to two dollars. Virtually all the work you don't see—taking an order from a retailer or wholesaler, processing orders, scientists working in research centers—is all run collaboratively in back rooms with partners. So our operating margin increases, even though we're still spending on R&D and branding and capital to support innovation.

On Retirement

C'mon, I'm not even 62. I've got some runway left. Right now I'm focused like a laser on P&G and P&G stakeholders. It will probably be something a lot different at 65 and beyond. But this is a seven-day-a-week job, and I still feel young.

Questions for Discussion

1. What kind of business-level strategy is Procter & Gamble pursuing?
2. What kind of competencies does it possess that allow it to pursue this strategy?
3. In what ways is it using other kinds of strategies, such as acquisitions and business partnerships, to build its competitive advantage?

Source: Roger O. Crockett, "How Procter & Gamble Plans to Clean Up." Reprinted from April 2, 2009 issue of *Bloomberg Businessweek* by special permission, copyright © 2009 by Bloomberg L.P.

CHAPTER 9

Value Chain Management: Functional Strategies for Competitive Advantage

Learning Objectives

After studying this chapter, you should be able to:

LO9-1 Explain the role of functional strategy and value chain management in achieving superior quality, efficiency, innovation, and responsiveness to customers.

LO9-2 Describe what customers want, and explain why it is so important for managers to be responsive to their needs.

LO9-3 Explain why achieving superior quality is so important, and understand the challenges facing managers and organizations that seek to implement total quality management.

LO9-4 Explain why achieving superior efficiency is so important, and understand the different kinds of techniques that need to be employed to increase efficiency.

LO9-5 Differentiate between two forms of innovation, and explain why innovation and product development are crucial components of the search for competitive advantage.

A MANAGER'S CHALLENGE

Dell Is Battling with HP and Apple to Create Value for Customers

How can managers increase operating performance? In 2005 Dell had a market value of over $100 billion, more than HP and Apple combined; but by March 2010 its value had dropped to $30 billion while Apple's was $210 billion and HP's was $125 billion![1] Why? The major reason was that Dell's value chain management practices failed in the 2000s because it lost its focus on the customer and its managers could not innovate the kinds of PCs and mobile computing devices that they desired. Dell became the leading global PC maker because its mastery in materials management and supply chain management allowed it to obtain computer components, assemble them into final products, and sell them to customers far more efficiently than its competitors. At its peak, for example, it had a 20% cost advantage over HP and Apple because it assembled its computers at low-cost global locations and instructed its suppliers to open parts warehouses next to its factories to take advantage of "just-in-time" inventory systems that lowered its production costs.

Dell, however, was able to achieve this enormous efficiency advantage only by sacrificing its ability to customize its PCs to the needs of its customers—that is, to be flexible in meeting their needs. Just as Henry Ford told customers they could have any Model T car color they wanted "as long as it is black," so Dell's computers were uniformly a color such as beige or black because such standardization is an important way to keep costs low. At the same time it increases quality and reliability because workers become expert at assembling a product when they continuously perform the same work tasks, such as assembling the same set of PC components into the final product. Customers were happy to purchase Dell's products because they were much less expensive than those of its rivals; and recall

Michael Dell (far left) returned to his troubled company in 2007 and attempted to inject new life with the appointment of Ronald Garriques (far right). Time will tell if their new approach appeals to consumers.

from Chapter 1 that Dell also pioneered direct phone sales to sell its computers at rock-bottom prices.

Dell's problems steadily increased in the 2000s because its rivals learned how to manage their supply chains and outsourced PC manufacturing to reduce costs. And unlike Dell, HP and Apple have always made innovation an important component of their value chain management strategies. These companies have consistently spent billions of dollars to innovate new and improved components and products. Although this put them at a cost disadvantage in the past (because R&D increases total costs), today their competence in innovation allows them to satisfy customer needs for more stylish, powerful, and versatile PCs and portable digital devices. This has given them a competitive advantage over Dell—hence the dramatic change in the values of these companies over the 2000s.

Michael Dell returned as CEO in 2007 when he realized that his company was quickly losing its competitive advantage because Apple and HP could manage their values chains while being more responsive to customers by offering them innovative, customized products that better satisfied their needs. To help him turn around the company, Dell brought in a new team of value chain management experts from companies such as IBM, GE, and Motorola. In particular, from Motorola he hired Ronald Garriques, the former head of its mobile devices division, who had led the successful launch of the Razr cell phone, to head Dell's consumer division. Michael Dell realized that control of the new world of mobile digital computing would be key to Dell's future success; he asked Garriques to develop innovative new lines of desktop, laptop, and mobile digital devices that could compete successfully against those of Apple and HP.

Garriques immediately ended projects he felt would not result in the flexible computing solutions customers wanted, and he formed new teams of engineers and instructed them to design a new generation of innovative computing products. He also began to manage Dell's value chain to focus on meeting customer needs, and he demanded that engineers design products that could be increasingly customized. At the same time, Dell could not lose its focus on efficiency; so Garriques also changed how it managed its supply chain. Dell has closed down many of its global and U.S. factories and has outsourced production to Asian companies. Garriques also decided Dell had to find new ways to distribute its products; in 2007 it began to sell its PCs to retailers such as Walmart to reach more customers and compete with HP. HP had found this to be a highly profitable distribution strategy even though it meant lower profit margins.

When Microsoft launched Windows 7 in October 2009, Dell simultaneously introduced the thinnest laptop computer then available, the Adamo, to show it now had the competence in innovation to compete with its rivals; it has since introduced new lines of desktops and laptops. It has also announced a new Dell cell phone and tablet computer to compete with Apple. However, in the spring of 2010, although its sales and profits had improved, they still did not meet analysts' estimates—and its market value did not increase.[2] Some analysts worried that Dell lacked strong value chain skills in R&D and marketing to compete with Apple and HP; others believed its low-cost rivals like Acer and Lenovo would be able to offer customers the lowest prices in the future. The question was whether Dell and his top management team could find ways to develop new competencies in value chain management to regain its competitive advantage and once again become the leading global PC maker.

Overview

Dell is working to develop many strategies to encourage managers in value-creating functions like manufacturing, materials management, and product development to improve how functional activities are performed to promote the organization's competitive advantage. In this chapter we focus on the functional-level strategies managers can use to achieve superior efficiency, quality, innovation, and responsiveness to customers and so build competitive advantage. We also examine the nature of an organization's value chain and discuss how the combined or cooperative efforts of managers across the value chain are required if an organization is to achieve its mission and goal of maximizing the amount of value its products provide customers. By the end of this chapter, you will understand the vital role value chain management plays in building competitive advantage and creating a high-performing organization.

Functional Strategies, the Value Chain, and Competitive Advantage

LO9-1 Explain the role of functional strategy and value chain management in achieving superior quality, efficiency, innovation, and responsiveness to customers.

As we noted in Chapter 8, managers can use two basic business-level strategies to add value to an organization's products and achieve a competitive advantage over industry rivals. First, managers can pursue a *low-cost strategy* and lower the costs of creating value to attract customers by keeping product prices as low as or lower than competitors' prices. Second, managers can pursue a *differentiation strategy* and add value to a product by finding ways to make it superior in some way to the products of other companies. If they are successful, and customers see greater value in the product, then like Apple they can charge a premium or higher price for the product. The four specific ways in which managers can lower costs and/or increase differentiation to obtain a competitive advantage were mentioned in Chapter 1 and are reviewed here; how organizations seek to achieve them is the topic of this chapter. (See Figure 9.1.)

1. *Achieve superior efficiency.* Efficiency is a measure of the amount of inputs required to produce a given amount of outputs. The fewer the inputs required to produce a given output, the higher is efficiency and the lower the cost of outputs. For example, in the 1990s Dell was the leader in global supply chain management and had a major cost advantage over its rivals, but in the 2000s its rivals adopted more efficient manufacturing methods and significantly reduced their costs.
2. *Achieve superior quality.* Quality means producing goods and services that have attributes–such as design, styling, performance, and reliability–that customers perceive as being superior to those found in competing products.[3] Providing high-quality products creates a brand-name reputation for an organization's products, and this enhanced reputation allows it to charge higher prices. In the PC industry, for example, Dell's reputation for making reliable PCs allowed it to outperform its rivals, and even today this still gives it some advantage over them.
3. *Achieve superior innovation, speed, and flexibility.* Anything new or better about the way an organization operates or the goods and services it produces is the result of innovation. Successful innovation gives an organization something *unique* or

Figure 9.1
Four Ways to Create a Competitive Advantage

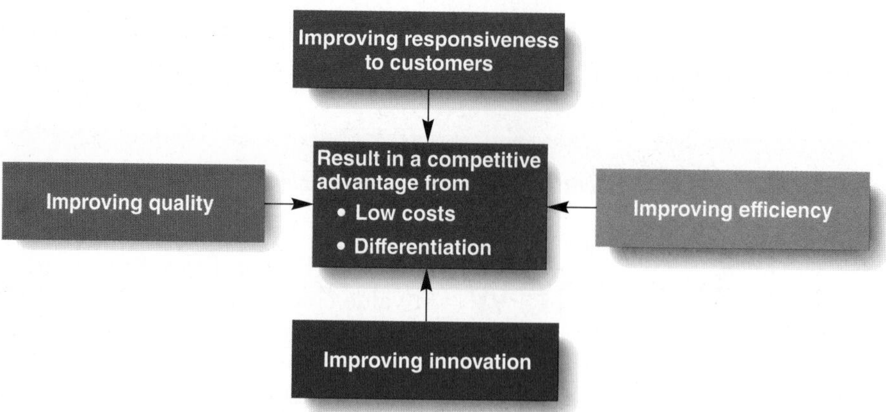

different about its products that rivals lack–more sophisticated products, production processes, or strategies and structures that strengthen its competitive advantage. Innovation adds value to products and allows the organization to further differentiate itself from rivals and attract customers willing to pay a premium price for unique products. Today Dell's competitive advantage has been eroded because companies like Apple and HP now make some of the most innovative PCs.

4. *Attain superior responsiveness to customers.* An organization that is responsive to customers tries to satisfy their needs and give them *exactly* what they want. An organization that treats customers better than its rivals do also provides a valuable service some customers may be willing to pay a higher price for. Managers can increase responsiveness by providing excellent after-sales service and support and by working to provide improved products or services to customers in the future. Today Dell, like Apple and HP, is searching for ways to satisfy changing customer needs, and as "A Manager's Challenge" described, managers across its functions are working to develop new value chain strategies to design and make computers and mobile digital devices to better meet those needs.

functional-level strategy A plan of action to improve the ability of each of an organization's functions to perform its task-specific activities in ways that add value to an organization's goods and services.

value chain The coordinated series or sequence of functional activities necessary to transform inputs such as new product concepts, raw materials, component parts, or professional skills into the finished goods or services customers value and want to buy.

value chain management The development of a set of functional-level strategies that support a company's business-level strategy and strengthen its competitive advantage.

Functional Strategies and Value Chain Management

Functional-level strategy is a plan of action to improve the ability of each of an organization's functions or departments (such as manufacturing or marketing) to perform its task-specific activities in ways that add value to an organization's goods and services. A company's **value chain** is the coordinated series or sequence of functional activities necessary to transform inputs such as new product concepts, raw materials, component parts, or professional skills into the finished goods or services customers value and want to buy (see Figure 9.2). Each functional activity along the chain *adds value* to the product when it lowers costs or gives the product differentiated qualities that increase the price a company can charge for it.

Value chain management is the development of a set of functional-level strategies that support a company's business-level strategy and strengthen its competitive advantage. Functional managers develop the strategies that increase efficiency, quality, innovation, and/or responsiveness to customers and thus strengthen an organization's competitive advantage. So the better the fit between functional- and business-level strategies, the greater will be the organization's competitive advantage, and the better able the organization is to achieve its mission and goal of maximizing the amount of value it gives customers. Each function along the value chain has an important role to play in value creation.

Figure 9.2
Functional Activities and the Value Chain

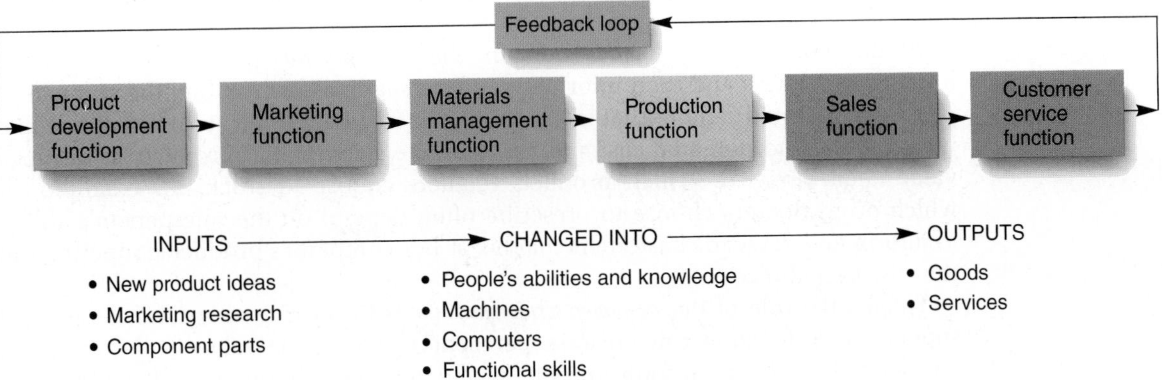

As Figure 9.2 suggests, the starting point of the value chain is often the search for new and improved products that will better appeal to customers, so the activities of the product development and marketing functions become important. *Product development* is the engineering and scientific research activities involved in innovating new or improved products that add value to a product. For example, Apple has been a leader in developing new kinds of mobile digital devices that have become so popular among buyers that its products are rapidly imitated by its competitors. Once a new product has been developed, the *marketing function's* task is to persuade customers that the product meets their needs and convince them to buy it. Marketing can help create value through brand positioning and advertising that increase customer perceptions of the utility of a company's product. For example, the French company Perrier persuaded U.S. customers that carbonated bottled water is worth $2 per liter–much more than the 75 cents it costs to purchase a gallon of spring water. Perrier's marketing function developed strategies that made customers want to buy the product, and major U.S. companies such as Coca-Cola and PepsiCo rushed to bring out their own bottled water labels to capitalize on customers' growing appetite for "differentiated" bottled water.

Even the best-designed product can fail if the marketing function hasn't devised a careful plan to persuade people to buy it and try it out–or to make sure customers really want it. For this reason, marketing often conducts consumer research to discover unmet customer product needs and to find better ways to tailor existing products to satisfy customer needs. Marketing then presents its suggestions to product development, which performs its own research to discover how best to design and make the new or improved products.

At the next stage of the value chain, the *materials management function* controls the movement of physical materials from the procurement of inputs through production and to distribution and delivery to the customer. The efficiency with which this is carried out can significantly lower costs and create more value. Walmart has the most efficient materials management function in the retail industry. By tightly controlling the flow of goods from its suppliers through its stores and into the hands of customers, Walmart has eliminated the need to hold large inventories of goods. Lower inventories mean lower costs and hence greater value creation. Similarly, Dell once insisted that its suppliers establish computer warehouses close to its factories so it did not have to hold a large inventory of components–a major cost saving.

The *production function* is responsible for creating, assembling, or providing a good or service–for transforming inputs into outputs. For physical products, when we talk about production, we generally mean manufacturing and assembly. For services such as banking or retailing, production takes place when the service is actually provided or delivered to the customer (for example, when a bank originates a loan for a customer, it is engaged in "production" of the loan). By performing its activities efficiently, the production function helps to lower costs. For example, the efficient production operations of Honda and Toyota have made them more profitable than competitors such as Renault, Volkswagen, and Chrysler. The production function can also perform its activities in a way that is consistent with high product quality, which leads to differentiation (and higher value) and to lower costs.

At the next stage in the value chain, the *sales function* plays a crucial role in locating customers and then informing and persuading them to buy the company's products. Personal selling–that is, direct face-to-face communication by salespeople with existing and potential customers to promote a company's products–is a crucial value chain activity. Which products retailers choose to stock, for example, or which drugs doctors choose to prescribe often depend on the salesperson's ability to inform and persuade customers that his or her company's product is superior and thus the best choice.

Finally, the role of the *customer service function* is to provide after-sales service and support. This function can create a perception of superior value in the minds of customers by solving customer problems and supporting customers after they have purchased the product. For example, FedEx can get its customers' parcels to any point in the world within 24 hours, thereby lowering the cost of its own value creation activities. Finally, customer service controls the electronic systems for tracking sales and inventory, pricing products, selling products, dealing with customer inquiries, and so on, all of which can greatly increase responsiveness to customers. Indeed, an important activity of sales and customer service is to tell product development and marketing why a product is meeting or not meeting customers' needs so the product can be redesigned or improved. Hence a feedback loop links the end of the value chain to its beginning (see Figure 9.2).

In the rest of this chapter we examine the functional strategies used to manage the value chain to improve quality, efficiency, innovation, and responsiveness to customers. Notice, however, that achieving superior quality, efficiency, and innovation is *part* of attaining superior responsiveness to customers. Customers want value for their money, and managers who develop functional strategies that result in a value chain capable of creating innovative, high-quality, low-cost products best deliver this value to customers. For this reason, we begin by discussing how functional managers can increase responsiveness to customers.

Improving Responsiveness to Customers

All organizations produce outputs–goods or services–that are consumed by customers, who, in buying these products, provide the monetary resources most organizations need to survive. Because customers are vital to organizational survival, managers must correctly identify their customers and pursue strategies that result in products that best meet their needs. This is why the marketing function plays such an important part in the value chain, and good value chain management requires that marketing managers focus on defining their company's business in terms of the customer *needs* it is satisfying and not by the *type of products* it makes–or the result can be disaster.[4] For example, Kodak's managers said "no thanks" when the company was offered the rights to "instant photography," which was later marketed by Polaroid. Why did they make this mistake? Because the managers adopted a product-oriented approach to their business that didn't put the needs of customers first. Kodak's managers believed their job was to sell high-quality, glossy photographs to people; why would they want to become involved in instant photography, which results in inferior-quality photographs? In reality, Kodak was not satisfying people's needs for high-quality photographs; it was satisfying the need customers had to *capture and record the images of their lives*–their birthday parties, weddings, graduations, and so on. And people wanted those images quickly so they could share them right away with other people–which is why today digital photography has taken off. In the 2000s Kodak was in serious trouble because

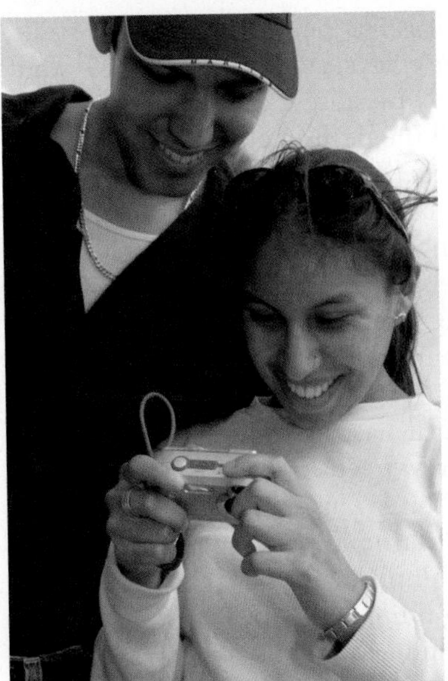

Kodak fell behind in the digital camera market by focusing more on products than on customers.

its film-based photographic business had declined sharply; it lost billions while striving to position itself in the digital market to give customers what they want.

What Do Customers Want?

Given that satisfying customer demand is central to the survival of an organization, an important question is "What do customers want?" Although specifying *exactly* what customers want is not possible because their needs vary from product to product, it is possible to identify some general product attributes or qualities that most customers prefer:

1. A lower price to a higher price.
2. High-quality products to low-quality products.
3. Quick service and good after-sales service to slow service and poor after-sales support.
4. Products with many useful or valuable features to products with few features.
5. Products that are, as far as possible, customized or tailored to their unique needs.

LO9-2 Describe what customers want, and explain why it is so important for managers to be responsive to their needs.

Managers know that the more desired product attributes a company's value chain builds into its products, the higher the price that must be charged to cover the costs of developing and making the product. So what do managers of a customer-responsive organization do? They try to develop functional strategies that allow the organization's value chain to deliver to customers either *more* desired product attributes for the *same price* or the *same* product attributes for a *lower price*.[5] For example, Walmart's "price rollbacks" or reductions are possible because it constantly searches for lower-cost suppliers or more efficient ways to manage its product inventory and deliver it to stores. It told its suppliers, for example, that if they did not put on their products new radio frequency tags (RFTs) that allow inventory to be monitored electronically as it is distributed globally, it would cease to buy from them.[6] In general, new IT has allowed many organizations to offer new models of products with more attributes at a price similar to or even lower than that of earlier models, and so in the last decade customers have been able to choose from a wider variety of higher-quality products and receive quicker customer service.

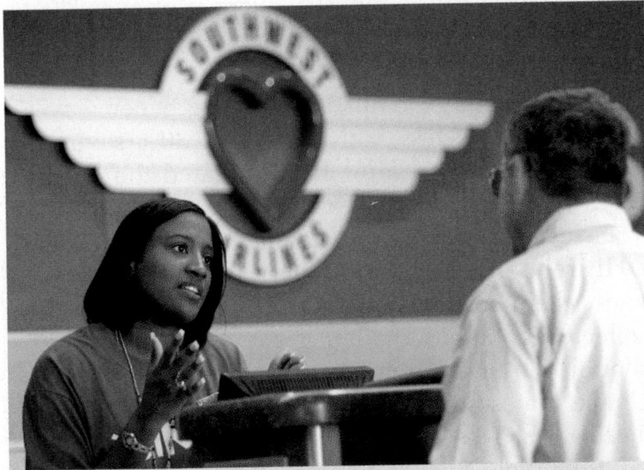

A Southwest ticket agent may assist a customer and then turn around to load her or his baggage as part of the organization's emphasis on cross-training workers for multiple tasks. Southwest's operating system is geared toward satisfying customer demand for low-priced, reliable, and convenient air travel, making it one of the most consistently successful airlines in recent years.

Managing the Value Chain to Increase Responsiveness to Customers

Because satisfying customers is so important, managers try to design and improve the way their value chains operate so they can supply products that have the desired attributes–quality, cost, and features. For example, the need to respond to customer demand for competitively priced, quality cars drove U.S. carmakers like Ford and GM to imitate Japanese companies and copy how Toyota and Honda perform their value chain activities. Today the imperative of satisfying customer needs shapes the activities of U.S. carmakers materials management and manufacturing functions. As an example of the link between responsiveness to customers and an organization's value chain, consider how Southwest Airlines, the most profitable U.S. airline, operates.[7]

The major reason for Southwest's success is that it has pursued functional strategies that improve how its value chain operates to give customers what they want. Southwest commands high customer loyalty precisely because it can deliver products, such as flights from Houston to Dallas, that have all the desired attributes: reliability, convenience, and low price. In each of its functions, Southwest's strategies revolve around finding ways to lower costs. For example, Southwest offers a no-frills approach to in-flight customer service; no meals are served onboard, and there are no first-class seats. Southwest does not subscribe to the big reservation computers used by travel agents because the booking fees are too costly. Also, the airline flies only one aircraft, the fuel-efficient Boeing 737, which keeps training and maintenance costs down. All this translates into low prices for customers.

Southwest's reliability derives from the fact that it has the quickest aircraft turnaround time in the industry. A Southwest ground crew needs only 15 minutes to turn around an incoming aircraft and prepare it for departure. This speedy operation helps keep flights on time. Southwest has such a quick turnaround because it has a flexible workforce that has been cross-trained to perform multiple tasks. Thus the person who checks tickets might also help with baggage loading if time is short.

Southwest's convenience comes from its scheduling multiple flights every day between its popular locations, such as Dallas and Houston, and its use of airports that are close to downtown areas (Hobby at Houston and Love Field at Dallas) instead of using more distant, major airports.[8] In sum, Southwest's excellent value chain management has given it a competitive advantage in the airline industry. Another company that has found a way to be responsive to customers by offering them faster service is First Global Xpress, which is profiled in the following "Management Insight" box.

Management Insight

First Global Xpress Delivers Packages Faster, Cheaper, and Greener

First Global Xpress (FGX) is a small, \$10 million global package shipping company that claims it can ship packages from the 12 largest U.S. cities on the East Coast anywhere around the globe 24 hours faster and more reliably (its package loss rate is 1% to compared to the industry average of over 8%) than large competitors such as FedEx and UPS. Also, FGX claims it can ship its over 400 customers' packages at a 20% lower cost than its large rivals and in a "greener way" because it uses less fuel oil with a 30% savings in CO_2 emissions.[9] How has it created the value chain strategies to achieve this?

Can upstart company FGX successfully compete with FedEx and co.? Direct shipping routes and alliances with major airlines are two of the ways FGX believes it can become a major player in the industry.

First, large shipping companies like FedEx and DHL rely on a "hub-and-spoke" package distribution system so that no matter where a package is collected or its destination it has to go through a central hub first, where packages from all over the United States are sorted for shipment to their final destination. This means that a customer's shipment, say from New York to London, has to take two different flights–one to get to a hub, such as FedEx's hub in Memphis, Tennessee, and then another to get to England. FGX does not own aircraft; it has been rapidly forming alliances with over 100 different global airlines that can ship its customers' packages directly from city to city–from New York to London, for example, which saves time and money.

Of course commercial airlines charge a fee for this service, but when demand for global air travel is declining and fuel costs are rising, forming an alliance with FGX is profitable for their bottom lines. As a result, airlines such as Continental, Virgin Atlantic, and Air France are willing to work closely with FGX to ensure that its packages are shipped directly and reliably to their destination cities. Because its flights are direct, FGX can also claim that it is providing this service "in a more socially responsible, greener way."

FGX hopes to grow quickly and offer its service from other large U.S. cities such as Chicago, Houston, and Los Angeles. And its CEO claims, "Over the next five years FGX plans to keep growing, replicating its model for clients worldwide. Every day, FGX offers you the chance to save money, cut time off of your deliveries, and reduce your carbon footprint–all through the simple solution of shipping direct." The challenge facing its managers is to keep its value chain operations lean and efficient–just as Southwest does in the passenger segment of the airline business.[10]

Although managers must seek to improve their responsiveness to customers by improving how the value chain operates, they should not offer a level of responsiveness to customers that results in costs becoming *too high*–something that threatens an organization's future performance and survival. For example, a company that customizes every product to the unique demands of individual customers is likely to see its costs grow out of control.

Customer Relationship Management

customer relationship management (CRM) A technique that uses IT to develop an ongoing relationship with customers to maximize the value an organization can deliver to them over time.

One functional strategy managers can use to get close to customers and understand their needs is **customer relationship management (CRM).** CRM is a technique that uses IT to develop an ongoing relationship with customers to maximize the value an organization can deliver to them over time. In the 2000s most large companies had installed sophisticated CRM IT to track customers' changing demands for a company's products; this became a vital tool to maximize responsiveness to customers. CRM IT monitors, controls, and links each of the functional activities involved in marketing, selling, and delivering products to customers, such as monitoring the delivery of products through the distribution channel, monitoring salespeople's selling activities, setting product pricing, and coordinating after-sales service. CRM systems have three interconnected components: sales and selling, after-sales service and support, and marketing.

Suppose a sales manager has access only to sales data that show the total sales revenue each salesperson generated in the last 30 days. This information does not break down how much revenue came from sales to existing customers versus sales to new customers. What important knowledge is being lost? First, if most revenues are earned from sales to existing customers, this suggests that the money being spent by a company to advertise and promote its products is not attracting new customers and so is being wasted. Second, important dimensions involved in sales are pricing, financing, and order processing. In many companies, to close a deal, a salesperson has to send the paperwork to a central sales office that handles matters such as approving the customer for special financing and determining specific shipping and delivery dates. In some companies, different departments handle these activities, and it can take a long time to get a response from them; this keeps customers waiting–something that often leads to lost sales. Until CRM systems were introduced, these kinds of problems were widespread and resulted in missed sales and higher operating costs. Today the sales and selling CRM software contains *best sales practices* that analyze this information and then recommend ways to improve how the sales process operates.

One company that has improved its sales and after-sales practices by implementing CRM is Empire HealthChoice Inc., the largest health insurance provider in New York, which sells its policies through 1,800 sales agents. For years these agents were responsible for collecting all the customer-specific information needed to determine the price of each policy. Once they had collected the necessary information, the agents called Empire to get price quotes. After waiting days for these quotes, the agents relayed them back to customers, who often then modified their requests to reduce the cost of their policies. When this occurred, the agents had to telephone Empire again to get revised price quotes. Because this frequently happened several times with each transaction, it often took more than 20 days to close a sale and another 10 days for customers to get their insurance cards.[11]

Recognizing that these delays were causing lost sales, Empire decided to examine how a CRM system could improve the sales process. Its managers chose a Web-based system so agents themselves could calculate the insurance quotes online. Once an agent enters a customer's data, a quote is generated in just a few seconds. The agent can continually modify a policy while sitting face-to-face with the customer until the policy and price are agreed upon. As a result, the sales process can now be completed in a few hours, and customers receive their insurance cards in 2 to 3 days rather than 10.[12]

When a company implements after-sales service and support CRM software, salespeople are required to input detailed information about their follow-up visits to customers. Because the system tracks and documents every customer's case history, salespeople have instant access to a record of everything that occurred during previous phone calls or visits. They are in a much better position to respond to customers' needs and build customer loyalty, so a company's after-sales service improves. Cell phone companies like T-Mobile and Sprint, for example, require that telephone sales reps collect information about all customers' inquiries, complaints, and requests, and this is recorded electronically in customer logs. The CRM module can analyze the information in these logs to evaluate whether the customer service reps are meeting or exceeding the company's required service standards.

A CRM system can also identify the top 10 reasons for customer complaints. Sales managers can then work to eliminate the sources of these problems and improve after-sales support procedures. The CRM system also identifies the top 10 best service and support practices, which can then be taught to all sales reps.

Finally, as a CRM system processes information about changing customer needs, this improves marketing in many ways. Marketing managers, for example, have access to detailed customer profiles, including data about purchases and the reasons why individuals were or were not attracted to a company's products. Armed with this knowledge, marketing can better identify customers and the specific product attributes they desire. It may become clear, for example, that a targeted customer group has a specific need that is not satisfied by a product–such as a need for a cell phone containing a 20-megapixel video camera and a GPS system. With real-time information, marketing can work with product development to redesign the product to better meet customer needs. In sum, a CRM system is a comprehensive method of gathering crucial information about how customers respond to a company's products. It is a powerful functional strategy used to align a company's products with customer needs.

Improving Quality

LO9-3 Explain why achieving superior quality is so important, and understand the challenges facing managers and organizations that seek to implement total quality management.

As noted earlier, high-quality products possess attributes such as superior design, features, reliability, and after-sales support; these products are designed to better meet customer requirements.[13] Quality is a concept that can be applied to the products of both manufacturing and service organizations–goods such as a Dell computer or services such as Southwest Airlines flight service or customer service in a Citibank branch. Why do managers seek to control and improve the quality of their organizations' products?[14] There are two reasons (see Figure 9.3).

First, customers usually prefer a higher-quality product to a lower-quality product. So an organization able to provide, *for the same price,* a product of higher quality than a competitor's product is serving its customers better–it is being more responsive to its customers. Often providing high-quality products creates a brand-name reputation

Figure 9.3
The Impact of Increased Quality on Organizational Performance

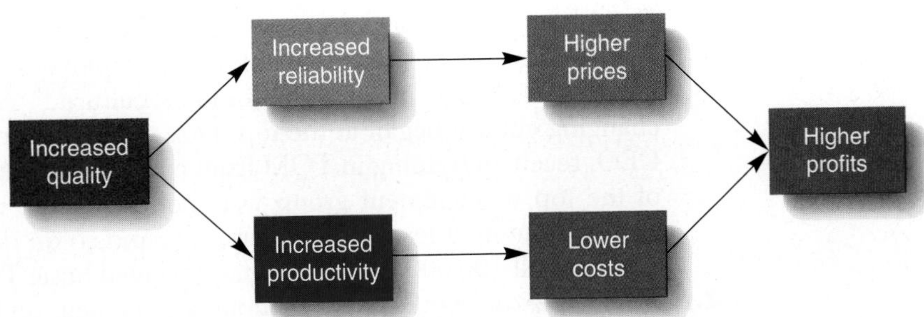

for an organization's products. This enhanced reputation may allow the organization to charge more for its products than its competitors can charge, and thus it makes greater profits. For example, in 2009 Lexus was ranked number one, as it has been for over a decade, on the J. D. Power list of the 10 most reliable carmakers.[15] The high quality of Lexus vehicles enables the company to charge higher prices for its cars than the prices charged by rival carmakers.

The second reason for trying to boost product quality is that higher product quality can increase efficiency and thereby lower operating costs and boost profits. Achieving high product quality lowers operating costs because of the effect of quality on employee productivity: Higher product quality means less employee time is wasted in making defective products that must be discarded or in providing substandard services, and thus less time has to be spent fixing mistakes. This translates into higher employee productivity, which means lower costs.

Total Quality Management

total quality management (TQM) A management technique that focuses on improving the quality of an organization's products and services.

At the forefront of the drive to improve product quality is a functional strategy known as total quality management.[16] **Total quality management (TQM)** focuses on improving the quality of an organization's products and stresses that *all* of an organization's value chain activities should be directed toward this goal. TQM requires the cooperation of managers in every function of an organization and across functions.[17] To show how TQM works, we next describe the way that Citibank used the technique. Then, using Citibank as an example, we look at the 10 steps that are necessary for managers to implement a successful TQM program.

In the 2000s Citibank's top managers decided the bank could retain and expand its customer base only if it could increase customer loyalty, so they decided to implement a TQM program to better satisfy customer needs. As the first step in its TQM effort, Citibank identified the factors that dissatisfy its customers. When analyzing the complaints, it found that most concerned the time it took to complete a customer's request, such as responding to an account problem or getting a loan. So Citibank's managers began to examine how they handled each kind of customer request. For each distinct request, they formed a cross-functional team that broke down the request into the steps required, between people and departments, to complete the response. In analyzing the steps, teams found that many of them were unnecessary and could be replaced by using the right information systems. They also found that delays often occurred because employees did not know how to handle a request. They were not being given the right kind of training, and when they couldn't handle a request, they simply put it aside until a supervisor could deal with it.

Citibank's second step to increase its responsiveness was to implement an organizationwide TQM program. Managers and supervisors were charged with reducing the complexity of the work process and finding the most effective way to process each particular request, such as a request for a loan. Managers were also charged with training employees to answer each specific request. The results were remarkable. For example, in the loan department the TQM program reduced by 75% the number of handoffs necessary to process a request. The department's average response time dropped from several hours to 30 minutes. What are the 10 steps in TQM that made this possible?

1. *Build organizational commitment to quality.* TQM will do little to improve the performance of an organization unless all employees embrace it, and this often requires a change in an organization's culture.[18] At Citibank the process of changing culture began at the top. First a group of top managers, including the CEO, received training in TQM from consultants from Motorola. Each member of the top management group was then given the responsibility of training a group at the next level in the hierarchy, and so on down through the organization until all 100,000 employees had received basic TQM training.
2. *Focus on the customer.* TQM practitioners see a focus on the customer as the starting point.[19] According to TQM philosophy, the customer, not managers in quality control or engineering, defines what quality is. The challenge is fourfold: (1) to identify what customers want from the good or service that the company provides; (2) to identify what the company actually provides to customers; (3) to identify any gap between what customers want and what they actually get (the quality gap); and (4) to formulate a plan for closing the quality gap. The efforts of Citibank managers to increase responsiveness to customers illustrate this aspect of TQM well.
3. *Find ways to measure quality.* Another crucial element of TQM is the development of a measuring system that managers can use to evaluate quality. Devising appropriate measures is relatively easy in manufacturing companies, where quality can be measured by criteria such as defects per million parts. It is more difficult in service companies, where outputs are less tangible. However, with a little creativity, suitable quality measures can be devised as they were by managers at Citibank. Similarly, at L. L. Bean, the mail-order retailer, managers use the percentage of orders that are correctly filled as one of their quality measures.
4. *Set goals and create incentives.* Once a measure has been devised, managers' next step is to set a challenging quality goal and to create incentives for reaching that goal. At Citibank the CEO set an initial goal of reducing customer complaints by 50%. One way of creating incentives to attain a goal is to link rewards, such as bonus pay and promotional opportunities, to the goal.
5. *Solicit input from employees.* Employees are a major source of information about the causes of poor quality, so it is important that managers establish a system for soliciting employee suggestions about improvements that can be made. At most companies, like Citibank, this is an ongoing endeavor–the process never stops.
6. *Identify defects and trace them to their source.* A major source of product defects is the production system; a major source of service defects is poor customer service procedures. TQM preaches the need for managers to identify defects in the work process, trace those defects back to their source, find out why they occurred, and make corrections so they do not occur again. Today IT makes quality measurement much easier.
7. *Introduce just-in-time inventory systems.* **Inventory** is the stock of raw materials, inputs, and component parts that an organization has on hand at a particular time. When the materials management function designs a **just-in-time (JIT) inventory system,** parts or supplies arrive at the organization when they are needed, not before. Also, under a JIT inventory system, defective parts enter an organization's operating system immediately; they are not warehoused for months before use. This means defective inputs can be quickly spotted. JIT is discussed more later in the chapter.
8. *Work closely with suppliers.* A major cause of poor-quality finished goods is poor-quality component parts. To decrease product defects, materials managers must work closely with suppliers to improve the quality of the parts they supply. Managers at Xerox worked closely with suppliers to get them to adopt TQM programs, and the result was a huge reduction in the defect rate of component parts. Managers also need to work closely with suppliers to get them to adopt a JIT inventory system, also required for high quality.

inventory The stock of raw materials, inputs, and component parts that an organization has on hand at a particular time.

just-in-time (JIT) inventory system A system in which parts or supplies arrive at an organization when they are needed, not before.

9. *Design for ease of production.* The more steps required to assemble a product or provide a service, the more opportunities there are for making a mistake. It follows that designing products that have fewer parts or finding ways to simplify providing a service should be linked to fewer defects or customer complaints. For example, Dell continually redesigns the way it assembles its computers to reduce the number of assembly steps required, and it constantly searches for new ways to reduce the number of components that have to be linked together. The consequence of these redesign efforts was a continuous fall in assembly costs and marked improvement in product quality during the 1990s.

10. *Break down barriers between functions.* Successful implementation of TQM requires substantial cooperation between the different value chain functions. Materials managers have to cooperate with manufacturing managers to find high-quality inputs that reduce manufacturing costs; marketing managers have to cooperate with manufacturing so customer problems identified by marketing can be acted on; information systems have to cooperate with all other functions of the company to devise suitable IT training programs; and so on.

In essence, to increase quality, all functional managers need to cooperate to develop goals and spell out exactly how they will be achieved. Managers should embrace the philosophy that mistakes, defects, and poor-quality materials are not acceptable and should be eliminated. Functional managers should spend more time working with employees and providing them with the tools they need to do the job. Managers should create an environment in which employees will not be afraid to report problems or recommend improvements. Output goals and targets need to include not only numbers or quotas but also some indicators of quality to promote the production of defect-free output. Functional managers also need to train employees in new skills to keep pace with changes in the workplace. Finally, achieving better quality requires that managers develop organizational values and norms centered on improving quality.

Six Sigma A technique used to improve quality by systematically improving how value chain activities are performed and then using statistical methods to measure the improvement.

SIX SIGMA One TQM technique called **Six Sigma** has gained increasing popularity in the last decade, particularly because of the well-publicized success GE enjoyed as a result of implementing it across its operating divisions. The goal of Six Sigma is to improve a company's quality to only three defects per million by systematically altering the way all the processes involved in value chain activities are performed, and then carefully measuring how much improvement has been made using statistical methods. Six Sigma shares with TQM its focus on improving value chain processes to increase quality; but it differs because TQM emphasizes top-down organizationwide employee involvement, whereas the Six Sigma approach is to create teams of expert change agents, known as "green belts and black belts," to take control of the problem-finding and problem-solving process and then to train other employees in implementing solutions. The following "Management Insight" box shows how Six Sigma works at the Starwood hotel chain.

Management Insight

How Starwood Uses Six Sigma to Improve Hotel Performance

Starwood Hotels & Resorts, based in White Plains, New Jersey, is one of the largest global hotel chains and one of the most profitable–its profit margins are nearly 15% higher than rivals such as Hilton and Marriott. Why? Starwood attributes a significant part of its high performance to its use of Six Sigma, which it began to use in 2001 to improve the quality of service it provides its guests.[20]

The company's Six Sigma group is led by Brian Mayer, the vice president of "Six Sigma Operations Management & Room Support," whose father and grandfather both worked in the hospitality industry. Mayer, a Six Sigma expert,

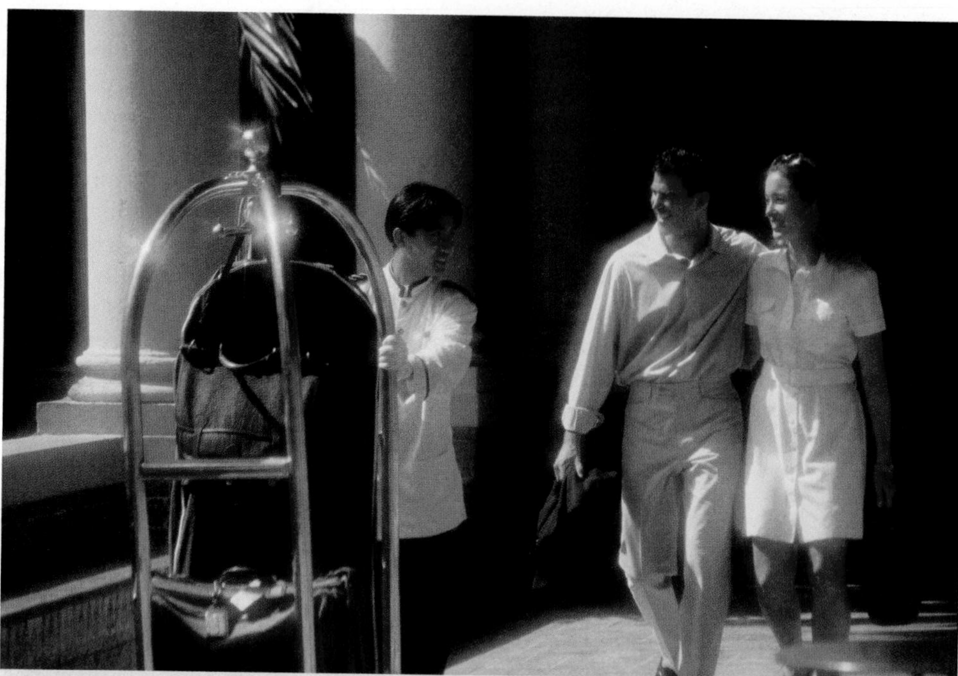

Guests and a bellhop share a laugh at a Starwood resort. The Starwood company remains one of the most highly profitable in the entire industry based on its rigorous Six Sigma program, listening ear toward customers, and attention to employee needs.

helped by a small group of other experts he recruited, implemented the program in 2001. Since then they have trained 150 Starwood employees as "black belts" and another 2,700 as "green belts" in the practices of Six Sigma. Black belts are the lead change agents in Starwood hotels who take responsibility for managing the change process to meet its main objectives–increasing quality customer service and responsiveness.[21] Green belts are the employees trained by Mayer's experts and each hotel's black belt to become the Six Sigma team in each hotel who work together to develop new ideas or programs that will improve customer responsiveness, and to find the work procedures and processes that will implement the new programs most effectively to improve customer service quality.

Almost all the new initiatives that have permeated the thousands of individual hotels in the Starwood chain come from these Six Sigma teams–whose work has improved the company's performance by hundreds of millions of dollars. For example, the "Unwind Program" was an initiative developed to cater to the interests of the 34% of hotel guests that a study found felt lonely and isolated in overnight hotel stays. Its purpose was to make guests feel at home so they would become return customers. The chain's Six Sigma teams began brainstorming ideas for new kinds of activities and services that would encourage nightly guests to leave their rooms and gather in the lobby, where they could meet and mingle with other guests and so feel more at home. They came up with hundreds of potential new programs. An initial concept was to offer guests short complimentary massages in the lobby that they hoped would encourage them to book massage sessions that would boost hotel revenues. Teams at each hotel then dreamed up other programs that they felt would best meet guest needs. These ranged from fire dancing in hotels in Fiji to Chinese watercolor painting in hotels in Beijing.[22] These ideas are shared across all the hotels in the chain using Starwood's proprietary "E-Tool," which contains thousands of successful projects that have worked–and the specific work procedures needed to perform them successfully.

In another major project, Starwood's managers were concerned about the number of injuries hotel employees sustained during their work, such as back strain injuries common among the housekeepers who cleaned rooms. The black and green belt teams studied how housekeepers worked in the various hotels and, pooling their knowledge, realized several changes could reduce injuries. For example, they found a large number of back strains occurred early in housekeepers' shifts because they were not "warmed up," so one central coordinating team developed a series of job-related stretching exercises. This team also looked at the cleaning tools used, and after experimenting with different sizes and types found that curved, longer-handled tools, which required less bending and stretching, could significantly reduce injuries. To date the program has reduced the accident rate from 12 to 2 for every 200,000 work hours–a major achievement.

As Starwood has found, having teams of Six Sigma specialists trained to always be alert for opportunities to improve the tens of thousands of different work procedures that help create high-quality customer service pays off. For guests and employees, the result is greater satisfaction and loyalty to the hotel chain in the form of both repeat guest visits and reduced employee turnover.

Improving Efficiency

LO9-4 Explain why achieving superior efficiency is so important, and understand the different kinds of techniques that need to be employed to increase efficiency.

The third goal of value chain management is to increase the efficiency of the various functional activities. The fewer the input resources required to produce a given volume of output, the higher will be the efficiency of the operating system. So efficiency is a useful measure of how well an organization uses all its resources–such as labor, capital, materials, or energy–to produce its outputs, or goods and services. Developing functional strategies to improve efficiency is an extremely important issue for managers because increased efficiency lowers production costs, which lets an organization make a greater profit or attract more customers by lowering its price. Several important functional strategies are discussed here.

Facilities Layout, Flexible Manufacturing, and Efficiency

facilities layout The strategy of designing the machine–worker interface to increase operating system efficiency.

flexible manufacturing The set of techniques that attempt to reduce the costs associated with the product assembly process or the way services are delivered to customers.

The strategies managers use to lay out or design an organization's physical work facilities also determine its efficiency. First, the way in which machines and workers are organized or grouped together into workstations affects the efficiency of the operating system. Second, a major determinant of efficiency is the cost associated with setting up the equipment needed to make a particular product. **Facilities layout** is the strategy of designing the machine–worker interface to increase operating system efficiency. **Flexible manufacturing** is a strategy based on the use of IT to reduce the costs associated with the product assembly process or the way services are delivered to customers. For example, this might be how computers are made on a production line or how patients are routed through a hospital.

FACILITIES LAYOUT The way in which machines, robots, and people are grouped together affects how productive they can be. Figure 9.4 shows three basic ways of arranging workstations: product layout, process layout, and fixed-position layout.

In a *product layout,* machines are organized so that each operation needed to manufacture a product or process a patient is performed at workstations arranged in a fixed sequence. In manufacturing, workers are stationary in this arrangement, and a moving conveyor belt takes the product being worked on to the next workstation so that it is progressively assembled. Mass production is the familiar name for this layout; car assembly lines are probably the best-known example. It used to be that product layout was efficient only when products were created in large quantities; however, the introduction of modular assembly lines controlled by computers is making it efficient to make products in small batches.

In a *process layout,* workstations are not organized in a fixed sequence. Rather, each workstation is relatively self-contained, and a product goes to whichever workstation is needed to perform the next operation to complete the product. Process layout is often suited to manufacturing settings that produce a variety of custom-made

Figure 9.4
Three Facilities Layouts

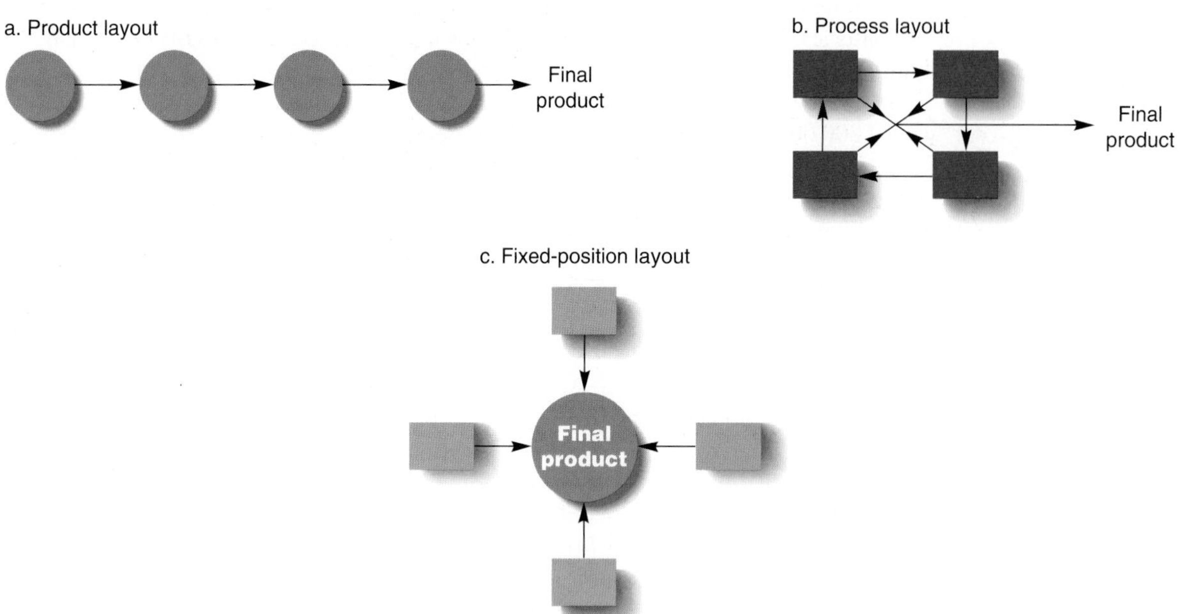

products, each tailored to the needs of a different kind of customer. For example, a custom furniture manufacturer might use a process layout so different teams of workers can produce different styles of chairs or tables made from different kinds of woods and finishes. Such a layout also describes how a patient might go through a hospital from emergency room to X-ray room, to operating room, and so on. A process layout provides the flexibility needed to change a product, whether it is a PC or a patient's treatment. Such flexibility, however, often reduces efficiency because it is expensive.

In a *fixed-position layout,* the product stays in a fixed position. Its component parts are produced in remote workstations and brought to the production area for final assembly. Increasingly, self-managed teams are using fixed-position layouts. Different teams assemble each component part and then send the parts to the final assembly team, which makes the final product. A fixed-position layout is commonly used for products such as jet airliners, mainframe computers, and gas turbines–products that are complex and difficult to assemble or so large that moving them from one workstation to another would be difficult. The effects of moving from one facilities layout to another can be dramatic, as the following "Manager as a Person" box suggests.

Manager as a Person

Paddy Hopkirk Improves Facilities Layout

Paddy Hopkirk established his car accessories business in Bedfordshire, England, shortly after he had shot to car-racing fame by winning the famous Monte Carlo Rally. Sales of Hopkirk's accessories, such as bicycle racks and axle stands, were always brisk; but Hopkirk was the first to admit that his operating system left a lot to be desired, so he invited consultants to help reorganize the system.

After analyzing his factory's operating system, the consultants realized that the source of the problem was the facilities layout Hopkirk had established.

Figure 9.5
Changing a Facilities Layout[23]

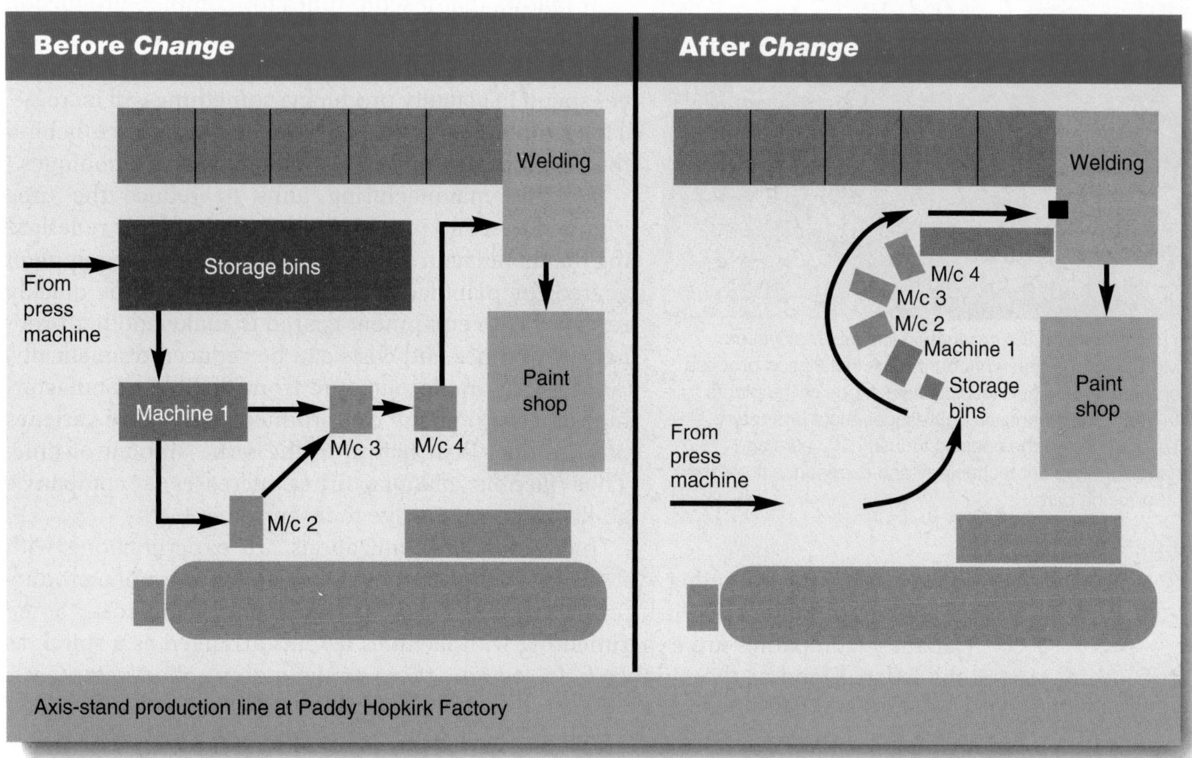

Over time, as sales grew, Hopkirk simply added new workstations to the operating system as they were needed. The result was a process layout in which the product being assembled moved in the irregular sequences shown in the "Before Change" half of Figure 9.5. The consultants suggested that to save time and effort, the workstations should be reorganized into the sequential product layout shown in the "After Change" illustration.

Once this change was made, the results were dramatic. One morning the factory was an untidy sprawl of workstations surrounded by piles of crates holding semi-finished components. Two days later, when the 170-person workforce came back to work, the machines had been brought together into tightly grouped workstations arranged in the fixed sequence shown in the illustration. The piles of components had disappeared, and the newly cleared floor space was neatly marked with color-coded lines mapping out the new flow of materials between workstations.

In the first full day of production, efficiency increased by as much as 30%. The space needed for some operations had been cut in half, and work in progress had been cut considerably. Moreover, the improved layout allowed some jobs to be combined, freeing operators for deployment elsewhere in the factory. An amazed Hopkirk exclaimed, "I was expecting a change but nothing as dramatic as this . . . it is fantastic."[24]

FLEXIBLE MANUFACTURING In a manufacturing company, a major source of costs is setting up the equipment needed to make a particular product. One of these costs is that of production forgone because nothing is produced while the equipment is being set up. For example, components manufacturers often need as much as half a day to set up automated production equipment when switching from production of one component part (such as a washer ring for the steering column of a car) to another (such as a washer

Housing units move on the production line as employees of Toyota Motor Corporation work during the installation process at the company's Kasugai Housing Works, one of the plants of Toyota home-brand houses on Kasugai, Aichi Prefecture, Japan. Toyota entered the housing industry 30 years ago where it applies the plant technology and experience it gained through producing cars.

ring for the steering column of a truck). During this half-day, a manufacturing plant is not producing anything, but employees are paid for this "nonproductive" time.

It follows that if setup times for complex production equipment can be reduced, so can setup costs, and efficiency will rise; that is, the time that plant and employees spend in actually producing something will increase. This simple insight has been the driving force behind the development of flexible manufacturing techniques.

Flexible manufacturing aims to reduce the time required to set up production equipment.[25] By redesigning the manufacturing process so production equipment geared for manufacturing one product can be quickly replaced with equipment geared to make another product, setup times and costs can be reduced dramatically. Another favorable outcome from flexible manufacturing is that a company can produce many more varieties of a product than before in the same amount of time. Thus flexible manufacturing increases a company's ability to be responsive to its customers.

Increasingly, organizations are experimenting with new designs for operating systems that not only allow workers to be more productive but also make the work process more flexible, thus reducing setup costs. Some Japanese companies are experimenting with facilities layouts arranged as a spiral, as the letter *Y*, and as the number 6, to see how these configurations affect setup costs and worker productivity. At a camcorder plant in Kohda, Japan, for example, Sony changed from a fixed-position layout in which 50 workers sequentially built a camcorder to a flexible spiral process design in which 4 workers perform all the operations necessary to produce the camcorder. This new layout lets the most efficient workers work at the highest pace, and it reduces setup costs because workers can easily switch from one model to another, increasing efficiency by 10%.[26]

An interesting example of a company that built a new factory to obtain the benefits from flexible manufacturing is the German company Igus Inc. Igus makes over 28,000 polymer bearings and energy supply cable products used in applications the world over. Increasing global competition led Igus managers to realize they needed to build a new factory that could handle the company's rapidly growing product line. At Igus new products are often introduced daily, so flexibility is the company's prime requirement. Moreover, because many of its products are highly customized, the specific and changing needs of its customers drive new product development.

Igus's new factory was designed for flexibility. As big as three football fields, the factory has nothing tied down or bolted to the floor. All the machines, computers, and equipment can be moved and repositioned to suit changing product requirements. Moreover, all Igus employees are trained to be flexible and can perform many of the necessary production tasks. For example, when one new product line proved popular with customers, its employees and production operations were relocated four times as it grew into larger spaces. Igus can change its operating system at a moment's notice and with minimal disruption; and because the company operates seven days a week, 24 hours a day, these changes are constant. Igus's decision to create a flexible factory of the future has paid off as its global sales have more than tripled in the 2000s.

Just-in-Time Inventory and Efficiency

As noted earlier, a just-in-time inventory system gets components to the assembly line just as they are needed and thus drives down costs. In a JIT inventory system, component parts travel from suppliers to the assembly line in a small wheeled container known as a *kanban*. Assembly-line workers empty the kanbans, which are sent back to the suppliers as the signal to produce another small batch of component parts, and so the process repeats itself. This system can be contrasted with a just-in-case view of inventory, which leads an organization to stockpile excess inputs in a warehouse in case it needs them to meet sudden upturns in demand.

JIT inventory systems have major implications for efficiency. Great cost savings can result from increasing inventory turnover and reducing inventory holding costs, such as warehousing and storage costs and the cost of capital tied up in inventory. Although companies that manufacture and assemble products can obviously use JIT to great advantage, so can service organizations.[27] Walmart, the biggest retailer in the United States, uses JIT systems to replenish the stock in its stores at least twice a week. Many Walmart stores receive daily deliveries. Walmart's main competitors typically restock every two weeks. Walmart can maintain the same service levels as these competitors but at one-fourth the inventory holding cost. Faster inventory turnover has helped Walmart achieve an efficiency-based competitive advantage in the retailing industry.[28] Even a small company can benefit from a kanban, as the experience of United Electric suggests in the following "Management Insight" box.

Management Insight

United Electric's Kanban System

United Electric Controls, headquartered in Watertown, Massachusetts, is the market leader in the application of threshold detection and switching technology. At one time the company simply warehoused its inputs and dispensed them as needed. Then it decided to reduce costs by storing these inputs at their point of use in the production system. However, this also caused problems because inventories of some inputs started to increase while other inputs were used up without anyone knowing which input stopped production.

United Electric's kanban system involves suppliers in automatic checking and restocking, shortening production time and lowering costs.

So managers decided to experiment with a supplier kanban system even though United Electric had fewer than 40 suppliers and they were up to date with its input requirements. Managers decided to store a three-week supply of parts in a central storeroom–a supply large enough to avoid unexpected shortages.[29] They began by asking their casting supplier to deliver inputs in kanbans and bins. Once a week, this supplier checks the bins to determine how much stock needs to be delivered the following week. Other suppliers were then asked to participate in this system, and now more than 35 major suppliers operate some form of the kanban system.

By all measures of performance, the kanban system has succeeded. Inventory holding costs have fallen sharply. Products are delivered to all customers on time. And new products' design-to-production cycles have dropped by 50% because suppliers are now involved much earlier in the design process so they can supply new inputs as needed.

Self-Managed Work Teams and Efficiency

Another functional strategy to increase efficiency is the use of self-managed work teams.[30] A typical self-managed team consists of 5 to 15 employees who produce an entire product instead of just parts of it.[31] Team members learn all team tasks and move from job to job. The result is a flexible workforce because team members can fill in for absent coworkers. The members of each team also assume responsibility for scheduling work and vacations, ordering materials, and hiring new members–previously all responsibilities of first-line managers. Because people often respond well to greater autonomy and responsibility, the use of empowered self-managed teams can increase productivity and efficiency. Moreover, cost savings arise from eliminating supervisors and creating a flatter organizational hierarchy, which further increase efficiency.

The effect of introducing self-managed teams is often an increase in efficiency of 30% or sometimes much more. After the introduction of flexible manufacturing technology and self-managed teams, a GE plant in Salisbury, North Carolina, increased efficiency by 250% compared with other GE plants producing the same products.[32]

Process Reengineering and Efficiency

process reengineering The fundamental rethinking and radical redesign of business processes to achieve dramatic improvement in critical measures of performance such as cost, quality, service, and speed.

The value chain is a collection of functional activities or business processes that transforms one or more kinds of inputs to create an output that is of value to the customer.[33] **Process reengineering** involves the fundamental rethinking and radical redesign of business processes (and thus the *value chain*) to achieve dramatic improvements in critical measures of performance such as cost, quality, service, and speed.[34] Order fulfillment, for example, can be thought of as a business process: When a customer's order is received (the input), many different functional tasks must be performed as necessary to process the order, and then the ordered goods are delivered to the customer (the output). Process reengineering boosts efficiency when it reduces the number of order fulfillment tasks that must be performed, or reduces the time they take, and so reduces operating costs.

For an example of process reengineering in practice, consider how Ford used it. One day a manager from Ford was working at its Japanese partner Mazda and discovered that Mazda had only five people in its accounts payable department. The Ford manager was shocked because Ford's U.S. operation had 500 employees in accounts payable. He reported his discovery to Ford's U.S. managers, who decided to form a task force to study this difference.

Ford managers discovered that procurement began when the purchasing department sent a purchase order to a supplier and sent a copy of the purchase order to Ford's accounts payable department. When the supplier shipped the goods and they arrived at Ford, a clerk at the receiving dock completed a form describing the goods and sent the form to accounts payable. The supplier, meanwhile, sent accounts payable an invoice. Thus accounts payable received three documents relating to these goods: a copy of the original purchase order, the receiving document, and the invoice. If the information in all three was in agreement (most of the time it was), a clerk in accounts payable issued payment. Occasionally, however, all three documents did not agree. And Ford discovered that accounts payable clerks spent most of their time straightening out the 1% of instances in which the purchase order, receiving document, and invoice contained conflicting information.[35]

Ford managers decided to reengineer the procurement process to simplify it. Now when a buyer in the purchasing department issues a purchase order to a supplier, that buyer also enters the order into an online database. As before, suppliers send goods to the receiving dock. When the goods arrive, the clerk at the receiving dock checks a computer terminal to see whether the received shipment matches the description on the purchase order. If it does, the clerk accepts the goods and pushes a button on the terminal keyboard that tells the database the goods have arrived. Receipt of the goods is recorded in the database, and a computer automatically issues and sends a check to the supplier. If the goods do not correspond to the description on the purchase order in the database, the clerk at the dock refuses the shipment and sends it back to the supplier.

Payment authorization, which used to be performed by accounts payable, is now accomplished at the receiving dock. The new process has come close to eliminating the need for an accounts payable department. In some parts of Ford, the size of the accounts payable department has been cut by 95%. By reducing the head count in accounts payable, the reengineering effort reduced the amount of time wasted on unproductive activities, thereby increasing the efficiency of the total organization.

Information Systems, the Internet, and Efficiency

With the rapid spread of computers, the explosive growth of the Internet and corporate intranets, and high-speed digital Internet technology, the information systems function is moving to center stage in the quest for operating efficiencies and a lower cost structure. The impact of information systems on productivity is wide-ranging and potentially affects all other activities of a company. For example, Cisco Systems has been able to realize significant cost savings by moving its ordering and customer service functions online. The company has just 300 service agents handling all its customer accounts, compared to the 900 it would need if sales were not handled online. The difference represents an annual savings of $30 million a year. Moreover, without automated customer service functions, Cisco calculates that it would need at least 1,000 additional service engineers, which would cost around $75 million.

All large companies today use the Internet to manage the value chain, feeding real-time information about order flow to suppliers, which use this information to schedule their own production to provide components on a just-in-time basis. This approach reduces the costs of coordination both between the company and its customers and between the company and its suppliers. Using the Internet to automate customer and supplier interactions substantially reduces the number of employees required to manage these interfaces, which significantly reduces costs. This trend extends beyond high-tech companies. Banks and financial service companies are finding that they can substantially reduce costs by moving customer accounts and support functions online. Such a move reduces the need for customer service representatives, bank tellers, stockbrokers, insurance agents, and others. For example, it costs about $1 when a customer executes a transaction at a bank, such as shifting money from one account to another; over the Internet the same transaction costs about $0.01.

Improving Innovation

As discussed in Chapter 6, *technology* comprises the skills, know-how, experience, body of scientific knowledge, tools, machines, computers, and equipment used in the design, production, and distribution of goods and services. Technology is involved in all functional activities, and the rapid advance of technology today is a significant factor in managers' attempts to improve how their value chains innovate new kinds of goods and services or ways to provide them–as Dell has discovered.

LO9-5 Differentiate between two forms of innovation, and explain why innovation and product development are crucial components of the search for competitive advantage.

Two Kinds of Innovation

quantum product innovation The development of new, often radically different, kinds of goods and services because of fundamental shifts in technology brought about by pioneering discoveries.

incremental product innovation The gradual improvement and refinement of existing products that occurs over time as existing technologies are perfected.

Two principal kinds of innovation can be identified based on the nature of the technological change that brings them about. **Quantum product innovation** results in the development of new, often radically different, kinds of goods and services because of fundamental shifts in technology brought about by pioneering discoveries. Examples are the creation of the Internet and the World Wide Web that have revolutionized the computer, cell phone, and media/music industries, and biotechnology, which has transformed the treatment of illness by creating new, genetically engineered medicines. McDonald's development of the principles behind the provision of fast food also qualifies as a quantum product innovation.

Incremental product innovation results in gradual improvements and refinements of existing products over time as existing technologies are perfected and functional managers, like those at Dell, Toyota, and McDonald's, learn how to perform value chain activities in better ways–ways that add more value to products. For example, since their debut, Google's staffers have made thousands of incremental improvements to the company's search engine, Chrome Internet browser, and Android operating system–changes that have enhanced their capabilities enormously such as by giving them the ability to work on all kinds of mobile devices and making them available in many different languages.

Quantum product innovations are relatively rare; most managers' activities focus on incremental product innovations that result from ongoing technological advances. For example, every time Dell or HP puts a new, faster Intel or AMD chip into a PC, or Google improves its search engine's capability, the company is making incremental product innovations. Similarly, every time car engineers redesign a car model, and every time McDonald's managers work to improve the flavor and texture of burgers, fries, and salads, their product development efforts are intended to lead to incremental product innovations. Incremental innovation is frequently as important as–or even more important than–quantum innovation in raising a company's performance. Indeed, as discussed next, it is often managers' ability to successfully manage incremental product development that results in success or failure in an industry–as Dell found out to its cost.

The need to speed innovation and quickly develop new and improved products becomes especially important when the technology behind the product is advancing rapidly. This is because the first companies in an industry to adopt the new technology will be able to develop products that better meet customer needs and gain a "first-mover" advantage over their rivals. Indeed, managers who do not quickly adopt and apply new technologies to innovate products may soon find they have no customers for their products–and destroy their organizations. In sum, the greater the rate of technological change in an industry, the more important it is for managers to innovate.

Strategies to Promote Innovation and Speed Product Development

product development The management of the value chain activities involved in bringing new or improved goods and services to the market.

There are several ways in which managers can promote innovation and encourage the development of new products. **Product development** is the management of the value chain activities involved in bringing new or improved goods and services to the market. The steps that Monte Peterson, former CEO of Thermos, took to develop a new barbecue grill show how good product development should proceed. Peterson had no doubt about how to increase Thermos's sales of barbecue grills: Motivate Thermos's functional managers to create new and improved models. So Peterson assembled a cross-functional product development team of five functional managers (from marketing, engineering, manufacturing, sales, and finance) and told them to develop a new barbecue grill within 18 months. To ensure that they were not spread too thin, he assigned them to this team only. Peterson also arranged for leadership of the team to rotate. Initially, to focus on what customers wanted, the marketing manager would take the lead; then, when technical developments became the main consideration, leadership would switch to engineering; and so on.

Team members christened the group the "lifestyle team." To find out what people really wanted in a grill, the marketing manager and nine subordinates spent a month on the road, visiting customers. What they found surprised them. The stereotype of Dad slaving over a smoky barbecue grill was wrong–more women were barbecuing. Many cooks were tired of messy charcoal, and many homeowners did not like rusty grills that spoiled the appearance of their decks. Moreover, environmental and safety issues were increasing in importance. In California charcoal starter fluid is considered a pollutant and is banned; in New Jersey the use of charcoal and gas grills on the balconies of condos and apartments has been prohibited to avoid fires. Based on these findings, the team decided Thermos had to produce a barbecue grill that not only made the food taste good but also looked attractive, used no pollutants, and was safe for balcony use (which meant it had to be electric).

Within one year the basic attributes of the product were defined, and leadership of the team moved to engineering. The critical task for engineering was to design a grill that gave food the cookout taste that conventional electric grills could not provide because they did not get hot enough. To raise the cooking temperature, Thermos's engineers designed a domed vacuum top that trapped heat inside the grill, and they built electric heat rods directly into the surface of the grill. These features made the grill hot enough to sear meat and give it brown barbecue lines and a barbecue taste.

Manufacturing had been active from the early days of the development process, making sure any proposed design could be produced economically. Because manufacturing was involved from the beginning, the team avoided some costly mistakes. At one critical team meeting the engineers said they wanted tapered legs on the grill. Manufacturing explained that tapered legs would have to be custom-made–and would raise manufacturing costs–and persuaded the team to go with straight legs.

When the new grill was introduced on schedule, it was an immediate success. The study of many product development successes, such as that of Thermos's lifestyle team, suggests three strategies managers can implement to increase the likelihood that their product development efforts will result in innovative and successful new products.

INVOLVE BOTH CUSTOMERS AND SUPPLIERS Many new products fail when they reach the marketplace because they were designed with scant attention to customer needs. Successful product development requires inputs from more than just an organization's members; also needed are inputs from customers and suppliers. Thermos team members spent a month on the road, visiting customers to identify their needs. The revolutionary electric barbecue grill was a direct result of this process. In other cases companies have found it worthwhile to include customer representatives as peripheral members of their product development teams. Boeing, for example, has included its customers, the major airlines, in the design of its most recent commercial jet aircraft, the 787 Dreamliner. Boeing builds a mockup of the aircraft's cabin and then, over a period of months, allows each airline's representatives to experiment with repositioning the galleys, seating, aisles, and bathrooms to best meet the needs of their particular airline. Boeing has learned a great deal from this process.

ESTABLISH A STAGE-GATE DEVELOPMENT FUNNEL One of the most common mistakes managers make in product development is trying to fund too many new projects at any one time. This approach spreads the activities of the different value chain functions too thinly over too many different projects. As a consequence, no single project is given the functional resources and attention required.

stage-gate development funnel A planning model that forces managers to choose among competing projects so organizational resources are not spread thinly over too many projects.

One strategy for solving this problem is for managers to develop a structured process for evaluating product development proposals and deciding which to support and which to reject. A common solution is to establish a **stage-gate development funnel,** a technique that forces managers to choose among competing projects so functional resources are not spread thinly over too many projects. The funnel gives functional managers control over product development and allows them to intervene and take corrective action quickly and appropriately (see Figure 9.6).

Cross-functionality at its best. Here, two research scientists, an executive, and a marketing manager put their heads together to figure out what's next.

At stage 1 the development funnel has a wide mouth, so top managers initially can encourage employees to come up with as many new product ideas as possible. Managers can create incentives for employees to come up with ideas. Many organizations run "bright-idea programs" that reward employees whose ideas eventually make it through the development process. Other organizations allow research scientists to devote a certain amount of work time to their own projects. Top managers at 3M, for example, have a 15% rule: They expect a research scientist to spend 15% of the workweek working on a project of his or her own choosing. Ideas may be submitted by individuals or by groups. Brainstorming (see Chapter 7) is a technique that managers frequently use to encourage new ideas.

Figure 9.6
A Stage–Gate Development Funnel

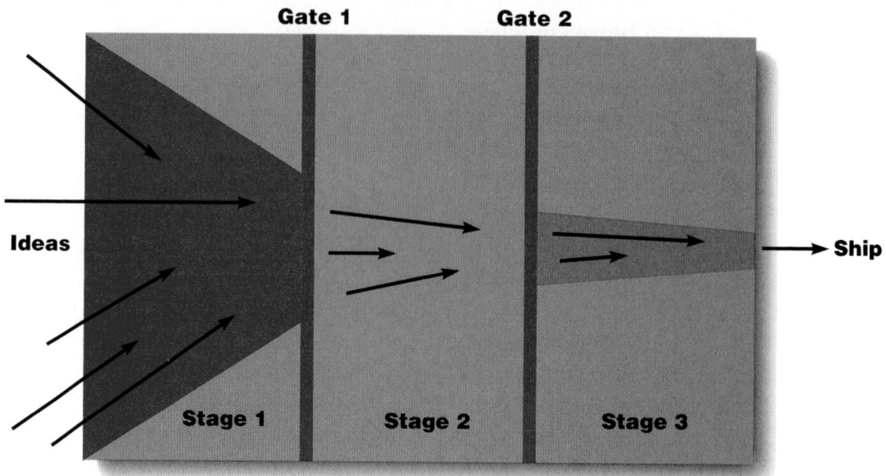

New product ideas are written up as brief proposals. The proposals are submitted to a cross-functional team of managers, who evaluate each proposal at gate 1. The cross-functional team considers a proposal's fit with the organization's strategy and its technical feasibility. Proposals that are consistent with the strategy of the organization and are judged technically feasible pass through gate 1 and into stage 2. Other proposals are turned down (although the door is often left open for reconsidering a proposal later).

The primary goal in stage 2 is to draft a detailed product development plan. The **product development plan** specifies all of the relevant information that managers need to decide whether to go ahead with a full-blown product development effort. The product development plan should include strategic and financial objectives, an analysis of the product's market potential, a list of desired product features, a list of technological requirements, a list of financial and human resource requirements, a detailed development budget, and a time line that contains specific milestones (for example, dates for prototype completion and final launch).

product development plan A plan that specifies all of the relevant information that managers need in order to decide whether to proceed with a full-blown product development effort.

A cross-functional team of managers normally drafts this plan. Good planning requires a good strategic analysis (see Chapter 8), and team members must be prepared to spend considerable time in the field with customers, trying to understand their needs. Drafting a product development plan generally takes about three months. Once completed, the plan is reviewed by a senior management committee at gate 2 (see Figure 9.6). These managers focus on the details of the plan to see whether the proposal is attractive (given its market potential) and viable (given the technological, financial, and human resources that would be needed to develop the product). Senior managers making this review keep in mind all other product development efforts currently being undertaken by the organization. One goal at this point is to ensure that limited organizational resources are used to their maximum effect.

At gate 2 projects are rejected, sent back for revision, or allowed to pass through to stage 3, the development phase. Product development starts with the formation of a cross-functional team that is given primary responsibility for developing the product. In some companies, at the beginning of stage 3 top managers and cross-functional team members sign a **contract book,** a written agreement that details factors such as responsibilities, resource commitments, budgets, time lines, and development milestones. Signing the contract book is viewed as the symbolic launch of a product development effort. The contract book is also a document against which actual development progress can be measured. At 3M, for example, team members and top management negotiate a contract and sign a contract book at the launch of a development effort, thereby signaling their commitment to the objectives contained in the contract.

contract book A written agreement that details product development factors such as responsibilities, resource commitments, budgets, time lines, and development milestones.

The stage 3 development effort can last anywhere from 6 months to 10 years, depending on the industry and type of product. Some electronics products have development cycles of 6 months, but it takes from 3 to 5 years to develop a new car, about 5 years to develop a new jet aircraft, and as long as 10 years to develop a new medical drug.

ESTABLISH CROSS-FUNCTIONAL TEAMS A smooth-running cross-functional team also seems to be a critical component of successful product development, as the experience of Thermos suggests. Marketing, engineering, and manufacturing personnel are **core members** of a successful product development team–the people who have primary responsibility for the product development effort. Other people besides core members work on the project when the need arises, but the core members (generally from three to six individuals) stay with the project from inception to completion of the development effort (see Figure 9.7).

core members The members of a team who bear primary responsibility for the success of a project and who stay with a project from inception to completion.

The reason for using a cross-functional team is to ensure a high level of coordination and communication among managers in different functions. Input from both marketing and manufacturing members of Thermos's lifestyle team determined the characteristics of the barbecue that the engineers on the team ended up designing.

If a cross-functional team is to succeed, it must have the right kind of leadership and it must be managed effectively. To be successful, a product development team needs a team leader who can rise above a functional background and take a cross-functional view. In addition to having effective leadership, successful cross-functional product development teams have several other key characteristics. Often core members of successful teams are located close to one another, in the same office space, to foster a sense of shared mission and commitment to a development program. Successful teams develop a clear sense of their objectives and how they will be achieved, the purpose again being to create a sense of shared mission. The way in which Google uses many of these strategies to promote innovation is discussed in the following "Management Insight" box.

Figure 9.7
Members of a Cross-Functional Product Development Team

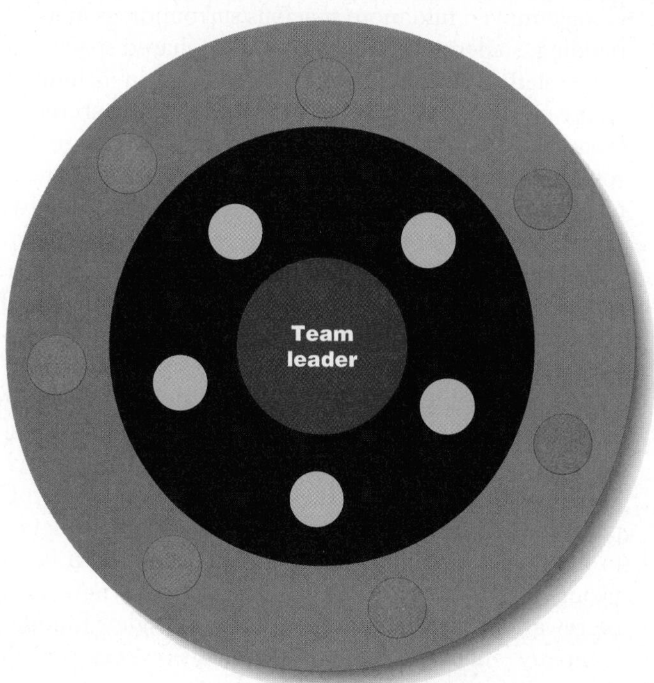

Management Insight

Innovation and Product Development Are Google's Major Imperative

The history of Google, the Internet search engine company, began in 1995 when two Stanford graduate computer science students, Sergey Brin and Larry Page, decided to collaborate to develop a new kind of search engine technology.[36] They understood the limitations of existing search engines, and by 1998 they had developed a superior engine that they felt was ready to go online. They raised $1 million from family, friends, and risk-taking "angel" investors to buy the hardware necessary to connect Google to the Internet.

At first Google answered 10,000 inquiries a day, but in a few months it was answering 500,000. By fall 1999 it was handling 3 million; by fall 2000, 60 million; and by spring 2001, 100 million per day. In the 2000s Google became the dominant search engine, handling around 75% of inquiries by 2010; it is one of the top five most used Internet companies, and rivals like Microsoft are working hard to catch up and beat Google at its own game.

From the beginning, Google employees have worked in "high-density clusters," which contributes to their camaraderie and cooperative innovations—whether they're sitting on therapeutic bouncy balls or ergonomic office chairs.

Google's explosive growth is largely due to the culture of innovation its founders cultivated from the start. Although by 2010 Google had grown to 15,000 employees worldwide, its founders claim that Google still maintains a small-company feel because its culture empowers its employees, who are called staffers or "Googlers," to create the best software possible. Brin and Page created Google's innovative culture in several ways.

From the beginning, lacking space and seeking to keep operating costs low, Google staffers worked in "high-density clusters." Three or four employees, each equipped with a high-powered Linux workstation, shared a desk, couch, and chairs that were large rubber balls, working together to improve the company's technology. Even when Google moved into more spacious surroundings at its "Googleplex" headquarters building, staffers continued to work in shared spaces. Google designed the building so staffers constantly meet one another in its funky lobby; in its Google Café, where everyone eats together; in its state-of-the-art recreational facilities; and in its "snack rooms," equipped with bins packed with cereals, gummi bears, yogurt, carrots, and make-your-own cappuccino. Google also created many social gatherings of employees, such as a TGIF open meetings and a twice weekly outdoor roller hockey game where staffers are encouraged to bring down the founders.[37]

All this attention to creating what might be the "grooviest" company headquarters in the world did not come about by chance. Brin and Page knew that Google's most important strength would be its ability to attract the best software engineers in the world and then motivate them to perform well. Common offices, lobbies, cafés, and so on bring staffers into close contact with one another, develop collegiality, and encourage them to share new ideas with their colleagues and to constantly improve Google's search engine technology and find new ways to expand the company. The freedom Google gives its staffers to pursue new ideas is a clear indication of its founders' desire to empower them to be innovative and to look off the beaten path for new ideas. Finally, recognizing that staffers who innovate important new software applications should be rewarded for their achievements, Google's founders give them stock in the company, effectively making staffers its owners as well.

Their focus on innovation did not blind Brin and Page to the need to build a viable competitive strategy so Google could compete effectively in the cutthroat search engine market. They recognized, however, that they lacked business experience; they had never had to craft strategies to compete with giants like Microsoft and Yahoo. Moreover, they also had never been responsible for building a strong set of value chain functions. So they recruited a team of talented and experienced functional managers to help them manage their company. They also decided to give responsibility for the company's value chain management to a new CEO, Eric Schmidt, who came from Novell, where he had been in charge of strategic planning and technology development.

Brin and Page's understanding that successful product development requires building a strong organizational architecture has paid off. In August 2004 Google went public, and its shares, which were sold at $85, were worth over $100 each by the end of the first day of trading, $500 by 2006, and a staggering $750 in 2007 before falling back to around $550 in spring 2010 after the recession. This has made Brin and Page's stake in the company worth billions; clearly it can pay to focus on innovation.

Google prospers because of its founders' ability to create a culture that encourages staffers to be innovative and because of their willingness to delegate authority for product development to managers and staffers. Managing innovation is an increasingly important aspect of a manager's job in an era of dramatic changes in advanced IT. Promoting successful new product development is difficult and challenging, and some product development efforts are much more successful than others. Google is performing at a high level, while thousands of other dot-coms, including many search engine companies such as Magellan and Openfind, have gone out of business.

In sum, managers need to recognize that successful innovation and product development cut across roles and functions and require a high level of cooperation. They should recognize the importance of common values and norms in promoting the high levels of cooperation and cohesiveness necessary to build a culture for innovation. They also should reward successful innovators and make heroes of the employees and teams who develop successful new products. Finally, managers should fully utilize the product development techniques just discussed to guide the process.

Summary and Review

LO9-1 **VALUE CHAIN MANAGEMENT AND COMPETITIVE ADVANTAGE** To achieve high performance, managers try to improve their responsiveness to customers, the quality of their products, and the efficiency of their organization. To achieve these goals, managers can use a number of value chain management techniques to improve the way an organization operates.

LO9-2 **IMPROVING RESPONSIVENESS TO CUSTOMERS** To achieve high performance in a competitive environment, it is imperative that the organization's value chain be managed to produce outputs that have the attributes customers desire. A central task of value chain management is to develop new and improved operating systems that enhance the ability of the organization to economically deliver more of the product attributes that customers desire for the same price. Techniques such as CRM and TQM, JIT, flexible manufacturing, and process reengineering are popular because they promise to do this. As important as responsiveness to customers is, however, managers need to recognize that there are limits to how responsive an organization can be and still cover its costs.

LO9-3 **IMPROVING QUALITY** Managers seek to improve the quality of their organization's output because doing so enables them to better serve customers, to raise prices, and to lower production costs. Total quality management focuses on improving the quality of an organization's products and services and stresses that all of an organization's operations should be directed toward this goal. Putting TQM into practice requires having an organizationwide commitment to TQM, having a strong customer focus, finding ways to measure quality, setting quality improvement goals, soliciting input from employees about how to improve product quality, identifying defects and tracing them to their source, introducing just-in-time inventory systems, getting suppliers to adopt TQM practices, designing products for ease of manufacture, and breaking down barriers between functional departments.

LO9-4 **IMPROVING EFFICIENCY** Improving efficiency requires one or more of the following: the introduction of a TQM program, the adoption of flexible manufacturing technologies, the introduction of just-in-time inventory systems, the establishment of self-managed work teams, and the application of process reengineering. Top management is responsible for setting the context within which efficiency improvements can take place by, for example, emphasizing the need for continuous improvement. Functional-level managers bear prime responsibility for identifying and implementing efficiency-enhancing improvements in operating systems.

LO9-5 **IMPROVING PRODUCT INNOVATION** When technology is changing, managers must quickly innovate new and improved products to protect their competitive advantage. Some value chain strategies managers can use to achieve this are (1) involving both customers and suppliers in the development process; (1) establishing a stage–gate development funnel for evaluating and controlling different product development efforts; and (3) establishing cross-functional teams composed of individuals from different functional departments, and giving each team a leader who can rise above his or her functional background.

Management in Action

Topics for Discussion and Action

Discussion

1. What is CRM, and how can it help improve responsiveness to customers? [LO9-2]
2. What are the main challenges in implementing a successful total quality management program? [LO9-3]
3. What is efficiency, and what are some strategies managers can use to increase it? [LO9-4]
4. Why is it important for managers to pay close attention to value chain management if they wish to be responsive to their customers? [LO9-1, 9-2]
5. What is innovation, and what are some strategies managers can use to develop successful new products? [LO9-5]

Action

6. Ask a manager how responsiveness to customers, quality, efficiency, and innovation are defined and measured in his or her organization. [LO9-1, 9-2]
7. Go to a local store, restaurant, or supermarket, observe how customers are treated, and list the ways in which you think the organization is being responsive or unresponsive to the needs of its customers. How could this business improve its responsiveness to customers? [LO9-1, 9-2]

Building Management Skills

Managing the Value Chain [LO9-1, 9-2]

Choose an organization with which you are familiar—one that you have worked in or patronized or one that has received extensive coverage in the popular press. The organization should be involved in only one industry or business. Answer these questions about the organization:

1. What is the output of the organization?
2. Describe the value chain activities that the organization uses to produce this output.
3. What product attributes do customers of the organization desire?
4. Try to identify improvements that might be made to the organization's value chain to boost its responsiveness to customers, quality, efficiency, and innovation.

Managing Ethically [LO9-1, 9-4]

After implementing efficiency-improving techniques, many companies commonly lay off hundreds or thousands of employees whose services are no longer required. And frequently remaining employees must perform more tasks more quickly—a situation that can generate employee stress and other work-related problems. Also, these employees may experience guilt because they stayed while many of their colleagues and friends were fired.

Questions

1. Either by yourself or in a group, think through the ethical implications of using a new functional strategy to improve organizational performance.
2. What criteria would you use to decide which kind of strategy is ethical to adopt and how far to push employees to raise the level of their performance?
3. How big a layoff, if any, is acceptable? If layoffs are acceptable, what could be done to reduce their harm to employees?

Small Group Breakout Exercise

How to Compete in the Sandwich Business [LO9-1, 9-2]

Form groups of three or four people, and appoint one member as the spokesperson who will communicate your findings to the class when called on by the instructor. Then discuss the following scenario:

You and your partners are thinking about opening a new kind of sandwich shop that will compete head-to-head with Subway and Thundercloud Subs. Because these chains have good brand-name recognition, it is vital that you find some source of competitive advantage for your new sandwich shop, and you are meeting to brainstorm ways of obtaining one.

1. Identify the product attributes that a typical sandwich shop customer wants the most.
2. In what ways do you think you will be able to improve on the operations and processes of existing sandwich shops and increase responsiveness to customers through better product quality, efficiency, or innovation?

Exploring the World Wide Web [LO9-3, 9-4]

In 2010 Toyota was accused of allowing its desire for rapid global growth to undermine its commitment to quality and safety in the design of its vehicles, creating problems such as the design failure of the acceleration and braking systems in some of its vehicles. Search the Web for articles about the Toyota recalls and investigations.

1. How have the recalls that Toyota announced in early 2010 affected current public opinion about the company's record for quality and reliability?
2. How has Toyota changed its strategies toward value chain management as a result of these quality and safety problems?

Be the Manager [LO9-1, 9-3, 9-4, 9-5]

How to Build Flat-Panel Displays

You are the top manager of a start-up company that will produce innovative new flat-screen displays for PC makers like Dell and HP. The flat-screen display market is highly competitive, so there is considerable pressure to reduce costs. Also, PC makers are demanding ever-higher quality and better features to please customers. In addition, they demand that delivery of your product meets their production schedule needs. Functional managers want your advice on how to best meet these requirements, especially because they are in the process of recruiting new workers and building a production facility.

Questions

1. What kinds of techniques discussed in the chapter can help your functional managers to increase efficiency?
2. In what ways can these managers develop a program to increase quality and innovation?
3. What critical lessons do these managers need to learn about value chain management?

Case in the News [LO9-1, 9-2]

Customer Service in a Shrinking Economy

Hertz couldn't ask for a better customer than Richard M. Garber. The Cleveland-based business development manager typically rents cars from the chain 20 to 40 times a year when traveling on business for materials manufacturer FLEXcon. But now Garber is rethinking that loyalty. In the past month he has returned Hertz cars to the Boston and Minneapolis airports only to find nobody waiting with a handheld check-in device. In Minneapolis, Garber had to drag his bags to the counter to return his car; in Boston, he finally tracked down an employee who came out and explained that some colleagues had just been laid off. "When you're

rushing for an airplane, every minute counts," says Garber. "The less convenient they are, the more likely I am to try someone else." As the economy plunges deeper into recession, many companies are confronting the same brutal choices Hertz faced when it announced layoffs of some 4,000 people on January 16. While businesses may feel forced to trim costs, cutting too deeply can drive away customers. Across the business world, managers are trying to pull off the same perilous high-wire act. Just as companies are dealing with plummeting sales and sinking employee morale, skittish customers want more attention, better quality, and greater value for their money. Those same customers are also acutely aware that their patronage is of growing importance to companies as others decrease their spending.

The reality, of course, is that the opposite is often true. From retailers such as Talbots, which have stiffened their rules on returns, to airlines that now charge for checked bags, companies are stretching budgets in ways that can make things tougher for customers. But the best performers are actually doing more to safeguard service in this recession. Top performers are treating their best customers better than ever, even if that means doing less to wow new ones. While cutting back-office expenses, they're trying to preserve frontline jobs and investing in cheap technology to improve service. If anything, the tough economy has made starker the difference between companies that put customers first and those that sacrifice loyalty for short-term gain. Smart players have learned from previous downturns. Companies used to go after customer reps with the same blunt ax used elsewhere. Now managers are starting to understand the long-term damage created by such moves, from eroded market share to diminished brand value.

A better strategy is to get more out of the people you have. USAA, the insurance and financial services giant that caters to military families and ranks at No. 2 on our list, started cross-training its call center reps in 2007. Some 60% of the agents who answer investment queries can now respond to insurance-related calls. Not only did such training curb call transfers between agents, which drive up the cost of running a call center, but it also improved productivity. Reps are more empowered to deal with customers, even if they may also have to do more work. For those that slash costs, the challenge is keeping customers from noticing. Putting call center reps under one roof, for example, can eventually save as much as 35%. USAA announced it will combine its six call centers into four, for example, and companies such as KeyBank and Ace Hardware have also consolidated operations in the past year.

Hoteliers also are trying to trim in ways customers are unlikely to detect. They're increasingly combining purchasing power to get better deals across properties that are within the same chain but may have different owners. Some hotels in the Four Seasons chain are joining up to buy goods and services such as coffee, valet parking agreements, and overnight cleaning contracts that each hotel once bought on its own. JW Marriott hotels are teaming up to buy landscaping services that would be costlier if contracted for separately. The Ritz-Carlton is doing laundry at night to save electricity and replacing fresh flowers at posh properties with potted plants as occupancy rates fall. As the game changes from acquiring new customers to keeping old ones, companies are shifting more resources to their steady patrons. They're the ones who pay the bills. And while first-time guests may not miss the fresh flowers, repeat customers probably will.

Some companies are experimenting more with cheap technology, such as responding to customers via Twitter after they broadcast their complaints to the world. Other tech upgrades for customers can deliver unexpected cost savings. When BMW rolled out Wi-Fi service at its dealerships last year, the move was intended to give customers a cheap way to pass the time while their cars were serviced. The cost was next to nothing since BMW just expanded the broadband dealers already used to run their businesses. But now that customers can use their waiting time productively, fewer are opting for free loaner cars, which are pricey for dealers to maintain. BMW's Alan Harris says Wi-Fi, along with software that helps dealers better estimate loaner needs, has helped BMW cut its monthly loaner expenses by 10% to 15%. When companies come up with simple, low-cost ways to trim costs while improving life for customers, they're likely to win in good times and bad.

Questions for Discussion

1. List the various value chain strategies the companies discussed here used to increase efficiency and effectiveness.
2. How can companies best increase responsiveness to customers while controlling costs to increase efficiency?
3. Search the Web for more examples of companies who are finding ways to manage their value chains to increase responsiveness to customers.

Source: J. McGregor, A. McConnon, and D. Kiley, "Customer Service in a Shrinking Economy," *BusinessWeek*, February 19, 2009. Reprinted from February 19, 2009 issue of *Bloomberg Businessweek* by special permission, copyright © 2009 by Bloomberg L.P.

CHAPTER 10

Managing Organizational Structure and Culture

Learning Objectives

After studying this chapter, you should be able to:

LO10-1 Identify the factors that influence managers' choice of an organizational structure.

LO10-2 Explain how managers group tasks into jobs that are motivating and satisfying for employees.

LO10-3 Describe the types of organizational structures managers can design, and explain why they choose one structure over another.

LO10-4 Explain why managers must coordinate jobs, functions, and divisions using the hierarchy of authority and integrating mechanisms.

LO10-5 List the four sources of organizational culture, and explain why and how a company's culture can lead to competitive advantage.

A MANAGER'S CHALLENGE

Andrea Jung Reorganizes Avon's Global Structure

How should managers organize to improve performance? After a decade of profitable growth under its CEO Andrea Jung, Avon suddenly began to experience falling global sales in the mid-2000s both in developing markets in Central Europe, Russia, and China, a major source of its rising sales, and in the United States and Mexico. Avon's booming stock price plunged by 2007, and Jung was shocked by this turn of events. For the first time as CEO she faced the problem of having to solve the crisis it now was experiencing—rather than searching for new ways to add to its success.[1]

After several months jetting around the globe to visit the managers of its worldwide divisions, she came to a surprising conclusion: Avon's rapid global expansion had given these managers too much autonomy. They had gained so much authority to control operations in their respective countries and world regions that they had made decisions to benefit their own divisions—and these decisions had hurt the performance of the whole company. Avon's country-level managers from Poland to Mexico ran their own factories, made their own product development decisions, and developed their own advertising campaigns. And these decisions were often based on poor marketing knowledge and with little concern for operating costs; their goal was to increase sales as fast as possible. Also, when too much authority is decentralized to managers lower in an organization's hierarchy, these managers often recruit more managers to help them build their country "empires." The result was that Avon's global organizational hierarchy had exploded—it had risen from 7 levels to 15 levels of managers in a decade as tens of thousands of extra managers were hired around the globe.[2] Because Avon's profits were rising fast,

Andrea Jung, here addressing a stellar group of women leaders in the White House, has seen her tough streamlining decisions in the short term begin to pay off over the longer haul.

Jung had not paid enough attention to the way Avon's organizational structure was becoming taller and taller—just as it was getting wider and wider as it established new divisions in new countries to expand cosmetics sales.

By 2008 Jung realized she had to lay off thousands of Avon's global managers and restructure its organizational hierarchy to reduce costs and increase profitability. She embarked on a program to take away the authority of Avon's country-level managers and to transfer authority to global regional and corporate headquarters managers to streamline decision making and reduce costs. She cut out seven levels of management and laid off 25% of Avon's global managers in its 114 worldwide markets. Then, using teams of expert managers from corporate headquarters, she examined all of Avon's functional activities, country by country, to find out why its costs had risen so quickly and what could be done to bring them under control. The duplication of marketing efforts in countries around the world was one source of these high costs. In Mexico one team found that country managers' desire to expand their empires led to the development of a staggering 13,000 different products! Not only had this led product development costs to soar; it had also caused major marketing problems—how could Avon's Mexican sales reps learn about the differences between so many products to help customers choose the right ones for them?

In Avon's new structure, the goal is to centralize all major new product development. Avon still develops over 1,000 new products a year, but in the future while the input from different country managers will be used to customize products to country needs in terms of fragrance, packaging, and so on, R&D will be performed in the United States. Similarly, Avon's present strategy is to develop marketing campaigns targeted toward the average global customer but that can be easily customized to a particular country or world region by, for example, using the appropriate language or nationality of the models. Other initiatives have been to increase the money spent on global marketing, which had not kept pace with Avon's rapid global expansion, and to hire more Avon salespeople in developing nations to attract more customers. Today Avon has recruited over 400,000 reps in China alone![3]

Country-level managers now are responsible for managing this army of Avon reps and for making sure that marketing dollars are directed toward the right channels for maximum impact. However, they no longer have authority to engage in major product development or build new manufacturing capacity—or to hire new managers without the agreement of regional or corporate level managers. The balance of control has changed at Avon, and Jung and all her managers are now firmly focused on making operational decisions in the best interests of the whole company.

Jung's efforts to streamline the company's organizational structure have worked; but the recession necessitated more restructuring, and the company began another program of downsizing. Jung's focus has been on realigning its global value chain operations, particularly in Western Europe and Latin America; and Avon has increased its use of outsourcing, such as by outsourcing its call centers and transaction processing functions. As a result of these initiatives, approximately 4,000 more global positions will be lost by 2012; but Jung hopes that by then with its new streamlined structure Avon will be able to expand rapidly again when the economy has recovered—analysts claim the prospects for the company in China alone are "outstanding." Avon's share price had recovered by 2010. Clearly, paying attention to organizing is important in determining a company's long-term profitability.

Overview

As the example of Avon suggests, when the environment changes because, for example, customer tastes change, or because agile competitors have developed new strategies to outperform their rivals, a company often has to change its organizational structure and move to one better suited to its new environment. How an organization is designed also affects employees' behavior and how well the organization operates; and with competition heating up in the cosmetics industry, the challenge facing Avon's Andrea Jung was to identify the best way to organize people and resources to increase efficiency and effectiveness.

organizational architecture The organizational structure, control systems, culture, and human resource management systems that together determine how efficiently and effectively organizational resources are used.

organizational structure A formal system of task and reporting relationships that coordinates and motivates organizational members so they work together to achieve organizational goals.

In Part 4 of this book, we examine how managers can organize and control human and other resources to create high-performing organizations. To organize and control (two of the four tasks of management identified in Chapter 1), managers must design an organizational architecture that makes the best use of resources to produce the goods and services customers want. **Organizational architecture** is the combination of organizational structure, culture, control systems, and human resource management (HRM) systems that together determine how efficiently and effectively organizational resources are used.

By the end of this chapter, you will be familiar not only with various forms of organizational structures and cultures but also with various factors that determine the organizational design choices that managers make. Then, in Chapters 11 and 12, we examine issues surrounding the design of an organization's control systems and HRM systems.

Designing Organizational Structure

LO10-1 Identify the factors that influence managers' choice of an organizational structure.

organizational design The process by which managers make specific organizing choices that result in a particular kind of organizational structure.

Organizing is the process by which managers establish the structure of working relationships among employees to allow them to achieve organizational goals efficiently and effectively. **Organizational structure** is the formal system of task and job reporting relationships that determines how employees use resources to achieve organizational goals.[4] *Organizational culture,* discussed in Chapter 3, is the shared set of beliefs, values, and norms that influence how people and groups work together to achieve organizational goals. **Organizational design** is the process by which managers create a specific type of organizational structure and culture so a company can operate in the most efficient and effective way–as Andrea Jung did for Avon.[5]

Once a company decides what kind of work attitudes and behaviors it wants from its employees, managers create a particular arrangement of task and authority relationships, and promote specific cultural values and norms, to obtain these desired attitudes and behaviors. The challenge facing all companies is to design a structure and culture that (1) *motivate* managers and employees to work hard and to develop supportive job behaviors and attitudes and (2) *coordinate* the actions of employees, groups, functions, and divisions to ensure they work together efficiently and effectively.

As noted in Chapter 2, according to contingency theory, managers design organizational structures to fit the factors or circumstances that are affecting the company the most and causing the most uncertainty.[6] Thus there is no one best way to design an organization: Design reflects each organization's specific situation, and researchers have argued that in some situations stable, mechanistic structures may be most appropriate while in others flexible, organic structures might be the most effective. Four factors are important determinants of the type of organizational structure or culture managers select: the nature of the organizational environment, the type of strategy the organization pursues, the technology (and particularly information technology) the organization uses, and the characteristics of the organization's human resources (see Figure 10.1).[7]

The Organizational Environment

In general, the more quickly the external environment is changing and the greater the uncertainty within it, the greater are the problems managers face in trying to gain access to scarce resources. In this situation, to speed decision making and communication and make it easier to obtain resources, managers typically make organizing choices that result in more flexible structures and entrepreneurial cultures.[8] They are likely to decentralize authority, empower lower-level employees to make important operating decisions, and encourage values and norms that emphasize change and innovation–a more organic from of organizing.

In contrast, if the external environment is stable, resources are readily available, and uncertainty is low, then less coordination and communication among people and functions are needed to obtain resources. Managers can make organizing choices that bring more stability or formality to the organizational structure and can establish values and norms that emphasize obedience and being a team player. Managers in this situation prefer to make decisions within a clearly defined hierarchy of authority and to use detailed rules, standard operating procedures (SOPs), and restrictive norms to guide and govern employees' activities–a more mechanistic form of organizing.

As we discussed in Chapter 6, change is rapid in today's marketplace, and increasing competition both at home and abroad is putting greater pressure on managers to attract customers and increase efficiency and effectiveness. Consequently, interest in finding ways to structure organizations–such as through empowerment and self-managed teams–to allow people and departments to behave flexibly has been increasing.

Figure 10.1
Factors Affecting Organizational Structure

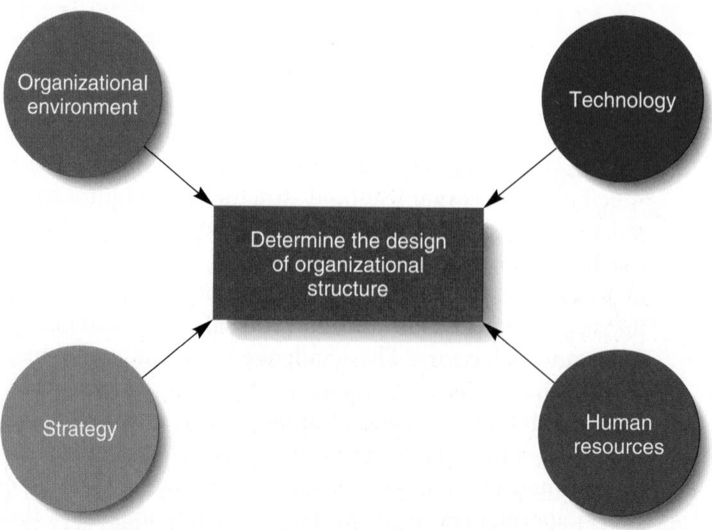

Strategy

Chapter 8 suggests that once managers decide on a strategy, they must choose the right means to implement it. Different strategies often call for the use of different organizational structures and cultures. For example, a differentiation strategy aimed at increasing the value customers perceive in an organization's goods and services usually succeeds best in a flexible structure with a culture that values innovation; flexibility facilitates a differentiation strategy because managers can develop new or innovative products quickly–an activity that requires extensive cooperation among functions or departments. In contrast, a low-cost strategy that is aimed at driving down costs in all functions usually fares best in a more formal structure with more conservative norms, which gives managers greater control over the activities of an organization's various departments.[9]

In addition, at the corporate level, when managers decide to expand the scope of organizational activities by vertical integration or diversification, for example, they need to design a flexible structure to provide sufficient coordination among the different business divisions.[10] As discussed in Chapter 8, many companies have been divesting businesses because managers have been unable to create a competitive advantage to keep them up to speed in fast-changing industries. By moving to a more flexible structure, managers gain more control over their different businesses. Finally, expanding internationally and operating in many different countries challenges managers to create organizational structures that allow organizations to be flexible on a global level.[11] As we discuss later, managers can group their departments or divisions in several ways to allow them to effectively pursue an international strategy.

Technology

Recall that technology is the combination of skills, knowledge, machines, and computers that are used to design, make, and distribute goods and services. As a rule, the more complicated the technology that an organization uses, the more difficult it is to regulate or control it because more unexpected events can arise. Thus the more complicated the technology, the greater is the need for a flexible structure and progressive culture to enhance managers' ability to respond to unexpected situations–and give them the freedom and desire to work out new solutions to the problems they encounter. In contrast, the more routine the technology, the more appropriate is a formal structure because tasks are simple and the steps needed to produce goods and services have been worked out in advance.

What makes a technology routine or complicated? One researcher who investigated this issue, Charles Perrow, argued that two factors determine how complicated or nonroutine technology is: task variety and task analyzability.[12] *Task variety* is the number of new or unexpected problems or situations that a person or function encounters in performing tasks or jobs. *Task analyzability* is the degree to which programmed solutions are available to people or functions to solve the problems they encounter. Nonroutine or complicated technologies are characterized by high task variety and low task analyzability; this means many varied problems occur and solving these problems requires significant nonprogrammed decision making. In contrast, routine technologies are characterized by low task variety and high task analyzability; this means the problems encountered do not vary much and are easily resolved through programmed decision making.

Examples of nonroutine technology are found in the work of scientists in an R&D laboratory who develop new products or discover new drugs, and they are seen in the planning exercises an organization's top management team uses to chart the organization's future strategy. Examples of routine technology include typical mass-production or assembly operations, where workers perform the same task repeatedly and where managers have already identified the programmed solutions necessary to perform a task efficiently. Similarly, in service organizations such as fast-food restaurants, the tasks that crew members perform in making and serving fast food are routine.

Human Resources

LO10-2 Explain how managers group tasks into jobs that are motivating and satisfying for employees.

A final important factor affecting an organization's choice of structure and culture is the characteristics of the human resources it employs. In general, the more highly skilled its workforce, and the greater the number of employees who work together in groups or teams, the more likely an organization is to use a flexible, decentralized structure and a professional culture based on values and norms that foster employee autonomy and self-control. Highly skilled employees, or employees who have internalized strong professional values and norms of behavior as part of their training, usually desire greater freedom and autonomy and dislike close supervision.

Flexible structures, characterized by decentralized authority and empowered employees, are well suited to the needs of highly skilled people. Similarly, when people work in teams, they must be allowed to interact freely and develop norms to guide their own work interactions, which also is possible in a flexible organizational structure. Thus, when designing organizational structure and culture, managers must pay close attention to the needs of the workforce and to the complexity and kind of work employees perform.

In summary, an organization's external environment, strategy, technology, and human resources are the factors to be considered by managers seeking to design the best structure and culture for an organization. The greater the level of uncertainty in the organization's environment, the more complex its strategy and technologies, and the more highly qualified and skilled its workforce, the more likely managers are to design a structure and a culture that are flexible, can change quickly, and allow employees to be innovative in their responses to problems, customer needs, and so on. The more stable the organization's environment, the less complex and more well understood its strategy or technology, and the less skilled its workforce, the more likely managers are to design an organizational structure that is formal and controlling and a culture whose values and norms prescribe how employees should act in particular situations.

Later in the chapter we discuss how managers can create different kinds of organizational cultures. First, however, we discuss how managers can design flexible or formal organizational structures. The way an organization's structure works depends on the organizing choices managers make about three issues:

- How to group tasks into individual jobs.
- How to group jobs into functions and divisions.
- How to allocate authority and coordinate or integrate functions and divisions.

Grouping Tasks into Jobs: Job Design

The first step in organizational design is **job design,** the process by which managers decide how to divide into specific jobs the tasks that have to be performed to provide customers with goods and services. Managers at McDonald's, for example, have decided how best to divide the tasks required to provide customers with fast, cheap food in each McDonald's restaurant. After experimenting with different job arrangements, McDonald's managers decided on a basic division of labor among chefs and food servers. Managers allocated all the tasks involved in actually cooking the food (putting oil in the fat fryers, opening packages of frozen french fries, putting beef patties on the grill, making salads, and so on) to the job of chef. They allocated all the tasks involved in giving the food to customers (such as greeting customers, taking orders, putting fries and burgers into bags, adding salt, pepper, and napkins, and taking money) to food servers. In addition, they created other jobs–the job of dealing with drive-through customers, the job of keeping the restaurant clean, and the job of overseeing employees and responding to unexpected events. The result of the job design process is a *division of labor* among employees, one that McDonald's managers have discovered through experience is most efficient.

job design The process by which managers decide how to divide tasks into specific jobs.

At Subway, the roles of chef and server are combined into one, making the job "larger" than the jobs of McDonald's more specialized food servers. The idea behind job enlargement is that increasing the range of tasks performed by the worker will reduce boredom.

Establishing an appropriate division of labor among employees is a critical part of the organizing process, one that is vital to increasing efficiency and effectiveness. At McDonald's, the tasks associated with chef and food server were split into different jobs because managers found that, for the kind of food McDonald's serves, this approach was most efficient. It is efficient because when each employee is given fewer tasks to perform (so that each job becomes more specialized), employees become more productive at performing the tasks that constitute each job.

At Subway sandwich shops, however, managers chose a different kind of job design. At Subway there is no division of labor among the people who make the sandwiches, wrap the sandwiches, give them to customers, and take the money. The roles of chef and food server are combined into one. This different division of tasks and jobs is efficient for Subway and not for McDonald's because Subway serves a limited menu of mostly submarine-style sandwiches that are prepared to order. Subway's production system is far simpler than McDonald's; McDonald's menu is much more varied, and its chefs must cook many different kinds of foods. In 2010, however, Subway announced that it would start its own breakfast menu to increase its product sales.

job simplification The process of reducing the number of tasks that each worker performs.

Managers of every organization must analyze the range of tasks to be performed and then create jobs that best allow the organization to give customers the goods and services they want. In deciding how to assign tasks to individual jobs, however, managers must be careful not to take **job simplification,** the process of reducing the number of tasks that each worker performs, too far.[13] Too much job simplification may reduce efficiency rather than increase it if workers find their simplified jobs boring and monotonous, become demotivated and unhappy, and, as a result, perform at a low level.

Job Enlargement and Job Enrichment

In an attempt to create a division of labor and design individual jobs to encourage workers to perform at a higher level and be more satisfied with their work, several researchers have proposed ways other than job simplification to group tasks into jobs: job enlargement and job enrichment.

job enlargement Increasing the number of different tasks in a given job by changing the division of labor.

Job enlargement is increasing the number of different tasks in a given job by changing the division of labor.[14] For example, because Subway food servers make the food as well as serve it, their jobs are "larger" than the jobs of McDonald's food servers. The idea behind job enlargement is that increasing the range of tasks performed by a worker will reduce boredom and fatigue and may increase motivation to perform at a high level–increasing both the quantity and the quality of goods and services provided.

job enrichment Increasing the degree of responsibility a worker has over his or her job.

Job enrichment is increasing the degree of responsibility a worker has over a job by, for example, (1) empowering workers to experiment to find new or better ways of doing the job, (2) encouraging workers to develop new skills, (3) allowing workers to decide how to do the work and giving them the responsibility for deciding how to respond to unexpected situations, and (4) allowing workers to monitor and measure their own performance.[15] The idea behind job enrichment is that increasing workers' responsibility increases their involvement in their jobs and thus improves their interest in the quality of the goods they make or the services they provide.

In general, managers who make design choices that increase job enrichment and job enlargement are likely to increase the degree to which people behave flexibly rather than rigidly or mechanically. Narrow, specialized jobs are likely to lead people to behave in predictable ways; workers who perform a variety of tasks and who are allowed and encouraged to discover new and better ways to perform their jobs are likely to act flexibly and creatively. Thus managers who enlarge and enrich jobs create a flexible organizational structure, and those who simplify jobs create a more formal structure. If workers are grouped into self-managed work teams, the organization is likely to be flexible because team members provide support for each other and can learn from one another.

LO10-3 Describe the types of organizational structures managers can design, and explain why they choose one structure over another.

The Job Characteristics Model

J. R. Hackman and G. R. Oldham's job characteristics model is an influential model of job design that explains in detail how managers can make jobs more interesting and motivating.[16] Hackman and Oldham's model (see Figure 10.2) also describes the likely personal and organizational outcomes that will result from enriched and enlarged jobs.

According to Hackman and Oldham, every job has five characteristics that determine how motivating the job is. These characteristics determine how employees react to their work and lead to outcomes such as high performance and satisfaction and low absenteeism and turnover:

- *Skill variety:* The extent to which a job requires that an employee use a wide range of different skills, abilities, or knowledge. Example: The skill variety required by the job of a research scientist is higher than that called for by the job of a McDonald's food server.
- *Task identity:* The extent to which a job requires that a worker perform all the tasks necessary to complete the job, from the beginning to the end of the production process. Example: A craftsworker who takes a piece of wood and transforms it into a custom-made desk has higher task identity than does a worker who performs only one of the numerous operations required to assemble a flat-screen TV.
- *Task significance:* The degree to which a worker feels his or her job is meaningful because of its effect on people inside the organization, such as coworkers, or on people outside the organization, such as customers. Example: A teacher who sees the effect of his or her efforts in a well-educated and well-adjusted student enjoys high task significance compared to a dishwasher who monotonously washes dishes as they come to the kitchen.
- *Autonomy:* The degree to which a job gives an employee the freedom and discretion needed to schedule different tasks and decide how to carry them out. Example: Salespeople who have to plan their schedules and decide how to allocate

Figure 10.2
The Job Characteristics Model

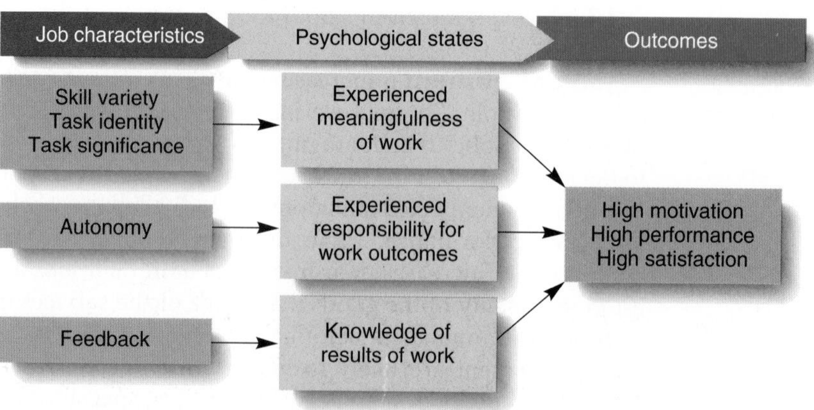

Source: J. Richard Hackman and Greg R. Oldham, *Work Redesign*, 1st edition, © 1980. Reproduced by permission of Pearson Education, Inc., Upper Saddle River, New Jersey.

their time among different customers have relatively high autonomy compared to assembly-line workers, whose actions are determined by the speed of the production line.

- *Feedback:* The extent to which actually doing a job provides a worker with clear and direct information about how well he or she has performed the job. Example: An air traffic controller whose mistakes may result in a midair collision receives immediate feedback on job performance; a person who compiles statistics for a business magazine often has little idea of when he or she makes a mistake or does a particularly good job.

Hackman and Oldham argue that these five job characteristics affect an employee's motivation because they affect three critical psychological states (see Figure 10.2). The more employees feel that their work is *meaningful* and that they are *responsible for work outcomes and responsible for knowing how those outcomes affect others,* the more motivating work becomes and the more likely employees are to be satisfied and to perform at a high level. Moreover, employees who have jobs that are highly motivating are called on to use their skills more and to perform more tasks, and they are given more responsibility for doing the job. All of the foregoing are characteristic of jobs and employees in flexible structures where authority is decentralized and where employees commonly work with others and must learn new skills to complete the range of tasks for which their group is responsible.

Grouping Jobs into Functions and Divisions: Designing Organizational Structure

Once managers have decided which tasks to allocate to which jobs, they face the next organizing decision: how to group jobs together to best match the needs of the organization's environment, strategy, technology, and human resources. Typically managers first decide to group jobs into departments and then design a *functional structure* to use organizational resources effectively. As an organization grows and becomes more difficult to control, managers must choose a more complex organizational design, such as a divisional structure or a matrix or product team structure. The different way in which managers can design organizational structure are discussed next. Selecting and designing an organizational structure to increase efficiency and effectiveness is a significant challenge. As noted in Chapter 8, managers reap the rewards of a well-thought-out strategy only if they choose the right type of structure to implement the strategy. The ability to make the right kinds of organizing choices is often what differentiates effective from ineffective managers and creates a high-performing organization.

Functional Structure

A *function* is a group of people, working together, who possess similar skills or use the same kind of knowledge, tools, or techniques to perform their jobs. Manufacturing, sales, and research and development are often organized into functional departments. A **functional structure** is an organizational structure composed of all the departments that an organization requires to produce its goods or services. Figure 10.3 shows the functional structure that Pier 1 Imports, the home furnishings company, uses to supply its customers with a range of goods from around the world to satisfy their desires for new and innovative products.

functional structure An organizational structure composed of all the departments that an organization requires to produce its goods or services.

Pier 1's main functions are finance and administration, merchandising (purchasing the goods), stores (managing the retail outlets), planning and allocations (managing marketing, credit, and product distribution), and human resources. Each job inside a function exists because it helps the function perform the activities necessary for high organizational performance. Thus within the planning and allocations function are all

Figure 10.3
The Functional Structure of Pier 1 Imports

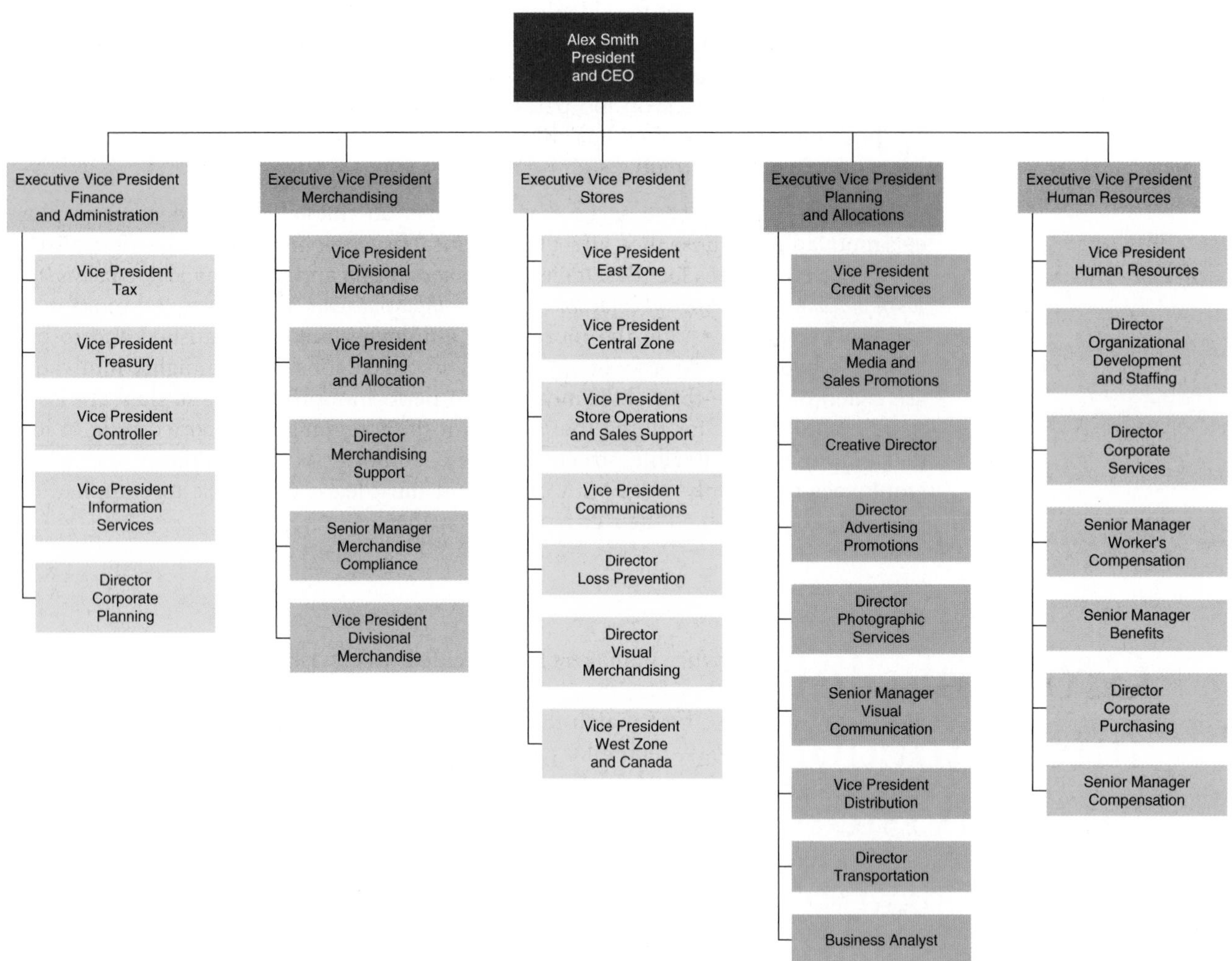

the jobs necessary to efficiently advertise Pier 1's products to increase their appeal to customers (such as promotion, photography, and visual communication) and then to distribute and transport the products to stores.

There are several advantages to grouping jobs according to function. First, when people who perform similar jobs are grouped together, they can learn from observing one another and thus become more specialized and can perform at a higher level. The tasks associated with one job often are related to the tasks associated with another job, which encourages cooperation within a function. In Pier 1's planning department, for example, the person designing the photography program for an ad campaign works closely with the person responsible for designing store layouts and with visual communication experts. As a result, Pier 1 is able to develop a strong, focused marketing campaign to differentiate its products.

Second, when people who perform similar jobs are grouped together, it is easier for managers to monitor and evaluate their performance.[17] Imagine if marketing experts, purchasing experts, and real estate experts were grouped together in one function and supervised by a manager from merchandising. Obviously the merchandising manager would not have the expertise to evaluate all these different people appropriately. A functional structure allows workers to evaluate how well coworkers are performing their jobs, and if some workers are performing poorly, more experienced workers can help them develop new skills.

Pier 1 organizes its operations by function, which means that employees can more easily learn from one another and improve the service they provide to its customers.

Finally, managers appreciate functional structure because it lets them create the set of functions they need to scan and monitor the competitive environment and obtain information about how it is changing.[18] With the right set of functions in place, managers are in a good position to develop a strategy that allows the organization to respond to its changing situation. Employees in the marketing group can specialize in monitoring new marketing developments that will allow Pier 1 to better target its customers. Employees in merchandising can monitor all potential suppliers of home furnishings both at home and abroad to find the goods most likely to appeal to Pier 1's customers and manage Pier 1's global supply chain.

As an organization grows, and particularly as its task environment and strategy change because it is beginning to produce a wider range of goods and services for different kinds of customers, several problems can make a functional structure less efficient and effective.[19] First, managers in different functions may find it more difficult to communicate and coordinate with one another when they are responsible for several different kinds of products, especially as the organization grows both domestically and internationally. Second, functional managers may become so preoccupied with supervising their own specific departments and achieving their departmental goals that they lose sight of organizational goals. If that happens, organizational effectiveness will suffer because managers will be viewing issues and problems facing the organization only from their own, relatively narrow, departmental perspectives.[20] Both of these problems can reduce efficiency and effectiveness.

Divisional Structures: Product, Market, and Geographic

divisional structure An organizational structure composed of separate business units within which are the functions that work together to produce a specific product for a specific customer.

As the problems associated with growth and diversification increase over time, managers must search for new ways to organize their activities to overcome the problems associated with a functional structure. Most managers of large organizations choose a **divisional structure** and create a series of business units to produce a specific kind of product for a specific kind of customer. Each *division* is a collection of functions or departments that work together to produce the product. The goal behind the change to a divisional structure is to create smaller, more manageable units within the organization. There are three forms of divisional structure (see Figure 10.4).[21] When managers organize divisions according to the *type of good or service* they provide, they adopt a product structure. When managers organize divisions according to the *area of the country or world* they operate in, they adopt a geographic structure. When managers organize divisions according to *the type of customer* they focus on, they adopt a market structure.

PRODUCT STRUCTURE Imagine the problems that managers at Pier 1 would encounter if they decided to diversify into producing and selling cars, fast food, and health insurance–in addition to home furnishings–and tried to use their existing set of functional managers to oversee the production of all four kinds of products. No manager would have the necessary skills or abilities to oversee those four products. No individual marketing manager, for example, could effectively market cars, fast food, health insurance, and home furnishings at the same time. To perform a functional activity successfully, managers must have experience in specific markets or industries. Consequently, if managers decide to diversify into new industries or to expand their range of products, they commonly design a product structure to organize their operations (see Figure 10.4a).

Figure 10.4
Product, Market, and Geographic Structures

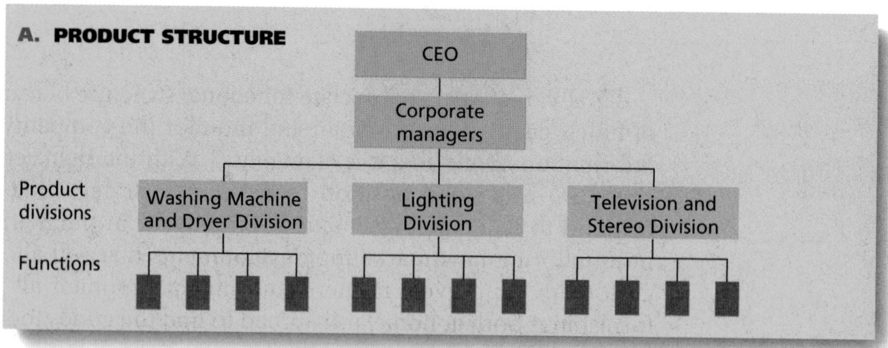

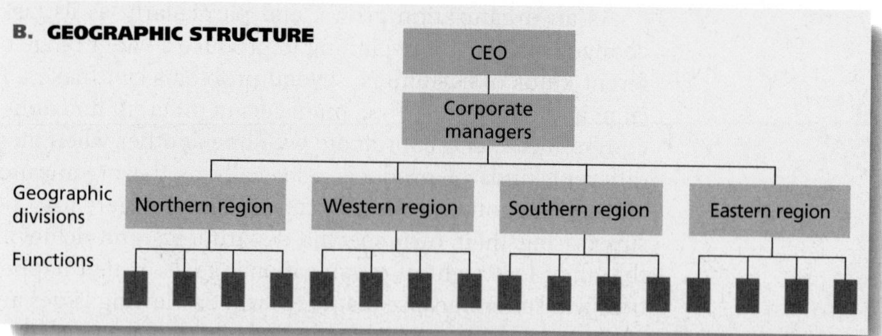

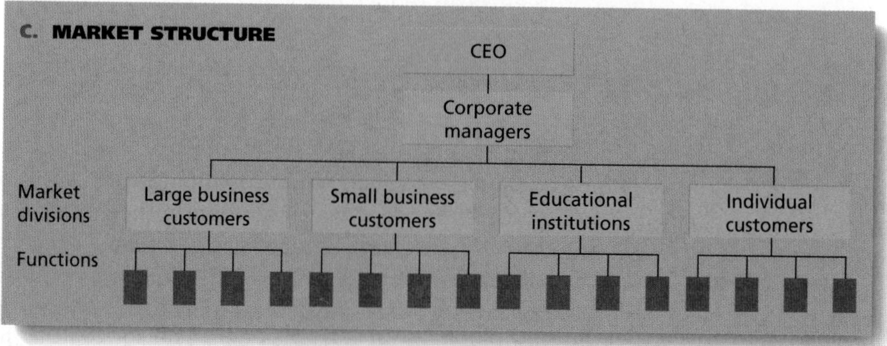

product structure An organizational structure in which each product line or business is handled by a self-contained division.

Using a **product structure,** managers place each distinct product line or business in its own self-contained division and give divisional managers the responsibility for devising an appropriate business-level strategy to allow the division to compete effectively in its industry or market.[22] Each division is self-contained because it has a complete set of all the functions–marketing, R&D, finance, and so on–that it needs to produce or provide goods or services efficiently and effectively. Functional managers report to divisional managers, and divisional managers report to top or corporate managers.

Grouping functions into divisions focused on particular products has several advantages for managers at all levels in the organization. First, a product structure allows functional managers to specialize in only one product area, so they can build expertise and fine-tune their skills in this particular area. Second, each division's managers can become experts in their industry; this expertise helps them choose and develop a business-level strategy to differentiate their products or lower their costs while meeting the needs of customers. Third, a product structure frees corporate managers from the need to supervise directly each division's day-to-day operations; this latitude lets corporate managers create the best corporate-level strategy to maximize the organization's future growth and ability to create value. Corporate managers are likely to make fewer mistakes about which businesses to diversify into or how to best expand internationally, for example, because they can take an organizationwide view.[23] Corporate managers also are likely to evaluate better how well divisional managers are doing, and they can intervene and take corrective action as needed.

The extra layer of management, the divisional management layer, can improve the use of organizational resources. Moreover, a product structure puts divisional managers close to their customers and lets them respond quickly and appropriately to the changing task environment. One pharmaceutical company that successfully adopted a new product structure to better organize its activities is GlaxoSmithKline. The need to innovate new kinds of prescription drugs to boost performance is a continual battle for pharmaceutical companies. In the 2000s many of these companies have been merging to try to increase their research productivity, and one of them, GlaxoSmithKline, was created from the merger between Glaxo Wellcome and SmithKline Beecham.[24] Prior to the merger, both companies experienced a steep decline in the number of new prescription drugs their scientists were able to invent. The problem facing the new company's top managers was how to best use and combine the talents of the scientists and researchers from both of the former companies to allow them to quickly innovate exciting new drugs.

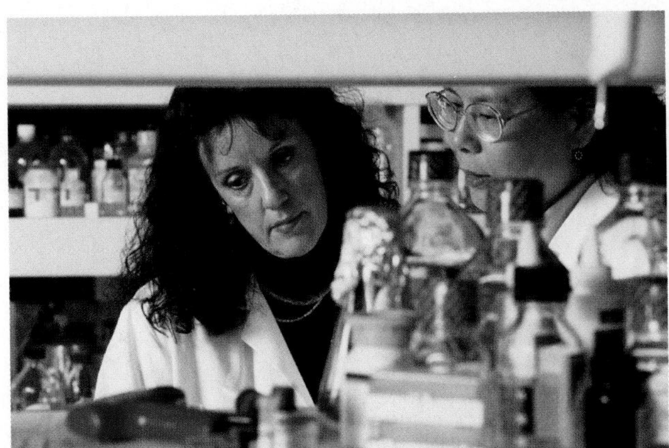

When Glaxo Wellcome and SmithKline Beecham merged, managers resolved the problem of how to coordinate the activities of thousands of research scientists by organizing them into product divisions focusing on clusters of diseases.

Top managers realized that after the merger there would be enormous problems associated with coordinating the activities of the thousands of research scientists who were working on hundreds of different kinds of drug research programs. Understanding the problems associated with large size, the top managers decided to group the researchers into eight product divisions to allow them to focus on particular clusters of diseases such as heart disease or viral infections. The members of each product division were told they would be rewarded based on the number of new prescription drugs they were able to invent and the speed with which they could bring these new drugs to the market. GlaxoSmithKline's new product structure worked well; its research productivity doubled after the reorganization, and a record number of new drugs moved into clinical trials.[25]

GEOGRAPHIC STRUCTURE When organizations expand rapidly both at home and abroad, functional structures can create special problems because managers in one central location may find it increasingly difficult to deal with the different

geographic structure An organizational structure in which each region of a country or area of the world is served by a self-contained division.

problems and issues that may arise in each region of a country or area of the world. In these cases, a **geographic structure,** in which divisions are broken down by geographic location, is often chosen (see Figure 10.4b). To achieve the corporate mission of providing next-day mail service, Fred Smith, CEO of FedEx, chose a geographic structure and divided up operations by creating a division in each region. Large retailers such as Macy's, Neiman Marcus, and Brooks Brothers also use a geographic structure. Because the needs of retail customers differ by region–for example, shorts in California and down parkas in the Midwest–a geographic structure gives retail regional managers the flexibility they need to choose the range of products that best meets the needs of regional customers.

In adopting a *global geographic structure,* such as shown in Figure 10.5a, managers locate different divisions in each of the world regions where the organization operates. Managers are most likely to do this when they pursue a multidomestic strategy because customer needs vary widely by country or world region. For example, if products that appeal to U.S. customers do not sell in Europe, the Pacific Rim, or South America, managers must customize the products to meet the needs of customers in those different world regions; a global geographic structure with global divisions will allow them to do this.

In contrast, to the degree that customers abroad are willing to buy the same kind of product or slight variations thereof, managers are more likely to pursue a global strategy. In this case they are more likely to use a global product structure. In a *global product structure,* each product division, not the country and regional managers, takes responsibility for deciding where to manufacture its products and how to market them in countries worldwide (see Figure 10.5b). Product division managers manage their own global value chains and decide where to establish foreign subsidiaries to distribute and sell their products to customers in foreign countries. As we noted at

Figure 10.5
Global Geographic and Global Product Structures

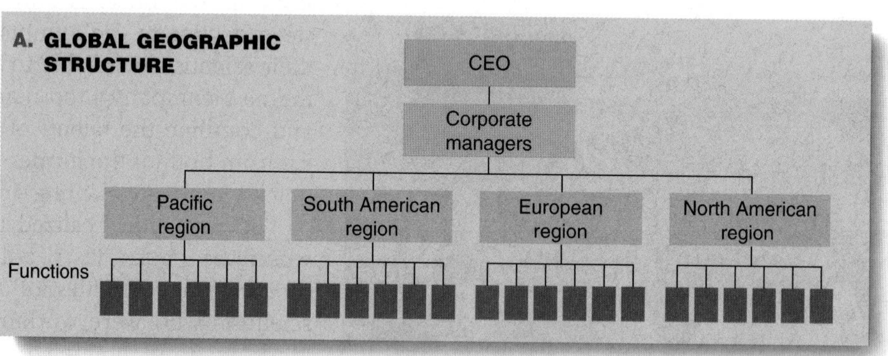

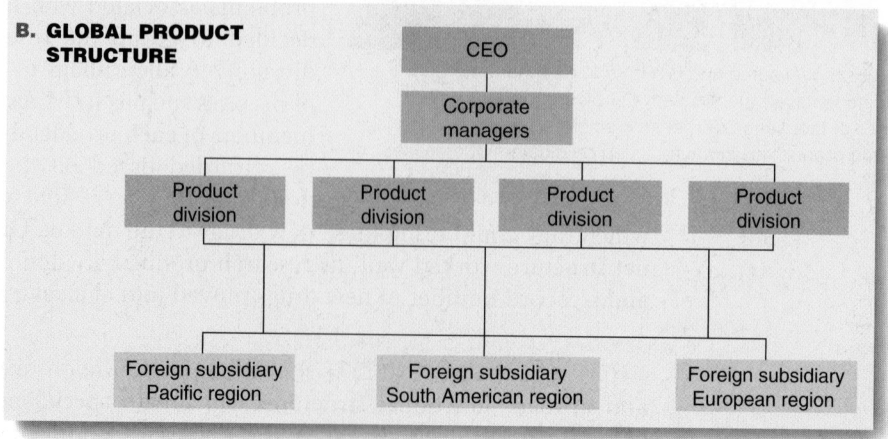

the beginning of this chapter, an organization's strategy is a major determinant of its structure both at home and abroad; and in Chapter 6 we discussed how Nokia took a commanding lead in global cell phone sales because of its strategy of customizing phones to the needs of local users and assembling the phones in a factory located in a country within the world region where the phones are to be sold. Nokia's most important function is its design and engineering function, which spearheads its global new product development efforts. And to allow this function, and the company, to perform most effectively, Nokia adopted a global structure to organize its design activities.

Nokia was the first cell phone manufacturer to recognize that the needs of customers differ markedly in different countries of the world. In Western countries, for example, the style of the phone is paramount, as is its ability to offer users services like e-mail and video downloading, and Nokia is developing advanced smartphones to compete with Apple. In India customers also value style, and they buy a cell phone as a status symbol and so are willing to pay a premium price for it. But in China customers want a bargain–the phone has to be at the right price point if customers are to buy the entry-level version or be enticed to spend more for premium features. How did Nokia discover how much needs diverge among customers in different countries?

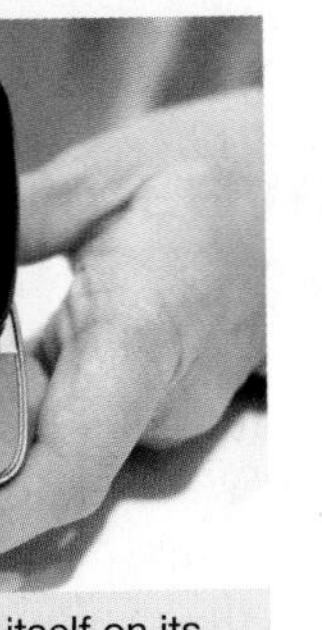

Click, click, click. Nokia can pride itself on its forward-thinking momentum, which prompted it to develop regionally based products.

Its top managers decided that the engineers in its vast central design studio in Finland should be in charge of basic cell phone R&D and monitoring changing global forces in technology and changing customer demand for services such as video downloads, touch screens, colors, and so forth. However, to get close to customers in different countries, top managers decided to open nine different geographic design studios in various world regions and countries, such as India and China, where Nokia hopes to generate the most sales revenues. Engineers in these geographic studios, aided by marketing experts, determine the most important country-specific customer preferences.[26] These preferences are then transmitted back to Nokia's Finnish design headquarters, where they are incorporated into the studio's knowledge about changing global preferences for faster Internet service, touch screens, and so on. The result is a range of phones that share much in common but that can be highly customized to the needs of customers in different regions and countries. So Nokia uses a global divisional structure to facilitate its global design and manufacturing competencies as it attempts to remain ahead in the fiercely competitive global cell phone market.

MARKET STRUCTURE Sometimes the pressing issue facing managers is to group functions according to the type of customer buying the product in order to tailor the products the organization offers to each customer's unique demands. A PC maker such as Dell, for example, has several kinds of customers, including large businesses (which might demand networks of computers linked to a mainframe computer), small companies (which may need just a few PCs linked together), educational users in schools and universities (which might want thousands of independent PCs for their students), and individual users (who may want a high-quality multimedia PC so they can play the latest video games).

market structure An organizational structure in which each kind of customer is served by a self-contained division; also called *customer structure.*

To satisfy the needs of diverse customers, a company might adopt a **market structure,** which groups divisions according to the particular kinds of customers they serve (see Figure 10.4c). A market structure lets managers be responsive to the needs of their customers and allows them to act flexibly in making decisions in response to customers' changing needs. To spearhead its turnaround, for example, Dell, as discussed in "A Manager's Challenge" in Chapter 9, has also changed its structure, which like Avon's had become too complex as it expanded globally. Today it has four streamlined market divisions that each focus on being responsive to one particular type of customer: individual consumers (headed by Ronald Garriques), small businesses, large companies, and government and state agencies. All kinds of organizations need to continually evaluate their structures, as is suggested in the following "Management Insight" box, which examines how a major school district increased its performance.

Matrix and Product Team Designs

Moving to a product, market, or geographic divisional structure allows managers to respond more quickly and flexibly to the particular circumstances they confront. However, when information technology or customer needs are changing rapidly and the environment is uncertain, even a divisional structure may not give managers enough flexibility to respond to the environment quickly. To operate effectively under these conditions, managers must design the most flexible kind of organizational structure available: a matrix structure or a product team structure (see Figure 10.6).

Management Insight

A School District Moves from a Geographic to a Market Structure

Like all organizations, state and city government agencies such as school districts may become too tall and bureaucratic over time and, as they grow, develop ineffective and inefficient organizational structures. This happened to the Houston Independent School District (HISD) when the explosive growth of the city during the last decades added over a million new students to school rolls. As Houston expanded many miles in every direction to become the fourth largest U.S. city, successive HISD superintendents adopted a geographic structure to coordinate and control all the teaching functions involved in creating high-performing elementary, middle, and high schools. The HISD eventually created five different geographic regions or regional school districts. And over time each regional district sought to control more of its own functional activities and became increasingly critical of HISD's central administration. The result was a slowdown in decision making, infighting between districts, an increasingly in-effectual team of district administrators, and falling student academic test scores across the city.

In 2010 a new HISD superintendent was appointed who, working on the suggestions of HISD's top managers, decided to reorganize HISD into a market structure. HISD's new organizational structure is now grouped by the needs of its customers–its students–and three "chief officers" oversee all of Houston's high schools, middle schools, and elementary schools, respectively. The focus will now be on the needs of its three types of students, not on the needs of the former five regional managers. Over 270 positions were eliminated in this restructuring, saving over $8 million per year, and many observers hope to see more cost savings ahead.

Many important support functions were recentralized to HISD's headquarters office to eliminate redundancies and reduce costs, including teacher professional development. Also, a new support function called school improvement was formed with managers charged to share ideas and information between schools and oversee their performance on many dimensions to improve service and student performance. HISD administrators also hope that eliminating the regional geographic structure will encourage schools to share best practices and cooperate so student education and test scores will improve over time.

Figure 10.6
Matrix and Product Team Structures

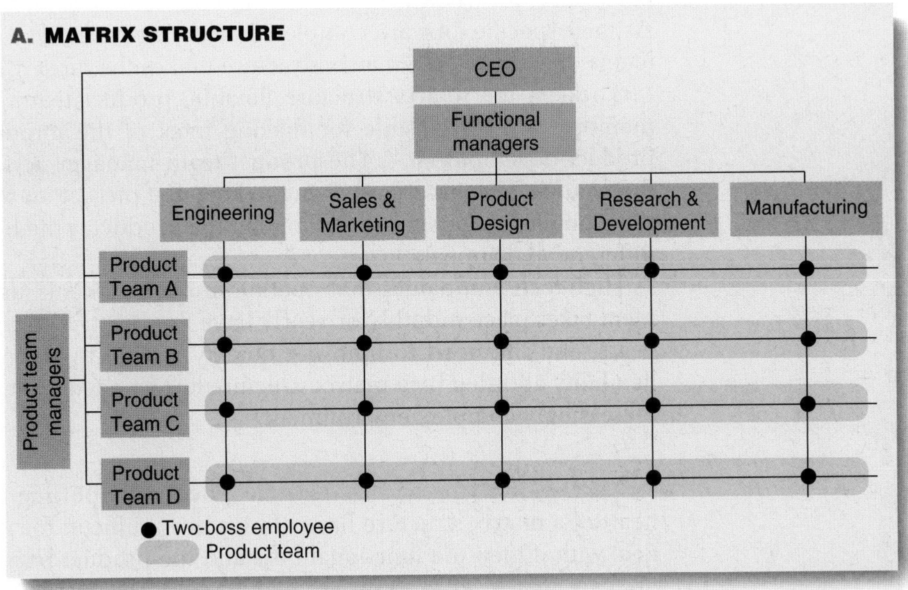

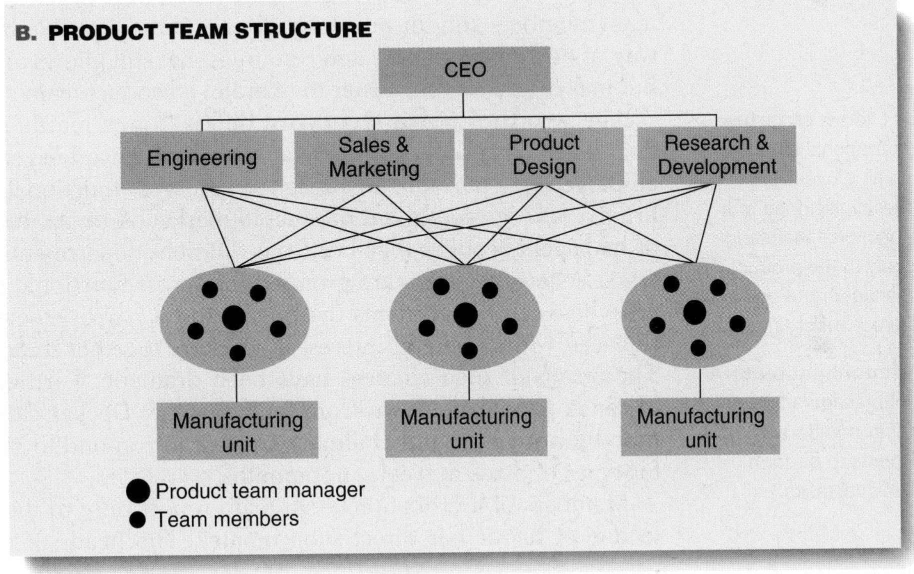

matrix structure An organizational structure that simultaneously groups people and resources by function and by product.

MATRIX STRUCTURE In a **matrix structure,** managers group people and resources in two ways simultaneously: by function and by product.[27] Employees are grouped by *functions* to allow them to learn from one another and become more skilled and productive. In addition, employees are grouped into *product teams* in which members of different functions work together to develop a specific product. The result is a complex network of reporting relationships among product teams and functions that makes the matrix structure very flexible (see Figure 10.6a). Each person in a product team reports to two managers: (1) a functional boss, who assigns individuals to a team and evaluates their performance from a functional perspective, and (2) the boss of the product team, who evaluates their performance on the team. Thus team members are known as *two-boss employees.* The functional employees assigned to product teams change over time as the specific skills that the team needs change. At the beginning of the product development process, for example, engineers and R&D specialists are assigned to a product team because their skills are needed to develop new products. When a provisional design has been established, marketing experts are assigned to the team to gauge how customers will respond to the new product. Manufacturing personnel join when it is time to find the most efficient way to produce the product. As their specific jobs are completed, team members leave and are reassigned to new teams. In this way the matrix structure makes the most use of human resources.

To keep the matrix structure flexible, product teams are empowered and team members are responsible for making most of the important decisions involved in product development.[28] The product team manager acts as a facilitator, controlling the financial resources and trying to keep the project on time and within budget. The functional managers try to ensure that the product is the best it can be to maximize its differentiated appeal.

High-tech companies that operate in environments where new product development takes place monthly or yearly have used matrix structures successfully for many years, and the need to innovate quickly is vital to the organization's survival. The flexibility afforded by a matrix structure lets managers keep pace with a changing and increasingly complex environment.[29]

PRODUCT TEAM STRUCTURE The dual reporting relationships that are at the heart of a matrix structure have always been difficult for managers and employees to deal with. Often the functional boss and the product boss make conflicting demands on team members, who do not know which boss to satisfy first. Also, functional and product team bosses may come into conflict over precisely who is in charge of which team members and for how long. To avoid these problems, managers have devised a way of organizing people and resources that still allows an organization to be flexible but makes its structure easier to operate: a product team structure.

product team structure An organizational structure in which employees are permanently assigned to a cross-functional team and report only to the product team manager or to one of his or her direct subordinates.

cross-functional team A group of managers brought together from different departments to perform organizational tasks.

The **product team structure** differs from a matrix structure in two ways: (1) It does away with dual reporting relationships and two-boss employees, and (2) functional employees are permanently assigned to a cross-functional team that is empowered to bring a new or redesigned product to market. A **cross-functional team** is a group of managers brought together from different departments to perform organizational tasks. When managers are grouped into cross-functional teams, the artificial boundaries between departments disappear, and a narrow focus on departmental goals is replaced with a general interest in working together to achieve organizational goals. The results of such changes have been dramatic: Ford can introduce a new model of car in two years, down from four; Black & Decker can innovate new products in months, not years; and Hallmark Cards can respond to changing customer demands for types of cards in weeks, not months.

Members of a cross-functional team report only to the product team manager or to one of his or her direct subordinates. The heads of the functions have only an informal, advisory relationship with members of the product teams–the role of functional managers is only to counsel and help team members, share knowledge among teams, and provide new technological developments that can help improve each team's performance (see Figure 10.6b).[30]

A committee looks over an artist's work during a meeting at Hallmark in Kansas City. At Hallmark, cross-functional teams like this one can respond quickly to changing customer needs.

Increasingly, organizations are making empowered cross-functional teams an essential part of their organizational architecture to help them gain a competitive advantage in fast-changing organizational environments. For example, Newell Rubbermaid, the well-known maker of more than 5,000 household products, moved to a product team structure because its managers wanted to speed up the rate of product innovation. Managers created 20 cross-functional teams composed of five to seven people from marketing, manufacturing, R&D, and other functions.[31] Each team focuses its energies on a particular product line, such as garden products, bathroom products, or kitchen products. These teams develop more than 365 new products a year.

Coordinating Functions and Divisions

The more complex the structure a company uses to group its activities, the greater are the problems of *linking and coordinating* its different functions and divisions. Coordination becomes a problem because each function or division develops a different orientation toward the other groups that affects how it interacts with them. Each function or division comes to view the problems facing the company from its own perspective; for example, they may develop different views about the major goals, problems, or issues facing a company.

At the functional level, the manufacturing function typically has a short-term view; its major goal is to keep costs under control and get the product out the factory door on time. By contrast, the product development function has a long-term viewpoint because developing a new product is a relatively slow process and high product quality is seen as more important than low costs. Such differences in viewpoint may make manufacturing and product development managers reluctant to cooperate and coordinate their activities to meet company goals. At the divisional level, in a company with a product structure, employees may become concerned more with making *their* division's products a success than with the profitability of the entire company. They may refuse, or simply not see, the need to cooperate and share information or knowledge with other divisions.

The problem of linking and coordinating the activities of different functions and divisions becomes more acute as the number of functions and divisions increases. We look first at how managers design the hierarchy of authority to coordinate functions and divisions so they work together effectively. Then we focus on integration and examine the different integrating mechanisms managers can use to coordinate functions and divisions.

Allocating Authority

authority The power to hold people accountable for their actions and to make decisions concerning the use of organizational resources.

hierarchy of authority An organization's chain of command, specifying the relative authority of each manager.

span of control The number of subordinates who report directly to a manager.

As organizations grow and produce a wider range of goods and services, the size and number of their functions and divisions increase. To coordinate the activities of people, functions, and divisions and to allow them to work together effectively, managers must develop a clear hierarchy of authority.[32] **Authority** is the power vested in a manager to make decisions and use resources to achieve organizational goals by virtue of his or her position in an organization. The **hierarchy of authority** is an organization's *chain of command*–the relative authority that each manager has–extending from the CEO at the top, down through the middle managers and first-line managers, to the nonmanagerial employees who actually make goods or provide services. Every manager, at every level of the hierarchy, supervises one or more subordinates. The term **span of control** refers to the number of subordinates who report directly to a manager.

Figure 10.7 shows a simplified picture of the hierarchy of authority and the span of control of managers in McDonald's in 2008. At the top of the hierarchy is Jim Skinner, CEO and vice chairman of McDonald's board of directors, who took control in 2004.[33] Skinner is the manager who has ultimate responsibility for McDonald's performance, and he has the authority to decide how to use organizational resources to benefit McDonald's stakeholders.[34] Don Thompson, next in line, is president and COO and is responsible for overseeing all of McDonald's global restaurant operations. Thompson reports directly to Skinner, as does chief financial officer Peter Bensen. Unlike the other managers, Bensen is not a **line manager,** someone in the direct line or chain of command who has formal authority over people and resources. Rather, Bensen is a **staff manager,** responsible for one of McDonald's specialist functions, finance. Worldwide chief operations officer Jeff Stratton is responsible

Figure 10.7
The Hierarchy of Authority and Span of Control at McDonald's Corporation

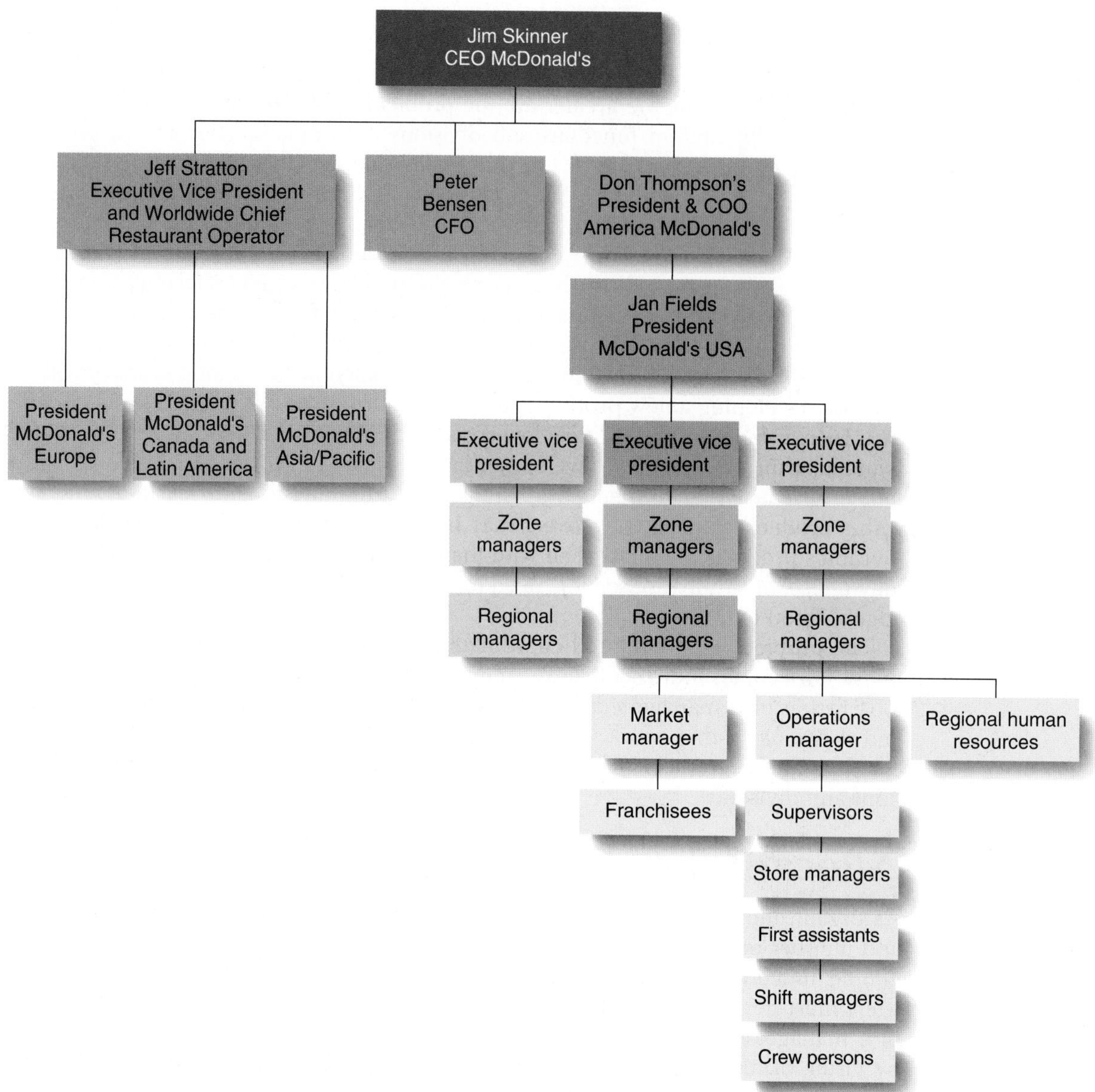

for overseeing all functional aspects of McDonald's overseas operations, which are headed by the presidents of world regions: Europe; Canada and Latin America; and Asia/Pacific, Middle East, and Africa. Jan Fields is president of McDonald's U.S. operations and reports to Thompson.

Managers at each level of the hierarchy confer on managers at the next level down the authority to decide how to use organizational resources. Accepting this authority, those lower-level managers are accountable for how well they make those decisions. Managers who make the right decisions are typically promoted, and organizations motivate managers with the prospects of promotion and increased responsibility within the chain of command.

Below Fields are the other main levels or layers in the McDonald's domestic chain of command–executive vice presidents of its West, Central, and East regions, zone managers, regional managers, and supervisors. A hierarchy is also evident in each company-owned McDonald's restaurant. At the top is the store manager; at lower levels are the first assistant, shift managers, and crew personnel. McDonald's managers have decided that this hierarchy of authority best allows the company to pursue its business-level strategy of providing fast food at reasonable prices–and its stock price has exploded in the 2000s as its performance has increased.

TALL AND FLAT ORGANIZATIONS As an organization grows in size (normally measured by the number of its managers and employees), its hierarchy of authority normally lengthens, making the organizational structure taller. A *tall* organization has many levels of authority relative to company size; a *flat* organization has fewer levels relative to company size (see Figure 10.8).[35] As a hierarchy becomes taller, problems that make the organization's structure less flexible and slow managers' response to changes in the organizational environment may result.

Communication problems may arise when an organization has many levels in the hierarchy. It can take a long time for the decisions and orders of upper-level managers to reach managers further down in the hierarchy, and it can take a long time for top managers to learn how well their decisions worked. Feeling out of touch, top managers may want to verify that lower-level managers are following orders and may require written confirmation from them. Middle managers, who know they will be held strictly accountable for their actions, start devoting too much time to the process of making decisions to improve their chances of being right. They might even try to avoid responsibility by making top managers decide what actions to take.

Figure 10.8
Tall and Flat Organizations

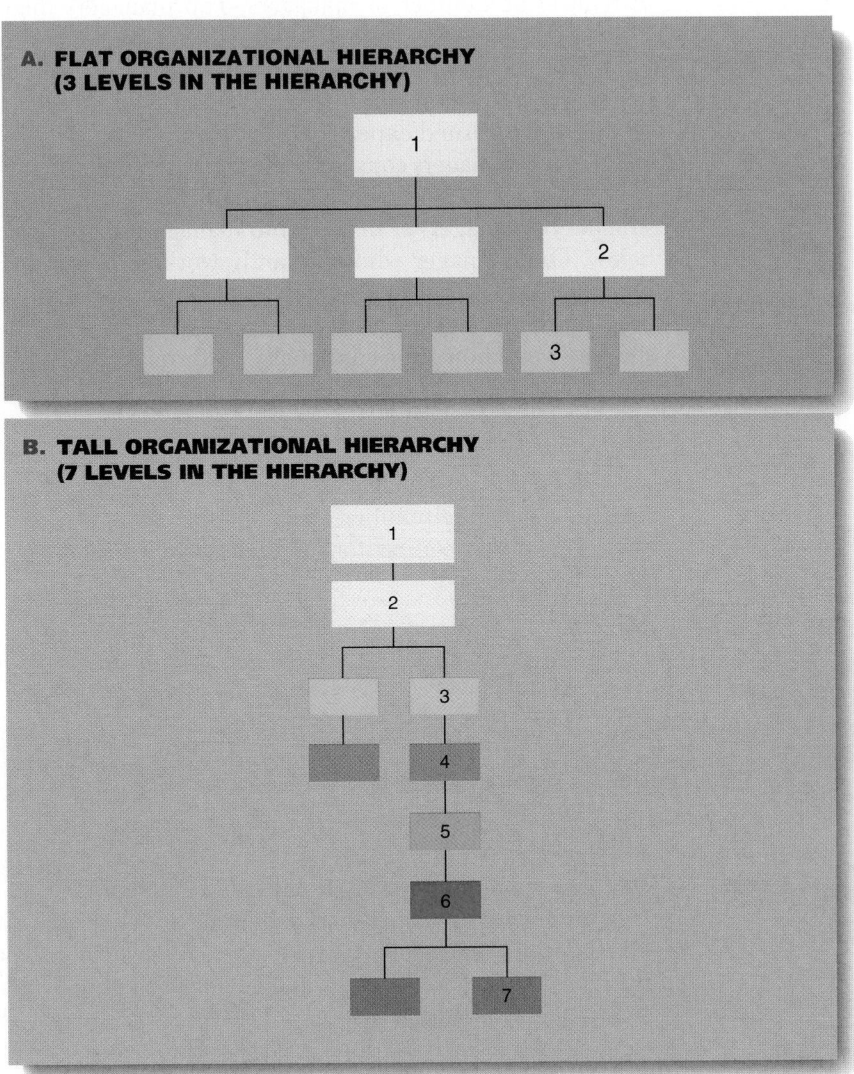

Another communication problem that can result is the distortion of commands and messages being transmitted up and down the hierarchy, which causes managers at different levels to interpret what is happening differently. Distortion of orders and messages can be accidental, occurring because different managers interpret messages from their own narrow, functional perspectives. Or distortion can be intentional, occurring because managers low in the hierarchy decide to interpret information in a way that increases their own personal advantage.

Another problem with tall hierarchies is that they usually indicate that an organization is employing many managers, and managers are expensive. Managerial salaries, benefits, offices, and secretaries are a huge expense for organizations. Large companies such as IBM and GM pay their managers millions of dollars a year. During the recession that started in 2007, hundreds of thousands of managers were laid off as companies restructured and downsized their workforces to reduce costs, and they were still doing this in 2010. For example, Walmart's Sam's Club cut 10,000 of its temporary in-store "food-sampling" employees and outsourced their jobs to a specialized company. Companies such as IBM, Microsoft, and Merck also laid off tens of thousands of employees to streamline their cost structures in order to respond rapidly as the global economy recovered; for example, in February 2010 Merck laid off 16,000 sales, R&D, and support employees despite rapidly rising profits.

THE MINIMUM CHAIN OF COMMAND To ward off the problems that result when an organization becomes too tall and employs too many managers, top managers need to ascertain whether they are employing the right number of middle and first-line managers and whether they can redesign their organizational architecture to reduce the number of managers. Top managers might well follow a basic organizing principle–the principle of the minimum chain of command–which states that top managers should always construct a hierarchy with the fewest levels of authority necessary to efficiently and effectively use organizational resources. This is something Andrea Jung learned expensively at Avon.

Effective managers constantly scrutinize their hierarchies to see whether the number of levels can be reduced–for example, by eliminating one level and giving the responsibilities of managers at that level to managers above and by empowering employees below. One manager who constantly worked to empower employees and keep the hierarchy flat is Colleen C. Barrett, the highest-ranking woman in the airline industry until she stepped down to become its "president emeritus" in 2008.[36] At Southwest she was well known for continually reaffirming Southwest's message that employees should feel free to go above and beyond their prescribed roles to provide better customer service. Her central message was that Southwest values, trusts, and empowers its employees, who should not look to supervisors for guidance but find their own ways to do the job better. The need to empower workers is increasing as companies work to reduce the number of middle managers to lower costs and to compete with low-cost overseas competitors, as the following "Managing Globally" box suggests.

Managing Globally

Empowered Self-Managed Teams Can Help Many Companies

In the United States over 5 million manufacturing jobs have been lost to factories in low-cost countries abroad in the 2000s. While many large U.S. manufacturing companies have given up the battle, some companies such as electronics maker Plexus Corp., based in Neenah, Wisconsin, have been able to find ways of organizing that allow them to survive and prosper in a low-cost manufacturing world. They have done this by creating empowered work teams.

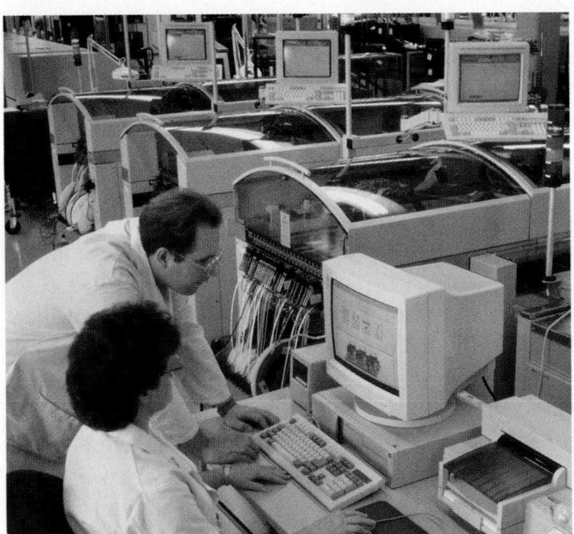

These two employees monitoring the progress of a circuit board production line embody cross-functional empowerment. If problems occur, they have the authority and expertise to make any changes necessary to keep the production line at full speed.

By 2000 Plexus saw the writing on the wall as more and more of its customers began to outsource the production of electronic components or whole products to manufacturers abroad. U.S. companies cannot match the efficiency of manufacturers abroad in producing high volumes of a single product, such as millions of a particular circuit board used in a laptop computer. So Plexus's managers decided to focus their efforts on developing a manufacturing technology called "low–high" that could efficiently produce low volumes of many different kinds of products. Plexus's managers formed a team to design an organizational structure based on creating four "focused factories" in which control over production decisions is given to the workers, who perform all the operations involved in making a product. The managers cross-trained workers so they can perform any particular operation in their "factory." With this approach, when work slows down at any point in the production of a particular product, a worker further along the production process can move back to help solve the problem that has arisen at the earlier stage.[37]

Furthermore, managers organized workers into self-managed teams that are empowered to make all the decisions necessary to make a particular product in one of the four factories. Because each product is different, these teams have to make their decisions quickly if they are to assemble the product in a cost-effective way. The ability of the teams to make rapid decisions and respond to unexpected contingencies is vital on a production line, where time is money–every minute a production line is not moving adds hundreds or thousands of dollars to production costs. Also, a second reason for empowering teams is that when a changeover takes place from making one product to making another, nothing is produced, so it is vital that changeover time be kept to a minimum. At Plexus managers, by allowing teams to experiment and by providing guidance, have reduced changeover time from hours to as little as 30 minutes, so the line is making products over 80% of the time.[38] This incredible flexibility, brought about by the way employees are organized, is why Plexus is so efficient and can compete against low-cost manufacturers abroad.

decentralizing authority Giving lower-level managers and nonmanagerial employees the right to make important decisions about how to use organizational resources.

CENTRALIZATION AND DECENTRALIZATION OF AUTHORITY Another way in which managers can keep the organizational hierarchy flat is by **decentralizing authority**–that is, by giving lower-level managers and nonmanagerial employees the right to make important decisions about how to use organizational resources.[39] If managers at higher levels give lower-level employees the responsibility of making important decisions and only *manage by exception,* then the problems of slow and distorted communication noted previously are kept to a minimum. Moreover, fewer managers are needed because their role is not to make decisions but to act as coach and facilitator and to help other employees make the best decisions. In addition, when decision-making authority is low in the organization and near the customer, employees are better able to recognize and respond to customer needs.

Decentralizing authority allows an organization and its employees to behave in a flexible way even as the organization grows and becomes taller. This is why managers are so interested in empowering employees, creating self-managed work teams, establishing cross-functional teams, and even moving to a product team structure. These design innovations help keep the organizational architecture flexible and responsive to complex task and general environments, complex technologies, and complex strategies.

Although more and more organizations are taking steps to decentralize authority, *too much* decentralization has certain disadvantages. If divisions, functions, or teams are given too much decision-making authority, they may begin to pursue their own goals at the expense of organizational goals. Managers in engineering design or R&D, for example, may become so focused on making the best possible product they fail to realize that the best product may be so expensive few people are willing or able to buy it. Also, too much decentralization can cause lack of communication among functions or divisions; this prevents the synergies of cooperation from ever materializing, and organizational performance suffers.

Top managers must seek the balance between centralization and decentralization of authority that best meets the four major contingencies an organization faces (see Figure 10.1). If managers are in a stable environment, are using well-understood technology, and are producing stable kinds of products (such as cereal, canned soup, or books), there is no pressing need to decentralize authority, and managers at the top can maintain control of much of organizational decision making.[40] However, in uncertain, changing environments where high-tech companies are producing state-of-the-art products, top managers must often empower employees and allow teams to make important strategic decisions so the organization can keep up with the changes taking place. No matter what its environment, a company that fails to control the balance between centralization and decentralization will find its performance suffering, as the example of the companies profiled in the following "Management Insight" box suggests.

Management Insight

To Decentralize and Centralize: Union Pacific and Yahoo!

Union Pacific (UP), one of the biggest railroad freight carriers in the United States, faced a crisis when an economic boom in the early 2000s led to a record increase in the amount of freight the railroad had to transport–but at the same time the railroad was experiencing record delays in moving this freight. UP's customers complained bitterly about the problem, and the delays cost the company tens of millions of dollars in penalty payments. Why the problem? UP's top managers decided to centralize authority high in the organization and to standardize operations to cut operating costs. All scheduling and route planning were handled centrally at headquarters to increase efficiency. The job of regional managers was largely to ensure the smooth flow of freight through their regions.

Recognizing that efficiency had to be balanced by the need to be responsive to customers, UP announced a sweeping reorganization. Regional managers would have the authority to make everyday operational decisions; they could alter scheduling and routing to accommodate customer requests even if it raised costs. UP's goal was to "return to excellent performance by simplifying our processes and becoming easier to deal with." In deciding to decentralize authority, UP was following the lead of its competitors that had already decentralized their operations. Its managers would continue to "decentralize decision making into the field, while fostering improved customer responsiveness, operational excellence, and personal accountability." The result has been continued success for the company; in fact, in 2010 Union Pacific was recognized as the top railroad in on-time service performance and customer service by several large companies.

Yahoo! has been forced by circumstances to pursue a different approach to decentralization. In 2009, after Microsoft failed to take over Yahoo! because of the resistance of Jerry Wang, a company founder, the company's stock price plunged. Wang, who had come under intense criticism for preventing the merger, resigned as CEO and was replaced by Carol Bartz, who had a long history of success in managing online companies. Bartz moved quickly to find ways to reduce Yahoo!'s cost structure and simplify its operations to maintain its strong online brand identity. Intense competition from the growing popularity of online companies such as Google, Facebook, and Twitter also threatened its popularity.

Bartz decided the best way to restructure Yahoo! was to recentralize authority. To gain more control over its different business units and reduce operating costs, she decided to centralize functions that had previously been performed by Yahoo!'s different business units, such as product development and marketing activities. For example, all the company's publishing and advertising functions were centralized and put under the control of a single executive. Yahoo!'s European, Asian, and emerging markets divisions were centralized, and another top executive took control. Bartz's goal was to find out how she could make the company's resources perform better. While she was centralizing authority she was also holding many "town hall" meetings asking Yahoo! employees from all functions, "What would you do if you were me?" Even as she centralized authority to help Yahoo! recover its dominant industry position, she was looking for the input of employees at every level in the hierarchy.

Nevertheless, in 2010 Yahoo! was still in a precarious position. It had signed a search agreement with Microsoft to use the latter's search technology; Bartz had focused on selling off Yahoo!'s noncore business assets to reduce costs and gain the money for strategic acquisitions. But the company was still in an intense battle with other dot-coms that had more resources, such as Google, and in 2010 Bartz announced the company was still for sale–at the right price.

LO10-4 Explain why managers must coordinate jobs, functions, and divisions using the hierarchy of authority and integrating mechanisms.

Integrating and Coordinating Mechanisms

Much coordination takes place through the hierarchy of authority. However, several problems are associated with establishing contact among managers in different functions or divisions. As discussed earlier, managers from different functions and divisions may have different views about what must be done to achieve organizational goals. But if the managers have equal authority (as functional managers typically do), the only manager who can tell them what to do is the CEO, who has the ultimate authority to resolve conflicts. The need to solve everyday conflicts, however, wastes top management time and slows strategic decision making; indeed, one sign of a poorly performing structure is the number of problems sent up the hierarchy for top managers to solve.

integrating mechanisms Organizing tools that managers can use to increase communication and coordination among functions and divisions.

To increase communication and coordination among functions or between divisions and to prevent these problems from emerging, top managers incorporate various **integrating mechanisms** into their organizational architecture. The greater the complexity of an organization's structure, the greater is the need for coordination among people, functions, and divisions to make the organizational structure work efficiently and effectively.[41] Thus when managers adopt a divisional, matrix, or product team structure, they must use complex integrating mechanisms to achieve organizational goals. Several integrating mechanisms are available to managers to increase communication and coordination.[42] Figure 10.9 lists these mechanisms, as well as examples of the individuals or groups who might use them.

LIAISON ROLES Managers can increase coordination among functions and divisions by establishing liaison roles. When the volume of contacts between two functions increases, one way to improve coordination is to give one manager in each function or division the responsibility for coordinating with the other. These managers may meet daily, weekly, monthly, or as needed. A liaison role is illustrated in Figure 10.9; the small dot represents the person within a function who has responsibility for coordinating with the other function. Coordinating is part of the liaison's full-time job, and usually an informal relationship develops between the people involved, greatly easing

Figure 10.9
Types and Examples of Integrating Mechanisms

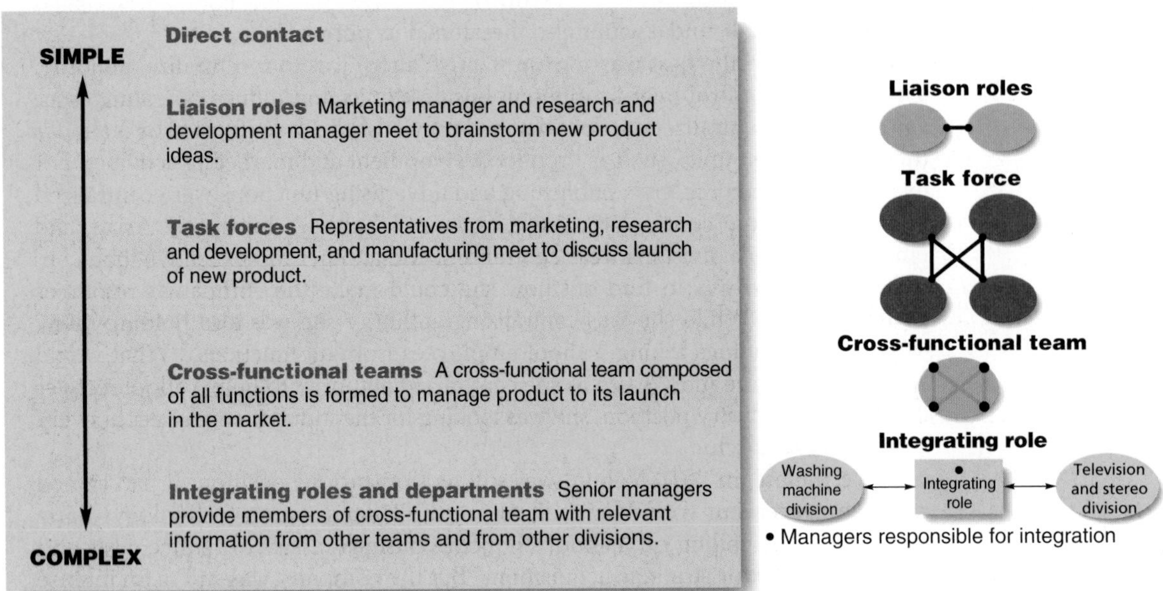

strains between functions. Furthermore, liaison roles provide a way of transmitting information across an organization, which is important in large organizations whose employees may know no one outside their immediate function or division.

task force A committee of managers from various functions or divisions who meet to solve a specific, mutual problem; also called *ad hoc committee.*

TASK FORCES When more than two functions or divisions share many common problems, direct contact and liaison roles may not provide sufficient coordination. In these cases, a more complex integrating mechanism, a **task force,** may be appropriate (see Figure 10.9). One manager from each relevant function or division is assigned to a task force that meets to solve a specific, mutual problem; members are responsible for reporting to their departments on the issues addressed and the solutions recommended. Task forces are often called *ad hoc committees* because they are temporary; they may meet on a regular basis or only a few times. When the problem or issue is solved, the task force is no longer needed; members return to their normal roles in their departments or are assigned to other task forces. Typically task force members also perform many of their normal duties while serving on the task force.

CROSS-FUNCTIONAL TEAMS In many cases the issues addressed by a task force are recurring problems, such as the need to develop new products or find new kinds of customers. To address recurring problems effectively, managers are increasingly using permanent integrating mechanisms such as cross-functional teams. An example of a cross-functional team is a new product development committee that is responsible for the choice, design, manufacturing, and marketing of a new product. Such an activity obviously requires a great deal of integration among functions if new products are to be successfully introduced, and using a complex integrating mechanism such as a cross-functional team accomplishes this. As discussed earlier, in a product team structure people and resources are grouped into permanent cross-functional teams to speed products to market. These teams assume long-term responsibility for all aspects of development and making the product.

INTEGRATING ROLES An integrating role is a role whose only function is to increase coordination and integration among functions or divisions to achieve performance gains from synergies. Usually managers who perform integrating roles are experienced senior managers who can envisage how to use the resources of the functions or divisions to obtain new synergies. One study found that DuPont, the giant chemical company, had created 160 integrating roles to coordinate the different divisions of the company and improve corporate performance.[43] The more complex an organization and the greater the number of its divisions, the more important integrating roles are.

In summary, to keep an organization responsive to changes in its task and general environments as it grows and becomes more complex, managers must increase coordination among functions and divisions by using complex integrating mechanisms. Managers must decide on the best way to organize their structures–that is, choose the structure that allows them to make the best use of organizational resources.

Organizational Culture

organizational culture The shared set of beliefs, expectations, values, and norms that influence how members of an organization relate to one another and cooperate to achieve organizational goals.

The second principal issue in organizational design is to create, develop, and maintain an organization's culture. As we discussed in Chapter 3, **organizational culture** is the shared set of beliefs, expectations, values, and norms that influence how members of an organization relate to one another and cooperate to achieve organizational goals. Culture influences the work behaviors and attitudes of individuals and groups in an organization because its members adhere to shared values, norms, and expected standards of behavior. Employees *internalize* organizational values and norms and then let these values and norms guide their decisions and actions.[44]

A company's culture is a result of its pivotal or guiding values and norms. A company's *values* are the shared standards that its members use to evaluate whether they have helped the company achieve its vision and goals. The values a company might adopt include any or all of the following standards: excellence, stability, predictability, profitability, economy, creativity, morality, and usefulness. A company's *norms* specify or prescribe the kinds of shared beliefs, attitudes, and behaviors that its members should observe and follow. Norms are informal, but powerful, rules about how employees should behave or conduct themselves in a company if they are to be accepted and help it to achieve its goals. Norms can be equally as constraining as the formal written rules contained in a company's handbook. Companies might encourage workers to adopt norms such as working hard, respecting traditions and authority, and being courteous to others; being conservative, cautious, and a "team player"; being creative and courageous and taking risks; or being honest and frugal and maintaining high personal standards. Norms may also prescribe certain specific behaviors such as keeping one's desk tidy, cleaning up at the end of the day, taking one's turn to bring doughnuts, and even wearing jeans on Fridays.

Ideally a company's norms help the company achieve its values. For example, a new computer company whose culture is based on values of excellence and innovation may try to attain this high standard by encouraging workers to adopt norms about being creative, taking risks, and working hard now and looking long-term for rewards (this combination of values and norms leads to an *entrepreneurial* culture in a company). On the other hand, a bank or insurance company that has values of stability and predictability may emphasize norms of cautiousness and obedience to authority (the result of adopting these values and norms would be a *stable, conservative* culture in a company).

Over time, members of a company learn from one another how to perceive and interpret various events that happen in the work setting and to respond to them in ways that reflect the company's guiding values and norms. This is why organizational culture is so important: When a strong and cohesive set of organizational values and norms is in place, employees focus on what is best for the organization in the long run–all their decisions and actions become oriented toward helping the organization perform well. For example, a teacher spends personal time after school coaching and counseling students; an R&D scientist works 80 hours a week, evenings, and weekends to help speed up a late project; or a salesclerk at a department store runs after a customer who left a credit card at the cash register. An interesting example of a manager who has been working hard to change a company's dysfunctional culture is profiled in the following "Manager as a Person" box.

Manager as a Person

Alan Mulally Transforms Ford's Culture

After a loss of more than $13 billion in 2006, William Ford III, who had been Ford Motor's CEO for five years, decided he was not the right person to turn around the company's performance.[45] In fact, it became apparent that he was a part of Ford's problems because he and other Ford top managers tried to build and protect their own corporate empires, and none would ever admit that mistakes had occurred over the years. As a result the whole company's performance had suffered; its future was in doubt. Finally Ford's board of directors realized they needed an outsider to change Ford's culture and the way it operated, and they recruited Alan Mulally from Boeing to become Ford's new CEO.

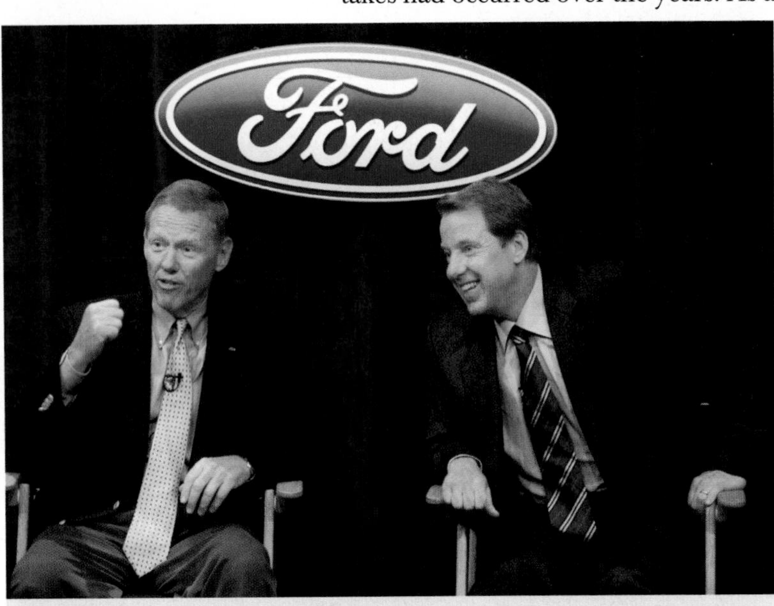

New Ford CEO Alan Mulally (left), with former CEO Bill Ford (right), who realized the company needed an outsider at the helm to change Ford's insular, self-protective culture.

After arriving at Ford, Mulally attended hundreds of executive meetings with his new managers; and at one meeting he became confused why one top division manager, who obviously did not know the answer to one of Mulally's questions concerning the performance of his car division, had rambled on for several minutes trying to disguise his ignorance. Mulally turned to his second-in-command Mark Fields and asked him why the manager had done that. Fields explained that "at Ford you never admit when you don't know something." He also told Mulally that when he arrived as a middle manager at Ford and wanted to ask his boss to lunch to gain information about divisional operations, he was told, "What rank are you at Ford? Don't you know that a subordinate never asks a superior to lunch?"[46]

It turned out that over the years Ford had develop a tall hierarchy composed of managers whose main goal was to protect their turf and avoid any direct blame for its plunging car sales. When asked why car sales were falling, they did not admit to bad design and poor quality issues in their divisions; instead they hid in the details. They brought thick notebooks and binders to meetings, listing the high prices of components and labor costs to explain why their own particular car models were not selling well–or even why they had to be sold at a loss. Why, Mulally wondered, did Ford's top executives have this inward-looking, destructive mind-set?

Mulally soon realized the problem was the values and norms in Ford's culture that had created a situation in which the managers of its different divisions and functions thought the best way to maintain their jobs, salaries, and status was to hoard, rather than share, information. Thus values and norms of secrecy and ambiguity, and of emphasizing status and rank, to protect their information had developed. The reason only the boss could ask a subordinate to lunch was to allow superiors to protect their information and positions. Ford's culture allowed managers to hide their problems and poor performance. What could Mulally do? He issued a direct order that the managers of every division should share with every other Ford division a detailed statement of the costs they incurred to build each of its vehicles. He insisted that each of Ford's divisional presidents should attend a weekly (rather than a monthly) meeting to share and discuss openly the problems all the company's division's faced. He also told them they should bring a different subordinate with them to each meeting so every manager in the hierarchy would learn of the problems that had been kept hidden.[47]

Essentially, Mulally's goal was to demolish the dysfunctional values and norms of Ford's culture that focused managers' attention on their own empires at the expense of the whole company. No longer would they be allowed to protect their own careers at the expense of customers. Mulally's goal was to create new values and norms that it was fine to admit mistakes, share information about all aspects of model design and costs, and of course find ways to speed development and reduce costs. He also wanted to emphasize norms of cooperation within and across divisions to improve performance.

How could this situation have gone unchanged in a major car company that has been experiencing increased competition since the mid-1970s? The answer is that the norms and values of an organization's culture are difficult to change; and despite Ford's major problems, no CEO had been able to change the mind-set of the top managers in the company. Ford had become more hierarchical and bureaucratic over time as its problems increased because poor performance led managers to become more defensive and concerned with defending their empires.

By 2010 it was clear that Mulally had changed Ford's values and norms; the company finally reported a profit in the spring of 2010, for which Mulally received over $17 million in salary and other bonuses. Many managers who could not or would not conform to the new Ford culture were gone; the others were still learning to adjust their behavior to the new culture oriented to satisfying the needs of customers, not the needs of top managers.

LO10-5 List the four sources of organizational culture, and explain why and how a company's culture can lead to competitive advantage.

Where Does Organizational Culture Come From?

In managing organizational architecture, some important questions that arise are these: Where does organizational culture come from? Why do different companies have different cultures? Why might a culture that for many years helped an organization achieve its goals suddenly harm the organization?

Organizational culture is shaped by the interaction of four main factors: the personal and professional characteristics of people within the organization, organizational ethics, the nature of the employment relationship, and the design of its organizational structure (see Figure 10.10). These factors work together to produce different cultures in different organizations and cause changes in culture over time.

CHARACTERISTICS OF ORGANIZATIONAL MEMBERS The ultimate source of organizational culture is the people who make up the organization. If you want to know why organizational cultures differ, look at how the characteristics of their members differ. Organizations A, B, and C develop distinctly different cultures because they attract, select, and retain people who have different values, personalities, and ethics.[48] Recall the attraction–selection–attrition model from Chapter 3. People may be attracted to an organization whose values match theirs; similarly, an organization selects people who share its values. Over time, people who do not fit in leave. The result is that people inside the organization become more similar, the values of the organization become more pronounced and clear-cut, and the culture becomes distinct from those of similar organizations.[49]

The fact that an organization's members become similar over time and come to share the same values may actually hinder their ability to adapt and respond to changes in the environment.[50] This happens when the organization's values and norms become so strong and promote so much cohesiveness in members' attitudes

Figure 10.10
Sources of an Organization's Culture

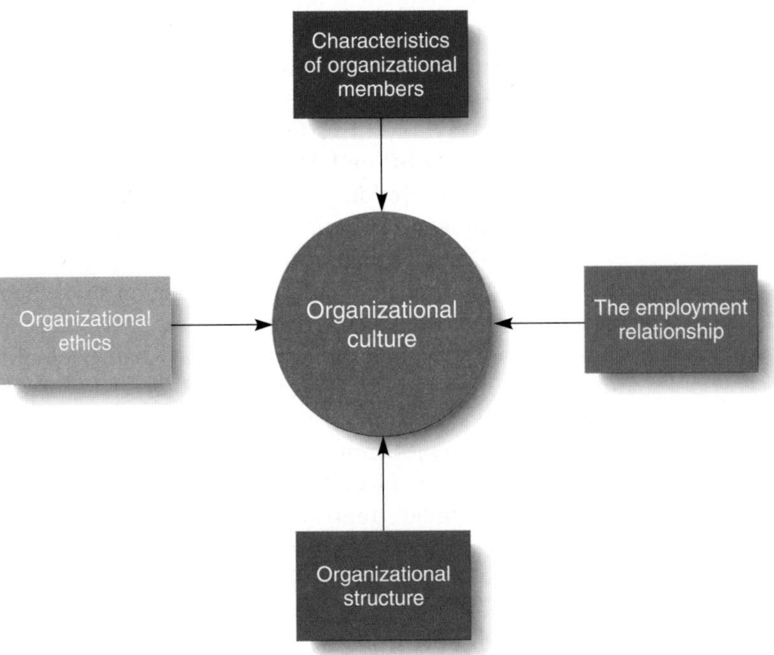

that the members begin to misperceive the environment, as did Ford's top managers.[51] Companies such as Ford, Google, Apple, and Microsoft need a strong set of values that emphasize innovation and hard work; they also need to be careful their success doesn't lead members to believe their company is the best in the business. Companies frequently make this mistake. One famous example is the CEO of Digital Equipment, who in the 1990s laughed off the potential threat posed by PCs to his powerful minicomputers, claiming, "Personal computers are just toys." This company no longer exists.

organizational ethics The moral values, beliefs, and rules that establish the appropriate way for an organization and its members to deal with each other and with people outside the organization.

ORGANIZATIONAL ETHICS The managers of an organization can set out purposefully to develop specific cultural values and norms to control how its members behave. One important class of values in this category stems from **organizational ethics,** which are the moral values, beliefs, and rules that establish the appropriate way for an organization and its members to deal with each other and with people outside the organization. Recall from Chapter 4 that ethical values rest on principles stressing the importance of treating organizational stakeholders fairly and equitably. Managers and employees are constantly making choices about the right, or ethical, thing to do; and to help them make ethical decisions, top managers purposefully implant ethical values into an organization's culture.[52] Consequently ethical values, and the rules and norms that embody them, become an integral part of an organization's culture and determine how its members will manage situations and make decisions.

THE EMPLOYMENT RELATIONSHIP A third factor shaping organizational culture is the nature of the employment relationship a company establishes with its employees via its human resource policies and practices. Recall from Chapter 1 our discussion of the changing relationship between organizations and their employees due to the growth of outsourcing and employment of contingent workers. Like a company's hiring, promotion, and layoff policies, human resource policies, along with pay and benefits, can influence how hard employees will work to achieve the organization's goals, how attached they will be to the organization, and whether they will buy into its values and norms.[53] As we discuss in Chapter 12, an organization's human resource policies are a good indicator of the values in its culture concerning its responsibilities to employees. Consider the effects of a company's promotion policy, for example: A company with a policy of promoting from within will fill higher-level positions with employees who already work for the organization. On the other hand, a company with a policy of promotion from without will fill its open positions with qualified outsiders. What does this say about each organization's culture?

Promoting from within will bolster strong values and norms that build loyalty, align employees' goals with the organization, and encourage employees to work hard to advance within the organization. If employees see no prospect of being promoted from within, they are likely to look for better opportunities elsewhere, cultural values and norms result in self-interested behavior, and cooperation and cohesiveness fall. The tech sector has gone through great turmoil in recent years, and over 2 million U.S. tech employees lost their jobs during the 2000s because of outsourcing and the recession. Apple, HP, and IBM–known for their strong employee-oriented values that emphasized long-term employment and respect for employees–were among the many companies forced to lay off employees, and their cultures have changed as a result. To rebuild their cultures, and make their remaining employees feel like "owners," many companies have HRM pay policies that reward superior performance with bonuses and stock options.[54] For example, Southwest Airlines and Google established companywide stock option systems that encourage their employees to be innovative and responsive to customers.

ORGANIZATIONAL STRUCTURE We have seen how the values and norms that shape employee work attitudes and behaviors derive from an organization's people, ethics, and HRM policies. A fourth source of cultural values comes from the organization's structure. *Different kinds of structure give rise to different kinds of culture;* so to create a certain culture, managers often need to design a particular type of structure. Tall and highly centralized structures give rise to totally different sets of norms, rules, and cultural values than do structures that are flat and decentralized. In a tall, centralized organization people have little personal autonomy, and norms that focus on being cautious, obeying authority, and respecting traditions emerge because predictability and stability are desired goals. In a flat, decentralized structure people have more freedom to choose and control their own activities, and norms that focus on being creative and courageous and taking risks appear, giving rise to a culture in which innovation and flexibility are desired goals.

Whether a company is centralized or decentralized also leads to the development of different kinds of cultural values. By decentralizing authority and empowering employees, an organization can establish values that encourage and reward creativity or innovation. In doing this, an organization signals employees that it's okay to be innovative and do things their own way–as long as their actions are consistent with the good of the organization. Conversely, in some organizations it is important that employees do not make decisions on their own and that their actions be open to the scrutiny of superiors. In cases like this, centralization can be used to create cultural values that reinforce obedience and accountability. For example, in nuclear power plants, values that promote stability, predictability, and obedience to authority are deliberately fostered to prevent disasters.[55] Through norms and rules, employees are taught the importance of behaving consistently and honestly, and they learn that sharing information with supervisors, especially information about mistakes or errors, is the only acceptable form of behavior.[56]

An organization that seeks to manage and change its culture must take a hard look at all four factors that shape culture: the characteristics of its members, its ethical values, its human resource policies, and its organizational structure. However, changing a culture can be difficult because of the way these factors interact and affect one another.[57] Often a major reorganization is necessary for a cultural change to occur, as we discuss in the next chapter.

Strong, Adaptive Cultures versus Weak, Inert Cultures

Many researchers and managers believe that employees of some organizations go out of their way to help the organization because it has a strong and cohesive organizational culture–an adaptive culture that controls employee attitudes and behaviors. *Adaptive cultures* are those whose values and norms help an organization to build momentum and to grow and change as needed to achieve its goals and be effective. By contrast, *inert cultures* are those whose values and norms fail to motivate or inspire employees; they lead to stagnation and, often, failure over time. What leads to a strong adaptive culture or one that is inert and hard to change?

Researchers have found that organizations with strong adaptive cultures, like 3M, UPS, Microsoft, and IBM, invest in their employees. They demonstrate their commitment to their members by, for example, emphasizing the long-term nature of the employment relationship and trying to avoid layoffs. These companies develop long-term career paths for their employees and spend a lot of money on training and development to increase employees' value to the organization. In these ways, terminal and instrumental values pertaining to the worth of human resources encourage the development of supportive work attitudes and behaviors.

In adaptive cultures employees often receive rewards linked directly to their performance and to the performance of the company as a whole. Sometimes employee stock ownership plans (ESOPs) are developed in which workers as a group are allowed to buy a significant percentage of their company's stock. Workers who are owners of the company have additional incentive to develop skills that allow them to perform highly and search actively for ways to improve quality, efficiency, and performance. At Dell, for example, employees may still buy Dell stock at a steep 15% discount, and this will allow them to build a sizable stake in the company over time if its performance recovers.

Some organizations, however, develop cultures with values that do not include protecting and increasing the worth of their human resources as a major goal. Their employment practices are based on short-term employment according to the needs of the organization and on minimal investment in employees who perform simple, routine tasks. Moreover, employees are not often rewarded on the basis of their performance and thus have little incentive to improve their skills or otherwise invest in the organization to help it achieve goals. If a company has an inert culture, poor working relationships frequently develop between the organization and its employees, and instrumental values of noncooperation, laziness, and loafing and work norms of output restriction are common.

Moreover, an adaptive culture develops an emphasis on entrepreneurship and respect for the employee and allows the use of organizational structures, such as the cross-functional team structure, that empower employees to make decisions and motivate them to succeed. By contrast, in an inert culture, employees are content to be told what to do and have little incentive or motivation to perform beyond minimum work requirements. As you might expect, the emphasis is on close supervision and hierarchical authority, which result in a culture that makes it difficult to adapt to a changing environment.

Nokia, discussed earlier, is a good example of a company in which managers strive to create an adaptive culture.[58] Nokia's top managers, including its present CEO Jorma Ollila, have always believed that Nokia's cultural values are based on the Finnish character: Finns are down-to-earth, rational, straightforward people. They are also friendly and democratic people who do not believe in a rigid hierarchy based either on a person's authority or on social class. Nokia's culture reflects these values because innovation and decision making are pushed right down to the bottom line, to teams of employees who take up the challenge of developing the ever-smaller and more sophisticated phones for which the company is known. Bureaucracy is kept to a minimum at Nokia; its adaptive culture is based on informal and personal relationships and norms of cooperation and teamwork.

To help strengthen its culture, Nokia built a futuristic open-plan steel and glass building just outside Helsinki. Here, in an open environment, its R&D employees can work together to innovate new kinds of cell phones focused on Nokia's company mission to produce phones that are more versatile, cheaper, and easier to use than competitor's phones. This is the "Nokia Way"–a system of cultural values and norms that can't be written down but is always present in the values that cement people together and in the language and stories its members use to orient themselves to the company. Yet, as we noted before, Nokia is the cell phone company that is most sensitive to the need to appreciate the values, norms, and tastes of other nations. So the Nokia Way is not just confined to Finland; the company has taken it to every country around the globe in which it operates.

Another company with an adaptive culture is GlaxoSmithKline, the prescription drug maker discussed earlier in the chapter. Much of GSK's success can be attributed to its ability to recruit the best research scientists because its adaptive culture nurtures scientists and emphasizes values and norms of innovation. Scientists are given great freedom to pursue intriguing ideas even if the commercial payoff is questionable. Moreover, researchers are inspired to think of their work as a quest to alleviate human disease and suffering worldwide, and GSK has a reputation as an ethical company whose values put people above profits.

Although the experience of Nokia and GSK suggests that organizational culture can give rise to managerial actions that ultimately benefit the organization, this is not always the case. The cultures of some organizations become dysfunctional, encouraging managerial actions that harm the organization and discouraging actions that might improve performance.[59] For example, Sunflower Electric Power, an electricity generation and transmission cooperative, almost went bankrupt in the early 2000s. A committee of inquiry set up to find the source of the problem put the blame on Sunflower's CEO and decided he had created an abusive culture based on fear and blame that encouraged managers to fight over and protect their turf–an inert culture. The CEO was fired, and a new CEO was appointed to change the cooperative's culture, which he found hard to do because his top managers were so used to the old values and norms. With the help of consultants, he changed values and norms to emphasize cooperation, teamwork, and respect for others–which involved firing many top managers. Clearly, managers can influence how their organizational culture develops over time.

Summary and Review

DESIGNING ORGANIZATIONAL STRUCTURE The four main determinants of organizational structure are the external environment, strategy, technology, and human resources. In general, the higher the level of uncertainty associated with these factors, the more appropriate is a flexible, adaptable structure as opposed to a formal, rigid one.

LO10-1 LO10-2 **GROUPING TASKS INTO JOBS** Job design is the process by which managers group tasks into jobs. To create more interesting jobs, and to get workers to act flexibly, managers can enlarge and enrich jobs. The job characteristics model is a tool that managers can use to measure how motivating or satisfying a particular job is.

LO10-3 **ORGANIZATIONAL STRUCTURE: GROUPING JOBS INTO FUNCTIONS AND DIVISIONS** Managers can choose from many kinds of organizational structures to make the best use of organizational resources. Depending on the specific organizing problems they face, managers can choose from functional, product, geographic, market, matrix, product team, and hybrid structures.

LO10-4 **COORDINATING FUNCTIONS AND DIVISIONS** No matter which structure managers choose, they must decide how to distribute authority in the organization, how many levels to have in the hierarchy of authority, and what balance to strike between centralization and decentralization to keep the number of levels in the hierarchy to a minimum. As organizations grow, managers must increase integration and coordination among functions and divisions. Four integrating mechanisms that facilitate this are liaison roles, task forces, cross-functional teams, and integrating roles.

LO10-5 **ORGANIZATIONAL CULTURE** Organizational culture is the set of values, norms, and standards of behavior that control how individuals and groups in an organization interact with one another and work to achieve organizational goals. The four main sources of organizational culture are member characteristics, organizational ethics, the nature of the employment relationship, and the design of organizational structure. How managers work to influence these four factors determines whether an organization's culture is strong and adaptive or is inert and difficult to change.

Management in Action

Topics for Discussion and Action

Discussion

1. Would a flexible or a more formal structure be appropriate for these organizations? (a) A large department store, (b) a Big Five accounting firm, (c) a biotechnology company. Explain your reasoning. **[LO10-1, 10-2]**

2. Using the job characteristics model as a guide, discuss how a manager can enrich or enlarge subordinates' jobs. **[LO10-2]**

3. How might a salesperson's job or a secretary's job be enlarged or enriched to make it more motivating? **[LO10-2, 10-3]**

4. When and under what conditions might managers change from a functional to (a) a product, (b) a geographic, or (c) a market structure? **[LO10-1, 10-3]**

5. How do matrix structure and product team structure differ? Why is product team structure more widely used? **[LO10-1, 10-3, 10-4]**

6. What is organizational culture, and how does it affect the way employees behave? **[LO10-5]**

Action

7. Find and interview a manager and identify the kind of organizational structure that his or her organization uses to coordinate its people and resources. Why is the organization using that structure? Do you think a different structure would be more appropriate? Which one? **[LO10-1, 10-3, 10-4]**

8. With the same or another manager, discuss the distribution of authority in the organization. Does the manager think that decentralizing authority and empowering employees is appropriate? **[LO10-1, 10-3]**

9. Interview some employees of an organization, and ask them about the organization's values and norms, the typical characteristics of employees, and the organization's ethical values and socialization practices. Using this information, try to describe the organization's culture and the way it affects how people and groups behave. **[LO10-1, 10-5]**

Building Management Skills

Understanding Organizing [LO10-1, 10-2, 10-3]

Think of an organization with which you are familiar, perhaps one you have worked for—such as a store, restaurant, office, church, or school. Then answer the following questions:

1. Which contingencies are most important in explaining how the organization is organized? Do you think it is organized in the best way?

2. Using the job characteristics model, how motivating do you think the job of a typical employee in this organization is?

3. Can you think of any ways in which a typical job could be enlarged or enriched?

4. What kind of organizational structure does the organization use? If it is part of a chain, what kind of structure does the entire organization use? What other structures discussed in the chapter might allow the organization to operate more effectively? For example, would the move to a product team structure lead to greater efficiency or effectiveness? Why or why not?

5. How many levels are there in the organization's hierarchy? Is authority centralized or decentralized? Describe the span of control of the top manager and of middle or first-line managers.

6. Is the distribution of authority appropriate for the organization and its activities? Would it be possible to flatten the hierarchy by decentralizing authority and empowering employees?

7. What are the principal integrating mechanisms used in the organization? Do they provide sufficient coordination among individuals and functions? How might they be improved?

8. Now that you have analyzed the way this organization is structured, what advice would you give its managers to help them improve how it operates?

Managing Ethically [LO10-1, 10-3, 10-5]

Suppose an organization is downsizing and laying off many of its middle managers. Some top managers charged with deciding whom to terminate might decide to keep the subordinates they like, and who are obedient to them, rather than the ones who are difficult or the best performers. They might also decide to lay off the most highly paid subordinates even if they are high performers. Think of the ethical issues involved in designing a hierarchy, and discuss the following issues.

Questions

1. What ethical rules (see Chapter 4) should managers use to decide which employees to terminate when redesigning their hierarchy?
2. Some people argue that employees who have worked for an organization for many years have a claim on the organization at least as strong as that of its shareholders. What do you think of the ethics of this position—can employees claim to "own" their jobs if they have contributed significantly to the organization's past success? How does a socially responsible organization behave in this situation?

Small Group Breakout Exercise

Bob's Appliances [LO10-1, 10-3]

Form groups of three or four people, and appoint one member as the spokesperson who will communicate your findings to the class when called on by the instructor. Then discuss the following scenario:

Bob's Appliances sells and services household appliances such as washing machines, dishwashers, ranges, and refrigerators. Over the years, the company has developed a good reputation for the quality of its customer service, and many local builders patronize the store. However, large retailers such as Best Buy, Walmart, and Costco are also providing an increasing range of appliances. Moreover, to attract more customers these stores also carry a complete range of consumer electronics products—LCD TVs, computers, and digital devices. Bob Lange, the owner of Bob's Appliances, has decided that if he is to stay in business, he must widen his product range and compete directly with the chains.

In 2007 he decided to build a 20,000-square-foot store and service center, and he is now hiring new employees to sell and service the new line of consumer electronics. Because of his company's increased size, Lange is not sure of the best way to organize the employees. Currently he uses a functional structure; employees are divided into sales, purchasing and accounting, and repair. Bob is wondering whether selling and servicing consumer electronics is so different from selling and servicing appliances that he should move to a product structure (see the accompanying figure) and create separate sets of functions for each of his two lines of business.[60]

You are a team of local consultants whom Bob has called in to advise him as he makes this crucial choice. Which structure do you recommend? Why?

FUNCTIONAL STRUCTURE

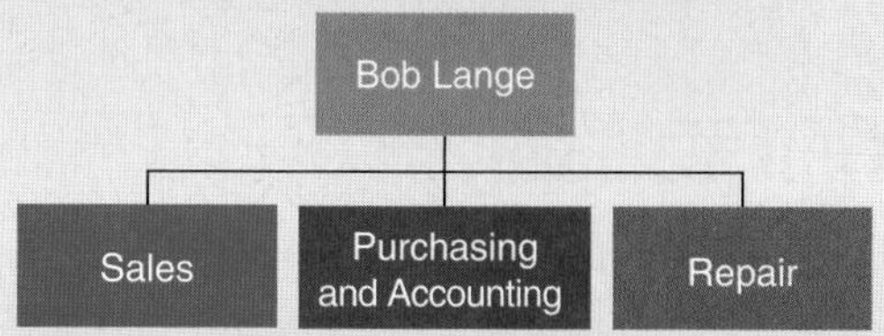

PRODUCT STRUCTURE

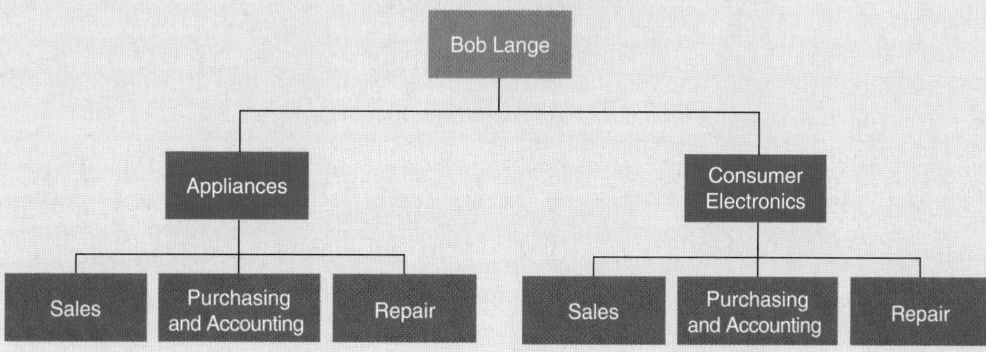

Exploring the World Wide Web [LO10-3]

Go to the Web site of Kraft, the food services company (www.kraft.com). Click on "Corporate Information" and then explore its brands—especially its takeover of Cadbury's.

1. Given the way it describes its brands, what kind of divisional structure do you think Kraft uses? Why do you think it uses this structure?
2. Click on featured brands, and look at products like its Oreo cookies. How is Kraft managing its different brands to increase global sales? What do you think are the main challenges Kraft faces in managing its global food business to improve performance?

Be the Manager [LO10-1, 10-3, 10-5]

Speeding Up Web Site Design

You have been hired by a Web site design, production, and hosting company whose new animated Web site designs are attracting a lot of attention and many customers. Currently employees are organized into different functions such as hardware, software design, graphic art, and Web site hosting, as well as functions such as marketing and human resources. Each function takes its turn to work on a new project from initial customer request to final online Web site hosting.

The problem the company is experiencing is that it typically takes one year from the initial idea stage to the time a Web site is up and running; the company wants to shorten this time by half to protect and expand its market niche. In talking to other managers, you discover that they believe the company's current functional structure is the source of the problem—it is not allowing employees to develop Web sites fast enough to satisfy customers' demands. They want you to design a better structure.

Questions

1. Discuss how you can improve the way the current functional structure operates so it speeds Web site development.
2. Discuss the pros and cons of moving to a (a) multidivisional, (b) matrix, and (c) product team structure to reduce Web site development time.
3. Which of these structures do you think is most appropriate, and why?
4. What kind of culture would you help create to make the company's structure work more effectively?

Case in the News [LO10-3, 10-4]

GSK and Pfizer Create New HIV Company

The ink is barely dry on its $68 billion merger with Wyeth, but that hasn't stopped Pfizer from launching yet another deal. On April 16 Pfizer announced it will join forces with Britain's GlaxoSmithKline to pool their HIV operations to create a new company devoted to marketing the two companies' existing HIV medicines and developing new ones. The new venture, which will be 85% owned by GSK, will have a 19% share of the HIV market.

"This creates the focus of a specialist company with the support of two big parents," GSK CEO Andrew Witty said in a conference call. "It gives us a huge portfolio of 11 medicines on the market and 6 in the clinic."

The news comes just a day after Pfizer's head of worldwide research Rod MacKenzie told a conference in New York that "the big research organization model really doesn't work particularly well." MacKenzie said the "old model" (of which Pfizer was the industry's biggest proponent) was too unwieldy, lacking accountability, and overly bureaucratic.

After years of endless mergers and acquisitions to get bigger, now big pharma is intent on getting smaller. The new venture is an attempt by the world's two biggest drug companies to replicate the energy and drive of a small biotech. Witty calls it an opportunity to "create a specialist company . . . with real independence that will have the flexibility to do other deals and license in other products just as a specialist biotech would."

While the new company will centralize sales, marketing, and administration from a new headquarters in London, research and development teams will remain within each parent's organization. They will be contracted out to the new company. This seems at odds with the stated goal of creating the culture of a biotech.

It will, however, lead to cost savings of $89 million, most of which will be delivered in 2010, Witty said. The new company will be headquartered in London with $373 million in working capital, although Witty did not disclose exactly how much each company will contribute.

For GSK, which created some of the world's first and best-selling HIV drugs such as AZT and Epivir, many of which are set to lose patent protection in the coming years, the deal offers access to Pfizer's portfolio of new medicines in clinical development. Pfizer gets the benefit of GSK's strong marketing and distribution in HIV.

Witty, who has repeatedly said he is not interested in megamergers, says the new company "is a good example of the way in which we want to create value and generate efficiency in our business." He noted that GSK is looking at various parts of its businesses where it might be possible to create similar alliances.

After years of megadeals, will hiving off research areas to create smaller stand-alone businesses become the new template for pharma? The jury is out. It's clearly a way for both companies to reduce risks and costs.

The way the new company plans to incentivize new drug development, however, does offer an interesting new model. Describing the model as innovative, Witty said the rewards will go to developers of new medicines if they make it to market. If those new medicines come only from GSK, its equity share in the venture will increase; or conversely if Pfizer is more successful, its interest will increase.

Questions for Discussion

1. Why are GSK and Pfizer creating a new "specialist organization" to manage the sales and development of their HIV drugs?
2. How will the new company be organized? In what ways will it help speed the development of new drugs and reduce costs?
3. Go to the Internet and find some articles about the performance of the new venture.

Source: K. Capell, "GSK and Pfizer Create New HIV Company," *BusinessWeek,* April 16, 2009. Reprinted from April 16, 2009 issue of *Bloomberg Businessweek* by special permission,

CHAPTER 11

Organizational Control and Change

Learning Objectives

After studying this chapter, you should be able to:

LO11-1 Define organizational control and explain how it increases organizational effectiveness.

LO11-2 Describe the four steps in the control process and the way it operates over time.

LO11-3 Identify the main output controls, and discuss their advantages and disadvantages as means of coordinating and motivating employees.

LO11-4 Identify the main behavior controls, and discuss their advantages and disadvantages as a means of coordinating and motivating employees.

LO11-5 Discuss the relationship between organizational control and change, and explain why managing change is a vital management task.

A MANAGER'S CHALLENGE

Toyota Needs a Major Fix to Its Quality Control System

What is the best way to control people and resources? Toyota has long been known as a company that strives to improve its car design and production systems to enhance efficiency, quality, innovation, and customer responsiveness. It pioneered the system of "lean production" that changed how cars are assembled and has been imitated by all global carmakers because it dramatically improves vehicle reliability. Also, Toyota pursues total quality management that makes production-line employees responsible for continuously finding incremental improvements to work procedures that drive down costs and drive up quality. In the 2000s, under the leadership of Toyota's president, Katsuaki Watanabe, the company developed new control systems to further improve efficiency and quality and to strengthen its competitive advantage over rivals such as Volkswagen, Ford, and Honda. For example, it implemented an advanced TQM program to improve control over various functions as its global operations grew rapidly. One new TQM manufacturing strategy was "pokayoke," or mistake-proofing, an initiative that focuses on the assembly process stages that produce the most quality problems; employees double- and triple-check operating procedures at a particular stage to discover defective parts or fix improper assembly operations that might lead to subsequent customer complaints. Another strategy was "CCC21," which involves working with suppliers to jointly develop control systems that would lower the cost of Toyota's car components by 30%; this program saved over $10 billion by 2007. Toyota also implemented a new manufacturing process called GBL that allowed it to build factories that can assemble several different car models on the same production line with no loss in efficiency or quality—a major competitive advantage.

Akio Toyoda finally has something to smile about: after the firestorm over defective accelerators in Toyota vehicles prompted the company to reevaluate its focus, customers are coming back and the future of the company is looking up.

Although Toyota is a world leader in developing control systems that improve value chain management, it would be a mistake to believe that its record is perfect. Over the years it made many mistakes and errors as it searched for new ways to increase innovation, quality, and efficiency. On the quality front, for example, it made mistakes when its engineers designed parts such as air-conditioning systems and airbags that proved defective, and many vehicle recalls were necessary to correct them. On the efficiency front, vehicles became more difficult to assemble in the 2000s because both components and work processes became increasingly complex. And during the 2000s Toyota's managers increasingly failed to realize the need to train employees to improve their work performance and so prevent vehicle recalls. One reason was because of rapid expansion around the globe.[1] Between 2004 and 2008, for example, Toyota recalled 9.3 million vehicles in the United States and Japan, almost three times its previous rate. Its president, Katsuaki Watanabe, publicly apologized in 2007 for these increasing errors and affirmed that Toyota was now back on the right track with many new global quality and manufacturing initiatives in place. All carmakers experience recall problems from time to time, and Toyota almost always tops the quality list as the best global carmaker.[2]

So it came as a tremendous shock to Toyota when in January 2010 increasing reports of uncontrolled acceleration in some of its vehicles, particularly the Prius hybrid, were publicized in the global media. Stories said hundreds of drivers of Toyota vehicles had experienced this problem, and several deaths were attributed to this problem. Toyota was forced to recall more than 6 million U.S. vehicles, because of problems with accelerator pedals and braking. At first the problems were attributed to floor mats becoming stuck under accelerator pedals; however, within weeks it was discovered that the design of the accelerator pedals was also faulty. By March 2010 Toyota dealers had repaired over 2 million recalled U.S. cars and trucks (50,000 a day) by shaving and adding metal shims to accelerator pedals to prevent their sticking.

The current president of Toyota, Akio Toyoda, a member of the founding family, who took up his post in 1999, publicly apologized to Toyota customers in the United States and around the world, admitting that the company had been slow to respond to the braking problems that it had been aware of for months—and which it had been working to solve. Toyoda vowed to revamp Toyota's sprawling organizational structure to improve its ability to control vital issues such as quality and safety—although these product development problems had supposedly been fixed three years earlier under the quality push by former president Watanabe.

President Toyoda admitted that Toyota's control problems have proved difficult to solve because its push to become the world's largest carmaker (it overtook GM as the global leader in 2008) had let it drift away from its core value of focusing on the customer. And in March 2010 Toyoda, in a major meeting on global vehicle quality, revealed a new companywide control system to improve quality and reliability. Toyota announced that it would increase the number of its technology centers in North America to seven from one, as well as around the world, and recruit hundreds of new engineers to uncover potential problems with vehicle quality. Under the new management structure, quality officers at Toyota headquarters in Japan will decide with their counterparts in each global region how to address quality issues, and the chief quality officers in each region will share information about complaints raised by local customers. Previously headquarters told each region what to do; now Toyota is decentralizing control to engineers at the front line to speed decision making so it can react more quickly to emerging problems.[3]

Although its quality problems led to plunging car sales in January, by March sales were up by 40% after Toyota offered some of its steepest discounts to rebuild customer sales and trust after the fallout from millions of recalled vehicles. Clearly customers believe that Toyota has learned from its mistakes and that its improved systems of output and bureaucratic control will help to reduce or prevent such design quality problems in the future.

Overview

As we discussed in Chapter 10, the first task facing managers is to establish a structure of task and job reporting relationships that allows organizational members to use resources most efficiently and effectively. Structure alone, however, does not provide the incentive or motivation for people to behave in ways that help achieve organizational goals. When managers choose how to influence, shape, and regulate the activities of organizational divisions, functions, and employees to achieve the organization's mission and goals, they establish the second foundation of organizational architecture: organizational control. An organization's structure provides the organization with a skeleton, but its control systems give it the muscles, sinews, nerves, and sensations that allow managers to regulate and govern its activities. The control systems also give managers specific feedback on how well the organization and its members are performing. The managerial functions of organizing and controlling are inseparable, and effective managers must learn to make them work together in a harmonious way.

In this chapter, we look in detail at the nature of organizational control and describe the main steps in the control process. We also discuss the different types of control systems that are available to managers to shape and influence organizational activities–*output control, behavior control,* and *clan control.*[4] Finally, we discuss the important issue of organizational change, which is possible only when managers have put in place a control system that allows them to adjust the way people and groups behave and alter or transform the way the organization operates–something Akio Toyoda is currently trying to achieve across Toyota's global operations. Control is the essential ingredient that is needed to bring about and manage organizational change efficiently and effectively. By the end of this chapter, you will appreciate the different forms of control available to managers and understand why developing an appropriate control system is vital to increasing organizational performance.

What Is Organizational Control?

As noted in Chapter 1, *controlling* is the process whereby managers monitor and regulate how efficiently and effectively an organization and its members are performing the activities necessary to achieve organizational goals. As discussed in previous chapters, when planning and organizing, managers develop the organizational strategy and structure that they hope will allow the organization to use resources most effectively to create value for customers. In controlling, managers monitor and evaluate whether the organization's strategy and structure are working as intended, how they could be improved, and how they might be changed if they are not working.

LO11-1 Define organizational control and explain how it increases organizational effectiveness.

Control, however, does not mean just reacting to events after they have occurred. It also means keeping an organization on track, anticipating events that might occur, and then changing the organization to respond to whatever opportunities or threats have been identified. Control is concerned with keeping employees motivated, focused on the important problems confronting the organization, and working together to make the changes that will help an organization improve its performance over time.

The Importance of Organizational Control

To understand the importance of organizational control, consider how it helps managers obtain superior efficiency, quality, responsiveness to customers, and innovation–the four building blocks of competitive advantage.

To determine how efficiently they are using their resources, managers must be able to accurately measure how many units of inputs (raw materials, human resources, and so on) are being used to produce a unit of output, such as a Toyota vehicle. Managers also must be able to measure how many units of outputs (goods and services) are being produced. A control system contains the measures or yardsticks that let managers assess how efficiently the organization is producing goods and services. Moreover, if managers experiment with changing how the organization produces goods and services to find a more efficient way of producing them, these measures tell managers how successful they have been. For example, when managers at Toyota decided to adopt GBL to manufacture different cars on the same production line, they used measures such as time taken to change over from one car to another, and cost savings per car produced, to evaluate how well the new method worked. Without a control system in place, managers have no idea how well their organization is performing and how its performance can be improved–information that is becoming increasingly important in today's highly competitive environment.

Today much of the competition among organizations centers on increasing the quality of goods and services. In the car industry, for example, cars within each price range compete in features, design, and reliability. Thus whether a customer will buy a Ford Taurus, GM Grand Prix, Chrysler Sebring, Toyota Camry, or Honda Accord depends significantly on the quality of each product. Organizational control is important in determining the quality of goods and services because it gives managers feedback on product quality. If the managers of carmakers consistently measure the number of customer complaints and the number of new cars returned for repairs, or if school principals measure how many students drop out of school or how achievement scores on nationally based tests vary over time, they have a good indication of how much quality they have built into their product–be it an educated student or a car that does not break down. Effective managers create a control system that consistently monitors the quality of goods and services so they can continuously improve quality–an approach to change that gives them a competitive advantage.

Managers can help make their organizations more responsive to customers if they develop a control system, such as a CRM system, that allows them to evaluate how well customer contact employees perform their jobs. Monitoring employee behavior can help managers find ways to increase employees' performance levels, perhaps by revealing areas in which skill training can help employees or in which new procedures can allow employees to perform their jobs better–as Toyota discovered. Also, when employees know their behaviors are being monitored, they have more incentive to be helpful and consistent in how they act toward customers. To improve customer service, for example, Toyota regularly surveys customers about their experiences with particular Toyota dealers. If a dealership receives too many customer complaints, Toyota's managers investigate the dealership to uncover the sources of the problems and suggest solutions; if necessary, they might even threaten to reduce the number of

Who would you rather buy a new car from? A company that reinforces and rewards employee responsiveness, consistency, and know-how in customer care, or a company that doesn't? Toyota bets you'll pick the former.

cars a dealership receives to force the dealer to improve the quality of its customer service.

Finally, controlling can raise the level of innovation in an organization. Successful innovation takes place when managers create an organizational setting in which employees feel empowered to be creative and in which authority is decentralized to employees so they feel free to experiment and take control of their work activities. Deciding on the appropriate control systems to encourage risk taking is an important management challenge; organizational culture is vital in this regard. To encourage work teams at Toyota to perform at a high level, top managers monitored the performance of each team, for example, by examining how each team reduced costs or increased quality–and used a bonus system related to performance to reward each team. The team manager then evaluated each team member's individual performance, and the most innovative employees received promotions and rewards based on their superior performance.

Control Systems and IT

control systems Formal target-setting, monitoring, evaluation, and feedback systems that provide managers with information about how well the organization's strategy and structure are working.

Control systems are formal target-setting, monitoring, evaluation, and feedback systems that provide managers with information about whether the organization's strategy and structure are working efficiently and effectively.[5] Effective control systems alert managers when something is going wrong and give them time to respond to opportunities and threats. An effective control system has three characteristics: It is flexible enough to allow managers to respond as necessary to unexpected events; it provides accurate information about organizational performance; and it gives managers information in a timely manner because making decisions on the basis of outdated information is a recipe for failure.

New forms of IT have revolutionized control systems because they facilitate the flow of accurate and timely information up and down the organizational hierarchy and between functions and divisions. Today employees at all levels of the organization routinely feed information into a company's information system or network and start the chain of events that affect decision making in some other part of the organization. This could be the department store clerk whose scanning of purchased clothing tells merchandise managers what kinds of clothing need to be reordered or the salesperson in the field who feeds into a wireless laptop the CRM information necessary to inform marketing about customers' changing needs.

feedforward control Control that allows managers to anticipate problems before they arise.

Control and information systems are developed to measure performance at each stage in the process of transforming inputs into finished goods and services (see Figure 11.1). At the input stage, managers use **feedforward control** to anticipate problems before they arise so problems do not occur later during the conversion process.[6] For example, by giving stringent product specifications to suppliers in advance (a form of performance target), an organization can control the quality of the inputs it receives from its suppliers and thus avoid potential problems during the conversion process. Also, IT can be used to keep in contact with suppliers and to monitor their progress. Similarly, by screening job applicants, often by viewing their résumés electronically and using several interviews to select the most highly skilled people, managers can lessen the chance that they will hire people who lack the necessary skills or experience to perform effectively. In general, the development of management information systems promotes feedforward control that gives managers timely information about changes in the task and general environments that may impact their organization later on. Effective managers always monitor trends and changes in the external environment to try to anticipate problems. (We discuss management information systems in detail in Chapter 18.)

Figure 11.1
Three Types of Control

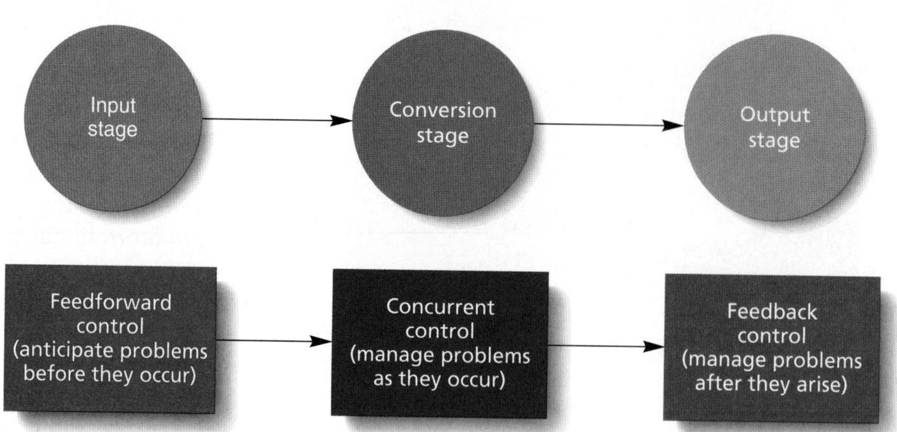

concurrent control Control that gives managers immediate feedback on how efficiently inputs are being transformed into outputs so managers can correct problems as they arise.

At the conversion stage, **concurrent control** gives managers immediate feedback on how efficiently inputs are being transformed into outputs so managers can correct problems as they arise. Concurrent control through IT alerts managers to the need to react quickly to whatever is the source of the problem, be it a defective batch of inputs, a machine that is out of alignment, or a worker who lacks the skills necessary to perform a task efficiently. Concurrent control is at the heart of total quality management programs (discussed in Chapter 9), in which workers are expected to constantly monitor the quality of the goods or services they provide at every step of the production process and inform managers as soon as they discover problems. One of the strengths of Toyota's production system, for example, is that individual workers have the authority to push a button to stop the assembly line whenever they discover a quality problem. When all problems are corrected the result is a finished product that is much more reliable.

feedback control Control that gives managers information about customers' reactions to goods and services so corrective action can be taken if necessary.

At the output stage, managers use **feedback control** to provide information about customers' reactions to goods and services so corrective action can be taken if necessary. For example, a feedback control system that monitors the number of customer returns alerts managers when defective products are being produced, and a management information system (MIS) that measures increases or decreases in relative sales of different products alerts managers to changes in customer tastes so they can increase or reduce the production of specific products.

The Control Process

LO11-2 Describe the four steps in the control process and the way it operates over time.

The control process, whether at the input, conversion, or output stage, can be broken down into four steps: establishing standards of performance, and then measuring, comparing, and evaluating actual performance (see Figure 11.2).[7]

- Step 1: *Establish the standards of performance, goals, or targets against which performance is to be evaluated.*

At step 1 in the control process managers decide on the standards of performance, goals, or targets that they will use in the future to evaluate the performance of the entire organization or part of it (such as a division, a function, or an individual). The standards of performance that managers select measure efficiency, quality, responsiveness to customers, and innovation.[8] If managers decide to pursue a low-cost strategy, for example, they need to measure efficiency at all levels in the organization.

At the corporate level, a standard of performance that measures efficiency is operating costs, the actual costs associated with producing goods and services, including all employee-related costs. Top managers might set a corporate goal of "reducing operating costs by 10% for the next three years" to increase efficiency. Corporate

Figure 11.2
Four Steps in Organizational Control

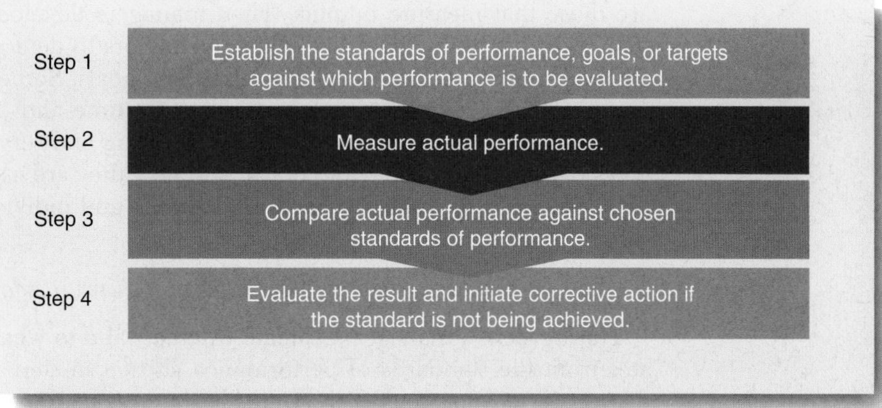
Step 1
Establish the standards of performance, goals, or targets against which performance is to be evaluated.
Step 2
Measure actual performance.
Step 3
Compare actual performance against chosen standards of performance.
Step 4
Evaluate the result and initiate corrective action if the standard is not being achieved.

managers might then evaluate divisional managers for their ability to reduce operating costs within their respective divisions, and divisional managers might set cost-saving targets for functional managers. Thus performance standards selected at one level affect those at the other levels, and ultimately the performance of individual managers is evaluated in terms of their ability to reduce costs.

The number of standards or indicators of performance that an organization's managers use to evaluate efficiency, quality, and so on can run into the thousands or hundreds of thousands. Managers at each level are responsible for selecting standards that will best allow them to evaluate how well the part of the organization they are responsible for is performing.[9] Managers must be careful to choose standards of performance that let them assess how well they are doing with all four building blocks of competitive advantage. If managers focus on just one standard (such as efficiency), and ignore others (such as determining what customers really want and innovating a new line of products to satisfy them), managers may end up hurting their organization's performance.

- Step 2: *Measure actual performance.*

Once managers have decided which standards or targets they will use to evaluate performance, the next step in the control process is to measure actual performance. In practice, managers can measure or evaluate two things: (1) the actual *outputs* that result from the behavior of their members and (2) the *behaviors* themselves (hence the terms *output control* and *behavior control* used in this chapter).[10]

Sometimes both outputs and behaviors can be easily measured. Measuring outputs and evaluating behavior is relatively easy in a fast-food restaurant, for example, because employees are performing routine tasks. Managers at Home Depot are rigorous in using output control to measure how fast inventory flows through stores. Similarly, managers of a fast-food restaurant can easily measure outputs by counting how many customers their employees serve, the time each transaction takes, and how much money each customer spends. Managers can easily observe each employee's behavior and quickly take action to solve any problems that may arise.

When an organization and its members perform complex, nonroutine activities that are intrinsically hard to measure, it is more challenging for managers to measure outputs or behavior.[11] It is difficult, for example, for managers in charge of R&D departments at Intel or AMD, or at Microsoft or Google, to measure performance or to evaluate the performance of individual members because it can take several years to determine whether the new products that engineers and scientists are developing will be profitable. Moreover, it is impossible for a manager to measure how creative an engineer or scientist is by watching his or her actions.

In general, the more nonroutine or complex organizational activities are, the harder it is for managers to measure outputs or behaviors.[12] Outputs, however, are usually easier to measure than behaviors because they are more tangible and objective. Therefore, the first kind of performance measures that managers tend to use are those that measure outputs. Then managers develop performance measures or standards that allow them to evaluate behaviors to determine whether employees at all levels are working toward organizational goals. Some simple behavior measures are (1) whether employees come to work on time and (2) whether employees consistently follow the established rules for greeting and serving customers. The various types of output and behavior control and how they are used at the different organizational levels–corporate, divisional, functional, and individual–are discussed in detail subsequently.

- Step 3: *Compare actual performance against chosen standards of performance.*

During step 3, managers evaluate whether–and to what extent–performance deviates from the standards of performance chosen in step 1. If performance is higher than expected, managers might decide they set performance standards too low and may raise them for the next period to challenge their subordinates.[13] Managers at Japanese companies are well known for the way they try to improve performance in manufacturing settings by constantly raising performance standards to motivate managers and workers to find new ways to reduce costs or increase quality; Chapter 9 discussed how companies can use TQM from an organizational control perspective.

However, if performance is too low and standards were not reached, or if standards were set so high that employees could not achieve them, managers must decide whether to take corrective action.[14] It is easy to take corrective action when the reasons for poor performance can be identified–for instance, high labor costs. To reduce costs, managers can search for low-cost overseas suppliers, invest more in technology, or implement cross-functional teams. More often, however, the reasons for poor performance are hard to identify. Changes in the environment, such as the emergence of a new global competitor, a recession, or an increase in interest rates, might be the source of the problem. Within an organization, perhaps the R&D function underestimated the problems it would encounter in developing a new product or the extra costs of doing unforeseen research–or as at Toyota, the faulty design of just one component in thousands slipped through the cracks. If managers are to take any form of corrective action, step 4 is necessary.

- Step 4: *Evaluate the result and initiate corrective action (that is, make changes) if the standard is not being achieved.*

The final step in the control process is to evaluate the results and bring about change as appropriate. Whether or not performance standards have been met, managers can learn a great deal during this step. If managers decide the level of performance is unacceptable, they must try to change how work activities are performed to solve the problem. Sometimes performance problems occur because the work standard was too high–for example, a sales target was too optimistic and impossible to achieve. In this case, adopting more realistic standards can reduce the gap between actual performance and desired performance.

However, if managers determine that something in the situation is causing the problem, then to raise performance they will need to change how resources are utilized.[15] Perhaps the latest technology is not being used; perhaps workers lack the advanced training needed to perform at a higher level; perhaps the organization needs to buy its inputs or assemble its products abroad to compete against low-cost rivals; perhaps it needs to restructure itself or reengineer its work processes using Six Sigma to increase efficiency.

The simplest example of a control system is the thermostat in a home. By setting the thermostat, you establish the standard of performance with which actual temperature is to be compared. The thermostat contains a sensing or monitoring device, which measures the actual temperature against the desired temperature. Whenever

Figure 11.3
Three Organizational Control Systems

Type of control	Mechanisms of control
Output control	Financial measures of performance Organizational goals Operating budgets
Behavior control	Direct supervision Management by objectives Rules and standard operating procedures
Clan control	Values Norms Socialization

there is a difference between them, the furnace or air-conditioning unit is activated to bring the temperature back to the standard. In other words, corrective action is initiated. This is a simple control system: It is entirely self-contained, and the target (temperature) is easy to measure.

Establishing targets and designing measurement systems are much more difficult for managers because the high level of uncertainty in the organizational environment means managers rarely know what might happen in the future. Thus it is vital for managers to design control systems to alert them to problems quickly so they can be dealt with before they become threatening. Obviously Toyota was too slow to react to its accelerator pedal problem, which has cost it billions of dollars in vehicle recalls, lawsuits, and lost business. Another issue is that managers are not just concerned about bringing the organization's performance up to some predetermined standard; they want to push that standard forward to encourage employees at all levels to find new ways to raise performance. This is something that Toyota has traditionally excelled at, which is why customers are not afraid to buy its vehicles.

In the following sections, we consider three important types of control systems that managers use to coordinate and motivate employees to ensure that they pursue superior efficiency, quality, innovation, and responsiveness to customers: output control, behavior control, and clan control (see Figure 11.3). Managers use all three to shape, regulate, and govern organizational activities, no matter what specific organizational structure is in place. However, as Figure 11.3 suggests, an important element of control is embedded in organizational culture, which is discussed later.

Output Control

All managers develop a system of output control for their organizations. First they choose the goals or output performance standards or targets that they think will best measure efficiency, quality, innovation, and responsiveness to customers. Then they measure to see whether the performance goals and standards are being achieved at the corporate, divisional, functional, and individual employee levels of the organization. The three main mechanisms that managers use to assess output or performance are financial measures, organizational goals, and operating budgets.

LO11-3 Identify the main output controls, and discuss their advantages and disadvantages as means of coordinating and motivating employees.

Financial Measures of Performance

Top managers are most concerned with overall organizational performance and use various financial measures to evaluate it. The most common are profit ratios, liquidity ratios, leverage ratios, and activity ratios. They are discussed here and summarized in Table 11.1.[16]

Table 11.1
Four Measures of Financial Performance

Ratio		Formula	Description
Profit Ratios			
Return on investment	=	$\frac{\text{Net profit before taxes}}{\text{Total assets}}$	Measures how well managers are using the organization's resources to generate profits.
Operating margin	=	$\frac{\text{Total operating profit}}{\text{Sales revenues}}$	A measure of how much percentage profit a company is earning on sales; the higher the percentage, the better a company is using its resources to make and sell the product.
Liquidity Ratios			
Current ratio	=	$\frac{\text{Current assets}}{\text{Current liabilities}}$	Do managers have resources available to meet claims of short-term creditors?
Quick ratio	=	$\frac{\text{Current assets} - \text{Inventory}}{\text{Current liabilities}}$	Can managers pay off claims of short-term creditors without selling inventory?
Leverage Ratios			
Debt-to-assets ratio	=	$\frac{\text{Total debt}}{\text{Total assets}}$	To what extent have managers used borrowed funds to finance investments?
Times-covered ratio	=	$\frac{\text{Profit before interest and taxes}}{\text{Total interest charges}}$	Measures how far profits can decline before managers cannot meet interest changes. If this ratio declines to less than 1, the organization is technically insolvent.
Activity Ratios			
Inventory turnover	=	$\frac{\text{Cost of good sold}}{\text{Inventory}}$	Measures how efficiently managers are turning inventory over so that excess inventory is not carried.
Days sales outstanding	=	$\frac{\text{Current accounts receivable}}{\text{Sales for period divided by days in period}}$	Measures how efficiently managers are collecting revenues from customers to pay expenses.

- *Profit ratios* measure how efficiently managers are using the organization's resources to generate profits. *Return on investment (ROI),* an organization's net income before taxes divided by its total assets, is the most commonly used financial performance measure because it allows managers of one organization to compare performance with that of other organizations. ROI lets managers assess an organization's competitive advantage. *Operating margin* is calculated by dividing a company's operating profit (the amount it has left after all the costs of making the product and running the business have been deducted) by sales revenues. This measure tells managers how efficiently an organization is using its resources; every successful attempt to reduce costs will be reflected in increased operating profit, for example. Also, operating margin is a means of comparing one year's performance to another; for example, if managers discover operating margin has improved by 5% from one year to the next, they know their organization is building a competitive advantage.
- *Liquidity ratios* measure how well managers have protected organizational resources to be able to meet short-term obligations. The *current ratio* (current assets divided by current liabilities) tells managers whether they have the resources available to meet the claims of short-term creditors. The *quick ratio* shows whether they can pay these claims without selling inventory.
- *Leverage ratios,* such as the *debt-to-assets ratio* and the *times-covered ratio,* measure the degree to which managers use debt (borrow money) or equity (issue new shares) to finance ongoing operations. An organization is highly leveraged if it uses more debt than equity. Debt can be risky when net income or profit fails to cover the interest on the debt–as some people learn too late when their paychecks do not allow them to pay off their credit cards.

- *Activity ratios* show how well managers are creating value from organizational assets. *Inventory turnover* measures how efficiently managers are turning inventory over so excess inventory is not carried. *Days sales outstanding* reveals how efficiently managers are collecting revenue from customers to pay expenses.

The objectivity of financial measures of performance is the reason why so many managers use them to assess the efficiency and effectiveness of their organizations. When an organization fails to meet performance standards such as ROI, revenue, or stock price targets, managers know they must take corrective action. Thus financial controls tell managers when a corporate reorganization might be necessary, when they should sell off divisions and exit businesses, or when they should rethink their corporate-level strategies.[17] Today financial controls are taught to all organizational employees, as the following "Management Insight" box describes.

Management Insight

Making the Financial Figures Come Alive

You might think financial control is the province of top managers and employees lower in the organization don't need to worry about the numbers or about how their specific activities affect those numbers. However, some top managers make a point of showing employees exactly how their activities affect financial ratios, and they do so because employees' activities directly affect a company's costs and its sales revenues. One of those managers is Michael Dell, who was a focus in Chapter 9.

Dell goes to enormous lengths to convince employees that they need to watch every dime spent in making the PCs that have made his company so prosperous, as well as in saying every word or making every phone call or service call that is needed to sell or repair them. Dell believes all his managers need to have at their fingertips detailed information about Dell's cost structure, including assembly costs, selling costs, and after-sales costs, in order to squeeze out every cent of operating costs. One good reason for this is that Dell puts a heavy emphasis on the operating margin financial ratio in measuring his company's performance. Dell doesn't care about how much profits or sales are growing individually; he cares about how these two figures work together because only if profits are growing faster than sales is the company increasing its long-run profitability by operating more efficiently and effectively.

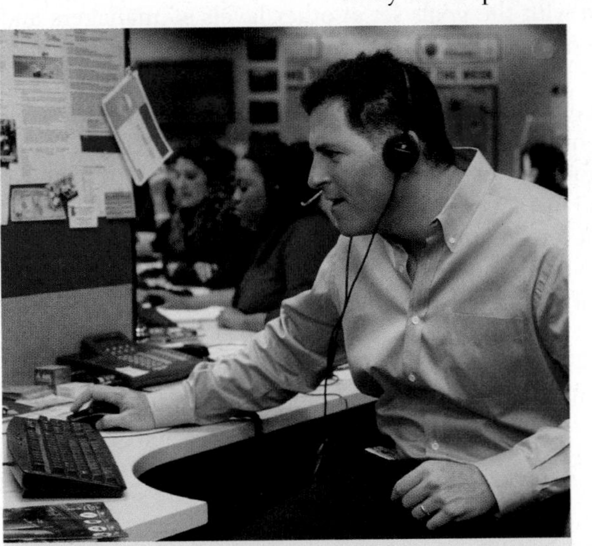

Michael Dell prepares to work the phone lines at Dell's U.S. customer service call center. Dell's emphasis on productivity everywhere means he has no qualms about sitting in an entry-level position for a day both to learn what his employees face and to better teach them.

So he insists that his managers search for every way possible to reduce costs or make customers happier and then help employees learn the new procedures to achieve these goals. At Dell's boot camp for new employees in Austin, Texas, he has been known to bring financial charts that show employees how each minute spent on performing some job activity, or how each mistake made in assembling or packing a PC, affects bottom-line profitability. In the early 2000s Dell's repeated efforts to reduce costs and build customer loyalty boosted its efficiency and operating margins; today, as it battles rivals such as HP and Acer, it is even more important that its employees understand how their specific behaviors affect Dell's bottom-line financial performance. In the 2000s all kinds of companies are training employees at all levels in how their specific job activities, and the way their functions operate, affect the financial ratios used to judge how well an organization is performing.

Although financial information is an important output control, financial information by itself does not tell managers all they need to know about the four building blocks of competitive advantage. Financial results inform managers about the results of decisions they have already made; they do not tell managers how to find new opportunities to build competitive advantage in the future. To encourage a future-oriented approach, top managers must establish organizational goals that encourage middle and first-line managers to achieve superior efficiency, quality, innovation, and responsiveness to customers.

Organizational Goals

Once top managers consult with lower-level managers and set the organization's overall goals, they establish performance standards for the divisions and functions. These standards specify for divisional and functional managers the level at which their units must perform if the organization is to achieve its overall goals.[18] Each division is given a set of specific goals to achieve (see Figure 11.4). We saw in Chapter 8, for example, that Jeffrey Immelt, CEO of GE, has established the goal of having each GE division be first or second in its industry in profit. Divisional managers then develop a business-level strategy (based on achieving superior efficiency or innovation) that they hope will allow them to achieve that goal.[19] In consultation with functional managers, they specify the functional goals that the managers of different functions need to achieve to allow the division to achieve its goals. For example, sales managers might be evaluated for their ability to increase sales; materials management managers, for their ability to increase the quality of inputs or lower their costs; R&D managers, for the number of products they innovate or the number of patents they receive. In turn, functional managers establish goals that first-line managers and nonmanagerial employees need to achieve to allow the function to achieve its goals.

Output control is used at every level of the organization, and it is vital that the goals set at each level harmonize with the goals set at other levels so managers and other employees throughout the organization work together to attain the corporate goals that top managers have set.[20] It is also important that goals be set appropriately so managers are motivated to accomplish them. If goals are set at an impossibly high level, managers might work only half-heartedly to achieve them because they are certain they will fail. In contrast, if goals are set so low that they are too easy to achieve, managers will not be motivated to use all their resources as efficiently and effectively as possible. Research suggests that the best goals are specific, difficult goals–goals that challenge and stretch managers' ability but are not out of reach and do not require an impossibly high expenditure of managerial time and energy. Such goals are often called *stretch goals.*

Deciding what is a specific, difficult goal and what is a goal that is too difficult or too easy is a skill that managers must develop. Based on their own judgment and work

Figure 11.4
Organizationwide Goal Setting

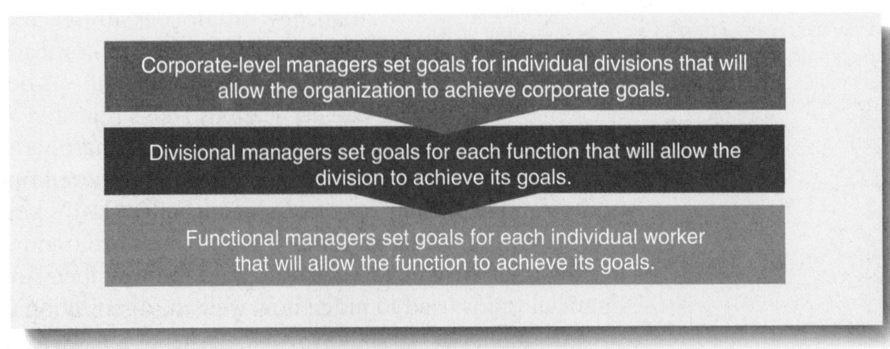

Corporate-level managers set goals for individual divisions that will allow the organization to achieve corporate goals.
Divisional managers set goals for each function that will allow the division to achieve its goals.
Functional managers set goals for each individual worker that will allow the function to achieve its goals.

experience, managers at all levels must assess how difficult a certain task is, and they must assess the ability of a particular subordinate manager to achieve the goal. If they do so successfully, challenging, interrelated goals–goals that reinforce one another and focus on achieving overall corporate objectives–will energize the organization.

Operating Budgets

operating budget A budget that states how managers intend to use organizational resources to achieve organizational goals.

Once managers at each level have been given a goal or target to achieve, the next step in developing an output control system is to establish operating budgets that regulate how managers and workers attain their goals. An **operating budget** is a blueprint that states how managers intend to use organizational resources to achieve organizational goals efficiently. Typically managers at one level allocate to subordinate managers a specific amount of resources to produce goods and services. Once they have been given a budget, these lower-level managers must decide how to allocate money for different organizational activities. They are then evaluated for their ability to stay within the budget and to make the best use of available resources. For example, managers at GE's washing machine division might have a budget of $50 million to spend on developing and selling a new line of washing machines. They must decide how much money to allocate to the various functions such as R&D, engineering, and sales so the division generates the most customer revenue and makes the biggest profit.

Large organizations often treat each division as a singular or stand-alone responsibility center. Corporate managers then evaluate each division's contribution to corporate performance. Managers of a division may be given a fixed budget for resources and be evaluated on the amount of goods or services they can produce using those resources (this is a cost or expense budget approach). Alternatively, managers may be asked to maximize the revenues from the sales of goods and services produced (a revenue budget approach). Or managers may be evaluated on the difference between the revenues generated by the sales of goods and services and the budgeted cost of making those goods and services (a profit budget approach). Japanese companies' use of operating budgets and challenging goals to increase efficiency is instructive in this context.

In summary, three components–objective financial measures, challenging goals and performance standards, and appropriate operating budgets–are the essence of effective output control. Most organizations develop sophisticated output control systems to allow managers at all levels to keep accurate account of the organization so they can move quickly to take corrective action as needed.[21] Output control is an essential part of management.

Problems with Output Control

When designing an output control system, managers must be careful to avoid some pitfalls. For example, they must be sure the output standards they create motivate managers at all levels and do not cause managers to behave in inappropriate ways to achieve organizational goals.

Suppose top managers give divisional managers the goal of doubling profits over a three-year period. This goal seems challenging and reachable when it is jointly agreed upon, and in the first two years profits go up by 70%. In the third year, however, an economic recession hits and sales plummet. Divisional managers think it is increasingly unlikely that they will meet their profit goal. Failure will mean losing the substantial monetary bonus tied to achieving the goal. How might managers behave to try to preserve their bonuses?

Perhaps they might find ways to reduce costs because profit can be increased either by raising sales revenues or reducing costs. Thus divisional managers might cut back on expensive research activities, delay machinery maintenance, reduce marketing expenditures, and lay off middle managers and workers to reduce costs so that at the end of the year they will make their target of doubling profits and receive their bonuses. This tactic might help them achieve a short-run goal–doubling profits–but such actions could hurt long-term profitability or ROI (because a cutback in R&D can reduce the rate of product innovation, a cutback in marketing will lead to the loss of customers, and so on).

The message is clear: Although output control is a useful tool for keeping managers and employees at all levels motivated and the organization on track, it is only a guide to appropriate action. Managers must be sensitive in how they use output control and must constantly monitor its effects at all levels in the organization–and on customers and other stakeholders.

Behavior Control

LO11-4 Identify the main behavior controls, and discuss their advantages and disadvantages as a means of coordinating and motivating employees.

Organizational structure by itself does not provide any mechanism that motivates managers and nonmanagerial employees to behave in ways that make the structure work–or even improve how it works–hence the need for control. Put another way, managers can develop an organizational structure that has the right grouping of divisions and functions, and an effective chain of command, but it will work as designed *only* if managers also establish control systems that motivate and shape employee behavior in ways that *match* this structure.[22] Output control is one method of motivating employees; behavior control is another method. This section examines three mechanisms of behavior control that managers can use to keep subordinates on track and make organizational structures work as they are designed to work: direct supervision, management by objectives, and rules and standard operating procedures (see Figure 11.3).

Direct Supervision

The most immediate and potent form of behavior control is direct supervision by managers who actively monitor and observe the behavior of their subordinates, teach subordinates the behaviors that are appropriate and inappropriate, and intervene to take corrective action as needed. Moreover, when managers personally supervise subordinates, they lead by example and in this way can help subordinates develop and increase their own skill levels. (Leadership is the subject of Chapter 14.)

Direct supervision allows managers at all levels to become personally involved with their subordinates and allows them to mentor subordinates and develop their management skills. Thus control through personal supervision can be an effective way of motivating employees and promoting behaviors that increase efficiency and effectiveness.[23]

Nevertheless, certain problems are associated with direct supervision. First, it is expensive because a manager can personally manage only a relatively small number of subordinates effectively. Therefore, if direct supervision is the main kind of control being used in an organization, a lot of managers will be needed and costs will increase. For this reason, output control is usually preferred to behavior control; indeed, output control tends to be the first type of control that managers at all levels use to evaluate performance. Second, direct supervision can *demotivate* subordinates. This occurs if employees feel they are under such close scrutiny that they are not free to make their own decisions or if they feel they are not being evaluated in an accurate and impartial way. Team members and other employees may start to pass the buck, avoid responsibility, and cease to cooperate with other team members if they feel their manager is not accurately evaluating their performance and is favoring some people over others.

Third, as noted previously, for many jobs personal control through direct supervision is simply not feasible. The more complex a job is, the more difficult it is for a manager to evaluate how well a subordinate is performing. The performance of divisional and functional managers, for example, can be evaluated only over relatively long periods (which is why an output control system is developed), so it makes little sense for top managers to continually monitor their performance. However, managers can still communicate the organization's mission and goals to their subordinates and reinforce the values and norms in the organization's culture through their own personal style.

Management by Objectives

management by objectives (MBO) A goal-setting process in which a manager and each of his or her subordinates negotiate specific goals and objectives for the subordinate to achieve and then periodically evaluate the extent to which the subordinate is achieving those goals.

To provide a framework within which to evaluate subordinates' behavior and, in particular, to allow managers to monitor progress toward achieving goals, many organizations implement some version of management by objectives. **Management by objectives (MBO)** is a formal system of evaluating subordinates on their ability to achieve specific organizational goals or performance standards and to meet operating budgets.[24] Most organizations use some form of MBO system because it is pointless to establish goals and then fail to evaluate whether they are being achieved. Management by objectives involves three specific steps:

- Step 1: *Specific goals and objectives are established at each level of the organization.*

MBO starts when top managers establish overall organizational objectives, such as specific financial performance goals or targets. Then objective setting cascades down throughout the organization as managers at the divisional and functional levels set their goals to achieve corporate objectives.[25] Finally first-level managers and employees jointly set goals that will contribute to achieving functional objectives.

- Step 2: *Managers and their subordinates together determine the subordinates' goals.*

An important characteristic of management by objectives is its participatory nature. Managers at every level sit down with each of the subordinate managers who report directly to them, and together they determine appropriate and feasible goals for the subordinate and bargain over the budget that the subordinate will need to achieve his or her goals. The participation of subordinates in the objective-setting process is a way of strengthening their commitment to achieving their goals and meeting their budgets.[26] Another reason why it is so important for subordinates (both individuals and teams) to participate in goal setting is that doing so enables them to tell managers what they think they can realistically achieve.[27]

- Step 3: *Managers and their subordinates periodically review the subordinates' progress toward meeting goals.*

Once specific objectives have been agreed on for managers at each level, managers are accountable for meeting those objectives. Periodically they sit down with their subordinates to evaluate their progress. Normally salary raises and promotions are linked to the goal-setting process, and managers who achieve their goals receive greater rewards than those who fall short. (The issue of how to design reward systems to motivate managers and other organizational employees is discussed in Chapter 13.)

In the companies that have decentralized responsibility for the production of goods and services to empowered teams and cross-functional teams, management by objectives works somewhat differently. Managers ask each team to develop a set of goals and performance targets that the team hopes to achieve–goals that are consistent with organizational objectives. Managers then negotiate with each team to establish its final goals and the budget the team will need to achieve them. The reward system is linked to team performance, not to the performance of any one team member.

Cypress Semiconductor offers an interesting example of how IT can be used to manage the MBO process quickly and effectively. In the fast-moving semiconductor business, a premium is placed on organizational adaptability. At Cypress, CEO T. J. Rodgers was facing a problem: How could he control his growing, 1,500-employee organization without developing a bureaucratic management hierarchy? Rodgers believed that a tall hierarchy hinders the ability of an organization to adapt to changing conditions. He was committed to maintaining a flat and decentralized organizational structure with a minimum of management layers. At the same time he needed to control his employees to ensure that they performed in a manner consistent with the goals of the company.[28] How could he achieve this without resorting to direct supervision and the lengthy management hierarchy that it implies?

To solve this problem, Rodgers implemented an online information system through which he can monitor what every employee and team is doing in his fast-moving and decentralized organization. Each employee maintains a list of 10 to 15 goals, such as "Meet with marketing for new product launch" or "Make sure to check with customer X." Noted next to each goal are when it was agreed upon, when it is due to be finished, and whether it has been finished. All this information is stored on a central computer. Rodgers claims that he can review the goals of all employees in about four hours and that he does so each week.[29] How is this possible? He *manages by exception* and looks only for employees who are falling behind. He then calls them, not to scold but to ask whether there is anything he can do to help them get the job done. It takes only about half an hour each week for employees to review and update their lists. This system allows Rodgers to exercise control over his organization without resorting to the expensive layers of a management hierarchy and direct supervision.

MBO does not always work out as planned, however. Managers and their subordinates at all levels must believe that performance evaluations are accurate and fair. Any suggestion that personal biases and political objectives play a part in the evaluation process can lower or even destroy MBO's effectiveness as a control system. This is why many organizations work so hard to protect the integrity of their systems. Microsoft has experienced problems with its performance evaluation system, as the following "Management Insight" box suggests.

Management Insight

Microsoft Has Problems Evaluating Its Employees

From its beginning, Microsoft organized its software engineers into small work groups and teams so team members could cooperate, learning from and helping each other, and so speed the development of innovative software. Each team works on a subset of the thousands of programs that together make up its Windows operating system and applications software, which is loaded on over 90% of PCs today.[30] In the past, much of Microsoft's reward system was based on team performance; employees of successful teams that quickly developed innovative software received valuable stock options and other benefits. Microsoft's team-based reward system encouraged team members to work together intensively and cooperate to meet team goals. At the same time, the contributions of exceptional team members were recognized; these individuals received rewards such as promotion to become the managers or leaders of new teams as the company grew.

Microsoft ran into serious problems when it was developing its Vista operating system. Vista was scheduled to come out in the summer of 2006, but unforeseen delays had put the project six months behind schedule, delaying its planned launch until spring 2007. Why? Many analysts blamed the delay on the new performance evaluation system Microsoft had introduced, which, because it was primarily based on individual performance contributions, was hurting team performance. As Microsoft grew over time (it now employs over 100,000 people), it developed a more and more rigid performance evaluation system that became increasingly based on each engineer's individual performance. The manager of each team was expected to rate the performance of each team member on a scale of 2.5, 3.0, and so on to 5, the highest individual performance rating. Microsoft adopted this system to try to increase the perceived fairness of its evaluation system.

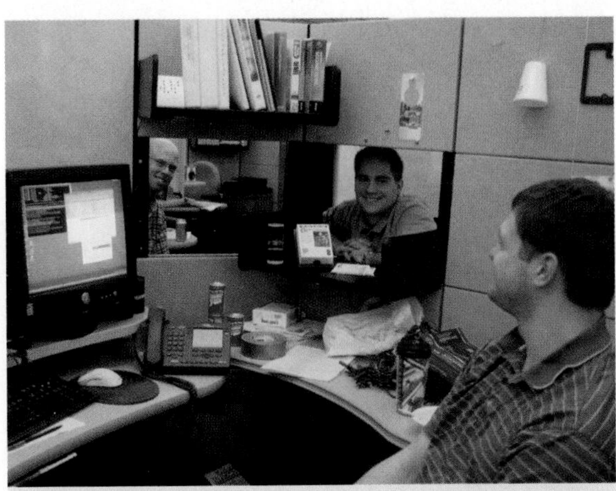
Microsoft employees revamped their work cubicles to allow for greater face-to-face contact and better communication, which improves their ability to cooperate with each other to achieve team goals.

Employees still worked principally in teams, however, and the new emphasis on individual performance negatively affected the relationships among team members because members were aware that they were in competition for the highest ratings. For example, when confronted with a situation in which they could help other team members but doing so might hurt their own personal performance evaluations, they behaved self-interestedly, and this hurt overall team performance. Moreover, Microsoft is highly secretive about employees' performance evaluations, current salaries, and raises: Employees are told *not* to share such information and can get fired if they do.[31] To make matters worse, the way these evaluations were made by team managers was also highly secretive. And employees believed that when the managers of different teams met to discuss which teams (as a unit) had achieved the highest level of team performance, these evaluations were distorted by favoritism. Specifically, leaders of the teams who were liked by *their* managers (often because the leaders actively support their managers) received higher team evaluations than did leaders of teams who were not perceived as supportive by their managers. Because evaluations were biased by personal likes and dislikes, the performance evaluation system was regarded as being highly political.

Increasingly, engineers and teams perceived that they were being evaluated not objectively–by the results achieved–but subjectively, by the ability of an engineer or team leader to "make the right pitch" and gain the favor of his or her direct superior. As a result, team members increasingly pursued their own interests at the expense of others, and so team performance was declining across the organization.[32] As you can imagine, when team members feel that their personal performance contributions are not being adequately recognized, and that even the performance of different teams is not being judged fairly, many performance problems arise. And one of these problems was that many of Microsoft's best software engineers left to join rivals such as Google or create their own start-up organizations as a result of their failure to achieve the recognition they thought they deserved at Microsoft.[33]

In developing its new Windows 7 operating system Microsoft was careful to make team performance a more important element of its promotion and reward evaluations. Indeed, it now lets team members contribute to the evaluation process and allows them to evaluate their team leaders' performance using the 360-degree performance appraisal technique discussed in the next chapter.

Clearly, when people work in teams, each member's contribution to the team, and each team's contribution to the goals of the organization, must be fairly evaluated. This is no easy thing to do. It depends on managers' ability to create an organizational control system that measures performance accurately and fairly and links performance evaluations to rewards so employees stay motivated and coordinate their activities to achieve the organization's mission and goals. Microsoft's problem was that the changes it made to its control system (new performance evaluation measures) as the company grew hurt its ability to motivate its employees.

Bureaucratic Control

bureaucratic control
Control of behavior by means of a comprehensive system of rules and standard operating procedures.

When direct supervision is too expensive and management by objectives is inappropriate, managers might turn to another mechanism to shape and motivate employee behavior: bureaucratic control. **Bureaucratic control** is control by means of a comprehensive system of rules and standard operating procedures (SOPs) that shapes and regulates the behavior of divisions, functions, and individuals. In Chapter 2 we discussed Weber's theory of bureaucracy and noted that all organizations use bureaucratic rules and procedures but some use them more than others.[34] Recall that rules and SOPs are formal, written instructions that specify a series of actions that employees should follow to achieve a given end; in other words, if *A* happens, then do *B* and *C*. For example, a simple set of rules developed by the supervisor of some custodial workers (Crew G) at a Texas A&M University building clearly established task responsibilities and clarified expectations (see Table 11.2).

Rules and SOPs guide behavior and specify what employees are to do when they confront a problem that needs a solution. It is the responsibility of a manager to develop rules that allow employees to perform their activities efficiently and effectively. Rules and SOPs also clarify people's expectations about one another and prevent misunderstandings over responsibility or the use of power. Such guidelines can prevent a supervisor from arbitrarily increasing a subordinate's workload and prevent a subordinate from ignoring tasks that are a legitimate part of the job.

When employees follow the rules that managers have developed, their behavior is *standardized*–actions are performed the same way time and time again–and the outcomes of their work are predictable. And to the degree that managers can make employees' behavior predictable, there is no need to monitor the outputs of behavior because *standardized behavior leads to standardized outputs,* such as goods and services of the same uniform quality. Suppose a worker at Toyota comes up with a way to attach exhaust pipes that reduces the number of steps in the assembly process and increases efficiency. Always on the lookout for ways to standardize and improve procedures, managers make this idea the basis of a new rule that says, "From now on, the procedure for attaching the exhaust pipe to the car is as follows." If all workers follow the rule to the letter, every car will come off the assembly line with its exhaust pipe attached in the new way, and there will be no need to check exhaust pipes at the end of the line.

Table 11.2
Team Rules of Conduct

1. All employees must call their supervisor or leader before 5:55 a.m. to notify of absence or tardiness.
2. Disciplinary action will be issued to any employee who abuses sick leave policy.
3. Disciplinary action will be issued to any employee whose assigned area is not up to custodial standards.
4. If a door is locked when you go in to clean an office, it's your responsibility to lock it back up.
5. Name tags and uniforms must be worn daily.
6. Each employee is responsible for buffing hallways and offices. Hallways must be buffed weekly, offices periodically.
7. All equipment must be put in closets during 9:00 a.m. and 11 a.m. breaks.
8. Do not use the elevator to move trash or equipment from 8:50 to 9:05, 9:50 to 10:05, 11:50 to 12:05, or 1:50 to 2:05 to avoid breaks between classes.
9. Try to mop hallways when students are in classrooms, or mop floors as you go down to each office.
10. Closets must be kept clean, and all equipment must be clean and operative.
11. Each employee is expected to greet building occupants with "Good morning."
12. Always knock before entering offices and conference rooms.
13. Loud talking, profanity, and horseplay will not be tolerated inside buildings.
14. All custodial carts must be kept uniform and cleaned daily.
15. You must have excellent "public relations" with occupants at all times.

In practice, mistakes and lapses of attention happen, so output control is used at the end of the line, and each car's exhaust system is given a routine inspection. However, the number of quality problems with the exhaust system is minimized because the rule (bureaucratic control) is being followed. Service organizations such as retail stores, fast-food restaurants, and home improvement stores also attempt to standardize employee behavior, such as customer service quality, by instructing employees in the correct way to greet customers or the appropriate way to serve and bag food. Employees are trained to follow the rules that have proved to be most effective in a particular situation, and the better trained the employees are, the more standardized is their behavior and the more trust managers can have that outputs (such as food quality) will be consistent. An interesting example of how creating the wrong rules can reduce performance occurred at Gateway (now part of PC maker Acer), which saw its customer satisfaction rating plummet as a result of its new rules. Managers at Gateway discovered that the reason for rising customer dissatisfaction was the new rules they had created to reduce the increasing costs of after-sales service. When customers installed additional software on their new Gateway computers, this often caused problems with the software already installed on the PC. It often took customer reps considerable time to iron out the problems, and Gateway was spending millions of dollars in employee time to solve these problems. To reduce costs, managers told its service reps to inform customers that if they installed any other software on their machines, this would invalidate Gateway's warranty. This infuriated customers who obviously had the right to install other software. Gateway also began to reward customer reps based on how quickly they handled customer calls; the more calls they handled in an hour or day, the higher their bonuses. The effect of these changes was to motivate customer reps to keep service calls short. Customers resented this treatment, and when Gateway's managers realized what was happening, they went back to the old system and customer satisfaction soared. As Gateway's and Toyota's managers discovered, to prevent unexpected problems, it is necessary to carefully choose and evaluate the rules and policies used to control employees' behavior.

In contrast to the situation at Gateway, Dave Lilly, an ex-nuclear submarine commander, chose the right rules for siteROCK, whose business is hosting and managing other companies' Web sites to keep them running and error-free. A customer's Web site that goes down or runs haywire is the enemy. To maximize his employees' performance and increase their ability to respond to unexpected online events, Lilly decided they needed a comprehensive set of rules and SOPs to cover the main known problems.[35] Lilly insisted that every problem-solving procedure should be written down and recorded. siteROCK's employees developed over 30 thick binders that list all the processes and checklists they need to follow when an unexpected event happens. Moreover, again drawing from his military experience, Lilly instituted a "two-person rule": Whenever the unexpected happens, each employee must immediately tell a coworker and the two together should attempt to solve the problem. The goal is simple: Use the rules to achieve a quick resolution of a complex issue. If the existing rules don't work, employees must experiment; and when they find a solution, it is turned into a new rule to be included in the procedures book to aid the future decision making of all employees in the organization.

Problems with Bureaucratic Control

Like all organizations, Toyota, Gateway, and siteROCK make extensive use of bureaucratic control because rules and SOPs effectively control routine organizational activities. With a bureaucratic control system in place, managers can manage by exception and intervene and take corrective action only when necessary. However, managers need to be aware of a number of problems associated with bureaucratic control because such problems can reduce organizational effectiveness.[36]

Looks like even Mickey Mouse approves! Bob Iger's redesign of Disney's methods of innovation and planning lets employees get moving faster on new ideas.

First, establishing rules is always easier than discarding them. Organizations tend to become overly bureaucratic over time as managers do everything according to the rule book. If the amount of red tape becomes too great, decision making slows and managers react sluggishly to changing conditions. This can imperil an organization's survival if agile new competitors emerge. Once a siteROCK employee has found a better rule, the old one is discarded.

Second, because rules constrain and standardize behavior and lead people to behave in predictable ways, people might become so used to automatically following rules that they stop thinking for themselves. Thus too much standardization can actually *reduce* the level of learning taking place in an organization and get the organization off track if managers and workers focus on the wrong issues. An organization thrives when its members are constantly thinking of new ways to increase efficiency, quality, and customer responsiveness. By definition, new ideas do not come from blindly following standardized procedures. Similarly, the pursuit of innovation implies a commitment by managers to discover new ways of doing things; innovation, however, is incompatible with extensive bureaucratic control.

Consider, for example, what happened at Walt Disney in 2006 when Bob Iger became CEO of the troubled company. Bob Iger had been COO of Disney under CEO Michael Eisner, and he had noticed how Disney was plagued by slow decision making that had led to made many mistakes in putting its new strategies into action. Its Disney stores were losing money; its Internet properties were flops; and even its theme parks seemed to have lost their luster as few new rides or attractions were introduced. Iger believed one of the main reasons for Disney's declining performance was that it had become too tall and bureaucratic and its top managers were following financial rules that did not lead to innovative strategies.

One of Iger's first moves to turn around the performance of the poorly performing company was to dismantle Disney's central strategic planning office. In this office several levels of managers were responsible for sifting through all the new ideas and innovations sent up by Disney's different business divisions, such as theme parks, movies, and gaming, and then deciding which ones to present to the CEO. Iger saw the strategic planning office as a bureaucratic bottleneck that reduced the number of ideas coming from below. So he dissolved the office and reassigned its managers back to the different business units.[37] The result of cutting an unnecessary layer in Disney's hierarchy has been that more new ideas are generated by its different business units. The level of innovation has increased because managers are more willing to speak out and champion their ideas when they know they are dealing directly with the CEO and a top management team searching for innovative ways to improve performance–rather than a layer of strategic planning bureaucrats concerned only with the bottom line.[38]

Managers must always be sensitive about the way they use bureaucratic control. It is most useful when organizational activities are routine and well understood and when employees are making programmed decisions–for example, in mass-production settings such as Ford or in routine service settings such as stores like Target or Midas Muffler. Bureaucratic control is much less useful in situations where nonprogrammed decisions have to be made and managers have to react quickly to changes in the task environment. There are also ethical issues involved in the way managers create and enforce bureaucratic rules and SOPs, as the following "Ethics in Action" box suggests.

To use output control and behavior control, managers must be able to identify the outcomes they want to achieve and the behaviors they want employees to perform

Ethics in Action

How Does Apple Enforce Its Rules for Product Secrecy against Its Rules for Employee Working Conditions?

Apple has rules that govern all its value chain activities, but consider how it enforces the rules about protecting the secrets of its innovative new products compared to how it enforces the rules about protecting the rights of its employees overseas who make those products. Today all Apple products are assembled by huge specialist outsourcing companies abroad, such as Foxconn International, which operates several huge factories in mainland China, some of which employ over 300,000 employees. Foxconn is a subsidiary of Taiwan's giant outsourcer, Hon Hai Precision Industry.

Your iPhone's cool new features may entail more than you think; Apple's emphasis on secrecy and isolation within its outsourced factories appears to also open the door to unsavory labor practices.

Apple has long been known for its concern with protecting the details of its new products until their launch. Its concern for secrecy led it to sue a college student who published a Web site that contained details of its future products; it has also brought legal action against many bloggers who reveal details about its new products. Even in its own U.S. product development units, Apple is known for its strict rules preventing engineers from discussing their own projects with other engineers not involved in those projects to stop the flow of information across its employees. Apple has also developed stern rules governing how its outsourcers behave to protect the secrecy of its products.

To keep its business, outsourcers like Foxconn have to go to extreme lengths to follow Apple's rules protecting the details of its new products and follow stringent security guidelines in their manufacturing plants. For example, Apple dictates that the final product should not be assembled until as late as possible to meet its launch date; so while workers learn how to assemble each component, they have no idea what collection of final components will go into the final product. Also, outsourcers control their factories to make it easier to enforce such rules. For example, Foxconn's massive plant in Longhua, China, employs over 350,000 workers who are discouraged from leaving the plant because it offers them a full array of inexpensive services such as canteens, dormitories, and recreational facilities. If they leave the plant they are searched, and metal detectors are used to ensure they do not take components with them. Workers are scanned when they return as well, as are the truck drivers who bring components to the plant and anyone else who wishes to enter. Apple's contracts always include a confidentiality clause with stiff penalties in the event of a security breach, and Apple performs surprise factory inspections to ensure that outsourcers follow its rules.

To protect the security of its products Apple insists on elaborate operating rules to build walls around the assembly plants of its contractors. But these same walls make it much more difficult to enforce the extensive and well-publicized rules Apple has developed regarding the fair and equitable treatment of employees who work in these gigantic "sweatshops." For example, in 2006, after reporters claimed Hon Hai, Foxconn's owner, was not following Apple's rules regarding employee treatment, Apple audited Hon Hai's facilities. It found many violations whose nature was never publicly disclosed. The company has been repeatedly criticized for allowing its products to be made at plants with poor employment practices–despite the fact that it claims to enforce many rules governing how they should be treated. In 2010 Apple announced that new audits had revealed that child labor had been used in Chinese factories that made its iPods and other electronic devices: "In each of the three facilities, we required a review of all employment records for the year as well as a complete analysis of the hiring process to clarify how under-age people had been able to gain employment." Also, Apple admitted that sweatshop conditions existed inside the factories making its products, and at least 55 of the 102 factories had ignored Apple's rule that employees should not work more than 60 hours per week. Apple said one of its factories had repeatedly falsified its records to conceal child labor practices and long employee hours; it terminated all contracts with that factory: "When we investigated, we uncovered records and conducted worker interviews that revealed excessive working hours and seven days of continuous work."

The bottom line is that Apple likes to develop rules to govern how its various functions operate; but which rules does it spend the most time and effort to enforce? The rules protecting the secrecy of its products or the rules that protect the basic rights of the workers who labor in factories to make those products?

to achieve those outcomes. For many of the most important and significant organizational activities, however, output control and behavior control are inappropriate for several reasons:

- A manager cannot evaluate the performance of workers such as doctors, research scientists, or engineers by observing their daily behavior.
- Rules and SOPs are of little use in telling a doctor how to respond to an emergency situation or a scientist how to discover something new.
- Output controls such as the amount of time a surgeon takes for each operation or the costs of making a discovery are crude measures of the quality of performance.

How can managers attempt to control and regulate the behavior of their subordinates when personal supervision is of little use, when rules cannot be developed to tell employees what to do, and when outputs and goals cannot be measured at all or can be measured usefully only over long periods?

Clan Control

clan control The control exerted on individuals and groups in an organization by shared values, norms, standards of behavior, and expectations.

One source of control increasingly being used by organizations is **clan control,** which takes advantage of the power of internalized values and norms to guide and constrain employee attitudes and behavior in ways that increase organizational performance.[39] The first function of a control system is to shape the behavior of organizational members to ensure that they are working toward organizational goals and to take corrective action if those goals are not being met. The second function of control, however, is to keep organizational members focused on thinking about what is best for their organization in the future and to keep them looking for new opportunities to use organizational resources to create value. Clan control serves this dual function of keeping organizational members goal-directed while open to new opportunities because it takes advantage of the power of organizational culture, discussed in the previous chapter.

Organizational culture functions as a kind of control system because managers can deliberately try to influence the kind of values and norms that develop in an organization–values and norms that specify appropriate and inappropriate behaviors and so determine the way its members behave.[40] We discussed the sources of organizational culture and the way managers can help create different kinds of cultures in

Chapter 10, so there is no need to repeat this discussion here. Instead the following "Manager as a Person" box describes how two CEOs created specific kinds of company culture that survive to this day.

Manager as a Person

James Casey and Sam Walton Create Cultures That Live On

United Parcel Service (UPS) was founded as a bicycle messenger service in 1907 by James E. Casey. Today it controls more than three-fourths of the U.S. ground and air parcel service, delivering over 10 million packages a day in its fleet of 150,000 trucks.[41] It is also the most profitable company in its industry and employs over 250,000 people. Walmart, the largest retailer in the world, was founded by Sam Walton; today it employs over a million people and is the most profitable company in its industry. What do these companies have in common? They were both founded by managers who wanted their employees to take a hands-on approach to their jobs and be completely committed to their mission–total customer satisfaction. And to achieve this both these founders created strong values and norms about how employees should behave and in the process created performance-enhancing organizational cultures.

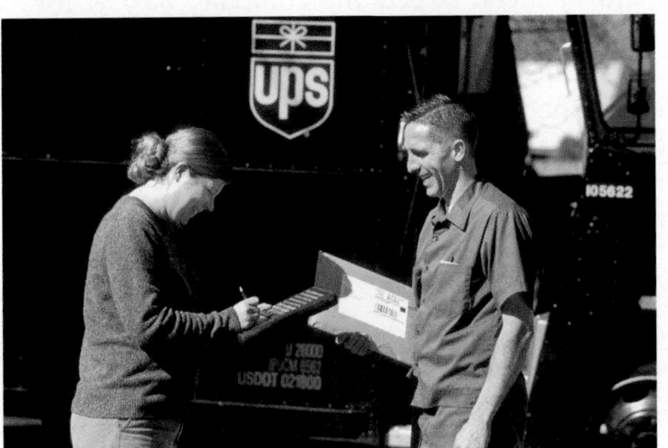

UPS drivers must follow strict guidelines regarding appearance, job performance, and customer interactions.

While its other human resource issues may remain, greeters, check-out attendants, and floor associates alike all practice the Walmart brand of hospitality.

At UPS, from the beginning Casey made efficiency and economy the company's driving values and loyalty, humility, discipline, dependability, and intense effort the key norms its employees should adopt. UPS has always gone to extraordinary lengths to develop and maintain these values and norms in its workforce. First, its control systems from the top of the company down to its trucking operations are the subject of intense scrutiny by the company's 3,000 industrial engineers, who continually search for ways to measure outputs and behaviors to improve efficiency. They time every part of an employee's job. Truck drivers, for example, are told in extraordinary detail how to perform their tasks: They must step from their truck with their right foot first, fold their money face-up, carry packages under their left arm, walk at a pace of 3 feet per second, and slip the key ring holding their truck keys over their third finger.[42] Employees are not allowed to have beards, must be carefully groomed, and are instructed in how to deal with customers. Drivers who perform below average receive visits from training supervisors who accompany them on their delivery routes and teach how to raise their performance level. Not surprisingly, because of this intensive training and close behavior control, UPS employees internalize the company's strong norms about the appropriate ways to behave to help the organization achieve its values of economy and efficiency. In fact, today UPS offers a consulting service to other companies in global supply chain management to teach them how to recreate its values and norms of efficiency and economy that the company has pursued for the last hundred years because these were the values of its founder.

In a similar way, to involve employees at all levels, who are called "associates," and encourage them to develop work behaviors focused on providing quality customer service, Walton established strong cultural values and norms for Walmart. One of the norms associates are expected to follow is the "10-foot attitude." This norm encourages associates, in Walton's words, to "promise that whenever you come within 10 feet of a customer, you will look him in the eye, greet him, and ask him if you can help him." The "sundown rule" states that employees should strive to answer customer requests by sundown of the day they are made. The Walmart cheer ("Give me a W, give me an A," and so on) is used in all its stores.[43]

The strong customer-oriented values that Walton created are exemplified in the stories Walmart members tell one another about associates' concern for customers. They include stories like the one about Sheila, who risked her own safety when she jumped in front of a car to prevent a little boy from being struck; about Phyllis, who administered CPR to a customer who had suffered a heart attack in her store; and about Annette, who gave up the Power Ranger she had on layaway for her own son to fulfill the birthday wish of a customer's son.[44] The strong Walmart culture helps control and motivate employees to achieve the stringent output and financial targets the company has set for itself.[45]

Although both founders are long gone, their companies still seem governed by the values and norms they established. Their new managers take seriously their charge to provide efficient service to customers, and in any delivery by a UPS employee or visit to a Walmart store, it is possible to observe how employees still buy into these values and are rewarded for doing so.

Organizational Change

As we have discussed, many problems can arise if an organization's control systems are not designed correctly. One of these problems is that an organization cannot change or adapt in response to a changing environment unless it has effective control over its activities. Companies can lose this control over time, as happened to Toyota, discussed in the opening case; or they can change in ways that make them more effective, as happened to UPS and Walmart. **Organizational change** is the movement of an organization away from its present state toward some preferred future state to increase its efficiency and effectiveness.

organizational change The movement of an organization away from its present state and toward some preferred future state to increase its efficiency and effectiveness.

Interestingly enough, there is a fundamental tension or need to balance two opposing forces in the control process that influences how organizations change. As just noted, organizations and their managers need to be able to control their activities and make their operations routine and predictable. At the same time, however, organizations have to be responsive to the need to change, and managers and employees have to "think on their feet" and realize when they need to depart from routines to be responsive to unpredictable events. In other words, even though adopting the right set of output and behavior controls is essential for improving efficiency, because the environment is dynamic and uncertain employees also need to feel that they have the autonomy to depart from routines as necessary to increase effectiveness. (See Figure 11.5.)

LO11-5 Discuss the relationship between organizational control and change, and explain why managing change is a vital management task.

For this reason many researchers believe that the highest-performing organizations are those that are constantly changing–and thus become experienced at doing so–in their search to become more efficient and effective. Companies like UPS, Toyota, and Walmart are constantly changing the mix of their activities to move forward even as they seek to make their existing operations more efficient. For example, UPS entered the air express parcel market, bought a chain of mailbox stores, and began offering a consulting service. At the same time it has been increasing the efficiency of its ground and global air transport network.

Figure 11.5
Organizational Control and Change

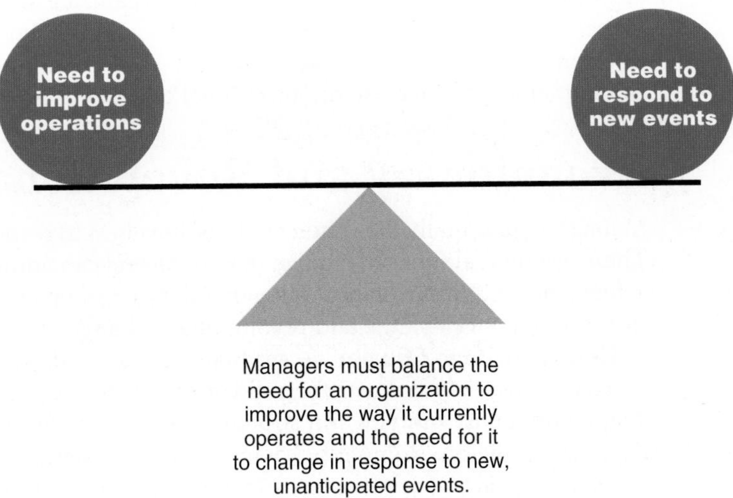

Lewin's Force-Field Theory of Change

Researcher Kurt Lewin developed a theory about organizational change. According to his *force-field theory,* a wide variety of forces arise from the way an organization operates–from its structure, culture, and control systems–that make organizations resistant to change. At the same time a wide variety of forces arise from changing task and general environments that push organizations toward change. These two sets of forces are always in opposition in an organization.[46] When the forces are evenly balanced, the organization is in a state of inertia and does not change. To get an organization to change, managers must find a way to *increase* the forces for change, *reduce* resistance to change, or do *both* simultaneously. Any of these strategies will overcome inertia and cause an organization to change.

Figure 11.6 illustrates Lewin's theory. An organization at performance level P1 is in balance: Forces for change and resistance to change are equal. Management, however, decides that the organization should strive to achieve performance level P2.

Figure 11.6
Lewin's Force-Field Model of Change

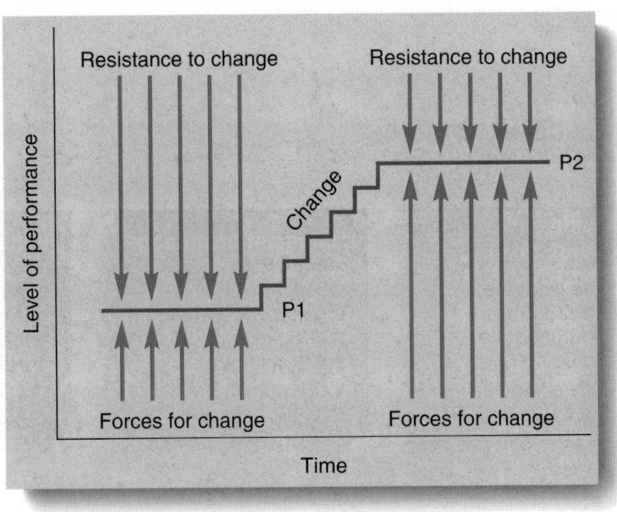

To get to level P2, managers must *increase* the forces for change (the increase is represented by the lengthening of the up arrows), *reduce* resistance to change (the reduction is represented by the shortening of the down arrows), or both. If managers pursue any of the three strategies successfully, the organization will change and reach performance level P2. Before we look in more detail at the techniques managers can use to overcome resistance and facilitate change, we need to look at the types of change they can implement to increase organizational effectiveness.

Evolutionary and Revolutionary Change

Managers continually face choices about how best to respond to the forces for change. There are several types of change that managers can adopt to help their organizations achieve desired future states.[47] In general, types of change fall into two broad categories: evolutionary change and revolutionary change.[48]

evolutionary change Change that is gradual, incremental, and narrowly focused.

Evolutionary change is gradual, incremental, and narrowly focused. Evolutionary change is not drastic or sudden but, rather, is a constant attempt to improve, adapt, and adjust strategy and structure incrementally to accommodate changes taking place in the environment.[49] Sociotechnical systems theory and total quality management, or kaizen, are two instruments of evolutionary change. Such improvements might entail using technology in a better way or reorganizing the work process.

Some organizations, however, need to make major changes quickly. Faced with drastic, unexpected changes in the environment (for example, a new technological breakthrough) or with an impending disaster resulting from mismanagement, an organization might need to act quickly and decisively. In this case, revolutionary change is called for.

revolutionary change Change that is rapid, dramatic, and broadly focused.

Revolutionary change is rapid, dramatic, and broadly focused. Revolutionary change involves a bold attempt to quickly find new ways to be effective. It is likely to result in a radical shift in ways of doing things, new goals, and a new structure for the organization. The process has repercussions at all levels in the organization–corporate, divisional, functional, group, and individual. Reengineering, restructuring, and innovation are three important instruments of revolutionary change.

Managing Change

The need to constantly search for ways to improve efficiency and effectiveness makes it vital that managers develop the skills necessary to manage change effectively. Several experts have proposed a model of change that managers can follow to implement change successfully–that is, to move an organization away from its present state and toward some desired future state to increase its efficiency and effectiveness.[50] Figure 11.7 outlines the steps in this process. In the rest of this section we examine each one.

Figure 11.7
Four Steps in the Organizational Change Process

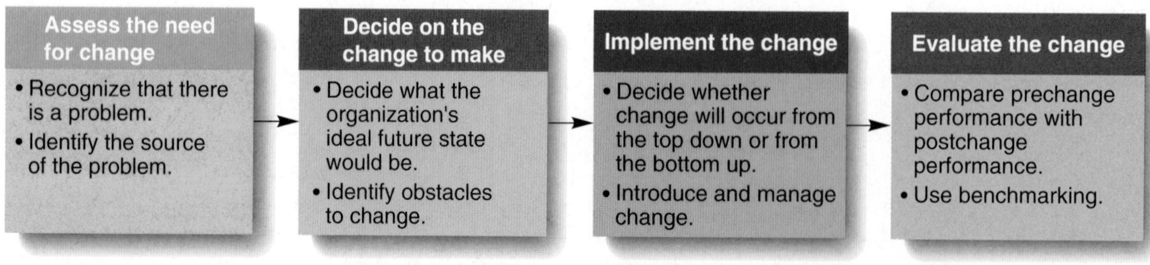

Assess the need for change
• Recognize that there is a problem.
• Identify the source of the problem.
Decide on the change to make
• Decide what the organization's ideal future state would be.
• Identify obstacles to change.
Implement the change
• Decide whether change will occur from the top down or from the bottom up.
• Introduce and manage change.
Evaluate the change
• Compare prechange performance with postchange performance.
• Use benchmarking.

ASSESSING THE NEED FOR CHANGE Organizational change can affect practically all aspects of organizational functioning, including organizational structure, culture, strategies, control systems, and groups and teams, as well as the human resource management system and critical organizational processes such as communication, motivation, and leadership. Organizational change can alter how managers carry out the critical tasks of planning, organizing, leading, and controlling and the ways they perform their managerial roles.

Deciding how to change an organization is a complex matter because change disrupts the status quo and poses a threat, prompting employees to resist attempts to alter work relationships and procedures. Organizational learning–the process through which managers try to increase organizational members' abilities to understand and appropriately respond to changing conditions–can be an important impetus for change and can help all members of an organization, including managers, effectively make decisions about needed changes.

Assessing the need for change calls for two important activities: recognizing that there is a problem and identifying its source. Sometimes the need for change is obvious, such as when an organization's performance is suffering. Often, however, managers have trouble determining that something is going wrong because problems develop gradually; organizational performance may slip for a number of years before a problem becomes obvious. Thus during the first step in the change process, managers need to recognize that there is a problem that requires change.

Often the problems that managers detect have produced a gap between desired performance and actual performance. To detect such a gap, managers need to look at performance measures–such as falling market share or profits, rising costs, or employees' failure to meet their established goals or stay within budgets–which indicate whether change is needed. These measures are provided by organizational control systems, discussed earlier in the chapter.

To discover the source of the problem, managers need to look both inside and outside the organization. Outside the organization, they must examine how changing environmental forces may be creating opportunities and threats that are affecting internal work relationships. Perhaps the emergence of low-cost competitors abroad has led to conflict among different departments that are trying to find new ways to gain a competitive advantage. Managers also need to look within the organization to see whether its structure is causing problems between departments. Perhaps a company does not have integrating mechanisms in place to allow different departments to respond to low-cost competition.

DECIDING ON THE CHANGE TO MAKE Once managers have identified the source of the problem, they must decide what they think the organization's ideal future state would be. In other words, they must decide where they would like their organization to be in the future–what kinds of goods and services it should be making, what its business-level strategy should be, how the organizational structure should be changed, and so on. During this step, managers also must plan how to attain the organization's ideal future state.

This step in the change process also includes identifying obstacles or sources of resistance to change. Managers must analyze the factors that may prevent the company from reaching its ideal future state. Obstacles to change are found at the corporate, divisional, departmental, and individual levels of the organization.

Corporate-level changes in an organization's strategy or structure, even seemingly trivial changes, may significantly affect how divisional and departmental managers behave. Suppose that to compete with low-cost foreign competitors, top managers decide to increase the resources spent on state-of-the-art machinery and reduce the resources spent on marketing or R&D. The power of manufacturing managers would increase, and the power of marketing and R&D managers would fall. This decision would alter the balance of power among departments and might increase conflict as departments fight to retain their status in the organization. An organization's present strategy and structure are powerful obstacles to change.

Whether a company's culture is adaptive or inert facilitates or obstructs change. Organizations with entrepreneurial, flexible cultures, such as high-tech companies, are much easier to change than are organizations with more rigid cultures, such as those sometimes found in large, bureaucratic organizations like the military or GM.

The same obstacles to change exist at the divisional and departmental levels. Division managers may differ in their attitudes toward the changes that top managers propose and, if their interests and power seem threatened, will resist those changes. Managers at all levels usually fight to protect their power and control over resources. Given that departments have different goals and time horizons, they may also react differently to the changes other managers propose. When top managers are trying to reduce costs, for example, sales managers may resist attempts to cut back on sales expenditures if they believe that problems stem from manufacturing managers' inefficiencies.

At the individual level, too, people often resist change because it brings uncertainty and stress. For example, individuals may resist the introduction of a new technology because they are uncertain about their abilities to learn it and effectively use it.

These obstacles make organizational change a slow process. Managers must recognize the potential obstacles to change and take them into consideration. Some obstacles can be overcome by improving communication so all organizational members are aware of the need for change and of the nature of the changes being made. Empowering employees and inviting them to participate in planning for change also can help overcome resistance and allay employees' fears. In addition, managers can sometimes overcome resistance by emphasizing group or shared goals such as increased organizational efficiency and effectiveness. The larger and more complex an organization is, the more complex is the change process.

top-down change A fast, revolutionary approach to change in which top managers identify what needs to be changed and then move quickly to implement the changes throughout the organization.

bottom-up change A gradual or evolutionary approach to change in which managers at all levels work together to develop a detailed plan for change.

IMPLEMENTING THE CHANGE Generally managers implement–that is, introduce and manage–change from the top down or from the bottom up.[51] **Top-down change** is implemented quickly: Top managers identify the need for change, decide what to do, and then move quickly to implement the changes throughout the organization. For example, top managers may decide to restructure and downsize the organization and then give divisional and departmental managers specific goals to achieve. With top-down change, the emphasis is on making the changes quickly and dealing with problems as they arise; it is revolutionary in nature.

Bottom-up change is typically more gradual or evolutionary. Top managers consult with middle and first-line managers about the need for change. Then, over time, managers at all levels work to develop a detailed plan for change. A major advantage of bottom-up change is that it can co-opt resistance to change from employees. Because the emphasis in bottom-up change is on participation and on keeping people informed about what is going on, uncertainty and resistance are minimized. Pfizer's new chief of research did not have the luxury of adopting an evolutionary approach; he had to take swift action to turn around the company, as the following "Manager as a Person" box describes.

Manager as a Person

Pfizer's Big Push to Create Blockbuster Drugs

Pfizer is the largest global pharmaceuticals company with sales of almost $50 billion in 2009. In the past Pfizer's researchers have innovated some of the most successful and profitable drugs in the market, such as its leading cholesterol reducer Lipitor, which earns $13 billion a year. In the 2000s, however, it has run into major roadblocks in innovating new blockbuster drugs. Although many of the drugs in its new product development seemed to be winners, when Pfizer's scientists tested them on groups of people they failed to work as planned; this was a major crisis for Pfizer. With no new drugs in its pipeline, and with blockbusters like Lipitor due to lose their patent protection in a few years, Pfizer desperately needed to find ways to make its product development pipeline work. And one manager, Martin Mackay, believed he knew how to do it.

When Pfizer's longtime R&D chief retired, Mackay, his deputy, made it clear to CEO Jeffrey Kindler that he wanted the job. Kindler made it equally clear he thought the company could use some fresh ideas, and he began to bring in outsiders to interview for the job. So Mackay quickly created a detailed plan for changing Pfizer's organizational structure and culture as he believed the company needed. Kindler reviewed the plan and was so impressed he promoted Mackay to the top R&D position in 2008. What was Mackay's plan?

Mackay had watched how Pfizer's organizational structure had become taller and taller over time as a result of huge mergers with pharmaceutical companies Warner Lambert and Pharmacia. After every merger, with more managers and levels in the hierarchy, there was a much greater need for committees to integrate across all their activities. Mackay felt that too many managers and committees had resulted in Pfizer's R&D function developing a bureaucratic culture, in which scientists had to follow more and more rules and procedures to perform and report on their work. His plan was to change this situation.

Mackay slashed the number of management layers between top managers and scientists from 14 to 7. He abolished the scores of product development committees that he felt hampered, not helped, the process of transforming innovative ideas into blockbuster drugs. After streamlining the hierarchy of authority, he focused his efforts on reducing the number of bureaucratic rules scientists had to follow, many of which he thought unnecessary. He and his team examined all the types of reports in which scientists were supposed to report the results of their work for evaluation. He then eliminated every kind of report that he considered superfluous and that merely slowed down the innovation process. For example, scientists had been in the habit of submitting quarterly and monthly reports to executives explaining each drug's progress; Mackay told them to pick which one they wanted to keep, and the other would be eliminated.

Mackay's goal was to move the company to more of an organic structure, which (as you recall from Chapter 2) is flat and decentralized, and in which teams of scientists can develop the norms and values that encourage a culture of innovation and entrepreneurship. Certainly Pfizer's scientists reported that they felt "liberated" by the new structure, and in 2008 drugs were moving faster along the pipeline. However, new drugs can take seven to eight years from idea stage to market, so only time will tell. Meanwhile Mackay looked outside the company and formed alliances with small drug start-up companies to bring in new outside talent and open up the R&D function to new ideas and approaches. Often companies like Pfizer end up taking over these start-ups and integrating them into their structure, so this is one more avenue he is using to help create a new culture of innovation at the company.

EVALUATING THE CHANGE The last step in the change process is to evaluate how successful the change effort has been in improving organizational performance.[52] Using measures such as changes in market share, in profits, or in Pfizer's case the ability of its scientists to innovate new drugs, managers compare how well an organization is performing after the change with how well it was performing before. Managers also can use **benchmarking,** comparing their performance on specific dimensions with the performance of high-performing organizations to decide how successful a change effort has been. For example, when Xerox was performing poorly in the 1980s, it benchmarked the efficiency of its distribution operations against that of L.L. Bean,

benchmarking The process of comparing one company's performance on specific dimensions with the performance of other, high-performing organizations.

the efficiency of its central computer operations against that of John Deere, and the efficiency of its marketing abilities against that of Procter & Gamble. Those three companies are renowned for their skills in these different areas, and by studying how they performed Xerox was able to dramatically increase its own performance. Benchmarking is a key tool in total quality management, an important change program discussed in Chapter 9.

In summary, organizational control and change are closely linked because organizations operate in environments that are constantly changing; so managers must be alert to the need to change their strategies and structures. Managers of high-performing organizations are attuned to the need to continually modify the way they operate, and they adopt techniques like empowered work groups and teams, benchmarking, and global outsourcing to remain competitive in a global world.

Summary and Review

LO11-1, 11-2 **WHAT IS ORGANIZATIONAL CONTROL?** Controlling is the process whereby managers monitor and regulate how efficiently and effectively an organization and its members are performing the activities necessary to achieve organizational goals. Controlling is a four-step process: (1) establishing performance standards, (2) measuring actual performance, (3) comparing actual performance against performance standards, and (4) evaluating the results and initiating corrective action if needed.

LO11-3 **OUTPUT CONTROL** To monitor output or performance, managers choose goals or performance standards that they think will best measure efficiency, quality, innovation, and responsiveness to customers at the corporate, divisional, departmental or functional, and individual levels. The main mechanisms that managers use to monitor output are financial measures of performance, organizational goals, and operating budgets.

LO11-4 **BEHAVIOR CONTROL** In an attempt to shape behavior and induce employees to work toward achieving organizational goals, managers use direct supervision, management by objectives, and bureaucratic control by means of rules and standard operating procedures.

CLAN CONTROL Clan control is the control exerted on individuals and groups by shared values, norms, and prescribed standards of behavior. An organization's culture is deliberately fashioned to emphasize the values and norms top managers believe will lead to high performance.

LO11-5 **ORGANIZATIONAL CHANGE** There is a need to balance two opposing forces in the control process that influences the way organizations change. On one hand, managers need to be able to control organizational activities and make their operations routine and predictable. On the other hand, organizations have to be responsive to the need to change, and managers must understand when they need to depart from routines to be responsive to unpredictable events. The four steps in managing change are (1) assessing the need for change, (2) deciding on the changes to make, (3) implementing change, and (4) evaluating the results of change.

Management in Action

Topics for Discussion and Action

Discussion

1. What is the relationship between organizing and controlling? [LO11-1]
2. How do output control and behavior control differ? [LO11-2, 11-3]
3. Why is it important for managers to involve subordinates in the control process? [LO11-3, 11-4]
4. What kind of controls would you expect to find most used in (a) a hospital, (b) the Navy, and (c) a city police force? Why? [LO11-2, 11-3, 11-4]
5. What are the main obstacles to organizational change? What techniques can managers use to overcome these obstacles? [LO11-1, 11-5]

Action

6. Ask a manager to list the main performance measures that he or she uses to evaluate how well the organization is achieving its goals. [LO11-1, 11-3, 11-4]
7. Ask the same or a different manager to list the main forms of output control and behavior control that he or she uses to monitor and evaluate employee behavior. [LO11-3, 11-4]

Building Management Skills

Understanding Controlling [LO11-1, 11-3, 11-4]

For this exercise you will analyze the control systems used by a real organization such as a department store, restaurant, hospital, police department, or small business. It can be the organization that you investigated in Chapter 10 or a different one. Your objective is to uncover all the different ways in which managers monitor and evaluate the performance of the organization and employees.

1. At what levels does control take place in this organization?
2. Which output performance standards (such as financial measures and organizational goals) do managers use most often to evaluate performance at each level?
3. Does the organization have a management by objectives system in place? If it does, describe it. If it does not, speculate about why not.
4. How important is behavior control in this organization? For example, how much of managers' time is spent directly supervising employees? How formalized is the organization? Do employees receive a book of rules to teach them how to perform their jobs?
5. What kind of culture does the organization have? What are the values and norms? What effect does the organizational culture have on the way employees behave or treat customers?
6. Based on this analysis, do you think there is a fit between the organization's control systems and its culture? What is the nature of this fit? How could it be improved?

Managing Ethically [LO11-1, 11-5]

Some managers and organizations go to great lengths to monitor their employees' behavior, and they keep extensive records about employees' behavior and performance. Some organizations also seem to possess norms and values that cause their employees to behave in certain ways.

Questions

1. Either by yourself or in a group, think about the ethical implications of organizations' monitoring and collecting information about their employees. What kinds of information is it ethical or unethical to

collect? Why? Should managers and organizations tell subordinates they are collecting such information?

2. Similarly, some organizations' cultures seem to develop norms and values that cause their members to behave in unethical ways. When and why does a strong norm that encourages high performance become one that can cause people to act unethically? How can organizations keep their values and norms from becoming "too strong"?

Small Group Breakout Exercise

How Best to Control the Sales Force? [LO11-1, 11-3, 11-5]

Form groups of three or four people, and appoint one member as the spokesperson who will communicate your findings to the class when called on by the instructor. Then discuss the following scenario:

You are the regional sales managers of an organization that supplies high-quality windows and doors to building supply centers nationwide. Over the last three years, the rate of sales growth has slackened. There is increasing evidence that, to make their jobs easier, salespeople are primarily servicing large customer accounts and ignoring small accounts. In addition, the salespeople are not dealing promptly with customer questions and complaints, and this inattention has resulted in poor after-sales service. You have talked about these problems, and you are meeting to design a control system to increase both the amount of sales and the quality of customer service.

1. Design a control system that you think will best motivate salespeople to achieve these goals.
2. What relative importance do you put on (a) output control, (b) behavior control, and (c) organizational culture in this design?

Exploring the World Wide Web [LO11-1, 11-5]

Go to the Web site of Google. Look at pages such as "Jobs at Google," "Life at Google," "Company Overview," and "Our Culture."

1. How would you expect Google's values and norms to affect its employees' behavior?
2. How does Google design its organizational structure and workspace to shape its culture?

Be the Manager

You have been asked by your company's CEO to find a way to improve the performance of its teams of Web design and Web hosting specialists and programmers. Each team works on a different aspect of Web site production; and while each is responsible for the quality of its own performance, its performance also depends on how well the other teams perform. Your task is to create a control system that will help to increase the performance of each team separately and facilitate cooperation among the teams. This is necessary because the various projects are interlinked and affect one another just as the different parts of a car must fit together. Because competition in the Web site production market is intense, it is imperative that each Web site is up and running as quickly as possible and incorporates all the latest advances in Web site software technology.

Questions

1. What kind of output controls will best facilitate positive interactions both within the teams and among the teams?
2. What kind of behavior controls will best facilitate positive interactions both within the teams and among the teams?
3. How would you help managers develop a culture to promote high team performance?

Case in the News [LO11-1, 11-3, 11-5]

Hospitals: Radical Cost Surgery

Walk into most hospitals, and you'll see patients scattered about the halls on gurneys or wheelchairs. They're waiting to be moved from intensive care to a standard ward, or to an X-ray room, or to physical therapy. Each journey adds to the patient's discomfort and increases the risk of infections and other complications. Tally up a single patient's migrations over 24 hours, and they may consume as much as half a day of staff time.

Walk into Providence Regional Medical Center in Everett, Washington, and you will see a hospital trying something different: It brings the equipment to the patient. In 2003 Providence opened one of the few "single stay" wards in the nation. After heart surgery, cardiac patients remain in one room throughout their recovery; only the gear and staff are in motion. As the patient's condition stabilizes, the beeping machines of intensive care are removed and physical therapy equipment is added. Testing gear is wheeled to the patient, not the other way around. Patient satisfaction with the "single stay" ward has soared, and the average length of a hospital stay has dropped by a day or more.

This is just one of many changes—some radical, many quite small—that have enabled Providence Regional to join a special subset of American hospitals: those that do not lose money on Medicare patients.

Almost 60% of U.S. hospitals report losing 20 cents on the dollar for every elderly patient who comes through their doors. They make up the difference by charging the under-65s far higher fees. But Providence breaks even on the elderly, even though Medicare pays about $1,000 less per enrollee in the hospital's region than the national average. The hospital accomplishes this feat while winning a doctor's satchel full of national awards for top-notch care, placing it among the elite 5% of all U.S. hospitals.

High quality at a low price. Every other industry strives for that combination, but a hospital that does both is all too rare. Providence and its cost-efficient brethren demonstrate that quality care can be delivered at an affordable price, provided hospitals can be persuaded to rethink decades-old practices.

The crazy world of hospital economics does not offer a lot of incentives to change. Both Medicare and private insurers reimburse on a piecework basis—known as fee-for-service—that encourages hospitals to treat more, prescribe more, and test more. Economists refer to this arrangement as a "value-blind" payment system because no premium is paid for quality.

Consequently, hospitals have no financial motivation to invest in productivity-enhancing computer technology, management experts, or efficiency research—and by and large, they don't. Columbia University economist Frank Lichtenberg calculates that productivity growth for the hospital industry has increased at less than half the rate of the general economy. The nonprofit Institute for Health Care Improvement last year identified 70 regions around the country, out of a total of 306, where high-quality care is delivered at a reasonable cost. One of those regions is Everett, home of Providence Regional. Providence is the only hospital in this coastal city of 98,000 people located 20 miles north of Seattle. It is the third largest hospital in Washington, with two campuses serving 25,000 overnight patients a year, and operates the second busiest emergency room in the state. It's building a $500 million, 368-bed tower, due to open next year, that will double its capacity.

What sets Providence apart from its peers is not size or location but its ability to operate within a Medicare-designated budget. The majority of U.S. hospitals have the market power to demand higher reimbursements from private insurers to make up for what they see as insufficient payments by Medicare. Because of a wave of consolidation in the 1990s, when more than 900 hospitals merged (including the two medical centers that created Providence Regional), some 90% of the U.S. population that lives in metropolitan areas is now served by just one or two hospital networks. "Hospitals simply don't need to be efficient," says Dr. Robert A. Berenson, a leading health care economist and member of MedPAC, an independent agency that advises Congress on Medicare. "They are able to get payment differentials from the private sector of 30% to 35% over what Medicare pays." In some markets, it's 50% to 100%, he says.

Providence doesn't have enough private payers to engage in such fee shifting. Forty percent of its annual revenues come from Medicare, and an additional 13% from Medicaid. Commercial insurers account for only 39%. Dependence on Medicare has forced it to focus on taking costs out of its operation rather than maximizing revenues.

To get those savings, the hospital tries to standardize best practices whenever possible. "There is a tremendous variation in medical delivery that is not quality driven," complains Dr. James Brevig, director of cardiac surgery at Providence. Doctors and nurses are often reluctant to analyze and change their methods because it would mean revamping long-accepted treatments or routines. As a result, says Brevig, "there are no standards in hospitals. Why is that? It's crazy. No other industry is like this."

Providence took a different path after picketing by workers nine years ago reflected a shattered morale. A new administration decided to attack the internal staff divisions and foster collaboration among doctors, nurses, and administrators. Everyone is encouraged to contribute ideas on driving down costs and improving patient outcomes. "I'm eligible for retirement, and under the prior leadership I would have left," says pediatric nurse Kathy Elder, a 34-year veteran of Providence. "They were very hierarchical, very closed. There was a lack of trust all around."

The current CEO, 48-year-old David T. Brooks, a fast-talking Detroit native, took over two years ago. He says the administration is open to suggestions from any and all staffers. "We have scorecards for everything around here, which measure both quality and efficiency. If all we had were great clinical outcomes but costs kept rising, that just wouldn't be good enough."

The staff embraced the challenge to innovate. The nursing team came up with the idea of checking on patients every two hours without waiting for a call button, to see if they need help walking to the bathroom or moving about their rooms. Ten percent of fatal falls by the elderly in the U.S. occur in hospitals. This one change at Providence reduced falls by 25%, according to chief nursing officer Kim Williams. "We believe we'll see more improvement over the next six months.

One of the bigger changes at Providence, implemented in 2003, is to place the day-to-day care of almost all its inpatients in the hands of hospitalists, a new type of doctor that has emerged in the last decade. Unlike primary care physicians, who usually visit their patients only early in the morning or late at night, hospitalists are available around the clock, checking that medications are administered properly, chart orders followed, and infection risks minimized. About 37% of Medicare inpatients are attended by hospitalists nationwide, and several studies have associated their use with better outcomes. Providence has also published data showing that infections, lengths of stay, and surgical complications have dropped since starting its own program. But hospitalists are still controversial in many communities because primary care physicians are wary of giving up control of their patients, along with their share of inpatient fees. Dr. Joanne C. Roberts, one of the first hospitalists at Providence, has not seen this conflict in Everett, possibly because most of the hospitalists and primary care doctors are associates at one large medical practice, Everett Clinic.

It also helps that Providence has no competition nearby. "We don't have to engage in a medical arms race," says Dr. Lawrence M. Schecter, chief medical officer. Instead a 20-member Value Analysis Committee consisting of doctors, nurses, and administrators scrutinizes every proposal for a major equipment purchase to determine if it is warranted in terms of patient need, rather than to keep up with the competition or to increase billings. Providence's savings efforts don't stop at the hospital doors. It offers financial training courses to the 800 independent doctors affiliated with the hospital in an effort to get them thinking about cost efficiencies. That's no easy task, however, because savings don't necessarily flow into their pockets. Cutting back on unnecessary services may be better for the bill payer, but it lowers the income of doctors and hospitals.

Brooks says Providence's 2009 operating margins were 6% despite its heavy dependence on Medicare. Reaching that level is a challenge. As the only major hospital in a fast-growing county, Providence must provide every kind of medical service. Thus its lucrative cardiology unit and high-tech cancer centers are offset by an obstetrics ward that delivers 4,000 babies a year. The hospital loses money on almost every one of those births. Providence also has to absorb some $16 million in unpaid bills each year, more than any other Washington hospital except a public facility in Seattle. Charity care fulfills a moral mission at Providence that sometimes trumps economics. The hospital is owned by the Sisters of Providence, a Canadian order of Catholic nuns founded in 1843 to minister to the poor. "Everything we do has to uphold our core values," says Brooks. "Our mission doesn't end with our business goals."

When Providence can't find standard medical practices, it innovates. That was the case with blood transfusions. Cardiac and orthopedic surgeons realized a few years ago that there were no widely accepted data on the optimal amount of blood to give patients during surgery, despite the $240 cost per bag. Dr. Brevig started looking around and found several studies that correlated greater transfusion volumes with longer patient stays and higher infection rates. He was particularly surprised that transfusion rates varied greatly from hospital to hospital, regardless of the patient's status. "The variations were related to the culture of the hospital, not the decisions of the doctor," he says. Brevig set out to create a low-transfusion culture at Providence. He got surgeons to slow down because speedy operations cause more blood loss. Settings were changed on heart bypass machines to save blood, and the hospital hired a blood conservation coordinator. In a study of 2,531 operations at Providence, Brevig reported that the incidence of transfusions was reduced to just 18% in 2007 down from 43% in 2003 while the average patient stay was reduced by half a day. The changes saved Providence $4.5 million.

However, there is a fear that cutbacks in services will lead to accusations of rationing. Dr. Donald Berwick, president of the Institute for Health Care Improvement and a longtime campaigner for better, safer hospitals, says this attitude must be revamped. In a recent speech he called on hospitals to reduce costs by 10% over the next three years without harming care. In almost every case, he noted, fewer interventions and adherence to standards lead to better medical outcomes. "Doctors and patients alike need to realize that the best health care is the very least health care that we need," he said. "The best hospital bed is empty, not full."

Questions

1. What kind of control systems are being used to measure the performance of hospitals and their different kinds of employees such as doctors and nurses?
2. What are the pros and cons of these control systems?
3. How could hospital control systems be improved to increase efficiency and effectiveness?

Source: C. Arnst, "Hospitals: Radical Cost Surgery," *BusinessWeek,* January 7, 2010. Reprinted from January 7, 2010 issue of *Bloomberg Businessweek* by special permission,

CHAPTER 12

Human Resource Management

Learning Objectives

After studying this chapter, you should be able to:

LO12-1 Explain why strategic human resource management can help an organization gain a competitive advantage.

LO12-2 Describe the steps managers take to recruit and select organizational members.

LO12-3 Discuss the training and development options that ensure organizational members can effectively perform their jobs.

LO12-4 Explain why performance appraisal and feedback is such a crucial activity, and list the choices managers must make in designing effective performance appraisal and feedback procedures.

LO12-5 Explain the issues managers face in determining levels of pay and benefits.

LO12-6 Understand the role that labor relations play in the effective management of human resources.

A MANAGER'S CHALLENGE

Happy Employees Provide Exceptional Service at Zappos

How can managers ensure that employees will provide excellent service and be happy doing so? Nothing is conventional about the online retailer Zappos. Think accountants running Pinewood Derby car races during the workday, a conference room that a team decorated to simulate a log cabin, employees ringing cowbells and blowing horns during visitor tours, managers spending 10–20 percent of their time socializing with their subordinates, and the CEO working from a small, messy cubicle.[1] And the list could go on. Yet Zappos, founded in 1999 as a struggling online shoe shop, rode out the dot-com bust to earn $1 billion in sales in 2008 and be ranked 15th on *Fortune* magazine's list of the One Hundred Best Companies to Work For in 2010; in 2009 Zappos was ranked 23rd.[2] In 2009 Amazon.com purchased Zappos for shares worth $1.2 billion.[3] As a wholly owned subsidiary of Amazon, Zappos continues to be led by its long-standing CEO Tony Hsieh; Hsieh was the initial primary investor who kept Zappos afloat as a start-up and became its CEO in 2000.[4]

Key to Zappos's success is a focus on people—having happy employees provide exceptional service to customers.[5] In fact, Hsieh's own experiences helped him realize the importance of employees being happy and having fun at work. Hsieh, who has a computer science degree from Harvard, started his first company, LinkExchange, when he was in his early 20s. This company enabled small Web publishers to trade advertising on each other's sites and also sold advertising. When he was 24, Hsieh sold LinkExchange to Microsoft for $265 million. Despite this phenomenal early success, Hsieh felt uneasy because he no longer much enjoyed going to work, and the people around him seemed more interested in cashing out than building something long-term.[6]

Mission: create fun and a little weirdness, accomplished! If you'd like to work in a T-shirt surrounded by your favorite plants, a plastic skull, and personalized balloons while getting the chance to develop your business savvy, check out Zappos's job openings.

Hseih decided to build something long-lasting and a workplace in which happy employees wanted to come to work each day. Zappos was one of 27 start-ups that Hseih invested in along with his partner and former classmate, Alfred Lin, through their venture capital fund Venture Frogs. Although some of these succeeded (such as Ask.com and OpenTable), many did not live through the dot-com bust. When Zappos was struggling, Hseih stepped in with more funds and became involved in running the company.[7]

Zappos has expanded from selling shoes to selling a wide range of products ranging from clothing and handbags to housewares, watches, and jewelry.[8] What is distinctive about Zappos is not so much the products it sells but rather the exceptional service it provides customers.[9] Customers receive free shipping on products both ways (for purchases and returns), and Zappos has a 365-day return policy. Its Web site prominently displays a toll-free telephone number that customers can call to speak to a member of the Customer Loyalty Team (CLT) 24 hours a day, seven days a week.[10] CLT members have great autonomy to keep customers happy the way they think is best. Their call times are not monitored, and they do not read from scripts. They make decisions on their own, such as providing refunds for defective goods or sending flowers to a customer who had a death in the family, without having to consult a manager. And they strive to make personal connections with their customers. Some calls last for hours, and team members regularly send personal notes to customers.[11] Providing exceptional service that leads to repeat business from happy customers and good word-of-mouth advertising is central to Zappos's approach to business.[12]

Equally central is having a happy workforce of satisfied employees who actually want to come to work each day and have fun on and off the job.[13] Thus Hsieh and other managers at Zappos go to great lengths to ensure that the Zappos core values and unique culture are maintained and strengthened. The core values of Zappos are these: "1. Deliver WOW through Service; 2. Embrace and Drive Change; 3. Create Fun and a Little Weirdness; 4. Be Adventurous, Creative, and Open-Minded; 5. Pursue Growth and Learning; 6. Build Open and Honest Relationships with Communication; 7. Build a Positive Team and Family Spirit; 8. Do More with Less; 9. Be Passionate and Determined; 10. Be Humble."[14]

Because of the importance of having happy employees, Zappos goes to great lengths to effectively manage human resources. Potential new hires are interviewed by human resources, to make sure they will work well in Zappos's culture and support its values, as well as by the department doing the hiring, to determine their suitability for the position they are interviewing for. If human resources and the hiring manager disagree in their assessments of an applicant, Hsieh interviews the applicant himself and makes the final decision.[15]

Newly hired employees receive extensive training. For example, the CLT new hires who answer calls have two weeks of classroom training followed by two weeks of training in answering calls. Once the training is completed, they are given the opportunity to receive $2,000 and pay for the time they spent in training if they want to quit.[16] This way only new hires who want to stay with the company remain.

Experienced employees are encouraged to continue to grow and develop on the job. For example, employees who have worked at Zappos for two or fewer years have over 200 hours of classroom training and development during their work hours and are required to read nine books about business. More experienced employees receive training and development in such areas as financial planning and speaking in public. Zappos has a company library well stocked with multiple copies of business books and books about personal growth and development for employees to borrow and read. As Hseih indicates, "The vision is that three years from now, almost all our hires will be entry-level people. . . . We'll provide them with training and mentorship, so that within five to seven years, they can become senior leaders within the company."[17]

Although pay for entry-level employees is not high, Zappos pays for all their health care; and upon announcing that Zappos would become a subsidiary of Amazon.com, employees were told they would each receive a retention bonus equivalent to 40% of their yearly salary and a Kindle.[18] In any case, Zappos's phenomenal growth in revenues and being ranked 15th among the 100 Best Companies to Work For suggest that human resources are being effectively managed to promote happiness among customers and employees alike.[19]

Overview

LO12-1 Explain why strategic human resource management can help an organization gain a competitive advantage.

Managers are responsible for acquiring, developing, protecting, and utilizing the resources an organization needs to be efficient and effective. One of the most important resources in all organizations is human resources–the people involved in producing and distributing goods and services. Human resources include all members of an organization, ranging from top managers to entry-level employees. Effective managers like Tony Hsieh in "A Manager's Challenge" realize how valuable human resources are and take active steps to make sure their organizations build and fully utilize their human resources to gain a competitive advantage.

This chapter examines how managers can tailor their human resource management system to their organization's strategy and structure. We discuss in particular the major components of human resource management: recruitment and selection, training and development, performance appraisal, pay and benefits, and labor relations. By the end of this chapter you will understand the central role human resource management plays in creating a high-performing organization.

human resource management (HRM) Activities that managers engage in to attract and retain employees and to ensure that they perform at a high level and contribute to the accomplishment of organizational goals.

Strategic Human Resource Management

Organizational architecture (see Chapter 10) is the combination of organizational structure, control systems, culture, and a human resource management system that managers develop to use resources efficiently and effectively. **Human resource management (HRM)** includes all the activities managers engage in to attract and retain employees and to ensure that they perform at a high level and contribute to the accomplishment of organizational goals. These activities make up an organization's human resource management system, which has five major components: recruitment and selection, training and development, performance appraisal and feedback, pay and benefits, and labor relations (see Figure 12.1).

Figure 12.1
Components of a Human Resource Management System

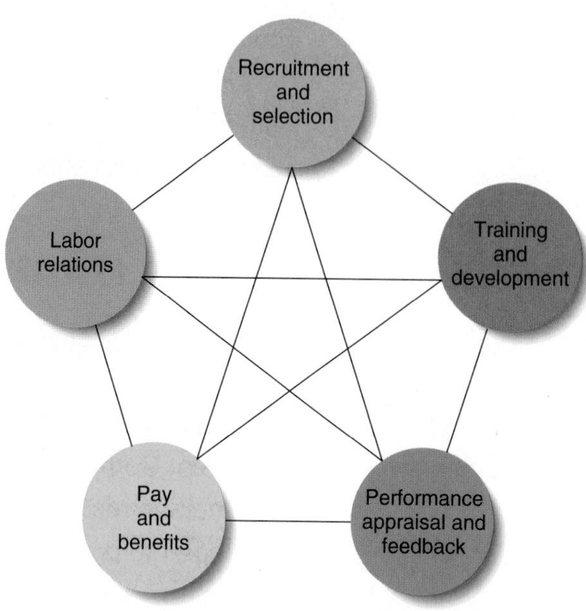

Each component of an HRM system influences the others, and all five must fit together.

strategic human resource management The process by which managers design the components of an HRM system to be consistent with each other, with other elements of organizational architecture, and with the organization's strategy and goals.

Strategic human resource management is the process by which managers design the components of an HRM system to be consistent with each other, with other elements of organizational architecture, and with the organization's strategy and goals.[20] The objective of strategic HRM is the development of an HRM system that enhances an organization's efficiency, quality, innovation, and responsiveness to customers–the four building blocks of competitive advantage. At Zappos in "A Manager's Challenge," HRM practices ensure that all employees provide excellent customer service.

As part of strategic human resource management, some managers have adopted "Six Sigma" quality improvement plans. These plans ensure that an organization's products and services are as free of errors or defects as possible through a variety of human resource–related initiatives. Jack Welch, former CEO of General Electric Company, has indicated that these initiatives have saved his company millions of dollars; and other companies, such as Whirlpool and Motorola, also have implemented Six Sigma initiatives. For such initiatives to be effective, however, top managers have to be committed to Six Sigma, employees must be motivated, and there must be demand for the products or services of the organization in the first place. David Fitzpatrick, head of Deloitte Consulting's Lean Enterprise Practice, estimates that most Six Sigma plans are not effective because the conditions for effective Six Sigma are not in place. For example, if top managers are not committed to the quality initiative, they may not devote the necessary time and resources to make it work and may lose interest in it prematurely.[21]

Overview of the Components of HRM

Managers use *recruitment and selection,* the first component of an HRM system, to attract and hire new employees who have the abilities, skills, and experiences that will help an organization achieve its goals. Microsoft Corporation, for example, has the goal of remaining the premier computer software company in the world. To achieve this goal, managers at Microsoft realize the importance of hiring only the best software designers: Hundreds of highly qualified candidates are interviewed and rigorously tested. This careful attention to selection has contributed to Microsoft's competitive advantage. Microsoft has little trouble recruiting top programmers because candidates know they will be at the forefront of the industry if they work for Microsoft.[22]

After recruiting and selecting employees, managers use the second component, *training and development,* to ensure that organizational members develop the skills and abilities that will enable them to perform their jobs effectively in the present and the future. Training and development compose an ongoing process; changes in technology and the environment, as well as in an organization's goals and strategies, often require that organizational members learn new techniques and ways of working. At Microsoft, newly hired program designers receive on-the-job training by joining small teams that include experienced employees who serve as mentors or advisers. New recruits learn firsthand from team members how to go about developing computer systems that are responsive to customers' programming needs.[23]

The third component, *performance appraisal and feedback,* serves two different purposes in HRM. First, performance appraisal can give managers the information they need to make good human resources decisions–decisions about how to train, motivate, and reward organizational members.[24] Thus the performance appraisal and feedback component is a kind of *control system* that can be used with management by objectives (discussed in Chapter 11). Second, feedback from performance appraisal serves a developmental purpose for members of an organization. When managers regularly evaluate their subordinates' performance, they can provide employees with valuable information about their strengths and weaknesses and the areas in which they need to concentrate.

On the basis of performance appraisals, managers distribute *pay* to employees, which is part of the fourth component of an HRM system. By rewarding high-performing organizational members with pay raises, bonuses, and the like, managers increase the likelihood that an organization's most valued human resources will be motivated to continue their high levels of contribution to the organization. Moreover, if pay is linked to performance, high-performing employees are more likely to stay with the organization, and managers are more likely to fill positions that become open with highly talented individuals. *Benefits* such as health insurance are important outcomes that employees receive by virtue of their membership in an organization.

Last, but not least, *labor relations* encompass the steps that managers take to develop and maintain good working relationships with the labor unions that may represent their employees' interests. For example, an organization's labor relations component can help managers establish safe working conditions and fair labor practices in their offices and plants.

Managers must ensure that all five of these components fit together and complement their company's structure and control systems.[25] For example, if managers decide to decentralize authority and empower employees, they need to invest in training and development to ensure that lower-level employees have the knowledge and expertise they need to make the decisions that top managers would make in a more centralized structure.

Each of the five components of HRM influences the others (see Figure 12.1).[26] The kinds of people that the organization attracts and hires through recruitment and selection, for example, determine (1) the kinds of training and development that are necessary, (2) the way performance is appraised, and (3) the appropriate levels of pay and benefits. Managers at Microsoft ensure that their organization has highly qualified program designers by (1) recruiting and selecting the best candidates, (2) guiding new hires with experienced team members, (3) appraising program designers' performance in terms of their individual contributions and their teams' performance, and (4) basing programmers' pay on individual and team performance.

Effectively managing human resources helps ensure that both customers and employees are satisfied and loyal, as illustrated in the following "Managing Globally" box.

Managing Globally

Managing Human Resources at Semco

Ricardo Semler was 21 years old (and one of the youngest graduates from the Harvard Business School MBA program) when he took his father's place as head of the family business, Semco, based in São Paolo, Brazil, in 1984.[27] His father, Antonio, had founded Semco in 1954 as a machine shop; the company went on to become a manufacturer of marine pumps for the shipbuilding industry, with $4 million a year in revenues when Ricardo Semler took over. Today Semco's revenues are over $200 million a year from a diverse set of businesses ranging from industrial machinery, cooling towers, and facility management to environmental consulting and Web-based HRM outsourcing and inventory management services. Semco prides itself on being a premier provider of goods and services in its markets and has loyal customers.[28]

Richard Semler recognizes that Semco's success hinges on its employees.

Semler is the first to admit that Semco's track record of success is due to its human resources–its employees. In fact, Semler so firmly believes in Semco's employees that he and the other top managers are reluctant to tell employees what to do. Semco has no rules, regulations, or organizational charts; hierarchy is eschewed; and workplace democracy rules the day. Employees have levels of autonomy unheard of in other companies, and flexibility and trust are built into every aspect of human resource management at Semco.[29]

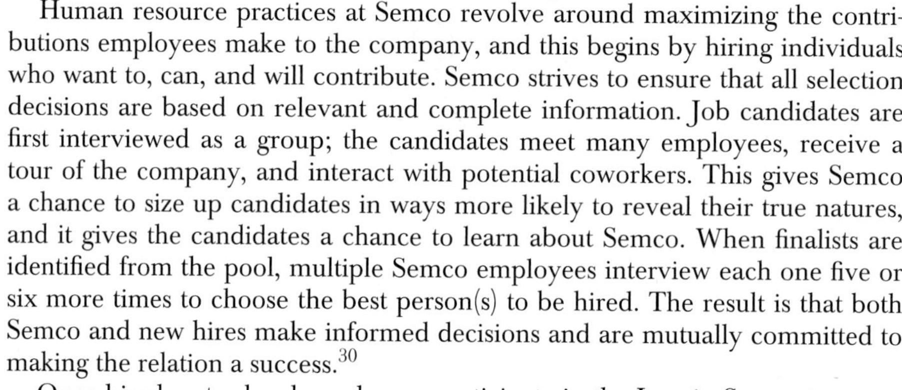

Human resource practices at Semco revolve around maximizing the contributions employees make to the company, and this begins by hiring individuals who want to, can, and will contribute. Semco strives to ensure that all selection decisions are based on relevant and complete information. Job candidates are first interviewed as a group; the candidates meet many employees, receive a tour of the company, and interact with potential coworkers. This gives Semco a chance to size up candidates in ways more likely to reveal their true natures, and it gives the candidates a chance to learn about Semco. When finalists are identified from the pool, multiple Semco employees interview each one five or six more times to choose the best person(s) to be hired. The result is that both Semco and new hires make informed decisions and are mutually committed to making the relation a success.[30]

Once hired, entry-level employees participate in the Lost in Space program, in which they rotate through different positions and units of their own choosing for about a year.[31] In this way, the new hires learn about their options and can decide where their interests lie, and the units they work in learn about the new hires. At the end of the year, the new employees may be offered a job in one of the units in which they worked, or they may seek a position elsewhere in Semco. Seasoned Semco employees are also encouraged to rotate positions and work in different parts of the company to keep them fresh, energized, and motivated and to give them the opportunity to contribute in new ways as their interests change.[32]

Performance is appraised at Semco in terms of results; all employees and managers must demonstrate that they are making valuable contributions and deserve to be "rehired." For example, each manager's performance is anonymously appraised by all the employees who report to him or her, and the appraisals are made publicly available in Semco. Employees also can choose how they are paid from a combination of 11 different compensation options, ranging from fixed salaries, bonuses, and profit sharing to royalties on sales or profits and arrangements based on meeting annual self-set goals. Flexibility in compensation promotes risk taking and innovation, according to Semler, and maximizes returns to employees in terms of their pay and to the company in terms of revenues and profitability.[33] Flexibility, autonomy, the ability to change jobs often, and control of working hours and even compensation are some of the ways by which Semler strives to ensure that employees are loyal and involved in their work because they *want* to be; turnover at Semco is less than 1% annually.[34] And with human resource practices geared toward maximizing contributions and performance, Semco is well poised to continue to provide value to its customers.

The Legal Environment of HRM

In the rest of this chapter we focus in detail on the choices managers must make in strategically managing human resources to attain organizational goals and gain a competitive advantage. Effectively managing human resources is a complex undertaking for managers, and we provide an overview of some major issues they face. First, however, we need to look at how the legal environment affects human resource management.

equal employment opportunity (EEO) The equal right of all citizens to the opportunity to obtain employment regardless of their gender, age, race, country of origin, religion, or disabilities.

The local, state, and national laws and regulations that managers and organizations must abide by add to the complexity of HRM. For example, the U.S. government's commitment to **equal employment opportunity (EEO)** has resulted in the creation and enforcement of a number of laws that managers must abide by. The goal of EEO is to ensure that all citizens have an equal opportunity to obtain employment regardless of their gender, race, country of origin, religion, age, or disabilities. Table 12.1 summarizes some of the major EEO laws affecting HRM. Other laws, such as the Occupational Safety and Health Act of 1970, require that managers ensure that employees are protected from workplace hazards and safety standards are met.

Table 12.1
Major Equal Employment Opportunity Laws Affecting HRM

Year	Law	Description
1963	Equal Pay Act	Requires that men and women be paid equally if they are performing equal work.
1964	Title VII of the Civil Rights Act	Prohibits employment discrimination on the basis of race, religion, sex, color, or national origin; covers a wide range of employment decisions, including hiring, firing, pay, promotion, and working conditions.
1967	Age Discrimination in Employment Act	Prohibits discrimination against workers over the age of 40 and restricts mandatory retirement.
1978	Pregnancy Discrimination Act	Prohibits employment discrimination against women on the basis of pregnancy, childbirth, and related medical decisions.
1990	Americans with Disabilities Act	Prohibits employment discrimination against individuals with disabilities and requires that employers make accommodations for such workers to enable them to perform their jobs.
1991	Civil Rights Act	Prohibits discrimination (as does Title VII) and allows the awarding of punitive and compensatory damages, in addition to back pay, in cases of intentional discrimination.
1993	Family and Medical Leave Act	Requires that employers provide 12 weeks of unpaid leave for medical and family reasons including paternity and illness of a family member.

In Chapter 5 we explained how effectively managing diversity is an ethical and business imperative, and we discussed the many issues surrounding diversity. EEO laws and their enforcement make the effective management of diversity a legal imperative as well. The Equal Employment Opportunity Commission (EEOC) is the division of the Department of Justice that enforces most EEO laws and handles discrimination complaints. In addition, the EEOC issues guidelines for managers to follow to ensure that they are abiding by EEO laws. For example, the Uniform Guidelines on Employee Selection Procedures issued by the EEOC (in conjunction with the Departments of Labor and Justice and the Civil Service Commission) guide managers on how to ensure that the recruitment and selection component of human resource management complies with Title VII of the Civil Rights Act (which prohibits discrimination based on gender, race, color, religion, and national origin).[35]

Contemporary challenges that managers face related to the legal environment include how to eliminate sexual harassment (see Chapter 5 for an in-depth discussion of sexual harassment), how to accommodate employees with disabilities, how to deal with employees who have substance abuse problems, and how to manage HIV-positive employees and employees with AIDS.[36] HIV-positive employees are infected with the virus that causes AIDS but may show no AIDS symptoms and may not develop AIDS in the near future. Often such employees are able to perform their jobs effectively, and managers must take steps to ensure that they are allowed to do so and are not discriminated against in the workplace.[37] Employees with AIDS may or may not be able to perform their jobs effectively, and, once again, managers need to ensure that they are not unfairly discriminated against.[38] Many organizations have instituted AIDS awareness training programs to educate organizational members about HIV and AIDS, dispel myths about how HIV is spread, and ensure that individuals infected with the HIV virus are treated fairly and are able to be productive as long as they can be while not putting others at risk.[39]

Recruitment and Selection

LO12-2 Describe the steps managers take to recruit and select organizational members.

Recruitment includes all the activities managers engage in to develop a pool of qualified candidates for open positions.[40] **Selection** is the process by which managers determine the relative qualifications of job applicants and their potential for performing well in a particular job. Before actually recruiting and selecting employees, managers need to engage in two important activities: human resource planning and job analysis (Figure 12.2).

Human Resource Planning

recruitment Activities that managers engage in to develop a pool of qualified candidates for open positions.

selection The process that managers use to determine the relative qualifications of job applicants and their potential for performing well in a particular job.

human resource planning Activities that managers engage in to forecast their current and future needs for human resources.

Human resource planning includes all the activities managers engage in to forecast their current and future human resource needs. Current human resources are the employees an organization needs today to provide high-quality goods and services to customers. Future human resource needs are the employees the organization will need at some later date to achieve its longer-term goals.

Figure 12.2
The Recruitment and Selection System

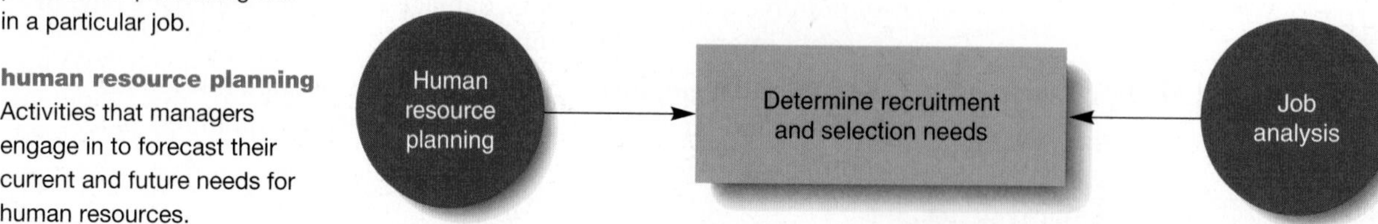

outsource To use outside suppliers and manufacturers to produce goods and services.

Produce goods

As part of human resource planning, managers must make both demand forecasts and supply forecasts. *Demand forecasts* estimate the qualifications and numbers of employees an organization will need given its goals and strategies. *Supply forecasts* estimate the availability and qualifications of current employees now and in the future, as well as the supply of qualified workers in the external labor market.

As a result of their human resource planning, managers sometimes decide to **outsource** to fill some of their human resource needs. Instead of recruiting and selecting employees to produce goods and services, managers contract with people who are not members of their organization to produce goods and services. Managers in publishing companies, for example, frequently contract with freelance editors to copyedit books that they intend to publish. Kelly Services is an organization that provides temporary typing, clerical, and secretarial workers to managers who want to use outsourcing to fill some of their human resource requirements in these areas.

Two reasons why human resource planning sometimes leads managers to outsource are flexibility and cost. First, outsourcing can give managers increased flexibility, especially when accurately forecasting human resource needs is difficult, human resource needs fluctuate over time, or finding skilled workers in a particular area is difficult. Second, outsourcing can sometimes allow managers to use human resources at a lower cost. When work is outsourced, costs can be lower for a number of reasons: The organization does not have to provide benefits to workers; managers can contract for work only when the work is needed; and managers do not have to invest in training. Outsourcing can be used for functional activities such as after-sales service on appliances and equipment, legal work, and the management of information systems.[41]

Outsourcing has disadvantages, however.[42] When work is outsourced, managers may lose some control over the quality of goods and services. Also, individuals performing outsourced work may have less knowledge of organizational practices, procedures, and goals and less commitment to an organization than regular employees. In addition, unions resist outsourcing because it has the potential to eliminate some of their members. To gain some of the flexibility and cost savings of outsourcing and avoid some of its disadvantages, a number of organizations, such as Microsoft and IBM, rely on a pool of temporary employees to, for example, debug programs.

A major trend reflecting the increasing globalization of business is the outsourcing of office work, computer programming, and technical jobs from the United States and countries in western Europe, with high labor costs, to countries like India and China, with low labor costs.[43] For example, computer programmers in India and China earn a fraction of what their U.S. counterparts earn. Outsourcing (or *offshoring,* as it is also called when work is outsourced to other countries) has also expanded into knowledge-intensive work such as engineering, research and development, and the development of computer software. According to a recent study conducted by The Conference Board and Duke University's Offshoring Research Network, more than half of U.S. companies surveyed have some kind of offshoring strategy related to knowledge-intensive work and innovation.[44] Why are so many companies engaged in offshoring, and why are companies that already offshore work planning to increase the extent of offshoring? While cost savings continue to be a major motivation for offshoring, managers also want to take advantage of an increasingly talented global workforce and be closer to the growing global marketplace for goods and services.[45]

Major U.S. companies often earn a substantial portion of their revenues overseas. For example, Hewlett-Packard, Caterpillar, and IBM earn over 60% of their revenues from overseas markets. And many large companies employ thousands of workers overseas. For example, IBM employs close to 100,000 workers in India and Hewlett-Packard over 25,000.[46] Managers at some smaller companies have offshored work to Brazil, Sri Lanka, Russia, and Egypt.[47] Key challenges for managers who offshore are retaining sufficient managerial control over activities and employee turnover.[48]

Job Analysis

job analysis Identifying the tasks, duties, and responsibilities that make up a job and the knowledge, skills, and abilities needed to perform the job.

Job analysis is a second important activity that managers need to undertake prior to recruitment and selection.[49] **Job analysis** is the process of identifying (1) the tasks, duties, and responsibilities that make up a job (the *job description*) and (2) the knowledge, skills, and abilities needed to perform the job (the *job specifications*).[50] For each job in an organization, a job analysis needs to be done.

Job analysis can be done in a number of ways, including observing current employees as they perform the job or interviewing them. Often managers rely on questionnaires compiled by jobholders and their managers. The questionnaires ask about the skills and abilities needed to perform the job, job tasks and the amount of time spent on them, responsibilities, supervisory activities, equipment used, reports prepared, and decisions made.[51] The Position Analysis Questionnaire (PAQ) is a comprehensive standardized questionnaire that many managers rely on to conduct job analyses.[52] It focuses on behaviors jobholders perform, working conditions, and job characteristics and can be used for a variety of jobs.[53] The PAQ contains 194 items organized into six divisions: (1) information input (where and how the jobholder acquires information to perform the job), (2) mental processes (reasoning, decision making, planning, and information processing activities that are part of the job), (3) work output (physical activities performed on the job and machines and devices used), (4) relationships with others (interactions with other people that are necessary to perform the job), (5) job context (the physical and social environment of the job), and (6) other job characteristics (such as work pace).[54] A trend, in some organizations, is toward more flexible jobs in which tasks and responsibilities change and cannot be clearly specified in advance. For these kinds of jobs, job analysis focuses more on determining the skills and knowledge workers need to be effective and less on specific duties.

After managers have completed human resource planning and job analyses for all jobs in an organization, they will know their human resource needs and the jobs they need to fill. They will also know what knowledge, skills, and abilities potential employees need to perform those jobs. At this point, recruitment and selection can begin.

External and Internal Recruitment

As noted earlier, recruitment is what managers do to develop a pool of qualified candidates for open positions.[55] They traditionally have used two main types of recruiting: external and internal, which are now supplemented by recruiting over the Internet.

EXTERNAL RECRUITING When managers recruit externally to fill open positions, they look outside the organization for people who have not worked for the organization previously. There are multiple means through which managers can recruit externally: advertisements in newspapers and magazines, open houses for students and career counselors at high schools and colleges or on-site at the organization, career fairs at colleges, and recruitment meetings with groups in the local community.

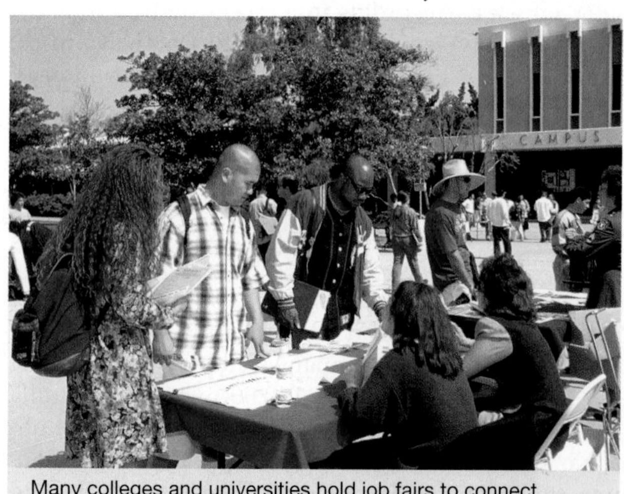

Many colleges and universities hold job fairs to connect employers with students looking for jobs.

Many large organizations send teams of interviewers to college campuses to recruit new employees. External recruitment can also take place through informal networks, as occurs when current employees inform friends about open positions in their companies or recommend people they know to fill vacant spots. Some organizations use employment agencies for external recruitment, and some external recruitment takes place simply through walk-ins–job hunters coming to an organization and inquiring about employment possibilities.

With all the downsizing and corporate layoffs that have taken place in recent years, you might think external recruiting would be a relatively easy task for managers. However, it often is not, because even though many people may be looking for jobs, many jobs that are open require skills and abilities that these job hunters do not have. Managers needing to fill vacant positions and job hunters seeking employment opportunities are increasingly relying on the Internet to connect with each other through employment Web sites such as Monster.com[56] and JobLine International.[57] Major corporations such as Coca-Cola, Cisco, Ernst & Young, Canon, and Telia have relied on JobLine to fill global positions.[58]

External recruiting has both advantages and disadvantages for managers. Advantages include having access to a potentially large applicant pool, being able to attract people who have the skills, knowledge, and abilities that an organization needs to achieve its goals, and being able to bring in newcomers who may have a fresh approach to problems and be up to date on the latest technology. These advantages have to be weighed against the disadvantages, including the relatively high costs of external recruitment. Employees recruited externally also lack knowledge about the inner workings of the organization and may need to receive more training than those recruited internally. Finally, when employees are recruited externally, there is always uncertainty concerning whether they will actually be good performers. Nonetheless, there are steps managers can take to reduce some of the uncertainty surrounding external recruitment, as profiled in the following "Information Technology Byte" box.

Information Technology Byte

Fog Creek Software's Approach to Recruiting

Fog Creek Software is a small, privately owned software company founded in 2000 by Joel Spolsky and Michael Pryor in a renovated loft in the Fashion District of New York City.[59] Fog Creek has earned a profit each year since its founding.[60] Hiring great computer software developers is essential for a company like Fog Creek; according to Spolsky, the top 1% of software developers outperform average developers by a ratio of around 10:1. And the top 1% are the inventive types who can successfully develop new products while also being highly efficient.[61]

Fog Creek Software uses paid summer internships to help identify and attract promising software developers.

Finding, never mind recruiting, the top 1% is a real challenge for a small company like Fog Creek because many of these people already have great jobs and are not looking to switch employers. Realizing that the top 1% of developers might rarely apply for positions with Fog Creek (or any other company), Fog Creek uses paid summer internships to recruit over 50% of its developers while they are still in college; they are hired full-time after graduation.[62]

In the fall of every year, Spolsky sends personalized letters to computer science majors across the country who have the potential to be top developers in the future, contacts professors at leading computer science programs for recommendations, and also seeks applications through his blog.[63] This process yields hundreds of applicants for internships, the best of whom are then given a phone interview. During the interview, the candidates describe themselves and their classes, are asked how they would go about solving a software development problem or challenge, and then can ask Spolsky anything they want about the company or living in New York City.[64]

Those who do well in the phone interview are flown to New York for an all-expense paid visit to Fog Creek–they are met at the airport in a limousine, stay in a hip hotel, receive welcoming gifts in their room, have a full day of interviews at Fog Creek, and then are given the option of staying two extra nights (at no cost to themselves) to get a feel for New York City. Typically only one out of every three recruits who have an on-site visit receives an internship offer.[65]

Interns perform real software development work–several summers ago, a team of four interns developed a new successful technology support product called Fog Creek Copilot.[66] This both motivates the interns and helps managers decide which interns they would like to hire. The interns are treated well–in addition to being paid, they receive free housing and are invited to outings, parties, and cultural events in New York City. At the conclusion of the internships, managers have a good sense of which interns are great programmers. These top programmers are offered jobs upon graduation with generous salaries, excellent working conditions, and great benefits. Although Fog Creek's approach to external recruitment is lengthy and expensive, it more than pays for itself by identifying and attracting top programmers. As Spolsky indicates, "An internship program creates a pipeline for great employees. It's a pretty long pipeline, so you need to have a long-term perspective, but it pays off in spades."[67]

lateral move A job change that entails no major changes in responsibility or authority levels.

INTERNAL RECRUITING When recruiting is internal, managers turn to existing employees to fill open positions. Employees recruited internally are either seeking **lateral moves** (job changes that entail no major changes in responsibility or authority levels) or promotions. Internal recruiting has several advantages. First, internal applicants are already familiar with the organization (including its goals, structure, culture, rules, and norms). Second, managers already know the candidates; they have considerable information about their skills and abilities and actual behavior on the job. Third, internal recruiting can help boost levels of employee motivation and morale, both for the employee who gets the job and for other workers. Those who are not seeking a promotion or who may not be ready for one can see that promotion is a possibility in the future; or a lateral move can alleviate boredom once a job has been fully mastered and can also be a useful way to learn new skills. Finally, internal recruiting is normally less time-consuming and expensive than external recruiting.

Given the advantages of internal recruiting, why do managers rely on external recruiting as much as they do? The answer lies in the disadvantages of internal recruiting–among them, a limited pool of candidates and a tendency among those candidates to be set in the organization's ways. Often the organization simply does not have suitable internal candidates. Sometimes, even when suitable internal applicants are available, managers may rely on external recruiting to find the very best candidate or to help bring new ideas and approaches into their organization. When organizations are in trouble and performing poorly, external recruiting is often relied on to bring in managerial talent with a fresh approach.

HONESTY IN RECRUITING At times, when trying to recruit the most qualified applicants, managers may be tempted to paint rosy pictures of both the open positions and the organization as a whole. They may worry that if they are honest about advantages and disadvantages, they either will not be able to fill positions or will have fewer or less qualified applicants. A manager trying to fill a secretarial position, for example, may emphasize the high level of pay and benefits the job offers and fail to mention the fact that the position is usually a dead-end job offering few opportunities for promotion.

realistic job preview (RJP) An honest assessment of the advantages and disadvantages of a job and organization.

Research suggests that painting a rosy picture of a job and the organization is not a wise recruiting strategy. Recruitment is more likely to be effective when managers give potential applicants an honest assessment of both the advantages and the disadvantages of the job and organization. Such an assessment is called a **realistic job preview (RJP).**[68] RJPs can reduce the number of new hires who quit when their jobs and organizations fail to meet their unrealistic expectations, and they help applicants decide for themselves whether a job is right for them.

Take the earlier example of the manager trying to recruit a secretary. The manager who paints a rosy picture of the job might have an easy time filling it but might hire a secretary who expects to be promoted quickly to an administrative assistant position. After a few weeks on the job, the secretary may realize that a promotion is unlikely no matter how good his or her performance, become dissatisfied, and look for and accept another job. The manager then has to recruit, select, and train another new secretary. The manager could have avoided this waste of valuable organizational resources by using a realistic job preview. The RJP would have increased the likelihood of hiring a secretary who was comfortable with few promotional opportunities and subsequently would have been satisfied to remain on the job.

The Selection Process

Once managers develop a pool of applicants for open positions through the recruitment process, they need to find out whether each applicant is qualified for the position and likely to be a good performer. If more than one applicant meets these two conditions, managers must further determine which applicants are likely to be better performers than others. They have several selection tools to help them sort out the relative qualifications of job applicants and appraise their potential for being good performers in a particular job. These tools include background information, interviews, paper-and-pencil tests, physical ability tests, performance tests, and references (see Figure 12.3).[69]

BACKGROUND INFORMATION To aid in the selection process, managers obtain background information from job applications and from résumés. Such information might include the highest levels of education obtained, college majors and minors, type of college or university attended, years and type of work experience, and mastery of foreign languages. Background information can be helpful both to screen out applicants who are lacking key qualifications (such as a college degree) and to determine which qualified applicants are more promising than others. For example, applicants with a BS may be acceptable, but those who also have an MBA may be preferable.

Figure 12.3
Selection Tools

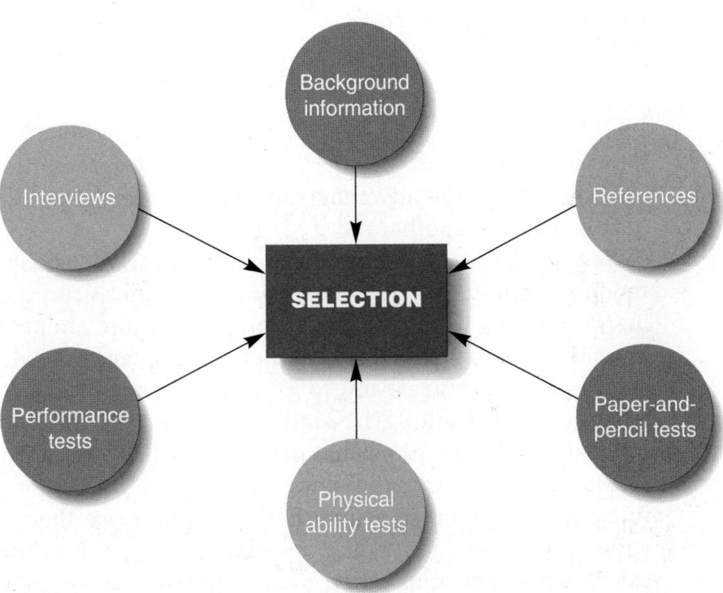

Increasing numbers of organizations are performing background checks to verify the background information prospective employees provide (and also to uncover any negative information such as crime convictions).[70] According to ADP Employer Services, an outsourcing company that performs payroll and human resource functions for organizations, more and more companies are performing background checks on prospective employees and are uncovering inaccuracies, inconsistencies, and negative information such as prior convictions or driving violations.[71] According to a recent survey ADP conducted, about half of all background checks turn up an inconsistency between the education and credentials applicants list and the information other sources (such as universities or prior employers) provide. And in some cases, background checks reveal convictions and driving violations.[72]

INTERVIEWS Virtually all organizations use interviews during the selection process, as is true at Zappos in "A Manager's Challenge." Interviews may be structured or unstructured. In a *structured interview,* managers ask each applicant the same standard questions (such as "What are your unique qualifications for this position?" and "What characteristics of a job are most important to you?"). Particularly informative questions may be those that prompt an interviewee to demonstrate skills and abilities needed for the job by answering the question. Sometimes called *situational interview questions,* these often present interviewees with a scenario they would likely encounter on the job and ask them to indicate how they would handle it.[73] For example, applicants for a sales job may be asked to indicate how they would respond to a customer who complains about waiting too long for service, a customer who is indecisive, and a customer whose order is lost.

An *unstructured interview* proceeds more like an ordinary conversation. The interviewer feels free to ask probing questions to discover what the applicant is like and does not ask a fixed set of questions determined in advance. In general, structured interviews are superior to unstructured interviews because they are more likely to yield information that will help identify qualified candidates, are less subjective, and may be less influenced by the interviewer's biases.

Practically all organizations use some kind of interview during the selection process.

Even when structured interviews are used, however, the potential exists for the interviewer's biases to influence his or her judgment. Recall from Chapter 5 how the similar-to-me effect can cause people to perceive others who are similar to themselves more positively than those who are different and how stereotypes can result in inaccurate perceptions. Interviewers must be trained to avoid these biases and sources of inaccurate perceptions as much as possible. Many of the approaches to increasing diversity awareness and diversity skills described in Chapter 5 are used to train interviewers to avoid the effects of biases and stereotypes. In addition, using multiple interviewers can be advantageous because their individual biases and idiosyncrasies may cancel one another out.[74]

When conducting interviews, managers cannot ask questions that are irrelevant to the job in question; otherwise their organizations run the risk of costly lawsuits. It is inappropriate and illegal, for example, to inquire about an interviewee's spouse or to ask questions about whether an interviewee plans to have children. Because questions such as these are irrelevant to job performance, they are discriminatory and violate EEO laws (see Table 12.1). Thus interviewers need to be instructed in EEO laws and informed about questions that may violate those laws.

Managers can use interviews at various stages in the selection process. Some use interviews as initial screening devices; others use them as a final hurdle that applicants must jump. Regardless of when they are used, managers typically use other selection tools in conjunction with interviews because of the potential for bias and for inaccurate assessments of interviewees. Even though training and structured interviews can eliminate the effects of some biases, interviewers can still come to erroneous conclusions about interviewees' qualifications. Interviewees, for example, who make a bad initial impression or are overly nervous in the first minute or two of an interview tend to be judged more harshly than less nervous candidates, even if the rest of the interview goes well.

PAPER-AND-PENCIL TESTS The two main kinds of paper-and-pencil tests used for selection purposes are ability tests and personality tests. *Ability tests* assess the extent to which applicants possess the skills necessary for job performance, such as verbal comprehension or numerical skills. Autoworkers hired by General Motors, Chrysler, and Ford, for example, are typically tested for their ability to read and to do mathematics.[75]

Personality tests measure personality traits and characteristics relevant to job performance. Some retail organizations, for example, give job applicants honesty tests to determine how trustworthy they are. The use of personality tests (including honesty tests) for hiring purposes is controversial. Some critics maintain that honesty tests do not really measure honesty (that is, they are not valid) and can be faked by job applicants. Before using any paper-and-pencil tests for selection purposes, managers must have sound evidence that the tests are actually good predictors of performance on the job in question. Managers who use tests without such evidence may be subject to costly discrimination lawsuits.

PHYSICAL ABILITY TESTS For jobs requiring physical abilities, such as firefighting, garbage collecting, and package delivery, managers use physical ability tests that measure physical strength and stamina as selection tools. Autoworkers are typically tested for mechanical dexterity because this physical ability is an important skill for high job performance in many auto plants.[76]

PERFORMANCE TESTS *Performance tests* measure job applicants' performance on actual job tasks. Applicants for secretarial positions, for example, typically are required to complete a keyboarding test that measures how quickly and accurately they type. Applicants for middle and top management positions are sometimes given short-term projects to complete–projects that mirror the kinds of situations that arise in the job being filled–to assess their knowledge and problem-solving capabilities.[77]

Assessment centers, first used by AT&T, take performance tests one step further. In a typical assessment center, about 10 to 15 candidates for managerial positions participate in a variety of activities over a few days. During this time they are assessed for the skills an effective manager needs–problem-solving, organizational, communication, and conflict resolution skills. Some of the activities are performed individually; others are performed in groups. Throughout the process, current managers observe the candidates' behavior and measure performance. Summary evaluations are then used as a selection tool.

REFERENCES Applicants for many jobs are required to provide references from former employers or other knowledgeable sources (such as a college instructor or adviser) who know the applicants' skills, abilities, and other personal characteristics. These individuals are asked to provide candid information about the applicant. References are often used at the end of the selection process to confirm a decision to hire. Yet the fact that many former employers are reluctant to provide negative information in references sometimes makes it difficult to interpret what a reference is really saying about an applicant.

In fact, several recent lawsuits filed by applicants who felt that they were unfairly denigrated or had their privacy invaded by unfavorable references from former employers have caused managers to be increasingly wary of providing any negative information in a reference, even if it is accurate. For jobs in which the jobholder is responsible for the safety and lives of other people, however, failing to provide accurate negative information in a reference does not just mean that the wrong person might get hired; it may also mean that other people's lives will be at stake.

reliability The degree to which a tool or test measures the same thing each time it is used.

THE IMPORTANCE OF RELIABILITY AND VALIDITY Whatever selection tools a manager uses need to be both reliable and valid. **Reliability** is the degree to which a tool or test measures the same thing each time it is administered. Scores on a selection test should be similar if the same person is assessed with the same tool on two different days; if there is quite a bit of variability, the tool is unreliable. For interviews, determining reliability is more complex because the dynamic is personal interpretation. That is why the reliability of interviews can be increased if two or more different qualified interviewers interview the same candidate. If the interviews are reliable, the interviewers should come to similar conclusions about the interviewee's qualifications.

validity The degree to which a tool or test measures what it purports to measure.

Validity is the degree to which a tool measures what it purports to measure–for selection tools, it is the degree to which the test predicts performance on the tasks or job in question. Does a physical ability test used to select firefighters, for example, actually predict on-the-job performance? Do assessment center ratings actually predict managerial performance? Do keyboarding tests predict secretarial performance? These are all questions of validity. Honesty tests, for example, are controversial because it is not clear that they validly predict honesty in such jobs as retailing and banking.

LO12-3 Discuss the training and development options that ensure organizational members can effectively perform their jobs.

Managers have an ethical and legal obligation to use reliable and valid selection tools. Yet reliability and validity are matters of degree rather than all-or-nothing characteristics. Thus managers should strive to use selection tools in such a way that they can achieve the greatest degree of reliability and validity. For ability tests of a particular skill, managers should keep up to date on the latest advances in the development of valid paper-and-pencil tests and use the test with the highest reliability and validity ratings for their purposes. Regarding interviews, managers can improve reliability by having more than one person interview job candidates.

Training and Development

Training and development help to ensure that organizational members have the knowledge and skills needed to perform jobs effectively, take on new responsibilities, and adapt to changing conditions. **Training** focuses primarily on teaching organizational members how to perform their current jobs and helping them acquire the knowledge and skills they need to be effective performers. **Development** focuses on building the knowledge and skills of organizational members so they are prepared to take on new responsibilities and challenges. Training tends to be used more frequently at lower levels of an organization; development tends to be used more frequently with professionals and managers.

training Teaching organizational members how to perform their current jobs and helping them acquire the knowledge and skills they need to be effective performers.

development Building the knowledge and skills of organizational members so they are prepared to take on new responsibilities and challenges.

needs assessment An assessment of which employees need training or development and what type of skills or knowledge they need to acquire.

Before creating training and development programs, managers should perform a **needs assessment** to determine which employees need training or development and what type of skills or knowledge they need to acquire (see Figure 12.4).[78]

Types of Training

There are two types of training: classroom instruction and on-the-job training.

CLASSROOM INSTRUCTION Through classroom instruction, employees acquire knowledge and skills in a classroom setting. This instruction may take place within the organization or outside it, such as through courses at local colleges and universities. Many organizations establish their own formal instructional divisions–some are even called "colleges"–to provide needed classroom instruction.

At Ethan Allen Interiors Inc., for example, employees from stores around the country attend Ethan Allen College at company headquarters in Danbury, Connecticut. During classes, employees acquire in-depth knowledge about the company's products and learn how to listen to customers and accurately assess their needs. In addition, the college provides instruction on such diverse topics as floor plans and window treatments. Training at Ethan Allen is an ongoing process. Veteran employees attend two- or three-day sessions at the college to brush up on their skills and keep abreast

Figure 12.4
Training and Development

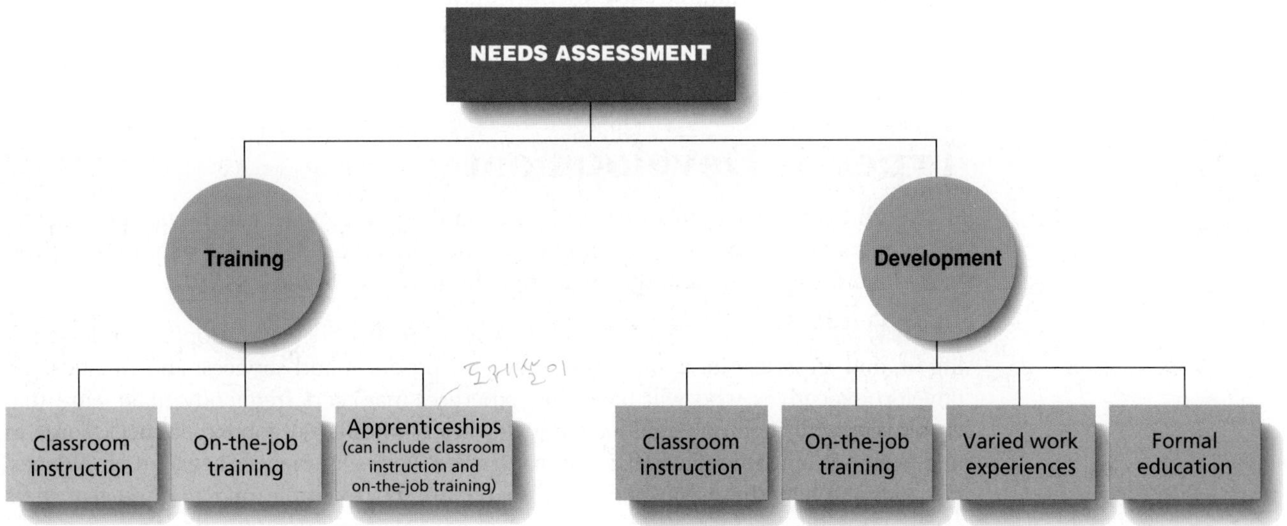

of the latest developments. M. Farooq Kathwari, chairman and CEO of Ethan Allen, believes the classroom instruction employees receive at Ethan Allen College has contributed significantly to his company's competitive advantage.[79]

Classroom instruction frequently uses videos and role playing in addition to traditional written materials, lectures, and group discussions. *Videos* can demonstrate appropriate and inappropriate job behaviors. For example, by watching an experienced salesperson effectively deal with a loud and angry customer, inexperienced salespeople can develop skills in handling similar situations. During *role playing,* trainees either directly participate in or watch others perform actual job activities in a simulated setting. At McDonald's Hamburger University, for example, role playing helps franchisees acquire the knowledge and skills they need to manage their restaurants.

Simulations also can be part of classroom instruction, particularly for complicated jobs that require an extensive amount of learning and in which errors carry a high cost. In a simulation, key aspects of the work situation and job tasks are duplicated as closely as possible in an artificial setting. For example, air traffic controllers are trained by simulations because of the complicated nature of the work, the extensive amount of learning involved, and the very high costs of air traffic control errors.

on-the-job training
Training that takes place in the work setting as employees perform their job tasks.

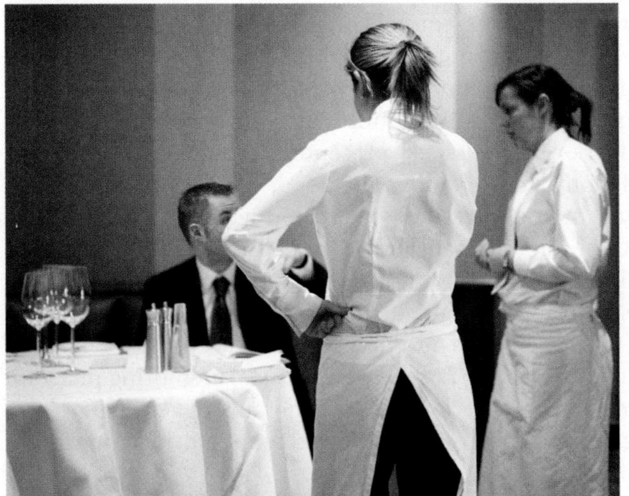
At many restaurants, new employees receive on-the-job training by shadowing more experienced waiters and waitresses as they go about their work.

ON-THE-JOB TRAINING In **on-the-job training,** learning occurs in the work setting as employees perform their job tasks. On-the-job training can be provided by coworkers or supervisors or can occur simply as jobholders gain experience and knowledge from doing the work. Newly hired waiters and waitresses in chains such as Red Lobster or the Olive Garden often receive on-the-job training from experienced employees. The supervisor of a new bus driver for a campus bus system may ride the bus for a week to ensure that the driver has learned the routes and follows safety procedures. Chefs learn to create new and innovative dishes by experimenting with different combinations of ingredients and cooking techniques. For all on-the-job training, employees learn by doing.

Managers often use on-the-job training on a continuing basis to ensure that their subordinates keep up to date with changes in goals, technology, products, or customer needs and desires. For example, sales representatives at Mary Kay Cosmetics Inc. receive ongoing training so they not only know about new cosmetic products and currently popular colors but also are reminded of Mary Kay's guiding principles. Mary Kay's expansion into Russia has succeeded in part because of the ongoing training that Mary Kay's Russian salespeople receive.[80]

Types of Development

Although both classroom instruction and on-the-job training can be used for development as well as training, development often includes additional activities such as varied work experiences and formal education.

VARIED WORK EXPERIENCES Top managers need to develop an understanding of, and expertise in, a variety of functions, products and services, and markets. To develop executives who will have this expertise, managers frequently make sure that employees with high potential have a wide variety of different job experiences, some in line positions and some in staff positions. Varied work experiences broaden employees' horizons and help them think about the big picture. For example, one- to three-year stints overseas are being used increasingly to provide managers with international work experiences. With organizations becoming more global, managers need to understand the different values, beliefs, cultures, regions, and ways of doing business in different countries.

Another development approach is mentoring. (Recall from Chapter 5 that a *mentor* is an experienced member of an organization who provides advice and guidance to a less experienced member, called a *protégé*.) Having a mentor can help managers seek out work experiences and assignments that will contribute to their development and can enable them to gain the most possible from varied work experiences.[81] Although some mentors and protégés hook up informally, organizations have found that formal mentoring programs can be valuable ways to contribute to the development of managers and all employees.

Formal mentoring programs ensure that mentoring takes place in an organization, structure the process, and make sure diverse organizational members have equal access to mentors. Participants receive training, efforts are focused on matching mentors and protégés so meaningful developmental relationships ensue, and organizations can track reactions and assess the potential benefits of mentoring. Formal mentoring programs can also ensure that diverse members of an organization receive the benefits of mentoring. A study conducted by David A. Thomas, a professor at the Harvard Business School, found that members of racial minority groups at three large corporations who were very successful in their careers had the benefit of mentors. Formal mentoring programs help organizations make this valuable development tool available to all employees.[82]

When diverse members of an organization lack mentors, their progress in the organization and advancement to high-level positions can be hampered. Ida Abott, a lawyer and consultant on work-related issues, presented a paper to the Minority Corporate Counsel Association in which she concluded, "The lack of adequate mentoring has held women and minority lawyers back from achieving professional success and has led to high rates of career dissatisfaction and attrition."[83]

Mentoring can benefit all kinds of employees in all kinds of work.[84] John Washko, a manager at the Four Seasons hotel chain, benefited from the mentoring he received from Stan Bromley on interpersonal relations and how to deal with employees; mentor Bromley, in turn, found that participating in the Four Seasons' mentoring program helped him develop his own management style.[85] More generally, development is an ongoing process for all managers, and mentors often find that mentoring contributes to their own personal development.

FORMAL EDUCATION Many large corporations reimburse employees for tuition expenses they incur while taking college courses and obtaining advanced degrees. This is not just benevolence on the part of the employer or even a simple reward given to the employee; it is an effective way to develop employees who can take on new responsibilities and more challenging positions. For similar reasons, corporations spend thousands of dollars sending managers to executive development programs such as executive MBA programs. In these programs, experts teach managers the latest in business and management techniques and practices.

performance appraisal The evaluation of employees' job performance and contributions to their organization.

To save time and travel costs, some managers rely on *long-distance learning* to formally educate and develop employees. Using videoconferencing technologies, business schools such as the Harvard Business School, the University of Michigan, and Babson College teach courses on video screens in corporate conference rooms. Business schools also customize courses and degrees to fit the development needs of employees in a particular company and/or a particular geographic region.[86]

LO12-4 Explain why performance appraisal and feedback is such a crucial activity, and list the choices managers must make in designing effective performance appraisal and feedback procedures.

Transfer of Training and Development

Whenever training and development take place off the job or in a classroom setting, it is vital for managers to promote the transfer of the knowledge and skills acquired *to the actual work situation.* Trainees should be encouraged and expected to use their newfound expertise on the job.

Performance Appraisal and Feedback

The recruitment/selection and training/development components of a human resource management system ensure that employees have the knowledge and skills needed to be effective now and in the future. Performance appraisal and feedback complement recruitment, selection, training, and development. **Performance appraisal** is the evaluation of employees' job performance and contributions to the organization. **Performance feedback** is the process through which managers share performance appraisal information with their subordinates, give subordinates an opportunity to reflect on their own performance, and develop, with subordinates, plans for the future. Before performance feedback, performance appraisal must take place. Performance appraisal could take place without providing performance feedback, but wise managers are careful to provide feedback because it can contribute to employee motivation and performance.

performance feedback The process through which managers share performance appraisal information with subordinates, give subordinates an opportunity to reflect on their own performance, and develop, with subordinates, plans for the future.

Performance appraisal and feedback contribute to the effective management of human resources in several ways. Performance appraisal gives managers important information on which to base human resource decisions.[87] Decisions about pay raises, bonuses, promotions, and job moves all hinge on the accurate appraisal of performance. Performance appraisal can also help managers determine which workers are candidates for training and development and in what areas. Performance feedback encourages high levels of employee motivation and performance. It lets good performers know that their efforts are valued and appreciated. It also lets poor performers know that their lackluster performance needs improvement. Performance feedback can give both good and poor performers insight on their strengths and weaknesses and ways in which they can improve their performance in the future.

How'm I doing? Sitting down for an honest and open performance appraisal with your immediate supervisor can help keep you on track.

Types of Performance Appraisal

Performance appraisal focuses on the evaluation of traits, behaviors, and results.[88]

TRAIT APPRAISALS When trait appraisals are used, managers assess subordinates on personal characteristics that are relevant to job performance, such as skills, abilities, or personality. A factory worker, for example, may be evaluated based on her ability to use computerized equipment and perform numerical calculations. A social worker may be appraised based on his empathy and communication skills.

Three disadvantages of trait appraisals often lead managers to rely on other appraisal methods. First, possessing a certain personal characteristic does not ensure that the personal characteristic will actually be used on the job and result in high performance. For example, a factory worker may possess superior computer and numerical skills but be a poor performer due to low motivation. The second disadvantage of trait appraisals is linked to the first. Because traits do not always show a direct association with performance, workers and courts of law may view them as unfair and potentially discriminatory. The third disadvantage of trait appraisals is that they often do not enable managers to give employees feedback they can use to improve performance. Because trait appraisals focus on relatively enduring human characteristics that change only over the long term, employees can do little to change their behavior in response to performance feedback from a trait appraisal. Telling a social worker that he lacks empathy says little about how he can improve his interactions with clients, for example. These disadvantages suggest that managers should use trait appraisals only when they can demonstrate that the assessed traits are accurate and important indicators of job performance.

BEHAVIOR APPRAISALS Through behavior appraisals, managers assess how workers perform their jobs–the actual actions and behaviors that workers exhibit on the job. Whereas trait appraisals assess what workers *are like,* behavior appraisals assess what workers *do.* For example, with a behavior appraisal, a manager might evaluate a social worker on the extent to which he looks clients in the eye when talking with them, expresses sympathy when they are upset, and refers them to community counseling and support groups geared toward the specific problems they are encountering. Behavior appraisals are especially useful when *how* workers perform their jobs is important. In educational organizations such as high schools, for example, the numbers of classes and students taught are important, but also important is how they are taught or the methods teachers use to ensure that learning takes place.

Behavior appraisals have the advantage of giving employees clear information about what they are doing right and wrong and how they can improve their performance. And because behaviors are much easier for employees to change than traits, performance feedback from behavior appraisals is more likely to lead to improve performance.

RESULTS APPRAISALS For some jobs, *how* people perform the job is not as important as *what* they accomplish or the results they obtain. With results appraisals, managers appraise performance by the results or the actual outcomes of work behaviors. Take the case of two new car salespeople. One salesperson strives to develop personal relationships with her customers. She spends hours talking to them and frequently calls them to see how their decision-making process is going. The other salesperson has a much more hands-off approach. He is very knowledgeable, answers customers' questions, and then waits for them to come to him. Both salespersons sell, on average, the same number of cars, and the customers of both are satisfied with the service they receive, according to postcards the dealership mails to customers asking for an assessment of their satisfaction. The manager of the dealership appropriately uses results appraisals (sales and customer satisfaction) to evaluate the salespeople's performance because it does not matter which behavior salespeople use to sell cars as long as they sell the desired number and satisfy customers. If one salesperson sells too few cars, however, the manager can give that person performance feedback about his or her low sales.

objective appraisal An appraisal that is based on facts and is likely to be numerical.

OBJECTIVE AND SUBJECTIVE APPRAISALS Whether managers appraise performance in terms of traits, behaviors, or results, the information they assess is either *objective* or *subjective.* **Objective appraisals** are based on facts and are likely to be numerical–the number of cars sold, the number of meals prepared, the number of times late, the number of audits completed. Managers often use objective appraisals when results are being appraised because results tend to be easier to quantify than traits or behaviors. When *how* workers perform their jobs is important, however, subjective behavior appraisals are more appropriate than results appraisals.

subjective appraisal An appraisal that is based on perceptions of traits, behaviors, or results.

Subjective appraisals are based on managers' perceptions of traits, behaviors, or results. Because subjective appraisals rest on managers' perceptions, there is always the chance that they are inaccurate (see Chapter 5). This is why both researchers and managers have spent considerable time and effort on determining the best way to develop reliable and valid subjective measures of performance.

Some of the more popular subjective measures such as the graphic rating scale, the behaviorally anchored rating scale (BARS), and the behavior observation scale (BOS) are illustrated in Figure 12.5.[89] When graphic rating scales are used, performance is assessed along a continuum with specified intervals. With a BARS, performance is assessed along a scale with clearly defined scale points containing examples

Figure 12.5
Subjective Measures of Performance

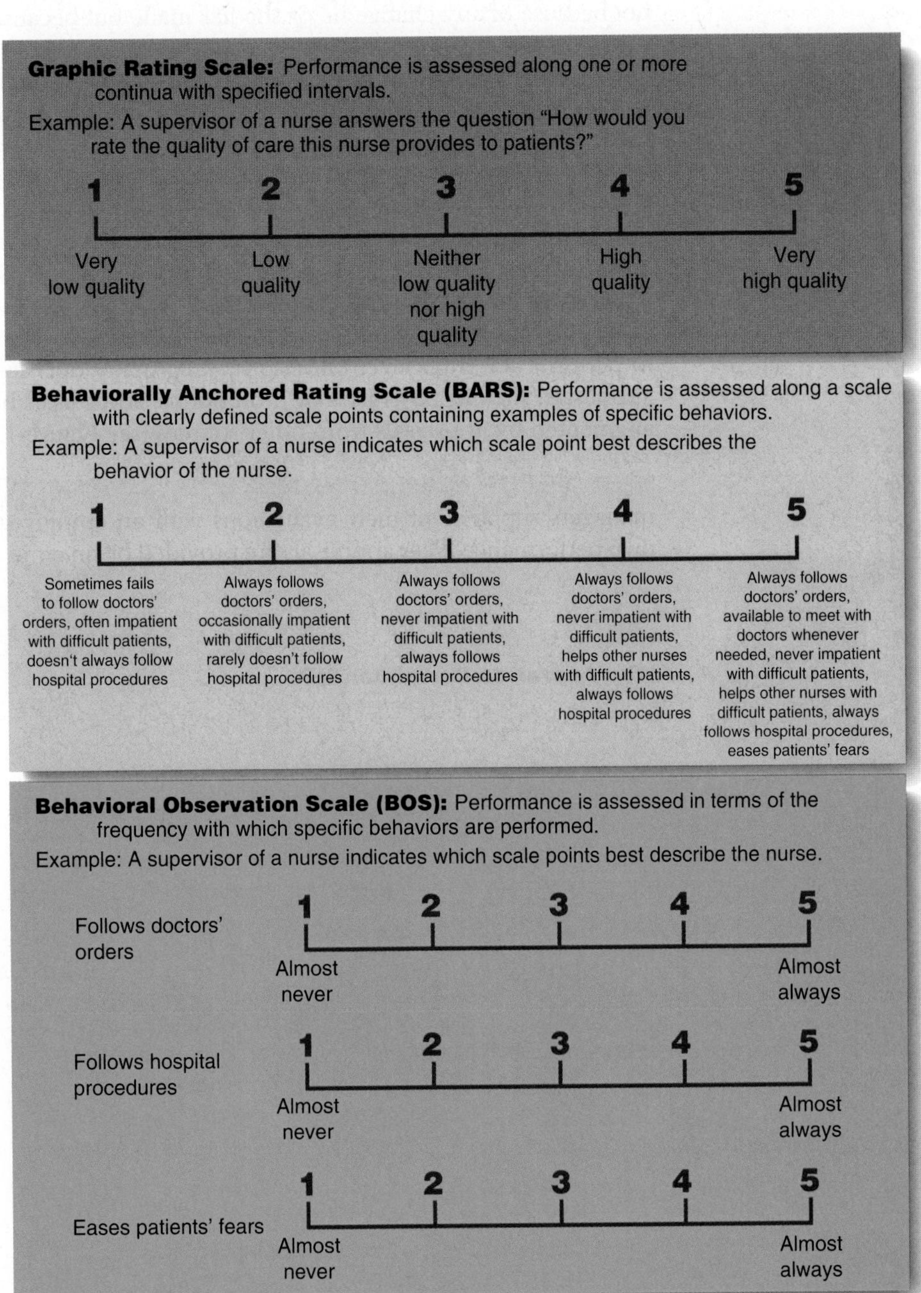

of specific behaviors. A BOS assesses performance by how often specific behaviors are performed. Many managers may use both objective and subjective appraisals. For example, a salesperson may be appraised both on the dollar value of sales (objective) and the quality of customer service (subjective).

In addition to subjective appraisals, some organizations employ *forced rankings* whereby supervisors must rank their subordinates and assign them to different categories according to their performance (which is subjectively appraised). For example, middle managers at Ford Motor Company are ranked by their supervisors in a forced distribution from A to C, with 10% of them receiving A ratings, 80% receiving B ratings, and 10% receiving C ratings.[90] The first year an employee receives a C, he or she does not receive a bonus, and after two years of C performance, a demotion or even firing is possible. Employees tend to not like these systems because they believe they are unfair. For example, managers at Ford have filed a class action lawsuit because they feel Ford's ranking system is unfair.[91] Relying on relative performance through ranking systems can force managers to rate some of their subordinates as unsatisfactory even if this might not be true and can also result in an employee's performance being downgraded not because of any change he or she has made but because coworkers have improved their performance. In other organizations that use ranking systems, employees tend to voice similar concerns. For example, forced ranking systems can result in a zero-sum, competitive environment that can discourage cooperation and teamwork.[92]

Who Appraises Performance?

We have been assuming that managers or the supervisors of employees evaluate performance. This is a reasonable assumption: Supervisors are the most common appraisers of performance.[93] Performance appraisal is an important part of most managers' job duties. Managers are responsible for not only motivating their subordinates to perform at a high level but also making many decisions hinging on performance appraisals, such as pay raises or promotions. Appraisals by managers can be usefully augmented by appraisals from other sources (see Figure 12.6).

SELF, PEERS, SUBORDINATES, AND CLIENTS When self-appraisals are used, managers supplement their evaluations with an employee's assessment of his or her own performance. Peer appraisals are provided by an employee's coworkers. Especially

Figure 12.6
Who Appraises Performance?

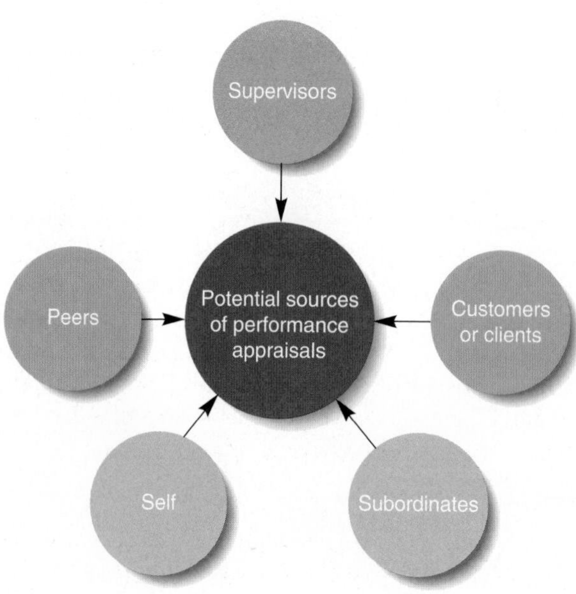

when subordinates work in groups or teams, feedback from peer appraisals can motivate team members while giving managers important information for decision making. A growing number of companies are having subordinates appraise their managers' performance and leadership as well. And sometimes customers or clients assess employee performance in terms of responsiveness to customers and quality of service. Although appraisals from these sources can be useful, managers need to be aware of potential issues that may arise when they are used. Subordinates sometimes may be inclined to inflate self-appraisals, especially if organizations are downsizing and they are worried about job security. Managers who are appraised by their subordinates may fail to take needed but unpopular actions out of fear that their subordinates will appraise them negatively. Some of these potential issues can be mitigated to the extent that there are high levels of trust in an organization.

360-DEGREE PERFORMANCE APPRAISALS To improve motivation and performance, some organizations include 360-degree appraisals and feedback in their performance appraisal systems, especially for managers. In a **360-degree appraisal** a variety of people, beginning with the manager and including peers or coworkers, subordinates, superiors, and sometimes even customers or clients, appraise a manager's performance. The manager receives feedback based on evaluations from these multiple sources.

360-degree appraisal A performance appraisal by peers, subordinates, superiors, and sometimes clients who are in a position to evaluate a manager's performance.

The growing number of companies using 360-degree appraisals and feedback include AT&T Corp., Allied Signal Inc., Eastman Chemical Co., and Baxter International Inc.[94] For 360-degree appraisals and feedback to be effective, there has to be trust throughout an organization. More generally, trust is a critical ingredient in any performance appraisal and feedback procedure. In addition, research suggests that 360-degree appraisals should focus on behaviors rather than traits or results and that managers need to carefully select appropriate raters. Moreover, appraisals tend to be more honest when made anonymously and when raters have been trained in how to use 360-degree appraisal forms.[95] Additionally, managers need to think carefully about the extent to which 360-degree appraisals are appropriate for certain jobs and be willing to modify any appraisal system they implement if they become aware of unintended problems it creates.[96]

Even when 360-degree appraisals are used, it is sometimes difficult to design an effective process by which subordinates' feedback can be communicated to their managers; but advances in information technology can solve this problem. For example, ImproveNow.com has online questionnaires that subordinates fill out to evaluate the performance of their managers and give the managers feedback. Each subordinate of a particular manager completes the questionnaire independently, all responses are tabulated, and the manager is given specific feedback on behaviors in a variety of areas, such as rewarding good performance, looking out for subordinates' best interests and being supportive, and having a vision for the future.[97]

Effective Performance Feedback

For the appraisal and feedback component of a human resource management system to encourage and motivate high performance, managers must give their subordinates feedback. To generate useful information to feed back to their subordinates, managers can use both formal and informal appraisals. **Formal appraisals** are conducted at set times during the year and are based on performance dimensions and measures that have been specified in advance. A salesperson, for example, may be evaluated by his or her manager twice a year on the performance dimensions of sales and customer service, sales being objectively measured from sales reports, and customer service being measured with a BARS (see Figure 12.5).

formal appraisal An appraisal conducted at a set time during the year and based on performance dimensions and measures that were specified in advance.

Managers in most large organizations use formal performance appraisals on a fixed schedule dictated by company policy, such as every six months or every year. An integral part of a formal appraisal is a meeting between the manager and the subordinate in which the subordinate is given feedback on performance.

Performance feedback lets subordinates know which areas they are excelling in and which areas need improvement; it should also tell them *how* they can improve their performance.

Realizing the value of formal appraisals, managers in many large corporations have committed substantial resources to updating their performance appraisal procedures and training low-level managers in how to use them and provide accurate feedback to employees. Top managers at the pharmaceutical company Hoffmann-La Roche Inc., for example, spent $1.5 million updating and improving their performance appraisal procedures. Alan Rubino, vice president of human resources for Hoffmann-La Roche, believes this was money well spent because "people need to know exactly where they stand and what's required of them." Before Hoffmann-La Roche's new system was implemented, managers attended a three-day training and development session to improve their performance appraisal skills. The new procedures call for every manager and subordinate to develop a performance plan for subordinates for the coming year–a plan that is linked to the company's strategy and goals and approved by the manager's own superiors. Formal performance appraisals are conducted every six months, during which actual performance is compared to planned performance.[98]

informal appraisal An unscheduled appraisal of ongoing progress and areas for improvement.

Formal performance appraisals supply both managers and subordinates with valuable information; but subordinates often want more frequent feedback, and managers often want to motivate subordinates as the need arises. For these reasons many companies, including Hoffman-La Roche, supplement formal performance appraisal with frequent **informal appraisals,** for which managers and their subordinates meet as the need arises to discuss ongoing progress and areas for improvement. Moreover, when job duties, assignments, or goals change, informal appraisals can give workers timely feedback concerning how they are handling their new responsibilities.

Managers often dislike providing performance feedback, especially when the feedback is negative, but doing so is an important managerial activity.[99] Here are some guidelines for giving effective performance feedback that contributes to employee motivation and performance:

- *Be specific and focus on behaviors or outcomes that are correctable and within a worker's ability to improve.* Example: Telling a salesperson that he is too shy when interacting with customers is likely to lower his self-confidence and prompt him to become defensive. A more effective approach would be to give the salesperson feedback about specific behaviors to engage in–greeting customers as soon as they enter the department, asking customers whether they need help, and volunteering to help customers find items.
- *Approach performance appraisal as an exercise in problem solving and solution finding, not criticizing.* Example: Rather than criticizing a financial analyst for turning in reports late, the manager helps the analyst determine why the reports are late and identify ways to better manage her time.
- *Express confidence in a subordinate's ability to improve.* Example: Instead of being skeptical, a first-level manager tells a subordinate that he is confident that the subordinate can increase quality levels.
- *Provide performance feedback both formally and informally.* Example: The staff of a preschool receives feedback from formal performance appraisals twice a year. The school director also provides frequent informal feedback such as complimenting staff members on creative ideas for special projects, noticing when they do a particularly good job handling a difficult child, and pointing out when they provide inadequate supervision.
- *Praise instances of high performance and areas of a job in which a worker excels.* Example: Rather than focusing on just the negative, a manager discusses the areas her subordinate excels in as well as the areas in need of improvement.
- *Avoid personal criticisms and treat subordinates with respect.* Example: An engineering manager acknowledges her subordinates' expertise and treats them as

professionals. Even when the manager points out performance problems to subordinates, she refrains from criticizing them personally.

- *Agree to a timetable for performance improvements.* Example: A first-level manager and his subordinate decide to meet again in one month to determine whether quality levels have improved.

In following these guidelines, managers need to remember *why* they are giving performance feedback: to encourage high levels of motivation and performance. Moreover, the information that managers gather through performance appraisal and feedback helps them determine how to distribute pay raises and bonuses.

Pay and Benefits

LO12-5 Explain the issues managers face in determining levels of pay and benefits.

Pay includes employees' base salaries, pay raises, and bonuses and is determined by a number of factors such as characteristics of the organization and the job and levels of performance. Employee *benefits* are based on membership in an organization (and not necessarily on the particular job held) and include sick days, vacation days, and medical and life insurance. In Chapter 13 we discuss how pay can motivate organizational members to perform at a high level, as well as the different kinds of pay plans managers can use to help an organization achieve its goals and gain a competitive advantage. As you will learn, it is important to link pay to behaviors or results that contribute to organizational effectiveness. Next we focus on establishing an organization's pay level and pay structure.

Pay Level

pay level The relative position of an organization's pay incentives in comparison with those of other organizations in the same industry employing similar kinds of workers.

Pay level is a broad comparative concept that refers to how an organization's pay incentives compare, in general, to those of other organizations in the same industry employing similar kinds of workers. Managers must decide if they want to offer relatively high wages, average wages, or relatively low wages. High wages help ensure that an organization is going to be able to recruit, select, and retain high performers, but high wages also raise costs. Low wages give an organization a cost advantage but may undermine the organization's ability to select and recruit high performers and to motivate current employees to perform at a high level. Either of these situations may lead to inferior quality or inadequate customer service.

In determining pay levels, managers should take into account their organization's strategy. A high pay level may prohibit managers from effectively pursuing a low-cost strategy. But a high pay level may be worth the added costs in an organization whose competitive advantage lies in superior quality and excellent customer service. As one might expect, hotel and motel chains with a low-cost strategy, such as Days Inn and Hampton Inns, have lower pay levels than chains striving to provide high-quality rooms and services, such as the Four Seasons. In fact, the Four Seasons treats and pays its employees very well, as profiled in the following "Management Insight" box.

Management Insight

Treating Employees Well Leads to Satisfied Customers

Four Seasons Hotels and Resorts is one of only 13 companies to be ranked one of the "100 Best Companies to Work For" every year since *Fortune* magazine started this annual ranking of companies.[100] And the Four Seasons often receives other awards and recognition such as being named the "Best Hotel Group Worldwide" by *Gallivanter's Guide* and dominating *Travel + Leisure's* World's Best Awards Readers' Poll and Condé Nast *Traveler's* Readers' Choice Awards

At Four Seasons, individualized attention for employees enables them to pass the care on to customers. Everyone wins!

based on customers' responses.[101] In an industry in which annual turnover rates are over 35%, the Four Seasons' is around 18%.[102] Evidently employees and customers alike are satisfied with how they are treated at the Four Seasons. Understanding that the two are causally linked is perhaps the key to the Four Seasons' success. As the Four Seasons' founder, chairman of the board, and CEO Isadore Sharp[103] suggests, "How you treat your employees is how you expect them to treat the customer."[104]

The Four Seasons was founded by Sharp in 1961 when he opened his first hotel called the Four Seasons Motor Hotel in a less-than-desirable area outside downtown Toronto. Whereas his first hotel had 125 inexpensively priced rooms appealing to the individual traveler, his fourth hotel was built to appeal to business travelers and conventions with 1,600 rooms, conference facilities, several restaurants, banquet halls, and shops in an arcade. Both these hotels were successful, but Sharp decided he could provide customers with a different kind of hotel experience by combining the best features of both kinds of hotel experiences–the sense of closeness and personal attention that a small hotel brings with the amenities of a big hotel to suit the needs of business travelers.[105]

Sharp sought to provide the kind of personal service that would really help business travelers on the road–giving them the amenities they have at home and in the office and miss when traveling on business. Thus the Four Seasons was the first hotel chain to provide bathrobes, shampoo, round-the-clock room service, laundry and dry cleaning services, large desks in every room, two-line phones, and round-the-clock secretarial assistance.[106] While these are relatively concrete ways of personalizing the hotel experience, Sharp realized that how employees treat customers is just as, or perhaps even more, important. When employees view each customer as an individual with his or her own needs and desires, and empathetically try to meet these needs and desires and help customers both overcome any problems or challenges they face and truly enjoy their hotel experience, a hotel can indeed serve the purposes of a home away from home (and an office away from office), and customers are likely to be both loyal and highly satisfied.[107]

Sharp has always realized that for employees to treat customers well, the Four Seasons needs to treat its employees well. Salaries are relatively high at the Four Seasons by industry standards (between the 75th and 90th percentiles); employees participate in a profit sharing plan; and the company contributes to their 401(k) plans. Four Seasons pays 78% of employees' health insurance premiums and provides free dental insurance.[108] All employees get free meals in the hotel cafeteria, have access to staff showers and a locker room, and receive an additional highly attractive benefit–once a new employee has worked for the Four Seasons for six months, he or she can stay for three nights free at any Four Seasons hotel or resort in the world. After a year of employment, this benefit increases to six free nights, and it continues to grow as tenure with the company increases. Employees like waitress Michelle De Rochemont love this benefit. As she indicates, "You're never treated like just an employee. You're a guest. . . . You come back from those trips on fire. You want to do so much for the guest."[109]

The Four Seasons also tends to promote from within.[110] For example, while recent college graduates may start out as assistant managers, those who do well and have high aspirations could potentially become general managers in less than 15 years. This helps to ensure that managers have empathy and respect for those in lower-level positions as well as the ingrained ethos of treating others (employees, subordinates, coworkers, and customers) as they would like to be treated. All in all, treating employees well leads to satisfied customers at the Four Seasons.[111]

Pay Structure

pay structure The arrangement of jobs into categories reflecting their relative importance to the organization and its goals, levels of skill required, and other characteristics.

After deciding on a pay level, managers have to establish a pay structure for the different jobs in the organization. A **pay structure** clusters jobs into categories reflecting their relative importance to the organization and its goals, levels of skill required, and other characteristics managers consider important. Pay ranges are established for each job category. Individual jobholders' pay within job categories is then determined by factors such as performance, seniority, and skill levels.

There are some interesting global differences in pay structures. Large corporations based in the United States tend to pay their CEOs and top managers higher salaries than do their European or Japanese counterparts. Also, the pay differential between employees at the bottom of the corporate hierarchy and those higher up is much greater in U.S. companies than in European or Japanese companies.[112]

Concerns have been raised over whether it is equitable or fair for CEOs of large companies in the United States to be making millions of dollars in years when their companies are restructuring and laying off a large portion of their workforces.[113] Additionally, the average CEO in the United States typically earns over 360 times what the average hourly worker earns.[114] Is a pay structure with such a huge pay differential ethical? Shareholders and the public are increasingly asking this very question and asking large corporations to rethink their pay structures.[115] Also troubling are the millions of dollars in severance packages that some CEOs receive when they leave their organizations. When many workers are struggling to find and keep jobs and make ends meet, more and more people are questioning whether it is ethical for some top managers to be making so much money.[116]

Benefits

Organizations are legally required to provide certain benefits to their employees, including workers' compensation, Social Security, and unemployment insurance. Workers' compensation helps employees financially if they become unable to work due to a work-related injury or illness. Social Security provides financial assistance to retirees and disabled former employees. Unemployment insurance provides financial assistance to workers who lose their jobs due to no fault of their own. The legal system in the United States views these three benefits as ethical requirements for organizations and thus mandates that they be provided.

Some organizations seek to promote employee wellness by providing on-site fitness centers.

Other benefits such as health insurance, dental insurance, vacation time, pension plans, life insurance, flexible working hours, company-provided day care, and employee assistance and wellness programs have traditionally been provided at the option of employers. The Health Care Reform Bill signed by President Barack Obama in March 2010 contains provisions whereby, starting in 2014, employers with 50 or more employees may face fines if they don't provide their employees with health insurance coverage.[117] Recall that an attractive benefit at Zappos in "A Manager's Challenge" is that Zappos pays for all health care costs. Benefits enabling workers to balance the demands of their jobs and of their lives away from the office or factory are of growing importance for many workers who have competing demands on their scarce time and energy.

In some organizations, top managers determine which benefits might best suit the employees and organization and offer the same benefit package to all

cafeteria-style benefit plan A plan from which employees can choose the benefits they want.

employees. Other organizations, realizing that employees' needs and desires might differ, offer **cafeteria-style benefit plans** that let employees themselves choose the benefits they want. Cafeteria-style benefit plans sometimes help managers deal with employees who feel unfairly treated because they are unable to take advantage of certain benefits available to other employees who, for example, have children. Some organizations have success with cafeteria-style benefit plans; others find them difficult to manage.

As health care costs escalate and overstretched employees find it hard to take time to exercise and take care of their health, more companies are providing benefits and incentives to promote employee wellness. AstraZeneca International offers its employees on-site counseling with a nutritionist and pays employees $125 for voluntarily taking a health risk assessment that covers wellness-related factors such as weight and nutrition.[118] Dole Food Company rewards employees with points toward gift certificates for participating in wellness activities provided on-site, such as yoga classes.[119]

For working parents, family-friendly benefits are especially attractive, as profiled in the following "Focus on Diversity" box.

Focus on Diversity

Family-Friendly Benefits at Guerra DeBerry Coody

Guerra DeBerry Coody is a small public relations and advertising firm based in San Antonio, Texas.[120] Founded in 1995, the firm has 61 employees and over $50 million in annual revenues. Recently Guerra DeBerry Coody was named a "Top Small Workplace" by *The Wall Street Journal* and Winning Workplaces, a nonprofit organization. Employees at Guerra DeBerry Coody nominated their employer for this award; and given the family-friendly benefits this firm provides, it is easy to understand why.[121]

Guerra DeBerry Coody offers family-friendly benefits such as child care.

Guerra DeBerry Coody provides on-site employee child care until employees' children enter kindergarten, with the firm covering 85% of the cost and employees paying $20 per day per child.[122] Employees can spend time with their children during the workday–employees often eat with their children, play with them, and settle them down for naps. The on-site child care center has a ratio of 1 child care worker for every 2 children enrolled, and around 11 children are currently enrolled. Employees with older children can bring their children to work after school if they wish. Senior account supervisor Patti Tanner sometimes has her two young teenage children come to the office after school. She indicates, "I don't even have any angst about having them here because I know it's completely and totally accepted."[123]

Guerra DeBerry Coody provides other benefits that help employees deal with the multiple demands and obligations in their lives. For example, employees can apply for interest-free loans from the company. Employees also have the options of working from home, telecommuting, and adopting flexible work schedules. Guerra DeBerry Coody provides free health insurance for all its employees, and those with dependents needing coverage can purchase it for around $125–$200 per month. The company also contributes to a 401(k) retirement plan for its employees.[124] As Frank Guerra, one of the founding partners of Guerra DeBerry Coody and its current CEO, indicated upon the firm being named a "Top Small Workplace," "With or without this recognition we are so proud that we have the ability to offer our employees a family-friendly work environment where everyone has a vested interest in each other and in the business, caring for one another like family."[125]

Same-sex domestic partner benefits are also being used to attract and retain valued employees. Gay and lesbian workers are reluctant to work for companies that do not provide the same kinds of benefits for their partners as those provided for partners of the opposite sex.[126]

LO12-6 Understand the role that labor relations play in the effective management of human resources.

Labor Relations

Labor relations are the activities managers engage in to ensure that they have effective working relationships with the labor unions that represent their employees' interests. Although the U.S. government has responded to the potential for unethical and unfair treatment of workers by creating and enforcing laws regulating employment (including the EEO laws listed in Table 12.1), some workers believe a union will ensure that their interests are fairly represented in their organizations.

labor relations The activities managers engage in to ensure that they have effective working relationships with the labor unions that represent their employees' interests.

Before we describe unions in more detail, let's take a look at some examples of important employment legislation. In 1938 the government passed the Fair Labor Standards Act, which prohibited child labor and provided for minimum wages, overtime pay, and maximum working hours to protect workers' rights. In 1963 the Equal Pay Act mandated that men and women performing equal work (work requiring the same levels of skill, responsibility, and effort performed in the same kind of working conditions) receive equal pay (see Table 12.1). In 1970 the Occupational Safety and Health Act mandated procedures for managers to follow to ensure workplace safety. These are just a few of the U.S. government's efforts to protect workers' rights. State legislatures also have been active in promoting safe, ethical, and fair workplaces.

Unions

Unions exist to represent workers' interests in organizations. Given that managers have more power than rank-and-file workers and that organizations have multiple stakeholders, there is always the potential that managers might take steps that benefit one set of stakeholders such as shareholders while hurting another such as employees. For example, managers may decide to speed up a production line to lower costs and increase production in the hopes of increasing returns to shareholders. Speeding up the line, however, could hurt employees forced to work at a rapid pace and may increase the risk of injuries. Also, employees receive no additional pay for the extra work they are performing. Unions would represent workers' interests in a scenario such as this one.

Congress acknowledged the role that unions could play in ensuring safe and fair workplaces when it passed the National Labor Relations Act of 1935. This act made it legal for workers to organize into unions to protect their rights and interests and declared certain unfair or unethical organizational practices to be illegal. The act also established the National Labor Relations Board (NLRB) to oversee union activity. Currently the NLRB conducts certification elections, which are held among the employees of an organization to determine whether they want a union to represent their interests. The NLRB also makes judgments concerning unfair labor practices and specifies practices that managers must refrain from.

Employees might vote to have a union represent them for any number of reasons.[127] They may think their wages and working conditions need improvement. They may believe managers are not treating them with respect. They may think their working hours are unfair or they need more job security or a safer work environment. Or they may be dissatisfied with management and find it difficult to communicate their concerns to their bosses. Regardless of the specific reason, one overriding reason is power: A united group inevitably wields more power than an individual, and this type of power may be especially helpful to employees in some organizations.

Although these would seem to be potent forces for unionization, some workers are reluctant to join unions. Sometimes this reluctance is due to the perception that union leaders are corrupt. Some workers may simply believe that belonging to a union might not do them much good or may actually cause more harm than good while costing them money in membership dues. Employees also might not want to be forced into doing something they do not want to, such as striking because the union thinks it is in their best interest. Moreover, although unions can be a positive force in organizations, sometimes they also can be a negative force, impairing organizational effectiveness. For example, when union leaders resist needed changes in an organization or are corrupt, organizational performance can suffer.

The percentage of U.S. workers represented by unions today is smaller than it was in the 1950s, an era when unions were especially strong.[128] In the 1950s, around 35% of U.S. workers were union members; in 2009, 12.3% of workers were members of unions.[129] The American Federation of Labor–Congress of Industrial Organizations (AFL-CIO) includes 57 voluntary member unions representing 11.5 million workers.[130] Overall, approximately 15.3 million workers in the United States belong to unions.[131] Union influence in manufacturing and heavy industries has been on the decline; approximately 11% of manufacturing workers are union members.[132] However, over 35% of government workers belong to unions.[133] Unions have made inroads in other segments of the workforce, particularly the low-wage end. Garbage collectors in New Jersey, poultry plant workers in North Carolina, and janitors in Baltimore are among the growing numbers of low-paid workers who are currently finding union membership attractive. North Carolina poultry workers voted in a union partly because they thought it was unfair that they had to buy their own gloves and hairnets used on the job and had to ask their supervisors' permission to go to the restroom.[134]

Union membership and leadership, traditionally dominated by white men, are becoming increasingly diverse. For example, Linda Chavez-Thompson was the executive vice president of the AFL-CIO from 1995 to 2007 and was the first woman and

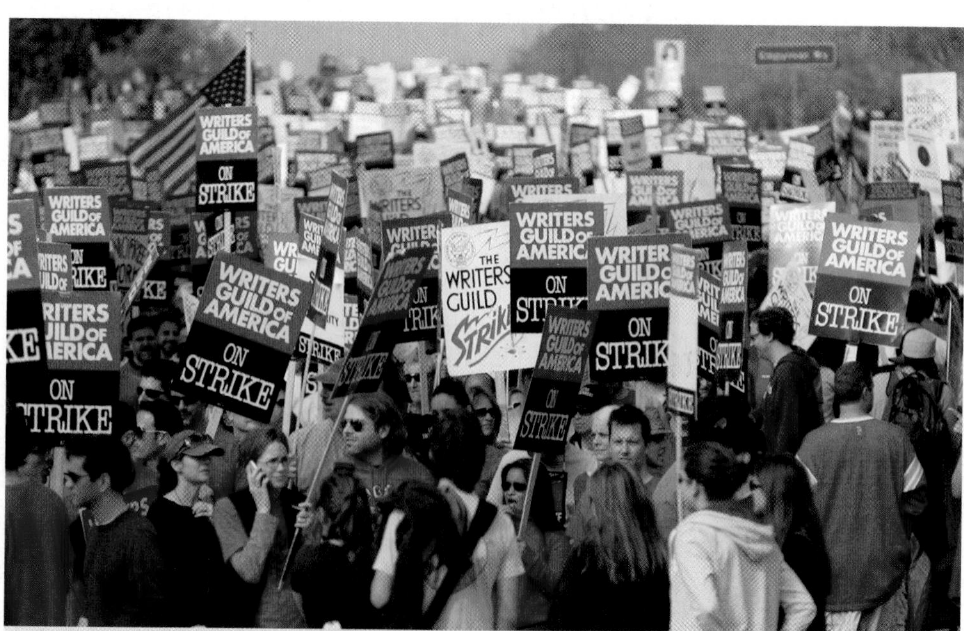

The Writer's Guild of America strike lasted for 100 days.

Hispanic to hold a top management position in the federation.[135] Labor officials in Washington, DC, also are becoming increasingly diverse. Elaine L. Chao, the 24th U.S. secretary of labor,[136] was the first Asian-American woman to hold an appointment in a U.S. president's cabinet.[137] In terms of union membership, women now make up over 45% of unionized workers.[138]

Collective Bargaining

collective bargaining Negotiations between labor unions and managers to resolve conflicts and disputes about issues such as working hours, wages, benefits, working conditions, and job security.

Collective bargaining is negotiation between labor unions and managers to resolve conflicts and disputes about important issues such as working hours, wages, working conditions, and job security. Before sitting down with management to negotiate, union members sometimes go on strike to drive home their concerns to managers. Once an agreement that union members support has been reached (sometimes with the help of a neutral third party called a *mediator*), union leaders and managers sign a contract spelling out the terms of the collective bargaining agreement. We discuss conflict and negotiation in depth in Chapter 17, but some brief observations are in order here because collective bargaining is an ongoing consideration in labor relations.

The signing of a contract, for example, does not finish the collective bargaining process. Disagreement and conflicts can arise over the interpretation of the contract. In such cases, a neutral third party called an *arbitrator* is usually called in to resolve the conflict. An important component of a collective bargaining agreement is a *grievance procedure* through which workers who believe they are not being fairly treated are allowed to voice their concerns and have their interests represented by the union. Workers who think they were unjustly fired in violation of a union contract, for example, may file a grievance, have the union represent them, and get their jobs back if an arbitrator agrees with them. Union members sometimes go on strike when managers make decisions that the members think will hurt them and are not in their best interests.

Summary and Review

LO12-1 **STRATEGIC HUMAN RESOURCE MANAGEMENT** Human resource management (HRM) includes all the activities managers engage in to ensure that their organizations can attract, retain, and effectively use human resources. Strategic HRM is the process by which managers design the components of a human resource management system to be consistent with each other, with other elements of organizational architecture, and with the organization's strategies and goals.

LO12-2 **RECRUITMENT AND SELECTION** Before recruiting and selecting employees, managers must engage in human resource planning and job analysis. Human resource planning includes all the activities managers engage in to forecast their current and future needs for human resources. Job analysis is the process of identifying (1) the tasks, duties, and responsibilities that make up a job and (2) the knowledge, skills, and abilities needed to perform the job. Recruitment includes all the activities managers engage in to develop a pool of qualified applicants for open positions. Selection is the process by which managers determine the relative qualifications of job applicants and their potential for performing well in a particular job.

LO12-3 **TRAINING AND DEVELOPMENT** Training focuses on teaching organizational members how to perform effectively in their current jobs. Development focuses on broadening organizational members' knowledge and skills so they are prepared to take on new responsibilities and challenges.

LO12-4 **PERFORMANCE APPRAISAL AND FEEDBACK** Performance appraisal is the evaluation of employees' job performance and contributions to the organization. Performance feedback is the process through which managers share performance appraisal information with their subordinates, give them an opportunity to reflect on their own performance, and develop with them plans for the future. Performance appraisal gives managers useful information for decision making. Performance feedback can encourage high levels of motivation and performance.

LO12-5 **PAY AND BENEFITS** Pay level is the relative position of an organization's pay incentives in comparison with those of other organizations in the same industry employing similar workers. A pay structure clusters jobs into categories according to their relative importance to the organization and its goals, the levels of skill required, and other characteristics. Pay ranges are then established for each job category. Organizations are legally required to provide certain benefits to their employees; other benefits are provided at the discretion of employers.

LO12-6 **LABOR RELATIONS** Labor relations include all the activities managers engage in to ensure that they have effective working relationships with the labor unions that represent their employees' interests. The National Labor Relations Board oversees union activity. Collective bargaining is the process through which labor unions and managers resolve conflicts and disputes and negotiate agreements.

Management in Action

Topics for Discussion and Action

Discussion

1. Discuss why it is important for human resource management systems to be in sync with an organization's strategy and goals and with each other. [LO12-1]
2. Discuss why training and development are ongoing activities for all organizations. [LO12-3]
3. Describe the type of development activities you think middle managers are most in need of. [LO12-3]
4. Evaluate the pros and cons of 360-degree performance appraisals and feedback. Would you like your performance to be appraised in this manner? Why or why not? [LO12-4]
5. Discuss why two restaurants in the same community might have different pay levels. [LO12-5]
6. Explain why union membership is becoming more diverse. [LO12-6]

Action

7. Interview a manager in a local organization to determine how that organization recruits and selects employees. [LO12-2]

Building Management Skills

Analyzing Human Resource Systems [LO12-1, 12-2, 12-3, 12-4, 12-5]

Think about your current job or a job you have had in the past. If you have never had a job, interview a friend or family member who is currently working. Answer the following questions about the job you have chosen:

1. How are people recruited and selected for this job? Are the recruitment and selection procedures the organization uses effective or ineffective? Why?
2. What training and development do people who hold this job receive? Are the training and development appropriate? Why or why not?
3. How is performance of this job appraised? Does performance feedback contribute to motivation and high performance on this job?
4. What levels of pay and benefits are provided on this job? Are these levels appropriate? Why or why not?

Managing Ethically [LO12-4, 12-5]

Some managers do not want to become overly friendly with their subordinates because they are afraid that if they do so, their objectivity when conducting performance appraisals and making decisions about pay raises and promotions will be impaired. Some subordinates resent it when they see one or more of their coworkers being very friendly with the boss; they are concerned about the potential for favoritism. Their reasoning runs something like this: If two subordinates are equally qualified for a promotion and one is a good friend of the boss and the other is a mere acquaintance, who is more likely to receive the promotion?

Questions

1. Either individually or in a group, think about the ethical implications of managers' becoming friendly with their subordinates.
2. Do you think managers should feel free to socialize and become good friends with their subordinates outside the workplace if they so desire? Why or why not?

Small Group Breakout Exercise [LO12-1, 12-2, 12-3, 12-4, 12-5]

Building a Human Resource Management System

Form groups of three or four people, and appoint one group member as the spokesperson who will communicate your findings to the class when called on by the instructor. Then discuss the following scenario:

You and your three partners are engineers who minored in business at college and have decided to start a consulting business. Your goal is to provide manufacturing process engineering and other engineering services to large and small organizations. You forecast that there will be an increased use of outsourcing for these activities. You discussed with managers in several large organizations the services you plan to offer, and they expressed considerable interest. You have secured funding to start your business and now are building the HRM system. Your human resource planning suggests that you need to hire between five and eight experienced engineers with good communication skills, two clerical/secretarial workers, and two MBAs who between them have financial, accounting, and human resource skills. You are striving to develop your human resources in a way that will enable your new business to prosper.

1. Describe the steps you will take to recruit and select (a) the engineers, (b) the clerical/secretarial workers, and (c) the MBAs.
2. Describe the training and development the engineers, the clerical/secretarial workers, and the MBAs will receive.
3. Describe how you will appraise the performance of each group of employees and how you will provide feedback.
4. Describe the pay level and pay structure of your consulting firm.

Exploring the World Wide Web [LO12-2]

Go to www.net-temps.com, a Web site geared toward temporary employment. Imagine that you have to take a year off from college and are seeking a one-year position. Guided by your own interests, use this Web site to learn about your options and possible employment opportunities.

1. What are the potential advantages of online job searching and recruiting? What are the potential disadvantages?
2. Would you ever rely on a Web site like this to help you find a position? Why or why not?

Be the Manager [LO12-4]

You are Walter Michaels and have just received some disturbing feedback. You are the director of human resources for Maxi Vision Inc., a medium-size window and glass door manufacturer. You recently initiated a 360-degree performance appraisal system for all middle and upper managers at Maxi Vision, including yourself but excluding the most senior executives and the top management team.

You were eagerly awaiting the feedback you would receive from the managers who report to you; you had recently implemented several important initiatives that affected them and their subordinates, including a complete overhaul of the organization's performance appraisal system. While the managers who report to you were evaluated based on 360-degree appraisals, their subordinates were evaluated using a 20-question BARS scale you recently created that focuses on behaviors. Conducted annually, appraisals are an important input into pay raise and bonus decisions.

You were so convinced that the new performance appraisal procedures were highly effective that you hoped your own subordinates would mention them in their feedback to you. And boy did they! You were amazed to learn that the managers *and* their subordinates thought the new BARS scales were unfair, inappropriate, and a waste of time. In fact, the managers' feedback to you was that their own performance was suffering, based on the 360-degree appraisals they received, because their subordinates hated the new appraisal system and partially blamed their bosses, who were part of management. Some managers even admitted giving all their subordinates approximately the same scores on the scales so their pay raises and bonuses would not be affected by their performance appraisals.

You couldn't believe your eyes when you read these comments. You spent so much time developing what you thought was the ideal rating scale for this group of employees. Evidently, for some unknown reason, they wouldn't give it a chance. Your own supervisor is aware of these complaints and said that it was a top priority for you to fix "this mess" (with the implication that you were responsible for creating it). What are you going to do?

Case in the News [LO12-1, 12-2, 12-3, 12-5]

The Best Places to Launch a Career

Miranda Azzam's title at Aflac's Columbus (Georgia) headquarters is college recruiter, but that doesn't begin to describe what she does for the $16.6 billion insurer. Like all recruiters, she spends a lot of time talking to students and running career fairs. But she also manages a new Web ad campaign and tracks everything from how long it takes to fill each opening to what it costs to bring new employees on board. In fact, she heads the insurance company's entire campus recruiting effort. And, oh yes—she just turned 26.

Oddly enough, Azzam has the recession to thank for her success. She landed a job at Aflac after graduating from the business program at the University of Texas at Tyler in 2006, long before the economy began unraveling. But she assumed her new supervisory responsibilities in March, when her boss moved to another position within Aflac and the company chose not to hire a replacement. Without the downturn, Azzam might have waited much longer for her big break. "We're operating very lean," says Azzam. "When we had a supervisor over our team, she made the final decisions. Learning to lead people and delegate is something I've never been able to do until now."

With the economy shedding 6.7 million jobs since the recession began in December 2007 and college graduates facing the most difficult labor market in many years, it's easy to conclude that for many young people this is the worst of times. But for those like Azzam who are already employed and for any young graduate who manages to beat the odds and follow her into the labor force this year, it could well be the best of times. With companies everywhere trimming payrolls to cut costs, many new grads will likely find themselves filling the shoes of the recently departed and taking on bigger responsibilities faster than they ever imagined. Most will not get big raises or fancy new titles as a result. But when the recovery comes, those same grads will be well positioned for promotions, as boomer retirements create openings in middle management. It's a recession dividend that can be found at many of the employers in *BusinessWeek*'s fourth annual Best Places to Launch a Career ranking. "There are more opportunities than there were a few years ago," says Craig A. Johnson, president of Philip Morris USA/Altria. "Many companies have streamlined their operations, so there's a greater chance for people to stand out."

And standing out may be the only chance they have to get ahead. The time-honored method for reaching the second rung on the career ladder—switching employers—will be difficult. Going back to school piles debt on top of debt and offers no guarantees. "The voluntary mobility they expected is not there now, and it's not going to happen for the next few years," says Edward E. Lawler III, director of the Center for Effective Organizations at the University of Southern California's Marshall School of Business. "[Work] is about battling and hunkering down and trying to hang on."

All well and good for the gainfully employed, but getting a job in the first place is no slam dunk. Many companies have been cutting back on entry-level hiring—one survey of 2009 college grads found that only 1 out of 5 who applied for a job succeeded in landing one—and the employers in our ranking are no different. Entry-level hiring in the first half of the year was down across the board, with at least 50 of the 69 employers who took part in our survey reporting an average decrease of more than 20%. At many companies, including AT&T, Macy's, and Microsoft, the employment picture was far worse, with entry-level hiring down well more than 50%.

Big Shakeup

To compile this ranking, *BusinessWeek* polled 60 college career services directors across the country; collected data from a survey of 60,000 U.S. undergrads by Universum USA, a Philadelphia research company; and required employers to submit statistics on everything from pay and benefits to training programs and retention. The number of ranked employers is down sharply this year, owing to our decision to raise the bar on eligibility. And the tougher competition—combined with a handful of new employers and shifts in sentiment among students and career services directors—resulted in a shakeup in the standings. Some companies, including No. 11 Accenture and No. 19 Prudential, moved up more than 35 spots, while No. 34 Marriott and No. 48 Lockheed Martin were down 28 and 40 spots, respectively.

Even the top 10 underwent big changes this year. Marriott and Lockheed were out, as was Google, which declined to participate. But three new employers entered the winner's circle. The State Department and Teach For America, which places college grads in troubled school districts, are both in the midst of ramped-up recruiting campaigns, while J.P. Morgan, a unit of JPMorgan Chase, reaped a survivor's benefit: It's one of the few big investment banks left standing.

For the Big Four accounting firms, which have dominated the top of the ranking since its inception in 2006, this was a business-as-usual year. The group once again took all four top spots, though Deloitte unseated rival Ernst & Young at No. 1. With rich benefits, extensive training programs, and a combined recruiting effort that makes more than 10,000 hires even in a tough year, the Big Four are hard to beat, and Deloitte is harder than most. With substantially higher pay—18% of Deloitte's entry-level hires this year will earn north of \$65,000—plus the industry's biggest signing bonuses and most generous time-off policy, it's no wonder Deloitte is a favorite of students and career services directors. It doesn't hurt that Deloitte's entry-level hiring took the smallest hit this year, down just 1.1% in the first half compared with double-digit drops for No. 2 Ernst & Young and No. 4 KPMG.

Deloitte, like most of the companies in the ranking, is not immune to the effects of the downturn—it reduced its U.S. workforce about 2% last year, citing "the overall slowdown in the U.S. and global economies." To make do with less, Deloitte is tapping its brightest young employees for cost-cutting ideas—then tossing them the keys. "When people come in with an innovative idea that's cost-effective, they may get a chance to implement it," says Diane Borhani, Deloitte's national campus recruiting leader.

And not just at Deloitte. Just ask Justin Welke, a 26-year-old who started as an operations management trainee at Nestlé's Bloomington (Illinois) factory, where he put a number of cost-cutting initiatives of his own invention in place. "We're having a war on waste," says Welke, who joined the company in 2007 after graduating from Michigan State University with a degree in packaging. Welke sensed an opportunity—and found that minor tweaks to packaging and design can make a big difference. One of his ideas, restacking cases to make room for 10 more on a single pallet, is saving the company an estimated \$60,000 a year. He also supervised a team of 20 in the factory.

Welke's performance got him noticed—and a new assignment at the Springville (Utah) plant. He now manages 44 hourly workers, some of whom are more than twice his age, something he much prefers to a headquarters job. "I thought, 'Wow, I have a chance to get front-line leadership experience.' That's something you wouldn't get in a corporate role," says Welke. "The best learning experience is when they just throw you in there."

Welke, who wakes up at 3 a.m. to get to work an hour before the start of his 5:15 a.m. shift—and often stays late—is a good example of what it takes for young people unaccustomed to drudgery to get ahead these days: hard work, long hours, and a willingness to make sacrifices. At Deloitte, Cedric Nabe, 26, travels extensively to work with his IT consulting clients. It's a job he loves, even though it makes training for this Olympics hopeful a challenge. In a few weeks he'll be on assignment in France, where he'll need to work in two hours of training each day if he's going to have a shot at the 100-meter dash. "I don't want to give up on track," Nabe says. "But I also want to be a great performer at work."

For Generation Y, all this represents a dilemma. As a generation, it never suffered from lack of ambition. But to get the responsibilities they covet, millennials will need a new outlook on work. Often criticized for a sense of entitlement, members of this cohort will have to knuckle down and pay their dues. And though often seen as needing direction, they'll have to make do without hand-holding. Plus, the search for work–life balance that Gen Y considers a priority will be more elusive than ever.

The new rules of work will, for many, be a rude awakening. "I think some are kind of frustrated and angry about having to take on more work," says Jennifer Kushell, a consultant who advises companies on managing Gen Y. "The ones who are clinging to 'business as usual' as the world crumbles around them are in trouble."

Unfortunately, that seems to be exactly what many are doing. A recent employee survey by research firm Development Dimensions International found that more than half the 223 Gen Yers in the sample felt their careers were in limbo, but fully 93% of those said they were unlikely to push for more responsibility. Forty-four percent said they would look for another job when the economy improved, 30% said they'd go back to school, and 11% said they would "do what I'm told, nothing more, nothing less"—not a recipe for success. "It's easy to excel in a good economy," says Deloitte's Borhani. "Those really willing to do what it takes and say, 'this too shall pass,' are the ones people will remember."

Indeed, Gen Y's best and brightest are counting on their bosses having good memories. When Pathik Soni, 24, joined drug and medical device maker Abbott Laboratories' training program in January 2008, the financial crisis was in full swing. Soni, a University of Wisconsin electrical engineering grad, expected difficult challenges ahead and less job security, but he saw opportunity, too. During his first rotation he suggested changes to one Abbott building to make it more environmentally friendly, including installing more energy-efficient lighting. If adopted companywide, such changes could save millions—cost reductions he hopes will help him land his choice of jobs when his training ends in December. "I feel pretty secure," Soni says.

While many members of Gen Y who are being propelled up today's corporate ladder have the recession to thank, Soni could likely benefit from a different trend. With more than half of Abbott's senior executives set to retire in the next five years, the company's senior vice president for human resources, Stephen R. Fussell, says a talent vacuum at the top will create opportunities in middle management for the most qualified young workers—a situation likely to repeat itself elsewhere. As a result, says Fussell, Abbott's top-performing Gen Y employees can expect to be promoted 50% faster than boomers and 20% faster than Gen Xers early in their careers. Says Fussell, "They're going to reach bigger jobs earlier in their career, and they're going to get there in a less hierarchical manner."

That message hasn't been lost on Amber Brown. Since starting at Walt Disney's Imagineering division in 2007 (after earning three master's degrees and starting on a PhD), the 31-year-old research scientist has been analyzing visitor satisfaction at the company's theme parks—everything from the architecture to the ability of guests to take memorable pictures. But that's hardly all she does. At last count, the Glendale (California)-based Brown was involved in seven different projects, several of which she pitched herself. One of them involves the Epcot Test Track ride that hurtles people down bumpy roads and hairpin turns. Her analysis of a feature that photographs passengers during the ride involves overseeing six teams throughout the organization. By immersing herself in projects outside her own division, she hopes to guarantee her survival and advance her career. "In a company this large," she says, "you never know what's going to spring up a year down the line."

As the recovery gains a foothold, young employees will be able to begin breathing more easily. But for those who are willing to put in the extra effort, rapid advancement may come sooner than they think. And the economic clouds may not be so dark after all.

Questions for Discussion

1. What human resource challenges did the recession that started in December 2007 present managers with?
2. How did some managers respond to these challenges?
3. What are likely to be some of the long-term implications of these challenges?
4. How can managers effectively respond to these long-term implications?

Source: "The Best Places to Launch a Career," *BusinessWeek,* September 14, 2009, 32–39. Reprinted from September 14, 2009 issue of *Bloomberg Businessweek* by special permission,

CHAPTER 13

Motivation and Performance

Learning Objectives

After studying this chapter, you should be able to:

LO13-1 Explain what motivation is and why managers need to be concerned about it.

LO13-2 Describe from the perspectives of expectancy theory and equity theory what managers should do to have a highly motivated workforce.

LO13-3 Explain how goals and needs motivate people and what kinds of goals are especially likely to result in high performance.

LO13-4 Identify the motivation lessons that managers can learn from operant conditioning theory and social learning theory.

LO13-5 Explain why and how managers can use pay as a major motivation tool.

A MANAGER'S CHALLENGE

Keeping Employees Highly Motivated at SAS

How can managers create and sustain high levels of employee motivation? SAS is in the enviable position of being listed on *Fortune* magazine's annual ranking of the "100 Best Companies to Work For" for 13 years in a row; in 2010 SAS was ranked first.[1] SAS is the world's largest privately owned software company, with over 11,000 employees worldwide and approximately $2.3 billion in revenues.[2] In fact, revenues have increased at SAS every year since the company was founded in 1976. SAS software is used at over 45,000 locations in more than 100 countries; over 90 of the top 100 companies on the *Fortune* Global 500 list use SAS software. Headquartered in Cary, North Carolina, SAS also has offices in Europe, the Middle East, Africa, Asia Pacific, Latin America, and Canada.[3]

Every indicator suggests that SAS employees are highly motivated and perform well while also working 35-hour weeks.[4] Since its founding, SAS has strived to ensure that employees enjoy and are motivated by the work they perform. Managers approach motivation from the perspective that all employees should be interested and involved in the work they are performing and have the sense that they are making meaningful contributions to SAS and its customers. While some software companies that seek to develop new products buy companies that are already making these products, SAS develops its new products internally, and employees can engage in interesting work at the forefront of technology.[5] Creativity is encouraged at SAS, and employees experience the excitement of developing a new product and seeing it succeed.[6] Overall, employees exert high levels of effort and persist in the face of setbacks to develop and provide the outstanding software solutions for businesses that SAS is renowned for.

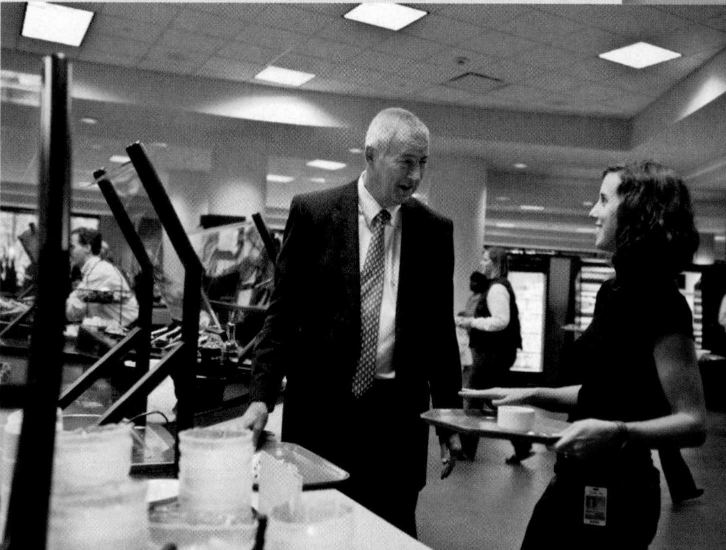

Can you joke around with the president while grabbing the lunch of your choice at the subsidized company cafeteria before taking a short walk to say hi to your kids, playing happily in the company day care center? James Goodnight (at left) thinks this is the way work should be.

Over 20% of annual revenues are committed to research and development at SAS, consistent with its long-term focus.[7] This long-term focus also helps ensure that SAS can weather economic downturns. For example, as a result of the recession that started in 2007, many technology companies laid off employees in 2009—which was not the case at SAS. As SAS cofounder and CEO James Goodnight puts it, "I've got a two-year pipeline of projects in R&D. . . . Why would I lay anyone off?"[8]

Recognizing that sometimes employees might lose interest in the type of work they are doing or just need a change of pace, SAS employees can change jobs to prevent becoming bored with their work. SAS gives employees any additional training they might need when they change jobs. By encouraging these lateral moves, managers help sustain high levels of motivation at SAS.[9] Although annual turnover rates in the software industry are around 22%, SAS's turnover rate in 2009 was 2%, and the average tenure at SAS is 10 years.[10]

Managers at SAS fairly and equitably reward employees for a job well done. Moreover, Goodnight and other managers recognize that SAS's employees are its biggest asset and go to great lengths to satisfy their needs and create a work environment that will be conducive to creativity, high motivation, and well-being for employees and their families. At headquarters in North Carolina, SAS subsidizes two employee child care centers, a summer camp, three cafeterias, a 66,000-square-foot fitness and recreation center including an Olympic-size pool, and all kinds of services ranging from dry cleaning and car detailing to massages and a book exchange. Google (as SAS customers) used SAS as a prototype to develop its own suite of employee benefits and perks.[11]

An on-campus health care center with an annual budget of $4.5 million and staff of 56 gives SAS employees and their families free basic care clinic services.[12] The center is open 10 hours most days and has four physicians, 10 nurse practitioners, physical therapists, lab technicians, and a psychologist on hand to attend to health needs and problems. In 2009 about 90% of headquarters employees and their families had 40,000 appointments at the center. SAS estimates that the center saves the company about $5 million per year because employees are not losing valuable time traveling to doctors' offices and waiting to see them. Moreover, employees are more likely to get care when they need it, and SAS can provide the care they need at lower costs.[13]

Wellness and work–life centers offer a variety of programs to help employees achieve a sense of balance in their lives and days. Programs range from Pilates, Zumba, and partner yoga to weight management, salsa aerobics, cooking classes, harmonic sound healing, and movies that employees can watch while floating in the pool. Employees with children are encouraged to have lunch with their kids in the subsidized cafeterias, which are complete with high chairs.[14]

Employees have their own offices, and the headquarters' work environment is rich in pleasant vistas, ranging from artwork on the walls to views of the rolling hills of Cary, North Carolina. SAS has two artists on its staff with the thinking being that exposure to beautiful artwork and surroundings can spur creativity.[15] Employees and their families are encouraged to use the 200 acres that surround company headquarters for family walks and picnics.[16]

SAS trusts its employees to do what is right for the company. Thus many employees determine their own work schedules, and there are unlimited sick days.[17] With so many benefits and facilities, employees do not have to interrupt their work days or leave the campus for a doctor's appointment or to run an errand. And SAS realizes that to sustain high levels of motivation over time, employees need balanced lives—hence the 35-hour workweek. Of course, because SAS is a truly global company, sometimes employees on global teams with a tight new product development schedule need to work long hours, and some employees check work e-mail at home. Nonetheless, employees at SAS are not expected to work excessive hours as is common at some other companies.[18]

Since the company was founded, CEO James Goodnight has been committed to motivating employees to develop creative and high-quality products that meet customers' needs. Today hundreds of companies use SAS products for a wide variety of purposes including risk management, monitoring and measuring performance, managing relations with suppliers and customers, and detecting fraud.[19] SAS also donates educational software to schools and teachers through SAS in School.[20] Clearly, motivating employees and helping to satisfy their needs is a win–win situation for SAS. And trusting employees and treating them well motivates them to do what is best for SAS. As Bev Brown, an SAS employee in external communications, puts it, "Some may think that because SAS is family-friendly and has great benefits that we don't work hard. . . . But people do work hard here, because they're motivated to take care of a company that takes care of them."[21]

Overview

Even with the best strategy in place and an appropriate organizational architecture, an organization will be effective only if its members are motivated to perform at a high level. James Goodnight of SAS in "A Manager's Challenge" clearly realizes this. One reason why leading is such an important managerial activity is that it entails ensuring that each member of an organization is motivated to perform highly and help the organization achieve its goals. When managers are effective, the outcome of the leading process is a highly motivated workforce. A key challenge for managers of organizations both large and small is to encourage employees to perform at a high level.

In this chapter we describe what motivation is, where it comes from, and why managers need to promote high levels of it for an organization to be effective and achieve its goals. We examine important theories of motivation: expectancy theory, need theories, equity theory, goal-setting theory, and learning theories. Each gives managers important insights about how to motivate organizational members. The theories are complementary in that each focuses on a different aspect of motivation. Considering all the theories together helps managers gain a rich understanding of the many issues and problems involved in encouraging high levels of motivation throughout an organization. Last, we consider the use of pay as a motivation tool. By the end of this chapter you will understand what it takes to have a highly motivated workforce.

The Nature of Motivation

LO13-1 Explain what motivation is and why managers need to be concerned about it.

Motivation may be defined as psychological forces that determine the direction of a person's behavior in an organization, a person's level of effort, and a person's level of persistence in the face of obstacles.[22] The *direction of a person's behavior* refers to the many possible behaviors a person could engage in. For example, employees at SAS are encouraged to be creative and develop new software that will meet customers' future needs. *Effort* refers to how hard people work. Employees at SAS exert high levels of effort to provide superior software solutions for business customers. *Persistence* refers to whether, when faced with roadblocks and obstacles, people keep trying or give up. Setbacks and obstacles are part of research and development work; at SAS, employees persist through these difficulties to develop new sophisticated software.

motivation Psychological forces that determine the direction of a person's behavior in an organization, a person's level of effort, and a person's level of persistence.

Motivation is central to management because it explains *why* people behave the way they do in organizations[23]–why employees at SAS continue to develop new software that is used by SAS customers around the world. Motivation also explains why a waiter is polite or rude and why a kindergarten teacher really tries to get children to enjoy learning or just goes through the motions. It explains why some managers truly put their organizations' best interests first whereas others are more concerned with maximizing their salaries and why–more generally–some workers put forth twice as much effort as others.

intrinsically motivated behavior Behavior that is performed for its own sake.

Motivation can come from *intrinsic* or *extrinsic* sources. **Intrinsically motivated behavior** is behavior that is performed for its own sake; the source of motivation is actually performing the behavior, and motivation comes from doing the work itself. Many managers are intrinsically motivated; they derive a sense of accomplishment and achievement from helping the organization achieve its goals and gain competitive advantages. Jobs that are interesting and challenging or high on the five characteristics described by the job characteristics model (see Chapter 10) are more likely to lead to intrinsic motivation than are jobs that are boring or do not use a person's skills and abilities. An elementary school teacher who really enjoys teaching children, a computer programmer who loves solving programming problems, and a commercial photographer who relishes taking creative photographs are all intrinsically motivated. For these individuals, motivation comes from performing their jobs–teaching children, finding bugs in computer programs, and taking pictures.

extrinsically motivated behavior Behavior that is performed to acquire material or social rewards or to avoid punishment.

Extrinsically motivated behavior is behavior that is performed to acquire material or social rewards or to avoid punishment; the source of motivation is the consequences of the behavior, not the behavior itself. A car salesperson who is motivated by receiving a commission on all cars sold, a lawyer who is motivated by the high salary and status that go along with the job, and a factory worker who is motivated by the opportunity to earn a secure income are all extrinsically motivated. Their motivation comes from the consequences they receive as a result of their work behaviors.

Child care often attracts those with a highly intrinsic motivation, such as the preschool worker above.

People can be intrinsically motivated, extrinsically motivated, or both intrinsically and extrinsically motivated.[24] A top manager who derives a sense of accomplishment and achievement from managing a large corporation and strives to reach year-end targets to obtain a hefty bonus is both intrinsically and extrinsically motivated. Similarly, a nurse who enjoys helping and taking care of patients and is motivated by having a secure job with good benefits is both intrinsically and extrinsically motivated. At SAS, employees are both extrinsically motivated, because of equitable pay and outstanding benefits, and intrinsically motivated, because of the opportunity to do interesting work. Whether workers are intrinsically motivated, extrinsically motivated, or both depends on a wide variety of factors: (1) workers' own personal characteristics (such as their personalities, abilities, values, attitudes, and needs), (2) the nature of their jobs (such as whether they have been enriched or where they are on the five core characteristics of the job characteristics model), and (3) the nature of the organization (such as its structure, its culture, its control systems, its human resource management system, and the ways in which rewards such as pay are distributed to employees).

prosocially motivated behavior Behavior that is performed to benefit or help others.

In addition to being intrinsically or extrinsically motivated, some people are prosocially motivated by their work.[25] **Prosocially motivated behavior** is behavior that is performed to benefit or help others.[26] Behavior can be prosocially motivated in addition to being extrinsically and/or intrinsically motivated. An elementary school teacher who not only enjoys the process of teaching young children (has high intrinsic motivation) but also has a strong desire to give children the best learning experience possible and help those with learning disabilities overcome their challenges, and who keeps up with the latest research on child development and teaching methods in an effort to continually improve the effectiveness of his teaching, has high prosocial motivation in addition to high intrinsic motivation. A surgeon who specializes in organ transplants and enjoys the challenge of performing complex operations, has a strong desire to help her patients regain their health and extend their lives through successful organ transplants, and also is motivated by the relatively high income she earns has high intrinsic, prosocial, and extrinsic motivation. Recent preliminary research suggests that when workers have high prosocial motivation, also having high intrinsic motivation can be especially beneficial for job performance.[27]

outcome Anything a person gets from a job or organization.

Regardless of whether people are intrinsically, extrinsically, or prosocially motivated, they join and are motivated to work in organizations to obtain certain outcomes. An **outcome** is anything a person gets from a job or organization. Some outcomes, such as autonomy, responsibility, a feeling of accomplishment, and the pleasure of doing interesting or enjoyable work, result in intrinsically motivated behavior. Outcomes such as improving the lives or well-being of other people and doing good by helping others result in prosocially motivated behavior. Other outcomes, such as pay, job security, benefits, and vacation time, result in extrinsically motivated behavior.

input Anything a person contributes to his or her job or organization.

Organizations hire people to obtain important inputs. An **input** is anything a person contributes to the job or organization, such as time, effort, education, experience, skills, knowledge, and actual work behaviors. Inputs such as these are necessary for an organization to achieve its goals. Managers strive to motivate members of an organization to contribute inputs–through their behavior, effort, and persistence–that help the organization achieve its goals. How do managers do this? They ensure that members of an organization obtain the outcomes they desire when they make valuable contributions to the organization. Managers use outcomes to motivate people to contribute their inputs to the organization. Giving people outcomes when they contribute inputs and perform well aligns the interests of employees with the goals of the organization as a whole because when employees do what is good for the organization, they personally benefit.

This alignment between employees and organizational goals as a whole can be described by the motivation equation depicted in Figure 13.1. Managers seek to ensure that people are motivated to contribute important inputs to the organization, that these inputs are put to good use or focused in the direction of high performance, and that high performance results in workers' obtaining the outcomes they desire.

Each of the theories of motivation discussed in this chapter focuses on one or more aspects of this equation. Each theory focuses on a different set of issues that managers need to address to have a highly motivated workforce. Together, the theories provide a comprehensive set of guidelines for managers to follow to promote high levels of employee motivation. Effective managers, such as James Goodnight in "A Manager's Challenge," tend to follow many of these guidelines, whereas ineffective managers often fail to follow them and seem to have trouble motivating organizational members.

Figure 13.1
The Motivation Equation

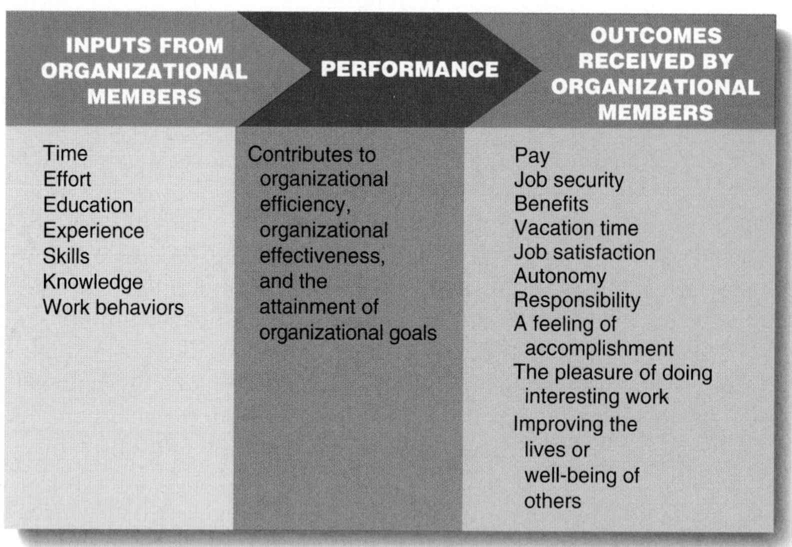

Expectancy Theory

LO13-2 Describe from the perspectives of expectancy theory and equity theory what managers should do to have a highly motivated workforce.

Expectancy theory, formulated by Victor H. Vroom in the 1960s, posits that motivation is high when workers believe that high levels of effort lead to high performance and high performance leads to the attainment of desired outcomes. Expectancy theory is one of the most popular theories of work motivation because it focuses on all three parts of the motivation equation: inputs, performance, and outcomes. Expectancy theory identifies three major factors that determine a person's motivation: *expectancy, instrumentality,* and *valence* (see Figure 13.2).[28]

expectancy theory The theory that motivation will be high when workers believe that high levels of effort lead to high performance and high performance leads to the attainment of desired outcomes.

Figure 13.2
Expectancy, Instrumentality, and Valence

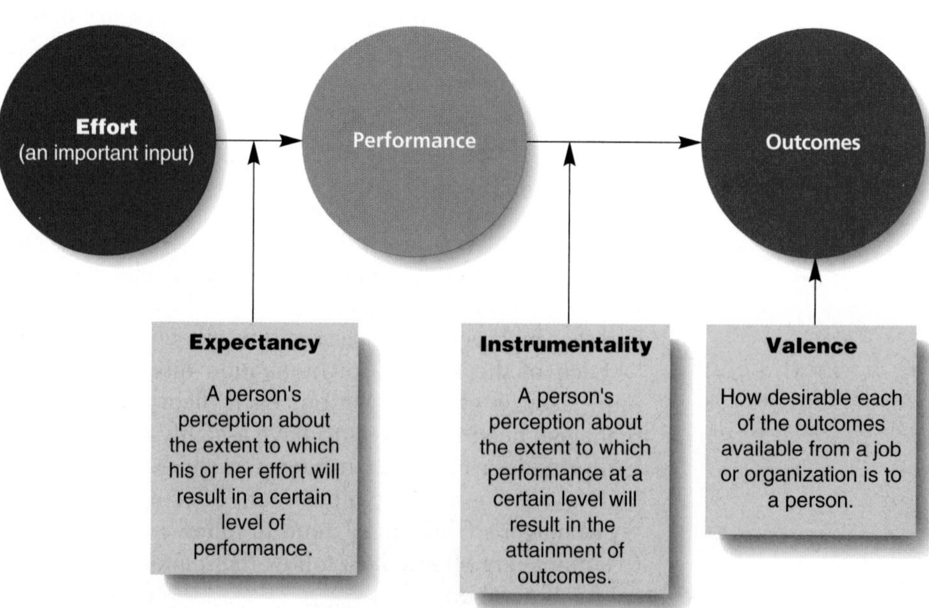

Expectancy

expectancy In expectancy theory, a perception about the extent to which effort results in a certain level of performance.

Expectancy is a person's perception about the extent to which effort (an input) results in a certain level of performance. A person's level of expectancy determines whether he or she believes that a high level of effort results in a high level of performance. People are motivated to put forth a lot of effort on their jobs only if they think that their effort will pay off in high performance–that is, if they have high expectancy. Think about how motivated you would be to study for a test if you thought that no matter how hard you tried, you would get a D. Think about how motivated a marketing manager would be who thought that no matter how hard he or she worked, there was no way to increase sales of an unpopular product. In these cases, expectancy is low, so overall motivation is also low.

Members of an organization are motivated to put forth a high level of effort only if they think that doing so leads to high performance.[29] In other words, in order for people's motivation to be high, expectancy must be high. Thus, in attempting to influence motivation, managers need to make sure their subordinates believe that if they do try hard, they can actually succeed. One way managers can boost expectancies is through expressing confidence in their subordinates' capabilities. Managers at the Container Store, for example, express high levels of confidence in their subordinates. As Container Store cofounder Garrett Boone put it, "Everybody we hire, we hire as a leader. Anybody in our store can take an action that you might think of typically being a manager's action."[30]

If you know how it works, you can sell it more easily to the person who needs it. Best Buy puts this common sense into practice with its extensive salesperson training.

In addition to expressing confidence in subordinates, other ways for managers to boost subordinates' expectancy levels and motivation is by providing training so people have the expertise needed for high performance and increasing their levels of autonomy and responsibility as they gain experience so they have the freedom to do what it takes to perform at a high level. For example, the Best Buy chain of over 629 stores selling electronics, computers, music and movies, and gadgets of all sorts boosts salespeople's expectancies by giving them extensive training in on-site meetings and online. Electronic learning terminals in each department not only help salespeople learn how different systems work and can be sold as an integrated package but also enable them to keep up to date with the latest advances in technology and products. Salespeople also receive extensive training in how to determine customers' needs.[31] At SAS in "A Manager's Challenge," employees who change jobs receive any additional training they might need to be effective in their new positions, which boosts their expectancy.

Instrumentality

instrumentality In expectancy theory, a perception about the extent to which performance results in the attainment of outcomes.

Expectancy captures a person's perceptions about the relationship between effort and performance. **Instrumentality,** the second major concept in expectancy theory, is a person's perception about the extent to which performance at a certain level results in the attainment of outcomes (see Figure 13.2). According to expectancy theory, employees are motivated to perform at a high level only if they think high performance will lead to (or is *instrumental* for attaining) outcomes such as pay, job security, interesting job assignments, bonuses, or a feeling of accomplishment. In other words, instrumentalities must be high for motivation to be high–people must perceive that because of their high performance they will receive outcomes.[32]

Managers promote high levels of instrumentality when they link performance to desired outcomes. In addition, managers must clearly communicate this linkage to subordinates. By making sure that outcomes available in an organization are distributed to organizational members on the basis of their performance, managers promote high instrumentality and motivation. When outcomes are linked to performance in this way, high performers receive more outcomes than low performers. In "A Manager's Challenge," managers raise levels of instrumentality and motivation for SAS employees by rewarding employees for a job well done.

Another example of high instrumentality contributing to high motivation can be found in the Cambodian immigrants who own, manage, and work in more than 80% of the doughnut shops in California.[33] These immigrants see high performance as leading to many important outcomes such as income, a comfortable existence, family security, and the autonomy provided by working in a small business. Their high instrumentality contributes to their high motivation to succeed.

Valence

valence In expectancy theory, how desirable each of the outcomes available from a job or organization is to a person.

Although all members of an organization must have high expectancies and instrumentalities, expectancy theory acknowledges that people differ in their preferences for outcomes. For many people, pay is the most important outcome of working. For others, a feeling of accomplishment or enjoying one's work is more important than pay. The term **valence** refers to how desirable each of the outcomes available from a job or organization is to a person. To motivate organizational members, managers need to determine which outcomes have high valence for them–are highly desired–and make sure that those outcomes are provided when members perform at a high level.

Providing employees with highly valent outcomes not only can contribute to high levels of motivation but also has the potential to reduce turnover, as indicated in the following "Management Insight" box.

Management Insight

Motivating and Retaining Employees at the Container Store

Kip Tindell and Garrett Boone founded the Container Store in Dallas, Texas, in 1978, and Tindell currently serves as CEO and chairman (Boone is chairman emeritus).[34] When they opened their first store, they were out on the floor trying to sell customers their storage and organization products that would economize on space and time and make purchasers' lives a little less complicated. The Container Store has grown to include 47 stores in 20 U.S. markets from coast to coast; although the original store in Dallas had only 1,600 square feet, the stores today average around 25,000 square feet.[35] The phenomenal growth in the size of the stores has been matched by impressive growth rates in sales and profits.[36] Surprisingly enough, Tindell can still be found on the shop floor tidying shelves and helping customers carry out their purchases.[37] And that, perhaps, is an important clue to the secret of their success. The Container Store has been consistently ranked among *Fortune* magazine's "100 Best Companies to Work For" for nine years running.[38] In 2010 the Container Store was 36th on this list.[39]

Early on, Tindell and Boone recognized that people are the Container Store's most valuable asset and that after hiring great people, one of the most important managerial tasks is motivating them. One would think motivating employees might be especially challenging in the retail industry, which has an average

The Container Store's motivational approach means that each employee works as a leader—and that those in managerial positions still walk the floor to tidy displays. Results are extremely positive, with the retail chain boasting significantly lower turnover rates than other chains in the industry.

annual turnover rate of 100% or more.[40] At the Container Store annual turnover is less than 10%, a testament to Tindell's ability to motivate.[41]

Tindell and Boone have long recognized the importance of rewarding employees for a job well done with highly valent outcomes. For example, starting salaries for salespeople are around $40,000, which is significantly higher than retail averages; and employees receive merit pay increases for superior sales performance. To encourage high individual performance as well as teamwork and cooperation, both individual and team-based rewards are given at the Container Store. Some high-performing salespeople earn more than their store managers, which suits the store managers fine as long as equitable procedures are used and rewards are distributed fairly.[42]

Professional development is another valent outcome employees obtain from working at the Container Store. Full-time salespeople receive over 240 hours of training their first year, and all employees have ongoing opportunities for additional training and development.[43] Employees also have flexible work options and flexible benefits; medical, dental, and 401(k) retirement plans; job security; a casual dress code; and access to a variety of wellness programs ranging from yoga classes and chair massages to a personalized, Web-based nutrition and exercise planner.[44] Another valent outcome is the opportunity to work with other highly motivated individuals in an environment that exudes enthusiasm and excitement. Not only are the Container Store's employees motivated, but they also look forward to coming to work and feel as if their coworkers and managers are part of their family. Employees feel pride in what they do–helping customers organize their lives, save space and time, and have a better sense of well-being. Hence they not only personally benefit from high performance by receiving highly valent outcomes but also feel good about the products they sell and the help they give customers.[45] Tindell evidently has never lost sight of the importance of motivation for both organizations and their members.

Bringing It All Together

According to expectancy theory, high motivation results from high levels of expectancy, instrumentality, and valence (see Figure 13.3). If any one of these factors is low, motivation is likely to be low. No matter how tightly desired outcomes are linked to performance, if a person thinks it is practically impossible to perform at a high level, motivation to perform at a high level will be exceedingly low. Similarly, if a person does not think outcomes are linked to high performance, or if a person does not desire the outcomes that are linked to high performance, motivation to perform at a high level will be low.

Effective managers realize the importance of high levels of expectancy, instrumentality, and valence and take concrete steps to ensure that their employees are highly motivated. This has certainly been the case at Enterprise Rent-A-Car, as profiled in the following "Management Insight" box.

Figure 13.3
Expectancy Theory

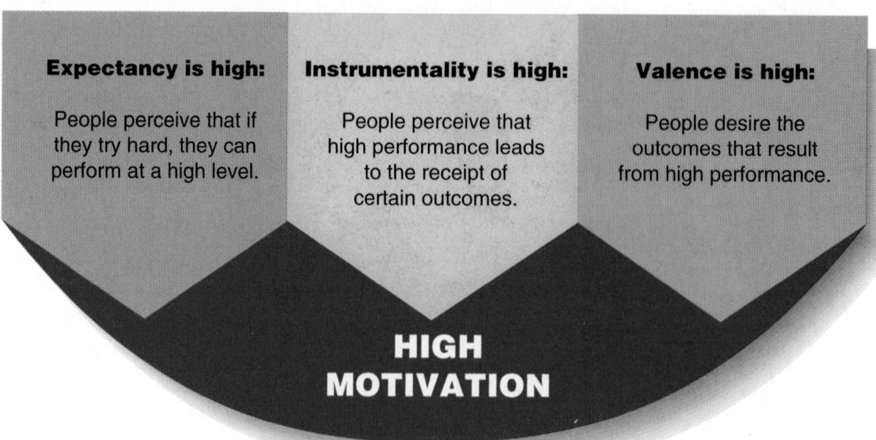
Expectancy is high:
People perceive that if they try hard, they can perform at a high level.
Instrumentality is high:
People perceive that high performance leads to the receipt of certain outcomes.
Valence is high:
People desire the outcomes that result from high performance.
HIGH MOTIVATION

Management Insight

Motivating Employees at Enterprise Rent-A-Car

Enterprise Rent-A-Car was founded by Jack Taylor in 1957 in St. Louis, Missouri, as a small auto leasing business.[46] Today Enterprise is the biggest car rental company in North America with over $9 billion in revenues and more than 64,000 employees. Enterprise has over 6,900 locations in the United States, Canada, the United Kingdom, Ireland, and Germany.[47] One of the biggest employers of new college graduates in the United States, Enterprise has been ranked among the top 50 best companies for new college graduates to launch their careers by *BusinessWeek* magazine.[48]

One key to Enterprise's success is how it motivates its employees to provide excellent customer service.[49] Practically all entry-level hires participate in Enterprise's management training program.[50] As part of the program, new hires learn all aspects of the company's business and how to provide excellent customer service. Management trainees first have a four-day training session focused on Enterprise's culture. They are then assigned to a branch office for around 8–12 months, where they learn all aspects of the business from negotiating with body shops to helping customers to washing cars. As part of this training, they learn how important high-quality customer service is to Enterprise and how they can personally provide great service, increasing their expectancy levels.[51]

Enterprise
1 800 rent-a-car

Enterprise's emphasis on top-notch customer care wraps around all other aspects of employee training, giving workers incentives to take good care of themselves by effectively serving the client.

All those who do well in the program are promoted after about a year to the position of management assistant. Management assistants who do well are promoted to become assistant branch managers with responsibility for mentoring and supervising employees. Assistant managers who do well can be promoted to become branch managers, who are responsible for managing a branch's employees and provision of customer service, rental car fleet, and financial performance. Branch managers who do well and have about five years of experience in the position often move on to take up management positions at headquarters or assume the position of area manager overseeing all the branches in a certain geographic region.[52] Promotions are highly valent outcomes for many Enterprise employees; and because performance is closely linked to promotions, employees have high instrumentality. As Patrick Farrell, vice president of corporate communications, indicated, "What's unique about our company is that everyone came up through the same system, from the CEOs on down . . . 100% of our operations personnel started as management trainees."[53]

In addition to motivating high performance and excellent customer service through training and promotional opportunities, Enterprise also uses financial incentives to motivate employees. Essentially each branch is considered a profit center, and the managers overseeing the branch and in charge of all aspects of its functioning have the autonomy and responsibility for the branch's profitability–almost as if the branch were their own small business or franchise.[54] All branch employees at the rank of assistant manager and higher earn incentive compensation, whereby their monthly pay depends on the profitability of their branch. Managers at higher levels, such as area managers, have their monthly pay linked to the profitability of the region they oversee. Thus managers at all levels know their pay is linked to the profitability of the parts of Enterprise for which they are responsible. And they have the autonomy to make decisions ranging from buying and selling cars to opening new branches.[55]

All in all, Enterprise's employees are highly motivated because of their high levels of expectancy, instrumentality, and valence. Contributing to high levels of expectancy is the training all new hires receive in all aspects of the business, including the provision of excellent customer service, and the ongoing valuable experiences employees receive with increasing levels of responsibility and empowerment. Linking two highly valent outcomes, pay and promotions, to performance leads to high instrumentality. And the highly motivated employees at Enterprise provide excellent service to their customers.

LO13-3 Explain how goals and needs motivate people and what kinds of goals are especially likely to result in high performance.

Need Theories

A **need** is a requirement or necessity for survival and well-being. The basic premise of **need theories** is that people are motivated to obtain outcomes at work that will satisfy their needs. Need theory complements expectancy theory by exploring in depth which outcomes motivate people to perform at a high level. Need theories suggest that to motivate a person to contribute valuable inputs to a job and perform at a high level, a manager must determine what needs the person is trying to satisfy at work and ensure that the person receives outcomes that help to satisfy those needs when the person performs at a high level and helps the organization achieve its goals.

need A requirement or necessity for survival and well-being.

need theories Theories of motivation that focus on what needs people are trying to satisfy at work and what outcomes will satisfy those needs.

There are several need theories. Here we discuss Abraham Maslow's hierarchy of needs, Clayton Alderfer's ERG theory, Frederick Herzberg's motivator-hygiene theory, and David McClelland's needs for achievement, affiliation, and power. These theories describe needs that people try to satisfy at work. In doing so, they give managers insights about what outcomes motivate members of an organization to perform at a high level and contribute inputs to help the organization achieve its goals.

Maslow's Hierarchy of Needs

Maslow's hierarchy of needs An arrangement of five basic needs that, according to Maslow, motivate behavior. Maslow proposed that the lowest level of unmet needs is the prime motivator and that only one level of needs is motivational at a time.

Psychologist Abraham Maslow proposed that all people seek to satisfy five basic kinds of needs: physiological needs, safety needs, belongingness needs, esteem needs, and self-actualization needs (see Table 13.1).[56] He suggested that these needs constitute a **hierarchy of needs,** with the most basic or compelling needs–physiological and safety needs–at the bottom. Maslow argued that these lowest-level needs must be met before a person strives to satisfy needs higher up in the hierarchy, such as self-esteem needs.

Table 13.1
Maslow's Hierarchy of Needs

	Needs	Description	Examples of How Managers Can Help People Satisfy These Needs at Work
Highest-level needs	**Self-actualization needs**	The needs to realize one's full potential as a human being.	By giving people the opportunity to use their skills and abilities to the fullest extent possible.
↑	**Esteem needs**	The needs to feel good about one-self and one's capabilities, to be respected by others, and to receive recognition and appreciation.	By granting promotions and recog-nizing accomplishments.
	Belongingness needs	Needs for social interaction, friend-ship, affection, and love.	By promoting good interpersonal relations and organizing social functions such as company picnics and holiday parties.
↓	**Safety needs**	Needs for security, stability, and a safe environment.	By providing job security, ade-quate medical benefits, and safe working conditions.
Lowest-level needs (most basic or compelling)	**Physiological needs**	Basic needs for things such as food, water, and shelter that must be met in order for a person to survive.	By providing a level of pay that enables a person to buy food and clothing and have adequate housing.

The lowest level of unsatisfied needs motivates behavior; once this level of needs is satisfied, a person tries to satisfy the needs at the next level.

Once a need is satisfied, Maslow proposed, it ceases to operate as a source of motivation. The lowest level of *unmet* needs in the hierarchy is the prime motivator of behavior; if and when this level is satisfied, needs at the next highest level in the hierarchy motivate behavior.

Although this theory identifies needs that are likely to be important sources of motivation for many people, research does not support Maslow's contention that there is a need hierarchy or his notion that only one level of needs is motivational at a time.[57] Nevertheless, a key conclusion can be drawn from Maslow's theory: People try to satisfy different needs at work. To have a motivated workforce, managers must determine which needs employees are trying to satisfy in organizations and then make sure that individuals receive outcomes that satisfy their needs when they perform at a high level and contribute to organizational effectiveness. By doing this, managers align the interests of individual members with the interests of the organization as a whole. By doing what is good for the organization (that is, performing at a high level), employees receive outcomes that satisfy their needs.

In our increasingly global economy, managers must realize that citizens of different countries might differ in the needs they seek to satisfy through work.[58] Some research suggests, for example, that people in Greece and Japan are especially motivated by safety needs and that people in Sweden, Norway, and Denmark are motivated by belongingness needs.[59] In less developed countries with low standards of living, physiological and safety needs are likely to be the prime motivators of behavior. As countries become wealthier and have higher standards of living, needs related to personal growth and accomplishment (such as esteem and self-actualization) become important motivators of behavior.

Alderfer's ERG Theory

Alderfer's ERG theory The theory that three universal needs—for existence, relatedness, and growth—constitute a hierarchy of needs and motivate behavior. Alderfer proposed that needs at more than one level can be motivational at the same time.

Clayton **Alderfer's ERG theory** collapsed the five categories of needs in Maslow's hierarchy into three universal categories–existence, relatedness, and growth–also arranged in a hierarchy (see Table 13.2). Alderfer agreed with Maslow that as lower-level needs become satisfied, a person seeks to satisfy higher-level needs. Unlike Maslow, however, Alderfer believed that a person can be motivated by needs at more than one level at the same time. A cashier in a supermarket, for example, may be motivated by both existence needs and relatedness needs. The existence needs motivate the cashier to come to work regularly and not make mistakes so his job will be secure and he will be able to pay his rent and buy food. The relatedness needs motivate the cashier to become friends with some of the other cashiers and have a good relationship with the store manager. Alderfer also suggested that when people experience *need frustration* or are unable to satisfy needs at a certain level, they will focus more intently on satisfying the needs at the next lowest level in the hierarchy.[60]

As with Maslow's theory, research does not support some of the specific ideas outlined in ERG theory, such as the existence of the three-level need hierarchy that Alderfer proposed.[61] However, for managers, the important message from ERG theory is the same as that from Maslow's theory: Determine what needs your subordinates are trying to satisfy at work, and make sure they receive outcomes that satisfy these needs when they perform at a high level to help the organization achieve its goals.

Herzberg's Motivator-Hygiene Theory

Herzberg's motivator-hygiene theory A need theory that distinguishes between motivator needs (related to the nature of the work itself) and hygiene needs (related to the physical and psychological context in which the work is performed) and proposes that motivator needs must be met for motivation and job satisfaction to be high.

Adopting an approach different from Maslow's and Alderfer's, Frederick Herzberg focused on two factors: (1) outcomes that can lead to high levels of motivation and job satisfaction and (2) outcomes that can prevent people from being dissatisfied. According to **Herzberg's motivator-hygiene theory,** people have two sets of needs or requirements: motivator needs and hygiene needs.[62] *Motivator needs* are related to the nature of the work itself and how challenging it is. Outcomes such as interesting work, autonomy, responsibility, being able to grow and develop on the job, and a sense of accomplishment and achievement help to satisfy motivator needs. To have a highly motivated and satisfied workforce, Herzberg suggested, managers should take steps to ensure that employees' motivator needs are being met.

Table 13.2
Alderfer's ERG Theory

	Needs	Description	Examples of How Managers Can Help People Satisfy These Needs at Work
Highest-level needs ↑	**Growth needs**	The needs for self-development and creative and productive work.	By allowing people to continually improve their skills and abilities and engage in meaningful work.
	Relatedness needs	The needs to have good interpersonal relations, to share thoughts and feelings, and to have open two-way communication.	By promoting good interpersonal relations and by providing accurate feedback.
Lowest-level needs ↓	**Existence needs**	Basic needs for food, water, clothing, shelter, and a secure and safe environment.	By promoting enough pay to provide for the basic necessities of life and safe working conditions.

As lower-level needs are satisfied, a person is motivated to satisfy higher-level needs. When a person is unable to satisfy higher-level needs (or is frustrated), motivation to satisfy lower-level needs increases.

Hygiene needs are related to the physical and psychological context in which the work is performed. Hygiene needs are satisfied by outcomes such as pleasant and comfortable working conditions, pay, job security, good relationships with coworkers, and effective supervision. According to Herzberg, when hygiene needs are not met, workers are dissatisfied, and when hygiene needs are met, workers are not dissatisfied. Satisfying hygiene needs, however, does not result in high levels of motivation or even high levels of job satisfaction. For motivation and job satisfaction to be high, motivator needs must be met.

Many research studies have tested Herzberg's propositions, and, by and large, the theory fails to receive support.[63] Nevertheless, Herzberg's formulations have contributed to our understanding of motivation in at least two ways. First, Herzberg helped to focus researchers' and managers' attention on the important distinction between intrinsic motivation (related to motivator needs) and extrinsic motivation (related to hygiene needs), covered earlier in the chapter. Second, his theory prompted researchers and managers to study how jobs could be designed or redesigned so they are intrinsically motivating.

McClelland's Needs for Achievement, Affiliation, and Power

need for achievement The extent to which an individual has a strong desire to perform challenging tasks well and to meet personal standards for excellence.

need for affiliation The extent to which an individual is concerned about establishing and maintaining good interpersonal relations, being liked, and having the people around him or her get along with each other.

need for power The extent to which an individual desires to control or influence others.

Psychologist David McClelland extensively researched the needs for achievement, affiliation, and power.[64] The **need for achievement** is the extent to which an individual has a strong desire to perform challenging tasks well and to meet personal standards for excellence. People with a high need for achievement often set clear goals for themselves and like to receive performance feedback. The **need for affiliation** is the extent to which an individual is concerned about establishing and maintaining good interpersonal relations, being liked, and having the people around him or her get along with each other. The **need for power** is the extent to which an individual desires to control or influence others.[65]

Although each of these needs is present in each of us to some degree, their importance in the workplace depends on the position one occupies. For example, research suggests that high needs for achievement and for power are assets for first-line and middle managers and that a high need for power is especially important for upper managers.[66] One study found that U.S. presidents with a relatively high need for power tended to be especially effective during their terms of office.[67] A high need for affiliation may not always be desirable in managers and other leaders because it might lead them to try too hard to be liked by others (including subordinates) rather than doing all they can to ensure that performance is as high as it can and should be. Although most research on these needs has been done in the United States, some studies suggest that the findings may be applicable to people in other countries as well, such as India and New Zealand.[68]

Other Needs

Clearly more needs motivate workers than the needs described by these four theories. For example, more and more workers are feeling the need for work–life balance and time to take care of their loved ones while simultaneously being highly motivated at work. Recall from "A Management Challenge" how SAS recognizes and seeks to satisfy these needs. Interestingly enough, recent research suggests that being exposed to nature (even just being able to see some trees from an office window) has many salutary effects, and a lack of such exposure can impair well-being and performance.[69] Thus having some time during the day when one can at least see nature may be another important need. Managers of successful companies often strive to ensure that as many of their valued employees' needs as possible are satisfied in the workplace.

Equity Theory

LO13-2 Describe from the perspectives of expectancy theory and equity theory what managers should do to have a highly motivated workforce.

Equity theory is a theory of motivation that concentrates on people's perceptions of the fairness of their work *outcomes* relative to, or in proportion to, their work *inputs.* Equity theory complements expectancy and need theories by focusing on how people perceive the relationship between the outcomes they receive from their jobs and organizations and the inputs they contribute. Equity theory was formulated in the 1960s by J. Stacy Adams, who stressed that what is important in determining motivation is the *relative* rather than the *absolute* levels of outcomes a person receives and inputs a person contributes. Specifically, motivation is influenced by the comparison of one's own outcome–input ratio with the outcome–input ratio of a referent.[70] The *referent* could be another person or a group of people who are perceived to be similar to oneself; the referent also could be oneself in a previous job or one's expectations about what outcome–input ratios should be. In a comparison of one's own outcome–input ratio to a referent's ratio, one's *perceptions* of outcomes and inputs (not any objective indicator of them) are key.

equity theory A theory of motivation that focuses on people's perceptions of the fairness of their work outcomes relative to their work inputs.

Equity

equity The justice, impartiality, and fairness to which all organizational members are entitled.

Equity exists when a person perceives his or her own outcome–input ratio to be equal to a referent's outcome–input ratio. Under conditions of equity (see Table 13.3), if a referent receives more outcomes than you receive, the referent contributes proportionally more inputs to the organization, so his or her outcome–input ratio still equals your ratio. Maria Sanchez and Claudia King, for example, both work in a shoe store in a large mall. Sanchez is paid more per hour than King but also contributes more inputs, including being responsible for some of the store's bookkeeping, closing the store, and periodically depositing cash in the bank. When King compares her outcome–input ratio to Sanchez's (her referent's), she perceives the ratios to be equitable because Sanchez's higher level of pay (an outcome) is proportional to her higher level of inputs (bookkeeping, closing the store, and going to the bank).

Similarly, under conditions of equity, if you receive more outcomes than a referent, your inputs are perceived to be proportionally higher. Continuing with our example, when Sanchez compares her outcome–input ratio to King's (her referent's) ratio, she perceives them to be equitable because her higher level of pay is proportional to her higher level of inputs.

When equity exists, people are motivated to continue contributing their current levels of inputs to their organizations to receive their current levels of outcomes. If people wish to increase their outcomes under conditions of equity, they are motivated to increase their inputs.

Table 13.3
Equity Theory

Condition	Person		Referent	Example
Equity	$\frac{\text{Outcomes}}{\text{Inputs}}$	=	$\frac{\text{Outcomes}}{\text{Inputs}}$	An engineer perceives that he contributes more inputs (time and effort) and receives proportionally more outcomes (a higher salary and choice job assignments) than his referent.
Underpayment inequity	$\frac{\text{Outcomes}}{\text{Inputs}}$	< (less than)	$\frac{\text{Outcomes}}{\text{Inputs}}$	An engineer perceives that he contributes more inputs but receives the same outcomes as his referent.
Overpayment inequity	$\frac{\text{Outcomes}}{\text{Inputs}}$	> (greater than)	$\frac{\text{Outcomes}}{\text{Inputs}}$	An engineer perceives that he contributes the same inputs but receives more outcomes than his referent.

Inequity

inequity Lack of fairness.

Inequity, or lack of fairness, exists when a person's outcome–input ratio is not perceived to be equal to a referent's. Inequity creates pressure or tension inside people and motivates them to restore equity by bringing the two ratios back into balance.

underpayment inequity The inequity that exists when a person perceives that his or her own outcome–input ratio is less than the ratio of a referent.

overpayment inequity The inequity that exists when a person perceives that his or her own outcome–input ratio is greater than the ratio of a referent.

There are two types of inequity: underpayment inequity and overpayment inequity (see Table 13.3). **Underpayment inequity** exists when a person's own outcome–input ratio is perceived to be *less* than that of a referent. In comparing yourself to a referent, you think you are *not* receiving the outcomes you should be, given your inputs. **Overpayment inequity** exists when a person perceives that his or her own outcome–input ratio is *greater* than that of a referent. In comparing yourself to a referent, you think you are receiving *more* outcomes than you should be, given your inputs.

Ways to Restore Equity

According to equity theory, both underpayment inequity and overpayment inequity create tension that motivates most people to restore equity by bringing the ratios back into balance.[71] When people experience *underpayment* inequity, they may be motivated to lower their inputs by reducing their working hours, putting forth less effort on the job, or being absent; or they may be motivated to increase their outcomes by asking for a raise or a promotion. Susan Richie, a financial analyst at a large corporation, noticed that she was working longer hours and getting more work accomplished than a coworker who had the same position, yet they both received the exact same pay and other outcomes. To restore equity, Richie decided to stop coming in early and staying late. Alternatively, she could have tried to restore equity by trying to increase her outcomes, perhaps by asking her boss for a raise.

When people experience underpayment inequity and other means of equity restoration fail, they can change their perceptions of their own or the referent's inputs or outcomes. For example, they may realize that their referent is really working on more difficult projects than they are or that they really take more time off from work than their referent does. Alternatively, if people who feel they are underpaid have other employment options, they may leave the organization. As an example, John Steinberg, an assistant principal in a high school, experienced underpayment inequity when he realized all the other assistant principals of high schools in his school district had received promotions to the position of principal even though they had been in their jobs for a shorter time than he had. Steinberg's performance had always been appraised as being high, so after his repeated requests for a promotion went unheeded, he found a job as a principal in a different school district.

When people experience *overpayment* inequity, they may try to restore equity by changing their perceptions of their own or their referent's inputs or outcomes. Equity can be restored when people realize they are contributing more inputs than they originally thought. Equity also can be restored by perceiving the referent's inputs to be lower or the referent's outcomes to be higher than one originally thought. When equity is restored in this way, actual inputs and outcomes are unchanged, and the person being overpaid takes no real action. What is changed is how people think about or view their or the referent's inputs and outcomes. For instance, Mary McMann experienced overpayment inequity when she realized she was being paid $2 an hour more than a coworker who had the same job as she did in a record store and who contributed the same amount of inputs. McMann restored equity by changing her perceptions of her inputs. She realized she worked harder than her coworker and solved more problems that came up in the store.

Experiencing either overpayment or underpayment inequity, you might decide that your referent is not appropriate because, for example, the referent is too different from yourself. Choosing a more appropriate referent may bring the ratios back into balance. Angela Martinez, a middle manager in the engineering department of a chemical company, experienced overpayment inequity when she realized she was being paid quite a bit more than her friend, who was a middle manager in the marketing department of the same company. After thinking about the discrepancy for a while, Martinez decided that engineering and marketing were so different that she should not be comparing her job to her friend's job even though they were both middle managers. Martinez restored equity by changing her referent; she picked a middle manager in the engineering department as a new referent.

Motivation is highest when as many people as possible in an organization perceive that they are being equitably treated–their outcomes and inputs are in balance. Top contributors and performers are motivated to continue contributing a high level of inputs because they are receiving the outcomes they deserve. Mediocre contributors and performers realize that if they want to increase their outcomes, they have to increase their inputs. Managers of effective organizations, like SAS, realize the importance of equity for motivation and performance and continually strive to ensure that employees believe they are being equitably treated.

The dot-com boom, its subsequent bust, and two recessions, along with increased global competition, have resulted in some workers putting in longer and longer working hours (increasing their inputs) without any increase in their outcomes. For those whose referents are not experiencing a similar change, perceptions of inequity are likely. According to Jill Andresky Fraser, author of *White Collar Sweatshop,* over 25 million U.S. workers work more than 49 hours per week in the office, almost 11 million work more than 60 hours per week in the office, and many also put in additional work hours at home. Moreover, advances in information technology, such as e-mail and cell phones, have resulted in work intruding on home time, vacation time, and even special occasions.[72]

Goal-Setting Theory

LO13-3 Explain how goals and needs motivate people and what kinds of goals are especially likely to result in high performance.

goal-setting theory A theory that focuses on identifying the types of goals that are most effective in producing high levels of motivation and performance and explaining why goals have these effects.

Goal-setting theory focuses on motivating workers to contribute their inputs to their jobs and organizations; in this way it is similar to expectancy theory and equity theory. But goal-setting theory takes this focus a step further by considering as well how managers can ensure that organizational members focus their inputs in the direction of high performance and the achievement of organizational goals.

Ed Locke and Gary Latham, the leading researchers for goal-setting theory, suggested that the goals organizational members strive to attain are prime determinants of their motivation and subsequent performance. A *goal* is what a person is trying to accomplish through his or her efforts and behaviors.[73] Just as you may have a goal to get a good grade in this course, so do members of an organization have goals they strive to meet. For example, salespeople at Neiman Marcus strive to meet sales goals, while top managers pursue market share and profitability goals.

Goal-setting theory suggests that to stimulate high motivation and performance, goals must be *specific* and *difficult.*[74] Specific goals are often quantitative–a salesperson's goal to sell $200 worth of merchandise per day, a scientist's goal to finish a project in one year, a CEO's goal to reduce debt by 40% and increase revenues by 20%, a restaurant manager's goal to serve 150 customers per evening. In contrast to specific goals, vague goals such as "doing your best" or "selling as much as you can" do not have much motivational impact.

Difficult goals are hard but not impossible to attain. In contrast to difficult goals, easy goals are those that practically everyone can attain, and moderate goals are goals that about one-half of the people can attain. Both easy and moderate goals have less motivational power than difficult goals.

Regardless of whether specific, difficult goals are set by managers, workers, or teams of managers and workers, they lead to high levels of motivation and performance. When managers set goals for their subordinates, their subordinates must accept the goals or agree to work toward them; also, they should be committed to them or really want to attain them. Some managers find that having subordinates participate in the actual setting of goals boosts their acceptance of and commitment to the goals. In addition, organizational members need to receive *feedback* about

Specific, difficult goals can encourage people to exert high levels of effort and to focus efforts in the right direction.

how they are doing; feedback can often be provided by the performance appraisal and feedback component of an organization's human resource management system (see Chapter 12). More generally, goals and feedback are integral components of performance management systems such as management by objectives (see Chapter 11).

Specific, difficult goals affect motivation in two ways. First, they motivate people to contribute more inputs to their jobs. Specific, difficult goals cause people to put forth high levels of effort, for example. Just as you would study harder if you were trying to get an A in a course instead of a C, so too will a salesperson work harder to reach a $200 sales goal instead of a $100 sales goal. Specific, difficult goals also cause people to be more persistent than easy, moderate, or vague goals when they run into difficulties. Salespeople who are told to sell as much as possible might stop trying on a slow day, whereas having a specific, difficult goal to reach causes them to keep trying.

A second way in which specific, difficult goals affect motivation is by helping people focus their inputs in the right direction. These goals let people know what they should be focusing their attention on, be it increasing the quality of customer service or sales or lowering new product development times. The fact that the goals are specific and difficult also frequently causes people to develop *action plans* for reaching them.[75] Action plans can include the strategies to attain the goals and timetables or schedules for the completion of different activities crucial to goal attainment. Like the goals themselves, action plans also help ensure that efforts are focused in the right direction and that people do not get sidetracked along the way.

learning theories Theories that focus on increasing employee motivation and performance by linking the outcomes that employees receive to the performance of desired behaviors and the attainment of goals.

Although specific, difficult goals have been found to increase motivation and performance in a wide variety of jobs and organizations both in the United States and abroad, recent research suggests that they may detract from performance under certain conditions. When people are performing complicated and challenging tasks that require them to focus on a considerable amount of learning, specific, difficult goals may actually impair performance.[76] Striving to reach such goals may direct some of a person's attention away from learning about the task and toward trying to figure out how to achieve the goal. Once a person has learned the task and it no longer seems complicated or difficult, then the assignment of specific, difficult goals is likely to have its usual effects. Additionally, for work that is very creative and uncertain, specific, difficult goals may be detrimental.

LO13-4 Identify the motivation lessons that managers can learn from operant conditioning theory and social learning theory.

Learning Theories

The basic premise of **learning theories** as applied to organizations is that managers can increase employee motivation and performance by how they link the outcomes that employees receive to the performance of desired behaviors and the attainment of goals. Thus learning theory focuses on the linkage between performance and outcomes in the motivation equation (see Figure 13.1).

learning A relatively permanent change in knowledge or behavior that results from practice or experience.

Learning can be defined as a relatively permanent change in a person's knowledge or behavior that results from practice or experience.[77] Learning takes place in organizations when people learn to perform certain behaviors to receive certain outcomes. For example, a person learns to perform at a higher level than in the past or to come to work earlier because he or she is motivated to obtain the outcomes that result from these behaviors, such as a pay raise or praise from a supervisor.

Tough economic times can sometimes propel people to learn new skills and behaviors so as to keep their jobs and help their employers stay afloat, as illustrated in the following "Information Technology Byte" box.

Information Technology Byte

Tough Times Spur Learning

Hero Arts, based in Richmond, California, is a small company that makes decorative rubber stamps.[78] As a result of the recession and economic downtown in 2008, Aaron Leventhal, the CEO of Hero Arts, told his staff of 100 that business was down and that layoffs might be on the horizon. Lay Luangrath, a Hero Arts employee whose job responsibilities were taking phone calls and answering customer questions, volunteered to take on information technology responsibilities such as maintenance of Hero Arts' computer systems in addition to his regular job duties to help Hero Arts cut costs. When a server broke down, he volunteered to try to fix it himself rather than have a consultant called in.[79]

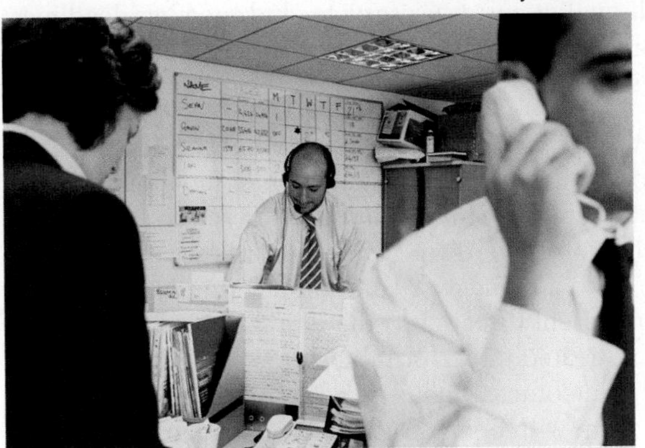

Multitasking and working across functional areas takes on a new urgency when the company faces learner times.

Luangrath didn't have all the knowledge and skills needed to take on this information technology work when he volunteered. However, he did research on the Internet, sought advice from experts, and learned new skills that he has put to use to not only fix the server but also to modernize Hero Arts' data retention system. As he puts it, "I could have failed and blown everything up. . . . But it worked, and I was pretty proud of myself."[80] Although sometimes Hero Arts still needs to call in technical support consultants for IT problems that Luangrath can't solve, he has saved Hero Arts thousands of dollars.[81]

Catherine Bissett, a manager with operations responsibilities at Xantrion Inc., an Oakland, California, company that provides computer services for small businesses, is an engineer by training.[82] Having no background in sales, she was a bit taken aback when Xantrion's president Anne Bisagno asked her and another manager in engineering to start helping out with sales to help the company maintain its revenue base during the economic downturn. After learning some basic selling skills as well as learning about Xantrion's customer base and sales process and objectives, Bissett and the other manager started attending events to network with potential new customers. Both managers sales' efforts have paid off, and Xantrion has attracted new customers.[83]

As a result of a temporary halt in new hiring at Southwest Airlines during the downturn, recruiters learned new skills and worked in a variety of departments including the legal department and flight operations.[84] When employees learn new skills and take on new or additional responsibilities, they not only help their companies to weather an economic downturn but also increase their own employability.

Of the different learning theories, operant conditioning theory and social learning theory provide the most guidance to managers in their efforts to have a highly motivated workforce.

Operant Conditioning Theory

operant conditioning theory The theory that people learn to perform behaviors that lead to desired consequences and learn not to perform behaviors that lead to undesired consequences.

According to **operant conditioning theory,** developed by psychologist B. F. Skinner, people learn to perform behaviors that lead to desired consequences and learn not to perform behaviors that lead to undesired consequences.[85] Translated into motivation terms, Skinner's theory means that people will be motivated to perform at a high level and attain their work goals to the extent that high performance and goal attainment allow them to obtain outcomes they desire. Similarly, people avoid performing behaviors that lead to outcomes they do not desire. By linking the performance of *specific behaviors* to the attainment of *specific outcomes,* managers can motivate organizational members to perform in ways that help an organization achieve its goals.

Operant conditioning theory provides four tools that managers can use to motivate high performance and prevent workers from engaging in absenteeism and other behaviors that detract from organizational effectiveness. These tools are positive reinforcement, negative reinforcement, extinction, and punishment.[86]

positive reinforcement Giving people outcomes they desire when they perform organizationally functional behaviors.

POSITIVE REINFORCEMENT **Positive reinforcement** gives people outcomes they desire when they perform organizationally functional behaviors. These desired outcomes, called *positive reinforcers,* include any outcomes that a person desires, such as pay, praise, or a promotion. Organizationally functional behaviors are behaviors that contribute to organizational effectiveness; they can include producing high-quality goods and services, providing high-quality customer service, and meeting deadlines. By linking positive reinforcers to the performance of functional behaviors, managers motivate people to perform the desired behaviors.

negative reinforcement Eliminating or removing undesired outcomes when people perform organizationally functional behaviors.

NEGATIVE REINFORCEMENT **Negative reinforcement** also can encourage members of an organization to perform desired or organizationally functional behaviors. Managers using negative reinforcement actually eliminate or remove undesired outcomes once the functional behavior is performed. These undesired outcomes, called *negative reinforcers,* can range from a manager's constant nagging or criticism to unpleasant assignments or the ever-present threat of losing one's job. When negative reinforcement is used, people are motivated to perform behaviors because they want to stop receiving or avoid undesired outcomes. Managers who try to encourage salespeople to sell more by threatening them with being fired are using negative reinforcement. In this case, the negative reinforcer is the threat of job loss, which is removed once the functional behavior is performed.

Whenever possible, managers should try to use positive reinforcement. Negative reinforcement can create a very unpleasant work environment and even a negative culture in an organization. No one likes to be nagged, threatened, or exposed to other kinds of negative outcomes. The use of negative reinforcement sometimes causes subordinates to resent managers and try to get back at them.

IDENTIFYING THE RIGHT BEHAVIORS FOR REINFORCEMENT Even managers who use positive reinforcement (and refrain from using negative reinforcement) can get into trouble if they are not careful to identify the right behaviors to reinforce–behaviors that are truly functional for the organization. Doing this is not always as straightforward as it might seem. First, it is crucial for managers to choose behaviors over which subordinates have control; in other words, subordinates must have the freedom and opportunity to perform the behaviors that are being reinforced. Second, it is crucial that these behaviors contribute to organizational effectiveness.

EXTINCTION Sometimes members of an organization are motivated to perform behaviors that detract from organizational effectiveness. According to operant conditioning theory, all behavior is controlled or determined by its consequences; one way for managers to curtail the performance of dysfunctional behaviors is to eliminate whatever is reinforcing the behaviors. This process is called **extinction.**

extinction Curtailing the performance of dysfunctional behaviors by eliminating whatever is reinforcing them.

Suppose a manager has a subordinate who frequently stops by his office to chat–sometimes about work-related matters but at other times about various topics ranging from politics to last night's football game. The manager and the subordinate share certain interests and views, so these conversations can get quite involved, and both seem to enjoy them. The manager, however, realizes that these frequent and sometimes lengthy conversations are causing him to stay at work later in the evenings to make up for the time he loses during the day. The manager also realizes that he is reinforcing his subordinate's behavior by acting interested in the topics the subordinate brings up and responding at length to them. To extinguish this behavior, the manager stops acting interested in these non-work-related conversations and keeps his responses polite and friendly but brief. No longer being reinforced with a pleasurable conversation, the subordinate eventually ceases to be motivated to interrupt the manager during working hours to discuss non-work-related issues.

PUNISHMENT Sometimes managers cannot rely on extinction to eliminate dysfunctional behaviors because they do not have control over whatever is reinforcing the behavior or because they cannot afford the time needed for extinction to work. When employees are performing dangerous behaviors or behaviors that are illegal or unethical, the behavior needs to be eliminated immediately. Sexual harassment, for example, is an organizationally dysfunctional behavior that cannot be tolerated. In such cases managers often rely on **punishment,** which is administering an undesired or negative consequence to subordinates when they perform the dysfunctional behavior. Punishments used by organizations range from verbal reprimands to pay cuts, temporary suspensions, demotions, and firings. Punishment, however, can have some unintended side effects–resentment, loss of self-respect, a desire for retaliation–and should be used only when necessary.

punishment Administering an undesired or negative consequence when dysfunctional behavior occurs.

To avoid the unintended side effects of punishment, managers should keep in mind these guidelines:

- Downplay the emotional element involved in punishment. Make it clear that you are punishing a person's performance of a dysfunctional behavior, not the person himself or herself.
- Try to punish dysfunctional behaviors as soon after they occur as possible, and make sure the negative consequence is a source of punishment for the individuals involved. Be certain that organizational members know exactly why they are being punished.
- Try to avoid punishing someone in front of others because this can hurt a person's self-respect and lower esteem in the eyes of coworkers as well as make coworkers feel uncomfortable.[87] Even so, making organizational members aware that an individual who has committed a serious infraction has been punished can sometimes be effective in preventing future infractions and teaching all members of the organization that certain behaviors are unacceptable. For example, when organizational members are informed that a manager who has sexually harassed subordinates has been punished, they learn or are reminded of the fact that sexual harassment is not tolerated in the organization.

Managers and students alike often confuse negative reinforcement and punishment. To avoid such confusion, keep in mind the two major differences between them. First, negative reinforcement is used to promote the performance of functional behaviors in organizations; punishment is used to stop the performance of dysfunctional behaviors. Second, negative reinforcement entails the *removal* of a negative consequence when functional behaviors are performed; punishment entails the *administration* of negative consequences when dysfunctional behaviors are performed.

ORGANIZATIONAL BEHAVIOR MODIFICATION When managers systematically apply operant conditioning techniques to promote the performance of organizationally functional behaviors and discourage the performance of dysfunctional behaviors, they are engaging in **organizational behavior modification (OB MOD).**[88] OB MOD has been successfully used to improve productivity, efficiency, attendance, punctuality, safe work practices, customer service, and other important behaviors in a wide variety of organizations such as banks, department stores, factories, hospitals, and construction sites.[89] The five basic steps in OB MOD are described in Figure 13.4.

organizational behavior modification (OB MOD) The systematic application of operant conditioning techniques to promote the performance of organizationally functional behaviors and discourage the performance of dysfunctional behaviors.

OB MOD works best for behaviors that are specific, objective, and countable, such as attendance and punctuality, making sales, or putting telephones together, all of which lend themselves to careful scrutiny and control. OB MOD may be questioned because of its lack of relevance to certain work behaviors (for example, the many work behaviors that are not specific, objective, and countable). Some people also

Figure 13.4
Five Steps in OB MOD

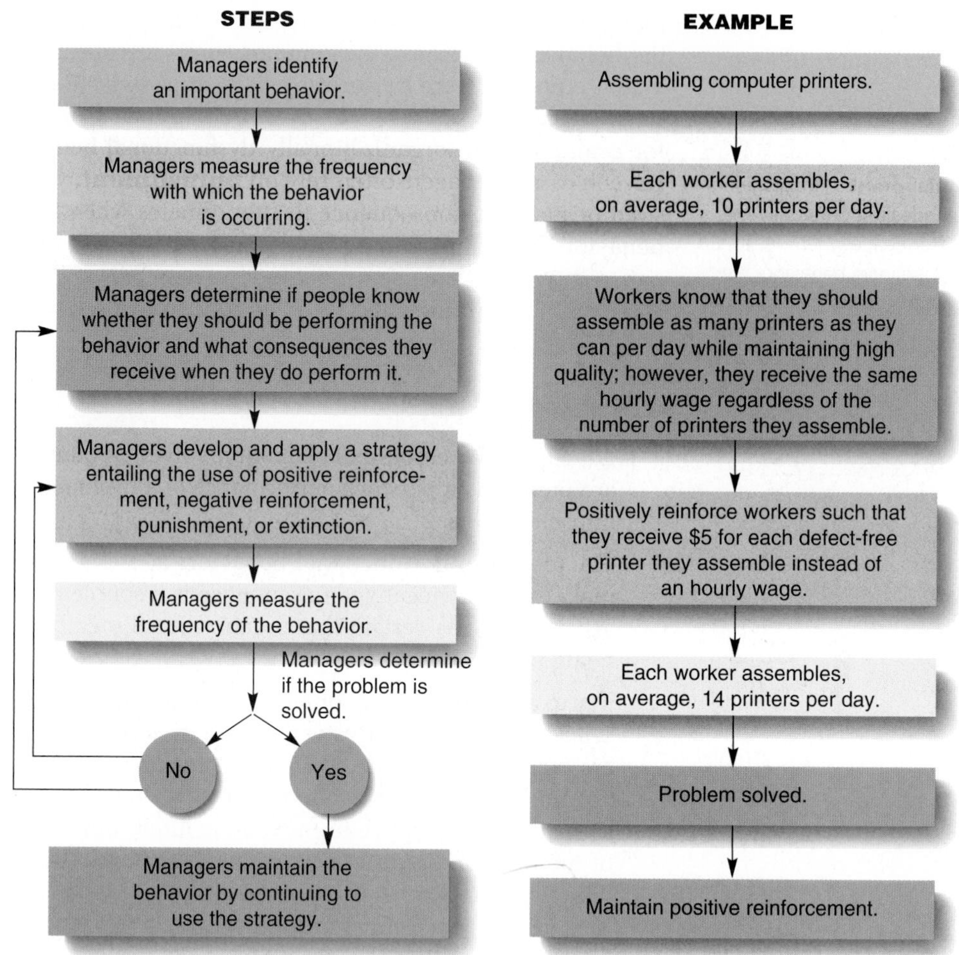

Source: Adapted from *Organizational Behavior Modification and Beyond* by F. Luthans and R. Kreitner (Scott, Foresman, 1985). With permission of the authors.

have questioned it on ethical grounds. Critics of OB MOD suggest that it is overly controlling and robs workers of their dignity, individuality, freedom of choice, and even creativity. Supporters counter that OB MOD is a highly effective means of promoting organizational efficiency. There is some merit to both sides of this argument. What is clear, however, is that when used appropriately, OB MOD gives managers a technique to motivate the performance of at least some organizationally functional behaviors.[90]

Social Learning Theory

social learning theory A theory that takes into account how learning and motivation are influenced by people's thoughts and beliefs and their observations of other people's behavior.

Social learning theory proposes that motivation results not only from direct experience of rewards and punishments but also from a person's thoughts and beliefs. Social learning theory extends operant conditioning's contribution to managers' understanding of motivation by explaining (1) how people can be motivated by observing other people performing a behavior and being reinforced for doing so (*vicarious learning*), (2) how people can be motivated to control their behavior themselves (*self-reinforcement*), and (3) how people's beliefs about their ability to successfully perform a behavior affect motivation (*self-efficacy*).[91] We look briefly at each of these motivators.

vicarious learning Learning that occurs when the learner becomes motivated to perform a behavior by watching another person performing it and being reinforced for doing so; also called *observational learning.*

VICARIOUS LEARNING **Vicarious learning,** often called *observational learning,* occurs when a person (the learner) becomes motivated to perform a behavior by watching another person (the model) performing the behavior and being positively reinforced for doing so. Vicarious learning is a powerful source of motivation on many jobs in which people learn to perform functional behaviors by watching others. Salespeople learn how to help customers, medical school students learn how to treat patients, law clerks learn how to practice law, and nonmanagers learn how to be managers, in part, by observing experienced members of an organization perform these behaviors properly and be reinforced for them. In general, people are more likely to be motivated to imitate the behavior of models who are highly competent, are (to some extent) experts in the behavior, have high status, receive attractive reinforcers, and are friendly or approachable.[92]

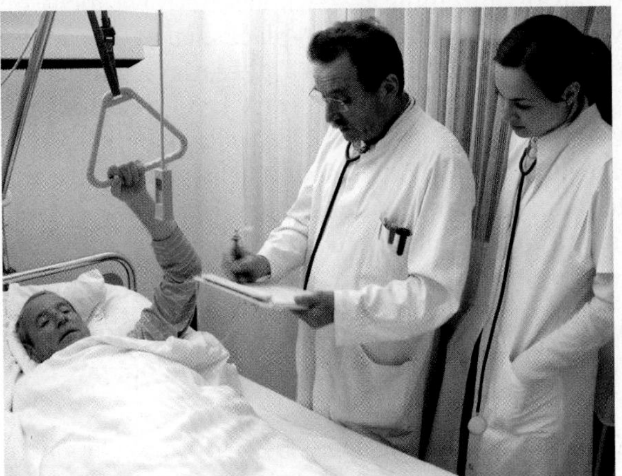

How do you treat *that*? When medical students enter residency, their education becomes entirely vicarious, as they shadow a full physician on his or her rounds.

To promote vicarious learning, managers should strive to have the learner meet the following conditions:

- The learner observes the model performing the behavior.
- The learner accurately perceives the model's behavior.
- The learner remembers the behavior.
- The learner has the skills and abilities needed to perform the behavior.
- The learner sees or knows that the model is positively reinforced for the behavior.[93]

self-reinforcer Any desired or attractive outcome or reward that a person gives to himself or herself for good performance.

SELF-REINFORCEMENT Although managers are often the providers of reinforcement in organizations, sometimes people motivate themselves through self-reinforcement. People can control their own behavior by setting goals for themselves and then reinforcing themselves when they achieve the goals.[94] **Self-reinforcers** are any desired or attractive outcomes or rewards that people can give to themselves for good performance, such as a feeling of accomplishment, going to a movie, having dinner out, buying a new CD, or taking time out for a golf game. When members of an organization control their own behavior through self-reinforcement, managers do not need to spend as much time as they ordinarily would trying to motivate and control behavior through the administration of consequences because subordinates are controlling and motivating themselves. In fact, this self-control is often referred to as the *self-management of behavior.*

When employees are highly skilled and are responsible for creating new goods and services, managers typically rely on self-control and self-management of behavior, as is the case at Google. Employees at Google are given the flexibility and autonomy to experiment, take risks, and sometimes fail as they work on new projects. They are encouraged to learn from their failures and apply what they learn to subsequent projects.[95] Google's engineers are given one day a week to work on their own projects that they are highly involved with, and new products such as Google News often emerge from these projects.[96]

self-efficacy A person's belief about his or her ability to perform a behavior successfully.

SELF-EFFICACY **Self-efficacy** is a person's belief about his or her ability to perform a behavior successfully.[97] Even with all the most attractive consequences or reinforcers hinging on high performance, people are not going to be motivated if they do not think they can actually perform at a high level. Similarly, when people control their own behavior, they are likely to set for themselves difficult goals that will lead to outstanding accomplishments only if they think they can reach those goals. Thus self-efficacy influences motivation both when managers provide reinforcement and when workers themselves provide it.[98] The greater the self-efficacy, the greater is the motivation and performance. Verbal persuasion such as a manager expressing confidence in an employee's ability to reach a challenging goal, as well as a person's own past performance and accomplishments and the accomplishments of other people, plays a role in determining a person's self-efficacy.

Pay and Motivation

LO13-5 Explain why and how managers can use pay as a major motivation tool.

In Chapter 12 we discussed how managers establish a pay level and structure for an organization as a whole. Here we focus on how, once a pay level and structure are in place, managers can use pay to motivate employees to perform at a high level and attain their work goals. Pay is used to motivate entry-level workers, first-line and middle managers, and even top managers such as CEOs. Pay can be used to motivate people to perform behaviors that help an organization achieve its goals, and it can be used to motivate people to join and remain with an organization.

Each of the theories described in this chapter alludes to the importance of pay and suggests that pay should be based on performance:

- *Expectancy theory:* Instrumentality, the association between performance and outcomes such as pay, must be high for motivation to be high. In addition, pay is an outcome that has high valence for many people.
- *Need theories:* People should be able to satisfy their needs by performing at a high level; pay can be used to satisfy several different kinds of needs.
- *Equity theory:* Outcomes such as pay should be distributed in proportion to inputs (including performance levels).
- *Goal-setting theory:* Outcomes such as pay should be linked to the attainment of goals.
- *Learning theories:* The distribution of outcomes such as pay should be contingent on the performance of organizationally functional behaviors.

As these theories suggest, to promote high motivation, managers should base the distribution of pay to organizational members on performance levels so that high performers receive more pay than low performers (other things being equal).[99] At General Mills, for example, the pay of all employees, ranging from mailroom clerks to senior managers, is based, at least in part, on performance.[100] A compensation plan basing pay on performance is often called a **merit pay plan.**

merit pay plan
A compensation plan that bases pay on performance.

In tough economic times, when organizations lay off employees and pay levels and benefits of those who are at least able to keep their jobs may be cut while their responsibilities are often increased,[101] managers are often limited in the extent to which they can use merit pay, if at all.[102] Nonetheless, in such times, managers can still try to recognize top performers, as indicated in the following "Management Insight" box.

Management Insight

Recognizing Top Performers in Tough Economic Times

Jenny Miller, manager of 170 engineers in the commercial systems engineering department at Rockwell Collins, an aerospace electronics company in Cedar Rapids, Iowa, has experienced firsthand the challenge of not being able to recognize top performers with merit pay during tough economic times.[103] Rockwell Collins laid off 8% of its workforce, and the workloads for the engineers Miller manages increased by about 15%. The engineers were working longer hours without receiving any additional pay; there was a salary freeze, so they knew raises

Gift cards, watches, medals, ceremonies: whatever you do to recognize an employee's hard work only increases his or her motivation to keep up the trend.

were not in store. With a deadline approaching for flight deck software for a customer, she needed some engineers to work over the Thanksgiving holiday and so sent out an e-mail request for volunteers. Approximately 20 employees volunteered. In recognition of their contributions, Miller gave them each a $100 gift card.[104]

A $100 gift card might not seem like much for an employee, who is already working long hours, to come to work over the Thanksgiving holiday for no additional pay or time off. Yet Steve Nieuwsma, division vice president at Rockwell Collins, indicates that the gift cards at least signal that managers recognize and appreciate employees' efforts and seek to thank them for it. Not being able to give his employees raises, Nieuwsma has also given gift cards to recognize contributions and top performers in amounts varying between $25 and $500.[105]

Craig Chiulli, a manager at Sanofi-Aventis in Ohio, sends e-mail messages to his employees recognizing and congratulating them on their accomplishments.[106] His company also laid off employees, and the remaining employees have found their workloads increased. Not being able to give pay raises in 2009, Elise Lelon, owner of a New York consulting firm, gave her employees higher-status job titles, flexible working hours, and the opportunity to work from home. As Lelon indicates, "You've got to think outside the money box when it comes to motivating your employees in this economic environment."[107] Clearly, when managers cannot use merit pay to reward performance and accomplishments, there are other ways in which they can recognize employees' contributions.

Once managers have decided to use a merit pay plan, they face two important choices: whether to base pay on individual, group, or organizational performance and whether to use salary increases or bonuses.

Basing Merit Pay on Individual, Group, or Organizational Performance

Managers can base merit pay on individual, group, or organizational performance. When individual performance (such as the dollar value of merchandise a salesperson sells, the number of loudspeakers a factory worker assembles, and a lawyer's billable hours) can be accurately determined, individual motivation is likely to be highest when pay is based on individual performance.[108] When members of an organization work closely together and individual performance cannot be accurately determined (as in a team of computer programmers developing a single software package), pay cannot be based on individual performance, and a group- or organization-based plan must be used. When the attainment of organizational goals hinges on members' working closely together and cooperating with each other (as in a small construction company that builds custom homes), group- or organization-based plans may be more appropriate than individual-based plans.[109]

It is possible to combine elements of an individual-based plan with a group- or organization-based plan to motivate each individual to perform highly and, at the same time, motivate all individuals to work well together, cooperate with one another, and help one another as needed. Lincoln Electric, a very successful company and a leading manufacturer of welding machines, uses a combination individual- and organization-based plan.[110] Pay is based on individual performance. In addition, each year the size of a bonus fund depends on organizational performance. Money from the bonus fund is distributed to people on the basis of their contributions to the organization, attendance, levels of cooperation, and other indications of performance.

Employees of Lincoln Electric are motivated to cooperate and help one another because when the firm as a whole performs well, everybody benefits by having a larger bonus fund. Employees also are motivated to contribute their inputs to the organization because their contributions determine their share of the bonus fund.

Salary Increase or Bonus?

Managers can distribute merit pay to people in the form of a salary increase or a bonus on top of regular salaries. Although the dollar amount of a salary increase or bonus might be identical, bonuses tend to have more motivational impact for at least three reasons. First, salary levels are typically based on performance levels, cost-of-living increases, and so forth, from the day people start working in an organization, which means the absolute level of the salary is based largely on factors unrelated to *current* performance. A 5% merit increase in salary, for example, may seem relatively small in comparison to one's total salary. Second, a current salary increase may be affected by other factors in addition to performance, such as cost-of-living increases or across-the-board market adjustments. Third, because organizations rarely reduce salaries, salary levels tend to vary less than performance levels do. Related to this point is the fact that bonuses give managers more flexibility in distributing outcomes. If an organization is doing well, bonuses can be relatively high to reward employees for their contributions. However, unlike salary increases, bonus levels can be reduced when an organization's performance lags. All in all, bonus plans have more motivational impact than salary increases because the amount of the bonus can be directly and exclusively based on performance.[111]

Consistent with the lessons from motivation theories, bonuses can be linked directly to performance and vary from year to year and employee to employee, as at Gradient Corporation, a Cambridge, Massachusetts, environmental consulting firm.[112] Another organization that successfully uses bonuses is Nucor Corporation. Steelworkers at Nucor tend to be much more productive than steelworkers in other companies–probably because they can receive bonuses tied to performance and quality that can range from 130% to 150% of their regular base pay.[113] During the economic downturn in 2007–2009, Nucor struggled as did many other companies, and bonus pay for steelworkers dropped considerably. However, managers at Nucor avoided having to lay off employees by finding ways to cut costs and having employees work on maintenance activities and safety manuals, along with taking on tasks that used to be performed by independent contractors, such as producing specialty parts and mowing the grass.[114]

employee stock option A financial instrument that entitles the bearer to buy shares of an organization's stock at a certain price during a certain period or under certain conditions.

In addition to receiving pay raises and bonuses, high-level managers and executives are sometimes granted employee stock options. **Employee stock options** are financial instruments that entitle the bearer to buy shares of an organization's stock at a certain price during a certain period or under certain conditions.[115] For example, in addition to salaries, stock options are sometimes used to attract high-level managers. The exercise price is the stock price at which the bearer can buy the stock, and the vesting conditions specify when the bearer can actually buy the stock at the exercise price. The option's exercise price is generally set equal to the market price of the stock on the date it is granted, and the vesting conditions might specify that the manager has to have worked at the organization for 12 months or perhaps met some performance target (perhaps an increase in profits) before being able to exercise the option. In high-technology firms and start-ups, options are sometimes used in a similar fashion for employees at various levels in the organization.[116]

From a motivation standpoint, stock options are used not so much to reward past individual performance but, rather, to motivate employees to work in the future for the good of the company as a whole. This is true because stock options issued at current stock prices have value in the future only if an organization does well and its stock price appreciates; thus giving employees stock options should encourage them to help the organization improve its performance over time.[117] At high-technology start-ups and dot-coms, stock options have often motivated potential employees to leave promising jobs in larger companies and work for the start-ups. In the late 1990s and early 2000s, many dot-commers were devastated to learn not only that their stock options were worthless, because their companies went out of business or were doing poorly, but also that they were unemployed. Unfortunately stock options have also led to unethical behavior; for example, sometimes individuals seek to artificially inflate the value of a company's stock to increase the value of stock options.

Examples of Merit Pay Plans

Managers can choose among several merit pay plans, depending on the work that employees perform and other considerations. Using *piece-rate pay,* an individual-based merit plan, managers base employees' pay on the number of units each employee produces, whether televisions, computer components, or welded auto parts. Managers at Lincoln Electric use piece-rate pay to determine individual pay levels. Advances in information technology are currently simplifying the administration of piece-rate pay in a variety of industries. For example, farmers typically allocated piece-rate pay to farmworkers through a laborious, time-consuming process. Now they can rely on metal buttons the size of a dime that farmworkers clip to their shirts or put in their pockets. Made by Dallas Semiconductor Corporation, these buttons are customized for use in farming by Agricultural Data Systems, based in Laguna Niguel, California.[118] Each button contains a semiconductor linked to payroll computers by a wandlike probe in the field.[119] The wand relays the number of boxes of fruit or vegetables that each worker picks as well as the type and quality of the produce picked, the location it was picked in, and the time and the date. The buttons are activated by touching them with the probe; hence they are called Touch Memory Buttons. Managers generally find that the buttons save time, improve accuracy, and provide valuable information about their crops and yields.[120]

Using *commission pay,* another individual-based merit pay plan, managers base pay on a percentage of sales. Managers at the successful real estate company Re/Max International Inc. use commission pay for their agents, who are paid a percentage of their sales. Some department stores, such as Neiman Marcus, use commission pay for their salespeople.

Examples of organizational-based merit pay plans include the Scanlon plan and profit sharing. The *Scanlon plan* (developed by Joseph Scanlon, a union leader in a steel and tin plant in the 1920s) focuses on reducing expenses or cutting costs; members of an organization are motivated to come up with and implement cost-cutting strategies because a percentage of the cost savings achieved during a specified time is distributed to the employees.[121] Under *profit sharing,* employees receive a share of an organization's profits. Regardless of the specific kind of plan that is used, managers should always strive to link pay to the performance of behaviors that help an organization achieve its goals.

Japanese managers in large corporations have long shunned merit pay plans in favor of plans that reward seniority. However, more and more Japanese companies are adopting merit-based pay due to its motivational benefits; among such companies are SiteDesign,[122] Tokio Marine and Fire Insurance, and Hissho Iwai, a trading organization.[123]

Summary and Review

THE NATURE OF MOTIVATION Motivation encompasses the psychological forces within a person that determine the direction of the person's behavior in an organization, the person's level of effort, and the person's level of persistence in the face of obstacles. Managers strive to motivate people to contribute their inputs to an
LO13-1 organization, to focus these inputs in the direction of high performance, and to ensure that people receive the outcomes they desire when they perform at a high level.

LO13-2 **EXPECTANCY THEORY** According to expectancy theory, managers can promote high levels of motivation in their organizations by taking steps to ensure that expectancy is high (people think that if they try, they can perform at a high level), instrumentality is high (people think that if they perform at a high level, they will receive certain outcomes), and valence is high (people desire these outcomes).

LO13-3 **NEED THEORIES** Need theories suggest that to motivate their workforces, managers should determine what needs people are trying to satisfy in organizations and then ensure that people receive outcomes that satisfy these needs when they perform at a high level and contribute to organizational effectiveness.

LO13-2 **EQUITY THEORY** According to equity theory, managers can promote high levels of motivation by ensuring that people perceive that there is equity in the organization or that outcomes are distributed in proportion to inputs. Equity exists when a person perceives that his or her own outcome–input ratio equals the outcome–input ratio of a referent. Inequity motivates people to try to restore equity.

LO13-3 **GOAL-SETTING THEORY** Goal-setting theory suggests that managers can promote high motivation and performance by ensuring that people are striving to achieve specific, difficult goals. It is important for people to accept the goals, be committed to them, and receive feedback about how they are doing.

LO13-4 **LEARNING THEORIES** Operant conditioning theory suggests that managers can motivate people to perform highly by using positive reinforcement or negative reinforcement (positive reinforcement being the preferred strategy). Managers can motivate people to avoid performing dysfunctional behaviors by using extinction or punishment. Social learning theory suggests that people can also be motivated by observing how others perform behaviors and receive rewards, by engaging in self-reinforcement, and by having high levels of self-efficacy.

LO13-5 **PAY AND MOTIVATION** Each of the motivation theories discussed in this chapter alludes to the importance of pay and suggests that pay should be based on performance. Merit pay plans can be individual-, group-, or organization-based and can entail the use of salary increases or bonuses.

Management in Action

Topics for Discussion and Action

Discussion

1. Discuss why two people with similar abilities may have very different expectancies for performing at a high level. [LO13-2]
2. Describe why some people have low instrumentalities even when their managers distribute outcomes based on performance. [LO13-2]
3. Analyze how professors try to promote equity to motivate students. [LO13-2]
4. Describe three techniques or procedures that managers can use to determine whether a goal is difficult. [LO13-3]
5. Discuss why managers should always try to use positive reinforcement instead of negative reinforcement. [LO13-4]

Action

6. Interview three people who have the same kind of job (such as salesperson, waiter/waitress, or teacher), and determine what kinds of needs each is trying to satisfy at work. [LO13-3]
7. Interview a manager in an organization in your community to determine the extent to which the manager takes advantage of vicarious learning to promote high motivation among subordinates. [LO13-3]

Building Management Skills

Diagnosing Motivation [LO13-1, 13-2, 13-3, 13-4]

Think about the ideal job that you would like to obtain upon graduation. Describe this job, the kind of manager you would like to report to, and the kind of organization you would be working in. Then answer the following questions:

1. What would be your levels of expectancy and instrumentality on this job? Which outcomes would have high valence for you on this job? What steps would your manager take to influence your levels of expectancy, instrumentality, and valence?
2. Whom would you choose as a referent on this job? What steps would your manager take to make you feel that you were being equitably treated? What would you do if, after a year on the job, you experienced underpayment inequity?
3. What goals would you strive to achieve on this job? Why? What role would your manager play in determining your goals?
4. What needs would you strive to satisfy on this job? Why? What role would your manager play in helping you satisfy these needs?
5. What behaviors would your manager positively reinforce on this job? Why? What positive reinforcers would your manager use?
6. Would there be any vicarious learning on this job? Why or why not?
7. To what extent would you be motivated by self-control on this job? Why?
8. What would be your level of self-efficacy on this job? Why would your self-efficacy be at this level? Should your manager take steps to boost your self-efficacy? If not, why not? If so, what would these steps be?

Managing Ethically [LO13-5]

Sometimes pay is so contingent upon performance that it creates stress for employees. Imagine a salesperson who knows that if sales targets are not met, she or he will not be able to make a house mortgage payment or pay the rent.

Questions

1. Either individually or in a group, think about the ethical implications of closely linking pay to performance.
2. Under what conditions might contingent pay be most stressful, and what steps can managers take to try to help their subordinates perform effectively and not experience excessive amounts of stress?

Small Group Breakout Exercise

Increasing Motivation [LO13-1, 13-2, 13-3, 13-4, 13-5]

Form groups of three or four people, and appoint one member as the spokesperson who will communicate your findings to the class when called on by the instructor. Then discuss the following scenario:

You and your partners own a chain of 15 dry-cleaning stores in a medium-size town. All of you are concerned about a problem in customer service that has surfaced recently. When any one of you spends the day, or even part of the day, in a particular store, clerks seem to provide excellent customer service, spotters make sure all stains are removed from garments, and pressers do a good job of pressing difficult items such as silk blouses. Yet during those same visits customers complain to you about such things as stains not being removed and items being poorly pressed in some of their previous orders; indeed, several customers have brought garments in to be redone. Customers also sometimes comment on having waited too long for service on previous visits. You and your partners are meeting today to address this problem.

1. Discuss the extent to which you believe that you have a motivation problem in your stores.
2. Given what you have learned in this chapter, design a plan to increase the motivation of clerks to provide prompt service to customers even when they are not being watched by a partner.
3. Design a plan to increase the motivation of spotters to remove as many stains as possible even when they are not being watched by a partner.
4. Design a plan to increase the motivation of pressers to do a top-notch job on all clothes they press, no matter how difficult.

Exploring the World Wide Web [LO13-1, 13-2, 13-3, 13-4, 13-5]

If you had the chance to choose which well-known corporation you would work for, which would it be? Now go to the Web site of that company and find out as much as you can about how it motivates employees. Also, using Google and other search engines, try to find articles in the news about this company. Based on what you have learned, would this company still be your top choice? Why or why not?

Be the Manager [LO13-1, 13-2, 13-3, 13-4, 13-5]

You supervise a team of marketing analysts who work on different snack products in a large food products company. The marketing analysts have recently received undergraduate degrees in business or liberal arts and have been on the job between one and three years. Their responsibilities include analyzing the market for their respective products, including competitors; tracking current marketing initiatives; and planning future marketing campaigns. They also need to prepare quarterly sales and expense reports for their products and estimated budgets for the next three quarters; to prepare these reports, they need to obtain data from financial and accounting analysts assigned to their products.

When they first started on the job, you took each marketing analyst through the reporting cycle, explaining what needs to be done and how to accomplish it and emphasizing the need for timely reports. Although preparing the reports can be tedious, you think the task is pretty straightforward and easily accomplished if the analysts plan ahead and allocate sufficient time for it. When reporting time approaches, you remind the analysts through e-mail messages and emphasize the need for accurate and timely reports in team meetings.

You believe this element of the analysts' jobs couldn't be more straightforward. However, at the end of each quarter, the majority of the analysts turn their reports in a day or two late, and, worse yet, your own supervisor (to whom the reports are eventually turned in) has indicated that information is often missing and sometimes the reports contain errors. Once you started getting flak from your supervisor about this problem, you decided you had better fix things quickly. You met with the marketing analysts, explained the problem, told them to turn the reports in to you a day or two early so you could look them over, and more generally emphasized that they really needed to get their act together. Unfortunately things have not improved much, and you are spending more and more of your own time doing the reports. What are you going to do?

Case in the News

Customer Service Champs: USAA's Battle Plan

When Staff Sergeant Corey Mason wants to deposit a check, he doesn't use an ATM, a teller at a branch, or even a stamped envelope and deposit slip. Rather, the 37-year-old GPS systems specialist takes a picture of the check with his iPhone, uses an app to send it to his bank, and within minutes the money shows up in his account. Although he's now stationed at Fort Knox, Kentucky, it's the kind of service Mason knows his fellow troops in Iraq, where he served in 2004, surely appreciate. "The mail over there is extremely slow," he says. "They know what it's like."

By "they," Mason means his bank and insurance company, USAA, which counts military members and their families as the bulk of its clients. But he also means the 23% of USAA's top management and new hires that have served in the military. Says Mason, "It's not every day I get addressed 'sergeant' by a customer service agent."

In almost everything it does, the financial services outfit puts itself in the spit-shined shoes of its often highly mobile customers, many of whom face unique financial challenges. USAA was the first bank to allow iPhone deposits; it routinely texts balances to soldiers in the field; and it heavily discounts customers' car insurance while they are deployed overseas. "They do all this really creative stuff that applies to guys and gals who are in Afghanistan," says Karen Pauli, a research director at consulting firm TowerGroup. "There is nobody on this earth who understands their customer better than USAA."

Although few large companies have such a specialized focus, managers everywhere could learn plenty from USAA about coddling customers. A private company with $68.3 billion in assets, USAA has unrivaled staying power atop *Bloomberg BusinessWeek*'s annual Customer Service Champs ranking. Since we first produced the list in 2007 with our research partner, J.D. Power & Associates, no other company has come close to achieving USAA's feat: a No. 1 or No. 2 spot for four years running. No fewer than 87% of respondents to J.D. Power's syndicated surveys say they will definitely buy from the company again—far higher than the average, which is just 36%. Its client retention rate? A near-perfect 97.8%.

For USAA, though, maintaining that track record could become a bigger challenge. In November its insurance business scrapped some of its eligibility requirements, more than doubling its potential customer base, from 26 million to 61 million. USAA's property and casualty insurance is now open to anyone who has ever served honorably in the military; in the past, customers had to have served or signed up for USAA between certain dates. And while most of its banking and brokerage units have sold to anyone for years, it began advertising those services widely only last year.

While the company has no plans to offer insurance to the general public, expanding beyond its traditional customer could make it harder to provide the same lauded service. For one thing, a broader membership could lead to more consumers who present a greater insurance risk, which may mean service reps will need to be more skeptical about claims, says Brian Sullivan, editor of *Auto Insurance Report.* "If you rarely question the claim, you don't create any conflict," he says.

And while new members may be armed forces veterans and their families, their needs may be different, says Bruce Temkin, who heads up Forrester Research's customer experience practice and has studied USAA. "The real trick for USAA will be how they continue to serve their core military customer while serving this broader set," he says. "It can get really messy if they grow too fast." A USAA spokesperson contends the insurer's pricing will correct for any greater risks that come from expansion.

For now, USAA is focusing on what it knows best: its armed forces customers and the unique financial issues they face. That focus goes back to its roots, when 25 army officers got together in 1922 to insure each other's vehicles. By 1972 five out of six military officers belonged to USAA, and in 1996 the company expanded its membership to active-duty enlisted soldiers, too.

So it's little surprise that training for USAA employees is steeped in the military experience. New reps attend sessions where they dine on MREs, or "meals ready to eat," which troops consume in the field. They try on Kevlar vests and flak helmets. And each rep is handed a bona fide deployment letter—with the names changed, of course—to get them thinking about the financial decisions customers face at such an emotional time. Colleen Williams, a Phoenix-based service rep who joined the company in 2008, says the training clued her in to family issues that help her when answering calls. "I speak to women who haven't talked to their husbands in six weeks," she says. "It never really registered to me, the real disconnect" deployed soldiers have from their families.

Training isn't the only thing USAA lavishes on employees. After all, it takes satisfied workers to get satisfied customers. In 2009 even call center agents at USAA saw bonuses of nearing 19% of their pay, up from 13.5% the year before. A new $5-an-hour concierge service lets employees outsource errands on the cheap during the workday. And when the company closed two call centers in 2009, it offered every employee a company-paid relocation package to jobs at other locations, even helping staffers burdened with underwater mortgages unload their homes. Of the 1,200 affected workers, 50% accepted move offers—far more than the fewer than 20% USAA expected.

Staffers get time to do their jobs, too. Employees aren't rushed through calls with customers or evaluated on how fast they handle the inquiries. "Member satisfaction trumps every single metric," says Forrester's Temkin. Other call centers "may relax things like average handle time, but they still measure it, and still you get in trouble if you're out of bounds."

Reps are also armed with software that lets them view a history of the online screens a particular customer has viewed on USAA's Web site, letting them know what policies or business lines the customer was perusing—and may be ready to buy.

The mobile lives of its core consumers—troops stationed in distant locales or military families constantly on the move—have made the company an unlikely innovator in the world of personal finance. Because USAA has just one physical bank branch, at its headquarters in San Antonio, deposit-by-iPhone is a logical step. (It also launched an app for Android users on January 22.) Since August, more than $260 million in deposits have been made using the mobile service, as USAA's customers, whether in Camp Pendleton, California, or Iraq, send in checks. Giants like Bank of America are just testing a similar service.

Lieutenant Randall Blakeslee, a plans and operations officer stationed at Fort Sam Houston, Texas, is on two-hour standby to depart for Haiti, where he'll stay at least 90 days to help with relief efforts. That means his mail will be forwarded to him there, and he fully expects to use the mobile deposit service to submit checks from his job at home or when family sends him money. He already used the service to deposit checks when he was based in El Salvador. USAA is "really ahead of the game when it comes to technology," says Blakeslee, 34. "If I'm on the run, I can text a command and within seconds get a message back with my balance."

Blakeslee is referring to another high-tech service USAA rolled out in 2008 that lets its far-flung customers—a sizable number of whom are young, tech-savvy, and living paycheck to paycheck—get text messages about their account balances before, say, making a big purchase. Later in 2010, USAA is planning mobile peer-to-peer payments, which let customers e-mail or text-message money to friends or family for immediate deposit, no matter where they are at the time.

USAA was among the first to let customers initiate an insurance claim using their phones from the scene of an accident. And it soon will expand that app so policyholders can attach photos to the claim and complete the entire process via phone. By 2011 customers will even be able to attach voice recordings to their file, immediately retelling exactly what happened.

Also coming this year: a mobile car-buying service that lets customers standing at a dealership snap an iPhone pic of a vehicle's VIN number and instantly get back insurance quotes, loan terms, and prenegotiated rates at approved dealerships. "The idea is you can turn that phone around to the salesman," says Bob Otis, USAA's vice president for auto product management, "and say 'this is the price I'm going to pay.'"

Besides helping policyholders, such technology benefits USAA. As it adds customers, both through advertising banking services for the first time and vastly expanding the pool of vets who can buy its insurance, such self-service tools could mean it won't have to increase the size of its 13,000-strong army of reps at the same rate as its membership. "If you can have the member self-serve on certain parts of the claim, or the entire claim," says Ken Rosen, senior vice president for claims service, "clearly there's an efficiency gain."

If USAA leans too much on self-service, of course, its vaunted reputation could suffer. Widening its risk pool and taking on more customers could have the same impact. But USAA's executive vice president for member experience, Wayne Peacock, isn't worried. He says expanding USAA's customer ranks is "gradual and purposeful." And that's something the company has done incrementally since 1996, continually racking up top service scores along the way.

Questions for Discussion

1. How does USAA motivate its employees?
2. What are some potential sources of intrinsic motivation for USAA employees? What are some potential sources of prosocial motivation?
3. What are some potential sources of extrinsic motivation for USAA employees?
4. How do managers at USAA boost levels of expectancy?

Source: J. McGregor, "Customer Service Champs: USAA's Battle Plan," *BusinessWeek*, March 1, 2010, 40–43. Reprinted from March 1, 2010 issue of *Bloomberg Businessweek* by special permission, copyright © 2010 by Bloomberg L.P.

CHAPTER 14

Leadership

Learning Objectives

After studying this chapter, you should be able to:

LO14-1 Explain what leadership is, when leaders are effective and ineffective, and the sources of power that enable managers to be effective leaders.

LO14-2 Identify the traits that show the strongest relationship to leadership, the behaviors leaders engage in, and the limitations of the trait and behavior models of leadership.

LO14-3 Explain how contingency models of leadership enhance our understanding of effective leadership and management in organizations.

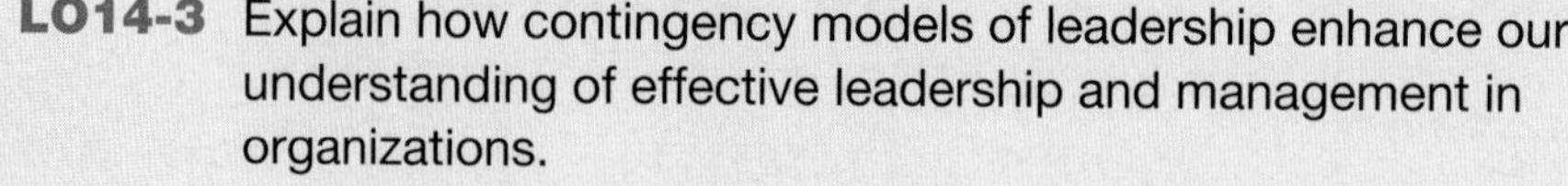

LO14-4 Describe what transformational leadership is, and explain how managers can engage in it.

LO14-5 Characterize the relationship between gender and leadership and explain how emotional intelligence may contribute to leadership effectiveness.

A MANAGER'S CHALLENGE

Judy McGrath Leads MTV Networks

How can a manager continuously transform a hip company in a rapidly changing environment? As chairperson and CEO of MTV Networks, Judy McGrath has one of the most challenging and encompassing leadership positions in the media industry.[1] MTV Networks, a unit of Viacom, is home to the original MTV as well as MTV2, mtvU, MTV Tr3s, Nickelodeon, VH1, VH1 Classic, VH1 Soul, CMT, Comedy Central, LOGO, Nick at Nite, Noggin, TV Land, CMT, the N, Spike TV, Atom, AddictingGames.com, Shockwave.com, GameTrailers.com, Harmonix, Neopets, Quizilla, Xfire, Y2M, and MTVN International.[2] MTV Networks is accessed by more than 440 million households in over 165 viewing territories. Operating in an industry and markets whose rate of change is parallel to none, MTV Networks presents a daunting task to a manager wanting to keep it hip and maintain its appeal in an ever-changing digital landscape.[3]

McGrath certainly seems up to the challenge. She is one of only five women that has been included on *Fortune* magazine's list of the "50 Most Powerful Women in Business" every year since the magazine started the list; in 2009 she was ranked 20th.[4] In 2009 she also made *Forbes'* list of "The 100 Most Powerful Women in Business," was awarded the AWRT Achievement Award, and topped the list of the 2009 Billboard Women In Music Power Players list.[5] Interestingly enough, McGrath, who was born in Scranton, Pennsylvania, first came to New York City in the late 1970s with hopes of combining her love of rock music with her college degree in English literature to write for *Rolling Stone* magazine. Instead McGrath started writing for *Mademoiselle* magazine and later for *Glamour.* In 1981 friends told her about the newly launched MTV, and she took a job there writing promotional pieces. And the rest has been history. With MTV from its earliest days, McGrath is now in the top post.[6]

Chairperson and CEO Judy McGrath successfully leads the complex organization that is MTV Networks.

McGrath is far from what comes to some people's minds when they think of a traditional CEO. Widely read, she is very attuned to pop culture, is nurturing of employees and talent alike, and is a creative leader who encourages the same in others; she has been credited with creating an inclusive culture at MTV, where all employees are listened to and heard. She is down to earth, as comfortable planning strategies with top managers as she is interacting with hip-hoppers or seeing live indie music acts. McGrath's confidence and high energy are matched by her knowledge of the industry, creativity, and integrity.[7]

Her personal leadership style emphasizes empowering all members of the MTV organization as well as its viewers. According to McGrath, creativity and innovation stem from employees at all ranks, leaders and managers should listen to employees' ideas, and change must be the rule of the day in a dynamic environment.[8] She has also strived to empower the MTV viewing audience and raise viewers' awareness about important social concerns with award-winning programming such as the *Fight For Your Rights* series [for example, "Take a Stand against Violence," "Protect Yourself" (an AIDS awareness initiative), and "Take a Stand against Discrimination"].[9]

McGrath networks daily with wide-ranging contacts, keeping up with the latest developments in the industry and pop culture and always on the lookout for new ideas and opportunities. She is visionary and can see possibilities and opportunities where others might see just risks or potential downsides. She works hard, perseveres, and believes that anything is possible. Under her leadership, MTV has launched scores of successful new programs, all of which were risky and could have failed. As she puts it, "Falling flat on your face is a great motivator. The smartest thing we can do when confronted by something truly creative is to get out of the way."[10] That is what McGrath did when two producers came to her with the idea of filming people going through their day-to-day lives (with a soundtrack, of course, of new music); so started reality TV and MTV's *The Real World* series, which is in its 23rd season.[11]

McGrath faces new challenges as she leads MTV forward. MTV's programming is now part of the media establishment, and in an era of broadband, iPods, and online everything, she realizes that MTV cannot rest on its laurels: It must continually transform itself to maintain its hip and edgy focus and continue to appeal to its audience. Thus McGrath has pushed MTV to deliver services from multiple digital platforms ranging from cell phones to new broadband channels to video games.[12]

To spearhead this digital transformation, McGrath is expanding from MTV's tradition of developing its own offerings to seeking partnerships and acquisitions. For example, MTV Networks has partnered with Microsoft to offer a digital music download service called URGE.[13] MTV has purchased Web sites such as IFILM, which is devoted to amateur short movies, and Neopets (popular with the younger set). McGrath is seeking synergies between digital acquisitions such as these and MTV's existing lineup. For example, IFILM debuted a show on VH1, and Nickelodeon has developed products for Neopets.[14]

Clearly, challenging times lie ahead for McGrath as she seeks to transform MTV in the digital era. Her vision and decisiveness, combined with her style of empowering employees, encouraging risk taking and creativity, and making sure that all enjoy the ride suggest that MTV is in good hands.[15]

Overview

LO14-1 Explain what leadership is, when leaders are effective and ineffective, and the sources of power that enable managers to be effective leaders.

Judy McGrath exemplifies the many facets of effective leadership. In Chapter 1 we explained that one of the four primary tasks of managers is leading. Thus it should come as no surprise that leadership is a key ingredient in effective management. When leaders are effective, their subordinates or followers are highly motivated, committed, and high-performing. When leaders are ineffective, chances are good that their subordinates do not perform up to their capabilities, are demotivated, and may be dissatisfied as well. CEO Judy McGrath is a leader at the very top of an organization, but leadership is an important ingredient for managerial success at all levels of organizations: top management, middle management, and first-line management. Moreover, leadership is a key ingredient of managerial success for organizations large and small.

In this chapter we describe what leadership is and examine the major leadership models that shed light on the factors that contribute to a manager's being an effective leader. We look at trait and behavior models, which focus on what leaders are like and what they do, and contingency models–Fiedler's contingency model, path–goal theory, and the leader substitutes model–each of which takes into account the complexity surrounding leadership and the role of the situation in leader effectiveness. We also describe how managers can use transformational leadership to dramatically affect their organizations. By the end of this chapter, you will appreciate the many factors and issues that managers face in their quest to be effective leaders.

The Nature of Leadership

leadership The process by which an individual exerts influence over other people and inspires, motivates, and directs their activities to help achieve group or organizational goals.

leader An individual who is able to exert influence over other people to help achieve group or organizational goals.

Leadership is the process by which a person exerts influence over other people and inspires, motivates, and directs their activities to help achieve group or organizational goals.[16] The person who exerts such influence is a **leader.** When leaders are effective, the influence they exert over others helps a group or organization achieve its performance goals. When leaders are ineffective, their influence does not contribute to, and often detracts from, goal attainment. As "A Manager's Challenge" makes clear, Judy McGrath is taking multiple steps to inspire and motivate MTV's employees so they help MTV achieve its goals.

Beyond facilitating the attainment of performance goals, effective leadership increases an organization's ability to meet all the contemporary challenges discussed throughout this book, including the need to obtain a competitive advantage, the need to foster ethical behavior, and the need to manage a diverse workforce fairly and equitably. Leaders who exert influence over organizational members to help meet these goals increase their organizations' chances of success.

In considering the nature of leadership, we first look at leadership styles and how they affect managerial tasks and at the influence of culture on leadership styles. We then focus on the key to leadership, *power,* which can come from a variety of sources. Finally we consider the contemporary dynamic of empowerment and how it relates to effective leadership.

Personal Leadership Style and Managerial Tasks

A manager's *personal leadership style*–that is, the specific ways in which a manager chooses to influence other people–shapes how that manager approaches planning, organizing, and controlling (the other principal tasks of managing). Consider Judy McGrath's personal leadership style in "A Manager's Challenge": She is down to earth, nurturing of employees and talent, and at the same time decisive and visionary. She empowers employees, encourages them to be creative and take risks, and fosters an inclusive culture at MTV Networks.[17]

Managers at all levels and in all kinds of organizations have their own personal leadership styles that determine not only how they lead their subordinates but also how they perform the other management tasks. Michael Kraus, owner and manager of a dry cleaning store in the northeastern United States, for example, takes a hands-on approach to leadership. He has the sole authority for determining work schedules and job assignments for the 15 employees in his store (an organizing task), makes all important decisions by himself (a planning task), and closely monitors his employees' performance and rewards top performers with pay increases (a control task). Kraus's personal leadership style is effective in his organization. His employees generally are motivated, perform highly, and are satisfied, and his store is highly profitable.

Developing an effective personal leadership style often is a challenge for managers at all levels in an organization. This challenge is often exacerbated when times are tough, due, for example, to an economic downturn or a decline in customer demand. The recession in the late 2000s provided many managers with just such a challenge.

Although leading is one of the four principal tasks of managing, a distinction is often made between managers and leaders. When this distinction is made, managers are thought of as those organizational members who establish and implement procedures and processes to ensure smooth functioning and who are accountable for goal accomplishment.[18] Leaders look to the future, chart the course for the organization, and attract, retain, motivate, inspire, and develop relationships with employees based on trust and mutual respect.[19] Leaders provide meaning and purpose, seek innovation rather than stability, and impassion employees to work together to achieve the leaders' vision.[20]

servant leader A leader who has a strong desire to serve and work for the benefit of others.

As part of their personal leadership style, some leaders strive to truly serve others. Robert Greenleaf, who was director of management research at AT&T and upon his retirement in 1964 embarked on a second career focused on writing, speaking, and consulting, came up with the term *servant leadership* to describe these leaders.[21] **Servant leaders,** above all else, have a strong desire to serve and work for the benefit of others.[22] Servant leaders share power with followers and strive to ensure that followers' most important needs are met, they are able to develop as individuals, and their well-being is enhanced, and that attention is paid to those who are least well-off in a society.[23] Greenleaf founded a nonprofit organization called the Greenleaf Center for Servant Leadership (formerly called the Center for Applied Ethics) to foster leadership focused on service to others, power sharing, and a sense of community between organizations and their multiple stakeholders.[24] Some entrepreneurs strive to incorporate servant leadership into their personal leadership styles, as profiled in the following "Ethics in Action" box.

Leadership Styles across Cultures

Some evidence suggests that leadership styles vary not only among individuals but also among countries or cultures. Some research indicates that European managers tend to be more humanistic or people-oriented than both Japanese and American managers. The collectivistic culture in Japan places prime emphasis on the group rather than the individual, so the importance of individuals' own personalities, needs, and desires

Ethics in Action

Servant Leadership at Zingerman's

Ari Weinzweig and Paul Saginaw founded Zingerman's Delicatessen in Ann Arbor, Michigan, in 1982.[25] Food lovers at heart, Weinzweig and Saginaw delighted in finding both traditional and exotic foods from around the world, making delicious sandwiches to order, and having extensive selections of food items ranging from olives, oils, and vinegars to cheeses, smoked fish, and salami. As their business grew, and to maintain an intimate atmosphere with excellent customer service, Weinzweig and Saginaw expanded from their original deli into a community of related businesses called Zingerman's Community of Businesses. In addition to the original deli, Zingerman's Community of Businesses now includes a mail-order business, a bakery, a catering business, a creamery, a restaurant, a wholesale coffee business, and a training business and has combined annual revenues of about $30 million.[26] From the start, Weinzweig and Saginaw have been devoted to excellent customer service, great food, and a commitment to people and community.[27]

As part of their commitment to people and community, Weinzweig and Saginaw have incorporated servant leadership into their personal leadership styles. As their business has grown and prospered, they have realized that increasing success means greater responsibility to serve others. They strive to treat their employees as well as they treat their customers and give their employees opportunities for growth and development on the job. They have also realized that when their own needs or desires differ from what is best for their company, they should do what is best for the company.[28]

To this day, the cofounders encourage their employees to let them know how they can help them and what they can do for them. And given Zingerman's culture of mutual respect and trust, employees do not hesitate to communicate how their leaders can serve them in many and varied ways. For example, when Weinzweig visits the Zingerman's Roadhouse restaurant and the staff is very

Paul Saginaw (left) and Ari Weinzweig have incorporated servant leadership into their personal leadership styles at Zingerman's.

busy, they may ask him to help out by serving customers or cleaning off tables. As he indicates, "People give me assignments all the time. Sometimes I'm the note-taker. Sometimes I'm the cleaner-upper. . . . Sometimes I'm on my hands and knees wiping up what people spilled."[29]

Weinzweig and Saginaw also have a strong sense of commitment to serving the local community; Zingerman's founded the nonprofit organization Food Gatherers to eliminate hunger and distribute food to the needy, and Food Gatherers is now an independent nonprofit responsible for the Washtenaw County Food Bank with over 5,000 volunteers and a 19-member staff.[30] On Zingerman's 20th anniversary, 13 nonprofit community organizations in Ann Arbor erected a plaque next to Zingerman's Delicatessen with a dedication that read, "Thank you for feeding, sheltering, educating, uplifting, and inspiring an entire community."[31] Clearly, for Weinzweig and Saginaw, leadership entails being of service to others.[32]

is minimized. Organizations in the United States tend to be very profit-oriented and thus tend to downplay the importance of individual employees' needs and desires. Many countries in Europe have a more individualistic perspective than Japan and a more humanistic perspective than the United States, and this may result in some European managers' being more people-oriented than their Japanese or American counterparts. European managers, for example, tend to be reluctant to lay off employees, and when a layoff is absolutely necessary, they take careful steps to make it as painless as possible.[33]

Another cross-cultural difference occurs in time horizons. While managers in any one country often differ in their time horizons, there are also national differences. For example, U.S. organizations tend to have a short-term profit orientation, and thus U.S. managers' personal leadership styles emphasize short-term performance. Japanese organizations tend to have a long-term growth orientation, so Japanese managers' personal leadership styles emphasize long-term performance. Justus Mische, a personnel manager at the European organization Hoechst, suggests that "Europe, at least the big international firms in Europe, have a philosophy between the Japanese, long term, and the United States, short term."[34] Research on these and other global aspects of leadership is in its infancy; as it continues, more cultural differences in managers' personal leadership styles may be discovered.

Power: The Key to Leadership

No matter what one's leadership style, a key component of effective leadership is found in the *power* the leader has to affect other people's behavior and get them to act in certain ways.[35] There are several types of power: legitimate, reward, coercive, expert, and referent power (see Figure 14.1).[36] Effective leaders take steps to ensure that they have sufficient levels of each type and that they use the power they have in beneficial ways.

legitimate power The authority that a manager has by virtue of his or her position in an organization's hierarchy.

LEGITIMATE POWER **Legitimate power** is the authority a manager has by virtue of his or her position in an organization's hierarchy. Personal leadership style often influences how a manager exercises legitimate power. Take the case of Carol Loray, who is a first-line manager in a greeting card company and leads a group of 15 artists and designers. Loray has the legitimate power to hire new employees, assign projects to the artists and designers, monitor their work, and appraise their performance. She uses this power effectively. She always makes sure her project assignments match the interests of her subordinates as much as possible so they will enjoy their work. She monitors their work to make sure they are on track but does not engage in close supervision, which can hamper creativity. She makes sure her performance appraisals are developmental, providing concrete advice for areas where improvements could be

Figure 14.1
Source of Managerial Power

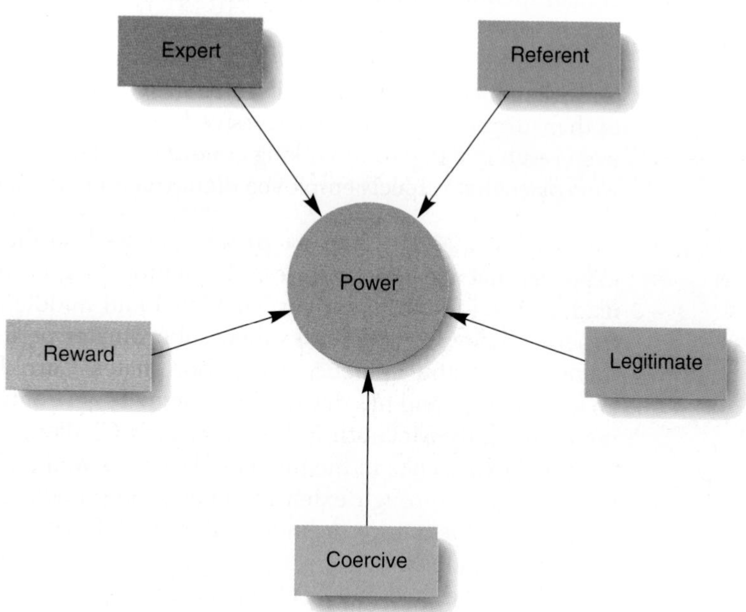

made. Recently Loray negotiated with her manager to increase her legitimate power so she can now initiate and develop proposals for new card lines.

reward power The ability of a manager to give or withhold tangible and intangible rewards.

REWARD POWER **Reward power** is the ability of a manager to give or withhold tangible rewards (pay raises, bonuses, choice job assignments) and intangible rewards (verbal praise, a pat on the back, respect). As you learned in Chapter 13, members of an organization are motivated to perform at a high level by a variety of rewards. Being able to give or withhold rewards based on performance is a major source of power that allows managers to have a highly motivated workforce. Managers of salespeople in retail organizations like Neiman Marcus, Nordstrom, and Macy's[37] and in car dealerships such as Mazda, Ford, and Volvo often use their reward power to motivate their subordinates. Subordinates in organizations such as these often receive commissions on whatever they sell and rewards for the quality of their customer service, which motivate them to do the best they can.

Effective managers use their reward power in to show appreciation for subordinates' good work and efforts. Ineffective managers use rewards in a more controlling manner (wielding the "stick" instead of offering the "carrot") that signals to subordinates that the manager has the upper hand. Managers also can take steps to increase their reward power. Carol Loray had the legitimate power to appraise her subordinates' performance, but she lacked the reward power to distribute raises and end-of-year bonuses until she discussed with her own manager why this would be a valuable motivational tool for her to use. Loray now receives a pool of money each year for salary increases and bonuses and has the reward power to distribute them as she sees fit.

coercive power The ability of a manager to punish others.

COERCIVE POWER **Coercive power** is the ability of a manager to punish others. Punishment can range from verbal reprimands to reductions in pay or working hours to actual dismissal. In the previous chapter we discussed how punishment can have negative side effects, such as resentment and retaliation, and should be used only when necessary (for example, to curtail a dangerous behavior). Managers who rely heavily on coercive power tend to be ineffective as leaders and sometimes even get fired themselves. William J. Fife is one example; he was fired from his position as CEO of Giddings and Lewis Inc., a manufacturer of factory equipment, because of his overreliance on coercive power. In meetings Fife often verbally criticized, attacked, and embarrassed top managers. Realizing how destructive Fife's use of punishment was for them and the company, these managers complained to the board of directors, who, after a careful consideration of the issues, asked Fife to resign.[38]

Excessive use of coercive power seldom produces high performance and is questionable ethically. Sometimes it amounts to a form of mental abuse, robbing workers of their dignity and causing excessive levels of stress. Overuse of coercive power can even result in dangerous working conditions. Better results and, importantly, an ethical workplace that respects employee dignity can be obtained by using reward power.

expert power Power that is based on the special knowledge, skills, and expertise that a leader possesses.

EXPERT POWER **Expert power** is based on the special knowledge, skills, and expertise that a leader possesses. The nature of expert power varies, depending on the leader's level in the hierarchy. First-level and middle managers often have technical expertise relevant to the tasks their subordinates perform. Their expert power gives them considerable influence over subordinates. Carol Loray has expert power: She is an artist herself and has drawn and designed some of her company's top-selling greeting cards. Judy McGrath in "A Manager's Challenge" has expert power from over 25 years' experience in the media industry, as well as from her efforts to stay attuned to pop culture through extensive networking, reading, and ever-ready openness for the new and the quirky. As indicated in the following "Manager as a Person" box, the kinds of positions that leaders with expert power assume depends on who they are as individuals and the kinds of challenges that appeal to them.

Manager as a Person

Liane Pelletier Uses Her Expert Power in Alaska

Liane Pelletier exemplifies leadership: rather than simply pushing the needed changes into place in ACS, she won legitimacy for her ideas by embracing the Alaskan culture of her employees and customers.

Liane Pelletier was a senior vice president at Sprint when a recruiting firm called her to see if she was interested in becoming CEO of Alaska Communications Systems (ACS).[39] With over 15 years' experience in the telecommunications industry, she definitely had the skills, knowledge, and expertise to head ACS. Like many top managers, Connecticut-born Pelletier hesitated about making a move to Alaska–but she didn't hesitate for long.[40]

Pelletier loves adventure and new experiences; the opportunity to leverage her industry experience and take on the challenge of transforming ACS made her decision an easy one. For Pelletier, Alaska was not such a far-flung place to move to: She had traveled widely, on excursions ranging from hiking the Appalachian Trail to boating down the Amazon River. And now snowshoeing in Alaska is one of her new leisure activities.[41]

ACS is Alaska's largest local exchange carrier and the only in-state provider with its own local, long distance, wireless, and Internet infrastructure.[42] As an experienced top manager in telecommunications, Pelletier sees her role at ACS as an exciting opportunity.[43] When she came to ACS, she realized the company was focused on products rather than customers: Different divisions would provide different kinds of services to customers without taking into account that the same customers might be using other services provided by other parts of the company. Pelletier restructured ACS around customers and how to better meet their needs through the multiple products and services ACS offers. Now sales and service at ACS are integrated across product lines, and employees receive training so they are knowledgeable about all of ACS's products and services.[44] Pelletier's vision for ACS revolves around customer-focused growth and improved wireless services. Already her efforts have paid off for the company in terms of increases in ACS's earnings and stock price.[45] Clearly ACS is fortunate that Pelletier assumed the top post and is applying her expertise to enable the company to better serve its customers and expand its range of products.[46]

Some top managers derive expert power from their technical expertise. Craig Barrett, chairman of the board of directors of Intel from 2005 to 2009, has a PhD in materials science from Stanford University and is very knowledgeable about the ins and outs of Intel's business–producing semiconductors and microprocessors.[47] Similarly, Bill Gates, chairman of Microsoft, and CEO Steve Ballmer have expertise in software design; and Tachi Yamada, president of the Bill and Melinda Gates Foundation's Global Health Program, has an MD and was previously chairman of research and development at GlaxoSmithKline.[48] Many top-level managers, however, lack technical expertise and derive their expert power from their abilities as decision makers, planners, and strategists. Jack Welch, the former well-known leader and CEO of General Electric, summed it up this way: "The basic thing that we at the top of the company know is that we don't know the business. What we have, I hope, is the ability to allocate resources, people, and dollars."[49]

Effective leaders take steps to ensure that they have an adequate amount of expert power to perform their leadership roles. They may obtain additional training or education in their fields, make sure they keep up with the latest developments and changes in technology, stay abreast of changes in their fields through involvement in professional associations, and read widely to be aware of momentous changes in the organization's task and general environments. Expert power tends to be best used in a guiding or coaching manner rather than in an arrogant, high-handed manner.

referent power Power that comes from subordinates' and coworkers' respect, admiration, and loyalty.

REFERENT POWER **Referent power** is more informal than the other kinds of power. Referent power is a function of the personal characteristics of a leader; it is the power that comes from subordinates' and coworkers' respect, admiration, and loyalty. Leaders who are likable and whom subordinates wish to use as a role model are especially likely to possess referent power, as is true of Judy McGrath in "A Manager's Challenge."

In addition to being a valuable asset for top managers like McGrath, referent power can help first-line and middle managers be effective leaders as well. Sally Carruthers, for example, is the first-level manager of a group of secretaries in the finance department of a large state university. Carruthers's secretaries are known to be among the best in the university. Much of their willingness to go above and beyond the call of duty has been attributed to Carruthers's warm and caring nature, which makes each of them feel important and valued. Managers can take steps to increase their referent power, such as taking time to get to know their subordinates and showing interest in and concern for them.

Empowerment: An Ingredient in Modern Management

empowerment The expansion of employees' knowledge, tasks, and decision-making responsibilities.

More and more managers today are incorporating into their personal leadership styles an aspect that at first glance seems to be the opposite of being a leader. In Chapter 1 we described how **empowerment**–the process of giving employees at all levels the authority to make decisions, be responsible for their outcomes, improve quality, and cut costs–is becoming increasingly popular in organizations. When leaders empower their subordinates, the subordinates typically take over some responsibilities and

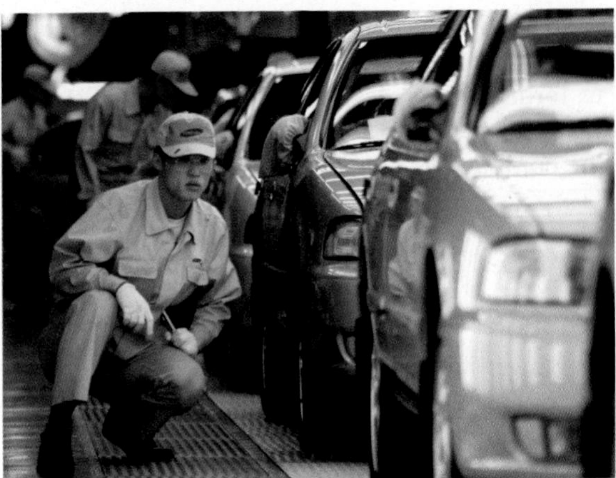
An empowered employee, like this auto assembly line worker, can halt the production process to correct an error rather than wasting time and money by waiting for a supervisor.

authority that used to reside with the leader or manager, such as the right to reject parts that do not meet quality standards, the right to check one's own work, and the right to schedule work activities. Empowered subordinates are given the power to make some decisions that their leaders or supervisors used to make.

Empowerment might seem to be the opposite of effective leadership because managers are allowing subordinates to take a more active role in leading themselves. In actuality, however, empowerment can contribute to effective leadership for several reasons:

- Empowerment increases a manager's ability to get things done because the manager has the support and help of subordinates who may have special knowledge of work tasks.
- Empowerment often increases workers' involvement, motivation, and commitment, and this helps ensure that they are working toward organizational goals.
- Empowerment gives managers more time to concentrate on their pressing concerns because they spend less time on day-to-day supervision.

Effective managers like Judy McGrath realize the benefits of empowerment. The personal leadership style of managers who empower subordinates often entails developing subordinates' ability to make good decisions as well as being their guide, coach, and source of inspiration. Empowerment is a popular trend in the United States at companies as diverse as United Parcel Service (a package delivery company) and Coram Healthcare Corporation (a provider of medical equipment and services) and is a part of servant leadership. Empowerment is also taking off around the world.[50] For instance, companies in South Korea (such as Samsung, Hyundai, and Daewoo), in which decision making typically was centralized with the founding families, are now empowering managers at lower levels to make decisions.[51]

Trait and Behavior Models of Leadership

Leading is such an important process in all organizations–nonprofit organizations, government agencies, and schools, as well as for-profit corporations–that it has been researched for decades. Early approaches to leadership, called the *trait model* and the *behavior model,* sought to determine what effective leaders are like as people and what they do that makes them so effective.

The Trait Model

LO14-2 Identify the traits that show the strongest relationship to leadership, the behaviors leaders engage in, and the limitations of the trait and behavior models of leadership.

The trait model of leadership focused on identifying the personal characteristics that cause effective leadership. Researchers thought effective leaders must have certain personal qualities that set them apart from ineffective leaders and from people who never become leaders. Decades of research (beginning in the 1930s) and hundreds of studies indicate that certain personal characteristics do appear to be associated with effective leadership. (See Table 14.1 for a list of these.)[52] Notice that although this model is called the "trait" model, some of the personal characteristics that it identifies are not personality traits per se but, rather, are concerned with a leader's skills, abilities, knowledge, and expertise. As "A Manager's Challenge" shows, Judy McGrath certainly appears to possess many of these characteristics (such as intelligence, knowledge and expertise, self-confidence, high energy, and integrity and honesty). Leaders who do not possess these traits may be ineffective.

Table 14.1
Traits and Personal Characteristics Related to Effective Leadership

Trait	Description
Intelligence	Helps managers understand complex issues and solve problems.
Knowledge and expertise	Help managers make good decisions and discover ways to increase efficiency and effectiveness.
Dominance	Helps managers influence their subordinates to achieve organizational goals.
Self-confidence	Contributes to managers' effectively influencing subordinates and persisting when faced with obstacles or difficulties.
High energy	Helps managers deal with the many demands they face.
Tolerance for stress	Helps managers deal with uncertainty and make difficult decisions.
Integrity and honesty	Help managers behave ethically and earn their subordinates' trust and confidence.
Maturity	Helps managers avoid acting selfishly, control their feelings, and admit when they have made a mistake.

Traits alone are not the key to understanding leader effectiveness, however. Some effective leaders do not possess all these traits, and some leaders who possess them are not effective in their leadership roles. This lack of a consistent relationship between leader traits and leader effectiveness led researchers to shift their attention away from traits and to search for new explanations for effective leadership. Rather than focusing on what leaders are like (the traits they possess), researchers began looking at what effective leaders actually do–in other words, at the behaviors that allow effective leaders to influence their subordinates to achieve group and organizational goals.

The Behavior Model

After extensive study in the 1940s and 1950s, researchers at The Ohio State University identified two basic kinds of leader behaviors that many leaders in the United States, Germany, and other countries engaged in to influence their subordinates: *consideration* and *initiating structure*.[53]

consideration Behavior indicating that a manager trusts, respects, and cares about subordinates.

CONSIDERATION Leaders engage in **consideration** when they show their subordinates that they trust, respect, and care about them. Managers who truly look out for the well-being of their subordinates, and do what they can to help subordinates feel good and enjoy their work, perform consideration behaviors. In "A Manager's Challenge," Judy McGrath engages in consideration when she listens to employees and fosters an inclusive, nurturing culture at MTV Networks.

At Costco Wholesale Corporation, CEO Jim Senegal believes that consideration not only is an ethical imperative but also makes good business sense,[54] as indicated in the following "Ethics in Action" box.

initiating structure Behavior that managers engage in to ensure that work gets done, subordinates perform their jobs acceptably, and the organization is efficient and effective.

INITIATING STRUCTURE Leaders engage in **initiating structure** when they take steps to make sure that work gets done, subordinates perform their jobs acceptably, and the organization is efficient and effective. Assigning tasks to individuals or work groups, letting subordinates know what is expected of them, deciding how work should be done, making schedules, encouraging adherence to rules and regulations, and motivating subordinates to do a good job are all examples of initiating structure.[69]

Ethics in Action

Consideration at Costco

Managers at Costco, including CEO Jim Senegal, believe consideration is so important that one of the principles in Costco's code of ethics is "Take Care of Our Employees."[55] Costco Wholesale Corporation is the fifth largest retailer, and the top warehouse retailer, in the United States.[56] Wages at Costco are an average of $17 per hour–over 40% higher than the average hourly wage at Walmart, Costco's major competitor.[57] Costco pays the majority of health insurance costs for its employees (employees pay around 8% of health insurance costs compared to an industry average of around 25%), and part-time employees receive health

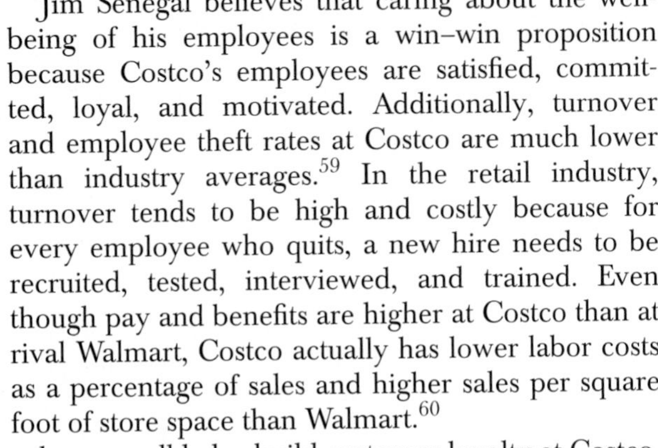

insurance after they have been with the company six months. Overall, about 85% of Costco employees are covered by health insurance, compared with fewer than 45% of employees at Target and Walmart.[58]

Jim Senegal believes that caring about the well-being of his employees is a win–win proposition because Costco's employees are satisfied, committed, loyal, and motivated. Additionally, turnover and employee theft rates at Costco are much lower than industry averages.[59] In the retail industry, turnover tends to be high and costly because for every employee who quits, a new hire needs to be recruited, tested, interviewed, and trained. Even though pay and benefits are higher at Costco than at rival Walmart, Costco actually has lower labor costs as a percentage of sales and higher sales per square foot of store space than Walmart.[60]

Loyal Costco customers like these know that their bargains don't come at the expense of employees' paychecks and benefits.

Additionally, treating employees well helps build customer loyalty at Costco. Surely customers enjoy the bargains and low prices that come from shopping in a warehouse store, the relatively high quality of the goods Costco stocks, and Costco's policy of not marking up prices by more than 14% or 15% (relatively low markups for retail) even if the goods would sell with higher markups. However, customers are also loyal to Costco because they know the company treats its employees well and their bargains are not coming at the expense of employees' paychecks and benefits.[61]

Costco started out as a single warehouse store in Seattle, Washington, in 1983. Now the company has 566 stores (including stores in South Korea, Taiwan, Japan, Canada, and Britain) and over 50 million members who pay an annual fee to shop at Costco stores.[62] Costco's growth and financial performance are enviable.[63] For example, annual revenues for the 2009 fiscal year were $64.4 billion.[64] Clearly consideration has paid off for Costco and for its employees.[65]

True to caring for the well-being of employees, Costco did not lay off any employees during the recession in the late 2000s.[66] However, some female employees have filed a class action lawsuit alleging gender discrimination at Costco.[67] Costco denies that discrimination has taken place, and in a recent interview Jim Senegal indicated that Costco has had relatively few lawsuits for an organization of its size.[68] Determining whether discrimination took place at Costco will be a matter for the courts to decide.

Michael Teckel, the manager of an upscale store selling imported men's and women's shoes in a midwestern city, engages in initiating structure when he establishes weekly work, lunch, and break schedules to ensure that the store has enough salespeople on the floor. Teckle also initiates structure when he discusses the latest shoe designs with his subordinates so they are knowledgeable with customers, when he encourages adherence to the store's refund and exchange policies, and when he encourages his staff to provide high-quality customer service and to avoid a hard-sell approach.

Initiating structure and consideration are independent leader behaviors. Leaders can be high on both, low on both, or high on one and low on the other. Many effective leaders, like Judy McGrath of MTV Networks, engage in both of these behaviors.

Leadership researchers have identified leader behaviors similar to consideration and initiating structure. Researchers at the University of Michigan, for example, identified two categories of leadership behaviors, *employee-centered behaviors* and *job-oriented behaviors,* that correspond roughly to consideration and initiating structure, respectively.[70] Models of leadership popular with consultants also tend to zero in on these two kinds of behaviors. For example, Robert Blake and Jane Mouton's Managerial Grid focuses on *concern for people* (similar to consideration) and *concern for production* (similar to initiating structure). Blake and Mouton advise that effective leadership often requires both a high level of concern for people and a high level of concern for production.[71] As another example, Paul Hersey and Kenneth Blanchard's model focuses on *supportive behaviors* (similar to consideration) and *task-oriented behaviors* (similar to initiating structure). According to Hersey and Blanchard, leaders need to consider the nature of their subordinates when trying to determine the extent to which they should perform these two behaviors.[72]

You might expect that effective leaders and managers would perform both kinds of behaviors, but research has found that this is not necessarily the case. The relationship between performance of consideration and initiating-structure behaviors and leader effectiveness is not clear-cut. Some leaders are effective even when they do not perform consideration or initiating-structure behaviors, and some leaders are ineffective even when they perform both kinds of behaviors. Like the trait model of leadership, the behavior model alone cannot explain leader effectiveness. Realizing this, researchers began building more complicated models of leadership, focused not only on the leader and what he or she does but also on the situation or context in which leadership occurs.

Contingency Models of Leadership

LO14-3 Explain how contingency models of leadership enhance our understanding of effective leadership and management in organizations.

Simply possessing certain traits or performing certain behaviors does not ensure that a manager will be an effective leader in all situations calling for leadership. Some managers who seem to possess the right traits and perform the right behaviors turn out to be ineffective leaders. Managers lead in a wide variety of situations and organizations and have various kinds of subordinates performing diverse tasks in a multiplicity of environmental contexts. Given the wide variety of situations in which leadership occurs, what makes a manager an effective leader in one situation (such as certain traits or behaviors) is not necessarily what that manager needs to be equally effective in a different situation. An effective army general might not be an effective university president; an effective restaurant manager might not be an effective clothing store manager; an effective football team coach might not be an effective fitness center manager; and an effective first-line manager in a manufacturing company might not be an effective middle manager. The traits or behaviors that may contribute to a manager's being an effective leader in one situation might actually result in the same manager being an ineffective leader in another situation.

Contingency models of leadership take into account the situation or context within which leadership occurs. According to contingency models, whether or not a manager is an effective leader is the result of the interplay between what the manager is like, what he or she does, and the situation in which leadership takes place. Contingency models propose that whether a leader who possesses certain traits or performs certain behaviors is effective depends on, or is contingent on, the situation or context. In this section we discuss three prominent contingency models developed to shed light on what makes managers effective leaders: Fred Fiedler's contingency model, Robert House's path–goal theory, and the leader substitutes model. As you will see, these leadership models are complementary; each focuses on a somewhat different aspect of effective leadership in organizations.

Fiedler's Contingency Model

Fred E. Fiedler was among the first leadership researchers to acknowledge that effective leadership is contingent on, or depends on, the characteristics of the leader *and* of the situation. Fiedler's contingency model helps explain why a manager may be an effective leader in one situation and ineffective in another; it also suggests which kinds of managers are likely to be most effective in which situations.[73]

LEADER STYLE As with the trait approach, Fiedler hypothesized that personal characteristics can influence leader effectiveness. He used the term *leader style* to refer to a manager's characteristic approach to leadership and identified two basic leader styles: *relationship-oriented* and *task-oriented.* All managers can be described as having one style or the other.

relationship-oriented leaders Leaders whose primary concern is to develop good relationships with their subordinates and to be liked by them.

task-oriented leaders Leaders whose primary concern is to ensure that subordinates perform at a high level.

Relationship-oriented leaders are primarily concerned with developing good relationships with their subordinates and being liked by them. Relationship-oriented managers focus on having high-quality interpersonal relationships with subordinates. This does not mean, however, that the job does not get done when such leaders are at the helm. But it does mean that the quality of interpersonal relationships with subordinates is a prime concern for relationship-oriented leaders.

Task-oriented leaders are primarily concerned with ensuring that subordinates perform at a high level and focus on task accomplishment. While task-oriented leaders also may be concerned about having good interpersonal relationships with their subordinates, task accomplishment is their prime concern.

In his research, Fiedler measured leader style by asking leaders to rate the coworker with whom they have had the most difficulty working (called the least preferred coworker or LPC) on a number of dimensions, such as whether the person is boring or interesting, gloomy or cheerful, enthusiastic or unenthusiastic, cooperative or uncooperative. Relationship-oriented leaders tend to describe the LPC in relatively positive terms; their concern for good relationships leads them to think well of others. Task-oriented leaders tend to describe the LPC in negative terms; their concern for task accomplishment causes them to think badly about others who make getting the job done difficult. Thus relationship-oriented and task-oriented leaders are sometimes referred to as high-LPC and low-LPC leaders, respectively.

SITUATIONAL CHARACTERISTICS According to Fiedler, leadership style is an enduring characteristic; managers cannot change their style, nor can they adopt different styles in different kinds of situations. With this in mind, Fiedler identified three situational characteristics that are important determinants of how favorable a situation is for leading: leader–member relations, task structure, and position power. When a situation is favorable for leading, it is relatively easy for a manager to influence subordinates so they perform at a high level and contribute to organizational efficiency and effectiveness. In a situation unfavorable for leading, it is much more difficult for a manager to exert influence.

leader–member relations The extent to which followers like, trust, and are loyal to their leader; a determinant of how favorable a situation is for leading.

LEADER–MEMBER RELATIONS The first situational characteristic Fiedler described, **leader–member relations,** is the extent to which followers like, trust, and are loyal to their leader. Situations are more favorable for leading when leader–member relations are good.

task structure The extent to which the work to be performed is clear-cut so that a leader's subordinates know what needs to be accomplished and how to go about doing it; a determinant of how favorable a situation is for leading.

TASK STRUCTURE The second situational characteristic Fiedler described, **task structure,** is the extent to which the work to be performed is clear-cut so that a leader's subordinates know what needs to be accomplished and how to go about doing it. When task structure is high, the situation is favorable for leading. When task structure is low, goals may be vague, subordinates may be unsure of what they should be doing or how they should do it, and the situation is unfavorable for leading.

Task structure was low for Geraldine Laybourne when she was a top manager at Nickelodeon, the children's television network. It was never precisely clear what would appeal to her young viewers, whose tastes can change dramatically, or how to motivate her subordinates to come up with creative and novel ideas.[74] In contrast, Herman Mashaba, founder of Black Like Me, a hair care products company based

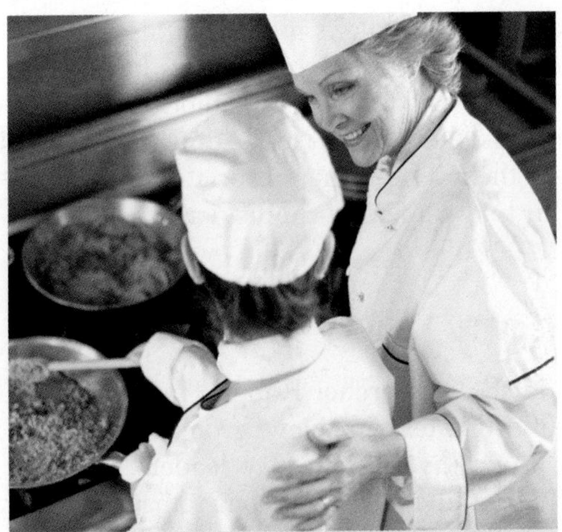

Developing good relations with employees can make the "situation" more favorable for leading.

in South Africa, seemed to have relatively high task structure when he started his company. His company's goals were to produce and sell inexpensive hair care products to native Africans, and managers accomplished these goals by using simple yet appealing packaging and distributing the products through neighborhood beauty salons.[75]

POSITION POWER The third situational characteristic Fiedler described, **position power,** is the amount of legitimate, reward, and coercive power a leader has by virtue of his or her position in an organization. Leadership situations are more favorable for leading when position power is strong.

position power The amount of legitimate, reward, and coercive power that a leader has by virtue of his or her position in an organization; a determinant of how favorable a situation is for leading.

COMBINING LEADER STYLE AND THE SITUATION By considering all possible combinations of good and poor leader–member relations, high and low task structure, and strong and weak position power, Fiedler identified eight leadership situations, which vary in their favorability for leading (see Figure 14.2). After extensive research, he determined that relationship-oriented leaders are most effective in moderately favorable situations (IV, V, VI, and VII in Figure 14.2) and task-oriented leaders are most effective in situations that are either very favorable (I, II, and III) or very unfavorable (VIII).

PUTTING THE CONTINGENCY MODEL INTO PRACTICE Recall that, according to Fiedler, leader style is an enduring characteristic that managers cannot change. This suggests that for managers to be effective, either managers need to be placed in leadership situations that fit their style or situations need to be changed to suit the managers. Situations can be changed, for example, by giving a manager more position power or taking steps to increase task structure, such as by clarifying goals.

Take the case of Mark Compton, a relationship-oriented leader employed by a small construction company, who was in a very unfavorable situation and was having a rough time leading his construction crew. His subordinates did not trust him to look out for their well-being (poor leader–member relations); the construction jobs he supervised tended to be novel and complex (low task structure); and he had no control over the rewards and disciplinary actions his subordinates received (weak position power). Recognizing the need to improve matters, Compton's supervisor gave him the power to reward crew members with bonuses and overtime work as he saw fit and to discipline crew members for poor-quality work and unsafe on-the-job behavior. As his leadership situation improved to moderately favorable, so too did Compton's effectiveness as a leader and the performance of his crew.

Figure 14.2
Fielder's Contingency Theory of Leadership

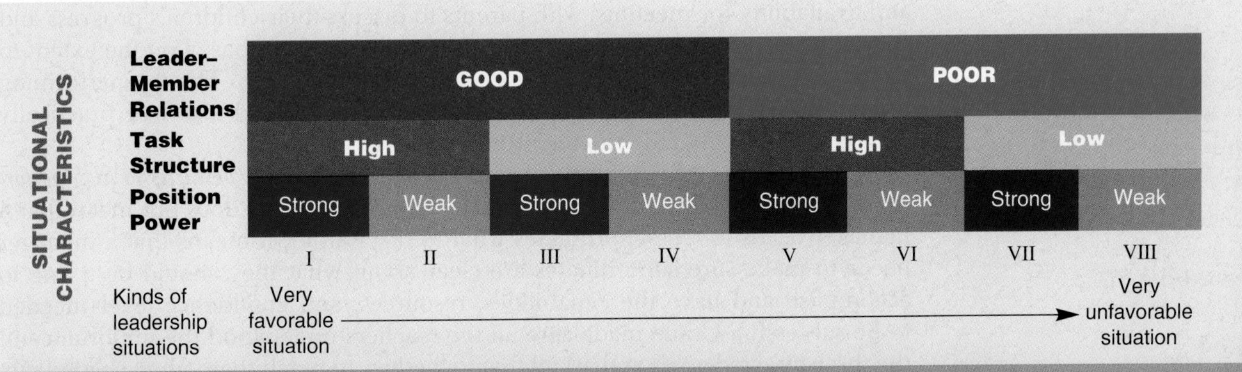

Relationship-oriented leaders are most effective in moderately favorable situations for leading (IV, V, VI, VII).
Task-oriented leaders are most effective in very favorable situations (I, II, III) or very unfavorable situations (VIII) for leading.

Research studies tend to support some aspects of Fiedler's model but also suggest that, like most theories, it needs some modifications.[76] Some researchers have questioned what the LPC scale really measures. Others find fault with the model's premise that leaders cannot alter their styles. That is, it is likely that at least some leaders can diagnose the situation they are in and, when their style is inappropriate for the situation, modify their style so that it is more in line with what the leadership situation calls for.

House's Path–Goal Theory

path–goal theory A contingency model of leadership proposing that leaders can motivate subordinates by identifying their desired outcomes, rewarding them for high performance and the attainment of work goals with these desired outcomes, and clarifying for them the paths leading to the attainment of work goals.

In what he called **path–goal theory,** leadership researcher Robert House focused on what leaders can do to motivate their subordinates to achieve group and organizational goals.[77] The premise of path–goal theory is that effective leaders motivate subordinates to achieve goals by (1) clearly identifying the outcomes that subordinates are trying to obtain from the workplace, (2) rewarding subordinates with these outcomes for high performance and the attainment of work goals, and (3) clarifying for subordinates the *paths* leading to the attainment of work *goals.* Path–goal theory is a contingency model because it proposes that the steps managers should take to motivate subordinates depend on both the nature of the subordinates and the type of work they do.

Based on the expectancy theory of motivation (see Chapter 13), path–goal theory gives managers three guidelines to being effective leaders:

1. *Find out what outcomes your subordinates are trying to obtain from their jobs and the organization.* These outcomes can range from satisfactory pay and job security to reasonable working hours and interesting and challenging job assignments. After identifying these outcomes, the manager should have the *reward power* needed to distribute or withhold the outcomes. Mark Crane, for example, is the vice principal of a large elementary school. Crane determined that the teachers he leads are trying to obtain the following outcomes from their jobs: pay raises, autonomy in the classroom, and the choice of which grades they teach. Crane had reward power for the latter two outcomes, but the school's principal determined how the pool of money for raises was to be distributed each year. Because Crane was the first-line manager who led the teachers and was most familiar with their performance, he asked the principal (his boss) to give him some say in determining pay raises. Realizing that this made a lot of sense, his principal gave Crane full power to distribute raises and requested only that Crane review his decisions with him before informing the teachers about them.
2. *Reward subordinates for high performance and goal attainment with the outcomes they desire.* The teachers and administrators at Crane's school considered several dimensions of teacher performance to be critical to achieving their goal of providing high-quality education: excellent in-class instruction, special programs to enhance student interest and learning (such as science and computer projects), and availability for meetings with parents to discuss their children's progress and special needs. Crane distributed pay raises to the teachers based on the extent to which they performed highly on each of these dimensions. The top-performing teachers were given first choice of grade assignments and also had practically complete autonomy in their classrooms.
3. *Clarify the paths to goal attainment for subordinates, remove any obstacles to high performance, and express confidence in subordinates' capabilities.* This does not mean that a manager needs to tell subordinates what to do. Rather, it means that a manager needs to make sure subordinates are clear about what they should be trying to accomplish and have the capabilities, resources, and confidence levels needed to be successful. Crane made sure all the teachers understood the importance of the three targeted goals and asked them whether, to reach them, they needed any special resources or supplies for their classes. Crane also gave additional coaching and guidance to teachers who seemed to be struggling. For example, Patrick Conolly, in his first year of teaching after graduate school, was unsure how to

use special projects in a third grade class and how to react to parents who were critical. Conolly's teaching was excellent, but he felt insecure about how he was doing on this dimension. To help build Conolly's confidence, Crane told Conolly that he thought he could be one of the school's top teachers (which was true). He gave Conolly some ideas about special projects that worked particularly well with the third grade, such as a writing project. Crane also role-played teacher–parent interactions with Conolly. Conolly played the role of a particularly dissatisfied or troubled parent, while Crane played the role of a teacher trying to solve the underlying problem while making the parent feel that his or her child's needs were being met. Crane's efforts to clarify the paths to goal attainment for Conolly paid off: Within two years the local PTS voted Conolly teacher of the year.

Path–goal theory identifies four kinds of leadership behaviors that motivate subordinates:

- *Directive behaviors* are similar to initiating structure and include setting goals, assigning tasks, showing subordinates how to complete tasks, and taking concrete steps to improve performance.
- *Supportive behaviors* are similar to consideration and include expressing concern for subordinates and looking out for their best interests.
- *Participative behaviors* give subordinates a say in matters and decisions that affect them.
- *Achievement-oriented behaviors* motivate subordinates to perform at the highest level possible by, for example, setting challenging goals, expecting that they be met, and believing in subordinates' capabilities.

Which of these behaviors should managers use to lead effectively? The answer to this question depends, or is contingent on, the nature of the subordinates and the kind of work they do.

Directive behaviors may be beneficial when subordinates are having difficulty completing assigned tasks, but they might be detrimental when subordinates are independent thinkers who work best when left alone. *Supportive* behaviors are often advisable when subordinates are experiencing high levels of stress. *Participative* behaviors can be particularly effective when subordinates' support of a decision is required. *Achievement-oriented* behaviors may increase motivation levels of highly capable subordinates who are bored from having too few challenges, but they might backfire if used with subordinates who are already pushed to their limit.

The Leader Substitutes Model

leadership substitute A characteristic of a subordinate or of a situation or context that acts in place of the influence of a leader and makes leadership unnecessary.

The leader substitutes model suggests that leadership is sometimes unnecessary because substitutes for leadership are present. A **leadership substitute** is something that acts in place of the influence of a leader and makes leadership unnecessary. This model suggests that under certain conditions managers do not have to play a leadership role–members of an organization sometimes can perform at a high level without a manager exerting influence over them.[78] The leader substitutes model is a contingency model because it suggests that in some situations leadership is unnecessary.

Take the case of David Cotsonas, who teaches English at a foreign language school in Cyprus, an island in the Mediterranean Sea. Cotsonas is fluent in Greek, English, and French; is an excellent teacher; and is highly motivated. Many of his students are businesspeople who have some rudimentary English skills and wish to increase their fluency to be able to conduct more of their business in English. He enjoys not only teaching them English but also learning about the work they do, and he often keeps in touch with his students after they finish his classes. Cotsonas meets with the director of the school twice a year to discuss semiannual class schedules and enrollments.

With practically no influence from a leader, Cotsonas is a highly motivated top performer at the school. In his situation, leadership is unnecessary because substitutes for leadership are present. Cotsonas's teaching expertise, his motivation, and his enjoyment of his work all are substitutes for the influence of a leader–in this case the school's director. If the school's director were to try to influence how Cotsonas performs his job, Cotsonas would probably resent this infringement on his autonomy, and it is unlikely that his performance would improve because he is already one of the school's best teachers.

As in Cotsonas's case, *characteristics of subordinates*–such as their skills, abilities, experience, knowledge, and motivation–can be substitutes for leadership.[79] *Characteristics of the situation or context*–such as the extent to which the work is interesting and enjoyable–also can be substitutes. When work is interesting and enjoyable, as it is for Cotsonas, jobholders do not need to be coaxed into performing because performing is rewarding in its own right. Similarly, when managers *empower* their subordinates or use *self-managed work teams* (discussed in detail in Chapter 15), the need for leadership influence from a manager is decreased because team members manage themselves.

Substitutes for leadership can increase organizational efficiency and effectiveness because they free up some of managers' valuable time and allow managers to focus their efforts on discovering new ways to improve organizational effectiveness. The director of the language school, for example, was able to spend much of his time making arrangements to open a second school in Rhodes, an island in the Aegean Sea, because of the presence of leadership substitutes, not only for Cotsonas but for most other teachers at the school as well.

Bringing It All Together

Effective leadership in organizations occurs when managers take steps to lead in a way that is appropriate for the situation or context in which leadership occurs and for the subordinates who are being led. The three contingency models of leadership just discussed help managers focus on the necessary ingredients for effective leadership. They are complementary in that each one looks at the leadership question from a different angle. Fiedler's contingency model explores how a manager's leadership style needs to be matched to that person's leadership situation for maximum effectiveness. House's path–goal theory focuses on how managers should motivate subordinates and describes the specific kinds of behaviors managers can engage in to have a highly motivated workforce. The leadership substitutes model alerts managers to the fact that sometimes they do not need to exert influence over subordinates and thus can free up their time for other important activities. Table 14.2 recaps these three contingency models of leadership.

Table 14.2
Contingency Models of Leadership

Model	Focus	Key Contingencies
Fiedler's contingency model	Describes two leader styles, relationship-oriented and task-oriented, and the kinds of situations in which each kind of leader will be most effective.	Whether a relationship-oriented or a task-oriented leader is effective is contingent on the situation.
House's path–goal theory	Describes how effective leaders motivate their followers.	The behaviors that managers should engage in to be effective leaders are contingent on the nature of the subordinates and the work they do.
Leader substitutes model	Describes when leadership is unnecessary.	Whether leadership is necessary for subordinates to perform highly is contingent on characteristics of the subordinates and the situation.

Transformational Leadership

LO14-4 Describe what transformational leadership is, and explain how managers can engage in it.

Time and time again, throughout business history, certain leaders seem to literally transform their organizations, making sweeping changes to revitalize and renew operations. For example, when Sue Nokes became senior vice president of sales and customer service at T-Mobile USA in 2002, the quality of T-Mobile's customer service was lower than that of its major competitors; on average, 12% of employees were absent on any day; and annual employee turnover was over 100%.[80] T-Mobile USA is a subsidiary of Deutsche Telekom, has 36,000 employees, and provides wireless voice, messaging, and data services.[81] When Nokes arrived at T-Mobile, valuable employees were quitting their jobs and customers weren't receiving high-quality service; neither employees nor customers were satisfied with their experience with the company.[82] However, by the late 2000s T-Mobile was regularly receiving highest rankings for customer care and satisfaction in the wireless category by J. D. Power and Associates, absence and turnover rates substantially declined, and around 80% of employees indicated that they were satisfied with their jobs.[83] In fact, when Nokes visited call centers, it was not uncommon for employees to greet her with cheers and accolades.[84]

Nokes transformed T-Mobile into a company in which satisfied employees provide excellent service to customers.[85] When managers have such dramatic effects on their subordinates and on an organization as a whole, they are engaging in transformational leadership. **Transformational leadership** occurs when managers change (or transform) their subordinates in three important ways:[86]

transformational leadership Leadership that makes subordinates aware of the importance of their jobs and performance to the organization and aware of their own needs for personal growth and that motivates subordinates to work for the good of the organization.

1. *Transformational managers make subordinates aware of how important their jobs are for the organization and how necessary it is for them to perform those jobs as best they can so the organization can attain its goals.* At T-Mobile, Nokes visited call centers, conducted focus groups, and had town hall meetings to find out what employees and customers were unhappy with and what steps she could take to improve matters.[87] Her philosophy was that when employees are satisfied with their jobs and view their work as important, they are much more likely to provide high-quality customer service. She made employees aware of how important their jobs were by the many steps she took to improve their working conditions, ranging from providing them with their own workspaces to substantially raising their salaries.[88] She emphasized the importance of providing excellent customer service by periodically asking employees what was working well and what was not working well, asking them what steps could be taken to improve problem areas, and taking actions to ensure that employees were able to provide excellent customer service. Nokes also instituted a performance measurement system to track performance in key areas such as quality of service and speed of problem resolution.[89] She sincerely told employees, "You are No. 1, and the customer is why."[90]
2. *Transformational managers make their subordinates aware of the subordinates' own needs for personal growth, development, and accomplishment.* Nokes made T-Mobile's employees aware of their own needs in this regard by transforming training and development at T-Mobile and increasing opportunities for promotions to more responsible positions. Employees now spend over 130 hours per year in training and development programs and team meetings. Nokes also instituted a promote-from-within policy, and around 80% of promotions are given to current employees.[91]
3. *Transformational managers motivate their subordinates to work for the good of the organization as a whole, not just for their own personal gain or benefit.* Nokes emphasized that employees should focus on what matters to customers, coworkers, and T-Mobile as a whole. She let

Sue Nokes exhibits transformational leadership at T-Mobile, turning around their sales and customer service one call center at a time.

employees know that when they were unnecessarily absent from their jobs, they were not doing right by their coworkers. And she emphasized the need to try to resolve customer problems in a single phone call so customers can get on with their busy lives.[92]

When managers transform their subordinates in these three ways, subordinates trust the managers, are highly motivated, and help the organization achieve its goals. How do managers such as Nokes transform subordinates and produce dramatic effects in their organizations? There are at least three ways in which transformational leaders can influence their followers: by being a charismatic leader, by intellectually stimulating subordinates, and by engaging in developmental consideration (see Table 14.3).

Being a Charismatic Leader

charismatic leader An enthusiastic, self-confident leader who is able to clearly communicate his or her vision of how good things could be.

Transformational managers such as Nokes are **charismatic leaders.** They have a vision of how good things could be in their work groups and organizations that is in contrast with the status quo. Their vision usually entails dramatic improvements in group and organizational performance as a result of changes in the organization's structure, culture, strategy, decision making, and other critical processes and factors. This vision paves the way for gaining a competitive advantage. From "A Manager's Challenge," it is clear that part of Judy McGrath's vision for MTV Networks is increasing its digital offerings and transforming MTV into a truly digital company.

Charismatic leaders are excited and enthusiastic about their vision and clearly communicate it to their subordinates, as does Judy McGrath. The excitement, enthusiasm, and self-confidence of a charismatic leader contribute to the leader's being able to inspire followers to enthusiastically support his or her vision.[93] People often think of charismatic leaders or managers as being "larger than life." The essence of charisma, however, is having a vision and enthusiastically communicating it to others. Thus managers who appear to be quiet and earnest can also be charismatic.

Stimulating Subordinates Intellectually

intellectual stimulation Behavior a leader engages in to make followers be aware of problems and view these problems in new ways, consistent with the leader's vision.

Transformational managers openly share information with their subordinates so they are aware of problems and the need for change. The manager causes subordinates to view problems in their groups and throughout the organization from a different perspective, consistent with the manager's vision. Whereas in the past subordinates might not have been aware of some problems, may have viewed problems as a "management issue" beyond their concern, or may have viewed problems as insurmountable, the transformational manager's **intellectual stimulation** leads subordinates to view problems as challenges that they can and will meet and conquer.

Table 14.3
Transformational Leadership

Transformational managers

- Are charismatic.
- Intellectually stimulate subordinates.
- Engage in developmental consideration.

Subordinates of transformational managers

- Have increased awareness of the importance of their jobs and high performance.
- Are aware of their own needs for growth, development, and accomplishment.
- Work for the good of the organization and not just their own personal benefit.

The manager engages and empowers subordinates to take personal responsibility for helping to solve problems, as did Nokes at T-Mobile.[94]

Engaging in Developmental Consideration

developmental consideration Behavior a leader engages in to support and encourage followers and help them develop and grow on the job.

When managers engage in **developmental consideration,** they not only perform the consideration behaviors described earlier, such as demonstrating true concern for the well-being of subordinates, but go one step further. The manager goes out of his or her way to support and encourage subordinates, giving them opportunities to enhance their skills and capabilities and to grow and excel on the job.[95] As mentioned earlier, Nokes did this in numerous ways. In fact, after she first met with employees in a call center in Albuquerque, New Mexico, Karen Viola, the manager of the call center, said, "Everyone came out crying. The people said that they had never felt so inspired in their lives, and that they had never met with any leader at that level who [they felt] cared."[96]

All organizations, no matter how large or small, successful or unsuccessful, can benefit when their managers engage in transformational leadership. Moreover, while the benefits of transformational leadership are often most apparent when an organization is in trouble, transformational leadership can be an enduring approach to leadership, leading to long-term organizational effectiveness.

The Distinction between Transformational and Transactional Leadership

transactional leadership Leadership that motivates subordinates by rewarding them for high performance and reprimanding them for low performance.

Transformational leadership is often contrasted with transactional leadership. In **transactional leadership,** managers use their reward and coercive powers to encourage high performance. When managers reward high performers, reprimand or otherwise punish low performers, and motivate subordinates by reinforcing desired behaviors and extinguishing or punishing undesired ones, they are engaging in transactional leadership.[97] Managers who effectively influence their subordinates to achieve goals, yet do not seem to be making the kind of dramatic changes that are part of transformational leadership, are engaging in transactional leadership.

Many transformational leaders engage in transactional leadership. They reward subordinates for a job well done and notice and respond to substandard performance. But they also have their eyes on the bigger picture of how much better things could be in their organizations, how much more their subordinates are capable of achieving, and how important it is to treat their subordinates with respect and help them reach their full potential.

Research has found that when leaders engage in transformational leadership, their subordinates tend to have higher levels of job satisfaction and performance.[98] Additionally, subordinates of transformational leaders may be more likely to trust their leaders and their organizations and feel that they are being fairly treated, and this, in turn, may positively influence their work motivation (see Chapter 13).[99]

LO14-5 Characterize the relationship between gender and leadership and explain how emotional intelligence may contribute to leadership effectiveness.

Gender and Leadership

The increasing number of women entering the ranks of management, as well as the problems some women face in their efforts to be hired as managers or promoted into management positions, has prompted researchers to explore the relationship between gender and leadership. Although there are relatively more women in management positions today than there were 10 years ago, there are still relatively few women in top management and, in some organizations, even in middle management.

When women do advance to top management positions, special attention often is focused on them and the fact that they are women. For example, women CEOs of large companies are still rare; those who make it to the top post, such as Indra

Nooyi of PepsiCo,[100] Judy McGrath of MTV Networks, and Andrea Jung of Avon,[101] are salient. As business writer Linda Tischler puts it, "In a workplace where women CEOs of major companies are so scarce . . . they can be identified, like rock stars, by first name only."[102] Although women have certainly made inroads into leadership positions in organizations, they continue to be underrepresented in top leadership posts. For example, as was indicated in Chapter 5, while around 50.5% of the employees in managerial and professional jobs in the United States are women, only about 15.4% of corporate officers in the *Fortune* 500 are women, and only 6.7% of the top earners are women.[103]

A widespread stereotype of women is that they are nurturing, supportive, and concerned with interpersonal relations. Men are stereotypically viewed as being directive and focused on task accomplishment. Such stereotypes suggest that women tend to be more relationship-oriented as managers and engage in more consideration behaviors, whereas men are more task-oriented and engage in more initiating-structure behaviors. Does the behavior of actual male and female managers bear out these stereotypes? Do women managers lead in different ways than men do? Are male or female managers more effective as leaders?

Research suggests that male and female managers who have leadership positions in organizations behave in similar ways.[104] Women do not engage in more consideration than men, and men do not engage in more initiating structure than women. Research does suggest, however, that leadership style may vary between women and men. Women tend to be somewhat more participative as leaders than are men, involving subordinates in decision making and seeking their input.[105] Male managers tend to be less participative than are female managers, making more decisions on their own and wanting to do things their own way. Moreover, research suggests that men tend to be harsher when they punish their subordinates than do women.[106]

There are at least two reasons why female managers may be more participative as leaders than are male managers.[107] First, subordinates may try to resist the influence of female managers more than they do the influence of male managers. Some subordinates may never have reported to a woman before; some may incorrectly see a management role as being more appropriate for a man than for a woman; and some may just resist being led by a woman. To overcome this resistance and encourage subordinates' trust and respect, women managers may adopt a participative approach.

A second reason why female managers may be more participative is that they sometimes have better interpersonal skills than male managers.[108] A participative approach to leadership requires high levels of interaction and involvement between a manager and his or her subordinates, sensitivity to subordinates' feelings, and the ability to make decisions that may be unpopular with subordinates but necessary for goal attainment. Good interpersonal skills may help female managers have the effective interactions with their subordinates that are crucial to a participative approach.[109] To the extent that male managers have more difficulty managing interpersonal relationships, they may shy away from the high levels of interaction with subordinates necessary for true participation.

The key finding from research on leader behaviors, however, is that male and female managers do *not* differ significantly in their propensities to perform different leader behaviors. Even though they may be more participative, female managers do not engage in more consideration or less initiating structure than male managers.

Perhaps a question even more important than whether male and female managers differ in the leadership behaviors they perform is whether they differ in effectiveness. Consistent with the findings for leader behaviors, research suggests that across different kinds of organizational settings, male and female managers tend to be *equally effective* as leaders.[110] Thus there is no logical basis for stereotypes favoring male managers and leaders or for the existence of the "glass ceiling" (an invisible barrier that seems to prevent women from advancing as far as they should in some organizations). Because women and men are equally effective as leaders, the increasing number of women in the workforce should result in a larger pool of highly qualified candidates for management positions in organizations, ultimately enhancing organizational effectiveness.[111]

Emotional Intelligence and Leadership

Do the moods and emotions leaders experience on the job influence their behavior and effectiveness as leaders? Research suggests this is likely to be the case. For example, one study found that when store managers experienced positive moods at work, salespeople in their stores provided high-quality customer service and were less likely to quit.[112] Another study found that groups whose leaders experienced positive moods had better coordination, whereas groups whose leaders experienced negative moods exerted more effort; members of groups with leaders in positive moods also tended to experience more positive moods themselves; and members of groups with leaders in negative moods tended to experience more negative moods.[113]

A leader's level of emotional intelligence (see Chapter 3) may play a particularly important role in leadership effectiveness.[114] For example, emotional intelligence may help leaders develop a vision for their organizations, motivate their subordinates to commit to this vision, and energize them to enthusiastically work to achieve this vision. Moreover, emotional intelligence may enable leaders to develop a significant identity for their organization and instill high levels of trust and cooperation throughout the organization while maintaining the flexibility needed to respond to changing conditions.[115]

Emotional intelligence also plays a crucial role in how leaders relate to and deal with their followers, particularly when it comes to encouraging followers to be creative.[116] Creativity in organizations is an emotion-laden process; it often entails challenging the status quo, being willing to take risks and accept and learn from failures, and doing much hard work to bring creative ideas to fruition in terms of new products, services, or procedures and processes when uncertainty is bound to be high.[117] Leaders who are high on emotional intelligence are more likely to understand all the emotions surrounding creative endeavors, to be able to awaken and support the creative pursuits of their followers, and to provide the kind of support that enables creativity to flourish in organizations.[118]

Leaders, like people everywhere, sometimes make mistakes. Emotional intelligence may also help leaders respond appropriately when they realize they have made a mistake. Recognizing, admitting, and learning from mistakes can be especially important for entrepreneurs who start their own businesses, as profiled in the following "Focus on Diversity" box.

Focus on Diversity

Admitting a Mistake Helps Small Business Leader

Things seemed to be going well for Maureen Borzacchiello, CEO of Creative Display Solutions, located in Garden City, New York.[119] She founded her small business in 2001 to provide displays, graphics, and exhibits for use in trade shows and at events for companies ranging from American Express, FedEx, and General Electric to JetBlue Airways, AIG, and The Weather Channel.[120] Her company was growing, and she had received an award from the nonprofit organization, Count Me In for Women's Economic Independence.[121]

However, in 2006 she realized she had overextended her business financially. A large investment in inventory coupled with a sizable lease commitment, the need for office space renovations, the purchase of new furniture, and the addition of three new employees brought her to the point where she lacked the cash to pay her employees their regular salaries. When she had made these decisions, she thought she and her husband (who also works in the company) would be able to generate the revenues to cover the expenditures. But her

Leadership means taking on responsibility for one's (and one's company's) mistakes, learning how to do better, and maintaining honesty with employees, as Maureen Borzacchiello exemplifies.

brother-in-law unexpectedly passed away, and their involvement in family matters meant they weren't able to get new accounts as quickly as she had thought they would.[122]

Still confident that if she could get through this tough period, she would be able to get her business back on track, Borzacchiello decided to be honest with her employees about the company's current financial problems, why they occurred, and how she would strive to prevent such problems in the future. She met with her employees and told them, "All I can tell you is that I apologize. . . . We were so focused on accelerating growth that I didn't see it coming."[123] She admitted she needed to better understand her company's financial situation and daily cash flow, reassured employees that the company would be back on square footing in two to three months, and promised she would pay much more attention to ongoing financial performance and cash flow in the future.[124]

Borzacchiello also told employees that she and her husband would take no money out of the business for their own salaries until the financial problems were resolved. By being honest and open with employees, Borzacchiello gained their commitment and support. All employees decided to work shorter hours, and two employees were willing to have their hourly pay rates cut.[125] True to her promise, within two months all employees were able to return to their regular work hours; and by the beginning of 2007, Creative Display Solutions had over $1 million in revenues (which was more than double its revenues at the time of the financial problems).[126] To this day Creative Display Solutions remains a profitable business; and by 2010 its list of clients included more than 600 companies.[127] Clearly Borzacchiello effectively handled the temporary crisis her company faced by admitting and apologizing for her mistake and being open and honest with employees about her company's future prospects.[128]

Summary and Review

THE NATURE OF LEADERSHIP Leadership is the process by which a person exerts influence over other people and inspires, motivates, and directs their activities to help achieve group or organizational goals. Leaders can influence others because they possess power. The five types of power available to managers are

LO14-1 legitimate power, reward power, coercive power, expert power, and referent power. Many managers are using empowerment as a tool to increase their effectiveness as leaders.

LO14-2 **TRAIT AND BEHAVIOR MODELS OF LEADERSHIP** The trait model of leadership describes personal characteristics or traits that contribute to effective leadership. However, some managers who possess these traits are not effective leaders, and some managers who do not possess all the traits are nevertheless effective leaders. The behavior model of leadership describes two kinds of behavior that most leaders engage in: consideration and initiating structure.

LO14-3 **CONTINGENCY MODELS OF LEADERSHIP** Contingency models take into account the complexity surrounding leadership and the role of the situation in determining whether a manager is an effective leader. Fiedler's contingency model explains why managers may be effective leaders in one situation and ineffective in another. According to Fiedler's model, relationship-oriented leaders are most effective in situations that are moderately favorable for leading, and task-oriented leaders are most effective in situations that are very favorable or very unfavorable for leading. House's path–goal theory describes how effective managers motivate their subordinates by determining what outcomes their subordinates want, rewarding subordinates with these outcomes when they achieve their goals and perform at a high level, and clarifying the paths to goal attainment. Managers can engage in four kinds of behaviors to motivate subordinates: directive, supportive, participative, and achievement-oriented behaviors. The leader substitutes model suggests that sometimes managers do not have to play a leadership role because their subordinates perform at a high level without the manager having to exert influence over them.

LO14-4 **TRANSFORMATIONAL LEADERSHIP** Transformational leadership occurs when managers have dramatic effects on their subordinates and on the organization as a whole, and inspire and energize subordinates to solve problems and improve performance. These effects include making subordinates aware of the importance of their own jobs and high performance; making subordinates aware of their own needs for personal growth, development, and accomplishment; and motivating subordinates to work for the good of the organization and not just their own personal gain. Managers can engage in transformational leadership by being charismatic leaders, by intellectually stimulating subordinates, and by engaging in developmental consideration. Transformational managers also often engage in transactional leadership by using their reward and coercive powers to encourage high performance.

LO14-5 **GENDER AND LEADERSHIP** Female and male managers do not differ in the leadership behaviors they perform, contrary to stereotypes suggesting that women are more relationship-oriented and men more task-oriented. Female managers sometimes are more participative than male managers, however. Research has found that women and men are equally effective as managers and leaders.

LO14-5 **EMOTIONAL INTELLIGENCE AND LEADERSHIP** The moods and emotions leaders experience on the job, and their ability to effectively manage these feelings, can influence their effectiveness as leaders. Moreover, emotional intelligence can contribute to leadership effectiveness in multiple ways, including encouraging and supporting creativity among followers.

Management in Action

Topics for Discussion and Action

Discussion

1. Describe the steps managers can take to increase their power and ability to be effective leaders. **[LO14-1]**
2. Think of specific situations in which it might be especially important for a manager to engage in consideration and in initiating structure. **[LO14-2]**
3. For your current job or for a future job you expect to hold, describe what your supervisor could do to strongly motivate you to be a top performer. **[LO14-3]**
4. Discuss why managers might want to change the behaviors they engage in, given their situation, their subordinates, and the nature of the work being done. Do you think managers can readily change their leadership behaviors? Why or why not? **[LO14-3]**
5. Discuss why substitutes for leadership can contribute to organizational effectiveness. **[LO14-3]**
6. Describe what transformational leadership is, and explain how managers can engage in it. **[LO14-4]**
7. Discuss why some people still think men make better managers than women even though research indicates that men and women are equally effective as managers and leaders. **[LO14-5]**
8. Imagine that you are working in an organization in an entry-level position after graduation and have come up with what you think is a great idea for improving a critical process in the organization that relates to your job. In what ways might your supervisor encourage you to implement your idea? How might your supervisor discourage you from even sharing your idea with others? **[LO14-4, 14-5]**

Action

9. Interview a manager to find out how the three situational characteristics that Fiedler identified affect his or her ability to provide leadership. **[LO14-3]**
10. Find a company that has dramatically turned around its fortunes and improved its performance. Determine whether a transformational manager was behind the turnaround and, if one was, what this manager did. **[LO14-4]**

Building Management Skills

Analyzing Failures of Leadership [LO14-1, 14-2, 14-3, 14-4]

Think about a situation you are familiar with in which a leader was very ineffective. Then answer the following questions:

1. What sources of power did this leader have? Did the leader have enough power to influence his or her followers?
2. What kinds of behaviors did this leader engage in? Were they appropriate for the situation? Why or why not?
3. From what you know, do you think this leader was a task-oriented leader or a relationship-oriented leader? How favorable was this leader's situation for leading?
4. What steps did this leader take to motivate his or her followers? Were these steps appropriate or inappropriate? Why?
5. What signs, if any, did this leader show of being a transformational leader?

Managing Ethically [LO14-1]

Managers who verbally criticize their subordinates, put them down in front of their coworkers, or use the threat of job loss to influence behavior are exercising coercive power. Some employees subject to coercive power believe that using it is unethical.

Questions

1. Either alone or in a group, think about the ethical implications of the use of coercive power.
2. To what extent do managers and organizations have an ethical obligation to put limits on the amount of coercive power that is exercised?

Small Group Breakout Exercise

Improving Leadership Effectiveness [LO14-1, 14-2, 14-3, 14-4]

Form groups of three to five people, and appoint one member as the spokesperson who will communicate your findings and conclusions to the class when called on by the instructor. Then discuss the following scenario:

You are a team of human resource consultants who have been hired by Carla Caruso, an entrepreneur who has started her own interior decorating business. A highly competent and creative interior decorator, Caruso has established a working relationship with most of the major home builders in her community. At first she worked on her own as an independent contractor. Then because of a dramatic increase in the number of new homes being built, she became swamped with requests for her services and decided to start her own company.

She hired a secretary–bookkeeper and four interior decorators, all of whom are highly competent. Caruso still does decorating jobs herself and has adopted a hands-off approach to leading the four decorators who report to her because she feels that interior design is a very personal, creative endeavor. Rather than pay the decorators on some kind of commission basis (such as a percentage of their customers' total billings), she pays them a premium salary, higher than average, so they are motivated to do what's best for a customer's needs and not what will result in higher billings and commissions.

Caruso thought everything was going smoothly until customer complaints started coming in. The complaints ranged from the decorators' being hard to reach, promising unrealistic delivery times, and being late for or failing to keep appointments to their being impatient and rude when customers had trouble making up their minds. Caruso knows her decorators are competent and is concerned that she is not effectively leading and managing them. She wonders, in particular, if her hands-off approach is to blame and if she should change the manner in which she rewards or pays her decorators. She has asked for your advice.

1. Analyze the sources of power that Caruso has available to her to influence the decorators. What advice can you give her to either increase her power base or use her existing power more effectively?
2. Given what you have learned in this chapter (for example, from the behavior model and path–goal theory), does Caruso seem to be performing appropriate leader behaviors in this situation? What advice can you give her about the kinds of behaviors she should perform?
3. What steps would you advise Caruso to take to increase the decorators' motivation to deliver high-quality customer service?
4. Would you advise Caruso to try to engage in transformational leadership in this situation? If not, why not? If so, what steps would you advise her to take?

Exploring the World Wide Web [LO14-1, 14-2, 14-3, 14-4, 14-5]

Go to the Web site of the Center for Creative Leadership (www.ccl.org). Spend some time browsing through the site to learn more about this organization, which specializes in leadership. Then click on "Customized Services" and then "Coaching Services." Read about the different coaching programs and options the center provides. How do you think leaders might benefit from coaching? What kinds of leaders/managers may find coaching especially beneficial? Do you think coaching services such as those provided by the Center for Creative Leadership can help leaders become more effective? Why or why not?

Be the Manager [LO14-1, 14-2, 14-3, 14-4, 14-5]

You are the CEO of a medium-size company that makes window coverings similar to Hunter Douglas blinds and Duettes. Your company has a real cost advantage in terms of being able to make custom window coverings at costs that are relatively low in the industry. However, the performance of your company has been lackluster. To make needed changes and improve performance, you met with the eight other top managers in your company and charged them with identifying problems and missed opportunities in each of their areas and coming up with an action plan to address the problems and take advantage of opportunities.

Once you gave the managers the okay, they were charged with implementing their action plans in a timely fashion and monitoring the effects of their initiatives monthly for the next 8 to 12 months.

You approved each of the managers' action plans, and a year later most of the managers were reporting that their initiatives had been successful in addressing the problems and opportunities they had identified a year ago. However, overall company performance continues to be lackluster and shows no signs of improvement. You are confused and starting to question your leadership capabilities and approach to change. What are you going to do to improve the performance and effectiveness of your company?

Case in the News [LO14-1, 14-2, 14-3, 14-4]

Kraft's Sugar Rush

Irene Rosenfeld hasn't been around Kraft Foods' suburban Chicago headquarters much lately. The door to her wood-paneled office is kept closed. Her desk is bare. Rosenfeld has grabbed her leather folders of meticulously compiled research and is traveling to London and around the United States in Kraft's Gulfstream jet. These trips weren't supposed to be urgent or secretive, but they've become both as Rosenfeld scrambles to reassure shareholders that her surprising $17 billion hostile bid to buy British candy maker Cadbury will be good for them.

Rosenfeld, 56, has led Kraft since 2006 and has worked there for almost her entire professional life. She can be pretty persuasive. Early on she told her bosses that commercials for Kool-Aid should be aimed at kids (not mothers) and that Jell-O could be made modern with new flavors. In the late 1990s she turned around Kraft's business in Canada; troubled as it was when she arrived, the first thing she had to do was show skeptical colleagues that an American could understand Canadian consumers. As chief executive, she has won most employees' cooperation for a wrenching reorganization. "When she is trying to persuade you of something, she will be relentless in coming back with facts and showing you she has the support of other people," says John Bowlin, who ran Kraft North America in the mid-1990s. "She will be totally emotionally and intellectually committed to her idea."

Now Rosenfeld must summon all of her powers as she takes on her biggest marketing challenge yet: selling the Cadbury deal to shareholders. Her task is all the more difficult because she has alienated her biggest shareholder and one of the world's most influential investors, Warren Buffett.

So confident was Rosenfeld of the deal's potential to transform Kraft into a global juggernaut that she told investors on December 18 she planned to issue new stock to help pay for the purchase. The subtext: She might be willing to raise her original $17 billion bid, which Cadbury management had complained was too low. But Buffett didn't like the idea of paying more. On January 5 he issued a press release warning Rosenfeld not to sell more stock or increase her price, even if other bidders emerge. It was an unusually public smackdown for an investor used to operating behind closed doors. Rosenfeld and Buffett declined to comment.

Now, to save the deal, Rosenfeld is traveling the world to placate two groups of shareholders: Kraft's, who are increasingly worried that she'll pay too much, and Cadbury's, who are being told she's offering too little. She has until January 19 to make her final offer and until February 2 to persuade them all. Win or lose, says former Kraft CEO Robert S. Morrison, the Cadbury affair "will be defining for her career."

Kraft is the world's No. 2 food company after Nestlé, selling $42 billion worth of Kraft Macaroni & Cheese, Oreos, Oscar Mayer cold cuts, and hundreds of other brands each year. It is the product of two decades of deal making. Philip Morris International, seeking to broaden its reach beyond cigarettes, bought General Foods (which had among its brands Jell-O, Minute Rice, and Kool-Aid) in 1985, succeeded in a hostile takeover of Kraft in 1988, merged the two companies by 1995, and five years later bought Nabisco.

Midnight Brainstorming

During the 1980s General Foods, which was based in Westchester County, New York, had a reputation as an intellectually challenging workplace where debate was encouraged. It was here, in 1981, that Rosenfeld got her start in market research. She had spent most of the previous decade at Cornell University completing an undergraduate degree in psychology, an MBA, and a PhD in marketing and statistics. Her thesis adviser, Vithala R. Rao, recalls that even though she was working and pregnant she was determined to finish her dissertation on how consumers make decisions about purchases.

"She knew a PhD would give her an edge in the business world," says Rao. "And her husband was getting one. They were a little competitive."

When Rosenfeld presented her bosses at General Foods with research showing that Kool-Aid should be marketed directly to kids, the pitch won her a job working on the brand full-time. It was an unexpected turn for a researcher. After a presentation at one of her first meetings with Grey Advertising, Rosenfeld was so excited that she applauded. Back then, junior employees were expected to stay silent. "We were all so shocked and amused by her reaction," says Carol Herman, who worked at Grey and remains a close friend of Rosenfeld's.

As Rosenfeld came up through the ranks at General Foods and Kraft—eventually overseeing the Nabisco integration and serving as president of Kraft North America—she developed a reputation as a tough and insistent boss. She would call people with ideas, however big or small, late into the night. Conversations about kids turned into discussions about Kraft products. "I can't tell you how many midnight talks we had about Minute Rice and Stove Top stuffing," says Herman, who worked on various accounts for Kraft through the 1990s. Says James M. Kilts, a former Kraft president who later ran Gillette, "Irene didn't need a lot of advice. That's why I liked her. She was giving me the right answers." Yet her intensity and self-confidence didn't always endear her to colleagues. One former executive recalls a time when Rosenfeld provided helpful insight into a business she had once managed. When the executive offered to return the favor, Rosenfeld took a pass.

In 2001 Rosenfeld suffered her first big professional setback when a contemporary, Betsy D. Holden, was appointed co-chief executive alongside Roger Deromedi. Rosenfeld stayed on almost two more years, then left to join Frito-Lay, a Kraft rival more global in its outlook and more local in its decision making. "Irene thought about the marketing agenda and innovation much more aggressively" than the company was used to, says Indra Nooyi, the CEO of PepsiCo, which owns Frito-Lay. "She was fearless in what she did."

"Rewire for Growth"

Rosenfeld gave every impression that she was committed to Frito-Lay for the long term. But when Kraft asked her to return as CEO in June 2006, she jumped. The dual leader experiment had failed; Kraft was faltering amid high commodity prices, increasing competition from private labels, and a misplaced focus on cost-cutting. She told Kraft's nearly 100,000 employees that the company had lost its heart and soul and needed to "rewire for growth." In a speech at Cornell in 2007, Rosenfeld described her return to Kraft. "The staff was tired, raw, disillusioned," she told the audience. "My slogan was, 'let's get growing.' It's not a warm and fuzzy strategy." She replaced half of her executive team and half of those in the next two levels down. She reorganized the structure of the company, changed how people receive their bonuses, and told everyone "to stop apologizing for our categories and make them more relevant." She concluded her talk, "Sometimes I lie awake thinking, 'Should we?' And then I think, 'How can we not?'"

Rosenfeld wasn't alone in wanting change—activist investor Nelson Peltz was demanding it. She learned that engagement and conciliation were the best ways to handle powerful dissenters. When Peltz pushed her to sell some brands, she did, unloading Veryfine fruit juice and Post cereals. And when she asked him not to purchase more than 10% of the company, he agreed.

Peltz was also a big investor in Cadbury Schweppes, and he persuaded the British food giant to sell its soft drink division in 2008 and become purely a candy company. That would set the stage for Rosenfeld's eventual hostile takeover bid and provide Cadbury its philosophical defense: It didn't want to lose focus on its core business by becoming part of a conglomerate.

As the Great Recession took hold, Kraft should have thrived. But even though consumers ate at home more often and ingredient prices fell, the company was forced to cut prices to compete with private label products. Kraft stock, which went public at $31 a share in 2001, fell as low as $21 last March. (It has been hovering at about $29 this year.) The company introduced items such as Bagelfuls, bagels stuffed with Philadelphia cream cheese. The products did well, but not well enough to have a major impact. Rosenfeld also devoted considerable resources to creating premium toppings for Kraft's DiGiorno frozen pizza and frequently pointed to the brand's success.

With the recession abating, Rosenfeld started thinking of ways to transform the company. "She wanted to capture the imagination of the world about what Kraft could be," says Shelly Lazarus, chairperson of ad agency Ogilvy & Mather Worldwide, which works with Kraft. Rosenfeld began studying the possibility of buying Cadbury, which sells Trident gum and chocolate in 60 countries and has sales of about $8 billion. It's a fast-growing global business with high profit margins.

Eventually she fixed on a price, and in early August decided to approach Cadbury Chairman Roger Carr with an offer. On August 28 she met with Carr in London to lay out her plan. "She was brisk, efficient, delivered her proposal and left quite quickly," says Carr. The two haven't spoken since, he says.

They have, however, exchanged a few letters. In the first, which Carr sent to Rosenfeld the next week, he called the offer "derisory." Then on Labor Day, Rosenfeld announced Kraft's bid in a news release on the corporate Web site, hoping to win over shareholders directly. She spoke to several British newspapers about her admiration for Cadbury and the great promise of a merger. In a video interview posted on the Kraft site, she expressed her enthusiasm for Cadbury's products in a way only a marketer could appreciate: "I am a heavy, heavy user of Trident gum and, on a seasonal basis, I love those Cadbury eggs." But after receiving no encouragement from the candy maker, Rosenfeld launched a hostile bid on November 9. "We believe that our proposal offers the best immediate and long-term value for Cadbury's shareholders and for the company itself compared with any other option currently available, including Cadbury remaining independent," she wrote in the formal offer.

Meanwhile Rosenfeld was juggling another deal that would determine how much Kraft could spend for Cadbury. In early 2009 Nestlé made a surprise offer to buy DiGiorno and the rest of Kraft's pizza business. Rosenfeld concluded that selling the unit made sense: Frozen pizza wouldn't do well outside of North America, and within the company it was an isolated brand. Next she had to persuade the board. "It was a difficult decision. But once we got our heads around the strategic and financial rationale for the deal, it became clear," says Perry Yeatman, a Kraft spokeswoman. Closing the sale proved difficult; it wasn't until January 5 that Kraft announced it would sell the pizza business to Nestlé for $3.7 billion. Some investors thought the price was too low. But the deal would give Rosenfeld the cash she'd need to pursue Cadbury. And there was another benefit: Nestlé, Kraft's main rival for Cadbury, said it wouldn't bid.

Whatever sense of relief Rosenfeld might have felt didn't last long. On the same day, Buffett went public with his concerns, calling Rosenfeld's proposal to issue more shares a "blank check." He noted that while the company had bought back shares at a price of $33 apiece in 2007, it would be selling the new shares for the Cadbury transaction for far less. He did say, though, that he would support an offer that "does not destroy value for Kraft shareholders." Other investors share Buffett's skepticism. "What is she wasting our money for?" asks John Kornitzer, founder of Kornitzer Capital Management in Shawnee Mission, Kansas. "To chase after these guys is ridiculous." Alice Schroeder, a former Wall Street analyst and author of a biography of Buffett who also writes a column for Bloomberg News, says even if Rosenfeld had consulted with Buffett it might serve his purposes to take a public stand. He can take credit for reining her in and defending shareholders. "No matter how this turns out, Warren looks great," she says.

Rosenfeld, however, is under attack from all sides. On January 12 Carr released a stinging "defense document" on Cadbury's Web site, saying "the bid is even more unattractive today than it was when Kraft made its formal offer." Kraft called the argument "underwhelming." Carr responds, "I think the clarity with which we reviewed Kraft's own record must have been disturbing for them and illuminating for our shareholders."

Kraft shareholders will vote on whether to issue more stock on February 1; the next day Cadbury stockholders will vote on the offer. Rosenfeld spent January 12 with Cadbury investors in the United States before jetting to London to talk with Cadbury shareholders there. Some refused her visit, says Carr. While Rosenfeld remains determined to make Kraft bigger and more global, finding a price for Cadbury that works for everyone might be impossible. "Rosenfeld has made it clear that she's disciplined, that she won't overpay," says Donald Yacktman, president of Yacktman Asset Management, a longtime investor. "I guess we'll find out how much she really means what she says."

Questions for Discussion

1. How would you describe the personal leadership style of Irene Rosenfeld?
2. What are Rosenfeld's sources of power?
3. What behaviors does Rosenfeld appear to engage in?
4. Do you think Rosenfeld is a transformational leader? If so, in what ways has she been a transformational leader? If not, why not?

Source: S. Berfield and M. Arndt, "Kraft's Sugar Rush," http://www.businessweek.com/magazine/content/10_04/b4164036495789.htm, January 14, 2010. Reprinted from January 14, 2010 issue of *Bloomberg Businessweek* by special permission, copyright © 2010 by Bloomberg L.P.

CHAPTER 15

Effective Groups and Teams

Learning Objectives

After studying this chapter, you should be able to:

LO15-1 Explain why groups and teams are key contributors to organizational effectiveness.

LO15-2 Identify the different types of groups and teams that help managers and organizations achieve their goals.

LO15-3 Explain how different elements of group dynamics influence the functioning and effectiveness of groups and teams.

LO15-4 Explain why it is important for groups and teams to have a balance of conformity and deviance and a moderate level of cohesiveness.

LO15-5 Describe how managers can motivate group members to achieve organizational goals and reduce social loafing in groups and teams.

A MANAGER'S CHALLENGE

Teams Innovate at Cisco

How can managers promote innovation in rapidly changing industries? In 2010 Cisco Systems was ranked 17th on *Fast Company*'s list of the "World's Most Innovative Companies."[1] Cisco is a global leader in providing networking solutions for the Internet. Cisco designs and produces Internet Protocol (IP)–based networking products, solutions, and services for businesses, governments, academic institutions, and consumers.[2] Cisco focuses on improving the speed and efficiency of Internet collaboration, data transmission, and video applications. In this rapidly changing industry, Cisco prides itself on innovation.[3] For example, on November 9, 2009, Cisco announced over 60 new collaboration technologies.[4] As another example, on March 9, 2010, Cisco introduced the Cisco® CRS-3 Carrier Routing System designed to greatly accelerate the pace of broadband communication including data, voice, and video transmission.[5] Innovating in its existing markets and expanding into new markets around the world are major priorities for Cisco.

In the 2000s John Chambers, Cisco's CEO and chairman of the board, realized that for Cisco to continue to innovate in a rapidly changing industry amid perilous economic times, he would need to change how decisions were made at Cisco. Like many other large corporations (Cisco has over 60,000 employees),[6] decisions at Cisco used to be made in a top-down manner by Chambers and over key executives. Recognizing that it is next to impossible for a small number of top decision makers to fuel large-scale innovation in multiple markets simultaneously, Chambers realized that Cisco needed to involve many more employees in decision making.[7]

How did he do this? Essentially by creating a system of teams that do everything from charting the future direction of the company to working on individual projects. In terms of charting the overall direction of the company, Chambers is a member of a team

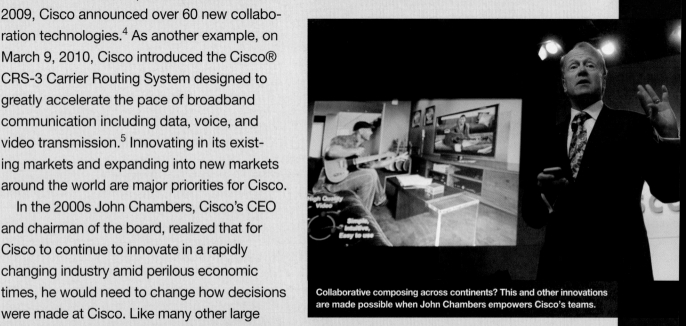

Collaborative composing across continents? This and other innovations are made possible when John Chambers empowers Cisco's teams.

called the Operating Committee, which includes 15 other high-level executives.[8] The Operating Committee, however, does not make all major decisions at Cisco. Some teams, called councils, are empowered to decide on potential opportunities in the range of $10 billion. Each council has about 14 members, with 2 members being either senior or executive vice presidents of the company. Other teams, called boards, are empowered to decide on potential opportunities in the range of $1 billion. Each board has about 14 members, with 2 members being either vice presidents or senior vice presidents. Smaller teams of between 2 and 10 members are formed temporarily to work on specific projects or issues. Opportunities uncovered or developed by these working groups are presented to one of the boards for consideration. By involving more employees in decisions, Chambers hopes to spur innovation in multiple businesses at Cisco.[9] As Chambers puts it, "When you have command and control by the top 10 people, you can only do one or two things at a time. . . . The future is about collaboration and teamwork and making decisions with a replicable process that offers scale, speed, and flexibility."[10]

Councils and boards include members from different functional areas, businesses, and even sometimes countries to gain a variety of perspectives on issues and opportunities.[11] They are organized around key initiatives or product lines, and employees who have skills that could contribute to the teams are asked (and required) to join them.[12] For example, Ron Ricci, a vice president at Cisco, formed a board of sports enthusiasts to focus on how Cisco might get more involved in the sports field. Ricci's 16-member board worked intensely to develop a new product called StadiumVision, which enables sports venues to give fans multiple high-definition video screens that provide customized live videos of games, programming, advertising, promotions, and other relevant and timely information.[13] In collaboration with marketing and sales teams at Cisco, the board won contracts with major sports teams and venues, and a multimillion-dollar business was launched in under four months.[14]

Cisco uses teams to collaborate for innovation as well as respond to problems that might arise. For example, teams helped Cisco rapidly respond with aid to China after a devastating earthquake in 2007.[15]

Teams are also used at Cisco to expand into emerging markets. While Cisco is headquartered in San Jose, California, Executive Vice President and Chief Globalization Officer Wim Elfrink created a second headquarters in Bangalore, India, to help staff teams focus on developing and selling products in emerging markets.[16] In Bangalore Elfrink recruits teams of qualified engineers from emerging markets to develop networks and infrastructures for companies and governments in a variety of countries such as Russia and Chile. Once a team has developed a product for a customer in another country, the team heads back to Bangalore to transform the customized solution it provided for a specific customer's needs into a more generalized product that can be sold to other customers in multiple countries.[17]

Financial incentives at Cisco are aimed at encouraging collaboration both across teams and within teams. Thus members of teams not only want their own teams to succeed but also try to contribute to the success of other teams for the good of the company. Clearly the use of teams is integral to Chambers's quest for Cisco to innovate around the world.[18]

Overview

Cisco Systems is not alone in using groups and teams to improve organizational effectiveness. Managers in companies large and small are using groups and teams to enhance performance, increase responsiveness to customers, spur innovation, and motivate employees. In this chapter we look in detail at how groups and teams can contribute to organizational effectiveness and the types of groups and teams used in organizations. We discuss how different elements of group dynamics influence the functioning and effectiveness of groups, and we describe how managers can motivate group members to achieve organizational goals and reduce social loafing in groups and teams. By the end of this chapter you will appreciate why the effective management of groups and teams is a key ingredient for organizational performance and effectiveness.

Groups, Teams, and Organizational Effectiveness

LO15-1 Explain why groups and teams are key contributors to organizational effectiveness.

group Two or more people who interact with each other to accomplish certain goals or meet certain needs.

team A group whose members work intensely with one another to achieve a specific common goal or objective.

A **group** may be defined as two or more people who interact with each other to accomplish certain goals or meet certain needs.[19] A **team** is a group whose members work *intensely* with one another to achieve a specific common goal or objective. As these definitions imply, all teams are groups, but not all groups are teams. The two characteristics that distinguish teams from groups are the *intensity with which team members work together* and the presence of a *specific, overriding team goal or objective.*

Recall from "A Manager's Challenge" how the team Ron Ricci formed at Cisco Systems worked intensely together to achieve the goal of developing a new product for the sports business and was able to launch a multimillion-dollar new business in under four months. In contrast, the accountants who work in a small CPA firm are a group: They may interact with one another to achieve goals such as keeping up to date on the latest changes in accounting rules and regulations, maintaining a smoothly functioning office, satisfying clients, and attracting new clients. But they are not a team because they do not work intensely with one another. Each accountant concentrates on serving the needs of his or her own clients.

Because all teams are also groups, whenever we use the term *group* in this chapter, we are referring to both groups *and* teams. As you might imagine, because members of teams work intensely together, teams can sometimes be difficult to form, and it may take time for members to learn how to effectively work together. Groups and teams can help an organization gain a competitive advantage because they can (1) enhance its performance, (2) increase its responsiveness to customers, (3) increase innovation, and (4) increase employees' motivation and satisfaction (see Figure 15.1). In this section we look at each of these contributions in turn.

Groups and Teams as Performance Enhancers

synergy Performance gains that result when individuals and departments coordinate their actions.

One of the main advantages of using groups is the opportunity to obtain a type of **synergy:** People working in a group can produce more or higher-quality outputs than would have been produced if each person had worked separately and all their individual efforts were later combined. The essence of synergy is captured in the saying "The whole is more than the sum of its parts." Factors that can contribute to synergy in groups include the ability of group members to bounce ideas off one another, to correct one another's mistakes, to solve problems immediately as they arise, to bring a diverse knowledge base to bear on a problem or goal, and to accomplish work that is too vast or all-encompassing for any individual to achieve on his or her own.

To take advantage of the potential for synergy in groups, managers need to make sure that groups are composed of members who have complementary skills and

Figure 15.1

Groups' and Teams' Contributions to Organizational Effectiveness

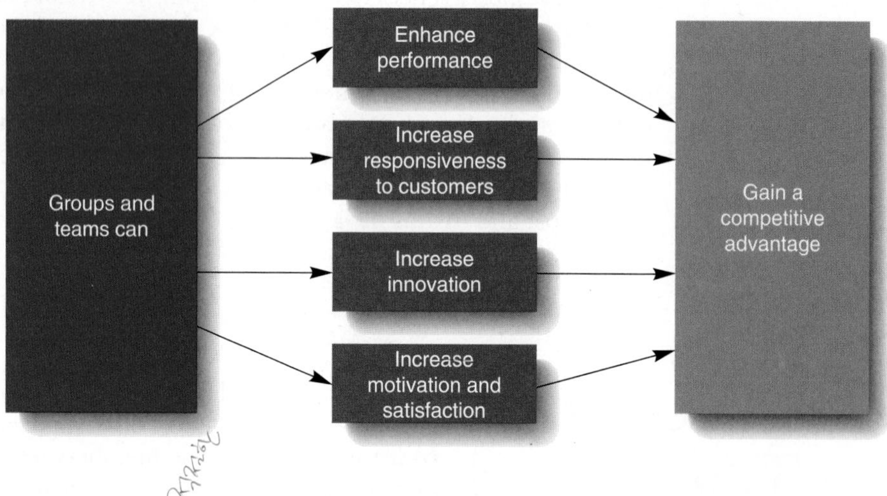

knowledge relevant to the group's work. For example, at Hallmark Cards synergies are created by bringing together all the different functions needed to create and produce a greeting card in a cross-functional team (a team composed of members from different departments or functions; see Chapter 10). For instance, artists, writers, designers, and marketing experts work together as team members to develop new cards.[20]

At Hallmark the skills and expertise of the artists complement the contributions of the writers and vice versa. Managers also need to give groups enough autonomy so the groups, rather than the manager, are solving problems and determining how to achieve goals and objectives, as is true in the cross-functional teams at Hallmark and the teams at Cisco Systems in "A Manager's Challenge." To promote synergy, managers need to empower their subordinates and be coaches, guides, and resources for groups while refraining from playing a more directive or supervisory role. The potential for synergy in groups may be why more and more managers are incorporating empowerment into their personal leadership styles (see Chapter 14).

Getting multiple perspectives and departmental inputs on one project at once unravels snafus before they start and gets a better product out the door faster.

When tasks are complex and involve highly sophisticated and rapidly changing technologies, achieving synergies in teams often hinges on having the appropriate mix of backgrounds and areas of expertise represented on the team. In large organizations with operations in many states and countries, managers can rely on databases and software applications to determine which employees might have the expertise needed on a particular team or for a certain project.

Groups, Teams, and Responsiveness to Customers

Being responsive to customers is not always easy. In manufacturing organizations, for example, customers' needs and desires for new and improved products have to be balanced against engineering constraints, production costs and feasibilities, government safety regulations, and marketing challenges. In service organizations such as health maintenance organizations (HMOs), being responsive to patients' needs and desires for prompt, high-quality medical care and treatment has to be balanced against meeting physicians' needs and desires and keeping health care costs under control. Being responsive to customers often requires the wide variety of skills and expertise found in different departments and at different levels in an organization's hierarchy. Sometimes, for example, employees at lower levels in an organization's hierarchy, such as sales representatives for a computer company, are closest to its customers and the most attuned to their needs. However, lower-level employees like salespeople often lack the technical expertise needed for new product ideas; such expertise is found in the research and development department. Bringing salespeople, research and development experts, and members of other departments together in a group or cross-functional team can enhance responsiveness to customers. Consequently, when managers form a team, they must make sure the diversity of expertise and knowledge needed to be responsive to customers exists within the team; this is why cross-functional teams are so popular.

In a cross-functional team, the expertise and knowledge in different organizational departments are brought together in the skills and knowledge of the team members. Managers of high-performing organizations are careful to determine which types of expertise and knowledge are required for teams to be responsive to customers, and they use this information in forming teams.

Teams and Innovation

Innovation–the creative development of new products, new technologies, new services, or even new organizational structures–is a topic we discuss in detail in Chapter 18. Often an individual working alone does not possess the extensive and diverse skills, knowledge, and expertise required for successful innovation. Managers can better encourage innovation by creating teams of diverse individuals who together have the knowledge relevant to a particular type of innovation, as has been the case at Cisco Systems, rather than by relying on individuals working alone.

Using teams to innovate has other advantages. First, team members can often uncover one another's errors or false assumptions; an individual acting alone would not be able to do this. Second, team members can critique one another's approaches and build off one another's strengths while compensating for weaknesses–an advantage of devil's advocacy and dialectical inquiry, discussed in Chapter 7.

To further promote innovation, managers can empower teams and make their members fully responsible and accountable for the innovation process. The manager's role is to provide guidance, assistance, coaching, and the resources team members need and *not* to closely direct or supervise their activities. To speed innovation, managers also need to form teams in which each member brings some unique resource to the team, such as engineering prowess, knowledge of production, marketing expertise, or financial savvy. Successful innovation sometimes requires that managers form teams with members from different countries and cultures.

Amazon uses teams to spur innovation, and many of the unique features on its Web site that enable it to be responsive to customers and meet their needs have been developed by teams, as indicated in the following "Information Technology Byte" box.

Information Technology Byte

Pizza Teams Innovate at Amazon

Jeff Bezos, founder, CEO, and chairman of the board of Amazon, is a firm believer in the power of teams to spur innovation.[21] At Amazon, teams have considerable autonomy to develop their ideas and experiment without interference from managers or other groups. And teams are kept deliberately small. According to Bezos, no team should need more than two pizzas to feed its members. If more than two pizzas are needed to nourish a team, the team is too

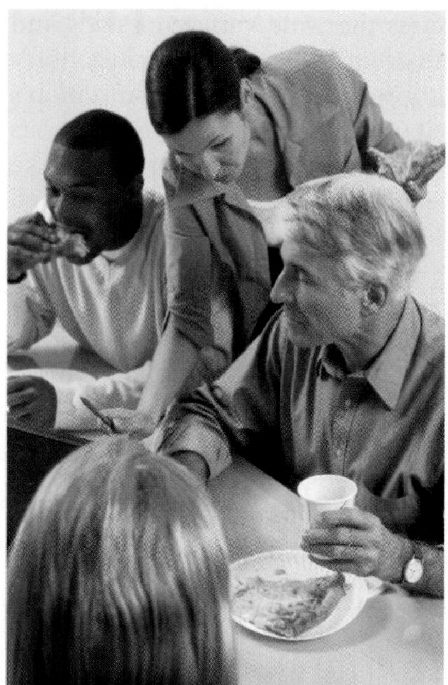

Pepperoni or plain cheese? When your pizza team is small enough to need just one of each, you're more likely to come up with an innovation like the Kindle.

large. Thus teams at Amazon typically have no more than about five to seven members.[22]

"Pizza teams" have come up with unique and popular innovations that individuals working alone might never have thought of. A team developed the "Gold Box" icon that customers can click on to receive special offers that expire within an hour of opening the treasure chest. Another team developed "Search Inside This Book," which allows customers to search and read content from over 100,000 books.[23] And a team developed the Amazon Kindle, a wireless reader that weighs 10.2 ounces, can hold over 1,500 titles, can receive automatic delivery of major newspapers and blogs, and has a high-resolution screen that looks like and can be read like paper.[24]

While Bezos gives teams autonomy to develop and run with their ideas, he also believes in careful analysis and testing of ideas. A great advocate of the power of facts, data, and analysis, Bezos feels that whenever an idea can be tested through analysis, analysis should rule the day. When an undertaking is just too large or too uncertain or when data are lacking, Bezos and other experienced top managers make the final call.[25] But to make such judgment calls about implementing new ideas (either by data analysis or expert judgment), truly creative ideas are needed. To date, teams have played a very important role in generating ideas that have helped Amazon be responsive to its customers, have a widely known Internet brand name, and be the highly successful and innovative company it is today.[26]

Groups and Teams as Motivators

Managers often form groups and teams to accomplish organizational goals and then find that using groups and teams brings additional benefits. Members of groups, and especially members of teams (because of the higher intensity of interaction in teams), are likely to be more satisfied than they would have been if they were working on their own. The experience of working alongside other highly charged and motivated people can be stimulating and motivating: Team members can see how their efforts and expertise directly contribute to the achievement of team and organizational goals, and they feel personally responsible for the outcomes or results of their work. This has been the case at Hallmark Cards.

The increased motivation and satisfaction that can accompany the use of teams can also lead to other outcomes, such as lower turnover. This has been Frank B. Day's experience as founder and chairman of the board of Rock Bottom Restaurants Inc.[27] To provide high-quality customer service, Day has organized the restaurants' employees into waitstaff teams, whose members work together to refill beers, take orders, bring hot chicken enchiladas to the tables, or clear off the tables. Team members share the burden of undesirable activities and unpopular shift times, and customers no longer have to wait until a particular waitress or waiter is available. Motivation and satisfaction levels in Rock Bottom restaurants seem to be higher than in other restaurants, and turnover is about half that experienced in other U.S. restaurant chains.[28]

Working in a group or team can also satisfy organizational members' needs for engaging in social interaction and feeling connected to other people. For workers who perform highly stressful jobs, such as hospital emergency and operating room staff, group membership can be an important source of social support and motivation. Family members or friends may not be able to fully understand or appreciate some sources of work stress that these group members experience firsthand. Moreover, group members may cope better with work stressors when they can share them with other members of their group. In addition, groups often devise techniques to relieve stress, such as the telling of jokes among hospital operating room staff.

Why do managers in all kinds of organizations rely so heavily on groups and teams? Effectively managed groups and teams can help managers in their quest for high performance, responsiveness to customers, and employee motivation. Before explaining how managers can effectively manage groups, however, we will describe the types of groups that are formed in organizations.

Types of Groups and Teams

LO15-2 Identify the different types of groups and teams that help managers and organizations achieve their goals.

To achieve their goals of high performance, responsiveness to customers, innovation, and employee motivation, managers can form various types of groups and teams (see Figure 15.2). **Formal groups** are those managers establish to achieve organizational goals. The formal work groups are *cross-functional* teams composed of members from different departments, such as those at Hallmark Cards, and *cross-cultural* teams composed of members from different cultures or countries, such as the teams at global carmakers. As you will see, some of the groups discussed in this section also can be considered to be cross-functional (if they are composed of members from different departments) or cross-cultural (if they are composed of members from different countries or cultures).

formal group A group that managers establish to achieve organizational goals.

informal group A group that managers or nonmanagerial employees form to help achieve their own goals or meet their own needs.

top management team A group composed of the CEO, the president, and the heads of the most important departments.

Sometimes organizational members, managers or nonmanagers, form groups because they feel that groups will help them achieve their own goals or meet their own needs (for example, the need for social interaction). Groups formed in this way are **informal groups.** Four nurses who work in a hospital and have lunch together twice a week constitute an informal group.

The Top Management Team

A central concern of the CEO and president of a company is to form a **top management team** to help the organization achieve its mission and goals. Top management teams are responsible for developing the strategies that result in an organization's competitive advantage; most have between five and seven members. In forming their top management teams, CEOs are well advised to stress diversity in expertise, skills, knowledge, and experience. Thus many top management teams are also cross-functional teams: They are composed of members from different departments, such as finance, marketing, production, and engineering. Diversity helps ensure that the top management team will have all the background and resources it needs to make good decisions. Diversity also helps guard against *groupthink*–faulty group decision making that results when group members strive for agreement at the expense of an accurate assessment of the situation (see Chapter 7).

Figure 15.2
Types of Groups and Teams in Organizations

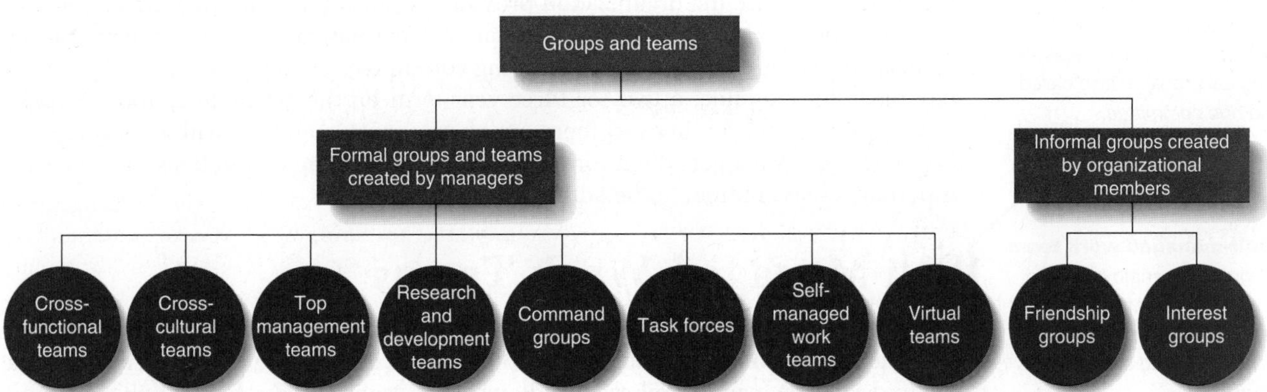

Research and Development Teams

research and development team A team whose members have the expertise and experience needed to develop new products.

Managers in pharmaceuticals, computers, electronics, electronic imaging, and other high-tech industries often create **research and development teams** to develop new products. Managers select R&D team members on the basis of their expertise and experience in a certain area. Sometimes R&D teams are cross-functional teams with members from departments such as engineering, marketing, and production in addition to members from the research and development department.

Command Groups

command group A group composed of subordinates who report to the same supervisor; also called *department* or *unit.*

Subordinates who report to the same supervisor compose a **command group.** When top managers design an organization's structure and establish reporting relationships and a chain of command, they are essentially creating command groups. Command groups, often called *departments* or *units,* perform a significant amount of the work in many organizations. In order to have command groups that help an organization gain a competitive advantage, managers not only need to motivate group members to perform at a high level but also need to be effective leaders. Examples of command groups include the salespeople in a large department store in New York who report to the same supervisor, the employees of a small swimming pool sales and maintenance company in Florida who report to a general manager, the telephone operators at the MetLife insurance company who report to the same supervisor, and workers on an automobile assembly line in the Ford Motor Company who report to the same first-line manager.

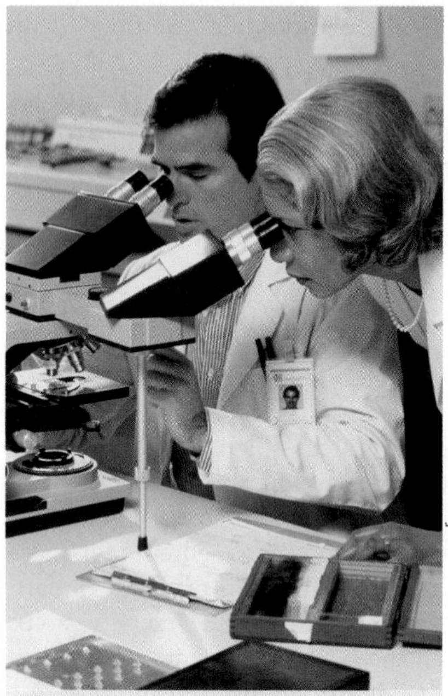

Figuring out if the new pharmaceutical drug is a go takes a strong R&D team made up of medical experts who know the science as well as the market needs.

Task Forces

task force A committee of managers or nonmanagerial employees from various departments or divisions who meet to solve a specific, mutual problem; also called *ad hoc committee.*

Managers form **task forces** to accomplish specific goals or solve problems in a certain time period; task forces are sometimes called *ad hoc committees.* For example, Michael Rider, owner and top manager of a chain of six gyms and fitness centers in the Midwest, created a task force composed of the general managers of the six gyms to determine whether the fitness centers should institute a separate fee schedule for customers who wanted to use the centers only for aerobics classes (and not use other facilities such as weights, steps, tracks, and swimming pools). The task force was given three months to prepare a report summarizing the pros and cons of the proposed change in fee schedules. After the task force completed its report and reached the conclusion that the change in fee structure probably would reduce revenues rather than increase them and thus should not be implemented, it was disbanded. As in Rider's case, task forces can be a valuable tool for busy managers who do not have the time to personally explore an important issue in depth.

Sometimes managers need to form task forces whose work, so to speak, is never done. The task force may be addressing a long-term or enduring problem or issue facing an organization, such as how to most usefully contribute to the local community or how to make sure the organization provides opportunities for potential employees with disabilities. Task forces that are relatively permanent are often referred to as *standing committees.* Membership in standing committees changes over time. Members may have, for example, a two- or three-year term on the committee, and memberships expire at varying times so there are always some members with experience on the committee. Managers often form and maintain standing committees to make sure important issues continue to be addressed.

Self-Managed Work Teams

self-managed work team A group of employees who supervise their own activities and monitor the quality of the goods and services they provide.

Self-managed work teams are teams in which members are empowered and have the responsibility and autonomy to complete identifiable pieces of work. On a day-to-day basis, team members decide what the team will do, how it will do it, and which members will perform which specific tasks.[29] Managers assign self-managed work teams' overall goals (such as assembling defect-free computer keyboards) but let team members decide how to meet those goals. Managers usually form self-managed work teams to improve quality, increase motivation and satisfaction, and lower costs. Often, by creating self-managed work teams, they combine tasks that individuals working separately used to perform, so the team is responsible for the whole set of tasks that yields an identifiable output or end product.

Managers can take a number of steps to ensure that self-managed work teams are effective and help an organization achieve its goals:[30]

- Give teams enough responsibility and autonomy to be truly self-managing. Refrain from telling team members what to do or solving problems for them even if you (as a manager) know what should be done.
- Make sure a team's work is sufficiently complex so it entails a number of different steps or procedures that must be performed and results in some kind of finished end product.
- Carefully select members of self-managed work teams. Team members should have the diversity of skills needed to complete the team's work, have the ability to work with others, and want to be part of a team.
- As a manager, realize that your role vis-à-vis self-managed work teams calls for guidance, coaching, and supporting, not supervising. You are a resource for teams to turn to when needed.
- Analyze what type of training team members need, and provide it. Working in a self-managed work team often requires that employees have more extensive technical and interpersonal skills.

Managers in a wide variety of organizations have found that self-managed work teams help the organization achieve its goals,[31] as profiled in the following "Management Insight" box.

Management Insight

Self-Managed Teams at Louis Vuitton and Nucor Corporation

Managers at Louis Vuitton, the most profitable luxury brand in the world, and managers at Nucor Corporation, the largest producer of steel and biggest recycler in the United States, have succeeded in effectively using self-managed teams to produce luxury accessories and steel, respectively. Self-managed teams at both companies not only are effective but truly excel and have helped make the companies leaders in their respective industries.[32]

Teams with between 20 and 30 members make Vuitton handbags and accessories. The teams work on only one product at a time; a team with 24 members might produce about 120 handbags per day. Team members are empowered to take ownership of the goods they produce, are encouraged to suggest improvements, and are kept up to date on key facts such as products' selling prices and popularity. As Thierry Nogues, a team leader at a Vuitton factory in Ducey, France, puts it, "Our goal is to make everyone as multiskilled and autonomous as possible."[33]

Production workers at Nucor are organized into teams ranging in size from 8 to 40 members based on the kind of work the team is responsible for, such as rolling steel or operating a furnace. Team members have considerable autonomy to make decisions and creatively respond to problems and opportunities,

A team member assembles classic Louis Vuitton bags at the company's fine leather goods factory in the Normandy town of Ducey in France.

and there are relatively few layers in the corporate hierarchy, supporting the empowerment of teams.[34] Teams develop their own informal rules for behavior and make their own decisions. As long as team members follow organizational rules and policies (such as those for safety) and meet quality standards, they are free to govern themselves. Managers act as coaches or advisers rather than supervisors, helping teams when needed.[35]

To ensure that production teams are motivated to help Nucor achieve its goals, team members are eligible for weekly bonuses based on the team's performance. Essentially, these production workers receive base pay that does not vary and are eligible to receive weekly bonus pay that can average from 80% to 150% of their regular pay.[36] The bonus rate is predetermined by the work a team performs and the capabilities of the machinery they use. Given the immediacy of the bonus and its potential magnitude, team members are motivated to perform at a high level, develop informal rules that support high performance, and strive to help Nucor reach its goals. Moreover, because all members of a team receive the same amount of weekly bonus money, they are motivated to do their best for the team, cooperate, and help one another out.[37] Of course, in tough economic times such as the recession in the late 2000s, Nucor's production workers' bonuses fall as demand for Nucor's products drops. Nonetheless, Nucor has been able to avoid laying off employees (unlike a lot of other large corporations).[38]

Crafting a luxury handbag and making steel joists couldn't be more different from each other in certain ways. Yet the highly effective self-managed teams at Louis Vuitton and Nucor share some fundamental qualities. These teams really do take ownership of their work and are highly motivated to perform effectively. Team members have the skills and knowledge they need to be effective, they are empowered to make decisions about their work, and they know their teams are making vital contributions to their organizations.[39]

Sometimes employees have individual jobs but also are part of a self-managed team that is formed to accomplish a specific goal or work on an important project. Employees need to perform their own individual job tasks and also actively contribute to the self-managed team so the team achieves its goal.

Sometimes self-managed work teams can run into trouble. Members may be reluctant to discipline one another by withholding bonuses from members who are not performing up to par or by firing members.[40] Buster Jarrell, a manager who oversaw self-managed work teams in AES Corporation's Houston plant, found that although the self-managed work teams were highly effective, they had a difficult time firing team members who were performing poorly.[41]

The Dallas office of the New York Life Insurance Co. experimented with having members of self-managed teams evaluate one another's performance and determine pay levels. Team members did not feel comfortable assuming this role, however, and managers ended up handling these tasks.[42] One reason for team members' discomfort may be the close personal relationships they sometimes develop with one another. In addition, members of self-managed work teams may sometimes take longer to accomplish tasks, such as when team members have difficulties coordinating their efforts.

Virtual Teams

virtual team A team whose members rarely or never meet face-to-face but, rather, interact by using various forms of information technology such as e-mail, computer networks, telephone, fax, and videoconferences.

Virtual teams are teams whose members rarely or never meet face-to-face but, rather, interact by using various forms of information technology such as e-mail, text messaging, computer networks, telephone, fax, and videoconferences. As organizations become increasingly global, and as the need for specialized knowledge increases due to advances in technology, managers can create virtual teams to solve problems or explore opportunities without being limited by team members needing to work in the same geographic location.[43]

Take the case of an organization that has manufacturing facilities in Australia, Canada, the United States, and Mexico and is encountering a quality problem in a complex manufacturing process. Each of its facilities has a quality control team headed by a quality control manager. The vice president for production does not try to solve the problem by forming and leading a team at one of the four manufacturing facilities; instead she forms and leads a virtual team composed of the quality control managers of the four plants and the plants' general managers. When these team members communicate via e-mail, the company's networking site, and videoconferencing, a wide array of knowledge and experience is brought to solve the problem.

The principal advantage of virtual teams is that they enable managers to disregard geographic distances and form teams whose members have the knowledge, expertise, and experience to tackle a particular problem or take advantage of a specific opportunity.[44] Virtual teams also can include members who are not actually employees of the organization itself; a virtual team might include members of a company that is used for outsourcing. More and more companies, including BP PLC, Nokia Corporation, and Ogilvy & Mather, are using virtual teams.[45]

Members of virtual teams rely on two forms of information technology: synchronous technologies and asynchronous technologies.[46] *Synchronous technologies* let virtual team members communicate and interact with one another in real time simultaneously and include videoconferencing, teleconferencing, and electronic meetings. *Asynchronous technologies* delay communication and include e-mail, electronic bulletin boards, and Internet Web sites. Many virtual teams use both kinds of technology depending on what projects they are working on.

Increasing globalization is likely to result in more organizations relying on virtual teams to a greater extent.[47] One challenge members of virtual teams face is building a sense of camaraderie and trust among team members who rarely, if ever, meet face-to-face. To address this challenge, some organizations schedule recreational activities, such as ski trips, so virtual team members can get together. Other organizations make sure virtual team members have a chance to meet in person soon after the team is formed and then schedule periodic face-to-face meetings to promote trust, understanding, and cooperation in the teams.[48] The need for such meetings is underscored by research suggesting that while some virtual teams can be as effective as teams that meet face-to-face, virtual team members might be less satisfied with teamwork efforts and have fewer feelings of camaraderie or cohesion. (Group cohesiveness is discussed in more detail later in the chapter.)[49]

Research also suggests that it is important for managers to keep track of virtual teams and intervene when necessary by, for example, encouraging members of teams who do not communicate often enough to monitor their team's progress and making sure team members actually have the time, and are recognized for, their virtual teamwork.[50] Additionally, when virtual teams are experiencing downtime or rough spots, managers might try to schedule face-to-face team time to bring team members together and help them focus on their goals.[51]

Researchers at the London Business School, including Professor Lynda Gratton, recently studied global virtual teams to try to identify factors that might help such teams be effective.[52] Based on their research, Gratton suggests that when forming virtual teams, it is helpful to include a few members who already know each other, other members who are well connected to people outside the team, and when possible, members who have volunteered to be a part of the team.[53] It is also advantageous for companies to have some kind of online site where team members can learn more about each other and the kinds of work they are engaged in, and in particular, a shared online workspace that team members can access around the clock.[54] Frequent communication is beneficial. Additionally, virtual team projects should be perceived as meaningful, interesting, and important by their members to promote and sustain their motivation.[55]

friendship group An informal group composed of employees who enjoy one another's company and socialize with one another.

Friendship Groups

The groups described so far are formal groups created by managers. **Friendship groups** are informal groups composed of employees who enjoy one another's company and socialize with one another. Members of friendship groups may have lunch together, take breaks together, or meet after work for meals, sports, or other activities. Friendship groups help satisfy employees' needs for interpersonal interaction, can provide needed social support in times of stress, and can contribute to people's feeling good at work and being satisfied with their jobs. Managers themselves often form friendship groups. The informal relationships that managers build in friendship groups can often help them solve work-related problems because members of these groups typically discuss work-related matters and offer advice.

A recycling interest group organizes like-minded colleagues to help pick up the slack where formal organization may be lacking.

Interest Groups

Employees form informal **interest groups** when they seek to achieve a common goal related to their membership in an organization. Employees may form interest groups, for example, to encourage managers to consider instituting flexible working hours, providing on-site child care, improving working conditions, or more proactively supporting environmental protection. Interest groups can give managers valuable insights into the issues and concerns that are foremost in employees' minds. They also can signal the need for change.

interest group An informal group composed of employees seeking to achieve a common goal related to their membership in an organization.

Group Dynamics

How groups function and, ultimately, their effectiveness hinge on group characteristics and processes known collectively as *group dynamics*. In this section we discuss five key elements of group dynamics: group size, tasks, and roles; group leadership; group development; group norms; and group cohesiveness.

Group Size, Tasks, and Roles

LO15-3 Explain how different elements of group dynamics influence the functioning and effectiveness of groups and teams.

Managers need to take group size, group tasks, and group roles into account as they create and maintain high-performing groups and teams.

GROUP SIZE The number of members in a group can be an important determinant of members' motivation and commitment and group performance. There are several advantages to keeping a group relatively small–between two and nine members. Compared with members of large groups, members of small groups tend to (1) interact more with each other and find it easier to coordinate their efforts, (2) be more motivated, satisfied, and committed, (3) find it easier to share information, and (4) be better able to see the importance of their personal contributions for group success. A disadvantage of small rather than large groups is that members of small groups have fewer resources available to accomplish their goals.

Large groups—with 10 or more members—also offer some advantages. They have more resources at their disposal to achieve group goals than small groups do. These resources include the knowledge, experience, skills, and abilities of group members as well as their actual time and effort. Large groups also let managers obtain the advantages stemming from the **division of labor**—splitting the work to be performed into particular tasks and assigning tasks to individual workers. Workers who specialize in particular tasks are likely to become skilled at performing those tasks and contribute significantly to high group performance.

division of labor Splitting the work to be performed into particular tasks and assigning tasks to individual workers.

The disadvantages of large groups include the problems of communication and coordination and the lower levels of motivation, satisfaction, and commitment that members of large groups sometimes experience. It is clearly more difficult to share information with, and coordinate the activities of, 16 people rather than 8 people. Moreover, members of large groups might not think their efforts are really needed and sometimes might not even feel a part of the group.

In deciding on the appropriate size for any group, managers attempt to gain the advantages of small group size and, at the same time, form groups with sufficient resources to accomplish their goals and have a well-developed division of labor. As a general rule of thumb, groups should have no more members than necessary to achieve a division of labor and provide the resources needed to achieve group goals. In R&D teams, for example, group size is too large when (1) members spend more time communicating what they know to others than applying what they know to solve problems and create new products, (2) individual productivity decreases, and (3) group performance suffers.[56]

GROUP TASKS The appropriate size of a high-performing group is affected by the kind of tasks the group is to perform. An important characteristic of group tasks that affects performance is **task interdependence**—the degree to which the work performed by one member of a group influences the work performed by other members.[57] As task interdependence increases, group members need to interact more frequently and intensely with one another, and their efforts have to be more closely coordinated if they are to perform at a high level. Management expert James D. Thompson identified three types of task interdependence: pooled, sequential, and reciprocal (see Figure 15.3).[58]

task interdependence The degree to which the work performed by one member of a group influences the work performed by other members.

POOLED TASK INTERDEPENDENCE **Pooled task interdependence** exists when group members make separate and independent contributions to group performance; overall group performance is the sum of the performance of the individual members (see Figure 15.3a). Examples of groups that have pooled task interdependence include a group of teachers in an elementary school, a group of salespeople in a department store, a group of secretaries in an office, and a group of custodians in an office building. In these examples, group performance, whether it be the number of children who are taught and the quality of their education, the dollar value of sales, the amount of secretarial work completed, or the number of offices cleaned, is determined by summing the individual contributions of group members.

pooled task interdependence The task interdependence that exists when group members make separate and independent contributions to group performance.

For groups with pooled interdependence, managers should determine the appropriate group size primarily from the amount of work to be accomplished. Large groups can be effective because group members work independently and do not have to interact frequently with one another. Motivation in groups with pooled interdependence will be highest when managers reward group members based on individual performance.

SEQUENTIAL TASK INTERDEPENDENCE **Sequential task interdependence** exists when group members must perform specific tasks in a predetermined order; certain tasks have to be performed before others, and what one worker does affects the work of others (see Figure 15.3b). Assembly lines and mass-production processes are characterized by sequential task interdependence.

sequential task interdependence The task interdependence that exists when group members must perform specific tasks in a predetermined order.

When group members are sequentially interdependent, group size is usually dictated by the needs of the production process—for example, the number of steps needed in an assembly line to efficiently produce a DVD player. With sequential interdependence,

Figure 15.3
Types of Task Interdependence

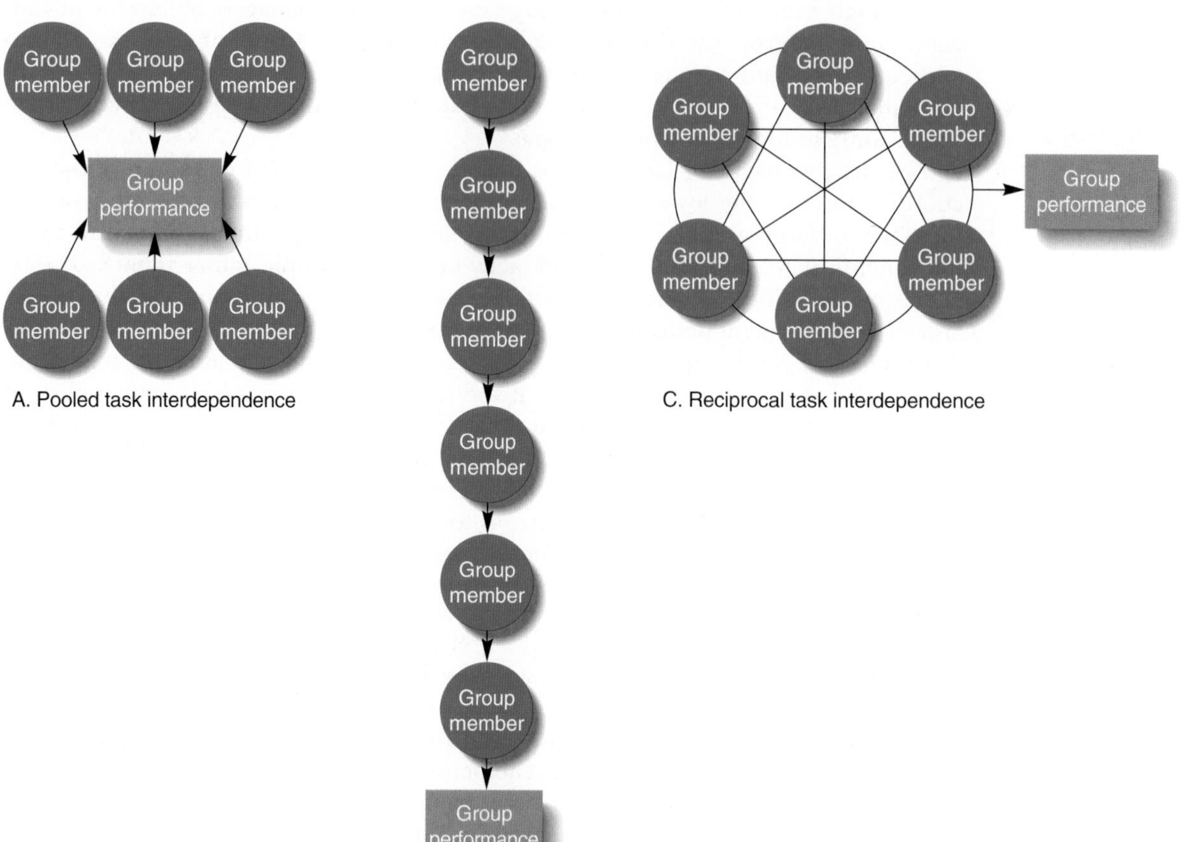

it is difficult to identify individual performance because one group member's performance depends on how well others perform their tasks. A slow worker at the start of an assembly line, for example, causes all workers further down to work slowly. Thus managers are often advised to reward group members for group performance. Group members will be motivated to perform at a high level because if the group performs well, each member will benefit. In addition, group members may put pressure on poor performers to improve so group performance and rewards do not suffer.

reciprocal task interdependence The task interdependence that exists when the work performed by each group member is fully dependent on the work performed by other group members.

RECIPROCAL TASK INTERDEPENDENCE **Reciprocal task interdependence** exists when the work performed by each group member is fully dependent on the work performed by other group members; group members have to share information, intensely interact with one another, and coordinate their efforts in order for the group to achieve its goals (see Figure 15.3c). In general, reciprocal task interdependence characterizes the operation of teams, rather than other kinds of groups. The task interdependence of R&D teams, top management teams, and many self-managed work teams is reciprocal.

When group members are reciprocally interdependent, managers are advised to keep group size relatively small because of the necessity of coordinating team members' activities. Communication difficulties can arise in teams with reciprocally interdependent tasks because team members need to interact frequently with one another and be available when needed. As group size increases, communication difficulties increase and can impair team performance.

When a group's members are reciprocally interdependent, managers also are advised to reward group members on the basis of group performance. Individual

First the steak, then the green beans, then the carefully drizzled béarnaise; gourmet kitchens where the presentation is an integral part of the experience exemplify sequential task interdependence.

levels of performance are often difficult for managers to identify, and group-based rewards help ensure that group members will be motivated to perform at a high level and make valuable contributions to the group. Of course, if a manager can identify instances of individual performance in such groups, they too can be rewarded to maintain high levels of motivation. Microsoft and many other companies reward group members for their individual performance as well as for the performance of their group.

GROUP ROLES A **group role** is a set of behaviors and tasks that a member of a group is expected to perform because of his or her position in the group. Members of cross-functional teams, for example, are expected to perform roles relevant to their special areas of expertise. In our earlier example of cross-functional teams at Hallmark Cards, it is the role of writers on the teams to create verses for new cards, the role of artists to draw illustrations, and the role of designers to put verse and artwork together in an attractive and appealing card design. The roles of members of top management teams are shaped primarily by their areas of expertise–production, marketing, finance, research and development–but members of top management teams also typically draw on their broad expertise as planners and strategists.

In forming groups and teams, managers need to clearly communicate to group members the expectations for their roles in the group, what is required of them, and how the different roles in the group fit together to accomplish group goals. Managers also need to realize that group roles often change and evolve as a group's tasks and goals change and as group members gain experience and knowledge. Thus, to get the performance gains that come from experience or "learning by doing," managers should encourage group members to take the initiative to assume additional responsibilities as they see fit and modify their assigned roles. This process, called **role making,** can enhance individual and group performance.

group role A set of behaviors and tasks that a member of a group is expected to perform because of his or her position in the group.

role making Taking the initiative to modify an assigned role by assuming additional responsibilities.

In self-managed work teams and some other groups, group members themselves are responsible for creating and assigning roles. Many self-managed work teams also pick their own team leaders. When group members create their own roles, managers should be available to group members in an advisory capacity, helping them effectively settle conflicts and disagreements. At Johnsonville Foods, for example, the position titles of first-line managers have been changed to "advisory coach" to reflect the managers' new role vis-à-vis the self-managed work teams they oversee.[59]

Group Leadership

All groups and teams need leadership. Indeed, as we discussed in detail in Chapter 14, effective leadership is a key ingredient for high-performing groups, teams, and organizations. Sometimes managers assume the leadership role in groups and teams, as is the case in many command groups and top management teams. Or a manager may appoint a member of a group who is not a manager to be group leader or chairperson, as is the case in a task force or standing committee. In other cases, group or team members may choose their own leaders, or a leader may emerge naturally as group members work together to achieve group goals. When managers empower members of self-managed work teams, they often let group members choose their own leaders. Some self-managed work teams find it effective to rotate the leadership role among their members. Whether or not leaders of groups and teams are managers, and whether they are appointed by managers (often referred to as *formal leaders*) or emerge naturally in a group (often referred to as *informal leaders*), they play an important role in ensuring that groups and teams perform up to their potential.

When teams do not live up to their promise, sometimes the problem is a lack of team leadership, as illustrated in the following "Ethics in Action" box.

Ethics in Action

Leadership in Teams at ICU Medical

Dr. George Lopez, an internal medicine physician, founded ICU Medical in San Clemente, California, in 1984 after a patient of his accidentally died when an intravenous (IV) line became inadvertently disconnected.[60] Lopez thought there must be a better way to design components of IV lines so these kinds of tragic accidents didn't happen. He developed a product called the Click Lock, which has both a locking mechanism for IV systems and also a protected needle so health care workers are protected from accidental needle pricks.[61] Today ICU Medical has over 1,400 employees, and in 2009 net sales were over $210 million.[62] Lopez is CEO of the company, which in 2009 made *Forbes* magazine's list of "The 200 Best Small Companies."[63] ICU Medical continues to focus on the development and manufacture of products that improve the functioning of IV lines and systems while protecting health care workers from accidental needle pricks.[64] For example, the CLAVE NeedleFree Connector for IV lines is one of ICU Medical's top-selling products.[65]

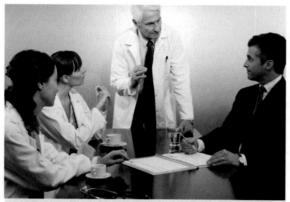

Self-managed teams with strong leaders and carefully thought-out guidelines for how to evaluate group decisions make all the difference for such companies as ICU Medical.

In the early 1990s Lopez experienced something not uncommon to successful entrepreneurs as their businesses grow. As the entrepreneur–CEO, he continued to make the majority of important decisions himself; yet he had close to 100 employees, demand for the CLAVE was very high, and he was starting to feel overloaded to the point where he would often sleep at nights in the office.[66] After watching one of his son's hockey games, he realized that a well-functioning team could work wonders; in the case of the hockey game, although the opposing team had an outstanding player, his son's team really pulled together as a team and was able to win the game despite the rival team's outstanding member. Lopez decided to empower employees to form teams to work on a pressing goal for ICU Medical: increasing production.[67] While employees did form teams and spent a lot of time in team interactions, the teams did not seem to come up with any real tangible results, perhaps because there were no team leaders in place and the teams had no guidelines to help them accomplish their goals.[68]

In an effort to improve team effectiveness, Lopez told employees that teams should elect team leaders. And together with Jim Reitz, ICU Medical's director of human resources, Lopez came up with rules or guidelines teams should follow, such as "challenge the issue, not the person" and "stand up for your position, but never argue against the facts."[69] ICU Medical also started to reward team members for their team's contributions to organizational effectiveness. With these changes, Reitz and Lopez were striving to ensure that teams had leaders, had some guidelines for team member behavior, and were rewarded for their contributions to organizational effectiveness but, at the same time, were not bogged down by unnecessary constraints and structures and were truly self-managing.[70]

With these changes in place, teams at ICU Medical began to live up to their promise. Today any ICU Medical employee can create a team to address a problem, seize an opportunity, or work on a project ranging from developing a new product to making improvements in the physical work environment.[71] The teams have leaders and are self-managing.

Recognizing that self-managed teams still need rules, guidelines, leadership, and structure, a team of employees developed a 25-page guidebook for effective team functioning. And to ensure that teams learn from each other as well as get feedback, teams are required to put up notes from each of their meetings on ICU Medical's intranet, and any employee can provide feedback to any of the teams.[72] All in all, effectively led teams have helped ICU Medical prosper in its efforts to develop and manufacture products that protect the safety of both patients and health care workers.

Group Development over Time

As many managers overseeing self-managed teams have learned, it sometimes takes a self-managed work team two or three years to perform up to its true capabilities.[73] As their experience suggests, what a group is capable of achieving depends in part on its stage of development. Knowing that it takes considerable time for self-managed work teams to get up and running has helped managers have realistic expectations for new teams and know that they need to give new team members considerable training and guidance.

Although every group's development over time is unique, researchers have identified five stages of group development that many groups seem to pass through (see Figure 15.4).[74] In the first stage, *forming,* members try to get to know one another and reach a common understanding of what the group is trying to accomplish and how group members should behave. During this stage, managers should strive to make each member feel that he or she is a valued part of the group.

In the second stage, *storming,* group members experience conflict and disagreements because some members do not wish to submit to the demands of other group members. Disputes may arise over who should lead the group. Self-managed work teams can be particularly vulnerable during the storming stage. Managers need to keep an eye on groups at this stage to make sure conflict does not get out of hand.

During the third stage, *norming,* close ties between group members develop, and feelings of friendship and camaraderie emerge. Group members arrive at a consensus about what goals they should seek to achieve and how group members should behave toward one another. In the fourth stage, *performing,* the real work of the group gets accomplished. Depending on the type of group in question, managers need to take different steps at this stage to help ensure that groups are effective. Managers of command groups need to make sure that group members are motivated and that they are effectively leading group members. Managers overseeing self-managed work teams have to empower team members and make sure teams are given enough responsibility and autonomy at the performing stage.

The last stage, *adjourning,* applies only to groups that eventually are disbanded, such as task forces. During adjourning a group is dispersed. Sometimes adjourning takes place when a group completes a finished product, such as when a task force evaluating the pros and cons of providing on-site child care produces a report supporting its recommendation.

Managers should have a flexible approach to group development and should keep attuned to the different needs and requirements of groups at the various stages.[75] Above all else, and regardless of the stage of development, managers need to think of themselves as *resources* for groups. Thus managers always should strive to find ways to help groups and teams function more effectively.

Figure 15.4
Five Stages of Group Development

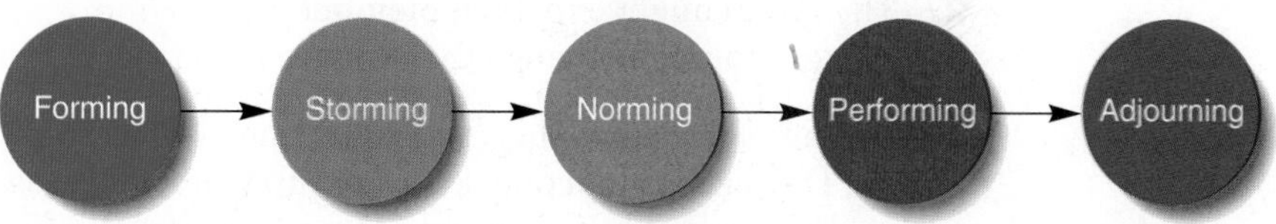

LO15-4 Explain why it is important for groups and teams to have a balance of conformity and deviance and a moderate level of cohesiveness.

Group Norms

All groups, whether top management teams, self-managed work teams, or command groups, need to control their members' behaviors to ensure that the group performs at a high level and meets its goals. Assigning roles to each group member is one way to control behavior in groups. Another important way in which groups influence members' behavior is through the development and enforcement of group norms.[76] **Group norms** are shared guidelines or rules for behavior that most group members follow. Groups develop norms concerning a wide variety of behaviors, including working hours, the sharing of information among group members, how certain group tasks should be performed, and even how members of a group should dress.

group norms Shared guidelines or rules for behavior that most group members follow.

Managers should encourage members of a group to develop norms that contribute to group performance and the attainment of group goals. For example, group norms dictating that each member of a cross-functional team should always be available for the rest of the team when his or her input is needed, return phone calls as soon as possible, inform other team members of travel plans, and give team members a phone number at which he or she can be reached when traveling on business help to ensure that the team is efficient, performs at a high level, and achieves its goals. A norm in a command group of secretaries that dictates that secretaries who happen to have a light workload in any given week should help out secretaries with heavier workloads helps to ensure that the group completes all assignments in a timely and efficient manner. And a norm in a top management team that dictates that team members should always consult with one another before making major decisions helps to ensure that good decisions are made with a minimum of errors.

CONFORMITY AND DEVIANCE Group members conform to norms for three reasons: (1) They want to obtain rewards and avoid punishments. (2) They want to imitate group members whom they like and admire. (3) They have internalized the norm and believe it is the right and proper way to behave.[77] Consider the case of Robert King, who conformed to his department's norm of attending a fund-raiser for a community food bank. King's conformity could be due to (1) his desire to be a member of the group in good standing and to have friendly relationships with other group members (rewards), (2) his copying the behavior of other members of the department whom he respects and who always attend the fund-raiser (imitating other group members), or (3) his belief in the merits of supporting the activities of the food bank (believing that is the right and proper way to behave).

Failure to conform, or deviance, occurs when a member of a group violates a group norm. Deviance signals that a group is not controlling one of its member's behaviors. Groups generally respond to members who behave defiantly in one of three ways:[78]

1. The group might try to get the member to change his or her deviant ways and conform to the norm. Group members might try to convince the member of the need to conform, or they might ignore or even punish the deviant. For example, in a Jacksonville Foods plant Liz Senkbiel, a member of a self-managed work team responsible for weighing sausages, failed to conform to a group norm dictating that group members should periodically clean up an untidy interview room. Because Senkbiel refused to take part in the team's cleanup efforts, team members reduced her monthly bonus by about $225 for a two-month period.[79] Senkbiel clearly learned the costs of deviant behavior in her team.
2. The group might expel the member.
3. The group might change the norm to be consistent with the member's behavior.

This last alternative suggests that some deviant behavior can be functional for groups. Deviance is functional for a group when it causes group members to evaluate norms that may be dysfunctional but are taken for granted by the group. Often group members do not think about why they behave in a certain way or why they follow certain norms.(Deviance can cause group members to reflect on their norms and change them when appropriate.)

Consider a group of receptionists in a beauty salon who followed the norm that all appointments would be handwritten in an appointment book and, at the end of each day, the receptionist on duty would enter the appointments into the salon's computer system, which printed out the hairdressers' daily schedules. One day a receptionist decided to enter appointments directly into the computer system when they were being made, bypassing the appointment book. This deviant behavior caused the other receptionists to think about why they were using the appointment book at all. After consulting with the owner of the salon, the group changed its norm. Now appointments are entered directly into the computer, which saves time and reduces scheduling errors.

ENCOURAGING A BALANCE OF CONFORMITY AND DEVIANCE To effectively help an organization gain a competitive advantage, groups and teams need the right balance of conformity and deviance (see Figure 15.5). A group needs a certain level of conformity to ensure that it can control members' behavior and channel it in the direction of high performance and group goal accomplishment. A group also needs a certain level of deviance to ensure that dysfunctional norms are discarded and replaced with functional ones. Balancing conformity and deviance is a pressing concern for all groups, whether they are top management teams, R&D teams, command groups, or self-managed work teams.

The extent of conformity and reactions to deviance within groups are determined by group members themselves. The three bases for conformity just described are powerful forces that more often than not result in group members' conforming to

Figure 15.5
Balancing Conformity and Deviance in Groups

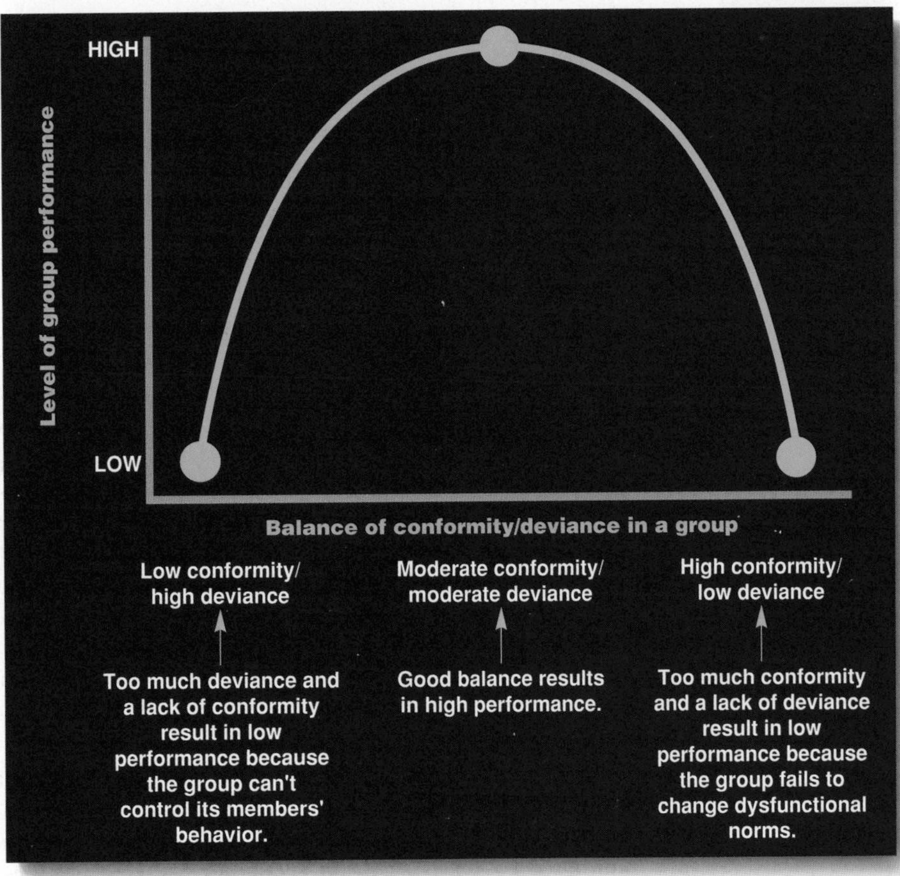

norms. Sometimes these forces are so strong that deviance rarely occurs in groups, and when it does, it is stamped out.

Managers can take several steps to ensure adequate tolerance of deviance in groups so group members are willing to deviate from dysfunctional norms and, when deviance occurs in their group, reflect on the appropriateness of the violated norm and change the norm if necessary. First, managers can be role models for the groups and teams they oversee. When managers encourage and accept employees' suggestions for changes in procedures, do not rigidly insist that tasks be accomplished in a certain way, and admit when a norm they once supported is no longer functional, they signal to group members that conformity should not come at the expense of needed changes and improvements. Second, managers should let employees know that there are always ways to improve group processes and performance levels and thus opportunities to replace existing norms with norms that will better enable a group to achieve its goals and perform at a high level. Third, managers should encourage members of groups and teams to periodically assess the appropriateness of their norms.

Managers in the innovative design firm IDEO, based in Palo Alto, California (IDEO's culture is described in Chapter 3), have excelled at ensuring that design teams have the right mix of conformity and deviance, resulting in IDEO's designing products in fields ranging from medicine to space travel to computing and personal hygiene, as indicated in the following "Management Insight" box.

Management Insight

Teams Benefit from Deviance and Conformity at IDEO

IDEO has designed many products we now take for granted: the first Apple mouse, the Palm handheld organizer, stand-up toothpaste containers, flexible shelving for offices, self-sealing drink bottles for sports, blood analyzers, and even equipment used in space travel.[80] Managers and designers at IDEO take pride in being experts at the process of innovation in general, rather than in any particular domain. Of course the company has technical design experts, such as mechanical and electrical engineers, who work on products requiring specialized knowledge; but on the same teams with the engineers might be an anthropologist, a biologist, and a social scientist.[81]

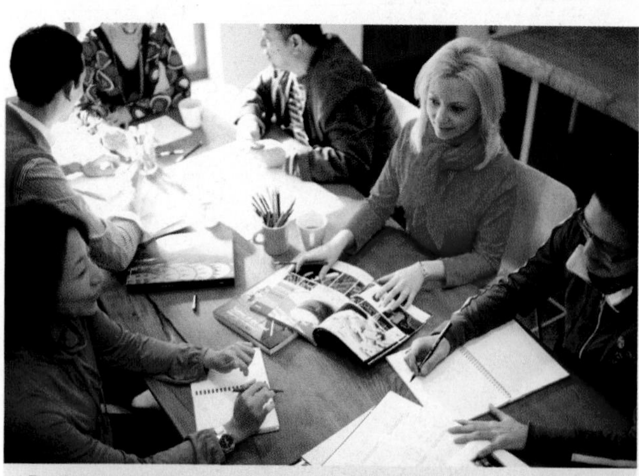

Deviance, or the capacity to think differently from the status quo, is promoted by IDEO's diverse employee teams, which might include artists, biologists, and anthropologists.

A guiding principle at IDEO is that innovation comes in many shapes and sizes, and it is only through diversity in thought that people can recognize opportunities for innovation. To promote such diversity in thought, new product development at IDEO is a team effort.[82] Moreover, both conformity and deviance are encouraged on IDEO teams.

Deviance, thinking differently, and not conforming to expected ways of doing things and mind-sets are encouraged at IDEO. In fact, innovative ideas often flow when designers try to see things as they really are and are not blinded by thoughts of what is appropriate, what is possible, or how things should be. Often constraints on new product design are created by designers themselves conforming to a certain mind-set about the nature of a product or what a product can or should do and look like. IDEO designers are encouraged to actively break down these constraints in their design teams.[83]

Managers at IDEO realize the need for a certain amount of conformity so members of design teams can work effectively together and achieve their goals. Thus conformity to a few central norms is emphasized in IDEO teams. These norms include understanding what the team is working on (the product, market, or client need), observing real people in their natural environments, visualizing how new products might work and be used, evaluating and refining product prototypes, encouraging wild ideas, and never rejecting an idea simply because it sounds too crazy.[84] As long as these norms are followed, diversity of thought and even deviance promote innovation at IDEO. In fact, another norm at IDEO is to study "rule breakers"–people who don't follow instructions for products, for example, or who try to put products to different uses–because these individuals might help designers identify problems with existing products and unmet consumer needs.[85] All in all, IDEO's focus on encouraging both deviance and conformity in design teams has benefited all of us–we use IDEO-designed products that seem so familiar we take them for granted. We forget these products did not exist until a design team at IDEO was called on by a client to develop a new product or improve an existing one.[86]

Group Cohesiveness

group cohesiveness The degree to which members are attracted to or loyal to their group.

Another important element of group dynamics that affects group performance and effectiveness is **group cohesiveness,** which is the degree to which members are attracted to or loyal to their group or team.[87] When group cohesiveness is high, individuals strongly value their group membership, find the group appealing, and have strong desires to remain a part of the group. When group cohesiveness is low, group members do not find their group particularly appealing and have little desire to retain their group membership. Research suggests that managers should strive to have a moderate level of cohesiveness in the groups and teams they manage because that is most likely to contribute to an organization's competitive advantage.

CONSEQUENCES OF GROUP COHESIVENESS There are three major consequences of group cohesiveness: level of participation within a group, level of conformity to group norms, and emphasis on group goal accomplishment (see Figure 15.6).[88]

LEVEL OF PARTICIPATION WITHIN A GROUP As group cohesiveness increases, the extent of group members' participation within the group increases. Participation contributes to group effectiveness because group members are actively involved in the group, ensure that group tasks get accomplished, readily share information with each other, and have frequent and open communication (the important topic of communication is covered in depth in Chapter 16).

A moderate level of group cohesiveness helps ensure that group members actively participate in the group and communicate effectively with one another. The reason why managers may not want to encourage high levels of cohesiveness is illustrated by the example of two cross-functional teams responsible for developing new toys. Members of the highly cohesive Team Alpha often have lengthy meetings that usually start with non-work-related conversations and jokes, meet more often than most of the other cross-functional teams in the company, and spend a good portion of their time communicating the ins and outs of their department's contribution to toy development to other team members. Members of the moderately cohesive Team Beta generally have efficient meetings in which ideas are communicated and discussed as needed, do not meet more often than necessary, and share the ins and outs of their expertise with one another to the extent needed for the development process. Teams Alpha and Beta have both developed some top-selling toys. However, it generally takes Team Alpha 30% longer to do so than Team Beta. This is why too much cohesiveness can be too much of a good thing.

LEVEL OF CONFORMITY TO GROUP NORMS Increasing levels of group cohesiveness result in increasing levels of conformity to group norms, and when cohesiveness becomes high, there may be so little deviance in groups that group members conform to norms even when they are dysfunctional. In contrast, low cohesiveness can result in too much deviance and undermine the ability of a group to control its members' behaviors to get things done.

Teams Alpha and Beta in the toy company both had the same norm for toy development. It dictated that members of each team would discuss potential ideas for new toys, decide on a line of toys to pursue, and then have the team member from R&D design a prototype. Recently a new animated movie featuring a family of rabbits produced by a small film company was an unexpected hit, and major toy companies were scrambling to reach licensing agreements to produce toy lines featuring the rabbits. The top management team in the toy company assigned Teams Alpha and Beta to develop the new toy lines quickly to beat the competition.

Members of Team Alpha followed their usual toy development norm even though the marketing expert on the team believed the process could have been streamlined to save time. The marketing expert on Team Beta urged the team to deviate from its toy development norm. She suggested that the team not have R&D develop prototypes but, instead, modify top-selling toys the company already made to feature rabbits and then reach a licensing agreement with the film company based on the high sales potential (given the company's prior success). Once the licensing agreement was signed, the company could take the time needed to develop innovative and unique rabbit toys with more input from R&D.

As a result of the willingness of the marketing expert on Team Beta to deviate from the norm for toy development, the toy company obtained an exclusive licensing agreement with the film company and had its first rabbit toys on the shelves of stores in a record three months. Groups need a balance of conformity and deviance, so a moderate level of cohesiveness often yields the best outcome, as it did in the case of Team Beta.

EMPHASIS ON GROUP GOAL ACCOMPLISHMENT As group cohesiveness increases, the emphasis placed on group goal accomplishment also increases within a group. A strong emphasis on group goal accomplishment, however, does not always lead to organizational effectiveness. For an organization to be effective and gain a competitive advantage, the different groups and teams in the organization must cooperate with one another and be motivated to achieve *organizational goals,* even if doing so sometimes comes at the expense of the achievement of group goals. A moderate level of cohesiveness motivates group members to accomplish both group and organizational goals. High levels of cohesiveness can cause group members to be so focused on group goal accomplishment that they may strive to achieve group goals no matter what–even when doing so jeopardizes organizational performance.

At the toy company, the major goal of the cross-functional teams was to develop new toy lines that were truly innovative, utilized the latest in technology, and were in some way fundamentally distinct from other toys on the market. When it came to the rabbit project, Team Alpha's high level of cohesiveness contributed to its continued emphasis on its group goal of developing an innovative line of toys; thus the team stuck with its usual design process. Team Beta, in contrast, realized that developing the new line of toys quickly was an important organizational goal that should take precedence over the group's goal of developing groundbreaking new toys, at least in the short term. Team Beta's moderate level of cohesiveness contributed to team members' doing what was best for the toy company in this case.

FACTORS LEADING TO GROUP COHESIVENESS Four factors contribute to the level of group cohesiveness (see Figure 15.6).[89] By influencing these *determinants of group cohesiveness,* managers can raise or lower the level of cohesiveness to promote moderate levels of cohesiveness in groups and teams.

GROUP SIZE As we mentioned earlier, members of small groups tend to be more motivated and committed than members of large groups. Thus to promote

Figure 15.6
Sources and Consequences of Group Cohesiveness

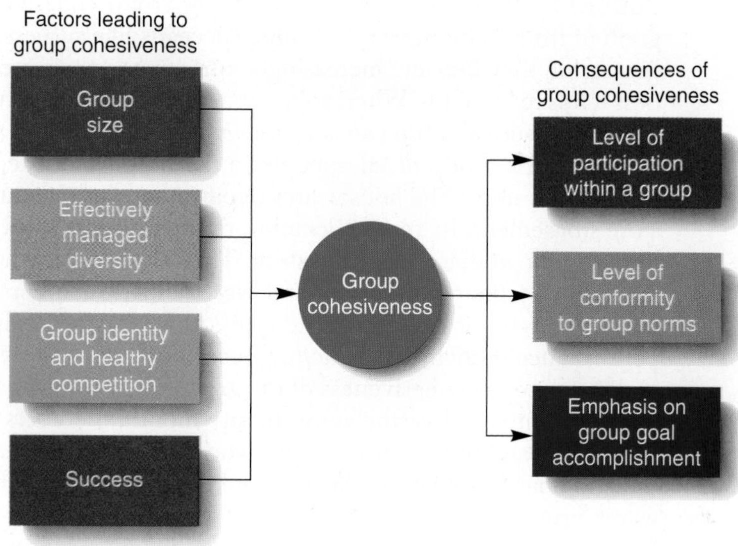

cohesiveness in groups, when feasible, managers should form groups that are small to medium in size (about 2 to 15 members). If a group is low in cohesiveness and large in size, managers might want to consider dividing the group in half and assigning different tasks and goals to the two newly formed groups.

EFFECTIVELY MANAGED DIVERSITY In general, people tend to like and get along with others who are similar to themselves. It is easier to communicate with someone, for example, who shares your values, has a similar background, and has had similar experiences. However, as discussed in Chapter 5, diversity in groups, teams, and organizations can help an organization gain a competitive advantage. Diverse groups often come up with more innovative and creative ideas. One reason why cross-functional teams are so popular in organizations like Hallmark Cards is that the diverse expertise represented in the teams results in higher levels of team performance.

In forming groups and teams, managers need to make sure the diversity in knowledge, experience, expertise, and other characteristics necessary for group goal accomplishment is represented in the new groups. Managers then have to make sure this diversity in group membership is effectively managed so groups will be cohesive (see Chapter 5).

GROUP IDENTITY AND HEALTHY COMPETITION When group cohesiveness is low, managers can often increase it by encouraging groups to develop their own identities or personalities and engage in healthy competition. This is precisely what managers at Eaton Corporation's manufacturing facility in Lincoln, Illinois, did. Eaton's employees manufacture products such as engine valves, gears, truck axles, and circuit breakers. Managers at Eaton created self-managed work teams to cut costs and improve performance. They realized, however, that the teams would have to be cohesive to ensure that they would strive to achieve their goals. Managers promoted group identity by having the teams give themselves names such as "The Hoods," "The Worms," and "Scrap Attack" (a team striving to reduce costly scrap metal waste by 50%). Healthy competition among groups was promoted by displaying measures of each team's performance and the extent to which teams met their goals on a large TV screen in the cafeteria and by rewarding team members for team performance.[90]

If groups are too cohesive, managers can try to decrease cohesiveness by promoting organizational (rather than group) identity and making the organization as a whole the focus of the group's efforts. Organizational identity can be promoted by making group members feel that they are valued members of the organization and by stressing cooperation across groups to promote the achievement of organizational goals. Excessive levels of cohesiveness also can be reduced by reducing or eliminating competition among groups and rewarding cooperation.

SUCCESS When it comes to promoting group cohesiveness, there is more than a grain of truth to the saying "Nothing succeeds like success." As groups become more successful, they become increasingly attractive to their members, and their cohesiveness tends to increase. When cohesiveness is low, managers can increase cohesiveness by making sure a group can achieve some noticeable and visible successes.

Consider a group of salespeople in the housewares department of a medium-size department store. The housewares department was recently moved to a corner of the store's basement. Its remote location resulted in low sales because of infrequent customer traffic in that part of the store. The salespeople, who were generally evaluated favorably by their supervisors and were valued members of the store, tried various initiatives to boost sales, but to no avail. As a result of this lack of success and the poor performance of their department, their cohesiveness started to plummet. To increase and preserve the cohesiveness of the group, the store manager implemented a group-based incentive across the store. In any month, members of the group with the best attendance and punctuality records would have their names and pictures posted on a bulletin board in the cafeteria and would each receive a $50 gift certificate. The housewares group frequently had the best records, and their success on this dimension helped to build and maintain their cohesiveness. Moreover, this initiative boosted attendance and discouraged lateness throughout the store.

Managing Groups and Teams for High Performance

Now that you understand why groups and teams are so important for organizations, the types of groups managers create, and group dynamics, we consider some additional steps managers can take to make sure groups and teams perform at a high level and contribute to organizational effectiveness. Managers striving to have top-performing groups and teams need to (1) motivate group members to work toward the achievement of organizational goals, (2) reduce social loafing, and (3) help groups manage conflict effectively.

LO15-5 Describe how managers can motivate group members to achieve organizational goals and reduce social loafing in groups and teams.

Motivating Group Members to Achieve Organizational Goals

When work is difficult, tedious, or requires a high level of commitment and energy, managers cannot assume group members will always be motivated to work toward the achievement of organizational goals. Consider a group of house painters who paint the interiors and exteriors of new homes for a construction company and are paid on an hourly basis. Why should they strive to complete painting jobs quickly and efficiently if doing so will just make them feel more tired at the end of the day and they will not receive any tangible benefits? It makes more sense for the painters to adopt a relaxed approach, to take frequent breaks, and to work at a leisurely pace. This relaxed approach, however, impairs the construction company's ability to gain a competitive advantage because it raises costs and increases the time needed to complete a new home.

Managers can motivate members of groups and teams to achieve organizational goals by making sure the members themselves benefit when the group or team performs highly. For example, if members of a self-managed work team know they will receive a weekly bonus based on team performance, they will be motivated to perform at a high level.

Managers often rely on some combination of individual and group-based incentives to motivate members of groups and teams to work toward the achievement of organizational goals. When individual performance within a group can be assessed, pay is often determined by individual performance or by both individual and group performance. When individual performance within a group cannot be accurately assessed, group performance should be the key determinant of pay levels. Many companies that use self-managed work teams base team members' pay in part on team performance.[91] A major challenge for managers is to develop a fair pay system that will lead to both high individual motivation and high group or team performance.

Other benefits managers can make available to high-performance group members–in addition to monetary rewards–include extra resources such as equipment and computer software, awards and other forms of recognition, and choice of future work assignments. For example, members of self-managed work teams that develop new software at companies such as Microsoft often value working on interesting and important projects; members of teams that have performed at a high level are rewarded by being assigned to interesting and important new projects.

At IDEO (profiled earlier in a "Management Insight" box), managers motivate team members by making them feel important. As Tom Kelley, IDEO's general manager, puts it, "When people feel special, they'll perform beyond your wildest dreams."[92] To make IDEO team members feel special, IDEO managers plan unique and fun year-end parties, give teams the opportunity to take time off if they feel they need or want to, encourage teams to take field trips, and see pranks as a way to incorporate fun into the workplace.[93]

Valero Energy motivates groups and teams to achieve organizational goals by valuing its employees, looking out for their well-being, and standing by them in crisis situations.[94] For example, employees with medical emergencies can use Valero's corporate jet if they need to, and Valero covers the complete cost of employee's health insurance premiums.[95] In turn, group members put forth high levels of effort to help Valero achieve its goals. As former Valero CEO and chairman Bill Greehey put it, "The more you do for your employees, the more they do for shareholders and the more they do for the community."[96]

Valero Energy Corporation helped workers like Ronald Lewis get back on their feet in the wake of Hurricane Katrina, which damaged many homes and communities in Louisiana.

When Hurricane Katrina hit the Louisiana coastline in 2005, the way Valero stood by employees in its St. Charles oil refinery near New Orleans, and the way employees stood by each other and the company, brought plant manager Jonathan Stuart to tears as he was briefing Greehey and other top managers a few days after the hurricane hit.[97] Stuart led a 50-person crew that rode out the hurricane in the shut-down refinery. The day before the storm hit, a supervisor used his personal credit card to buy supplies and stayed up all night preparing meals for the crew. Crew members worked round the clock, putting up new power poles, repairing power lines, and replacing motors. The refinery was up and running within eight days (while a Shell refinery close by was still shut down), and the crew had located all of the plant's 570 employees.[98]

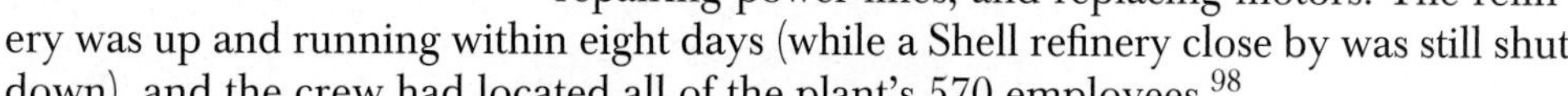

Valero's headquarters had supplies delivered to employees whose homes were damaged; trucks brought in food, water, generators, chain saws, refrigerators, shovels, and Nextel phones (the only cell phone system that was still working). Sixty mobile homes were brought in for employees whose houses were unlivable. Employees and law enforcement personnel were given free fuel, and employees were given up to $10,000 in aide from Valero's SAFE fund. Valero continued issuing paychecks to its employees while other affected refineries did not.[99]

Reducing Social Loafing in Groups

We have been focusing on the steps managers can take to encourage high levels of performance in groups. Managers, however, need to be aware of an important downside to group and team work: the potential for social loafing, which reduces group

social loafing The tendency of individuals to put forth less effort when they work in groups than when they work alone.

performance. **Social loafing** is the tendency of individuals to put forth less effort when they work in groups than when they work alone.[100] Have you ever worked on a group project in which one or two group members never seemed to be pulling their weight? Have you ever worked in a student club or committee in which some members always seemed to be missing meetings and never volunteered for activities? Have you ever had a job in which one or two of your coworkers seemed to be slacking off because they knew you or other members of your work group would make up for their low levels of effort? If so, you have witnessed social loafing in action.

Social loafing can occur in all kinds of groups and teams and in all kinds of organizations. It can result in lower group performance and may even prevent a group from attaining its goals. Fortunately managers can take steps to reduce social loafing and sometimes completely eliminate it; we will look at three (see Figure 15.7):

1. *Make individual contributions to a group identifiable.* Some people may engage in social loafing when they work in groups because they think they can hide in the crowd–no one will notice if they put forth less effort than they should. Other people may think if they put forth high levels of effort and make substantial contributions to the group, their contributions will not be noticed and they will receive no rewards for their work–so why bother.[101]

One way that managers can effectively eliminate social loafing is by making individual contributions to a group identifiable so group members perceive that low and high levels of effort will be noticed and individual contributions evaluated.[102] Managers can accomplish this by assigning specific tasks to group members and holding them accountable for their completion. Take the case of a group of eight employees responsible for reshelving returned books in a large public library in New York. The head librarian was concerned that there was always a backlog of seven or eight carts of books to be reshelved, even though the employees never seemed to be particularly busy and some even found time to sit down and read newspapers and magazines. The librarian decided to try to eliminate the apparent social loafing by assigning each employee sole responsibility for reshelving a particular section of the library. Because the library's front desk employees sorted the books by section on the carts as they were returned, holding the shelvers responsible for particular sections was easily accomplished. Once the shelvers knew the librarian could identify their effort or lack thereof, there were rarely any backlogs of books to be reshelved.

Sometimes the members of a group can cooperate to eliminate social loafing by making individual contributions identifiable. For example, in a small security

Figure 15.7
Three Ways to Reduce Social Loafing

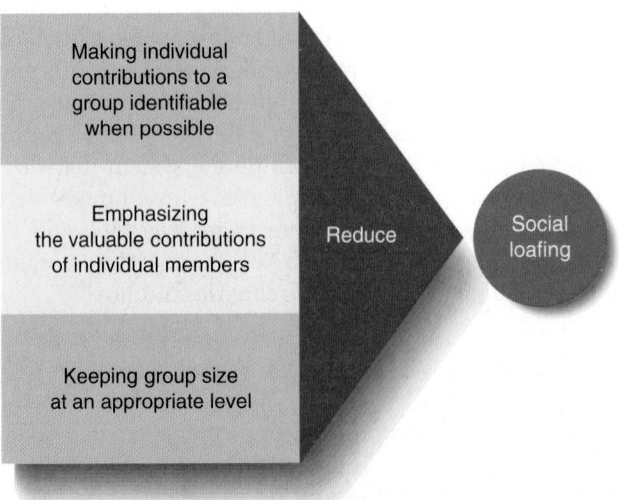

company, members of a self-managed work team who assemble control boxes for home alarm systems start each day by deciding who will perform which tasks that day and how much work each member and the group as a whole should strive to accomplish. Each team member knows that, at the end of the day, the other team members will know exactly how much he or she has accomplished. With this system in place, social loafing never occurs in the team. Remember, however, that in some teams, individual contributions cannot be made identifiable, as in teams whose members are reciprocally interdependent.

2. *Emphasize the valuable contributions of individual members.* Another reason why social loafing may occur is that people sometimes think their efforts are unnecessary or unimportant when they work in a group. They feel the group will accomplish its goals and perform at an acceptable level whether or not they personally perform at a high level. To counteract this belief, when managers form groups, they should assign individuals to a group on the basis of the valuable contributions that *each* person can make to the group as a whole. Clearly communicating to group members why each person's contributions are valuable to the group is an effective means by which managers and group members themselves can reduce or eliminate social loafing.[103] This is most clearly illustrated in cross-functional teams, where each member's valuable contribution to the team derives from a personal area of expertise. By emphasizing why each member's skills are important, managers can reduce social loafing in such teams.
3. *Keep group size at an appropriate level.* Group size is related to the causes of social loafing we just described. As size increases, identifying individual contributions becomes increasingly difficult, and members are increasingly likely to think their individual contributions are not important. To overcome this, managers should form groups with no more members than are needed to accomplish group goals and perform at a high level.[104]

Helping Groups to Manage Conflict Effectively

At some point or other, practically all groups experience conflict either within the group (*intragroup* conflict) or with other groups (*intergroup* conflict). In Chapter 17 we discuss conflict in depth and explore ways to manage it effectively. As you will learn, managers can take several steps to help groups manage conflict and disagreements.

Summary and Review

LO15-1 **GROUPS, TEAMS, AND ORGANIZATIONAL EFFECTIVENESS** A group is two or more people who interact with each other to accomplish certain goals or meet certain needs. A team is a group whose members work intensely with one another to achieve a specific common goal or objective. Groups and teams can contribute to organizational effectiveness by enhancing performance, increasing responsiveness to customers, increasing innovation, and being a source of motivation for their members.

LO15-2 **TYPES OF GROUPS AND TEAMS** Formal groups are groups that managers establish to achieve organizational goals; they include cross-functional teams, cross-cultural teams, top management teams, research and development teams, command groups, task forces, self-managed work teams, and virtual teams. Informal groups are groups that employees form because they believe the groups will help them achieve their own goals or meet their needs; they include friendship groups and interest groups.

LO15-3 **GROUP DYNAMICS** Key elements of group dynamics are group size, tasks, and roles; group leadership; group development; group norms; and group cohesiveness.

The advantages and disadvantages of large and small groups suggest that managers should form groups with no more members than are needed to provide the group with the human resources it needs to achieve its goals and use a division of labor. The type of task interdependence that characterizes a group's work gives managers a clue about the appropriate size of the group. A group role is a set of behaviors and tasks that a member of a group is expected to perform because of his or her position in the group. All groups and teams need leadership.

LO15-3, 15-4 Five stages of development that many groups pass through are forming, storming, norming, performing, and adjourning. Group norms are shared rules for behavior that most group members follow. To be effective, groups need a balance of conformity and deviance. Conformity allows a group to control its members' behavior to achieve group goals; deviance provides the impetus for needed change.

LO15-4 Group cohesiveness is the attractiveness of a group or team to its members. As group cohesiveness increases, so do the level of participation and communication within a group, the level of conformity to group norms, and the emphasis on group goal accomplishment. Managers should strive to achieve a moderate level of group cohesiveness in the groups and teams they manage.

LO15-5 **MANAGING GROUPS AND TEAMS FOR HIGH PERFORMANCE** To make sure groups and teams perform at a high level, managers need to motivate group members to work toward the achievement of organizational goals, reduce social loafing, and help groups to effectively manage conflict. Managers can motivate members of groups and teams to work toward the achievement of organizational goals by making sure members personally benefit when the group or team performs at a high level.

Management in Action

Topics for Discussion and Action

Discussion

1. Why do all organizations need to rely on groups and teams to achieve their goals and gain a competitive advantage? [LO15-1]
2. What kinds of employees would prefer to work in a virtual team? What kinds of employees would prefer to work in a team that meets face-to-face? [LO15-2]
3. Think about a group that you are a member of, and describe that group's current stage of development. Does the development of this group seem to be following the forming, storming, norming, performing, and adjourning stages described in the chapter? [LO15-3]
4. Think about a group of employees who work in a McDonald's restaurant. What type of task interdependence characterizes this group? What potential problems in the group should the restaurant manager be aware of and take steps to avoid? [LO15-3]
5. Discuss the reasons why too much conformity can hurt groups and their organizations. [LO15-4]
6. Why do some groups have very low levels of cohesiveness? [LO15-4]
7. Imagine that you are the manager of a hotel. What steps will you take to reduce social loafing by members of the cleaning staff who are responsible for keeping all common areas and guest rooms spotless? [LO15-5]

Action

8. Interview one or more managers in an organization in your local community to identify the types of groups and teams that the organization uses to achieve its goals. What challenges do these groups and teams face? [LO15-2]

Building Management Skills

Diagnosing Group Failures [LO15-1, 15-2, 15-3, 15-4, 15-5]

Think about the last dissatisfying or discouraging experience you had as a member of a group or team. Perhaps the group did not accomplish its goals, perhaps group members could agree about nothing, or perhaps there was too much social loafing. Now answer the following questions:

1. What type of group was this?
2. Were group members motivated to achieve group goals? Why or why not?
3. How large was the group, what type of task interdependence existed in the group, and what group roles did members play?
4. What were the group's norms? How much conformity and deviance existed in the group?
5. How cohesive was the group? Why do you think the group's cohesiveness was at this level? What consequences did this level of group cohesiveness have for the group and its members?
6. Was social loafing a problem in this group? Why or why not?
7. What could the group's leader or manager have done differently to increase group effectiveness?
8. What could group members have done differently to increase group effectiveness?

Managing Ethically [LO15-1, 15-2, 15-3, 15-4, 15-5]

Some self-managed teams encounter a vexing problem: One or more members engage in social loafing, and other members are reluctant to try to rectify the situation. Social loafing can be especially troubling if team members' pay is based on team performance and social loafing reduces the team's performance and thus the pay of all members (even the highest performers). Even if managers are aware of the problem, they may be reluctant to take action because the team is supposedly self-managing.

Questions

1. Either individually or in a group, think about the ethical implications of social loafing in a self-managed team.
2. Do managers have an ethical obligation to step in when they are aware of social loafing in a self-managed team? Why or why not? Do other team members have an obligation to try to curtail the social loafing? Why or why not?

Small Group Breakout Exercise

Creating a Cross-Functional Team [LO15-1, 15-2, 15-3, 15-4, 15-5]

Form groups of three or four people, and appoint one member as the spokesperson who will communicate your findings to the class when called on by the instructor. Then discuss the following scenario:

You are a group of managers in charge of food services for a large state university in the Midwest. Recently a survey of students, faculty, and staff was conducted to evaluate customer satisfaction with the food services provided by the university's eight cafeterias. The results were disappointing, to put it mildly. Complaints ranged from dissatisfaction with the type and range of meals and snacks provided, operating hours, and food temperature to frustration about unresponsiveness to current concerns about healthful diets and the needs of vegetarians. You have decided to form a cross-functional team that will further evaluate reactions to the food services and will develop a proposal for changes to be made to increase customer satisfaction.

1. Indicate who should be on this important cross-functional team, and explain why.
2. Describe the goals the team should strive to achieve.
3. Describe the different roles that will need to be performed on this team.
4. Describe the steps you will take to help ensure that the team has a good balance between conformity and deviance and has a moderate level of cohesiveness.

Exploring the World Wide Web [LO15-1, 15-2, 15-3, 15-4, 15-5]

Many consultants and organizations provide team-building services to organizations. Although some managers and teams have found these services to be helpful, others have found them to be a waste of time and money—another consulting fad that provides no real performance benefits. Search online for team-building services, and examine the Web sites of a few consultants/companies. Based on what you have read, what might be some advantages and disadvantages of team-building services? For what kinds of problems/issues might these services be beneficial, and when might they have little benefit or perhaps even do more harm than good?

Be the Manager [LO15-1, 15-2, 15-3, 15-4, 15-5]

You were recently hired in a boundary-spanning role for the global unit of an educational and professional publishing company. The company is headquartered in New York (where you work) and has divisions in multiple countries. Each division is responsible for translating, manufacturing, marketing, and selling a set of books in its country. Your responsibilities include interfacing with managers in each of the divisions in your region (Central and South America), overseeing their budgeting and financial reporting to headquarters, and leading a virtual team consisting of the top managers in charge of each of the divisions in your region. The virtual team's mission is to promote global learning, explore new potential opportunities and markets, and address ongoing problems. You communicate directly with division managers via telephone and e-mail, as well as written reports, memos, and faxes. When virtual team meetings are convened, videoconferencing is often used.

After your first few virtual team meetings, you noticed that the managers seemed to be reticent about speaking up. Interestingly enough, when each manager communicates with you individually, primarily in telephone conversations and e-mails, she or he tends to be forthcoming and frank, and you feel you have a good rapport with each of them. However, getting the managers to communicate with one another as a virtual team has been a real challenge. At the last meeting you tried to prompt some of the managers to raise issues relevant to the agenda that you knew were on their minds from your individual conversations with them. Surprisingly, the managers skillfully avoided informing their teammates about the heart of the issues in question. You are confused and troubled. Although you feel your other responsibilities are going well, you know your virtual team is not operating like a team at all; and no matter what you try, discussions in virtual team meetings are forced and generally unproductive. What are you going to do to address this problem?

Case in the News [LO15-1, 15-2, 15-3, 15-4, 15-5]

Putting Ford on Fast-Forward

Adam Gryglak had what seemed like an impossible task: deliver an all-new Ford diesel engine in 36 months. Ford was way behind schedule, so the time frame was a year faster than usual. Gryglak, the chief diesel engineer, knew he'd never meet his deadline without short-circuiting the usual development process. So he put together a team, moved off campus, and kept his second-guessing bosses at bay. Gryglak called the project Scorpion (after the heavy metal band the Scorpions) and came up with a logo featuring a menacing mechanical insect.

In mid-September, on schedule and to strong reviews, Ford unveiled the new Super Duty pickup—powered by Project Scorpion's engine—at the Texas State Fair. Gryglak had shown that the classic skunkworks model pioneered by Lockheed-Martin in the 1930s could help Ford protect its flank—in this case the highly lucrative market for contractor-grade pickup trucks. "We have a good product development system," Gryglak says. "The key was to respect what we have and the people who run it, deconstruct it a bit, and make it better to suit our target."

Gryglak's task was doubly difficult. For one thing, Ford had previously outsourced the design and manufacture of the engine, known as the Powerstroke, to truck and engine maker Navistar. What's more, the Powerstroke brand had eroded in recent years because of quality problems. Gryglak didn't just need to design and build an engine in-house from scratch—he needed to vastly improve it if Ford were to keep dominating the market for large pickups, which in good years have generated much of its overall profit.

Like all big companies, Ford has a strict product development hierarchy. It works well enough nowadays that the carmaker can get new models from blueprint to showroom as fast as or faster than its rivals. Going off-site inevitably made executives anxious. But Gryglak's pitch got a better reception than it might have, say, five years ago, when turf-obsessed managers tended to look unkindly on heterodoxy.

In October 2006 Gryglak began recruiting his team of engineers. He discovered that not everyone was eager to work beyond the bounds of Ford's familiar environment. Some engineers craved structure. "We had people self-select out because they weren't comfortable working outside their comfort zone," says Gryglak. But others couldn't wait to be asked. Ken Pumford, an engineer from Ford's Kentucky truck plant, moved from Louisville to Dearborn, Michigan, to join the project.

It wasn't long before the benefits began to emerge. Specialists used to working only with their own kind became more familiar with what other engineers were up to. "We saved months by knowing hourly what the other guys were thinking and what their problems were," says Pat Morgan, a veteran Ford engineer. "The result was that the engine fit into the truck perfectly the first time, and that almost never happens."

The team also let go of certain Fordisms. The company has long forced suppliers to adapt their technology in hundreds of time-consuming ways to Ford specifications. Engineers, after all, justify their paychecks by coming up with engineering tweaks. With time short, the team learned to trust suppliers more. For example, Ford let the German company Bosch work on the engine's antipollution device with minimal reengineering for its own sake.

Fun and Games

Freed from the rigid atmosphere of Ford's tech center, the engineers let themselves have fun. They played jokes on each other, building full-size snowmen, decorated with machine parts, on one another's desks. Gryglak also encouraged friendly competition. In August 2007, after months of R&D but before starting to build the engine, the team organized a Pinewood Derby competition. Design and mechanical engineers, of course, weren't about to whittle cars from wood the way Cub Scouts do. They milled cars out of aluminum. Some had remote controls and electric motors.

As the team worked in isolation, Gryglak's bosses had a hard time staying in the background. Bob Fascetti, Ford's chief engineer of big engines, forced himself to check in with the team only every four to six weeks instead of the usual weekly or biweekly intervals. "It was tough for me to do," he says. "But to keep [the project] on track, I convinced my bosses it would be better to leave them alone." Fascetti says things got tense when Team Scorpion decided to build the engine out of a lighter material that would make the truck more fuel-efficient. Doing so was more expensive, with a greater risk of failure. By the time Fascetti and his own bosses found out, the decision had been made. Gryglak faced some tough questioning, but he got the green light.

The new Super Duty truck goes on sale in the spring. Ford says the engine will be the first of its kind to use state-of-the-art antipollution technology that meets new federal regulations. The truck also will have the best fuel economy in its category and won't need significant maintenance for 300,000 miles. The best part, says Tony Hudson, a Project Scorpion engineer, is that the team pulled off what initially had seemed impossible. "That," he says, "will give us license to do it again."

Questions for Discussion

1. What factors contributed to the success of the team that Adam Gryglak formed to develop a new Ford diesel engine?
2. Why did the team move off campus?
3. How were synergies achieved in the team?
4. How would you characterize the group dynamics of the team?

Source: D. Kiley, "Putting Ford on Fast-Forward," *BusinessWeek,* October 26, 2009, 56–57. Reprinted from October 26, 2009 issue of *Bloomberg Businessweek* by special permission, copyright © 2009 by Bloomberg L.P.

CHAPTER 16

Promoting Effective Communication

Learning Objectives

After studying this chapter, you should be able to:

LO16-1 Explain why effective communication helps an organization gain a competitive advantage.

LO16-2 Describe the communication process, and explain the role of perception in communication.

LO16-3 Define information richness, and describe the information richness of communication media available to managers.

LO16-4 Describe the communication networks that exist in groups and teams.

LO16-5 Explain how advances in technology have given managers new options for managing communication.

LO16-6 Describe important communication skills that managers need as senders and as receivers of messages and why it is important to understand differences in linguistic styles.

A MANAGER'S CHALLENGE

Managers in Diverse Industries Need Feedback from Employees

How can managers ensure that they get needed feedback from employees? As managers advance in the corporate hierarchy and assume positions with increased responsibility, they often become removed from the day-to-day operations of their organizations. Thus they are less likely to notice or become aware of problems with existing processes and procedures and sources of inefficiencies as well as how customers and clients are reacting to the goods and services the organization provides. Moreover, ideas for ways to improve goods and services sometimes occur to those who are most closely and immediately linked to producing and delivering products and services. Some of these ideas may rarely occur to upper-level managers who are not engaged in these daily activities.[1]

Thus it is crucial that managers receive and listen to feedback from employees, regardless of the industry in which they operate. Although this might seem straightforward and easily accomplished, managers are sometimes the last ones to know about problems for a number of reasons. Employees sometimes fear that they will be blamed for problems they make their bosses aware of, that they will be seen as troublemakers, or that managers will perceive their well-intentioned feedback as a personal criticism or attack.[2]

"I'm all ears." Yogesh Gupta knows from experience that asking for feedback and actually receiving it are two different things. His work at FatWire demonstrates a commitment to hearing others out.

Moreover, if employees feel that their feedback, even suggestions for improvements or ways to seize new opportunities, will be ignored, they will be reluctant to speak up.

Effective managers recognize the importance of receiving feedback from employees and take active steps to ensure that this happens. When Yogesh Gupta accepted the position of president and CEO of FatWire Software, one of his priorities was to ensure that his employees provided him with ongoing feedback.[3] FatWire Software, headquartered in Mineola, New York, is a privately owned Web content management company with around 200 employees, offices in over 10 countries, and over 500 customers ranging from 3M, *The New York Times,* and Best Buy to the Flemish government, Dutch railways, and TDC cable TV.[4] An experienced manager who, prior to assuming the top position at FatWire Software, was senior vice president and chief technology strategist at CA, Inc., one of the largest information technology management software companies in the world, Gupta often witnessed managers inadvertently discouraging employees from providing them with feedback, even when the managers desired it.[5] As he indicates, "I've heard so many executives tell employees to be candid and then jump down their throats if they bring up a problem or ask a critical question."[6]

Gupta spends a lot of time talking with FatWire employees and its managers to get their perspectives and feedback on how the company is doing. He often has individual meetings with managers so they will feel more comfortable giving him frank and honest feedback. And he explicitly asks them if he is doing anything wrong, if there is a better way for him to do things, and what kinds of obstacles interfere with their own performance. He also asks them how the company could be doing better. Early on, as a result of listening to the feedback he received, Gupta realized that FatWire might benefit from having more employees focused on product development and marketing and also that customer support services and processes could be enhanced.[7]

When Gupta receives valuable feedback, he makes it a point to positively reinforce the manager or employee who provided it in a public fashion, so other employees realize he is open to, and really wants, their feedback. As he indicates, "I know I have to say 'You did the right thing to speak up' again and again, because employees fear they'll get blamed if they say anything negative."[8]

At Intuit Inc., a major provider of accounting and financial software, managers receive valuable feedback from employees in a number of ways. An annual employee survey is used to find out what employees think about Intuit's practices and procedures.[9] Managers are advised to have what are called "skip level" meetings throughout the year, whereby they meet with the subordinates of the managers who report to them to get their feedback on how things are going.[10] Managers also are encouraged to take part in what Intuit calls a "learn, teach, learn" process whereby employees give managers feedback about some issue, problem, or situation (the manager learns about the issue); the manager comes up with a course of action to deal with the issue and communicates it to the employees (the manager instructs or teaches the employees about the course of action); and then the employees give the manager more feedback (the manager learns if the course of action is viable or should be modified).[11] Jim Grenier, vice president for human resources at Intuit, suggests that obtaining employee feedback through this process leads to improved decision making. As he puts it, "You're looking for more input so you can make a better decision. Employees know that we are serious about asking for their feedback, and we listen and we do something about it."[12]

To obtain feedback from his employees, Jonathan McDaniel, manager of a Kentucky Fried Chicken restaurant in Houston, Texas, surveys them around four times a year.[13] More important, he listens to and acts on the feedback employees provide in the surveys. For example, from one of his periodic surveys, McDaniel learned that employees were unhappy about their working hours; some employees thought they should be working more hours per week while others thought they were working too many hours. Based on this feedback, McDaniel now communicates more frequently with employees to get their input on scheduling and working hours.[14] Clearly, and in organizations large and small, managers need to receive feedback from their employees to be effective, make good decisions, and help the organization achieve its goals.[15]

Overview

Even with all the advances in information technology that are available to managers, ineffective communication continues to take place in organizations. Ineffective communication is detrimental for managers, employees, and organizations; it can lead to poor performance, strained interpersonal relations, poor service, and dissatisfied customers. For an organization to be effective and gain a competitive advantage, managers at all levels need to be good communicators. As illustrated in "A Manager's Challenge," an important part of being a good communicator is obtaining and listening to feedback from others; this is sometimes more challenging than it seems.

In this chapter we describe the nature of communication and the communication process and explain why all managers and their subordinates need to be effective communicators. We describe the communication media available to managers and the factors they need to consider in selecting a communication medium for each message they send. We consider the communication networks organizational members rely on, and we explore how advances in information technology have expanded managers' range of communication options. We describe the communication skills that help managers be effective senders and receivers of messages. By the end of this chapter you will appreciate the nature of communication and the steps managers can take to ensure that they are effective communicators.

LO16-1 Explain why effective communication helps an organization gain a competitive advantage.

Communication and Management

Communication is the sharing of information between two or more individuals or groups to reach a common understanding.[16] First and foremost, no matter how electronically based, communication is a human endeavor and involves individuals and groups. Second, communication does not take place unless a common understanding is reached. Thus when you call a business to speak to a person in customer service or billing and are bounced between endless automated messages and menu options and eventually hang up in frustration, communication has not taken place.

communication The sharing of information between two or more individuals or groups to reach a common understanding.

The Importance of Good Communication

In Chapter 1 we described how an organization can gain a competitive advantage when managers strive to increase efficiency, quality, responsiveness to customers, and innovation. Good communication is essential for attaining each of these four goals and thus is a necessity for gaining a competitive advantage.

Managers can *increase efficiency* by updating the production process to take advantage of new and more efficient technologies and by training workers to operate the new technologies and to expand their skills. Good communication is necessary for managers to learn about new technologies, implement them in their organizations, and train workers in how to use them. Similarly, *improving quality* hinges on effective communication. Managers need to communicate to all members of an organization the meaning and importance of high quality and the routes to attaining it. Subordinates need to communicate quality problems and suggestions for increasing quality to their superiors, and members of self-managed work teams need to share their ideas on improving quality with one another.

Good communication can also help increase *responsiveness to customers.* When the organizational members who are closest to customers, such as department store salespeople and bank tellers, are empowered to communicate customers' needs and desires to managers, managers can better respond to these needs. Managers, in turn, must communicate with other organizational members to determine how best to respond to changing customer preferences.

Innovation, which often takes place in cross-functional teams, also requires effective communication. Members of a cross-functional team developing a new electronic game, for example, must effectively communicate with one another to develop a game that customers will want to play; that will be engaging, interesting, and fun; and that can potentially lead to sequels. Members of the team also must communicate with managers to secure the resources they need for developing the game and to keep managers informed of progress on the project. Innovation in organizations is increasingly taking place on a global level, making effective communication all the more important, as illustrated in the following "Managing Globally" box.

Managing Globally

Global Communication for Global Innovation

GE Healthcare (headquartered in the United Kingdom) is a provider of medical technology and services and makes medical imaging, diagnostic, and monitoring systems such as CT scanners. With over 46,000 employees around the world, GE Healthcare has approximately $17 billion in revenues.[17] To make the best scanners that meet the needs of doctors and patients around the world with next-generation technology, new product development and manufacture are truly global endeavors at GE Healthcare Technologies. Consider the LightSpeed VCT scanner series (*VCT* stands for "volume controlled tomography"), which costs in the millions and is among the quickest and highest-resolution scanners available in the world.[18] The LightSpeed can perform a full-body scan in under 10 seconds and yields a three-dimensional picture of patients' hearts within five heartbeats.[19]

The LightSpeed was developed through global collaboration. GE managers not only spoke with doctors (including cardiologists and radiologists) around the world to find out what their needs were and what kinds of tests they would perform with the LightSpeed but also gathered information about differences among patients in various countries. Engineers in Hino (Japan), Buc (France),

As GE Healthcare learned, conference calls and e-mails can stand in the gap, but nothing replaces getting managers together for face-to-face conversations and problem solving.

and Waukesha, Wisconsin, developed the electronics for the LightSpeed. Other parts, such as the automated table that patients lie on, are made in Beijing (China) and Hino. Software for the LightSpeed was written in Haifa (Israel), Bangalore (India), Buc, and Waukesha.[20]

Effective global communication was a challenge and a necessity to successfully develop the LightSpeed series. As Brian Duchinsky, GE's general manager for global CT, put it, "If we sat around in this cornfield west of Milwaukee, we wouldn't come up with the same breadth of good ideas. But yet, getting six countries on the phone to make a decision can be a pain."[21]

GE managers facilitated effective communication in a number of ways–participating in daily conference calls, making sure teams in different countries depended on one another, developing an internal Web site devoted to the LightSpeed, encouraging teams to ask one another for help, and holding face-to-face meetings in different locations. Although much communication took place electronically, such as through conference calls, face-to-face meetings were also important. As Bob Armstrong, GE's general manager for engineering, indicated, "You need to get your people together in one place if you want them to really appreciate how good everyone is, and how good you are as a team."[22]

LO16-2 Describe the communication process, and explain the role of perception in communication.

Effective communication is necessary for managers and all members of an organization to increase efficiency, quality, responsiveness to customers, and innovation and thus gain a competitive advantage for the organization. Managers therefore must understand the communication process well if they are to perform effectively.

The Communication Process

The communication process consists of two phases. In the *transmission phase,* information is shared between two or more individuals or groups. In the *feedback phase,* a common understanding is ensured. In both phases, a number of distinct stages must occur for communication to take place (see Figure 16.1).[23]

sender The person or group wishing to share information.

message The information that a sender wants to share.

Starting the transmission phase, the **sender,** the person or group wishing to share information with some other person or group, decides on the **message,** what information to communicate. Then the sender translates the message into symbols or

Figure 16.1
The Communication Process

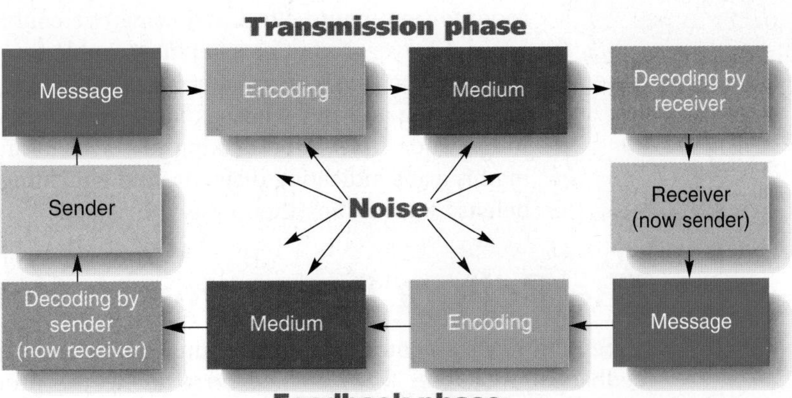

encoding Translating a message into understandable symbols or language.

noise Anything that hampers any stage of the communication process.

receiver The person or group for which a message is intended.

medium The pathway through which an encoded message is transmitted to a receiver.

decoding Interpreting and trying to make sense of a message.

verbal communication The encoding of messages into words, either written or spoken.

nonverbal communication The encoding of messages by means of facial expressions, body language, and styles of dress.

language, a process called **encoding;** often messages are encoded into words. **Noise** is a general term that refers to anything that hampers any stage of the communication process.

Once encoded, a message is transmitted through a medium to the **receiver,** the person or group for which the message is intended. A **medium** is simply the pathway, such as a phone call, a letter, a memo, or face-to-face communication in a meeting, through which an encoded message is transmitted to a receiver. At the next stage, the receiver interprets and tries to make sense of the message, a process called **decoding.** This is a critical point in communication.

The feedback phase is initiated by the receiver (who becomes a sender). The receiver decides what message to send to the original sender (who becomes a receiver), encodes it, and transmits it through a chosen medium (see Figure 16.1). The message might contain a confirmation that the original message was received and understood or a restatement of the original message to make sure it has been correctly interpreted, or it might include a request for more information. The original sender decodes the message and makes sure a common understanding has been reached. If the original sender determines that a common understanding has not been reached, sender and receiver cycle through the whole process as many times as needed to reach a common understanding. Feedback eliminates misunderstandings, ensures that messages are correctly interpreted, and enables senders and receivers to reach a common understanding.

The encoding of messages into words, written or spoken, is **verbal communication.** We can also encode messages without using written or spoken language. **Nonverbal communication** shares information by means of facial expressions (smiling, raising an eyebrow, frowning, dropping one's jaw), body language (posture, gestures, nods, and shrugs), and even style of dress (casual, formal, conservative, trendy). The trend toward increasing empowerment of the workforce has led some managers to dress informally to communicate that all employees of an organization are team members, working together to create value for customers.

If a picture is worth a thousand words, so too is nonverbal communication; facial expressions, body language, posture, and eye contact all send powerful messages.

Nonverbal communication can be used to back up or reinforce verbal communication. Just as a warm and genuine smile can back up words of appreciation for a job well done, a concerned facial expression can back up words of sympathy for a personal problem. In such cases, the congruence between the verbal and the nonverbal communication helps to ensure that a common understanding is reached.

Sometimes when members of an organization decide not to express a message verbally, they inadvertently do so nonverbally. People tend to have less control over nonverbal communication, and often a verbal message that is withheld gets expressed through body language or facial expressions. A manager who agrees to a proposal that she or he actually does not like may unintentionally communicate her or his disfavor by grimacing.

Sometimes nonverbal communication is used to send messages that cannot be sent through verbal channels. Many lawyers are well aware of this communication tactic. Lawyers are often schooled in techniques of nonverbal communication, such as choosing where to stand in the courtroom for maximum effect and using eye contact during different stages of a trial. Lawyers sometimes get into trouble for using inappropriate nonverbal communication in an attempt to influence juries. In a Louisiana court, prosecuting attorney Thomas Pirtle was admonished and fined $2,500 by Judge Yada Magee for shaking his head in an expression of doubt, waving his arms indicating disfavor, and chuckling when the attorneys for the defense were stating their case.[24]

The Role of Perception in Communication

Perception plays a central role in communication and affects both transmission and feedback. In Chapter 5 we defined *perception* as the process through which people select, organize, and interpret sensory input to give meaning and order to the world around them. We mentioned that perception is inherently subjective and is influenced by people's personalities, values, attitudes, and moods as well as by their experience and knowledge. When senders and receivers communicate with each other, they are doing so based on their own subjective perceptions. The encoding and decoding of messages and even the choice of a medium hinge on the perceptions of senders and receivers.

In addition, perceptual biases can hamper effective communication. Recall from Chapter 5 that *biases* are systematic tendencies to use information about others in ways that result in inaccurate perceptions. In Chapter 5 we described a number of biases that can cause unfair treatment of diverse members of an organization. The same biases also can lead to ineffective communication. For example, *stereotypes*–simplified and often inaccurate beliefs about the characteristics of particular groups of people–can interfere with the encoding and decoding of messages.

Suppose a manager stereotypes older workers as being fearful of change. When this manager encodes a message to an older worker about an upcoming change in the organization, she may downplay the extent of the change so as not to make the older worker feel stressed. The older worker, however, fears change no more than do his younger colleagues and thus decodes the message to mean that only a minor change is going to be made. The older worker fails to adequately prepare for the change, and his performance subsequently suffers because of his lack of preparation for the change. Clearly this ineffective communication was due to the manager's inaccurate assumptions about older workers. Instead of relying on stereotypes, effective managers strive to perceive other people accurately by focusing on their actual behaviors, knowledge, skills, and abilities. Accurate perceptions, in turn, contribute to effective communication.

The Dangers of Ineffective Communication

Because managers must communicate with others to perform their various roles and tasks, managers spend most of their time communicating, whether in meetings, in telephone conversations, through e-mail, or in face-to-face interactions. Indeed, some experts estimate that managers spend approximately 85% of their time engaged in some form of communication.[25]

Effective communication is so important that managers cannot just be concerned that they themselves are effective communicators; they also have to help their subordinates be effective communicators. When all members of an organization can communicate effectively with one another and with people outside the organization, the organization is much more likely to perform highly and gain a competitive advantage.

When managers and other members of an organization are ineffective communicators, organizational performance suffers and any competitive advantage the organization might have is likely to be lost. Moreover, poor communication sometimes can be downright dangerous and even lead to tragic and unnecessary loss of human life. For example, researchers from Harvard University recently studied the causes of mistakes, such as a patient receiving the wrong medication, in two large hospitals in the Boston area. They discovered that some mistakes in hospitals occur because of communication problems–physicians' not having the information they need to correctly order medications for their patients or nurses' not having the information they need to correctly administer medications. The researchers concluded that some of the responsibility for these mistakes lies with hospital management, which has not taken active steps to improve communication.[26]

Communication problems in airplane cockpits and between flying crews and air traffic controllers are unfortunately all too common, sometimes with deadly consequences. In the late 1970s two jets collided in Tenerife (one of the Canary Islands) because of miscommunication between a pilot and the control tower, and 600 people were killed. The tower radioed to the pilot, "Clipper 1736 report clear of runway." The pilot mistakenly interpreted this message to mean that he was cleared for takeoff.[27] Unfortunately communication problems persist in the airline industry.

In 2009 a Northwest Airlines Airbus A320 flew 150 miles past its Minneapolis destination while the crew of the airplane was out of contact with air traffic controllers for over an hour.[28] A safety group at NASA tracked more than 6,000 unsafe flying incidents and found that communication difficulties caused approximately 529 of them.[29] And NASA has its own communication difficulties.[30] In 2004 NASA released a report detailing communication problems at the International Space Station jointly managed and staffed by NASA and the Russian space agency; the problems included inadequate record keeping, missing information, and failure to keep data current.[31]

Information Richness and Communication Media

LO16-3 Define information richness, and describe the information richness of communication media available to managers.

To be effective communicators, managers (and other members of an organization) need to select an appropriate communication medium for each message they send. Should a change in procedures be communicated to subordinates in a memo sent through e-mail? Should a congratulatory message about a major accomplishment be communicated in a letter, in a phone call, or over lunch? Should a layoff announcement be made in a memo or at a plant meeting? Should the members of a purchasing team travel to Europe to cement a major agreement with a new supplier, or should they do so through faxes? Managers deal with these questions day in and day out.

information richness The amount of information that a communication medium can carry and the extent to which the medium enables the sender and receiver to reach a common understanding.

There is no one best communication medium for managers to rely on. In choosing a communication medium for any message, managers need to consider three factors. The first and most important is the level of information richness that is needed. **Information richness** is the amount of information a communication medium can carry and the extent to which the medium enables the sender and receiver to reach a common understanding.[32] The communication media that managers use vary in their information richness (see Figure 16.2).[33] Media high in information richness can carry an extensive amount of information and generally enable receivers and senders to come to a common understanding.

The second factor that managers need to take into account in selecting a communication medium is the *time* needed for communication because managers' and

Figure 16.2
The Information Richness of Communication Media

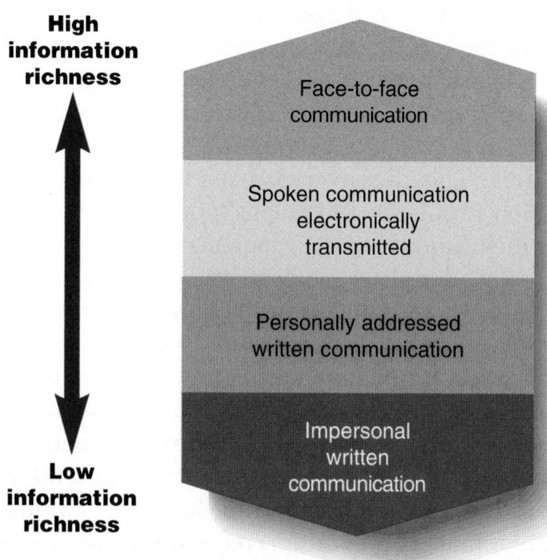

other organizational members' time is valuable. Managers at United Parcel Service, for example, dramatically reduced the amount of time they spent on communicating by using videoconferences instead of face-to-face communication, which required that managers travel overseas.[34]

The third factor that affects the choice of a communication medium is the *need for a paper or electronic trail* or some kind of written documentation that a message was sent and received. A manager may wish to document in writing, for example, that a subordinate was given a formal warning about excessive lateness.

In the remainder of this section we examine four types of communication media that vary along these three dimensions (information richness, time, and paper or electronic trail).[35]

Face-to-Face Communication

Face-to-face communication is the medium that is highest in information richness. When managers communicate face-to-face, they not only can take advantage of verbal communication but also can interpret each other's nonverbal signals such as facial expressions and body language. A look of concern or puzzlement can sometimes say more than a thousand words, and managers can respond to such nonverbal signals on the spot. Face-to-face communication also enables managers to receive instant feedback. Points of confusion, ambiguity, or misunderstanding can be resolved, and managers can cycle through the communication process as many times as needed to reach a common understanding.

With the growing proliferation of electronic forms of communication, such as e-mail, some managers fear that face-to-face communication is being shortchanged to the detriment of building common understandings and rapport.[36] Moreover, some messages that really should be communicated face-to-face or at least in a phone conversation, and messages that are more efficiently communicated in this manner, are nonetheless sent electronically.[37] As indicated in the following "Management Insight" box, managers need to carefully consider whether face-to-face communication is being shortchanged in their organizations and, if it is, take steps to rectify the situation.

Management Insight

When Face-to-Face Communication Is Called For

Anyone who has participated in one of those frustrating e-mail exchanges where messages shoot back and forth and it seems to take forever to resolve a problem or reach a common understanding knows there must be a better way. In such cases a face-to-face conversation (or if that is not possible, a phone conversation) often will lead to better outcomes all around.

According to Ron McMillan, a consultant to managers at all ranks and coauthor of best-selling books on communication, e-mail should not be relied on to communicate information that is complex, important, or sensitive.[38] In such cases face-to-face communication (or even a phone conversation) can convey more information than e-mail can, and it is much more effective at generating a common understanding. Research conducted by Professor Albert Mehrabian at UCLA suggests that more meaning is conveyed by nonverbal communication from facial expressions and body language and from tone of voice and vocal inflection than is conveyed by the actual words that are used when communicating.[39] And of course nonverbal communication, tone of voice, and vocal inflection are all missing when e-mail is used. JoAnne Yates, a professor at the Sloan

"No E-mail Friday" bolsters in-person conversations and strengthens employee ties.

School of Management at MIT, suggests that e-mail is best for simple information that will be readily understood.[40]

Sara Roberts, founder and president of Roberts Golden Consulting in San Francisco, recognizes the value of face-to-face communication. Although consultants in her firm regularly communicate with each other, clients, and suppliers via e-mail and this is often efficient and effective, Roberts believes rapport and collaboration can suffer when e-mail is used extensively. So she instituted "No E-mail Fridays" at her firm; on Fridays employees are not to use e-mail unless it is clearly necessary (such as to reply to a client who wants an urgent e-mail response).[41] As Roberts puts it, "No E-mail Friday helps us to remember we really could go over to that person sitting right over there and collaborate more."[42] In fact a growing number of organizations are experimenting with "no e-mail Fridays" to encourage more face-to-face communication and phone conversations.[43]

Allowing opportunities for face-to-face communication can be especially important when trying to effectively communicate with employees located in other countries. For example, Greg Caltabiano, CEO of Teknovus Inc., which is based in Petaluma, California, and has offices in Asia, arranges for U.S. employees to go to Asia and Asian employees to come to the United States to engage in face-to-face communication to build mutual understanding.[44]

management by wandering around A face-to-face communication technique in which a manager walks around a work area and talks informally with employees about issues and concerns.

Management by wandering around is a face-to-face communication technique that is effective for many managers at all levels in an organization.[45] Rather than scheduling formal meetings with subordinates, managers walk around work areas and talk informally with employees about issues and concerns that both employees and managers may have. These informal conversations give managers and subordinates important information and at the same time foster the development of positive relationships. William Hewlett and David Packard, founders and former top managers of Hewlett-Packard, found management by wandering around to be a highly effective way of communicating with their employees.

Because face-to-face communication is highest in information richness, you might think it should always be the medium of choice for managers. This is not the case, however, because of the amount of time it can take and the lack of a paper or electronic trail resulting from it. For messages that are important, personal, or likely to be misunderstood, it is often well worth managers' time to use face-to-face communication and, if need be, supplement it with some form of written communication documenting the message.

Advances in information technology are giving managers new communication media that are close substitutes for face-to-face communication. Many organizations, such as American Greetings Corp. and Hewlett-Packard, are using *videoconferences* to capture some of the advantages of face-to-face communication (such as access to facial expressions) while saving time and money because managers in different locations do not have to travel to meet with one another. During a videoconference, managers in two or more locations communicate with each other over large TV or video screens; they not only hear each other but also see each other throughout the meeting.

In addition to saving travel costs, videoconferences sometimes have other advantages. Managers at American Greetings have found that decisions get made more quickly when videoconferences are used because more managers can be involved in the decision-making process and therefore fewer managers have to be consulted outside the meeting itself. Managers at Hewlett-Packard have found that videoconferences have shortened new product development time by 30% for similar

Videoconferencing allows these remotely based teams to see each other around the conference table, the next best thing to actually being in the same office space.

reasons. Videoconferences also seem to lead to more efficient meetings. Some managers have found that their meetings are 20% to 30% shorter when videoconferences are used instead of face-to-face meetings.[46]

Taking videoconferences a leap forward, Cisco Systems has developed its TelePresence line of products, enabling individuals and teams in different locations to communicate live and in real time over the Internet with high-definition, life-size video and excellent audio that make it feel like all participants, no matter where they are, are in the same room.[47] One morning Cisco CEO John Chambers was able to participate in meetings with employees and teams in India, Japan, Cleveland, and London in less than four hours by using TelePresence.[48] Other companies, such as HP, have developed similar products. What distinguishes these products from older videoconferencing systems is the lack of transmission delay and the sharp, clear, life-size video quality.[49]

Spoken Communication Electronically Transmitted

After face-to-face communication, spoken communication electronically transmitted over phone lines (and the World Wide Web) is second highest in information richness (see Figure 16.2). Although managers communicating over the telephone do not have access to body language and facial expressions, they do have access to the tone of voice in which a message is delivered, the parts of the message the sender emphasizes, and the general manner in which the message is spoken, in addition to the actual words themselves. Thus telephone conversations can convey extensive amounts of information. Managers can ensure that mutual understanding is reached because they can get quick feedback over the phone and answer questions. When Greg Caltabiano, CEO of Teknovus Inc., wanted to improve communication between engineers in California who design semiconductors for fiber optic networks and employees and customers in Asia, he encouraged the engineers to communicate via the telephone instead of by e-mail.[50]

Voice mail systems and answering machines also allow managers to send and receive verbal electronic messages over telephone lines. Voice mail systems are companywide systems that let senders record messages for members of an organization who are away from their desks and allow receivers to access their messages even when hundreds of miles away from the office. Such systems are obviously a necessity when managers are frequently out of the office, and managers on the road are well advised to periodically check their voice mail.

Personally Addressed Written Communication

Lower in information richness than electronically transmitted verbal communication is personally addressed written communication (see Figure 16.2). One advantage of face-to-face communication and electronically transmitted verbal communication is that they both tend to demand attention, which helps ensure that receivers pay attention. Personally addressed written communications, such as memos and letters, also have this advantage. Because they are addressed to a particular person, the chances are good that the person will actually pay attention to (and read) them. Moreover, the sender can write the message in a way that the receiver is most likely to understand. Like voice mail, written communication does not enable a receiver to have his or her questions answered immediately; but when messages are clearly written and feedback is provided, common understandings can still be reached.

Even if managers use face-to-face communication, sending a follow-up in writing is often necessary for messages that are important or complicated and need to be referred to later on. This is precisely what Karen Stracker, a hospital administrator, did when she needed to tell one of her subordinates about an important change in how the hospital would be handling denials of insurance benefits. Stracker met with the subordinate and described the changes face-to-face. Once she was sure the subordinate understood them, she handed her a sheet of instructions to follow, which essentially summarized the information they had discussed.

E-mail also fits into this category of communication media because senders and receivers are communicating through personally addressed written words. The words, however, appear on their computer screens rather than on paper. E-mail is so widespread in the business world that some managers find they have to deliberately take time out from managing their e-mail to get their work done, think about pressing concerns, and come up with new and innovative ideas.[51] According to the Radacati Group, an independent market research firm, the average e-mail account in corporations today receives about 18 megabytes of e-mail and attachments per workday; the volume of e-mail is expected to increase over time.[52] To help their employees effectively manage e-mail, a growing number of organizations are instituting training programs to help employees learn how to more effectively use e-mail by sending clearer messages, avoiding e-mail copies to multiple parties who do not really need to see it, and writing clear and informative subject lines.[53] For example, Capital One trains employees to (1) write clear subject lines so recipients know why they are receiving a message and can easily search for it and retrieve it later, and (2) convey information clearly and effectively in the e-mail body.[54]

Ultimately, for messages that are sensitive or potentially misunderstood, or that require the give-and-take of a face-to-face or telephone conversation, relying on e-mail can take considerably more time to reach a common understanding.[55] Additionally, given the lack of nonverbal cues, tone of voice, and intonation in e-mail, senders need to be aware of the potential for misunderstandings.[56] For example, Kristin Byron, a professor of management at Syracuse University, suggests that recipients may have a tendency to perceive some of the e-mail they receive as more negative than the senders intended, based on her research.[57] Senders who are rushed, for example, may send short, curt messages lacking greeting and closing lines because they are so busy.[58] Recipients, however, might read something more negative into messages like these.[59]

The growing popularity of e-mail has also enabled many workers and managers to become *telecommuters*–people who are employed by organizations and work out of offices in their own homes. There are over 34 million telecommuters in the United States.[60] Many telecommuters indicate that the flexibility of working at home lets them be more productive and, at the same time, be closer to their families and not waste time traveling to and from the office.[61] In a study conducted by Georgetown University, 75% of the telecommuters surveyed said their productivity increased, and 83% said their home life improved once they started telecommuting.[62]

Unfortunately the widespread use of e-mail has been accompanied by growing abuse of e-mail. There have been cases of employees sexually harassing coworkers through e-mail, sending pornographic content via e-mail, and sending messages that disparage certain employees or groups.[63] To counter disparaging remarks making their way to employees' in-boxes (and being copied to coworkers), Mark Stevens, CEO of MSCO, a 40-person marketing firm in Purchase, New York, instituted a policy that forbids employees to use e-mail or BlackBerrys to communicate messages that criticize someone else.[64]

Managers need to develop a clear, written policy specifying what company e-mail can and should be used for and what is out of bounds. Managers also should clearly communicate this policy to all members of the organization, as well as tell them what procedures will be used when e-mail abuse is suspected and what consequences will result if the abuse is confirmed. According to a survey conducted by the ePolicy

Institute, of the 79% of companies that have an e-mail policy, only about 54% actually give employees training and education to ensure that they understand it.[65] Training and education are important to ensure that employees know not only what the policy is but also what it means for their own e-mail use.

Additionally, e-mail policies should specify how much personal e-mail is appropriate and when the bounds of appropriateness have been overstepped. Just as employees make personal phone calls while on the job (and sometimes have to), so too do they send and receive personal e-mail. In fact, according to Waterford Technologies, a provider of e-mail management and archive services based in Irvine, California, about one-third of e-mail to and from companies is personal or not work-related.[66] Clearly, banning all personal e-mail is impractical and likely to have negative consequences for employees and their organizations (such as lower levels of job satisfaction and increased personal phone conversations). Some companies limit personal e-mail to certain times of the day or a certain amount of time per day; others have employees create lists of contacts from whom they want to receive e-mail at work (family members, children, baby-sitters); still others want personal e-mail to be sent and received through Web-based systems like Gmail and Hotmail rather than the corporate e-mail system.[67]

According to the American Management Association, while the majority of organizations have a written policy about e-mail use, some do not have written guidelines for instant messaging.[68] *Instant messaging* allows people who are online and linked through a buddy or contact list to send instant messages back and forth through a small window on their computer screens without having to go through the steps of sending and receiving e-mail.[69]

What about surfing the Internet on company time? According to a study conducted by Websense, approximately half of the employees surveyed indicated that they surfed the Web at work, averaging about two hours per week.[70] Most visited news and travel sites, but about 22% of the male respondents and 12% of the female respondents indicated that they visited pornographic Web sites.[71] Of all those surveyed, 56% said they sent personal e-mail at work. The majority of those surveyed felt that sending personal e-mail and surfing the Web had no effect on their performance, and 27% thought that doing so improved their productivity.[72] Other statistics suggest that while overall there is more Internet use at home than at work, individuals who use the Internet at work spend more time on it and visit more sites than do those who use it at home.[73] As indicated in the following "Ethics in Action" box, personal e-mail and Internet surfing at work present managers with some challenging ethical dilemmas.

Ethics in Action

Monitoring E-mail and Internet Use

A growing number of companies provide managers and organizations with tools to track the Web sites their employees visit and the e-mail they send. For example, Stellar Technologies Inc., based in Naples, Florida, sells software that managers can access anywhere to find out exactly how much time employees have spent at specific Web sites.[74] Currently a majority of large corporations in the United States monitor their employees' e-mail; the percentage is higher among high-technology organizations. Most of the organizations that monitor e-mail tell their employees about the monitoring.[75] However, the means by which they let employees know are not necessarily effective. For example, putting information about e-mail monitoring in an employee handbook might be ineffective if most employees do not read the handbook.[76]

Monitoring employees raises concerns about privacy.[77] Most employees would not like to have their bosses listening to their phone conversations; similarly, some believe that monitoring e-mail and tracking Internet use are an invasion of privacy.[78]

Surf YouTube or finish that spreadsheet? The spreadsheet might just win out, especially when companies realize that intrusive monitoring policies often backfire on employee performance.

Given the increasingly long working hours of many employees, should personal e-mail and Internet use be closely scrutinized? Clearly, when illegal and unethical e-mail use is suspected, such as sexually harassing coworkers or divulging confidential company information, monitoring may be called for. But should it be a normal part of organizational life, even when there are no indications of a real problem?

Essentially this dilemma involves issues of trust. Procter & Gamble does not monitor individuals unless there appears to be a need to do so. P&G has close to 140,000 employees working in 80 countries, and the different countries have different laws and different internal organizational rules and norms.[79] Rather than monitoring individuals to see if they are abiding by the particular standards of the location where they work, P&G monitors electronic communication at its work sites in the aggregate to spot patterns. As Sandy Hughes, head of P&G's Global Privacy Council, puts it, "At some level, you have to trust your employees are going to be doing the right things."[80] Interestingly, some research suggests that people are less likely to lie in e-mail than they are in phone calls or face-to-face conversations.[81]

Impersonal Written Communication

Impersonal written communication is lowest in information richness but is well suited for messages that need to reach many receivers. Because such messages are not addressed to particular receivers, feedback is unlikely, so managers must make sure messages sent by this medium are written clearly in language that all receivers will understand.

Managers often find company newsletters useful vehicles for reaching large numbers of employees. Many managers give their newsletters catchy names to spark employee interest and also to inject a bit of humor into the workplace.[82] Increasing numbers of companies are distributing their newsletters online. For example, IBM's employee newsletter w3 is distributed to employees online and is updated daily.[83]

Managers can use impersonal written communication for various messages, including announcements of rules, regulations, policies, newsworthy information, changes in procedures, and the arrival of new organizational members. Impersonal written communication also can convey instructions about how to use machinery or how to process work orders or customer requests. For these kinds of messages, the paper or electronic trail left by this communication medium can be valuable for employees.

Just as with personal written communication, impersonal written communication can be delivered and retrieved electronically, and this is increasingly the case in companies large and small. Unfortunately the ease with which electronic messages can spread has led to their proliferation. Many managers' and workers' electronic in-boxes are so backlogged that often they do not have time to read all the electronic work-related information available to them. The problem with such **information overload** is the potential for important information to be ignored or overlooked (even that which is personally addressed) while tangential information receives attention. Moreover, information overload can result in thousands of hours and millions of dollars in lost productivity.

information overload The potential for important information to be ignored or overlooked while tangential information receives attention.

blog A Web site on which an individual, group, or organization posts information, commentary, and opinions and to which readers can often respond with their own commentary and opinions.

Some managers and organizations use blogs to communicate with employees, investors, customers, and the general public.[84] A **blog** is a Web site on which an individual, group, or organization posts information, commentary, and opinions and to which readers can often respond with their own commentary and opinions.[85] Some top managers write their own blogs, and some companies such as Cisco Systems and

Oracle have corporate blogs.[86] Just as organizations have rules and guidelines about employee e-mail and Internet use, a growing number of organizations are instituting employee guidelines for blogs.[87] At IBM over 25,000 employees have blogs on IBM's internal computer network.[88] Guidelines for the use of blogs include following IBM's code of conduct (especially with regard to confidentiality, respect, and privacy), refraining from criticizing competitors, and refraining from mentioning customers' names without obtaining prior permission; bloggers must also reveal their own identity on their blogs (anonymous blogs are not permitted).[89]

social networking site A Web site that enables people to communicate with others with whom they have some common interest or connection.

A **social networking site** such as Facebook or Twitter is a Web site that enables people to communicate with others with whom they might have some common interest or connection. Participants in these sites create customized profiles and communicate with networks of other participants.[90] Millions of people in the United States and other countries communicate via social networking sites.[91] While communication through social networking sites can be work-related, some managers are concerned that their employees are wasting valuable time at work communicating with their friends through these sites. According to a recent study sponsored by Robert Half Technology, over 50% of the U.S. companies included in the study prohibit employees from accessing social networking sites such as Twitter, MySpace, LinkedIn, and Facebook while at work.[92] Around 19% of the companies permit communicating through social networking sites for work-related reasons, and 16% permit some personal communication through these sites. Just 10% of the companies surveyed permit full use of social networking sites while on the job.[93]

LO16-4 Describe the communication networks that exist in groups and teams.

Communication Networks

Although various communication media are used, communication in organizations tends to flow in certain patterns. The pathways along which information flows in groups and teams and throughout an organization are called **communication networks.** The type of communication network that exists in a group depends on the nature of the group's tasks and the extent to which group members need to communicate with one another to achieve group goals.

communication networks The pathways along which information flows in groups and teams and throughout the organization.

Communication Networks in Groups and Teams

As you learned in Chapter 15, groups and teams, whether they are cross-functional teams, top management teams, command groups, self-managed work teams, or task forces, are the building blocks of organizations. Four kinds of communication networks can develop in groups and teams: the wheel, the chain, the circle, and the all-channel network (see Figure 16.3).

WHEEL NETWORK In a wheel network, information flows to and from one central member of the group. Other group members do not need to communicate with one another to perform at a high level, so the group can accomplish its goals by directing all communication to and from the central member. Wheel networks are often found in command groups with pooled task interdependence. Picture a group of taxi drivers who report to the same dispatcher, who is also their supervisor. Each driver needs to communicate with the dispatcher, but the drivers do not need to communicate with one another. In groups such as this, the wheel network results in efficient communication, saving time without compromising performance. Although found in groups, wheel networks are not found in teams because they do not allow the intense interactions characteristic of teamwork.

CHAIN NETWORK In a chain network, members communicate with one another in a predetermined sequence. Chain networks are found in groups with sequential task interdependence, such as in assembly-line groups. When group work has to be

Figure 16.3
Communication Networks in Groups and Teams

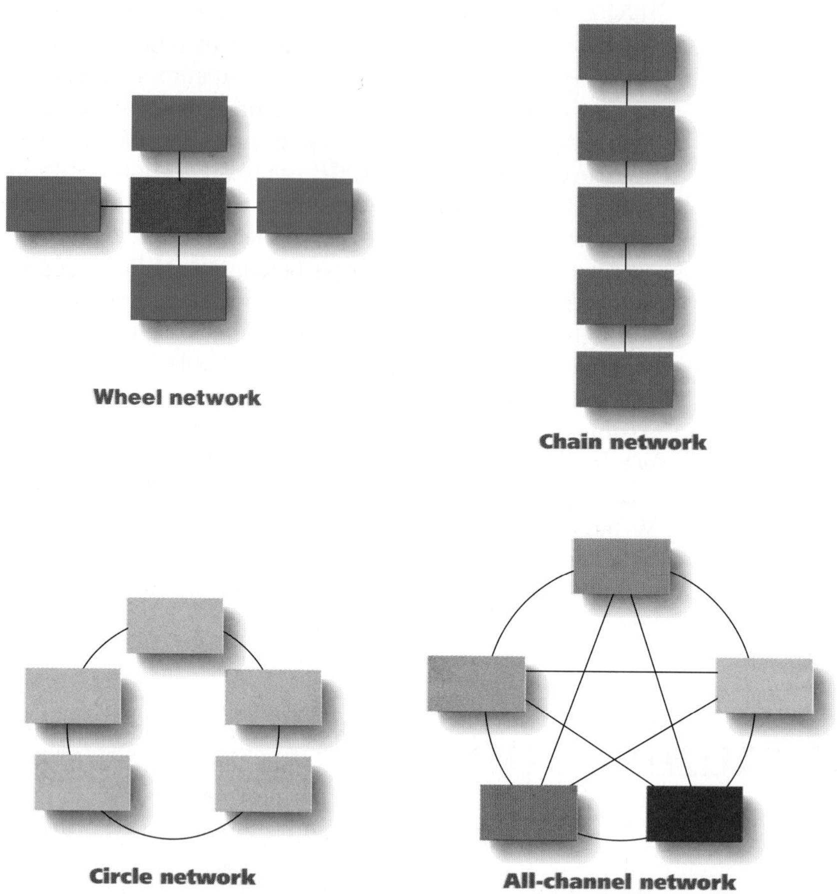

performed in a predetermined order, the chain network is often found because group members need to communicate with those whose work directly precedes and follows their own. Like wheel networks, chain networks tend not to exist in teams because of the limited amount of interaction among group members.

CIRCLE NETWORK In a circle network, group members communicate with others who are similar to them in experiences, beliefs, areas of expertise, background, office location, or even where they sit when the group meets. Members of task forces and standing committees, for example, tend to communicate with others who have similar experiences or backgrounds. People also tend to communicate with people whose offices are next to their own. Like wheel and chain networks, circle networks are most often found in groups that are not teams.

All-channel networks, like this team, are structured around the premise that in a small enough group, if everyone talks with everyone else, things can get done faster.

ALL-CHANNEL NETWORK An all-channel network is found in teams. It is characterized by high levels of communication: Every team member communicates with every other team member. Top management teams, cross-functional teams, and self-managed work teams frequently have all-channel networks. The reciprocal task interdependence often found in such teams requires information flows in all directions. Computer software specially designed for use by work groups can help maintain effective communication in teams with all-channel networks because it gives team members an efficient way to share information.

Organizational Communication Networks

An organization chart may seem to be a good summary of an organization's communication network, but often it is not. An organization chart summarizes the *formal* reporting relationships in an organization and the formal pathways along which communication takes place. Often, however, communication is *informal* and flows around issues, goals, projects, and ideas instead of moving up and down the organizational hierarchy in an orderly fashion. Thus an organization's communication network includes not only the formal communication pathways summarized in an organization chart but also informal communication pathways along which a great deal of communication takes place (see Figure 16.4).

Communication can and should occur across departments and groups as well as within them and up and down and sideways in the corporate hierarchy. Communication up and down the corporate hierarchy is often called *vertical* communication. Communication among employees at the same level in the hierarchy, or sideways, is called *horizontal* communication. Managers obviously cannot determine in advance what an organization's communication network will be, nor should they try to. Instead, to accomplish goals and perform at a high level, organizational members should be free to communicate with whomever they need to contact. Because organizational goals change over time, so too do organizational communication networks. Informal communication networks can contribute to an organization's competitive advantage because they help ensure that organizational members have the information they need when they need it to accomplish their goals.

grapevine An informal communication network along which unofficial information flows.

The **grapevine** is an informal organizational communication network along which unofficial information flows quickly, if not always accurately.[94] People in an organization who seem to know everything about everyone are prominent in the grapevine. Information spread over the grapevine can be about issues of either a business nature (an impending takeover) or a personal nature (the CEO's separation from his wife).

Figure 16.4
Formal and Informal Communication Networks in an Organization

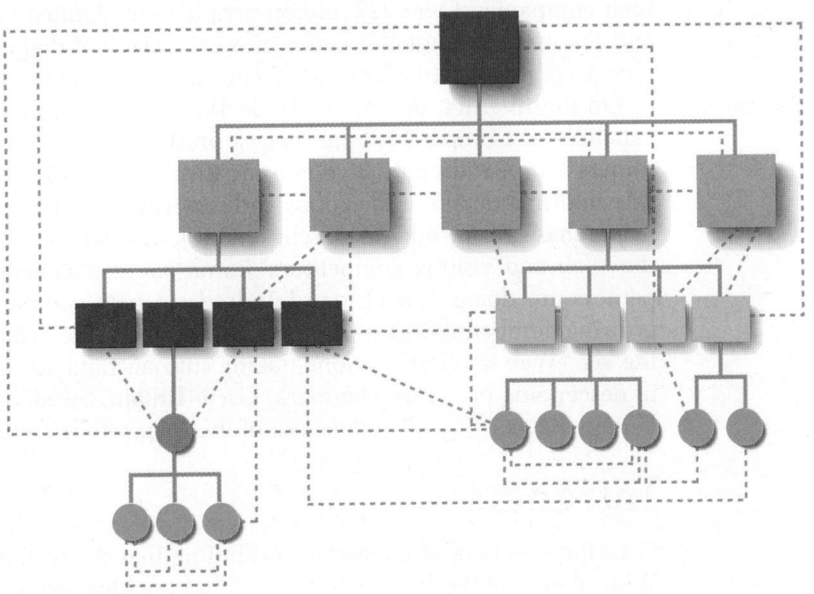

Formal pathways of communication summarized in an organization chart.

Informal pathways along which a great deal of communication takes place.

External Networks

In addition to participating in networks within an organization, managers, professional employees, and those with work-related ties outside their employing organization often are part of external networks whose members span a variety of companies. For example, scientists working in universities and in corporations often communicate in networks formed around common underlying interests in a particular topic or subfield. As another example, physicians working throughout the country belong to specialty professional associations that help them keep up to date on the latest advances in their fields. For some managers and professionals, participation in such interest-oriented networks is as important as, or even more important than, participation in internal company networks. Networks of contacts who are working in the same discipline or field or who have similar expertise and knowledge can be very helpful, for example, when an individual wants to change jobs or find a job after a layoff. Unfortunately, as a result of discrimination and stereotypes, some of these networks are off-limits to certain individuals due to gender or race. For example, the term *old boys' network* alludes to the fact that networks of contacts for job leads, government contracts, or venture capital funding have sometimes been dominated by men and less welcoming of women.[95]

Information Technology and Communication

Advances in information technology have dramatically increased managers' abilities to communicate with others as well as to quickly access information to make decisions. Advances that are having major impacts on managerial communication include the Internet, intranets, groupware, and collaboration software. However, managers must not forget that communication is essentially a human endeavor, no matter how much it may be facilitated by information technology.

LO16-5 Explain how advances in technology have given managers new options for managing communication.

The Internet

Internet A global system of computer networks.

The **Internet** is a global system of computer networks that is easy to join and is used by employees of organizations around the world to communicate inside and outside their companies. Over 227 million people in the United States alone use the Internet, and the use of broadband connections (in place of dial-up service) has dramatically increased.[96] Table 16.1 lists the 20 countries with the most Internet users.[97]

On the Internet, the World Wide Web is the "business district" with multimedia capabilities. Companies' home pages on the Web are like offices that potential customers can visit. In attractive graphic displays on home pages, managers communicate information about the goods and services they offer, why customers should want to purchase them, how to purchase them, and where to purchase them. By surfing the Web and visiting competitors' home pages, managers can see what their competitors are doing.[98] Each day hundreds of new companies add themselves to the growing number of organizations on the World Wide Web.[99] According to one study, the six "Web-savviest" nations (taking into account use of broadband connections) in descending order are Denmark, Great Britain, Sweden, Norway, Finland, and the United States.[100] By all counts, use of the Internet for communication is burgeoning.

Intranets

intranet A companywide system of computer networks.

Growing numbers of managers are finding that the technology on which the World Wide Web and the Internet are based has enabled them to improve communication within their own companies. These managers use this technology to share information within their own companies through company networks called **intranets.** Intranets are being used at many companies including Chevron, Goodyear, Levi Strauss, Pfizer, Chrysler, Motorola, and Ford.[101]

Table 16.1
Top 20 Countries in Internet Usage as of September 30, 2009

Country	Internet Users
China	360,000,000
United States	227,719,000
Japan	95,979,000
India	81,000,000
Brazil	67,510,400
Germany	54,229,325
United Kingdom	46,683,900
Russia	45,250,000
France	43,100,134
South Korea	37,475,800
Iran	32,200,000
Italy	30,026,400
Indonesia	30,000,000
Spain	29,093,984
Mexico	27,600,000
Turkey	26,500,000
Canada	25,086,000
Philippines	24,000,000
Vietnam	21,963,117
Poland	20,020,362

Source: "Top 20 Countries with the Highest Number of Internet Users," Internet World Stats Usage and Population Statistics, www.internetworldstats.com/top20.htm, March 15, 2010. Used by permission.

Intranets allow employees to have many kinds of information at their fingertips. Directories, manuals, inventory figures, product specifications, information about customers, biographies of top managers and the board of directors, global sales figures, meeting minutes, annual reports, delivery schedules, and up-to-the-minute revenue, cost, and profit figures are just a few examples of the information that can be shared through intranets. Intranets can be accessed with different kinds of computers so that all members of an organization can be linked together. Intranets are protected from unwanted intrusions, by hackers or by competitors, by firewall security systems that ask users to provide passwords and other identification before they are allowed access.[102]

The advantage of intranets lies in their versatility as a communication medium. They can be used for a number of different purposes by people who may have little expertise in computer software and programming. While some managers complain that the Internet is too crowded and the World Wide Web too glitzy, informed managers are realizing that using the Internet's technology to create their own computer networks may be one of the Internet's biggest contributions to organizational effectiveness.

Groupware and Collaboration Software

groupware Computer software that enables members of groups and teams to share information with one another.

Groupware is computer software that enables members of groups and teams to share information with one another to improve their communication and performance. In some organizations, such as the Bank of Montreal, managers have had success in introducing groupware into the organization; in other organizations, such as the advertising agency Young & Rubicam, managers have encountered considerable resistance to groupware.[103] Even in companies where the introduction of groupware has been successful, some employees resist using it. Some clerical and secretarial workers at the Bank of Montreal, for example, were dismayed to find that their neat and accurate files were being consolidated into computer files that would be accessible to many of their coworkers.

Managers are most likely to be able to successfully use groupware as a communication medium in their organizations when certain conditions are met:[104]

1. The work is group- or team-based, and members are rewarded, at least in part, for group performance.
2. Groupware has the full support of top management.
3. The culture of the organization stresses flexibility and knowledge sharing, and the organization does not have a rigid hierarchy of authority.
4. Groupware is used for a specific purpose and is viewed as a tool that enables group or team members to work more effectively together, not as a personal source of power or advantage.
5. Employees receive adequate training in the use of computers and groupware.[105]

Employees are likely to resist using groupware and managers are likely to have a difficult time implementing it when people are working primarily on their own and are rewarded for individual performance.[106] Under these circumstances, information is often viewed as a source of power, and people are reluctant to share information with others by means of groupware.

Consider three salespeople who sell insurance policies in the same geographic area; each is paid based on the number of policies he or she sells and on his or her retention of customers. Their supervisor invested in groupware and encouraged them to use it to share information about their sales, sales tactics, customers, insurance providers, and claim histories. The supervisor told the salespeople that having all this information at their fingertips would allow them to be more efficient as well as sell more policies and provide better service to customers.

Even though they received extensive training in how to use the groupware, the salespeople never got around to using it. Why? They all were afraid that giving away their secrets to their coworkers might reduce their own commissions. In this situation, the salespeople were essentially competing with one another and thus had no incentive to share information. Under such circumstances, a groupware system may not be a wise choice of communication medium. Conversely, had the salespeople been working as a team and had they received bonuses based on team performance, groupware might have been an effective communication medium.

For an organization to gain a competitive advantage, managers need to keep up to date on advances in information technology such as groupware. But managers should not adopt these or other advances without first considering carefully how the advance in question might improve communication and performance in their particular groups, teams, or whole organization. Moreover, managers need to keep in mind that all of these advances in IT are tools for people to use to facilitate effective communication; they are not replacements for face-to-face communication.

collaboration software Groupware that promotes and facilitates collaborative, highly interdependent interactions and provides an electronic meeting site for communication among team members.

Collaboration software is groupware that aims to promote collaborative, highly interdependent interactions among members of a team and provide the team with an electronic meeting site for communication.[107] Collaboration software gives members of a team an online work site where they can post, share, and save data, reports, sketches, and other documents; keep calendars; have team-based online conferences; and send and receive messages. The software can also keep and update progress reports, survey team members about different issues, forward documents to managers, and let users know which of their team members are also online and at the site.[108] Having an integrated online work area can help organize and centralize the work of a team, help ensure that information is readily available as needed, and also help team members make sure important information is not overlooked.

Collaboration software can be much more efficient than e-mail or instant messaging for managing ongoing team collaboration and interaction that is not face-to-face. Moreover, when a team does meet face-to-face, all documents the team might need in the meeting are just a click away.[109]

For work that is truly team-based, entails a number of highly interdependent yet distinct components, and involves team members with distinct areas of expertise who need to closely coordinate their efforts, collaboration software can be a powerful communication tool. The New York–based public relations company Ketchum Inc. uses collaboration software for some of its projects. For example, Ketchum managed public relations, marketing, and advertising for a new charitable program that Fireman's Fund Insurance Co. undertook. By using the eRoom software provided by Documentum (a part of EMC Corporation), Ketchum employees working on the project at six different locations, employee representatives from Fireman's, and a graphics company that was designing a Web site for the program were able to share plans, documents, graphic designs, and calendars at an online work site.[110] Members of the Ketchum–Fireman team got e-mail alerts when something had been modified or added to the site. As Ketchum's chief information officer Andy Roach puts it, "The fact that everyone has access to the same document means Ketchum isn't going to waste time on the logistics and can focus on the creative side."[111]

Another company taking advantage of collaboration software is Honeywell International Inc. Managers at Honeywell decided to use the SharePoint collaboration software provided by Microsoft, in part because it can be integrated with other Microsoft software such as Outlook.[112] For example, if a team using SharePoint makes a change to the team's calendar, that change will be automatically made in team members' Outlook calendars.[113] Clearly collaboration software has the potential to enhance communication efficiency and effectiveness in teams.

Wikis, a result of the open-source software movement, are a free or very low-cost form of collaboration software that a growing number of organizations are using. Wikis enable the organizations not only to promote collaboration and better communication but also to cut back on the use of e-mail,[114] as indicated in the following "Information Technology Byte" box.

Information Technology Byte

Collaborating with Wikis

According to Postini Inc., an e-mail filtering company in Redwood, California, approximately 10% of all e-mail sent and received is legitimate.[115] And while many organizations have invested in filtering software to keep spam from flooding employees' in-boxes, according to the Gartner Group (an Internet research firm), 60% of messages that make their way into employees' in-boxes are spam.[116] Darren Lennard, a managing director at Dresdner Kleinwort Wasserstein, an investment bank in London, was receiving approximately 250 e-mail messages a day, of which only 15% were relevant to his job. Every day Lennard's first and last activities were to clear out his in-box on his BlackBerry–until frustration got the better of him, after a long and grueling workday, and he smashed his BlackBerry on the kitchen countertop in his home.[117]

Lennard is not alone in his frustration. J. P. Rangaswani, global chief information officer at Dresdner, who particularly dislikes use of copies on e-mail, wants to reduce the reliance on e-mail communication at the bank. He is taking steps to implement the use of collaboration software and other electronic forms of communication such as instant messaging and RSS (really simple syndication, which enables users to subscribe for information they require). In fact many organizations such as Yahoo!, Eastman Kodak, Walt Disney, and the U.S. government are trying to reduce their reliance on e-mail by turning to other software tools that promote effective communication and collaboration.[118] While e-mail is likely to continue to be extensively used for one-on-one communication, for communication that involves collaboration within and between groups and teams, the use of other, more efficient and effective software tools is likely to dramatically increase in the coming years.[119]

In particular, wikis (in Hawaiian, the word *wiki* means "fast"), which are relatively easy to use and low-cost or free, are becoming increasingly popular as collaborative communication tools.[120] A wiki uses server software to enable users to create and revise Web pages quickly on a company intranet or through a hosted Internet site. Users who are authorized to access a wiki can log on to it and edit and update data, as well as see what other authorized users have contributed. Wikis enable collaboration in real time, and they keep a history so users can see what changes were made to, for example, a spreadsheet or a proposal.[121] Some Web-based collaboration software providers such as Basecamp provide customers with a wiki as part of their services.[122]

Soar Technology Inc., an artificial intelligence company in Ann Arbor, Michigan, that does work for the U.S. Office of Naval Research, has found that relying on wikis for collaboration has reduced the time it takes to complete projects by 50%.[123] According to Jacob Crossman, an engineer at Soar, wikis save time because they do away with the need for multiple e-mail messages with attachments and eliminate the typical confusion that surrounds multiple iterations of the same document.[124] Dresdner has found that e-mail pertaining to projects that use wikis has been reduced by about 75%, and even meeting times have been significantly lowered.[125] Lennard recently created a wiki to figure out how to increase profits on a certain kind of trade. In the past he would send e-mail with attachments to multiple colleagues, have to integrate and make sense of all the responses he received back from them, and then perhaps follow up with subsequent e-mail. Instead, on the wiki page he created, colleagues contributed ideas, commented on each others' ideas, and revised and edited in real time. Lennard estimates that what would have taken about two weeks to accomplish through e-mail took about two days using a wiki.[126]

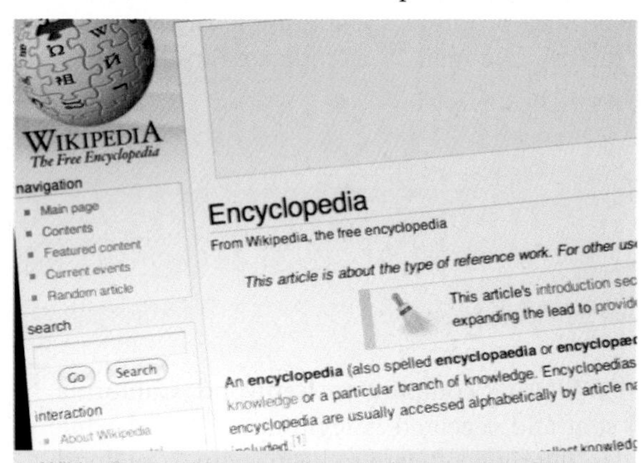

Wikis allow a wide range of people from multiple locations to contribute their specific skills and knowledge to the same task, resulting in a truly collaborative process.

Even though IBM has its own collaboration software, Lotus Notes, IBM employees rely on wikis for collaboration to such a great extent that IBM created Wiki Central to manage the wikis. Wiki Central manages over 20,000 IBM wikis and has over 100,000 users.[127] For example, some teams use wikis to coordinate the development of computer software. Wiki Central also gives employees tools to improve and enhance the functioning of their wikis, such as the "polling widget" (used for electronic voting) and the "rating widget" (used to evaluate proposals).[128] Clearly managers have multiple options to ensure efficient, effective, and collaborative communication.[129]

Communication Skills for Managers

Some of the barriers to effective communication in organizations have their origins in senders. When messages are unclear, incomplete, or difficult to understand, when they are sent over an inappropriate medium, or when no provision for feedback is made, communication suffers. Other communication barriers have their origins in receivers. When receivers pay no attention to or do not listen to messages or when they make no effort to understand the meaning of a message, communication is likely to be ineffective. Sometimes advanced information technology, such as automated phone systems, can hamper effective communication to the extent that the human element is missing.

To overcome these barriers and effectively communicate with others, managers (as well as other organizational members) must possess or develop certain communication skills. Some of these skills are particularly important when managers *send* messages; others are critical when managers *receive* messages. These skills help ensure that managers will be able to share information, will have the information they need to make good decisions and take action, and will be able to reach a common understanding with others.

Communication Skills for Managers as Senders

LO16-6 Describe important communication skills that managers need as senders and as receivers of messages and why it is important to understand differences in linguistic styles.

Organizational effectiveness depends on the ability of managers (as well as other organizational members) to effectively send messages to people both inside and outside the organization. Table 16.2 summarizes seven communication skills that help ensure that when managers send messages, they are properly understood and the transmission phase of the communication process is effective. Let's see what each skill entails.

SEND CLEAR AND COMPLETE MESSAGES Managers need to learn how to send a message that is clear and complete. A message is clear when it is easy for the receiver to understand and interpret, and it is complete when it contains all the information that the sender and receiver need to reach a common understanding. In striving to send messages that are both clear and complete, managers must learn to anticipate how receivers will interpret messages and must adjust messages to eliminate sources of misunderstanding or confusion.

ENCODE MESSAGES IN SYMBOLS THE RECEIVER UNDERSTANDS Managers need to appreciate that when they encode messages, they should use symbols or language that the receiver understands. When sending messages in English to receivers whose native language is not English, for example, it is important to use common vocabulary and to avoid using clichés that, when translated, may make little sense and sometimes are either comical or insulting. **Jargon,** specialized language that members of an occupation, group, or organization develop to facilitate communication among themselves, should never be used when communicating with people outside the occupation, group, or organization.

jargon Specialized language that members of an occupation, group, or organization develop to facilitate communication among themselves.

SELECT A MEDIUM APPROPRIATE FOR THE MESSAGE As you have learned, when relying on verbal communication, managers can choose from a variety of communication media, including face-to-face communication in person, written letters, memos, newsletters, phone conversations, e-mail, voice mail, faxes, and videoconferences. When choosing among these media, managers need to take into account the level of information richness required, time constraints, and the need for a paper or electronic trail. A primary concern in choosing an appropriate medium is the nature of the message. Is it personal, important, nonroutine, and likely to be misunderstood and in need of further clarification? If it is, face-to-face communication is likely to be in order.

Table 16.2
Seven Communication Skills for Managers as Senders of Messages

- Send messages that are clear and complete.
- Encode messages in symbols that the receiver understands.
- Select a medium that is appropriate for the message.
- Select a medium that the receiver monitors.
- Avoid filtering and information distortion.
- Ensure that a feedback mechanism is built into messages.
- Provide accurate information to ensure that misleading rumors are not spread.

SELECT A MEDIUM THE RECEIVER MONITORS Another factor that managers need to take into account when selecting a communication medium is whether the medium is one that the receiver monitors. Managers differ in the communication media they pay attention to. Many managers simply select the medium that they themselves use the most and are most comfortable with, but doing this can often lead to ineffective communication. Managers who dislike telephone conversations and too many face-to-face interactions may prefer to use e-mail, send many e-mail messages per day, and check their own e-mail often. Managers who prefer to communicate with people in person or over the phone may have e-mail addresses but may be less likely to respond to e-mail messages. No matter how much a manager likes e-mail, sending e-mail to someone who does not respond to e-mail may be futile. Learning which managers like things in writing and which prefer face-to-face interactions and then using the appropriate medium enhances the chance that receivers will actually receive and pay attention to messages.

A related consideration is whether receivers have disabilities that hamper their ability to decode certain messages. A blind receiver, for example, cannot read a written message. Managers should ensure that employees with disabilities have resources available to communicate effectively with others. For example, deaf employees can effectively communicate over the telephone by using text-typewriters that have a screen and a keyboard on which senders can type messages. The message travels along the phone lines to special operators called *communication assistants,* who translate the typed message into words that the receiver can listen to. The receiver's spoken replies are translated into typewritten text by the communication assistants and appear on the sender's screen. The communication assistants relay messages back and forth to each sender and receiver.[130] Additionally, use of fax and e-mail instead of phone conversations can aid deaf employees.

filtering Withholding part of a message because of the mistaken belief that the receiver does not need or will not want the information.

AVOID FILTERING AND INFORMATION DISTORTION **Filtering** occurs when senders withhold part of a message because they (mistakenly) think the receiver does not need the information or will not want to receive it. Filtering can occur at all levels in an organization and in both vertical and horizontal communication. Rank-and-file workers may filter messages they send to first-line managers, first-line managers may filter messages to middle managers, and middle managers may filter messages to top managers. Such filtering is most likely to take place when messages contain bad news or problems that subordinates are afraid they will be blamed for. As indicated in "A Manager's Challenge," managers need to hear bad news and be aware of problems as soon as they occur so they can take swift steps to rectify the problem and limit the damage it may have caused.

Some filtering takes place because of internal competition in organizations or because organizational members fear their power and influence will be diminished if others have access to some of their specialized knowledge. By increasing levels of trust in an organization, taking steps to motivate all employees (and the groups and teams they belong to) to work together to achieve organizational goals, and ensuring that employees realize that when the organization reaches its goals and performs effectively, they too will benefit, this kind of filtering can be reduced.

information distortion Changes in the meaning of a message as the message passes through a series of senders and receivers.

Information distortion occurs when the meaning of a message changes as the message passes through a series of senders and receivers. Some information distortion is accidental–due to faulty encoding and decoding or to a lack of feedback. Other information distortion is deliberate. Senders may alter a message to make themselves or their groups look good and to receive special treatment.

Managers themselves should avoid filtering and distorting information. But how can they eliminate these barriers to effective communication throughout their organization? They need to establish trust throughout the organization. Subordinates who trust their managers believe they will not be blamed for things beyond their control and will be treated fairly. Managers who trust their subordinates give them clear and complete information and do not hold things back.

INCLUDE A FEEDBACK MECHANISM IN MESSAGES Because feedback is essential for effective communication, managers should build a feedback mechanism into the messages they send. They either should include a request for feedback or indicate when and how they will follow up on the message to make sure it was received and understood. When managers write letters and memos or send faxes, they can request that the receiver respond with comments and suggestions in a letter, memo, or fax; schedule a meeting to discuss the issue; or follow up with a phone call. By building feedback mechanisms such as these into their messages, managers ensure that they get heard and are understood.

rumors Unofficial pieces of information of interest to organizational members but with no identifiable source.

PROVIDE ACCURATE INFORMATION **Rumors** are unofficial pieces of information of interest to organizational members but with no identifiable source. Rumors spread quickly once they are started, and usually they concern topics that organizational members think are important, interesting, or amusing. Rumors, however, can be misleading and can harm individual employees and their organizations when they are false, malicious, or unfounded. Managers can halt the spread of misleading rumors by giving organizational members accurate information about matters that concern them.

Providing accurate information is especially important in tough economic times like the recession in the late 2000s.[131] During a recession, employees are sometimes laid off or find their working hours or pay levels cut back and often experience high levels of stress. When managers give employees accurate information, this can help reduce their stress levels as well as motivate them to find ways to help their companies weather the tough times.[132] Moreover, when the economy does turn around, employees who received accurate information from their bosses may be more likely to remain with their organizations rather than pursue other opportunities.

Communication Skills for Managers as Receivers

Table 16.3
Three Communication Skills for Managers as Receivers of Messages

- Pay attention.
- Be a good listener.
- Be empathetic.

Managers receive as many messages as they send. Thus managers must possess or develop communication skills that allow them to be effective receivers of messages. Table 16.3 summarizes three of these important skills, which we examine here in greater detail.

PAY ATTENTION Because of their multiple roles and tasks, managers often are overloaded and forced to think about several things at once. Pulled in many different directions, they sometimes do not pay sufficient attention to the messages they receive. To be effective, however, managers should always pay attention to messages they receive, no matter how busy they are. When discussing a project with a subordinate, an effective manager focuses on the project and not on an upcoming meeting with his or her own boss. Similarly, when managers are reading written communication, they should focus on understanding what they are reading; they should not be sidetracked into thinking about other issues.

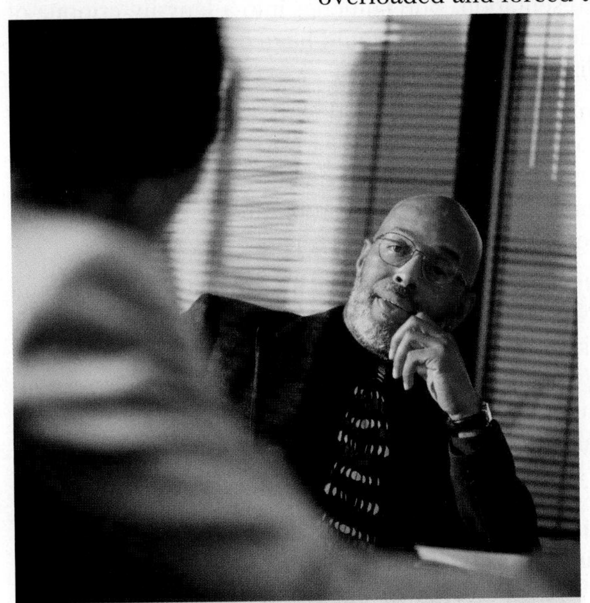

This manager demonstrates that he is paying attention to what his employee is asking for with his eye contact, engaged posture, and focus.

BE A GOOD LISTENER Managers (and all other members of an organization) can do several things to be good listeners. First, managers should refrain from interrupting senders in the middle of a message so senders do not lose their train of thought and managers do not jump to erroneous conclusions based on incomplete information. Second, managers should maintain eye contact with senders so senders feel their listeners are paying attention; doing this also helps managers focus on what they are hearing. Third, after receiving a message, managers should ask questions to clarify points of ambiguity or confusion. Fourth, managers should paraphrase, or restate in their own words, points senders make that are important, complex, or open to alternative interpretations; this is the feedback component so critical to successful communication.

Managers, like most people, often like to hear themselves talk rather than listen to others. Part of being a good communicator, however, is being a good listener–an essential communication skill for managers as receivers of messages transmitted face-to-face and over the telephone.

BE EMPATHETIC Receivers are empathetic when they try to understand how the sender feels and try to interpret a message from the sender's perspective, rather than viewing the message from only their own point of view. Marcia Mazulo, the chief psychologist in a public school system in the Northwest, recently learned this lesson after interacting with Karen Sanchez, a new psychologist on her staff. Sanchez was distraught after meeting with the parent of a child she had been working with extensively. The parent was difficult to talk to and argumentative and was not supportive of her own child. Sanchez told Mazulo how upset she was, and Mazulo responded by reminding Sanchez that she was a professional and that dealing with such a situation was part of her job. This feedback upset Sanchez further and caused her to storm out of the room.

In hindsight, Mazulo realized that her response had been inappropriate. She had failed to empathize with Sanchez, who had spent so much time with the child and was deeply concerned about the child's well-being. Rather than dismissing Sanchez's concerns, Mazulo realized, she should have tried to understand how Sanchez felt and given her some support and advice for dealing positively with the situation.

Understanding Linguistic Styles

Consider the following scenarios:

- A manager from New York is having a conversation with a manager from Iowa City. The Iowa City manager never seems to get a chance to talk. He keeps waiting for a pause to signal his turn to talk, but the New York manager never pauses long enough. The New York manager wonders why the Iowa City manager does not say much. He feels uncomfortable when he pauses and the Iowa City manager says nothing, so he starts talking again.
- Elizabeth compliments Bob on his presentation to upper management and asks Bob what he thought of her presentation. Bob launches into a lengthy critique of Elizabeth's presentation and describes how he would have handled it differently. This is hardly the response Elizabeth expected.
- Catherine shares with co-members of a self-managed work team a new way to cut costs. Michael, another team member, thinks her idea is a good one and encourages the rest of the team to support it. Catherine is quietly pleased by Michael's support. The group implements "Michael's" suggestion, and it is written up as such in the company newsletter.
- Robert was recently promoted and transferred from his company's Oklahoma office to its headquarters in New Jersey. Robert is perplexed because he never seems to get a chance to talk in management meetings; someone else always seems to get the floor. Robert's new boss wonders whether Robert's new responsibilities are too much for him, although Robert's supervisor in Oklahoma rated him highly and said he is a real "go-getter." Robert is timid in management meetings and rarely says a word.

What do these scenarios have in common? Essentially, they all describe situations in which a misunderstanding of linguistic styles leads to a breakdown in communication. The scenarios are based on the research of linguist Deborah Tannen, who describes **linguistic style** as a person's characteristic way of speaking. Elements of linguistic style include tone of voice, speed, volume, use of pauses, directness or indirectness, choice of words, credit taking, and use of questions, jokes, and other

linguistic style A person's characteristic way of speaking.

manners of speech.[133] When people's linguistic styles differ and these differences are not understood, ineffective communication is likely.

The first and last scenarios illustrate regional differences in linguistic style.[134] The Iowa City manager and Robert from Oklahoma expect the pauses that signal turn taking in conversations to be longer than the pauses made by their colleagues in New York and New Jersey. This difference causes communication problems. The Iowan and transplanted Oklahoman think their Eastern colleagues never let them get a word in edgewise, and the Easterners cannot figure out why their colleagues from the Midwest and South do not get more actively involved in conversations.

Differences in linguistic style can be a particularly insidious source of communication problems because linguistic style is often taken for granted. People rarely think about their own linguistic styles and often are unaware of how linguistic styles can differ. In the example here, Robert did not realize that when dealing with his New Jersey colleagues, he could and should jump into conversations more quickly than he used to do in Oklahoma, and his boss never realized that Robert felt he was not being given a chance to speak in meetings.

The aspect of linguistic style just described, length of pauses, differs by region in the United States. Much more dramatic differences in linguistic style occur cross-culturally.

CROSS-CULTURAL DIFFERENCES Managers from Japan tend to be more formal in their conversations and more deferential toward upper-level managers and people with high status than are managers from the United States. Japanese managers do not mind extensive pauses in conversations when they are thinking things through or when they think further conversation might be detrimental. In contrast, U.S. managers (even managers from regions of the United States where pauses tend to be long) find lengthy pauses disconcerting and feel obligated to talk to fill the silence.[135]

Another cross-cultural difference in linguistic style concerns the appropriate physical distance separating speakers and listeners in business-oriented conversations.[136] The distance between speakers and listeners is greater in the United States, for example, than it is in Brazil or Saudi Arabia. Citizens of different countries also vary in how direct or indirect they are in conversations and the extent to which they take

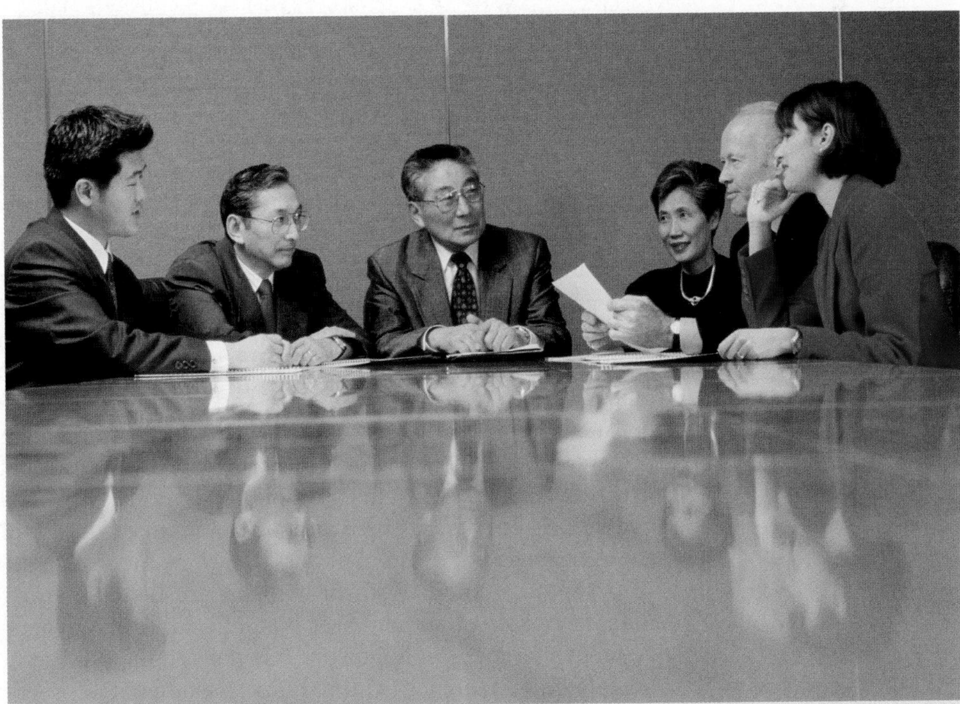

Cross-cultural differences in linguistic style can lead to misunderstandings.

individual credit for accomplishments. Japanese culture, with its collectivist or group orientation, tends to encourage linguistic styles in which group rather than individual accomplishments are emphasized. The opposite tends to be true in the United States.

These and other cross-cultural differences in linguistic style can and often do lead to misunderstandings. For example, when a team of American managers presented a proposal for a joint venture to Japanese managers, the Japanese managers were silent as they thought about the implications of what they had just heard. The American managers took this silence as a sign that the Japanese managers wanted more information, so they went into more detail about the proposal. When they finished, the Japanese were silent again, not only frustrating the Americans but also making them wonder whether the Japanese were interested in the project. The American managers suggested that if the Japanese already had decided they did not want to pursue the project, there was no reason for the meeting to continue. The Japanese were bewildered. They were trying to carefully think out the proposal, yet the Americans thought they were not interested!

Communication misunderstandings and problems like this can be overcome if managers learn about cross-cultural differences in linguistic styles. If the American managers and the Japanese managers had realized that periods of silence are viewed differently in Japan and in the United States, their different linguistic styles might have been less troublesome barriers to communication. Before managers communicate with people from abroad, they should try to find out as much as they can about the aspects of linguistic style that are specific to the country or culture in question. Expatriate managers who have lived in the country in question for an extended time can be good sources of information about linguistic styles because they are likely to have experienced firsthand some of the differences that citizens of a country are not aware of. Finding out as much as possible about cultural differences also can help managers learn about differences in linguistic styles because the two are often closely linked.

GENDER DIFFERENCES Referring again to the four scenarios that open this section, you may be wondering why Bob launched into a lengthy critique of Elizabeth's presentation after she paid him a routine compliment on his presentation, or you may be wondering why Michael got the credit for Catherine's idea in the self-managed work team. Research conducted by Tannen and other linguists has found that the linguistic styles of men and women differ in practically every culture or language.[137] Men and women take their own linguistic styles for granted and thus do not realize when they are talking with someone of a different gender that differences in their styles may lead to ineffective communication.

In the United States, women tend to downplay differences between people, are not overly concerned about receiving credit for their own accomplishments, and want to make everyone feel more or less on an equal footing so that even poor performers or low-status individuals feel valued. Men, in contrast, tend to emphasize their own superiority and are not reluctant to acknowledge differences in status. These differences in linguistic style led Elizabeth to routinely compliment Bob on his presentation even though she thought he had not done a particularly good job. She asked him how her presentation was so he could reciprocate and give her a routine compliment, putting them on an equal footing. Bob took Elizabeth's compliment and question about her own presentation as an opportunity to confirm his superiority, never realizing that all she was expecting was a routine compliment. Similarly, Michael's enthusiastic support for Catherine's cost-cutting idea and her apparent surrender of ownership of the idea after she described it led team members to assume incorrectly that the idea was Michael's.[138]

Do some women try to prove they are better than everyone else, and are some men unconcerned about taking credit for ideas and accomplishments? Of course. The gender differences in linguistic style that Tannen and other linguists have uncovered are general tendencies evident in *many* women and men, not in *all* women and men.

Where do gender differences in linguistic style come from? Tannen suggests they begin developing in early childhood. Girls and boys tend to play with children of their own gender, and the ways in which girls and boys play are quite different. Girls play in small groups, engage in a lot of close conversation, emphasize how similar they are to one another, and view boastfulness negatively. Boys play in large groups, emphasize status differences, expect leaders to emerge who boss others around, and give one another challenges to try to meet. These differences in styles of play and interaction result in different linguistic styles when boys and girls grow up and communicate as adults. The ways in which men communicate emphasize status differences and play up relative strengths; the ways in which women communicate emphasize similarities and downplay individual strengths.[139]

Interestingly, gender differences are also turning up in how women and men use e-mail and electronic forms of communication. For example, Susan Herring, a researcher at Indiana University, has found that in public electronic forums such as message boards and chat rooms, men tend to make stronger assertions, be more sarcastic, and be more likely to use insults and profanity than women, whereas women are more likely to be supportive, agreeable, and polite.[140] David Silver, a researcher at the University of Washington, has found that women are more expressive electronic communicators and encourage others to express their thoughts and feelings, while men are briefer and more to the point.[141] Interestingly enough, some men find e-mail to be a welcome way to express their feelings to people they care about. For example, real estate broker Mike Murname finds it easier to communicate with, and express his love for, his grown children via e-mail.[142]

MANAGING DIFFERENCES IN LINGUISTIC STYLES Managers should not expect to change people's linguistic styles and should not try to. To be effective, managers need to understand differences in linguistic styles. Knowing, for example, that some women are reluctant to speak up in meetings not because they have nothing to contribute but because of their linguistic style should lead managers to ensure that these women have a chance to talk. And a manager who knows certain people are reluctant to take credit for ideas can be careful to give credit where it is deserved. As Tannen points out, "Talk is the lifeblood of managerial work, and understanding that different people have different ways of saying what they mean will make it possible to take advantage of the talents of people with a broad range of linguistic styles."[143]

Summary and Review

COMMUNICATION AND MANAGEMENT Communication is the sharing of information between two or more individuals or groups to reach a common understanding. Good communication is necessary for an organization to gain a competitive advantage. Communication occurs in a cyclical process that entails two
LO16-1, 16-2 phases, transmission and feedback.

LO16-3 **INFORMATION RICHNESS AND COMMUNICATION MEDIA** Information richness is the amount of information a communication medium can carry and the extent to which the medium enables the sender and receiver to reach a common understanding. Four categories of communication media, in descending order of information richness, are face-to-face communication (includes videoconferences), electronically transmitted spoken communication (includes voice mail), personally addressed written communication (includes e-mail), and impersonal written communication.

LO16-4 **COMMUNICATION NETWORKS** Communication networks are the pathways along which information flows in an organization. Four communication networks found in groups and teams are the wheel, the chain, the circle, and the all-channel network. An organization chart summarizes formal pathways of communication, but communication in organizations is often informal, as is true of communication through the grapevine.

LO16-5 **INFORMATION TECHNOLOGY AND COMMUNICATION** The Internet is a global system of computer networks that managers around the world use to communicate within and outside their companies. The World Wide Web is the multimedia business district on the Internet. Intranets are internal communication networks that managers can create to improve communication, performance, and customer service. Intranets use the same technology that the Internet and World Wide Web are based on. Groupware is computer software that enables members of groups and teams to share information with one another to improve their communication and performance.

LO16-6 **COMMUNICATION SKILLS FOR MANAGERS** There are various barriers to effective communication in organizations. To overcome these barriers and effectively communicate with others, managers must possess or develop certain communication skills. As senders of messages, managers should send messages that are clear and complete, encode messages in symbols the receiver understands, choose a medium appropriate for the message and monitored by the receiver, avoid filtering and information distortion, include a feedback mechanism in the message, and provide accurate information to ensure that misleading rumors are not spread. Communication skills for managers as receivers of messages include paying attention, being a good listener, and being empathetic. Understanding linguistic styles is also an essential communication skill for managers. Linguistic styles can vary by geographic region, gender, and country or culture. When these differences are not understood, ineffective communication can occur.

Management in Action

Topics for Discussion and Action

Discussion

1. Which medium (or media) do you think would be appropriate for each of the following kinds of messages that a subordinate could receive from his or her boss: (a) a raise, (b) not receiving a promotion, (c) an error in a report prepared by the subordinate, (d) additional job responsibilities, and (e) the schedule for company holidays for the upcoming year? Explain your choices. [LO16-3]
2. Discuss the pros and cons of using the Internet and World Wide Web for communication within and between organizations. [LO16-1, 16-2, 16-3, 16-5]
3. Why do some organizational members resist using groupware? [LO16-5]
4. Why do some managers find it difficult to be good listeners? [LO16-6]
5. Explain why subordinates might filter and distort information about problems and performance shortfalls when communicating with their bosses. What steps can managers take to eliminate filtering and information distortion? [LO16-6]
6. Explain why differences in linguistic style, when not understood by senders and receivers of messages, can lead to ineffective communication. [LO16-6]

Action

7. Interview a manager in an organization in your community to determine with whom he or she communicates on a typical day, what communication media he or she uses, and which typical communication problems the manager experiences. [LO16-1, 16-2, 16-3, 16-4, 16-5, 16-6]

Building Management Skills

Diagnosing Ineffective Communication [LO16-1, 16-2, 16-3, 16-4, 16-5, 16-6]

Think about the last time you experienced very ineffective communication with another person—someone you work with, a classmate, a friend, a member of your family. Describe the incident. Then answer the following questions:

1. Why was your communication ineffective in this incident?
2. What stages of the communication process were particularly problematic and why?
3. Describe any filtering or information distortion that occurred.
4. Do you think differences in linguistic styles adversely affected the communication that took place? Why or why not?
5. How could you have handled this situation differently so communication would have been effective?

Managing Ethically [LO16-3, 16-5]

Many employees use their company's Internet connections and e-mail systems to visit Web sites and send personal e-mail and instant messages.

Questions

1. Either individually or in a group, explore the ethics of using an organization's Internet connection and e-mail system for personal purposes at work and while away from the office. Should employees have some rights to use this resource? When does their behavior become unethical?
2. Some companies track how their employees use the company's Internet connection and e-mail system. Is it ethical for managers to read employees' personal e-mail or to record Web sites that employees visit? Why or why not?

Small Group Breakout Exercise

Reducing Resistance to Advances in Information Technology [LO16-5]

Form groups of three or four people, and appoint one member as the spokesperson who will communicate your findings to the class when called on by the instructor. Then discuss the following scenario:

You are a team of managers in charge of information and communication in a large consumer products corporation. Your company has already implemented many advances in information technology. Managers and workers have access to e-mail, the Internet, your company's own intranet, groupware, and collaboration software.

Many employees use the technology, but the resistance of some is causing communication problems. A case in point is the use of groupware and collaboration software. Many teams in your organization have access to groupware and are encouraged to use it. While some teams welcome this communication tool and actually have made suggestions for improvements, others are highly resistant to sharing documents in their teams' online workspaces.

Although you do not want to force people to use the technology, you want them to at least try it and give it a chance. You are meeting today to develop strategies for reducing resistance to the new technologies.

1. One resistant group of employees is made up of top managers. Some of them seem computer-phobic and are highly resistant to sharing information online, even with sophisticated security precautions in place. What steps will you take to get these managers to have more confidence in electronic communication?
2. A second group of resistant employees consists of middle managers. Some middle managers resist using your company's intranet. Although these managers do not resist the technology per se and do use electronic communication for multiple purposes, they seem to distrust the intranet as a viable way to communicate and get things done. What steps will you take to get these managers to take advantage of the intranet?
3. A third group of resistant employees is made up of members of groups and teams who do not want to use the groupware that has been provided to them. You think the groupware could improve their communication and performance, but they seem to think otherwise. What steps will you take to get these members of groups and teams to start using groupware?

Exploring the World Wide Web [LO16-5]

Atos Origin is a global information technology company that provides IT services to major corporations to improve, facilitate, integrate, and manage operations, information, and communication across multiple locations. Visit Atos Origin's Web site at www.atosorigin.com, and read about this company and the services it provides to improve communication. Then read the case studies on the Web site (listed under "Business Insights"). How can companies like Atos Origin help managers improve communication effectiveness in their organizations? What kinds of organizations and groups are most likely to benefit from services provided by Atos Origin? Why is it beneficial for some organizations to contract with firms like Atos Origin for their IT and communication needs rather than meet these needs internally with their own employees?

Be the Manager [LO16-1, 16-2, 16-3, 16-6]

You supervise support staff for an Internet merchandising organization that sells furniture over the Internet. You always thought that you needed to expand your staff, and just when you were about to approach your boss with such a request, business slowed. Thus your plan to try to add new employees to your staff is on hold.

However, you have noticed a troubling pattern of communication with your staff. Ordinarily, when you want a staff member to work on a task, you e-mail that subordinate the pertinent information. For the last few months, your e-mail requests have gone unheeded, and your subordinates seem to respond to your requests only after you visit them in person and give them a specific deadline. Each time they apologize for not getting to the task sooner but say they are so overloaded with requests that they sometimes even stop answering their phones. Unless someone asks for something more than once, your staff seems to feel the request is not that urgent and can be put on hold. You think this state of affairs is dysfunctional and could lead to serious problems down the road. Also, you are starting to realize that your subordinates seem to have no way of prioritizing tasks—hence some very important projects you asked them to complete were put on hold until you followed up with them about the tasks. Knowing you cannot add employees to your staff in the short term, what are you going to do to improve communication with your overloaded staff?

Case in the News [LO16-1, 16-2, 16-3, 16-4, 16-5, 16-6]

A Method to the Madness

Think you're busy? The consummate multitasker? Well, meet Brenda Grigsby. Grigsby owns five businesses, and 6 a.m. finds her happily in bed, typing e-mail with one hand and working a cup of coffee with the other. "It's my way of finding out what my day is going to look like and what I need to prioritize," says Grigsby. "For me, it's actually relaxing."

If only we could all conquer the madness as serenely as Grigsby. Basex, a New York–based business research firm, estimates information overload costs the U.S. economy $900 billion a year in lost productivity and stifled innovation. "It's not just e-mail overload, it's too much content, not being able to find things when you search, and interruptions, which is one of the largest culprits," says Jonathan Spira, chief analyst for Basex. "You can lose more than 25% of the day from interruptions alone." While a simple 30-second interruption may seem trivial, the real time-waster comes when you try to retrain your attention on the task at hand. Research from Basex shows that recovery time from a seemingly minor interruption is 10 to 20 times longer than the interruption itself. Even if you're dealing with only a half-dozen interruptions in your day—well, there goes an hour.

Yet some entrepreneurs excel at finding the calm at the center of the storm. Or storms. We found a number of business owners, each of whom owns at least two businesses, who have developed a methodology to wring order out of chaos. If they can do it, we figured, so can the rest of us.

There is some evidence, however, that entrepreneurs who thrive while running two or more businesses are hardwired to handle multiple information streams in a way that others may not be. Entrepreneurs who own more than one company "need more stimulation, more brain food, more challenges that will allow them to really stretch their imagination," says Debra Condren, a business psychologist. "It keeps them feeling passionate about their work as opposed to feeling sated, like eating the same food every day. They want variety." In other words, one man's hopeless confusion is another man's smorgasbord.

But even if they're naturally more comfortable being bombarded with information than their peers, these entrepreneurs consciously delegate, structure their day, and leverage technology to keep the work flowing smoothly. In the following pages, we'll show you how they do it. Finding a method that works for you can help your business reclaim hours you never even knew were gone.

Choreograph the Day

Grigsby manages her five companies as if she were born to juggle. Her largest venture is Moonlight Mailing & Printing—a $4.3 million, 22-employee firm—followed by Northwest Design Group, a four-employee, $1.3 million commercial interior design firm. Grigsby also owns a pet boarding facility, a drive-through coffee shop, and a residential construction company. All are within 20 miles of her home in Bend, Oregon. "I love having a lot going on," she says. "It's fun, mentally stimulating, and challenging."

Grigsby carefully structures her days to manage the streams of information coming at her from five different directions. By sunrise, she's already digging into scores of e-mail messages—likening the morning habit to perusing the newspaper. "I can see if there were any crises overnight that I need to address before getting to work in the morning," she says.

By 9 a.m. Grigsby is at the desk in her office, surrounded by tall bookcases stacked with binders of financial reports for her various companies. She runs daily meetings with each department head at Moonlight Mailing & Printing. Her bookkeeper, who manages all five companies, provides a daily cash report. Grigsby holds weekly huddles with managers of the other four companies to stay abreast of finances, marketing ideas, and any other pressing issues. By 4 p.m., she's reviewing the next day's production schedules for Moonlight.

All five companies use the same lawyer and accountant. Grigsby tries to let her managers handle most of the day-to-day operations so she can focus on keeping the companies growing. She's preparing to start an offshoot of Moonlight Mailing to serve corporate and international clients, and she has developed a patent-pending postcard product for direct-mail marketing that she's just rolling out. And if a test of chuck wagon-style barbecue goes well at Espresso Junction, she'll make a significant investment there, plus try to package and sell a brand of barbecue sauces and rubs. "I like to maintain contact and control, but I really try not to micromanage," says Grigsby. "I have great employees, and I could not have done this without them."

That said, video cameras at Moonlight Mailing and Espresso Junction are crucial in allowing her to bounce more easily among her various businesses—and keep tabs on her great employees. "I can view them online at any given time of the day," she says. "It's mainly for security purposes, and it helps with [employee] accountability. I can see who's doing what and what's going on, anywhere I am in the world." Employees think differently about having friends hang out with them on the job if they know their boss is watching, she says. And waste at both businesses has decreased dramatically since the cameras were installed. Employees do a better job monitoring the printing machines, she says, because now if there's a mistake, Grigsby will see them throwing the paper out before they start the job over. And the drinks are made more carefully at Espresso Junction, again because Grigsby could see them being tossed if they're wrong.

Prioritize

Mike Mothner's $10 million, 50-person search engine marketing company, Wpromote, had been operating for six years when he decided to launch ScanDigital, a photo and home movie transfer company, in 2007. Partly because he'd enlisted a partner to work with him in his new endeavor, he mistakenly thought starting the second business would be easier than launching the first had been. "I underestimated what it would take," the El Segundo (California)–based entrepreneur says. "In the beginning, if anybody e-mailed or popped up on instant messenger, I responded and dealt with it. But it became overwhelming, and we needed to give it some structure."

Now problems that don't need a fast fix are tabled until the weekly lunch with Andrew Schoenrock, Mothner's partner at ScanDigital, which has grown to become an 18-employee, $1.8 million company. To manage incessant and distracting calls, Mothner uses software called PhoneTag, which converts voicemail into e-mail and then sends it directly to his in-box, where it becomes his "to-do" list. "I'm far more efficient by e-mail," explains Mothner, who receives upward of 300 e-mail messages each day and sends out about 75. "Now, I can turn even a short call into a 15-second e-mail response."

But before an e-mail gets even 15 seconds, Mothner mentally gives it a priority from one (immediate) to five (least important), based on how critical it is and how long it will take him to deal with it. Those that rate a one he deals with first and moves on to those of lesser priority. "It's about resource management, whether it's money or time," he says, "it's something you have to be vigilantly aware of."

Delegate

Barry Hamilton is quick to admit that organizational management is not his strong suit. But when his two companies began to outgrow his ability to bounce from one to the other, he knew he needed a better method to his entrepreneurial madness. His companies are in different industries, and at first Hamilton was the only common link between his $1.6 million, eight-employee BareRose Real Estate, which buys, rehabs, and sells homes, and his $3.4 million Red Canyon Software, whose 29 employees work with Lockheed Martin to write the flight software for Mars satellite missions and for *Orion,* the spacecraft that will replace the space shuttle in 2014.

In 2007 Hamilton brought in a chief financial officer to manage the finances of both companies. The CFO doubles as chief operating officer for both businesses, managing tax and estate planning, overseeing the companies' accountants, negotiating property leases and collections, and helping with hiring and recruitment. He even has been able to handle property tax disputes in-house.

In June Hamilton hired an office manager, who culls his e-mail clutter. She handles what she can, then passes on items that require Hamilton's attention. "Letting go of stuff is somewhat difficult," he says, "but it frees up time for me to look at growing the companies." To help do that, the Denver-based entrepreneur uses Tuesdays to hold a two-hour meeting with his BareRose team, immediately followed by a two-hour session with his Red Canyon employees.

Technology helps, too. Hamilton uses rentmanager.com to manage his properties under BareRose Real Estate. At Red Canyon he has started using software from Salesforce.com to manage the recruitment process and customer relationships.

His new hires and the right technology let Hamilton enjoy the variety he craves in business. "From my perspective, that's what I have to have," he says.

Take Four Steps

Paul Holstein knows how to organize, and has built a $13.1 million, 45-employee company based on exactly that. He founded CableOrganizer.com, which sells products that help get rid of cord clutter in homes and offices. Then Holstein went further, launching LifeOrganizers.com, an informational Web site that offers tips for organizing every aspect of life. One year after launching CableOrganizer.com he enlisted a partner to start Ultimatewasher.com, now a $3.1 million, five-employee pressure washer retailer in Jupiter, Florida. "Ultimatewasher is located 100 miles away, but I speak to my partner there at least once a day," Holstein says. "I also send my accounting department up there once a month, and I visit several times a year."

Thanks to his passion for organization, you'll find only two things on Holstein's desk at any given time: the immediate task that he is working on and his to-do list. For everything else, he has a four-step system. "I'll either handle it, file it, delegate it, or throw it away," says the Fort Lauderdale–based entrepreneur. He learned about the four-step system from a consultant while he was working for another company, and insists that he tables absolutely nothing for later.

Holstein also relies on his iPhone to help organize his businesses. He especially likes an app called Evernote, which lets him easily store important lists, such as credit card numbers and frequent flier numbers. Another favorite is Toodledo, which lets him create to-do lists with alerts that remind him of items at specific dates and times. Every other month, Holstein brings in a professional organizer, who tackles paperwork that doesn't require any particular action (such as bank statements) but needs to be filed.

Just last year, Holstein decided to start yet another business,

RezClick.com, a software company that provides schools with online reservation systems for classes. RezClick is based in Fort Lauderdale and so far has two employees and about $50,000 in revenues. With a third company, information overload could easily loom large, but Holstein says focusing intently on one item at a time, via his four-step system, ensures that everything will be taken care of at the end of the day. "That's the only way I can sleep at night," he says.

Questions for Discussion

1. Why is information overload a growing problem for many entrepreneurs, managers, and employees?
2. How does each of the four entrepreneurs profiled in the case manage information overload?
3. What are the pros and cons to each of their approaches?
4. In what ways do advances in information technology both contribute to the information overload problem and at the same time give people tools to manage information overload?

Source: T. Evans, "A Method to the Madness," *BusinessWeek SmallBiz,* December 2009/January 2010, 52–55. Reprinted from December 2009/January 2010 issue of *Bloomberg Businessweek SmallBiz* by special permission, copyright © 2010 by Bloomberg L.P.

CHAPTER 17

Managing Conflict, Politics, and Negotiation

Learning Objectives

After studying this chapter, you should be able to:

LO17-1 Explain why conflict arises, and identify the types and sources of conflict in organizations.

LO17-2 Describe conflict management strategies that managers can use to resolve conflict effectively.

LO17-3 Understand the nature of negotiation and why integrative bargaining is more effective than distributive negotiation.

LO17-4 Describe ways in which managers can promote integrative bargaining in organizations.

LO17-5 Explain why managers need to be attuned to organizational politics, and describe the political strategies that managers can use to become politically skilled.

A MANAGER'S CHALLENGE

Bart Becht Effectively Manages Conflict at Reckitt Benckiser

How can managers effectively manage conflict while promoting innovation in global organizations? When Reckitt & Colman, a British company that made cleaning products for household use, merged with Benckiser, a Dutch company that made consumer products, Reckitt Benckiser came into existence and has been led ever since by Bart Becht, its current CEO.[1] Reckitt Benckiser, headquartered in Slough, England, is a truly global company that makes and sells products for personal care, household use, and health. Although some people have never heard of this company, many are familiar with what it calls its Powerbrands—brands like Vanish, Calgon, Woolite, Lysol, Air Wick, Muxinex, and Clearasil.[2] Employing 23,000 people in over 60 countries, Reckitt Benckiser sells its products in approximately 80 countries.[3]

Often mergers run into problems because employees from the different companies are used to working in different organizational cultures, have different perspectives and outlooks, and find it difficult to work synergistically together.[4] When two companies are based in different countries with different national cultures, potential problems and conflicts can be exacerbated. After the merger Becht deliberately assigned managers to work in countries other than those of their origin and continues to do so to this day. For example, an American manager oversees operations in Germany, an Italian manager oversees operations in the United Kingdom, a Dutch manager oversees operations in the United States, and an Indian manager oversees operations in China. In each country in which Reckitt Benckiser has operations, multiple nationalities are represented along with local citizens. The 400 top managers at Reckitt Benckiser are from 53 different countries.[5]

Essentially, working in a variety of countries over one's career is normal at Reckitt

Bart Becht relocates managers at Reckitt Benckiser to oversee operations in countries other than their place of origin, believing that doing so can eliminate turf battles and promote cross-cultural innovation.

Benckiser. Becht believes that experience working and living in other countries promotes creativity, innovation, and global entrepreneurship as well as ongoing learning and development. And it also can help prevent dysfunctional conflict and an "us versus them" mentality between employees of different nationalities. By living and working in several different countries, and by having several nationalities represented in every location, employees not only learn to respect and appreciate each other but also come up with new ideas based on their different perspectives and experiences.[6]

Even though Becht is Dutch, he does not speak his native language when he is with other Dutch employees at Reckitt Benckiser because this would make other employees feel left out.[7] Since so many nationalities and languages are represented in Reckitt Benckiser, Becht felt the need to have one language—English—used in all meetings. As he puts it, "We are one team with one language. English isn't most people's native language, and often our English isn't pretty. But the way we see it, it doesn't matter as long as you give a view."[8]

While recognizing that conflict due to cultural misunderstanding is dysfunctional, Becht believes in constructive conflict and everyone speaking his or her mind on work-related matters. Employees are expected and encouraged to come to meetings prepared with facts, speak their minds, and defend their positions. Becht knows that sometimes those who might disagree with the majority on a project or idea for a new product might have the best insights and be sources of real creativity and innovation.[9]

Becht strives to achieve win–win solutions to conflicts and disagreements whereby all parties can express and defend their positions, everyone's voice is listened to, and real collaboration takes place. When conflicts occur, rather than strive for consensus by convincing those in the minority to accept the majority's decision, Becht strives for consensus in terms of implementation. Thus once a decision has been made, everyone works together to effectively implement it, including those who might have been in the minority by not supporting it. Those in the minority, however, are permitted to continue to develop their ideas and run small experiments to determine if they are on the right track for an innovative product that will be appealing to Reckitt Benckiser's consumers.[10]

For example, around 2003 there was much conflict over a potential new product called Air Wick Freshmatic that automatically emits air freshener on a predetermined schedule.[11] A Korean brand manager had noticed a similar automatic dispenser of scents available in Korean stores and thought that while that product had design problems, it was an interesting concept. At headquarters the Korean manager met with other managers to discuss the idea, and dissenting views and conflict ensued. Some managers at the meeting thought it might be a good idea for European markets, whereas other managers thought the product would never appeal to many consumers. Concerns were raised that consumers would not want to pay for an automatic dispenser that would cost more to produce; Reckitt Benckiser had no experience with the technology involved; and ultimately a new manufacturing plant would be needed to make this kind of product for a large market. Nonetheless, two managers at the meeting thought the automatic air freshener was a great idea and continued to push for it.[12]

Becht gave the two managers funding to develop the idea on a small scale.[13] Initial testing of a prototype with consumers in the United Kingdom went well. By the end of 2004 the product was being sold in over 30 countries, and a new factory was built in China to manufacture it. By 2010 a variety of types of Air Wick Freshmatic were being sold in 85 countries, generating hundreds of millions of dollars in revenues. By managing conflict through collaboration and permitting those in the minority to run with an idea that others disagreed with, Reckitt Benckiser had an extremely successful launch of a new product.[14]

Of course sometimes ideas for new products don't turn out that well, regardless of whether they were supported by the majority or the minority. However, by ensuring that all opinions and perspectives are heard and experimenting on a small scale, Reckitt Benckiser reaps the benefits of new ideas and innovation while finding out quickly when consumers don't like a new product and it should be dropped.[15]

All in all, Reckitt Benckiser is a truly global company in which managers and employees from many different countries can work together to develop innovative products. For example, products launched in the last three years make up 35–40% of Reckitt Benckiser's revenues.[16] And without effectively managed conflict, some of these new products might never have seen the light of day.

Overview

Successful leaders such as Bart Becht in "A Manager's Challenge" can effectively use their power to influence others and to manage conflict to achieve win–win solutions. In Chapter 14 we described how managers, as leaders, influence other people to achieve group and organizational goals and how managers' sources of power enable them to exert such influence. In this chapter we describe why managers need to develop the skills necessary to manage organizational conflict, politics, and negotiation if they are going to be effective and achieve their goals, as does Bart Becht.

We describe conflict and the strategies managers can use to resolve it effectively. We discuss one major conflict resolution technique, negotiation, in detail, outlining the steps managers can take to be good negotiators. Then we discuss the nature of organizational politics and the political strategies managers can use to maintain and expand their power and use it effectively. By the end of this chapter, you will appreciate why managers must develop the skills necessary to manage these important organizational processes if they are to be effective and achieve organizational goals.

Organizational Conflict

LO17-1 Explain why conflict arises, and identify the types and sources of conflict in organizations.

Organizational conflict is the discord that arises when the goals, interests, or values of different individuals or groups are incompatible and those individuals or groups block or thwart one another's attempts to achieve their objectives.[17] Conflict is an inevitable part of organizational life because the goals of different stakeholders such as managers and workers are often incompatible. Organizational conflict also can exist between departments and divisions that compete for resources or even between managers who may be competing for promotion to the next level in the organizational hierarchy.

organizational conflict The discord that arises when the goals, interests, or values of different individuals or groups are incompatible and those individuals or groups block or thwart one another's attempts to achieve their objectives.

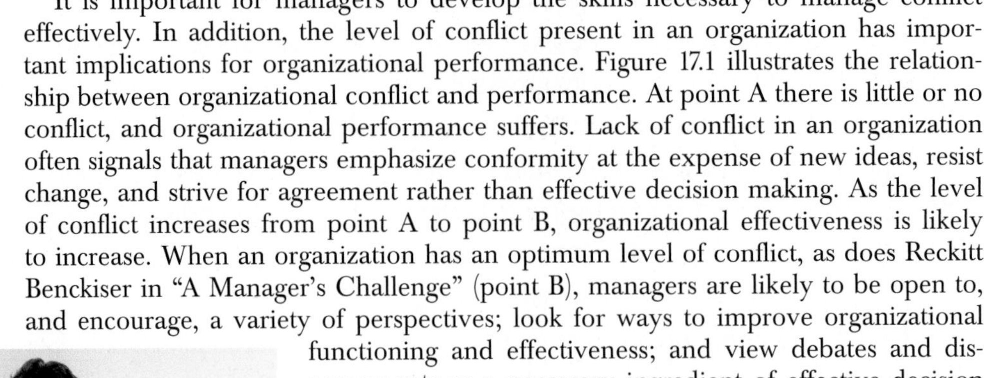

It is important for managers to develop the skills necessary to manage conflict effectively. In addition, the level of conflict present in an organization has important implications for organizational performance. Figure 17.1 illustrates the relationship between organizational conflict and performance. At point A there is little or no conflict, and organizational performance suffers. Lack of conflict in an organization often signals that managers emphasize conformity at the expense of new ideas, resist change, and strive for agreement rather than effective decision making. As the level of conflict increases from point A to point B, organizational effectiveness is likely to increase. When an organization has an optimum level of conflict, as does Reckitt Benckiser in "A Manager's Challenge" (point B), managers are likely to be open to, and encourage, a variety of perspectives; look for ways to improve organizational functioning and effectiveness; and view debates and disagreements as a necessary ingredient of effective decision making and innovation. As the level of conflict increases from point B to point C, conflict escalates to the point where organizational performance suffers. When an organization has a dysfunctionally high level of conflict, managers are likely to waste organizational resources to achieve their own ends, to be more concerned about winning political battles than about doing what will lead to a competitive advantage for their organization, and to try to get even with their opponents rather than make good decisions.

Just another manic Monday? Inappropriately handling legitimate conflict can create lasting damage within one's work group.

Conflict is a force that needs to be managed rather than eliminated.[18] Managers should never try to eliminate all conflict but, rather, should try to keep conflict at a moderate and functional level to promote change efforts that benefit the organization. Additionally, managers should

Figure 17.1
The Effect of Conflict on Organizational Performance

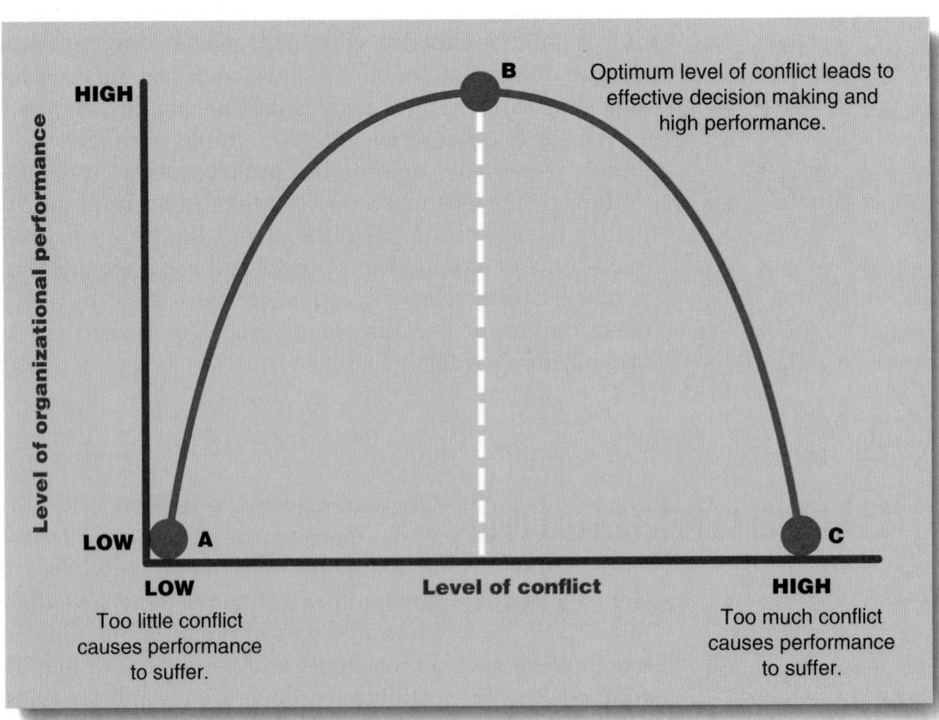

strive to keep conflict focused on substantive, task-based issues and minimize conflict based on personal disagreements and animosities. To manage conflict,[19] managers must understand the types and sources of conflict and be familiar with strategies that can be effective in dealing with it.

Types of Conflict

There are several types of conflict in organizations: interpersonal, intragroup, intergroup, and interorganizational (see Figure 17.2).[20] Understanding how these types differ can help managers deal with conflict.

INTERPERSONAL CONFLICT Interpersonal conflict is conflict between individual members of an organization, occurring because of differences in their goals or values. Two managers may experience interpersonal conflict when their values concerning protection of the environment differ. One manager may argue that the organization should do only what is required by law. The other manager may counter that the organization should invest in equipment to reduce emissions even though the organization's current level of emissions is below the legal limit.

INTRAGROUP CONFLICT Intragroup conflict arises within a group, team, or department. When members of the marketing department in a clothing company disagree about how they should spend budgeted advertising dollars for a new line of men's designer jeans, they are experiencing intragroup conflict. Some of the members want to spend all the money on advertisements in magazines. Others want to devote half of the money to billboards and ads in city buses and subways.

INTERGROUP CONFLICT Intergroup conflict occurs between groups, teams, or departments. R&D departments, for example, sometimes experience intergroup conflict with production departments. Members of the R&D department may develop a new product that they think production can make inexpensively by using existing manufacturing capabilities. Members of the production department, however, may disagree and believe that the costs of making the product will be much higher. Managers of departments usually play a key role in managing intergroup conflicts such as this.

INTERORGANIZATIONAL CONFLICT Interorganizational conflict arises across organizations. Sometimes interorganizational conflict occurs when managers in one organization feel that another organization is not behaving ethically and is threatening the well-being of certain stakeholder groups.

Figure 17.2
Types of Conflict in Organizations

Sources of Conflict

Conflict in organizations springs from a variety of sources. The ones we examine here are different goals and time horizons, overlapping authority, task interdependencies, different evaluation or reward systems, scarce resources, and status inconsistencies (see Figure 17.3).[21]

DIFFERENT GOALS AND TIME HORIZONS Recall from Chapter 10 that an important managerial activity is organizing people and tasks into departments and divisions to accomplish an organization's goals. Almost inevitably this grouping creates departments and divisions that have different goals and time horizons, and the result can be conflict. Production managers, for example, usually concentrate on efficiency and cost cutting; they have a relatively short time horizon and focus on producing quality goods or services in a timely and efficient manner. In contrast, marketing managers focus on sales and responsiveness to customers. Their time horizon is longer than that of production because they are trying to be responsive not only to customers' needs today but also to their changing needs in the future to build long-term customer loyalty. These fundamental differences between marketing and production often breed conflict.

Suppose production is behind schedule in its plan to produce a specialized product for a key customer. The marketing manager believes the delay will reduce sales of the product and therefore insists that the product be delivered on time even if saving the production schedule means increasing costs by paying production workers overtime. The production manager says that she will happily schedule overtime if marketing will pay for it. Both managers' positions are reasonable from the perspective of their own departments, and conflict is likely.

OVERLAPPING AUTHORITY When two or more managers, departments, or functions claim authority for the same activities or tasks, conflict is likely.[22] This is precisely what happened when heirs of the Forman liquor distribution company, based in Washington, D.C., inherited the company from their parents. One of the heirs, Barry Forman, wanted to control the company and was reluctant to share power with the other heirs. Several of the heirs felt they had authority over certain tasks crucial to Forman's success (such as maintaining good relationships with the top managers

Figure 17.3
Sources of Conflict in Organizations

of liquor companies). What emerged was a battle of wills and considerable conflict, which escalated to the point of being dysfunctional, requiring that the family hire a consulting firm to help resolve it.[23]

TASK INTERDEPENDENCIES Have you ever been assigned a group project for one of your classes and had one group member who consistently failed to get things done on time? This probably created some conflict in your group because other group members were dependent on the late member's contributions to complete the project. Whenever individuals, groups, teams, or departments are interdependent, the potential for conflict exists.[24] With differing goals and time horizons, the managers of marketing and production come into conflict precisely because the departments are interdependent. Marketing is dependent on production for the goods it markets and sells, and production is dependent on marketing to create demand for the things it makes.

DIFFERENT EVALUATION OR REWARD SYSTEMS How interdependent groups, teams, or departments are evaluated and rewarded can be another source of conflict.[25] Production managers, for example, are evaluated and rewarded for their success in staying within budget or lowering costs while maintaining quality. So they are reluctant to take any steps that will increase costs, such as paying workers high overtime rates to finish a late order for an important customer. Marketing managers, in contrast, are evaluated and rewarded for their success in generating sales and satisfying customers. So they often think overtime pay is a small price to pay for responsiveness to customers. Thus conflict between production and marketing is rarely unexpected.

Whenever groups or teams are interdependent, the potential for conflict exists.

SCARCE RESOURCES Management is the process of acquiring, developing, protecting, and using the resources that allow an organization to be efficient and effective (see Chapter 1). When resources are scarce, management is more difficult and conflict is likely.[26] For example, divisional managers may be in conflict over who has access to financial capital, and organizational members at all levels may be in conflict over who gets raises and promotions.

STATUS INCONSISTENCIES The fact that some individuals, groups, teams, or departments within an organization are more highly regarded than others in the organization can also create conflict. In some restaurants, for example, the chefs have relatively higher status than the people who wait on tables. Nevertheless, the chefs receive customers' orders from the waitstaff, and the waitstaff can return to the chefs food that their customers or they think is not acceptable. This status inconsistency–high-status chefs taking orders from low-status waitstaff–can be the source of considerable conflict between chefs and the waitstaff. For this reason, some restaurants require that the waitstaff put orders on a spindle, thereby reducing the amount of direct order giving from the waitstaff to the chefs.[27]

LO17-2 Describe conflict management strategies that managers can use to resolve conflict effectively.

Conflict Management Strategies

compromise A way of managing conflict in which each party is concerned about not only its own goal accomplishment but also the goal accomplishment of the other party and is willing to engage in a give-and-take exchange and make concessions.

If an organization is to achieve its goals, managers must be able to resolve conflicts in a functional manner. *Functional conflict resolution* means the conflict is settled by compromise or by collaboration between the parties in conflict (later in the chapter we discuss other, typically less functional ways in which conflicts are sometimes resolved).[28] **Compromise** is possible when each party is concerned about not only its own goal accomplishment but also the goal accomplishment of the other party and is willing to engage in a give-and-take exchange and to make concessions until a

collaboration A way of managing conflict in which both parties try to satisfy their goals by coming up with an approach that leaves them both better off and does not require concessions on issues that are important to either party.

reasonable resolution of the conflict is reached. **Collaboration** is a way of handling conflict in which the parties try to satisfy their goals without making any concessions but, instead, come up with a way to resolve their differences that leaves them both better off.[29] Bart Becht, from "A Manager's Challenge," excels at using collaboration to resolve conflicts; so does Ravi Kant, Managing Director of Tata Motors Ltd.,[30] as profiled in the following "Managing Globally" box.

Managing Globally

Ravi Kant Excels at Collaboration

Ravi Kant, managing director of Tata Motors Ltd., used collaboration to address a conflict he faced as executive director of Tata Motors' commercial vehicles unit.[31] The commercial vehicles unit of Tata Motors, the biggest automobile manufacturer in India, was interested in acquiring Daewoo's truck division based in Gunsan, South Korea, to increase its capabilities.[32] The Korean truck division was doing poorly, and an auction was being held in Korea to sell off the unit. When Kant traveled to Korea, he realized that there was resistance among some managers and employees at the Daewoo truck division to being potentially taken over by Tata Motors; they were concerned about what such a takeover would mean for the future of their company.[33]

Ravi Kant lowered cross-cultural tensions in the Tata Motors' acquisition of Daewoo's truck division by meeting the Korean company's employees on their own turf.

Kant arranged for Tata managers who were trying to negotiate the deal to take lessons in the Korean language so they could better communicate with the Koreans.[34] He had brochures and other documents about Tata translated into Korean. Tata managers made presentations to multiple parties involved in the auction, including Daewoo managers and employees, the head of the local auto association, Gunsun's mayor, and government decision makers in Seoul, Korea, including the prime minister. In these presentations, Tata managers indicated that if Tata were to win the auction, Daewoo employees would be able to keep their jobs, and efforts would focus on building the Daewoo truck unit into a key exporter while integrating it into Tata Motors (and the larger Tata Group of which it is a part). Kant and Tata's efforts paid off; Tata purchased Daewoo's truck division for $102 million.[35] As Kwang-Ok Chae, CEO of Tata Daewoo,[36] indicated, "Tata had done its homework in everything needed to do business here."[37]

Throughout the process, Tata managers showed respect for Daewoo employees and managers.[38] At Tata Daewoo a joint board of directors was created, and Kwang-Ok Chae retained his top management position as CEO of the company.[39] When Kant requested that two Tata top managers advise him, Chae made them a part of his top management team. Together Indian and Korean managers focused on ways to increase Tata Daewoo's product line and exports. Although Daewoo had focused on the Korean market, today Tata Daewoo is a major exporter of heavy trucks, and its revenues have increased substantially since the acquisition.[40] Tata Daewoo is the second biggest manufacturer of heavy-duty trucks in Korea and now exports trucks to over 60 countries, including countries in the Middle East, South Africa, Eastern Europe, and Southeast Asia.[41]

Clearly, the process of acquiring a company can be fraught with the potential for conflict, which if not effectively managed can harm both the acquiring company and the company being acquired. The collaborative way in which the acquisition that created Tata Daewoo was handled made both parties better off. Tata Daewoo is now a successful company, employees' and managers' jobs are secure, and the Tata Group as a whole is better off as a result of the acquisition. As Choi Jai Choon, a South Korean labor union leader, indicated, "It's turned out to be a win–win situation."[42]

accommodation An ineffective conflict-handling approach in which one party, typically with weaker power, gives in to the demands of the other, typically more powerful, party.

avoidance An ineffective conflict handling approach in which the parties try to ignore the problem and do nothing to resolve their differences.

competition An ineffective conflict handling approach in which each party tries to maximize its own gain and has little interest in understanding the other party's position and arriving at a solution that will allow both parties to achieve their goals.

In addition to compromise and collaboration, there are three other ways in which conflicts are sometimes handled: accommodation, avoidance, and competition.[43] When **accommodation** takes place, one party to the conflict simply gives in to the demands of the other party. Accommodation typically takes place when one party has more power than the other and can pursue its goal attainment at the expense of the weaker party. From an organizational perspective, accommodation is often ineffective: The two parties are not cooperating with each other, they are unlikely to want to cooperate in the future, and the weaker party who gives in or accommodates the more powerful party might look for ways to get back at the stronger party in the future.

When conflicts are handled by **avoidance,** the parties to a conflict try to ignore the problem and do nothing to resolve the disagreement. Avoidance is often ineffective because the real source of the disagreement has not been addressed, conflict is likely to continue, and communication and cooperation are hindered.

Competition occurs when each party to a conflict tries to maximize its own gain and has little interest in understanding the other party's position and arriving at a solution that will allow both parties to achieve their goals. Competition can actually escalate levels of conflict as each party tries to outmaneuver the other. As a way of handling conflict, competition is ineffective for the organization because the two sides to a conflict are more concerned about winning the battle than cooperating to arrive at a solution that is best for the organization and acceptable to both sides. Handling conflicts through accommodation, avoidance, or competition is ineffective from an organizational point of view because the parties do not cooperate with each other and work toward a mutually acceptable solution to their differences.

When the parties to a conflict are willing to cooperate with each other and, through compromise or collaboration, devise a solution that each finds acceptable, an organization is more likely to achieve its goals.[44] Conflict management strategies that managers can use to ensure that conflicts are resolved in a functional manner focus on individuals and on the organization as a whole. Next we describe four strategies that focus on individuals: increasing awareness of the sources of conflict, increasing diversity awareness and skills, practicing job rotation or temporary assignments, and using permanent transfers or dismissals when necessary. We also describe two strategies that focus on the organization as a whole: changing an organization's structure or culture and directly altering the source of conflict.

STRATEGIES FOCUSED ON INDIVIDUALS

INCREASING AWARENESS OF THE SOURCES OF CONFLICT Sometimes conflict arises because of communication problems and interpersonal misunderstandings. For example, different linguistic styles (see Chapter 16) may lead some men in work teams to talk more, and take more credit for ideas, than women in those teams. These communication differences can cause conflict when the men incorrectly assume that the women are uninterested or less capable because they participate less and the women incorrectly assume that the men are bossy and are not interested in their ideas because they seem to do all the talking. By increasing people's awareness of this source of conflict, managers can help resolve conflict functionally. Once men and women realize that the source of their conflict is different linguistic styles, they can take steps to interact with each other more effectively. The men can give the women more chances to provide input, and the women can be more proactive in providing this input.

Sometimes personalities clash in an organization. In these situations, too, managers can help resolve conflicts functionally by increasing organizational members' awareness of the source of their difficulties. For example, some people who are not inclined to take risks may come into conflict with those who are prone to taking risks. The non-risk takers might complain that those who welcome risk propose outlandish ideas without justification, whereas the risk takers might complain that their innovative ideas are always getting shot down. When both types of people are made aware that their conflicts are due to fundamental differences in their ways of approaching problems, they will likely be better able to cooperate in coming up with innovative ideas that entail only moderate levels of risk.

INCREASING DIVERSITY AWARENESS AND SKILLS Interpersonal conflicts also can arise because of diversity. Older workers may feel uncomfortable or resentful about reporting to a younger supervisor, a Hispanic may feel singled out in a group of non-Hispanic workers, or a female top manager may feel that members of her predominantly male top management team band together whenever one of them disagrees with one of her proposals. Whether or not these feelings are justified, they are likely to cause recurring conflicts. Many of the techniques we described in Chapter 5 for increasing diversity awareness and skills can help managers effectively manage diversity and resolve conflicts that originate in differences among organizational members.

Increasing diversity awareness and skills can be especially important when organizations expand globally and seek to successfully integrate operations in other countries, as illustrated in the following "Managing Globally" box.

Managing Globally

Xplane Integrates Operations in Spain

Xplane is a small consulting and design firm with global headquarters in Portland, Oregon, and an additional U.S. office in St. Louis, Missouri.[45] When Dave Gray, founder and chairman of the company, decided to expand operations by acquiring a small firm in Madrid, Spain, with around six employees, in the hopes of expanding operations in Europe as well as building capabilities to serve companies in Spanish-speaking countries, he learned firsthand the importance of increasing diversity awareness and skills. Misunderstandings and conflict arose, ranging from a St. Louis employee inadvertently insulting Spanish employees during a dinner in Madrid to Spanish employees feeling excluded from communications and not integrated within Xplane's operations.[46] For example, Stephen O'Flynn, who is a project manager in the Madrid office and originally came from Ireland, felt that some employees in the two U.S. offices almost seemed to forget that the company had a third office in Spain.[47]

Gray realized that given cultural differences and the geographic distance between the U.S. and Spanish offices, it was vital to both improve communication across offices and provide more opportunities for employees in the different offices to interact with each other and establish a common understanding. Company e-mail, for example, should not be sent just to U.S. employees but also to employees in Spain. The company changed to a Web-based phone system so employees would need to dial only 4 digits (rather than 13) to make calls between Spain and the United States.[48] Wikis were created with photos of all employees. O'Flynn frequently called employees in Portland and St. Louis to discuss projects with them and encouraged other employees in the Madrid office to similarly reach out. As he indicates, "I did a lot of brokering to get people talking."[49]

Xplane learned that plane tickets plus technology were needed to integrate Spanish and American workers; this infrastructure enables the company to continue expanding in Europe.

Gray also realized that it was important for U.S. and Spanish employees to have a chance to interact face-to-face and for more extended periods than a phone conversation, a dinner, or one-shot meeting in either country. To accomplish this, he created an exchange program for employees.[50] As part of the program, employees in each country can visit and work with their counterparts in the other country to build relationships, increase their diversity awareness and skills, and learn from each other. For example, a U.S. employee can stay in an apartment rented by Xplane in Madrid for a week and work with employees in the Spanish office. Similarly, a Spanish employee can stay in an apartment rented by Xplane in Portland and work with employees in Portland for a week.[51] As Xplane CEO Aric Wood indicated, "We tried to close the gap through technology, but ultimately we had to buy a lot of airline tickets."[52] By taking steps to increase diversity awareness and skills and foster effective communication, managers like Wood not only help alleviate sources of misunderstanding and potential conflict but also increase their chances of reaping the benefits that different perspectives and points of view can bring. The Madrid office is now Xplane's global headquarters; on April 1, 2010, Xplane opened an additional European office in Amsterdam in the Netherlands.[53]

PRACTICING JOB ROTATION OR TEMPORARY ASSIGNMENTS Sometimes conflicts arise because individual organizational members simply do not understand the work activities and demands that others in an organization face. A financial analyst, for example, may be required to submit monthly reports to a member of the accounting department. These reports have a low priority for the analyst, who typically turns them in a couple of days late. On each due date the accountant calls the financial analyst, and conflict ensues as the accountant describes in detail why she must have the reports on time and the financial analyst describes everything else he needs to do. In situations such as this, job rotation or temporary assignments, which expand organizational members' knowledge base and appreciation of other departments, can be a useful way of resolving the conflict. If the financial analyst spends some time working in the accounting department, he may appreciate better the need for timely reports. Similarly, a temporary assignment in the finance department may help the accountant realize the demands a financial analyst faces and the need to streamline unnecessary aspects of reporting.

USING PERMANENT TRANSFERS OR DISMISSALS WHEN NECESSARY Sometimes when other conflict resolution strategies do not work, managers may need to take more drastic steps, including permanent transfers or dismissals.

Suppose two first-line managers who work in the same department are always at each other's throats; frequent bitter conflicts arise between them even though they both seem to get along well with other employees. No matter what their supervisor does to increase their understanding of each other, the conflicts keep occurring. In this case the supervisor may want to transfer one or both managers so they do not have to interact as frequently.

When dysfunctionally high levels of conflict occur among top managers who cannot resolve their differences and understand each other, it may be necessary for one of them to leave the company. This is how Gerald Levin managed such conflict among top managers when he was chairman of Time Warner. Robert Daly and Terry Semel, one of the most respected management teams in Hollywood at the time and top managers in the Warner Brothers film company, had been in conflict with Michael Fuchs, a long-time veteran of Time Warner and head of the music division, for two years. As Semel described it, the company "was running like a dysfunctional family, and it needed one management team to run it."[54] Levin realized that Time Warner's future success rested on resolving this conflict, that it was unlikely that Fuchs would ever be able to work effectively with Daly and Semel, and that he risked losing Daly and Semel to another company if he did not resolve the conflict. Faced with that scenario, Levin asked Fuchs to resign.[55]

STRATEGIES FOCUSED ON THE WHOLE ORGANIZATION

CHANGING AN ORGANIZATION'S STRUCTURE OR CULTURE Conflict can signal the need for changes in an organization's structure or culture. Sometimes managers can effectively resolve conflict by changing the organizational structure they use to group people and tasks.[56] As an organization grows, for example, the *functional structure* (composed of departments such as marketing, finance, and production) that was effective when the organization was small may cease to be effective, and a shift to a *product structure* might effectively resolve conflicts (see Chapter 10).

Managers also can effectively resolve conflicts by increasing levels of integration in an organization. Recall from Chapter 15 that Hallmark Cards increased integration by using cross-functional teams to produce new cards. The use of cross-functional teams sped new card development and helped resolve conflicts between different departments. Now when a writer and an artist have a conflict over the appropriateness of the artist's illustrations, they do not pass criticisms back and forth from one department to another because they are on the same team and can directly resolve the issue on the spot.

Sometimes managers may need to take steps to change an organization's culture to resolve conflict (see Chapter 3). Norms and values in an organizational culture might inadvertently promote dysfunctionally high levels of conflict that are difficult to resolve. For instance, norms that stress respect for formal authority may create conflict that is difficult to resolve when an organization creates self-managed work teams and managers' roles and the structure of authority in the organization change. Values stressing individual competition may make it difficult to resolve conflicts when organizational members need to put others' interests ahead of their own. In circumstances such as these, taking steps to change norms and values can be an effective conflict resolution strategy.

negotiation A method of conflict resolution in which the parties consider various alternative ways to allocate resources to come up with a solution acceptable to all of them.

third-party negotiator An impartial individual with expertise in handling conflicts and negotiations who helps parties in conflict reach an acceptable solution.

ALTERING THE SOURCE OF CONFLICT When the source of conflict is overlapping authority, different evaluation or reward systems, or status inconsistencies, managers can sometimes effectively resolve the conflict by directly altering its source. For example, managers can clarify the chain of command and reassign tasks and responsibilities to resolve conflicts due to overlapping authority.

Negotiation

LO17-3 Understand the nature of negotiation and why integrative bargaining is more effective than distributive negotiation.

mediator A third-party negotiator who facilitates negotiations but has no authority to impose a solution.

Negotiation is a particularly important conflict resolution technique for managers and other organizational members in situations where the parties to a conflict have approximately equal levels of power. During **negotiation** the parties to a conflict try to come up with a solution acceptable to themselves by considering various alternative ways to allocate resources to each other.[57] Sometimes the sides involved in a conflict negotiate directly with each other. Other times a **third-party negotiator** is relied on. Third-party negotiators are impartial individuals who are not directly involved in the conflict and have special expertise in handling conflicts and negotiations;[58] they are relied on to help the two negotiating parties reach an acceptable resolution of their conflict.[59] When a third-party negotiator acts as a **mediator,** his or her role in the negotiation process is to facilitate an effective negotiation between the two parties; mediators do not force either party to make concessions, nor can they force an agreement

arbitrator A third-party negotiator who can impose what he or she thinks is a fair solution to a conflict that both parties are obligated to abide by.

to resolve a conflict. **Arbitrators,** on the other hand, are third-party negotiators who can impose what they believe is a fair solution to a dispute that both parties are obligated to abide by.[60]

Distributive Negotiation and Integrative Bargaining

distributive negotiation Adversarial negotiation in which the parties in conflict compete to win the most resources while conceding as little as possible.

integrative bargaining Cooperative negotiation in which the parties in conflict work together to achieve a resolution that is good for them both.

There are two major types of negotiation–distributive negotiation and integrative bargaining.[61] In **distributive negotiation,** the two parties perceive that they have a "fixed pie" of resources that they need to divide.[62] They take a competitive, adversarial stance. Each party realizes that he or she must concede something but is out to get the lion's share of the resources.[63] The parties see no need to interact with each other in the future and do not care if their interpersonal relationship is damaged or destroyed by their competitive negotiation.[64] In distributive negotiations, conflicts are handled by competition.

In **integrative bargaining,** the parties perceive that they might be able to increase the resource pie by trying to come up with a creative solution to the conflict. They do not view the conflict competitively, as a win-or-lose situation; instead they view it cooperatively, as a win–win situation in which both parties can gain. Trust, information sharing, and the desire of both parties to achieve a good resolution of the conflict characterize integrative bargaining.[65] In integrative bargaining, conflicts are handled through collaboration and/or compromise.

Consider how Adrian Hofbeck and Joseph Steinberg, partners in a successful German restaurant in the Midwest, resolved their recent conflict. Hofbeck and Steinberg founded the restaurant 15 years ago, share management responsibilities, and share equally in the restaurant's profits. Hofbeck recently decided that he wanted to retire and sell the restaurant, but retirement was the last thing Steinberg had in mind; he wanted to continue to own and manage the restaurant. Distributive negotiation was out of the question, for Hofbeck and Steinberg were close friends and valued their friendship; neither wanted to do something that would hurt the other or their continuing relationship. So they opted for integrative bargaining, which they thought would help them resolve their conflict so both could achieve their goals and maintain their friendship.

LO17-4 Describe ways in which managers can promote integrative bargaining in organizations.

Strategies to Encourage Integrative Bargaining

Managers in all kinds of organizations can rely on five strategies to facilitate integrative bargaining and avoid distributive negotiation: emphasizing superordinate goals; focusing on the problem, not the people; focusing on interests, not demands; creating new options for joint gain; and focusing on what is fair (see Table 17.1).[66] Hofbeck and Steinberg used each of these strategies to resolve their conflict.

EMPHASIZING SUPERORDINATE GOALS *Superordinate goals* are goals that both parties agree to regardless of the source of their conflict. Increasing organizational effectiveness, increasing responsiveness to customers, and gaining a competitive

Table 17.1
Negotiation Strategies for Integrative Bargaining

- Emphasize superordinate goals.
- Focus on the problem, not the people.
- Focus on interests, not demands.
- Create new options for joint gain.
- Focus on what is fair.

advantage are just a few of the many superordinate goals that members of an organization can emphasize during integrative bargaining. Superordinate goals help parties in conflict to keep in mind the big picture and the fact that they are working together for a larger purpose or goal despite their disagreements. Hofbeck and Steinberg emphasized three superordinate goals during their bargaining: ensuring that the restaurant continued to survive and prosper, allowing Hofbeck to retire, and allowing Steinberg to remain an owner and manager as long as he wished.

FOCUSING ON THE PROBLEM, NOT THE PEOPLE People who are in conflict may not be able to resist the temptation to focus on the other party's shortcomings and weaknesses, thereby personalizing the conflict. Instead of attacking the problem, the parties to the conflict attack each other. This approach is inconsistent with integrative bargaining and can easily lead both parties into a distributive negotiation mode. All parties to a conflict need to keep focused on the problem or on the source of the conflict and avoid the temptation to discredit one another.

Integrative bargaining brings all parties to the table in order to create a solution based on honest assessment of the problem and a willingness to honor others' interests and values.

Given their strong friendship, this was not much of an issue for Hofbeck and Steinberg, but they still had to be on their guard to avoid personalizing the conflict. Steinberg recalls that when they were having a hard time coming up with a solution, he started thinking that Hofbeck, a healthy 57-year-old, was lazy to want to retire so young: "If only he wasn't so lazy, we would never be in the mess we're in right now." Steinberg never mentioned these thoughts to Hofbeck (who later admitted that sometimes he was annoyed with Steinberg for being such a workaholic) because he realized that doing so would hurt their chances for reaching an integrative solution.

FOCUSING ON INTERESTS, NOT DEMANDS Demands are *what* a person wants; interests are *why* the person wants them. When two people are in conflict, it is unlikely that the demands of both can be met. Their underlying interests, however, can be met, and meeting them is what integrative bargaining is all about.

Hofbeck's demand was that they sell the restaurant and split the proceeds. Steinberg's demand was that they keep the restaurant and maintain the status quo. Obviously both demands could not be met, but perhaps their interests could be. Hofbeck wanted to be able to retire, invest his share of the money from the restaurant, and live off the returns on the investment. Steinberg wanted to continue managing, owning, and deriving income from the restaurant.

CREATING NEW OPTIONS FOR JOINT GAIN Once two parties to a conflict focus on their interests, they are on the road to achieving creative solutions to the conflict that will benefit them both. This win–win scenario means that rather than having a fixed set of alternatives from which to choose, the two parties can come up with new alternatives that might even expand the resource pie.

Hofbeck and Steinberg came up with three such alternatives. First, even though Steinberg did not have the capital, he could buy out Hofbeck's share of the restaurant. Hofbeck would provide the financing for the purchase, and in return Steinberg would pay him a reasonable return on his investment (the same kind of return he could have obtained had he taken his money out of the restaurant and invested it). Second, the partners could seek to sell Hofbeck's share in the restaurant to a third party under the stipulation that Steinberg would continue to manage the restaurant and receive income for his services. Third, the partners could continue to jointly own the restaurant. Steinberg would manage it and receive a proportionally greater share of its profits than Hofbeck, who would be an absentee owner not involved in day-to-day operations but would still receive a return on his investment in the restaurant.

FOCUSING ON WHAT IS FAIR Focusing on what is fair is consistent with the principle of distributive justice, which emphasizes the fair distribution of outcomes based on the meaningful contributions that people make to organizations (see Chapter 5). It is likely that two parties in conflict will disagree on certain points and prefer different alternatives that each party believes may better serve his or her own interests or maximize his or her own outcomes. Emphasizing fairness and distributive justice will help the two parties come to a mutual agreement about what the best solution is to the problem.

Steinberg and Hofbeck agreed that Hofbeck should be able to cut his ties with the restaurant if he chose to do so. They thus decided to pursue the second alternative described and seek a suitable buyer for Hofbeck's share. They were successful in finding an investor who was willing to buy out Hofbeck's share and let Steinberg continue managing the restaurant. And they remained good friends.

When managers pursue these five strategies and encourage other organizational members to do so, they are more likely to be able to effectively resolve their conflicts through integrative bargaining. In addition, throughout the negotiation process, managers and other organizational members need to be aware of, and on their guard against, the biases that can lead to faulty decision making (see Chapter 7).[67]

Organizational Politics

LO17-5 Explain why managers need to be attuned to organizational politics, and describe the political strategies that managers can use to become politically skilled.

Managers must develop the skills necessary to manage organizational conflict for an organization to be effective. Suppose, however, that top managers are in conflict over the best strategy for an organization to pursue or the best structure to adopt to use organizational resources efficiently. In such situations resolving conflict is often difficult, and the parties to the conflict resort to organizational politics and political strategies to try to resolve the conflict in their favor.

Organizational politics are the activities that managers (and other members of an organization) engage in to increase their power and to use power effectively to achieve their goals and overcome resistance or opposition.[68] Managers often engage in organizational politics to resolve conflicts in their favor.

organizational politics Activities that managers engage in to increase their power and to use power effectively to achieve their goals and overcome resistance or opposition.

political strategies Tactics that managers use to increase their power and to use power effectively to influence and gain the support of other people while overcoming resistance or opposition.

Political strategies are the specific tactics that managers (and other members of an organization) use to increase their power and to use power effectively to influence and gain the support of other people while overcoming resistance or opposition. Political strategies are especially important when managers are planning and implementing major changes in an organization: Managers need not only to gain support for their change initiatives and influence organizational members to behave in new ways but also to overcome often strong opposition from people who feel threatened by the change and prefer the status quo. By increasing their power, managers are better able to make needed changes. In addition to increasing their power, managers also must make sure they use their power in a way that actually enables them to influence others.

The Importance of Organizational Politics

The term *politics* has a negative connotation for many people. Some may think that managers who are political have risen to the top not because of their own merit and capabilities but because of whom they know. Or people may think that political managers are self-interested and wield power to benefit themselves, not their organization. There is a grain of truth to this negative connotation. Some managers do appear to misuse their power for personal benefit at the expense of their organization's effectiveness.

Nevertheless, organizational politics are often a positive force. Managers striving to make needed changes often encounter resistance from individuals and groups who feel threatened and wish to preserve the status quo. Effective managers engage in politics to gain support for and implement needed changes. Similarly, managers often face resistance from other managers who disagree with their goals for a group or for the organization and with what they are trying to accomplish. Engaging in organizational politics can help managers overcome this resistance and achieve their goals.

Indeed, managers cannot afford to ignore organizational politics. Everyone engages in politics to a degree–other managers, coworkers, and subordinates, as well as people outside an organization, such as suppliers. Those who try to ignore politics might as well bury their heads in the sand because in all likelihood they will be unable to gain support for their initiatives and goals.

Political Strategies for Gaining and Maintaining Power

Managers who use political strategies to increase and maintain their power are better able to influence others to work toward the achievement of group and organizational goals. (Recall from Chapter 14 that legitimate, reward, coercive, expert, and referent powers help managers influence others as leaders.) By controlling uncertainty, making themselves irreplaceable, being in a central position, generating resources, and building alliances, managers can increase their power (see Figure 17.4).[69] We next look at each of these strategies.

CONTROLLING UNCERTAINTY Uncertainty is a threat for individuals, groups, and whole organizations and can interfere with effective performance and goal attainment. For example, uncertainty about job security is threatening for many workers and may cause top performers (who have the best chance of finding another job)

Figure 17.4
Political Strategies for Increasing Power

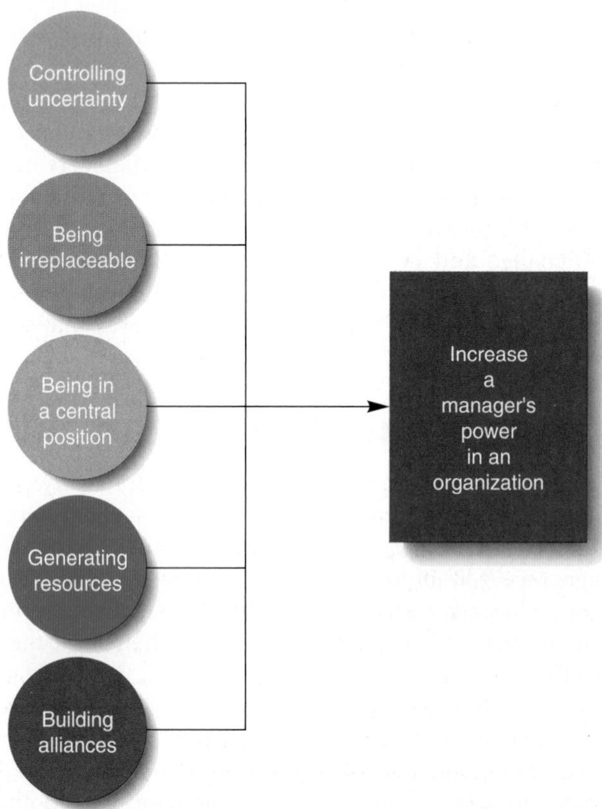

to quit and take a more secure position with another organization. When an R&D department faces uncertainty about customer preferences, its members may waste valuable resources to develop a product, such as smokeless cigarettes, that customers do not want. When top managers face uncertainty about global demand, they may fail to export products to countries that want them and thus may lose a source of competitive advantage.

Managers who can control and reduce uncertainty for other managers, teams, departments, and the organization as a whole are likely to see their power increase.[70] Managers of labor unions gain power when they can eliminate uncertainty over job security for workers. Marketing and sales managers gain power when they can eliminate uncertainty for other departments such as R&D by accurately forecasting customers' changing preferences. Top managers gain power when they are knowledgeable about global demand for an organization's products. Managers who can control uncertainty are likely to be in demand and be sought after by other organizations.

MAKING ONESELF IRREPLACEABLE Managers gain power when they have valuable knowledge and expertise that allow them to perform activities no one else can handle. This is the essence of being irreplaceable.[71] The more central these activities are to organizational effectiveness, the more power managers gain from being irreplaceable.

BEING IN A CENTRAL POSITION Managers in central positions are responsible for activities that are directly connected to an organization's goals and sources of competitive advantage and often are located in central positions in important communication networks in an organization.[72] Managers in key positions have control over crucial organizational activities and initiatives and have access to important information. Other organizational members depend on them for their knowledge, expertise, advice, and support, and the success of the organization as a whole is seen as riding on these managers. These consequences of being in a central position are likely to increase managers' power.

Managers who are outstanding performers, have a wide knowledge base, and have made important and visible contributions to their organizations are likely to be offered central positions that will increase their power.

GENERATING RESOURCES Organizations need three kinds of resources to be effective: (1) input resources such as raw materials, skilled workers, and financial capital; (2) technical resources such as machinery and computers; and (3) knowledge resources such as marketing, information technology, or engineering expertise. To the extent that a manager can generate one or more of these kinds of resources for an organization, that manager's power is likely to increase.[73] In universities, for example, professors who win large grants to fund their research, from associations such as the National Science Foundation and the Army Research Institute, gain power because of the financial resources they generate for their departments and the university as a whole.

BUILDING ALLIANCES When managers build alliances, they develop mutually beneficial relationships with people both inside and outside the organization. The parties to an alliance support one another because doing so is in their best interests, and all parties benefit from the alliance. Alliances give managers power because they provide the managers with support for their initiatives. Partners to alliances provide support because they know the managers will reciprocate when their partners need support. Alliances can help managers achieve their goals and implement needed changes in organizations because they increase managers' levels of power. As illustrated in the following "Focus on Diversity" box, many powerful top managers such as Indra Nooyi, chair and CEO of PepsiCo, are particularly skilled when it comes to building alliances.[74]

Focus on Diversity

Indra Nooyi Builds Alliances

By all counts Indra Nooyi is a powerful business leader.[75] As CEO and chair of PepsiCo, she oversees a company with over $43 billion in revenues and over 198,000 employees; Pepsi-Cola, Lay's, Doritos, Tropicana, Mountain Dew, Gatorade, and Quaker are among Pepsi's many well-known brands.[76] She effectively uses her vision for PepsiCo, "Performance with Purpose," both to motivate and guide Pepsi employees and to communicate PepsiCo's stance on important issues such as health, obesity, and protecting the natural environment around the world.[77] In 2008 she was included in *Time* magazine's list of "The World's Most Influential People";[78] in 2007, 2008, and 2009 she was ranked the most powerful woman in business by *Fortune* magazine.[79]

Nooyi, born and raised in India, was senior vice president of strategic planning at PepsiCo before assuming the top post on October 1, 2006.[80] When the PepsiCo board of directors was deciding who would be the next CEO of the company, two senior executives at PepsiCo were under consideration, Nooyi and Michael White, vice chairman.[81] When Nooyi found out the board had chosen her, one of her top priorities was to ensure that White would stay at PepsiCo, the two would maintain the great relationship they had with each other that had evolved from years of working together, and she would have his support and advice.[82] At the time White was on vacation at his beach house in Cape Cod, Massachusetts. Nooyi flew to Cape Cod and the two walked on the beach, had ice cream together, and even played a duet (Nooyi and White both are fond of music, and in this case he played the piano and she sang). Prior to leaving Cape Cod, she told White, "Tell me whatever I need to do to keep you, and I will."[83] Ultimately White decided to remain at PepsiCo as CEO of PepsiCo International as well as vice chairman of PepsiCo.[84] At a meeting announcing Nooyi's appointment, Nooyi told employees, "I treat Mike as my partner. He could easily have been CEO." White said, "I play the piano and Indra sings."[85] In 2009 White retired from PepsiCo.[86]

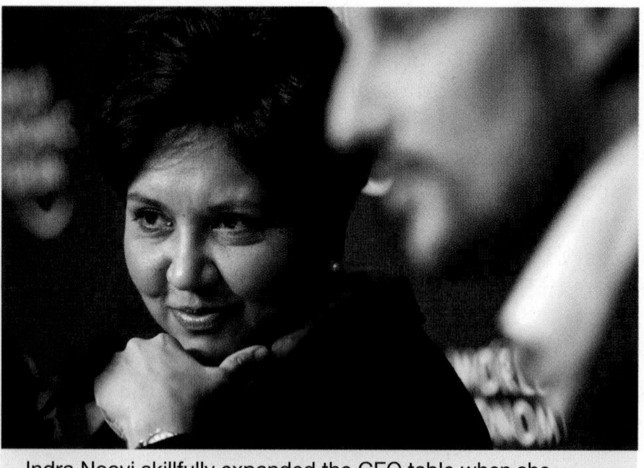

Indra Nooyi skillfully expanded the CEO table when she assumed the reins at PepsiCo; by openly asking for help from other key executives and previous CEOs, she has ensured that she isn't flying blind.

Nooyi excels at building alliances both inside and outside of PepsiCo. Given the breadth of her responsibilities, she decided to increase the team of top managers she works closely with to 29 (which is around double the size of the team before she became CEO). She has good relations with key decision makers around the world in both government and business. And she frequently consults with and seeks the advice of three former CEOs of PepsiCo, Stephen Reinemund, Roger Enrico, and Don Kendall, whom she considers her friends.[87]

Nooyi also excels at gaining the support of PepsiCo's employees.[88] She is down-to-earth, sincere, and genuine in her interactions with employees and also comfortable just being herself; she has been known to walk barefoot in the halls of PepsiCo on occasion and sometimes sings at gatherings. Celebrations for employees' birthdays include a cake. Nooyi, as a mother of two daughters, also recognizes how employees' families are affected by their work and what a great source of support families can be.[89]

Of course Nooyi faces a number of challenges at PepsiCo as she strives to make the company more globally focused (and less focused on the United

States), make more healthful food products, protect the natural environment, and look out for the well-being of employees in a troubled economy with rising prices for ingredients in PepsiCo's products.[90] Her exceptional skills at building alliances and gaining support will help. As she indicates, ". . . you give the team of people a set of objectives and goals and get them all to buy into it, and they can move mountains."[91]

Many powerful top managers focus on building alliances not only inside their organizations but also with individuals, groups, and organizations in the task and general environments on which their organizations depend for resources. These individuals, groups, and organizations enter alliances with managers because doing so is in their best interests and they know they can count on the managers' support when they need it. When managers build alliances, they need to be on their guard to ensure that everything is aboveboard, ethical, and legal.

Political Strategies for Exercising Power

Politically skilled managers not only understand, and can use, the five strategies to increase their power; they also appreciate strategies for exercising their power. These strategies generally focus on how managers can use their power *unobtrusively*.[92] When managers exercise power unobtrusively, other members of an organization may not be aware that the managers are using their power to influence them. They may think they support these managers for a variety of reasons: because they believe it is the rational or logical thing to do, because they believe doing so is in their own best interests, or because they believe the position or decision the managers are advocating is legitimate or appropriate.

The unobtrusive use of power may sound devious, but managers typically use this strategy to bring about change and achieve organizational goals. Political strategies for exercising power to gain the support and concurrence of others include relying on objective information, bringing in an outside expert, controlling the agenda, and making everyone a winner (see Figure 17.5).[93]

RELYING ON OBJECTIVE INFORMATION Managers require the support of others to achieve their goals, implement changes, and overcome opposition. One way for a manager to gain this support and overcome opposition is to rely on objective information that supports the manager's initiatives. Reliance on objective information leads others to support the manager because of the facts; objective information causes others to believe that what the manager is proposing is the proper course of action. By relying on objective information, politically skilled managers unobtrusively exercise their power to influence others.

Take the case of Mary Callahan, vice president of Better Built Cabinets, a small cabinet company in the Southeast. Callahan is extremely influential in the company; practically every new initiative that she proposes to the president and owner of the company is implemented. Why is Callahan able to use her power in the company so effectively? Whenever she has an idea for a new initiative that she thinks the company might pursue, she and her subordinates begin by collecting objective information supporting the initiative. Recently Callahan decided that Better Built should develop a line of high-priced European-style kitchen cabinets. Before presenting her proposal to Better Built's president, she compiled objective information showing that (1) there was strong unmet demand for these kinds of cabinets, (2) Better Built could manufacture them in its existing production facilities, and (3) the new line had the potential to increase Better Built's sales by 20% while not detracting from sales of the company's other cabinets. Presented with this information, the president agreed to Callahan's proposal. Moreover, the president and other members of Better Built whose cooperation

Figure 17.5
Political Strategies for Exercising Power

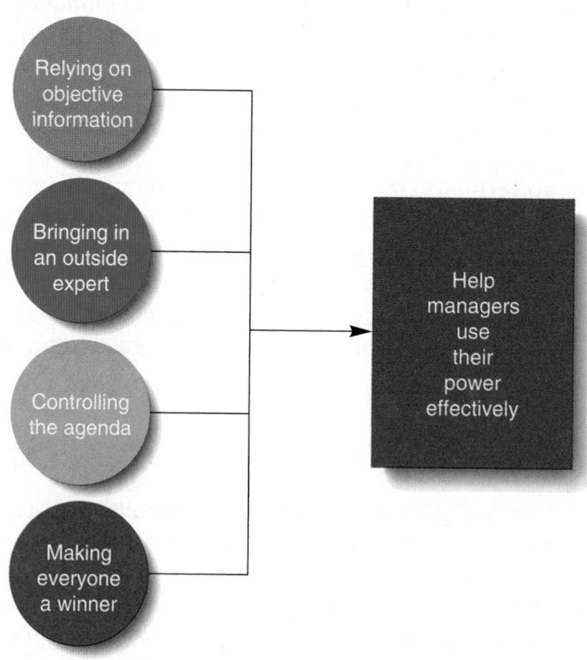

was needed to implement the proposal supported it because they thought it would help Better Built gain a competitive advantage. Using objective information to support her position enabled Callahan to unobtrusively exercise her power and influence others to support her proposal.

BRINGING IN AN OUTSIDE EXPERT Bringing in an outside expert to support a proposal or decision can, at times, provide managers with some of the same benefits that the use of objective information does. It lends credibility to a manager's initiatives and causes others to believe that what the manager is proposing is the appropriate or rational thing to do. Suppose Callahan had hired a consultant to evaluate whether her idea was a good one. The consultant reports back to the president that the new European-style cabinets are likely to fulfill Callahan's promises and increase Better Built's sales and profits. As with objective information, this information provided by an objective expert can lend a sense of legitimacy to Callahan's proposal and allow her to unobtrusively exercise power to influence others.

Although you might think consultants and other outside experts are neutral or objective, they sometimes are hired by managers who want them to support a certain position or decision in an organization. For instance, when managers face strong opposition from others who fear that a decision will harm their interests, the managers may bring in an outside expert. They hope this expert will be perceived as a neutral observer to lend credibility and "objectivity" to their point of view. The support of an outside expert may cause others to believe that a decision is indeed the right one. Of course sometimes consultants and other outside experts actually are brought into organizations *to be* objective and guide managers on the appropriate course of action.

CONTROLLING THE AGENDA Managers also can exercise power unobtrusively by controlling the agenda–influencing which alternatives are considered or even whether a decision is made.[94] When managers influence the alternatives that are considered, they can make sure that each considered alternative is acceptable to them and that undesirable alternatives are not in the feasible set. In a hiring context, for example, managers can exert their power unobtrusively by ensuring that job candidates whom they do not find acceptable do not make their way onto the list of finalists for an open position. They do this by making sure that these candidates' drawbacks or deficiencies are communicated to everyone involved in making the hiring decision. When three finalists for an open position are discussed and evaluated in a hiring meeting, a manager may seem to exert little power or influence and just go along with what the rest of the group wants. However, the manager may have exerted power in the hiring process unobtrusively by controlling which candidates made it to the final stage.

Sometimes managers can prevent a decision from being made. A manager in charge of a community relations committee, for example, may not favor a proposal for the organization to become more involved in local youth groups such as the Boy Scouts and the Girl Scouts. The manager can exert influence in this situation by not including the proposal on the agenda for the committee's next meeting. Alternatively, the manager could place the proposal at the end of the agenda for the meeting and feel confident that the committee will run out of time and not get to the last items on the agenda because that is what always happens. Either approach enables the manager to unobtrusively exercise power. Committee members do not perceive this manager as trying to influence them to turn down the proposal. Rather, the manager has made the proposal into a nonissue that is not even considered.

MAKING EVERYONE A WINNER Often, politically skilled managers can exercise their power unobtrusively because they make sure that everyone whose support they need benefits personally from providing that support. By making everyone a winner, a manager can influence other organizational members because these members see supporting the manager as being in their best interest.

When top managers turn around troubled companies, some organizational members and parts of the organization are bound to suffer due to restructurings that often entail painful layoffs. However, the power of the turnaround CEO often accelerates as it becomes clear that the future of the company is on surer footing and the organization and its stakeholders are winners as a result of the change effort.

Making everyone a winner not only is an effective way of exercising power but, when used consistently and forthrightly, can increase managers' power and influence over time. That is, when a manager actually does make everyone a winner, all stakeholders will see it as in their best interests to support the manager and his or her initiatives. When managers who make everyone a winner have strong ethical values, everyone really is a winner, as profiled in the following "Ethics in Action" box.

Ethics in Action

El Faro Benefits Multiple Stakeholders

When Estuardo Porras was taking business classes at Pepperdine University in Malibu, California, in the 1990s, he was surprised to see the high prices that Starbucks charged for coffee.[95] In his native country of Guatemala, coffee used to be the major export until prices declined in the 1980s due to a large influx of low-cost coffee beans coming on the market from countries like Vietnam. Porras had a vision of returning to Guatemala, resurrecting an old coffee plantation, and operating it in a socially responsible way that protected the natural environment, looked out for and contributed to the well-being of the workers who operated it and the local community, and produced high-quality coffee beans that a socially responsible organization like Starbucks would be interested in purchasing.[96]

Porras returned to Guatemala, borrowed $1.25 million from his father, who had recently sold a Coca-Cola bottling company, and transformed an abandoned plantation called El Faro into a marvel of environmental sustainability, social responsibility, and effectiveness.[97] El Faro protects the natural environment, helps a poor community, and produces high-quality arabica coffee used by specialty coffee companies like Starbucks. And because of Starbucks' commitment to purchasing coffee beans from growers that abide by ethical social and environmental values, El Faro can sell all the coffee beans it grows that meet Starbucks' standards for more than the beans would sell for on the general commodity export market.[98]

El Faro is located near a volcano, and the ash from the volcano provides excellent soil for growing coffee. Coffee beans are fermented in recycled water, and the casings from the beans are eaten by earthworms, yielding an organic fertilizer. Much of the work on the plantation is done by hand.[99] El Faro supports a free elementary school for children in the local community and buses older children to a high school in the vicinity. Employees receive free health care after they have been with El Faro for three months; the care is provided in the plantation's medical office, staffed by a part-time doctor and full-time nurse. They also receive 15 days of paid vacation annually. Many of El Faro's full-time employees and their families live on the plantation; El Faro also has part-time employees.[100]

Fermenting coffee beans in recycled water is just one of the many areas in which Estuardo Porras has transformed El Faro into a productive, environmentally responsible enterprise.

Porras initially sold El Faro's coffee beans on the commodity export market while persistently trying to make inroads at Starbucks by sending letters and coffee samples to no avail. Eventually an exporter who bought beans from El Faro persuaded two coffee buyers from Starbucks to visit the plantation. After a tour and coffee tasting, the buyers were so delighted with what they saw and tasted that they ordered coffee from El Faro that day and gave Porras the opportunity to participate in a program that gives long-terms contracts to growers who are socially responsible.[101]

Today El Faro Estate Coffee is sold exclusively to Starbucks, and Finca El Faro is a Starbucks's C.A.F.E. Practices supplier.[102] Clearly Porras has made everyone a winner and, in the process, has created a sustainable and thriving business.[103]

Summary and Review

LO17-1, 17-2 **ORGANIZATIONAL CONFLICT** Organizational conflict is the discord that arises when the goals, interests, or values of different individuals or groups are incompatible and those individuals or groups block or thwart each other's attempts to achieve their objectives. Four types of conflict arising in organizations are interpersonal conflict, intragroup conflict, intergroup conflict, and interorganizational conflict. Sources of conflict in organizations include different goals and time horizons, overlapping authority, task interdependencies, different evaluation or reward systems, scarce resources, and status inconsistencies. Conflict management strategies focused on individuals include increasing awareness of the sources of conflict, increasing diversity awareness and skills, practicing job rotation or temporary assignments, and using permanent transfers or dismissals when necessary. Strategies focused on the whole organization include changing an organization's structure or culture and altering the source of conflict.

LO17-3, 17-4 **NEGOTIATION** Negotiation is a conflict resolution technique used when parties to a conflict have approximately equal levels of power and try to come up with an acceptable way to allocate resources to each other. In distributive negotiation, the parties perceive that there is a fixed level of resources for them to allocate, and they compete to receive as much as possible at the expense of the other party, not caring about their relationship in the future. In integrative bargaining, both parties perceive that they may be able to increase the resource pie by coming up with a creative solution to the conflict, trusting each other, and cooperating with each other to achieve a win–win resolution. Five strategies that managers can use to facilitate integrative bargaining are to emphasize superordinate goals; focus on the problem, not the people; focus on interests, not demands; create new options for joint gain; and focus on what is fair.

LO17-5 **ORGANIZATIONAL POLITICS** Organizational politics are the activities that managers (and other members of an organization) engage in to increase their power and to use power effectively to achieve their goals and overcome resistance or opposition. Effective managers realize that politics can be a positive force that enables them to make needed changes in an organization. Five important political strategies for gaining and maintaining power are controlling uncertainty, making oneself irreplaceable, being in a central position, generating resources, and building alliances. Political strategies for effectively exercising power focus on how to use power unobtrusively and include relying on objective information, bringing in an outside expert, controlling the agenda, and making everyone a winner.

Management in Action

Topics for Discussion and Action

Discussion

1. Discuss why too little conflict in an organization can be just as detrimental as too much conflict. [LO17-1]
2. Why are compromise and collaboration more effective ways of handling conflict than accommodation, avoidance, and competition? [LO17-2]
3. Why should managers promote integrative bargaining rather than distributive negotiation? [LO17-3]
4. How can managers promote integrative bargaining? [LO17-4]
5. Why do organizational politics affect practically every organization? [LO17-5]
6. Why do effective managers need good political skills? [LO17-5]
7. What steps can managers take to ensure that organizational politics are a positive force leading to a competitive advantage, not a negative force leading to personal advantage at the expense of organizational goal attainment? [LO17-5]
8. Think of a member of an organization whom you know and who is particularly powerful. What political strategies does this person use to increase his or her power? [LO17-5]
9. Why is it best to use power unobtrusively? How are people likely to react to power that is exercised obtrusively? [LO17-5]

Action

10. Interview a manager in a local organization to determine the kinds of conflicts that occur in his or her organization and the strategies that are used to manage them. [LO17-1, 17-2]

Building Management Skills [LO17-1, 17-2]

Effective and Ineffective Conflict Resolution

Think about two recent conflicts that you had with other people—one conflict that you felt was effectively resolved (C1) and one that you felt was ineffectively resolved (C2). The other people involved could be coworkers, students, family members, friends, or members of an organization that you are a member of. Answer the following questions:

1. Briefly describe C1 and C2. What type of conflict was involved in each of these incidents?
2. What was the source of the conflict in C1 and in C2?
3. What conflict management strategies were used in C1 and in C2?
4. What could you have done differently to more effectively manage conflict in C2?
5. How was the conflict resolved in C1 and in C2?

Managing Ethically [LO17-5]

One political strategy managers can engage in is controlling the agenda by subtly influencing which alternatives are considered or even whether a decision is up for discussion. Some employees believe this can be unethical and can prevent important issues from being raised and points of view from being expressed.

Questions

1. Either individually or in a group, think about the ethical implications of controlling the agenda as a political strategy.
2. What steps can managers and organizations take to ensure that this strategy does not result in important issues and differing points of view being suppressed in an organization?

Small Group Breakout Exercise [LO17-3, 17-4]

Negotiating a Solution

Form groups of three or four people. One member of your group will play the role of Jane Rister, one member will play the role of Michael Schwartz, and one or two members will be observer(s) and spokesperson(s) for your group.

Jane Rister and Michael Schwartz are assistant managers in a large department store. They report directly to the store manager. Today they are meeting to discuss some important problems they need to solve but about which they disagree.

The first problem hinges on the fact that either Rister or Schwartz needs to be on duty whenever the store is open. For the last six months, Rister has taken most of the least desirable hours (nights and weekends). They are planning their schedules for the next six months. Rister thought Schwartz would take more of the undesirable times, but Schwartz has informed Rister that his wife has just gotten a nursing job that requires her to work weekends, so he needs to stay home weekends to take care of their infant daughter.

The second problem concerns a department manager who has had a hard time retaining salespeople in his department. The turnover rate in his department is twice that in the other store departments. Rister thinks the manager is ineffective and wants to fire him. Schwartz thinks the high turnover is just a fluke and the manager is effective.

The last problem concerns Rister's and Schwartz's vacation schedules. Both managers want to take off the week of July 4, but one of them needs to be in the store whenever it is open.

1. The group members playing Rister and Schwartz assume their roles and negotiate a solution to these three problems.
2. Observers take notes on how Rister and Schwartz negotiate solutions to their problems.
3. Observers determine the extent to which Rister and Schwartz use distributive negotiation or integrative bargaining to resolve their conflicts.
4. When called on by the instructor, observers communicate to the rest of the class how Rister and Schwartz resolved their conflicts, whether they used distributive negotiation or integrative bargaining, and their actual solutions.

Exploring the World Wide Web [LO17-1, 17-2]

Think of a major conflict in the business world that you have read about in the newspaper in the past few weeks. Then search on the Web for magazine and newspaper articles presenting differing viewpoints and perspectives on the conflict. Based on what you have read, how are the parties to this conflict handling it? Is their approach functional or dysfunctional, and why?

Be the Manager [LO17-1, 17-2, 17-3, 17-4, 17-5]

You are a middle manager in a large corporation, and lately you feel that you are caught between a rock and a hard place. Times are tough; your unit has experienced layoffs; your surviving subordinates are overworked and demoralized; and you feel that you have no meaningful rewards, such as the chance for a pay raise, bonus, or promotion, to motivate them with. Your boss keeps increasing the demands on your unit as well as the unit's responsibilities. Moreover, you believe that you and your subordinates are being unfairly blamed for certain problems beyond your control. You believe that you have the expertise and skills to perform your job effectively and also that your subordinates are capable and effective in their jobs. Yet you feel that you are on shaky ground and powerless given the current state of affairs. What are you going to do?

Case in the News [LO17-1, 17-2, 17-5]

Tough Love at Chrysler

When Fiat-Chrysler Chief Executive Officer Sergio Marchionne spoke for the first time to his new U.S. employees in June, he quickly dispensed with the rah-rah rhetoric. Standing in the four-story atrium at Chrysler's Auburn Hills (Michigan) headquarters, a couple thousand people hanging on his every word, the new chief thanked U.S. taxpayers for their forbearance and praised Chrysler veterans for their fortitude. Shortly after that, Marchionne, a rumpled figure in slacks and a black polo shirt sporting a Chrysler logo, cut to the chase. "In this business," he said, "mediocrity will kill you. We can't accept it."

For the third time in 11 years, Chrysler is bracing for the vagaries of new ownership. First it was the Germans, then the private equity guys, now the Italians. Many executives who watched Marchionne that day express relief that he and Fiat want to revive an automaker many had given up for dead. On the other hand, they have heard about the new boss's operating style. Marchionne, who declined to comment, demands teamwork while pitting divisions against each other. He isn't afraid to promote from deep in the ranks, and he expects executives to put in seven-day weeks as he does. That's how he brought Fiat back from the brink. "Only two people have turned around car companies [recently], Sergio and Nissan's Carlos Ghosn," says Ron Bloom, who heads the U.S. Treasury Department's Auto Task Force. "His decision making moves quickly. He's a firm believer in meritocracy."

Man in a Hurry

There is little time to waste. Bankruptcy harmed a company that already had lost much of the buying public. Chrysler's models are older and less fuel-efficient than rivals'; not one vehicle gets the Consumer Reports seal of approval. Then there are the gaping holes in the lineup.

Marchionne will have to restore luster to Jeep, Chrysler, and Dodge, and plug those holes with small, fuel-efficient vehicles designed by Fiat. His biggest challenge will be replacing misfires such as the Sebring sedan, Jeep Compass, and Dodge Caliber—with the kind of mass-market vehicles that will make or break Chrysler. "Getting that right is where a lot of energy is being poured because that's the cake and the rest is icing," says a Chrysler executive, who expects Marchionne to approve a five-year product plan this month.

It doesn't help that Marchionne, 57, is inheriting a company suffering a crisis of confidence. The Chrysler of yore was a swaggering place—agile and unafraid of taking chances. In 1998 Daimler bought the company and over the next nine years managed to squelch much of the Chrysler esprit de corps. Two years ago Cerberus Capital Management gained control. Faced with a far worse market than anyone had predicted, Cerberus cut and cut—and then cut some more.

Marchionne assumed Chrysler still had a brain trust. He wasn't about to bring in a bunch of outsiders. "He thinks there are good people at Chrysler," says Stefano Aversa, co-chief of the consultancy Alix Partners, who has worked with Marchionne. "He wants to retain the U.S. culture." Of Marchionne's 23 direct reports at Chrysler, 3 came from Fiat.

Rather than rely on suggestions from top management, Marchionne asked more than 100 middle- and lower-ranked staffers what they thought of their bosses. Then, say people familiar with the process, he picked people most respected by their subordinates. "If he didn't hear expressions of leadership voluntarily from people, he took it as a sign that they didn't view the executive as a leader," says a staffer Marchionne interviewed. Several senior people have since left, including the sales and marketing chief and the product development czar.

Marchionne then reached deep into the company to find talent. For example, he grabbed Peter L. Fong, who was running sales for the mid-Atlantic states, and made him president and CEO of the Chrysler brand. An outside executive who was privy to the process says Marchionne had heard Fong was a great sales guy and well-respected.

To help strengthen and focus Chrysler's brands, Marchionne decided they should compete with each other for marketing and development resources. He has turned Dodge, Jeep, and Chrysler into separate companies, each with its own CEO. The risk is that the brand chiefs wind up undermining each other. To prevent that, Marchionne gave these executives corporate responsibilities, too. For example, Fong runs the Chrysler brand but is also in charge of sales for the whole company. The Dodge chief is responsible for the marketing strategy of all three brands.

No lover of hierarchy and process, Marchionne has stripped people of fancy titles and moved the CEO's office from the 15th story to the ground floor, where designers and engineers dream up new cars. He encourages low- and midlevel staff to keep the work moving even if they have to bypass a supervisor to get a project or expenditure approved. Before, says a Chrysler executive, "People guarded the chain of command and their titles like mother lions."

Marchionne is at heart a delegator. He sets goals and expects his reports to tell him how to proceed. For example, the chief was set on quickly bringing Fiat to the United States and ditching the Chrysler brand. His team persuaded him that doing so would be too expensive right now. But there is one area where Marchionne gets deeply hands-on: marketing, a discipline that Chrysler desperately needs to get right. Marchionne personally approves every ad and already has been meeting with BBDO, the automaker's long-time advertising agency.

Marchionne's plan to combine the best of Fiat (small cars) with the best of Chrysler (pickups, minivans, and SUVs) makes sense in theory. But today's auto market is every bit as Darwinian as Marchionne's management philosophy. As he told his troops in June, "We have been given this incredible second chance to rethink everything we do. There will not be a third."

Questions for Discussion

1. To what extent do you think Sergio Marchionne is effectively managing conflict at Fiat-Chrysler?
2. What steps is he taking to try to ensure that the company has an optimal level of conflict?
3. How is he trying to promote collaboration at Fiat-Chrysler?
4. In what ways has he tried to make everyone a winner?

Source: D. Welch, D. Kiley, and C. Matlack, "Tough Love at Chrysler," *BusinessWeek,* August 24 and 31, 2009, 26–28. Reprinted from August 24, 2009 and August 31, 2009 issue of *Bloomberg Businessweek* by special permission, copyright © 2009 by Bloomberg L.P.

CHAPTER 18

Using Advanced Information Technology to Increase Performance

Learning Objectives

After studying this chapter, you should be able to:

LO18-1 Differentiate between data and information, and explain how the attributes of useful information allow managers to make better decisions.

LO18-2 Describe three reasons why managers must have access to information to perform their tasks and roles effectively.

LO18-3 Describe the computer hardware and software innovations that created the IT revolution and changed the way managers behave.

LO18-4 Differentiate among seven performance-enhancing kinds of management information systems.

LO18-5 Explain how IT is helping managers build strategic alliances and network structures to increase efficiency and effectiveness.

A MANAGER'S CHALLENGE

Cloud Computing, Bricks and Mortar, and Mobile Container Data Center Storage Solutions

How can managers create competitive advantage through IT? Server computers (servers) are designed to provide powerful, information-intensive computing solutions that in the past could have been executed only on huge, expensive mainframe computers. Servers also link networks of desktop and laptop PCs, and they link to wireless personal digital assistants (PDAs) such as netbooks, tablet computers, and smartphones. Using this array of computing devices, a company's employees can access its installed software applications and databases to obtain the real-time information they need to manage ongoing activities. In the 2000s the computing power of servers increased enormously as Intel and AMD competed to develop ever more advanced microprocessors (chips). Today servers can process staggering amounts of data to execute highly complex software applications, and they can access and store amazing amounts of information. Server sales have increased greatly over time (the server market was $30 billion in 2009) because of their ever-increasing computing power and low cost compared to mainframes—although most large companies still use a single mainframe as the "brain" that stores the most essential, secret, and important operating routines and to coordinate the companywide computing network.

Blackbox server racks, such as this one created by Sun Microsystems, offer a significant safeguard to companies looking for cost- and space-conscious ways to back up their information.

As large companies began to buy hundreds and then thousands of servers to meet their increasing need to process and store information, server makers such as HP, Dell, and Sun designed *rack servers* that link individual servers together to increase their joint power. For example, a rack server links an individual server into a rack of 10 connected servers; then 10 racks create a network of 100 servers; 100 racks create a network of a thousand servers, and so on. Using software from specialized companies such as IBM and Oracle to link the operations of these server racks, large companies developed "server farms," which are bricks and mortar (B&M) operating facilities that are remote and physically separate from company headquarters. Server farms are database centers composed of thousands of networked server racks that are constantly monitored, maintained, and upgraded by a company's IT engineers (or specialized outsourcers such as IBM) to protect a company's information and databases. Should a company lose such information, it would be helpless; it would have no record of its transactions with its employees, customers, suppliers, and so on. IT and database storage are the lifeblood of a global company, which cannot function without them. But a growing concern of managers today is how to reduce the costs of database storage, which are hundreds of millions of dollars for large companies.

In the late 2000s a new way to offer companies a quick, efficient way to enlarge and upgrade their database center capabilities to respond to the vast increase in Internet use was to house these server racks in standard-size storage containers—the same kind of containers hauled on trucks or stacked on cargo ships. The first U.S. server maker to offer such a mobile database solution was Sun, which launched its "Blackbox" data center containing its proprietary Solaris rack servers in a 20-foot shipping container. Each Blackbox contained a mobile data center that could deliver the computing capability of a 9,000-square-foot physical data center but would cost only about one-fifth as much. Another company called SGI quickly announced its own new "Concentro" mobile server container—the first self-contained data center based on custom-designed, high-density server racks and data storage housed in a larger 40 × 20-foot shipping container.[1] Because SGI's space-saving rack servers are half as deep as standard servers, it could cram in twice as many individual servers into a 40-foot container as could its competitors. The immense processing power of SGI's Concentro containers, equivalent to a 30,000-square-foot B&M data center, allowed companies to rethink their need for high-cost bricks-and-mortar data centers, especially given the relatively low operating costs of SGI containers compared to physical data centers. Mobile data centers offered companies a low-cost solution and were snapped up by companies such as Google, Yahoo!, and Amazon.

Also in the late 2000s the term *cloud computing* was popularized by companies like IBM, Microsoft, and Google to refer to a new way to offer companies computing and data storage service similar to how they used and paid for utilities like water or electricity. The strategy behind cloud computing was to create (1) a cost-effective Internet-based global platform of hardware and software provided by (2) a network of thousands of interlinked IT companies that had (3) the capability to provide a full range of on-demand software applications, computing services, and database storage to millions of companies and individuals around the world. The advantage of cloud-based Web services was that the cost of running applications or storing data through the Internet was much less than the cost of purchasing hardware and installing software on in-house servers. Cloud computing was like an alliance in which IT companies pooled their resources to share processing power and applications that let them offer better prices to customers. For example, installing and managing the software and hardware to operate a specialized software application might cost $50,000 a year; in cloud computing the same service could be rented for $500 a month—this is why Amazon, Google, and Microsoft pushed cloud computing so vigorously.

In sum, cloud computing offered outsourced, pay-as-you-go, on-demand, Internet software capabilities to companies for a fee. Of course a major concern of users is information reliability and security. If cloud computing expands, even the largest companies may cease to operate their own database centers and outsource all their information and computing operations to Web-based IT providers because they can perform these IT activities at a significantly lower cost than any particular company.

But even cloud computing providers must house their operations in B&M or mobile container data center facilities. So this will also help companies like SGI, whose mobile storage containers are bought not only by companies that wish to reduce the costs of managing their own data centers but also by outsourcers. Obviously outsourcers will search for the lowest-cost mobile server rack solutions; and demand for storage server containers has increased so much that Dell, HP, and IBM have all announced new mobile server-based solutions. The problems facing managers is to choose the most efficient and effective method to manage their companywide computing networks and database storage operations to reduce operating costs by millions or billions of dollars a year.

Overview

In a world in which business activities of all kinds are increasingly conducted through the Internet, the challenge facing managers is to continually update and improve their use of advancing IT to increase organizational performance. Managers must work to adopt the most effective IT solutions for their employees and customers or risk being surpassed by more effective rivals who have developed superior IT competencies. Google and Apple have become two of the most valuable companies in the world because they provide advanced IT solutions that increase people's ability to access, search, and use the potential of the World Wide Web and communicate with others. The most successful B&M and online companies, such as Walmart, Best Buy, Amazon.com, and eBay, excel in developing improved company-specific IT solutions. The implication is clear: There are enormous opportunities for managers of all kinds of organizations to find new ways to use IT to use organizational resources more efficiently and effectively.

In this chapter we begin by looking at the relationship between information and the manager's job and then examine the ongoing IT revolution. Then we discuss six types of management information systems, each of which is based on a different sort of IT, which can help managers perform their jobs more efficiently and effectively. Next we examine the impact of rapidly evolving IT on managers' jobs and on an organization's competitive advantage. By the end of this chapter, you will understand how new developments in IT are profoundly shaping managers' tasks and roles and the way organizations operate.

Information and the Manager's Job

Managers cannot plan, organize, lead, and control effectively unless they have access to information. Information is the source of the knowledge and intelligence they need to make the right decisions. Information, however, is not the same as data.[2] **Data** are raw, unsummarized, and unanalyzed facts such as volume of sales, level of costs, or number of customers. **Information** is data that are organized in a meaningful fashion, such as in a graph showing the changes in sales volume or costs over time. Data alone do not tell managers anything; information, in contrast, can communicate a great deal of useful knowledge to the person who receives it–such as a manager who sees sales falling or costs rising. The distinction between data and information is important because one purpose of IT is to help managers transform data into information to make better managerial decisions.

data Raw, unsummarized, and unanalyzed facts.

information Data that are organized in a meaningful fashion.

To further clarify the difference between data and information, consider a supermarket manager who must decide how much shelf space to allocate to two breakfast cereal brands: Dentist's Delight and Sugar Supreme. Most supermarkets use checkout scanners to record individual sales and store the data on a computer. Accessing this computer, the manager might find that Dentist's Delight sells 50 boxes per day and Sugar Supreme sells 25 boxes per day. These raw data, however, are of little help in helping the manager decide how to allocate shelf space. The manager also needs to know how much shelf space each cereal currently occupies and how much profit each cereal generates for the supermarket.

LO18-1 Differentiate between data and information, and explain how the attributes of useful information allow managers to make better decisions.

Suppose the manager discovers that Dentist's Delight occupies 10 feet of shelf space and Sugar Supreme occupies 4 feet and that Dentist's Delight generates 20 cents of profit a box while Sugar Supreme generates 40 cents of profit a box. By putting these three bits of data together (number of boxes sold, amount of shelf space, and profit per box), the manager gets some useful information on which to base a decision: Dentist's Delight generates $1 of profit per foot of shelf space per day [(50 boxes × $.20)/10 feet], and Sugar Supreme generates $2.50 of profit per foot of shelf space per day [(25 boxes × $.40)/4 feet]. Armed with this information, the manager might decide to allocate less shelf space to Dentist's Delight and more to Sugar Supreme.

Attributes of Useful Information

Four factors determine the usefulness of information to a manager: quality, timeliness, completeness, and relevance (see Figure 18.1).

Figure 18.1
Factors Affecting the Usefulness of Information

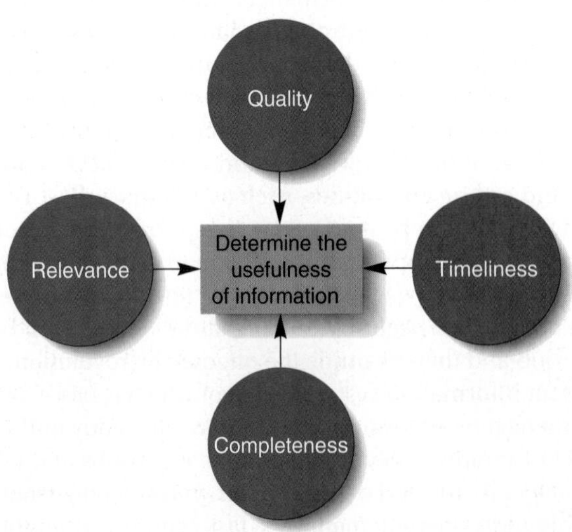

QUALITY Accuracy and reliability determine the quality of information.[3] The greater its accuracy and reliability, the higher is the quality of information. Modern IT gives managers access to high-quality real-time information that they can use to improve long-term decision making and alter short-term operating decisions, such as how much of a particular product to make daily or monthly. Supermarket managers, for example, use handheld bar code readers linked to a server to monitor and record how demand for particular products such as milk, chicken, or bread changes daily so they know how to restock their shelves to ensure the products are always available.

TIMELINESS Information that is timely is available when it is required to allow managers to make the optimal decision–not after the decision has been made. In today's rapidly changing world, the need for timely information often means information must be available on a real-time basis–hence the enormous growth in the demand for PDAs such as smartphones.[4] **Real-time information** is information that reflects current changes in business conditions. In an industry that experiences rapid changes, real-time information may need to be updated frequently.

real-time information Frequently updated information that reflects current conditions.

Airlines use real-time information about the number of flight bookings and competitors' prices to adjust their prices hourly to maximize their revenues. Thus, for example, the fare for flights from New York to Seattle might change from one hour to the next as fares are reduced to fill empty seats and raised when most seats have been sold. Airlines use real-time information about reservations to adjust fares at the last possible moment to fill planes and maximize revenues. U.S. airlines make more than 100,000 fare changes each day.[5] Obviously the managers who make such pricing decisions need real-time information about current market demand.

COMPLETENESS Information that is complete gives managers all the information they need to exercise control, achieve coordination, or make an effective decision. Recall from Chapter 7, however, that managers rarely have access to complete information. Instead, because of uncertainty, ambiguity, and bounded rationality, they have to make do with incomplete information.[6] One function of IT is to increase the completeness of managers' information.

RELEVANCE Information that is relevant is useful and suits a manager's particular needs and circumstances. Irrelevant information is useless and may actually hurt the performance of a busy manager who has to spend valuable time determining whether information is relevant. Given the massive amounts of information that managers are now exposed to and their limited information-processing capabilities, a company's information systems designers need to ensure that managers receive only relevant information.

information technology The set of methods or techniques for acquiring, organizing, storing, manipulating, and transmitting information.

management information system (MIS) A specific form of IT that managers utilize to generate the specific, detailed information they need to perform their roles effectively.

What Is Information Technology?

Information technology (IT) is the set of methods or techniques for acquiring, organizing, storing, manipulating, and transmitting information.[7] A **management information system (MIS)** is a specific form of IT that managers select and use to generate the specific, detailed information they need to perform their roles effectively. Management information systems have existed for as long as there have been organizations, which is a long time indeed–merchants in ancient Egypt used clay tablets to record their transactions. Before the computing age, most systems were paper-based: Clerks recorded important information on paper documents (often in duplicate or triplicate) in words and numbers; sent copies of the documents to superiors, customers, or suppliers; and stored other copies in filing cabinets for future reference.

Rapid advances in the power of IT–specifically the development of ever more powerful and sophisticated computer hardware and software–have had a fundamental impact on organizations and managers, as suggested by the developments in the server data center storage business discussed in "A Manager's Challenge."[8] Some recent IT developments, such as inventory management and customer relationship management (CRM) systems, contribute so much to performance that organizations that do

LO18-2 Describe three reasons why managers must have access to information to perform their tasks and roles effectively.

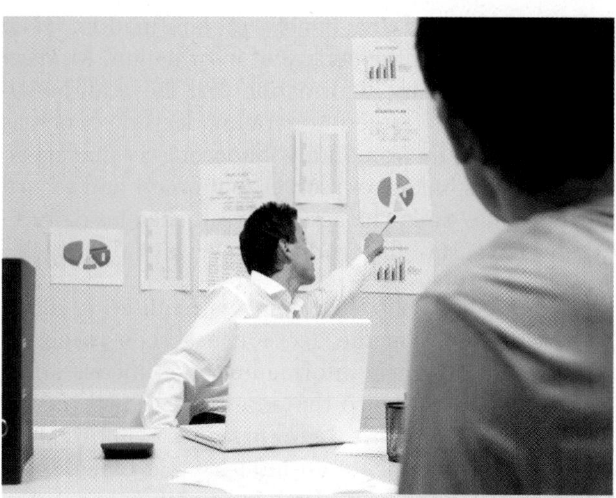

Charts and graphs may be the clichéd centerpieces of managerial meetings, but the data they represent are key for making informed decisions.

not adopt it, or that implement it ineffectively, become uncompetitive compared with organizations that do adopt it.[9] In the 2000s much of the increasing productivity and efficiency of business in general has been attributed to the way organizations and their employees use advancing IT to improve their performance.

Managers need information for three reasons: to make effective decisions, to control the activities of the organization, and to coordinate the activities of the organization. Next we examine these uses of information in detail.

Information and Decisions

Much of management (planning, organizing, leading, and controlling) is about making decisions. For example, the marketing manager must decide what price to charge for a product, what distribution channels to use, and what promotional messages to emphasize to maximize sales. The manufacturing manager must decide how much of a product to make and how to make it. The purchasing manager must decide from whom to purchase inputs and what inventory of inputs to hold. The human relations manager must decide how much employees should be paid, how they should be trained, and what benefits they should be given. The engineering manager must make decisions about new product design. Top managers must decide how to allocate scarce financial resources among competing projects, how best to structure and control the organization, and what business-level strategy the organization should be pursuing. And regardless of their functional orientation, all managers have to make decisions about matters such as what performance evaluation to give to a subordinate.

To make effective decisions, managers need information both from inside the organization and from external stakeholders. When deciding how to price a product, for example, marketing managers need information about how consumers will react to different prices. They need information about unit costs because they do not want to set the price below the cost of production. And they need information about competitive strategy because pricing strategy should be consistent with an organization's competitive strategy. Some of this information will come from outside the organization (for example, from consumer surveys) and some from inside the organization (information about production costs comes from manufacturing). As this example suggests, managers' ability to make effective decisions rests on their ability to acquire and process information.

Information and Control

As discussed in Chapter 11, controlling is the process through which managers regulate how efficiently and effectively an organization and its members perform the activities necessary to achieve its stated goals.[10] Managers achieve control over organizational activities by taking four steps (see Figure 11.2 on page 359): (1) They establish measurable standards of performance or goals; (2) they measure actual performance; (3) they compare actual performance against established goals; and (4) they evaluate the results and take corrective action if necessary.[11] The package delivery company UPS, for example, has a delivery goal: to deliver 95% of the overnight packages it picks up by noon the next day.[12] UPS has thousands of U.S. ground stations (branch offices that coordinate the pickup and delivery of packages in a particular area) that are responsible for the physical pickup and delivery of packages. UPS managers monitor the delivery performance of these stations regularly; if they find that the 95% goal is not being attained, they determine why and take corrective action if necessary.

To achieve control over any organizational activity, managers must have information. To control ground station activities, a UPS manager might need to know what percentage of packages each station delivers by noon. To obtain this information the manager uses UPS's own IT; UPS is also a leader in developing proprietary in-house IT. All packages to be shipped to the stations have been scanned with handheld scanners by the UPS drivers who pick them up; then all this information is sent wirelessly through UPS servers to its headquarter's mainframe computer. When the packages are scanned again at delivery, this information is also transmitted through its computer network. Managers can access this information to quickly discover what percentage of packages were delivered by noon of the day after they were picked up, and also how this information breaks down station by station so they can take corrective action if necessary.

Management information systems are used to control all divisional and functional operations. In accounting, for example, information systems are used to monitor expenditures and compare them against budgets.[13] To track expenditures against budgets, managers need information about current expenditures, broken down by relevant organizational units; accounting IT is designed to give managers this information. An example of IT used to monitor and control the daily activities of employees is the online MBO information system used by T. J. Rodgers at Cypress Semiconductor, discussed in Chapter 11. Rodgers implemented IT that allows him to review the goals of all his employees in about four hours.[14] At first glance it might seem that advances in IT would have a limited impact on the business of an office furniture maker; however, this assumption would be incorrect, as the following "Management Insight" box suggests.

Management Insight

Herman Miller's Office of the Future

Managers at Herman Miller have been finding countless ways to use IT and the Internet to give their company a competitive advantage over rival office furniture makers (OFMs) such as Steelcase and Hon.[15] Early on, Miller's managers saw the potential of the Internet for selling its furniture to business customers. Other furniture companies' Web sites were simply online advertisements for their products, services, and other marketing information. But Miller's managers quickly realized the true potential of using both the company's intranet and the Internet to reach customers to gain competitive advantage.

First Miller's managers developed IT that linked all the company's dealers and salespeople to its manufacturing hub so sales orders could be coordinated with the custom design department and with manufacturing, enabling customers to receive pricing and scheduling information promptly. Then, with this customer delivery system in place, Miller developed IT to link its manufacturing operations with its network of suppliers so its input supply chain would be coordinated with its customer needs.

When Miller's managers noticed that competitors were imitating its IT, they searched for new ways to maintain their competitive advantage. Soon they realized IT could transform the office furniture business itself. When they began to define Herman Miller as a digital enterprise infused with e-business, they realized IT could not only improve efficiency but also change how the customer experienced Herman Miller and increase value for the customer. A major Web initiative was the establishment of an e-learning tool, Uknowit.com, which became Herman Miller's online university. Via the Web thousands of Miller's employees and dealers are currently enrolled in Uknowit.com, where they choose from 85 courses covering technology, products and services, product applications, selling

Herman Miller's custom-made ergonomic office furniture arrives on time due to the company's use of IT that links its dealers with its manufacturing hub.

skills, and industry competitive knowledge. The benefits to Miller and its dealers and customers from this IT initiative are improved speed to market and ability to respond to competitors' tactics. Salespeople and dealers now have the information and tools they need to better compete for and keep customers.

Moreover, the office furniture business offers highly customized solutions to its customers. A main source of competitive advantage is the ability to give customers exactly what they want at the right price. Using its new IT, Miller's salespeople give design and manufacturing more accurate and timely information, which has reduced specification errors during the selling process. Also, with the new systems time to market has been reduced, and Miller is committed to being able to offer customers highly customized furniture in 10 or fewer business days.

Of course all these IT initiatives have been costly to Herman Miller. Thousands of hours of management time have been spent developing the IT and providing content, such as information about competitors, for the company's online classes. Herman Miller's managers are looking at the long term; they believe they have created a real source of competitive advantage for their company that will sustain it in the years ahead. And the company was voted as one of the most admired companies by *Fortune* in 2010 because its managers try to keep their IT one step ahead of its competitors.[16]

Information and Coordination

Coordinating department and divisional activities to achieve organizational goals is another basic task of management. As an example of the size of the coordination task that managers face, consider the coordination effort necessary to build Boeing's 787 Dreamliner jet aircraft, which is assembled from over 3 million individual parts.[17] Managers at Boeing have to coordinate the production and delivery of all these parts so every part arrives at Boeing's Everett, Washington, facility exactly when it is needed (for example, the wings should arrive before the engines). To achieve this high level of coordination, managers need information about which global supplier is producing what part, and when it will be produced. To meet this need, managers at Boeing created global IT that links Boeing to all its suppliers and can track the flow of 3 million components through the production process around the world in real time–an immense task. Indeed, as we noted in earlier chapters Boeing's IT system could not match the enormous complexity of the task, and the launch of its new airliner was delayed until 2010 because of IT glitches that affected communication with suppliers.

Managers face increasing coordination problems in managing their global supply chains to take advantage of national differences in production costs. As a result, managers must adopt ever more sophisticated IT that helps them coordinate the flow of materials, semifinished goods, and finished products throughout the world. Consider, for example, how Bose, which manufactures some of the world's highest-quality speakers, manages its global supply chain. Bose purchases almost all the components for its speakers, and about half of these components come from overseas suppliers, mainly in Asia. The challenge for managers is to coordinate this global supply chain to minimize Bose's inventory and transportation costs, which is achieved when components arrive at Bose's assembly plant just in time to enter the production process. Bose also has to remain responsive to customer demands, which means its suppliers have to be able to respond quickly to changes in Bose's demand for specific kinds of components and increase or decrease production as needed.

The responsibility for coordinating the supply chain to simultaneously minimize inventory and transportation costs and respond quickly to changing customer demands belongs to Bose's logistics managers. They contracted with W. N. Procter, a Boston-based supply chain manager, to use its proprietary logistics IT, ProcterLink, to give Bose the real-time information it needs to track components parts as they move through the global supply chain.[18] When a shipment leaves a supplier it is logged into ProcterLink, and from this point on Bose can track the supplies as they move around the globe toward Massachusetts, which allows Bose to fine-tune its production scheduling so components enter the assembly process exactly when they are needed.

How well this system works was illustrated when one Japanese customer unexpectedly doubled its order for Bose speakers. Bose had to gear up its manufacturing in a hurry, but many of its components were stretched out across long distances. By using ProcterLink, Bose was able to locate the needed parts in its supply chain. It broke them out of the normal delivery chain and moved them by air freight to get them to the assembly line in time to meet the accelerated schedule so Bose could meet the needs of its customer.

The IT Revolution

Advances in IT have enabled managers to make gigantic leaps in the way they can collect more timely, complete, relevant, and high-quality information and use it in more effective ways. To better understand the ongoing revolution in IT that has transformed companies such as Herman Miller and Bose, allowing them to improve their responsiveness to customers, minimize costs, and improve their competitive position, we need to examine several key aspects of advanced IT.

LO18-3 Describe the computer hardware and software innovations that created the IT revolution and changed the way managers behave.

The Effects of Advancing IT

The IT revolution began with the development of the first computers–the hardware of IT–in the 1950s. The language of computers is a digital language of zeros and ones. Words, numbers, images, and sound can all be expressed in zeros and ones. Each letter in the alphabet has its own unique code of zeros and ones, as does each number, each color, and each sound. For example, the digital code for the number 20 is 10100. In the language of computers it takes a lot of zeros and ones to express even a simple sentence, to say nothing of complex color graphics or moving video images. Nevertheless, modern computers can read, process, and store trillions of instructions per second (an *instruction* is a line of software code) and thus vast amounts of zeros and ones. This awesome number-crunching power forms the foundation of the ongoing IT revolution.

The products and services that result from advancing IT are all around us–ever more powerful microprocessors and PCs, high-bandwidth wireless smartphones, sophisticated word-processing software, ever-expanding computer networks, inexpensive digital cameras and camcorders, and more and more useful online information and retailing services that did not exist a generation ago. These products are commonplace and are being continuously improved. Many managers and companies that helped develop the new IT have reaped enormous gains.

However, while many companies have benefited from advancing IT, others have been threatened. Traditional landline telephone companies such as AT&T, Verizon, and other long-distance companies the world over have seen their market dominance threatened by new companies offering Internet, broadband, and wireless telephone technology. They have been forced to respond by buying wireless cell phone companies, building their own high-powered broadband networks, and forming alliances with companies such as Apple, which was making a version of its iPhone to run on Verizon's network in 2010. So advancing IT is both an opportunity and a threat, and managers have to move quickly to protect their companies and maintain their competitive advantage.[19] In 2010 Sprint, which had lost millions of customers to its rivals (especially AT&T with its iPhone franchise), began to champion its new WiMAX, 4G broadband network and new Android-based smartphones from Samsung. Sprint claimed its new IT would give customers much faster Internet service than AT&T's iPhone customers have received because AT&T's outdated broadband network could not keep up with customer demands for access to the Web. To fight back, in 2010 AT&T announced it would spend $2 billion more to upgrade its U.S. network and was working with Apple to make software changes that would allow iPhone and iPad applications to work faster on its network to improve the quality of customer service. Clearly, developing the right strategies to provide advanced IT solutions is a complicated process.

On one hand, IT helps create new product opportunities that managers and their organizations can take advantage of–such as online travel and vacation booking. On the other hand, IT creates new and improved products that reduce or destroy demand for older, established products–such as the services provided by bricks-and-mortar travel agents. Walmart, by developing its own sophisticated proprietary IT, has been able to reduce retailing costs so much that it has put hundreds of thousands of small and medium-size stores out of business. Similarly, thousands of small, specialized U.S. bookstores have closed in the last decade as a result of advances in IT that made online bookselling possible.

IT and the Product Life Cycle

product life cycle The way demand for a product changes in a predictable pattern over time.

When IT is advancing, organizational survival requires that managers quickly adopt and apply it. One reason for this is how IT affects the length of the **product life cycle,** which is the way demand for a product changes in a predictable pattern over time.[20] In general, the product life cycle consists of four stages: the embryonic, growth, maturity, and decline stages (see Figure 18.2). In the *embryonic stage* a product has yet to gain widespread acceptance; customers are unsure what a product, such as a new smartphone, has to offer, and demand for it is minimal. As a product, like Apple's iPod, becomes accepted by customers (although many products do

Figure 18.2
A Product Life Cycle

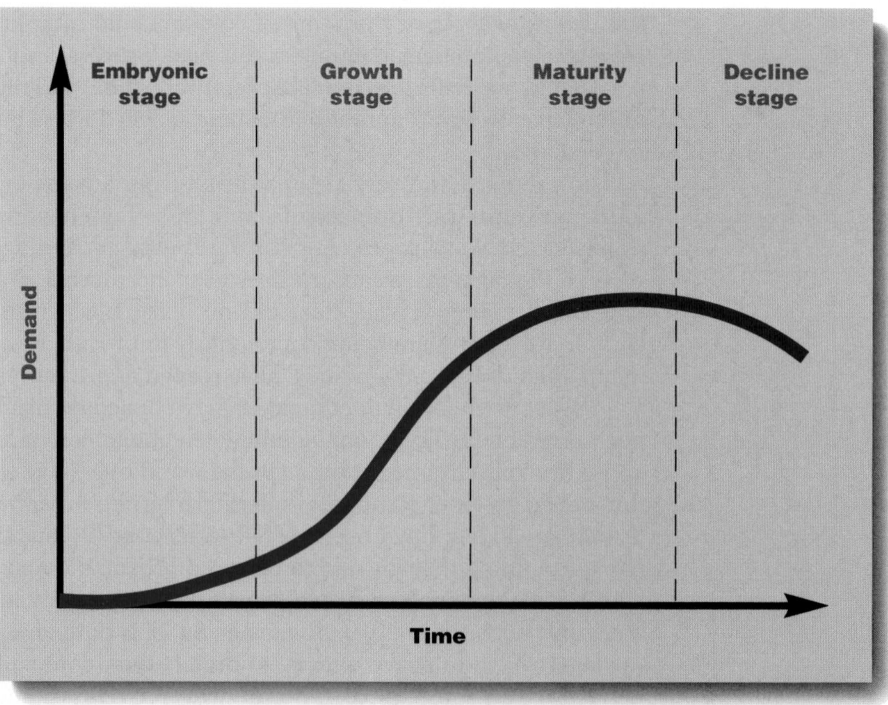

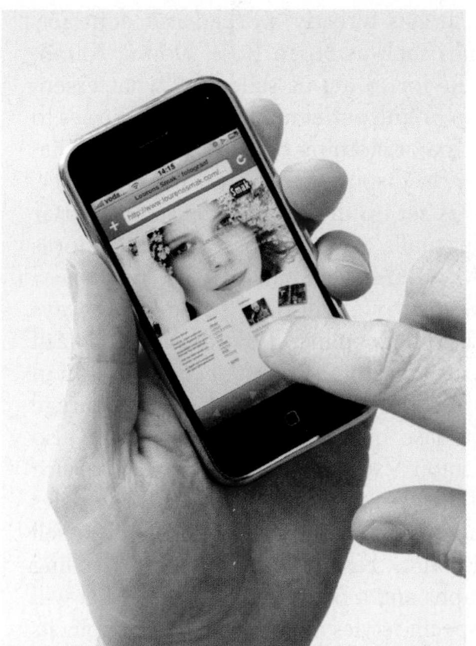

Apple's iPhone 4 claims that it changes everything, again. Boasting the revolutionary FaceTime app and HD video, Steve Jobs may not be exaggerating. Need one in your hot little hands? Get ready to fork over $200–$300.

not, like Dell's defunct MP3 player), demand takes off and the product enters its growth stage. In the *growth stage* many consumers are entering the market and buying the product for the first time, and demand increases rapidly. This is the stage Apple iPods were in and its iPhones are currently in–and Apple hopes its new iPad (launched in April 2010) will quickly reach the growth stage. Of course this will depend on the value customers see in the collection of IT applications that the iPad offers them–and how fast competitors move to offer similar and less expensive tablet computers.

The growth stage ends and the *maturity stage* begins when market demand peaks because most customers have already bought the product (there are relatively few first-time buyers left). At this stage, demand is typically replacement demand. In the PC market, for example, people who already have a PC trade up to a more powerful model. The iPod is currently in this stage; its users decide whether or not to trade up to a more powerful version that offer greater capabilities. Products such as laptops and smartphones and services such as Internet broadband and digital TV services are currently in this stage; for example, AT&T, Comcast, and Direct TV are battling to increase their market share.

Once demand for a product starts to fall, the *decline stage* begins; this typically occurs when advancing IT leads to the development of a more advanced product, making the old one obsolete, such as when the iPod destroyed Sony's Walkman franchise. In general, demand for every generation of a digital device such as a PC, cell phone, or MP3 music player falls off when the current leaders' technology is superseded by new products that incorporate the most recent IT advances. For example, 3G or 4G smartphones and tablet computers with broadband capability permit superfast Web browsing and downloading of videos, books, and all kinds of digital media. Thus one reason the IT revolution has been so important for managers is that advances in IT are one of the most significant determinants of the length of a product's life cycle, and therefore of competition in an industry.[21] In more and more industries advances in IT are shortening product life cycles as customers jump on the latest fad or fashion–such as the iPad in 2010. Will iPad technology hurt Amazon.com's Kindle book reader, which was the leader in book downloading and reading in 2009? In the clothing industry, which also has a short product life cycle because of quickly changing customer tastes, IT makes it possible to introduce new fashions much more quickly–or dispose of outdated clothing, as the following "Information Technology Byte" feature discusses.

Information Technology Byte

eBay Uses IT to Develop New Ways to Sell Out-of-Fashion Clothing

eBay Inc. is the world's largest online clothing seller; every year it sells millions of articles of new and used clothing in all shapes and sizes–it sold $7.1 billion worth of clothing in 2009 to over 10 million buyers. Until now the merchandise provided by its sellers has determined the choice of clothing it can offer its customers. And with an average of 20 million listings in the clothing category, eBay's site can be hard to navigate and search, which makes it difficult for customers to find what they want. Recognizing its growing problems in April 2010, eBay announced a major new initiative to drive up its online clothing sales.

eBay planned to launch a new fashion "microsite," Fashion.ebay.com, and work with the major fashion brands and clothing makers to sell their overstocked

eBay's Fashion Vault Web site is just one of the IT initiatives the company is rolling out in order to compete with other online fashion retailers.

merchandise. It has already worked out contracts with companies such as Hugo Boss, Donna Karan, and Lord & Taylor to act as sellers in what essentially will be an online outlet mall, and eBay hopes to encourage all major clothing brands to join its initiative. Currently, to dispose of their excess inventory, clothing makers set up their own bricks-and-mortar stores in outlet malls or sell to discount retail stores such as T. J. Maxx and Marshalls.

eBay's new microsite will offer several new ways of selling to customers online. It has developed "flash sales," which are sales of a small selection of fashion merchandise for only short periods to encourage buyers to purchase quickly. In March 2010 it also launched "Fashion Vault," which is a fashion service that allows it to compete with online private sales companies such as Gilt.com and Ruelala.com to sell trendy clothing and accessories at deep discounts. Fashion.ebay.com uses a selling format that employs gallery-style photographs and a better search engine that will make it easier for customers to search for specific styles of fashion. For example, its new IT features an improved search engine to allow shoppers to better find brands, fashion trends, and prices; its gallery photographs let buyers see the items they are interested in–but also offer them photographs of similar competing products to improve their buying experience. "We're really transforming the experience," said Lorrie Norrington, president of eBay marketplaces, which also include such e-commerce sites as Shopping.com and Kijiji and accounted for 61% of the company's revenue of $8.7 billion last year. "We're playing to our strengths" in clothing, she said.[22] In 2010 fixed-price selling accounted for over half of eBay's revenues, up from 35% two years ago, and Norrington expects it to grow as much as 70%.

eBay's new approach to online fashion retailing will put it in direct competition with Amazon.com and traditional retailers like Macy's and Target. The company plans to transfer all the IT innovations it has made to develop and launch its fashion microsite into other product categories, including home and garden, technology, and media, to increase sales. So far, early signs from its big push into fashion have been positive. According to eBay managers, many clothing makers have expressed interest in its new outlet mall because they see the site as a more efficient way to get rid of excess inventory in the clothing market–where the life cycles of fashions are very short, often only months, so that cost savings from fast inventory turnaround are substantial.

The message for managers is clear: The shorter a product's life cycle because of advancing IT, the more important it is to innovate products quickly and continuously. A PC company that cannot develop a new and improved product line every three to six months will soon find itself in trouble. Increasingly managers are trying to outdo their rivals by being the first to market with a product that incorporates some advance in IT, such as advanced stability or steering control that prevents vehicle wrecks.[23] In sum, the tumbling price of information brought about by advances in IT is at the heart of the IT revolution. So how can managers use all this computing power to their advantage?

The Network of Computing Power

The tumbling price of computing power and applications has allowed all kinds of organizations, large and small, to invest more to develop the network of computer servers described in the opening case. Companies can buy networks of server racks that are customized with the mix of hardware and software applications that best meets the

network Interlinked computers that exchange information.

needs of their current value chain management activities. As "A Manager's Challenge" discusses, the typical organizationwide computing **network** that has emerged over time is a four-tier network solution that consists of "external" PDAs such as netbooks, smartphones, and tablet computers, connected to desktops and laptops, and then through "internal" rack servers to a company's mainframe (see Figure 18.3). Through wireless and wired communication an employee with the necessary permissions can hook into a company's IT system from any location–in the office, at home, on a boat, on the beach, in the air–anywhere a wireless or wired link can be established.

The internal network is composed of "client" desktop and laptop PCs connected by Ethernet to the company's system of rack servers. The client computers that are linked directly to a server constitute a *local area network* (LAN), and most companies have many LANs–for example, one in every division and function. Large companies that need immense processing power have a mainframe computer at the center or hub of the network that can quickly process vast amounts of information, issue commands, and coordinate computing devices at the other levels. The mainframe can also handle electronic communications between servers and PCs situated in different LANs, and the mainframe can connect to the mainframes of other companies. The mainframe is the master computer that controls the operations of all the other types of computers and digital devices as needed and can link them into one integrated system. It also provides the connection to the *external* IT networks outside the organization; for example, it gives a user access to an organization's cloud computing services–but

Figure 18.3
A Four-Tier Information System with Cloud Computing

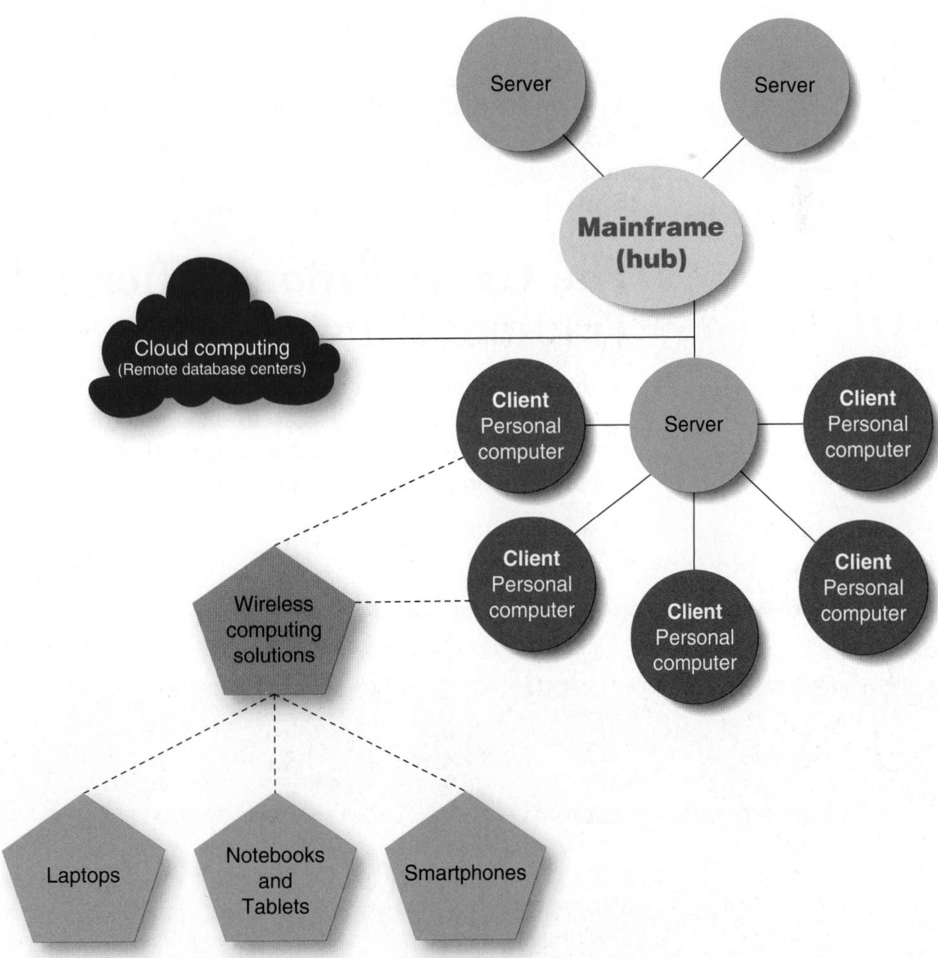

with high security and reliability and only from recognized and protected computing devices. For instance, a manager with a PDA or PC hooked into a four-tier system can access data and software stored in the local server, in the mainframe, or through the Internet to a cloud-based computing solution hosted by an outsourcer whose B&M database might be located anywhere in the world.

Just as computer hardware has been advancing rapidly, so has computer software. *Operating system software* tells the computer hardware how to run. *Applications software,* such as programs for word processing, spreadsheets, graphics, and database management, is developed for a specific task or use. The increase in the power of computer hardware has allowed software developers to write increasingly powerful programs that are also increasingly user-friendly. By harnessing the rapidly growing power of microprocessors, applications software has vastly increased the ability of managers to acquire, organize, and transmit information. In doing so, it also has improved the ability of managers to coordinate and control the activities of their organization and to make better decisions, as discussed earlier.

LO18-4 Differentiate among seven performance-enhancing kinds of management information systems.

Types of Management Information Systems

Advances in IT have continuously increased managers' ability to obtain the information they need to make better decisions and coordinate and control organizational resources. Next we discuss six types of management information systems (MIS) that have been particularly helpful to managers as they perform their management tasks: transaction-processing systems, operations information systems, decision support systems, expert systems, enterprise resource planning systems, and e-commerce systems (see Figure 18.4). These MIS systems are arranged along a continuum according to the sophistication of the IT they are based on–IT that determines their ability to give managers the information they need to make nonprogrammed decisions. (Recall from Chapter 7 that nonprogrammed decision making occurs in response to unusual, unpredictable opportunities and threats.) We examine each of these systems after focusing on the management information system that preceded them all: the organizational hierarchy.

The Organizational Hierarchy: The Traditional Information System

Traditionally managers have used the organizational hierarchy as the main way to gather the information necessary to make decisions and coordinate and control organizational activities (see Chapter 10 for a detailed discussion of organizational structure and hierarchy). According to business historian Alfred Chandler, the use of the

Figure 18.4
Six Computer-Based Management Information Systems

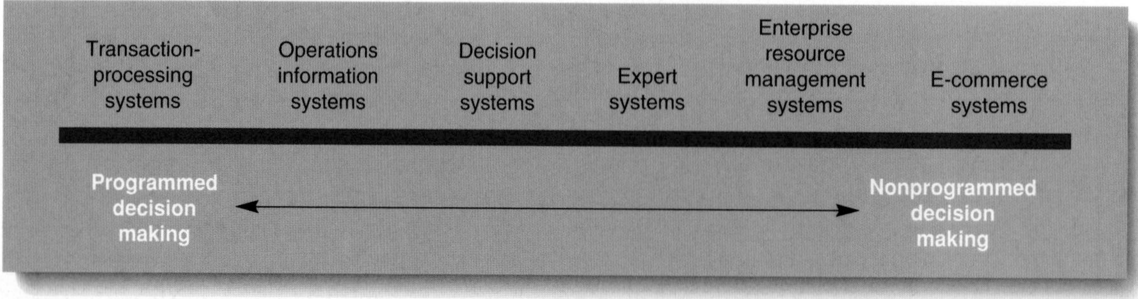

hierarchy as an information network was perfected by U.S. railroad companies in the 1850s.[24] At that time railroads were among the largest U.S. companies, and because of the size of their geographic footprint they faced unique problems of coordination and control. Railroad companies started to solve these problems by designing hierarchical management structures that gave top managers the information they needed to coordinate and control their nationwide operations.

Daniel McCallum, superintendent of the Erie Railroad, realized that the lines of authority and responsibility that defined Erie's management hierarchy also were channels of communication along which information traveled. McCallum established what was perhaps the first modern management information system when he ordered that regular daily and monthly reports should be sent up the hierarchy to top managers so they could make the best decisions about, for example, controlling costs and setting freight rates. Decisions were then sent back down the hierarchy to be carried out by lower-level managers. When the performance gains from this system were publicized, many organizations imitated the railroads by using their hierarchies to collect, channel, and process information.

Although hierarchy is a useful information system, it has several drawbacks, as we noted in Chapter 10. First, when too many layers of managers exist it takes a long time for information and requests to travel up the hierarchy and for decisions and answers to travel back down. The slow communication can reduce the timeliness and usefulness of the information and prevent a quick response to changing market conditions.[25] Second, information can be distorted as it moves from one layer of management to another, and information distortion reduces the quality of information.[26] Third, managers have only a limited span of control; so as an organization grows larger and its hierarchy lengthens, more managers must be hired, and this makes the hierarchy an expensive information system. The popular idea that companies with tall management hierarchies are bureaucratic and unresponsive to the needs of their customers arises from the inability of tall hierarchies to effectively process data and give managers timely, complete, relevant, and high-quality information. The management hierarchy is still the best information system available today–the one that results in the best decisions–*if* managers have access to the other kinds of MIS systems discussed next.

Transaction-Processing Systems

transaction-processing system A management information system designed to handle large volumes of routine, recurring transactions.

A **transaction-processing system** is an MIS designed to handle large volumes of routine, recurring transactions (see Figure 18.4). Transaction-processing systems began to appear in the early 1960s with the advent of commercially available mainframe computers. They were the first type of computer-based IT adopted by many organizations, and today they are commonplace. Bank managers use a transaction-processing system to record deposits into, and payments out of, bank accounts. Supermarket managers use a transaction-processing system to record the sale of items and to track inventory levels. More generally, most managers in large organizations use a transaction-processing system to handle tasks such as payroll preparation and payment, customer billing, and payment of suppliers.

Operations Information Systems

operations information system A management information system that gathers, organizes, and summarizes comprehensive data in a form that managers can use in their nonroutine coordinating, controlling, and decision-making tasks.

Many types of MIS followed hard on the heels of transaction-processing systems in the 1960s as companies like IBM advanced IT. An **operations information system** is an MIS that gathers comprehensive data, organizes them, and summarizes them in a form that is of value to managers. Whereas a transaction-processing system processes routine transactions, an operations information system gives managers information they can use in their nonroutine coordinating, controlling, and decision-making tasks. Most operations information systems are coupled with a transaction-processing system. An operations information system typically accesses data gathered by a transaction-processing system, processes those data into useful information, and organizes that information into a form accessible to managers. Managers often use an operations information system to get sales, inventory, accounting, and other performance-related information. For example, the information that T. J. Rodgers at Cypress Semiconductors gets about individual employee goals and performance is provided by an operations information system.

UPS uses an operations information system to track the performance of its thousands of ground stations. Each ground station is evaluated according to four criteria: delivery (to deliver 95% of all packages within the agreed upon time period), productivity (measured by the number of packages shipped per employee-hour), cost control and efficiency, and station profitability. Each ground station also has specific delivery, efficiency, cost, and profitability targets that it must attain. Every month UPS's operations information system gathers information about these four criteria and summarizes it for top managers, who can then compare the performance of each station against its previously established targets. The system quickly alerts senior managers to underperforming ground stations so they can intervene selectively to help solve any problems that may have given rise to the poor performance.

Decision Support Systems

decision support system An interactive computer-based management information system that managers can use to make nonroutine decisions.

A **decision support system** provides computer-built models that help managers make better nonprogrammed decisions.[27] Recall from Chapter 7 that nonprogrammed decisions are those that are relatively unusual or novel, such as decisions to invest in new productive capacity, develop a new product, launch a new promotional campaign, enter a new market, or expand internationally. Whereas an operations information system organizes important information for managers, a decision support system gives managers model-building capability and the chance to manipulate information in a variety of ways. Managers might use a decision support system to help them decide whether to cut prices for a product. The decision support system might contain models of how customers and competitors would respond to a price cut. Managers could run these models and use the results as an *aid* to decision making.

The stress on the word *aid* is important–in the final analysis a decision support system is not meant to make decisions for managers. Rather, its function is to give managers valuable information they can use to improve the quality of their decisions. A good example of a sophisticated decision support system, one developed by Judy Lewent, the first woman to become the chief financial officer of a major U.S. company, is profiled in the following "Manager as a Person" box.

Manager as a Person

How Judy Lewent Became One of the Most Powerful Women in Corporate America

With annual sales of over $27 billion, Merck is one of the world's largest developers and marketers of advanced pharmaceuticals.[28] The company spends over $3 billion a year on R&D to develop new drugs–an expensive and difficult process that is fraught with risks. Most new drug ideas fail to make it through the development process. It takes an average of $300 million and 10 years to bring a new drug to market, and 7 out of 10 new drugs fail to make a profit for the developing company.

Given the costs, risks, and uncertainties involved in the new drug development process, Judy Lewent, the former director of capital analysis at Merck, decided to develop a decision support system that could help managers make more effective R&D investment decisions. Her aim was to give Merck's top

Judy Lewent's Research Planning Model has allowed Merck to more strategically develop promising new drugs while avoiding pitfalls, thus sharpening the company's focus and allowing it to roll out such programs as an HIV/AIDS prevention initiative in China, pictured here.

managers the information they needed to evaluate proposed R&D projects on a case-by-case basis. The system that Lewent and her staff developed is referred to in Merck as the "Research Planning Model."[29] At the heart of this decision support system is a sophisticated model. The input variables to the model include data on R&D spending, manufacturing costs, selling costs, and demand conditions. The relationships among the input variables are modeled by several equations that factor in the probability of a drug's making it through the development process and to market. The outputs of this modeling process are the revenues, cash flows, and profits that a project might generate.

The model Lewent developed did not use a single value for an input variable, nor did it compute a single value for each output. Rather, a range is specified for each input variable (such as high, medium, and low R&D spending); then the computer randomly samples repeatedly from the range of values for each input variable to produce a probability distribution of values for each output. So, for example, instead of reporting that a proposed R&D project will yield a profit of $500 million, the decision support system produces a probability distribution. It might state that although $500 million is the most likely profit, there is a 25% chance that the profit will be less than $300 million and a 25% chance that it will be greater than $700 million.

Merck used Lewent's decision support system to evaluate all its proposed R&D investment decisions; of course, in recent years as IT advances have become commonplace, it has improved upon and refined her system. But Lewent's reward for her innovation was promotion to the chief financial officer of Merck, and she became one of the most powerful women in corporate America.

Most decision support systems are geared toward aiding middle managers in the decision-making process. For example, a loan manager at a bank might use a decision support system to evaluate the credit risk involved in lending money to a particular client. Rarely does a top manager use a decision support system. One reason for this is that most electronic management information systems have not yet become sophisticated enough to handle effectively the ambiguous types of problems facing top managers. To improve this situation, IT experts have been developing a variant of the decision support system: an executive support system.

executive support system A sophisticated version of a decision support system that is designed to meet the needs of top managers.

An **executive support system** is a sophisticated version of a decision support system that is designed to meet the needs of top managers. One defining characteristic of executive support systems is user-friendliness. Many of them include simple pull-down menus to take a manager through a decision analysis problem. Moreover, they may contain stunning graphics and other visual and interactive features to encourage top managers to use them.[30] Increasingly, executive support systems are used to link top managers virtually so they can function as a team; this type of executive support system is called a **group decision support system.**

group decision support system An executive support system that links top managers so they can function as a team.

Ultimately top managers' intuition, judgment, and integrity will always be needed to decide whether to pursue the course of action suggested by an MIS. There are always many different issues to be factored into a decision, not least of which are its ethical implications.

Artificial Intelligence and Expert Systems

artificial intelligence Behavior performed by a machine that, if performed by a human being, would be called "intelligent."

expert system A management information system that employs human knowledge, embedded in a computer, to solve problems that ordinarily require human expertise.

Artificial intelligence has been defined as behavior by a machine that, if performed by a human being, would be called "intelligent."[31] Artificial intelligence has already made it possible to write programs that can solve problems and perform simple tasks. For example, software programs variously called *software agents, softbots,* or *knowbots* can be used to perform simple managerial tasks such as sorting through reams of data or incoming e-mail messages to look for important ones. The interesting feature of these programs is that from "watching" a manager sort through such data they can "learn" what his or her preferences are. Having done this, they can take over some of this work from the manager, freeing time for the manager to work on other tasks. Most of these programs are still in the development stage, but they may be commonplace within a decade.[32]

Expert systems, the most advanced management information systems available, incorporate artificial intelligence in their design.[33] An **expert system** is a system that employs human knowledge, embedded in computer software, to solve problems that ordinarily require human expertise.[34] Mimicking human expertise (and intelligence) requires IT that can at a minimum (1) recognize, formulate, and solve a problem; (2) explain the solution; and (3) learn from experience.

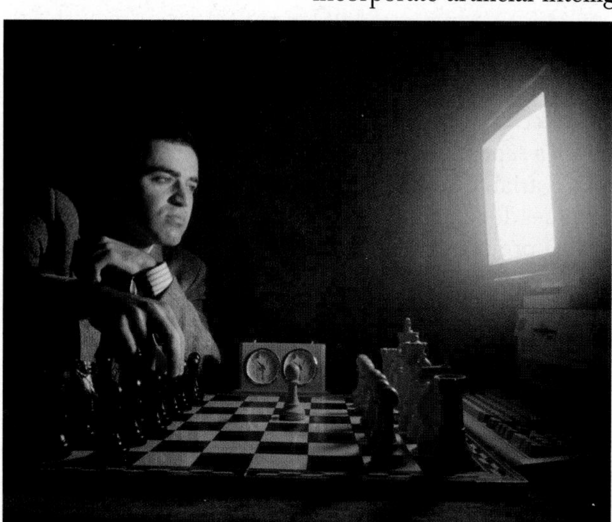

Artificial intelligence takes to the boards. Chess expert Garry Kasparov squares off against IBM's chess-playing computer Deep Blue. In 1997 Deep Blue and Kasparov traded wins, ending in a decisive victory for the computer—after it had been reprogrammed.

Recent developments in artificial intelligence that go by names such as "fuzzy logic" and "neural networks" have resulted in computer programs that, in a primitive way, try to mimic human thought processes. Although artificial intelligence is still at an early stage of development, an increasing number of business applications are beginning to emerge in the form of expert systems.

Enterprise Resource Planning Systems

To achieve high performance, it is not sufficient just to develop an MIS inside each of a company's functions or divisions to provide better information and knowledge. It is also vital that managers in the different functions and divisions have access to information about the activities of managers in other functions and divisions. The greater the flow of information and knowledge among functions and divisions, the more learning can take place, and this builds a company's stock of knowledge and expertise. This knowledge and expertise are the source of its competitive advantage and profitability.

enterprise resource planning (ERP) systems Multimodule application software packages that coordinate the functional activities necessary to move products from the design stage to the final customer stage.

In the last 25 years, another revolution has taken place in IT as software companies have worked to develop enterprise resource planning systems, which essentially incorporate most MIS aspects just discussed, as well as much more. **Enterprise resource planning (ERP) systems** are multimodule application software packages that allow a company to link and coordinate the entire set of functional activities and operations necessary to move products from the initial design stage to the final customer stage. Essentially ERP systems (1) help each individual function improve its functional-level skills and (2) improve integration among all functions so they work together to build a competitive advantage for the company. Today choosing and designing an ERP system to improve how a company operates is the biggest challenge facing the IT function inside a company. To understand why almost every large global company has installed an ERP system in the last few decades, it is necessary to return to the concept of the value chain, introduced in Chapter 8.

Recall that a company's value chain is composed of the sequence of functional activities that are necessary to make and sell a product. The value chain idea focuses attention on the fact that each function, in sequence, performs its activities to add or contribute value to a product. After one function has made its contribution, it hands the product over to the next function, which makes its own contribution, and so on down the line.

The primary activity of marketing, for example, is to uncover new or changing customer needs or new groups of customers and then decide what kinds of products should be developed to appeal to those customers. It shares or "hands off" its information to product development, where engineers and scientists work to develop and design the new products. In turn, manufacturing and materials management work to find ways to make the new products as efficiently as possible. Then sales is responsible for finding the best way to convince customers to buy these products.

The value chain is useful in demonstrating the sequence of activities necessary to bring products to the market successfully. In an IT context, however, it suggests the enormous amount of information and communication that needs to link and coordinate the activities of all the various functions. Installing an ERP system for a large company can cost tens of millions of dollars. The following "Information Technology Byte" feature discusses the ERP system designed and sold by the German IT company SAP.

Information Technology Byte

SAP's ERP System

SAP, the world's leading supplier of ERP software, introduced the world's first ERP system in 1973. So great was the demand for its software that it had to train thousands of consultants from companies like IBM, HP, Accenture, and Cap Gemini to install and customize its software to meet the needs of companies in different industries throughout the world. Why?

SAP's ERP was demanded by companies because it can manage all the stages of the value chain, and strengthen them both individually and jointly when they work together. SAP's software has modules specifically devoted to each of a company's core functional activities. Each module contains a set of "best practices," the optimum way to perform a specific functional activity that increases efficiency, quality, innovation, and responsiveness to customers. SAP's ERP is therefore "the expert system of expert systems." SAP claims that when a company reconfigures its IT system to make SAP's software work, it can achieve productivity gains of 30% to 50%, which amounts to many billions of dollars of savings for large companies.[35]

For each function in the value chain, SAP installs its software module on a function's LAN. Each function then inputs its data into that module in the way specified by SAP. For example, the sales function inputs all the information about customer needs required by SAP's sales module, and the materials management function inputs information about the product specifications it requires from suppliers into SAP's materials management module. These modules give functional managers real-time feedback on ongoing developments in their particular functional activity, such as daily changes in sales of leading products. Each SAP module functions as an expert system that can reason through the information functional employees continually input into it through their laptops or other computers. It recommends new strategies that managers can use to improve functional operations. However, the magic of ERP does not stop there.

SAP's ERP software also connects across functions. Managers in all functions have access to other functions' expert systems, and SAP's software is designed to alert managers when their functional activities will be affected by changes taking place in another function. Thus SAP's ERP system lets managers across the organization better coordinate their activities–a major source of competitive advantage. Moreover, SAP software on corporate mainframe computers takes the information from all the different functional and divisional expert systems and creates a companywide ERP system that shows top managers an overview of the operations of the whole company.

In sum, SAP's ERP system creates a sophisticated top-level expert system that can reason through the huge volume of information provided by the company's functions. It can recognize and diagnose common problems and issues in that information and develop and recommend organizationwide solutions for those problems. Using this information, top managers can improve the fit between their strategies and the changing environment.

As an example of how an ERP system works, let's examine how SAP's software helps managers coordinate their activities to speed product development. Suppose marketing has discovered some new unmet customer need, has suggested what kind of product needs to be developed, and forecasts that the demand for the product will be 40,000 units a year. With SAP's IT, engineers in product development use their expert system to work out how to design the new product in a way that builds in quality at the lowest possible cost. Manufacturing managers, watching product development's progress, work simultaneously to find the best way to make the product, and thus use their expert system to find out how to keep operating costs at a minimum.

Remember that SAP's IT gives all the other functions access to this information; they can tap into what is going on between marketing and manufacturing in real time. So materials management managers watching manufacturing make its plans can simultaneously plan how to order supplies of inputs or components from global suppliers or how and when to ship the final product to customers to keep costs at a minimum. At the same time, HRM is tied into the ERP system and uses its expert system to forecast the type and cost of the labor that will be required to carry out the activities in the other functions–for example, the number of manufacturing employees who will be required to make the product or the number of salespeople who will be needed to sell the product to achieve the 40,000 sales forecast.

How does this build competitive advantage and profitability? First, it speeds up product development; companies can bring products to market much more quickly, thereby generating higher sales revenues. Second, SAP's IT focuses on how to drive down operating costs while keeping quality high. Third, SAP's IT is oriented toward the final customer; its CRM module watches how customers respond to the new product and then feeds back this information quickly to the other functions.

To see what this means in practice, let's jump ahead three months and suppose that the CRM component of SAP's ERP software reports that actual sales are 20% below target. Further, the software has reasoned that the problem is occurring because the product lacks a crucial feature that customers want. The product is a smartphone, for example, and customers demand a built-in digital camera. Sales decides this issue deserves major priority and alerts managers in all the other functions about the problem. Now managers can begin to decide how to manage this unexpected situation.

Engineers in product development, for example, use their expert system to work out how much it would cost, and how long it would take, to modify the product so it includes the missing feature, the digital camera, that customers require. Managers in other functions watch the engineers' progress through the ERP system and can make suggestions for improvement. In the meantime, manufacturing managers know about the slow sales and have already cut back on production to avoid a buildup of the unsold product in the company's warehouse. They are also planning how to phase out this product and introduce the next version, with the digital camera, to keep costs as low as possible. Similarly, materials management managers are contacting digital camera makers to find out how much such a camera will cost and when it can be supplied. Meanwhile marketing managers are researching how they missed this crucial product feature and are developing new sales forecasts to estimate demand for the modified product. They announce a revised sales forecast of 75,000 units of the modified product.

It takes the engineers one month to modify the product; but because SAP's IT has been providing information about the modified product to managers in manufacturing and materials management, the product reaches the market only two months later. Within weeks, the sales function reports that early sales figures for the product have greatly exceeded even marketing's revised forecast. The company knows it has a winning product, and top managers give the go-ahead for manufacturing to build a second production line to double production of the product. All the other functions are expecting this decision; in fact, they have already been experimenting with their SAP modules to find out how long it will take them to respond to such a move. Each function gives the others its latest information so they can all adjust their functional activities accordingly.

This quick and responsive action is possible because of the ERP system that gives a company better control of its manufacturing and materials management activities. Quality is increased because a greater flow of information between functions allows a better-designed product. Innovation is speeded because a company can rapidly change its products to suit the needs of customers. Finally, responsiveness to customers improves because using its CRM software module, sales can better manage and react to customers' changing needs and provide better service and support to back up the sales of the product. ERP's ability to promote competitive advantage is the reason why managers in so many companies, large and small, are moving to find the best ERP solution for their particular companies.

E-Commerce Systems

e-commerce Trade that takes place between companies, and between companies and individual customers, using IT and the Internet.

E-commerce is trade that takes place between companies, and between companies and individual customers, using IT and the Internet. **Business-to-business (B2B) commerce** is trade that takes place between companies using IT and the Internet to link and coordinate the value chains of different companies. (See Figure 18.5.) The goal of B2B commerce is to increase the profitability of making and selling goods and services. B2B commerce increases profitability because it lets companies reduce operating costs and may improve product quality. A principal B2B software

Figure 18.5
Types of E-Commerce

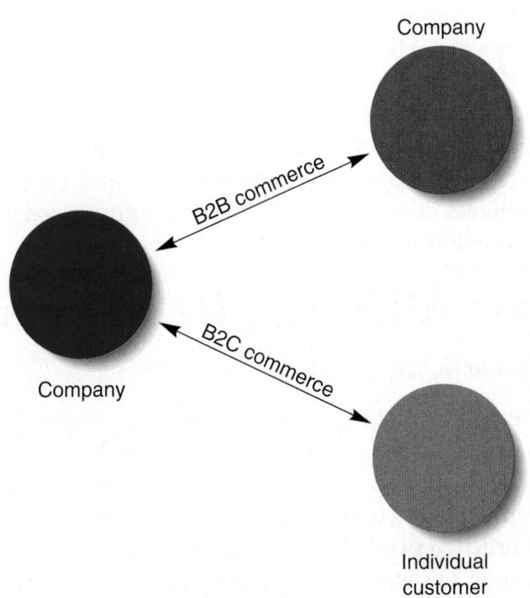

business-to-business (B2B) commerce Trade that takes place between companies using IT and the Internet to link and coordinate the value chains of different companies.

B2B marketplace An Internet-based trading platform set up to connect buyers and sellers in an industry.

business-to-customer (B2C) commerce Trade that takes place between a company and individual customers using IT and the Internet.

application is **B2B marketplaces,** which are Internet-based trading platforms that have been set up in many industries to connect buyers and sellers. To participate in a B2B marketplace, companies adopt a common software standard that allows them to search for and share information with one another. Then companies can work together over time to find ways to reduce costs or improve quality.

Business-to-customer (B2C) commerce is trade that takes place between a company and individual customers using IT and the Internet. Using IT to connect directly to the customer means companies can avoid having to use intermediaries, such as wholesalers and retailers, who capture a significant part of the profit in the value chain. The use of Web sites and online stores also lets companies give their customers much more information about the value of their products. This often allows them to attract more customers and thus generate higher sales revenues.

In the 2000s computer software makers, including Microsoft, Oracle, SAP, and IBM, have rushed to make their products work seamlessly with the Internet to respond to global companies' growing demand for e-commerce software. Previously their software was configured to work only on a particular company's intranet; today their software must be able to network a company's IT systems to other companies, such as their suppliers and distributors.

The challenge facing managers now is to select e-commerce software that allows seamless exchange of information between companies anywhere in the world. The stakes are high because global competitive advantage goes to the company first with a major new technological advance. For example, SAP rushed to update its ERP modules to allow transactions over the Internet, and today all its modules have full Internet capability. However, Oracle, IBM, and many small specialist companies have also developed ways to provide advanced Internet applications at a lower price, so SAP faces increased global competition.

LO18-5 Explain how IT is helping managers build strategic alliances and network structures to increase efficiency and effectiveness.

In summary, by using advanced types of MIS, managers have more control over a company's activities and operations and can work to improve its competitive advantage and profitability. Today the IT function is becoming increasingly important because IT managers select which kind of hardware and software a company will use and then train other functional managers and employees how to use it.

The Impact and Limitations of Information Technology

Advances in IT and management information systems are having important effects on managers and organizations. By improving the ability of managers to coordinate and control the activities of the organization and by helping managers make more effective decisions, modern IT has become a central component of any organization's structure. And evidence that IT can be a source of competitive advantage is growing; organizations that do not adopt leading-edge IT are likely to be at a competitive disadvantage. In this section we examine how the rapid advances in IT are affecting organizational structure and competitive advantage. We also examine problems associated with implementing management information systems effectively, as well as the limitations of MIS.

Strategic Alliances, B2B Network Structures, and IT

strategic alliance An agreement in which managers pool or share their organization's resources and know-how with a foreign company, and the two organizations share the rewards and risks of starting a new venture.

Recently, increasing globalization and the use of new IT have brought about two innovations that are sweeping through U.S. and European companies: electronically managed strategic alliances and B2B network structures. A **strategic alliance** is a formal agreement that commits two or more companies to exchange or share their resources in order to produce and market a product.[36] Most commonly, strategic alliances are formed because the companies share similar interests and believe they can benefit from cooperating. For example, global carmakers such as Honda and GM have formed many strategic alliances with particular suppliers of inputs such as car axles, gearboxes, and air-conditioning systems. Over time these car companies work closely with their suppliers to improve the efficiency and effectiveness of the inputs so that the final product–the car produced–is of higher quality and often can be produced at lower cost. Honda and GM have also established alliances with many different global suppliers because both companies now make several car models that are assembled and sold in many countries around the world.

B2B network structure A series of global strategic alliances that an organization creates with suppliers, manufacturers, and distributors to produce and market a product.

Throughout the 1990s, the growing sophistication of IT with global intranets and teleconferencing made it much easier to manage strategic alliances and allow managers to share information and cooperate. One outcome of this has been the growth of strategic alliances into an IT-based network structure. A **B2B network structure** is a formal series of global strategic alliances that one or several organizations create with suppliers, manufacturers, and distributors to produce and market a product. Network structures allow an organization to manage its global value chain in order to find new ways to reduce costs and increase the quality of products–without incurring the high costs of operating a complex organizational structure (such as the costs of employing many managers). More and more U.S. and European companies are relying on global network structures to gain access to low-cost foreign sources of inputs, as discussed in Chapter 6. Shoemakers such as Nike and Adidas are two companies that have used this approach extensively.

Nike is the largest and most profitable sports shoe manufacturer in the world. The key to Nike's success is the network structure that Nike founder and CEO Philip Knight created to allow his company to produce and market shoes. As noted in Chapter 8, the most successful companies today are trying to pursue simultaneously a low-cost and a differentiation strategy. Knight decided early that to do this at Nike he needed to focus his company's efforts on the most important functional activities, such as product design and engineering, and leave the others, such as manufacturing, to other organizations.

By far the largest function at Nike's Oregon headquarters is the design and engineering function, whose members pioneered innovations in sports shoe design such as the air pump and Air Jordans that Nike introduced so successfully. Designers use computer-aided design (CAD) to design Nike shoes, and they electronically store all new product information, including manufacturing instructions. When the designers have finished their work, they electronically transmit the blueprints for the new products to a network of Southeast Asian suppliers and manufacturers with which Nike has formed strategic alliances.[37] Instructions for the design of a new sole may be sent to a supplier in Taiwan; instructions for the leather uppers, to a supplier in Malaysia. The suppliers produce the shoe parts and send them for final assembly to a manufacturer in China with which Nike has established another strategic alliance. From China the shoes are shipped to distributors throughout the world. Ninety-nine percent of the over 100 million pairs of shoes that Nike makes each year are made in Southeast Asia.

This network structure gives Nike two important advantages. First, Nike can quickly respond to changes in sports shoe fashion. Using its global IT system, Nike literally can change the instructions it gives each of its suppliers overnight, so that within a few weeks its foreign manufacturers are producing new kinds of shoes.[38] Any alliance partners that fail to perform up to Nike's standards are replaced with new partners through the regular B2B marketplace.

Second, Nike's costs are low because wages in Southeast Asia are a fraction of what they are in the United States, and this difference gives Nike a low-cost advantage. Also, Nike's ability to outsource and use foreign manufacturers to produce all its shoes abroad allows Knight to keep the organization's U.S. structure flat and flexible. Nike can use a relatively inexpensive functional structure to organize its activities.

The use of network structures is increasing rapidly as organizations recognize the many opportunities they offer to reduce costs and increase organizational flexibility. U.S. companies spent $300 billion on global supply chain management each year in the 2000s. The push to lower costs has led to the development of B2B marketplaces in which most or all of the companies in an industry (for example, carmakers) use the same software platform to link to each other and establish industry specifications and standards. Then these companies jointly list the quantity and specifications of the inputs they require and invite bids from the thousands of potential suppliers around the world. Suppliers also use the same software platform, so electronic bidding, auctions, and transactions are possible between buyers and sellers around the world. The idea is that high-volume standardized transactions can help drive down costs at the industry level. Also, quality will increase as these relationships become more stable as a B2B network structure develops.

Flatter Structures and Horizontal Information Flows

Rapid advances in IT have been associated with a "delayering" (flattening) of the organizational hierarchy, a move toward greater decentralization and horizontal information flows within organizations, and the concept of the boundaryless organization.[39] By electronically giving managers high-quality, timely, relevant, and relatively complete information, modern management information systems have reduced the need for tall management hierarchies.

Modern IT has reduced the need for a hierarchy to function as a means of coordinating and controlling organizational activities. Also, by reducing the need for hierarchy, modern IT can directly increase an organization's efficiency because fewer employees are required to perform organizational activities. At one time, for example, 13 layers of management separated Kodak's general manager of manufacturing and factory workers; with IT the number of layers has been cut to 4. Similarly, Intel found that by increasing the sophistication of its own MIS, it could cut the number of hierarchical layers in the organization from 10 to 5.[40]

The ability of IT to flatten structure and facilitate the flow of horizontal information between employees has led many researchers and consultants to popularize the idea of a **boundaryless organization.** Such an organization is composed of people linked by IT–computers, faxes, computer-aided design systems, and video teleconferencing–who may rarely, if ever, see one another face-to-face. People are utilized when their services are needed, but they are not formal members of an organization; they are functional experts who form an alliance with an organization, fulfill their contractual obligations, and then move on to the next project.

boundaryless organization An organization whose members are linked by computers, faxes, computer-aided design systems, and video teleconferencing and who rarely, if ever, see one another face-to-face.

Large consulting companies, such as Accenture and McKinsey & Co., use their global consultants in this way. Consultants are connected by laptops to an organization's **knowledge management system**–its company-specific virtual information system that systematizes the knowledge of its employees and facilitates the sharing and integrating of expertise within and between functions and divisions through real-time, interconnected IT. Knowledge management systems let employees share their knowledge and expertise and give them virtual access to other employees who have the expertise to solve the problems they encounter as they perform their jobs.

knowledge management system A company-specific virtual information system that systematizes the knowledge of its employees and facilitates the sharing and integrating of their expertise.

Despite their usefulness, IT in general and management information systems in particular have some limitations. A serious potential problem is that in all the enthusiasm for MIS, communication via computer networks might lose the vital human element of communication. There is a strong argument that electronic communication should support face-to-face communication rather than replacing it. For example, it would be wrong to make a judgment about an individual's performance merely by "reading the numbers" provided by an MIS. Instead the numbers should be used to alert managers to individuals who may have a performance problem. The nature of this problem should then be explored in a face-to-face meeting, during which more detailed information can be gathered. One drawback of using IT, such as e-mail and teleconferencing, is that employees may spend too much time watching their computer screens and communicating electronically–and little time interacting directly with other employees.[41] If this occurs, important and relevant information may not be obtained because of the lack of face-to-face contact, and the quality of decision making may fall. As the following "Management Insight" box suggests, the experience of George Lucas and his high-tech digital media illustrates how IT must be woven with personal face-to-face contact to get the most performance-enhancing benefits.

Management Insight

The *Star Wars* Studio Reorganizes

The *Star Wars* movies are some of the best known in the world, and George Lucas, the director who writes and produces them, is famous for pioneering special effects. But in the 2000s competition from other special effects companies intensified, and there is a huge market for new video games; thus pressure is increasing on all companies to make the best use of their resources. So what do you do if you manage a special effects company that has many different units staffed by talented engineers who are so distant from each other that they have no incentive to cooperate and share their knowledge? This was the problem confronting CEO Lucas and Micheline Chua, the president and COO of Lucas Arts: how to better use the talents of their creative digital artists and engineers who worked autonomously–often connected to their coworkers mainly by videoconferencing systems.[42]

George Lucas with a pair of storm troopers from *Star Wars*. Lucas's special effects studio faced real challenges in getting his company's digital artists and special effects crews to work together to compete in the video game industry.

By 2008 Lucas and Chau realized they were losing valuable synergies between their various groups. They especially needed to make more use of the Industrial Light & Magic (ILM) Group, the unit responsible for the special effects behind the *Star Wars* movies and many other movies whose directors rely on its services to make their state-of-the-art special effects. How do you make different groups cooperate, especially when they each contain hundreds of talented design artists who value their autonomy and are proud of their own achievements?

The answer for Lucas was to build a new state-of-the-art $250 million office complex in the Presidio, a former army base and now a national park that has spectacular views of San Francisco Bay. In this modernistic, futuristic building everything–its rooms, facilities, and recreational areas–has been designed to facilitate communication and cooperation between people, but especially between different units.[43] Both the ILM and Lucas Arts units have been thrust together, for example, and their members who now work face-to-face have been told to build a common digital platform that will allow each unit to learn from and take advantage of the skills and knowledge of the other. To increase its performance, Lucas Arts needs these experts to collaborate to develop the state-of-the-art movies, and especially video games, on which its future profitability depends. Indeed, the gaming market is booming in the 2000s as the Nintendo Wii and its competitors compete to develop games that customers want, and these often rely on state-of-the-art graphics that only companies like Lucas can produce.

Apparently both units have learned to work together and take advantage of the open, inviting lounges and work areas where designers can meet personally to share their skills and knowledge. One recent result of their cooperation was the video game *Star Wars: The Force Unleashed.* The gaming group credits the ILM group with providing the technology for the incredible lighting, facial, and movement effects that have made the game so popular. Who knows what might happen as the members of these units develop the personal relationships and networks necessary to create the next generation of digital technology for movies and gaming? One result has been the special effects in the blockbuster Iron Man 2 movie in 2010.

Summary and Review

LO18-1, 18-2 **INFORMATION AND THE MANAGER'S JOB** Computer-based IT is central to the operation of most organizations. By giving managers high-quality, timely, relevant, and relatively complete information, properly implemented IT can improve managers' ability to coordinate and control the operations of an organization and to make effective decisions. Moreover, IT can help the organization attain a competitive advantage through its beneficial impact on productivity, quality, innovation, and responsiveness to customers. Thus modern IT is an indispensable management tool.

LO18-3 **THE IT REVOLUTION** Over the last 30 years there have been rapid advances in the power, and rapid declines in the cost, of IT. Falling prices, wireless communication, computer networks, and software developments have all radically improved the power and efficacy of computer-based IT.

LO18-4 **TYPES OF MANAGEMENT INFORMATION SYSTEMS** Traditionally managers used the organizational hierarchy as the main system for gathering the information they needed to coordinate and control the organization and to make effective decisions. Today managers use six main types of computer-based information systems. Listed in ascending order of sophistication, they are transaction-processing systems, operations information systems, decision support systems, expert systems, enterprise resource planning systems, and e-commerce systems.

LO18-5 **THE IMPACT AND LIMITATIONS OF IT** Modern IT has changed organizational structure in many ways. Using IT, managers can create electronic strategic alliances and form a B2B network structure. A network structure, based on some shared form of IT, can be formed around one company, or a number of companies can join together to create an industry B2B network. Modern IT also makes organizations flatter and encourages more horizontal cross-functional communication. As this increasingly happens across the organizational boundary, the term *boundaryless organizations* has been coined to refer to virtual organizations whose members are linked electronically.

Management in Action

Topics for Discussion and Action

Discussion

1. To be useful, information must be of high quality, be timely, be relevant, and be as complete as possible. Why does a tall management hierarchy, when used as a management information system, have negative effects on these desirable attributes? [LO18-1]
2. What is the relationship between IT and competitive advantage? [LO18-2]
3. Because of the growth of high-powered, low-cost wireless communications and IT such as videoconferencing, many managers soon may not need to come into the office to do their jobs. They will be able to work at home. What are the pros and cons of such an arrangement? [LO18-3, 18-4]
4. Many companies have reported that it is difficult to implement advanced management information systems such as ERP systems. Why do you think this is so? How might the roadblocks to implementation be removed? [LO18-4]
5. How can IT help in the new product development process? [LO18-4]
6. Why is face-to-face communication between managers still important in an organization? [LO18-4, 18-5]

Action

7. Ask a manager to describe the main kinds of IT that he or she uses on a routine basis at work. [LO18-1, 18-4]
8. Compare the pros and cons of using a network structure to perform organizational activities versus performing all activities in-house or within one organizational hierarchy. [LO18-3, 18-4, 18-5]
9. What are the advantages and disadvantages of business-to-business networks? [LO18-5]

Building Management Skills

Analyzing Management Information Systems [LO18-3, 18-4]

Pick an organization about which you have some direct knowledge. It may be an organization you worked for in the past or are in contact with now (such as the college or school you attend). For this organization, answer the following questions:

1. Describe the management information systems that are used to coordinate and control organizational activities and to help make decisions.
2. Do you think that the organization's existing MIS gives managers high-quality, timely, relevant, and relatively complete information? Why or why not?
3. How might advanced IT improve the competitive position of this organization? In particular, try to identify the impact that a new MIS might have on the organization's efficiency, quality, innovation, and responsiveness to customers.

Managing Ethically [LO18-1, 18-2]

The use of management information systems, such as ERPs, often gives employees access to confidential information from all functions and levels of an organization. Employees can see important information about the company's products that is of great value to competitors. As a result, many companies monitor employees' use of the intranet and Internet to prevent an employee from acting unethically, such as by selling this information to competitors. On the other hand, with access to this information employees might discover that their company has been engaging in unethical or even illegal practices.

Questions

1. Ethically speaking, how far should a company go to protect its proprietary information, given that it needs to also protect the privacy of its employees? What steps can it take?
2. When is it ethical for employees to give information about a company's unethical or illegal practices to a third party, such as a newspaper or government agency?

Small Group Breakout Exercise

Using New Management Information Systems [LO18-2, 18-4]

Form groups of three or four people, and appoint one member as the spokesperson who will communicate your findings to the class when called on by the instructor. Then discuss the following scenario:

You are a team of managing partners of a large management consulting company. You are responsible for auditing your firm's MIS to determine whether it is appropriate and up to date. To your surprise, you find that although your organization has a wireless e-mail system in place and consultants are connected into a powerful local area network (LAN) at all times, most of the consultants (including partners) are not using this technology. It seems that most important decision making still takes place through the organizational hierarchy.

Given this situation, you are concerned that your organization is not exploiting the opportunities offered by new IT to obtain a competitive advantage. You have discussed this issue and are meeting to develop an action plan to get consultants to appreciate the need to learn about and use the new IT.

1. What advantages can you tell consultants they will obtain when they use the new IT?
2. What problems do you think you may encounter in convincing consultants to use the new IT?
3. What steps might you take to motivate consultants to learn to use the new technology?

Exploring the World Wide Web [LO18-2, 18-5]

Go to UPS's Web site (the specific page is http://www.ups-scs.com/solutions/case_consumer.html). Scroll through the featured case studies including Adidas, Crown premiums, and so on. Read about how UPS used its IT and logistic systems to help these companies, and answer the following questions:

1. What are the main ways in which UPS can use its IT and logistics skills to help its clients?
2. In what specific ways does UPS's IT help these companies improve their efficiency, quality, innovation, and responsiveness to customers, and performance?

Be the Manager [LO18-4]

You are one of the managers of a small specialty maker of custom tables, chairs, and cabinets. You have been charged with finding ways to use IT and the Internet to identify new business opportunities that can improve your company's competitive advantage, such as ways to reduce costs or attract customers.

Questions

1. What are the various forces in a specialty furniture maker's task environment that have the most effect on its performance?
2. What kinds of IT or MIS can help the company better manage these forces?
3. In what ways can the Internet help this organization improve its competitive position?

Case in the News [LO18-2, 18-4, 18-5]

How B&M Retailers Use IT to Attract Customers

The growing popularity of online shopping at Internet retailers such as Amazon.com, as well as at the online stores of bricks-and-mortar (B&M) retailers such as Walmart and Best Buy, is causing major changes in how managers use IT in retail settings and in how they use the skills of retail employees.[44] Today more and more potential buyers are taking advantage of the limitless information they can find on the World Wide Web to become informed customers. Buyers can search online for information about and reviews of the different qualities of competing products; they can then go to specific sites that specialize in providing up-to-date prices being charged for these products by different B&M and online retailers. The availability of so much information online poses huge challenges for all retailers, but especially B&M retailers because their sales reps are dealing with highly informed customers, and the ability to complete a sale often depends on the retailer being able to offer extra information or customer service compared to an online retailer.

A main challenge confronting managers of B&M retailers is to use IT to improve the quality of the shopping experience and to better train their employees to provide higher-quality customer service. In the past, for example, one attraction of shopping at exclusive high-priced department stores was that salespeople would go to great lengths to satisfy customers. For example, sales reps would phone other branches to locate the right size of a dress that a client wanted and have the item shipped overnight. But today, when customers are often as knowledgeable as employees because of their use of the Web, they may just ask a sales rep, "Why don't you look online?" assuming that any retailer today would have IT that provides real-time information about where such items are located. In reality, many retail stores have not kept up with the need to use IT to improve customer service; nor have they thought about how they can improve employee training to make better use of their skills. The result has been falling store performance and the loss of customers to online stores.

So how does a retailer attempt to catch up and use advanced retailing IT, combined with better customer relationship management (CRM) practices, to attract customers back to the B&M world? One way is to invest in state-of-the-art retail IT such as touch-screen terminals, LCD monitors, and high-tech interactive TVs that (1) tell customers detailed information about all the important features of the products on hand, (2) help speed up customer service and checkout, and (3) "involve" customers and help convince them they have made the best buying decisions. For example, Bloomingdale's linked up with a specialty IT company in 2007 to run a three-day experiment to use IT to help salespeople aid customers in purchasing decisions. As usual, salespeople helped customers select new clothing; but after the customers tried on the clothing, they paraded before an interactive three-way mirror connected to the Internet. This lets family members and friends who were online see and comment on the different clothing selections, and the customers could use their extra input to make final clothing choices.[45] In 2010 retailers were expected to spend over $1 billion on new in-store IT to improve the shopping experience and keep customers coming back to B&M stores. Another way B&M stores can use IT to better serve customers is to find ways to link their stores' online sites to the B&M stores to encourage customers to think of both kinds of stores as two integrated parts of the same business. Similarly, Bloom Supermarkets, owned by Food Lion, has adopted a novel approach to suit its food business: It has developed an interactive wireless shopping cart that records the nature and dollar value of the items customers put into their carts so they can keep track of their purchases.

The other main way B&M companies can compete with online retailers is to make better use of their employees—especially by training employees so they have more information than IT-savvy customers and can provide services that online stores cannot—such as profitable extra services like home setup, service, and repair. Best Buy, for example, decided to retrain 30% of its top salespeople so they would not only possess detailed information about the products in their own departments (for example, PCs or flat-screen TVs) but also know how to match products across departments (for example, to help customers decide which printer is best for a PC that has a certain kind of graphics card). The goal is to give customers extra information that makes a difference and so encourage them to make their purchases in B&M stores as well as to believe it is worth their while to come back in the future.

Indeed, another advantage of investing in high-quality customer service is that using IT to bring customers into the store, either to pick up products or to gain better advice, is a major source of extra sales. Why? Customer reps are trained to inform customers about the accessories that will help them better enjoy their purchases (type of protective case for a laptop, or newest video games for a game console). And in B&M stores that offer a wide array of products, such as Best Buy or Walmart, customers often explore different departments and make extra purchases—such as a pack of $10 energy-efficient lightbulbs or a $2,000 HDTV. These extra purchases contribute significantly to a store's performance. Walmart, for example, which developed an online-to-B&M store program in select stores in 2007, found that it increased the number of customers by 20% and that they spent an extra $60 during their pick-up visits![46]

Questions for Discussion

1. In what ways can B&M stores develop new IT to help improve customers' shopping experience?
2. Which kinds of IT systems discussed in the chapter are most likely to help online companies develop new ways to attract customers and increase their sales?
3. Search the Web to discover how Amazon.com has recently adopted methods to increase its level of customer service.

CREDITS

Notes

Chapter 1

1. www.apple.com, 2010.
2. Ibid.
3. G. R. Jones, *Organizational Theory, Design, and Change* (Upper Saddle River, NJ: Pearson, 2008).
4. J. P. Campbell, "On the Nature of Organizational Effectiveness," in P. S. Goodman, J. M. Pennings, et al., *New Perspectives on Organizational Effectiveness* (San Francisco: Jossey-Bass, 1977).
5. M. J. Provitera, "What Management Is: How It Works and Why It's Everyone's Business," *Academy of Management Executive* 17 (August 2003), 152–54.
6. J. McGuire and E. Matta, "CEO Stock Options: The Silent Dimension of Ownership," *Academy of Management Journal* 46 (April 2003), 255–66.
7. www.apple.com, press releases, 2000, 2001, 2003, 2006, 2008, 2009, 2010.
8. www2.goldmansachs.com, 2010; www.jpmorganchase.com, 2010.
9. J. G. Combs and M. S. Skill, "Managerialist and Human Capital Explanations for Key Executive Pay Premium: A Contingency Perspective," *Academy of Management Journal* 46 (February 2003), 63–74.
10. H. Fayol, *General and Industrial Management* (New York: IEEE Press, 1984). Fayol actually identified five different managerial tasks, but most scholars today believe these four capture the essence of Fayol's ideas.
11. P. F. Drucker, *Management Tasks, Responsibilities, and Practices* (New York: Harper & Row, 1974).
12. www.apple.com, press release, 2003.
13. G. McWilliams, "Lean Machine–How Dell Fine-Tunes Its PC Pricing to Gain Edge in a Slow Market," *The Wall Street Journal,* June 8, 2001, A1.
14. R. H. Guest, "Of Time and the Foreman," *Personnel* 32 (1955), 478–86.
15. L. Hill, *Becoming a Manager: Mastery of a New Identity* (Boston: Harvard Business School Press, 1992).
16. Ibid.
17. H. Mintzberg, "The Manager's Job: Folklore and Fact," *Harvard Business Review,* July–August 1975, 56–62.
18. H. Mintzberg, *The Nature of Managerial Work* (New York: Harper & Row, 1973).
19. J. Kotter, *The General Managers* (New York: Free Press, 1992).
20. C. P. Hales, "What Do Managers Do? A Critical Review of the Evidence," *Journal of Management Studies,* January 1986, 88–115; A. I. Kraul, P. R. Pedigo, D. D. McKenna, and M. D. Dunnette, "The Role of the Manager: What's Really Important in Different Management Jobs," *Academy of Management Executive,* November 1989, 286–93.
21. A. K. Gupta, "Contingency Perspectives on Strategic Leadership," in D. C. Hambrick, ed., *The Executive Effect: Concepts and Methods for Studying Top Managers* (Greenwich, CT: JAI Press, 1988), 147–78.
22. D. G. Ancona, "Top Management Teams: Preparing for the Revolution," in J. S. Carroll, ed., *Applied Social Psychology and Organizational Settings* (Hillsdale, NJ: Erlbaum, 1990); D. C. Hambrick and P. A. Mason, "Upper Echelons: The Organization as a Reflection of Its Top Managers," *Academy of Management Journal* 9 (1984), 193–206.
23. T. A. Mahony, T. H. Jerdee, and S. J. Carroll, "The Jobs of Management," *Industrial Relations* 4 (1965), 97–110; L. Gomez-Mejia, J. McCann, and R. C. Page, "The Structure of Managerial Behaviors and Rewards," *Industrial Relations* 24 (1985), 147–54.
24. W. R. Nord and M. J. Waller, "The Human Organization of Time: Temporal Realities and Experiences," *Academy of Management Review* 29 (January 2004), 137–40.
25. R. L. Katz, "Skills of an Effective Administrator," *Harvard Business Review,* September–October 1974, 90–102.
26. Ibid.
27. P. Tharenou, "Going Up? Do Traits and Informal Social Processes Predict Advancing in Management," *Academy of Management Journal* 44 (October 2001), 1005–18.
28. C. J. Collins and K. D. Clark, "Strategic Human Resource Practices, Top Management Team Social Networks, and Firm Performance: The Role of Human Resource Practices in Creating Organizational Competitive Advantage," *Academy of Management Journal* 46 (December 2003), 740–52.
29. R. Stewart, "Middle Managers: Their Jobs and Behaviors," in J. W. Lorsch, ed., *Handbook of Organizational Behavior* (Englewood Cliffs, NJ: Prentice-Hall, 1987), 385–91.
30. S. C. de Janasz, S. E. Sullivan, and V. Whiting, "Mentor Networks and Career Success: Lessons for Turbulent Times," *Academy of Management Executive* 17 (November 2003), 78–92.
31. K. Labich, "Making Over Middle Managers," *Fortune,* May 8, 1989, 58–64.
32. B. Wysocki, "Some Companies Cut Costs Too Far, Suffer from Corporate Anorexia," *The Wall Street Journal,* July 5, 1995, A1.
33. www.dell.com, 2008, 2010.
34. V. U. Druskat and J. V. Wheeler, "Managing from the Boundary: The Effective Leadership of Self-Managing Work Teams," *Academy of Management Journal* 46 (August 2003), 435–58.
35. S. R. Parker, T. D. Wall, and P. R. Jackson, "That's Not My Job: Developing Flexible Work Orientations," *Academy of Management Journal* 40 (1997), 899–929.
36. B. Dumaine, "The New Non-Manager," *Fortune,* February 22, 1993, 80–84.
37. H. G. Baum, A. C. Joel, and E. A. Mannix, "Management Challenges in a New Time," *Academy of Management Journal* 45 (October 2002), 916–31.
38. A. Shama, "Management under Fire: The Transformation of Management in the Soviet Union and Eastern Europe," *Academy of Management Executive* 10 (1993), 22–35.
39. www.apple.com, 2010; www.nike.com, 2010.
40. K. Seiders and L. L. Berry, "Service Fairness: What It Is and Why It Matters," *Academy of Management Executive* 12 (1998), 8–20.
41. T. Donaldson, "Editor's Comments: Taking Ethics Seriously–A Mission Now More Possible," *Academy of Management Review* 28 (July 2003), 363–67.
42. C. Anderson, "Values-Based Management," *Academy of Management Executive* 11 (1997), 25–46.
43. W. H. Shaw and V. Barry, *Moral Issues in Business,* 6th ed. (Belmont, CA: Wadsworth, 1995); T. Donaldson, *Corporations and Morality* (Englewood Cliffs, NJ: Prentice-Hall, 1982).

44. www.apple.com, press release, 2010.
45. www.sec.gov, 2010.
46. D. Janoski, "Conohan, Ciavarella Face New Charges," www.thetimestribune.com, September 10, 2009.
47. D. Janoski, "Conohan, Ciavarella Deny New Charges," www.thetimestribune.com, September 15, 2009.
48. S. Jackson et al., *Diversity in the Workplace: Human Resource Initiatives* (New York: Guilford Press, 1992).
49. G. Robinson and C. S. Daus, "Building a Case for Diversity," *Academy of Management Executive* 3 (1997), 21–31; S. J. Bunderson and K. M. Sutcliffe, "Comparing Alternative Conceptualizations of Functional Diversity in Management Teams: Process and Performance Effects," *Academy of Management Journal* 45 (October 2002), 875–94.
50. D. Jamieson and J. O'Mara, *Managing Workforce 2000: Gaining a Diversity Advantage* (San Francisco: Jossey-Bass, 1991).
51. http://digital.virtualmarketingpartners.com/vmp/accenture/diversity-inclusion/index.php, 2010.
52. Press release, "Dell CEO Kevin Rollins Cites Workforce Diversity as Key to Gaining Competitive Advantages in Business," www.dell.com, March 6, 2006.
53. "Union Bank of California Honored by U.S. Labor Department for Employment Practices," press release, September 11, 2000.

Chapter 2

1. H. Ford, "Progressive Manufacture," *Encyclopedia Britannica,* 13th ed. (New York: Encyclopedia Co., 1926).
2. R. Edwards, *Contested Terrain: The Transformation of the Workplace in the Twentieth Century* (New York: Basic Books, 1979).
3. A. Smith, *The Wealth of Nations* (London: Penguin, 1982).
4. Ibid., 110.
5. J. G. March and H. A. Simon, *Organizations* (New York: Wiley, 1958).
6. L. W. Fry, "The Maligned F. W. Taylor: A Reply to His Many Critics," *Academy of Management Review* 1 (1976), 124–29.
7. F. W. Taylor, *Shop Management* (New York: Harper, 1903); F. W. Taylor, *The Principles of Scientific Management* (New York: Harper, 1911).
8. J. A. Litterer, *The Emergence of Systematic Management as Shown by the Literature from 1870–1900* (New York: Garland, 1986).
9. H. R. Pollard, *Developments in Management Thought* (New York: Crane, 1974).
10. D. Wren, *The Evolution of Management Thought* (New York: Wiley, 1994), 134.
11. Edwards, *Contested Terrain.*
12. J. M. Staudenmaier Jr., "Henry Ford's Big Flaw," *Invention and Technology* 10 (1994), 34–44.
13. H. Beynon, *Working for Ford* (London: Penguin, 1975).
14. Taylor, *The Principles of Scientific Management.*
15. F. B. Gilbreth, *Primer of Scientific Management* (New York: Van Nostrand Reinhold, 1912).
16. F. B. Gilbreth Jr. and E. G. Gilbreth, *Cheaper by the Dozen* (New York: Crowell, 1948).
17. D. Roy, "Efficiency and the Fix: Informal Intergroup Relations in a Piece Work Setting," *American Journal of Sociology* 60 (1954), 255–66.
18. M. Weber, *From Max Weber: Essays in Sociology,* ed. H. H. Gerth and C. W. Mills (New York: Oxford University Press, 1946); M. Weber, *Economy and Society,* ed. G. Roth and C. Wittich (Berkeley: University of California Press, 1978).
19. C. Perrow, *Complex Organizations,* 2nd ed. (Glenview, IL: Scott, Foresman, 1979).
20. Weber, *From Max Weber,* 331.
21. See Perrow, *Complex Organizations,* chap. 1, for a detailed discussion of these issues.
22. H. Fayol, *General and Industrial Management* (New York: IEEE Press, 1984).
23. Ibid., 79.
24. T. J. Peters and R. H. Waterman Jr., *In Search of Excellence: Lessons from America's Best-Run Companies* (New York: Harper & Row, 1982).
25. R. E. Eccles and N. Nohira, *Beyond the Hype: Rediscovering the Essence of Management* (Boston: Harvard Business School Press, 1992).
26. L. D. Parker, "Control in Organizational Life: The Contribution of Mary Parker Follett," *Academy of Management Review* 9 (1984), 736–45.
27. P. Graham, *M. P. Follett–Prophet of Management: A Celebration of Writings from the 1920s* (Boston: Harvard Business School Press, 1995).
28. M. P. Follett, *Creative Experience* (London: Longmans, 1924).
29. E. Mayo, *The Human Problems of Industrial Civilization* (New York: Macmillan, 1933); F. J. Roethlisberger and W. J. Dickson, *Management and the Worker* (Cambridge: Harvard University Press, 1947).
30. D. W. Organ, "Review of *Management and the Worker,* by F. J. Roethlisberger and W. J. Dickson," *Academy of Management Review* 13 (1986), 460–64.
31. D. Roy, "Banana Time: Job Satisfaction and Informal Interaction," *Human Organization* 18 (1960), 158–61.
32. For an analysis of the problems in distinguishing cause from effect in the Hawthorne studies and in social settings in general, see A. Carey, "The Hawthorne Studies: A Radical Criticism," *American Sociological Review* 33 (1967), 403–16.
33. D. McGregor, *The Human Side of Enterprise* (New York: McGraw-Hill, 1960).
34. Ibid., 48.
35. Peters and Waterman, *In Search of Excellence.*
36. J. Pitta, "It Had to Be Done and We Did It," *Forbes,* April 26, 1993, 148–52.
37. Press release, www.hp.com, June 2001.
38. T. Dewett and G. R. Jones, "The Role of Information Technology in the Organization: A Review, Model, and Assessment," *Journal of Management* 27 (2001), 313–46.
39. W. E. Deming, *Out of the Crisis* (Cambridge: MIT Press, 1986).
40. J. D. Thompson, *Organizations in Action* (New York: McGraw-Hill, 1967).
41. D. Katz and R. L. Kahn, *The Social Psychology of Organizations* (New York: Wiley, 1966); Thompson, *Organizations in Action.*
42. T. Burns and G. M. Stalker, *The Management of Innovation* (London: Tavistock, 1961); P. R. Lawrence and J. R. Lorsch, *Organization and Environment* (Boston: Graduate School of Business Administration, Harvard University, 1967).
43. Burns and Stalker, *The Management of Innovation.*
44. C. W. L. Hill and G. R. Jones, *Strategic Management: An Integrated Approach,* 8th ed. (Florence, KY: Cengage, 2010).
45. J. Bohr, "Deadly Roses," The Battalion, February 13, 2006, 3.

Chapter 3

1. "PAETEC Signs Exclusive Agreement with Los Angeles Area Hotel and Lodging Association," PAETEC News Current Press Releases, February 18, 2004; "Markets Served–PAETEC Communications, Inc.," www.paetec.com/2_1/2_1_5_2.html, May 27, 2006; "Media Center–2005 Press Releases–PAETEC Communications, Inc.," www.paetec.com/3/2005_news.html, May 27, 2006; "PAETEC SECURETEC MPLS Now Has a World–Reach," www.paetec.com, May 27, 2006; "Markets Served," http://www.paetec.com/strategic/markets_served.html, January 25, 2008; PAETEC, "Company Profile," http://www.paetec.com/about-us, February 3, 2010; *The New York Times,* "PAETEC Holding Corporation," http://topics.nytimes.com/topics/news/business/companies/paetec-holding-corporation/index . . . , February 3, 2010.

2. "Partnership Pays Off for OSS Player," in Ray Le Maistre, International (ed.), *Boardwatch,* January 28, 2004, www.boardwatch.com; "PAETEC Communications, Inc.: 2005 Year in Review," http://www.paetec.com, May 27, 2006; "PAETEC Communications," http://en.wikipedia.org/wiki/PAETEC_Communications, May 27, 2006; PAETEC Holding Corp.: Private Company Information–*BusinessWeek,* http://investing.businessweek.com/research/stocks/private/snapshop.asp?privcapId=32638, February 3, 2010.
3. "Offering the PAETEC Solutions Portfolio," www.paetec.com, March 8, 2004.
4. D. Dorsey, "Happiness Pays," *Inc. Magazine,* February 2004, 89–94; 2009 Technology Fast 500 Ranking/Technology Fast 500/Deloitte LLP, "2009 Technology Fast™ 500 Ranking, http://www.deloitte.com/view/en_US/us/Industries/Technology/technology fast500/article/1 . . . , February 3, 2010.
5. "Company Profile," http://www.paetec.com/strategic/PAETEC_profile.html, January 25, 2008.
6. "PAETEC Communications, Inc.: 2005 Year in Review"; "Company Profile," http://www.paetec.com/strategic/PAETEC_profile.html, January 25, 2008.
7. D. Dorsey, "Happiness Pays."
8. "Company Profile about PAETEC," www.paetec.com, March 8, 2004; "Company Profile," http://www.paetec.com/strategic/PAETEC_profile.html, January 25, 2008.
9. "Company Profile," http://www.paetec.com/strategic/PAETEC_profile.html, January 25, 2008.
10. Dorsey, "Happiness Pays."
11. "PAETEC Receives 2005 American Business Ethics Award," www.paetec.com, May 27, 2006.
12. PAETEC, "January 5, 2010–PAETEC Named to Best Large Company to Work For Ranking for Second Consecutive Year," http://www.paetec.com/about-us/media-center/press-releases/PAETEC-Named-to-Best-Lar . . . , February 3, 2010.
13. A. A. Chesonis & D. Dorsey, *It Isn't Just Business It's Personal* (Rochester, NY: RIT Cary Graphics Art Press, 2006).
14. R News Staff, "Paetec Gives Bonuses," www.rnews.com, March 8, 2004.
15. "PAETEC Communications, Inc.: 2005 Year in Review."
16. Dorsey, "Happiness Pays."
17. Dorsey, "Happiness Pays."
18. Dorsey, "Happiness Pays."
19. Dorsey, "Happiness Pays."
20. "Company Profile about PAETEC"; "Company Profile," http://www.paetec.com/strategic/PAETEC_profile.html, January 25, 2008; Our People–About Us–PAETEC, PAETEC, "Our People," http://www.paetec.com/about-us/our-people. February 3, 2010.
21. S. Carpenter, "Different Dispositions, Different Brains," *Monitor on Psychology,* February 2001, 66–68.
22. J. M. Digman, "Personality Structure: Emergence of the Five-Factor Model," *Annual Review of Psychology* 41 (1990), 417–40; R. R. McCrae and P. T. Costa, "Validation of the Five-Factor Model of Personality across Instruments and Observers," *Journal of Personality and Social Psychology* 52 (1987), 81–90; R. R. McCrae and P. T. Costa, "Discriminant Validity of NEO-PIR Facet Scales," *Educational and Psychological Measurement* 52 (1992), 229–37.
23. Digman, "Personality Structure"; McCrae and Costa, "Validation of the Five-Factor Model"; McCrae and Costa, "Discriminant Validity"; R. P. Tett and D. D. Burnett, "A Personality Trait-Based Interactionist Model of Job Performance," *Journal of Applied Psychology* 88, no. 3 (2003), 500–17; J. M. George, "Personality, Five-Factor Model," in S. Clegg and J. R. Bailey, eds., *International Encyclopedia of Organization Studies* (Thousand Oaks, CA: Sage, 2007).
24. L. A. Witt and G. R. Ferris, "Social Skills as Moderator of Conscientiousness–Performance Relationship: Convergent Results across Four Studies," *Journal of Applied Psychology* 88, no. 5 (2003), 809–20; M. J. Simmering, J. A. Colquitte, R. A. Noe, and C. O. L. H. Porter, "Conscientiousness, Autonomy Fit, and Development: A Longitudinal Study," *Journal of Applied Psychology* 88, no. 5 (2003), 954–63.
25. M. R. Barrick and M. K. Mount, "The Big Five Personality Dimensions and Job Performance: A Meta-Analysis," *Personnel Psychology* 44 (1991), 1–26; S. Komar, D. J. Brown, J. A. Komar, and C. Robie, "Faking and the Validity of Conscientiousness: A Monte Carlo Investigation," *Journal of Applied Psychology* 93 (2008), 140–54.
26. Digman, "Personality Structure"; McCrae and Costa, "Validation of the Five-Factor Model"; McCrae and Costa, "Discriminant Validity."
27. E. McGirt, "The Dirtiest Mind in Business: How Filth Met Opportunity and Created a Franchise," *Fast Company* 122 (February 2008), 64, www.fastcompany.com/magazine/122/the-dirtiest-mind-in-business_Printer_Friendl . . . , January 23, 2008; Dirty Jobs: About the Show; Discovery Channel, "Get Down and Dirty," http://dsc.discovery.com/fansites/dirtyjobs/about/about-print.html, February 3, 2010.
28. "Mike Rowe's World: Mike's Bio: Discovery Channel," http://dsc.discovery.com/fansites/dirtyjobs/bio/bio-print.html, January 23, 2008.
29. McGirt, "The Dirtiest Mind in Business."
30. "Dirty Jobs: Season 1 DVD Set–Discovery Channel Store–754317," http://shopping.discovery.com/product-60948.html?jzid=40588004-66-0, January 25, 2008; "Mike Rowe's World: Mike's Bio: Discovery Channel."
31. McGirt, "The Dirtiest Mind in Business."
32. McGirt, "The Dirtiest Mind in Business"; Dirty Jobs: About the Show; Discovery Channel, "Get Down and Dirty," http://dsc.discovery.com/fansites/dirtyjobs/about/about-print.html, February 3, 2010.
33. McGirt, "The Dirtiest Mind in Business."
34. McGirt, "The Dirtiest Mind in Business"; M. Rowe, "Seven Dirty Habits of Highly Effluent People: Mike Rose's Seven Rules for Job Satisfaction," *Fast Company* 122 (February 2008), 69, www.fastcompany.com/magazine/122/seven-dirty-habits-of-highly-effluent-people_ . . . , January 23, 2008.
35. J. B. Rotter, "Generalized Expectancies for Internal versus External Control of Reinforcement," *Psychological Monographs* 80 (1966), 1–28; P. Spector, "Behaviors in Organizations as a Function of Employees' Locus of Control," *Psychological Bulletin* 91 (1982), 482–97.
36. J. Brockner, *Self-Esteem at Work* (Lexington, MA: Lexington Books, 1988).
37. D. C. McClelland, *Human Motivation* (Glenview, IL: Scott, Foresman, 1985); D. C. McClelland, "How Motives, Skills, and Values Determine What People Do," *American Psychologist* 40 (1985), 812–25; D. C. McClelland, "Managing Motivation to Expand Human Freedom," *American Psychologist* 33 (1978), 201–10.
38. D. G. Winter, *The Power Motive* (New York: Free Press 1973).
39. M. J. Stahl, "Achievement, Power, and Managerial Motivation: Selecting Managerial Talent with the Job Choice Exercise," *Personnel Psychology* 36 (1983), 775–89; D. C. McClelland and D. H. Burnham, "Power Is the Great Motivator," *Harvard Business Review* 54 (1976), 100–10.
40. R. J. House, W. D. Spangler, and J. Woycke, "Personality and Charisma in the U.S. Presidency: A Psychological Theory of Leader Effectiveness," *Administrative Science Quarterly* 36 (1991), 364–96.

41. G. H. Hines, "Achievement, Motivation, Occupations and Labor Turnover in New Zealand," *Journal of Applied Psychology* 58 (1973), 313–17; P. S. Hundal, "A Study of Entrepreneurial Motivation: Comparison of Fast- and Slow-Progressing Small Scale Industrial Entrepreneurs in Punjab, India," *Journal of Applied Psychology* 55 (1971), 317–23.
42. M. Rokeach, *The Nature of Human Values* (New York: Free Press 1973).
43. Rokeach, *The Nature of Human Values.*
44. Rokeach, *The Nature of Human Values.*
45. K. K. Spors, "Top Small Workplaces 2007: Gentle Giant Moving," *The Wall Street Journal,* October 1, 2007, R4–R5; "Gentle Giant Sees Revenue Boost, *Boston Business Journal,* January 15, 2008, www.gentlegiant.com/news-011508-1.htm, February 5, 2008; Company History: Gentle Giant Moving Company, "Company History," http://www.gentlegiant.com/history.php, February 3, 2010; "Massachusetts Moving Company Gentle Giant Moving Company Celebrates 30 Years in Operation," January 25, 2010, http://www.gentlegiant.com/press/press20100125.php, February 3, 2010.
46. Spors, "Top Small Workplaces 2007: Gentle Giant Moving."
47. Spors, "Top Small Workplaces 2007: Gentle Giant Moving."
48. Spors, "Top Small Workplaces 2007: Gentle Giant Moving."
49. Spors, "Top Small Workplaces 2007: Gentle Giant Moving"; "Gentle Giant Receives Top Small Workplace Award," www.gentlegiant.com/topsmallworkplace.htm, January 5, 2008; "Corporate Overview," http://www.gentlegiant.com/company.php, February 3, 2010.
50. Spors, "Top Small Workplaces 2007: Gentle Giant Moving."
51. Spors, "Top Small Workplaces 2007: Gentle Giant Moving."
52. A. P. Brief, *Attitudes In and Around Organizations* (Thousand Oaks, CA: Sage, 1998).
53. P. S. Goodman, "U.S. Job Losses in December Dim Hopes for Quick Upswing," *The New York Times,* http://www.nytimes.com/2010/01/09/business/economy/09jobs.html?pagewanted=print, February 3, 2010; U.S. Bureau of Labor Statistics, Economic News Release Employment Situations Summary, http://data.bls.gov/cgi-bin/print.pl/news.release/empsit.nr0.htm, February 3, 2010; B. Steverman, "Layoffs: Short-Term Profits, Long-Term Problems," *BusinessWeek,* http://www.businessweek.com/print/investor/content/jan2010/pi20100113_133780.htm, February 3, 2010.
54. J. Aversa, "Americans' Job Satisfaction Falls to Record Low," http://news.yahoo.com/s/ap/20100105/ap_on_bi_ge/us_unhappy_workers/print, February 3, 2010.
55. The Conference Board, Press Release/News, "U.S. Job Satisfaction at Lowest Level in Two Decades," January 5, 2010, http://www.conference-board.org/utilities/pressPrinterFriendly.cfm?press_ID=3820, February 3, 2010.
56. Aversa, "Americans' Job Satisfaction Falls to Record Low"; The Conference Board, Press Release/News, "U.S. Job Satisfaction at Lowest Level in Two Decades."
57. Aversa, "Americans' Job Satisfaction Falls to Record Low"; The Conference Board, Press Release/News, "U.S. Job Satisfaction at Lowest Level in Two Decades."
58. Aversa, "Americans' Job Satisfaction Falls to Record Low"; The Conference Board, Press Release/News, "U.S. Job Satisfaction at Lowest Level in Two Decades."
59. Aversa, "Americans' Job Satisfaction Falls to Record Low"; The Conference Board, Press Release/News, "U.S. Job Satisfaction at Lowest Level in Two Decades."
60. The Conference Board, Press Release/News, "U.S. Job Satisfaction at Lowest Level in Two Decades."
61. D. W. Organ, *Organizational Citizenship Behavior: The Good Soldier Syndrome* (Lexington, MA: Lexington Books, 1988).
62. J. M. George and A. P. Brief, "Feeling Good–Doing Good: A Conceptual Analysis of the Mood at Work–Organizational Spontaneity Relationship," *Psychological Bulletin* 112 (1992), 310–29.
63. W. H. Mobley, "Intermediate Linkages in the Relationship between Job Satisfaction and Employee Turnover," *Journal of Applied Psychology* 62 (1977), 237–40.
64. C. Hymowitz, "Though Now Routine, Bosses Still Stumble during Layoff Process," *The Wall Street Journal,* June 25, 2007, B1; J. Brockner, "The Effects of Work Layoffs on Survivors: Research, Theory and Practice," in B. M. Staw and L. L. Cummings, eds., *Research in Organizational Behavior,* vol. 10 (Greenwich, CT: JAI Press, 1988), 213–55.
65. Hymowitz, "Though Now Routine, Bosses Still Stumble during Layoff Process."
66. Hymowitz, "Though Now Routine, Bosses Still Stumble during Layoff Process."
67. Hymowitz, "Though Now Routine, Bosses Still Stumble during Layoff Process."
68. Goodman, "U.S. Job Losses in December Dim Hopes for Quick Upswing."
69. M. Luo, "For Small Employers, Rounds of Shedding Workers and Tears," *The New York Times,* May 7, 2009, A1, A3.
70. Luo, "For Small Employers, Rounds of Shedding Workers and Tears."
71. Luo, "For Small Employers, Rounds of Shedding Workers and Tears."
72. N. Solinger, W. van Olffen, and R. A. Roe, "Beyond the Three-Component Model of Organizational Commitment," *Journal of Applied Psychology* 93 (2008), 70–83.
73. J. E. Mathieu and D. M. Zajac, "A Review and Meta-Analysis of the Antecedents, Correlates, and Consequences of Organizational Commitment," *Psychological Bulletin* 108 (1990), 171–94.
74. D. Watson and A. Tellegen, "Toward a Consensual Structure of Mood," *Psychological Bulletin* 98 (1985), 219–35.
75. Watson and Tellegen, "Toward a Consensual Structure of Mood."
76. J. M. George, "The Role of Personality in Organizational Life: Issues and Evidence," *Journal of Management* 18 (1992), 185–213.
77. H. A. Elfenbein, "Emotion in Organizations: A Review and Theoretical Integration," in J. P. Walsh and A. P. Brief, eds., *The Academy of Management Annals,* vol. 1 (New York: Lawrence Erlbaum Associates, 2008), 315–86.
78. J. P. Forgas, "Affect in Social Judgments and Decisions: A Multi-Process Model," in M. Zanna, ed., *Advances in Experimental and Social Psychology,* vol. 25 (San Diego, CA: Academic Press, 1992), 227–75; J. P. Forgas and J. M. George, "Affective Influences on Judgments and Behavior in Organizations: An Information Processing Perspective," *Organizational Behavior and Human Decision Processes* 86 (2001), 3–34; J. M. George, "Emotions and Leadership: The Role of Emotional Intelligence," *Human Relations* 53 (2000), 1027–55; W. N. Morris, *Mood: The Frame of Mind* (New York: Springer-Verlag, 1989).
79. George, "Emotions and Leadership."
80. J. M. George and K. Bettenhausen, "Understanding Prosocial Behavior, Sales Performance, and Turnover: A Group Level Analysis in a Service Context," *Journal of Applied Psychology* 75 (1990), 698–709.
81. George and Brief, "Feeling Good–Doing Good"; J. M. George and J. Zhou, "Understanding When Bad Moods Foster Creativity and Good Ones Don't: The Role of Context and Clarity of Feelings," paper presented at the Academy of Management Annual Meeting, 2001; A. M. Isen and R. A. Baron, "Positive Affect as a

Factor in Organizational Behavior," in B. M. Staw and L. L. Cummings, eds., *Research in Organizational Behavior,* vol. 13 (Greenwich, CT: JAI Press, 1991), 1–53.

82. J. M. George and J. Zhou, "Dual Tuning in a Supportive Context: Joint Contributions of Positive Mood, Negative Mood, and Supervisory Behaviors to Employee Creativity," *Academy of Management Journal,* 50 (2007), 605–22; J. M. George, "Creativity in Organizations," in J. P. Walsh and A. P. Brief, eds., *The Academy of Management Annals,* vol. 1 (New York: Lawrence Erlbaum Associates, 2008), 439–77.
83. J. D. Greene, R. B. Sommerville, L. E. Nystrom, J. M. Darley, and J. D. Cohen, "An FMRI Investigation of Emotional Engagement in Moral Judgment," *Science,* September 14, 2001, 2105–08; L. Neergaard, "Brain Scans Show Emotions Key to Resolving Ethical Dilemmas," *Houston Chronicle,* September 14, 2001, 13A.
84. George and Zhou, "Dual Tuning in a Supportive Context."
85. George and Zhou, "Dual Tuning in a Supportive Context."
86. R. C. Sinclair, "Mood, Categorization Breadth, and Performance Appraisal: The Effects of Order of Information Acquisition and Affective State on Halo, Accuracy, Informational Retrieval, and Evaluations," *Organizational Behavior and Human Decision Processes* 42 (1988), 22–46.
87. D. Goleman, *Emotional Intelligence* (New York: Bantam Books, 1994); J. D. Mayer and P. Salovey, "The Intelligence of Emotional Intelligence," *Intelligence* 17 (1993), 433–42; J. D. Mayer and P. Salovey, "What Is Emotional Intelligence?" in P. Salovey and D. Sluyter, eds., *Emotional Development and Emotional Intelligence: Implications for Education* (New York: Basic Books, 1997); P. Salovey and J. D. Mayer, "Emotional Intelligence," *Imagination, Cognition, and Personality* 9 (1989–1990), 185–211.
88. S. Epstein, *Constructive Thinking* (Westport, CT: Praeger, 1998).
89. "Leading by Feel," *Inside the Mind of the Leader,* January 2004, 27–37.
90. P. C. Early and R. S. Peterson, "The Elusive Cultural Chameleon: Cultural Intelligence as a New Approach to Intercultural Training for the Global Manger," *Academy of Management Learning and Education* 3, no. 1 (2004), 100–15.
91. George, "Emotions and Leadership"; S. Begley, "The Boss Feels Your Pain," *Newsweek,* October 12, 1998, 74; D. Goleman, *Working with Emotional Intelligence* (New York: Bantam Books, 1998).
92. J. Bercovici, "Remembering Bernie Goldhirsh," www.medialifemagazine.com/news2003/jun03/jun30/4_thurs/news1thursday.html, April 15, 2004.
93. B. Burlingham, "Legacy: The Creative Spirit," *INC.,* September 2003, 11–12.
94. Burlingham, "Legacy: The Creative Spirit"; "Inc. magazine," www.inc.com/magazine, May 28, 2006.
95. Burlingham, "Legacy: The Creative Spirit"; "Inc. magazine," www.inc.com/magazine, May 28, 2006; www.inc.com, February 5, 2008.
96. "Leading by Feel," *Inside the Mind of the Leader,* January 2004, 27–37.
97. George, "Emotions and Leadership."
98. J. Zhou and J. M. George, "Awakening Employee Creativity: The Role of Leader Emotional Intelligence," *Leadership Quarterly* 14 (2003), 545–68.
99. A. Jung, "Leading by Feel: Seek Frank Feedback," *Inside the Mind of the Leader,* January 2004, 31.
100. H. M. Trice and J. M. Beyer, *The Cultures of Work Organizations* (Englewood Cliffs, NJ: Prentice-Hall, 1993).
101. J. B. Sørensen, "The Strength of Corporate Culture and the Reliability of Firm Performance," *Administrative Science Quarterly* 47 (2002), 70–91.
102. "Personality and Organizational Culture," in B. Schneider and D. B. Smith, eds., *Personality and Organizations* (Mahway, NJ: Lawrence Erlbaum, 2004), 347–69; J. E. Slaughter, M. J. Zickar, S. Highhouse, and D. C. Mohr, "Personality Trait Inferences about Organizations: Development of a Measure and Assessment of Construct Validity," *Journal of Applied Psychology* 89, no. 1 (2004), 85–103.
103. T. Kelley, *The Art of Innovation: Lessons in Creativity from IDEO, America's Leading Design Firm* (New York: Random House, 2001).
104. "Personality and Organizational Culture."
105. B. Schneider, "The People Make the Place," *Personnel Psychology* 40 (1987), 437–53.
106. "Personality and Organizational Culture."
107. "Personality and Organizational Culture."
108. B. Schneider, H. B. Goldstein, and D. B. Smith, "The ASA Framework: An Update," *Personnel Psychology* 48 (1995), 747–73; J. Schaubroeck, D. C. Ganster, and J. R. Jones, "Organizational and Occupational Influences in the Attraction–Selection–Attrition Process," *Journal of Applied Psychology* 83 (1998), 869–91.
109. Kelley, *The Art of Innovation.*
110. www.ideo.com, February 5, 2008.
111. Kelley, *The Art of Innovation.*
112. "Personality and Organizational Culture."
113. Kelley, *The Art of Innovation.*
114. George, "Emotions and Leadership."
115. Kelley, *The Art of Innovation.*
116. Kelley, *The Art of Innovation.*
117. D. C. Feldman, "The Development and Enforcement of Group Norms," *Academy of Management Review* 9 (1984), 47–53.
118. G. R. Jones, *Organizational Theory, Design, and Change* (Upper Saddle River, NJ: Prentice-Hall, 2003).
119. H. Schein, "The Role of the Founder in Creating Organizational Culture," *Organizational Dynamics* 12 (1983), 13–28.
120. S. Covel, "Telemarketer Bucks High Turnover Trend," *The Wall Street Journal,* November 19, 2007, B4; "Ryla History & Culture!" www.rylateleservices.com/print.asp?level=2&id=166, January 24, 2008.
121. Covel, "Telemarketer Bucks High Turnover Trend."
122. Covel, "Telemarketer Bucks High Turnover Trend"; "Ryla History & Culture!"; Ryla, Inc., "Outsourced Customer Contact Center Solutions, about us," "The RYLA Difference," http://ryla.com/difference.html, February 5, 2010.
123. Covel, "Telemarketer Bucks High Turnover Trend"; Ryla, Inc., "Outsourced Customer Contact Center Solutions, about us," "The RYLA Difference," http://ryla.com/difference.html, February 5, 2010.
124. "Company Culture," www.rylateleservices.com/print.asp?level=2&id=98, January 24, 2008.
125. Covel, "Telemarketer Bucks High Turnover Trend."
126. Covel, "Telemarketer Bucks High Turnover Trend."
127. "A Great Career Is Waiting for You at Ryla," www.rylateleservices.com/print.asp?level=1&id=13, January 25, 2008.
128. Covel, "Telemarketer Bucks High Turnover Trend."
129. Covel, "Telemarketer Bucks High Turnover Trend."
130. "Ryla Named by The Wall Street Journal and Winning Workplaces as a Top Small Workplace in US," October 1, 2007, www.rylateleservices.com/print.asp?level=2&id=168, January 24, 2008.
131. "Ryla Named by The Wall Street Journal and Winning Workplaces as a Top Small Workplace in US."

132. Covel, "Telemarketer Bucks High Turnover Trend."
133. J. M. George, "Personality, Affect, and Behavior in Groups," *Journal of Applied Psychology* 75 (1990), 107–16.
134. J. Van Maanen, "Police Socialization: A Longitudinal Examination of Job Attitudes in an Urban Police Department," *Administrative Science Quarterly* 20 (1975), 207–28.
135. www.intercotwest.com/Disney; M. N. Martinez, "Disney Training Works Magic," *HRMagazine,* May 1992, 53–57.
136. P. L. Berger and T. Luckman, *The Social Construction of Reality* (Garden City, NY: Anchor Books, 1967).
137. H. M. Trice and J. M. Beyer, "Studying Organizational Culture through Rites and Ceremonials," *Academy of Management Review* 9 (1984), 653–69.
138. Kelley, *The Art of Innovation.*
139. H. M. Trice and J. M. Beyer, *The Cultures of Work Organizations* (Englewood Cliffs, NJ: Prentice-Hall, 1993).
140. B. Ortega, "Wal-Mart's Meeting Is a Reason to Party," *The Wall Street Journal,* June 3, 1994, A1.
141. Kelley, *The Art of Innovation.*
142. www.ibm.com; IBM Investor Relations–Corporate Governance, Executive Officers, "Executive Officers," http://www.ibm.com/investor/governance/executive-officers.wss, February 5, 2010.
143. K. E. Weick, *The Social Psychology of Organization* (Reading, MA: Addison Wesley, 1979).
144. B. McLean and P. Elkind, *The Smartest Guys in the Room: The Amazing Rise and Scandalous Fall of Enron* (New York: Penguin Books, 2003); R. Smith and J. R. Emshwiller, *24 Days: How Two Wall Street Journal Reporters Uncovered the Lies That Destroyed Faith in Corporate America* (New York: HarperCollins, 2003); M. Swartz and S. Watkins, *Power Failure: The Inside Story of the Collapse of ENRON* (New York: Doubleday, 2003).

Chapter 4

1. www.fda.org, press release, 2009.
2. Ibid.
3. B. J. Blackledge and S. Lindsey, "Peanut Plant Owner Becomes Recluse after Outbreak," ap.com, February 19, 2009.
4. A. E. Tenbrunsel, "Misrepresentation and Expectations of Misrepresentation in an Ethical Dilemma: The Role of Incentives and Temptation," *Academy of Management Journal* 41 (June 1998), 330–40.
5. D. Kravets, "Supreme Court to Hear Case on Medical Pot," www.yahoo.com, June 29, 2004; C. Lane, "A Defeat for Users of Medical Marihuana," www.washingtonpost.com, June 7, 2005.
6. www.yahoo.com, 2003; www.mci.com, 2004.
7. J. Child, "The International Crisis of Confidence in Corporations," *Academy of Management Executive* 16 (August 2002), 145–48.
8. T. Donaldson, "Editor's Comments: Taking Ethics Seriously–A Mission Now More Possible," *Academy of Management Review* 28 (July 2003), 463–67.
9. R. E. Freeman, *Strategic Management: A Stakeholder Approach* (Marshfield, MA: Pitman, 1984).
10. J. A. Pearce, "The Company Mission as a Strategic Tool," *Sloan Management Review,* Spring 1982, 15–24.
11. J. Robertson, "Ex-Brocade CEO Sentenced to 21 Months, www.yahoo.com, January 16, 2008.
12. C. I. Barnard, *The Functions of the Executive* (Cambridge, MA: Harvard University Press, 1948).
13. Freeman, *Strategic Management.*
14. P. S. Adler, "Corporate Scandals: It's Time for Reflection in Business Schools," *Academy of Management Executive* 16 (August 2002), 148–50.
15. W. G. Sanders and D. C. Hambrick, "Swinging for the Fences: The Effects of CEO Stock Options on Company Risk Taking and Performance," *Academy of Management Journal* 53, no. 5 (2007), 1055–78.
16. "The Green Machine," *Newsweek,* March 21, 2005, E8–E10.
17. www.wholefoodsmarket.com, 2010.
18. "John Mackey's Blog: 20 Questions with Sunni's Salon," www.wholefoodsmarket.com, 2006.
19. Ibid.
20. T. L. Beauchamp and N. E. Bowie, eds., *Ethical Theory and Business* (Englewood Cliffs, NJ: Prentice-Hall, 1979); A. MacIntyre, *After Virtue* (South Bend, IN: University of Notre Dame Press, 1981).
21. R. E. Goodin, "How to Determine Who Should Get What," *Ethics,* July 1975, 310–21.
22. E. P. Kelly, "A Better Way to Think about Business" (book review), *Academy of Management Executive* 14 (May 2000), 127–29.
23. T. M. Jones, "Ethical Decision Making by Individuals in Organizations: An Issue Contingent Model," *Academy of Management Journal* 16 (1991), 366–95; G. F. Cavanaugh, D. J. Moberg, and M. Velasquez, "The Ethics of Organizational Politics," *Academy of Management Review* 6 (1981), 363–74.
24. L. K. Trevino, "Ethical Decision Making in Organizations: A Person–Situation Interactionist Model," *Academy of Management Review* 11 (1986), 601–17; W. H. Shaw and V. Barry, *Moral Issues in Business,* 6th ed. (Belmont, CA: Wadsworth, 1995).
25. T. M. Jones, "Instrumental Stakeholder Theory: A Synthesis of Ethics and Economics," *Academy of Management Review* 20 (1995), 404–37.
26. B. Victor and J. B. Cullen, "The Organizational Bases of Ethical Work Climates," *Administrative Science Quarterly* 33 (1988), 101–25.
27. www.yahoo.com, 2010.
28. www.napster.com, 2010; bestbuy.com, 2010.
29. C. W. L. Hill, "Napster," in C. W. L. Hill and G. R. Jones, *Strategic Management: An Integrated Approach* (Boston: Houghton Mifflin, 2010).
30. D. Collins, "Organizational Harm, Legal Consequences and Stakeholder Retaliation," *Journal of Business Ethics* 8 (1988), 1–13.
31. R. C. Soloman, *Ethics and Excellence* (New York: Oxford University Press, 1992).
32. T. E. Becker, "Integrity in Organizations: Beyond Honesty and Conscientiousness," *Academy of Management Review* 23 (January 1998), 154–62.
33. S. W. Gellerman, "Why Good Managers Make Bad Decisions," in K. R. Andrews, ed., *Ethics in Practice: Managing the Moral Corporation* (Boston: Harvard Business School Press, 1989).
34. J. Dobson, "Corporate Reputation: A Free Market Solution to Unethical Behavior," *Business and Society* 28 (1989), 1–5.
35. M. S. Baucus and J. P. Near, "Can Illegal Corporate Behavior Be Predicted? An Event History Analysis," *Academy of Management Journal* 34 (1991), 9–36.
36. Trevino, "Ethical Decision Making in Organizations."
37. "GSK, Merck, and Bristol Myers Squibb Are the World's Most Ethical Companies, across All Sectors, Swiss Study," www.medicalnewstoday.com, January 8, 2006.
38. A. S. Waterman, "On the Uses of Psychological Theory and Research in the Process of Ethical Inquiry," *Psychological Bulletin* 103, no. 3 (1988), 283–98.
39. P. Engardio and R. Dexter, "How to Makes Factories Play Fair," www.businessweek.com, November 27, 2006.
40. M. S. Frankel, "Professional Codes: Why, How, and with What Impact?" *Ethics* 8 (1989), 109–15.

41. J. Van Maanen and S. R. Barley, "Occupational Communities: Culture and Control in Organizations," in B. Staw and L. Cummings, eds., *Research in Organizational Behavior,* vol. 6 (Greenwich, CT: JAI Press, 1984), 287–365.
42. Jones, "Ethical Decision Making by Individuals in Organizations."
43. www.bbc.co.uk, press release, January 10, 2010.
44. A. Soke, "Jimmy Carter Helps Build 1000th and 1001st Home," www.typepad.com, May 22, 2007.
45. www.habitat.org, press release, March 2010.
46. E. Gatewood and A. B. Carroll, "The Anatomy of Corporate Social Response," *Business Horizons,* September–October 1981, 9–16.
47. www.yahoo.com, June 7, 2006.
48. M. Friedman, "A Friedman Doctrine: The Social Responsibility of Business Is to Increase Its Profits," *New York Times Magazine,* September 13, 1970, 33.
49. P. Engardio and M. Arndt, "What Price Reputation?" www.businessweek.com, July 9, 2007.
50. M. Conlin, "Where Layoffs Are a Last Resort," www.businessweek.com, October 8, 2001; Southwest Airlines Fact Sheet, www.southwest.com, 2004.
51. G. R. Jones, *Organizational Theory: Text and Cases* (Englewood Cliffs, NJ: Prentice-Hall, 2008).
52. P. E. Murphy, "Creating Ethical Corporate Structure," *Sloan Management Review,* Winter 1989, 81–87.
53. C. Stavraka, "Strong Corporate Reputation at J&J Boosts Diversity Recruiting Efforts," DiversityInc.com, February 16, 2001.
54. "Our Credo," www.jj.com, 2010.
55. Ibid.
56. L. L. Nash, *Good Intentions Aside* (Boston: Harvard Business School Press, 1993).
57. Ibid.; L. L. Nash, "Johnson & Johnson's Credo," in *Corporate Ethics: A Prime Business Asset* (New York: Business Roundtable, February 1988).
58. Nash, *Good Intentions Aside.*
59. Stavraka, "Strong Corporate Reputation."
60. Nash, *Good Intentions Aside.*
61. R. Johnson, "Ralston to Buy Beechnut, Gambling It Can Overcome Apple Juice Scandal," *The Wall Street Journal,* September 18, 1989, B11.

Chapter 5

1. P. Dvorak, "Firms Push New Methods to Promote Diversity," *The Wall Street Journal,* December 18, 2006, B3; www.sodexhousa.com/, February 7, 2008, About Us, http:/www.sodexousa.com/usen/aboutus/aboutus.asp; February 8, 2010.
2. Dvorak, "Firms Push New Methods to Promote Diversity."
3. Dvorak, "Firms Push New Methods to Promote Diversity."
4. Dvorak, "Firms Push New Methods to Promote Diversity."
5. Dvorak, "Firms Push New Methods to Promote Diversity."
6. "Sodexho Named Large Employer of the Year by Pike Area (Alabama) Committee," www.sodexhousa.com/press-releases/pr110907_2.asp, February 6, 2008; No. 6 Sodexo–DiversityInc.com, http:/www.diversityinc.com/content/1757/article/5454/?No_6_Sodexo, February 9, 2010; Sodexo Tops 2009 HACR List of Most Inclusive Companies for Hispanics, http://www.sodexousa.com/usen/newsroom/press/press10/hacrcorporateinclusion.asp, February 8, 2010.
7. "Corporate Diversity," www.sodexhousa.com/press-factsheets/press_fact_corporate.asp, February 6, 2008; "Sodexho Named to *Atlanta Tribune's* Top Companies for Minorities," www.sodexhousa.com/-press-releases/pr111207_1.asp, February 6, 2008; "Sodexho Recognized as Leader in Corporate Social Responsibility by Montgomery County Chamber of Commerce," www.sodexhousa.com/press-releases/pr111507.asp, February 6, 2008.
8. "Sodexho Chief Diversity Officer Named among Top 20 Diversity Champions," www.sodexhousa.com/press-releases/pr110907_3.asp, February 6, 2008; "Sodexho Receives Texas DiversityFirst Leadership Award," www.sodexhousa.com/press-releases/pr110907_1.asp, February 6, 2008; "Gutierrez Honored by the Hispanic Association on Corporate Responsibility," www.sodexhousa.com/press-releases/pr111207_2.asp, February 6, 2008.
9. Principal.com–About the Principal, http://www.principal.com/about/index.htm?print, February 8, 2010.
10. 100 Best Companies to Work For 2008: Principal Financial Group snapshot/FORTUNE, http://money.cnn.com/magazines/fortune/bestcompanies/2008/snapshots/21.html, February 8, 2010; 100 Best Companies to Work For 2009: Principal Financial Group–PFG–from *Fortune,* http://money.cnn.com/magazines/fortune/best-companies/2009/snapshots/17.html, February 8, 2010; Jessi Hempel, "In the Land of Women," *Fortune,* February 4, 2008, 68–69; Diversity: The Principal Financial Group Earns High Marks in 2010 Corporate Equality . . . , http://www.echelonmagazine.com/index.php?id=1123, February 8, 2010; Human Rights Campaign Foundation, Corporate Equality Index, 2010; HRC/Corporate Equality Index, http://www.hrc.org/issues/workplace/cei.htm, February 22, 2010.
11. Hempel, "In the Land of Women."
12. Hempel, "In the Land of Women."
13. Principal.com–Careers: Diversity, http://www.principal.com/careers/workinghere/diversity.htm?print, February 8, 2010; Principal.com–Careers at The Principal. http://www.principal.com/careers/workinghere/benefits_main.htm?print, February 8, 2010.
14. Principal.com–Careers: Employee Resource Groups, http://www.principal.com/careers/workinghere/resourcegroups.htm?print, February 8, 2010.
15. D. McCracken, "Winning the Talent War for Women," *Harvard Business Review,* November–December 2000, 159–67.
16. W. B. Swann, Jr., J. T. Polzer, D. C. Seyle, and S. J. Ko, "Finding Value in Diversity: Verification of Personal and Social Self-Views in Diverse Groups," *Academy of Management Review* 29, no. 1 (2004), 9–27.
17. "Usual Weekly Earnings Summary," *News: Bureau of Labor Statistics,* April 16, 2004 (www.bls.gov/news.release/whyeng.nr0.htm); "Facts on Affirmative Action in Employment and Contracting," *Americans for a Fair Chance,* January, 28, 2004 (fairchance.civilrights.org/research_center/details.cfm?id=18076); "Household Data Annual Averages," www.bls.gov, April 28, 2004.
18. "Prejudice: Still on the Menu," *BusinessWeek,* April 3, 1995, 42.
19. "She's a Woman, Offer Her Less," *BusinessWeek,* May 7, 2001, 34.
20. "Glass Ceiling Is a Heavy Barrier for Minorities, Blocking Them from Top Jobs," *The Wall Street Journal,* March 14, 1995, A1.
21. "Catalyst Report Outlines Unique Challenges Faced by African-American Women in Business," *Catalyst news release,* February 18, 2004.
22. C. Gibson, "Nation's Median Age Highest Ever, but 65-and-Over Population's Growth Lags, Census 2000 Shows," *U.S. Census Bureau News,* May 30, 2001 (www.census.gov); "U.S. Census Press Releases: Nation's Population One-Third Minority," *U.S. Census Bureau News,* May 10, 2006 (www.census.gov/Press-Release/www/releases/archives/population/006808.html).
23. "Table 2: United States Population Projections by Age and Sex: 2000–2050," *U.S. Census Board, International Data Base, 94,* April 28, 2004 (www.census.gov/ipc/www.idbprint.html).

24. U.S. Equal Employment Opportunity Commission, "Federal Laws Prohibiting Job Discrimination–Questions and Answers," www.eeoc.gov, June 20, 2001.
25. "Sex by Industry by Class of Worker for the Employed Civilian Population 16 Years and Over," *American FactFinder,* October 15, 2001 (factfinder.census.gov); "2002 Catalyst Census of Women Corporate Officers and Top Earners in the *Fortune* 500," www.catalystwomen.org, August 17, 2004; WB–Statistics & Data, http://www.dol.gov/wb/stats/main.htm?PrinterFriendly=true&, February 9, 2010.
26. "Profile of Selected Economic Characteristics: 2000," *American FactFinder,* October 15, 2001 (factfinder.census.gov); "Usual Weekly Earnings Summary," www.bls.gov/news.release, August 17, 2004; WB–Statistics & Data, http://www.dol.gov/wb/stats/main.htm?PrinterFriendly=true&, February 9, 2010.
27. "2000 Catalyst Census of Women Corporate Officers and Top Earners of the *Fortune* 500," www.catalystwomen.org, October 21, 2001; S. Wellington, M. Brumit Kropf, and P. R. Gerkovich, "What's Holding Women Back?" *Harvard Business Review,* June 2003, 18–19; D. Jones, "The Gender Factor," *USA Today.com,* December 30, 2003; "2002 Catalyst Census of Women Corporate Officers and Top Earners in the *Fortune* 500," www.catalystwomen.org, August 17, 2004; "2007 Catalyst Census of Women Corporate Officers and Top Earners of the *Fortune* 500," www.catalyst.org/knowledge/titles/title.php?page=cen_COTE_07, February 8, 2008.
28. T. Gutner, "Wanted: More Diverse Directors," *BusinessWeek,* April 30, 2001, 134; "2003 Catalyst Census of Women Board Directors," www.catalystwomen.org, August 17, 2004; "2007 Catalyst Census of Women Board Directors of the *Fortune* 500," www.catalyst.org/knowledge/titles/title.php?page+cen_WBD_07, February 8, 2008.
29. Gutner, "Wanted: More Diverse Directors"; "2003 Catalyst Census of Women Board Directors."
30. R. Sharpe, "As Leaders, Women Rule," *BusinessWeek,* November 20, 2000, 75–84.
31. Sharpe, "As Leaders, Women Rule."
32. "New Catalyst Study Reveals Financial Performance Is Higher for Companies with More Women at the Top," *Catalyst news release,* January 26, 2004.
33. P. Sellers, "Women on Boards (NOT!)," *Fortune,* October 15, 2007, 105.
34. United States Census 2010, U.S. Department of Commerce, U.S. Census Bureau.
35. United States Census 2010, U.S. Department of Commerce, U.S. Census Bureau
36. B. Guzman, "The Hispanic Population," U.S. Census Bureau, May 2001; U.S. Census Bureau, "Profiles of General Demographic Characteristics," May 2001; U.S. Census Bureau, "Revisions to the Standards for the Classification of Federal Data on Race and Ethnicity," November 2, 2000, 1–19.
37. L. Chavez, "Just Another Ethnic Group," *The Wall Street Journal,* May 14, 2001, A22.
38. Bureau of Labor Statistics, "Civilian Labor Force 16 and Older by Sex, Age, Race, and Hispanic Origin, 1978, 1988, 1998, and Projected 2008," stats.bls.gov/emp, October 16, 2001.
39. "U.S. Census Bureau, Profile of General Demographic Characteristics: 2000," *Census 2000,* www.census.gov; "U.S. Census Press Releases: Nation's Population One-Third Minority," *U.S. Census Bureau News,* May 10, 2006 (www.census.gov/Press-Release/www/releases/archives/population/006808.html).
40. *U.S. Census Bureau,* "Census Bureau Projects Tripling of Hispanic and Asian Populations in 50 Years; Non-Hispanic Whites May Drop to Half of Total Populations," www.census.gov/Press-Release/www/releases/archives/population/001720.html, March 18, 2004; "Asians Projected to Lead Next Population Growth Surge," *Houston Chronicle,* May 1, 2004, 3A.
41. "Report Says Disparities Abound between Blacks, Whites," *Houston Chronicle,* March 24, 2004, 7A.
42. "Report Says Disparities Abound between Blacks, Whites."
43. J. Flint, "NBC to Hire More Minorities on TV shows," *The Wall Street Journal,* January 6, 2000, B13.
44. J. Poniewozik, "What's Wrong with This Picture?" *Time,* June 1, 2001 (www.Time.com).
45. Poniewozik, "What's Wrong with This Picture?"
46. National Association of Realtors, "Real Estate Industry Adapting to Increasing Cultural Diversity," *PR Newswire,* May 16, 2001.
47. "Toyota Apologizes to African Americans over Controversial Ad," *Kyodo News Service,* Japan, May 23, 2001.
48. J. H. Coplan, "Putting a Little Faith in Diversity," *BusinessWeek Online,* December 21, 2000.
49. Coplan, "Putting a Little Faith in Diversity."
50. Coplan, "Putting a Little Faith in Diversity."
51. K. Holland, "When Religious Needs Test Company," *The New York Times,* February 25, 2007, BU17.
52. J. N. Cleveland, J. Barnes-Farrell, and J. M. Ratz, "Accommodation in the Workplace," *Human Resource Management Review* 7 (1997), 77–108; A. Colella, "Coworker Distributive Fairness Judgments of the Workplace Accommodations of Employees with Disabilities," *Academy of Management Review* 26 (2001), 100–16.
53. Colella, "Coworker Distributive Fairness Judgments"; D. Stamps, "Just How Scary Is the ADA," *Training* 32 (1995), 93–101; M. S. West and R. L. Cardy, "Accommodating Claims of Disability: The Potential Impact of Abuses," *Human Resource Management Review* 7 (1997), 233–46.
54. G. Koretz, "How to Enable the Disabled," *BusinessWeek,* November 6, 2000 (*BusinessWeek* Archives).
55. Colella, "Coworker Distributive Fairness Judgments."
56. "Notre Dame Disability Awareness Week 2004 Events," www.nd.edu/~bbuddies/daw.html, April 30, 2004.
57. P. Hewitt, "UH Highlights Abilities, Issues of the Disabled," *Houston Chronicle,* October 22, 2001, 24A.
58. "Notre Dame Disability Awareness Week 2004 Events"; Hewitt, "UH Highlights Abilities, Issues of the Disabled."
59. J. M. George, "AIDS/AIDS-Related Complex," in L. H. Peters, C. R. Greer, and S. A. Youngblood, eds., *The Blackwell Encyclopedic Dictionary of Human Resource Management* (Oxford, UK: Blackwell, 1997), 6–7.
60. J. M. George, "AIDS Awareness Training," in L. H. Peters, C. R. Greer, and S. A. Youngblood, eds., *The Blackwell Encyclopedic Dictionary of Human Resource Management* (Oxford, UK: Blackwell, 1997), 6.
61. S. Armour, "Firms Juggle Stigma, Needs of More Workers with HIV," *USA Today,* September 7, 2000, B1.
62. Armour, "Firms Juggle Stigma, Needs of More Workers with HIV."
63. Armour, "Firms Juggle Stigma, Needs of More Workers with HIV."; S. Vaughn, "Career Challenge; Companies' Work Not Over in HIV and AIDS Education," *Los Angeles Times,* July 8, 2001.
64. R. Brownstein, "Honoring Work Is Key to Ending Poverty," *Detroit News,* October 2, 2001, 9; G. Koretz, "How Welfare to Work Worked," *BusinessWeek,* September 24, 2001 (*BusinessWeek* Archives).

65. "As Ex-Welfare Recipients Lose Jobs, Offer Safety Net," *The Atlanta Constitution,* October 10, 2001, A18.
66. C. S. Rugaber, "Job Openings in a Squeeze," *Houston Chronicle,* February 10, 2010, D1.
67. Press Releases, U.S. Census Bureau, "Income, Poverty and Health Insurance Coverage in the United States: 2008," http://www.census.gov/Press-Release/www/releases/archives/income_wealth/014227.html, February 8, 2010; "The 2009 HHS Poverty Guidelines," http://aspe.hhs.gov/poverty/09poverty.shtml, February 8, 2010.
68. U.S. Census Bureau, "Poverty–How the Census Bureau Measures Poverty," *Census 2000,* September 25, 2001.
69. Press Releases, U.S. Census Bureau, "Income, Poverty and Health Insurance Coverage in the United States: 2008," http://www.census.gov/Press-Release/www/releases/archives/income_wealth/014227.html, February 8, 2010; "The 2009 HHS Poverty Guidelines," http://aspe.hhs.gov/poverty/09poverty.shtml, February 8, 2010.
70. I. Lelchuk, "Families Fear Hard Times Getting Worse/$30,000 in the Bay Area Won't Buy Necessities, Survey Says," *San Francisco Chronicle,* September 26, 2001, A13; S. R. Wheeler, "Activists: Welfare-to-Work Changes Needed," *Denver Post,* October 10, 2001, B6.
71. B. Carton, "Bedtime Stories: In 24-Hour Workplace, Day Care Is Moving to the Night Shift," *The Wall Street Journal,* July 6, 2001, A1, A4.
72. Carton, "Bedtime Stories: In 24-Hour Workplace, Day Care Is Moving to the Night Shift"; Mission, Core Values, and Philosophy, *Children's Choice Features,* http://childrenschoice.com/AboutUs/MissionCoreValuesandPhilosophy/tabid/59/Default.aspx, February 9, 2010.
73. Carton, "Bedtime Stories: In 24-Hour Workplace, Day Care Is Moving to the Night Shift."
74. Carton, "Bedtime Stories: In 24-Hour Workplace, Day Care Is Moving to the Night Shift."
75. "Google View Question: Q: Homosexual Statistics," answers.google.com/answers/threadview?id=271269, April 30, 2004; D. M. Smith and G. Gates, "Gay and Lesbian Families in the United States," *Urban Institute,* May 28, 2006 (www.urban.org/publications/1000491.html).
76. S. E. Needleman, "More Programs Move to Halt Bias against Gays," *The Wall Street Journal,* November 26, 2007, B3.
77. K. Fahim, "United Parcel Service Agrees to Benefits in Civil Unions," *The New York Times,* July 31, 2007, A19.
78. J. Hempel, "Coming Out in Corporate America," *BusinessWeek,* December 15, 2003, 64–72.
79. Hempel, "Coming Out in Corporate America."
80. J. Files, "Study Says Discharges Continue under 'Don't Ask, Don't Tell,' " *The New York Times,* March 24, 2004, A14; J. Files, "Gay Ex-Officers Say 'Don't Ask' Doesn't Work," *The New York Times,* December 10, 2003, A14.
81. Hempel, "Coming Out in Corporate America"; "DreamWorks Animation SKG Company History," www.dreamworksanimation.com/dwa/opencms/company/history/index.html, May 29, 2006; J. Chng, "Allan Gilmour: Former Vice-Chairman of Ford Speaks on Diversity," www.harbus.org/media/storage/paper343/news/2006/04/18/News/Allan.Gilmour.Former.ViceChairman.Of.Ford.Speaks.On.Diversity-1859600.shtml?nore write200606021800&sourcedomain=www.harbus.org, April 18, 2006.
82. Needleman, "More Programs Move to Halt Bias against Gays."
83. Hempel, "Coming Out in Corporate America."
84. Needleman, "More Programs Move to Halt Bias against Gays."
85. Needleman, "More Programs Move to Halt Bias against Gays."
86. "For Women, Weight May Affect Pay," *Houston Chronicle,* March 4, 2004, 12A.
87. V. Valian, *Why So Slow? The Advancement of Women* (Cambridge, MA: MIT Press, 2000).
88. S. T. Fiske and S. E. Taylor, *Social Cognition,* 2d ed. (New York: McGraw-Hill, 1991); Valian, *Why So Slow?*
89. Valian, *Why So Slow?*
90. S. Rynes and B. Rosen, "A Field Survey of Factors Affecting the Adoption and Perceived Success of Diversity Training," *Personnel Psychology* 48 (1995), 247–70; Valian, *Why So Slow?*
91. V. Brown and F. L. Geis, "Turning Lead into Gold: Leadership by Men and Women and the Alchemy of Social Consensus," *Journal of Personality and Social Psychology* 46 (1984), 811–24; Valian, *Why So Slow?*
92. Valian, *Why So Slow?*
93. J. Cole and B. Singer, "A Theory of Limited Differences: Explaining the Productivity Puzzle in Science," in H. Zuckerman, J. R. Cole, and J. T. Bruer, eds., *The Outer Circle: Women in the Scientific Community* (New York: Norton, 1991), 277–310; M. F. Fox, "Sex, Salary, and Achievement: Reward Dualism in Academia," *Sociology of Education* 54 (1981), 71–84; J. S. Long, "The Origins of Sex Differences in Science," *Social Forces* 68 (1990), 1297–1315; R. F. Martell, D. M. Lane, and C. Emrich, "Male–Female Differences: A Computer Simulation," *American Psychologist* 51 (1996), 157–58; Valian, *Why So Slow?*
94. Cole and Singer, "A Theory of Limited Differences"; Fox, "Sex, Salary, and Achievement: Reward Dualism in Academia"; Long, "The Origins of Sex Differences in Science"; Martell, Lane, and Emrich, "Male–Female Differences: A Computer Simulation"; Valian, *Why So Slow?*
95. R. Folger and M. A. Konovsky, "Effects of Procedural and Distributive Justice on Reactions to Pay Raise Decisions," *Academy of Management Journal* 32 (1989), 115–30; J. Greenberg, "Organizational Justice: Yesterday, Today, and Tomorrow," *Journal of Management* 16 (1990), 399–402; "O. Janssen, "How Fairness Perceptions Make Innovative Behavior More or Less Stressful," *Journal of Organizational Behavior* 25 (2004), 201–15.
96. Catalyst, "The Glass Ceiling in 2000: Where Are Women Now?" www.catalystwomen.org, October 21, 2001; Bureau of Labor Statistics, 1999, www.bls.gov; Catalyst, "1999 Census of Women Corporate Officers and Top Earners," www.catalystwomen.org; "1999 Census of Women Board Directors of the *Fortune* 1000," www.catalystwomen.org; Catalyst, "Women of Color in Corporate Management: Opportunities and Barriers, 1999," www.catalystwomen.org, October 21, 2001.
97. "Household Data Annual Averages," www.bls.gov, April 28, 2004; U.S. Bureau of Labor Statistics, Economic News Release, Table 7. *Median Usual Weekly Earnings of Full-Time Wage and Salary Workers by Occupation and Sex, Annual Averages,* http://data.bls.gov/cgi-bin/print.pl/news.release/wkyeng.t07.htm, February 9, 2010.
98. "Household Data Annual Averages," www.bls.gov, April 28, 2004.
99. A. M. Jaffe, "At Texaco, the Diversity Skeleton Still Stalks the Halls," *The New York Times,* December 11, 1994, sec. 3, p. 5.
100. Greenberg, "Organizational Justice"; M. G. Ehrhart, "Leadership and Procedural Justice Climate as Antecedents of Unit-Level Organizational Citizenship Behavior,"

Personnel Psychology 57 (2004), 61–94; A. Colella, R. L. Paetzold, and M. A. Belliveau, "Factors Affecting Coworkers' Procedural Justice Inferences of the Workplace Accommodations of Employees with Disabilities," *Personnel Psychology* 57 (2004), 1–23.

101. G. Robinson and K. Dechant, "Building a Case for Business Diversity," *Academy of Management Executive* 3 (1997), 32–47.
102. A. Patterson, "Target 'Micromarkets' Its Way to Success; No 2 Stores Are Alike," *The Wall Street Journal,* May 31, 1995, A1, A9.
103. "The Business Case for Diversity: Experts Tell What Counts, What Works," *DiversityInc.com,* October 23, 2001.
104. B. Hetzer, "Find a Niche–and Start Scratching," *BusinessWeek,* September 14, 1998 (*BusinessWeek* Archives).
105. K. Aaron, "Woman Laments Lack of Diversity on Boards of Major Companies," *The Times Union,* May 16, 2001 (www.timesunion.com).
106. "The Business Case for Diversity."
107. B. Frankel, "Measuring Diversity Is One Sure Way of Convincing CEOs of Its Value," *DiversityInc.com,* October 5, 2001.
108. A. Stevens, "Lawyers and Clients," *The Wall Street Journal,* June 19, 1995, B7.
109. J. Kahn, "Diversity Trumps the Downturn," *Fortune,* July 9, 2001, 114–16.
110. H. R. Schiffmann, *Sensation and Perception: An Integrated Approach* (New York: Wiley, 1990).
111. McDonald's Corporation, 2008 Annual Report.
112. A. E. Serwer, "McDonald's Conquers the World," *Fortune,* October 17, 1994, 103–16.
113. S. T. Fiske and S. E. Taylor, *Social Cognition* (Reading, MA: Addison-Wesley, 1984).
114. J. S. Bruner, "Going beyond the Information Given," in H. Gruber, G. Terrell, and M. Wertheimer, eds., *Contemporary Approaches to Cognition* (Cambridge, MA: Harvard University Press, 1957); Fiske and Taylor, *Social Cognition.*
115. Fiske and Taylor, *Social Cognition.*
116. Valian, *Why So Slow?*
117. D. Bakan, *The Duality of Human Existence* (Chicago: Rand McNally, 1966); J. T. Spence and R. L. Helmreich, *Masculinity and Femininity: Their Psychological Dimensions, Correlates, and Antecedents* (Austin: University of Texas Press, 1978); J. T. Spence and L. L. Sawin, "Images of Masculinity and Femininity: A Reconceptualization," in V. E. O'Leary, R. K. Unger, and B. B. Wallston, eds., *Women, Gender, and Social Psychology* (Hillsdale, NJ: Erlbaum, 1985), 35–66; Valian, *Why So Slow?*
118. Valian, *Why So Slow?*
119. Serwer, "McDonald's Conquers the World"; P. R. Sackett, C. M. Hardison, and M. J. Cullen, "On Interpreting Stereotype Threat as Accounting for African American–White Differences on Cognitive Tests," *American Psychologist* 59, no. 1 (January 2004), 7–13; C. M. Steele and J. A. Aronson, "Stereotype Threat Does Not Live by Steele and Aronson," *American Psychologist* 59, no. 1 (January 2004), 47–55; P. R. Sackett, C. M. Hardison, and M. J. Cullen, "On the Value of Correcting Mischaracterizations of Stereotype Threat Research," *American Psychologist* 59, no. 1 (January 2004), 47–49; D. M. Amodio, E. Harmon-Jones, P. G. Devine, J. J. Curtin, S. L. Hartley, and A. E. Covert, "Neural Signals for the Detection of Unintentional Race Bias," *Psychological Science* 15, no. 2 (2004), 88–93.
120. M. Loden and J. B. Rosener, *Workforce America! Managing Employee Diversity as a Vital Resource* (Burr Ridge, IL: Irwin, 1991).
121. M. E. Heilman and T. G. Okimoto, "Motherhood: A Potential Source of Bias in Employment Decisions," *Journal of Applied Psychology* 93, no. 1 (2008), 189–98.
122. L. Roberson, B. M. Galvin, and A. C. Charles, "Chapter 13, When Group Identities Matter: Bias in Performance Appraisal," in J. P. Walsh and A. P. Brief, eds., *The Academy of Management Annals* 1 (New York: Erlbaum, 2008, 617–50).
123. A. Stein Wellner, "The Disability Advantage," *Inc. Magazine,* October 2005, 29–31.
124. A. Merrick, "Erasing 'Un' From 'Unemployable,'" *The Wall Street Journal,* August 2, 2007, B6.
125. Merrick, "Erasing 'Un' From 'Unemployable.'"
126. Merrick, "Erasing 'Un' From 'Unemployable.'"
127. "Habitat International: Our Products," www.habitatint.com/products.htm, April 6, 2006; "Habitat International Home Page," www.habitatint.com, April 6, 2006.
128. Wellner, "The Disability Advantage."
129. "Habitat International: Our People," Habitat International–Our People, http://www.habitatint.com/people.htm, February 10, 2010.
130. Wellner, "The Disability Advantage."
131. "Habitat International: Our People"; Wellner, "The Disability Advantage."
132. "Habitat International: Our People"; Wellner, "The Disability Advantage."
133. "Habitat International: Our People"; Wellner, "The Disability Advantage."
134. "Habitat International: Our People"; Wellner, "The Disability Advantage."
135. E. D. Pulakos and K. N. Wexley, "The Relationship among Perceptual Similarity, Sex, and Performance Ratings in Manager Subordinate Dyads," *Academy of Management Journal* 26 (1983), 129–39.
136. Fiske and Taylor, *Social Cognition.*
137. "Hotel to Pay $8 Million in Settlement," *The Houston Chronicle,* March 22, 2000, 3A; M. France and T. Smart, "The Ugly Talk on the Texaco Tape," *BusinessWeek,* November 18, 1996, 58; J. S. Lublin, "Texaco Case Causes a Stir in Boardrooms," *The Wall Street Journal,* November 22, 1996, B1, B6; T. Smart, "Texaco: Lessons from a Crisis-in-Progress," *BusinessWeek,* December 2, 1996, 44; "Ford Settling Bias Case, Will Hire More Women, Minorities," *The Houston Chronicle,* February 19, 2000, 8C; C. Salter, "A Reformer Who Means Business," *Fast Company,* April 2003, 102–11; A. Zimmerman, "Wal-Mart Appeals Bias-Suit Ruling," *The Wall Street Journal,* August 8, 2005, B5: C. H. Deutsch, "Chief of Unit Files Lawsuit Accusing G.E. of Racial Bias," *The New York Times,* May 18, 2005, C3; "Nike Settles Discrimination Suit for $7.6 Million," *The Wall Street Journal,* July 31, 2007, B9; R. Parloff, "The War over Unconscious Bias," *Fortune,* October 15, 2007, 90–102.
138. N. Alster, "When Gray Heads Roll, Is Age Bias at Work?" *The New York Times,* January 30, 2005, BU3.
139. "Nike Settles Discrimination Suit for $7.6 Million," *The Wall Street Journal,* July 31, 2007, B9.
140. "Nike Settles Discrimination Suit for $7.6 Million."
141. "Nike Settles Discrimination Suit for $7.6 Million."
142. M. Fackler, "Career Women in Japan Find a Blocked Path," *The New York Times,* August 6, 2007, A6.
143. Fackler, "Career Women in Japan Find a Blocked Path"; www.un.org, February 11, 2008.
144. Fackler, "Career Women in Japan Find a Blocked Path."
145. www.nissanusa.com.
146. Fackler, "Career Women in Japan Find a Blocked Path."
147. Press Releases, U.S. Census Bureau, "Income, Poverty and Health Insurance Coverage in the United States:

2008," http://www.census.gov/Press-Release/www/releases/archives/income_wealth/014227.html, February 8, 2010.

148. Jennifer Levitz, "More Workers Cite Age Bias during Layoffs," *The Wall Street Journal,* March 11, 2009, pp. D1–2.

149. Levitz, "More Workers Cite Age Bias during Layoffs."

150. Levitz, "More Workers Cite Age Bias during Layoffs."

151. Levitz, "More Workers Cite Age Bias during Layoffs."

152. A. Raghavan, "Terminated: Why the Women of Wall Street Are Disappearing," Forbes.com–Magazine Article, ForbesWoman, by March 16, 2009, http://forbes.com/forbes/2009/0316-072_terminated_women_print.html, February 10, 2010.

153. A. Raghavan, "Terminated: Why the Women of Wall Street Are Disappearing."

154. G. Gross, "Dell Hit with Discrimination Class-Action Lawsuit," *The New York Times,* October 29, 2008, http://www.nytimes.com/external/idg/2008/10/29/29idg-Dell-hit-with-d.html?pagewanted . . . , February 10, 2010.

155. A. Gonsalves, "Dell Denies Discrimination In Layoffs," *InformationWeek,* November 3, 2008, http://www.informationweek.com/shared/printableArticleSrc.jhtml;jsessionid=5RQQTNK . . . , February 11, 2010.

156. A. G. Greenwald and M. Banaji, "Implicit Social Cognition: Attitudes, Self-Esteem, and Stereotypes," *Psychological Review* 102 (1995), 4–27.

157. A. Fisher, "Ask Annie: Five Ways to Promote Diversity in the Workplace," *Fortune,* April 23, 2004 (www.fortune.com/fortune/subs/print/0,15935,455997,00.html); E. Bonabeau, "Don't Trust Your Gut," *Harvard Business Review,* May 2003, 116–23.

158. A. P. Carnevale and S. C. Stone, "Diversity: Beyond the Golden Rule," *Training & Development,* October 1994, 22–39.

159. Fisher, "Ask Annie."

160. J. S. Lublin, "Top Brass Try Life in the Trenches," *The Wall Street Journal,* June 25, 2007, B1, B3.

161. www.davita.com, February 11, 2008; Company–About DaVita, http://www.davita.com/about/, February 11, 2010.

162. Lublin, "Top Brass Try Life in the Trenches."

163. Lublin, "Top Brass Try Life in the Trenches."

164. Lublin, "Top Brass Try Life in the Trenches."

165. Lublin, "Top Brass Try Life in the Trenches;" www.loews.com/loews.nsf/governance.htm, February 7, 2008; Lowes Hotel–Resorts, http://www.loewshotels.com/en/default.aspx?cm_mmc=Google-_-National-_-Paid%20Sea . . . , February 11, 2010.

166. Lublin, "Top Brass Try Life in the Trenches."

167. B. A. Battaglia, "Skills for Managing Multicultural Teams," *Cultural Diversity at Work* 4 (1992); Carnevale and Stone, "Diversity: Beyond the Golden Rule."

168. Swann et al., "Finding Value in Diversity."

169. Valian, *Why So Slow?*

170. A. P. Brief, R. T. Buttram, R. M. Reizenstein, S. D. Pugh, J. D. Callahan, R. L. McCline, and J. B. Vaslow, "Beyond Good Intentions: The Next Steps toward Racial Equality in the American Workplace," *Academy of Management Executive,* November 1997, 59–72.

171. Brief et al., "Beyond Good Intentions."

172. Brief et al., "Beyond Good Intentions."

173. Brief et al., "Beyond Good Intentions."

174. Y. Cole, "Linking Diversity to Executive Compensation," *Diversity Inc.,* August–September 2003, 58–62.

175. B. Mandell and S. Kohler-Gray, "Management Development That Values Diversity," *Personnel,* March 1990, 41–47.

176. "Online Extra: UPS Delivers an Eye-Opener," by Bremen Leak, *BusinessWeek,* October 10, 2005, http://www.businessweek.com/print/magazine/content/05_41/b3954012.htm?chan=gl, February 11, 2010; Community Internship Program–UPS Corporate Responsibility, "Community Internship Program," http://www.community.ups.com/Community/Community+Internship+Program, February 11, 2010.

177. B. Filipczak, "25 Years of Diversity at UPS," *Training,* August 1992, 42–46.

178. D. A. Thomas, "Race Matters: The Truth about Mentoring Minorities," *Harvard Business Review,* April 2001, 99–107.

179. Thomas, "Race Matters: The Truth about Mentoring Minorities."

180. S. N. Mehta, "Why Mentoring Works," *Fortune,* July 9, 2000.

181. Mehta, "Why Mentoring Works"; Thomas, "Race Matters."

182. "Chevron Settles Claims of 4 Women at Unit as Part of Sex Bias Suit," *The Wall Street Journal,* January 22, 1995, B12.

183. D. K. Berman, "TWA Settles Harassment Claims at JFK Airport for $2.6 Million," *The Wall Street Journal,* June 25, 2001, B6.

184. A. Lambert, "Insurers Help Clients Take Steps to Reduce Sexual Harassment," *Houston Business Journal,* March 19, 2004 (Houston.bizjournals.com/Houston/stories/2004/03/22/focus4.html).

185. T. Segal, "Getting Serious about Sexual Harassment," *BusinessWeek,* November 9, 1992, 78–82.

186. U.S. Equal Employment Opportunity Commission, "Facts about Sexual Harassment," www.eeoc.gov/facts/fs-sex.html, May 1, 2004.

187. B. Carton, "Muscled Out? At Jenny Craig, Men Are Ones Who Claim Sex Discrimination," *The Wall Street Journal,* November 29, 1994, A1, A7.

188. R. L. Paetzold and A. M. O'Leary-Kelly, "Organizational Communication and the Legal Dimensions of Hostile Work Environment Sexual Harassment," in G. L. Kreps, ed., *Sexual Harassment: Communication Implications* (Cresskill, NJ: Hampton Press, 1993).

189. M. Galen, J. Weber, and A. Z. Cuneo, "Sexual Harassment: Out of the Shadows," *Fortune,* October 28, 1991, 30–31.

190. A. M. O'Leary-Kelly, R. L. Paetzold, and R. W. Griffin, "Sexual Harassment as Aggressive Action: A Framework for Understanding Sexual Harassment," paper presented at the annual meeting of the Academy of Management, Vancouver, August 1995.

191. B. S. Roberts and R. A. Mann, "Sexual Harassment in the Workplace: A Primer," www3.uakron.edu/lawrev/robert1.html, May 1, 2004.

192. "Former FedEx Driver Wins EEOC Lawsuit," *Houston Chronicle,* February 26, 2004, 9B.

193. "Former FedEx Driver Wins EEOC Lawsuit."

194. J. Robertson, "California Jury Awards $61M for Harassment," http://news.Yahoo.com, June 4, 2006.

195. "2 FedEx Drivers Win Slur Lawsuit," *Houston Chronicle,* June 4, 2006, p. A9.

196. S. J. Bresler and R. Thacker, "Four-Point Plan Helps Solve Harassment Problems," *HR Magazine,* May 1993, 117–24.

197. "Du Pont's Solution," *Training,* March 1992, 29.

198. "Du Pont's Solution."

199. "Du Pont's Solution."

Chapter 6

1. www.sony.com, press release, 2010.
2. www.sony.com, press release, 2010.
3. L. J. Bourgeois, "Strategy and Environment: A Conceptual Integration," *Academy of Management Review* 5 (1985), 25–39.
4. M. E. Porter, *Competitive Strategy* (New York: Free Press, 1980).
5. "Coca-Cola versus Pepsi-Cola and the Soft Drink Industry," Harvard Business School Case 9-391-179.
6. www.splenda.com, 2010.
7. A. K. Gupta and V. Govindarajan, "Cultivating a Global Mind-Set," *Academy of Management Executive* 16 (February 2002), 116–27.
8. "Boeing's Worldwide Supplier Network," *Seattle Post-Intelligencer,* April 9, 1994, 13.
9. I. Metthee, "Playing a Large Part," *Seattle Post-Intelligencer,* April 9, 1994, 13.
10. "Business: Link in the Global Chain," *The Economist,* June 2, 2001, 62–63.
11. www.boeing.com, 2010.
12. www.hbi.com, 2010.
13. www.nokia.com, 2010.
14. M. E. Porter, *Competitive Advantage* (New York: Free Press, 1985).
15. www.walmart.com, 2010.
16. www.costco.com, 2010.
17. C. Harris, "Costco Loses State Case on Lowering Beer, Wine Prices," seattlepi .com, January 29, 2008.
18. www.amazon.com, 2010.
19. T. Levitt, "The Globalization of Markets," *Harvard Business Review,* May–June 1983, 92–102.
20. "Dell CEO Would Like 40 Percent PC Market Share," www.dailynews.yahoo .com, June 20, 2001.
21. For views on barriers to entry from an economics perspective, see Porter, *Competitive Strategy.* For the sociological perspective, see J. Pfeffer and G. R. Salancik, *The External Control of Organization: A Resource Dependence Perspective* (New York: Harper & Row, 1978).
22. Porter, *Competitive Strategy;* J. E. Bain, *Barriers to New Competition* (Cambridge, MA: Harvard University Press, 1956); R. J. Gilbert, "Mobility Barriers and the Value of Incumbency," in R. Schmalensee and R. D. Willig, eds., *Handbook of Industrial Organization,* vol. 1 (Amsterdam: North Holland, 1989).
23. Press release, www.amazon.com, May 2001.
24. C. W. L. Hill, "The Computer Industry: The New Industry of Industries," in Hill and Jones, *Strategic Management: An Integrated Approach* (Boston: Houghton Mifflin, 2003).
25. J. Schumpeter, *Capitalism, Socialism and Democracy* (London: Macmillan, 1950), 68. Also see R. R. Winter and S. G. Winter, *An Evolutionary Theory of Economic Change* (Cambridge, MA: Harvard University Press, 1982).
26. N. Goodman, *An Introduction to Sociology* (New York: HarperCollins, 1991); C. Nakane, *Japanese Society* (Berkeley: University of California Press, 1970).
27. For a detailed discussion of the importance of the structure of law as a factor explaining economic change and growth, see D. C. North, *Institutions, Institutional Change, and Economic Performance* (Cambridge: Cambridge University Press, 1990).
28. R. B. Reich, *The Work of Nations* (New York: Knopf, 1991).
29. J. Bhagwati, *Protectionism* (Cambridge, MA: MIT Press, 1988).
30. M. A. Carpenter and J. W. Fredrickson, "Top Management Teams, Global Strategic Posture, and the Moderating Role of Uncertainty," *Academy of Management Journal* 44 (June 2001), 533–46.
31. www.nestle.com, 2010.
32. 2009 Annual Report, www.nestle.com, 2010.
33. www.ikea.com, 2010.
34. Bhagwati, *Protectionism.*
35. For a summary of these theories, see P. Krugman and M. Obstfeld, *International Economics: Theory and Policy* (New York: HarperCollins, 1991). Also see C. W. L. Hill, *International Business* (New York: McGraw-Hill, 1997), chap. 4.
36. A. M. Rugman, "The Quest for Global Dominance," *Academy of Management Executive* 16 (August 2002), 157–60.
37. www.wto.org.com, 2004.
38. www.wto.org.com, 2010.
39. C. A. Bartlett and S. Ghoshal, *Managing across Borders* (Boston: Harvard Business School Press, 1989).
40. C. Arnst and G. Edmondson, "The Global Free-for-All," *BusinessWeek,* September 26, 1994, 118–26.
41. W. Konrads, "Why Leslie Wexner Shops Overseas," *BusinessWeek,* February 3, 1992, 30.
42. E. B. Tylor, *Primitive Culture* (London: Murray, 1971).
43. For details on the forces that shape culture, see Hill, *International Business,* chap. 2.
44. G. Hofstede, B. Neuijen, D. D. Ohayv, and G. Sanders, "Measuring Organizational Cultures: A Qualitative and Quantitative Study across Twenty Cases," *Administrative Science Quarterly* 35 (1990), 286–316.
45. M. H. Hoppe, "Introduction: Geert Hofstede's Culture's Consequences: International Differences in Work-Related Values," *Academy of Management Executive* 18 (February 2004), 73–75.
46. R. Bellah, *Habits of the Heart: Individualism and Commitment in American Life* (Berkeley: University of California Press, 1985).
47. R. Bellah, *The Tokugawa Religion* (New York: Free Press, 1957).
48. C. Nakane, *Japanese Society* (Berkeley: University of California Press, 1970).
49. Ibid.
50. G. Hofstede, "The Cultural Relativity of Organizational Practices and Theories," *Journal of International Business Studies,* Fall 1983, 75–89.
51. Hofstede et al., "Measuring Organizational Cultures."
52. J. Perlez, "GE Finds Tough Going in Hungary," *The New York Times,* July 25, 1994, C1, C3.
53. www.ge.com, 2004, 2010.
54. J. P. Fernandez and M. Barr, *The Diversity Advantage* (New York: Lexington Books, 1994).
55. www.ibm.com, 2010.

Chapter 7

1. D. Sacks, "The Catalyst," *Fast Company,* October 2006, 59–61.
2. About PUMA, http://about.puma.com/EN/1/, February 13, 2008.
3. Sacks, "The Catalyst."
4. Sacks, "The Catalyst."
5. "Puma Expects 2008 Sales, Profits to Rise–PPR CFO, Thursday, January 24, 2008, www.reuters.com/articlePrint?articleId=USL2491288920080124, February 13, 2008.
6. About PUMA, News, "PUMA Smashes Spring World Records with Usain Bolt at World Championships in Athletics in Berlin," Berlin, August 23, 2009, http://about.puma.com/?p=230, February 16, 2010.
7. About PUMA, "PUMA at a Glance," http://about.puma.com/?cat=4, February 16, 2010.
8. Sacks, "The Catalyst."
9. Sacks, "The Catalyst."
10. Sacks, "The Catalyst."
11. Sacks, "The Catalyst"; Fashion in Motion Africa 2005, Xuly Bet, www.vam.ac.uk/collections/fashion/fashion_motion/africa_05/index.html, February 14, 2008.
12. Sacks, "The Catalyst;" PUMA Online Shop, http://www.shop.puma.com/on/demandware.store/Sites-Puma-US-Site/en/Search-Show?q . . . , February 16, 2010.
13. Sacks, "The Catalyst."
14. Company Structure, http://about.puma.com/EN/1/9/9/, February 13, 2008.

15. Sacks, "The Catalyst."

16. G. P. Huber, *Managerial Decision Making* (Glenview, IL: Scott, Foresman, 1993).

17. Sacks, "The Catalyst."

18. Martin Cooper–History of Cell Phone and Martin Cooper, http://inventors.about.com/cs/inventorsalphabet/a/martin_cooper.htm?p=1, February 16, 2010; "Motorola Demonstrates Portable Telephone to Be Available for Public Use by 1976," April 3, 1973, www.motorola.com, February 17, 2009; "The Cellular Telephone Concept–An Overview," September 10, 1984, www.motorola.com, February 17, 2009;" "iPad," http://www.apple.com/, February 16, 2010.

19. H. A. Simon, *The New Science of Management* (Englewood Cliffs, NJ: Prentice-Hall, 1977).

20. N. A. Hira, "The Making of a UPS Driver," *Fortune,* November 12, 2007, 118–29.

21. Hira, "The Making of a UPS Driver"; J. Lovell, "Left-Hand Turn Elimination," *The New York Times,* December 9, 2007, www.nytimes.com/2007/12/09/magazine/09left-handturn.html?_r=2&oref=slogin&r, February 20, 2008.

22. Hira, "The Making of a UPS Driver."

23. L. Osburn, "Expecting the World on a Silver Platter," *Houston Chronicle,* September 17, 2007, D1, D6.

24. Hira, "The Making of a UPS Driver."

25. Hira, "The Making of a UPS Driver"; Welcome to UPS Careers, https://ups.managehr.com/Home.htm, February 20, 2008.

26. UPS Integrad–UPS Corporate Responsibility, http://www.community.ups.com/Safety/Training+For+Safety/UPS+Integrad.

27. Hira, "The Making of a UPS Driver."

28. Hira, "The Making of a UPS Driver."

29. Hira, "The Making of a UPS Driver."

30. Hira, "The Making of a UPS Driver."

31. Hira, "The Making of a UPS Driver."

32. D. Kahneman, "Maps of Bounded Rationality: A Perspective on Intuitive Judgment and Choice," Prize Lecture, December 8, 2002; E. Jaffe, "What Was I Thinking? Kahneman Explains How Intuition Leads Us Astray," *American Psychological Society* 17, no. 5 (May 2004), 23–26; E. Dane and M. Pratt, "Exploring Intuition and Its Role in Managerial Decision Making," *Academy of Management Review* 32 (2007), 33–54.

33. One should be careful not to generalize too much here, however; for as Peter Senge has shown, programmed decisions rely on the implicit assumption that the environment is in a steady state. If environmental conditions change, sticking to a routine decision rule can produce disastrous results. See P. Senge, *The Fifth Discipline: The Art and Practice of the Learning Organization* (New York: Doubleday, 1990).

34. Kahneman, "Maps of Bounded Rationality"; Jaffe, "What Was I Thinking?"

35. Kahneman, "Maps of Bounded Rationality"; Jaffe, "What Was I Thinking?"

36. J. Smutniak, "Freud, Finance and Folly: Human Intuition Is a Bad Guide to Handling Risk," *The Economist* 24 (January 2004), 5–6.

37. Kahneman, "Maps of Bounded Rationality"; Jaffe, "What Was I Thinking?"

38. Kahneman, "Maps of Bounded Rationality"; Jaffe, "What Was I Thinking?"

39. J. Pfeffer, "Curbing the Urge to Merge," *Business 2.0,* July 2003, 58; Smutniak, "Freud, Finance and Folly."

40. Kahneman, "Maps of Bounded Rationality"; Jaffe, "What Was I Thinking?"

41. Pfeffer, "Curbing the Urge to Merge"; Smutniak, "Freud, Finance and Folly."

42. M. Landler, "New Austerity for German Car Industry," *The New York Times,* September 29, 2005, C3; E. Taylor and C. Rauwald, "DaimlerChrysler to Cut 8,500 Jobs at Mercedes," *The Wall Street Journal,* September 29, 2005, A6; G. Edmondson, "On the Hot Seat at Daimler," *BusinessWeek Online,* February 17, 2006 (www.businessweek.com/autos/content/feb2006/bw20060217_187348.htm?campaign_id=search); Daimler AG News–*The New York Times,* http://topics.nytimes.com/topics/news/business/companies/daimler_ag/index.html., February 19, 2010.

43. "Hiring Freeze and Cost Cuts at Time Inc.," *The New York Times,* August 2005, B13.

44. Pfeffer, "Curbing the Urge to Merge."

45. Pfeffer, "Curbing the Urge to Merge."

46. H. A. Simon, *Administrative Behavior* (New York: Macmillan, 1947), 79.

47. H. A. Simon, *Models of Man* (New York: Wiley, 1957).

48. K. J. Arrow, *Aspects of the Theory of Risk Bearing* (Helsinki: Yrjo Johnssonis Saatio, 1965).

49. Arrow, *Aspects of the Theory of Risk Bearing.*

50. N. Gull, "Plan B (and C and D and . . .)," *Inc.,* March 2004, 40; C. Knouf, "Upgrading Your Office," *Orgeon Business,* January 2006, 36–37; D. McMillan, "Printer, Copier Dealer Grows by Doing Business in a Markedly Different Way," *Portland Business Journal,* January 20, 2006; "Associated Business Systems: News & Events," www.associatedbusiness.com/sw/common/custom/internet/custompage/asp, May 30, 2006.

51. Gull, "Plan B."

52. Gull, "Plan B."

53. B. Neill, "Nothing Sells a Printer Like the Promise of Good Service," *Business Journal of Portland,* January 5, 2004 (www.bizjournals.com/Portland/stories/2004/01/05/story4.html?t=printable); "Associated Business Systems Fact Sheet," www.associatedbusiness.com/news_detail.asp?id=6, May 11, 2004; McMillan, "Printer, Copier Dealer Grows."

54. "Associated Business Systems Ranks as One of America's Fastest Growing Private Companies," *Associated Business Systems News,* May 11, 2004 (www.associatedbusiness.com/news_detail.asp?id=7); "About Us," *Associated Business Systems,* www.associatedbusiness.com/sw/common/custom/internet/custompage.asp/SETSES, February 20, 2008.

55. "Associated Business Systems Merges with Ricoh Americas Corporation," May 6, 2008, www.associatedbusiness.com, February 16, 2010.

56. "Overview: Associated Business Systems and Ricoh," http://associatedbusiness.com/about-us-ricoh-portland.php, February 16, 2010.

57. Gull, "Plan B."

58. R. L. Daft and R. H. Lengel, "Organizational Information Requirements, Media Richness and Structural Design," *Management Science* 32 (1986), 554–71.

59. R. Cyert and J. March, *Behavioral Theory of the Firm* (Englewood Cliffs, NJ: Prentice-Hall, 1963).

60. J. G. March and H. A. Simon, *Organizations* (New York: Wiley, 1958).

61. H. A. Simon, "Making Management Decisions: The Role of Intuition and Emotion," *Academy of Management Executive* 1 (1987), 57–64.

62. M. H. Bazerman, *Judgment in Managerial Decision Making* (New York: Wiley, 1986). Also see Simon, *Administrative Behavior.*

63. Scott G. McNealy Profile–Forbes.com, http://people.forbes.com/profile/scott-g-mcnealy/75347, February 16, 2010; Sun Oracle, "Overview and Frequently Asked Questions," www.oracle.com, February 16, 2010.

64. "Sun Microsystems–Investor Relations: Officers and Directors," www.sun.com/aboutsun/investor/sun_facts/officers_directors.html, June 1, 2004; "How Sun Delivers Value to Customers," *Sun Microsystems–Investor Relations: Support & Training,* June 1, 2004 (www.sun.com/aboutsun/investor/sun_facts/core_strategies.html); "Sun at a Glance," *Sun Microsystems–Investor Relations: Sun Facts,* June 1, 2004

(www.sun.com/aboutsun/investor/sun_facts/index.html); "Plug in the System, and Everything Just Works," *Sun Microsystems–Investor Relations: Product Portfolio,* June 1, 2004 (www.sun.com/aboutsun/investor/sun_facts/portfolio/html).

65. N. J. Langowitz and S. C. Wheelright, "Sun Microsystems, Inc. (A)," Harvard Business School Case 686–133.
66. R. D. Hof, "How to Kick the Mainframe Habit," *BusinessWeek,* June 26, 1995, 102–104.
67. Bazerman, *Judgment in Managerial Decision Making;* Huber, *Managerial Decision Making;* J. E. Russo and P. J. Schoemaker, *Decision Traps* (New York: Simon & Schuster, 1989).
68. M. D. Cohen, J. G. March, and J. P. Olsen, "A Garbage Can Model of Organizational Choice," *Administrative Science Quarterly* 17 (1972), 1–25.
69. Cohen, March, and Olsen, "A Garbage Can Model of Organizational Choice."
70. Bazerman, *Judgment in Managerial Decision Making.*
71. Senge, *The Fifth Discipline.*
72. E. de Bono, *Lateral Thinking* (London: Penguin, 1968); Senge, *The Fifth Discipline.*
73. Russo and Schoemaker, *Decision Traps.*
74. Bazerman, *Judgment in Managerial Decision Making.*
75. B. Berger, "NASA: One Year after *Columbia*–Bush's New Vision Changes Agency's Course Midstream," *Space News Business Report,* January 26, 2004 (www.space.com/spacenews/businessmonday_040126.html).
76. J. Glanz and J. Schwartz, "Dogged Engineer's Effort to Assess Shuttle Damage," *The New York Times,* September 26, 2003, A1.
77. M. L. Wald and J. Schwartz, "NASA Chief Promises a Shift in Attitude," *The New York Times,* August 28, 2003, A23.
78. Russo and Schoemaker, *Decision Traps.*
79. Clifford, "Marc Shuman Was Determined to Expand Fast"; D. Kocieniewski, "After $12,000, There's Even Room to Park the Car," *The New York Times,* February 20, 2006; "The World's Cleanest Garage," www.garagetek.com, May 30, 2006 (www.garagetek.com/nav.asp); "What Is Garagetek?" www.garagetek.com, May 30, 2006 (www.garagetek.com/content_CNBC.asp); L. Christie, "7 Franchises: Riding the Housing Boom," CNNMoney.com, March 7, 2006 (http://money.cnn.com/2006/03/07/smbusiness/homefranchises/index.htm); "745 Businesses to Start Now!" *Entrepreneur,* January 2005, 88, 192, 193; "Franchise Opportunities Available," http://www.garagetek.com/FranchiseOpportunities/February 16, 2010; GarageTek Inc.: Private Company Information–*BusinessWeek,* http://investing.businessweek.com/research/stocks/private/snapshot.asp?privcapId=126174 . . . , February 15, 2010; "Garage Makover," *Inc.,* July 2007, p.53.
80. Clifford, "Marc Shuman Was Determined to Expand Fast."
81. Clifford, "Marc Shuman Was Determined to Expand Fast;" "Franchise Opportunities," *Garage Tek,* www.garagetek.com/FranchiseOpportunities/GarageTek-Opportunities.aspx, February 14, 2008.
82. Clifford, "Marc Shuman Was Determined to Expand Fast."
83. Clifford, "Marc Shuman Was Determined to Expand Fast."
84. Clifford, "Marc Shuman Was Determined to Expand Fast."
85. D. Kahneman and A. Tversky, "Judgment under Uncertainty: Heuristics and Biases," *Science* 185 (1974), 1124–31.
86. C. R. Schwenk, "Cognitive Simplification Processes in Strategic Decision Making," *Strategic Management Journal* 5 (1984), 111–28.
87. An interesting example of the illusion of control is Richard Roll's hubris hypothesis of takeovers. See R. Roll, "The Hubris Hypothesis of Corporate Takeovers," *Journal of Business* 59 (1986), 197–216.
88. J. Pfeffer and R. I. Sutton, *Hard Facts, Dangerous Half-Truths, and Total Nonsense: Profiting from Evidence-Based Management* (Boston: Harvard Business School Press, 2006).
89. B. M. Staw, "The Escalation of Commitment to a Course of Action," *Academy of Management Review* 6 (1981), 577–87.
90. Russo and Schoemaker, *Decision Traps.*
91. Russo and Schoemaker, *Decision Traps.*
92. I. L. Janis, *Groupthink: Psychological Studies of Policy Decisions and Disasters,* 2nd ed. (Boston: Houghton Mifflin, 1982).
93. C. R. Schwenk, *The Essence of Strategic Decision Making* (Lexington, MA: Lexington Books, 1988).
94. See R. O. Mason, "A Dialectic Approach to Strategic Planning," *Management Science* 13 (1969) 403–14; R. A. Cosier and J. C. Aplin, "A Critical View of Dialectic Inquiry in Strategic Planning," *Strategic Management Journal* 1 (1980), 343–56; I. I. Mitroff and R. O. Mason, "Structuring III–Structured Policy Issues: Further Explorations in a Methodology for Messy Problems," *Strategic Management Journal* 1 (1980), 331–42.
95. Mason, "A Dialectic Approach to Strategic Planning."
96. D. M. Schweiger and P. A. Finger, "The Comparative Effectiveness of Dialectic Inquiry and Devil's Advocacy," *Strategic Management Journal* 5 (1984), 335–50.
97. Mary C. Gentile, *Differences That Work: Organizational Excellence through Diversity* (Boston: Harvard Business School Press, 1994); F. Rice, "How to Make Diversity Pay," *Fortune,* August 8, 1994, 78–86.
98. B. Hedberg, "How Organizations Learn and Unlearn," in W. H. Starbuck and P. C. Nystrom, eds., *Handbook of Organizational Design,* vol. 1 (New York: Oxford University Press, 1981), 1–27.
99. Senge, *The Fifth Discipline.*
100. Senge, *The Fifth Discipline.*
101. P. M. Senge, "The Leader's New Work: Building Learning Organizations," *Sloan Management Review,* Fall 1990, 7–23.
102. W. Zellner, K. A. Schmidt, M. Ihlwan, and H. Dawley, "How Well Does Wal-Mart Travel?" *BusinessWeek,* September 3, 2001, 82–84.
103. J. P. Walsh and A. P. Brief (eds.), "Creativity in Organizations," *The Academy of Management Annals,* Volume 1, New York: Erlbaum, 439–77.
104. Walsh and Brief, "Creativity in Organizations."
105. C. Saltr, "FAST 50: The World's Most Innovative Companies," *Fast Company,* March 2008, 73–117.
106. R. W. Woodman, J. E. Sawyer, and R. W. Griffin, "Towards a Theory of Organizational Creativity," *Academy of Management Review* 18 (1993), 293–321.
107. T. Evans, "Entrepreneurs Seek to Elicit Workers' Ideas," *The Wall Street Journal,* December 22, 2009, B7; D. Dahl, "Rounding Up Staff Ideas," Inc.com, February 1, 2010, http://www.inc.com/magazine/20100201/rounding-up-staff-ideas_Printer_Friendly.html, February 12, 2010; "About Borrego Solar," http://www.borregosolar.com/solar-energy-company/solar-contractor.php, February 15, 2010.
108. T. J. Bouchard Jr., J. Barsaloux, and G. Drauden, "Brainstorming Procedure, Group Size, and Sex as Determinants of Problem Solving Effectiveness of Individuals and Groups," *Journal of Applied Psychology* 59 (1974), 135–38.

109. M. Diehl and W. Stroebe, "Productivity Loss in Brainstorming Groups: Towards the Solution of a Riddle," *Journal of Personality and Social Psychology* 53 (1987), 497–509.

110. D. H. Gustafson, R. K. Shulka, A. Delbecq, and W. G. Walster, "A Comparative Study of Differences in Subjective Likelihood Estimates Made by Individuals, Interacting Groups, Delphi Groups, and Nominal Groups," *Organizational Behavior and Human Performance* 9 (1973), 280–91.

111. N. Dalkey, *The Delphi Method: An Experimental Study of Group Decision Making* (Santa Monica, CA: Rand Corp., 1989).

112. T. Lonier, "Some Insights and Statistics on Working Solo," www.workingsolo.com.

113. I. N. Katsikis and L. P. Kyrgidou, "The Concept of Sustainable Entrepreneurship: A Conceptual Framework and Empirical Analysis," *Academy of Management Proceedings,* 2007, 1–6, web.ebscohost.com/ehost/delivery?vid=7&hid=102&sid=434afdf5-5ed9-45d4-993b-, January 24, 2008; "What Is a Social Entrepreneur?" http://ashoka.org/social_entrepreneur, February 20, 2008; C. Hsu, "Entrepreneur for Social Change," *U.S.News.com,* October 31, 2005, www.usnews.com/usnews/news/articles/051031/31drayton.htm; D. M. Sullivan, "Stimulating Social Entrepreneurship: Can Support from Cities Make a Difference?" *Academy of Management Perspectives,* February 2007, 78.

114. Katsikis and Kyrgidou, "The Concept of Sustainable Entrepreneurship"; "What Is a Social Entrepreneur?"; Hsu, "Entrepreneur for Social Change"; Sullivan, "Stimulating Social Entrepreneurship."

115. N. Tiku, "Do-Gooder Finance: How a New Crop of Investors is Helping Social Entrepreneurs," *Inc.,* February 2008.

116. World of Good, Inc., "Message from World of Good," http://worldofgoodinc.com/about/transition.php, February 17, 2010.

117. Tiku, "Do-Gooder Finance"; "About World of Good," *World of Good, Inc.,* www.worldofgoodinc.com/about/, February 20, 2008; "What Is Fair Trade?" *World of Good,* originalgood, www.originalgood.com/FT/, February 20, 2008.

118. Tiku, "Do-Gooder Finance."

119. Tiku, "Do-Gooder Finance"; Mission Research, "Our Mission Is to Support Your Mission," http://www.missionresearch.com/company.html, February 17, 2010.

120. Tiku, "Do-Gooder Finance."

121. Tiku, "Do-Gooder Finance."

122. Tiku, "Do-Gooder Finance."

Chapter 8

1. www.cisco.com, 2010.

2. A. Chandler, *Strategy and Structure: Chapters in the History of the American Enterprise* (Cambridge, MA: MIT Press, 1962).

3. Ibid.

4. H. Fayol, *General and Industrial Management* (1884; New York: IEEE Press, 1984).

5. Ibid., 18.

6. F. J. Aguilar, "General Electric: Reg Jones and Jack Welch," in *General Managers in Action* (Oxford: Oxford University Press, 1992).

7. Aguilar, "General Electric."

8. www.ge.com, 2010.

9. C. W. Hofer and D. Schendel, *Strategy Formulation: Analytical Concepts* (St. Paul, MN: West, 1978).

10. A. P. De Geus, "Planning as Learning," *Harvard Business Review,* March–April 1988, 70–74.

11. P. Wack, "Scenarios: Shooting the Rapids," *Harvard Business Review,* November–December 1985, 139–50.

12. R. Phelps, C. Chan, and S. C. Kapsalis, "Does Scenario Planning Affect Firm Performance?" *Journal of Business Research,* March 2001, 223–32.

13. J. A. Pearce, "The Company Mission as a Strategic Tool," *Sloan Management Review,* Spring 1992, 15–24.

14. D. F. Abell, *Defining the Business: The Starting Point of Strategic Planning* (Englewood Cliffs, NJ: Prentice-Hall, 1980).

15. www.mattel.com, 2010.

16. "Doll Wars," *Business Life,* May 2005, 40–42.

17. www.mattel.com, 2010.

18. www.mattel.com, 2010.

19. G. Hamel and C. K. Prahalad, "Strategic Intent," *Harvard Business Review,* May–June 1989, 63–73.

20. D. I. Jung and B. J. Avolio, "Opening the Black Box: An Experimental Investigation of the Mediating Effects of Trust and Value Congruence on Transformational and Transactional Leadership," *Journal of Organizational Behavior,* December 2000, 949–64; B. M. Bass and B. J. Avolio, "Transformational and Transactional Leadership: 1992 and Beyond," *Journal of European Industrial Training,* January 1990, 20–35.

21. J. Porras and J. Collins, *Built to Last: Successful Habits of Visionary Companies* (New York: HarperCollins, 1994).

22. E. A. Locke, G. P. Latham, and M. Erez, "The Determinants of Goal Commitment," *Academy of Management Review* 13 (1988), 23–39.

23. www.mattel.com, 2010.

24. K. R. Andrews, *The Concept of Corporate Strategy* (Homewood, IL: Irwin, 1971).

25. www.campbellsoup.com, 2001.

26. G. Mulvihill, "Campbell Is Really Cooking," *San Diego Tribune.com,* August 5, 2004.

27. W. D. Crotty, "Campbell Soup Is Not So Hot," www.MotleyFool.com, May 24, 2004.

28. A. Halperin, "Chicken Soup for the Investor's Soul," *BusinessWeek Online,* May 25, 2006 (www.businessweek.com).

29. A. Carter, "Lighting a Fire under Campbell," www.businessweek.com, December 4, 2006.

30. www.campbellsoupcompany.com, 2010.

31. "Campbell Completes $850M Godiva Sale," www.yahoo.com, March 18, 2008.

32. R. D. Aveni, *Hypercompetition* (New York: Free Press, 1994).

33. M. E. Porter, *Competitive Strategy* (New York: Free Press, 1980).

34. C. W. L. Hill, "Differentiation versus Low Cost or Differentiation and Low Cost: A Contingency Framework," *Academy of Management Review* 13 (1988), 401–12.

35. For details, see J. P. Womack, D. T. Jones, and D. Roos, *The Machine That Changed the World* (New York: Rawson Associates, 1990).

36. Porter, *Competitive Strategy.*

37. www.cott.com, 2010.

38. www.cocacola.com, 2010; www.pepsico.com, 2010.

39. www.zara.com, 2010.

40. C. Vitzthum, "Just-in-Time-Fashion," *The Wall Street Journal,* May 18, 2001, B1, B4.

41. www.zara.com, 2010.

42. M. K. Perry, "Vertical Integration: Determinants and Effects," in R. Schmalensee and R. D. Willig, *Handbook of Industrial Organization,* vol. 1 (New York: Elsevier Science, 1989).

43. "Matsushita Electric Industrial (MEI) in 1987," Harvard Business School Case 388-144.

44. P. Ghemawat, *Commitment: The Dynamic of Strategy* (New York: Free Press, 1991).

45. www.ibm.com, 2010.

46. E. Penrose, *The Theory of the Growth of the Firm* (Oxford: Oxford University Press, 1959).

47. M. E. Porter, "From Competitive Advantage to Corporate Strategy," *Harvard Business Review* 65 (1987), 43–59.

48. D. J. Teece, "Economies of Scope and the Scope of the Enterprise," *Journal of Economic Behavior and Organization* 3 (1980), 223–47.
49. M. E. Porter, *Competitive Advantage: Creating and Sustaining Superior Performance* (New York: Free Press, 1985).
50. www.3M.com, 2005, 2010.
51. www.3M.com, 2010.
52. C. Wyant, "Minnesota Companies Make *BusinessWeek*'s 'Most Innovative' List," *Minneapolis/St. Paul Business Journal*, April 18, 2008.
53. For a review of the evidence, see C. W. L. Hill and G. R. Jones, *Strategic Management: An Integrated Approach*, 5th ed. (Boston: Houghton Mifflin, 2003), chap. 10.
54. C. R. Christensen et al., *Business Policy Text and Cases* (Homewood, IL: Irwin, 1987), 778.
55. C. W. L. Hill, "Conglomerate Performance over the Economic Cycle," *Journal of Industrial Economics* 32 (1983), 197–213.
56. V. Ramanujam and P. Varadarajan, "Research on Corporate Diversification: A Synthesis," *Strategic Management Journal* 10 (1989), 523–51. Also see A. Shleifer and R. W. Vishny, "Takeovers in the 1960s and 1980s: Evidence and Implications," in R. P. Rumelt, D. E. Schendel, and D. J. Teece, eds., *Fundamental Issues in Strategy* (Boston: Harvard Business School Press, 1994).
57. J. R. Williams, B. L. Paez, and L. Sanders, "Conglomerates Revisited," *Strategic Management Journal* 9 (1988), 403–14.
58. G. Marcial, "As Tyco Splits into Three," www.businessweek.com, March 12, 2007.
59. www.tyco.com, 2008.
60. C. A. Bartlett and S. Ghoshal, *Managing across Borders* (Boston: Harvard Business School Press, 1989).
61. C. K. Prahalad and Y. L. Doz, *The Multinational Mission* (New York: Free Press, 1987).
62. "Gillette Co.'s New $40 Million Razor Blade Factory in St. Petersburg, Russia," *Boston Globe*, June 7, 2000, C6.
63. D. Sewell, "P&G Replaces Ex-Gillette CEO at Operations," www.yahoo.com, May 24, 2006.
64. www.pg.com, 2005, 2008, 2010.
65. R. E. Caves, *Multinational Enterprise and Economic Analysis* (Cambridge: Cambridge University Press, 1982).
66. B. Kogut, "Joint Ventures: Theoretical and Empirical Perspectives," *Strategic Management Journal* 9 (1988), 319–33.
67. "Venture with Nestlé SA Is Slated for Expansion," *The Wall Street Journal*, April 15, 2001, B2.
68. B. Bahree, "BP Amoco, Italy's ENI Plan $2.5 Billion Gas Plant," *The Wall Street Journal*, March 6, 2001, A16.
69. N. Hood and S. Young, *The Economics of the Multinational Enterprise* (London: Longman, 1979).
70. www.samsung.com, 2010.
71. Ibid.

Chapter 9

1. www.google.com/finance, March 26, 2010.
2. www.dell.com, 2010.
3. See D. Garvin, "What Does Product Quality Really Mean?" *Sloan Management Review* 26 (Fall 1984), 25–44; P. B. Crosby, *Quality Is Free* (New York: Mentor Books, 1980); A. Gabor, *The Man Who Discovered Quality* (New York: Times Books, 1990).
4. D. F. Abell, *Defining the Business: The Starting Point of Strategic Planning* (Englewood Cliffs, NJ: Prentice-Hall, 1980).
5. According to Richard D'Aveni, the process of pushing price–attribute curves to the right is a characteristic of the competitive process. See R. D'Aveni, *Hypercompetition* (New York: Free Press, 1994).
6. www.walmart.com, 2010.
7. www.southwest.com, 2010.
8. B. O'Brian, "Flying on the Cheap," *The Wall Street Journal*, October 26, 1992, A1; B. O'Reilly, "Where Service Flies Right," *Fortune*, August 24, 1992, 116–17; A. Salukis, "Hurt in Expansion, Airlines Cut Back and May Sell Hubs," *The Wall Street Journal*, April 1, 1993, A1, C8.
9. www.fgx.com, 2010.
10. www.fgx.com, company overview, 2010.
11. www.ciu.com, 2010.
12. www.crm.com, 2010.
13. The view of quality as reliability goes back to the work of Deming and Juran; see Gabor, *The Man Who Discovered Quality*.
14. See Garvin, "What Does Product Quality Really Mean?"; Crosby, *Quality Is Free;* Gabor, *The Man Who Discovered Quality*.
15. www.jdpa.com, 2009.
16. See J. W. Dean and D. E. Bowen, "Management Theory and Total Quality: Improving Research and Practice through Theory Development," *Academy of Management Review* 19 (1994), 392–418.
17. For general background information, see J. C. Anderson, M. Rungtusanatham, and R. G. Schroeder, "A Theory of Quality Management Underlying the Deming Management Method," *Academy of Management Review* 19 (1994), 472–509; "How to Build Quality," *The Economist*, September 23, 1989, 91–92; Gabor, *The Man Who Discovered Quality;* Crosby, *Quality Is Free.*
18. Bowles, "Is American Management Really Committed to Quality?" *Management Review*, April 1992, 42–46.
19. Gabor, *The Man Who Discovered Quality*.
20. www.starwood.com, 2010.
21. S.E. Ante, "Six Sigma Kick-Starts Starwood," www.businessweek.com, August 30, 2007.
22. Ibid.
23. "The Application of Kaizen to Facilities Layout," *Financial Times*, January 4, 1994, 12. Reprinted by permission of Financial Times Syndication, London.
24. R. Gourlay, "Back to Basics on the Factory Floor," *Financial Times*, January 4, 1994, 12.
25. P. Nemetz and L. Fry, "Flexible Manufacturing Organizations: Implications for Strategy Formulation," *Academy of Management Review* 13 (1988), 627–38; N. Greenwood, *Implementing Flexible Manufacturing Systems* (New York: Halstead Press, 1986).
26. M. Williams, "Back to the Past," *The Wall Street Journal*, October 24, 1994, A1.
27. For an interesting discussion of some other drawbacks of JIT and other "Japanese" manufacturing techniques, see S. M. Young, "A Framework for Successful Adoption and Performance of Japanese Manufacturing Practices in the United States," *Academy of Management Review* 17 (1992), 677–701.
28. G. Stalk and T. M. Hout, *Competing against Time* (New York: Free Press, 1990).
29. T. Stundza, "Massachusetts Switch Maker Switches to Kanban," *Purchasing*, November 16, 2000, 103.
30. B. Dumaine, "The Trouble with Teams," *Fortune*, September 5, 1994, 86–92.
31. See C. W. L. Hill, "Transaction Cost Economizing as a Source of National Competitive Advantage: The Case of Japan," *Organization Science*, 2 (1994); M. Aoki, *Information, Incentives, and Bargaining in the Japanese Economy* (Cambridge: Cambridge University Press, 1989).
32. J. Hoerr, "The Payoff from Teamwork," *BusinessWeek*, July 10, 1989, 56–62.
33. M. Hammer and J. Champy, *Reengineering the Corporation* (New York: HarperBusiness, 1993), 35.
34. Ibid., 46.
35. Ibid.
36. www.google.com, 2010.
37. Ibid.

Chapter 10

1. www.avon.com, 2010.
2. N. Byrnes, "Avon: More Than Just Cosmetic Changes," www.businessweek.com, March 12, 2007.
3. www.avon.com, 2010.
4. G. R. Jones, *Organizational Theory, Design, and Change: Text and Cases* (Upper Saddle River: Prentice-Hall, 2003).
5. J. Child, *Organization: A Guide for Managers and Administrators* (New York: Harper & Row, 1977).
6. P. R. Lawrence and J. W. Lorsch, *Organization and Environment* (Boston: Graduate School of Business Administration, Harvard University, 1967).
7. R. Duncan, "What Is the Right Organizational Design?" *Organizational Dynamics,* Winter 1979, 59–80.
8. T. Burns and G. R. Stalker, *The Management of Innovation* (London: Tavistock, 1966).
9. D. Miller, "Strategy Making and Structure: Analysis and Implications for Performance," *Academy of Management Journal* 30 (1987), 7–32.
10. A. D. Chandler, *Strategy and Structure* (Cambridge, MA: MIT Press, 1962).
11. J. Stopford and L. Wells, *Managing the Multinational Enterprise* (London: Longman, 1972).
12. C. Perrow, *Organizational Analysis: A Sociological View* (Belmont, CA: Wadsworth, 1970).
13. F. W. Taylor, *The Principles of Scientific Management* (New York: Harper, 1911).
14. R. W. Griffin, *Task Design: An Integrative Approach* (Glenview, IL: Scott, Foresman, 1982).
15. Ibid.
16. J. R. Hackman and G. R. Oldham, *Work Redesign* (Reading, MA: Addison-Wesley, 1980).
17. J. R. Galbraith and R. K. Kazanjian, *Strategy Implementation: Structure, System, and Process,* 2nd ed. (St. Paul, MN: West, 1986).
18. Lawrence and Lorsch, *Organization and Environment.*
19. Jones, *Organizational Theory.*
20. Lawrence and Lorsch, *Organization and Environment.*
21. R. H. Hall, *Organizations: Structure and Process* (Englewood Cliffs, NJ: Prentice-Hall, 1972); R. Miles, *Macro Organizational Behavior* (Santa Monica, CA: Goodyear, 1980).
22. Chandler, *Strategy and Structure.*
23. G. R. Jones and C. W. L. Hill, "Transaction Cost Analysis of Strategy–Structure Choice," *Strategic Management Journal* 9 (1988), 159–72.
24. www.gsk.com, 2006.
25. www.gsk.com, 2010.
26. www.nokia.com, 2010.
27. S. M. Davis and P. R. Lawrence, *Matrix* (Reading, MA: Addison-Wesley, 1977); J. R. Galbraith, "Matrix Organization Designs: How to Combine Functional and Project Forms," *Business Horizons* 14 (1971), 29–40.
28. L. R. Burns, "Matrix Management in Hospitals: Testing Theories of Matrix Structure and Development," *Administrative Science Quarterly* 34 (1989), 349–68.
29. C. W. L. Hill, *International Business* (Homewood, IL: Irwin, 2003).
30. Jones, *Organizational Theory.*
31. A. Farnham, "America's Most Admired Company," *Fortune,* February 7, 1994, 50–54.
32. P. Blau, "A Formal Theory of Differentiation in Organizations," *American Sociological Review* 35 (1970), 684–95.
33. S. Grey, "McDonald's CEO Announces Shifts of Top Executives," *The Wall Street Journal,* July 16, 2004, A11.
34. www.mcdonalds.com, 2010.
35. Child, *Organization.*
36. S. McCartney, "Airline Industry's Top-Ranked Woman Keeps Southwest's Small-Fry Spirit Alive," *The Wall Street Journal,* November 30, 1995, B1; www.swamedia.com, 2010.
37. www.plexus.com, 2010.
38. W. M. Bulkeley, "Plexus Strategy: Smaller Runs of More Things," *The Wall Street Journal,* October 8, 2003, B1, B12.
39. P. M. Blau and R. A. Schoenherr, *The Structure of Organizations* (New York: Basic Books, 1971).
40. Jones, *Organizational Theory.*
41. Lawrence and Lorsch, *Organization and Environment,* 50–55.
42. J. R. Galbraith, *Designing Complex Organizations* (Reading, MA: Addison-Wesley, 1977), chap. 1; Galbraith and Kazanjian, *Strategy Implementation,* chap. 7.
43. Lawrence and Lorsch, *Organization and Environment,* 55.
44. S. D. N. Cook and D. Yanow, "Culture and Organizational Learning." *Journal of Management Inquiry* 2 (1993), 373–90.
45. www.ford.com, 2010.
46. D. Kiley, "The New Heat on Ford," www.businessweek.com, June 4, 2007.
47. Ibid.
48. B. Schneider, "The People Make the Place," *Personnel Psychology* 40 (1987), 437–53.
49. J. E. Sheriden, "Organizational Culture and Employee Retention," *Academy of Management Journal* 35 (1992), 657–92.
50. M. Hannan and J. Freeman, "Structural Inertia and Organizational Change," *American Sociological Review* 49 (1984), 149–64.
51. C. A. O'Reilly, J. Chatman, and D. F. Caldwell, "People and Organizational Culture: Assessing Person–Organizational Fit," *Academy of Management Journal* 34 (1991), 487–517.
52. T. L. Beauchamp and N. E. Bowie, eds., *Ethical Theory and Business* (Englewood Cliffs, NJ: Prentice-Hall, 1979); A. MacIntyre, *After Virtue* (Notre Dame, IN: University of Notre Dame Press, 1981).
53. A. Sagie and D. Elizur, "Work Values: A Theoretical Overview and a Model of Their Effects," *Journal of Organizational Behavior* 17 (1996), 503–14.
54. G. R. Jones, "Transaction Costs, Property Rights, and Organizational Culture: An Exchange Perspective," *Administrative Science Quarterly* 28 (1983), 454–67.
55. C. Perrow, *Normal Accidents* (New York: Basic Books, 1984).
56. H. Mintzberg, *The Structuring of Organizational Structures* (Englewood Cliffs, NJ: Prentice-Hall, 1979).
57. G. Kunda, *Engineering Culture* (Philadelphia: Temple University Press, 1992).
58. www.nokia.com, 2010.
59. K. E. Weick, *The Social Psychology of Organization* (Reading, MA: Addison-Wesley, 1979).
60. Copyright © 2006, Gareth R. Jones.

Chapter 11

1. "Toyota Blames Rapid Growth for Quality Problems," www.iht.com, March 13, 2008.
2. I. Rowley, "Katsuaki Watanabe: Fighting to Stay Humble," www.businessweek.com, March 5, 2007.
3. Press release, www.toyota.com, March 30, 2010.
4. W. G. Ouchi, "Markets, Bureaucracies, and Clans," *Administrative Science Quarterly* 25 (1980), 129–41.
5. P. Lorange, M. Morton, and S. Ghoshal, *Strategic Control* (St. Paul, MN: West, 1986).
6. H. Koontz and R. W. Bradspies, "Managing through Feedforward Control," *Business Horizons,* June 1972, 25–36.
7. E. E. Lawler III and J. G. Rhode, *Information and Control in Organizations* (Pacific Palisades, CA: Goodyear, 1976).
8. C. W. L. Hill and G. R. Jones, *Strategic Management: An Integrated Approach,* 6th ed. (Boston: Houghton Mifflin, 2003).
9. E. Flamholtz, "Organizational Control Systems as a Management Tool,"

California Management Review, Winter 1979, 50–58.

10. W. G. Ouchi, "The Transmission of Control through Organizational Hierarchy," *Academy of Management Journal* 21 (1978), 173–92.
11. W. G. Ouchi, "The Relationship between Organizational Structure and Organizational Control," *Administrative Science Quarterly* 22 (1977), 95–113.
12. Ouchi, "Markets, Bureaucracies, and Clans."
13. W. H. Newman, *Constructive Control* (Englewood Cliffs, NJ: Prentice-Hall, 1975).
14. J. D. Thompson, *Organizations in Action* (New York: McGraw-Hill, 1967).
15. R. N. Anthony, *The Management Control Function* (Boston: Harvard Business School Press, 1988).
16. Ouchi, "Markets, Bureaucracies, and Clans."
17. Hill and Jones, *Strategic Management.*
18. R. Simons, "Strategic Orientation and Top Management Attention to Control Systems," *Strategic Management Journal* 12 (1991), 49–62.
19. G. Schreyogg and H. Steinmann, "Strategic Control: A New Perspective," *Academy of Management Review* 12 (1987), 91–103.
20. B. Woolridge and S. W. Floyd, "The Strategy Process, Middle Management Involvement, and Organizational Performance," *Strategic Management Journal* 11 (1990), 231–41.
21. J. A. Alexander, "Adaptive Changes in Corporate Control Practices," *Academy of Management Journal* 34 (1991), 162–93.
22. Hill and Jones, *Strategic Management.*
23. G. H. B. Ross, "Revolution in Management Control," *Management Accounting* 72 (1992), 23–27.
24. P. F. Drucker, *The Practice of Management* (New York: Harper & Row, 1954).
25. S. J. Carroll and H. L. Tosi, *Management by Objectives: Applications and Research* (New York: Macmillan, 1973).
26. R. Rodgers and J. E. Hunter, "Impact of Management by Objectives on Organizational Productivity," *Journal of Applied Psychology* 76 (1991), 322–26.
27. M. B. Gavin, S. G. Green, and G. T. Fairhurst, "Managerial Control–Strategies for Poor Performance over Time and the Impact on Subordinate Reactions," *Organizational Behavior and Human Decision Processes* 63 (1995), 207–21.
28. www.cypress.com, 2001, 2005, 2010.
29. B. Dumaine, "The Bureaucracy Busters," *Fortune,* June 17, 1991, 46.
30. www.microsoft.com, 2006, 2010.
31. O. Thomas, "Microsoft Employees Feel Maligned," www.money.cnn.com, March 10, 2006.
32. J. Nightingale, "Rising Frustration with Microsoft's Compensation and Review System," www.washtech.org, March 10, 2006.
33. "Microsoft's Departing Employees," www.yahoo.news.com, May 6, 2006.
34. D. S. Pugh, D. J. Hickson, C. R. Hinings, and C. Turner, "Dimensions of Organizational Structure," *Administrative Science Quarterly* 13 (1968), 65–91.
35. B. Elgin, "Running the Tightest Ships on the Net," *BusinessWeek,* January 29, 2001, 125–26.
36. P. M. Blau, *The Dynamics of Bureaucracy* (Chicago: University of Chicago Press, 1955).
37. J. McGregor, "The World's Most Innovative Companies," www.businessweek.com, May 4, 2007.
38. www.waltdisney.com, 2010.
39. Ouchi, "Markets, Bureaucracies, and Clans."
40. Ibid.
41. www.ups.com, 2010.
42. J. Van Maanen, "Police Socialization: A Longitudinal Examination of Job Attitudes in an Urban Police Department," *Administrative Science Quarterly* 20 (1975), 207–28.
43. "Associates Keystone to Structure," *Chain Store Age,* December 1999, 17.
44. www.walmart.com, 2010.
45. M. Troy, "The Culture Remains the Constant," *Discount Store News,* June 8, 1998, 95–98.
46. This section draws heavily on K. Lewin, *Field Theory in Social Science* (New York: Harper & Row, 1951).
47. L. Chung-Ming and R. W. Woodman, "Understanding Organizational Change: A Schematic Perspective," *Academy of Management Journal* 38, no. 2 (1995), 537–55.
48. D. Miller, "Evolution and Revolution: A Quantum View of Structural Change in Organizations," *Journal of Management Studies* 19 (1982), 11–151; D. Miller, "Momentum and Revolution in Organizational Adaptation," *Academy of Management Journal* 2 (1980), 591–614.
49. C. E. Lindblom, "The Science of Muddling Through," *Public Administration Review* 19 (1959), 79–88; P. C. Nystrom and W. H. Starbuck, "To Avoid Organizational Crises, Unlearn," *Organizational Dynamics* 12 (1984), 53–65.
50. L. Brown, "Research Action: Organizational Feedback, Understanding, and Change," *Journal of Applied Behavioral Research* 8 (1972), 697–711; P. A. Clark, *Action Research and Organizational Change* (New York: Harper & Row, 1972); N. Margulies and A. P. Raia, eds., *Conceptual Foundations of Organizational Development* (New York: McGraw-Hill, 1978).
51. W. L. French and C. H. Bell, *Organizational Development* (Englewood Cliffs, NJ: Prentice-Hall, 1990).
52. W. L. French, "A Checklist for Organizing and Implementing an OD Effort," in W. L. French, C. H. Bell, and R. A. Zawacki, eds., *Organizational Development and Transformation* (Homewood, IL: Irwin, 1994), 484–95.

Chapter 12

1. D. Garnick, "CEO Takes a Walk on the Whimsical Side," *Boston Herald,* Wednesday, May 20, 2009, http://about.zappos.com/press-center/media-coverage/ceo-takes-walk-whimsical-side, February 22, 2010; C. Palmeri, "Zappos Retails Its Culture," *BusinessWeek,* December 30, 2009, http://www.businessweek.com/print/magazine/content/10_02/b4162057120453.htm, February 22, 2010; "On a Scale of 1 to 10, How Weird Are You?" *The New York Times,* January 10, 2010, http://www.nytimes.com/2010/01/10/business/10corner.html?pagewanted=print, February 22, 2010; M. Chafkin, "Get Happy," *Inc.,* May 2009, 66–73; "Keeper of the Flame," *The Economist,* April 18, 2009, 75.
2. 100 Best Companies to Work For 2010: Zappos.com–AMZN–from FORTUNE, "15. Zappos.com," http://money.cnn.com/magazines/fortune/bestcompanies/2010/snapshots/15.html, February 22, 2010.
3. R. Wauters, "Amazon Closes Zappos Deal, Ends Up Paying $1.2 Billion," TechCrunch, November 2, 2009, http://techcrunch.com/2009/11/02/amazon-closes-zappos-deal-ends-up-paying-1-2-billion/, February 22, 2010.
4. J. McGregor, "Zappo's Secret: It's an Open Book," *BusinessWeek,* March 23 & 30, 2009, 62; "About.zappos.com," Tony Hsieh–CEO, http://about.zappos.com/meet-our-monkeys/tony-hsieh-ceo, February 22, 2010; Chafkin, "Get Happy."
5. Chafkin, "Get Happy"; "Keeper of the Flame."
6. "On a Scale of 1 to 10, How Weird Are You?"; Chafkin, "Get Happy."
7. Chafkin, "Get Happy."
8. Chafkin, "Get Happy"; "Keeper of the Flame."
9. In The Beginning–Let There Be Shoes/about.zappos.com, http://about.zappos.com/zappos-story/in-the-beginning-let-there-be-shoes, February 22, 2010; Looking Ahead–Let There

Be Anything and Everything/about.zappos.com, http://about.zappos.com/zappos-story/looking-ahead-let-there-be-anything-and-everything, February 22, 2010; J. B. Darin, "Curing Customer Service," *Fortune,* May 20, 2009, http://about.zappos.com/press-center/media-coverage/curing-customer-service, February 22, 2010.

10. "Happy Feet–Inside the Online Shoe Utopia," *The New Yorker,* September 14, 2009, http://about.zappos.com/press-center/media-coverage/happy-feet-inside-online-shoe-utopia, February 22, 2010.
11. "Happy Feet–Inside the Online Shoe Utopia."
12. Chafkin, "Get Happy"; "Keeper of the Flame."
13. Chafkin, "Get Happy"; "Keeper of the Flame."
14. Zappos Core Values/about.zappos.com, http://about.zappos.com/our-unique-culture/zappos-core-values, February 22, 2010.
15. "From Upstart to $1 Billion Behemoth, Zappos Marks 10 Years," *Las Vegas Sun,* Tuesday, June 16, 2009, http://about.zappos.com/press-center/media-coverage/upstart-1-billion-behemoth-zappos- . . . , February 22, 2010; Chafkin, "Get Happy"; "Keeper of the Flame."
16. "Keeper of the Flame"; Chafkin, "Get Happy."
17. Chafkin, "Get Happy."
18. 100 Best Companies to Work For 2010: Zappos.com; Chafkin, "Get Happy."
19. Chafkin, "Get Happy"; "Keeper of the Flame"; 100 Best Companies to Work For 2010: Zappos.com.
20. J. E. Butler, G. R. Ferris, and N. K. Napier, *Strategy and Human Resource Management* (Cincinnati: Southwestern Publishing, 1991); P. M. Wright and G. C. McMahan, "Theoretical Perspectives for Strategic Human Resource Management," *Journal of Management* 18 (1992), 295–320.
21. L. Clifford, "Why You Can Safely Ignore Six Sigma," *Fortune,* January 22, 2001, 140.
22. J. B. Quinn, P. Anderson, and S. Finkelstein, "Managing Professional Intellect: Making the Most of the Best," *Harvard Business Review,* March–April 1996, 71–80.
23. Quinn et al., "Managing Professional Intellect."
24. C. D. Fisher, L. F. Schoenfeldt, and J. B. Shaw, *Human Resource Management* (Boston: Houghton Mifflin, 1990).
25. Wright and McMahan, "Theoretical Perspectives."
26. L. Baird and I. Meshoulam, "Managing Two Fits for Strategic Human Resource Management," *Academy of Management Review* 14, 116–28; J. Milliman, M. Von Glinow, and M. Nathan, "Organizational Life Cycles and Strategic International Human Resource Management in Multinational Companies: Implications for Congruence Theory," *Academy of Management Review* 16 (1991), 318–39; R. S. Schuler and S. E. Jackson, "Linking Competitive Strategies with Human Resource Management Practices," *Academy of Management Executive* 1 (1987), 207–19; P. M. Wright and S. A. Snell, "Toward an Integrative View of Strategic Human Resource Management," *Human Resource Management Review* 1 (1991), 203–225.
27. "Who's in Charge Here? No One," *The Observer,* April 27, 2003 (http://observer.guardian.co.uk/business/story/0,6903,944138,00.html); "Ricardo Semler, CEO, Semco SA," cnn.com, June 29, 2004 (http://cnn.worldnews.printthis.clickability.com/pt/cpt&title=cnn.com); D. Kirkpatrick, "The Future of Work: An 'Apprentice' Style Office?" *Fortune,* April 14, 2004 (www.fortune.com/fortune/subs/print/0,15935,611068,00.html); A. Strutt and R. Van Der Beek, "Report from HR2004," www.mce.be/hr2004/reportd2.htm, July 2, 2004; R. Semler, "Seven-Day Weekend Returns Power to Employees," workopolis.com, May 26, 2004 (http://globeandmail.workopolis.com/servlet/content/qprinter/20040526/cabooks26); "SEMCO," http://semco.locaweb.com.br/ingles, May 31, 2006; "Ricardo Semler, Semco SA: What Are You Reading?" cnn.com, May 31, 2006. (www.cnn.com/2004/BUSINESS/06/29/semler.profile/index.html).
28. R. Semler, *The Seven-Day Weekend: Changing the Way Work Works* (New York: Penguin, 2003); "SEMCO."
29. Semler, *The Seven-Day Weekend;* "SEMCO"; G. Hamel, *The Future of Management* (Cambridge, MA: Harvard Business Press, 2007).
30. A. Strutt, "Interview with Ricardo Semler," *Management Centre Europe,* April 2004 (www.mce.be/knowledge/392/35).
31. Semler, *The Seven-Day Weekend.*
32. Semler, *The Seven-Day Weekend.*
33. R. Semler, "How We Went *Digital* without a *Strategy,*" *Harvard Business Review* 78, no. 5 (September–October 2000), 51–56.
34. Semler, *The Seven-Day Weekend.*
35. Equal Employment Opportunity Commission, "Uniform Guidelines on Employee Selection Procedures," *Federal Register* 43 (1978), 38290–315.
36. R. Stogdill II, R. Mitchell, K. Thurston, and C. Del Valle, "Why AIDS Policy Must Be a Special Policy," *BusinessWeek,* February 1, 1993, 53–54.
37. J. M. George, "AIDS/AIDS-Related Complex," in L. Peters, B. Greer, and S. Youngblood, eds., *The Blackwell Encyclopedic Dictionary of Human Resource Management* (Oxford, England: Blackwell Publishers, 1997).
38. George, "AIDS/AIDS-Related Complex."
39. George, "AIDS/AIDS-Related Complex"; Stogdill et al., "Why AIDS Policy Must Be a Special Policy"; K. Holland, "Out of Retirement and into Uncertainty," *The New York Times,* May 27, 2007, BU17.
40. S. L. Rynes, "Recruitment, Job Choice, and Post-Hire Consequences: A Call for New Research Directions," in M. D. Dunnette and L. M. Hough, eds., *Handbook of Industrial and Organizational Psychology,* vol. 2 (Palo Alto, CA: Consulting Psychologists Press, 1991), 399–444.
41. R. L. Sullivan, "Lawyers a la Carte," *Forbes,* September 11, 1995, 44.
42. E. Porter, "Send Jobs to India? U.S. Companies Say It's Not Always Best," *The New York Times,* April 28, 2004, A1, A7.
43. D. Wessel, "The Future of Jobs: New Ones Arise; Wage Gap Widens," *The Wall Street Journal,* April 2, 2004, A1, A5; "Relocating the Back Office," *The Economist,* December 13, 2003, 67–69.
44. The Conference Board, "Offshoring Evolving at a Rapid Pace, Report Duke University and The Conference Board," August 3, 2009, http://www.conference-board.org/utilities/pressPrinterFriendly.cfm?press_ID=3709, February 24, 2010; S. Minter, "Offshoring by U.S. Companies Doubles," *Industry Week,* August 19, 2009, http://www.industryweek.com/PrintArticle.aspx?ArticleID=19772&SectionID=3, February 24, 2010; AFP, "Offshoring by U.S. Companies Surges: Survey," August 3, 2009, http://www.google.com/hostednews/afp/article/ALeqM5iDaq1D2KZU16YfbKrMPdborD7 . . . , February 24, 2010; V. Wadhwa, "The Global Innovation Migration," *BusinessWeek,* November 9, 2009, http://www.businessweek.com/print/technology/content/nov2009/tc2009119_331698.htm, February 24, 2010; T. Heijmen, A. Y. Lewin, S. Manning, N. Perm-Ajchariyawong, and J. W. Russell, "Offshoring Research the C-Suite," 2007–2008 ORN Survey Report, *The Conference Board,* in collaboration with Duke University Offshoring Research Network.

45. The Conference Board, "Offshoring Evolving at a Rapid Pace"; Minter, "Offshoring by U.S. Companies Doubles"; AFP, "Offshoring by U.S. Companies Surges"; V. Wadhwa, "The Global Innovation Migration"; Heijmen et al., "Offshoring Research the C-Suite."
46. V. Wadhwa, "The Global Innovation Migration."
47. The Conference Board, "Offshoring Evolving at a Rapid Pace."
48. The Conference Board, "Offshoring Evolving at a Rapid Pace"; Minter, "Offshoring by U.S. Companies Doubles"; AFP, "Offshoring by U.S. Companies Surges"; Heijmen et al., "Offshoring Research the C-Suite."
49. R. J. Harvey, "Job Analysis," in Dunnette and Hough, *Handbook of Industrial and Organizational Psychology,* 71–163.
50. E. L. Levine, *Everything You Always Wanted to Know about Job Analysis: A Job Analysis Primer* (Tampa, FL: Mariner Publishing, 1983).
51. R. L. Mathis and J. H. Jackson, *Human Resource Management,* 7th ed. (Minneapolis: West, 1994).
52. E. J. McCormick, P. R. Jeannerette, and R. C. Mecham, *Position Analysis Questionnaire* (West Lafayette, IN: Occupational Research Center, Department of Psychological Sciences, Purdue University, 1969).
53. Fisher et al., *Human Resource Management;* Mathis and Jackson, *Human Resource Management;* R. A. Noe, J. R. Hollenbeck, B. Gerhart, and P. M. Wright, *Human Resource Management: Gaining a Competitive Advantage* (Burr Ridge, IL: Irwin, 1994).
54. Fisher et al., *Human Resource Management;* E. J. McCormick, *Job Analysis: Methods and Applications* (New York: American Management Association, 1979); E. J. McCormick and P. R. Jeannerette, "The Position Analysis Questionnaire," in S. Gael, ed., *The Job Analysis Handbook for Business, Industry, and Government* (New York: Wiley, 1988); Noe et al., *Human Resource Management.*
55. Rynes, "Recruitment, Job Choice, and Post-Hire Consequences."
56. R. Sharpe, "The Life of the Party? Can Jeff Taylor Keep the Good Times Rolling at Monster.com?" *BusinessWeek,* June 4, 2001 (*BusinessWeek* Archives); D. H. Freedman, "The Monster Dilemma," *Inc.,* May 2007, 77–78; P. Korkki, "So Easy to Apply, So Hard to Be Noticed," *The New York Times,* July 1, 2007, BU16.
57. Jobline International–Resume Vacancy Posting, Employment Resources, Job Searches, http://www.jobline.net, February 25, 2010.
58. www.jobline.org, Jobline press releases, May 8, 2001, accessed June 20, 2001.
59. J. Spolsky, "There Is a Better Way to Find and Hire the Very Best Employees," *Inc.,* May 2007, 81–82; "About the Company," www.fogcreek.com, March 5, 2008; "Fog Creek Software," www.fogcreek.com, March 5, 2008; Fog Creek Software–About the company, http://fogcreek.com/About.html, February 25, 2010.
60. Spolsky, "There Is a Better Way to Find and Hire the Very Best Employees"; "Fog Creek Software."
61. Spolsky, "There Is a Better Way to Find and Hire the Very Best Employees."
62. Spolsky, "There Is a Better Way to Find and Hire the Very Best Employees.
63. Spolsky, "There Is a Better Way to Find and Hire the Very Best Employees.
64. Spolsky, "There Is a Better Way to Find and Hire the Very Best Employees."
65. Spolsky, "There Is a Better Way to Find and Hire the Very Best Employees."
66. Spolsky, "There Is a Better Way to Find and Hire the Very Best Employees;" "About the Company"; "Fog Creek Software."
67. Spolsky, "There Is a Better Way to Find and Hire the Very Best Employees."
68. S. L. Premack and J. P. Wanous, "A Meta-Analysis of Realistic Job Preview Experiments," *Journal of Applied Psychology* 70 (1985), 706–19; J. P. Wanous, "Realistic Job Previews: Can a Procedure to Reduce Turnover also Influence the Relationship between Abilities and Performance?" *Personnel Psychology* 31 (1978), 249–58; J. P. Wanous, *Organizational Entry: Recruitment, Selection, and Socialization of Newcomers* (Reading, MA: Addison-Wesley, 1980).
69. R. M. Guion, "Personnel Assessment, Selection, and Placement," in Dunnette and Hough, *Handbook of Industrial and Organizational Psychology,* 327–97.
70. T. Joyner, "Job Background Checks Surge," *Houston Chronicle,* May 2, 2005, D6.
71. Joyner, "Job Background Checks Surge"; "ADP News Releases: Employer Services: ADP Hiring Index Reveals Background Checks Performed More Than Tripled since 1997," *Automatic Data Processing, Inc.,* June 3, 2006 (www.investquest.com/iq/a/aud/ne/news/adp042505background.htm).
72. "ADP News Releases."
73. Noe et al., *Human Resource Management;* J. A. Wheeler and J. A. Gier, "Reliability and Validity of the Situational Interview for a Sales Position," *Journal of Applied Psychology* 2 (1987), 484–87.
74. Noe et al., *Human Resource Management.*
75. J. Flint, "Can You Tell Applesauce from Pickles?" *Forbes,* October 9, 1995, 106–8.
76. Flint, "Can You Tell Applesauce from Pickles?"
77. "Wanted: Middle Managers, Audition Required," *The Wall Street Journal,* December 28, 1995, A1.
78. I. L. Goldstein, "Training in Work Organizations," in Dunnette and Hough, *Handbook of Industrial and Organizational Psychology,* 507–619.
79. S. Overman, "Ethan Allen's Secret Weapon," *HRMagazine,* May 1994, 61; Ethan Allen–Investor Relations–News Release, "Ethan Allen's Farooq Kathwari Inducted into American Furniture Hall of Fame," October 23, 2009, http://phx.corporate-ir.net/phoenix.zhtml?c=81552&p=irol-newsArticle_print&ID=134616 . . . , February 25, 2010.
80. N. Banerjee, "For Mary Kay Sales Reps in Russia, Hottest Shade Is the Color of Money," *The Wall Street Journal,* August 30, 1995, A8.
81. T. D. Allen, L. T. Eby, M. L. Poteet, E. Lentz, and L. Lima, "Career Benefits Associated with Mentoring for Protégés: A Meta-Analysis," *Journal of Applied Psychology* 89, no. 1 (2004), 127–36.
82. P. Garfinkel, "Putting a Formal Stamp on Mentoring," *The New York Times,* January 18, 2004, BU10.
83. Garfinkel, "Putting a Formal Stamp on Mentoring."
84. Allen et al., "Career Benefits Associated with Mentoring"; L. Levin, "Lesson Learned: Know Your Limits. Get Outside Help Sooner Rather Than Later," *BusinessWeek Online,* July 5, 2004 (www.businessweek.com); "Family, Inc.," *BusinessWeek Online,* November 10, 2003 (www.businessweek.com); J. Salamon, "A Year with a Mentor. Now Comes the Test," *The New York Times,* September 30, 2003, B1, B5; E. White, "Making Mentorships Work," *The Wall Street Journal,* October 23, 2007, B11.
85. Garfinkel, "Putting a Formal Stamp on Mentoring."
86. J. A. Byrne, "Virtual B-Schools," *BusinessWeek,* October 23, 1995, 64–68; Michigan Executive Education Locations around the Globe, http://exceed.bus.umich.edu/InternationalFacilities/default.aspx, February 25, 2010.
87. Fisher et al., *Human Resource Management.*

88. Fisher et al., *Human Resource Management;* G. P. Latham and K. N. Wexley, *Increasing Productivity through Performance Appraisal* (Reading, MA: Addison-Wesley, 1982).

89. T. A. DeCotiis, "An Analysis of the External Validity and Applied Relevance of Three Rating Formats," *Organizational Behavior and Human Performance* 19 (1977), 247–66; Fisher et al., *Human Resource Management.*

90. J. Muller, K. Kerwin, D. Welch, P. L. Moore, D. Brady, "Ford: It's Worse Than You Think," *BusinessWeek,* June 25, 2001 (*BusinessWeek* Archives).

91. Muller et al., "Ford: It's Worse Than You Think."

92. L. M. Sixel, "Enron Rating Setup Irks Many Workers," *Houston Chronicle,* February 26, 2001, 1C.

93. J. S. Lublin, "It's Shape-Up Time for Performance Reviews," *The Wall Street Journal,* October 3, 1994, B1, B2.

94. J. S. Lublin, "Turning the Tables: Underlings Evaluate Bosses," *The Wall Street Journal,* October 4, 1994, B1, B14; S. Shellenbarger, "Reviews from Peers Instruct–and Sting," *The Wall Street Journal,* October 4, 1994, B1, B4.

95. C. Borman and D. W. Bracken, "360 Degree Appraisals," in C. L. Cooper and C. Argyris, eds., *The Concise Blackwell Encyclopedia of Management* (Oxford, England: Blackwell Publishers, 1998), 17; D. W. Bracken, "Straight Talk about Multi-Rater Feedback," *Training and Development* 48 (1994), 44–51; M. R. Edwards, W. C. Borman, and J. R. Sproul, "Solving the Double Bind in Performance Appraisal: A Saga of Solves, Sloths, and Eagles," *Business Horizons* 85 (1985), 59–68.

96. M. A. Peiperl, "Getting 360 Degree Feedback Right," *Harvard Business Review,* January 2001, 142–47.

97. A. Harrington, "Workers of the World, Rate Your Boss!" *Fortune,* September 18, 2000, 340, 342; www.ImproveNow.com, June 2001.

98. Lublin, "It's Shape-Up Time for Performance Reviews."

99. S. E. Moss and J. I. Sanchez, "Are Your Employees Avoiding You? Managerial Strategies for Closing the Feedback Gap," *Academy of Management Executive* 18, no. 1 (2004), 32–46.

100. J. M. O'Brien, "100 Best Companies to Work For–A Perfect Season," *Fortune,* February 4, 2008, 64–66; "Four Seasons Employees Name Company to *Fortune* '100 Best Companies to Work For' List," www.fourseasons.com/about_us/press_release_280.html, February 22, 2008; "Four Seasons Hotels and Resort Named to *Fortune* List of the '100 Best Companies to Work For,'" http://press.fourseasons.com/news-releases/four-seasons-hotels-and-resorts-named-to-fortu . . . , February 24, 2010.

101. "Four Seasons Employees Name Company to *Fortune* '100 Best Companies to Work For' List."

102. O'Brien, "100 Best Companies to Work For–A Perfect Season."

103. Four Seasons Hotels and Resorts–About Us: Corporate Bios, http://www.fourseasons.com/about_us/corporate_bios/, February 24, 2010.

104. O'Brien, "100 Best Companies to Work For–A Perfect Season."

105. O'Brien, "100 Best Companies to Work For–A Perfect Season;" "Creating the Four Seasons Difference," www.businessweek.com/print/innovate/content/jan2008/id20080122_671354.htm, February 22, 2008.

106. O'Brien, "100 Best Companies to Work For–A Perfect Season."; "Creating the Four Seasons Difference."

107. "Creating the Four Seasons Difference"; "Four Seasons Employees Name Company to *Fortune* '100 Best Companies to Work For' List."

108. M. Moskowitz, R. Levering, and C. Tkaczyk, "The List," *Fortune,* February 8, 2010, pp. 75–88.

109. O'Brien, "100 Best Companies to Work For–A Perfect Season."

110. O'Brien, "100 Best Companies to Work For–A Perfect Season."

111. O'Brien, "100 Best Companies to Work For–A Perfect Season"; "Creating the Four Seasons Difference"; "Four Seasons Employees Name Company to *Fortune* '100 Best Companies to Work For' List."

112. J. Flynn and F. Nayeri, "Continental Divide over Executive Pay," *BusinessWeek,* July 3, 1995, 40–41.

113. J. A. Byrne, "How High Can CEO Pay Go?" *BusinessWeek,* April 22, 1996, 100–06.

114. A. Borrus, "A Battle Royal against Regal Paychecks," *BusinessWeek,* February 24, 2003, 127; "Too Many Turkeys," *The Economist,* November 26, 2005, 75–76; G. Morgenson, "How to Slow Runaway Executive Pay," *The New York Times,* October 23, 2005, 1, 4; S. Greenhouse, *The Big Squeeze: Tough Times for the American Worker* (New York: Alfred A. Knopf, 2008).

115. "Executive Pay," *BusinessWeek,* April 19, 2004, 106–110.

116. "Home Depot Chief's Pay in 2007 Could Reach $8.9m," *The New York Times,* Bloomberg News, January 25, 2007, C7; E. Carr, "The Stockpot," *The Economist, A Special Report on Executive Pay,* January 20, 2007, 6–10; E. Porter, "More Than Ever, It Pays to Be the Top Executive," *The New York Times,* May 25, 2007, A1, C7.

117. K. Garber, "What Is (and Isn't) in the Healthcare Bill," *U.S. News & World Report,* March 22, 2010, http://www.usnews.com/articles/news/politics/2010/02/22/what-is-and-isnt-in-the healthca . . . , March 29, 2010; S. Condon, "Health Care Bill Signed by Obama," Political Hotsheet-CBS News, http://www.cbsnews.com/8301-503544_162-20000981-503544.html, March 29, 2010; T. S. Bernard, "For Consumers, Clarity on Health Care Changes," *The New York Times,* March 21, 2010, http://www.nytimes.com/2010/03/22/your-money/health-insurance/22consumer.html?sq=h . . . , March 29, 2010; CBSNews.com, "Health Care Reform Bill Summary: A Look At What's in the Bill," March 23, 2009, http://www.cbsnews.com/8301-503544_162-20000846-503544.html, March 29, 2010; Reuters, "Factbox: Details of final healthcare bill", March 21, 2010, http://www.reuters.com/article/idUSTRE62K11V20100321, March 29, 2010.

118. E. Tahmincioglu, "Paths to Better Health (On the Boss's Nickel)," *The New York Times,* May 23, 2004, BU7.

119. Tahmincioglu, "Paths to Better Health."

120. K. K. Spors, "Top Small Workplaces 2007," *The Wall Street Journal,* October 1, 2007, R1–R6; K. K. Spors, "Guerra DeBerry Coody," *The Wall Street Journal,* October 1, 2007, R5; "Guerra DeBerry Coody Named One of the Nation's 15 Top Small Workplaces of 2007," *Business Wire,* http://findarticles.com/p/articles/mi_m0EIN/is_2007_Oct_1/ai_n20527510/print, March 6, 2008; "Guerra DeBerry Coody," www.gdc-co.com/, March 6, 2008; "Frank Guerra '83, Trish DeBerry-Mejia '87, and Tess Coody '93," *Trinity University, Alumni–Profiles,* www.trinity.edu/alumni/profiles/0503_guerra_deberry_coody.htm, March 6, 2008.

121. Spors, "Top Small Workplaces 2007"; Spors, "Guerra DeBerry Coody"; "Guerra DeBerry Coody Named One of the Nation's 15 Top Small Workplaces of 2007."

122. Spors, "Top Small Workplaces 2007"; Spors, "Guerra DeBerry Coody"; Guerra DeBerry Coody: Day Care, http://www.gdc-co.com/, February 25, 2010.

123. Spors, "Top Small Workplaces 2007"; Spors, "Guerra DeBerry Coody."

124. Spors, "Top Small Workplaces 2007"; Spors, "Guerra DeBerry Coody."

125. "Guerra DeBerry Coody Named One of the Nation's 15 Top Small Workplaces of 2007."

126. S. Shellenbarger, "Amid Gay Marriage Debate, Companies Offer More Benefits to Same-Sex Couples," *The Wall Street Journal,* March 18, 2004, D1.

127. S. Premack and J. E. Hunter, "Individual Unionization Decisions," *Psychological Bulletin* 103 (1988), 223–34.

128. M. B. Regan, "Shattering the AFL-CIO's Glass Ceiling," *BusinessWeek,* November 13, 1995, 46; S. Greenhouse, "The Hard Work of Reviving Labor," *The New York Times,* September 16, 2009, pp. B1, B7.

129. S. Greenhouse, "Survey Finds Deep Shift in the Makeup of Unions," *The New York Times,* November 11, 2009, p. B5.

130. www.aflcio.org, June 2001; About Us, AFL-CIO, http://www.aflcio.org/aboutus/, February 25, 2010; S. Greenhouse, "Most U.S. Union Members Are Working for the Government, New Data Shows," *The New York Times,* January 23, 2010, http://www.nytimes.com/2010/01/23/business/23labor.html?pagewanted=print, February 25, 2010.

131. Greenhouse, "Most U.S. Union Members Are Working for the Government."

132. Greenhouse, "Survey Finds Deep Shift in the Makeup of Unions."

133. Greenhouse, "Most U.S. Union Members Are Working for the Government."

134. G. P. Zachary, "Some Unions Step Up Organizing Campaigns and Get New Members," *The Wall Street Journal,* September 1, 1995, A1, A2.

135. Regan, "Shattering the AFL-CIO's Glass Ceiling"; www.aflcio.org, June 2001; R. S. Dunham, "Big Labor: So Out It's 'Off the Radar Screen,'" *BusinessWeek,* March 26, 2001 (*BusinessWeek* Archives); "Chavez-Thompson to Retire as Executive Vice President," *AFL-CIO Weblog,* http://blog.aflcio.org/2007/09/13/chavez-thompson-to-retire-as-executive-vice-president/print/, March 6, 2008.

136. "Secretary of Labor Elaine L. Chao," *U.S. Department of Labor–Office of the Secretary of Labor Elaine L. Chao (OSEC),* www.dol.gov/_sec/welcome.htm, March 6, 2008; S. Greenhouse, "Departing Secretary of Labor Fends Off Critics," *The New York Times,* January 10, 2009, http://www.nytimes.com/2009/01/10/washington/10chao.html?_r=1&pagewanted=print, February 25, 2010.

137. "The Honorable Elaine L. Chao United States Secretary of Labor," www.dol.gov/dol/sec/public/aboutosec/chao.htm, June 25, 2001.

138. Greenhouse, "Survey Finds Deep Shift in the Makeup of Unions."

Chapter 13

1. J. Schlosser and J. Sung, "The 100 Best Companies to Work For," *Fortune,* January 8, 2001, 148–68; R. Levering, M. Moskowitz, and S. Adams, "The 100 Best Companies to Work For," *Fortune* 149, no. 1 (2004), 56–78; "*Fortune* 100 Best Companies to Work For 2006," CNNMoney.com, June 5, 2006 (www.money.cnn.com/magazines/fortune/bestcompanies/snapshots/1181.html); "Awards," *SAS,* www.sas.com/awards/index.html, April 1, 2008; R. Levering and M. Moskowitz, "100 Best Companies to Work For: The Rankings," *Fortune,* February 4, 2008, 75–94; M. Moskowitz, R. Levering, and C. Tkaczyk, "100 best companies: The List," *Fortune,* February 8, 2010, 75–88.

2. E. P. Dalesio, "Quiet Giant Ready to Raise Its Profits," *Houston Chronicle,* May 6, 2001, 4D; Levering et al., "The 100 Best Companies to Work For"; J. Goodnight, "Welcome to SAS," www.sas.com/corporate/index.html, August 26, 2003; "SAS Press Center: SAS Corporate Statistics," www.sas.com/bin/pfp.pl?=fi, April 18, 2006; "SAS Continues Annual Revenue Growth Streak," www.sas.com/news/prelease/031003/newsl.html, August 28, 2003; Levering and Moskowitz, "100 Best Companies to Work For;" Corporate Statistics/SAS, Updated February 2010, http://www.sas.com/presscenter/bgndr_statistics.html, March 1, 2010.

3. About SAS/SAS, http://www.sas.com/corporate/overview/index.html, March 1, 2010; Corporate Statistics/SAS, Updated February 2010, http://www.sas.com/presscenter/bgndr_statistics.html, March 1, 2010.

4. J. Pfeffer, "SAS Institute: A Different Approach to Incentives and People Management Practices in the Software Industry," Harvard Business School Case HR-6, January 1998; "Saluting the Global Awards Recipients of Arthur Andersen's Best Practices Awards 2000," www.fortune.com, September 6, 2000; N. Stein, "Winning the War to Keep Top Talent," www.fortune.com, September 6, 2000; D. A. Kaplan, "The Best Company to Work For," *Fortune,* February 8, 2010, 57–64.

5. Pfeffer, "SAS Institute."

6. "Saluting the Global Awards Recipients of Arthur Andersen's Best Practices Awards 2000"; Stein, "Winning the War to Keep Top Talent."

7. Lahr, "At a Software Powerhouse, the Good Life Is under Siege," *The New York Times,* November 22, 2009, BU1, BU6.

8. Lahr, "At a Software Powerhouse, the Good Life Is under Siege."

9. Pfeffer, "SAS Institute"; Kaplan, "The Best Company to Work For."

10. Kaplan, "The Best Company to Work For."

11. Kaplan, "The Best Company to Work For"; Lahr, "At a Software Powerhouse, the Good Life Is under Siege."

12. Kaplan, "The Best Company to Work For"; Lahr, "At a Software Powerhouse, the Good Life Is under Siege."

13. Kaplan, "The Best Company to Work For"; Lahr, "At a Software Powerhouse, the Good Life Is under Siege."

14. Kaplan, "The Best Company to Work For."

15. Kaplan, "The Best Company to Work For."

16. "Saluting the Global Awards Recipients of Arthur Andersen's Best Practices Awards 2000"; Stein, "Winning the War to Keep Top Talent."

17. Kaplan, "The Best Company to Work For"; Lahr, "At a Software Powerhouse, the Good Life Is under Siege"; Pfeffer, "SAS Institute."

18. Kaplan, "The Best Company to Work For"; Lahr, "At a Software Powerhouse, the Good Life Is under Siege."

19. Goodnight, "Welcome to SAS"; "By Solution," www.sas.com/success/solution.html, August 26, 2003; www.sas.com, June 8, 2006.

20. S. H. Wildstrom, "Do Your Homework, Microsoft," *BusinessWeek Online,* August 8, 2005 (www.businessweek.com/print/magazine/content/05-b3946033-mz006.htm?chan); www.sas.com, June 8, 2006.

21. Kaplan, "The Best Company to Work For."

22. R. Kanfer, "Motivation Theory and Industrial and Organizational Psychology," in M. D. Dunnette and L. M. Hough, eds., *Handbook of Industrial and Organizational Psychology,* 2nd ed., vol. 1 (Palo Alto, CA: Consulting Psychologists Press, 1990), 75–170.

23. G. P. Latham & M. H. Budworth, "The Study of Work Motivation in the 20th Century," in L. L. Koppes, ed., *Historical Perspectives in Industrial and Organizational Psychology* (Hillsdale, NJ: Laurence Erlbaum, 2006).

24. N. Nicholson, "How to Motivate Your Problem People," *Harvard Business Review,* January 2003, 57–65.

25. A. M. Grant, "Does Intrinsic Motivation Fuel the Prosocial Fire? Motivational Synergy in Predicting Persistence, Performance, and Productivity," *Journal of Applied Psychology* 93, no. 1 (2008), 48–58.
26. Grant, "Does Intrinsic Motivation Fuel the Prosocial Fire?"; C. D. Batson, "Prosocial Motiviation: Is It Ever Truly Altruistic?" in L. Berkowitz, ed., *Advances in Experimental Social Psychology,* vol. 20 (New York: Academic Press, 1987), 65–122.
27. Grant, "Does Intrinsic Motivation Fuel the Prosocial Fire?"
28. J. P. Campbell and R. D. Pritchard, "Motivation Theory in Industrial and Organizational Psychology," in M. D. Dunnette, ed., *Handbook of Industrial and Organizational Psychology* (Chicago: Rand McNally, 1976), 63–130; T. R. Mitchell, "Expectancy Value Models in Organizational Psychology," in N. T. Feather, ed., *Expectations and Actions: Expectancy Value Models in Psychology* (Hillsdale, NJ: Erlbaum, 1982), 293–312; V. H. Vroom, *Work and Motivation* (New York: Wiley, 1964).
29. N. Shope Griffin, "Personalize Your Management Development," *Harvard Business Review* 8, no. 10 (2003), 113–119.
30. T. A. Stewart, "Just Think: No Permission Needed," *Fortune,* January 8, 2001 (www.fortune.com, June 26, 2001).
31. M. Copeland, "Best Buy's Selling Machine," *Business 2.0,* July 2004, 91–102; L. Heller, "Best Buy Still Turning on the Fun," *DSN Retailing Today* 43, no. 13 (July 5, 2004), 3; S. Pounds, "Big-Box Retailers Cash In on South Florida Demand for Home Computer Repair," *Knight Ridder Tribune Business News,* July 5, 2004 (gateway .proquest .com); J. Bloom, "Best Buy Reaps the Rewards of Risking Marketing Failure," *Advertising Age* 75, no. 25 (June 21, 2004), 16; L. Heller, "Discount Turns Up the Volume: PC Comeback, iPod Popularity Add Edge," *DSN Retailing Today* 43, no. 13 (July 5, 2004), 45; www.bestbuy.com, June 8, 2006.
32. T. J. Maurer, E. M. Weiss, and F. G. Barbeite, "A Model of Involvement in Work-Related Learning and Development Activity: The Effects of Individual, Situational, Motivational, and Age Variables," *Journal of Applied Psychology* 88, no. 4 (2003), 707–24.
33. J. Kaufman, "How Cambodians Came to Control California Doughnuts," *The Wall Street Journal,* February 22, 1995, A1, A8.
34. "Learn about Us," *The Container Store,* www.containerstore.com/learn/index .jhtml, April 1, 2008; The Container Store, "Welcome from Kip Tindell, Chairman & CEO," http://standfor .containerstore.com, March 3, 2010.
35. M. Duff, "Top-Shelf Employees Keep Container Store on Track," www. looksmart.com, www.findarticles.com, March 8, 2004; M. K. Ammenheuser, "The Container Store Helps People Think inside the Box," www.icsc.org, May 2004; "The Container Store: Store Location," www.containerstore .com/find/index/jhtml, June 5, 2006; "Store Locations," *The Container Store,* www.containerstore.com/find/index .jhtml, April 1, 2008; The Container Store–What We Stand For–Our Story, http:/standfor.containerstore.com/our-story/, March 3, 2010; "CEO Maxine Clark, of Build-a-Bear, Traded in Her Kid-Filled Existence for a Day in the Orderly Aisles of the Container Store, Doing the 'Closet Dance,'" *Fortune,* February 8, 2010, 68–72.
36. "Learn about Us," www.containerstore .com, June 26, 2001.
37. "Learn about Us," www.containerstore .com, June 26, 2001.
38. Schlosser and Sung, "The 100 Best Companies to Work For"; "Fortune 100 Best Companies to Work For 2006," cnn.com, June 5, 2006 (http:// money.cnn.com/magazines/fortune/ bestcompanies/snapshots/359.html); "Learn about Us," *The Container Store,* www.containerstore.com/learn/index .jhtml, April 1, 2008.
39. "The Container Store," www. careerbuilder.com, July 13, 2004; "Tom Takes Re-imagine to PBS," Case Studies, www.tompeters.com, March 15, 2004; "2004 Best Companies to Work For," www.fortune.com, July 12, 2004; "*Fortune* 100 Best Companies to Work For 2006," cnn.com, June 5, 2006; Levering and Moskowitz, "100 Best Companies to Work For: The Rankings"; Moskowitz, Levering, and Tkaczyk, "The List."
40. The Container Store–What We Stand For–Putting Our Employees First, http://standfor.containerstore.com puting-our-employees-first/, March 3, 2010.
41. D. Roth, "My Job at the Container Store," *Fortune,* January 10, 2000 (www. fortune.com, June 26, 2001); "*Fortune* 2004: 100 Best Companies to Work For," www.containerstore.com/careers/ FortunePR_2004.jhtml?message=/ repository/messages/fortuneCareer .jhtml, January 12, 2004; Levering, Moskowitz, and Adams, "The 100 Best Companies to Work For"; www. containerstore.com/careers/Fortune PR_2004.jhtml?message=/repository/ messages/fortuneCareer.jhtml, January 12, 2004.
42. Roth, "My Job at the Container Store."
43. "Learn about Us," *The Container Store,* http://www.containerstore.com/learn/ index.jhtml, April 1, 2008.
44. R. Yu, "Some Texas Firms Start Wellness Programs to Encourage Healthier Workers," *Knight Ridder Tribune Business News,* July 7, 2004 (gateway.proquest .com); Levering et al., "The 100 Best Companies to Work For."
45. Roth, "My Job at the Container Store"; "The Foundation Is Organization," *The Container Store,* June 5, 2006 (www. containerstore.com/careers/foundation .html).
46. C. J. Loomis, *Fortune* editor at large, "The Big Surprise Is Enterprise," *Fortune,* July 14, 2006, http://cnnmoney .printthis.clickability.com/pt/cpt?action= cpt&title=Fortune%3A+The+big . . . , March 31, 2008.
47. "Overview," *Enterprise Rent-A-Car Careers–Overview,* www.erac.com/ recruit/about_enterprise.asp?navID= overview, March 27, 2008; Enterprise Fact Sheet, http://aboutus.enterprise .com/what_we_do/rent_a_car.html, March 3, 2010.
48. "Enterprise Ranked in Top 10 of *BusinessWeek*'s 'Customer Service Champs,' " Thursday, February 22, 2007, *Enterprise Rent-A-Car Careers*–Enterprise in the News, www.erac.com/recruit/ news_detail.asp?navID=frontpage& RID=211, March 27, 2008; L. Gerdes, "The Best Places to Launch a Career," *BusinessWeek,* September 24, 2007, 49–60; P. Lehman, "A Clear Road to the Top," *BusinessWeek,* September 18, 2006, 72–82; 2009 "Best Places to Launch a Career," "15. Enterprise Rent-A-Car," *BusinessWeek,* February 24, 2010, http://www.businessweek .com/careers/first_jobs/2009/15.htm, March 1, 2010.
49. "Enterprise Ranked in Top 10 of *BusinessWeek*'s 'Customer Service Champs' "; Gerdes, "The Best Places to Launch a Career."
50. "It's Running a Business . . . Not Doing a Job," *Enterprise Rent-A-Car Careers–Opportunities,* www.erac.com/recruit/ opportunities.asp, March 27, 2008.
51. Loomis, "The Big Surprise Is Enterprise"; Lehman, "A Clear Road to the Top."
52. Loomis "The Big Surprise Is Enterprise"; Lehman, "A Clear Road to the Top."
53. Lehman, "A Clear Road to the Top."
54. Loomis, "The Big Surprise Is Enterprise."
55. Loomis, "The Big Surprise Is Enterprise"; Lehman, "A Clear Road to the Top."
56. A. H. Maslow, *Motivation and Personality* (New York: Harper & Row, 1954);

Campbell and Pritchard, "Motivation Theory in Industrial and Organizational Psychology."

57. Kanfer, "Motivation Theory and Industrial and Organizational Psychology."
58. S. Ronen, "An Underlying Structure of Motivational Need Taxonomies: A Cross-Cultural Confirmation," in H. C. Triandis, M. D. Dunnette, and L. M. Hough, eds., *Handbook of Industrial and Organizational Psychology,* vol. 4 (Palo Alto, CA: Consulting Psychologists Press, 1994), 241–69.
59. N. J. Adler, *International Dimensions of Organizational Behavior,* 2nd ed. (Boston: P.W.S. Kent, 1991); G. Hofstede, "Motivation, Leadership, and Organization: Do American Theories Apply Abroad?" *Organizational Dynamics,* Summer 1980, 42–63.
60. C. P. Alderfer, "An Empirical Test of a New Theory of Human Needs," *Organizational Behavior and Human Performance* 4 (1969), 142–75; C. P. Alderfer, *Existence, Relatedness, and Growth: Human Needs in Organizational Settings* (New York: Free Press, 1972); Campbell and Pritchard, "Motivation Theory in Industrial and Organizational Psychology."
61. Kanfer, "Motivation Theory and Industrial and Organizational Psychology."
62. F. Herzberg, *Work and the Nature of Man* (Cleveland: World, 1966).
63. N. King, "Clarification and Evaluation of the Two-Factor Theory of Job Satisfaction," *Psychological Bulletin* 74 (1970), 18–31; E. A. Locke, "The Nature and Causes of Job Satisfaction," in Dunnette, *Handbook of Industrial and Organizational Psychology,* 1297–1349.
64. D. C. McClelland, *Human Motivation* (Glenview, IL: Scott, Foresman, 1985); D. C. McClelland, "How Motives, Skills, and Values Determine What People Do," *American Psychologist* 40 (1985), 812–25; D. C. McClelland, "Managing Motivation to Expand Human Freedom," *American Psychologist* 33 (1978), 201–10.
65. D. G. Winter, *The Power Motive* (New York: Free Press, 1973).
66. M. J. Stahl, "Achievement, Power, and Managerial Motivation: Selecting Managerial Talent with the Job Choice Exercise," *Personnel Psychology* 36 (1983), 775–89; D. C. McClelland and D. H. Burnham, "Power Is the Great Motivator," *Harvard Business Review* 54 (1976), 100–10.
67. R. J. House, W. D. Spangler, and J. Woycke, "Personality and Charisma in the U.S. Presidency: A Psychological Theory of Leader Effectiveness," *Administrative Science Quarterly* 36 (1991), 364–96.
68. G. H. Hines, "Achievement, Motivation, Occupations, and Labor Turnover in New Zealand," *Journal of Applied Psychology* 58 (1973), 313–17; P. S. Hundal, "A Study of Entrepreneurial Motivation: Comparison of Fast- and Slow-Progressing Small Scale Industrial Entrepreneurs in Punjab, India," *Journal of Applied Psychology* 55 (1971), 317–23.
69. R. A. Clay, "Green Is Good for You," *Monitor on Psychology,* April 2001, 40–42.
70. J. S. Adams, "Toward an Understanding of Inequity," *Journal of Abnormal and Social Psychology* 67 (1963), 422–36.
71. Adams, "Toward an Understanding of Inequity"; J. Greenberg, "Approaching Equity and Avoiding Inequity in Groups and Organizations," in J. Greenberg and R. L. Cohen, eds., *Equity and Justice in Social Behavior* (New York: Academic Press, 1982), 389–435; J. Greenberg, "Equity and Workplace Status: A Field Experiment," *Journal of Applied Psychology* 73 (1988), 606–13; R. T. Mowday, "Equity Theory Predictions of Behavior in Organizations," in R. M. Steers and L. W. Porter, eds., *Motivation and Work Behavior* (New York: McGraw-Hill, 1987), 89–110.
72. A. Goldwasser, "Inhuman Resources," Ecompany.com, March 2001, 154–55.
73. E. A. Locke and G. P. Latham, *A Theory of Goal Setting and Task Performance* (Englewood Cliffs, NJ: Prentice-Hall, 1990).
74. Locke and Latham, *A Theory of Goal Setting and Task Performance;* J. J. Donovan and D. J. Radosevich, "The Moderating Role of Goal Commitment on the Goal Difficulty–Performance Relationship: A Meta-Analytic Review and Critical Analysis," *Journal of Applied Psychology* 83 (1998), 308–15; M. E. Tubbs, "Goal Setting: A Meta Analytic Examination of the Empirical Evidence," *Journal of Applied Psychology* 71 (1986), 474–83.
75. E. A. Locke, K. N. Shaw, L. M. Saari, and G. P. Latham, "Goal Setting and Task Performance: 1969–1980," *Psychological Bulletin* 90 (1981), 125–52.
76. P. C. Earley, T. Connolly, and G. Ekegren, "Goals, Strategy Development, and Task Performance: Some Limits on the Efficacy of Goal Setting," *Journal of Applied Psychology* 74 (1989), 24–33; R. Kanfer and P. L. Ackerman, "Motivation and Cognitive Abilities: An Integrative/Aptitude–Treatment Interaction Approach to Skill Acquisition," *Journal of Applied Psychology* 74 (1989), 657–90.
77. W. C. Hamner, "Reinforcement Theory and Contingency Management in Organizational Settings," in H. Tosi and W. C. Hamner, eds., *Organizational Behavior and Management: A Contingency Approach* (Chicago: St. Clair Press, 1974).
78. P. Dvorak, "Firms Shift Underused Workers," *The Wall Street Journal,* June 22, 2009, B2; http://www.heroarts.com/, March 3, 2010.
79. Dvorak, "Firms Shift Underused Workers."
80. Dvorak, "Firms Shift Underused Workers."
81. Dvorak, "Firms Shift Underused Workers."
82. Dvorak, "Firms Shift Underused Workers"; http://www.xantrion.com/, March 3, 2010.
83. Dvorak, "Firms Shift Underused Workers."
84. Dvorak, "Firms Shift Underused Workers"; Southwest Airlines–The Mission of Southwest Airlines, http://www.southwest.com/about_swa/?int=GFOOTER-ABOUT-ABOUT, March 3, 2010.
85. B. F. Skinner, *Contingencies of Reinforcement* (New York: Appleton-Century-Crofts, 1969).
86. H. W. Weiss, "Learning Theory and Industrial and Organizational Psychology," in Dunnette and Hough, *Handbook of Industrial and Organizational Psychology,* 171–221.
87. Hamner, "Reinforcement Theory and Contingency Management."
88. F. Luthans and R. Kreitner, *Organizational Behavior Modification and Beyond* (Glenview, IL: Scott, Foresman, 1985); A. D. Stajkovic and F. Luthans, "A Meta-Analysis of the Effects of Organizational Behavior Modification on Task Performance, 1975–95," *Academy of Management Journal* 40 (1997), 1122–49.
89. A. D. Stajkovic and F. Luthans, "Behavioral Management and Task Performance in Organizations: Conceptual Background, Meta Analysis, and Test of Alternative Models," *Personnel Psychology* 56 (2003), 155–94.
90. Stajkovic and Luthans, "Behavioral Management and Task Performance in Organizations"; Luthans and A. D. Stajkovic, "Reinforce for Performance: The Need to Go beyond Pay and Even Rewards," *Academy of Management Executive* 13, no. 2 (1999), 49–56; G. Billikopf Enciina and M. V. Norton, "Pay Method Affects Vineyard Pruner Performance," www.cnr.berkeley.edu/ucce50/ag-labor/7research/7calag05.htm.
91. A. Bandura, *Principles of Behavior Modification* (New York: Holt, Rinehart and Winston, 1969); A. Bandura, *Social Learning Theory* (Englewood Cliffs, NJ: Prentice-Hall, 1977); T. R. V. Davis and F. Luthans, "A Social Learning Approach to Organizational Behavior," *Academy of Management Review* 5 (1980), 281–90.

92. A. P. Goldstein and M. Sorcher, *Changing Supervisor Behaviors* (New York: Pergamon Press, 1974); Luthans and Kreitner, *Organizational Behavior Modification and Beyond.*

93. Bandura, *Social Learning Theory;* Davis and Luthans, "A Social Learning Approach to Organizational Behavior"; Luthans and Kreitner, *Organizational Behavior Modification and Beyond.*

94. A. Bandura, "Self-Reinforcement: Theoretical and Methodological Considerations," *Behaviorism* 4 (1976), 135–55.

95. K. H. Hammonds, "Growth Search," *Fast Company,* April, 2003, 74-81.

96. B. Elgin, "Managing Google's Idea Factory," *BusinessWeek,* October 3, 2005, 88–90.

97. A. Bandura, *Self-Efficacy: The Exercise of Control* (New York: W.H. Freeman, 1997); J. B. Vancouver, K. M. More, and R. J. Yoder, "Self-Efficacy and Resource Allocation: Support for a Nonmonotonic, Discontinuous Model," *Journal of Applied Psychology* 93, no. 1 (2008), 35–47.

98. A. Bandura, "Self-Efficacy Mechanism in Human Agency," *American Psychologist* 37 (1982), 122–27; M. E. Gist and T. R. Mitchell, "Self-Efficacy: A Theoretical Analysis of Its Determinants and Malleability," *Academy of Management Review* 17 (1992), 183–211.

99. E. E. Lawler III, *Pay and Organization Development* (Reading, MA: Addison-Wesley, 1981).

100. "The Risky New Bonuses," *Newsweek,* January 16, 1995, 42.

101. P. Dvorak and S. Thurm, "Slump Prods Firms to Seek New Compact with Workers," *The Wall Street Journal,* October 19, 2009, A1, A18.

102. D. Mattioli, "Rewards for Extra Work Come Cheap in Lean Times," *The Wall Street Journal,* January 4, 2010, B7.

103. Mattioli, "Rewards for Extra Work Come Cheap in Lean Times"; http://www.rockwellcollins.com/, March 3, 2010.

104. Mattioli, "Rewards for Extra Work Come Cheap in Lean Times."

105. Mattioli, "Rewards for Extra Work Come Cheap in Lean Times."

106. Mattioli, "Rewards for Extra Work Come Cheap in Lean Times"; http://en-sanofi-aventis.com/, March 3, 2010.

107. Mattioli, "Rewards for Extra Work Come Cheap in Lean Times."

108. Lawler, *Pay and Organization Development.*

109. Lawler, *Pay and Organization Development.*

110. J. F. Lincoln, *Incentive Management* (Cleveland: Lincoln Electric Company, 1951); R. Zager, "Managing Guaranteed Employment," *Harvard Business Review* 56 (1978), 103–15.

111. Lawler, *Pay and Organization Development.*

112. M. Gendron, "Gradient Named 'Small Business of Year,'" *Boston Herald,* May 11, 1994, 35; Gradient–Environmental Consulting, http://www.gradientcorp.com/index.php, March 3, 2010.

113. W. Zeller, R. D. Hof, R. Brandt, S. Baker, and D. Greising, "Go-Go Goliaths," *BusinessWeek,* February 13, 1995, 64–70.

114. N. Byrnes, "A Steely Resolve" *BusinessWeek,* April 6, 2009, 54.

115. "Stock Option," *Encarta World English Dictionary,* June 28, 2001 (www.dictionary.msn.com); personal interview with Professor Bala Dharan, Jones Graduate School of Business, Rice University, June 28, 2001.

116. Personal interview with Professor Bala Dharan.

117. Personal interview with Professor Bala Dharan.

118. A. J. Michels, "Dallas Semicoductor," *Fortune,* May 16, 1994, 81.

119. M. Betts, "Big Things Come in Small Buttons," *Computerworld,* August 3, 1992, 30.

120. M. Boslet, "Metal Buttons Toted by Crop Pickers Act as Mini Databases," *The Wall Street Journal,* June 1, 1994, B3.

121. C. D. Fisher, L. F. Schoenfeldt, and J. B. Shaw, *Human Resource Management* (Boston: Houghton Mifflin, 1990); B. E. Graham-Moore and T. L. Ross, *Productivity Gainsharing* (Englewood Cliffs, NJ: Prentice-Hall, 1983); A. J. Geare, "Productivity from Scanlon Type Plans," *Academy of Management Review* 1 (1976), 99–108.

122. K. Belson, "Japan's Net Generation," *BusinessWeek,* March 19, 2001 (*BusinessWeek* Archives, June 27, 2001).

123. K. Belson, "Taking a Hint from the Upstarts," *BusinessWeek,* March 19, 2001 (*BusinessWeek* Archives, June 27, 2001); "Going for the Gold," *BusinessWeek,* March 19, 2001 (*BusinessWeek* Archives, June 27, 2001); "What the Government Can Do to Promote a Flexible Workforce," *BusinessWeek,* March 19, 2001 (*BusinessWeek* Archives, June 27, 2001).

Chapter 14

1. T. Lowry, "Can MTV Stay Cool?" *BusinessWeek,* February 20, 2006, 51–60; "Senior Management," *VIACOM,* www.viacom.com/aboutviacom/Pages/seniormanagement.aspx, April 2, 2008.

2. www.viacom.com/2006/pdf/Viacom_Fact_Sheet_4_5_06.pdf, June 9, 2006; M. Gunther, "Mr. MTV Grows Up," CNNMoney.com, April 13, 2006, http://money.cnn.com/magazines/fortune/fortune_archive/2006/04/17/8374305/index.htm; "Viacom Completes Separation into CBS Corporation and 'New' Viacom," Viacom.com, January 1, 2006, www.viacom.com/view_release.jhtml?inID=10000040&inReleaseID=126683; "MTV Networks," http://www.viacom.com/ourbrands/medianetworks/mtvnetworks/Pages/default.aspx, March 3, 2010.

3. Lowry, "Can MTV Stay Cool?"; "VIACOM," *PULSE,* February 28, 2008, Fourth Quarter, 1, www.viacom.com/investorrelations/investor_relations_docs/pulse%20Q42007%20Final.pdf, April 2, 2008; A. Hampp, "Why It's Still Your MTV, According to Judy McGrath," *Advertising Age,* February 15, 2010, http://adage.com/mediaworks/article?article_id=142104, March 3, 2010.

4. J. H. Higgins, "A Rockin' Role: McGrath Keeps MTV Networks Plugged In and Focused," www.broadcastingcable.com, April 10, 2006, www.broadcastingcable.com/article/CA6323342.html?display=Search+Results&text=judy+mcgrath; "*Fortune* 50 Most Powerful Women in Business 2005," CNNMoney.com, November 14, 2005, http://money.cnn.com/magazines/fortune/mostpowerfulwomen/snapshots/10.html; E. Levenson, "Hall of Fame: Digging a Little Deeper into the List, We Salute the Highfliers and Share Some Facts to Inspire and Amuse," CNNMoney.com, November 14, 2005, http://money.cnn.com/magazines/fortune/fortune_archive/2005/11/14/8360698/index.html; "50 Most Powerful Women 2007: The Power 50," CNNMoney.com, *Fortune,* The Power 50–Judy McGrath (18)–FORTUNE, http://money.cnn.com/galleries/2007/fortune/0709/gallery.women_mostpowerful.fortune/18 . . . , April 2, 2008; "50 Most Powerful Women in Business," "All-Stars," http://money.cnn.com/magazines/fortune/mostpowerfulwomen/2009/allstars/index.html, March 3, 2010; "50 Most Powerful Women in Business 2009" Full List–*FORTUNE on CNNMoney.com,* http://money.cnn.com/magazines/fortune/mostpowerfulwomen/2009/full_list/, March 3, 2010.

5. "The 100 Most Powerful Women," *Forbes,* http://www.forbes.com/lists/2009/11/power-woman-09_Judy-McGrath_6J9A.html, March 3, 2010; "MTV Networks Chairman and CEO Judy McGrath Tops the 2009 Billboard Women in Music Power Players List," *Hip Hop Press,* October 2, 2009, http://www.hiphoppress.com/2009/10/mtv-networks-chairman-and-ceo-judy-mcgrath-tops-t . . . , March 3, 2010; "MTV Network's Chairman and CEO Judy McGrath to Receive Foundation of AWRT Achievement Award at 34th Annual Gracies Gala," May 21, 2009, *Gracies,* http://www.awrt.org/Gracies/pdfs/Press_Release_McGrath_2009.pdf, March 3, 2010.
6. Lowry, "Can MTV Stay Cool?"; "Welcome to Viacom–Senior Management," www.viacom.com/management.html, June 9, 2006.
7. Lowry, "Can MTV Stay Cool?"
8. Lowry, "Can MTV Stay Cool?"
9. "The 2006 National Show Mobile Edition–Judy McGrath," www.thenationalshoe.com/Mobile/SpeakerDetail.aspx?ID=199, June 9, 2006.
10. Lowry, "Can MTV Stay Cool?"
11. "Real World XX: Hollywood/Main," Real World XX: Hollywood/Show Cast, Episode Guides, Trailers, Aftershow & Preview . . . , www.mtv.com/ontv/dyn/realworld-season20/series.jhtml, April 2, 2008; New Music Videos, Reality TV Shows, Celebrity News, Top Stories / MTV, http://www.mtv.com, March 3, 2010.
12. Lowry, "Can MTV Stay Cool?"; "Viacom's MTV Networks Completes Acquisition of Xfire, Inc.," www.viacom.com/view_release.jhtml?inID=10000040&inReleaseID=227008, June 9, 2006; Nick.com/Kids Games, Kids Celebrity Video, Kids Shows/Nickelodeon, http://www.nick.com, March 3, 2010.
13. "MTV Networks Unveils URGE Digital Music Service on Microsoft's New Windows Media Player 11 Platform," *Microsoft,* May 17, 2006, www.microsoft.com/presspass/press/2006/may06/05-17URGEPR.mspx.
14. Lowry, "Can MTV Stay Cool?"
15. Lowry, "Can MTV Stay Cool?"
16. G. Yukl, *Leadership in Organizations,* 2nd ed. (New York: Academic Press, 1989); R. M. Stogdill, *Handbook of Leadership: A Survey of the Literature* (New York: Free Press, 1974).
17. Lowry, "Can MTV Stay Cool?"
18. W. D. Spangler, R. J. House, and R. Palrecha, "Personality and Leadership," in B. Schneider and D. B. Smith, eds., *Personality and Organizations* (Mahwah, NJ: Lawrence Erlbaum, 2004), 251–90.
19. W. D. Spangler, R. J. House, and R. Palrecha, "Personality and Leadership," in B. Schneider and D. B. Smith, eds., *Personality and Organizations* (Mahwah, NJ: Lawrence Erlbaum, 2004), 251–90; "Leaders vs. Managers: Leaders Master the Context of Their Mission, Managers Surrender to It," www.msue.msu.edu/msue/imp/modtd/visuals/tsld029.htm, July 28, 2004; "Leadership," Leadership Center at Washington State University; M. Maccoby, "Understanding the Difference between Management and Leadership," *Research Technology Management* 43, no. 1 (January–February 2000), 57–59, www.maccoby.com/articles/UtDBMaL.html; P. Coutts, "Leadership vs. Management," www.telusplanet.net/public/pdcoutts/leadership/LdrVsMgnt.htm, October 1, 2000; S. Robbins, "The Difference between Managing and Leading," www.Entrepreneur.com/article/0,4621,304743,00.html, November 18, 2002; W. Bennis, "The Leadership Advantage," *Leader to Leader* 12 (Spring 1999), www.pfdf.org/leaderbooks/121/spring99/bennis/html.
20. Spangler et al., "Personality and Leadership"; "Leaders vs. Managers"; "Leadership"; Maccoby, "Understanding the Difference between Management and Leadership"; Coutts, "Leadership vs. Management"; Robbins, "The Difference between Managing and Leading"; Bennis, "The Leadership Advantage."
21. "Greenleaf: Center for Servant Leadership: History," *Greenleaf Center for Servant Leadership,* www.greenleaf.org/aboutus/history.html, April 7, 2008.
22. "What Is Servant Leadership?" *Greenleaf: Center for Servant Leadership,* http://www.greenleaf.org/whatissl/index.html, April 2, 2008.
23. "What Is Servant Leadership?"; Review by F. Hamilton of L. Spears and M. Lawrence, *Practicing Servant Leadership: Succeeding through Trust, Bravery, and Forgiveness* (San Francisco: Jossey-Bass, 2004), in *Academy of Management Review* 30 (October 2005), 875–87; R. R. Washington, "Empirical Relationships between Theories of Servant, Transformational, and Transactional Leadership," *Academy of Management,* Best Paper Proceedings, 2007, 1–6.
24. "Greenleaf: Center for Servant Leadership: History"; "What Is Servant Leadership?"; "Greenleaf: Center for Servant Leadership: Our Mission," *Greenleaf Center for Servant Leadership,* www.greenleaf.org/aboutus/mission.html, April 7, 2008.
25. B. Burlingham, "The Coolest Small Company in America," *Inc.,* January 2003, www.inc.com/magazine/20030101/25036_Printer_Friendly.html, April 7, 2008.
26. Burlingham, "The Coolest Small Company in America"; "Zingerman's Community of Businesses," *About Us,* www.zingermans.com/AboutUs.aspx, April 7, 2008; L. Buchanan, "In Praise of Selflessness," *Inc.,* May 2007, 33–35; Zingerman's Community of Businesses, http://www.zingermanscommunity.com, March 3, 2010.
27. Burlingham, "The Coolest Small Company in America"; "Zingerman's Community of Businesses"; Buchanan, "In Praise of Selflessness."
28. Buchanan, "In Praise of Selflessness."
29. Buchanan, "In Praise of Selflessness."
30. Burlingham, "The Coolest Small Company in America"; "In a Nutshell," *food gatherers,* www.foodgatherers.org/about.htm, April 7, 2008; Food Gatherers, "In a Nutshell," http://www.foodgatherers.org/about.htm, March 3, 2010.
31. "In a Nutshell."
32. Buchanan, "In Praise of Selflessness."
33. R. Calori and B. Dufour, "Management European Style," *Academy of Management Executive* 9, no. 3 (1995), 61–70.
34. Calori and Dufour, "Management European Style."
35. H. Mintzberg, *Power in and around Organizations* (Englewood Cliffs, NJ: Prentice-Hall, 1983); J. Pfeffer, *Power in Organizations* (Marshfield, MA: Pitman, 1981).
36. R. P. French, Jr., and B. Raven, "The Bases of Social Power," in D. Cartwright and A. F. Zander, eds., *Group Dynamics* (Evanston, IL: Row, Peterson, 1960), 607–23.
37. C. Frey, "Nordstrom Salesman's Million-Dollar Secret Is in His Treasured Client List," *Seattle Post-Intelligencer,* Saturday, March 27, 2004, http://www.seattlepi.com/business/166571_retail27.html, March 5, 2010; "Macy's Herald Square, New York, NY: Retail Commission Sales Associate–Women's Shoes," http://jobview.monster.com/Macy's-Herald-Square-New-York-NY-Retail-Commission-Sale . . . , March 5, 2010.
38. R. L. Rose, "After Turning Around Giddings and Lewis, Fife Is Turned Out Himself," *The Wall Street Journal,* June 22, 1993, A1.
39. E. Olson, "Adventures as a Team Sport," *The New York Times,* October 23, 2005, 9; "Investor Relations–Alaska Communications System: Board of Directors," *ACS,* March 20, 2006, www.acsalaska.com/ALSK/en-US/Board+of+Directors/Liane+Pelletier.htm; About ACS, http://www.acsalaska.com/corporate/index.asp, March 3, 2010.

40. Olson, "Adventures as a Team Sport."
41. Olson, "Adventures as a Team Sport."
42. "Alaska's Premier Telecommunications Provider," ACS, *Alaska Communications Systems Group, Inc.,* Corporate Fact Sheet, www.acsalaska.com/NR/rdonlyres/47628010-7ADO-42BF-9484-0A7AE7E008AD/01ACSfactsheet031708.pdf, April 8, 2008; "People–Technology– Potential," *Alaska Communications Systems,* www.acsalaska.com/cultures/en-us/corporate%20information, April 8, 2008.
43. "Investor Relations–Alaska Communications System."
44. "Alaska Communications," *Corporate Spotlight,* March 21, 2006, www.redcoatpublishingcom/spotlights/s1_08_05_Alaska.asp.
45. G. G. Marcial, "Heading North to Alaska Communications," *BusinessWeek Online,* June 27, 2005, www.businessweek.com.
46. Olson, "Adventures as a Team Sport;" "Management Team," ACS, Alaska Communications Systems, www.acsalaska.com/ALSK/en-US/Management+Team/, April 8, 2008; Liane Pelletier: Executive Profile & Biography–*BusinessWeek,* http://investing.businessweek.com/businessweek/research/stocks/people/person.asp?personI . . . , March 3, 2010; Liane J. Pelletier Profile–Forbes.com, http://people.forbes.com/profile/print/liane-j-pelletier/2638, March 3, 2010.
47. A. Grove, "How Intel Makes Spending Pay Off," *Fortune,* February 22, 1993, 56–61; "Craig R. Barrett, Chief Executive Officer: Intel Corporation," *Intel,* July 28, 2004, www.intel.com/pressroom/kits/bios/barrett/bio.htm; Craig R. Barrett Bio, http://www.intel.com/pressroom/kits/bios/barrett.htm, March 3, 2010.
48. Craig R. Barrett Bio, www.intel.com/pressroom/kits/bios/barrett.htm, April 8, 2008; Microsoft Press Pass–Microsoft Board of Directors, www.microsoft.com/presspass/bod/default.mspx, April 8, 2008; "Tachi Yamada Selected to Lead Gates Foundation's Global Health Program," Announcements–Bill & Melinda Gates Foundation, February 6, 2006, www.gatesfoundation.org/GlobalHealth/Announcements/Announce-060106.htm, April 8, 2008; Microsoft PressPass–Microsoft Executives and Images, "Microsoft Board of Directors," http://www.microsoft.com/presspass/bod/bod.aspx, March 3, 2010; Tachi Yamada–Bill & Melinda Gates Foundation, http://www.gatesfoundation.org/leadership/Pages/tachi-yamada.aspx, March 3, 2010.
49. M. Loeb, "Jack Welch Lets Fly on Budgets, Bonuses, and Buddy Boards," *Fortune,* May 29, 1995, 146.
50. T. M. Burton, "Visionary's Reward: Combine 'Simple Ideas' and Some Failures; Result: Sweet Revenge," *The Wall Street Journal,* February 3, 1995, A1, A5.
51. L. Nakarmi, "A Flying Leap toward the 21st Century? Pressure from Competitors and Seoul May Transform the Chaebol," *BusinessWeek,* March 20, 1995, 78–80.
52. B. M. Bass, *Bass and Stogdill's Handbook of Leadership: Theory, Research, and Managerial Applications,* 3rd ed. (New York: Free Press, 1990); R. J. House and M. L. Baetz, "Leadership: Some Empirical Generalizations and New Research Directions," in B. M. Staw and L. L. Cummings, eds., *Research in Organizational Behavior,* vol. 1 (Greenwich, CT: JAI Press, 1979), 341–423; S. A. Kirpatrick and E. A. Locke, "Leadership: Do Traits Matter?" *Academy of Management Executive* 5, no. 2 (1991), 48–60; Yukl, *Leadership in Organizations;* G. Yukl and D. D. Van Fleet, "Theory and Research on Leadership in Organizations," in M. D. Dunnette and L. M. Hough, eds., *Handbook of Industrial and Organizational Psychology,* 2nd ed., vol. 3 (Palo Alto, CA: Consulting Psychologists Press, 1992), 147–97.
53. E. A. Fleishman, "Performance Assessment Based on an Empirically Derived Task Taxonomy," *Human Factors* 9 (1967), 349–66; E. A. Fleishman, "The Description of Supervisory Behavior," *Personnel Psychology* 37 (1953), 1–6; A. W. Halpin and B. J. Winer, "A Factorial Study of the Leader Behavior Descriptions," in R. M. Stogdill and A. I. Coons, eds., *Leader Behavior: Its Description and Measurement* (Columbus Bureau of Business Research, Ohio State University, 1957); D. Tscheulin, "Leader Behavior Measurement in German Industry," *Journal of Applied Psychology* 56 (1971), 28–31.
54. S. Greenhouse, "How Costco Became the Anti-Wal-Mart," *The New York Times,* July 17, 2005, BU1, BU8; "Directors," *Costco Wholesale, Investors Relations,* http://phx.corporate-ir.net/phoenix.zhtml?c=83830&p=irol-govBoard, April 8, 2008.
55. "Corporate Governance," *Costco Wholesale Investor Relations,* April 28, 2006, http://phx.corporate-ir.net/phoenix.zhtml?c=83830&p=irol-govhighlights.
56. Greenhouse, "How Costco Became the Anti-Wal-Mart."
57. Greenhouse, "How Costco Became the Anti-Wal-Mart."
58. Greenhouse, "How Costco Became the Anti-Wal-Mart."
59. Greenhouse, "How Costco Became the Anti-Wal-Mart;" S. Clifford, "Because Who Knew a Big-Box Chain Could Have a Generous Soul," *Inc.,* April 2005, 88.
60. S. Holmes and W. Zellner, "Commentary: The Costco Way," *BusinessWeek Online,* April 12, 2004, www.businessweek.com/print/magazine/content/04_15/b3878084_mz021.htm?chan . . . ; M. Herbst, "The Costco Challenge: An Alternative to Wal-Martization?" *LRA Online,* July 5, 2005, www.laborresearch.org/print.php?id=391.
61. Greenhouse, "How Costco Became the Anti-Wal-Mart."
62. Greenhouse, "How Costco Became the Anti-Wal-Mart;" "Company Profile," *Costco Wholesale, Investor Relations,* http://phx.corporate-ir.net/phoenix.zhtml?c=83830&p=irol-homeprofile, April 8, 2008; Costco–Company Profile, http://phx.corporate-ir.net/phoenix.zhtml?c=83830&p=irol-homeprofile, March 5, 2010.
63. A. Martinez and M. Allison, "Costco, Other Warehouse Clubs Holding Their Own during Recession," *The Seattle Times,* February 1, 2010, http://seattletimes.nwsource.com/cgi-bin/PrintStory.pl?document_id=2010922094&zsection . . . , March 3, 2010; S. Skidmore, "Wholesale Clubs' Profit Grows as Grocery Supermarkets Slide," *USA TODAY,* http://www.usatoday.com/cleanprint/?1267669249262, March 3, 2010.
64. Costco–Company Profile, http://phx.corporate-ir.net/phoenix.zhtml?c=83830&p=irol-homeprofile, March 5, 2010.
65. "Costco Wholesale Corporation Reports Second Quarter and Year-to-Date Operating Results Fiscal 2006 and February Sales Results," *Costco Wholesale Investor Relations: News Release,* April 28, 2006, http://phx.corporate-ir.net/phoenix.zhtml?c=83830&p=irol-newsArticle&ID=824344&highlight=; "Costco Wholesale Corporation Reports March Sales Results and Plans for Membership Fee Increase," *Costco Wholesale Investor Relations: News Release,* April 28, 2006, http://phx.corporate-ir.net/phoenix.zhtml?c=83830&p=irol-newsArticle&ID=839605&highlight=; "Wal-Mart Stores Post Higher January Sales," *BusinessWeek Online,* February 2, 2006, www.businessweek.com/print/investor/conent/feb2006/pi20060220732_pi004.htm.
66. Martinez and Allison, "Costco, Other Warehouse Clubs Holding Their Own during Recession."
67. "Costco Class Action Discrimination Lawsuit: Women Sue Costco," http://genderclassactionagainstcostco.com/costco94.pl, March 3, 2010; M. C. Fisk and K. Gullo, "Costco Ignored Sex Bias Warnings, Employees Say," http://www.seattlepi.com/

business/284317_costcobias08.html, March 3, 2010; "Costco Job-Bias Lawsuit Advances," *Los Angeles Times,* January 12, 2007, http://articles.latimes.com/2007/jan/12/business/fi-costco12, March 3, 2010.

68. "Costco Job-Bias Lawsuit Advances"; M. Allison, "Q&A: Costco CEO Jim Sinegal Talks about Recession, Succession," *The Seattle Times,* http://seattletimes.nwsource.com/cgi-bin/PrintStory.pl?document_id=2010271409&zsection . . . , March 3, 2010.

69. E. A. Fleishman and E. F. Harris, "Patterns of Leadership Behavior Related to Employee Grievances and Turnover," *Personnel Psychology* 15 (1962), 43–56.

70. R. Likert, *New Patterns of Management* (New York: McGraw-Hill, 1961); N. C. Morse and E. Reimer, "The Experimental Change of a Major Organizational Variable," *Journal of Abnormal and Social Psychology* 52 (1956), 120–29.

71. R. R. Blake and J. S. Mouton, *The New Managerial Grid* (Houston: Gulf, 1978).

72. P. Hersey and K. Blanchard, *Management of Organizational Behavior: Utilizing Human Resources* (Englewood Cliffs, NJ: Prentice-Hall, 1982).

73. F. E. Fiedler, *A Theory of Leadership Effectiveness* (New York: McGraw-Hill, 1967); F. E. Fiedler, "The Contingency Model and the Dynamics of the Leadership Process," in L. Berkowitz, ed., *Advances in Experimental Social Psychology* (New York: Academic Press, 1978).

74. J. Fierman, "Winning Ideas from Maverick Managers," *Fortune,* February 6, 1995, 66–80; "Laybourne, Geraldine, U.S. Media Executive," *Laybourne, Geraldine,* http://museum.tv/archives/etv/L/htmlL/laybournege/laybournege.htm, April 8, 2008.

75. M. Schuman, "Free to Be," *Forbes,* May 8, 1995, 78–80; "Profile–Herman Mashaba," *SAIE–Herman Mashaba,* www.entrepreneurship.co.za/page/herman_mashaba, April 8, 2008.

76. House and Baetz, "Leadership"; L. H. Peters, D. D. Hartke, and J. T. Pohlmann, "Fiedler's Contingency Theory of Leadership: An Application of the Meta-Analysis Procedures of Schmidt and Hunter," *Psychological Bulletin* 97 (1985), 274–85; C. A. Schriesheim, B. J. Tepper, and L. A. Tetrault, "Least Preferred Co-Worker Score, Situational Control, and Leadership Effectiveness: A Meta-Analysis of Contingency Model Performance Predictions," *Journal of Applied Psychology* 79 (1994), 561–73.

77. M. G. Evans, "The Effects of Supervisory Behavior on the Path–Goal Relationship," *Organizational Behavior and Human Performance* 5 (1970), 277–98; R. J. House, "A Path–Goal Theory of Leader Effectiveness," *Administrative Science Quarterly* 16 (1971), 321–38; J. C. Wofford and L. Z. Liska, "Path–Goal Theories of Leadership: A Meta-Analysis," *Journal of Management* 19 (1993), 857–76.

78. S. Kerr and J. M. Jermier, "Substitutes for Leadership: Their Meaning and Measurement," *Organizational Behavior and Human Performance* 22 (1978), 375–403; P. M. Podsakoff, B. P. Niehoff, S. B. MacKenzie, and M. L. Williams, "Do Substitutes for Leadership Really Substitute for Leadership? An Empirical Examination of Kerr and Jermier's Situational Leadership Model," *Organizational Behavior and Human Decision Processes* 54 (1993), 1–44.

79. Kerr and Jermier, "Substitutes for Leadership"; Podsakoff et al., "Do Substitutes for Leadership Really Substitute for Leadership?"

80. J. Reingold, "You Got Served," *Fortune,* October 1, 2007, 55–58; "News on Women," *News on Women: Sue Nokes SVP at T-Mobile,* http://newsonwomen.typepad.com/news_on_women/2007/09/sue-nokes-svp-a.html, April 8, 2008.

81. "Company Information," "T-Mobile Cell Phone Carrier Quick Facts," http://www.t-mobile/Company/CompanyInfo.aspx?tp=Abt_Tab_CompanyOverview, April 8, 2008; "T-Mobile Cell Phone Carrier Quick Facts," http://www.t-mobile.com/Company/CompanyInfo.aspx?tp=Abt_Tab_CompanyOverview, March 5, 2010.

82. Reingold, "You Got Served."

83. Reingold, "You Got Served"; "Company Information," "Highest Customer Satisfaction & Wireless Call Quality–J.D. Power Awards," http://www.t-mobile.com/Company/CompanyInfo.aspx?tp=Abt_Tab_Awards, April 8, 2008.

84. Reingold, "You Got Served."

85. Reingold, "You Got Served."

86. B. M. Bass, *Leadership and Performance beyond Expectations* (New York: Free Press, 1985); Bass, *Bass and Stogdill's Handbook of Leadership;* Yukl and Van Fleet, "Theory and Research on Leadership."

87. Reingold, "You Got Served."

88. Reingold, "You Got Served."

89. Reingold, "You Got Served."

90. Reingold, "You Got Served."

91. Reingold, "You Got Served."

92. Reingold, "You Got Served."

93. J. A. Conger and R. N. Kanungo, "Behavioral Dimensions of Charismatic Leadership," in J. A. Conger, R. N. Kanungo, and Associates, *Charismatic Leadership* (San Francisco: Jossey-Bass, 1988).

94. Bass, *Leadership and Performance beyond Expectations;* Bass, *Bass and Stogdill's Handbook of Leadership;* Yukl and Van Fleet, "Theory and Research on Leadership;" Reingold, "You Got Served."

95. Bass, *Leadership and Performance beyond Expectations;* Bass, *Bass and Stogdill's Handbook of Leadership;* Yukl and Van Fleet, "Theory and Research on Leadership."

96. Reingold, "You Got Served."

97. Bass, *Leadership and Performance beyond Expectations.*

98. Bass, *Bass and Stogdill's Handbook of Leadership;* B. M. Bass and B. J. Avolio, "Transformational Leadership: A Response to Critiques," in M. M. Chemers and R. Ayman, eds., *Leadership Theory and Research: Perspectives and Directions* (San Diego: Academic Press, 1993), 49–80; B. M. Bass, B. J. Avolio, and L. Goodheim, "Biography and the Assessment of Transformational Leadership at the World Class Level," *Journal of Management* 13 (1987), 7–20; J. J. Hater and B. M. Bass, "Supervisors' Evaluations and Subordinates' Perceptions of Transformational and Transactional Leadership," *Journal of Applied Psychology* 73 (1988), 695–702; R. Pillai, "Crisis and Emergence of Charismatic Leadership in Groups: An Experimental Investigation," *Journal of Applied Psychology* 26 (1996), 543–62; J. Seltzer and B. M. Bass, "Transformational Leadership: Beyond Initiation and Consideration," *Journal of Management* 16 (1990), 693–703; D. A. Waldman, B. M. Bass, and W. O. Einstein, "Effort, Performance, Transformational Leadership in Industrial and Military Service," *Journal of Occupation Psychology* 60 (1987), 1–10.

99. R. Pillai, C. A. Schriesheim, and E. S. Williams, "Fairness Perceptions and Trust as Mediators of Transformational and Transactional Leadership: A Two-Sample Study," *Journal of Management* 25 (1999), 897–933.

100. "50 Most Powerful Women–1. Indra Nooyi (1)–*Fortune,*" http://money.cnn.com/galleries/2009/fortune/0909/gallery.most_powerful_women.fortune/i . . . , March 5, 2010.

101. "50 Most Powerful Women–5. Andrea Jung (5)–*Fortune,*" http://money.cnn

.com/galleries/2009/fortune/0909/gallery.most_powerful_women.fortune/5 . . . , March 5, 2010.

102. L. Tischler, "Where Are the Women?" *Fast Company,* February 2004, 52–60.

103. "2000 Catalyst Census of Women Corporate Officers and Top Earners of the *Fortune* 500," www.catalystwomen.org, October 21, 2001; S. Wellington, M. Brumit Kropf, and P. R. Gerkovich, "What's Holding Women Back?" *Harvard Business Review,* June 2003, 18–19; D. Jones, "The Gender Factor," *USA Today.com,* December 30, 2003; "2002 Catalyst Census of Women Corporate Officers and Top Earners in the *Fortune* 500," www.catalystwomen.org, August 17, 2004; "2007 Catalyst Census of Women Corporate Officers and Top Earners of the *Fortune* 500," www.catalyst.org/knowledge/titles/title/php?page=cen_COTE_07, February 8, 2008.

104. A. H. Eagly and B. T. Johnson, "Gender and Leadership Style: A Meta-Analysis," *Psychological Bulletin* 108 (1990), 233–56.

105. Eagly and Johnson, "Gender and Leadership Style: A Meta-Analysis."

106. The Economist, "Workers Resent Scoldings from Female Bosses," *Houston Chronicle,* August 19, 2000, 1C.

107. The Economist, "Workers Resent Scoldings from Female Bosses."

108. The Economist, "Workers Resent Scoldings from Female Bosses."

109. The Economist, "Workers Resent Scoldings from Female Bosses."

110. A. H. Eagly, S. J. Karau, and M. G. Makhijani, "Gender and the Effectiveness of Leaders: A Meta-Analysis," *Psychological Bulletin* 117 (1995), 125–45.

111. Eagly, Karau, and Makhijani, "Gender and the Effectiveness of Leaders: A Meta-Analysis."

112. J. M. George and K. Bettenhausen, "Understanding Prosocial Behavior, Sales Performance, and Turnover: A Group-Level Analysis in a Service Context," *Journal of Applied Psychology* 75 (1990), 698–709.

113. T. Sy, S. Cote, and R. Saavedra, "The Contagious Leader: Impact of the Leader's Mood on the Mood of Group Members, Group Affective Tone, and Group Processes," *Journal of Applied Psychology* 90(2), (2005), 295–305.

114. J. M. George, "Emotions and Leadership: The Role of Emotional Intelligence," *Human Relations* 53 (2000), 1027–55.

115. George, "Emotions and Leadership."

116. J. Zhou and J. M. George, "Awakening Employee Creativity: The Role of Leader Emotional Intelligence," *The Leadership Quarterly* 14, no. 45 (August–October 2003), 545–68.

117. Zhou and George, "Awakening Employee Creativity."

118. Zhou and George, "Awakening Employee Creativity."

119. D. Fenn, "My Bad," *Inc.,* October 2007, 37–38; *Creative Display Solutions: About Us,* www.creativedisplaysolutions.com/pages/about/about.html, April 4, 2008; *Creative Display Solutions: About Us,* http://www.creativedisplaysolutions.com/pages/about/about.html, March 5, 2010.

120. Fenn, "My Bad"; *Creative Display Solutions: About Us,* www.creativedisplaysolutions.com/pages/about/about.html, April 4, 2008.

121. Fenn, "My Bad."

122. Fenn, "My Bad."

123. Fenn, "My Bad."

124. Fenn, "My Bad."

125. Fenn, "My Bad."

126. Fenn, "My Bad;" C. Mason-Draffen, "Inside Stories," "Feeling Like a Million," *Creative Display Solutions: CDS News,* www.creativedisplaysolutions.com/pages/about/news6.html, April 4, 2008.

127. D. Sonnenberg, "Mother Load: How to Balance Career and Family," July 30, 2007, *Creative Display Solutions: CDS News,* www.creativedisplaysolutions.com/pages/about/news8.html, April 4, 2008; C. Mason-Draffen, "Partnership at Work: Couples in Business Together Have Their Share of Sweet Rewards and Unique Challenges," February 13, 2007, *Creative Display Solutions, CDS News,* www.creativedisplaysolutions.com/pages/about/news7.html, April 4, 2008; "Client List," *Creative Display Solutions: About Us,* www.creativedisplaysolutions.com/pages/about/clients.html, April 8, 2008; Fenn, "My Bad;" "Client List," *Creative,* http://www.creativedisplaysolutions.com/pages/about/clients.html, March 5, 2010.

128. Fenn, "My Bad."

Chapter 15

1. "Most Innovative Companies–2010: Cisco Systems/Fast Company," http://www.fastcompany.com/mic/2010/profile/cisco-systems, March 8, 2010.

2. "News@Cisco–Fact Sheet," http://newsroom.cisco.com/dlls/corpinfo/factsheet.html, March 8, 2010; "Cisco Systems Inc. News," *The New York Times,* http://topics.nytimes.com/topics/news/business/companies/cisco_systems_inc/index.html, March 13, 2010; "Letter to Shareholders," Cisco Systems/Annual Report 2009.

3. "Letter to Shareholders," Cisco Systems/Annual Report 2009.

4. "Most Innovative Companies–2010: Cisco Systems/Fast Company."

5. "Cisco Introduces Foundation for Next-Generation Internet: The Cisco CRS-3 Carrier Routing System," http://newsroom.cisco.com/dlls/2010/prod_030910.html?print=true, March 13, 2010; R. Kim, "Cisco Unveils Blazing Fast Router," March 10, 2010, http://sfgate.com/cgi-bin/article.cgi?f=/c/a/2010/03/10/BUDQ1CD8NC.DTL&type= . . . , March 13, 2010.

6. "100 Best Companies to Work For 2010–CISCO," *Fortune,* http://money.cnn.com/magazines/fortune/bestcompanies/2010/snapshots/16.html, March 8, 2010.

7. B. Worthen, "Seeking Growth, Cisco Reroutes Decisions," *The Wall Street Journal,* August 6, 2009, B1; J. McGregor, "There Is No More Normal," *BusinessWeek,* March 23 & 30, 2009, 30–34; M. Kimes, "Cisco Systems Layers It On," *Fortune,* December 8, 2008, 24.

8. Worthen, "Seeking Growth, Cisco Reroutes Decisions"; McGregor, "There Is No More Normal."

9. Worthen, "Seeking Growth, Cisco Reroutes Decisions"; McGregor, "There Is No More Normal"; Kimes, "Cisco Systems Layers It On."

10. McGregor, "There Is No More Normal."

11. Kimes, "Cisco Systems Layers It On."

12. Worthen, "Seeking Growth, Cisco Reroutes Decisions"; McGregor, "There Is No More Normal"; E. McGirt, "How Cisco's CEO John Chambers Is Turning the Tech Giant Socialist," *FastCompany.com,* November 25, 2008, http://www.fastcompany.com/node/1093654/print, March 8, 2010.

13. "Cisco StadiumVision: A New Look at Sports and Entertainment," www.cisco.com/web/strategy/docs/. . . /Cisco_Connected_Sports.pdf, March 13, 2009.

14. McGirt, "How Cisco's CEO John Chambers Is Turning the Tech Giant Socialist."

15. McGirt, "How Cisco's CEO John Chambers Is Turning the Tech Giant Socialist."

16. P. Burrows, "Cisco: Turning a Workforce to Local Markets," *BusinessWeek,* March 23 & 30, 2009, 55; "Wim Elfrink Profile," *Forbes.com,* http://people.forbes.com/profile/print/wim-elfrink/19666, March 13, 2010.

17. Burrows, "Cisco: Turning a Workforce to Local Markets"

18. Worthen, "Seeking Growth, Cisco Reroutes Decisions"; McGregor, "There Is No More Normal"; McGirt, "How Cisco's CEO John Chambers Is Turning the Tech Giant Socialist."

19. T. M. Mills, *The Sociology of Small Groups* (Englewood Cliffs, NJ: Prentice-Hall, 1967); M. E. Shaw, *Group Dynamics* (New York: McGraw-Hill, 1981).

20. R. S. Buday, "Reengineering One Firm's Product Development and Another's Service Delivery," *Planning Review,* March–April 1993, 14–19; J. M. Burcke, "Hallmark's Quest for Quality Is a Job Never Done," *Business Insurance,* April 26, 1993, 122; M. Hammer and J. Champy, *Reengineering the Corporation* (New York: HarperBusiness, 1993); T. A. Stewart, "The Search for the Organization of Tomorrow," *Fortune,* May 18, 1992, 92–98; "Hallmark Corporate Information/About Hallmark," http://corporate.hallmark.com/Company, March 15, 2010.

21. "Amazon.com Investor Relations: Officers & Directors," http://phx.corporate-ir.net/phoenix.zhtml?c=97664&p=irol-gov Manage, June 19, 2006; "Amazon.com Investor Relations: Press Release," http://phx.corporate-ir.net/phoenix.zhtml?c=97664&p=irol-newsArticle&ID=1102342&hi . . . , April 17, 2008; "Amazon.com Investor Relations: Officers & Directors," http://phx.corporate-ir.net/phoenix.zhtml?c=97664&p=irol-govmanage_pf, March 14, 2010.

22. A. Deutschman, "Inside the Mind of Jeff Bezos," *Fast Company,* August 2004, 50–58.

23. Deutschman, "Inside the Mind of Jeff Bezos"; "Amazon.com Digital Media Technology," http://media-server.amazon.com/jobs/jobs.html, June 19, 2006.

24. "Amazon.com: Kindle: Amazon's New Wireless Reading Device: Kindle Store," www.amazon.com/gp/product/B000F173MA/ref=amb_link_6369712_2?pf_rd_m=A . . . , April 17, 2008; "Amazon.com: Kindle Wireless Reading Device (6" Display, U.S. Wireless): Kindle Store," http://www.amazon.com/Kindle-Wireless-Reading-Device-Display/dp/B00154JDAI, March 15, 2010.

25. Deutschman, "Inside the Mind of Jeff Bezos."

26. "Online Extra: Jeff Bezos on Word-of-Mouth Power," *BusinessWeek Online,* August 2, 2004, www.businessweek.com; R. D. Hof, "Reprogramming Amazon," *BusinessWeek Online,* December 22, 2003, www.businessweek.com; "About Amazon.com: Company Information," www.amazon.com/exec/obidos/tg/browsw/-/574562/104-0138839-3693547, June 19, 2006; "Amazon.com Investor Relations: Press Release."

27. "RockBottom Restaurants," www.rockbottom.com/RockBottomWeb/RBR/index.aspx?PageName=/RockBottom . . . , April 15, 2008.

28. S. Dallas, "Rock Bottom Restaurants: Brewing Up Solid Profits," *BusinessWeek,* May 22, 1995, 74.

29. J. A. Pearce II and E. C. Ravlin, "The Design and Activation of Self-Regulating Work Groups," *Human Relations* 11 (1987), 751–82.

30. B. Dumaine, "Who Needs a Boss?" *Fortune,* May 7, 1990, 52–60; Pearce and Ravlin, "The Design and Activation of Self-Regulating Work Groups."

31. Dumaine, "Who Needs a Boss?"; A. R. Montebello and V. R. Buzzotta, "Work Teams That Work," *Training and Development,* March 1993, 59–64.

32. C. Matlack, R. Tiplady, D. Brady, R. Berner, and H. Tashiro, "The Vuitton Machine," *BusinessWeek,* March 22, 2004, 98–102; "America's Most Admired Companies," *Fortune.com,* August 18, 2004, www.fortune.com/fortune/mostadmired/snapshot/0,15020,383,00.html; "Art Samberg's Ode to Steel," *Big Money Weekly,* June 29, 2004, http://trading.sina/com/trading/rightside/bigmoney_weekly_040629.b5.shtml; "Nucor Reports Record Results for First Quarter of 2004," www.nucor.com/financials.asp?finpage=news releases, August 18, 2004; "Nucor Reports Results for First Half and Second Quarter of 2004," www.nucor.com/financials.asp?finpage=newsreleases; J. C. Cooper, "The Price of Efficiency," *BusinessWeek Online,* March 22, 2004, www.businessweek.com/magazine/content/04_12/b3875603.htm; "LVHM–Fashion & Leather Goods," www.lvmh.com, June 18, 2006; C. Matlack, "Rich Times for the Luxury Sector," *BusinessWeek Online,* March 6, 2006, www.businessweek.com/globalbiz/content/mar2006/gb20060306_296309.htm? campaign_id=search; N. Byrnes, "The Art of Motivation," *BusinessWeek,* May 1, 2006, 56–62; "Nucor Steel," http://www.nucor.com/indexinner.aspx?finpage=aboutus, April 16, 2008; "Annual General Meetings–Group Investor Relations–Corporate Governance," http://www.lvmh.com/comfi/pg_home.asp?rub=6&srub=0, March 16, 2008.

33. Matlack et al., "The Vuitton Machine."

34. M. Arndt, "Out of the Forge and into the Fire," *BusinessWeek,* June 18, 2001, *BusinessWeek* Archives; Byrnes, "The Art of Motivation."

35. S. Baker, "The Minimill That Acts Like a Biggie," *BusinessWeek,* September 30, 1996, 101–104; S. Baker, "Nucor," *BusinessWeek,* February 13, 1995, 70; S. Overman, "No-Frills at Nucor," *HRMagazine,* July 1994, 56–60.

36. www.nucor.com, November 21, 2001; "Nucor: About Us."

37. Baker, "The Minimill That Acts Like a Biggie"; Baker, "Nucor"; Overman, "No-Frills at Nucor"; www.nucor.com; Byrnes, "The Art of Motivation"; "Nucor: About Us."

38. N. Byrnes, "A Steely Resolve," *BusinessWeek,* April 6, 2009, 54.

39. Matlack et al., "The Vuitton Machine"; "About Nucor"; "America's Most Admired Companies"; "Art Samberg's Ode to Steel"; "Nucor Reports Record Results for First Quarter of 2004"; "Nucor Reports Results for First Half and Second Quarter of 2004"; Byrnes, "The Art of Motivation."

40. T. D. Wall, N. J. Kemp, P. R. Jackson, and C. W. Clegg, "Outcomes of Autonomous Work Groups: A Long-Term Field Experiment," *Academy of Management Journal* 29 (1986), 280–304.

41. A. Markels, "A Power Producer Is Intent on Giving Power to Its People," *The Wall Street Journal,* July 3, 1995, A1, A12; "AES Corporation/The Power of Being Global," www.aes.com/aes/index?page=home, April 15, 2008.

42. J. S. Lublin, "My Colleague, My Boss," *The Wall Street Journal,* April 12, 1995, R4, R12.

43. W. R. Pape, "Group Insurance," *Inc.* (Technology Supplement), June 17, 1997, 29–31; A. M. Townsend, S. M. DeMarie, and A. R. Hendrickson, "Are You Ready for Virtual Teams?" *HR Magazine,* September 1996, 122–126; A. M. Townsend, S. M. DeMarie, and A. M. Hendrickson, "Virtual Teams: Technology and the Workplace of the Future," *Academy of Management Executive* 12, no. 3 (1998), 17–29.

44. Townsend et al., "Virtual Teams."

45. Pape, "Group Insurance"; Townsend et al., "Are You Ready for Virtual Teams?"; L. Gratton, "Working Together . . . When Apart," *The Wall Street Journal,* June 16–17, 2007, R4.

46. D. L. Duarte and N. T. Snyder, *Mastering Virtual Teams* (San Francisco: Jossey-Bass, 1999); K. A. Karl, "Book Reviews: *Mastering Virtual Teams,*" *Academy of Management Executive,* August 1999, 118–19.

47. B. Geber, "Virtual Teams," *Training* 32, no. 4 (August 1995), 36–40; T. Finholt and L. S. Sproull, "Electronic Groups at Work," *Organization Science* 1 (1990), 41–64.

48. Geber, "Virtual Teams."

49. E. J. Hill, B. C. Miller, S. P. Weiner, and J. Colihan, "Influences of the Virtual Office on Aspects of Work and Work/Life Balance," *Personnel Psychology* 31 (1998), 667–83; S. G. Strauss, "Technology, Group Process, and Group Outcomes: Testing the Connections in Computer-Mediated and Face-to-Face Groups," *Human Computer Interaction,* 12 (1997), 227–66; M. E. Warkentin, L. Sayeed, and R. Hightower, "Virtual Teams versus Face-to-Face Teams: An Exploratory Study of a Web-Based Conference System," *Decision Sciences* 28, no. 4 (Fall 1997), 975–96.
50. S. A. Furst, M. Reeves, B. Rosen, and R. S. Blackburn, "Managing the Life Cycle of Virtual Teams," *Academy of Management Executive* 18, no. 2 (May 2004), 6–20.
51. Furst et al., "Managing the Life Cycle of Virtual Teams."
52. Gratton, "Working Together . . . When Apart."
53. Gratton, "Working Together . . . When Apart."
54. Gratton, "Working Together . . . When Apart."
55. Gratton, "Working Together . . . When Apart."
56. A. Deutschman, "The Managing Wisdom of High-Tech Superstars," *Fortune,* October 17, 1994, 197–206.
57. J. D. Thompson, *Organizations in Action* (New York: McGraw-Hill, 1967).
58. Thompson, *Organizations in Action.*
59. Lublin, "My Colleague, My Boss."
60. "About ICU Medical, Inc.," www.icumed.com/about.asp, April 11, 2008.
61. "About ICU Medical, Inc."
62. "ICU Medical, Inc.–Fundamentals," http://phx.corporate-ir.net/phoenix.zhtml?c=86695&p=irol-fundamentals, April 11, 2008; "ICU Medical Inc. (ICUI): Stock Quote & Company Profile–BusinessWeek, *BusinessWeek,* http://investing.businessweek.com/research/stocks/snapshot/snapshot_article.asp?symbol= . . . , April 11, 2008; "The 200 Best Small Companies #80 ICU Medical," *Forbes.com,* http://www.forbes.com/lists/2009/23/small-companies-09_ICU-Medical_J1UO.html, March 14, 2010.
63. "ICU Medical, Inc.–Investor Relations Home," http://phx.corporate-ir.net/phoenix.zhtml?c=86695&p=irol-IRHome, April 11, 2008; "The 200 Best Small Companies #80 ICU Medical."
64. "About ICU Medical, Inc."
65. "Clave Connector," ICU Medical, Inc., www.icumend.com, April 11, 2008.
66. E. White, "How a Company Made Everyone a Team Player," *The Wall Street Journal,* August 13, 2007, B1, B7.
67. White, "How a Company Made Everyone a Team Player."
68. White, "How a Company Made Everyone a Team Player."
69. White, "How a Company Made Everyone a Team Player."
70. White, "How a Company Made Everyone a Team Player."
71. White, "How a Company Made Everyone a Team Player."
72. White, "How a Company Made Everyone a Team Player."
73. R. G. LeFauve and A. C. Hax, "Managerial and Technological Innovations at Saturn Corporation," *MIT Management,* Spring 1992, 8–19.
74. B. W. Tuckman, "Developmental Sequences in Small Groups," *Psychological Bulletin* 63 (1965), 384–99; B. W. Tuckman and M. C. Jensen, "Stages of Small Group Development," *Group and Organizational Studies* 2 (1977), 419–27.
75. C. J. G. Gersick, "Time and Transition in Work Teams: Toward a New Model of Group Development," *Academy of Management Journal* 31 (1988), 9–41; C. J. G. Gersick, "Marking Time: Predictable Transitions in Task Groups," *Academy of Management Journal* 32 (1989), 274–309.
76. J. R. Hackman, "Group Influences on Individuals in Organizations," in M. D. Dunnette and L. M. Hough, eds., *Handbook of Industrial and Organizational Psychology,* 2nd ed., vol. 3 (Palo Alto, CA: Consulting Psychologists Press, 1992), 199–267.
77. Hackman, "Group Influences on Individuals in Organizations."
78. Hackman, "Group Influences on Individuals in Organizations."
79. Lublin, "My Colleague, My Boss."
80. T. Kelley and J. Littman, *The Art of Innovation* (New York: Doubleday, 2001); "ideo.com: Our Work," www.ideo.com/portfolio, June 19, 2006.
81. B. Nussbaum, "The Power of Design," *BusinessWeek,* May 17, 2004, 86–94; "ideo.com: About Us: Teams," www.ideo.com/about/index.asp?x=1&y=1, June 19, 2006.
82. "ideo.com: About Us: Teams," www.ideo.com/about/index.asp?x=1&y=1, June 19, 2006; "ideo.com: About Us: Teams," www.ideo.com/about/index.asp?x=1&y=1, April 18, 2008; "Teams–IDEO," http://www.ideo.com/culture/teams/ March 15, 2010.
83. Nussbaum, "The Power of Design."
84. Kelley and Littman, *The Art of Innovation.*
85. Kelley and Littman, *The Art of Innovation;* www.ideo.com; "1999 Idea Winners," *BusinessWeek,* June 7, 1999, *BusinessWeek* Archives.
86. Nussbaum, "The Power of Design; "ideo.com: About Us: Teams."
87. L. Festinger, "Informal Social Communication," *Psychological Review* 57 (1950), 271–82; Shaw, *Group Dynamics.*
88. Hackman, "Group Influences on Individuals in Organizations"; Shaw, *Group Dynamics.*
89. D. Cartwright, "The Nature of Group Cohesiveness," in D. Cartwright and A. Zander, eds., *Group Dynamics,* 3rd ed. (New York: Harper & Row, 1968); L. Festinger, S. Schacter, and K. Black, *Social Pressures in Informal Groups* (New York: Harper & Row, 1950); Shaw, *Group Dynamics.*
90. T. F. O'Boyle, "A Manufacturer Grows Efficient by Soliciting Ideas from Employees," *The Wall Street Journal,* June 5, 1992, A1, A5.
91. Lublin, "My Colleague, My Boss."
92. Kelley and Littman, "The Art of Innovation," 93.
93. Kelley and Littman, "The Art of Innovation."
94. "Shared Commitment," www.valero.com/Work/SharedCommitment.htm, April 18, 2008.
95. R. Levering and M. Moskowitz, "100 Best Companies to Work For: The Rankings," *Fortune,* February 4, 2008, 75–94.
96. J. Guyon, "The Soul of a Moneymaking Machine," *Fortune,* October 3, 2005, 113–20.
97. Guyon, "The Soul of a Moneymaking Machine."
98. Guyon, "The Soul of a Moneymaking Machine."
99. Guyon, "The Soul of a Moneymaking Machine."
100. P. C. Earley, "Social Loafing and Collectivism: A Comparison of the United States and the People's Republic of China," *Administrative Science Quarterly* 34 (1989), 565–81; J. M. George, "Extrinsic and Intrinsic Origins of Perceived Social Loafing in Organizations," *Academy of Management Journal* 35 (1992), 191–202; S. G. Harkins, B. Latane, and K. Williams, "Social Loafing: Allocating Effort or Taking It Easy," *Journal of Experimental Social Psychology* 16 (1980), 457–65; B. Latane, K. D. Williams, and S. Harkins, "Many Hands Make Light the Work: The Causes and Consequences of Social Loafing," *Journal of Personality and Social Psychology*

37 (1979), 822–32; J. A. Shepperd, "Productivity Loss in Performance Groups: A Motivation Analysis," *Psychological Bulletin* 113 (1993), 67–81.

101. George, "Extrinsic and Intrinsic Origins"; G. R. Jones, "Task Visibility, Free Riding, and Shirking: Explaining the Effect of Structure and Technology on Employee Behavior," *Academy of Management Review* 9 (1984), 684–95; K. Williams, S. Harkins, and B. Latane, "Identifiability as a Deterrent to Social Loafing: Two Cheering Experiments," *Journal of Personality and Social Psychology* 40 (1981), 303–11.
102. S. Harkins and J. Jackson, "The Role of Evaluation in Eliminating Social Loafing," *Personality and Social Psychology Bulletin* 11 (1985), 457–65; N. L. Kerr and S. E. Bruun, "Ringelman Revisited: Alternative Explanations for the Social Loafing Effect," *Personality and Social Psychology Bulletin* 7 (1981), 224–31; Williams et al., "Identifiability as a Deterrent to Social Loafing"; Harkins and Jackson, "The Role of Evaluation in Eliminating Social Loafing"; Kerr and Bruun, "Ringelman Revisited."
103. M. A. Brickner, S. G. Harkins, and T. M. Ostrom, "Effects of Personal Involvement: Thought-Provoking Implications for Social Loafing," *Journal of Personality and Social Psychology* 51 (1986), 763–69; S. G. Harkins and R. E. Petty, "The Effects of Task Difficulty and Task Uniqueness on Social Loafing," *Journal of Personality and Social Psychology* 43 (1982), 1214–29.
104. B. Latane, "Responsibility and Effort in Organizations," in P. S. Goodman, ed., *Designing Effective Work Groups* (San Francisco: Jossey-Bass, 1986); Latane et al., "Many Hands Make Light the Work"; I. D. Steiner, *Group Process and Productivity* (New York: Academic Press, 1972).

Chapter 16

1. C. Hymowitz, "Sometimes, Moving Up Makes It Harder to See What Goes On Below," *The Wall Street Journal,* October 15, 2007, B1.
2. Hymowitz, "Sometimes, Moving Up Makes It Harder to See What Goes On Below"; J. Sandberg, "Shooting Messengers Makes Us Feel Better but Work Dumber," *The Wall Street Journal,* September 11, 2007, B1.
3. Hymowitz, "Sometimes, Moving Up Makes It Harder to See What Goes On Below"; "FatWire Software Appoints Former CA Executive Yogesh Gupta President and CEO," http://news.manta.com/press/description/200708070500230_66132700_1-0304, April 23, 2008; FatWire: Company–CEO Corner, http://www.fatwire.com/company/ceocorner, March 15, 2010.
4. Hymowitz, "Sometimes, Moving Up Makes It Harder to See What Goes On Below"; "FatWire Corporation," *FatWire Corporation: Private Company Information–Business Week,* http://investing.businessweek.com/businessweek/research/stocks/private/snapshot.asp?priv . . . , April 23, 2008; "Customers," *FatWire US: Customers–Customer Overview,* www.fatwire.com/cs/Satellite/CustomerOverviewPage_US.html, April 24, 2008; "Case Studies," *FatWire US: Customers–Case Studies,* www.fatwire.com/cs/Satellite/CustomerCaseStudiesPage_US.html, April 24, 2008; "FatWire Software Reports Record Growth," March 3, 2008, *FatWire Software,* www.fatwire.com/cs/Satellite?c=FW_C&cid=1202240759097&pagename=FW%2F . . . , April 23, 2008; "Company Overview," *FatWire U.S.: Company–Company Overview,* www.fatwire.com/cs/Satellite/CompanyOVPage_US.html, April 23, 2008; "About Us," *FatWire: Company,* http://www.fatwire.com/company/company, March 15, 2010.
5. "Management," *FatWire US: Company–Management,* www.fatwire.com/cs/Satellite/ManagementPage_US.html, April 23, 2008; "Company Overview," *Company Overview–CA,* www.ca.com/us/ca.aspx, April 24, 2008.
6. Hymowitz, "Sometimes, Moving Up Makes It Harder to See What Goes On Below."
7. Hymowitz, "Sometimes, Moving Up Makes It Harder to See What Goes On Below."
8. Hymowitz, "Sometimes, Moving Up Makes It Harder to See What Goes On Below."
9. K. Holland, "The Silent May Have Something to Say," *The New York Times,* November 5, 2006, http://www.nytimes.com/2006/11/05/business/yourmoney/05mgmt.html, June 29,2008; "About Intuit," *Intuit,* http://about.intuit.com/about_intuit/, March 15, 2010.
10. Holland, "The Silent May Have Something to Say."
11. Holland, "The Silent May Have Something to Say."
12. Holland, "The Silent May Have Something to Say."
13. E. White, "How Surveying Workers Can Pay Off," *The Wall Street Journal,* June 18, 2007, B3.
14. White, "How Surveying Workers Can Pay Off."
15. Hymowitz, "Sometimes, Moving Up Makes It Harder to See What Goes On Below."
16. C. A. O'Reilly and L. R. Pondy, "Organizational Communication," in S. Kerr, ed., *Organizational Behavior* (Columbus, OH: Grid, 1979).
17. "World's First Volume Computed Tomography (VCT) System, Developed by GE Healthcare, Scanning Patients at Froedtert," www.gehealthcare.com/company/pressroom/releases/pr_release_9722.html, June 18, 2004; "GE Healthcare Fact Sheet," *GE Healthcare Worldwide,* June 20, 2006, www.gehealthcare.com/usen/about/ge_factsheet.html; WTN News, "GE Healthcare Names New CEO," *Wisconsin Technology Network,* January 25, 2006, http://wistechnology.com/printarticle.php?id=2639, June 20, 2006; "About GE Healthcare," *GE Healthcare-Brochure–About GE Healthcare,* www.gehealthcare.com/usen/about/about.html, April 25, 2008; "About GE Healthcare," *GE Healthcare-Brochure–About GE Healthcare,* http://www.gehealthcare.com/usen/about/about.html, March 15, 2010.
18. S. Kirsner, "Time [Zone] Travelers," *Fast Company,* August 2004, 60–66; "LightSpeed VCT Series," *GE Healthcare Worldwide,* June 20, 2006, www.gehealthcare.com/usen/ct/products/vct.html.
19. "New CT Scanner by GE Healthcare Advances Imaging Technology," *Wisconsin Technology Network,* June 21, 2004, www.wistechnology.com.
20. Kirsner, "Time [Zone] Travelers."
21. Kirsner, "Time [Zone] Travelers."
22. Kirsner, "Time [Zone] Travelers."
23. E. M. Rogers and R. Agarwala-Rogers, *Communication in Organizations* (New York: Free Press, 1976).
24. R. B. Schmitt, "Judges Try Curbing Lawyers' Body Language Antics," *The Wall Street Journal,* September 11, 1997, B1, B7.
25. D. A. Adams, P. A. Todd, and R. R. Nelson, "A Comparative Evaluation of the Impact of Electronic and Voice Mail on Organizational Communication," *Information & Management* 24 (1993), 9–21.
26. R. Winslow, "Hospitals' Weak Systems Hurt Patients, Study Says," *The Wall Street Journal,* July 5, 1995, B1, B6.
27. B. Newman, "Global Chatter," *The Wall Street Journal,* March 22, 1995, A1, A15.
28. M. L. Wald, "Details Are Added on Pilots in Overflight," *The New York Times,* December 17, 2009, A34; "Pilots Who Missed Airport OK Deal," *Houston Chronicle,* Tuesday, March 16, 2010, p. A6.

29. "Miscommunications Plague Pilots and Air Traffic Controllers," *The Wall Street Journal,* August 22, 1995, A1.
30. P. Reinert, "Miscommunication Seen as Threat to Space Station," *Houston Chronicle,* September 24, 2003, 6A.
31. W. E. Leary, "NASA Report Says Problems Plague Space Station Program," *The New York Times,* February 28, 2004, A12.
32. R. L. Daft, R. H. Lengel, and L. K. Trevino, "Message Equivocality, Media Selection, and Manager Performance: Implications for Information Systems," *MIS Quarterly* 11 (1987), 355–66; R. L. Daft and R. H. Lengel, "Information Richness: A New Approach to Managerial Behavior and Organization Design," in B. M. Staw and L. L. Cummings, eds., *Research in Organizational Behavior* (Greenwich, CT: JAI Press, 1984).
33. R. L. Daft, *Organization Theory and Design* (St. Paul, MN: West, 1992).
34. "Lights, Camera, Meeting: Teleconferencing Becomes a Time-Saving Tool," *The Wall Street Journal,* February 21, 1995, A1.
35. Daft, *Organization Theory and Design.*
36. A. S. Wellner, "Lost in Translation," *Inc.,* September 2005, 37–38.
37. Wellner, "Lost in Translation."
38. Wellner, "Lost in Translation"; R. McMillan, "Business Communication Expert and *New York Times* Bestselling Author," www.vitalsmarts.com, June 20, 2006.
39. Wellner, "Lost in Translation."
40. Wellner, "Lost in Translation."
41. Wellner, "Lost in Translation"; S. Roberts, "Sara Roberts, President, Roberts Golden Consulting–Biographies," www.robertsgolden.com/bios.html, June 20, 2006; "Roberts Golden Consulting," www.robertsgolden.com, June 20, 2006; "Roberts Golden Consulting–About Us," "Management Team," http://www.robertsgolden.com/about_us/mgmt_team.html, March 15, 2010; "Roberts Golden Consulting–About Us," http://www.robertsgolden.com/about_us/index.html, March 15, 2010.
42. Wellner, "Lost in Translation."
43. S. Shellenbarger, "A Day without E-mail Is Like . . . ," *The Wall Street Journal,* October 11, 2007, D1, D2; D. Brady, "*!#?@ the E-Mail. Can We Talk?" *BusinessWeek,* December 4, 2006, 109.
44. P. Dvorak, "Frequent Contact Helps Bridge International Divide," *The Wall Street Journal,* June 1, 2009, B4.
45. T. J. Peters and R. H. Waterman, Jr., *In Search of Excellence* (New York: Harper & Row, 1982); T. Peters and N. Austin, *A Passion for Excellence: The Leadership Difference* (New York: Random House, 1985).
46. "Lights, Camera, Meeting."
47. R. Kirkland, "Cisco's Display of Strength," *Fortune,* November 12, 2007, 90–100; "Cisco TelePresence Overview," Overview *(TelePresence)–Cisco Systems,* www.cisco.com/en/US/solutions/ns669/networking_solutions_products_genericcont . . . , April 25, 2008.
48. R. Kirkland, "Cisco's Display of Strength."
49. Kirkland, "Cisco's Display of Strength"; "Cisco TelePresence Overview."
50. Dvorak, "Frequent Contact Helps Bridge International Divide."
51. C. Hymowitz, "Missing from Work: The Chance to Think, Even to Dream a Little," *The Wall Street Journal,* March 23, 2004, B1.
52. D. Beizer, "Email Is Dead . . . ," *Fast Company,* July–August 2007, 46; "The Radicati Group, Inc.," www.radicati.com, April 28, 2008.
53. J. Sandberg, "Employees Forsake Dreaded E-mail for the Beloved Phone," *The Wall Street Journal,* September 26, 2006, B1.
54. Beizer, "Email Is Dead . . ."
55. Sandberg, "Employees Forsake Dreaded E-mail for the Beloved Phone."
56. Sandberg, "Employees Forsake Dreaded E-mail for the Beloved Phone."
57. K. Byron, "Carrying Too Heavy a Load? The Communication and Miscommunication of Emotion by E-mail," *Academy of Management Review* 33, no. 2 (2008), 309–27.
58. "There's a Message in Every E-mail," *Fast Company,* September 2007, 43; Byron, "Carrying Too Heavy a Load?"
59. Byron, "Carrying Too Heavy a Load?"
60. "Telecommuters Bring Home Work and Broadband," www.emarketer.com/Article.aspx?1002943, July 20, 2004; "Annual Survey Shows Americans Are Working from Many Different Locations outside Their Employer's Office," *International Telework Association & Council,* May 10, 2006, www.workingfromanywhere.org/news; "Itac, the Telework Advisory Group for Worldat Work," www.workingfromanywhere.org, May 10, 2006; "Virtual Business Owners Community–FAQ Center: Telecommuting/Telework," www.vsscyberoffice.com/vfaq/25.html, May 10, 2006; T. Schadler, "US Telecommuting Forecast, 2009 to 2016: Telecommuting Will Rise to Include 43% of US Workers by 2016," March 11, 2009, http://www.forrester.com/rb/Research/us_telecommuting_forecast%2C_2009_to_2016/q/i . . . , March 15, 2010.
61. E. Baig, "Taking Care of Business–Without Leaving the House," *Business-Week,* April 17, 1995, 106–07.
62. "Life Is Good for Telecommuters, but Some Problems Persist," *The Wall Street Journal,* August 3, 1995, A1.
63. "E-Mail Abuse: Workers Discover High-Tech Ways to Cause Trouble in the Office," *The Wall Street Journal,* November 22, 1994, A1; "E-mail Alert: Companies Lag in Devising Policies on How It Should Be Used," *The Wall Street Journal,* December 29, 1994, A1.
64. Wellner, "Lost in Translation."
65. "The Most Important Part of an E-mail System Isn't the Software. It's the Rules You Make About Using It," *Inc. Magazine,* October 2005, 119–22.
66. "The Most Important Part of an E-mail System Isn't the Software."
67. "The Most Important Part of an E-mail System Isn't the Software."
68. American Management Association and the ePolicy Institute's N. Flynn, "2004 Workplace E-Mail and Instant Messaging Survey Summary," www.amanet.org, 2004; "2007 Electronic Monitoring & Surveillance Survey," *AMA/ePolicy Institute Research, American Management Association,* 2008.
69. J. Tyson, "How Instant Messaging Works," computer.howstuffworks.com, August 23, 2004.
70. "Study: Workers Are Surfing on Company Time," www.medialifemagazine.com/news2004/may04/may03/3_wed/news8wednesday.html, May 5, 2004; "Company Profile," *Websense,* www.websense.com/global/en/About Websense/, April 25, 2008.
71. "Study: Workers Are Surfing on Company Time."
72. "Study: Workers Are Surfing on Company Time."
73. ClikZ Stats staff, "U.S. Web Usage and Traffic, July 2004," www.clickz.com/stats/big_picture/traffic_patterns/article.php/3395351, August 23, 2004.
74. L. Conley, "The Privacy Arms Race," *Fast Company,* July 2004, 27–28; "Migrating to Microsoft Exchange . . . or Another Mail System?" www.stellarim.com, June 20, 2006; "About Stellar Technologies, Inc.," www.stellartechnologies.com/about_us.cfm, June 20, 2006.
75. Conley, "The Privacy Arms Race"; "2007 Electronic Monitoring & Surveillance Survey"; M. Villano, "The Risk Is All Yours in Office E-Mail," *The New York Times,* March 4, 2007, BU17.
76. "2007 Electronic Monitoring & Surveillance Survey."

77. J. Pfeffer, "It's Time to Start Trusting the Workforce," *Business 2.0,* December 2006, 68.
78. Conley, "The Privacy Arms Race."
79. "P & G Who We Are: Purpose, Values, and Principles," www.pg.com/company/who_we_are/ppv.jhtml, August 25, 2004; L. Conley, "Refusing to Gamble on Privacy," *Fast Company,* July 2004, http://pf.fastcompany.com/magazine/84.essay_hughes.html; "Who We Are," *P&G Global Operations,* June 20, 2006, www.pg.com/company/who_we_are/index.jhtml; "Company Who We Are," P&G, *PG .com–Who We Are,* www.pg.com/company/who_we_are/index.jhtml, April 28, 2008.
80. Conley, "The Privacy Arms Race;" "Privacy: Our Global Privacy Policy," *P&G,* http://www.pg.com/en_US/sustainability/point_of_view/privacy.shtml, March 15, 2010.
81. J. O'Neil, "E-Mail Doesn't Lie (That Much)," *The New York Times,* March 2, 2004, D6.
82. "Employee-Newsletter Names Include the Good, the Bad, and the Boring," *The Wall Street Journal,* July 18, 1995, A1.
83. W. M. Bulkeley, "Playing Well with Others," *The Wall Street Journal,* June 18, 2007, R10.
84. E. White, J. S. Lublin, and D. Kesmodel, "Executives Get the Blogging Bug," *The Wall Street Journal,* July 13, 2007, B1, B2.
85. *Blog–Wikipedia, the free encyclopedia,* http://en.wikipedia.org/wiki/Blog, April 28, 2008; White et al., "Executives Get the Blogging Bug."
86. *Blog–Wikipedia, the free encyclopedia;* White et al., "Executives Get the Blogging Bug"; "GM FastLane Blog: Lutz Biography," http://fastlane.gmblogs.com/archives/2005/01/lutz_biography_1.html, April 28, 2008.
87. "2006 Workplace E-Mail, Instant Messaging & Blog Survey: Bosses Battle Risk by Firing E-Mail, IM & Blog Violators," New York, July 11, 2006, *AMA Press Room,* http://press.amanet.org/press-releases/28/2006-workplace-e-mail-instant-messaging-blog-s . . . April 28, 2008.
88. Bulkeley, "Playing Well with Others."
89. Bulkeley, "Playing Well with Others."
90. D.M. Boyd and N.B. Ellison, "Social Network Sites: Definition, History, and Scholarship," *Journal of Computer-Mediated Communication* 13, no. 1 (2007), article 11, http://jcmc.indiana.edu/vol13/issue1/boyd.ellison.html, March 15, 2010; "Social Networking Site Definition from PC Magazine Encyclopedia," http://www.pcmag.com/encyclopedia_term/0,2542,t=social+networking&i=55316,00.asp, March 15, 2010; "Factsheet/Facebook," http://www.facebook.com/press/info.php?factsheet, March 15, 2010; "Statistics / Facebook," http://www.facebook.com/press/info.php?statistics, March 15, 2010; "Twitter News–*The New York Times,*" http://topics.nytimes.com/top/news/business/companies/twitter/index.html, March 15, 2010; "Twitter," http://twitter.com/about, March 15, 2010; "Facebook, Inc.: Private Company Information–*Business Week,*" http://investing.businessweek.com/research/stocks/private/snapshot.asp?privcapId=207654 . . . , March 15, 2010.
91. J. E. Vascellaro, "Why E-mail No Longer Rules," *The Wall Street Journal,* October 12, 2009, R1–3.
92. "Study: 54 Percent of Companies Ban Facebook, Twitter at Work/Epicenter/Wired.com," October 9, 2009, http://www.wired.com/epicenter/2009/10/study-54-of-companies-ban-facebook-twitter-at-. . . March 16, 2010.
93. "Study: 54 Percent of Companies Ban Facebook, Twitter at Work/Epicenter/Wired.com."
94. O. W. Baskin and C. E. Aronoff, *Interpersonal Communication in Organizations* (Santa Monica, CA: Goodyear, 1989).
95. T. Gutner, "Move Over, Bohemian Grove," *BusinessWeek,* February 19, 2001, 102.
96. "We've All Got Mail," *Newsweek,* May 15, 2001, 73K; "Diversity Deficit," *BusinessWeek Online,* May 14, 2001; "Dial-Up Users Converting to Broadband in Droves," www.emarketer.com/Article.aspx?1003009, August 23, 2004; "Top 20 Countries with the Highest Number of Internet Users," *Internet World Stats,* June 20, 2006, www.internetworldstats.com/top20.htm; "Top 20 Countries with the Highest Number of Internet Users," www.internetworldstats.com/top20.htm, April 29, 2008; "Top 20 Countries with the Highest Number of Internet Users," http://www.internetworldstats.com/top20.htm, March 15, 2010.
97. "Top 15 Countries in Internet Usage, 2002," www.infoplease.com/ipa/A0908185.html, August 25, 2004; "Top 20 Countries with the Highest Number of Internet Users," http://www.internetworldstats.com/top20.htm, April 29, 2008; "Top 20 Countries with the Highest Number of Internet Users," http://www.internetworldstats.com/top20.htm, March 15, 2010.
98. J. Sandberg, "Internet's Popularity in North America Appears to Be Soaring," *The Wall Street Journal,* October 30, 1995, B2.
99. "How to Research Companies," *Oxford Knowledge Company,* www.oxford-knowledge.co.uk, September 16, 2004.
100. "Survey: Denmark Is Web-Savviest Nation," MSNBC.com, April 19, 2004, www.msnbc.msn.com/id/4779944/1/displaymode/1098; L. Grinsven, "U.S. Drops on Lists of Internet Savvy," *Houston Chronicle,* April 20, 2004, 6B.
101. M. J. Cronin, "Ford's Intranet Success," *Fortune,* March 30, 1998, 158; M. J. Cronin, "Intranets Reach the Factory Floor," *Fortune,* June 10, 1997; A. L. Sprout, "The Internet inside Your Company," *Fortune,* November 27, 1995, 161–68; J. B. White, "Chrysler's Intranet: Promise vs. Reality," *The Wall Street Journal,* May 13, 1997, B1, B6.
102. White, "Chrysler's Intranet: Promise vs. Reality."
103. G. Rifkin, "A Skeptic's Guide to Groupware," *Forbes ASAP,* 1995, 76–91.
104. Rifkin, "A Skeptic's Guide to Groupware."
105. Rifkin, "A Skeptic's Guide to Groupware."
106. "Groupware Requires a Group Effort," *BusinessWeek,* June 26, 1995, 154.
107. M. Totty, "The Path to Better Teamwork," *The Wall Street Journal,* May 20, 2004, R4; "Collaborative Software," *Wikipedia,* August 25, 2004, en.wikipedia.org/wiki/Collaborative_software; "Collaborative Groupware Software," www.svpal.org/~grantbow/groupware.html, August 25, 2004.
108. Totty, "The Path to Better Teamwork"; "Collaborative Software."
109. Totty, "The Path to Better Teamwork"; "Collaborative Software"; "Collaborative Groupware Software."
110. Totty, "The Path to Better Teamwork"; "Collaborative Software."
111. Totty, "The Path to Better Teamwork"; "Collaborative Software."
112. Microsoft Windows SharePont Services Developer Center, "Windows SharePoint Service," http://msdn.microsoft.com/sharepoint, June 21, 2006.
113. Totty, "The Path to Better Teamwork"; "Collaborative Software."
114. M. Conlin, "E-mail Is So Five Minutes Ago," *BusinessWeek,* November 28, 2005, 111–12; D. Dahl, "The End of E-mail," *Inc.,* February 2006,

41–42; "Weaving a Secure Web around Education: A Guide to Technology Standards and Security," http://nces.ed.gov/pubs2003/secureweb/glossary.asp, June 21, 2006; "Wikis Make Collaboration Easier," *InformationWeek*, June 20, 2006, www.informationweek.com/shared/printableArticleSrc.jhtml?articleID=170100392.

115. "Postini," www.postini.com, April 28, 2008.
116. Conlin, "E-mail Is So Five Minutes Ago."
117. Conlin, "E-mail Is So Five Minutes Ago."
118. Conlin, "E-mail Is So Five Minutes Ago."
119. Conlin, "E-mail Is So Five Minutes Ago."
120. Dahl, "The End of E-mail"; "Wikis Make Collaboration Easier;" V. Vara, "Wikis at Work," *The Wall Street Journal*, June 18, 2007, R11.
121. Dahl, "The End of E-mail."
122. D. Dahl, "Connecting the Dots," *Inc.*, June 2009, 103–4; "Project Management, Collaboration, and Task Software: Basecamp," http://basecamphq.com/, March 15, 2010.
123. Conlin, "E-mail Is So Five Minutes Ago"; "Soar Technology, Thinking inside the Box," *Soar Technology, Inc.*, www.soartech.com/home.php, April 28, 2008.
124. Conlin, "E-mail Is So Five Minutes Ago."
125. Conlin, "E-mail Is So Five Minutes Ago."
126. Conlin, "E-mail Is So Five Minutes Ago."
127. Bulkeley, "Playing Well with Others."
128. Bulkeley, "Playing Well with Others."
129. Conlin, "E-mail Is So Five Minutes Ago"; Dahl, "The End of E-mail"; "Weaving a Secure Web around Education."
130. Wakizaka, "Faxes, E-Mail, Help the Deaf Get Office Jobs," *The Wall Street Journal*, October 3, 1995, B1, B5.
131. S. E. Needleman, "Business Owners Try to Motivate Employees," *The Wall Street Journal*, January 14, 2010, B5.
132. Needleman, "Business Owners Try to Motivate Employees."
133. D. Tannen, "The Power of Talk," *Harvard Business Review*, September–October 1995, 138–48; D. Tannen, *Talking from 9 to 5* (New York: Avon Books, 1995).
134. Tannen, "The Power of Talk."
135. Tannen, "The Power of Talk."
136. Tannen, "The Power of Talk."
137. Tannen, "The Power of Talk."
138. Tannen, "The Power of Talk"; Tannen, *Talking from 9 to 5.*
139. Tannen, *Talking from 9 to 5.*
140. J. Cohen, "He Writes, She Writes," *Houston Chronicle*, July 7, 2001, C1–C2.
141. Cohen, "He Writes, She Writes."
142. Cohen, "He Writes, She Writes."
143. Tannen, "The Power of Talk," 148.

Chapter 17

1. B. Becht, "Building a Company without Borders," *Harvard Business Review*, April 2010, 103–6; "Board of Directors," http://www.rb.com/RB-worldwide/The-Board, March 17, 2010.
2. "The Power behind the Powerbrands: A Quick Guide to Reckitt Benckiser," *Reckitt Benckiser*, http://www.rb.com, March 17, 2010.
3. Becht, "Building a Company without Borders"; "The Power behind the Powerbrands"; "Corporate Factsheet: ($ information)," *Reckitt Benckiser*, http://www.rb.com, March 17, 2010.
4. J. Pfeffer and R. I. Sutton, *Hard Facts, Dangerous Half-Truths, and Total Nonsense: Profiting from Evidence-Based Management*, (Boston: Harvard Business School Press, 2006).
5. Becht, "Building a Company without Borders."
6. Becht, "Building a Company without Borders."
7. Becht, "Building a Company without Borders."
8. Becht, "Building a Company without Borders."
9. Becht, "Building a Company without Borders."
10. Becht, "Building a Company without Borders."
11. Becht, "Building a Company without Borders."
12. Becht, "Building a Company without Borders."
13. Becht, "Building a Company without Borders."
14. Becht, "Building a Company without Borders."
15. Becht, "Building a Company without Borders."
16. Becht, "Building a Company without Borders."
17. J. A. Litterer, "Conflict in Organizations: A Reexamination," *Academy of Management Journal* 9 (1966), 178–86; S. M. Schmidt and T. A. Kochan, "Conflict: Towards Conceptual Clarity," *Administrative Science Quarterly* 13 (1972), 359–70; R. H. Miles, *Macro Organizational Behavior* (Santa Monica, CA: Goodyear, 1980).
18. S. P. Robbins, *Managing Organizational Conflict: A Nontraditional Approach* (Englewood Cliffs, NJ: Prentice-Hall, 1974); L. Coser, *The Functions of Social Conflict* (New York: Free Press, 1956).
19. K. A. Jehn, "A Qualitative Analysis of Conflict Types and Dimensions in Organizational Groups," Cornell University, 1997; K. A. Jehn, "A Multimethod Examination of the Benefits and Detriments of Intragroup Conflict," Cornell University, 1995.
20. L. L. Putnam and M. S. Poole, "Conflict and Negotiation," in F. M. Jablin, L. L. Putnam, K. H. Roberts, and L. W. Porter, eds., *Handbook of Organizational Communication: An Interdisciplinary Perspective* (Newbury Park, CA: Sage, 1987), 549–99.
21. L. R. Pondy, "Organizational Conflict: Concepts and Models," *Administrative Science Quarterly* 2 (1967), 296–320; R. E. Walton and J. M. Dutton, "The Management of Interdepartmental Conflict: A Model and Review," *Administrative Science Quarterly* 14 (1969), 62–73.
22. G. R. Jones and J. E. Butler, "Managing Internal Corporate Entrepreneurship: An Agency Theory Perspective," *Journal of Management* 18 (1992), 733–49.
23. T. Petzinger, Jr., "All Happy Businesses Are Alike, but Heirs Bring Unique Conflicts," *The Wall Street Journal*, November 17, 1995, B1.
24. J. A. Wall, Jr., "Conflict and Its Management," *Journal of Management* 21 (1995), 515–58.
25. Walton and Dutton, "The Management of Interdepartmental Conflict."
26. Pondy, "Organizational Conflict."
27. W. F. White, *Human Relations in the Restaurant Industry* (New York: McGraw-Hill, 1948).
28. R. L. Pinkley and G. B. Northcraft, "Conflict Frames of Reference: Implications for Dispute Processes and Outcomes," *Academy of Management Journal* 37 (February 1994), 193–206.
29. K. W. Thomas, "Conflict and Negotiation Processes in Organizations," in M. D. Dunnette and L. M. Hough, eds., *Handbook of Industrial and Organizational Psychology*, 2nd ed., vol. 3 (Palo Alto, CA: Consulting Psychologists Press, 1992), 651–717.
30. "Ravi Kant: Executive Profile & Biography," *BusinessWeek*, http://investing.businessweek.com/businessweek/research/stocks/people/person.asp?person. . ., March 18, 2010; "Ravi Kant Profile," Forbes.com, http://people.forbes.com/profile/print/ravi-kant/76754, March 18, 2010.

31. M. Kripalana, "Tata: Master of the Gentle Approach," *BusinessWeek,* February 25, 2008; "Ravi Kant," *Tata Group,* www.tata.com/scripts/print.asp, May 2, 2008; "Ravi Kant: Executive Profile & Biography," *Business Week,* http://investing.businessweek.com/businessweek/research/stocks/people/person.asp?person . . . , March 18, 2010; "Ravi Kant Profile," Forbes.com, http://people.forbes.com/profile/print/ravi-kant/76754, March 18, 2010.
32. Kripalana, "Tata: Master of the Gentle Approach"; "Profile," Tata Motors, www.tatamotors.com/our_world/profile.php, May 2, 2008; "Our Companies: Tata Motors," www.tata.com/tata_motors/index.htm, May 2, 2008.
33. Kripalana, "Tata: Master of the Gentle Approach."
34. Kripalana, "Tata: Master of the Gentle Approach."
35. Kripalana, "Tata: Master of the Gentle Approach."
36. K. Chae, "CEO Message," *Tata Daewoo,* www.tata-daewoo.com/ver3/eng/03_company/01_ceo.html, May 7, 2008; "Events and Happenings," *Tata,* www.tata.com/scripts/print.asp, May 7, 2008.
37. Kripalana, "Tata: Master of the Gentle Approach."
38. Kripalana, "Tata: Master of the Gentle Approach."
39. Kripalana, "Tata: Master of the Gentle Approach."
40. Kripalana, "Tata: Master of the Gentle Approach;" Tata Group/Our Businesses/Tata Companies/The Tata Daewoo Commercial Vehicle Co . . . , "Tata Daewoo Commercial Vehicle Company," http://www.tata.com/company/profile.aspx?sectid=HckEHljxqtM=, March 18, 2010.
41. "Sales Activities," *Tata Daewoo,* www.tata-daewoo.com/ver3/eng/08_center/01_faq.html, May 7, 2008; "Company," *Tata Daewoo,* www.tata-daewoo.com/ver3/eng/03_company/02_tata.html, May 7, 2008.
42. Kripalana, "Tata: Master of The Gentle Approach."
43. Thomas, "Conflict and Negotiation Processes in Organizations."
44. Pinkley and Northcraft, "Conflict Frames of Reference."
45. N. Heintz, "In Spanish, It's *Un Equipo,*" *Inc.,* April 2008; S. McAdams, "Putting Culture on the Map," *Ragan Report,* June 11, 2007, www.xplane.com/#/news/; S. Powers, "12 Revolutionary Companies Transforming the City That Works (and Yes, They're Hiring), *Portland Monthly,* October 2007, www.xplane.com/#/news/; About XPLANE/The visual thinking company, http://www.xplane.com/company/about/, March 18, 2010.
46. Heintz, "In Spanish, It's *Un Equipo.*"
47. Heintz, "In Spanish, It's *Un Equipo.*"
48. Heintz, "In Spanish, It's *Un Equipo.*"
49. Heintz, "In Spanish, It's *Un Equipo.*"
50. Heintz, "In Spanish, It's *Un Equipo.*"
51. Heintz, "In Spanish, It's *Un Equipo.*"
52. Heintz, "In Spanish, It's *Un Equipo.*"
53. XPLANE Expands, Opens Amsterdam Office/XPLANE/The Visual Thinking Company, March 17, 2010, http://www.xplane.com/company/news/2010/03/17/xplane-expands-opens-amsterdam-offi . . . , March 18, 2010.
54. E. Shapiro, J. A. Trachtenberg, and L. Landro, "Time Warner Settles Feud by Pushing Out Music Division's Fuchs," *The Wall Street Journal,* November 17, 1995, A1, A6.
55. Shapiro et al., "Time Warner Settles Feud."
56. P. R. Lawrence, L. B. Barnes, and J. W. Lorsch, *Organizational Behavior and Administration* (Homewood, IL: Irwin, 1976).
57. R. J. Lewicki and J. R. Litterer, *Negotiation* (Homewood, IL: Irwin, 1985); G. B. Northcraft and M. A. Neale, *Organizational Behavior* (Fort Worth, TX: Dryden, 1994); J. Z. Rubin and B. R. Brown, *The Social Psychology of Bargaining and Negotiation* (New York: Academic Press, 1975).
58. C. Bendersky, "Organizational Dispute Resolution Systems: A Complementarities Model," *Academy of Management Review* 28 (October 2003), 643–57.
59. R. E. Walton, "Third Party Roles in Interdepartmental Conflicts," *Industrial Relations* 7 (1967), 29–43.
60. "Meaning of Arbitrator," www.hyperdictionary.com, September 4, 2004; "Definitions of Arbitrator on the Web," www.google.com, September 4, 2004.
61. L. Thompson and R. Hastie, "Social Perception in Negotiation," *Organizational Behavior and Human Decision Processes* 47 (1990), 98–123.
62. Thomas, "Conflict and Negotiation Processes in Organizations."
63. R. J. Lewicki, S. E. Weiss, and D. Lewin, "Models of Conflict, Negotiation, and Third Party Intervention: A Review and Synthesis," *Journal of Organizational Behavior* 13 (1992), 209–52.
64. Northcraft and Neale, *Organizational Behavior.*
65. Lewicki et al., "Models of Conflict, Negotiation, and Third Party Intervention"; Northcraft and Neale, *Organizational Behavior;* D. G. Pruitt, "Integrative Agreements: Nature and Consequences," in M. H. Bazerman and R. J. Lewicki, eds., *Negotiating in Organizations* (Beverly Hills, CA: Sage, 1983).
66. R. Fischer and W. Ury, *Getting to Yes* (Boston: Houghton Mifflin, 1981); Northcraft and Neale, *Organizational Behavior.*
67. P. J. Carnevale and D. G. Pruitt, "Negotiation and Mediation," *Annual Review of Psychology* 43 (1992), 531–82.
68. A. M. Pettigrew, *The Politics of Organizational Decision Making* (London: Tavistock, 1973); Miles, *Macro Organizational Behavior.*
69. D. J. Hickson, C. R. Hinings, C. A. Lee, R. E. Schneck, and D. J. Pennings, "A Strategic Contingencies Theory of Intraorganizational Power," *Administrative Science Quarterly* 16 (1971), 216–27; C. R. Hinings, D. J. Hickson, J. M. Pennings, and R. E. Schneck, "Structural Conditions of Interorganizational Power," *Administrative Science Quarterly* 19 (1974), 22–44; J. Pfeffer, *Power in Organizations* (Boston: Pitman, 1981).
70. Pfeffer, *Power in Organizations.*
71. Pfeffer, *Power in Organizations.*
72. M. Crozier, "Sources of Power of Lower Level Participants in Complex Organizations," *Administrative Science Quarterly* 7 (1962), 349–64; A. M. Pettigrew, "Information Control as a Power Resource," *Sociology* 6 (1972), 187–204.
73. Pfeffer, *Power in Organizations;* G. R. Salancik and J. Pfeffer, "The Bases and Uses of Power in Organizational Decision Making," *Administrative Science Quarterly* 19 (1974), 453–73; J. Pfeffer and G. R. Salancik, *The External Control of Organizations: A Resource Dependence View* (New York: Harper & Row, 1978).
74. B. Morris, Senior Editor, "The Pepsi Challenge," *Fortune,* "What Makes Pepsi Great?" February 19, 2008, http://cnnmoney.printthis.clickability.com/pt/cpt?action=cpt&title=What+makes+Pepsi+gre . . . , April 8, 2008.
75. "The 100 Most Powerful Women #5 Indra K. Nooyi," Forbes.com, August 30, 2007, www.forbes.com/lists/2007/11/biz-07women_Indra-K-Nooyi_1S5D_print.html, April 23, 2008; "Indra K. Nooyi Profile," Forbes.com, http://people.forbes.com/profile/indra-k-nooyi/62917, March 17, 2010.
76. "PepsiCo–Investor Overview," http://phx.corporate-ir.net/phoenix.zhtml?c=78265&p=irol-irhome, May 2, 2008; "Indra Nooyi–News, Articles, Biography, Photos," WSJ.com, http://topics.wsj.com/person/n/indra-k-nooyi/247, March 17, 2010.

77. Morris, "The Pepsi Challenge"; D. Brady, "Indra Nooyi: Keeping Cool in Hot Water," *BusinessWeek,* June 11, 2007, www.businessweek.com/print/magazine/content/07_24/b4038067.htm?chan=gl, April 30, 2008; P. Maidment, "Re-Thinking Social Responsibility," Forbes.com, January 25, 2008, www.forbes.com/2008/01/25/davos-corporate-responsibility-lead-cx_pm_0125notes . . . , April 23, 2008; B. Saporito, "Indra Nooyi," *TIME in Partnership with CNN,* Monday, April 30, 2007, www.time.com/time/specials/2007/printout/0,29239,1595326_1615737_1615996,00 . . . , April 23, 2008.
78. "The World's Most Influential People," *The 2008 TIME 100,* www.time.com/time/specials/2007/0,28757,1733748,00.html, May 2, 2008.
79. "25 Most Powerful People in Business," *Fortune,* http://money.cnn.com/galleries/2007/fortune/0711/gallery.power_25.fortune/22.html, April 30, 2008; "50 Most Powerful Women 2007, The Power 50," CNNMoney.com, *Fortune,* http://money.cnn.com/galleries/2007/fortune/0709/gallery.women_mostpowerful.fortune/i . . . , April 23, 2008; "PepsiCo CEO Indra Nooyi Is the Queen of Pop," September, 10, 2009, http://cnnmoney.printthis.clickability.com/pt/cpt?action=cpt&title=PepsiCo+CEO+Indra+ . . . , March 17, 2010; "50 "Most Powerful Women–1. Indra Nooyi (1)," *Fortune,* http://money.cnn.com/galleries/2009/fortune/0909/gallery.most_powerful_women.fortune/ . . . , March 17, 2010.
80. Morris, "The Pepsi Challenge"; "PepsiCo's Board of Directors Appoints Indra K. Nooyi as Chief Executive Officer Effective October 1, 2006, Steve Reinemund to Retire as Chairman in May 2007," *PEPSICO,* News Release, http://phx.corporate-ir.net/phoenix.zhtml?c=78265&p=irol-newsArticle_print&ID=895346 . . . , May 8, 2008.
81. Morris, "The Pepsi Challenge."
82. Morris, "The Pepsi Challenge."
83. Morris, "The Pepsi Challenge."
84. "PEPSICO Officers and Directors," *PepsiCo,* http://www.pepsico.com/PEP_Company/OfficersDirectors/index.cfm, May 2, 2008.
85. Morris, "The Pepsi Challenge."
86. "PepsiCo Announces Upcoming Retirement of Michael White Chairman and PepsiCo International CEO," http://www.pepsico.com/PressRelease/PepsiCo-Announces-Upcoming-Retirement-of-Mic . . . , March 17, 2010.
87. Morris, "The Pepsi Challenge."
88. A. Moore, MarketWatch, "Indra Nooyi's Pepsi challenge, CEO puts her own brand on new products and global goals," December 6, 2007, www.marketwatch.com/news/story/indra-nooyi-puts-her-brand/story.aspx?guid=%7 . . . , April 23, 2008.
89. Morris, "The Pepsi Challenge."
90. Morris, "The Pepsi Challenge."
91. Morris, "The Pepsi Challenge."
92. Pfeffer, *Power in Organizations.*
93. Pfeffer, *Power in Organizations.*
94. Pfeffer, *Power in Organizations.*
95. L. Kramer, "Doing Well and Good: How Social Responsibility Helped One Coffee Grower Land a Deal with Starbucks," *Inc.,* June 2006, 55–56.
96. Kramer, "Doing Well and Good"; "Corporate Social Responsibility," www.starbucks.com/aboutus/csr.asp, June 25, 2006.
97. "The Exceptional Cup Participating Farms Finca El Faro," www.guatemalancoffees.com/GCContent/GCeng/auction_tec_fincas/FincaElFaro.asp, June 25, 2006.
98. Kramer, "Doing Well and Good."
99. Kramer, "Doing Well and Good."
100. Kramer, "Doing Well and Good."
101. Kramer, "Doing Well and Good."
102. "Welcome to El Faro Estate Website," *El Faro Estate Coffee,* www.elfaroestate.com/default.htm, May 7, 2008; "El Faro Today," El Faro Estate Coffee, www.elfaroestate.com/history/elFaro/ElFaroToday.htm, May 7, 2008; "C.A.F.E. Practices (Coffee and Farmer Equity Practices)," *Starbucks Coffee,* The Business of Coffee, www.starbucks.com/aboutus/sourcingcoffee.asp, May 7, 2008; "Welcome to El Faro Estate Website," http://www.elfaroestate.com/default.php, March 18, 2010; "El Faro Today," *El Faro Estate Coffee,* http://www.elfaroestate.com/history/elFaro/elFaroToday.php, March 18, 2010.
103. Kramer, "Doing Well and Good."

Chapter 18

1. www.sgi.com, 2010.
2. N. B. Macintosh, *The Social Software of Accounting Information Systems* (New York: Wiley, 1995).
3. C. A. O'Reilly, "Variations in Decision Makers' Use of Information: The Impact of Quality and Accessibility," *Academy of Management Journal* 25 (1982), 756–71.
4. G. Stalk and T. H. Hout, *Competing against Time* (New York: Free Press, 1990).
5. www.iata.com, 2010.
6. R. Cyert and J. March, *Behavioral Theory of the Firm* (Englewood Cliffs, NJ: Prentice-Hall, 1963).
7. E. Turban, *Decision Support and Expert Systems* (New York: Macmillan, 1988).
8. R. I. Benjamin and J. Blunt, "Critical IT Issues: The Next Ten Years," *Sloan Management Review,* Summer 1992, 7–19; W. H. Davidson and M. S. Malone, *The Virtual Corporation* (New York: Harper Business, 1992).
9. Davidow and Malone, *The Virtual Corporation;* M. E. Porter, *Competitive Advantage* (New York: Free Press, 1984).
10. S. M. Dornbusch and W. R. Scott, *Evaluation and the Exercise of Authority* (San Francisco: Jossey-Bass, 1975).
11. J. Child, *Organization: A Guide to Problems and Practice* (London: Harper & Row, 1984).
12. www.ups.com, 2010.
13. Macintosh, *The Social Software of Accounting Information Systems.*
14. www.cypress.com, 2010.
15. www.hermanmiller.com, 2010.
16. www.fortune.com, 2010.
17. www.boeing.com, 2010.
18. P. Bradley, "Global Sourcing Takes Split-Second Timing," *Purchasing,* July 20, 1989, 52–58.
19. J. A. Schumpeter, *Capitalism, Socialism, and Democracy* (New York: Harper, 1942).
20. V. P. Buell, *Marketing Management* (New York: McGraw-Hill, 1985).
21. See M. M. J. Berry and J. H. Taggart, "Managing Technology and Innovation: A Review," *R & D Management* 24 (1994), 341–53; K. B. Clark and S. C. Wheelwright, *Managing New Product and Process Development* (New York: Free Press, 1993).
22. www.ebay.com, March 2010.
23. See Berry and Taggart, "Managing Technology and Innovation"; M. Gort and J. Klepper, "Time Paths in the Diffusion of Product Innovations," *Economic Journal,* September 1982, 630–53. Looking at the history of 46 products, Gort and Klepper found that the length of time before other companies entered the markets created by a few inventive companies declined from an average of 14.4 years for products introduced before 1930 to 4.9 years for those introduced after 1949–implying that product life cycles were being compressed. Also see A. Griffin, "Metrics for Measuring Product Development Cycle Time," *Journal of Production and Innovation Management* 10 (1993), 112–25.
24. A. D. Chandler, *The Visible Hand* (Cambridge, MA: Harvard University Press, 1977).

25. C. W. L. Hill and J. F. Pickering, "Divisionalization, Decentralization, and Performance of Large United Kingdom Companies," *Journal of Management Studies* 23 (1986), 26–50.
26. O. E. Williamson, *Markets and Hierarchies: Analysis and Antitrust Implications* (New York: Free Press, 1975).
27. Turban, *Decision Support and Expert Systems.*
28. www.merck.com, 2008.
29. N. A. Nichols, "Scientific Management at Merck: An Interview with CFO Judy Lewent," *Harvard Business Review,* January–February 1994, 88–91.
30. Turban, *Decision Support and Expert Systems.*
31. E. Rich, *Artificial Intelligence* (New York: McGraw-Hill, 1983).
32. Brandt, "Agents and Artificial Life." *BusinessWeek,* June 13, 1994, 55–56.
33. Rich, *Artificial Intelligence.*
34. Ibid., 346.
35. G. R. Jones, "SAP and the Enterprise Resource Planning Industry," in C. W. L. Hill and G. R. Jones, *Strategic Management: An Integrated Approach,* 6th ed. (Boston: Houghton Mifflin, 2003).
36. B. Kogut, "Joint Ventures: Theoretical and Empirical Perspectives," *Strategic Management Journal* 9 (1988), 319–32.
37. G. S. Capowski, "Designing a Corporate Identity," *Management Review,* June 1993, 37–38.
38. J. Marcia, "Just Doing It," *Distribution,* January 1995, 36–40.
39. Davidow and Malone, *The Virtual Corporation.*
40. Ibid., 168.
41. Stewart, "Managing in a Wired Company," *Fortune,* July 11, 1994, 44–56.
42. www.lucasarts.com, 2010.
43. B. Hindo, "The Empire Strikes at Silos," www.businessweek.com, August 20, 2007.
44. www.bestbuy.com, 2010; www.walmart.com, 2010.
45. N. Byrnes, "Clicks and Bricks Retailers," www.businessweek.com, December 6, 2007.
46. www.walmart.com, 2010.

Photo Credits

Chapter 1

3 Bloomberg via Getty Images; **9** AP Photo/Harry Cabluck; **10** Courtesy of Xerox Corporation; **12** Mark Peterson 1998/Redux Pictures; **21** Tracy Hayes/ Bloomberg News/Landov; **26** Mark Moran/ ASSOCIATED PRESS; **27** Courtesy of Accenture; **28** Photo by James Berglie/ ZUMA Press. © Copyright 2006 by James Berglie; **29** WILLIAM PHILPOTT/AFP/ Getty Images

Chapter 2

39 (t)Austrian Archives/Corbis, (b)Chad Ehlers/International Stock; **43–46** Bettmann/ Corbis; **47** 20th Century Fox/Courtesy The Kobal Collection/Picture Desk; **48** Hulton-Deutsch Collection/Corbis; **51** The Granger Collection, New York; **53** Jacques Boyer/Roger Viollet/The Image Works; **56** Courtesy Regina A. Greenwood & Henley Management College; **57** Fox Photos/ Getty Images; **59** AP Photo/HO/Hewlett Packard; **61** Michael Nagle/Getty Images

Chapter 3

73 Courtesy of PAETEC Communications; **79** Paul Drinkwater/NBCU Photo Bank via AP Images; **81** Digital Vision; **83** Courtesy of Gentle Giant Moving Company; **86** Flying Colours Ltd./Getty Images; **89** BananaStock/ age footstock; **92** Courtesy of IDEO; **95** Ken Hawkins Photography; **97** Lana Sundman/Alamy

Chapter 4

105 Mark Wilson/Getty Images; **109** The Granger Collection, New York; **111** AP Photos; **115** AP Photo/Damian Dovarganes, file; **120** AP Photo/Paul Sakuma; **125** Darren McCollester/Getty Images; **126** Richard Carson/Reuters/ Corbis; **128** Robert K. Chin/Alamy; **130** Ricardo Arduengo/ASSOCIATED PRESS; **134** Courtesy of Google

Chapter 5

143 Courtesy of Sodexo; **147** Westend61/ Getty Images; **151** Ellen B. Senisi/The Image Works; **152** Courtesy of Chubb Group of Insurance Companies; **161** (t)Habitat International, Inc./Photo by Jim Madden, (b)Zia Soleil/Iconica/Getty Images; **163** Bloom Productions/Digital Vision/Getty Images; **166** Copyright ©, *Pittsburgh Post-Gazette,* 2010, all rights reserved. Reprinted with permission; **168** Somos/Veer/Getty Images

Chapter 6

177 AP Photo/Shizuo Kambayashi; **182** AP Photo/The News Tribune, Lui Kit Wong; **184** Copyright © Nokia 2010; **185** AP Photo/Paul Sakuma; **188** AP Photo/Itsuo Inouye; **190** Getty Images; **193** imagebroker/ Alamy; **195** AP Photo/Matt Houston; **203** Comstock/Getty Images

Chapter 7

211 AP Photo/Christof Stache; **214** Andersen Ross/Blend Images/Getty Images; **215** AP Photo/Nati Harnik; **220** Courtesy of ABS; **226** Courtesy of GarageTek; **229** Digital Vision/Punchstock; **233** Marc Romanelli/Workbook Stock/Getty Images; **235** Courtesy of World of Good, Inc.; **236** Radius Images/Getty Images

Chapter 8

245 Mark Leong 2001/Redux Pictures; **248** Ryan McVay/Getty Images; **253** AP Images/Tom Mihalek; **255** Stephen Hird/ Reuters/Corbis; **258** AP Photo/Mel Evans; **263** (t)Courtesy of Cott Corporation, (b)The McGraw-Hill Companies, Inc./Jill Braaten, photographer; **264** Bloomberg via Getty Images; **268** Bill Varie/Corbis; **271** (t)AP Images/Kasumi Kasahara, (b)Pablo Bartholomew/Getty News/Liaison; **274** Gene Blevins/LA Daily News/Corbis

Chapter 9

281 GRZEGORZ MICHALOWSKI/AFP/ Getty Images; **287** (t)Jeff Greenberg/ PhotoEdit, (b)AP Images/Joseph Kaczmarek; **288** Andy Sotiriou/Photodisc/Getty Images; **294** Corbis; **298** Junko Kimura/Getty Images; **299** Courtesy Toyota Motor Manufacturing, Kentucky, Inc.; **303** OJO Images Ltd/Alamy; **306** Erin Siegal/Redux Pictures

Chapter 10

313 Photo by Kevin Mazur/WireImage for Avon/Getty Images; **319** Jeffrey Allan Salter/Corbis; **323** Tim Boyle/Getty Images; **325** Kim Steele/Photodisc Green/ Getty Images; **327** Gene Blevins/LA Daily News/Corbis; **330** AP Images/Orlin Wagner; **335** Tom Raymond/Stone/Getty Images; **340** Fabrizio Costantini/The New York Times/Redux Pictures

Chapter 11

353 KAZUHIRO NOGI/AFP/Getty Images; **357** vario images GmbH & Co.KG/ Alamy; **363** AP Images/Harry Cabluck; **369** AP Images/Alyssa Hurst; **372** AP Photo/Disney, Gene Duncan; **373** STAFF/ Reuters/Corbis; **375** (t)David Frazier/The Image Works, (b)J.D. Pooley/Getty Images

Chapter 12

389 Ronda Churchill/Bloomberg via Getty Images; **394** James Leynse/Corbis; **398** Amy Etra/PhotoEdit; **399** Courtesy of Fog Creek Software; **402** Cabruken/Taxi/Getty Images; **405** Reza Estakhrian/Photographer's Choice/Getty Images; **407** Helen Ashford/ Workbook Stock/Getty Images; **414** Mark Peterson 2007/Redux Pictures; **415** AP Images/Ann Heisenfelt; **416** Photo by Jess Haessler/Courtesy Guerra DeBerry Coody; **418** AP Photo/Reed Saxon

Chapter 13

427 Jeremy M. Lange/The New York Times/Redux Pictures; **430** Jupiterimages/ Comstock Images/Getty Images; **433** AP Photo/Eugene Hoshiko; **435** Courtesy of The Container Store; **436** Duane A. Laverty/Bloomberg via Getty Images News; **444** Stockbyte/Punchstock Images; **445** Digital Vision/Getty Images; **449** vario images GmbH & Co.KG/Alamy; **451** altrendo images/Getty Images

Chapter 14

461 Neilson Barnard/Getty Images; **465** Courtesy of Zingerman's; **468** AP Photo/ Alaska Journal of Commerce, Melissa Campbell; **470** Yun Suk Bong/Reuters/ Corbis; **472** Tim Boyle/Getty Images; **475** Tim Pannell/Corbis; **479** D. Clarke Evans/NBAE via Getty Images; **484** Courtesy of Creative Display Solutions, Inc.

Chapter 15

493 Ethan Miller/Getty Images; **496** image100/Alamy; **498** Brand X Pictures/ PunchStock; **500** Comstock Images/ PictureQuest; **502** AP Images/Alexandra Boulat/VII; **504** David P. Hall/Corbis; **507** Getty Images/Digital Vision; **508** Latin-Stock Collection/Alamy; **512** hana/Datacraft/ Getty Images; **517** AP Images/Haraz/Ghanbari

Chapter 16

527 Courtesy of Fat Wire Software; **531** Doug Menuez/Getty Images; **532** Allan Danahar/Getty Images; **536** 2009 Jupiterimages Corporation; **537** Blend Images/ Getty Images; **540** David Lee/Alamy; **542** Royalty-Free/Corbis; **548** NetPhotos/ Alamy; **551** Duncan Smith/Getty Images; **553** Photodisc/Alamy

Chapter 17

563 Jiri Rezac 2008–All rights reserved; **566** avatra images/Alamy; **569** BananaStock/Jupiterimages; **570** KIM JAE-HWAN/AFP/Getty Images; **573** Doug Menuez/Getty Images; **576** Compassionate Eye Foundation/Robert Kent/Getty Images; **580** Andrew Harrer/Bloomberg via Getty Images; **584** Courtesy of El Faro Estate Coffee

Chapter 18

591 (t)Tetra Images/Alamy, (b)Courtesy of Sun Microsystems, Inc.; **596** Bill Freeman/PhotoEdit; **598** Courtesy of Herman Miller, Inc.; **601** Lourens Smak/Alamy; **602** Website screenshot courtesy of Ebay; **607** REUTERS/China Newsphoto/Landov; **608** Louie Psihoyos/Corbis; **615** AP Images/Matt Sayles

INDEX

Names

E

F

G

H

I

J

N

O

T

Organizations

Glossary/Subjects

A

B

E

J

K

N

O

Output control, 361–366
Outside expert, 582

Outsource *To use outside suppliers and manufacturers to produce goods and services,* 397

Outsourcing *Contracting with another company, usually abroad, to have it perform an activity the organization previously performed itself,* 20

Overconfidence, 217
Overlapping authority, 568–569

Overpayment inequity *The inequity that exists when a person perceives that his or her own outcome–input ratio is greater than the ratio of a referent,* 441, 442

Overt discrimination *Knowingly and willingly denying diverse individuals access to opportunities and outcomes in an organization,* 162

P

Paper-and-pencil tests, 403
PAQ, 398
Participative behavior, 477

Path–goal theory *A contingency model of leadership proposing that leaders can motivate subordinates by identifying their desired outcomes, rewarding them for high performance and the attainment of work goals with these desired outcomes, and clarifying for them the paths leading to the attainment of work goals,* 476–477, 478

Pay and benefits, 413–417
Pay and motivation, 450–453

Pay level *The relative position of an organization's pay incentives in comparison with those of other organizations in the same industry employing similar kinds of workers,* 413

Pay structures *The arrangement of jobs into categories reflecting their relative importance to the organization and its goals, levels of skill required, and other characteristics,* 415

Peer appraisal, 410–411

Perception *The process through which people select, organize, and interpret what they see, hear, touch, smell, and taste to give meaning and order to the world around them,* 158

Perceptual bias, 533

Performance appraisal *The evaluation of employees' job performance and contributions to their organization,* 407

Performance appraisal and feedback, 407–413

Performance feedback *The process through which managers share performance appraisal information with subordinates, give subordinates an opportunity to reflect on their own performance, and develop, with subordinates, plans for the future,* 407, 411–413

Performing stage, 509
Permanent transfers or dismissals, 573
Personal leadership style, 464
Personal selling, 286
Personality tests, 403

Personality traits *Enduring tendencies to feel, think, and act in certain ways,* 75–81

Personally addressed written communication, 537–539
PhoneTag, 560
Physical ability tests, 403
Physiological needs, 438
Piece-rate pay, 453

Planning *Identifying and selecting appropriate goals and courses of action; one of the four principal tasks of management,* 9–10, 247–253

- importance, 248–249
- levels/types, 249–251
- scenario planning, 252–253
- single-use plans, 252
- standing plans, 252
- time horizon, 251–252

Policy, 252

Political and legal forces *Outcomes of changes in laws and regulations, such as deregulation of industries, privatization of organizations, and increased emphasis on environmental protection,* 191–192

Political capital, 196

Political strategies *Tactics that managers use to increase their power and to use power effectively to influence and gain the support of other people while overcoming resistance or opposition,* 577

Politics. *See* Organizational politics

Pooled task interdependence *The task interdependence that exists when group members make separate and independent contributions to group performance,* 505

Pornographic Web sites, 539
Position analysis questionnaire (PAQ), 398

Position power *The amount of legitimate, reward, and coercive power that a leader has by virtue of his or her position in an organization; a determinant of how favorable a situation is for leading,* 475

Positive reinforcement *Giving people outcomes they desire when they perform organizationally functional behaviors,* 446

Potential competitors *Organizations that presently are not in a task environment but could enter if they so choose,* 187

Poverty, 151
Power, 466–469, 578–583

Power distance *The degree to which societies accept the idea that inequalities in the power and well-being of their citizens are due to differences in individuals' physical and intellectual capabilities and heritage,* 201

Practical rule *An ethical decision is one that a manager has no reluctance about communicating to people outside the company because the typical person in a society would think it is acceptable,* 119–120

Pregnancy Discrimination Act, 147, 395
Premium price, 261
Principles of Scientific Management, The (Taylor), 46

Prior-hypothesis bias *A cognitive bias resulting from the tendency to base decisions on strong prior beliefs even if evidence shows that those beliefs are wrong,* 227

Proactive approach *Companies and their managers actively embrace socially responsible behavior, going out of their way to learn about the needs of different stakeholder groups and using organizational resources to promote the interests of all stakeholders,* 133

Procedural justice *A moral principle calling for the use of fair procedures*

T

Tall hierarchy, 605
Tall organization, 333, 334

Tariff *A tax that a government imposes on imported or, occasionally, exported goods,* 197

Task analyzability, 317

Task environment *The set of forces and conditions that originate with suppliers, distributors, customers, and competitors and affect an organization's ability to obtain inputs and dispose of its outputs because they influence managers daily,* 180–188

Task force *A committee of managers or nonmanagerial employees from various departments or divisions who meet to solve a specific, mutual problem; also called ad hoc committee,* 338, 500

Task identity, 320

Task interdependence *The degree to which the work performed by one member of a group influences the work performed by other members,* 505–507, 569

Task-oriented behavior, 473

Task-oriented leaders *Leaders whose primary concern is to ensure that subordinates perform at a high level,* 474

Task significance, 320

Task structure *The extent to which the work to be performed is clear-cut so that a leader's subordinates know what needs to be accomplished and how to go about doing it; a determinant of how favorable a situation is for leading,* 474

Task variety, 317

Team *A group whose members work intensely with one another to achieve a specific common goal or objective,* 495. *See also* Groups and teams

Team learning, 231
Team rules of conduct, 370
Technical resources, 579

Technical skills *The job-specific knowledge and techniques required to perform an organizational role,* 18

Technological forces *Outcomes of changes in the technology that managers use to design, produce, or distribute goods and services,* 189–190

Technology *The combination of skills and equipment that managers use in designing, producing, and distributing goods and services,* 189, 317

Telecommuter, 538
TelePresence, 537
Temporary assignment, 573

Terminal value *A lifelong goal or objective that an individual seeks to achieve,* 82

Theory X *A set of negative assumptions about workers that leads to the conclusion that a manager's task is to supervise workers closely and control their behavior,* 58, 59

Theory Y *A set of positive assumptions about workers that leads to the conclusion that a manager's task is to create a work setting that encourages commitment to organizational goals and provides opportunities for workers to be imaginative and to exercise initiative and self-direction,* 58, 59

Thermostat, 360

Third-party negotiator *An impartial individual with expertise in handling conflicts and negotiations who helps parties in conflict reach an acceptable solution,* 574

360-degree appraisal *A performance appraisal by peers, subordinates, superiors, and sometimes clients who are in a position to evaluate a manager's performance,* 411

Time horizon *The intended duration of a plan,* 251, 568

Timeliness (of information), 595
Times-covered ratio, 362
Title VII of the Civil Rights Act of 1964, 147, 395
Tobacco companies, 190

Top-down change *A fast, revolutionary approach to change in which top managers identify what needs to be changed and then move quickly to implement the changes throughout the organization,* 380

Top management team *A group composed of the CEO, the COO, the president, and the heads of the most important departments,* 16, 499

Top manager *A manager who establishes organizational goals, decides how departments should interact, and monitors the performance of middle managers,* 16, 17

Total quality management (TQM) *A management technique that focuses on improving the quality of an organization's products and services,* 23, 62, 291–293, 378

Touch memory buttons, 453
TQM, 23, 62, 291–293, 378

Training *Teaching organizational members how to perform their current jobs and helping them acquire the knowledge and skills they need to be effective performers,* 404

Training and development, 404–407
Trait appraisal, 407–408
Trait model of leadership, 470–471

Transaction-processing system *A management information system designed to handle large volumes of routine, recurring transactions,* 605

Transactional leadership *Leadership that motivates subordinates by rewarding them for high performance and reprimanding them for low performance,* 481

Transformational leadership *Leadership that makes subordinates aware of the importance of their jobs and performance to the organization and aware of their own needs for personal growth and that motivates subordinates to work for the good of the organization,* 479–480, 481

Transmission phase, 531

Trust *The willingness of one person or group to have faith or confidence in the goodwill of another person, even though this puts them at risk,* 122–123

Turnaround management *The creation of a new vision for a struggling company based on a new approach to planning and organizing to make better use of a company's resources to allow it to survive and prosper,* 24

Twitter, 541
Two-boss employee, 329